Hotel Guide
2013

AA Lifestyle Guides

46th edition September 2012.
First published by the Automobile Association as the Hotel and Restaurant Guide, 1967

Assessments of AA inspected establishments are based on the experience of the Hotel and Restaurant Inspectors on the occasion(s) of their visit(s) and therefore descriptions given in this guide necessarily contain an element of subjective opinion which may not reflect or dictate a reader's own opinion on another occasion. See 'AA Star Classification' in the preliminary section for a clear explanation of how, based on our Inspectors' inspection experiences, establishments are graded. If the meal or meals experienced by an Inspector or Inspectors during an inspection fall between award levels the restaurant concerned may be awarded the lower of any award levels considered applicable.

AA Media Limited strives to ensure accuracy of the information in this guide at the time of printing. Due to the constantly evolving nature of the subject matter the information is subject to change. AA Media Limited will gratefully receive any advice from our readers of any necessary updated information.

Please contact:
Advertising Sales Department: advertisingsales@theAA.com
Editorial Department: lifestyleguides@theAA.com
AA Hotel Scheme Enquiries: 01256 844455

Web site addresses are included in some entries and specified by the respective establishment. Such web sites are not under the control of AA Media Limited and as such AA Media Limited has no control over them and will not accept any responsibility or liability in respect of any and all matters whatsoever relating to such web sites including access, content, material and functionality. By including the addresses of third party web sites the AA does not intend to solicit business or offer any security to any person in any country, directly or indirectly.

Every effort has been made to trace copyright holders, and we apologise in advance for any unintentional omisions or errors. We would be pleased to apply any corrections in a following edition of this publication.

Typeset/Repro: Servis Filmsetting Ltd, Stockport
Printed and bound by Graficas Estella, Spain

This directory is compiled by AA Lifestyle Guides; managed in the Librios Information Management System and generated by the AA establishment database system.

Published by AA Publishing, a trading name of AA Media Limited, whose registered office is Fanum House, Basing View, Basingstoke, Hampshire RG21 4EA.
Registered number 06112600
A CIP catalogue record for this book is available from the British Library
ISBN: 978-0-7495-7361-4
A04885

Maps prepared by the
Mapping Services Department of
AA Publishing.

Maps © AA Media Limited 2012.

Contains Ordnance Survey data
© Crown copyright and database right 2012.
Licence number 100021153.

 Land & This is based upon Crown
Property Copyright and is reproduced
Services. with the permission of Land &
Property Services under delegated authority from the
Controller of Her Majesty's Stationery Office.
© Crown copyright and database rights 2012
Licence number 100,363.
Permit number 110094

 Ordnance Republic of Ireland mapping based
Survey on © Ordnance Survey Ireland/
Ireland's National Mapping Agency Government of Ireland Copyright
Permit number MP000611

Information on National Parks in England provided by the Countryside Agency (Natural England).

Information on National Parks in Scotland provided by Scottish Natural Heritage.

Information on National Parks in Wales provided by The Countryside Council for Wales.

Contents

How to Use the Guide

1 LOCATION

Town listed alphabetically within country (the county name appears under the town name)

2 MAP REFERENCE

Map page number followed by a 2-figure National Grid reference (see also page 7)

3 HOTEL NAME

Where the name appears in *italic* type the information that follows has not been confirmed by the establishment for 2013

4 GRADING

Hotels are listed in star rating and merit score order within each location (for full explanation of ratings and awards see page 22)
★ Star rating
% Merit score
◉ Rosette award

5 TYPE OF HOTEL

(see opposite)

6 HOTEL LOGO

If a symbol appears here it represents a hotel group or consortium (See pages 27-35)

7 PICTURE

Optional photograph supplied by establishment

8 ADDRESS AND CONTACT DETAILS

9 DIRECTIONS

Brief details of how to find the hotel

10 DESCRIPTION

Written by the AA inspector at the time of the last visit

11 ROOMS

Number of rooms and prices (see page 6)

12 FACILITIES

Additional facilities including those for children and for leisure activities

13 CONFERENCE

Conference facilities as available (see page 6)

14 NOTES

Additional information (see pages 6-7)

1 **3** **4** **5** **7** **2** **6**

HELMSLEY
North Yorkshire   Map 19 SE66

Black Swan Hotel   LOGO
★★★★ 77% ◉◉ HOTEL

☎ 01439 770466
Market Place YO62 5BJ
8 **e-mail:** enquiries@blackswan-helmsley.co.uk
9 **web:** www.blackswan-helmsley.co.uk
dir: A1 junct 49, A168, A170 east, hotel 14m from Thirsk

10 People have been visiting this establishment for over 200 years and it has become a landmark that dominates the market square. The hotel is renowned for its hospitality and friendliness; many of the staff are long-serving and dedicated. The bedrooms are stylish and include a junior suite and feature rooms. Dinner in the award-winning restaurant is the highlight of any stay. The hotel has a Tearoom and Patisserie that is open daily.

11 **Rooms** 45 (4 fmly) 🐾 **S** £112-£206; **D** £142-£217 (incl. bkfst)* **Facilities** STV FTV Wi-fi Xmas New Year
12 **Conf** Class 30 Board 26 Thtr 50 Del from £165 to £200* **Parking** 50 **Notes** LB Civ Wed 130

13   **14**

KEY TO SYMBOLS AND ABBREVIATIONS	
★	Black stars
★	Red stars – indicate AA Inspectors' Choice
◉	AA Rosettes – indicate an AA award for food
%	Inspectors' Merit score (see page 6)
Ⓐ	Associate Hotels (see this page)
O	Hotel due to open during the currency of the guide
Ⓤ	Star rating not confirmed (see this page)
Fmly	Number of family rooms available
GF	Ground floors rooms available
⋔	Bedrooms with walk-in showers available
Smoking	Number of bedrooms allocated for smokers
pri facs	Bedroom with separate private facilities (Restaurant with Rooms only)
S	Single room
D	Double room
✳	2012 prices
fr	From
incl. bkfst	Breakfast included in the price
FTV	Freeview television
STV	Satellite television
Wi-fi	Wireless network connection
▷	High speed internet connection (bedrooms)
HL	Hearing loop installed
Air con	Air conditioning
⊛	Heated indoor swimming pool
⸛	Outdoor swimming pool
⸛	Heated outdoor swimming pool
♫	Entertainment
Child facilities	Children's facilities (see page 6)
Xmas/New Year	Special programme for Christmas/New Year
⚲	Tennis court
⚒	Croquet lawn
⚑	Golf course
CONF	Conference facilities
Thtr	Number of theatre style seats
Class	Number of classroom style seats
Board	Number of boardroom style seats
⊗	No dogs allowed (guide dogs for the blind and assist dogs should be allowed)
No children	Children cannot be accommodated
RS	Restricted opening time
Civ Wed	Establishment licensed for civil weddings (+ maximum number of guests at ceremony)
LB	Special leisure breaks available
Spa	Hotel has its own spa

TYPES OF HOTEL

The majority of establishments in this guide come under the category of Hotel; other categories are listed below.

TOWN HOUSE HOTEL A small, individual city or town centre property, which provides a high degree of personal service and privacy

COUNTRY HOUSE HOTEL These are quietly located in a rural area

SMALL HOTEL Has fewer than 20 bedrooms and is owner-managed

METRO HOTEL A hotel in an urban location that does not offer an evening meal

BUDGET HOTEL These are usually purpose built modern properties offering inexpensive accommodation. Often located near motorways and in town or city centres

RESTAURANT WITH ROOMS This category of accommodation is now assessed under the AA's Guest Accommodation scheme, therefore, although they continue to have an entry in this guide, we do not include their star rating. Most Restaurants with Rooms have been awarded AA Rosettes for their food and the rooms will meet the required AA standard. For more detailed information about any Restaurant with Rooms please consult The AA Bed and Breakfast Guide or see **theAA.com**

Ⓐ These are establishments that have not been inspected by the AA but which have been inspected by the national tourist boards in Britain and Northern Ireland. An establishment marked as "Associate" has paid to belong to the AA Associate Hotel Scheme and therefore receives a limited entry in the guide. Descriptions of these hotels can be found on the AA website.*

Ⓤ A small number of hotels in the guide have this symbol because their star classification was not confirmed at the time of going to press. This may be due to a change of ownership or because the hotel has only recently joined the AA rating scheme.

O These hotels were not open at the time of going to press, but will open in late 2012, or in 2013.

* Check the AA website **theAA.com** for current information and ratings

How to Use the Guide *continued*

Merit Score (%)

AA inspectors supplement their reports with an additional quality assessment of everything the hotel provides, including hospitality, based on their findings as a 'mystery guest'. This wider ranging quality assessment results in an overall Merit Score which is shown as a percentage beside the hotel name. When making your selection of hotel accommodation this enables you to see at a glance that a three star hotel with a Merit Score of 79% offers a higher standard overall than one in the same star classification but with a Merit Score of 69%. To gain AA recognition, a hotel must achieve a minimum score of 50%.

AA Awards

Every year the AA presents a range of awards to the finest AA-inspected and rated hotels from England, Scotland, Wales and the Republic of Ireland. The Hotel of the Year is our ultimate accolade and is awarded to those hotels that are recognised as outstanding examples in their field. Often innovative, the winning hotels always set high standards in hotel keeping. The winners for all the 2012-2013 awards are listed on pages 9-13.

Rooms

Each entry shows the total number of en suite rooms available (this total will include any annexe rooms). The total number may be followed by a breakdown of the type of rooms available, i.e. the number of annexe rooms; number of family rooms (fmly); number of ground-floor rooms (GF); number of rooms available for smokers.

Bedrooms in an annexe or extension are only noted if they are at least equivalent in quality to those in the main building, but facilities and prices may differ. In some hotels all bedrooms are in an annexe or extension.

If the hotel has high speed or broadband internet access in the bedrooms, this may be chargeable.

Prices

Prices are per room per night and are provided by the hoteliers in good faith. These prices are indications and not firm quotations. ✳ indicates 2012 prices. Perhaps due to the economic climate at the time we were collecting the data for this guide, fewer hotels were willing to tell us their room prices for 2013. Many hotels have introduced special rates so it is worth looking at their websites for the latest information.

Payment

Credit cards may be subject to a surcharge – check when booking if this is how you intend to pay.

Children

Child facilities may include baby intercom, baby sitting service, playroom, playground, laundry, drying/ironing facilities, cots, high chairs or special meals. In some hotels children can sleep in parents' rooms at no extra cost – check when booking.

If 'No children' is indicated a minimum age may be also given e.g. No children 4yrs indicates that no children under 4 years of age would be accepted.

Some hotels, although accepting children, may not have any special facilities for them.

Leisure breaks (LB)

Some hotels offer special leisure breaks, and these prices may differ from those quoted in this guide and the availability may vary through the year.

Parking

We indicate the number of parking spaces available for guests. This may include covered parking. Please note that some hotels make a charge to use their car park.

Civil Weddings (Civ Wed)

Indicates that the establishment holds a civil wedding licence, and we indicate the number of guests that can be accommodated at the ceremony.

Conference Facilities

We include three types of meeting layouts – Theatre, Classroom and Boardroom style and include the maximum number of delegates for each. The price shown is the maximum 24-hour rate per delegate. Please note that as arrangements vary between a hotel and a business client, VAT may or may not be included in the price quoted in the guide. We also show if Wi-fi connectivity is available, but please check with the hotel that this is suitable for your requirements.

Dogs

Although many hotels allow dogs, they may be excluded from some areas of the hotel and some breeds, particularly those requiring an exceptional licence, may not be acceptable at all. Under the Equality Act 2010 access should be allowed for guide dogs and assistance dogs. Please check the hotel's policy when making your booking.

Entertainment (♫)

This indicates that live entertainment should be available at least once a week all year. Some hotels provide live entertainment only in summer or on special occasions.

Hotel logos

If an establishment belongs to a hotel group or consortium their logo is included in their entry (see pages 27-35).

Map references

Each town is given a map reference – the map page number and a two-figure map reference based on the National Grid. For example: **Map 05 SU 48**:

05 refers to the page number of the map section at back of the guide

SU is the National Grid lettered square (representing 100,000sq metres) in which the location will be found

4 is the figure reading across the top or bottom of the map page

8 is the figure reading down at each side of the map page

Restricted service

Some hotels have restricted service (RS) during quieter months, usually during the winter, and at this time some of the listed facilities will not be available. If your booking is out-of-season, check with the hotel and enquire specifically.

Smoking regulations

If a bedroom has been allocated for smokers, the hotel is obliged to clearly indicate that this is the case. If either the freedom to smoke, or to be in a non-smoking environment is important to you, please check with the hotel when you book.

Spa

For the purposes of this guide the word **Spa** in an entry indicates that the hotel has its own spa which is either managed by themselves or outsourced to an external management company. Facilities will vary but will include a minimum of two treatment rooms. Any specific details are also given, and these are as provided to us by the establishment (i.e. steam room, beauty therapy etc).

Hotels of the Year

ENGLAND

LONDON

LIME WOOD
LYNDHURST, HAMPSHIRE Page 310

★★★★★ ◎◎◎

Situated in the heart of the New Forest National Park, this Regency country house has a new lease of life. Re-opening in 2009, this delightful hotel has a true country-house feeling with contemporary interior design by David Collins. It seems no expense has been spared, and the suites and bedrooms are stunning whether they be in the Main house, the Coach House, the Crescent or in one of the Pavilions in the grounds.

Food plays an important part at Lime Wood with excellent award-winning menus offered in the dining room, whilst the Scullery (fitted to resemble the original house kitchens) has more brasserie-style cuisine. The hotel has its own smokehouse and a forager is on site to seek out what is best throughout the seasons from the forest's own larder. Raw and Cured is the food bar offering natural, healthy food, including freshly made salads, cured fish and meat.

The world class Herb House Spa has treatment rooms and an impressive hydro pool and sauna. The perfect place to seek out for a bit of sunbathing or quiet reflection is The Herbery roof garden where fragrant herbs and gnarled olive trees have been planted to create an oasis of calm. This hotel truly sets the benchmark for country house hotels – flawless service, high tech, traditional, and unpretentious. The hotel is simply outstanding.

FOUR SEASONS HOTEL LONDON AT PARK LANE
LONDON W1 Page 294

★★★★★ ◎◎

This iconic hotel represents Park Lane at its finest. Following an impressive refurbishment, incorporating renowned artwork and stylish design, there has been a renaissance at this historic hotel. Hospitality here, as in all Four Seasons hotels, combines a home-from-home atmosphere with high standards of professionalism delivery by an extremely well-drilled team.

The stylishly designed accommodation includes over 40 suites, some with two or three bedrooms; some rooms have private terraces and a number enjoy wonderful views across the park. All rooms have been appointed to a very high standard with guest comfort in mind; in addition to the LCD TVs there are Blu-Ray DVD/CD players, iPod docks and MP3 player connection, and the high tech marble bathrooms have mirrors with integral TVs.

The Amaranto Restaurant menus have a strong Italian influence plus a taste of contemporary dishes from the Mediterranean. The concept is contemporary dining where lounge, bar and restaurant all meet, with the option to sit in the conservatory area, or if the weather is fine, relax on the terrace under the trees. The hotel has a glass-walled spa on the 10th floor offering luxury rejuvenating face and body treatments and many types of massages - it could be considered the ultimate way to chill out while gazing at the panoramic London views.

SCOTLAND

THE TORRIDON
TORRIDON, HIGHLAND Page 577

★★★★

This striking hotel enjoys an idyllic location in 58 acres of parkland with stunning views over a magnificent sea loch. A recipient of many awards, this property provides the ultimate in relaxation and tranquility, whilst offering guests the opportunity to partake in a number of outdoor activities such as clay pigeon shooting, kayaking, mountaineering, gorge scrambling, rock climbing, falconry, archery and mountain biking. It goes without saying that fly fishing is a possibility too. The countryside around is a birdwatcher's and wild life enthusiast's heaven, deer and golden eagles are a common sight.

Built as a grand shooting lodge in 1887, the building has been lovingly restored to its original splendour, and the 19 spacious bedrooms, including suites, are individually designed to offer the utmost comfort; many have fantastic views across the loch to the mountains. Expect to find luxury Egyptian linen, satellite TVs, FM radios and iPod docking stations plus Victorian-style bathrooms, some with free standing baths.

The cuisine under the watchful eye of award-winning head chef Jason 'Bruno' Birkbeck, is modern with classical roots and showcases the wonderful seasonal and locally sourced produce. Hands-on owners, Daniel and Rohaise Rose-Bristow joined Rohaise's parents in the family business in 1999 and this year the hotel celebrates 20 years of same-family ownership. This really is a special place, where guests will experience true Scottish hospitality in elegant and peaceful surroundings.

WALES

BODYSGALLEN HOTEL AND SPA
LLANDUDNO, CONWY Page 604

★★★★

This spectacular property, now handed to The National Trust, is located to the south of Llandudno and sits in over 200 acres of beautiful parkland and gardens, with spectacular views of Snowdonia and Conwy Castle.

The main house is a Grade I listed, and in parts dates back to the 17th century, however it is thought that the tower was built four centuries earlier. There are 15 individually designed bedrooms and suites located in the main house, whilst in the delightful grounds there are further cottage suites adapted from old farm buildings; some of the Hall Cottages have their own private gardens. Bedrooms are furnished with antiques, sofas and armchairs, and have bathrooms with power showers.

The Spa, as well as having a swimming pool, gym, steam room and sauna, also offers a wide range of treatments and spa day options.

The hotel has two restaurants - the more formal three-Rosette Dining Room, and the 1620 Bistro and its terrace for casual and alfresco dining. Traditional afternoon teas are also served in the beautiful oak-panelled day rooms or on the terrace when the weather permits. Guests are welcome to wander in the restored gardens where they will find a rare parterre of box hedges, a formal rose garden, a walled garden and several follies.

REPUBLIC OF IRELAND

KNOCKRANNY HOUSE HOTEL
WESTPORT, CO MAYO Page 656

★★★★ 84% ◉◉

Situated in an elevated position overlooking Westport, with Clew Bay and Croagh Patrick in the distance, this family-run hotel is set in well landscaped grounds. Step inside to find an inviting and relaxing atmosphere throughout the lounges, bar and restaurant.

The warmly decorated bedrooms are spacious, very well appointed and come in a number of styles; newly added are luxury suites including the Presidential Suite with its own kitchenette. Some of the rooms have four-posters and wonderful views, and grander rooms have DVD, CD players and MP3, iPod and game console capability, large bathrooms with Bose speakers and separate showers.

The award-winning La Fougère Restaurant is an elegant split-level dining room with breathtaking views through large windows. Here guests can expect to enjoy well presented, modern international cuisine. Tables are widely spaced and dressed for the occasion in white linen with high quality silverware and glasses. Alternatively there is The Brehon, a lounge bar where food is served throughout the day.

The hotel's much patronised Spa Salveo has a vitality pool, thermal suite and range of luxury treatments and packages to tempt anyone seeking relaxation and rejuvenation. Those with a rod and line will already know that County Mayo is famed as a top angling destination whether it be sea or course fishing on the rivers and lakes. The hotel is more than happy to arrange fishing trips for any guest keen to try their luck.

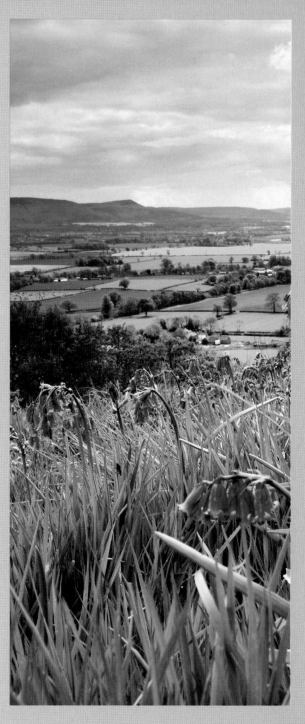

Hotel Group of the Year

HAND PICKED HOTELS

The Hand Picked portfolio of 17 properties is a unique collection of architecturally stunning and exquisitely refurbished country-house hotels set in beautifully maintained grounds that offers the highest standards of cuisine and service, making each guest's stay a memorable one. Eight of the hotels have Red Star status. For food excellence 16 have been awarded two AA Rosettes and one, Norton House Hotel, has three Rosettes.

ENGLAND

ALDERMINSTER, Warwickshire	Ettington Park Hotel
BASINGSTOKE, Hampshire	Audleys Wood Hotel
BRANDS HATCH, Kent	Brandshatch Place Hotel & Spa
BROCKENHURST, Hampshire	Rhinefield House Hotel
CRATHORNE, North Yorkshire	Crathorne Hall Hotel
EAST MIDLAND AIRPORT (Castle Donington)	The Priest House Hotel
LENHAM, Kent	Chilston Park Hotel
LONDON NW4	Hendon Hall Hotel
NANTWICH, Cheshire	Rookery Hall Hotel & Spa
REDHILL, Surrey	Nutfield Priory Hotel & Spa
STOKE D'ABERNON, Surrey	Woodlands Park Hotel
SUTTON COLDFIELD, West Midlands	New Hall Hotel & Spa
UCKFIELD, East Sussex	Buxted Park Hotel
WETHERBY, West Yorkshire	Wood Hall Hotel & Spa

CHANNEL ISLANDS

ST BRELADE, Jersey	L'Horizon Hotel & Spa

SCOTLAND

EDINBURGH	Norton House Hotel & Spa

WALES

CAERNARFON, Gwynedd	Seiont Manor Hotel

Ettington Park Hotel

Chilston Park Hotel

Rhinefield House Hotel

Small Hotel Group of the Year

COTSWOLD INNS & HOTELS

The Cotswold Inns & Hotels group comprises seven hotels all located in the beautiful Cotswolds. Privately owned, the individual style of the hotels is modelled on the quintessential English country home. The atmosphere at each is relaxing and friendly and there is an emphasis on good food and fine wine. The country settings of these hotels make them ideal venues for leisure breaks, weddings or business meetings.

ENGLAND

BIBURY, Gloucestershire	Swan Hotel
BROADWAY, Worcestershire	The Broadway Hotel
BURFORD, Oxfordshire	The Bay Tree Hotel
BURFORD, Oxfordshre	The Lamb Inn
MORETON-IN-MARSH, Gloucestershire	Manor House Hotel
STROUD, Gloucestershire	The Bear of Rodborough
TETBURY, Gloucestershire	Hare & Hounds Hotel

The Lamb Inn

Manor House Hotel

Swan Hotel

Be
inspired

The hotels in this guide range from one star to five stars, from small to large, from historic to modern and from town to country. If you have a particular interest or hobby one of them might just be the place for you.

Be inspired to...
...follow in royal footsteps

"Queen Elizabeth I never slept here." Such a sign, should it exist, can only be a tongue-in-cheek nod to any country-house hotel or inn that claims to have once plumped up the pillows for this famously itinerant monarch.

Actually, Elizabeth did sleep in many strange beds, and exploiting her patronage is a good marketing tool. Staying where a royal once stayed, perhaps even in the same bedroom, adds a certain frisson to a weekend away, and may well inspire our choice of destination.

One of her regular stop-offs, the last time in 1575, was Fawsley Hall near Daventry in Northamptonshire, now a country-house hotel surrounded by Lancelot 'Capability' Brown's landscaped parkland. She also once turned up at Seckford Hall in Woodbridge, Suffolk, today a luxury hotel and restaurant, where you can see the very chair in which King Edward VII is said to have died at Buckingham Palace in 1910. A little morbid maybe, but a royal connection nevertheless. During the English Civil War they say Charles II rested his head (maybe not so peacefully) at the Noel Arms, Chipping Campden. ▷

Fawsley Hall Hotel

"Charles Dickens seems to have stayed at as many places as Queen Elizabeth I"

Those looking to stay overnight in London might head for The Goring, purely because this was where Kate Middleton, now the Duchess of Cambridge, chose to stay on the eve of her 2011 wedding to HRH Prince William, or the Westleton Crown in Suffolk, where the royal couple stayed after attending a wedding nearby.

Royalty have also stayed at Thornbury Castle on the edge of the Cotswolds in Gloucestershire, the only Tudor castle in England that's also a hotel. This time the regal guests were Henry VIII and his short-lived (in both senses!) second wife, Anne Boleyn, while his daughter, later Mary I, lived here for several years too.

There are, of course, hotels in castles with no royal connection. In the South Tyne valley is Langley Castle Hotel, built in 1350, one of the very few English medieval castles to accommodate paying guests. Thirteenth-century Dalhousie Castle, a luxury hotel in wooded parkland on the banks of the River Esk near Edinburgh, is the archetypal Scottish fortress, one of a growing number of hotels now providing falconry packages. Others include 17th-century Lainston House Hotel, near Winchester, in Hampshire; the early 19th-century Peckforton Castle, in Cheshire; and in the pretty village of Straffan, Co Kildare, The K Club.

... find a hotel with a tale to tell

For some, a night at The Old Swan Hotel in Harrogate would appeal, because it was where Agatha Christie 'disappeared' for 11 days in 1926. Aviation aficionados might be drawn to the 200-year-old Ashburnham Hotel near Llanelli where, in 1928, after becoming the first woman to fly the Atlantic, Amelia Earhart recovered from whatever sort of lag existed before the jet variety. Charles Dickens seems to have stayed at as many places as Queen Elizabeth I – The Royal, Ross-on-Wye, The Angel Hotel, Bury St Edmunds where he penned part of *Pickwick Papers*, and Satis House Hotel, Yoxford where it is said the name for Miss Haversham's house in *Great Expectations* came from.

....wander in the grounds

When considering where to stay, you might find 'Capability' Brown's name cropping up, which isn't surprising since some of the 170 estates and parks he created are now the grounds of hotels. Among them are Grade 1 listed Luton Hoo Hotel, Golf and Spa, and Stoke Place, a modern country house hotel near Stoke Poges in Buckinghamshire. At Bowood Hotel, Spa and Golf Resort, Brown incorporated his trademark lake and cascade in the 100 acres of parkland surrounding the Wiltshire home of the Marquis and Marchioness of Lansdowne. Other gardens worthy of mention are those designed by Gertrude Jekyll at Tylney Hall, Rotherwick; the enchanting grounds and fascinating kitchen gardens at Le Manoir Aux Quat' Saisons, Great Milton, and the walled garden and 400-year-old yew hedge at Cringletie House Hotel, Peebles.

....cast your line

Now, if you can tell a fritz blob from a zonker, you might want to head for the

Arundell Arms, a top fly-fishing hotel in Devon, which owns 20 miles of the River Tamar and its tributaries. Or there's the The Izaak Walton Hotel in the Peak District National Park, with fishing rights on the Staffordshire bank of the Dove, a classic trout river that Walton featured in his famous work, *The Compleat Angler*. Then there's the Peacock at Rowsley where they can arrange for anglers to try their luck for trout and greyling on the Rivers Wye and Derwent; safe wading is possible in the latter.

Two-day fishing packages are available at the Lake Vyrnwy Hotel & Spa in mid-Wales and, in Ireland, the luxury Palladian-style Ritz Carlton Powerscourt Hotel outside Dublin will arrange close encounters with rainbow trout at nearby Tinnahinch Fly Fishing Centre, and with sea trout on the River Dargle.

...set sail

Whether you look at it, fish in it or sail on it, water is always an attraction. The owners of Toravaig House, a small, contemporary hotel on the Isle of Skye, will take guests on their yacht *Solus na Mara* across the Sound of Sleat to Lochs Nevis and Hourn, or out to the islands of Rhum and Eigg. Nearly 500 miles south, in Yarmouth, Isle of Wight, the strategically well placed, 17th-century George Hotel will arrange sailing trips on the Solent, or a good spot from which to sit back and watch the Round the Island Yacht Race.

...seek out the unusual

Choice is more limited if you want to stay in a lighthouse. One possibility is Corsewall Lighthouse Hotel near Stranraer, Dumfries & Galloway, built in 1815 and listed Category A (equivalent to English Grade 1 listed). Now automated, its light still warns ships approaching the mouth of Loch Ryan and from its galleries you can see the Kintyre Peninsula, the Firth of Clyde and even the coast of Ireland, while the beams of other Scottish and Irish lighthouses are visible on a clear night.

Hotels in former prisons are also thin on the ground, but one place where you can do time, admittedly in considerable luxury, is the Malmaison Oxford, the city's prison until 1996, and now a boutique hotel within the redeveloped Oxford Castle complex. The bedrooms were once the cells, although in consideration for guests' sensitivities, the cells associated with corporal or capital punishment became offices for staff.

...rediscover the age of steam

Finding an old railway building to stay in should prove easier. Following years of devoted restoration, a Victorian railway hotel that its saviour, Sir John Betjeman, once called "too beautiful and too romantic to survive", is now the St Pancras Renaissance London Hotel, one of London's architectural treasures. With glorious Gothic Revival metalwork, gold-leaf ceilings, hand-stencilled wall designs and a jaw-dropping grand staircase, it's probably more opulent than the day Queen Victoria opened it in 1873. ▷

St Pancras Renaissance London Hotel

Storrs Hall Hotel, Windermere

Prestonfield, Edinburgh

Another late-Victorian gem is The Landmark London at Marylebone station, which opened as The Great Central in 1899, the last of the great Victorian railway hotels built during 'the golden age of steam'. After only 40 years it closed, having fallen victim to the automobile, and during the next four decades it accommodated, among others, the British Railways Board, whose staff called it 'The Kremlin'. Now, with all its original fixtures and fittings revealed, it's hard to imagine how this elegant building could ever have acquired such an uncomplimentary soubriquet.

While St Pancras International and Marylebone are still working railway stations, the tracks no longer run through Kilmessan in Co Meath, only 20 minutes from Dublin. In 1981 Chris and Thelma Slattery bought the mid-19th-century village station to live in, then lovingly transformed it and the old signal box into the delightful, award-winning Station House Hotel.

...admire the views

Great views are another big attraction, a commodity the British Isles has in abundance; luckily it also has the hotels to take advantage of them. "The Best View in England," said a national newspaper of The Cottage in the Wood, high on the Malvern Hills in Worcestershire, with a 30-mile vista across the Severn Plain.

Views are a subjective business, however. You might prefer a bedroom looking out to sea, in which case try the cliff-top Land's End Hotel, right on the Atlantic Ocean with a panorama taking in the Longships Lighthouse and the Isles of Scilly. Or Glenapp Castle Hotel in 36 acres of

"Fabulous views usually go hand in hand with being off the beaten track"

gardens and woodland at Ballantrae on the rugged Ayrshire coast, with the island of Arran and the massive granite rock of Ailsa Craig firmly in its sights.

For upland scenery, the Lake District is up there with the best. Overlooking beautiful Windermere and the surrounding Lakeland fells is Linthwaite Country House Hotel, where guests in the Loft Suite are provided with a seriously good telescope for gazing at the stars in night skies almost completely unpolluted by light.

Fabulous views usually go hand in hand with being off the beaten track. For example, up in the far north-east of the Isle of Skye, in an area of unusual and dramatic rock formations known as the Quiraing, is the family-run Flodigarry Country House Hotel. Look across the Sound of Raasay to the Torridon mountains on the mainland and you can be sure nothing has changed since Scottish heroine Flora MacDonald lived in the cottage here in the mid-1700s.

On the harbourside in the tiny island of Herm in the Channel Islands, you'll find the White House Hotel easily enough, but you'll look in vain for TVs, clocks and telephones, which the owners consider inappropriate in such a tranquil location.▷

Dewentwater, Lake District National Park

"... the curriculum here features soufflés, chocolate Marquise and its famous lemon drizzle cake"

...find somewhere your children will love

The majority of hotels cater for families, of course, although some like to emphasise their child-friendliness.

Jersey's only AA five Red Star hotel, the Longueville Manor, in St Saviour, has no qualms about declaring that it "welcomes kids of all ages," while Satis House Hotel, Yoxford, Suffolk, sets aside two special guest rooms where "children can be children without disturbing other guests." Boredom is not an option at Calcot Manor, Tetbury – for the tinies there's Playzone (an Ofsted registered crèche), then for 8s and over, The Mez has every console game imaginable and a cinema to keep them entertained for hours, not to mention the outdoor opportunities.

... take tea, down a cocktail and relish a pud

The larger hotels usually cater for non-residents. The spectacular Palm Court at The Ritz in London's Piccadilly, for instance, has elevated the very British ritual of afternoon tea, with 17 types of leaf tea offered, to institutional status. The Dorchester, another iconic London hotel, serves afternoon tea in The Promenade, a room as long as Nelson's Column is tall, and also in what it calls The Spatisserie, an opulent, all-purpose room where the dress code ranges from normal day wear to bath robes. Both hotels are proud to be a member of the The Tea Guild, a prestigious organisation representing outlets dedicated to both brewing and serving tea to the high standards desired by the United Kingdom Tea Council. If something stronger is needed, try a cocktail at The Bar at The Dorchester, famed for its huge repertoire devised by award-winning Giuliano Morandin and his team.

In Chipping Campden, on the northern edge of the Cotswolds, is the privately owned Three Ways House Hotel, home of The Pudding Club. This esoteric body was founded in 1985 to prevent the feared demise of time-honoured, traditional British puddings such as syrup sponge and spotted dick, which are served on Club evenings, when everyone sits at large tables for a convivial dinner.

...learn to cook up a storm

Eating such puddings is one thing, but if you want to learn how to make them, you'd better consult Mrs Beeton rather than enrol for a course at Raymond Blanc Cookery School at Le Manoir aux Quat'Saisons, the celebrity chef's renowned Oxfordshire hotel and restaurant. Instead of jam roly poly, the curriculum here features soufflés, chocolate Marquise and its famous lemon drizzle cake. Lady Macdonald at Kinloch Lodge on the Isle of Skye runs inspirational three-day residential cookery courses whether you are a complete novice and or a more adept cook, while at the other end of the country Rick Stein's seafood school in Padstow will teach you the tricky art of cooking fish to perfection, and there's also a course for vegetarians. Swinton Park, Masham has a superb demonstration kitchen in converted stables where students can choose courses such as cooking game, making sushi and foraging for food. This hotel is a castle and although Elizabeth I might not have slept there, the grounds and gardens, restored in recent years, are inspirational too.

All these possibilities, and more, can be found in the guide. Take a look.

AA Star Classifications & Rosette Awards

AA Assessment

In collaboration with VisitBritain, VisitScotland and VisitWales, the AA developed Common Quality Standards for inspecting and rating accommodation. These standards and rating categories are now applied throughout the British Isles.

Any hotel applying for AA recognition receives an unannounced visit from an AA inspector to check standards. The hotels with full entries in this guide have all paid an annual fee for AA inspection, recognition and rating.

AA inspectors pay as a guest for their inspection visit, they do not accept free hospitality of any kind. Although AA inspectors do not stay overnight at Budget Hotels they do carry out regular visits to verify standards and procedures.

A guide to some of the general expectations for each star classification is as follows:

★ One Star

Polite, courteous staff providing a relatively informal yet competent style of service, available during the day and evening to receive guests
- At least one designated eating area open to residents for breakfast
- If dinner is offered it should be on at least five days a week, with last orders no earlier than 6.30pm
- Television in bedroom
- Majority of rooms en suite, bath or shower room available at all times

★★ Two Star

As for one star, plus
- At least one restaurant or dining room open to residents for breakfast (and for dinner at least five days a week)
- Last orders for dinner no earlier than 7pm
- En suite or private bath or shower and WC

★★★ Three Star

- Management and staff smartly and professionally presented and usually uniformed
- A dedicated receptionist on duty at peak times
- At least one restaurant or dining room open to residents and non-residents for breakfast and dinner whenever the hotel is open
- Last orders for dinner no earlier than 8pm
- Remote-control television, direct-dial telephone
- En suite bath or shower and WC.

★★★★ Four Star

- A formal, professional staffing structure with smartly presented, uniformed staff anticipating and responding to your needs or requests. Usually spacious, well-appointed public areas
- Reception staffed 24 hours by well-trained staff
- Express checkout facilities where appropriate
- Porterage available on request
- Night porter available
- At least one restaurant open to residents and non-residents for breakfast and dinner seven days per week, and lunch to be available in a designated eating area
- Last orders for dinner no earlier than 9pm
- En suite bath with fixed overhead shower and WC

restaurants in the UK, the AA identifies over 2,000 as the best. The following is an outline of what to expect from restaurants with AA Rosette Awards.

⊚ Excellent local restaurants serving food prepared with care, understanding and skill, using good quality ingredients.

⊚⊚ The best local restaurants, which aim for and achieve higher standards, better consistency and where a greater precision is apparent in the cooking. There will be obvious attention to the selection of quality ingredients.

⊚⊚⊚ Outstanding restaurants that demand recognition well beyond their local area.

⊚⊚⊚⊚ Amongst the very best restaurants in the British Isles, where the cooking demands national recognition.

⊚⊚⊚⊚⊚ The finest restaurants in the British Isles, where the cooking stands comparison with the best in the world.

★★★★★ Five Star

- Luxurious accommodation and public areas with a range of extra facilities. First time guests shown to their bedroom
- Multilingual service
- Guest accounts well explained and presented
- Porterage offered
- Guests greeted at hotel entrance, full concierge service provided
- At least one restaurant open to residents and non-residents for all meals seven days per week
- Last orders for dinner no earlier than 10pm
- High-quality menu and wine list
- Evening service to turn down the beds. Remote-control television, direct-dial telephone at bedside and desk, a range of luxury toiletries, bath sheets and robes. En suite bathroom incorporating fixed overhead shower and WC

★ Inspectors' Choice

Each year we select the best hotels in each rating. These hotels stand out as the very best in the British Isles, regardless of style. Red Star hotels appear in highlighted panels throughout the guide. Inspectors' Choice Restaurants with Rooms are establishments that have been awarded the highest accommodation rating under the AA Guest Accommodation scheme.

Additional information

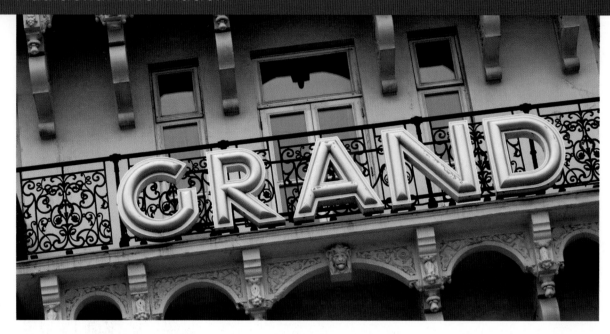

Hints on booking your stay

It's always worth booking as early as possible, particularly for the peak holiday period from the beginning of June to the end of September. Bear in mind that Easter and other public holidays may be busy too and in some parts of Scotland, the ski season is a peak holiday period.

Some hotels will ask for a deposit or full payment in advance, especially for one-night bookings. And some hotels charge half-board (bed, breakfast and dinner) whether you require the meals or not, while others may only accept full-board bookings. Not all hotels will accept advance bookings for bed and breakfast, overnight or short stays. Some will not take reservations from mid week.

Once a booking is confirmed, let the hotel know at once if you are unable to keep your reservation. If the hotel cannot re-let your room you may be liable to pay about two-thirds of the room price (a deposit will count towards this payment).

In Britain a legally binding contract is made when you accept an offer of accommodation, either in writing or by telephone, and illness is not accepted as a release from this contract. You are advised to take out insurance against possible cancellation, for example AA Single Trip Insurance (telephone 0800 975 5819).

Booking online

Locating and booking somewhere to stay can be a time-consuming process, but you can search quickly and easily online for a place that best suits your needs. Simply visit theAA.com to search for full details of over 5,800 quality rated hotels and B&Bs in Great Britain and Ireland. Check availability and click on the 'Book it' button.

Prices

The AA encourages the use of the Hotel Industry Voluntary Code of Booking Practice, which aims to ensure that guests know how much they will have to pay and what services and facilities are included, before entering a financially binding agreement. If the price has not previously been confirmed in writing, guests should be given a card stipulating the total obligatory charge when they register at reception.

Facilities for disabled guests

The Equality Act 2010 provides legal rights for disabled people including access to goods, services and facilities, and means that service providers may have to consider making adjustments to their premises. For more information about the Act see: www.equalities.gov.uk. or www.direct.gov.uk/en/DisabledPeople/RightsAndObligations/DisabilityRights/DG_4001068

The establishments in this guide should be aware of their obligations under the Act. We recommend that you always telephone in advance to ensure that the establishment you have chosen has appropriate facilities.

Please note: AA inspectors are not accredited to make inspections under the National Accessibility Scheme. We indicate in entries if an establishment has ground floor rooms, walk-in showers and whether the hotel has a hearing loop system; and if a hotel tells us that they have disabled facilities this is included in the description.

Licensing Laws

Licensing laws differ in England, Wales, Scotland, the Republic of Ireland, the Isle of Man, the Isles of Scilly and the Channel Islands. Public houses are generally open from mid morning to early afternoon, and from about 6 or 7pm until 11pm, although closing times may be earlier or later and some pubs are open all afternoon. Unless otherwise stated, establishments listed are licensed to serve alcohol. Hotel residents can obtain alcoholic drinks at all times, if the licensee is prepared to serve them. Non-residents eating at the hotel restaurant can have drinks with meals. Children under 14 may be excluded from bars where no food is served. Those under 18 may not purchase or consume alcoholic drinks.

Club licence means that drinks are served to club members only, 48 hours must lapse between joining and ordering.

The Fire Precautions Act does not apply to the Channel Islands, Republic of Ireland, or the Isle of Man, which have their own rules. As far as we are aware, all hotels listed in Great Britain have applied for and not been refused a fire certificate.

For information on Ireland see page 624.

Bank and Public Holidays 2013

New Year's Day	1st January
Good Friday	29th March
Easter Monday	1st April
Early May Bank Holiday	6th May
Spring Bank Holiday	27th May
Summer Bank Holiday (Scotland)	5th August
Summer Bank Holiday	26th August
St Andrew's Day (Scotland)	30th November
Christmas Day	25th December
Boxing Day	26th December

Hotel Groups Information

	Apex Hotels A group of contemporary four star hotels. One in Dundee, four in Edinburgh and three in London. Spa and gym facilities are available at a number of the hotels.	*0845 365 0000* *www.apexhotels.co.uk*
	Bespoke A growing group of personally managed three and four star hotels in leisure locations.	*0843 357 5555* *www.bespokehotels.com*
	Best Western Britain's largest consortia group has over 280 independently owned and managed hotels, modern and traditional, in the two, three and four star range. Many have leisure facilities and rosette awards.	*08457 76 76 76* *www.bestwestern.co.uk*
	Best Western Premier These hotels are selected for their beautiful settings, range of facilities and enhanced levels of service. There are currently 7 Best Western Great Britain hotels that have achieved Premier status. These join over 45 Best Western Premier accredited hotels across Europe and Asia.	*08457 76 76 76* *www.bestwestern.co.uk*
	Best Western Plus 13 independently owned and managed hotels that offer that little something extra in the three and four star range. Some of these hotels have AA Rosette awards.	*08457 76 76 76* *www.bestwestern.co.uk*
	Bewley's Hotels Part of the Moran Hotel Group. A privately owned group of high quality, contemporary three star hotels in key locations in the UK and Ireland.	*0845 234 5959* *www.bewleyshotels.com*
	Brend A privately owned group of 11 three and four star hotels in Devon and Cornwall.	*01271 344 496* *www.brend-hotels.co.uk*
	Campanile An American owned and French managed company, Campanile has 17 properties in the UK offering modern accommodation in budget hotels.	*www.campanile.com*
	Carlton Hotels An international hotel brand based in Ireland renowned for leisure, family and relaxing spa breaks, with hotels in major cities and scenic destinations throughout Ireland.	*+353 1 866 7555* *www.carlton.ie*
	Choice Choice has four different brands in the UK: Clarion and Quality Hotels are three and four star hotels, Comfort Inns are two and three star hotels, and Sleep Inns are budget hotels.	*0800 44 44 44* *www.choicehotelseurope.com*
	Classic British Hotels A consortium of four star and high-quality three star independent hotels marketed under the Classic British Hotels hallmark. Many have spas, health clubs and award-winning fine dining.	*0845 070 7090* *www.classicbritishhotels.com*
	Classic Lodges A small group of three and four star hotels.	*0845 603 8892* *www.classiclodges.co.uk*
	Copthorne Part of the Millennium and Copthorne group, with 12 three and four star hotels in primary provincial locations as well as London.	*0800 41 47 41* *www.millenniumhotels.com*
	Cotswold Inns & Hotels Charming three and four star small hotels located in the Cotswolds.	*www.cotswold-inns-hotels.co.uk*

Hotel Groups Information *continued*

Crowne Plaza Four star hotels predominantly found in key city centre locations.	0871 423 4876 www.crowneplaza.co.uk
Days Inn Good quality modern budget hotels with good coverage across the UK.	0800 028 0400 www.daysinn.com
De Vere Hotels & Resorts A group of four star hotels with good coverage across the UK.	0845 375 2808 www.devere.co.uk
English Lakes Hotels A collection of individually styled four star hotels located in and around the Lake District.	015394 33773 www.englishlakes.co.uk
Exclusive Hotels A small privately owned group of luxury five and four star hotels, all located in the south of England.	01276 471 774 www.exclusivehotels.co.uk
FBD Hotels An Irish owned and operated group offering quality hotels in convenient locations throughout Ireland.	353 (0)1 428 2400 www.fdbhotels.com
Focus Hotels A group of three star hotels in both city and country locations across England. All offer Wi-fi and a number have spa facilities.	0844 225 1625 www.focushotels.co.uk
Four Pillars Hotels A group of three and four star hotels in the Oxfordshire area.	0800 374 692 www.four-pillars.co.uk
Guoman Hotels A collection of large hotels in London, all four star, with the exception of The Royal Horseguards which has five stars.	www.gouman.com
Hallmark Hotels A collection of seven hotels that provide comfortable accommodation; some have leisure facilities.	0113 307 6760 www.hallmarkhotels.co.uk
Hand Picked Hotels A group of 17 predominantly four star, high quality country house hotels, with a real emphasis on quality food. Some provide stylish spa facilities.	0845 458 0901 www.handpickedhotels.co.uk
Holiday Inn A major international group with many hotels across the UK.	0871 423 4896 www.holidayinn.co.uk
Holiday Inn Express A major international hotel brand with over 100 hotels across the UK.	www.hiexpress.co.uk
Hotel du Vin A small expanding group of high quality four star hotels, that places a strong emphasis on its destination restaurant concept and appealing menus.	0845 365 4438 www.hotelduvin.com
Ibis A growing chain of modern budget hotels with properties across the UK.	www.ibishotel.com
Independents A consortium of independently owned, mainly two, three and four star hotels, across Britain.	0844 800 9965 www.theindependents.co.uk
Ireland's Blue Book A collection of country houses, historic hotels, castles and restaurants throughout Ireland.	00 353 1 676 9914 www.irelands-blue-book.ie

The Best of the British Seaside

A warm welcome awaits you at our Leisureplex Hotels

*Situated in stunning locations from St.Ives to Fort William, every one of our
20 Leisureplex hotels offers a prime location and quality service, at a very affordable price*

•Weston-Super-Mare •Ilfracombe •Newquay •St. Ives •Falmouth •Torquay
•Exmouth •Bournemouth •Isle of Wight •Bognor Regis •Eastbourne •Great Yarmouth
•Cromer •Blackpool •Scarborough •Llandudno •Criccieth •Porthcawl •Dunoon •Fort William

Leisureplex Hotels

AA ★★ Hotel

www.leisureplex.co.uk   08451 305888

(For Group Sales call 01257 248011)

Hotel Groups Information *continued*

IRISH COUNTRY HOTELS	**Irish Country Hotels** A collection of over 26 family run hotels, located all across Ireland.	*00 353 1 295 8900 (local)* *0818 281 281* *www.irishcountryhotels.com*
LAKE DISTRICT HOTELS	**Lake District Hotels** A small collection of hotels situated in some of the most beautiful parts of the Lake District countryside and in Lakeland towns.	*0800 840 1240* *www.lakedistricthotels.net*
LEGACY HOTELS	**Legacy Hotels** A small group of three and four star hotels growing its coverage across the UK.	*0844 411 9011* *www.legacy-hotels.co.uk*
Leisureplex	**Leisureplex** A group of 20 two star hotels located in many popular seaside resorts.	*08451 305 888* *www.leisureplex.co.uk*
MACDONALD HOTELS & RESORTS	**Macdonald** A large group of predominantly four star hotels, both traditional and modern in style and located across the UK. Many hotels enjoy rural settings and state-of-the-art spa facilities	*0844 879 9000* *www.macdonaldhotels.co.uk*
Malmaison	**Malmaison** A growing brand of modern, three star city centre hotels that provide deeply comfortable bedrooms, exciting restaurants and carefully selected wine lists.	*0845 365 4247* *www.malmaison.com*
MANOR HOUSE HOTELS	**Manor House** Located throughout Ireland, this group offers a selection of independent, high quality country and manor house hotels.	*00 353 1 295 8900 (local)* *0818 281 281* *www.manorhousehotels.com*
Marriott HOTELS & RESORTS	**Marriott** This international brand has four and five star hotels in primary locations. Most are modern and have leisure facilities with a focus on activities such as golf.	*00800 1927 1927* *www.marriott.co.uk*
MAYBOURNE HOTEL GROUP	**Maybourne Hotels** A hotel group representing the prestigious London five star hotels - The Berkeley, Claridge's and The Connaught.	*020 7107 8800 (Head Office)* *www.maybourne.com*
MenziesHotels	**Menzies Hotels** A group of predominantly four star hotels in key locations across the UK.	*0845 850 3013* *www.menzieshotels.co.uk*
Mercure	**Mercure Hotels** A large group of three and four star hotels throughout England, Scotland and Wales.	*0871 663 0627* *www.mercure.com*
MILLENNIUM MILLENNIUM + COPTHORNE	**Millennium** Part of the Millennium and Copthorne group with 7 high-quality four star hotels, mainly in central London.	*0800 41 47 41* *www.millenniumhotels.com*
MORAN HOTELS	**Moran Hotels** A privately owned group with 4 four star Moran Hotels, and 6 three star Bewley's Hotels. All have strategic locations in the UK and Ireland.	*00 353 1 459 3650* *www.moranhotels.com*
NEW FOREST HOTELS	**New Forest Hotels** A collection of properties situated in the New Forest National Park, each with its own distinct character. All have an AA Rosette award for culinary excellence.	*0800 44 44 41* *www.newforesthotels.co.uk*

famous for our welcome

With 33 unique luxury bedrooms, award winning food and a luxury spa it's no wonder The Feversham Arms Hotel & Verbena Spa is fast becoming a destination of choice for visitors to North Yorkshire. Nestled in the North Yorkshire Moors in the centre of picturesque Helmsley, we're only a stone's throw away from a variety of attractions, ranging from golf courses and historic castles to enjoyable moorland walks and stunning seaside vistas. So if you're looking for somewhere to relax and recharge, The Feversham Arms Hotel provides the perfect setting....we'll be ready and waiting with our famously warm Feversham welcome.

For more information about the hotel, restaurant or spa treatments available pick up the phone, or visit us online today.

01439 770766

Info@fevershamarmshotel.com

 ★★★★
Awarded by the AA

fevershamarmshotel.com

Helmsley, North Yorkshire, YO62 5AG

Rooms 33 (9 fmly) (8 GF) **S** £193-£473; **D** £260-£520 (incl bkfst & dinner). * **Facilities** Spa, Sauna Saunarium, Xmas New Year, Wi-Fi. **Conf** Class 20 Board 24 Thtr 35 Del from £65-£265* **Services** Lift **Parking** 50 **Notes** LB Civ Wed 50

Hotel Groups Information *continued*

Novotel Part of French group Accor, Novotel provides mainly modern three star hotels and a new generation of four star hotels in key locations throughout the UK.	*0871 663 0626* *www.novotel.com*	
Old English Inns A large collection of former coaching inns that are mainly graded at two and three stars.	*0845 608 6040* *www.oldenglishinns.co.uk*	
Oxford Hotels and Inns A large group of 25 hotels with good coverage across the UK, and particularly in Scotland. Each hotel has its own individual style and character.	*0871 376 9900* *www.oxfordhotelsandinns.com*	
Park Inn by Radisson A fresh, energetic hotel group suitable for business and leisure guests, offering comfortable accommodation and excellent meeting and conference facilities.	*www.parkinn.co.uk*	
Park Plaza Hotels A European based group increasing its presence in the UK with quality four star hotels in primary locations.	*0800 169 6128* *www.parkplaza.com*	
Peel Hotels A group of mainly three and four star hotels located across the UK.	*0845 601 7335* *www.peelhotels.co.uk*	
Premier Inns The largest and fastest growing budget hotel group with over 600 hotels offering quality, modern accommodation in key locations throughout the UK and Ireland. Each hotel is located adjacent to a family restaurant and bar.	*0871 527 8000* *www.premierinn.com*	
Pride of Britain A consortium of privately owned high quality British hotels, often in the country house style, many of which have been awarded Red Stars and AA Rosettes.	*0800 089 3929* *www.prideofbritainhotels.com*	
Prima Hotels A small hotel group which currently has 6 four star hotels. Five hotels are in England and one is in Scotland.	*www.primahotels.co.uk*	
Principal Hayley A small group of four star hotels currently represented by 13 hotels situated in prime city centre locations.	*0870 242 7474* *www.principal-hotels.com*	
Puma Hotels Formerly Barcelo UK, Puma Hotels Collection operates 20 four star hotels in locations across the UK.	*0800 652 8413* *www.pumahotels.co.uk*	
QHotels A hotel group with 21 individually styled four star hotels across the UK.	*0845 241 9783* *www.qhotels.co.uk*	
Radisson Blu A recognised international brand increasing its hotels in the UK and Ireland, and offering high-quality four star hotels in key locations. (Formerly known as Radisson SAS).	*0800 374 411* *www.radissonblu.com*	
Ramada A large hotel group with many properties throughout the UK in three brands - Ramada Plaza, Ramada and Ramada Hotel & Resort.	*0845 2070 100* *www.ramada.co.uk*	

Hotel Groups Information *continued*

RED CARNATION HOTEL COLLECTION	**Red Carnation** A unique collection of prestigious four and five star hotels in Dorset and the Channel Islands providing luxurious surroundings and attentive service.	*www.redcarnationhotels.com*
RELAIS & CHATEAUX	**Relais et Chateaux** An international consortium of rural, privately owned hotels, mainly in the country house style.	*00800 2000 0002* *www.relaischateaux.com*
RENAISSANCE HOTELS & RESORTS	**Renaissance** One of the Marriott brands, Renaissance is a collection of individual hotels offering comfortable guest rooms, quality cuisine and good levels of service.	*00800 1927 1927* *www.marriott.co.uk*
RICHARDSON HOTELS	**Richardson Hotels** A group of 5 three and four star hotels located in Cornwall and Devon, plus one hotel in Lancashire.	*www.richardsonhotels.co.uk*
THE ROCCO FORTE COLLECTION	**Rocco Forte Hotels** A small group of luxury hotels spread across Europe. Owned by Sir Rocco Forte, with three hotels in the UK, all situated in major city locations.	*0870 458 4040* *www.roccofortehotels.com*
	Scotland's Hotels of Distinction A consortium of independent Scottish hotels in the three and four star range.	*www.hotels-of-distinction.com*
Sheraton	**Sheraton** Represented in the UK by a small number of four and five star hotels in London and Scotland.	*www.starwoodhotels.com*
shire	**Shire** A small group of four star hotels which feature spa facilities and well-equipped bedrooms ideal for both business and leisure guests.	*01254 267 444 (Head Office)* *www.shirehotels.com*
SLH	**Small Luxury Hotels of the World** Part of an international consortium of mainly privately owned hotels, often in the country house style.	*0800 037 1888* *www.slh.com*
T A HOTEL COLLECTION	**TA Hotel Collection** A group of privately owned three and four star hotels in Suffolk.	*01728 452176* *www.tahotelcollection.co.uk*
THE CIRCLE	**The Circle** A consortium of independently owned, mainly two and three star hotels, across Britain.	*0845 345 1965* *www.circlehotels.co.uk*
thistle	**Thistle** A large group of 31 hotels across the UK with a significant number in London.	*0871 376 9099* *www.thistle.com*
Warner Leisure Hotels	**Warner Leisure Hotels** Exclusively for adults, a collection of four star country hotels.	*0844 871 4523* *www.warnerleisurehotels.co.uk*
WELCOMEBREAK	**Welcome Break** Good quality, modern, budget accommodation at motorway services.	*01908 299 700* *www.welcomebreak.co.uk*

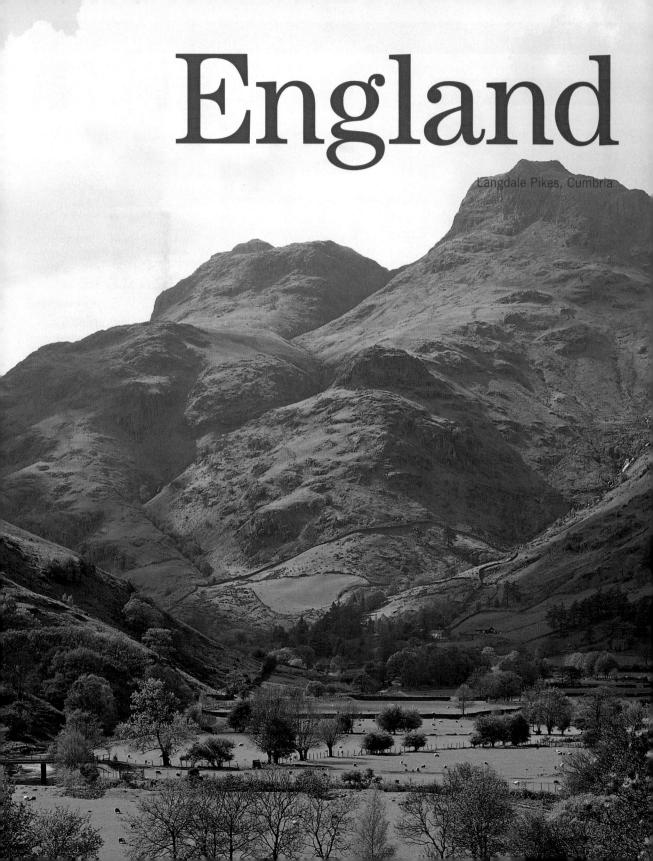

England

Langdale Pikes, Cumbria

A

ABBERLEY
Worcestershire   Map 10 SO76

The Elms Hotel
★★★ 88% ◎ ◎ HOTEL

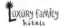

☎ 01299 896666
Stockton Rd WR6 6AT
e-mail: info@theelmshotel.co.uk
web: www.theelmshotel.co.uk
dir: On A443, 2m beyond Great Witley

This imposing Queen Anne mansion, set in delightful grounds, dates back to 1710 and offers a sophisticated yet relaxed atmosphere throughout. The spacious public rooms and generously proportioned bedrooms offer elegance and charm. The hotel is particularly well geared for families, with a host of child-friendly facilities including a crèche, a play area and wonderful high teas. Imaginative cooking is served in the elegant restaurant.

Rooms 23 (6 annexe) (1 fmly) (3 GF) �â€
S £127.50–£272; **D** £150–£320 (incl. bkfst)*
Facilities Spa FTV Wi-fi 🄌 ⌂ ⌁ Gym Xmas New Year Child facilities **Conf** Class 30 Board 22 Thtr 50 Del from £165 to £195* **Parking** 100 **Notes** LB Civ Wed 70

ABINGDON-ON-THAMES
Oxfordshire   Map 5 SU49

Oxford Abingdon Four Pillars Hotel
★★★ 77% HOTEL

☎ 0800 374 692 & 01235 553456
Marcham Rd OX14 1TZ
e-mail: abingdon@four-pillars.co.uk
web: www.four-pillars.co.uk/abingdon
dir: A34 at junct with A415, in Abingdon, turn right at rdbt, hotel on right

On the outskirts of Abingdon, this busy commercial hotel is well located for access to major roads. The

bedrooms are comfortable and well equipped with extras such as safes and trouser presses. All day refreshments are offered in the stylish lounge and conservatory.

Rooms 66 (5 fmly) (32 GF) 🌂 **S** £50–£140;
D £60–£150 **Facilities** FTV Wi-fi ⌁ Xmas New Year **Conf** Class 80 Board 40 Thtr 140 Del from £130 to £160 **Parking** 85 **Notes** LB ⊗ Civ Wed 120

Upper Reaches Hotel
★★★ 73% HOTEL

☎ 01235 522536 & 462143
Thames St OX14 3JA
e-mail:
reservations@upperreaches-abingdon.co.uk
web: www.upperreaches-abingdon.co.uk
dir: From A415 in Abingdon follow Dorchester signs, turn left just before bridge over Thames

Built from Abingdon Abbey's old corn mill, the hotel enjoys an attractive location. It offers well-appointed rooms, individually styled and with a wide range of amenities. The aptly named Millrace Restaurant is situated in the ancient mill house which still features a working wheel, and the river can be seen flowing beneath.

Rooms 31 (5 GF) **Facilities** FTV Fishing Xmas New Year **Parking** 60 **Notes** ⊗

Crown & Thistle Hotel
★★ 68% HOTEL

☎ 01235 522556
18 Bridge St OX14 3HS
e-mail: reception@crownandthistle.com
dir: A415 or A4183 to Abingdon-on-Thames. Hotel in town centre

A cosy hotel situated at the edge of a historical market town and a stone's throw from the Thames. There is a variety of bar and lounge areas and a maze of bright, airy corridors linking individually-styled bedrooms. The spacious reception leads to an outdoor courtyard for alfresco drinks and snacks. The Gallery Restaurant provides a pleasant atmosphere with satisfying cuisine served by friendly, efficient staff. Alternatively Stocks Bar offers pub dishes and a wide-screen TV for big sporting events.

Rooms 19 (3 fmly) **Facilities** Xmas **Conf** Class 8 Board 12 Thtr 12 **Parking** 35 **Notes** ⊗

Premier Inn Abingdon
BUDGET HOTEL

☎ 0871 527 8014
Marcham Rd OX14 1AD
web: www.premierinn.com
dir: On A415. Approx 0.5m from A34 at Abingdon South junct (Marcham Interchange)

High quality, budget accommodation ideal for both families and business travellers. Spacious, en suite bedrooms feature tea and coffee making facilities, and Freeview TV in most hotels. Internet access and Wi-fi are available for a small fee. The adjacent family restaurant features a wide and varied menu. See also the Hotel Groups pages.

Rooms 27

ACCRINGTON
Lancashire   Map 18 SD72

Mercure Blackburn Dunkenhalgh Hotel & Spa
★★★★ 74% HOTEL

☎ 01254 398021
Blackburn Rd, Clayton-le-Moors BB5 5JP
e-mail: H6617@accor.com
web: www.mercure.com
dir: M65 junct 7, left at rdbt, left at lights, hotel 100yds on left

Set in delightfully tended grounds yet only a stone's throw from the M65, this fine mansion has conference and banqueting facilities that attract the wedding and corporate markets. The state-of-the-art thermal suite allows guests to relax and take life easy. Bedrooms come in a variety of styles, sizes and standards; some are located away from the main hotel building.

Rooms 175 (119 annexe) (36 fmly) (43 GF) 🌂 **Facilities** Spa STV Wi-fi HL 🄌 Gym Thermal suite Aerobics studio Xmas New Year **Conf** Class 200 Board 100 Thtr 400 **Services** Lift **Parking** 400 **Notes** ⊗ Civ Wed 300

Sparth House Hotel
★★★ 74% SMALL HOTEL

☎ 01254 872263
Whalley Rd, Clayton Le Moors BB5 5RP
e-mail: mail.sparth@btinternet.com
web: www.sparthhousehotel.co.uk
dir: A6185 to Clitheroe along Dunkenhalgh Way, right at lights onto A678, left at next lights, A680 to Whalley. Hotel on left after 2 sets of lights

This 18th-century listed building sits in three acres of well-tended gardens. Bedrooms come in a choice of styles, from the cosy modern rooms ideal for business guests, to the spacious classical rooms - including one with furnishings from one of the great cruise liners. Public rooms feature a panelled restaurant and plush lounge bar.

Rooms 16 (3 fmly) **Facilities** FTV Wi-fi **Conf** Class 50 Board 40 Thtr 160 **Parking** 50 **Notes** ⊗ Civ Wed

---

ALCESTER　　　　　Map 10 SP05
Warwickshire

Kings Court Hotel

★★★ 77% HOTEL

☎ 01789 763111
Kings Coughton B49 5QQ
e-mail: info@kingscourthotel.co.uk
web: www.kingscourthotel.co.uk
dir: 1m N on A435

This privately owned hotel dates back to Tudor times and the bedrooms in the original house have oak beams. Most guests are accommodated in the well-appointed modern wings. The bar and restaurant offer very good dishes on interesting menus. The hotel is licensed to hold civil ceremonies and the pretty garden is ideal for summer weddings.

Rooms 61 (57 annexe) (2 fmly) (30 GF) ⋔ **S** £58-£68; **D** £80-£90 (incl. bkfst) **Facilities** FTV Wi-fi ⇘ Gym Xmas New Year **Conf** Class 60 Board 40 Thtr 100 Del from £104 to £125 **Parking** 200 **Notes** Civ Wed 100

ALDEBURGH　　　　　Map 13 TM45
Suffolk

Brudenell Hotel

T | A | HOTEL COLLECTION

★★★★ 85% ◉◉ HOTEL

☎ 01728 452071
The Parade IP15 5BU
e-mail: info@brudenellhotel.co.uk
web: www.brudenellhotel.co.uk
dir: A12, A1094. In town, right into High St. Hotel on seafront adjoining Fort Green car park

Situated at the far end of the town centre just a step away from the beach, this hotel has a contemporary appearance, enhanced by subtle lighting and quality soft furnishings. Many of the bedrooms have superb sea views; they include deluxe rooms with king-sized beds and superior rooms suitable for families. The informal restaurant showcases skilfully prepared dishes that use fresh, seasonal produce especially local fish, seafood and game.

Rooms 44 (17 fmly) ⋔ **S** £80-£120; **D** £150-£325 (incl. bkfst) **Facilities** Wi-fi Xmas New Year **Conf** Class 20 Board 20 Thtr 20 Del from £165 to £185 **Services** Lift **Parking** 18 **Notes** LB

Wentworth Hotel

A

★★★ 88% ◉◉ HOTEL

☎ 01728 452312
Wentworth Rd IP15 5BD
e-mail: stay@wentworth-aldeburgh.co.uk
web: www.wentworth-aldeburgh.com
dir: A12 onto A1094, 6m to Aldeburgh, with church on left, left at bottom of hill

A delightful privately owned hotel overlooking the beach. The attractive, well-maintained public rooms include three stylish lounges as well as a cocktail bar and elegant restaurant. Bedrooms are smartly decorated with co-ordinated fabrics and have many thoughtful touches; some rooms have superb sea views. Several very spacious Mediterranean-style rooms are located across the road.

Rooms 35 (7 annexe) (2 fmly) (5 GF) **Facilities** FTV Wi-fi Xmas New Year **Conf** Class 12 Board 12 Thtr 15 **Parking** 30

ALDEBURGH *continued*

The White Lion Hotel
T|A|HOTEL COLLECTION

★★★ 88% ® HOTEL

☎ 01728 452720
Market Cross Place IP15 5BJ
e-mail: info@whitelion.co.uk
web: www.whitelion.co.uk
dir: A12 onto A1094, follow signs to Aldeburgh at junct on left. Hotel on right

A popular 15th-century hotel situated at the quiet end of town overlooking the sea. Bedrooms are pleasantly decorated and thoughtfully equipped, many rooms have lovely sea views. Public areas include two lounges and an elegant restaurant, where locally-caught fish and seafood are served. There is also a modern brasserie.

Rooms 38 (1 fmly) **Facilities** STV Wi-fi Xmas New Year **Conf** Class 50 Board 50 Thtr 120 **Parking** 15 **Notes** Civ Wed 100

See advert on page 39

See advert on page 39

ALDERLEY EDGE   Map 16 SJ87
Cheshire

Alderley Edge Hotel

★★★★ 75% ®®® HOTEL

☎ 01625 583033
Macclesfield Rd SK9 7BJ
e-mail: sales@alderleyedgehotel.com
web: www.alderleyedgehotel.com
dir: From A34 in Alderley Edge onto B5087 towards Macclesfield. Hotel 200yds on right

This well-furnished hotel, with its charming grounds, was originally a country house built for one of the region's 'cotton kings'. The bedrooms and suites are attractively furnished, offering excellent quality and comfort. The welcoming bar and adjacent lounge lead into the conservatory restaurant where imaginative, memorable food and friendly, attentive service form highlights of any visit.

Rooms 50 (4 fmly) (6 GF) ⬟ **S** £99.50-£400;
D £135-£400* **Facilities** STV Wi-fi ⬟ Child facilities
Conf Class 40 Board 30 Thtr 120 Del £165*
Services Lift **Parking** 90 **Notes** LB ⊗ Closed 1 Jan
RS 25-26 Dec Civ Wed 114

Premier Inn Alderley Edge

BUDGET HOTEL

☎ 0871 527 8016
Congleton Rd SK9 7AA
web: www.premierinn.com
dir: From N: M56 junct 6, A538 towards Wilmslow, onto A34 towards Birmingham. From S: M6 junct 17, A534 towards Congleton, onto A34 towards Manchester. Hotel adjacent to De Trafford Arms

High quality, budget accommodation ideal for both families and business travellers. Spacious, en suite bedrooms feature tea and coffee making facilities, and Freeview TV in most hotels. Internet access and Wi-fi are available for a small fee. The adjacent family restaurant features a wide and varied menu. See also the Hotel Groups pages.

Rooms 37

ALDERMINSTER   Map 10 SP24
Warwickshire

INSPECTORS' CHOICE

Ettington Park Hotel
HandPICKED HOTELS · BUILT FOR PLEASURE

★★★★ ®®
COUNTRY HOUSE HOTEL

☎ 01789 450123 & 0845 072 7454
CV37 8BU
e-mail: ettingtonpark@handpicked.co.uk
web: www.handpickedhotels.co.uk/ettingtonpark
dir: Off A3400, 5m S of Stratford, just outside Alderminster

Set in 40-acre grounds in the picturesque Stour Valley, Ettington Park offers the best of both worlds - the peace of the countryside and easy access to main roads and motorway networks. Bedrooms are spacious and individually decorated; views include the delightful grounds and gardens, or the historic chapel. Luxurious day rooms extend to the period drawing room, the oak-panelled dining room with inlays of family crests, a range of contemporary meeting rooms and indoor leisure centre. Hand Picked Hotels — AA Hotel Group of the Year 2012-13.

Rooms 48 (20 annexe) (5 fmly) (10 GF)
Facilities STV Wi-fi ⬟ ⬟ ⬟ Clay pigeon shooting Archery Sauna Steam room Xmas New Year
Conf Class 48 Board 48 Thtr 90 **Services** Lift
Parking 100 **Notes** ⊗ Civ Wed 96

Save on hotels. Book at **theAA.com/hotel**

ALD – ALM 41 ENGLAND

A

ALDERSHOT Map 5 SU85
Hampshire

Potters International Hotel

★★★ 68% HOTEL

☎ 01252 344000
1 Fleet Rd GU11 2ET
e-mail: reservations@pottersinthotel.com
dir: Access via A325 & A321 towards Fleet

This modern hotel is located within easy reach of
Aldershot. Extensive air-conditioned public areas
include ample lounge areas, a pub and a more formal
restaurant; there are also conference rooms and a
very good leisure club. Bedrooms, mostly spacious,
are well equipped and have been attractively
decorated and furnished.

Rooms 103 (9 fmly) (9 GF) **Facilities** STV Wi-fi ⊗
Gym **Conf** Class 250 Board 100 Thtr 400 **Services** Lift
Parking 120 **Notes** ⊗

Premier Inn Aldershot

BUDGET HOTEL

☎ 0871 527 8018
7 Wellington Av GU11 1SQ
web: www.premierinn.com
dir: M3 junct 4, A331. A325 through Farnborough.
Pass Barons BMW then Queens Rdbt. Adjacent to
Willems Park Brewers Fayre

High quality, budget accommodation ideal for both
families and business travellers. Spacious, en suite
bedrooms feature tea and coffee making facilities,
and Freeview TV in most hotels. Internet access and
Wi-fi are available for a small fee. The adjacent
family restaurant features a wide and varied menu.
See also the Hotel Groups pages.

Rooms 60

ALDWARK Map 19 SE46
North Yorkshire

Aldwark Manor Golf & Spa Hotel

★★★★ 77% HOTEL

☎ 01347 838146
YO61 1UF
e-mail: aldwarkmanor@qhotels.co.uk
web: www.qhotels.co.uk
dir: A1/A59 towards Green Hammerton, then B6265
Little Ouseburn. Follow signs for Aldwark Bridge/
Manor. A19 through Linton-on-Ouse

Mature parkland forms the impressive backdrop for
this rambling 19th-century mansion, with the River
Ure flowing gently through the hotel's own 18-hole
golf course. Bedrooms vary - the main-house rooms
are traditional and those in the extension are modern
in design. Impressive conference and banqueting
facilities and a stylish, very well equipped leisure
club are available.

Rooms 54 (6 fmly) **Facilities** Spa FTV Wi-fi ⊗ ⅃ 18
Putt green Gym Health & beauty Xmas New Year
Conf Class 100 Board 80 Thtr 240 **Services** Lift
Parking 150 **Notes** ⊗ Civ Wed 140

ALFRISTON Map 6 TQ50
East Sussex

Deans Place

★★★ 86% ⊛⊛ HOTEL

CLASSIC
BRITISH HOTELS

☎ 01323 870248
Seaford Rd BN26 5TW
e-mail: mail@deansplacehotel.co.uk
web: www.deansplacehotel.co.uk
dir: Exit A27 between Eastbourne & Brighton, signed
Alfriston & Drusillas Zoo Park. S through village
towards Seaford

Situated on the southern fringe of the village, this
friendly hotel is set in attractive gardens. Bedrooms
vary in size and are well appointed with good

facilities. A wide range of food is offered including an
extensive bar menu and a fine dining option in
Harcourt's Restaurant.

Deans Place

Rooms 36 (4 fmly) (8 GF) **Facilities** STV FTV Wi-fi ⊀
Putt green ⊛ Boules Xmas New Year **Conf** Class 100
Board 60 Thtr 200 **Parking** 100 **Notes** Civ Wed 150

The Star Alfriston

★★★ 77% ⊛ HOTEL

☎ 01323 870495
BN26 5TA
e-mail: bookings@thestaralfriston.co.uk
dir: 2m from A27, at Drusillas rdbt follow Alfriston
signs. Hotel on right in centre of High St

Built in the 13th century and reputedly one of the
country's oldest inns, this charming establishment is
ideally situated for walking the South Downs or
exploring the Sussex coast. Bedrooms, including two
feature rooms and a mini suite, are traditionally
decorated but with comfortable, modern facilities.
Public areas include cosy lounges with open log fires,
a bar and a popular restaurant serving a wide choice
of dishes using mainly local produce. Guests can also
enjoy luxury spa treatments by appointment.

Rooms 37 (1 fmly) (11 GF) **S** £70-£85; **D** £115-£130
(incl. bkfst)* **Facilities** FTV Wi-fi Xmas New Year
Conf Class 60 Board 46 Thtr 85 Del from £125 to
£145* **Parking** 35 **Notes** LB Civ Wed 120

ALMONDSBURY Map 4 ST68
Gloucestershire

Aztec Hotel & Spa

shire
hotels & spas

★★★★ 80% ⊛ HOTEL

☎ 01454 201090
Aztec West Business Park, Almondsbury BS32 4TS
e-mail: aztec@shirehotels.com
web: www.aztechotelbristol.com

(For full entry see Bristol)

A

ALNWICK
Northumberland   Map 21 NU11

See also Embleton

White Swan Hotel
★★★ 80% HOTEL

☎ 01665 602109
Bondgate Within NE66 1TD
e-mail: info.whiteswan@classiclodges.co.uk
web: www.classiclodges.co.uk
dir: From A1 follow town centre signs. Hotel in town centre near Bondgate Tower

Situated in the heart of the historic town, this charming 300-year-old coaching inn still retains many authentic period features. The Olympic Suite Dining Room, with its original oak panelling and stained glass windows salvaged from the RMS Olympic (sister ship of the ill fated Titanic) blends well with the modern Hardy's bistro. All the bedrooms are stylishly appointed and well equipped.

Rooms 56 (5 fmly) (11 GF) **Facilities** Wi-fi Xmas New Year **Conf** Class 50 Board 40 Thtr 150 **Parking** 25 **Notes** ⊗ Civ Wed 150

ALSTON
Cumbria   Map 18 NY74

Lovelady Shield Country House Hotel
★★★ 82% ◉◉ COUNTRY HOUSE HOTEL

☎ 01434 381203 & 381305
CA9 3LF
e-mail: enquiries@lovelady.co.uk
dir: 2m E, signed off A689 at junct with B6294

Located in the heart of the Pennines close to England's highest market town, this delightful country house is set in three acres of landscaped gardens. Accommodation is provided in stylish, thoughtfully equipped bedrooms. Carefully prepared meals are served in the elegant dining room and there is a choice of appealing lounges with log fires in the cooler months.

Rooms 10 (1 fmly) **Facilities** Wi-fi Xmas New Year **Conf** Class 12 Board 12 **Parking** 20 **Notes** Civ Wed 100

Alston House
RESTAURANT WITH ROOMS

☎ 01434 382200
Townfoot CA9 3RN
e-mail: alstonhouse@fsmail.net
web: www.alstonhouse.co.uk
dir: On A686 opposite Spar garage

Located at the foot of the town, this family-owned restaurant with rooms provides well-equipped, stylish and comfortable accommodation. The kitchen serves both modern and traditional dishes with flair and creativity. Alston House runs a café during the day serving light meals and afternoon teas.

Rooms 7 (3 fmly)

ALTON
Hampshire   Map 5 SU73

The Anchor Inn
◉◉ RESTAURANT WITH ROOMS

☎ 01420 23261
Lower Froyle GU34 4NA
e-mail: info@anchorinnatlowerfroyle.co.uk
dir: From A3 follow Bentley signs & inn signs

The Anchor Inn is located in the tranquil village of Lower Froyle. Luxury rooms are designed to reflect the traditional English inn style with charming decor, pictures and a selection of books. The restaurant welcomes residents and the local population with classic pub cooking, and impressive surroundings, with wooden floors and period furnishings.

Rooms 5

ALTRINCHAM
Greater Manchester   Map 15 SJ78

Mercure Altrincham Bowden Hotel
★★★ 77% HOTEL

☎ 0161 928 7121 & 941 1866
Langham Rd, Bowdon WA14 2HT
e-mail: enquiries@hotels-altrincham.com
dir: A556 towards Manchester, into Park Rd at lights, hotel 1m on right

Situated within easy access of Manchester and the Airport, this hotel offers comfortable and well equipped bedrooms. Public areas include the Café Bar and The Restaurant, both serving a good choice of dishes. A well-equipped leisure centre has an indoor heated pool, spa, sauna and comprehensive air-condition gym. There is free Wi-fi throughout.

Rooms 87 (8 fmly) (13 GF) **Facilities** FTV Wi-fi ⊙ supervised Gym Sauna Steam room Xmas New Year **Conf** Board 40 Thtr 140 **Parking** 125 **Notes** Civ Wed 125

Premier Inn Manchester Altrincham
BUDGET HOTEL

☎ 0871 527 8738
Manchester Rd WA14 4PH
web: www.premierinn.com
dir: From N: M60 junct 7, A56 towards Altrincham. From S: M6 junct 19, A556 then A56 towards Sale

High quality, budget accommodation ideal for both families and business travellers. Spacious, en suite bedrooms feature tea and coffee making facilities, and Freeview TV in most hotels. Internet access and Wi-fi are available for a small fee. The adjacent family restaurant features a wide and varied menu. See also the Hotel Groups pages.

Rooms 46

ALVELEY
Shropshire   Map 10 SO78

Mill Hotel & Restaurant
★★★★ 78% HOTEL

☎ 01746 780437
WV15 6HL
e-mail: info@themill-hotel.co.uk
web: www.themill-hotel.co.uk
dir: Midway between Kidderminster & Bridgnorth, exit A442 signed Enville & Turley Green

Built around a 17th-century water mill, with the original water wheel still on display, this extended and renovated hotel is set in eight acres of landscaped grounds. Bedrooms are pleasant, well equipped and include some superior room, which have sitting areas. There are also some rooms with four-poster beds. The restaurant provides carefully prepared dishes and there are extensive wedding and function facilities.

Rooms 41 (5 fmly) ✦ S £65-£90; D £75-£95 (incl. bkfst) **Facilities** STV FTV Wi-fi Xmas New Year **Conf** Class 180 Board 80 Thtr 250 **Services** Lift **Parking** 212 **Notes** LB ⊗ Civ Wed 140

ALVESTON
Gloucestershire   Map 4 ST68

Alveston House Hotel

★★★ 81% ⓖ HOTEL

☎ 01454 415050
Davids Ln BS35 2LA
e-mail: info@alvestonhousehotel.co.uk
web: www.alvestonhousehotel.co.uk
dir: M5 junct 14 from N or junct 16 from S, on A38

In a quiet area with easy access to the city and a short drive from both the M4 and M5, this smartly presented hotel provides an impressive combination of good service, friendly hospitality and a relaxed atmosphere. The comfortable bedrooms are well equipped for both business and leisure guests. The restaurant offers carefully prepared fresh food, and the pleasant bar and conservatory area is perfect for enjoying a pre-dinner drink.

Rooms 30 (1 fmly) (6 GF) ⓡ **S** £75-£120; **D** £110-£140 (incl. bkfst)* **Facilities** FTV Wi-fi ⓑ Beauty treatments Xmas New Year **Conf** Class 48 Board 50 Thtr 85 Del from £125 to £145* **Parking** 75 **Notes** LB Civ Wed 75

AMBLESIDE
Cumbria   Map 18 NY30

See also Elterwater

Waterhead Hotel

English Lakes
Hotels Resorts & Venues

★★★★ 77% ⓖ TOWN HOUSE HOTEL

☎ 015394 32566
Lake Rd LA22 0ER
e-mail: waterhead@englishlakes.co.uk
web: www.englishlakes.co.uk
dir: A591 to Ambleside. Hotel opposite Waterhead Pier

With an enviable location opposite the bay, this well-established hotel offers contemporary and comfortable accommodation with CD/DVD players, plasma screens and internet access. There is a bar with a garden terrace overlooking the lake and a stylish restaurant serving classical cuisine with a modern twist. Staff are very attentive and friendly. Guests can enjoy full use of the leisure facilities at a nearby hotel.

Rooms 41 (3 fmly) (7 GF) **S** £86-£184; **D** £113-£308 (incl. bkfst)* **Facilities** FTV Wi-fi ⓑ Free use of leisure facilities at sister hotel (1m) Xmas New Year **Conf** Class 30 Board 26 Thtr 40 Del from £100 to £184* **Parking** 43 **Notes** LB Civ Wed 80

Rothay Manor

★★★ 83% ⓖ HOTEL

☎ 015394 33605
Rothay Bridge LA22 0EH
e-mail: hotel@rothaymanor.co.uk
web: www.rothaymanor.co.uk/aa
dir: In Ambleside follow signs for Coniston (A593). Hotel 0.25m SW of Ambleside opposite rugby pitch

A long-established hotel, this attractive listed building built in Regency style, is a short walk from both the town centre and Lake Windermere. Spacious bedrooms, including suites, family rooms and rooms with balconies, are comfortably equipped and furnished to a very high standard. Public areas include a choice of lounges, a spacious restaurant and conference facilities.

Rooms 19 (2 annexe) (7 fmly) (3 GF) ⓡ **S** £105; **D** £350-£470 (incl. bkfst)* **Facilities** STV Wi-fi Free use of nearby leisure centre Free fishing permit Xmas New Year **Conf** Board 18 Thtr 22 Del from £180* **Parking** 45 **Notes** LB ⓧ Closed 3-20 Jan

See advert on page 44

Best Western Ambleside Salutation Hotel

Best Western

★★★ 81% HOTEL

☎ 015394 32244
Lake Rd LA22 9BX
e-mail: ambleside@hotelslakedistrict.com
web: www.hotelslakedistrict.com
dir: A591 to Ambleside, onto one-way system, Wansfell Rd into Compston Rd. Right at lights into village

A former coaching inn, this hotel lies in the centre of the town. Bedrooms are tastefully appointed and thoughtfully equipped; many boast balconies and fine views. Inviting public areas include an attractive restaurant and a choice of comfortable lounges for relaxing, and for the more energetic there is a swimming pool and small gym, and for relaxation a spa and treatment rooms.

Rooms 52 (12 annexe) (4 fmly) (1 GF) ⓡ **S** £58-£106.50; **D** £116-£156 (incl. bkfst) **Facilities** Spa Wi-fi ⓩ Gym Sauna Steam room Xmas New Year **Conf** Class 36 Board 26 Thtr 80 Del from £81 to £130 **Services** Lift **Parking** 52 **Notes** LB

AMBLESIDE continued

Regent Hotel

★★★ 80% HOTEL

☎ 015394 32254

Waterhead Bay LA22 0ES

e-mail: info@regentlakes.co.uk

dir: 1m S on A591

This attractive holiday hotel, situated close to
Waterhead Bay, offers a warm welcome. Bedrooms
come in a variety of styles, including three suites and
five bedrooms in the garden wing. There is a modern
swimming pool and the restaurant offers a fine dining
experience in a contemporary setting.

Rooms 30 (7 fmly) (7 GF) ✿ **D** £93-£142 (incl. bkfst)
Facilities FTV Wi-fi New Year **Parking** 39
Notes Closed 19-27 Dec

The Log House

◉ RESTAURANT WITH ROOMS

☎ 015394 31077

Lake Rd LA22 0DN

e-mail: info@loghouse.co.uk

web: www.loghouse.co.uk

dir: From Windermere into Ambleside on A591. On left
after Hayes Garden Centre

This charming and historic Norwegian building is
located midway between the town centre and the
shore of Lake Windermere, just five minutes' walk to
each. Guests can enjoy delicious meals in the
attractive restaurant, which also has a bar area.
There are three comfortable bedrooms, each equipped
with thoughtful accessories such as DVD/VCR players
and hairdryers. Wi-fi is also available.

Rooms 3

AMESBURY
Wiltshire   Map 5 SU14

Holiday Inn Salisbury - Stonehenge

★★★★ 75% ◉ HOTEL

☎ 0845 241 3535

Midsummer Place, Solstice Park SP4 7SQ

e-mail:
reservations@hisalisbury-stonehenge.co.uk

web: www.hisalisbury-stonehenge.co.uk

dir: Exit A303, follow signs into Solstice Park. Hotel
adjacent to service area

This hotel of striking modern design is located on the
A303 very close to Stonehenge. All bedrooms have
been appointed to the highest standards with unique
headboards, air conditioning and broadband
connection included in the generous amenities. Fluffy
towels and powerful showers are provided in the
modern bathrooms. The Solstice Bar and Grill is open
from 7am-11pm and offers a range of snacks and
meals.

Rooms 103 (24 fmly) (8 GF) ✿ **S** £56-£131;
D £56-£131* **Facilities** FTV Wi-fi ⏶ Xmas New Year
Conf Class 20 Board 20 Thtr 25 Del from £120 to
£160* **Services** Lift Air con **Parking** 168 **Notes** ⊗

ANDOVER
Hampshire   Map 5 SU34

Esseborne Manor

★★★ 80% ◉◉ HOTEL

☎ 01264 736444

Hurstbourne Tarrant SP11 0ER

e-mail: info@esseborne-manor.co.uk

web: www.esseborne-manor.co.uk

dir: Halfway between Andover & Newbury on A343, 1m
N of Hurstbourne Tarrant

Set in two acres of well-tended gardens, this
attractive manor house is surrounded by the open
countryside of the North Wessex Downs. Bedrooms are
delightfully individual and are split between the main
house, an adjoining courtyard and separate garden
cottage. There's a wonderfully relaxed atmosphere
throughout, and public rooms combine elegance with
comfort.

Rooms 19 (8 annexe) (2 fmly) (6 GF) ✿ **S** £110-£130;
D £125-£180 (incl. bkfst) **Facilities** STV FTV Wi-fi ⏶
⏶ New Year Child facilities **Conf** Class 40 Board 30
Thtr 60 Del £135 **Parking** 50 **Notes** LB Civ Wed 100

Quality Hotel Andover

U

☎ 01264 369111
Micheldever Rd SP11 6LA
e-mail: andover@quality-hotels.co.uk
dir: At A303 & A3093 junct. At 1st rdbt 1st exit, at 2nd rdbt 1st exit. Left immediately before Total petrol station, left again

Currently the rating for this establishment is not confirmed. This may be due to a change of ownership or because it has only recently joined the AA rating scheme. For further details please see the AA website: theAA.com

Rooms 49 (36 annexe) (13 GF) **Facilities** Wi-fi
Conf Class 60 Board 60 Thtr 180 **Parking** 100
Notes Civ Wed 85

Premier Inn Andover

BUDGET HOTEL

☎ 0871 527 8020
West Portway Industrial Estate, Joule Rd SP10 3UX
web: www.premierinn.com
dir: From A303 follow A342/A343 signs. Hotel at rdbt junct of A342 & A343 adjacent to Portway Inn Brewers Fayre

High quality, budget accommodation ideal for both families and business travellers. Spacious, en suite bedrooms feature tea and coffee making facilities, and Freeview TV in most hotels. Internet access and Wi-fi are available for a small fee. The adjacent family restaurant features a wide and varied menu. See also the Hotel Groups pages.

Rooms 50

ANSTY   Map 11 SP48
Warwickshire

Macdonald Ansty Hall

★★★★ 76% ⊛ HOTEL

☎ 0844 879 9031
Main Rd CV7 9HZ
e-mail: ansty@macdonald-hotels.co.uk
web: www.macdonald-hotels.co.uk/anstyhall
dir: M6 junct 2 onto B4065 signed Ansty. Hotel 1.5m on left

Dating back to 1678, this Grade II listed Georgian house is set in eight acres of attractive grounds and woodland. The hotel enjoys a central yet tranquil location. Spacious bedrooms feature a traditional decorative style and a range of extras. Rooms are divided between the main house and the newer annexe.

Rooms 62 (39 annexe) (4 fmly) (22 GF) **S** £75-£179;
D £75-£179* **Facilities** FTV Wi-fi ⌕ Xmas New Year

Conf Class 60 Board 60 Thtr 150 Del from £140 to £175* **Services** Lift **Parking** 100 **Notes** LB Civ Wed 100

APPLEBY-IN-WESTMORLAND   Map 18 NY62
Cumbria

Appleby Manor Country House Hotel

★★★★ 78% ⊛ COUNTRY HOUSE HOTEL

☎ 017683 51571
Roman Rd CA16 6JB
e-mail: reception@applebymanor.co.uk
web: www.applebymanor.co.uk
dir: M6 junct 40, A66 towards Brough. Take Appleby turn, immediately right. 0.5m to hotel

This imposing country mansion is set in extensive grounds amid stunning Cumbrian scenery. The Dunbobbin family and their experienced staff ensure a warm welcome and attentive service. The thoughtfully equipped bedrooms vary in style and include the impressive Heelis Suite; some rooms also have patio areas. The bar offers a wide range of malt whiskies and the restaurant serves carefully prepared meals.

Rooms 30 (7 annexe) (9 fmly) (10 GF) ⚓
S £120-£150; **D** £150-£240 (incl. bkfst)*
Facilities FTV Wi-fi ⌕ ⚅ Putt green Steam room Spa bath Sauna Table tennis Pool table New Year
Conf Class 25 Board 28 Thtr 38 Del from £140 to £180* **Parking** 51 **Notes** LB ⊗ Closed 24-26 Dec RS 6-13 Jun Civ Wed 60

ARLINGHAM   Map 4 SO71
Gloucestershire

The Old Passage Inn

⊛⊛ RESTAURANT WITH ROOMS

☎ 01452 740547
Passage Rd GL2 7JR
e-mail: oldpassage@btconnect.com
dir: A38 onto B4071 through Frampton on Severn. 4m to Arlingham, through village to river

Delightfully located on the very edge of the River Severn, this relaxing restaurant with rooms combines high quality food with an air of tranquillity. Bedrooms and bathrooms are decorated in a modern style and include a range of welcome extras such as air conditioning and a well-stocked mini-bar. The menu offers a wide range of seafood and shellfish dishes including crab, oysters and lobsters from Cornwall (kept alive in seawater tanks). An outdoor terrace is available in warmer months.

Rooms 3

ARUNDEL   Map 6 TQ00
West Sussex

A

Premier Inn Arundel

BUDGET HOTEL

☎ 0871 527 8022
Crossbush Ln BN18 9PQ
web: www.premierinn.com
dir: At junct of A27 &A284, 1m E of Arundel

High quality, budget accommodation ideal for both families and business travellers. Spacious, en suite bedrooms feature tea and coffee making facilities, and Freeview TV in most hotels. Internet access and Wi-fi are available for a small fee. The adjacent family restaurant features a wide and varied menu. See also the Hotel Groups pages.

Rooms 30

The Town House

⊛⊛ RESTAURANT WITH ROOMS

☎ 01903 883847
65 High St BN18 9AJ
e-mail: enquiries@thetownhouse.co.uk
web: www.thetownhouse.co.uk
dir: A27 to Arundel, into High Street, establishment on left at top of hill

This is an elegant, Grade II-listed Regency building overlooking Arundel Castle, just a short walk from the shops and centre of the town. Bedrooms and public areas retain the building's unspoilt character. The ceiling in the dining room is particularly spectacular and originated in Florence in the 16th century. The owners can be justifiably proud of the enterprise they undertook just a few years ago.

Rooms 4

A

ASCOT
Berkshire   Map 6 SU96

Coworth Park
★★★★★ 86% COUNTRY HOUSE HOTEL

☎ 01344 876600
London Rd SL5 7SE
e-mail:
info.coworthpark@dorchestercollection.com
dir: M25 junct 13 S onto A30 to Sunningdale. Hotel on left 2 min past Wentworth Golf Club

Set in 240 acres of stunning parkland, Coworth Park is part of the luxury Dorchester Collection, sister to The Dorchester in London. The hotel offers luxurious guest rooms and suites, polo grounds, stables and a spa. Children are well cared for too, with a 'Kids Concierge' who can arrange a wide variety of activities for them. The hotel maintains a strong 'green' policy, as does the kitchen team where local quality suppliers are a priority. Casual dining is available in the popular Barn restaurant (1 AA Rosette), in a converted stable block. The AA Rosette award for the fine-dining Restaurant Coworth Park is suspended due to a change of chef. The award will be in place once our inspectors have assessed the food created by the new kitchen brigade.

Rooms 70 (40 fmly) (27 GF) ⁍ **D** £235-£520 (incl. bkfst)* **Facilities** Spa STV FTV Wi-fi ⓒ ⚂ ⚘ ⚒ Gym Polo Equestrian centre Archery Laser clays Falconry Duck herding ♫ Xmas New Year Child facilities **Conf** Class 54 Board 40 Thtr 100 Del from £325 to £545* **Services** Lift Air con **Parking** 100 **Notes** LB ⊗ Civ Wed 250

Macdonald Berystede Hotel & Spa
 MACDONALD HOTELS & RESORTS

★★★★ 78% ⊛ HOTEL

☎ 0844 879 9104
Bagshot Rd, Sunninghill SL5 9JH
e-mail: general.berystede@macdonald-hotels.co.uk
web: www.macdonald-hotels.co.uk/berystede
dir: A30, B3020 (Windmill Pub). 1.25m to hotel on left just before junct with A330

This impressive Victorian mansion, close to Ascot Racecourse, offers executive bedrooms that are spacious, comfortable and particularly well equipped. Public rooms include a cosy bar and an elegant restaurant in which creative dishes are served. An impressive self-contained conference centre and spa facility appeal to both conference and leisure guests.

Rooms 126 (61 fmly) (33 GF) **S** £95-£285; **D** £95-£285* **Facilities** Spa STV Wi-fi ⓒ ⚘ ⚒ Gym Leisure complex (thermal & beauty treatments) Outdoor garden spa Xmas New Year **Conf** Class 220 Board 150 Thtr 330 Del from £150 to £300* **Services** Lift **Parking** 200 **Notes** Civ Wed 300

Brockenhurst Hotel
★★ 67% HOTEL

☎ 01344 621912
Brockenhurst Rd SL5 9HA
e-mail: info@brockenhurst.com
dir: On A330 (near Ascot racecourse), pass course on left, right at mini rdbt, 0.5m, hotel on right

Sitting in well kept grounds and gardens, this hotel is in a convenient location in a leafy suburb in south Ascot, a short distance from the railway station. Bedrooms are comfortable and each is individually designed to reflect the hotel's unique character. Dinner is served in the contemporary dining room and offers a good range of home cooked dishes. Parking is available at this property.

Rooms 10 (3 fmly) **Facilities** Wi-fi **Parking** 30 **Notes** ⊗

Premier Inn Ascot
BUDGET HOTEL

☎ 0871 527 8024
London Rd SL5 8DR
web: www.premierinn.com
dir: M3 junct 3, A322 signed Bracknell & Ascot, follow Ascot signs. At next rdbt 1st exit to Bracknell. Hotel on right after lights. Or M4 junct 6 follow Ascot/A322 signs. Racecourse on left, at rdbt follow Bracknell/A329 signs. Hotel on right after lights

High quality, budget accommodation ideal for both families and business travellers. Spacious, en suite bedrooms feature tea and coffee making facilities, and Freeview TV in most hotels. Internet access and Wi-fi are available for a small fee. The adjacent family restaurant features a wide and varied menu. See also the Hotel Groups pages.

Rooms 28

ASENBY
North Yorkshire   Map 19 SE37

Crab Manor
⊛⊛ RESTAURANT WITH ROOMS

☎ 01845 577286
YO7 3QL
dir: A1(M) junct 49, on outskirts of village

This stunning 18th-century Grade II listed Georgian manor is located in the heart of the North Yorkshire Dales. Each bedroom is themed around the world's most famous hotels and each is uniquely designed with high quality furnishings, beautiful wallpaper, and thoughtful extras. Scandinavian log cabins are also available within the grounds, which have their own terrace with hot tubs. There is a comfortable lounge bar where guests can relax in the Manor

before enjoying dinner next door in the Crab & Lobster Restaurant, which specialises in fresh local seafood. The attractive gardens offer a lovely backdrop, and provide a pleasant place in which to relax.

Rooms 14 (6 annexe) (3 fmly)

ASHBOURNE
Derbyshire   Map 10 SK14

Callow Hall Hotel
★★★ 82% ⊛⊛ HOTEL

☎ 01335 300900
Mappleton Rd DE6 2AA
e-mail: info@callowhall.co.uk
dir: Telephone for directions

This delightful, creeper-clad, early Victorian house, set on a 44-acre estate, enjoys views over Bentley Brook and the Dove Valley. The atmosphere is relaxed and welcoming, and some of the bedrooms in the main house have comfortable sitting areas. Public rooms feature high ceilings, ornate plaster work and antique furniture. The elegant restaurant offers accomplished cuisine.

Rooms 16 **S** £105-£140; **D** £150-£210 (incl. bkfst)* **Conf** Class 40 Board 20 Thtr 40 Del from £140 to £190* **Parking** 21

ASHBY-DE-LA-ZOUCH
Leicestershire   Map 11 SK31

The Royal Hotel
★★★ 64% HOTEL

☎ 01530 412833
Station Rd LE65 2GP
e-mail: reservations@royalhotelashby.com
web: www.royalhotelashby.com
dir: A42 junct 13, A511 towards Ashby-de-la-Zouch. A511 on Nottingham Rd to Station Rd & Main Rd into town. Left at rdbt, left & left again

This Grade II listed Regency building retains much of its original character. The bedrooms, although varying in size are comfortable and well equipped; one room has a four-poster bed. The Castle Room Restaurant overlooks the lovely landscaped gardens. The staff are friendly and efficient.

Rooms 34 (4 fmly) **S** £50-£70; **D** £65-£110 (incl. bkfst)* **Facilities** STV Wi-fi **Conf** Class 26 Board 26 Thtr 70 Del from £120 to £145* **Parking** 200 **Notes** LB ⊗ Civ Wed 70

Premier Inn Ashby-De-La-Zouch

BUDGET HOTEL

☎ 0871 527 8026
Flagstaff Island LE65 1DS
web: www.premierinn.com
dir: M1 junct 23a, follow A42 (M42), Tamworth & Birmingham signs. Hotel at rdbt at A42 junct 13. (NB for Sat Nav use LE65 1JP)

High quality, budget accommodation ideal for both families and business travellers. Spacious, en suite bedrooms feature tea and coffee making facilities, and Freeview TV in most hotels. Internet access and Wi-fi are available for a small fee. The adjacent family restaurant features a wide and varied menu. See also the Hotel Groups pages.

Rooms 40

ASHFORD	Map 7 TR04
Kent	

INSPECTORS' CHOICE

Eastwell Manor

★★★★ ◉ HOTEL

☎ 01233 213000
Eastwell Park, Boughton Lees TN25 4HR
e-mail: enquiries@eastwellmanor.co.uk
dir: M20 junct 9, follow Faversham A251 signs. On A251 hotel on left on entering Boughton Lees

Set in 62 acres of landscaped grounds, this lovely hotel dates back to the Norman Conquest and boasts a number of interesting features, including carved wood-panelled rooms and huge baronial stone fireplaces. Accommodation is divided between the manor house and the courtyard mews cottages. The luxury Pavilion Spa in the grounds

has an all-day brasserie, and award-winning fine dining is offered in the main restaurant.

Eastwell Manor

Rooms 62 (39 annexe) (2 fmly) (15 GF) ☞
S £70-£335; **D** £100-£365 (incl. bkfst)*
Facilities Spa FTV Wi-fi ⊗ ⌇ ↧ 9 ☺ Putt green ☝ Gym Boules ♫ Xmas New Year **Conf** Class 70 Board 60 Thtr 180 Del from £160* **Services** Lift **Parking** 200 **Notes** LB ⊗ Civ Wed 450

Ashford International Hotel

★★★★ 80% HOTEL

☎ 01233 219988
Simone Weil Av TN24 8UX
e-mail: ashford@qhotels.co.uk
web: www.qhotels.co.uk
dir: M20 junct 9, exit for Ashford/Canterbury. Left at 1st rdbt, hotel 200mtrs on left

Situated just off the M20 and with easy links to the Eurotunnel, Eurostar and ferry terminals, this hotel has been stunningly appointed. The slick, stylishly presented bedrooms are equipped with the latest amenities. Public areas include the spacious Horizons Wine Bar and Restaurant serving a competitively priced menu, and Quench Sports Bar for relaxing drinks. The Reflections leisure club boasts a pool, fully-equipped gym, spa facilities and treatment rooms.

Rooms 179 (29 fmly) (57 GF) **S** £69-£199; **D** £79-£209 **Facilities** Spa Wi-fi ⊗ Gym Aroma steam room Rock sauna Feature shower Ice fountain Xmas New Year **Conf** Class 180 Board 26 Thtr 400 Del from £119 to £159* **Services** Lift Air con **Parking** 400 **Notes** Civ Wed 400

Holiday Inn Ashford - Central

★★★ 79% HOTEL

☎ 0870 400 9001
Canterbury Rd TN24 8QQ
e-mail: reservations-ashford@ihg.com
web: www.holidayinn.co.uk
dir: A28, at 2nd lights turn left. Hotel approx 90mtrs on right

Ideally situated within easy reach of Eurostar and Eurotunnel terminals and a short drive to historic Canterbury, this popular hotel offers stylish facilities for both business and leisure travellers. Comfortable, well-equipped bedrooms vary in size and include spacious family rooms with modern sofa beds. Public areas include a casual restaurant, lounges, bar and attractive garden area.

Rooms 103 (40 fmly) (50 GF) (12 smoking) **Facilities** STV Wi-fi Xmas **Conf** Class 64 Board 40 Thtr 120 **Parking** 120 **Notes** ⊗ Civ Wed 130

Holiday Inn Ashford - North A20

★★★ 74% HOTEL

☎ 01233 713333
Maidstone Rd, Hothfield TN26 1AR
e-mail: reception.ashford@hiashford.com
web: www.holidayinn.co.uk
dir: M20 junct 9, at rdbt take 3rd exit signed Ashford & Canterbury. At next rdbt 4th exit signed Lenham. Straight on at next rdbt. Hotel approx 3.5m on left just after Esso petrol station

This hotel is ideally situated to meet the needs of business and leisure travellers. It enjoys a rural outlook whilst occupying a convenient location for travel via the Eurostar terminal at Ashford, the channel port of Dover and the M20. There's a small bar, gym and restaurant with a 'local pub' in the grounds. Ample free parking is available.

Rooms 92 (5 fmly) (20 GF) (7 smoking) **Facilities** STV Wi-fi ⌇ Gym Xmas New Year **Conf** Class 28 Board 32 Thtr 125 **Services** Lift Air con **Parking** 140 **Notes** ⊗ Civ Wed 60

A

ASHFORD *continued*

Premier Inn Ashford Central

BUDGET HOTEL

☎ 0871 527 8030
Hall Av, Orbital Park, Sevington TN24 0GN
web: www.premierinn.com
dir: M20 junct 10 S'bound; 4th exit at rdbt. (N'bound: 1st exit onto A2070 signed Brenzett). Hotel on right at next rdbt

High quality, budget accommodation ideal for both families and business travellers. Spacious, en suite bedrooms feature tea and coffee making facilities, and Freeview TV in most hotels. Internet access and Wi-fi are available for a small fee. The adjacent family restaurant features a wide and varied menu. See also the Hotel Groups pages.

Rooms 60

Premier Inn Ashford (Eureka Leisure Park)

BUDGET HOTEL

☎ 0871 527 8028
Eureka Leisure Park TN25 4BN
web: www.premierinn.com
dir: M20 junct 9, take 1st exit on left

Rooms 74

Premier Inn Ashford North

BUDGET HOTEL

☎ 0871 527 8032
Maidstone Road (A20), Hothfield Common TN26 1AP
web: www.premierinn.com
dir: M20 junct 9, A20 follow Lenham signs. Hotel between Ashford & Charing

Rooms 60

The Wife of Bath

◉◉ RESTAURANT WITH ROOMS

☎ 01233 812232
4 Upper Bridge St, Wye TN25 5AF
e-mail: relax@thewifeofbath.com
dir: 4m NE of Ashford. M20 junct 9, A28 for Canterbury, 3m right to Wye

The Wife of Bath is set in the medieval village of Wye which is close to Dover, Canterbury and Ashford. Bedrooms are tastefully decorated and provide guests with comfortable accommodation; each is equipped with LCD TVs and DVD players (a range of DVDs is available). The stylish restaurant, with a small

separate bar area, is open for lunch and dinner daily; a cooked or continental breakfast is served here in the morning. Free Wi-fi is available throughout.

Rooms 5 (2 annexe)

ASHFORD IN THE WATER   Map 16 SK16
Derbyshire

Riverside House Hotel

★★★ 88% ◉◉ HOTEL

☎ 01629 814275
Fennel St DE45 1QF
e-mail: riversidehouse@enta.net
dir: From Bakewell towards Buxton on A6. 2m. Hotel at end of main street

This delightful and welcoming hotel, with outstanding service, is establishing a good reputation for its high quality accommodation and fine dining. In parts dating back to 1630, it enjoys a peaceful location by the River Wye. Individually styled bedrooms are thoughtfully equipped, and the smart public rooms include a bright conservatory, an oak-panelled lounge with inglenook fireplace, a drawing room and two dining rooms.

Rooms 14 (4 GF) 🌳 **S** £120-£155; **D** £145-£195 (incl. bkfst)* **Facilities** STV Wi-fi Xmas New Year **Conf** Class 15 Board 15 Thtr 15 Del £220* **Parking** 40 **Notes** LB ⊗ No children 16yrs Civ Wed 32

ASHINGTON   Map 21 NZ28
Northumberland

Premier Inn Ashington

BUDGET HOTEL

☎ 0871 527 8034
Queen Elizabeth Country Park, Woodhorn NE63 9AT
web: www.premierinn.com
dir: From A1 follow signs to Morpeth then Woodhorn Colliery Museum/Ashington. Through Ashington. Hotel in Queen Elizabeth II Country Park

High quality, budget accommodation ideal for both families and business travellers. Spacious, en suite bedrooms feature tea and coffee making facilities, and Freeview TV in most hotels. Internet access and Wi-fi are available for a small fee. The adjacent family restaurant features a wide and varied menu. See also the Hotel Groups pages.

Rooms 20

ASHWATER   Map 3 SX39
Devon

INSPECTORS' CHOICE

Blagdon Manor

◉◉ RESTAURANT WITH ROOMS

☎ 01409 211224
EX21 5DF
e-mail: stay@blagdon.com
web: www.blagdon.com
dir: A388 towards Launceston/Holsworthy. Approx 2m N of Chapman's Well take 2nd right for Ashwater. Next right beside Blagdon Lodge, 0.25m to manor

Located on the borders of Devon and Cornwall within easy reach of the coast, and set in its own beautifully kept natural gardens, this small and friendly restaurant with rooms offers a charming home-from-home atmosphere. The tranquillity of the secluded setting, the character and charm of the house and its unhurried pace ensure calm and relaxation. High levels of service, personal touches and thoughtful extras are all part of a stay here. Steve Morey cooks with passion and his commitment to using only the finest local ingredients speaks volumes.

Rooms 7

ASPLEY GUISE   Map 11 SP93
Bedfordshire

Best Western Moore Place Hotel

★★★ 78% HOTEL

☎ 01908 282000
The Square MK17 8DW
e-mail: manager@mooreplace.com
dir: M1 junct 13, A507 signed Aspley Guise & Woburn Sands. Hotel on left in village square

This impressive Georgian house, set in delightful gardens in the village centre, is very conveniently located for the M1. Bedrooms do vary in size, but consideration has been given to guest comfort, with many thoughtful extras provided. There is a wide range of meeting rooms and private dining options.

Rooms 62 (27 annexe) (16 GF) **S** £55-£99; **D** £79-£140* **Facilities** FTV Wi-fi 🐾 **Conf** Class 24 Board 20 Thtr 40 Del from £99 to £140* **Parking** 70 **Notes** LB Civ Wed 65

Save on hotels. Book at **theAA.com/hotel**

ASH – AYL   49   ENGLAND

A

ATHERSTONE   Map 10 SP39
Warwickshire

Chapel House Restaurant With Rooms

◉ RESTAURANT WITH ROOMS

☎ 01827 718949
Friar's Gate CV9 1EY
e-mail: info@chapelhouse.eu
web: www.chapelhouse.eu
dir: A5 to town centre, right into Church St. Right into Sheepy Rd, left into Friar's Gate

Sitting next to the church this 18th-century town house offers excellent hospitality and service while the cooking, using much local produce, is very notable. Bedrooms are well equipped and lounges are extensive; there is also a delightful walled garden for guests to use.

Rooms 11

AUSTWICK   Map 18 SD76
North Yorkshire

The Traddock

◉◉ RESTAURANT WITH ROOMS

☎ 015242 51224
LA2 8BY
e-mail: info@austwicktraddock.co.uk
dir: From Skipton take A65 towards Kendal, 3m after Settle turn right signed Austwick, cross hump back bridge, 100yds on left

Situated within the Yorkshire Dales National Park and a peaceful village environment, this fine Georgian country house with well-tended gardens offers a haven of calm and good hospitality. There are two comfortable lounges with real fires and fine furnishings, as well as a cosy bar and an elegant dining room serving fine cuisine. Bedrooms are individually styled with many homely touches.

Rooms 12 (2 fmly)

AXMINSTER   Map 4 SY29
Devon

See also Colyford

Fairwater Head Hotel

★★★ 77% ◉ HOTEL

☎ 01297 678349
Hawkchurch EX13 5TX
e-mail: stay@fairwaterheadhotel.co.uk
web: www.fairwaterheadhotel.co.uk
dir: From B3165 (Crewkerne to Lyme Regis road) follow Hawkchurch signs

This elegant Edwardian country house provides a perfect location for anyone looking for a peaceful break. Surrounded by extensive gardens and rolling countryside, the setting guarantees relaxation. Bedrooms are located both within the main house and the garden wing; all provide good levels of comfort. Public areas have much appeal and include lounge areas, a bar and an elegant restaurant. Food is a highlight with excellent local produce prepared with care and skill.

Rooms 16 (4 annexe) (8 GF) 🐾 **S** £67-£172; **D** £85-£190 (incl. bkfst) **Facilities** FTV Wi-fi Library Xmas New Year **Conf** Class 25 Board 20 Thtr 35 Del from £152 to £185 **Parking** 30 **Notes** LB Closed 1-30 Jan Civ Wed 50

AYCLIFFE   Map 19 NZ22
Co Durham

The County Restaurant with Rooms

RESTAURANT WITH ROOMS

☎ 01325 312273
12 The Green DL5 6LX
e-mail: info@thecountyaycliffevillage.com
dir: A1(M) junct 59, A167 towards Newton Aycliffe. In Aycliffe turn onto village green

Located overlooking the pretty village green yet convenient for the A1, the focus here is on fresh, home-cooked meals, real ales and friendly service. There is a relaxed atmosphere in the bar area, and the restaurant where attractive artwork is displayed. The bedrooms in the smart townhouse next door are all furnished to a high standard.

Rooms 7

AYLESBURY   Map 11 SP81
Buckinghamshire

Hartwell House Hotel, Restaurant & Spa

★★★★ ◉◉ HOTEL

☎ 01296 747444
Oxford Rd HP17 8NR
e-mail: info@hartwell-house.com
web: www.hartwell-house.com
dir: From S: M40 junct 7, A329 to Thame, then A418 towards Aylesbury. After 6m, through Stone, hotel on left. From N: M40 junct 9 for Bicester. A41 to Aylesbury, A418 to Oxford for 2m. Hotel on right

This beautiful, historic house is set in 90 acres of unspoilt parkland. The grand public rooms are truly magnificent, and feature many fine works of art. The service standards are very high; guests will find that the staff offer attentive and traditional hospitality without stuffiness. There is an elegant, award-winning restaurant where carefully prepared dishes use the best local produce. Bedrooms are spacious, elegant and very comfortable. Most are in the main house, but some, including suites, are in the nearby, renovated coach house, which also houses an excellent spa.

Rooms 46 (16 annexe) (3 fmly) (10 GF) 🐾 **S** £175; **D** £205-£290 (incl. bkfst)* **Facilities** Spa STV Wi-fi ⊿ ⊛ supervised 🎾 ⚓ Gym Sauna Beauty treatment rooms Steam rooms ♬ Xmas New Year **Conf** Class 40 Board 40 Thtr 100 Del from £225 to £295* **Services** Lift **Parking** 91 **Notes** LB No children 4yrs RS Xmas/New Year Civ Wed 120

AYLESBURY *continued*

Holiday Inn Aylesbury

★★★ 77% HOTEL *Holiday Inn*

☎ 01296 734000
Aston Clinton Rd HP22 5AA
e-mail: aylesbury@ihg.com
web: www.holidayinn.co.uk
dir: M25 junct 20, follow A41. Hotel on left on entering Aylesbury

Situated to the south of town, this hotel is conveniently located for local businesses and the town centre. Public areas are extensive including the well-equipped health club and a superb range of meeting rooms. Bedrooms are comfortable and are equipped with a host of extras.

Rooms 139 (45 fmly) (69 GF) (8 smoking)
Facilities Spa STV Wi-fi ⓢ supervised Gym Steam room Sauna Dance studio Gym New Year
Conf Class 50 Board 50 Thtr 120 **Services** Air con **Parking** 160 **Notes** Civ Wed 120

Premier Inn Aylesbury

BUDGET HOTEL *Premier Inn*

☎ 0871 527 8036
Buckingham Rd HP19 9QL
web: www.premierinn.com
dir: From Aylesbury on A413 towards Buckingham. Hotel in 1m on left adjacent to lights

High quality, budget accommodation ideal for both families and business travellers. Spacious, en suite bedrooms feature tea and coffee making facilities, and Freeview TV in most hotels. Internet access and Wi-fi are available for a small fee. The adjacent family restaurant features a wide and varied menu. See also the Hotel Groups pages.

Rooms 64

AYLESFORD
Kent   Map 6 TQ75

Hamlets Hotel & Restaurant

★★★ 62% HOTEL

☎ 01732 846858
802 London Rd ME20 6HJ
e-mail: reservations@hamletshotel.com
dir: M20 junct 4, A228, A20. Hotel on left adjacent to B&Q

This Georgian house was rebuilt in 1846 and retains much of traditional charm. It is conveniently located within easy reach of London as well as Gatwick and Heathrow airports, the south coast and the Channel Tunnel. The accommodation is comfortable and the public areas include a well-stocked, pub-style bar.

Rooms 52 (4 fmly) (9 GF) **S** £57-£89; **D** £138-£190 (incl. bkfst) **Facilities** FTV Wi-fi New Year **Conf** Class 35 Board 35 Thtr 90 Del from £125 to £155* **Parking** 45 **Notes** ⊗ Civ Wed 80

AYNHO
Northamptonshire   Map 11 SP53

Cartwright Hotel

★★★ 79% HOTEL

☎ 01869 811885
1-5 Croughton Rd OX17 3BE
e-mail: cartwright@oxfordshire-hotels.co.uk
dir: M40 junct 10, A43, B4100 to Aynho

This former coaching inn is located between Banbury and Oxford, making it ideally located for visiting the many tourist attractions the area has to offer including Blenheim Palace and the circuit at Silverstone. The hotel features individually designed bedrooms which range from double to executive, and premiere standards with flat-screen digital TVs and complimentary Wi-fi. Secure parking is available.

Rooms 21 (12 annexe) (2 fmly) (12 GF) ⓣ
S £75-£145; **D** £75-£175 (incl. bkfst)* **Facilities** FTV Wi-fi Xmas New Year **Conf** Class 40 Board 20 Thtr 60 Del from £140 to £160* **Parking** 15 **Notes** LB ⊗

BABBACOMBE

See Torquay

BACTON
Norfolk   Map 13 TG33

The Keswick Hotel

★★★ 70% ⓢ HOTEL

☎ 01692 650468
Walcott Rd NR12 0LS
e-mail: margaret@keswickhotelbacton.co.uk
web: www.keswickhotelbacton.co.uk
dir: On B1159 (coast road)

A small personally run hotel situated by the sea within easy driving distance of the Broads and north Norfolk coastline. The individually decorated bedrooms are pleasantly appointed, have modern facilities and either sea or countryside views. Public areas include a cosy lounge bar with plush sofas, a further lounge area, a restaurant and a conservatory.

Rooms 9 (1 fmly) (3 GF) **S** £39.95; **D** £69.95 (incl. bkfst)* **Facilities** FTV Wi-fi **Parking** 75

BAGSHOT
Surrey   Map 6 SU96

Pennyhill Park Hotel & The Spa

★★★★★ ⓢⓢⓢⓢⓢ
COUNTRY HOUSE HOTEL

☎ 01276 471774
London Rd GU19 5EU
e-mail: enquiries@pennyhillpark.co.uk
web: www.pennyhillpark.co.uk
dir: M3 junct 3, follow signs to Camberley. On A30 between Bagshot & Camberley

This delightful country-house hotel, set in 120-acre grounds, provides every modern comfort. The stylish bedrooms are individually designed and have impressive bathrooms. Leisure facilities include a jogging trail, a golf course and a state-of-the-art spa with a thermal sequencing experience, ozone treated swimming and hydrotherapy pools along with a comprehensive range of therapies and treatments. The Latymer restaurant, overseen by chef Michael Wignall, has become a true dining destination in its own right. The cooking is outstanding and great care is made to source first-rate ingredients, much from local suppliers. There is an eight-seater chef's table for enjoying the tasting menu while watching the action in the kitchen. In addition there are other eating options, and lounges and bars to relax in.

Rooms 123 (97 annexe) (6 fmly) (26 GF) ⓣ
D £195-£1350* **Facilities** Spa STV Wi-fi ⓢ ♨ ♪ 9 ♨ Fishing ♨ Gym Archery Clay shooting Plunge pool Turkish steam room Rugby/football pitch ♫ Xmas New Year **Conf** Class 108 Board 60 Thtr 140 Del from £280 to £425* **Services** Lift **Parking** 500 **Notes** LB Civ Wed 140

Save on hotels. Book at **theAA.com/hotel**

AYL – BAL   51   ENGLAND

Premier Inn Bagshot

BUDGET HOTEL

☎ 0871 527 8040
1 London Rd GU19 5HR
web: www.premierinn.com
dir: On A30 (London Rd) just before junct with A322 (Bracknell Rd). Adjacent to Cricketers Beefeater

High quality, budget accommodation ideal for both families and business travellers. Spacious, en suite bedrooms feature tea and coffee making facilities, and Freeview TV in most hotels. Internet access and Wi-fi are available for a small fee. The adjacent family restaurant features a wide and varied menu. See also the Hotel Groups pages.

Rooms 39

BAINBRIDGE   Map 18 SD99
North Yorkshire

Yorebridge House

◉◉ RESTAURANT WITH ROOMS

☎ 01969 652060
DL8 3EE
e-mail: enquiries@yorebridgehouse.co.uk
dir: A648 to Bainbridge. Yorebridge House N of centre on right before river

Yorebridge House is situated by the river on the edge of Bainbridge, in the heart of the North Yorkshire Dales. In the Victorian era this was a schoolmaster's house and school, but this building now offers luxury boutique-style accommodation. Each bedroom is individually designed with high quality furnishings and thoughtful extras. All rooms have stunning views of the Dales and some have their own terrace with hot tubs. There is a comfortable lounge bar where guests can relax before enjoying dinner in the attractive and elegant dining room.

Rooms 11 (4 annexe) (11 fmly)

BAKEWELL   Map 16 SK26
Derbyshire

Monsal Head Hotel

★★ 83% ◉ HOTEL

☎ 01629 640250 & 814275
Monsal Head DE45 1NL
e-mail: enquiries@monsalhead.com
web: www.monsalhead.com
dir: A6 from Bakewell to Buxton. In 2m turn into Ashford in the Water, take B6465 for 1m. Hotel on left through public car park entrance

Situated three miles from Bakewell and overlooking the picturesque Monsal Dale in the Peak District National Park, this hotel is full of charm and

character. The bedrooms have beautiful views, and public areas include the Ashford Room, a quiet residents' lounge, and Longstone Restaurant. The converted stables bar adjacent to the hotel has an excellent choice of cask ales and lagers.

Rooms 7 (1 fmly) ✺ **S** £70-£90; **D** £100-£160 (incl. bkfst & dinner) **Facilities** FTV Xmas New Year **Conf** Class 30 Board 20 Thtr 50 **Parking** 20 **Notes** LB RS 25 Dec

---

BALDOCK   Map 12 TL23
Hertfordshire

Days Inn Stevenage North - A1

BUDGET HOTEL

☎ 01462 730598
Baldock Extra Motorways, A1(M) Junction 10, Radwell SG7 5TR
e-mail: stevenage.hotel@welcomebreak.co.uk
dir: A1(M) junct 10 Baldock Extra Services

This modern, purpose built accommodation offers smartly appointed, well-equipped bedrooms, with good power showers. There is a choice of adjacent food outlets where guests may enjoy breakfast, snacks and meals. See also the Hotel Groups pages.

Rooms 62 (14 fmly) (30 GF) (8 smoking)
Conf Del from £49.95 to £125.95

BALSALL COMMON   Map 10 SP27
West Midlands

Nailcote Hall

★★★★ 76% ◉ HOTEL

☎ 024 7646 6174
Nailcote Ln, Berkswell CV7 7DE
e-mail: info@nailcotehall.co.uk
web: www.nailcotehall.co.uk
dir: On B4101

This 17th-century house, set in 15 acres of grounds, boasts a 9-hole championship golf course and Roman bath-style swimming pool amongst its many facilities. The bedrooms are spacious and elegantly furnished. The eating options are the fine dining restaurant where smart casual dress is required, or The Piano Bar where more informal meals are served.

Rooms 40 (19 annexe) (2 fmly) (15 GF) **Facilities** STV FTV Wi-fi ⊗ supervised ⌀ 9 ⚑ Putt green ⚑ Gym ♫ Xmas New Year **Conf** Class 80 Board 44 Thtr 140 Del from £135 to £165* **Services** Lift **Parking** 200 **Notes** ⊗ Civ Wed 120

Haigs Hotel

★★★ 73% HOTEL

☎ 01676 533004
Kenilworth Rd CV7 7EL
e-mail: info@haigshotel.co.uk
dir: A45 towards Coventry, at Stonebridge Island turn right, 4m S of M42 junct 6

Conveniently located just five miles from Birmingham Airport and twelve miles from Stratford-upon-Avon. This small family-run hotel offers its guests a comfortable stay. Enjoyable meals on a monthly changing menu can be taken in McKee's Restaurant.

Rooms 22 (2 fmly) (4 GF) **S** £55-£65; **D** £65-£75 (incl. bkfst) **Facilities** Wi-fi Xmas New Year **Conf** Board 20 Thtr 25 Del from £95.50* **Parking** 23 **Notes** LB Civ Wed 60

Premier Inn Balsall Common (Near NEC)

BUDGET HOTEL

☎ 0871 527 8042
Kenilworth Rd CV7 7EX
web: www.premierinn.com
dir: M42 junct 6, A45 towards Coventry for 0.5m. A452 signed Leamington/Kenilworth. In 3m hotel on right

High quality, budget accommodation ideal for both families and business travellers. Spacious, en suite bedrooms feature tea and coffee making facilities, and Freeview TV in most hotels. Internet access and Wi-fi are available for a small fee. The adjacent family restaurant features a wide and varied menu. See also the Hotel Groups pages.

Rooms 42

B

B

BAMBURGH
Northumberland | Map 21 NU13

Waren House Hotel
★★★ 85% ◉ COUNTRY HOUSE HOTEL

☎ 01668 214581
Waren Mill NE70 7EE
e-mail: enquiries@warenhousehotel.co.uk
web: www.warenhousehotel.co.uk
dir: 2m E of A1 turn onto B1342 to Waren Mill, at T-junct turn right, hotel 100yds on right

This delightful Georgian mansion is set in six acres of woodland and offers a welcoming atmosphere and views of the coast. The individually themed bedrooms and suites include many with large bathrooms. Good, home-cooked food is served in the elegant dining room. A comfortable lounge and library are also available.

Rooms 15 (4 annexe) (3 GF) **Facilities** FTV Wi-fi ↳ Xmas New Year **Conf** Class 16 Board 16 **Parking** 20 **Notes** No children 14yrs

Victoria Hotel
★★★ 81% ◉ HOTEL

☎ 01668 214431
Front St NE69 7BP
e-mail: chris@thevictoriahotelbamburgh.co.uk

Set on the delightful village green and overlooked by Bamburgh Castle, this hotel offers modern accommodation; all the bedrooms have high quality furnishings and modern conveniences including LCD TV, a hairdryer, trouser press and complimentary refreshment tray. Bailey's Bar and Restaurant offers locally sourced food on menus served throughout the day. The staff pay great attention to detail and the hotel makes an ideal base from which to tour this beautiful area of Northumberland.

Rooms 36 **S** £35-£60; **D** £65-£180 (incl. bkfst)* **Conf** Class 20 Board 12 Thtr 25 Del from £90 to £150*

The Lord Crewe
★★★ 81% HOTEL

☎ 01668 214243 & 214613
Front St NE69 7BL
e-mail: enquiries@lordcrewe.co.uk
dir: Just below castle

Located in the heart of the village in the shadow of impressive Bamburgh Castle, this hotel has been developed from an old inn. Public areas combine modern and traditional very well and include a choice of lounges, a cosy bar and a smart modern Italian restaurant. Bedrooms vary in size, but all are well equipped and offer modern amenities.

Rooms 17 **D** £105-£145 (incl. bkfst)* **Facilities** FTV Wi-fi **Parking** 20 **Notes** ⊗ No children 5yrs Closed 25-26 Dec & 6 Jan-1 Feb

BANBURY
Oxfordshire | Map 11 SP44

Best Western Plus Wroxton House Hotel
★★★ 82% ◉ HOTEL

☎ 01295 730777
Wroxton St Mary OX15 6QB
e-mail: reservations@wroxtonhousehotel.com
dir: M40 junct 11, A422 signed Banbury & Wroxton. Approx 3m, hotel on right on entering Wroxton

Dating in parts from 1649, this partially thatched hotel is set just off the main road. Bedrooms, either created from cottages or situated in a contemporary wing, are comfortable and well equipped with Wi-fi and LCD TVs. The public areas are open plan and the low-beamed Restaurant 1649 has a peaceful atmosphere for dining.

Rooms 32 (3 annexe) (5 fmly) (8 GF) ✿ **Facilities** FTV Wi-fi ↳ Xmas New Year **Conf** Class 40 Board 40 Thtr 80 Del from £125 to £142* **Parking** 60 **Notes** ⊗ Civ Wed 80

Mercure Banbury Whately Hall Hotel
★★★ 77% HOTEL

☎ 01295 253261
Banbury Cross OX16 0AN
e-mail: h6633@accor.com
web: www.mercure.com
dir: M40 junct 11, straight over 2 rdbts, left at 3rd, 0.25m to Banbury Cross, hotel on right

Dating back to 1677, this historic inn boasts many original features such as stone passages, priests' holes and a fine wooden staircase. Spacious public areas include the oak-panelled restaurant, which overlooks the attractive well-tended gardens, a choice of lounges and a traditional bar. Smartly appointed bedrooms vary in size and style but all are thoughtfully equipped.

Rooms 69 (6 fmly) (2 GF) **Facilities** FTV Wi-fi Xmas New Year **Conf** Class 40 Board 40 Thtr 120 **Services** Lift **Parking** 52 **Notes** ⊗ Civ Wed 150

Premier Inn Banbury
BUDGET HOTEL

☎ 0871 527 8044
Warwick Rd, Warmington OX17 1JJ
web: www.premierinn.com
dir: From N: M40 junct 12, B4451, B4100 towards Warmington. From S: M40 junct 11, A423, A422, B4100. Hotel adjacent to Wobbly Wheel Brewers Fayre

High quality, budget accommodation ideal for both families and business travellers. Spacious, en suite bedrooms feature tea and coffee making facilities, and Freeview TV in most hotels. Internet access and Wi-fi are available for a small fee. The adjacent family restaurant features a wide and varied menu. See also the Hotel Groups pages.

Rooms 39

BARFORD
Warwickshire | Map 10 SP26

The Glebe at Barford
★★★ 74% HOTEL

☎ 01926 624218
Church St CV35 8BS
e-mail: sales@glebehotel.co.uk
dir: M40 junct 15/A429 (Stow). At mini island turn left, hotel 500mtrs on right

The giant Lebanese cedar tree in front of this hotel was ancient even in 1820, when the original rectory was built. Public rooms within the house include a lounge bar and the aptly named Cedars Conservatory Restaurant which offers interesting cuisine. Individually appointed bedrooms are tastefully decorated in soft pastel fabrics, with coronet, tented ceiling or four-poster style beds.

Rooms 39 (3 fmly) (4 GF) **Facilities** STV Wi-fi ↳ ✪ Gym Beauty salon Xmas New Year **Conf** Class 40 Board 40 Thtr 120 **Services** Lift **Parking** 60 **Notes** Civ Wed 120

Save on hotels. Book at **theAA.com/hotel**

BAM – BAR 53 ENGLAND

B

BARKING
Greater London Map 6 TG48

Ibis London East Barking

BUDGET HOTEL

- -

☎ 020 8477 4100
Highbridge Rd IG11 7BA
e-mail: H2042@accor.com
web: www.ibishotel.com
dir: Exit Barking from A406 or A13

Modern, budget hotel offering comfortable accommodation in bright and practical bedrooms. Breakfast is self-service and dinner is available in the restaurant. See also the Hotel Groups pages.

Rooms 86 (26 GF) **S** £55-£180; **D** £55-£180*

Premier Inn Barking

BUDGET HOTEL

- -

☎ 0871 527 8048
Highbridge Rd IG11 7BA
web: www.premierinn.com
dir: A13 onto A406 signed Barking/Ilford. At Barking, exit at Tesco/A406 slip road. Hotel on left

High quality, budget accommodation ideal for both families and business travellers. Spacious, en suite bedrooms feature tea and coffee making facilities, and Freeview TV in most hotels. Internet access and Wi-fi are available for a small fee. The adjacent family restaurant features a wide and varied menu. See also the Hotel Groups pages.

Rooms 88

BARLBOROUGH
Derbyshire Map 16 SK47

Ibis Sheffield North

BUDGET HOTEL

- -

☎ 01246 813222
Tallys End, Chesterfield Rd S43 4TX
e-mail: H3157@accor.com
web: www.ibishotel.com
dir: M1 junct 30. Towards A619, right at rdbt towards Chesterfield. Hotel immediately left

Modern, budget hotel offering comfortable accommodation in bright and practical bedrooms. Breakfast is self-service and dinner is available in the restaurant. See also the Hotel Groups pages.

Rooms 86 (22 fmly) **Conf** Board 18 Thtr 35

BARNARD CASTLE
Co Durham Map 19 NZ01

The Morritt
★★★★ 80% ◉ HOTEL

- -

☎ 01833 627232
Greta Bridge DL12 9SE
e-mail: relax@themorritt.co.uk
web: www.themorritt.co.uk
dir: Exit A1 (A1(M)) at Scotch Corner onto A66 W'bound towards Penrith. Greta Bridge 9m on left

In the heart of beautiful Teesdale, this 17th-century former coaching house, with connections to Dickens, is full of character and is a popular meeting place for every occasion. The bar area is resplendent with two amazing Dickens murals - one newly created in 2012 to commemorate Dickens' 200th birthday. The hotel has equally impressive traditional values apparent in its service, locally-sourced food and individually styled rooms. Added relaxation in the way of unparalleled pampering and treatments in the adjoining new spa, The Garage, will be available from November 2012.

Rooms 27 (6 annexe) (3 fmly) (4 GF) ⚓ **S** £85-£110; **D** £95-£200 (incl. bkfst) **Facilities** Spa FTV Wi-fi ⚲ Xmas New Year **Conf** Class 60 Board 50 Thtr 200 Del from £115 **Parking** 40 **Notes** LB Civ Wed 200

BARNBY MOOR
Nottinghamshire Map 16 SK68

Ye Olde Bell Hotel & Restaurant
★★★★ 78% HOTEL

- -

☎ 01777 705121
DN22 8QS
e-mail: enquiries@yeoldebell-hotel.co.uk
web: www.yeoldebell-hotel.co.uk
dir: A1(M) south near junct 24, exit Barnby Moor or A1(M) north exit A620 Retford. Hotel on A638 between Retford & Bawtry

A 17th-century coaching inn situated in the rural village of Barnby Moor near Retford. Public rooms have a wealth of original character such as traditional log fires, ornate plaster work and wood panelling. The tastefully appointed bedrooms have

---

superb co-ordinated soft furnishings and many thoughtful touches.

Rooms 57 (8 annexe) (5 fmly) (8 GF) ⚓ **Facilities** FTV Wi-fi ⚲ Gym Hair & beauty salon Xmas New Year **Conf** Class 100 Board 50 Thtr 250 Del from £145 to £195* **Parking** 200 **Notes** ⊗ Civ Wed 250

BARNHAM BROOM
Norfolk Map 13 TG00

Barnham Broom Hotel, Golf & Restaurant
★★★★ 74% ◉◉ HOTEL

- -

☎ 01603 759393
NR9 4DD
e-mail: amortimer@barnham-broom.co.uk
web: www.barnham-broom.co.uk
dir: A11/A47 towards Swaffham, follow brown tourist signs

Situated in a peaceful rural location just a short drive from Norwich, this hotel offers contemporary style bedrooms that are tastefully furnished and thoughtfully equipped. The Sports Bar serves a range of snacks and meals throughout the day, or guests can choose from the a la carte menu in Flints Restaurant. There also are extensive leisure, conference and banqueting facilities.

Rooms 46 (11 fmly) (22 GF) **Facilities** Spa STV Wi-fi ⚲ ③ supervised ⚑ 36 ⛳ Putt green Gym Squash Sauna Steam room Personal trainers Xmas New Year **Conf** Class 100 Board 80 Thtr 250 Del from £125* **Parking** 150 **Notes** ⊗ Civ Wed 200

BARNSLEY
South Yorkshire Map 16 SE30

Tankersley Manor

★★★★ 77% HOTEL

- -

☎ 01226 744700
Church Ln S75 3DQ
e-mail: tankersleymanor@qhotels.co.uk
web: www.qhotels.co.uk

(For full entry see Tankersley)

B

BARNSLEY *continued*

Premier Inn Barnsley Central M1 Jct 37

BUDGET HOTEL

☎ 0871 527 9204
Gateway Plaza, Sackville St S70 2RD
web: www.premierinn.com
dir: M1 junct 37, A628 (Dodworth Rd) signed
Barnsley. In approx 1m 2nd exit at rdbt into Shambles
St, car park entrance on left

High quality, budget accommodation ideal for both
families and business travellers. Spacious, en suite
bedrooms feature tea and coffee making facilities,
and Freeview TV in most hotels. Internet access and
Wi-fi are available for a small fee. The adjacent
family restaurant features a wide and varied menu.
See also the Hotel Groups pages.

Rooms 110

BARNSTAPLE	Map 3 SS53
Devon	

The Imperial

★★★★ 75% HOTEL

☎ 01271 345861
Taw Vale Pde EX32 8NB
e-mail: reservations@brend-imperial.co.uk
web: www.brend-imperial.co.uk
dir: M5 junct 27/A361 to Barnstaple. Follow town
centre signs, passing Tesco. Straight on at next 2
rdbts. Hotel on right

This smart and attractive hotel is pleasantly located
at the centre of Barnstaple and overlooks the river.
The staff are friendly and offer attentive service. The
comfortable bedrooms are of various sizes; some have
balconies and many overlook the river. Afternoon tea
is available in the lounge, and the appetising cuisine
is freshly prepared.

The Imperial

Rooms 63 (9 fmly) (4 GF) ☞ **S** £87-£185;
D £97-£185* **Facilities** FTV Wi-fi ⓑ Leisure facilities
at sister hotel Xmas New Year **Conf** Class 40
Board 30 Thtr 60 **Services** Lift **Parking** 80 **Notes** LB
⊗ Civ Wed 50

See advert on opposite page

Barnstaple Hotel

★★★ 80% HOTEL

☎ 01271 376221
Braunton Rd EX31 1LE
e-mail: reservations@barnstaplehotel.co.uk
web: www.barnstaplehotel.co.uk
dir: Outskirts of Barnstaple on A361

This well-established hotel enjoys a convenient
location on the edge of town. Bedrooms are spacious
and well equipped, many with access to a balcony
overlooking the outdoor pool and garden. A wide
choice is offered from various menus based on local
produce, served in the Brasserie Restaurant. There is
an extensive range of leisure and conference
facilities.

Rooms 60 (4 fmly) (17 GF) ☞ **S** £67-£105;
D £72-£115* **Facilities** FTV Wi-fi ⓑ ⓧ ⚲ Gym
Beauty treatment room Saunas Barnstable health &
leisure club part of hotel Xmas New Year Child
facilities **Conf** Class 100 Board 50 Thtr 250
Parking 250 **Notes** LB ⊗ Civ Wed 150

Park Hotel

★★★ 78% HOTEL

☎ 01271 372166
Taw Vale EX32 9AE
e-mail: reservations@parkhotel.co.uk
web: www.parkhotel.co.uk
dir: A361 to Barnstable, 0.5m from town centre.
Opposite Rock Park

Enjoying views across the park and within easy
walking distance of the town centre, this modern
hotel offers a choice of bedrooms in both the main
building and the Garden Court, just across the car
park. Public rooms are open-plan in style and the
friendly staff offer attentive service in a relaxed
atmosphere.

Rooms 40 (17 annexe) (3 fmly) (2 GF) ☞ **S** £57-£72;
D £62-£82* **Facilities** FTV Wi-fi ⓑ Leisure facilities
available at sister hotel Xmas New Year
Conf Class 50 Board 30 Thtr 80 **Parking** 100
Notes LB ⊗ Civ Wed 100

Royal & Fortescue Hotel

★★★ 78% HOTEL

☎ 01271 342289
Boutport St EX31 1HG
e-mail: reservations@royalfortescue.co.uk
web: www.royalfortescue.co.uk
dir: From A361 onto Barbican Rd signed town centre,
right into Queen St, left into Boutport St, hotel on left

Formerly a coaching inn, this friendly and convivial
hotel is conveniently located in the centre of town.

Bedrooms vary in size and all are decorated and furnished to a consistently high standard. In addition to the formal restaurant, guests can take snacks in the popular coffee shop or dine more informally in The Bank, a bistro and café bar.

Rooms 49 (4 fmly) (4 GF) 🐾 **S** £60-£100; **D** £70-£150* **Facilities** FTV Wi-fi ⅃ Leisure facilities available at sister hotel Xmas New Year **Conf** Class 25 Board 25 Thtr 25 **Services** Lift **Parking** 40 **Notes** LB ⊗

Premier Inn Barnstaple

BUDGET HOTEL

☎ 0871 527 8052
Whiddon Dr, off Eastern Av EX32 8RY
web: www.premierinn.com
dir: Exit A361 (North Devon Link Rd) towards Barnstaple. Right at Portmore rdbt

High quality, budget accommodation ideal for both families and business travellers. Spacious, en suite bedrooms feature tea and coffee making facilities, and Freeview TV in most hotels. Internet access and Wi-fi are available for a small fee. The adjacent family restaurant features a wide and varied menu. See also the Hotel Groups pages.

Rooms 40

| **BARROW-IN-FURNESS** | **Map 18 SD26** |
| Cumbria | |

Clarence House Country Hotel & Restaurant

★★★ 82% ⊛ ⊛ HOTEL

☎ 01229 462508
Skelgate, Dalton-in-Furness LA15 8BQ
e-mail: clarencehsehotel@aol.com
web: www.clarencehouse-hotel.co.uk
dir: A590 through Ulverston & Lindal, 2nd exit at rdbt & 1st exit at next. Follow signs to Dalton, hotel at top of hill on right

This hotel is located in ornamental grounds with unrestricted countryside views. Bedrooms are individually themed with those in the main hotel being particularly stylish and comfortable. The public rooms are spacious and also furnished to a high standard. The popular conservatory restaurant and contemporary brasserie offer well-prepared dishes from extensive menus. There is a delightful barn conversion that is ideal for weddings.

Rooms 19 (12 annexe) (1 fmly) (5 GF) **Facilities** FTV Wi-fi ⅃ New Year **Conf** Class 40 Board 15 Thtr 100 **Parking** 40 **Notes** Closed 25-26 Dec Civ Wed 100

Abbey House Hotel

★★★ 78% HOTEL

☎ 01229 838282 & 0844 826 2091
Abbey Rd LA13 0PA
e-mail: enquiries@abbeyhousehotel.com
dir: From A590 follow signs for Furness General Hospital & Furness Abbey. Hotel approx 100yds on left

Set in its own gardens, this smart hotel provides stylish public areas, as well as extensive function and conference facilities. The well-equipped bedrooms vary in style - the more traditional rooms are in the main house and a more contemporary style of accommodation can be found in the extension. Service is friendly and helpful.

Rooms 61 (4 annexe) (6 fmly) (2 GF) 🐾 **Facilities** STV FTV Wi-fi ⅃ Xmas New Year **Conf** Class 120 Board 80 Thtr 300 Del from £75 to £150* **Services** Lift **Parking** 100 **Notes** Civ Wed 120

Clarke's Hotel

★★ 78% HOTEL

☎ 01229 820303
Rampside LA13 0PX
e-mail: bookings@clarkeshotel.co.uk
dir: A590 to Ulverston then A5087, take coast road for 8m, turn left at rdbt into Rampside

This smart, well-maintained hotel enjoys a peaceful location on the south Cumbrian coast, overlooking Morecambe Bay. The tastefully appointed bedrooms come in a variety of sizes and are thoughtfully equipped particularly for the business guest. Inviting public areas include an open-plan bar and brasserie offering freshly prepared food throughout the day.

Rooms 14 (1 fmly) **Facilities** FTV **Parking** 50

B

BARTON
Lancashire

Map 18 SD53

Barton Grange Hotel
★★★★ 77% HOTEL

☎ 01772 862551
Garstang Rd PR3 5AA
e-mail: stay@bartongrangehotel.com
web: www.bartongrangehotel.co.uk
dir: M6 junct 32, follow Garstang (A6) signs for 2.5m. Hotel on right

Situated close to the M6, this modern, stylish hotel benefits from extensive public areas that include leisure facilities with a swimming pool, sauna and gym. Comfortable, well-appointed bedrooms include executive rooms and family rooms, as well as attractive accommodation in an adjacent cottage. The unique Walled Garden Bistro offers all-day eating.

Rooms 51 (8 annexe) (4 fmly) (4 GF) ✆ **S** £60-£95; **D** £70-£120* **Facilities** STV Wi-fi ꜝ ⟲ Gym Sauna Xmas New Year **Conf** Class 100 Board 80 Thtr 300 Del from £105 to £150* **Services** Lift **Parking** 250 **Notes** LB ⊗ Civ Wed 300

BARTON-ON-SEA
Hampshire
Map 5 SZ29

Pebble Beach
◉ RESTAURANT WITH ROOMS

☎ 01425 627777
Marine Dr BH25 7DZ
e-mail: mail@pebblebeach-uk.com
dir: A35 from Southampton onto A337 to New Milton, left into Barton Court Ave to clifftop

Situated on the clifftop the restaurant at this establishment boasts stunning views towards The Needles. Bedrooms and bathrooms, situated above the restaurant, are well equipped and provide a range of accessories to enhance guest comfort. A freshly cooked breakfast is served in the main restaurant.

Rooms 4

BASILDON
Essex
Map 6 TQ78

Holiday Inn Basildon
★★★ 80% HOTEL

Holiday Inn

☎ 0871 942 9003 & 01268 824000
Waterfront Walk, Festival Leisure Park SS14 3DG
e-mail: reservations-basildon@ihg.com
web: www.hibasildonhotel.co.uk
dir: From A127 take A176/Basildon Billericay exit. Follow brown signs to Festival Leisure Park

This modern hotel sits alongside the river in a convenient location in the heart of town. It enjoys delightful views and is ideally placed for leisurely walks beside the river or for easy access to the town. The contemporary bedrooms are comfortable and particularly well equipped, with safes, Wi-fi and flat-screen TVs. There are a host of other facilities including a range of meeting rooms and leisure facilities, as well as a car park.

Rooms 148 (10 fmly) (8 GF) (16 smoking) **Facilities** STV Wi-fi ꜝ Use of nearby leisure club New Year **Conf** Class 80 Board 80 Thtr 300 **Services** Lift Air con **Parking** 152 **Notes** Civ Wed 300

Chichester Hotel
★★★ 77% HOTEL

☎ 01268 560555
Old London Rd, Wickford SS11 8UE
e-mail: reception@chichester-hotel.com
web: www.chichester-hotel.com
dir: Signed from A129 between Wickford & Rayleigh

Set in landscaped gardens and surrounded by farmland, this friendly hotel has been owned and run by the same family for over 25 years. Spacious bedrooms are located around an attractive courtyard, and each is pleasantly decorated and thoughtfully equipped. Public rooms include a cosy lounge bar and a smart restaurant.

Rooms 35 (32 annexe) (12 fmly) (17 GF) **S** £47-£69; **D** £47-£69* **Facilities** FTV Wi-fi **Parking** 150 **Notes** ⊗

Campanile Basildon
BUDGET HOTEL

☎ 01268 530810
Pipps Hill, Southend Arterial Rd SS14 3AE
e-mail: basildon@campanile.com
web: www.campanile.com
dir: M25 junct 29 Basildon exit, back under A127, then left at rdbt

This modern building offers accommodation in smart, well-equipped bedrooms, all with en suite bathrooms. Refreshments may be taken at the informal bistro. See also the Hotel Groups pages.

Rooms 97 (97 annexe) (8 fmly) (44 GF) **Conf** Class 18 Board 24 Thtr 35

Premier Inn Basildon (East Mayne)
BUDGET HOTEL

Premier Inn

☎ 0871 527 8054
Felmores, East Mayne SS13 1BW
web: www.premierinn.com
dir: M25 junct 29 , A127 towards Southend, take A132 S signed Basildon & Wickford at Neverdon exit. Hotel on left

High quality, budget accommodation ideal for both families and business travellers. Spacious, en suite bedrooms feature tea and coffee making facilities, and Freeview TV in most hotels. Internet access and Wi-fi are available for a small fee. The adjacent family restaurant features a wide and varied menu. See also the Hotel Groups pages.

Rooms 32

Save on hotels. Book at **theAA.com/hotel**

BAR – BAS 57 ENGLAND

Premier Inn Basildon (Festival Park)

BUDGET HOTEL

☎ 0871 527 8056
Festival Leisure Park, Pipps Hill Road South, Off Cranes Farm Rd SS14 3WB
web: www.premierinn.com
dir: M25 junct 9, A217 towards Basildon. Take A17. Hotel just off A1235 adjacent to David Lloyd Leisure Club

Rooms 64

Premier Inn Basildon South

BUDGET HOTEL

☎ 0871 527 8060
High Rd, Fobbing, Stanford-Le-Hope SS17 9NR
web: www.premierinn.com
dir: M2 junct 30/31, A13 towards Southend. 10m to Five Bells Rdbt junct with A176. Right into Fobbing High Rd. Hotel on left

Rooms 61

BASINGSTOKE Map 5 SU65
Hampshire

INSPECTORS' CHOICE

Tylney Hall Hotel

★★★★ ◉◉ HOTEL

☎ 01256 764881
RG27 9AZ
e-mail: sales@tylneyhall.com
web: www.tylneyhall.com

(For full entry see Rotherwick)

Oakley Hall Hotel

★★★★ 83% ◉ COUNTRY HOUSE HOTEL

☎ 01256 783350
Rectory Rd RG23 7EL
e-mail: enquiries@oakleyhall-park.com
web: www.oakleyhall-park.com
dir: M3 junct 7, follow Basingstoke signs. In 500yds before lights turn left onto A30 towards Oakley, immediately right onto unclass road towards Oakley. In 3m left at T-junct into Rectory Rd. Left onto B3400. Hotel signed 1st on left

An impressive drive leads to this country house which benefits from delightful country views across north Hampshire. Built in 1795, it was once owned by the Bramston family who were friends of Jane Austen. An ideal wedding venue, Oakley Hall also has an excellent range of conference facilities, and is a great place to spend a relaxing leisure break. The bedrooms

are spacious; many are located in the impressively restored courtyard and are particularly well equipped; there is also the delightful Garden Cottage. Service is delivered by a friendly team, and cuisine is contemporary and satisfying.

Rooms 18 (18 annexe) (8 fmly) (18 GF) 👀
Facilities FTV Wi-fi Clay pigeon shooting Xmas New Year **Conf** Class 82 Board 50 Thtr 300 Del from £145 to £245* **Services** Air con **Parking** 100 **Notes** ⊗ Civ Wed 100

Audleys Wood Hotel

HandPICKED HOTELS · BUILT FOR PLEASURE

★★★★ 80% ◉◉ HOTEL

☎ 01256 817555
Alton Rd RG25 2JT
e-mail: audleyswood@handpicked.co.uk
web: www.handpickedhotels.co.uk/audleyswood
dir: M3 junct 6. From Basingstoke take A339 towards Alton, hotel on right

A long sweeping drive leads to what was once a Victorian hunting lodge. This traditional country-house hotel offers bedrooms with flat-screen TVs and MP3 player connections. Smart and traditional public areas have log fires, and the dining options include the award-winning The Simonds Room and the contemporary conservatory with a small minstrels' gallery. Hand Picked Hotels – AA Hotel Group of the Year 2012-13.

Rooms 72 (23 fmly) (34 GF) **Facilities** STV FTV Wi-fi HL 🏊 Xmas New Year **Conf** Class 80 Board 60 Thtr 200 Del from £150 to £190* **Parking** 60 **Notes** ⊗ Civ Wed 100

The Hampshire Court Hotel

 QHOTELS

★★★★ 79% HOTEL

☎ 01256 319700
Centre Dr, Chineham RG24 8FY
e-mail: hampshirecourt@qhotels.co.uk
web: www.qhotels.co.uk
dir: Off A33 (Reading road) behind Chineham Shopping Centre via Great Binfields Rd

This hotel boasts a range of smart, comfortable and stylish bedrooms, and leisure facilities that are

unrivalled locally. Facilities include indoor and outdoor tennis courts, two swimming pools, a gym and a number of treatment rooms.

Rooms 90 (6 fmly) 👀 **Facilities** Spa STV Wi-fi ⚲ HL ⊡ 🏊 Gym Steam room Sauna Exercise studios Xmas New Year Child facilities **Conf** Class 800 Board 60 Thtr 1500 **Services** Lift **Parking** 220 **Notes** Civ Wed 220

Basingstoke Country Hotel

 PUMA HOTELS COLLECTION

★★★★ 75% ◉ HOTEL

☎ 01256 764161
Scures Hill, Nately Scures, Hook RG27 9JS
e-mail: basingstokecountry.mande@pumahotels.co.uk
web: www.pumahotels.co.uk
dir: M3 junct 5, A287 towards Newnham. Left at lights. Hotel 200mtrs on right

This popular hotel is close to Basingstoke and its country location ensures a peaceful stay. Bedrooms are available in a number of styles - all have air conditioning, Wi-fi, in-room safes and hairdryers. Guests have a choice of dining in the formal restaurant, or for lighter meals and snacks there is a relaxed café and a smart bar. Extensive wedding, conference and leisure facilities complete the picture.

Rooms 100 (26 GF) **Facilities** Spa STV Wi-fi ⊡ supervised Gym Sauna Solarium Steam room Dance studio Beauty treatments New Year **Conf** Class 85 Board 80 Thtr 240 **Services** Lift Air con **Parking** 200 **Notes** RS 24 Dec-2 Jan Civ Wed 90

Apollo Hotel

 CLASSIC BRITISH HOTELS

★★★★ 72% ◉ HOTEL

☎ 01256 796700
Aldermaston Roundabout RG24 9NU
e-mail: admin@apollohotels.com
web: www.apollohotels.com
dir: M3 junct 6. Follow ring road N towards Newbury. Follow A340 (Aldermaston) signs. Hotel on rdbt, 5th exit into Popley Way for access

This modern hotel provides well-equipped accommodation and spacious public areas, appealing to both the leisure and business guest. Facilities include a smartly appointed leisure club, a business centre, along with a good choice of formal and informal eating in two restaurants; Vespers is the fine dining option.

Rooms 125 (32 GF) **D** £170-£240* **Facilities** Spa FTV Wi-fi ⚲ ⊡ supervised Gym Sauna Steam room **Conf** Class 196 Board 30 Thtr 255 **Services** Lift Air con **Parking** 200 **Notes** LB ⊗ Civ Wed 100

BASINGSTOKE *continued*

Holiday Inn Basingstoke

★★★ 79% HOTEL

Holiday Inn

☎ 0871 942 9004
Grove Rd RG21 3EE
e-mail: reservations-basingstoke@ihg.com
web: www.hibasingstokehotel.co.uk
dir: On A339 (Alton road) S of Basingstoke

Located conveniently on the southern approach to Basingstoke and close to the M3, this modern, comfortable hotel offers well-equipped, air-conditioned bedrooms. There is a busy Conference Academy on site. The staff are friendly throughout the hotel. Free parking is available.

Rooms 86 (1 fmly) (43 GF) ⊀ **Facilities** STV FTV Wi-fi ⇘ Complimentary passes available at nearby leisure centre Xmas New Year **Conf** Class 70 Board 70 Thtr 140 Del from £99 to £160 **Services** Air con **Parking** 150 **Notes** ⊗ Civ Wed 140

Premier Inn Basingstoke Central

BUDGET HOTEL

☎ 0871 527 8062
Basingstoke Leisure Park, Worting Rd RG22 6PG
web: www.premierinn.com
dir: M3 junct 6, A339 towards Newbury. A340 follow brown Leisure Park signs. At next rdbt right onto B3400 (Churchill Way West). Right on next rdbt into Leisure Park. Hotel adjacent to Spruce Goose Beefeater

High quality, budget accommodation ideal for both families and business travellers. Spacious, en suite bedrooms feature tea and coffee making facilities, and Freeview TV in most hotels. Internet access and Wi-fi are available for a small fee. The adjacent family restaurant features a wide and varied menu. See also the Hotel Groups pages.

Rooms 71

BASLOW
Derbyshire
Map 16 SK27

Fischer's Baslow Hall

★★★ ◉◉◉ HOTEL

☎ 01246 583259
Calver Rd DE45 1RR
e-mail: reservations@fischers-baslowhall.co.uk
web: www.fischers-baslowhall.co.uk
dir: On A623 between Baslow & Calver

Located at the end of a chestnut tree-lined drive on the edge of the Chatsworth Estate, in marvellous gardens, this beautiful Derbyshire manor house offers sumptuous accommodation and facilities. Staff provide very friendly and personally attentive service. There are two styles of bedroom available - traditional, individually-themed rooms in the main house and spacious, more contemporary-styled rooms with Italian marble bathrooms in the Garden House. The cuisine is excellent and will prove the highlight of any stay.

Rooms 11 (5 annexe) (4 GF) ⊀ **S** £105-£140; **D** £155-£225 (incl. bkfst)* **Facilities** FTV Wi-fi ⇘ **Conf** Board 15 Thtr 20 Del from £205 to £225* **Parking** 40 **Notes** LB ⊗ No children 12 yrs Closed 25-26 Dec RS 31 Dec Civ Wed 38

Cavendish Hotel

★★★ 86% ◉◉ HOTEL

☎ 01246 582311
DE45 1SP
e-mail: info@cavendish-hotel.net
web: www.cavendish-hotel.net
dir: M1 junct 29/A617 W to Chesterfield & A619 to Baslow. Hotel in village centre, off main road

This stylish property, dating back to the 18th century, is delightfully situated on the outskirts of the Chatsworth Estate. Elegantly appointed bedrooms offer a host of thoughtful amenities, while comfortable public areas are furnished with period pieces and paintings. Guests have a choice of dining in either the informal conservatory Garden Room or the elegant Gallery Restaurant.

Rooms 24 (3 fmly) (2 GF) **S** £133-£177; **D** £169-£219* **Facilities** FTV Wi-fi ⇘ Putt green Xmas New Year **Conf** Class 8 Board 18 Thtr 25 Del £205* **Parking** 50 **Notes** LB ⊗ RS 25 Dec evening

BASSENTHWAITE   **Map 18 NY23**
Cumbria

INSPECTORS' CHOICE

Armathwaite Hall Country House & Spa

★★★★ ◉ COUNTRY HOUSE HOTEL

☎ 017687 76551
CA12 4RE
e-mail: reservations@armathwaite-hall.com
web: www.armathwaite-hall.com
dir: M6 junct 40/A66 to Keswick rdbt then A591 signed Carlisle. 8m to Castle Inn junct, turn left. Hotel 300yds

Enjoying fine views over Bassenthwaite Lake, this impressive mansion, dating from the 17th century, is situated amid 400 acres of deer park. The comfortably furnished bedrooms and well-appointed bathrooms are complemented by a choice of public rooms that have many original features. The spa is an outstanding asset to the leisure facilities; it offers an infinity pool, thermal suite, sauna, state-of-the-art gym, treatments, exercise classes and a hot tub overlooking the landscaped gardens.

Rooms 46 (8 fmly) (8 GF) ↳ **S** £135-£210; **D** £200-£370 (incl. bkfst)* **Facilities** Spa STV Wi-fi ⊗ supervised ⅃ Fishing ⅄ Gym Archery Clay shooting Quad & mountain bikes Falconry Xmas New Year **Conf** Class 50 Board 60 Thtr 200 Del from £165 to £250 **Services** Lift **Parking** 100 **Notes** LB Civ Wed 150

Best Western Plus Castle Inn

★★★★ 76% HOTEL

☎ 017687 76401
CA12 4RG
e-mail: reservations@castleinncumbria.co.uk
web: www.castleinncumbria.co.uk
dir: A591 to Carlisle, pass Bassenthwaite village on right. Hotel on left of T-junct

Overlooking some of England's highest fells and Bassenthwaite Lake, this fine hotel is ideally situated for exploring Bassenthwaite, Keswick and the Lake District. The accommodation, extensive leisure facilities and friendly service are certainly strong points here. Ritson's Restaurant and Laker's Lounge offer a range of dishes using locally sourced meats from the fells, managed, sustainable fish stocks plus international and seasonal ingredients.

Rooms 42 (4 fmly) (9 GF) ↳ **S** £85-£185; **D** £145-£205 (incl. bkfst)* **Facilities** FTV Wi-fi ⊗ supervised ⅃ Putt green Gym Sauna Steam room Xmas New Year **Conf** Class 108 Board 60 Thtr 200 Del from £139 to £147* **Parking** 120 **Notes** LB ⊗ Civ Wed 180

The Pheasant

★★★ 86% ◉ HOTEL

☎ 017687 76234
CA13 9YE
e-mail: info@the-pheasant.co.uk
web: www.the-pheasant.co.uk
dir: Midway between Keswick & Cockermouth, signed from A66

Enjoying a rural setting, within well-tended gardens, on the western side of Bassenthwaite Lake, this friendly 500-year-old inn is steeped in tradition. The attractive oak-panelled bar has seen few changes over the years and features log fires and a great selection of malt whiskies. The individually decorated bedrooms are stylish and thoughtfully equipped.

Rooms 15 (2 annexe) (2 GF) **Facilities** Wi-fi ⋈ New Year **Parking** 40 **Notes** No children 12yrs Closed 25 Dec

---

BATH   **Map 4 ST76**
Somerset

See also Colerne & Hinton Charterhouse   **B**

Macdonald Bath Spa

★★★★★ 87% ◉◉ HOTEL   MACDONALD HOTELS & RESORTS

☎ 0844 879 9106 & 01225 444424
Sydney Rd BA2 6JF
e-mail: sales.bathspa@macdonald-hotels.co.uk
web: www.macdonaldhotels.co.uk/bathspa
dir: A4, left onto A36 at 1st lights. Right at lights after pedestrian crossing left into Sydney Place. Hotel 200yds on right

A delightful Georgian mansion set amidst seven acres of pretty landscaped grounds, just a short walk from the many and varied delights of the city centre. A timeless elegance pervades the gracious public areas and bedrooms. Facilities include a popular leisure club, a choice of dining options and a number of meeting rooms.

Rooms 129 (3 fmly) (17 GF) ↳ **D** £215-£345 (incl. bkfst) **Facilities** Spa STV FTV Wi-fi ⊗ ⅄ Gym Beauty treatment Thermal suite Outdoor hydro pool Whirlpool Xmas New Year **Conf** Class 100 Board 50 Thtr 130 Del from £180 to £250 **Services** Lift Air con **Parking** 160 **Notes** LB ⊗ Civ Wed 130

The Bath Priory Hotel, Restaurant & Spa

★★★★★ 81% ◉◉◉ HOTEL

☎ 01225 331922
Weston Rd BA1 2XT
e-mail: mail@thebathpriory.co.uk
web: www.thebathpriory.co.uk
dir: Adjacent to Victoria Park

Set in delightful walled gardens, this attractive Georgian house provides peace and tranquillity, within easy reach of the city. An extensive display of paintings and fine art adorn the sumptuously furnished day rooms, whilst bedrooms are equally stylishly and boast beautifully appointed en suites. The stylish, award-winning restaurant is overseen by Michael Caines and offers memorable, classic dishes. The Garden Spa has extensive facilities including a pool, sauna, steam pod, treatment rooms and a fitness centre.

Rooms 31 (4 annexe) (6 fmly) (1 GF) **Facilities** Spa STV Wi-fi ⊗ ⋋ ⅄ Gym Xmas New Year **Conf** Class 25 Board 25 Thtr 32 **Parking** 40 **Notes** Civ Wed 70

BATH *continued*

Combe Grove Manor Hotel

PUMA HOTELS
COLLECTION

★★★★ 76% ◉◉ COUNTRY HOUSE HOTEL

☎ 01225 834644
Brassknocker Hill, Monkton Combe BA2 7HS
e-mail: combegrovemanor@pumahotels.co.uk
web: www.pumahotels.co.uk
dir: Exit A36 at Limpley Stoke onto Brassknocker Hill. Hotel 0.5m up hill on left

Set in over 80 acres of gardens, this Georgian mansion commands stunning views over Limpley Stoke Valley. Most bedrooms are in the Garden Lodge, a short walk from the main house. The superb range of indoor and outdoor leisure facilities includes a beauty clinic with holistic therapies, golf, tennis and two pools. The Eden Brasserie is in the cellar (please note that the narrow steps may prove a problem for less able guests).

Rooms 42 (33 annexe) (5 fmly) (8 GF) **Facilities** Spa STV Wi-fi ❄ supervised ❧ ♭ 5 ♨ Putt green ⛳ Gym Squash Driving range Xmas New Year **Conf** Class 60 Board 30 Thtr 90 **Parking** 150 **Notes** ⊗ Civ Wed 50

INSPECTORS' CHOICE
The Queensberry Hotel

★★★ ◉◉◉ HOTEL

☎ 01225 447928
Russel St BA1 2QF
e-mail: reservations@thequeensberry.co.uk
web: www.thequeensberry.co.uk
dir: 100mtrs from the Assembly Rooms

This charming family-run hotel, situated in a quiet residential street near the city centre, consists of four delightful townhouses. The spacious bedrooms offer deep armchairs, marble bathrooms and a range of modern comforts. Sumptuously furnished sitting rooms add to The Queensberry's appeal and allow access to the very attractive and peaceful walled gardens. The Olive Tree is a stylish restaurant that combines Georgian opulence with contemporary simplicity. Innovative menus are

based on best quality ingredients and competent cooking. Valet parking proves a useful service.

Rooms 29 (2 fmly) (2 GF) ↝ **S** £125-£190; **D** £130-£255* **Facilities** FTV Wi-fi **Conf** Class 12 Board 25 Thtr 35 Del from £225 to £280* **Services** Lift **Parking** 6 **Notes** ⊗

Dukes Hotel

★★★ 82% ◉◉ SMALL HOTEL

☎ 01225 787960
Great Pulteney St BA2 4DN
e-mail: info@dukesbath.co.uk
web: www.dukesbath.co.uk
dir: A46 to Bath, at rdbt right on A4. 4th set of lights turn left (A36), then right into Great Pulteney St. Hotel on left

An elegant, Grade I listed Georgian building, just a few minutes' walk from Pulteney Bridge. The well-equipped bedrooms, which differ in size and style, provide plenty of comfort and have flat-screen TVs; suites and ground-floor rooms are available. The staff are particularly friendly and attentive, and contribute to an engaging and welcoming atmosphere. There is a courtyard terrace leading from the lounge/bar, where guests can enjoy an aperitif or lunch in the summer months. The Cavendish Restaurant offers a very creative and interesting menu in a relaxed, light and airy environment.

Rooms 17 (5 fmly) (2 GF) **S** £99-£132; **D** £139-£251 (incl. bkfst)* **Facilities** FTV Wi-fi Xmas New Year **Conf** Board 20 Thtr 35 Del from £182 to £202* **Notes** LB

Haringtons Hotel

★★★ 78% METRO HOTEL

☎ 01225 461728 & 445883
8-10 Queen St BA1 1HE
e-mail: post@haringtonshotel.co.uk
web: www.haringtonshotel.co.uk
dir: A4 into George St, into Milsom St. 1st right into Quiet St, 1st left into Queen St

Dating back to the 18th century, this hotel is situated in the heart of the city and provides all the expected modern facilities and comforts. Although a full dinner in a restaurant is not offered, the comfortably furnished lounge is light and airy and open throughout the day for light snacks and refreshments. A warm welcome is assured from the proprietors and staff, making this a delightful place to stay.

Rooms 13 (3 fmly) ↝ **S** £88-£168; **D** £88-£168 (incl. bkfst)* **Facilities** STV FTV Wi-fi **Conf** Class 10 Board 12 Thtr 18 **Parking** 11 **Notes** LB ⊗

Mercure Bath Francis Hotel

Mercure

★★★ 77% HOTEL

☎ 01225 424105 & 338970
Queen Square BA1 2HH
e-mail: h6636@accor.com
web: www.mercure.com
dir: M4 junct 18/A46 to Bath junct. 3rd exit onto A4, right into George St, left into Gay St into Queen Sq. Hotel on left

Overlooking Queen Square in the centre of the city, this elegant Georgian hotel is within walking distance of Bath's many attractions. The public rooms provide a variety of areas where guests can eat, drink and relax - from the informal café-bar, a more formal restaurant to the traditional lounge. The bedrooms have air conditioning.

Rooms 95 (17 fmly) (5 smoking) **Facilities** Wi-fi Xmas New Year **Conf** Class 40 Board 30 Thtr 80 **Services** Lift **Parking** 40 **Notes** Civ Wed 100

Save on hotels. Book at **theAA.com/hotel**

BAT 61 ENGLAND

Wentworth House Hotel

★★ 69% HOTEL

☎ 01225 339193
106 Bloomfield Rd BA2 2AP
e-mail: stay@wentworthhouse.co.uk
web: www.wentworthhouse.co.uk
dir: A36 towards Bristol at railway arches, hotel on right

This hotel is located on the outskirts of Bath yet is within walking distance of the city centre. Bedrooms vary in size and style; ground-floor rooms have their own conservatory seating area, some have four-posters and one has superb city views. The dinner menu features authentic home-cooked Indian dishes. There is a garden, which has a pool to enjoy in fine weather.

Rooms 19 (2 fmly) (6 GF) **S** £65-£100; **D** £75-£130 (incl. bkfst) **Facilities** STV FTV Wi-fi ⚡ Xmas **Conf** Class 40 Board 35 Del from £125 to £175* **Parking** 19 **Notes** LB ⊗ No children 7yrs

Carfax Hotel

★★ TOWN HOUSE HOTEL

☎ 01225 462089
13-15 Great Pulteney St BA2 4BS
e-mail: reservations@carfaxhotel.co.uk
dir: A36 onto Great Pulteney St

Rooms 30 (5 fmly) (4 GF) **Facilities** FTV Wi-fi **Conf** Class 18 Board 12 Thtr 30 **Services** Lift **Parking** 13 **Notes** ⊗

The Royal Crescent Hotel

Ⓤ

☎ 01225 823333
16 Royal Crescent BA1 2LS
e-mail: info@royalcrescent.co.uk
dir: From A4, right at lights. 2nd left into Bennett St, into The Circus, 2nd exit into Brock St

Currently the rating for this establishment is not confirmed. This may be due to a change of ownership or because it has only recently joined the AA rating scheme. For further details please see the AA website: theAA.com

Rooms 45 (8 fmly) (7 GF) ⚡ **S** fr £179; (incl. bkfst)* **Facilities** Spa STV FTV Wi-fi ⚡ 🕲 💆 Gym 1920s river launch Xmas New Year **Conf** Class 20 Board 20 Thtr 50 Del from £284 to £384* **Services** Lift Air con **Parking** 27 **Notes** Civ Wed 50

Holiday Inn Express Bath

BUDGET HOTEL

☎ 01225 303000
Lower Bristol Rd, Brougham Hayes BA2 3QU
e-mail: info@expressbath.co.uk
web: www.hiexpress.co.uk/bath
dir: From A4, right into Bathwick St, over rdbt onto Pulteney Rd. Into Claverton St, straight over at next rdbt (Lower Bristol Rd). Hotel opposite Sainsburys

A modern hotel ideal for families and business travellers. Fresh and uncomplicated, the spacious rooms include Sky TV, power shower and tea and coffee-making facilities. Continental buffet breakfast is included in the room rate; other meals may be taken at the nearby family pub or restaurant. See also the Hotel Groups pages.

Rooms 126 (33 fmly) (31 GF) ⚡ **S** £79-£169; **D** £79-£169* **Conf** Class 10 Board 15 Thtr 15 Del £170*

Milsoms Bath

RESTAURANT WITH ROOMS

☎ 01225 750128
24 Milsom St BA1 1DG
e-mail: bath@milsomshotel.co.uk
dir: M4 junct 18, A46 (Bath), 3m, through Pennsylvania. 3rd exit at rdbt onto A420 (Bristol). 1st left signed Hamswell/Park & Ride, left at junct towards Lansdown. Right at next T-junct. 5th right into George St. 1st left into Milsom St

Located at the end of the main street in busy, central Bath, this stylish restaurant with rooms offers a range of comfortable, well-equipped accommodation. The ground-floor Loch Fyne Restaurant serves an excellent selection of dishes at both lunch and dinner with an emphasis on freshest quality fish and shellfish. A good selection of hot and cold items is also available in the same restaurant at breakfast.

Rooms 9

BATTLE

BATTLE Map 7 TQ71
East Sussex

B

Powder Mills Hotel

★★★ 81% ◉ HOTEL

☎ 01424 775511
Powdermill Ln TN33 0SP
e-mail: powdc@aol.com
web: www.powdermillshotel.com
dir: M25 junct 5, A21 towards Hastings. At St Johns Cross take A2100 to Battle. Pass Abbey on right, 1st right into Powdermills Ln. 1m, hotel on right

A delightful 18th-century country-house hotel set amidst 150 acres of landscaped grounds with lakes and woodland. The individually decorated bedrooms are tastefully furnished and thoughtfully equipped; some rooms have sun terraces with lovely views over the lake. Public rooms include a cosy lounge bar, music room, drawing room, library, restaurant and conservatory.

Rooms 40 (10 annexe) (5 GF) ⚡ **S** £90-£115; **D** £120-£350 (incl. bkfst) **Facilities** STV FTV Wi-fi ⚡ ⚡ 💆 Fishing Jogging trails Woodland walks Clay pigeon shooting Xmas New Year **Conf** Class 50 Board 16 Thtr 250 Del from £130 to £170 **Parking** 101 **Notes** LB Civ Wed 100

Brickwall Hotel

★★★ 78% HOTEL

☎ 01424 870253 & 870339
The Green, Sedlescombe TN33 0QA
e-mail: info@brickwallhotel.com
web: www.brickwallhotel.com
dir: A21 on B2244 at top of Sedlescombe Green

This is a well-maintained Tudor house, which is situated in the heart of this pretty village and overlooks the green. The spacious public rooms feature a lovely wood-panelled restaurant with a wealth of oak beams, a choice of lounges and a smart bar. Bedrooms are pleasantly decorated and some have garden views.

Rooms 25 (2 fmly) (17 GF) **Facilities** STV Wi-fi ⚡ ⚡ Xmas New Year **Conf** Class 40 Board 30 Thtr 30 **Parking** 40 **Notes** ⊗

B

BridgeHouse

★★★ 81% ◉◉ HOTEL

☎ 01308 862200
3 Prout Bridge DT8 3AY
e-mail: enquiries@bridge-house.co.uk
web: www.bridge-house.co.uk
dir: A3066 to Beaminster, hotel 100yds from town square

Dating back to the 13th century, this property offers friendly and attentive service. The stylish bedrooms feature finest Italian cotton linens, flat-screen TVs and Wi-fi. There are five types of room to choose from including four-poster and coach house rooms. Smartly presented public areas include the Georgian dining room, cosy bar and adjacent lounge, and a breakfast room together with the Beaminster Brasserie with its alfresco eating area under a canopy overlooking the attractive walled garden.

Rooms 13 (4 annexe) (2 fmly) (4 GF) ↟ **S** £95-£185; **D** £125-£215 (incl. bkfst)* **Facilities** FTV Wi-fi ↻ Xmas New Year Child facilities **Conf** Class 14 Board 10 Thtr 24 Del £195* **Parking** 20 **Notes** LB Civ Wed 100

Montagu Arms Hotel

★★★★ 82% ◉◉◉ HOTEL

☎ 01590 612324 & 624467
Palace Ln SO42 7ZL
e-mail: reservations@montaguarmshotel.co.uk
web: www.montaguarmshotel.co.uk
dir: M27 junct 2, follow signs for Beaulieu. In Dibden Purlieu right at rdbt. Hotel on left in Beaulieu

Situated at the heart of this charming village and surrounded by glorious New Forest scenery, this lovely hotel dates back to 1742 and still retains the character of a traditional country house. The individually designed bedrooms include some with four-posters. Public rooms include a choice of two dining options, the informal Monty's brasserie serving home-cooked classics, and the stylish, award-

winning Terrace Restaurant. Much produce comes from the kitchen garden project which saw a derelict piece of land to the rear transformed to produce organic fruit, vegetables and herbs plus free-range eggs from the hens. In warmer weather there is a sheltered alfresco eating area overlooking the pretty terraced garden. Complimentary use of leisure and spa facilities is available to guests at a sister hotel six miles away.

Rooms 22 (3 fmly) ↟ **D** £148-£348 (incl. bkfst)* **Facilities** FTV Wi-fi ↻ Complimentary use of spa in Brockenhurst Xmas New Year **Conf** Class 16 Board 26 Thtr 50 **Parking** 86 **Notes** LB ⊗ Civ Wed 100

Beaulieu Hotel

NEW FOREST HOTELS

★★★ 80% ◉ HOTEL

☎ 023 8029 3344
Beaulieu Rd SO42 7YQ
e-mail: beaulieu@newforesthotels.co.uk
web: www.newforesthotels.co.uk
dir: M27 junct 1, A337 towards Lyndhurst. Left at lights, through Lyndhurst, right onto B3056, hotel in 3m

Located in the heart of the beautiful New Forest National Park and close to Beaulieu Road railway station, this popular, small hotel provides an ideal base for exploring this remarkable area. Once a coaching inn, the hotel now particularly welcomes families; children will delight in seeing the ponies on the doorstep! Bedrooms, all with free Wi-fi and flat-screen TVs, range from cosy Keeper rooms to Crown rooms which also have four-posters and iPod docking stations. The relaxing Exbury Restaurant has doors that lead out onto the patio area and the landscaped gardens, and alfresco eating is possible in the summer.

Rooms 28 (7 annexe) (5 fmly) (4 GF) **S** £97-£130; **D** £132-£182 (incl. bkfst)* **Facilities** FTV Wi-fi ↻ HL ☽ Steam room Xmas New Year **Conf** Class 100 Board 100 Thtr 250 **Services** Lift **Parking** 60 **Notes** LB Civ Wed 205

The Master Builders at Bucklers Hard

★★★ 77% ◉ HOTEL

☎ 01590 616253
Buckler's Hard SO42 7XB
e-mail: enquiries@themasterbuilders.co.uk
web: www.themasterbuilders.co.uk
dir: M27 junct 2, follow Beaulieu signs. At T-junct left onto B3056, 1st left to Buckler's Hard. Hotel 2m on left before village

A tranquil historic riverside setting creates the backdrop for this delightful property. The main house bedrooms are full of historical features and of

individual design, and in addition there are some bedrooms in the newer wing. Public areas include a popular bar and guest lounge, whilst grounds are an ideal location for alfresco dining in the summer months. Award-winning cuisine is served in the stylish dining room.

Rooms 25 (17 annexe) (4 fmly) (8 GF) **Facilities** FTV Wi-fi Xmas New Year **Conf** Class 30 Board 20 Thtr 40 **Parking** 40

Waveney House Hotel

★★★ 83% HOTEL

☎ 01502 712270
Puddingmoor NR34 9PL
e-mail: enquiries@waveneyhousehotel.co.uk
web: www.waveneyhousehotel.co.uk
dir: From A146 onto Common Lane North, left into Pound Rd, left into Ravensmere, right onto Smallgate, right onto Old Market, continue to Puddingmoor

An exceptionally well presented, privately owned hotel situated by the River Waveney on the edge of this busy little market town. The stylish public rooms include a smart lounge bar and a contemporary-style restaurant with views over the river. The spacious bedrooms are attractively decorated with co-ordinated fabrics and have many thoughtful touches.

Rooms 12 (3 fmly) **Facilities** FTV Wi-fi Xmas New Year **Conf** Class 100 Board 50 Thtr 160 **Parking** 45 **Notes** ⊗ Civ Wed 80

The Bedford Swan Hotel

★★★★ 75% ◉◉ HOTEL

☎ 01234 346565
The Embankment MK40 1RW
e-mail: info@bedfordswanhotel.co.uk

This historic hotel successfully combines original features with modern comforts. The bedrooms ooze style and quality; the needs of the modern traveller are catered for. The award-winning River Room Restaurant offers a varied choice of freshly prepared dishes. The hotel also offers meeting and function rooms, spa facilities and secure parking.

Rooms 113 (10 fmly) (12 smoking) **S** £79-£199; **D** £89-£209* **Facilities** Spa STV FTV Wi-fi ↻ ☽ Xmas New Year **Conf** Class 40 Board 60 Thtr 250 **Services** Lift Air con **Parking** 80 **Notes** LB Civ Wed 250

B

The Barns Hotel

★★★★ 74% HOTEL

☎ 0844 855 9101

Cardington Rd MK44 3SA

e-mail: foh@barnshotelbedford.co.uk
web: www.barnshotelbedford.co.uk
dir: M1 junct 13, A421, approx 10m to A603 Sandy/
Bedford exit, hotel on right at 2nd rdbt

A tranquil location on the outskirts of Bedford, friendly staff and well-equipped bedrooms all combine to make this a good choice. Cosy day rooms and two informal bars add to the hotel's appeal, while large windows in the restaurant make the most of the view over the river. The original barn houses the conference and function suite.

Rooms 49 (18 GF) ⬈ **S** £72-£87; **D** £152-£167*
Facilities Wi-fi Free use of local leisure centre (1m)
New Year **Conf** Class 40 Board 40 Thtr 120
Del from £110 to £145* **Parking** 90 **Notes** LB ⊗
Civ Wed 90

Park Inn by Radisson Bedford

★★★ 68% HOTEL

☎ 01234 799988 & 799900

2 St Marys St MK40 1DZ

e-mail: info.bedford@rezidorparkinn.com
dir: B531, left A5141/Cauldwell St, right St Mary's St
then left into Duck Mill Lane

This modern hotel sits alongside the river in a convenient location in the heart of town and enjoys delightful views. The comfortable bedrooms are contemporary in style and particularly well equipped, with safes, Wi-fi and flat-screen TVs. The hotel also offers a host of other facilities including a leisure facilities and a range of meeting rooms.

Rooms 120 (1 fmly) (16 GF) **Facilities** FTV Wi-fi Gym
Treatment room Cardio vascular equipment Xmas
New Year **Conf** Class 200 Board 160 Thtr 450
Del from £110 to £150* **Services** Lift Air con
Parking 72 **Notes** ⊗ Civ Wed 100

Woodland Manor Hotel

★★★ 68% HOTEL

☎ 01234 363281

Green Ln, Clapham MK41 6EP

e-mail: reception@woodlandmanorhotel.co.uk
dir: A6 towards Kettering. Clapham N of town centre.
On entering village 1st right into Green Ln. Hotel
200mtrs on right

Sitting in acres of wooded grounds and gardens, this secluded Grade II listed, Victorian manor house offers a warm welcome. The hotel has spacious bedrooms, ample parking plus meeting rooms that are suitable for a variety of occasions. Traditional public areas include a cosy bar and a smart restaurant, where traditional English dishes, with a hint of French flair, are served.

Rooms 34 (3 annexe) (6 fmly) (3 GF) ⬈ **S** £65-£95;
D £85-£115 (incl. bkfst)* **Facilities** STV FTV Wi-fi ⬧
Conf Class 25 Board 22 Thtr 80 Del from £139 to
£159* **Parking** 60 **Notes** LB Civ Wed 80

Holiday Inn Express Bedford

BUDGET HOTEL

☎ 01234 224100

**Elstow Interchange A6/A421, Bedford Bypass
Junction, Wilstead Rd MK42 9BF**

e-mail: info@expressbedford.co.uk
web: www.expressbedford.co.uk
dir: 2m S of Bedford town centre at Elstow
interchange at junct of A421/A6

A modern hotel ideal for families and business travellers. Fresh and uncomplicated, the spacious rooms include Sky TV, power shower and tea and coffee-making facilities. Continental buffet breakfast is included in the room rate; other meals may be taken at the nearby family pub or restaurant. See also the Hotel Groups pages.

Rooms 80 (44 fmly) (18 GF) **Conf** Class 18 Board 20
Thtr 35

Premier Inn Bedford (Priory Marina)

BUDGET HOTEL

☎ 0871 527 8066

Priory Country Park, Barkers Ln MK41 9DJ

web: www.premierinn.com
dir: M1 junct 13, A421, A6, A428 signed Cambridge.
Cross River Ouse, right at next rdbt into Barkers Lane.
Follow Priory Country Park signs. Hotel adjacent to
Priory Marina Beefeater

High quality, budget accommodation ideal for both families and business travellers. Spacious, en suite bedrooms feature tea and coffee making facilities, and Freeview TV in most hotels. Internet access and Wi-fi are available for a small fee. The adjacent family restaurant features a wide and varied menu. See also the Hotel Groups pages.

Rooms 57

BELFORD   **Map 21 NU13**
Northumberland

Purdy Lodge

★★ 78% HOTEL

☎ 01668 213000

Adderstone Services NE70 7JU

e-mail: stay@purdylodge.co.uk
web: www.purdylodge.co.uk
dir: A1 onto B1341 then immediately left

Situated off the A1, this family-owned lodge provides modern bedrooms that look out over the fields towards Bamburgh Castle. Food is readily available in the attractive restaurant, Café One, and the lounge bar. This is a great stop-off hotel where a friendly welcome is guaranteed.

Rooms 20 (4 fmly) (10 GF) **S** £49.50-£69.50;
D £49.50-£79.50* **Facilities** FTV Wi-fi New Year
Parking 60 **Notes** Closed 25 Dec

BELTON   **Map 11 SK42**
Leicestershire

The Queen's Head

◉ RESTAURANT WITH ROOMS

☎ 01530 222359

2 Long St LE12 9TP

e-mail: enquiries@thequeenshead.org
dir: From Loughborough take A6 N, left onto B5324,
3m to Belton

Situated in the pretty village of Belton, close to East Midlands Airport, this popular restaurant with rooms offers good quality food and comfortable accommodation. All the bedrooms are en suite, individually decorated and well equipped - Wi-fi is available. Food is the focus with good quality locally sourced ingredients, blackboard specials and a range of ales from the local area.

Rooms 6 (2 fmly)

B

BELTON
Lincolnshire   Map 11 SK93

De Vere Belton Woods
★★★★ 75% HOTEL

DE VERE
Hotels & Resorts

☎ 01476 593200
NG32 2LN
e-mail: belton.woods@devere-hotels.com
web: www.devere.co.uk
dir: A1 to Gonerby Moor Services. B1174 towards
Great Gonerby. At top of hill turn left towards
Manthorpe/Belton. At T-junct turn left onto A607.
Hotel 0.25m on left

Beautifully located amidst 475 acres of picturesque
countryside, this is a destination venue for lovers of
sport, especially golf, as well as a relaxing executive
retreat for seminars. Comfortable and well-equipped
accommodation complements the elegant and
spacious public areas, which provide a good choice of
drinking and dining options.

Rooms 136 (136 fmly) (68 GF) **Facilities** Spa Wi-fi ⓢ
supervised ⌁ 45 ⚲ Putt green Fishing ⚲ Gym
Squash Outdoor activity centre Xmas New Year
Conf Class 180 Board 80 Thtr 245 **Services** Lift
Parking 350 **Notes** ⊗ Civ Wed 80

BEMBRIDGE
Isle of Wight   Map 5 SZ68

Bembridge Coast Hotel
★★★ 78% HOTEL

Warner Leisure Hotels
JUST FOR GROWN-UPS

☎ 01983 873931
Fishermans Walk PO35 5TH
dir: A3055 Ryde to Sandown, approx 1.5m, left at
lights into Carpenters Rd to St Helens. At mini-rdb
2nd exit onto A3395 signed Bembridge. In Bembridge
follow one-way system to right, left after bakery into
Forelands Rd. 1m, left into Lane End Rd. Follow to
end, right to hotel entrance

This hotel occupies a delightfully peaceful location on
the east coast of the Isle of Wight in 23-acre grounds.
The accommodation is comfortable, and there are a
number of rooms with sea views for which a small
supplementary charge applies. A full activities
itinerary ensures that guests can make the most of
what the hotel, and this beautiful island, has to offer.
The helpful reservations team can also arrange ferry
bookings from the UK mainland. Please note that this
is an adults-only (over 21 years) hotel.

Rooms 244 (70 GF) ⚲ **Facilities** FTV Wi-fi HL ⓢ ⚲
Putt green ⚲ Gym Beauty treatments rooms ♫ Xmas
New Year **Services** Lift **Parking** 244 **Notes** ⊗ No
children 21yrs

BERWICK-UPON-TWEED
Northumberland   Map 21 NT95

Queens Head
★★★ 75% SMALL HOTEL

☎ 01289 307852
Sandgate TD15 1EP
e-mail: info@queensheadberwick.co.uk
dir: A1 towards centre & town hall, into High St. Right
at bottom to Hide Hill

This small hotel is situated in the town centre, close
to the old walls of this former garrison town.
Bedrooms provide many thoughtful extras as
standard. Dining remains a strong aspect with a
carte menu that offers an impressive choice of tasty,
freshly prepared dishes served in the comfortable
lounge or dining room.

Rooms 6 (1 fmly) ⚲ **S** £57.50-£75; **D** £80-£90 (incl.
bkfst)* **Facilities** STV FTV Wi-fi ⚲ **Notes** LB ⊗

BEVERLEY
East Riding of Yorkshire   Map 17 TA03

Beverley Tickton Grange Hotel
★★★ 82% ◉◉ HOTEL

☎ 01964 543666
Tickton HU17 9SH
e-mail: info@ticktongrange.co.uk
dir: 3m NE on A1035

A charming Georgian country house situated in four
acres of private grounds and attractive gardens.
Bedrooms are individually designed and decorated to
a high specification. Pre-dinner drinks may be
enjoyed in the comfortable library lounge, prior to
enjoying fine, modern British cooking in the
restaurant. The hotel has excellent facilities for both
weddings and business conferences.

Rooms 20 (3 annexe) (2 fmly) (4 GF) **S** £85-£95;
D £112.50-£122.50 (incl. bkfst)* **Facilities** STV FTV
Wi-fi Gym **Conf** Class 100 Board 80 Thtr 200
Del from £108.95 to £121.95* **Parking** 90 **Notes** LB
⊗ RS 25-29 Dec Civ Wed 200

Best Western Lairgate Hotel
★★★ 72% HOTEL

Best Western

☎ 01482 882141
30/32 Lairgate HU17 8EP
e-mail: lairgate@bestwestern.co.uk
dir: A63 towards town centre. Hotel 220yds on left,
follow one-way system

Located just off the market square, this pleasing
Georgian hotel has been appointed to offer stylish
accommodation. Bedrooms are elegant and well
equipped, and public rooms include a comfortable
lounge, a lounge bar, and restaurant with a popular
sun terrace.

Rooms 30 (1 fmly) (8 GF) ⚲ **S** £70-£78; **D** £90-£98
(incl. bkfst)* **Facilities** FTV Wi-fi New Year
Conf Class 20 Board 20 Thtr 20 **Parking** 18 **Notes** LB
⊗ Closed 26 Dec & 1 Jan RS 25 Dec Civ Wed 70

BEXHILL
East Sussex   Map 6 TQ70

The Cooden Beach Hotel
★★★ 80% HOTEL

☎ 01424 842281
Cooden Beach TN39 4TT
e-mail: rooms@thecoodenbeachhotel.co.uk
web: www.thecoodenbeachhotel.co.uk
dir: A259 towards Bexhill. Signed at rdbt in Little
Common Village. Hotel at end of road in Cooden, just
past railway station

This privately owned hotel is situated in private
gardens which have direct access to the beach. With
a train station within walking distance the location is
perfectly suited for both business and leisure guests.
Bedrooms are comfortably appointed, and public
areas include a spacious restaurant, lounge, bar and
leisure centre with swimming pool.

Rooms 41 (8 annexe) (10 fmly) (4 GF) ⚲
Facilities FTV Wi-fi ⚲ ⓢ Gym Sauna Steam room Spa
bath ♫ Xmas New Year **Conf** Class 40 Board 40
Thtr 150 Del from £135* **Parking** 60
Notes Civ Wed 160

Save on hotels. Book at **theAA.com/hotel**

BEL – BIC 65 ENGLAND

BEXLEY
Greater London
Map 6 TQ47

Bexleyheath Marriott Hotel

Marriott
HOTELS & RESORTS

★★★★ 75% HOTEL

☎ 020 8298 1000
1 Broadway DA6 7JZ
e-mail: bexleyheath@marriotthotels.co.uk
web: www.bexleyheathmarriott.co.uk
dir: M25 junct 2/A2 towards London. Exit at Black Prince junct onto A220, signed Bexleyheath. Left at 2nd lights into hotel

Well positioned for access to major road networks, this large, modern hotel offers spacious, air-conditioned bedrooms with a comprehensive range of extra facilities. Planters Bar is a popular venue for pre-dinner drinks and offers guests a choice of lighter dining, whilst a more formal restaurant is also available. The hotel boasts a well-equipped leisure centre and undercover parking.

Rooms 142 (35 fmly) (26 GF) **Facilities** Spa STV FTV Wi-fi ⓑ ⓣ supervised Gym Steam room Xmas New Year **Conf** Class 120 Board 34 Thtr 250 **Services** Lift Air con **Parking** 77 **Notes** ⊗ Civ Wed 60

Holiday Inn London - Bexley
Holiday Inn

★★★ 80% HOTEL

☎ 0871 942 9006 & 01322 625513
Black Prince Interchange, Southwold Rd DA5 1ND
e-mail: bexley@ihg.com
web: www.hilondonbexleyhotel.co.uk
dir: M25 junct 2, A2 towards London. Exit at Black Prince Interchange (signed Bexley, Bexleyheath, A220, A223). Hotel on left

This hotel is within easy access of London and the Kent countryside; only 10 minutes from the famous Bluewater Shopping Centre and 15 minutes from Brands Hatch motor racing circuit. All bedrooms are air conditioned; suites are available. The hotel has a range of meeting rooms.

Rooms 107 (17 fmly) (33 GF) (10 smoking) **Facilities** STV FTV Wi-fi ⓑ Fitness room Xmas New Year **Conf** Class 42 Board 50 Thtr 120 Del from £120 to £170* **Services** Lift Air con **Parking** 200 **Notes** ⊗ Civ Wed 80

BIBURY
Gloucestershire
Map 5 SP10

Swan Hotel
COTSWOLD INNS & HOTELS

★★★★ 73% ⊛ HOTEL

☎ 01285 740695
GL7 5NW
e-mail: info@swanhotel.co.uk
web: www.cotswold-inns-hotels.co.uk/swan
dir: 9m S of Burford A40 onto B4425. 6m N of Cirencester A4179 onto B4425

This hotel, built in the 17th century as a coaching inn, is set in peaceful and picturesque surroundings. It provides well-equipped and smartly presented accommodation, including four luxury cottage suites set just outside the main hotel. The elegant public areas are comfortable and have feature fireplaces. There is a choice of dining options to suit all tastes. Cotswold Inns & Hotels – AA Small Hotel Group of the Year 2012-13.

Rooms 22 (4 annexe) (1 fmly) ✿ **Facilities** FTV Wi-fi ⓑ Fishing Xmas New Year **Conf** Class 50 Board 32 Thtr 80 **Services** Lift **Parking** 22 **Notes** Civ Wed 110

Bibury Court Hotel

★★★ 85% ⊛⊛ COUNTRY HOUSE HOTEL

☎ 01285 740337 & 741171
GL7 5NT
e-mail: info@biburycourt.com
web: www.biburycourt.com
dir: On B4425, 6m N of Cirencester (A4179). 8m S of Burford (A40), entrance by River Coln

Dating back to Tudor times, this elegant manor is the perfect antidote to the hustle and bustle of the modern world. Public areas have abundant charm and character. Bedrooms are spacious and offer traditional quality with modern comforts. A choice of interesting dishes is available in the conservatory at lunchtime, whereas dinner is served in the more formal restaurant. Staff are friendly and helpful.

Rooms 18 (3 fmly) (1 GF) **Facilities** FTV Wi-fi ⓑ Fishing ⤵ Xmas New Year **Conf** Class 50 Board 30 Thtr 50 **Parking** 40 **Notes** Civ Wed 80

BICESTER
Oxfordshire
Map 11 SP52

Bignell Park Hotel & Oaks Restaurant
THE INDEPENDENTS
HOTEL ASSOCIATION

★★★ 71% HOTEL

☎ 01869 326550
Chesterton OX26 1UE
e-mail: enq@bignellparkhotel.co.uk
web: www.bignellparkhotel.co.uk
dir: M40 junct 9/A41 to Bicester, over 1st & 2nd rdbts, left at mini-rdbt, follow signs to Witney A4095. Hotel 0.5m

This pleasant property is situated in the peaceful village of Chesterton, just a short drive from Bicester Village Retail Outlet, the M40 and Oxford. Public rooms feature an oak-beamed restaurant, a smart bar and a comfortable lounge with plush sofas. The bedrooms are smartly decorated, well maintained and equipped with modern facilities.

Rooms 23 (4 fmly) (9 GF) **Facilities** FTV Wi-fi Xmas New Year **Conf** Class 16 Board 60 Thtr 100 **Parking** 40 **Notes** ⊗ Civ Wed 60

BIDEFORD
Devon — Map 3 SS42

Yeoldon House Hotel

★★★ 77% ⊛ SMALL HOTEL

☎ 01237 474400
Durrant Ln, Northam EX39 2RL
e-mail: yeoldonhouse@aol.com
web: www.yeoldonhousehotel.co.uk
dir: A39 from Barnstaple over River Torridge Bridge. At rdbt right onto A386 towards Northam, 3rd right into Durrant Lane

In a tranquil location with superb views over attractive grounds and the River Torridge, this is a charming Victorian house. The well-equipped bedrooms are individually decorated and some have balconies with breathtaking views. The public rooms are full of character with many interesting features and artefacts. The daily-changing dinner menu offers imaginative dishes.

Rooms 10 **S** £80-£90; **D** £120-£140 (incl. bkfst) **Facilities** FTV Wi-fi **Parking** 20 **Notes** LB Closed 24-27 Dec Civ Wed 50

Royal Hotel

(Brend Hotels)

★★★ 74% HOTEL

☎ 01237 472005
Barnstaple St EX39 4AE
e-mail: reservations@royalbideford.co.uk
web: www.royalbideford.co.uk
dir: At eastern end of old Bideford Bridge

A quiet and relaxing hotel, the Royal is set near the river within a five-minute walk of the busy town

centre and the quay. The bright, well maintained public areas retain much of the charm and style of its 16th-century origins, particularly in the wood-panelled Kingsley Suite. Bedrooms are well equipped and comfortable. The meals at dinner and the lounge snacks are appetising.

Rooms 32 (2 fmly) (2 GF) **S** £59-£120; **D** £75-£120* **Facilities** FTV Wi-fi Xmas New Year **Conf** Class 100 Board 100 Thtr 100 **Services** Lift **Parking** 70 **Notes** LB ⊗ Civ Wed 130

Durrant House Hotel

★★★ Ⓐ HOTEL

☎ 01237 472361
Heywood Rd, Northam EX39 3QB
e-mail: info@durranthousehotel.com
dir: A39 to Bideford, over New Torridge Bridge, right at rdbt, hotel 500yds on right

Rooms 125 (25 fmly) (14 GF) **Facilities** FTV Wi-fi Gym Sauna Xmas New Year **Conf** Class 100 Board 80 Thtr 350 **Services** Lift **Parking** 200 **Notes** Civ Wed 100

BIGBURY-ON-SEA
Devon — Map 3 SX64

Henley Hotel

★★ 83% SMALL HOTEL

☎ 01548 810240
TQ7 4AR
e-mail: thehenleyhotel@btconnect.com
dir: Through Bigbury, past Golf Centre into Bigbury-on-Sea. Hotel on left

Built in Edwardian times and complete with its own private cliff path to a sandy beach, this small hotel boasts stunning views from an elevated position. Family run, it is a perfect choice for guests wishing to escape from the hurried pace of life to a peaceful retreat. Personal service, friendly hospitality and food cooked with care using local, fresh produce combine to make this an uncomplicated yet special place to stay.

Rooms 6 **S** £85; **D** £120-£144 (incl. bkfst)* **Facilities** FTV Wi-fi **Parking** 9 **Notes** LB No children 12yrs Closed Nov-Mar

BILDESTON
Suffolk — Map 13 TL94

The Bildeston Crown

★★★ ⊛⊛⊛ HOTEL

☎ 01449 740510
104 High St IP7 7EB
e-mail: hayley@thebildestoncrown.co.uk
web: www.thebildestoncrown.co.uk
dir: A12 junct 31, B1070 towards Hadleigh. At T-junct left onto A1141, right onto B1115. Hotel 0.5m

A charming Grade II former coaching inn situated in a peaceful village. Public areas feature beams, exposed brickwork and oak floors, with contemporary style decor; they include a choice of bars, a lounge and a restaurant. The individually designed bedrooms, including a romantic four-poster room, have lovely co-ordinated fabrics and modern facilities that include Musicast systems and internet access via Wi-fi and LAN. Food here is the real focus and certainly a draw; both the chef and the owner, who is a farmer, are very conscious of reducing 'food miles'; top quality produce such as Red Poll beef (from the owner's own farm), locally reared lamb, pork and seasonal game appear on the menus. Accomplished technical skills achieve award-winning results.

Rooms 13 **S** £70-£120; **D** £150-£195 (incl. bkfst) **Facilities** STV FTV Wi-fi Xmas New Year **Conf** Class 25 Board 16 Thtr 40 Del from £150 to £200 **Services** Lift **Parking** 30 **Notes** LB Civ Wed 50

Save on hotels. Book at **theAA.com/hotel**

BID – BIR 67 ENGLAND

B

BILLINGHAM
Co Durham   Map 19 NZ42

Wynyard Hall Hotel

★★★★ 83% ◉◉ HOTEL

☎ 01740 644811
Wynyard Village TS22 5NF
e-mail: enq@wynyardhall.co.uk
web: www.wynyardhall.co.uk
dir: A19, A1027 towards Stockton. At rdbt take B1274 (Junction Rd). At next rdbt take A177 (Durham Rd). Right onto Wynyard Rd signed Wolviston. Left into estate

Drive though the gates, over the lion bridge and Wynyard Hall will immediately impress with its grandeur and elegance. The opulent public areas are as much a feature of the property as are the grounds and gardens. The individually designed bedrooms and suites are stunning with a combination of modern and period style furniture. The elegant, award-winning Duke of Wellington restaurant is also impressive. The Essential Time Treatment Suite offers many relaxing therapies and beauty treatments. As a wedding venue the hall provides the option for a civil ceremony, or a religious service in the chapel, followed by a memorable reception.

Rooms 25 (9 annexe) (1 fmly) (9 GF) 🐾 **S** £180–£240; **D** £180–£240 (incl. bkfst)* **Facilities** Spa FTV Wi-fi 🦆 🌊 Clay pigeon shooting Archery Hawk walk Xmas New Year **Conf** Class 240 Board 50 Thtr 300 **Services** Lift **Parking** 500 **Notes** LB Civ Wed 150

BINGLEY
West Yorkshire   Map 19 SE13

Five Rise Locks Hotel & Restaurant

★★★ 75% ◉ SMALL HOTEL

☎ 01274 565296
Beck Ln BD16 4DD
e-mail: info@five-rise-locks.co.uk
dir: From Main St into Park Rd, in 0.5m left into Beck Ln

A warm welcome and comfortable accommodation awaits guests at this impressive Victorian building. Bedrooms are of a good size and feature homely extras. The restaurant offers imaginative dishes and the bright breakfast room overlooks open countryside.

Rooms 9 (2 GF) **S** £50–£69; **D** £80–£92 (incl. bkfst)* **Facilities** FTV Wi-fi **Conf** Class 16 Board 18 Thtr 25 Del from £95 to £120* **Parking** 20 **Notes** LB

BIRCHANGER GREEN MOTORWAY SERVICE AREA (M11)
Essex   Map 6 TL52

Days Inn Bishop's Stortford - M11

BUDGET HOTEL

☎ 01279 656477
CM23 5QZ
e-mail: birchanger.hotel@welcomebreak.co.uk
web: www.welcomebreak.co.uk
dir: M11 junct 8

This modern building offers accommodation in smart, spacious and well-equipped bedrooms, suitable for families and business travellers, and all with en suite bathrooms. Continental breakfast is available and other refreshments may be taken at the nearby family restaurant. See also the Hotel Groups pages.

Rooms 60 (12 fmly) (29 GF) (8 smoking) **S** £39.95–£59.95; **D** £49.95–£69.95*

BIRKENHEAD
Merseyside   Map 15 SJ38

The RiverHill Hotel

★★★ 82% HOTEL

☎ 0151 653 3773
Talbot Rd, Prenton CH43 2HJ
e-mail: reception@theriverhill.co.uk
web: www.theriverhill.co.uk
dir: M53 junct 3, A552. Left onto B5151 at lights, hotel 0.5m on right

Pretty lawns and gardens provide the setting for this friendly, privately owned hotel. Its convenient location and attractive grounds make it a popular wedding venue. The comfortable bedrooms are equipped with a wealth of extras; ground floor, family, and four-poster rooms are available. Well cooked meals and substantial breakfasts are served in the elegant restaurant overlooking the garden.

Rooms 15 (1 fmly) **Facilities** STV FTV Wi-fi Free use of local leisure facilities **Conf** Class 30 Board 52 Thtr 50 **Parking** 32 **Notes** ⊗ Civ Wed 40

Premier Inn Wirral (Greasby)

Premier Inn

BUDGET HOTEL

☎ 0871 527 9176
Greasby Rd, Greasby, Wirral CH49 2PP
web: www.premierinn.com
dir: 9m from Liverpool city centre. 2m from M53 junct 2. Just off B5139

High quality, budget accommodation ideal for both families and business travellers. Spacious, en suite bedrooms feature tea and coffee making facilities, and Freeview TV in most hotels. Internet access and Wi-fi are available for a small fee. The adjacent family restaurant features a wide and varied menu. See also the Hotel Groups pages.

Rooms 30

BIRMINGHAM
West Midlands   Map 10 SP08

See also Bromsgrove, Lea Marston, Oldbury & Sutton Coldfield

Birmingham Marriott Hotel

Marriott HOTELS & RESORTS

★★★★ 78% HOTEL

☎ 0121 452 1144
12 Hagley Rd, Five Ways B16 8SJ
e-mail: pascal.demarchi@marriotthotels.com
web: www.birminghammarriott.co.uk
dir: Leebank Middleway to Five Ways rdbt, 1st left then right. Follow signs for hotel

Situated in the suburb of Edgbaston, this Edwardian hotel is a prominent landmark on the outskirts of the city centre. Air-conditioned bedrooms are decorated in a comfortable, modern style and provide a comprehensive range of extra facilities. Public rooms include the contemporary, brasserie-style West 12 Bar and Restaurant.

Rooms 104 **Facilities** Spa STV Wi-fi 🦆 Gym Steam room **Conf** Board 35 Thtr 80 **Services** Lift Air con **Parking** 50 **Notes** ⊗ Civ Wed 60

B

BIRMINGHAM *continued*

Crowne Plaza Birmingham City Centre

★★★★ 78% HOTEL

☎ 0121 224 5000
Central Square, Holliday St B1 1HH
e-mail: enquiries@cpbhamcity.com
web: www.crowneplaza.com
dir: A38, follow city centre signs. After 2nd tunnel (Suffolk Queensway) into left slip road, follow signs for New St Station & The Mailbox. Hotel adjacent to The Mailbox

This hotel is ideally situated with cultural centres on its doorstep, and the city's heart just a stone's throw away. Accommodation is spacious and luxurious, with every home comfort provided. Well cooked meals are offered in the modern restaurant. Underground parking (separately owned) is provided.

Rooms 312 (115 fmly) **Facilities** STV FTV Wi-fi ↕ HL Gym **Conf** Class 150 Board 40 Thtr 300 **Services** Lift Air con **Notes** Civ Wed 200

Hotel du Vin Birmingham

★★★★ 76% ◉
TOWN HOUSE HOTEL

☎ 0121 200 0600
25 Church St B3 2NR
e-mail: info@birmingham.hotelduvin.com
web: www.hotelduvin.com
dir: M6 junct 6/A38(M) to city centre, over flyover. Keep left & exit at St Chads Circus signed Jewellery Quarter. At lights & rdbt take 1st exit, follow signs for Colmore Row, opposite cathedral. Right into Church St, across Barwick St. Hotel on right

The former Birmingham Eye Hospital has become a chic and sophisticated hotel. The stylish, high-ceilinged rooms, all with a wine theme, are luxuriously appointed and feature stunning bathrooms, sumptuous duvets and Egyptian cotton sheets. The Bistro offers relaxed dining and a top-notch wine list, while other attractions include a champagne bar, a wine boutique and a health club.

Rooms 66 **S** £125-£175; **D** £135-£195* **Facilities** Spa STV Wi-fi Gym Steam room Sauna Xmas New Year **Conf** Class 40 Board 40 Thtr 84 Del from £165 to £205 **Services** Lift Air con **Notes** LB Civ Wed 84

Macdonald Burlington Hotel

★★★★ 76% HOTEL

☎ 0844 879 9019 & 0121 643 9191
Burlington Arcade, 126 New St B2 4JQ
e-mail: events.burlington@macdonald-hotels.co.uk
web: www.macdonaldhotels.co.uk/burlington
dir: M6 junct 6, A38, follow city centre signs

The Burlington's original Victorian grandeur - the marble and iron staircases and the high ceilings - blend seamlessly with modern facilities. Bedrooms are equipped to a good standard and public areas include a stylish bar and coffee lounge. The Berlioz Restaurant specialises in innovative dishes using fresh produce.

Rooms 114 (6 fmly) ⚑ **Facilities** STV Wi-fi ↕ HL New Year **Conf** Class 200 Board 80 Thtr 500 Del from £120 to £165* **Services** Lift **Notes** Closed 24-26 Dec Civ Wed 400

Novotel Birmingham Centre

★★★★ 74% HOTEL

☎ 0121 643 2000
70 Broad St B1 2HT
e-mail: h1077@accor.com
web: www.novotel.com
dir: M6 junct 6, A38(M) (Aston Expressway), A456 towards Kidderminster

This large, modern, purpose-built hotel benefits from an excellent city centre location, with the bonus of secure parking. Bedrooms are spacious, modern and well equipped especially for business users; four rooms have facilities for less able guests. Public areas include the Garden Brasserie, function rooms and a fitness room.

Rooms 148 (148 fmly) ⚑ **S** £49-£235; **D** £49-£245* **Facilities** Wi-fi ↕ Gym Fitness room Cardiovascular equipment Sauna Steam room New Year **Conf** Class 120 Board 90 Thtr 300 Del from £99 to £265* **Services** Lift Air con **Parking** 53 **Notes** LB

Radisson Blu Hotel Birmingham

★★★★ 74% HOTEL

☎ 0121 654 6000
12 Holloway Circus, Queensway B1 1BT
e-mail: info.birmingham@radissonblu.com
dir: A3844, through A38 underpass, left, merge into Suffolk St Queensway. Hotel on corner of Holloway Circus Queensway

This modern glass structure of 39 floors sits in the heart of the city dominating the area with its concept design. The interior continues the modern look and feel - public areas have wooden floors, leather seating and a stylish Italian restaurant. The bedrooms are individually appointed with bold colours and designer pieces of furniture that create the wow factor. The small gym, sauna suite and spa areas add to the hotel's impressive facilities.

Rooms 211 (16 smoking) **Facilities** Spa STV FTV Wi-fi ↕ Gym **Conf** Class 48 Board 40 Thtr 130 **Services** Lift Air con **Notes** ⊗ Civ Wed 130

Menzies Strathallan

MenziesHotels

★★★★ 72% HOTEL

☎ 0121 455 9777
225 Hagley Rd, Edgbaston B16 9RY
e-mail: strathallan@menzieshotels.co.uk
web: www.menzies-hotels.co.uk
dir: From A38 follow signs for ICC into Broad St, towards Five Ways island, take underpass to Hagley Rd. Hotel 1m

Located just a few minutes from the city's central attractions and with the benefit of excellent parking, this hotel provides a range of comfortable and well-equipped bedrooms. A modern lounge bar and contemporary restaurant offer a good range of dining options.

Rooms 135 **Facilities** FTV Wi-fi ↕ Gym Xmas New Year **Conf** Class 90 Board 50 Thtr 170 **Services** Lift **Parking** 120 **Notes** ⊗ Civ Wed 100

Copthorne Hotel Birmingham

MILLENNIUM

★★★★ 70% HOTEL

☎ 0121 200 2727
Paradise Circus B3 3HJ
e-mail: reservations.birmingham@millenniumhotels.co.uk
web: www.millenniumhotels.co.uk
dir: M6 junct 6, city centre A38(M). After Queensway Tunnel follow International Convention Centre signs. At Paradise Circus island take right lane. Hotel in centre

This hotel is one of the few establishments in the city that benefits from its own car park. Bedrooms are spacious and come in a choice of styles, all with excellent facilities. Guests can choose to eat in the Bugis Street Brasserie which offers traditional Chinese, Singaporean and Malay cuisine.

Rooms 211 **Facilities** FTV Wi-fi ↕ Gym Xmas New Year **Conf** Class 120 Board 30 Thtr 200 Del from £105 to £139* **Services** Lift **Parking** 78 **Notes** ⊗ Civ Wed 150

B

Malmaison Birmingham

★★★ 85% ® HOTEL

☎ 0121 246 5000
1 Wharfside St, The Mailbox B1 1RD
e-mail: birmingham@malmaison.com
web: www.malmaison.com
dir: M6 junct 6, A38 towards Birmingham. Hotel within The Mailbox, signed from A38

The 'Mailbox' development, of which this stylish and contemporary hotel is a part, incorporates the very best in fashionable shopping outlets, an array of restaurants and ample parking. The air-conditioned bedrooms are stylishly decorated and feature comprehensive facilities. Public rooms include a contemporary bar and brasserie which prove a hit with guests and locals alike. Gymtonic, and a Petit Spa offering rejuvenating treatments are also available.

Rooms 189 **Facilities** Wi-fi Gym **Conf** Class 40 Board 24 Thtr 50 **Services** Lift Air con

Best Western Westley Hotel

★★★ 82% HOTEL

☎ 0121 706 4312
80-90 Westley Rd, Acocks Green B27 7UJ
e-mail: reservations@westley-hotel.co.uk
dir: A41 signed Birmingham on Solihull by-pass, to Acocks Green. At rdbt, 2nd exit B4146 (Westley Rd). Hotel 200yds on left

Situated in the city suburbs and conveniently located for the N.E.C. and the airport, this friendly hotel provides well-equipped, smartly presented bedrooms. In addition to the main restaurant, there is also a lively bar and brasserie together with a large function room.

Rooms 37 (11 annexe) (3 fmly) (3 GF) **Facilities** STV Wi-fi ⌨ New Year **Conf** Class 80 Board 50 Thtr 200 **Parking** 150 **Notes** ⊗ Civ Wed 200

Thistle Birmingham City

thistle

★★★ 81% HOTEL

☎ 0871 376 9005
St Chads, Queensway B4 6HY
e-mail: birminghamcity@thistle.co.uk
web: www.thistle.com/birminghamcity
dir: From M6 junct 6 onto Aston Expressway towards city centre, after 1m exit A38 signed Jewellery Quarter. Hotel on left

This hotel benefits from a central location and is convenient for both the motorway network and nearby extensive parking facilities. Bedrooms range in size and style with most bedrooms providing air conditioning, along with a host of thoughtful guest extras. A modern comfortable lounge bar links to a terrace area.

Rooms 133 (3 fmly) **Facilities** STV Wi-fi Xmas New Year **Conf** Class 90 Board 35 Thtr 180 **Services** Lift **Notes** ⊗ Civ Wed 170

Holiday Inn Birmingham City

★★★ 80% HOTEL

☎ 0871 942 9008
Smallbrook Queensway B5 4EW
e-mail: reservations-birminghamcity@ihg.com
web: www.holidayinn.co.uk
dir: M6 junct 6, A38(M) to city centre, keep left after flyover & two underpasses. 2nd left into Suffolk Place. 1st right into St Jude's Passage

This is a large hotel in the city centre with extensive meeting rooms and a business centre. The lounge bar with a roof terrace is a popular meeting place. The Albany Restaurant offers lunch and dinner, and room service is available.

Rooms 241 (8 fmly) ↻ **S** £50-£189; **D** £50-£189 **Facilities** FTV Wi-fi ⌨ Xmas New Year **Conf** Class 300 Board 150 Thtr 600 Del from £99 to £179 **Services** Lift Air con **Parking** 10 **Notes** LB Civ Wed 600

Holiday Inn Birmingham M6 Jct 7

★★★ 74% HOTEL

☎ 0871 942 9009 & 0121 357 7303
Chapel Ln, Great Barr B43 7BG
e-mail: birminghamgreatbarr@ihg.com
web: www.holidayinn.co.uk
dir: M6 junct 7, A34 signed Walsall. Hotel 200yds on right across carriageway in Chapel Ln

Situated in pleasant surroundings, this modern hotel offers well-equipped and comfortable bedrooms. Public areas include the popular Traders restaurant and a comfortable lounge where a menu is available to guests all day. There is also 24-hour room service; a courtyard patio and a garden.

Rooms 190 (45 fmly) (67 GF) (12 smoking) **Facilities** STV FTV Wi-fi ⌨ supervised Gym Xmas New Year **Conf** Class 75 Board 50 Thtr 160 **Services** Air con **Parking** 250 **Notes** Civ Wed 160

Edgbaston Palace Hotel

★★★ 72% HOTEL

☎ 0121 452 1577
198-200 Hagley Rd, Edgbaston B16 9PQ
e-mail: enquiries@edgbastonpalacehotel.com
dir: M5 junct 3 N, A456 for 4.3m. Hotel on right

Dating back to the 19th century, this Grade II listed Victorian property has bedrooms that are modern, well appointed and offer good comfort levels. The hospitality is warm, personal and refreshing. Supervised children under 18 are welcome.

Rooms 48 (21 annexe) (3 fmly) (16 GF) **Facilities** FTV Wi-fi **Conf** Class 70 Board 60 Thtr 200 **Parking** 70 **Notes** ⊗

Ramada Encore Birmingham City Centre

★★★ 72% HOTEL

☎ 0121 622 8800
Ernerst Street/Holloway Head B1 1NS
e-mail: reservations@encorebirmingham.co.uk
dir: M6 junct 6/A38, merge onto A5127, follow A38 onto A41 exit onto Suffolk Queensway, at rdbt take 4th exit onto Holloway Head

Located in the heart of the city, this hotel offers stylish and comfortable accommodation. 'The Hub' is a smart, modern, open plan bar and restaurant with a choice of seating areas and offers a full dining menu all day.

Rooms 131 (11 fmly) **Facilities** STV Wi-fi ⌨ Xmas New Year **Conf** Class 10 Board 20 Thtr 30 **Services** Lift **Parking** 24 **Notes** ⊗

BIRMINGHAM *continued*

Park Inn by Radisson Birmingham Walsall, M6 Jct 9

★★★ 67% HOTEL

☎ 01922 639100
Bescot Crescent WS1 4SE
e-mail: reservations.walsall@rezidorparkinn.com
dir: M6 junct 9 (signed Wednesbury), A461 (signed Walsall). At lights right onto A4148 (signed Ring Road, Birmingham, A34). At lights right into Bescot Cres (signed Bescot Stadium) pass stadium, hotel on left. (NB use WS1 4SA for Sat Nav)

This hotel is set just off the motorway and within easy reach of all the attractions around Birmingham, including the NEC. The bedrooms are bright and modern; all have air conditioning and spacious work desks. There are family rooms, twin rooms and double rooms. The spacious Hub Bar and Restaurant is the venue for a hot buffet breakfast. A meeting room and a fitness suite are also available.

Rooms 121

Great Barr Hotel & Conference Centre

★★★ 66% HOTEL

☎ 0121 357 1141
Pear Tree Dr, Newton Rd, Great Barr B43 6HS
e-mail: sales@thegreatbarrhotel.com
web: www.thegreatbarrhotel.com
dir: M6 junct 7, at Scott Arms x-rds right towards West Bromwich (A4010) Newton Rd. Hotel 1m on right

This busy hotel, situated in a leafy residential area, is particularly popular with business clients; the hotel has excellent, state-of-the-art training and seminar facilities. There is a traditional oak-panelled bar and formal restaurant. The bedrooms are appointed to a good standard and have the expected amenities.

Rooms 92 (6 fmly) **Facilities** STV Wi-fi
Conf Class 90 Board 60 Thtr 200 **Parking** 200
Notes ⊗ RS BH (restaurant may close) Civ Wed 200

Campanile Birmingham

BUDGET HOTEL

☎ 0121 359 3330
Chester St, Aston B6 4BE
e-mail: birmingham@campanile.com
web: www.campanile.com
dir: Adjacent to rdbt at junct of A4540 & A38

This modern building offers accommodation in smart, well-equipped bedrooms, all with en suite bathrooms.

Refreshments may be taken at the informal bistro. See also the Hotel Groups pages.

Rooms 110 (5 fmly) **Conf** Class 100 Board 100 Thtr 250

Holiday Inn Express Birmingham City Centre

BUDGET HOTEL

☎ 0845 1126151
65 Lionel St B3 1JE
e-mail: enquiries@hiexpressbirminghamcitycentre.co.uk
web: www.hiexpress.com/exb'minghamc
dir: A38 to City Centre until Paradise Circus, take 4th exit on Queensway, 1st left into Lionel St, hotel on right

A modern hotel ideal for families and business travellers. Fresh and uncomplicated, the spacious rooms include Sky TV, power shower and tea and coffee-making facilities. Continental buffet breakfast is included in the room rate; other meals may be taken at the nearby family pub or restaurant. See also the Hotel Groups pages.

Rooms 120 (80 fmly) ⇘ **S** £55-£145; **D** £55-£145 (incl. bkfst)* **Conf** Class 16 Board 16 Thtr 30 Del from £75 to £165*

Holiday Inn Express Birmingham - South A45

BUDGET HOTEL

☎ 0121 289 3333
1270 Coventry Rd, Yardley B25 8BS
e-mail: reservations@hiex-birmingham.co.uk

Rooms 83

Ibis Birmingham Bordesley Circus

BUDGET HOTEL

☎ 0121 506 2600
1 Bordesley Park Rd, Bordesley B10 0PD
e-mail: H2178@accor.com
web: www.ibishotel.com

Modern, budget hotel offering comfortable accommodation in bright and practical bedrooms. Breakfast is self-service and dinner is available in the restaurant. See also the Hotel Groups pages.

Rooms 87 (15 GF) ⇘

Ibis Birmingham City Centre

BUDGET HOTEL

☎ 0121 622 6010
Arcadian Centre, Ladywell Walk B5 4ST
e-mail: h1459@accor-hotels.com
web: www.ibishotel.com
dir: From motorways follow city centre signs. Then follow Bullring or Indoor Market signs. Hotel adjacent to market

Rooms 159 (5 fmly) **Conf** Class 60 Board 50 Thtr 120

Ibis Birmingham Holloway Circus

BUDGET HOTEL

☎ 0121 622 4925
55 Irving St B1 1DH
e-mail: H2092@accor.com
web: www.ibishotel.com
dir: From M6 take A38 (City Centre), left after 2nd tunnel. Right at rdbt, 4th left (Sutton St) into Irving St. Hotel on left

Rooms 51 (26 GF)

Premier Inn Birmingham Broad St Canal Side

BUDGET HOTEL

☎ 0871 527 8078
20 Bridge St B1 2JH
web: www.premierinn.com
dir: M6 junct 6, A38(M) towards city centre. Follow signs for city centre/ICC/A456 (Broad St). Left at Hyatt Hotel, hotel on right at bottom of Bridge St

High quality, budget accommodation ideal for both families and business travellers. Spacious, en suite bedrooms feature tea and coffee making facilities, and Freeview TV in most hotels. Internet access and Wi-fi are available for a small fee. The adjacent family restaurant features a wide and varied menu. See also the Hotel Groups pages.

Rooms 83

Premier Inn Birmingham Broad Street (Brindley Place)

BUDGET HOTEL

☎ 0871 527 8076
80 Broad St B15 1AU
web: www.premierinn.com
dir: M6 junct 6, A38(M) (Aston Expressway). Follow City Centre, ICC & NIA signs into Broad St. Right into Sheepcote St. 2nd left at rdbt into Essington St. Hotel on left. (NB for Sat Nav use B16 8AL)

Rooms 62

Save on hotels. Book at **theAA.com/hotel**

BIR 71 ENGLAND

B

Premier Inn Birmingham Central East

BUDGET HOTEL

☎ 0871 527 8080
Richard St, Aston, Waterlinks B7 4AA
web: www.premierinn.com
dir: M6 junct 6, signed city centre. A38(M) signed A4540 (ring road). At rdbt 1st exit 50mtrs left into Richard St, hotel on left (barrier access to car park)

Rooms 61

Premier Inn Birmingham Central (Hagley Road)

BUDGET HOTEL

☎ 0871 527 8082
Hagley Rd B16 9NY
web: www.premierinn.com
dir: M6 junct 6, A38(M) (Aston Express Way). Follow city centre, ICC & NIA signs, into Broad St. From M5 junct 3, A456 for approx 3m, hotel on left

Rooms 62

Premier Inn Birmingham City Centre (Waterloo Street)

BUDGET HOTEL

☎ 0871 527 8074
3-6 Waterloo St B2 5PG
web: www.premierinn.com
dir: M6 junct 6, A38 (Corporation St). Follow West Bromwich/A41 signs. Merge into St Chad's Queensway. 2nd exit for Great Charles St Queensway, becomes Livery St. Left into Waterloo St

Rooms 109

Premier Inn Birmingham (Great Barr/M6 Jct 7)

BUDGET HOTEL

☎ 0871 527 8072
Birmingham Rd, Great Barr B43 7AG
web: www.premierinn.com
dir: M6 junct 7, A34 towards Walsall. Hotel on left behind Beacon Harvester

Rooms 32

Premier Inn Birmingham South (Hall Green)

BUDGET HOTEL

☎ 0871 527 8092
Stratford Rd, Hall Green B28 9ES
web: www.premierinn.com
dir: M42 junct 4, A34 towards Shirley signed Birmingham. Straight on at 6 rdbts. At 7th rdbt 4th exit. Hotel on left

Rooms 51

BIRMINGHAM AIRPORT Map 10 SP08
West Midlands

Novotel Birmingham Airport

★★★★ 71% HOTEL

☎ 0121 782 7000 & 782 4111
B26 3QL
e-mail: H1158@accor.com
web: www.novotel.com
dir: M42 junct 6, A45 to Birmingham, signed to airport. Hotel opposite main terminal

This smartly decorated hotel with air conditioning throughout its public areas and bedrooms benefits from being less than a minute's walk from the main terminal of Birmingham International Airport. Spacious bedrooms are comfortable and modern bathrooms are stylish with powerful showers. The Elements bar and restaurant provides a great atmosphere for meals and a fitness room is available on site. Long stay car parking packages can be arranged at this location.

Rooms 195 (24 fmly) 🐾 S £89-£200; D £89-£200
Facilities STV Wi-fi 🐾 Gym Fitness room
Conf Class 10 Board 20 Thtr 35 Services Lift Air con

Ibis Birmingham Airport

BUDGET HOTEL

☎ 0121 780 5800
Ambassador Rd, Bickenhill, Solihull B26 3AW
e-mail: H6359@accor.com
dir: M42 junct 6, A45 follow signs to Birmingham Airport

Modern, budget hotel offering comfortable accommodation in bright and practical bedrooms. Breakfast is self-service and dinner is available in the restaurant. See also the Hotel Groups pages.

Rooms 162 (2 fmly)

BIRMINGHAM Map 10 SP18
(NATIONAL EXHIBITION CENTRE)
West Midlands

Best Western Premier Moor Hall Hotel & Spa

★★★★ 77% HOTEL

☎ 0121 308 3751
Moor Hall Dr, Four Oaks B75 6LN
e-mail: mail@moorhallhotel.co.uk
web: www.moorhallhotel.co.uk

(For full entry see Sutton Coldfield)

Nailcote Hall

★★★★ 76% ⊛ HOTEL

☎ 024 7646 6174
Nailcote Ln, Berkswell CV7 7DE
e-mail: info@nailcotehall.co.uk
web: www.nailcotehall.co.uk

(For full entry see Balsall Common)

Crowne Plaza Birmingham NEC

★★★★ 75% HOTEL

☎ 0871 942 9160
National Exhibition Centre, Pendigo Way B40 1PS
e-mail: necroomsales@ihg.com
web: www.crowneplaza.co.uk
dir: M42 junct 6, follow signs for NEC, take 2nd exit on left, South Way for hotel entrance 50mtrs on right

On the doorstep of the NEC and overlooking Pendigo Lake, this hotel has contemporary design and offers well-equipped bedrooms with air conditioning. Bedrooms have ample working space and high-speed internet access (for an additional charge). Eating options include the modern Pendigo Restaurant overlooking the lake, the bar and 24-hour room service.

Rooms 242 (12 fmly) (15 smoking) Facilities STV Wi-fi HL Gym Sauna Conf Class 140 Board 56 Thtr 200 Del from £129 to £189* Services Lift Air con Parking 348 Notes ⊗

B

BIRMINGHAM (NATIONAL EXHIBITION CENTRE) *continued*

Arden Hotel & Leisure Club

★★★ 74% HOTEL

☎ 01675 443221
Coventry Rd, Bickenhill B92 0EH
e-mail: enquiries@ardenhotel.co.uk
dir: M42 junct 6, A45 towards Birmingham. Hotel 0.25m on right, just off Birmingham International railway island

This smart hotel neighbouring the NEC offers modern rooms and well-equipped leisure facilities. After dinner in the formal restaurant, the place to relax is the spacious lounge area. A buffet breakfast is served in the bright and airy Meeting Place.

Rooms 216 (6 fmly) (6 GF) (12 smoking)
Facilities Spa STV Wi-fi 🕮 supervised Gym Beautician 🎵 New Year **Conf** Class 40 Board 60 Thtr 200 **Services** Lift **Parking** 300 **Notes** Closed 25-28 Dec Civ Wed 100

Haigs Hotel

★★★ 73% HOTEL

☎ 01676 533004
Kenilworth Rd CV7 7EL
e-mail: info@haigshotel.co.uk

(For full entry see Balsall Common)

Heath Lodge Hotel

★★ 74% HOTEL

☎ 0121 779 2218 & 07860 887212
117 Coleshill Rd, Marston Green B37 7HT
e-mail: enquiries@heathlodgehotel.co.uk
dir: 1m N of NEC or Birmingham International Airport & station. M6 junct 4, A446 signed North/Coleshill, 400yds, at rdbt left onto Coleshill Heath Rd. 0.5m, straight on at rdbt to Marston Green. Hotel at 2nd junct on right

This privately owned and personally run hotel is ideally located for visitors to the NEC and Birmingham Airport. Hospitality and service standards are high and while some bedrooms are compact, all are well equipped and comfortable. Public areas include a bar and a lounge, and a dining room that overlooks the pretty garden.

Rooms 23 (1 fmly) (6 GF) **Facilities** FTV Wi-fi Xmas **Conf** Class 30 Board 20 Thtr 35 **Parking** 23 **Notes** No children 2yrs

Holiday Inn Express Birmingham NEC

BUDGET HOTEL

☎ 0121 782 3222
Bickenhill Parkway, Bickenhill B40 1QA
e-mail: birmingham@morethanhotels.com
web: www.hiexpressbirminghamnec.co.uk
dir: M42 junct 6, follow signs for NEC

A modern hotel ideal for families and business travellers. Fresh and uncomplicated, the spacious rooms include Sky TV, power shower and tea and coffee-making facilities. Continental buffet breakfast is included in the room rate; other meals may be taken at the nearby family pub or restaurant. See also the Hotel Groups pages.

Rooms 179 (91 fmly) (23 GF) (3 smoking)
Conf Class 32 Board 32 Thtr 80

Premier Inn Birmingham NEC/Airport

BUDGET HOTEL

☎ 0871 527 8086
Off Bickenhill Parkway, National Exhibition Centre B40 1QA
web: www.premierinn.com
dir: M42 junct 6 signed NEC. Turn right towards North Way. Follow Premier Inn signs. Hotel on left at 5th rdbt

High quality, budget accommodation ideal for both families and business travellers. Spacious, en suite bedrooms feature tea and coffee making facilities, and Freeview TV in most hotels. Internet access and Wi-fi are available for a small fee. The adjacent family restaurant features a wide and varied menu. See also the Hotel Groups pages.

Rooms 199

Premier Inn Preston North

BUDGET HOTEL

☎ 0871 527 8912
Garstang Rd PR3 0RN
web: www.premierinn.com
dir: 4m from M6 junct 32 on A6 towards Garstang. 7m from Preston

High quality, budget accommodation ideal for both families and business travellers. Spacious, en suite bedrooms feature tea and coffee making facilities, and Freeview TV in most hotels. Internet access and Wi-fi are available for a small fee. The adjacent

family restaurant features a wide and varied menu. See also the Hotel Groups pages.

Rooms 40

Premier Inn Bishop Auckland

BUDGET HOTEL

☎ 0871 527 8096
West Auckland Rd DL14 9AP
web: www.premierinn.com
dir: From S: A1 junct 58, left onto A68 signed Corbridge/Bishop Auckland. At 1st rdbt 2nd exit onto A6072 signed Shildon. Straight on at 4 rdbts, follow Shildon/Bishop Auckland signs. Hotel approx 1m on left

High quality, budget accommodation ideal for both families and business travellers. Spacious, en suite bedrooms feature tea and coffee making facilities, and Freeview TV in most hotels. Internet access and Wi-fi are available for a small fee. The adjacent family restaurant features a wide and varied menu. See also the Hotel Groups pages.

Rooms 49

Down Hall Country House Hotel

★★★★ 77% HOTEL

☎ 01279 731441
Hatfield Heath CM22 7AS
e-mail: reservations@downhall.co.uk
web: www.downhall.co.uk
dir: A1060, at Hatfield Heath keep left. Right into lane opposite Hunters Meet restaurant, left at end, follow signs

Imposing country-house hotel set amidst 100 acres of mature grounds in a peaceful location just a short drive from Stansted Airport. Bedrooms are generally quite spacious; each one is pleasantly decorated, tastefully furnished and equipped with modern

Save on hotels. Book at **theAA.com/hotel**

BIR – BLA 73 ENGLAND

B

facilities. Public rooms include a choice of restaurants, a cocktail bar, two lounges and leisure facilities.

Down Hall Country House Hotel

Rooms 99 (20 GF) **D** £79-£169 (incl. bkfst)* **Facilities** FTV Wi-fi 🕸 ⚓ 🐬 Giant chess Whirlpool Sauna Snooker room Gym equipment Xmas New Year **Conf** Class 140 Board 68 Thtr 200 Del from £139 to £219* **Services** Lift **Parking** 150 **Notes** Civ Wed 150

Days Hotel London Stansted - M11

BUDGET HOTEL

☎ 01279 213900
M11 Motorway, Junction 8, Old Dunmow Rd CM23 5QZ
dir: Adjacent to M11 junct 8

This modern building offers accommodation in smart, spacious and well-equipped bedrooms, suitable for families and business travellers, and all with en suite bathrooms. There is an attractive lounge area and a dining room where breakfast is served and other refreshments may be taken. See also the Hotel Groups pages.

Rooms 77 (16 fmly) (16 GF) (8 smoking) 🐾
S £49.95-£99.95; **D** £52.95-£99.95*

BISHOPSTEIGNTON
Devon
Map 3 SX97

Cockhaven Manor Hotel

THE INDEPENDENTS
HOTEL ASSOCIATION

★★ 72% HOTEL

☎ 01626 775252
Cockhaven Rd TQ14 9RF
e-mail: cockhaven@btconnect.com
web: www.cockhavenmanor.com
dir: A380 towards Torquay, A381 towards Teignmouth. Left at Metro Motors. Hotel 500yds on left

A friendly, family-run inn that dates back to the 16th century. Bedrooms are well equipped and many enjoy views across the beautiful Teign estuary. A choice of dining options is offered, and traditional and interesting dishes, along with locally caught fish, prove popular.

Rooms 12 (2 fmly) **S** £50-£65; **D** £75-£90 (incl. bkfst)* **Facilities** FTV Wi-fi Petanque **Conf** Class 50 Board 30 Thtr 50 **Parking** 50 **Notes** LB Closed 25-26 Dec Civ Wed 100

BLACKBURN
Lancashire
Map 18 SD62

See also Langho

Mercure Blackburn Foxfields Country Hotel

★★★ 74% HOTEL

☎ 01254 822556
Whalley Rd, Billington, Clitheroe BB7 9HY
e-mail: enquiries@hotels-blackburn.com
dir: Just off A59

This modern hotel is easily accessible from major road networks. Bedrooms are comfortable and spacious, and include some suites and others with separate dressing areas. Facilities include a good-sized swimming pool, a small gym and conference suites. The traditional restaurant serves an interesting range of cuisine.

Rooms 44 (16 annexe) (27 fmly) (13 GF) (8 smoking) **Facilities** STV FTV Wi-fi 🕸 Gym Sauna Steam room Xmas New Year **Conf** Class 60 Board 60 Thtr 140 **Parking** 194 **Notes** Civ Wed 200

The Millstone at Mellor

★★ 85% ◉◉ HOTEL

☎ 01254 813333
Church Ln, Mellor BB2 7JR
e-mail: relax@millstonehotel.co.uk
web: www.millstonehotel.co.uk
dir: A677 from Blackburn (or from A59) follow signs to Mellor

Once a coaching inn, the Millstone is situated in a village just outside the town. The hotel provides a very high standard of accommodation, professional and friendly service and good food. Bedrooms, some in an adjacent house, are comfortable and generally spacious, and all are very well equipped. A room for less able guests is also available.

Rooms 23 (6 annexe) (5 fmly) (8 GF) 🐾 **S** £80-£112; **D** £89-£139 (incl. bkfst)* **Facilities** STV Wi-fi New Year **Parking** 40 **Notes** LB ⊗ Civ Wed 60

Premier Inn Blackburn North West

Premier Inn

BUDGET HOTEL

☎ 0871 527 8098
Myerscough Rd, Balderstone BB2 7LE
web: www.premierinn.com
dir: M6 junct 31, A59 towards Clitheroe. Hotel opposite British Aerospace, adjacent to Boddington Arms

High quality, budget accommodation ideal for both families and business travellers. Spacious, en suite bedrooms feature tea and coffee making facilities, and Freeview TV in most hotels. Internet access and Wi-fi are available for a small fee. The adjacent family restaurant features a wide and varied menu. See also the Hotel Groups pages.

Rooms 20

Premier Inn Blackburn South

BUDGET HOTEL

☎ 0871 527 8100
Off Eccleshill Rd, Riversway Dr, Lower Darwen BB3 0SN
web: www.premierinn.com
dir: At M65 junct 4

Rooms 43

BLACKPOOL
Lancashire
Map 18 SD33

The Imperial Hotel

PUMA HOTELS
COLLECTION

★★★★ 73% HOTEL

☎ 01253 623971
North Promenade FY1 2HB
e-mail: imperialblackpool@pumahotels.co.uk
web: www.pumahotels.co.uk
dir: M55 junct 2, A583 (North Shore), follow signs to North Promenade. Hotel on seafront, north of tower

Enjoying a prime seafront location, this grand Victorian hotel offers smartly appointed, well-equipped bedrooms and spacious, elegant public areas. Facilities include a smart leisure club, a comfortable lounge, the No.10 bar and an attractive split-level restaurant that overlooks the seafront. Conferences and functions are extremely well catered for.

Rooms 180 (16 fmly) **Facilities** Spa STV Wi-fi 🕸 supervised Gym Xmas New Year **Conf** Class 280 Board 70 Thtr 600 **Services** Lift **Parking** 150 **Notes** Civ Wed 200

BLACKPOOL *continued*

Best Western Carlton Hotel

★★★ 78% ◉ HOTEL

☎ 01253 628966

282-286 North Promenade FY1 2EZ
e-mail: mail@carltonhotelblackpool.co.uk
web: www.bw-carltonhotel.co.uk
dir: M6 junct 32, M55 follow signs for North Shore.
Between Blackpool Tower & Gynn Square

Enjoying a prime seafront location, this hotel offers
bedrooms that are attractively furnished in modern
style. Public areas include a choice of bar lounge and
seafront lounges. The fine dining Jali Indian
Restaurant is a contrast to the traditional dining
room; extensive function facilities are available and a
warm welcome is assured.

Rooms 58 (9 fmly) **S** £50-£76; **D** £60-£120 (incl.
bkfst) **Facilities** STV FTV Wi-fi ⤸ Xmas New Year
Conf Class 40 Board 40 Thtr 90 Del from £95 to
£135* **Services** Lift **Parking** 43 **Notes** LB ⊗
Civ Wed 80

Carousel Hotel

★★★ 77% HOTEL

☎ 01253 402642

663-671 New South Prom FY4 1RN
e-mail: carousel.reservations@sleepwellhotels.com
web: www.sleepwellhotels.com
dir: From M55 follow signs to airport, pass airport to
lights. Turn right, hotel 100yds on right

This friendly seafront hotel, close to the Pleasure
Beach, offers smart, contemporary accommodation.
Bedrooms are comfortably appointed and have a
modern, stylish feel to them. An airy restaurant and a
spacious bar/lounge both overlook the Promenade.
The hotel has good conference and meeting facilities
and its own car park.

Rooms 92 (22 fmly) **Facilities** FTV Wi-fi ⤸ ♫ Xmas
New Year **Conf** Class 30 Board 40 Thtr 100
Services Lift **Parking** 46 **Notes** ⊗ Civ Wed 150

The Claremont Hotel

★★ 75% HOTEL

☎ 0844 811 5570

270 North Promenade FY1 1SA
e-mail: reservations@choice-hotels.co.uk
dir: M55 junct 3 follow sign for promenade. Hotel
beyond North Pier

Conveniently situated this is a popular family holiday
hotel. The bedrooms are bright and attractively
decorated. The extensive public areas include a
spacious air-conditioned restaurant which offers a
good choice of dishes. There is a well equipped,

supervised children's play room, and entertainment is
provided during the season.

Rooms 143 (50 fmly) **S** £32-£55; **D** £64-£110 (incl.
bkfst & dinner) **Facilities** Wi-fi ☜ Beauty treatments
♫ Xmas New Year **Conf** Class 300 Board 75 Thtr 530
Del from £79 to £99.50* **Services** Lift **Parking** 40
Notes LB ⊗

The Viking Hotel

★★ 75% HOTEL

☎ 0844 811 5570

479 South Promenade FY4 1AY
e-mail: reservations@choice-hotels.co.uk
dir: M55 junct 3, follow Pleasure Beach signs

Located close to the centre of the South Promenade,
this establishment offers well equipped
accommodation and a warm welcome. Meals are
served in the attractive sea view restaurant and
entertainment is available in the renowned 'Talk of
the Coast' night club. Leisure facilities at sister
hotels are also available free of charge.

Rooms 101 (10 GF) (25 smoking) **S** £30-£80;
D £60-£120 (incl. bkfst & dinner) **Facilities** FTV Wi-fi
Cabaret club ♫ Xmas New Year **Services** Lift
Parking 50 **Notes** LB ⊗ No children 18yrs

The Cliffs Hotel

★★ 74% HOTEL

☎ 0844 811 5570 & 01253 595559
Queens Promenade FY2 9SG
e-mail: reservations@choice-hotels.co.uk
dir: M55 junct 3, follow Promenade signs. Hotel just
after Gynn rdbt

This large, privately owned and extremely popular
hotel is within easy reach of the town centre. The
bedrooms, including spacious family rooms, vary in
size. Public areas offer an all-day coffee shop, a
smart restaurant and a family room where children
are entertained.

Rooms 163 (53 fmly) ⟋ **S** £32-£55; **D** £64-£110 (incl.
bkfst & dinner) **Facilities** FTV Wi-fi ☜ supervised
Gym Beauty treatments ♫ Xmas New Year
Conf Class 210 Board 50 Thtr 475 Del from £79 to
£99.50* **Services** Lift **Parking** 30 **Notes** LB ⊗
Civ Wed 100

Hotel Sheraton

★★ 72% HOTEL

☎ 01253 352723

54-62 Queens Promenade FY2 9RP
e-mail: email@hotelsheraton.co.uk
web: www.hotelsheraton.co.uk
dir: 1m N from Blackpool Tower towards Fleetwood

This family-owned and run hotel is situated at the
quieter, northern end of the promenade. Public areas
include a choice of spacious lounges with sea views,
a large function suite where popular dancing and
cabaret evenings are held, and a heated indoor
swimming pool. The smartly appointed bedrooms
come in a range of sizes and styles.

Rooms 104 (45 fmly) (15 smoking) **Facilities** ☜
Table tennis Darts ♫ Xmas New Year **Conf** Class 100
Board 150 Thtr 200 **Services** Lift **Parking** 20
Notes ⊗

Headlands Hotel

★★ 71% HOTEL

☎ 01253 341179

611-613 South Promenade FY4 1NJ
e-mail: headlandshotel@aol.com
dir: From end of M55 follow South Promenade signs

This friendly, family owned hotel stands on the South
Promenade, close to the Pleasure Beach and many of
the town's major attractions. Bedrooms are
traditionally furnished and many enjoy sea views.
There is a choice of lounges and live entertainment is
provided regularly. Home cooked food is served in the
panelled dining room.

Rooms 41 (10 fmly) ⟋ **Facilities** Wi-fi Darts Games
room Pool Snooker ♫ Xmas New Year **Services** Lift
Parking 38 **Notes** Closed 2-15 Jan

Save on hotels. Book at **theAA.com/hotel**

BLA 75 **ENGLAND**

Lyndene Hotel

★★ **A** HOTEL

☎ 01253 346779
303/315 Promenade FY1 6AN
e-mail: enquiries@lyndenehotel.com
web: www.lyndenehotel.com

Rooms 140 (60 fmly) (12 GF) (140 smoking)
Facilities FTV Wi-fi ♫ Xmas New Year **Services** Lift
Parking 70 **Notes** ⊗ No children 5yrs

Queens Hotel

U   Leisureplex

☎ 01253 342015 & 336980
469-471 South Promendae FY4 1AY
e-mail: reservations@queenshotelblackpool.

Currently the rating for this establishment is not
confirmed. This may be due to a change of ownership
or because it has only recently joined the AA rating
scheme. For further details please see the AA website:
theAA.com

Rooms 107

Premier Inn Blackpool Airport

BUDGET HOTEL

☎ 0871 527 8106
Squire Gate Ln FY4 2QS
web: www.premierinn.com
dir: M55 junct 4, A5230, left at 1st rdbt towards
airport. Hotel just before Squires Gate rail station

High quality, budget accommodation ideal for both
families and business travellers. Spacious, en suite
bedrooms feature tea and coffee making facilities,
and Freeview TV in most hotels. Internet access and
Wi-fi are available for a small fee. The adjacent
family restaurant features a wide and varied menu.
See also the Hotel Groups pages.

Rooms 39

Premier Inn Blackpool (Bispham)

BUDGET HOTEL

☎ 0871 527 8102
Devonshire Rd, Bispham FY2 0AR
web: www.premierinn.com
dir: M55 junct 4, A583. At 5th lights turn right
(Whitegate Drive). Approx. 4.5m onto A587
(Devonshire Rd)

Rooms 40

Premier Inn Blackpool Central

BUDGET HOTEL

☎ 0871 527 8108
Yeadon Way, South Shore FY1 6BF
web: www.premierinn.com
dir: M55 junct 4 to Blackpool, straight on at last
island onto Yeaden Way. Follow signs for Central Car
Park/Coach Area. Left at Total garage

Rooms 82

Premier Inn Blackpool East (M55 Jct 4)

BUDGET HOTEL

☎ 0871 527 8110
Whitehills Park, Preston New Rd FY4 5NZ
web: www.premierinn.com
dir: Just off M55 junct 4. 1st left off rdbt. Hotel on
right

Rooms 81

BLAKENEY   Map 13 TG04
Norfolk

The Blakeney Hotel

★★★★ 76% ⊛ HOTEL

B

☎ 01263 740797
The Quay NR25 7NE
e-mail: reception@blakeneyhotel.co.uk
web: www.blakeneyhotel.co.uk
dir: From A148 between Fakenham & Holt, take
B1156 to Langham & Blakeney

A traditional, privately owned hotel situated on the
quayside with superb views across the estuary and
the salt marshes to Blakeney Point. Public rooms
feature an elegant restaurant, ground-floor lounge, a
bar and a first-floor sun lounge overlooking the
harbour. Bedrooms are smartly decorated and
equipped with modern facilities. The newly
refurbished leisure area is a real feature with pool,
sauna, steam room and mini gym.

Rooms 63 (16 annexe) (20 fmly) (17 GF)
S £91-£147; **D** £182-£318 (incl. bkfst & dinner)*
Facilities FTV Wi-fi ⊛ Gym Billiards Snooker Table
tennis Sauna Steam room Spa bath Xmas New Year
Conf Class 100 Board 100 Thtr 150 Del £145.20*
Services Lift **Parking** 60

BLAKENEY *continued*

INSPECTORS' CHOICE

Morston Hall

★★★ ◉◉◉ HOTEL

☎ 01263 741041
Morston, Holt NR25 7AA
e-mail: reception@morstonhall.com
web: www.morstonhall.com
dir: 1m W of Blakeney on A149 (King's Lynn to Cromer road)

This delightful 17th-century country-house hotel enjoys a tranquil setting amid well-tended gardens. The comfortable public rooms offer a choice of attractive lounges and a sunny conservatory, while the elegant dining room is the perfect setting to enjoy Galton Blackiston's award-winning cuisine. The spacious bedrooms are individually decorated and stylishly furnished with modern opulence.

Rooms 13 (6 annexe) (7 GF) ⟨ **S** £200-£280; **D** £340-£390 (incl. bkfst & dinner) **Facilities** STV FTV Wi-fi ⌇ New Year **Conf** Class 20 Board 16 Del from £310 to £360 **Parking** 40 **Notes** LB Closed 1 Jan-last Fri in Jan & 2 days Xmas

Blakeney Manor Hotel

★★ 78% HOTEL

☎ 01263 740376
The Quay, Holt NR25 7ND
e-mail: reception@blakeneymanor.co.uk
web: www.blakeneymanor.co.uk
dir: Exit A149 at Blakeney towards Blakeney Quay. Hotel at end of quay between Mariner's Hill & Friary Hills

An attractive Norfolk flint building overlooking Blakeney Marshes close to the town centre and quayside. The bedrooms are located in flint-faced barns in a courtyard adjacent to the main building. The spacious public rooms include a choice of lounges, a conservatory, a popular bar and a large restaurant offering an interesting choice of dishes.

Rooms 35 (28 annexe) (26 GF) **Facilities** Wi-fi Xmas New Year **Parking** 40 **Notes** No children 14yrs

BLEADON
Somerset — Map 4 ST35

Premier Inn Weston-Super-Mare

BUDGET HOTEL

☎ 0871 527 9154
Bridgwater Rd, Lympsham BS24 0BP
web: www.premierinn.com
dir: M5 junct 22, A38 (Bristol Rd) signed Weston-Super-Mare. At 1st rdbt take 1st exit into Bridgewater Rd (A370). Approx 2m to hotel

High quality, budget accommodation ideal for both families and business travellers. Spacious, en suite bedrooms feature tea and coffee making facilities, and Freeview TV in most hotels. Internet access and Wi-fi are available for a small fee. The adjacent family restaurant features a wide and varied menu. See also the Hotel Groups pages.

Rooms 24

BLETCHINGDON
Oxfordshire — Map 11 SP51

The Oxfordshire Inn

★★★ 64% HOTEL

☎ 01869 351444
Heathfield Village OX5 3DX
e-mail: staff@oxfordshireinn.co.uk
web: www.oxfordshireinn.co.uk
dir: M40 junct 9, A34 towards Oxford, A4027 towards Bletchingdon. Hotel signed 0.7m on right

A converted farmhouse with additional outbuildings that is located close to major motorway networks. The accommodation is set around an open courtyard, and includes suites that have four-poster beds. There is a spacious bar and restaurant.

Rooms 28 (4 fmly) (15 GF) **Facilities** Wi-fi Putt green Golf driving range Xmas New Year **Conf** Class 80 Board 30 Thtr 140 **Parking** 50

BODMIN
Cornwall — Map 2 SX06

Trehellas House Hotel & Restaurant

★★★ 74% ◉ SMALL HOTEL

☎ 01208 72700
Washaway PL30 3AD
e-mail: enquiries@trehellashouse.co.uk
web: www.trehellashouse.co.uk
dir: A389 from Bodmin towards Wadebridge. Hotel on right 0.5m beyond road to Camelford

This 18th-century former posting inn retains many original features and provides comfortable

accommodation. Bedrooms are located in both the main house and adjacent coach house - all provide the same high standards. An interesting choice of cuisine, with an emphasis on locally-sourced ingredients, is offered in the impressive slate-floored restaurant.

Rooms 12 (7 annexe) (2 fmly) (5 GF) **Facilities** FTV Wi-fi ⌇ Xmas New Year **Conf** Board 20 Thtr 20 **Parking** 32

Westberry Hotel

★★ 81% HOTEL

☎ 01208 72772
Rhind St PL31 2EL
e-mail: westberry@btconnect.com
web: www.westberryhotel.net
dir: On ring road off A30 & A38. St Petroc's Church on right, at mini rdbt turn right. Hotel on right

This popular hotel is conveniently located for both Bodmin town centre and the A30. The bedrooms are attractive and well equipped. A spacious bar lounge and a billiard room are also provided. The restaurant serves a variety of dishes, ranging from bar snacks to a more extensive carte menu.

Rooms 20 (8 annexe) (2 fmly) (6 GF) ⟨ **S** £38-£68; **D** £48-£78 (incl. bkfst) **Facilities** STV Wi-fi Full sized snooker table **Conf** Class 80 Board 80 Thtr 100 **Parking** 30 **Notes** LB

Premier Inn Bodmin

BUDGET HOTEL

☎ 0871 527 8112
Launceston Rd PL31 2AR
web: www.premierinn.com
dir: From A30 S'bound exit onto A389, hotel 0.5m on right. N'bound exit onto A38, follow A389 signs. Left at T-junct

High quality, budget accommodation ideal for both families and business travellers. Spacious, en suite bedrooms feature tea and coffee making facilities, and Freeview TV in most hotels. Internet access and Wi-fi are available for a small fee. The adjacent family restaurant features a wide and varied menu. See also the Hotel Groups pages.

Rooms 44

Save on hotels. Book at **theAA.com/hotel**

BLA – BOL   77   ENGLAND

BOGNOR REGIS
West Sussex   Map 6 SZ99

The Russell Hotel

★★★ 77% HOTEL

☎ 01243 871300
King's Pde PO21 2QP
e-mail: russell@visionhotels.co.uk
dir: A27 follow signs for town centre, hotel on seafront

Situated in a pleasant location close to the seafront, the Russell Hotel offers large and well-appointed bedrooms; some are fully accessible and many have sea views. This hotel also caters for visually impaired people, their families, friends and their guide dogs, as well as offering a warm welcome to business and leisure guests. There are of course special facilities for the guide dogs. Leisure facilities are also available.

Rooms 40 (5 fmly) ⸙ **D** £39-£149 (incl. bkfst)*
Facilities FTV Wi-fi ⬡ supervised Gym ♫ Xmas New Year **Conf** Class 60 Board 40 Thtr 100 Del from £69 to £99* **Services** Lift **Parking** 6 **Notes** LB

The Inglenook

★★★ 67% SMALL HOTEL

☎ 01243 262495 & 265411
255 Pagham Rd, Nyetimber PO21 3QB
e-mail: reception@the-inglenook.com
dir: A27 into Vinnetrow Rd, left at Walnut Tree, hotel 2.5m on right

This 16th-century inn retains much of its original character, including exposed beams throughout. Bedrooms are individually decorated and vary in size. There is a cosy lounge, a well-kept garden and a bar that offers a popular evening menu and convivial atmosphere. The restaurant, overlooking the garden, also serves enjoyable cuisine.

Rooms 18 (1 fmly) (2 GF) ⸙ **S** £55-£75; **D** £95-£210 (incl. bkfst)* **Facilities** STV FTV Wi-fi Xmas New Year **Conf** Class 50 Board 50 Thtr 100 **Parking** 35 **Notes** LB Civ Wed 80

The Royal Norfolk Hotel

★★ 74% HOTEL

☎ 01243 826222
The Esplanade PO21 2LH
e-mail: royalnorfolk@alfatravel.co.uk
web: www.leisureplex.co.uk
dir: From A259 follow Longford Rd through lights to Canada Grove to T-junct. Right, take 2nd exit at rdbt. Hotel on right

Located on the seafront, but set back behind well-tended lawns and gardens is this fine looking

Regency hotel. The bedrooms are traditionally furnished and provide guests with modern comforts. There are sea views from the bar and restaurant, as well as the lounges.

Rooms 60 (3 fmly) (7 GF) ⸙ **S** £38-£55; **D** £62-£96 (incl. bkfst)* **Facilities** FTV Wi-fi ♫ Xmas New Year **Services** Lift **Parking** 25 **Notes** LB ⊗ Closed 2 Jan-14 Feb

Premier Inn Bognor Regis

BUDGET HOTEL

☎ 0871 527 8114
Shripney Rd PO22 9PA
web: www.premierinn.com
dir: From A27 & A29 rdbt junct follow Bognor Regis signs. Approx 4m, hotel on left

High quality, budget accommodation ideal for both families and business travellers. Spacious, en suite bedrooms feature tea and coffee making facilities, and Freeview TV in most hotels. Internet access and Wi-fi are available for a small fee. The adjacent family restaurant features a wide and varied menu. See also the Hotel Groups pages.

Rooms 24

BOLTON
Greater Manchester   Map 15 SD70

Egerton House Hotel

★★★ 81% ⊛ HOTEL

☎ 01204 307171
Blackburn Rd, Egerton BL7 9SB
e-mail: reservation@egertonhouse-hotel.co.uk
web: www.egertonhouse-hotel.co.uk
dir: M61, A666 (Bolton road), pass ASDA on right. Hotel 2m on just after war memorial on right

Peace and relaxation come as standard at this popular, privately owned hotel, that sits in acres of well-tended woodland gardens. Public rooms are stylishly appointed and have an inviting, relaxing atmosphere. Many of the individually styled, attractive guest bedrooms enjoy delightful garden views. Conferences and meetings are well catered for.

Rooms 29 (7 fmly) **Facilities** FTV Wi-fi ⬡ Xmas New Year **Conf** Class 90 Board 60 Thtr 150 **Parking** 135 **Notes** ⊗ Civ Wed 140

Mercure Bolton Last Drop Village Hotel & Spa

★★★ 74% HOTEL

☎ 01204 591131
Hospital Rd, Bromley Cross BL7 9PZ
e-mail: h6634@accor.com
web: www.mercure.com
dir: 3m N of Bolton off B5472

A collection of 18th-century farmhouses set on cobbled streets with various shops and a pub. Extensive self-contained conference rooms, a modern health and beauty spa and breathtaking views of the West Pennine Moors make this a popular choice with both corporate and leisure guests. The bedrooms are well equipped and spacious.

Rooms 128 (10 annexe) (29 fmly) (20 GF) **Facilities** Spa FTV Wi-fi ⬡ Gym Craft shops Thermal suite Rock sauna Steam bath Bio sauna Xmas New Year **Conf** Class 300 Board 95 Thtr 700 Del from £99 to £145 **Services** Lift **Parking** 400 **Notes** Civ Wed 500

Premier Inn Bolton (Reebok Stadium)

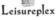

BUDGET HOTEL

☎ 0871 527 8116
Arena Approach 3, Horwich BL6 6LB
web: www.premierinn.com
dir: M61 junct 6, right at rdbt, left at 2nd rdbt

High quality, budget accommodation ideal for both families and business travellers. Spacious, en suite bedrooms feature tea and coffee making facilities, and Freeview TV in most hotels. Internet access and Wi-fi are available for a small fee. The adjacent family restaurant features a wide and varied menu. See also the Hotel Groups pages.

Rooms 74

Premier Inn Bolton West

BUDGET HOTEL

☎ 0871 527 8118
991 Chorley New Rd, Horwich BL6 4BA
web: www.premierinn.com
dir: M61 junct 6, follow dual carriageway signed Bolton/Horwich (Reebok Stadium on left). Hotel at 2nd rdbt

Rooms 60

B

BOLTON ABBEY — Map 19 SE05
North Yorkshire

The Devonshire Arms Country House Hotel & Spa

★★★★ ◉◉◉◉ HOTEL

☎ 01756 710441 & 718111
BD23 6AJ
e-mail: res@devonshirehotels.co.uk
web: www.thedevonshirearms.co.uk
dir: On B6160, 250yds N of junct with A59

With stunning views of the Wharfedale countryside this beautiful hotel, owned by the Duke and Duchess of Devonshire, dates back to the 17th century. Bedrooms are elegantly furnished; those in the old part of the house are particularly spacious and have four-posters and fine antiques. The sitting rooms are delightfully cosy with log fires, and the dedicated staff deliver service with a blend of friendliness and professionalism. The Burlington Restaurant offers award-winning, highly accomplished cuisine together with an impressive wine list, while the Brasserie provides a lighter alternative.

Rooms 40 (1 fmly) (17 GF) ⟨ **S** £190-£330; **D** £250-£485 (incl. bkfst)* **Facilities** Spa STV Wi-fi ↳ ⟨ supervised ⟨ Fishing ⟨ Gym Classic cars Falconry Laser pigeon shooting Fly fishing Cricket Xmas New Year **Conf** Class 80 Board 30 Thtr 90 **Parking** 150 **Notes** LB Civ Wed 90

BOREHAMWOOD — Map 6 TQ19
Hertfordshire

Ibis London Elstree Borehamwood

BUDGET HOTEL

☎ 020 8736 2600
Elstree Way WD6 1JY
e-mail: H6186@accor.com
dir: M25 junct 23, A1, exit at Borehamwood, take A5135 (Elstree Way)

Modern, budget hotel offering comfortable accommodation in bright and practical bedrooms. Breakfast is self-service and dinner is available in the restaurant. See also the Hotel Groups pages.

Rooms 122 (16 fmly) (16 GF)

Premier Inn London Elstree/Borehamwood

BUDGET HOTEL

☎ 0871 527 8654
Warwick Rd WD6 1US
web: www.premierinn.com
dir: Exit A1 signed Borehamwood onto A5135 (Elstree Way). Pass BP Garage, left into Warwick Rd

High quality, budget accommodation ideal for both families and business travellers. Spacious, en suite bedrooms feature tea and coffee making facilities, and Freeview TV in most hotels. Internet access and Wi-fi are available for a small fee. The adjacent family restaurant features a wide and varied menu. See also the Hotel Groups pages.

Rooms 120

BOROUGHBRIDGE — Map 19 SE36
North Yorkshire

Best Western Crown Hotel

★★★ 77% HOTEL

☎ 01423 322328
Horsefair YO51 9LB
e-mail: sales@crownboroughbridge.co.uk
web: www.crownboroughbridge.co.uk
dir: A1(M) junct 48 towards Boroughbridge. Hotel 1m

Situated in the centre of town but convenient for the A1(M), The Crown provides a full leisure complex, conference rooms and a secure car park. Bedrooms are well appointed. A wide range of well-prepared dishes can be enjoyed in both the restaurant and bar.

Rooms 37 (3 fmly) (2 GF) **Facilities** STV FTV Wi-fi ⟨ supervised Gym Xmas New Year **Conf** Class 80 Board 80 Thtr 150 **Services** Lift **Parking** 60 **Notes** ⊗ Civ Wed 120

The Crown Inn

◉ RESTAURANT WITH ROOMS

☎ 01423 322300
Roecliffe YO51 9LY
e-mail: info@crowninnroecliffe.com
web: www.crowninnroecliffe.com
dir: A1(M) junct 48, follow signs for Boroughbridge. At rdbt exit towards Roecliffe & brown tourist signs

The Crown is a 16th-century coaching inn provides an excellent combination of traditional charm and modern comforts. Service is friendly and professional and food is a highlight of any stay. Bedrooms are attractively furnished with stylish en suite bathrooms.

Rooms 4 (1 fmly)

Save on hotels. Book at **theAA.com/hotel**

BOL – BOS   79   ENGLAND

B

BORROWDALE
Cumbria
Map 18 NY21

See also Keswick & Rosthwaite

Lodore Falls Hotel
LAKE DISTRICT HOTELS

★★★★ 77% HOTEL

☎ 017687 77285 & 0800 840 1246
CA12 5UX
e-mail: lodorefalls@lakedistricthotels.net
web: www.lakedistricthotels.net/lodorefalls
dir: M6 junct 40, A66 to Keswick, B5289 to
Borrowdale. Hotel on left

This impressive hotel has an enviable location
overlooking Derwentwater. The bedrooms, many with
lake or fell views, are comfortably equipped; family
rooms and suites are also available. The dining room,
bar and lounge areas are appointed to a very high
standard. One of the treatments in the hotel's Elemis
Spa actually makes use of the Lodore Waterfall!

Rooms 69 (11 fmly) ✿ **S** £107-£113; **D** £180-£189
(incl. bkfst) **Facilities** Spa STV FTV Wi-fi ✚ ☜ ⎈
Fishing Gym Squash Sauna Xmas New Year
Conf Class 90 Board 45 Thtr 200 Del £145
Services Lift **Parking** 93 **Notes** LB Civ Wed 130

Leathes Head Hotel

★★★ 81% ◉ HOTEL

☎ 017687 77247 & 77650
CA12 5UY
e-mail: reservations@leatheshead.co.uk
web: www.leatheshead.co.uk
dir: 3.5m from Keswick on B5289 (Borrowdale road).
Hotel on left 0.25m before Grange Bridge

A fine Edwardian building, with lovely gardens, set in
the heart of the unspoilt Borrowdale Valley. The
hospitality and customer care are really outstanding
here. The bedrooms have commanding views and the
award-winning food, including a wonderful Cumbrian
breakfast, will not disappoint. New investment is
enhancing the property.

Rooms 11 (2 fmly) (3 GF) ✿ **D** £177-£235 (incl. bkfst
& dinner)* **Facilities** FTV Wi-fi **Parking** 16 **Notes** No
children 15yrs Closed late Nov-mid Feb

Borrowdale Gates Country House Hotel

★★★ 81% COUNTRY HOUSE HOTEL

☎ 017687 77204
CA12 5UQ
e-mail: hotel@borrowdale-gates.com
dir: From A66 follow B5289 for approx 4m. Turn right
over bridge, hotel 0.25m beyond village

This friendly hotel is peacefully located in the
Borrowdale Valley, close to the village but in its own
three acres of wooded grounds. Public rooms include
comfortable lounges and a restaurant with lovely
views. Bedrooms vary in size and style.

Rooms 25 (2 fmly) (9 GF) ✿ **S** £60-£90; **D** £120-£190
(incl. bkfst)* **Facilities** FTV Wi-fi ☜ Xmas New Year
Services Lift **Parking** 29 **Notes** Closed 3 Jan-4 Feb

Borrowdale Hotel
LAKE DISTRICT HOTELS

★★★ 80% HOTEL

☎ 017687 77224
CA12 5UY
e-mail: borrowdale@lakedistricthotels.net
dir: 3m from Keswick, on B5289 at S end of Lake
Derwentwater

Situated in the beautiful Borrowdale Valley
overlooking Derwentwater, this traditionally styled
hotel guarantees a friendly welcome. Extensive public
areas include a choice of lounges, traditional dining
room, lounge bar and popular conservatory which
serves more informal meals. Bedrooms vary in style
and size, including two that are suitable for less able
guests.

Rooms 40 (2 fmly) (4 GF) ✿ **S** £102-£127;
D £164-£254 (incl. bkfst)* **Facilities** STV FTV Wi-fi ☜
Leisure facilities available at nearby sister hotel
Xmas New Year **Conf** Class 30 Board 24 Thtr 80
Parking 30 **Notes** LB

BOSCASTLE
Cornwall
Map 2 SX09

The Wellington Hotel

★★ 82% ◉ HOTEL

☎ 01840 250202
The Harbour PL35 0AQ
e-mail: info@wellingtonhotelboscastle.com
web: www.wellingtonhotelboscastle.com
dir: A30/A395 at Davidstowe follow Boscastle signs.
B3266 to village. Right into Old Rd

This 16th-century coaching inn is very much a
landmark in Boscastle and has been providing rest
and relaxation for weary travellers for many a year.
There is character in abundance here which adds to
its engaging charm and personality. The Long Bar is
popular with visitors and locals alike and features a
delightful galleried area. The stylish bedrooms come
in varying sizes, including the spacious Tower Rooms;
all provide contemporary comforts and the expected
necessities. In addition to the bar menus, The
Waterloo Restaurant is the elegant setting for
accomplished cuisine.

Rooms 14 (1 fmly) **S** £40-£50; **D** £70-£145 (incl.
bkfst)* **Facilities** FTV Wi-fi ☜ Xmas New Year
Conf Class 40 Board 24 Thtr 50 **Parking** 14

BOSHAM
West Sussex
Map 5 SU80

The Millstream Hotel & Restaurant

★★★ 85% ◉◉ HOTEL

☎ 01243 573234
Bosham Ln PO18 8HL
e-mail: info@millstreamhotel.com
web: www.millstreamhotel.com
dir: 4m W of Chichester on A259, left at Bosham rdbt.
After 0.5m right at T-junct signed to church & quay.
Hotel 0.5m on right

Lying in the idyllic village of Bosham, this attractive
hotel provides comfortable, well-equipped and
tastefully decorated bedrooms. Many guests regularly
return here for the relaxed atmosphere created by the
notably efficient and friendly staff. Public rooms
include a cocktail bar that opens onto the garden,
and a pleasant award-winning restaurant where
varied and freshly prepared cuisine can be enjoyed.
The new Markwick's Brasserie Restaurant is open all
day for coffee, snacks and light lunches and dinners.

Rooms 35 (2 annexe) (2 fmly) (9 GF) **S** £95-£105;
D £155-£175 (incl. bkfst)* **Facilities** FTV Wi-fi
Painting & Bridge breaks Xmas New Year
Conf Class 20 Board 20 Thtr 45 Del from £129 to
£145* **Parking** 44 **Notes** LB ⊗ Civ Wed 75

B

BOSTON
Lincolnshire   Map 12 TF34

Poacher's Country Hotel

★★★ 82% HOTEL

☎ 01205 290310
Swineshead Rd, Kirton Holme PE20 1SQ
e-mail: enquiries@poachershotel.co.uk
dir: Just off A52, exit at A52/A17 rdbt

The Poachers, dating back to the 1800s, has
undergone a total transformation yet retains most of
its original character. The open-plan, contemporary
public areas are bright and inviting. The bedrooms
are smartly appointed and have flat-screen TVs and
many thoughtful touches.

Rooms 14 (1 fmly) (8 GF) **S** £45-£60; **D** £45-£80*
Facilities FTV Wi-fi Xmas New Year **Conf** Class 150
Board 50 Thtr 175 **Parking** 55 **Notes** LB ⊗
Civ Wed 200

Supreme Inns Boston

★★★ 78% HOTEL

☎ 01205 822804
Donnington Rd, Bicker Bar Roundabout PE20 3AN
e-mail: enquiries@supremeinns.co.uk
web: www.supremeinns.co.uk
dir: At rdbt junct of A52 & A17

Situated south west of Boston and surrounded by the
Lincolnshire Fens, this modern, purpose-built hotel
offers well equipped bedrooms that have flat-screen
TVs and internet access. Food is available in the
restaurant or all day in the relaxing bar area.
Wedding, private dinner and conference facilities are
all available.

Rooms 55 (27 GF) **S** £45-£60; **D** £45-£80*
Facilities FTV Wi-fi ⬗ Xmas New Year **Conf** Board 35
Thtr 60 Del from £80 to £95 **Parking** 65 **Notes** LB ⊗
Civ Wed 60

Boston West Hotel

★★★ 73% HOTEL

☎ 01205 292969 & 290670
Hubberts Bridge PE20 3QX
e-mail: info@bostonwesthotel.co.uk
dir: A1121 signed Boston, hotel on left after speed
camera

A modern, purpose-built hotel situated in a rural
location on the outskirts of town. The smartly
appointed bedrooms are spacious and thoughtfully
equipped; some rooms have balconies with stunning
countryside views. Public rooms include a restaurant
and a large open-plan lounge bar which overlooks the
golf course.

Rooms 24 (5 fmly) (12 GF) **Facilities** FTV Wi-fi ⅃ 18
Putt green Driving range New Year **Conf** Class 60
Board 40 Thtr 80 **Services** Lift **Parking** 24 **Notes** ⊗
Civ Wed 110

Premier Inn Boston

BUDGET HOTEL

☎ 0871 527 8120
Wainfleet Rd PE21 9RW
web: www.premierinn.com
dir: A52, 300yds E of junct with A16 (Boston/Grimsby
road)

High quality, budget accommodation ideal for both
families and business travellers. Spacious, en suite
bedrooms feature tea and coffee making facilities,
and Freeview TV in most hotels. Internet access and
Wi-fi are available for a small fee. The adjacent
family restaurant features a wide and varied menu.
See also the Hotel Groups pages.

Rooms 54

BOTLEY
Hampshire   Map 5 SU51

Macdonald Botley Park, Golf & Country Club

MACDONALD HOTELS & RESORTS

★★★★ 76% ⦿ COUNTRY HOUSE HOTEL

☎ 01489 780 888 & 0870 194 2132
Winchester Rd, Boorley Green SO32 2UA
e-mail: botleypark@macdonald-hotels.co.uk
web: www.macdonald-hotels.co.uk/botleypark
dir: M27 junct 7, A334 towards Botley. At 1st rdbt
left, pass M&S store, over at next 5 mini rdbts. At 6th
mini rdbt turn right. In 0.5m hotel on left

This modern and spacious hotel sits peacefully in the
midst of its own 176-acre parkland golf course.
Bedrooms are comfortably appointed with a good
range of extras and an extensive range of leisure
facilities is on offer. Attractive public areas include a
relaxing restaurant and the more informal Swing and
Divot Bar.

Rooms 130 (30 fmly) (44 GF) ✆ **S** £96-£275;
D £96-£275* **Facilities** Spa STV Wi-fi ⬗ ⊛ ⅃ 18 ⬗
Putt green Gym Squash Dance studio Xmas New Year
Conf Class 180 Board 100 Thtr 450 Del from £135 to
£210* **Services** Air con **Parking** 250 **Notes** ⊗
Civ Wed 400

BOURNEMOUTH
Dorset   Map 5 SZ19

See also Christchurch

Bournemouth Highcliff Marriott Hotel

Marriott HOTELS & RESORTS

★★★★ 80% ⦿⦿ HOTEL

☎ 01202 557702
St Michaels Rd, West Cliff BH2 5DU
e-mail: mhrs.bohbm.ays@marriotthotels.co.uk
web: www.bournemouthhighcliffmarriott.co.uk
dir: A338 into Bournemouth then BIC signs to West
Cliff Rd. 2nd right into St Michaels Rd. Hotel at end of
road on left

Originally built as a row of coastguard cottages, this
establishment has expanded over the years into a
very elegant and charming hotel. Impeccably
maintained throughout, many of the bedrooms have
sea views. An excellent range of leisure, business and
conference facilities are offered, as well as private
dining and banqueting rooms. The hotel also has
direct access to the Bournemouth International
Centre.

Save on hotels. Book at **theAA.com/hotel**

BOS – BOU 81 ENGLAND

B

Bournemouth Highcliff Marriott Hotel

Rooms 160 (19 annexe) (22 fmly) (4 GF) (8 smoking) ♣ **Facilities** STV FTV Wi-fi 🕸 ⚓ 🏊 Putt green Gym Beautician & beauty treatment room 🎵 Xmas New Year **Conf** Class 180 Board 90 Thtr 350 **Services** Lift Air con **Parking** 80 **Notes** LB ⊗ Civ Wed 250

Menzies East Cliff Court

MenziesHotels

★★★★ 79% HOTEL

☎ 01202 554545
East Overcliff Dr BH1 3AN
e-mail: eastcliff@menzieshotels.co.uk
web: www.menzieshotels.co.uk
dir: Telephone or check the website for directions

Enjoying panoramic views across the bay, this popular hotel offers bedrooms that are modern and contemporary in style; they are appointed to a very high standard, and may have the benefit of balconies and sea views. Stylish public areas include a range of inviting lounges, a spacious restaurant and a selection of conference rooms.

Rooms 67 (4 fmly) (2 GF) (5 smoking) **Facilities** FTV Wi-fi ⚓ Full leisure facilities at adjacent Menzies Carlton Xmas New Year **Conf** Class 80 Board 50 Thtr 200 **Services** Lift **Parking** 45 **Notes** Civ Wed 250

The Green House

★★★★ 77% TOWN HOUSE HOTEL

☎ 01202 498900
4 Grove Rd BH1 3AX
e-mail: reception@thegreenhousehotel.com

This hotel has a clear commitment to the environment which goes beyond just energy efficient lighting; everything has been designed and built to be sympathetic to the environment. The beautifully appointed bedrooms and bathrooms demonstrate the 'green' principle from the locally-made 100% wool carpets and solid wood furniture to the wallpapers and paint that have been used. The ingredients used for the menus are locally sourced and organic.

Rooms 32 (3 fmly) (6 GF) ♣ **Facilities** FTV Wi-fi ⇲ Xmas New Year **Conf** Class 40 Board 40 Thtr 100 **Services** Lift **Parking** 32 **Notes** ⊗ Civ Wed 100

BOURNEMOUTH *continued*

Menzies Carlton

MenziesHotels

★★★★ 75% ⊛ HOTEL

☎ 01202 552011
East Overcliff BH1 3DN
e-mail: carlton@menzieshotels.co.uk
web: www.menzieshotels.co.uk
dir: From M3, M27 towards Bournemouth on A338
(leads onto Wessex Way), follow signs to East Cliff,
hotel on seafront

Enjoying a prime location on the East Cliff, and with
views of the Isle of Wight and Dorset coastline, the
Carlton has attractive gardens and pool area. Most of
the spacious bedrooms enjoy sea views. Leisure
facilities include an indoor and outdoor pool as well
as a gym. Guests can enjoy an interesting range of
carefully prepared dishes in Frederick's restaurant.
The conference and banqueting facilities are varied.

Rooms 76 (17 fmly) (8 GF) (9 smoking) **Facilities** STV
FTV Wi-fi ◊ ⤳ Gym Hair & beauty salon Xmas
New Year **Conf** Class 120 Board 50 Thtr 250
Services Lift **Parking** 87 **Notes** ⊗ Civ Wed 200

Hermitage Hotel

★★★★ 73% ⊛ HOTEL

☎ 01202 557363
Exeter Rd BH2 5AH
e-mail: info@hermitage-hotel.co.uk
web: www.hermitage-hotel.co.uk
dir: A338 (Ringwood), follow signs for BIC & pier.
Hotel directly opposite

Occupying an impressive location overlooking the
seafront, at the heart of the town centre, the
Hermitage offers friendly and attentive service. The
majority of the smart bedrooms are comfortably
appointed and all are very well equipped; many rooms
have sea views. The wood-panelled lounge provides an
elegant and tranquil area, as does the restaurant
where well-prepared and interesting dishes are served.

Rooms 74 (11 annexe) (9 fmly) (7 GF) ⬧
Facilities FTV Wi-fi ◊ Xmas New Year **Conf** Class 60
Board 60 Thtr 180 Del from £84 to £130*
Services Lift **Parking** 58 **Notes** LB ⊗

See advert on page 81

Park Central Hotel

★★★★ 72% ⊛⊛ HOTEL

☎ 01202 203600
Exeter Rd BH2 5AJ
e-mail: reception@parkcentralhotel.co.uk
dir: A338, A35 (St Pauls Rd). At rdbt 3rd exit onto
B3066 (Holdenburst Rd). Straight on at 3 rdbts, hotel
on right opposite Bournemouth International Centre

Located opposite Bournemouth International Centre,
this modern, contemporary hotel is in a good location
and has sea views. The bedrooms are comfortable
and attractively furnished. The menu features
creative modern ideas based on intuitive
combinations of well-sourced raw materials
featuring, of course a great deal of seafood. A pre-
theatre menu is also available, but be sure to book as
this proves very popular.

Rooms 50 (6 fmly) (7 GF) ⬧ **D** £69-£162 (incl.
bkfst)* **Facilities** FTV Wi-fi ◊ ♫ Xmas New Year
Services Lift **Parking** 29 **Notes** ⊗

Norfolk Royale Hotel

★★★★ 72% HOTEL

PEEL HOTELS PLC

☎ 01202 551521
Richmond Hill BH2 6EN
e-mail: gm@norfolkroyale-hotel-bournemouth.com
web: www.norfolk-royale.co.uk
dir: A338 into Bournemouth take Richmond Hill exit to
A347 Wimborne, turn left at top into Richmond Hill.
Hotel on right

Easily recognisable by its wrought iron balconies, this
Edwardian hotel is conveniently located for the centre
of the town. Most of the bedrooms are contained in a
modern wing at the side of the building, overlooking
the pretty landscaped gardens. There is a car park at
rear of the hotel.

Rooms 95 (7 fmly) (9 GF) ⬧ **Facilities** Spa STV Wi-fi
◊ HL ⓧ Membership of nearby health club ♫ Xmas
New Year **Conf** Class 50 Board 40 Thtr 150
Del from £125 to £155 **Services** Lift **Parking** 95
Notes ⊗ Civ Wed 150

Hallmark Bournemouth

★★★★ 71% HOTEL

☎ 01202 751000
Durley Chine Rd, West Cliff BH2 5JS
e-mail: bournemouth.sales@hallmarkhotels.co.uk
dir: A338 follow signs to West Cliff & BIC, hotel on
right

This property is conveniently located and offers a
friendly atmosphere and attentive service. The
comfortable bedrooms are tastefully appointed and
are suitable for both business and leisure guests. The

restaurant and bar serve a good choice of dishes, and
the well-appointed leisure area is popular with both
residents and locals alike. There is also a good range
of conference facilities and meeting rooms.

Rooms 78 (12 annexe) ⬧ **Facilities** Spa FTV Wi-fi ⓧ
Gym Sauna Steam room Aromatherapy Ice zone Xmas
New Year **Conf** Class 80 Board 40 Thtr 250
Del from £99 to £155* **Services** Lift **Parking** 80
Notes Civ Wed 200

Cumberland Hotel

★★★ 88% ⊛⊛ HOTEL

☎ 01202 290722 & 298350
East Overcliff Dr BH1 3AF
e-mail: info@cumberlandbournemouth.co.uk
dir: A35 towards East Cliff & beaches, right onto
Holdenhurst Rd, straight over 2 rdbts, left at junct to
East Overcliff Drive, hotel on seafront

A purpose built, art deco hotel where many of the
bedrooms are appointed in keeping with the hotel's
original character. Front-facing bedrooms have
balconies with superb sea views. The comfortable
public areas are spacious and striking in their
design. The Mirabelle Restaurant and the Ventana
Bar offer cuisine prepared from local produce.

Rooms 102 (20 fmly) **S** £29.50-£79; **D** £59-£149
(incl. bkfst) **Facilities** FTV Wi-fi ◊ ⤳ Gym Squash
Sauna Xmas New Year **Conf** Class 180 Board 40
Thtr 250 Del from £59 to £99 **Services** Lift
Parking 50 **Notes** LB Civ Wed 100

Best Western The Connaught Hotel

★★★ 85% ⊛⊛ HOTEL

☎ 01202 298020
West Hill Rd, West Cliff BH2 5PH
e-mail: reception@theconnaught.co.uk
web: www.theconnaught.co.uk
dir: Follow Town Centre West & BIC signs

Conveniently located on the West Cliff, close to the
BIC, beaches and town centre, this privately-owned
hotel offers well equipped, neatly decorated rooms,
some with balconies. The hotel boasts a very well

Save on hotels. Book at **theAA.com/hotel**

BOU 83 ENGLAND

equipped leisure complex with a large pool and gym. Breakfast and dinner offer imaginative dishes made with quality local ingredients.

Best Western The Connaught Hotel

Rooms 82 (27 annexe) (9 fmly) ⬧ **S** £50-£80; **D** £70-£140 (incl. bkfst)* **Facilities** Spa FTV Wi-fi ⬧ supervised Gym Sauna Steam room Beauty therapies Xmas New Year **Conf** Class 60 Board 35 Thtr 180 Del from £130 to £145* **Services** Lift **Parking** 66 **Notes** ⊗ Civ Wed 200

See advert on this page

Hotel Miramar

★★★ 82% HOTEL

☎ 01202 556581

East Overcliff Dr, East Cliff BH1 3AL

e-mail: sales@miramar-bournemouth.com

web: www.miramar-bournemouth.com

dir: From Wessex Way rdbt into St Pauls Rd, right at next rdbt. 3rd exit at next rdbt, 2nd exit at next rdbt into Grove Rd. Hotel car park on right

Conveniently located on the East Cliff, this Edwardian hotel enjoys glorious sea views. The Miramar was a favoured destination of famed author JRR Tolkien, who often stayed here. The bedrooms are comfortable and well equipped, and there are spacious public areas and a choice of lounges. The friendly staff and a relaxing environment are noteworthy here.

Rooms 43 (6 fmly) ⬧ **Facilities** FTV Wi-fi HL ⬧ Xmas New Year **Conf** Class 50 Board 50 Thtr 200 Del from £80 to £125 **Services** Lift **Parking** 80 **Notes** Civ Wed 110

Langtry Manor - Lovenest of a King

★★★ 82% HOTEL

☎ 0844 3725 432 & 01202 553887

Derby Rd, East Cliff BH1 3QB

e-mail: lillie@langtrymanor.com

web: www.langtrymanor.co.uk

dir: A31/A338, 1st rdbt by rail station turn left. Over next rdbt, 1st left into Knyveton Rd. Hotel opposite

Retaining a stately air, this property was originally built in 1877 by Edward VII for his mistress Lillie Langtry. The individually furnished and decorated bedrooms include several with four-poster beds. Enjoyable cuisine is served in the magnificent dining hall that displays several large Tudor tapestries. There is an Edwardian banquet on Saturday evenings.

Rooms 20 (8 annexe) (2 fmly) (3 GF) **S** £95-£135; **D** £105-£305 (incl. bkfst) **Facilities** FTV Wi-fi Free use of health club (200yds) ⬧ Xmas New Year **Conf** Class 60 Board 40 Thtr 100 Del from £135 to £165 **Parking** 30 **Notes** Civ Wed 100

B

BOURNEMOUTH *continued*

The Chine

★★★ 81% ◉ HOTEL

☎ 01202 396234 & 0845 337 1550
Boscombe Spa Rd BH5 1AX
e-mail: reservations@fjbhotels.co.uk
web: www.fjbcollection.co.uk
dir: Follow BIC signs, A338/Wessex Way to St Pauls rdbt. 1st exit, to next rdbt, 2nd exit signed Eastcliff, Boscombe, Southbourne. Next rdbt, 1st exit into Christchurch Rd. After 2nd lights, right into Boscombe Spa Rd

Benefiting from superb views this popular hotel is set in delightful gardens with private access to the seafront and a sandy beach that stretches for miles; it is just a five-minute drive from the shops and entertainment of the town centre. The excellent range of facilities includes an indoor pool, a seasonal outdoor pool, jacuzzi, gym and sauna. There are also indoor and outdoor children's facilities and dedicated entertainers during the school holidays. The spacious bedrooms, some with balconies, are well appointed and thoughtfully equipped. The Seaview Restaurant and Gallery Brasserie are popular eating options.

Rooms 82 (23 annexe) (16 fmly) (8 GF) **Facilities** STV Wi-fi ⊗ supervised ⚡ supervised ⚡ Gym Games room Children's indoor play area Xmas New Year **Conf** Class 70 Board 40 Thtr 140 **Services** Lift Parking 55 **Notes** ⊗ Civ Wed 120

Best Western Hotel Royale

★★★ 80% HOTEL

☎ 01202 554794
16 Gervis Rd BH1 3EQ
e-mail: reservations@thehotelroyale.com
web: www.thehotelroyale.com
dir: M27 junct 1, A31 onto A338 to Bournemouth, follow signs for East Cliff & seafront. Over 2 rdbts into Gervis Rd. Hotel on right

Located on the East Cliff, just a short walk from the seafront and local shops and amenities, this is a

privately owned hotel. Public areas are contemporary in style, and facilities include a small health club and spacious function rooms. Bedrooms are comfortable and well furnished.

Rooms 64 (8 annexe) (22 fmly) (8 GF) ⚡ **S** £50–£75; **D** £65–£150 **Facilities** STV FTV Wi-fi ⊗ ⊗ Xmas New Year **Conf** Class 60 Board 40 Thtr 100 Del from £90 to £135 **Services** Lift **Parking** 80 **Notes** LB ⊗

Elstead Hotel

★★★ 80% HOTEL

☎ 01202 293071
Knyveton Rd BH1 3QP
e-mail: info@the-elstead.co.uk
web: www.the-elstead.co.uk
dir: A338 (Wessex Way) to St Pauls rdbt, left & left again

Ideal as a base for both business and leisure travellers, this popular hotel is conveniently located for the town centre, seafront and BIC. An impressive range of facilities is offered, including meeting rooms, an indoor leisure centre and comfortable lounges.

Rooms 50 (15 fmly) **Facilities** Wi-fi ⊗ supervised Gym Steam room Pool & snooker tables Xmas New Year **Conf** Class 60 Board 40 Thtr 80 **Services** Lift **Parking** 40 **Notes** Civ Wed 60

The Riviera Hotel

★★★ 79% HOTEL

☎ 01202 763653
Burnaby Rd, Alum Chine BH4 8JF
e-mail: info@rivierabournemouth.co.uk
web: www.rivierabournemouth.co.uk
dir: A338, follow signs to Alum Chine

The Riviera offers a range of comfortable, well-furnished bedrooms and bathrooms. Welcoming staff provide efficient service delivered in a friendly manner. In addition to a spacious lounge with regular entertainment, there is an indoor and an outdoor pool, and all just a short walk from the beach.

Rooms 73 (4 annexe) (25 fmly) (11 GF) **S** £29–£59; **D** £59–£179 (incl. bkfst)* **Facilities** FTV Wi-fi ⊗ ⚡ Games room Sauna Spa bath Beauty treatments available ♫ Xmas New Year **Conf** Class 120 Board 50 Thtr 180 Del from £59 to £119* **Services** Lift **Parking** 45 **Notes** LB Civ Wed 160

Royal Exeter Hotel

★★★ 79% HOTEL

☎ 01202 438000
Exeter Rd BH2 5AG
e-mail: enquiries@royalexeterhotel.com
web: www.royalexeterhotel.com
dir: Opposite Bournemouth International Centre

Ideally located opposite the Bournemouth International Centre, and convenient for the beach and town centre, this busy hotel caters for both business and leisure guests. Public areas are smart and there's a modern open-plan lounge bar and restaurant together with an exciting adjoining bar complex.

Rooms 54 (13 fmly) (12 smoking) **S** £35–£80; **D** £60–£140 **Facilities** FTV Wi-fi Gym ♫ **Conf** Class 40 Board 40 Thtr 100 Del from £70 to £150 **Services** Lift **Parking** 50 **Notes** LB ⊗

See advert on opposite page

B

Cliffeside Hotel

★★★ 77% HOTEL

☎ 01202 555724 & 298350
East Overcliff Dr BH1 3AQ
e-mail: info@cliffesidebournemouth.co.uk
dir: A35, A338 to East Cliff & beaches, right into
Holdenhurst Rd, over next 2 rdbts, at junct left into
East Overcliff Drive, hotel on left

Benefiting from an elevated position on the seafront
and just a short walk to town, it's no wonder that this
friendly hotel has many returning guests. Bedrooms
and public areas are attractively appointed, many
with sea views. The Atlantic Restaurant offers guests
a fixed-price menu.

Rooms 62 (5 fmly) (2 GF) **Facilities** Wi-fi ⊗ ☇ Gym
Squash Sauna ♫ Xmas New Year **Conf** Class 70
Board 40 Thtr 120 **Services** Lift **Parking** 32
Notes Civ Wed 120

Trouville Hotel

★★★ 77% HOTEL

☎ 01202 552262
Priory Rd BH2 5DH
e-mail: reception@trouvillehotel.com
dir: Follow Town Centre West signs. Exit at rdbt
signed BIC/West Cliff/Beaches. 2nd exit at next rdbt,
left at next rdbt. Hotel on left near end of Priory Rd

Located near Bournemouth International Centre, the
seafront and the shops, this hotel has the advantage
of indoor leisure facilities and a large car park.
Bedrooms are generally a good size with comfortable
furnishings; there are plenty of family rooms here. The
air-conditioned restaurant offers a daily changing
menu.

Rooms 99 (19 annexe) (21 fmly) (6 GF) 🐾
S £37.95-£64.95; **D** £75.90-£129.90* **Facilities** FTV
Wi-fi ⊾ ⊗ Gym Sauna ♫ Xmas New Year
Conf Class 100 Board 80 Thtr 250 **Services** Lift
Parking 70 **Notes** LB Civ Wed 130

Hotel Piccadilly

★★★ 75% HOTEL

☎ 01202 298024
25 Bath Rd BH1 2NN
e-mail: enquiries@hotelpiccadilly.co.uk
dir: From A338 take 1st exit rdbt, signed East Cliff.
3rd exit at next rdbt signed Lansdowne, 3rd exit at
next rdbt into Bath Rd

This hotel offers a friendly welcome to guests, many
of whom return on a regular basis, particularly for the
superb ballroom dancing facilities and small break
packages which are a feature here. Bedrooms are
smartly decorated, well maintained and comfortable.
Dining in the attractive restaurant is always popular
and dishes are freshly prepared and appetising.

Rooms 45 (2 fmly) (5 GF) **Facilities** FTV Wi-fi
Ballroom Xmas New Year **Conf** Class 11 Board 11
Thtr 140 **Services** Lift **Parking** 45 **Notes** ⊗ Civ Wed

Suncliff Hotel

★★★ 75% HOTEL

☎ 01202 291711 & 298350
29 East Overcliff Dr BH1 3AG
e-mail: info@suncliffbournemouth.co.uk
dir: A338/A35 towards East Cliff & beaches, right into
Holdenhurst Rd, straight over 2 rdbts, left at
junct into East Overcliff Drive, hotel on seafront

Enjoying splendid views from the East Cliff and
catering mainly for leisure guests, this friendly hotel
offers a range of facilities and services. Bedrooms are
well equipped and comfortable, and many have sea
views. Public areas include a large conservatory, an
attractive bar and pleasant lounges.

Rooms 97 (29 fmly) (14 GF) 🐾 **S** £32.50-£59;
D £69-£109 (incl. bkfst)* **Facilities** Wi-fi ⊗ ☇ Gym
Squash Sauna ♫ Xmas New Year **Conf** Class 70
Board 60 Thtr 100 Del from £39.50 to £89.50*
Services Lift **Parking** 62 **Notes** Civ Wed 80

BOURNEMOUTH *continued*

Hinton Firs Hotel

★★★ 74% HOTEL

☎ 01202 555409
Manor Rd, East Cliff BH1 3ET
e-mail: info@hintonfirshotel.co.uk
web: www.hintonfirshotel.co.uk
dir: A338, W at St Paul's rdbt, over next 2 rdbts, fork left to side of church. Hotel on next corner

This family owned and friendly hotel is conveniently located on East Cliff, just a short stroll from the sea. The smart, well-appointed bedrooms are light and airy; there are family rooms and also one bedroom, with a wet room, that is suitable for less able guests. The leisure facilities include indoor and outdoor pools, a sauna, beauty treatments and supervised children's activities in the school holidays. There is also a spacious lounge, a restaurant and bar.

Rooms 52 (6 annexe) (12 fmly) (6 GF) ☙
Facilities FTV Wi-fi ☜ ☈ Games room ♫ Xmas New Year **Conf** Class 40 Board 30 Thtr 50 **Services** Lift **Parking** 40 **Notes** ⊗

Mayfair Hotel

★★★ 74% HOTEL

☎ 01202 551983
27 Bath Rd BH1 2NW
e-mail: info@themayfair.com
web: www.themayfair.com
dir: Exit A338 at St Pauls Rd (Asda rdbt), right into Holdenhurst Rd, 3rd exit from Lansdowne rdbt

Occupying a central location in the heart of Bournemouth and within walking distance of both the town centre and the seafront, this hotel offers guests comfortable, modern accommodation. There is a spacious restaurant and bar area, plus a pleasant outdoor patio and function room.

Rooms 40 (6 fmly) (1 GF) **Facilities** Wi-fi Ballroom dancing programme on request Xmas New Year **Conf** Class 40 Board 30 Thtr 60 **Services** Lift **Parking** 30 **Notes** ⊗ Civ Wed 80

Hotel Collingwood

★★★ 70% HOTEL

☎ 01202 557575
11 Priory Rd, West Cliff BH2 5DF
e-mail: info@hotel-collingwood.co.uk
web: www.hotel-collingwood.co.uk
dir: A338 left at West Cliff sign, over 1st rdbt, left at 2nd rdbt. Hotel 500yds on left

This privately owned and managed hotel is situated close to the BIC. Bedrooms are airy, with the emphasis on comfort. An excellent range of leisure facilities is available and the public areas are spacious and welcoming. Pinks Restaurant offers carefully prepared cuisine and a fixed-price, five-course dinner.

Rooms 53 (16 fmly) (6 GF) ☙ **S** £50-£80;
D £100-£160 (incl. bkfst & dinner)* **Facilities** FTV Wi-fi ☜ Gym Steam room Sauna Games room Snooker room ♫ Xmas New Year **Conf** Class 60 Board 20 Thtr 100 Del from £120 to £170 **Services** Lift **Parking** 55

Durley Dean Hotel

★★★ 67% HOTEL

☎ 01202 557711
West Cliff Rd BH2 5HE
e-mail: reservations@durleydean.co.uk
dir: Into Bournemouth, follow signs for Westcliff. Onto Durley Chine Rd South to next rdbt, hotel at 2nd exit on left

Situated close to the seafront on the West Cliff, this modern hotel has bedrooms which vary in size and style. There is a restaurant, a comfortable bar and several meeting rooms. Parking is also a bonus.

Rooms 117 (36 fmly) (6 GF) **Facilities** FTV Wi-fi ☙ ☜ Gym ♫ Xmas New Year **Conf** Class 40 Board 40 Thtr 150 **Services** Lift **Parking** 30 **Notes** ⊗ Civ Wed 200

Burley Court Hotel

★★★ 63% HOTEL

☎ 01202 552824 & 556704
Bath Rd BH1 2NP
e-mail: info@burleycourthotel.co.uk
dir: Exit A338 at St Paul's rdbt, take 3rd exit at next rdbt into Holdenhurst Rd. 3rd exit at next rdbt into Bath Rd, over crossing, 1st left

Located on Bournemouth's West Cliff, this well-established hotel is well located and convenient for the town and beaches. Bedrooms are pleasantly furnished and decorated in bright colours. A daily-changing menu is served in the spacious dining room.

Rooms 38 (8 fmly) (4 GF) **Facilities** ☈ Xmas **Conf** Class 15 Board 15 Thtr 30 **Services** Lift **Parking** 35 **Notes** Closed 30 Dec-14 Jan RS 15-31 Jan

The Whitehall

★★ 78% HOTEL

☎ 01202 554682
Exeter Park Rd BH2 5AX
e-mail: reservations@thewhitehallhotel.co.uk
web: www.thewhitehallhotel.co.uk
dir: Follow BIC signs. From Exeter Rd into Exeter Park Rd

This friendly hotel enjoys an elevated position overlooking the park and is also close to the town centre and seafront. The spacious public areas include a choice of lounges, a cosy bar and a well-presented restaurant. The well-equipped and inviting bedrooms are spread over three floors.

Rooms 46 (5 fmly) (3 GF) **Facilities** ♫ Xmas **Conf** Class 40 Board 32 Thtr 70 **Services** Lift **Parking** 25

Tower House Hotel

★★ 76% HOTEL

☎ 01202 290742
West Cliff Gardens BH2 5HP
e-mail: towerhouse.hotel@btconnect.com

A popular family owned and run hotel on the West Cliff. The owners and their staff are friendly and helpful. The bedrooms are comfortable and well maintained and the hotel provides good off-road parking.

Rooms 32 (12 fmly) (3 GF) ☙ **Facilities** FTV Wi-fi Xmas New Year **Services** Lift **Parking** 30

B

Durley Grange Hotel

★★ 74% HOTEL

☎ 01202 554473
6 Durley Rd, West Cliff BH2 5JL
e-mail: reservations@durleygrange.com
web: www.durleygrange.com
dir: A338/Bournemouth West rdbt. Over next rdbt, 1st left into Sommerville Rd & right into Durley Rd

Located in a quiet area, with parking, the town and beaches are all in walking distance of this welcoming, friendly hotel. Bedrooms are brightly decorated, comfortable and well equipped. There is an indoor pool and sauna for all-year round use. Enjoyable meals are served in the smart dining room.

Rooms 52 (8 fmly) (4 GF) ♠ **Facilities** Wi-fi ⊗ Sauna ♬ Xmas New Year **Services** Lift **Parking** 35 **Notes** ⊗

Devon Towers Hotel

★★ 71% HOTEL   *Leisureplex*

☎ 01202 553863
58-62 St Michael's Rd, West Cliff BH2 5ED
e-mail:
devontowers.bournemouth@alfatravel.co.uk
dir: A338 into Bournemouth, follow signs for BIC. Left into St. Michaels Rd at top of hill. Hotel 100mtrs on left

Located in a quiet road within walking distance of the West Cliff and shops, this hotel appeals to the budget leisure market. The four-course menus offer plenty of choice and entertainment is featured most evenings. The bar and lobby area provide plenty of space for relaxing.

Rooms 62 (6 GF) **Facilities** FTV ♬ Xmas New Year **Services** Lift **Parking** 6 **Notes** ⊗ Closed Jan-mid Feb (ex Xmas) RS mid-end Feb, Mar & Nov

Ullswater Hotel

★★ 71% HOTEL

☎ 01202 555181
West Cliff Gardens BH2 5HW
e-mail: enquiries@ullswater-hotel.co.uk
web: www.ullswater-hotel.co.uk
dir: In Bournemouth follow signs to West Cliff. Hotel just off Westcliff Rd

A welcoming family run hotel conveniently located for the city and the seafront. This popular establishment attracts a loyal following. The well-equipped bedrooms vary in size, and the charming lounge bar and dining room are very smart. Cuisine is hearty and homemade offering a good choice from the daily-changing menu.

Rooms 42 (8 fmly) (2 GF) **S** £35-£46; **D** £49-£90 (incl. bkfst) **Facilities** FTV Wi-fi Snooker room Table tennis ♬ Xmas New Year **Conf** Class 30 Board 24 Thtr 40 Del from £45 to £65 **Services** Lift **Parking** 12 **Notes** LB

Arlington Hotel

★★ 69% HOTEL

☎ 01202 552879 & 553012
Exeter Park Rd BH2 5BD
e-mail: enquiries@arlingtonbournemouth.co.uk
dir: Follow BIC signs through Priory Rd, onto rdbt and exit at Royal Exeter Hotel sign

The well-equipped and comfortable accommodation, along with friendly hospitality are offered at this privately owned and run hotel. Conveniently located, midway between the square and the pier and ideally situated for the BIC, the Arlington has direct access to the Winter Gardens, which are overlooked from the hotel's lounge and terrace bar.

Rooms 28 (1 annexe) (6 fmly) **Facilities** Xmas **Services** Lift **Parking** 21 **Notes** ⊗ No children 2yrs Closed 4-15 Jan

Bourne Hall Hotel

★★ 62% HOTEL

☎ 01202 299715
14 Priory Rd, West Cliff BH2 5DN
e-mail: info@bournehall.co.uk
web: www.bournehall.co.uk
dir: M27, A31 from Ringwood into Bournemouth on A338 (Wessex Way). Follow signs to BIC, onto West Cliff. Hotel on right

This friendly, comfortable hotel is conveniently located close to the Bournemouth International Centre and the seafront. Bedrooms are well equipped, some located on the ground floor and some with sea views. In addition to the spacious lounge, there are two bars and a meeting room. A daily-changing menu is offered in the dining room.

Rooms 48 (9 fmly) (5 GF) ♠ **S** £30-£40; **D** £55-£70 **Facilities** FTV Wi-fi Free leisure facilities for guests at Marriott Highcliff Hotel ♬ Xmas New Year **Conf** Class 60 Board 40 Thtr 130 **Services** Lift **Parking** 35

Premier Inn Bournemouth Central

BUDGET HOTEL

☎ 0871 527 8124
Westover Rd BH1 2BZ
web: www.premierinn.com
dir: M27 junct 1, A31. Left at Ashley Heath junct. A338 towards Bournemouth. At rdbt 1st exit. At next rdbt 3rd exit (Holdenhurst Rd). At next rdbt 3rd exit (Bath Rd). At next rdbt 3rd exit onto Bath Hill. At next rdbt into Westover Rd, right into Hinton Rd, hotel on right

High quality, budget accommodation ideal for both families and business travellers. Spacious, en suite bedrooms feature tea and coffee making facilities, and Freeview TV in most hotels. Internet access and Wi-fi are available for a small fee. The adjacent family restaurant features a wide and varied menu. See also the Hotel Groups pages.

Rooms 120

Premier Inn Bournemouth East

BUDGET HOTEL

☎ 0871 527 8126
47 Christchurch Rd, Boscombe BH1 3PA
web: www.premierinn.com
dir: M27 junct 1, A31, 9m, left at Ashley Heath junct, take A338 signed Bournemouth. At 1st rdbt take 1st exit into Saint Paul's Rd. At 2nd rdbt 1st exit onto Christchurch Rd. Hotel on right

Rooms 20

B

BOURNEMOUTH *continued*

Premier Inn Bournemouth Westcliffe

BUDGET HOTEL

☎ 0871 527 8128
Poole Rd BH2 5QU
web: www.premierinn.com
dir: M27 junct 1, A31. At Ashley Heath junction, left.
Take A338 signed Bournemouth. At Bournemouth
West rdbt 1st exit signed Ring Road, West Cliff. At
next rdbt (St Michael's) 3rd exit (signed Westbourne)
into Poole Rd. Hotel on right

Rooms 101

BOURTON-ON-THE-WATER   Map 10 SP12
Gloucestershire

The Dial House Hotel

★★★ 80% ◉◉ SMALL HOTEL

☎ 01451 822244
The Chestnuts, High St GL54 2AN
e-mail: info@dialhousehotel.com
dir: Exit A429, 0.5m to village centre

Located in the main street of this popular Cotswold
town, The Dial House offers high quality and comfort
throughout. Bedrooms and bathrooms, in a wide
variety of shapes and sizes, are luxuriously decorated
and furnished. The building itself dates from 1698
and has intimate public areas full of character and
quality. Dinner, in the delightful award-winning
restaurant, utilises the finest produce and should not
be missed.

Rooms 15 (4 annexe) (7 GF) **Facilities** Wi-fi ✈ Xmas
New Year **Conf** Class 12 Board 12 Thtr 12 **Parking** 20
Notes No children 12yrs

Chester House Hotel

★★★ 72% SMALL HOTEL

☎ 01451 820286
Victoria St GL54 2BU
e-mail: info@chesterhousehotel.com
dir: On A429 between Northleach &
Stow-on-the-Wold

This hotel occupies a secluded but central location in
this delightful Cotswold village. Bedrooms, some at
ground floor level, are situated in the main house and
adjoining coach house. The public areas are stylish,
light and airy. Breakfast is taken in the main building
whereas dinner is served in the attractive restaurant
just a few yards away.

Rooms 22 (10 annexe) (3 fmly) (8 GF) ✾
Facilities FTV Wi-fi Beauty therapist New Year
Parking 18 **Notes** Closed 7 Jan-1 Feb

BOWNESS ON WINDERMERE

See Windermere

BOXWORTH   Map 12 TL36
Cambridgeshire

Days Inn Cambridge - A1

BUDGET HOTEL

☎ 01954 267176
**Cambridge Extra Services, Junction A14/M11
CB3 8WU**
e-mail: cambridge.hotel@welcomebreak.co.uk
dir: A14/M11 Cambridge Extra Services

This modern, purpose built accommodation offers
smartly appointed, well-equipped bedrooms, with
good power showers. There is a choice of adjacent
food outlets where guests may enjoy breakfast,
snacks and meals. See also the Hotel Groups pages.

Rooms 82 (14 fmly) (40 GF) (19 smoking)

BRACKNELL   Map 5 SU86
Berkshire

Coppid Beech

★★★★ 74% ◉ HOTEL

☎ 01344 303333
John Nike Way RG12 8TF
e-mail: sales@coppidbeech.com
web: www.coppidbeech.com
dir: M4 junct 10 take Wokingham/Bracknell onto
A329. In 2m take B3408 to Binfield, at lights turn
right. Hotel 200yds on right

This chalet designed hotel offers extensive facilities
and includes a ski-slope, ice rink, nightclub, health
club and Bier Keller. Bedrooms range from suites to
standard rooms - all are impressively equipped. A
choice of dining is offered; there's a full bistro menu
available in the Keller, and for more formal dining,
Rowan's restaurant provides award-winning cuisine.

Rooms 205 (6 fmly) (16 GF) **S** £70-£185; **D** £90-£245
(incl. bkfst)* **Facilities** STV Wi-fi ☺ Gym Beauty
treatment room Ice rink Dry ski slope Snow boarding
Freestyle park ♫ New Year **Conf** Class 161 Board 24
Thtr 350 Del from £135 to £250* **Services** Lift Air con
Parking 350 **Notes** LB ⊗ Civ Wed 200

Stirrups Country House

★★★ 82% HOTEL

☎ 01344 882284
Maidens Green RG42 6LD
e-mail: reception@stirrupshotel.co.uk
web: www.stirrupshotel.co.uk
dir: 3m N on B3022 towards Windsor

Situated in a peaceful location between Maidenhead,
Bracknell and Windsor, this hotel has high standards
of comfort particularly in the bedrooms; some rooms
have a small sitting room area. There is a popular
bar, a restaurant, function rooms and delightful
grounds.

Rooms 30 (4 fmly) (2 GF) ✾ **D** £112-£155 (incl.
bkfst)* **Facilities** STV Wi-fi ✎ New Year **Conf** Class 50
Board 40 Thtr 100 Del from £155 to £170*
Services Lift **Parking** 100 **Notes** LB ⊗ Civ Wed 100

Premier Inn Bracknell Central

BUDGET HOTEL

☎ 0871 527 8132
Wokingham Rd RG42 1NA
web: www.premierinn.com
dir: M4 junct 10, A329(M) (Bracknell) to lights. 1st
left, 3rd exit rdbt by Morrisons to town centre. Left at
rdbt, left at next rdbt. Hotel on left

High quality, budget accommodation ideal for both
families and business travellers. Spacious, en suite
bedrooms feature tea and coffee making facilities,
and Freeview TV in most hotels. Internet access and
Wi-fi are available for a small fee. The adjacent
family restaurant features a wide and varied menu.
See also the Hotel Groups pages.

Rooms 60

Premier Inn Bracknell (Twin Bridges)

BUDGET HOTEL

☎ 0871 527 8130
Downshire Way RG12 7AA
web: www.premierinn.com
dir: M4 junct 10, A329(M) towards Bracknell. Straight
on at mini rdbt. At Twin Bridges rdbt take 2nd exit.
Hotel on right adjacent to Downshire Arms Beefeater

Rooms 28

B

BRADFORD
West Yorkshire   Map 19 SE13

See also Gomersal & Shipley

Cedar Court Hotel

★★★★ 71% HOTEL

☎ 01274 406606 & 0845 409 0426
Mayo Av, Off Rooley Ln BD5 8HZ
e-mail: sales@cedarcourtbradford.co.uk
dir: M62 junct 26, M606, to end of motorway, take 1st left

This purpose built, modern hotel is conveniently located just off the motorway and close to the city centre and the airport. The hotel boasts extensive function and conference facilities, a well-equipped leisure club and an elegant restaurant. Bedrooms are comfortably appointed for both business and leisure guests.

Rooms 131 (7 fmly) (23 GF) (4 smoking)
Facilities STV FTV Wi-fi ☒ ☒ Gym Steam room Sauna Solarium New Year **Conf** Class 300 Board 100 Thtr 800 **Services** Lift **Parking** 350 **Notes** ☒ Civ Wed 550

Midland Hotel

★★★ 80% HOTEL   PEEL HOTELS PLC

☎ 01274 735735
Forster Square BD1 4HU
e-mail: info@midland-hotel-bradford.com
web: www.midland-hotel-bradford.com
dir: M62 junct 26, M606, left opposite ASDA, left at rdbt onto A650. Through 2 rdbts & 2 lights. Follow A6181/Haworth signs. Up hill, next left into Manor Row. Hotel 400mtrs

Ideally situated in the heart of the city, this grand Victorian hotel provides modern, very well equipped accommodation and comfortable, spacious day rooms. Ample parking is available in what was once the city's railway station, and a Victorian walkway linking the hotel to the old platform can still be used today.

Rooms 90 (5 fmly) (10 smoking) ☒
S £67.50-£107.50; **D** £77.50-£165 (incl. bkfst)*
Facilities STV FTV Wi-fi ☒ New Year **Conf** Class 150 Board 100 Thtr 450 **Services** Lift **Parking** 60
Notes LB Civ Wed 450

Best Western Guide Post Hotel

★★★ 75% HOTEL

☎ 0844 332 0459 & 01274 607866
Common Rd, Low Moor BD12 0ST
e-mail: sue.barnes@guideposthotel.net
web: www.guideposthotel.net
dir: From M606 rdbt take 2nd exit. At next rdbt take 1st exit (Cleckheaton Rd). 0.5m, turn right at bollard into Common Rd

Situated south of the city, this hotel offers attractively styled, modern, comfortable bedrooms. The restaurant offers an extensive range of food using fresh, local produce; lighter snack meals are served in the bar. There is also a choice of well-equipped meeting and function rooms. There is disabled access to the hotel, restaurant and one function room.

Rooms 42 (10 fmly) (13 GF) ☒ **Facilities** FTV Wi-fi ☒ Complimentary use of nearby swimming & gym facilities **Conf** Class 80 Board 60 Thtr 120 Del from £116.50 to £150 **Parking** 100
Notes Civ Wed 120

Campanile Bradford

Campanile

★★★ 73% HOTEL

☎ 01274 683683
6 Roydsdale Way, Euroway Estate BD4 6SA
e-mail: bradford@campanile.com
web: www.campanile.com
dir: M62 junct 26 into M606. Exit Euroway Estate East into Merrydale Rd, right onto Roydsdale Way

This modern building offers accommodation in smart, well-equipped bedrooms, all with en suite bathrooms. Refreshments may be taken at the informal bistro.

Rooms 130 (37 fmly) (22 GF) (8 smoking)
Facilities STV FTV Wi-fi **Conf** Class 100 Board 100 Thtr 300 **Services** Lift **Parking** 200
Notes Civ Wed 170

Holiday Inn Express Bradford City Centre

Holiday Inn Express

BUDGET HOTEL

☎ 01274 302100
Vicra Ln, Leisure Exchange BD1 5LD
e-mail: bradford@morethanhotels.com
web: www.hiexpress.com/exbradfordcc
dir: M62 junct 26, M606, A6177, 2nd left onto A650, follow signs for The Leisure Exchange

A modern hotel ideal for families and business travellers. Fresh and uncomplicated, the spacious rooms include Sky TV, power shower and tea and coffee-making facilities. Continental buffet breakfast is included in the room rate; other meals may be taken at the nearby family pub or restaurant. See also the Hotel Groups pages.

Rooms 120 (96 fmly) **Conf** Class 30 Board 30 Thtr 40

BRADFORD-ON-AVON
Wiltshire   Map 4 ST86

Widbrook Grange

★★★ 77% ☒ COUNTRY HOUSE HOTEL

☎ 01225 864750 & 863173
Trowbridge Rd, Widbrook BA15 1UH
e-mail: stay@widbrookgrange.com
web: www.widbrookgrange.com
dir: 1m SE from Bradford on A363, hotel diagonally opposite Bradford Marina & Arabian Stud

This former farmhouse, built as a model farm in the 18th century, has been carefully renovated to provide modern comforts, suitable for both business and leisure guests. Some bedrooms are in the main house, but most are in adjacent converted buildings, and these rooms have their own courtyard entrance and many are located on the ground floor. The lounges offer a good level of comfort. French influenced cuisine is served in the refurbished brasserie where friendly staff provide a personal and relaxed service.

Rooms 20 (15 annexe) (6 fmly) (13 GF) ☒
S £95-£125; **D** £135 (incl. bkfst)* **Facilities** FTV Wi-fi ☒ ☒ Gym Children's weekend play room Beauty treatments New Year Child facilities **Conf** Class 35 Board 25 Thtr 50 Del from £115 to £155* **Parking** 50
Notes LB ☒ Closed 24-30 Dec Civ Wed 50

B

BRAINTREE
Essex   Map 7 TL72

White Hart Hotel
★★★ 68% HOTEL OldEngl■sh

☎ 01376 321401
Bocking End CM7 9AB
e-mail: whitehart.braintree@greeneking.co.uk
web: www.oldenglish.co.uk
dir: Exit A120 towards town centre. Hotel at B1256 & Bocking Causeway junct

This 18th-century former coaching inn is conveniently located in the heart of the bustling town centre. The smartly appointed public rooms include a large lounge bar, a restaurant and meeting rooms. The pleasantly decorated bedrooms have co-ordinated fabrics and many thoughtful touches.

Rooms 31 (8 fmly) **Facilities** FTV Wi-fi Xmas New Year **Conf** Class 16 Board 24 Thtr 40 **Parking** 52 **Notes** ⊗ Civ Wed 35

Premier Inn Braintree (A120)

BUDGET HOTEL

☎ 0871 527 8138
Cressing Rd, Galley's Corner CM77 8GG
web: www.premierinn.com
dir: On A120 (Stansted to Braintree link road). Adjacent to Mulberry Tree Brewers Fayre

High quality, budget accommodation ideal for both families and business travellers. Spacious, en suite bedrooms feature tea and coffee making facilities, and Freeview TV in most hotels. Internet access and Wi-fi are available for a small fee. The adjacent family restaurant features a wide and varied menu. See also the Hotel Groups pages.

Rooms 60

Premier Inn Braintree (Freeport Village)
BUDGET HOTEL

☎ 0871 527 8140
Fowlers Farm, Cressing Rd CM77 8DH
web: www.premierinn.com
dir: M11 junct 8, follow signs to A120 Colchester & Freeport Shopping Village. At Galley's Corner rdbt, 4th exit, left into Wyevale Garden Centre. Hotel adjacent

Rooms 47

BRAITHWAITE
Cumbria   Map 18 NY22

The Cottage in the Wood
◉ ◉ RESTAURANT WITH ROOMS

☎ 017687 78409
Whinlatter Pass CA12 5TW
e-mail: relax@thecottageinthewood.co.uk
dir: M6 junct 40, A66 W. After Keswick exit for Braithwaite via Whinlatter Pass (B5292), establishment at top of pass

This charming property sits on wooded hills with striking views of Skiddaw, and it is in a conveniently placed for Keswick. The professional owners provide excellent hospitality in a relaxed manner. The award-winning food, freshly prepared and locally sourced, is served in the bright and welcoming conservatory restaurant that has stunning views. The comfortable bedrooms are well appointed and have many useful extras.

Rooms 9

BRAMPTON
Cumbria   Map 21 NY56

INSPECTORS' CHOICE

Farlam Hall Hotel
★★★ ◉ ◉ HOTEL

☎ 016977 46234
CA8 2NG
e-mail: farlam@relaischateaux.com
web: www.farlamhall.co.uk
dir: On A689 (Brampton to Alston). Hotel 2m on left (not in Farlam village)

This delightful country house has a history dating back to 1428, although the building today is very much the result of alterations carried out in the mid-19th century. The hotel is run by a friendly family team and their enthusiastic staff and is set in beautifully landscaped Victorian gardens complete with an ornamental lake and stream. Lovingly restored over many years, it provides the highest standards of comfort and hospitality. Gracious public rooms invite relaxation, whilst every thought has gone into the beautiful bedrooms,

many of which are simply stunning. Nearby are Hadrian's Wall and the Northern Pennines Area of Outstanding Natural Beauty which provide endless opportunities for walking and sightseeing.

Rooms 12 (1 annexe) (2 GF) ⚑ **S** £160-£190; **D** £300-£360 (incl. bkfst & dinner) **Facilities** FTV Wi-fi ⬥ New Year **Conf** Class 24 Board 12 Thtr 24 **Parking** 25 **Notes** LB No children 5yrs Closed 24-30 Dec & 4-17 Jan Civ Wed 45

BRANCASTER STAITHE
Norfolk   Map 13 TF74

The White Horse
★★★ 79% ◉ ◉ HOTEL

☎ 01485 210262
PE31 8BY
e-mail: reception@whitehorsebrancaster.co.uk
web: www.whitehorsebrancaster.co.uk
dir: On A149 (coast road) midway between Hunstanton & Wells-next-the-Sea

A charming hotel situated on the north Norfolk coast with contemporary bedrooms in two wings, some featuring an interesting cobbled fascia. Each room is attractively decorated and thoughtfully equipped. There is a large bar and a lounge area leading through to the conservatory restaurant, with stunning tidal marshland views across to Scolt Head Island.

Rooms 15 (8 annexe) (4 fmly) (8 GF) ⚑ **S** £47-£120; **D** £94-£180 (incl. bkfst)* **Facilities** FTV Wi-fi ⬥ Xmas New Year **Parking** 60

BRANDESBURTON
East Riding of Yorkshire   Map 17 TA14

Burton Lodge Hotel
★★ 71% HOTEL

☎ 01964 542847
YO25 8RU
e-mail: enquiries@burton-lodge.co.uk
dir: 7m from Beverley off A165, at Hainsworth Park Golf Club

A tennis court, sports play area and extensive lawns are features of this friendly hotel, which is situated in two acres of grounds adjoining a golf course. The modern bedrooms look out either onto the golf course or the countryside; there is a comfortable lounge with a small bar and a spacious restaurant that offers tasty home-style cooking.

Rooms 9 (2 annexe) (3 fmly) (2 GF) **Facilities** ⬥ 18 ⬥ Putt green Pitch and putt **Conf** Class 20 **Parking** 15 **Notes** Closed 25-26 Dec

B

BRANDON
Warwickshire — Map 11 SP47

Mercure Coventry Brandon Hall Hotel & Spa

★★★ 79% HOTEL

☎ 024 7654 6000
Main St CV8 3FW
e-mail: h6625@accor.com
web: www.mercure.com
dir: A45 towards Coventry S. After Peugeot-Citroen garage on left, at island take 5th exit to M1 South/London (back onto A45). After 200yds, immediately after Texaco garage, left into Brandon Ln, hotel after 2.5m

An impressive tree lined avenue leads to this 17th-century property which sits in 17 acres of grounds. The hotel provides a peaceful and friendly sanctuary away from the hustle and bustle. The bedrooms provide comfortable facilities and a good range of extras for guest comfort. There is a Spa Naturel with health, beauty and fitness facilities in a separate building.

Rooms 120 (30 annexe) (10 fmly) (50 GF) ↟ S £70-£180; D £70-£180 **Facilities** Spa STV Wi-fi Gym Steam room Sauna Xmas New Year **Conf** Class 120 Board 112 Thtr 280 Del from £125 to £185 **Services** Lift **Parking** 200 **Notes** Civ Wed 280

BRANDS HATCH
Kent — Map 6 TQ56

Brandshatch Place Hotel & Spa
HandPICKED HOTELS
★★★★ 80% ◉◉ HOTEL

☎ 01474 875000
Brands Hatch Rd, Fawkham DA3 8NQ
e-mail: brandshatchplace@handpicked.co.uk
web: www.handpickedhotels.co.uk/brandshatchplace
dir: M25 junct 3/A20 West Kingsdown. Left at paddock entrance/Fawkham Green sign. 3rd left signed Fawkham Rd. Hotel 500mtrs on right

This charming 18th-century Georgian country house close to the famous racing circuit offers stylish and elegant rooms. Bedrooms are appointed to a very high

standard, offering impressive facilities and excellent levels of comfort and quality. The hotel also features a comprehensive leisure club with substantial crèche facilities. Hand Picked Hotels — AA Hotel Group of the Year 2012-13.

Rooms 38 (12 annexe) (1 fmly) (6 GF) ↟ S £79-£173; D £89-£304 (incl. bkfst)* **Facilities** Spa FTV Wi-fi Gym Squash Aerobic dance studio Sauna Steam room Xmas New Year **Conf** Class 60 Board 50 Thtr 160 Del from £140 to £175* **Services** Lift **Parking** 100 **Notes** LB ⊗ Civ Wed 110

Thistle Brands Hatch
thistle
★★★★ 78% HOTEL

☎ 0871 376 9008
DA3 8PE
e-mail: brandshatch@thistle.co.uk
web: www.thistle.com/brandshatch
dir: M25 junct 3, follow signs for Brands Hatch. Hotel on left of racing circuit entrance

Ideally situated overlooking Brands Hatch race track and close to the major road networks (M20/M25). The open-plan public areas include a choice of bars, large lounge and a restaurant. Bedrooms are stylishly appointed and well equipped for both leisure and business guests. Extensive meeting rooms and Otium leisure facilities are also available.

Rooms 121 (5 fmly) (60 GF) (6 smoking) D £60-£140 (incl. bkfst) **Facilities** Spa STV FTV Wi-fi HL Gym Xmas New Year **Conf** Class 120 Board 60 Thtr 270 Del from £99 to £149 **Parking** 200 **Notes** LB Civ Wed 200

BRANKSOME

See Poole

BRANSCOMBE
Devon — Map 4 SY18

The Bulstone Hotel
★★ 71% HOTEL

☎ 01297 680446
High Bulstone EX12 3BL
e-mail: bulstone@aol.com
web: www.childfriendlyhotels.com
dir: A3052 (Exeter to Lyme Regis road) at Branscombe Cross follow brown hotel sign

Situated in a peaceful location close to the beautiful east Devon coast, this family-friendly hotel is ideally placed for a relaxing break with plenty of attractions within easy reach. All bedrooms comprise a main bedroom and separate children's room, each being practically furnished and equipped. Additional facilities include a playroom, a snug lounge, and the dining room where enjoyable home-cooked meals are

offered. There is no charge for children under ten, and children's tea is at 5pm.

Rooms 7 (7 fmly) (4 GF) **Facilities** FTV Wi-fi Children's playroom Xmas New Year **Conf** Class 25 Board 25 **Services** Air con **Parking** 25 **Notes** ⊗

BREADSALL
Derbyshire — Map 11 SK33

Breadsall Priory, A Marriott Hotel & Country Club
Marriott HOTELS & RESORTS
★★★★ 75% ◉ COUNTRY HOUSE HOTEL

☎ 01332 832235
Moor Rd, Morley DE7 6DL
web: www.marriottbreadsallpriory.co.uk
dir: A52 to Derby, at Pentagon rdbt 3rd exit towards A61/Chesterfield. At 3rd rdbt take 3rd exit & 1st left into village, left at church into Moor Rd. Hotel 1.5m on left

This extended mansion house is set in 400 acres of parkland and well-tended gardens. The smart bedrooms are mostly contained in the modern wing. There is a vibrant café-bar, a more formal restaurant and a large room-service menu. The extensive leisure facilities include two golf courses and a swimming pool. Dinner in the Priory Restaurant is a highlight.

Rooms 112 (100 annexe) (40 fmly) **Facilities** Spa STV Wi-fi 36 Putt green Gym Health, beauty & hair salon Dance studio Leisure club Xmas New Year **Conf** Class 50 Board 36 Thtr 120 **Services** Lift **Parking** 300 **Notes** ⊗ Civ Wed 100

BRENTFORD
Greater London

See London plan 1 C3

Premier Inn London Kew

BUDGET HOTEL

☎ 0871 527 8670
52 High St TW8 0BB
web: www.premierinn.com
dir: At junct of A4 (M4), A205 & A406, Chiswick rdbt, take A205 towards Kew & Brentford. 200yds right fork onto A315 (High St), for 0.5m. Hotel on left

High quality, budget accommodation ideal for both families and business travellers. Spacious, en suite bedrooms feature tea and coffee making facilities, and Freeview TV in most hotels. Internet access and Wi-fi are available for a small fee. The adjacent family restaurant features a wide and varied menu. See also the Hotel Groups pages.

Rooms 141

B

BRENT KNOLL
Somerset
Map 4 ST35

Brent Knoll Lodge & Fox & Goose Inn
★★ 78% HOTEL

☎ 01278 760008
Bristol Rd TA9 4HH
e-mail: reception@brentknolllodge.com
web: www.brentknolllodge.com
dir: On A38 approx 500mtrs N of M5 junct 22

The lodge is conveniently located just a few minutes drive from the M5 and is next door to the Fox & Goose Inn which offers a wide range of beverages and freshly prepared dishes. The American-style diner provides something that is distinctly different. Bedrooms, some at ground-floor level, are well equipped and spacious.

Rooms 14 (3 fmly) (7 GF) **Facilities** FTV Wi-fi Children's outdoor play area Xmas **Conf** Class 32 Board 20 Thtr 32 **Services** Lift Air con **Parking** 60

BRENTWOOD
Essex
Map 6 TQ59

Marygreen Manor Hotel
★★★★ 75% ◉ ◉ HOTEL

☎ 01277 225252
London Rd CM14 4NR
e-mail: info@marygreenmanor.co.uk
web: www.marygreenmanor.co.uk
dir: M25 junct 28, onto A1023 over 2 sets of lights, hotel on right

A 16th-century house which was built by Robert Wright, who named the house 'Manor of Mary Green' after his young bride. Public rooms exude character and have a wealth of original features that include exposed beams, carved panelling and the impressive Tudors Restaurant. Bedrooms are tastefully decorated and thoughtfully equipped.

Rooms 44 (40 annexe) (35 GF) (5 smoking) 🐾 **S** £97-£160; **D** £97-£160* **Facilities** STV FTV Wi-fi ♨ **Conf** Class 20 Board 25 Thtr 50 Del from £144.50 to £169.50* **Parking** 100 **Notes** ⊗ Civ Wed 60

De Rougemont Manor
★★★★ 74% HOTEL

☎ 01277 226418 & 220483
Great Warley St CM13 3JP
e-mail: info@derougemontmanor.co.uk
web: www.derougemontmanor.co.uk
dir: M25 junct 29, A127 to Southend then B186 towards Great Warley

Expect a warm welcome at this family owned and managed hotel, situated on the outskirts of

Brentwood just off the M25. The stylish bedrooms are divided between the main hotel and a bedroom wing; each one is tastefully appointed and well equipped. Public rooms include a smart lounge bar, restaurant and a choice of seating areas.

Rooms 74 (10 annexe) (8 fmly) (16 GF) 🐾 **S** £79-£109; **D** £99-£169* **Facilities** FTV Wi-fi ♨ ⚘ Gym 3-acre nature reserve Xmas New Year **Conf** Class 120 Board 16 Thtr 200 Del from £150 to £190* **Services** Lift Air con **Parking** 200 **Notes** ⊗ Civ Wed 90

Holiday Inn Brentwood
★★★ 80% HOTEL

☎ 0871 942 9012
Brook St CM14 5NF
e-mail: reservations-brentwoodm25@ihg.com
web: www.holidayinn.co.uk
dir: Exit M25 junct 28 (or A12 at M25 interchange). Follow signs to Brentwood/A1023. Hotel 200yds on left

Ideally located just off the M25, this hotel is only 40 minutes from central London and 25 minutes from Stansted Airport, making it the perfect choice for business and leisure travellers alike. The public areas are smartly appointed; the health and fitness club has an indoor swimming pool.

Rooms 149 (28 fmly) (43 GF) **Facilities** STV FTV Wi-fi ♨ HL ⚘ Gym Beauty treatment room New Year **Conf** Class 60 Board 50 Thtr 140 **Services** Lift Air con **Parking** 276 **Notes** ⊗ Civ Wed 70

Premier Inn Brentwood
BUDGET HOTEL

☎ 0871 527 8142
Brentwood House, 169 Kings Rd CM14 4EF
web: www.premierinn.com
dir: From S: M25 junct 28 take A1023 (or from N: at Brook Street rdbt 2nd exit onto A1023). Right at lights into Kings Rd, at rdbt 2nd exit into Kings Rd

High quality, budget accommodation ideal for both families and business travellers. Spacious, en suite bedrooms feature tea and coffee making facilities, and Freeview TV in most hotels. Internet access and Wi-fi are available for a small fee. The adjacent family restaurant features a wide and varied menu. See also the Hotel Groups pages.

Rooms 122

BRIDGNORTH
Shropshire
Map 10 SO79

Old Vicarage Hotel
★★★ 83% ◉ ◉ SMALL HOTEL

☎ 01746 716497
Worfield WV15 5JZ
e-mail: admin@oldvicarageworfield.co.uk
web: www.oldvicarageworfield.com
dir: Exit A454 approx 3.5m NE of Bridgnorth, 5m S of Telford's southern business area. Follow brown signs

This delightful property is set in acres of wooded farmland in a quiet and peaceful area of Shropshire. Service is friendly and helpful, and customer care is one the many strengths of this charming small hotel. The well-equipped bedrooms are individually appointed, and thoughtfully and luxuriously furnished. The lounge and conservatory are the perfect places to enjoy a pre-dinner drink or the complimentary afternoon tea. The elegant restaurant serves award-winning modern British cuisine.

Rooms 14 (4 annexe) (1 fmly) (2 GF) **Facilities** FTV Wi-fi ♨ ⚘ New Year **Conf** Class 40 Board 30 Thtr 60 **Parking** 30 **Notes** Civ Wed 60

BRIDGWATER
Somerset
Map 4 ST23

Walnut Tree Hotel
★★★ 77% ◉ HOTEL

☎ 01278 662255
North Petherton TA6 6QA
e-mail: reservations@walnuttreehotel.com
web: www.walnuttreehotel.com
dir: M5 junct 24. Follow North Petherton signs. 1.3m. Hotel in village centre

Popular with both business and leisure guests, this 18th-century former coaching inn is conveniently located within easy reach of the M5. The spacious and smartly decorated bedrooms are well furnished to ensure a comfortable and relaxing stay. An extensive selection of dishes is offered in either the restaurant, or the more informal setting of the bistro.

Save on hotels. Book at **theAA.com/hotel**

BRE – BRI 93 ENGLAND

Rooms 30 (3 fmly) (3 GF) ♦ S £69-£89; D £79-£99 (incl. bkfst)* Facilities FTV Wi-fi ♒ Gym Xmas New Year Conf Class 60 Board 50 Thtr 100 Del from £125 to £155* Parking 70 Notes LB ⊗ Civ Wed 100

Apple Tree Hotel

★★★ 70% HOTEL

☎ 01278 733238
Keenthorne TA5 1HZ
e-mail: reservations@appletreehotel.com
web: www.appletreehotel.com

(For full entry see Nether Stowey)

Premier Inn Bridgwater

BUDGET HOTEL

☎ 0871 527 8148
Express Park, Bristol Rd TA6 4RR
web: www.premierinn.com
dir: M5 junct 23, A38 to Bridgwater. Hotel on right in 2m

High quality, budget accommodation ideal for both families and business travellers. Spacious, en suite bedrooms feature tea and coffee making facilities, and Freeview TV in most hotels. Internet access and Wi-fi are available for a small fee. The adjacent family restaurant features a wide and varied menu. See also the Hotel Groups pages.

Rooms 40

Expanse Hotel

★★★ 75% HOTEL

☎ 01262 675347
North Marine Dr YO15 2LS
e-mail: reservations@expanse.co.uk
web: www.expanse.co.uk
dir: Follow North Beach signs, pass under railway arch for North Marine Drive. Hotel at bottom of hill

This traditional seaside hotel overlooks the bay and has been in the same family's ownership for many years. Service is relaxed and friendly and the modern bedrooms are well equipped. Comfortable public areas include a conference suite, a choice of bars and an inviting lounge.

Rooms 47 (5 fmly) Facilities FTV Wi-fi ♫ Xmas New Year Conf Class 50 Board 50 Thtr 180 Services Lift Parking 23 Notes ⊗ Civ Wed 140

Haddon House Hotel

★★★ 66% HOTEL

☎ 01308 423626 & 425323
West Bay DT6 4EL
e-mail: info@haddonhousehotel.co.uk
web: www.haddonhousehotel.co.uk
dir: At Crown Inn rdbt take B3157 (West Bay Rd), hotel 0.5m on right at mini-rdbt

This attractive, creeper-clad hotel offers good standards of accommodation and is situated a few minutes' walk from the seafront and the quay. A friendly and relaxed style of service is provided. An extensive range of dishes, from lighter bar snacks to main meals, is on offer in the Tudor-style restaurant.

Rooms 12 (2 fmly) (2 GF) Facilities FTV Wi-fi ♒ New Year Conf Class 20 Board 26 Thtr 60 Parking 40 Notes ⊗

Bridge House Hotel

THE INDEPENDENTS
HOTEL ASSOCIATION

★★ 78% HOTEL

☎ 01308 423371
115 East St DT6 3LB
e-mail: info@bridgehousebridport.co.uk
web: www.bridgehousebridport.co.uk
dir: From A35 follow town centre signs, hotel 200mtrs on right

A short stroll from the town centre, this 18th-century Grade II listed property offers well-equipped

bedrooms that vary in size. In addition to the main lounge, there is a small bar-lounge and a separate breakfast room. An interesting range of home-cooked meals is provided in the wine bar and brasserie.

Rooms 10 (3 fmly) S £75-£112; D £120-£164 (incl. bkfst)* Facilities FTV Wi-fi New Year Conf Class 20 Board 15 Thtr 36 Parking 13

Holiday Inn Leeds - Brighouse

Holiday Inn

★★★ 81% HOTEL

☎ 0871 942 9013
Clifton Village HD6 4HW
e-mail: brighouse@ihg.com
web: www.holidayinn.co.uk
dir: M62 junct 25, A644 signed Brighouse. Remain in right lane, 1st right, hotel at next left

A modern hotel built from traditional Yorkshire stone, and easily accessible from the M62. The bedrooms are spacious and include executive rooms. Other facilities include a leisure club, meeting rooms and ample parking.

Rooms 94 (14 fmly) (43 GF) Facilities STV Wi-fi ♒ ☜ supervised ♦ Gym Xmas New Year Conf Class 120 Board 50 Thtr 200 Services Air con Parking 197 Notes ⊗ Civ Wed 200

Premier Inn Huddersfield North

BUDGET HOTEL

☎ 0871 527 8530
Wakefield Rd HD6 4HA
web: www.premierinn.com
dir: M62 junct 25, A644 signed Huddersfield, Dewsbury & Wakefield. Hotel 500mtrs up hill on right

High quality, budget accommodation ideal for both families and business travellers. Spacious, en suite bedrooms feature tea and coffee making facilities, and Freeview TV in most hotels. Internet access and Wi-fi are available for a small fee. The adjacent family restaurant features a wide and varied menu. See also the Hotel Groups pages.

Rooms 71

B

BRIGHTON & HOVE
East Sussex
Map 6 TQ30

See also Steyning

Hotel du Vin Brighton

★★★★ 77% ◉ ◉
TOWN HOUSE HOTEL

☎ 01273 718588
2-6 Ship St BN1 1AD
e-mail: info@brighton.hotelduvin.com
web: www.hotelduvin.com
dir: From A23 follow seafront/city centre signs. Right at seafront, right into Middle St. Follow to end bear right into Ship St. Hotel on right

This tastefully converted mock-Tudor building occupies a convenient location in a quiet side street close to the seafront. The individually designed bedrooms have a wine theme, and all are comprehensively equipped. Public areas offer a spacious split-level bar, an atmospheric and locally popular restaurant, plus useful private dining and meeting facilities.

Rooms 49 (2 fmly) (4 GF) **Facilities** STV Wi-fi ♫ Xmas New Year **Conf** Class 50 Board 60 Thtr 80 **Services** Air con **Notes** Civ Wed 120

Thistle Brighton

thistle

★★★★ 77% HOTEL

☎ 01273 206700
King's Rd BN1 2GS
e-mail: brighton@thistle.co.uk
web: www.thistlehotels.com/brighton
dir: A23 to seafront. At rdbt turn right, hotel 200yds on right

Situated overlooking the sea and within easy reach of the town's many attractions this hotel is built around an atrium and offers air-conditioned rooms including luxury suites. The restaurant provides stunning sea views, and a comfortable, spacious lounge and bar offer a full range of drinks, light refreshments and meals. The Otium Health & Fitness Club has a pool, sauna and gym facilities plus health and beauty treatments.

Rooms 210 (29 fmly) **Facilities** STV FTV Wi-fi ⊛ supervised Sauna Solarium Beauty treatment room Xmas New Year **Conf** Class 180 Board 120 Thtr 300 **Services** Lift Air con **Parking** 68 **Notes** Civ Wed 300

The Old Ship Hotel

PUMA HOTELS
COLLECTION

★★★★ 75% HOTEL

☎ 01273 329001
King's Rd BN1 1NR
e-mail: oldship@pumahotels.co.uk
web: www.pumahotels.co.uk
dir: A23 to seafront, right at rdbt along Kings Rd. Hotel 200yds on right

This historic hotel enjoys a stunning seafront location and offers guests elegant surroundings to relax in. Bedrooms are well designed, with modern facilities ensuring comfort. Many original features have been retained, including the Paganini Ballroom. Facilities include a sleek bar, alfresco dining and a variety of conference rooms.

Rooms 152 **Facilities** STV Wi-fi Xmas New Year **Conf** Class 100 Board 35 Thtr 250 **Services** Lift **Parking** 40 **Notes** Civ Wed 150

Drakes

★★★★ 73% ◉ ◉ TOWN HOUSE HOTEL

☎ 01273 696934
43-44 Marine Pde BN2 1PE
e-mail: info@drakesofbrighton.com
dir: From A23 at Brighton Pier rdbt. Left into Marine Pde towards marina. Hotel on left before lights (ornate water feature at front)

This independently owned, double fronted Georgian townhouse is in a great location on the seafront and within walking distance of the pier and town centre. The interior design is stunning throughout and all bedrooms offer a touch of luxury - Egyptian cotton linen, goose and duckdown duvets and pillows, and velvet throws plus LCD satellite TV, DVD/CD players and Wi-fi; some rooms have free standing baths in front of large picture windows affording spectacular sea views, others have wet rooms. Dinner and breakfast can be enjoyed in the basement restaurant with an intimate yet relaxed atmosphere where staff offer friendly service.

Rooms 20 (2 GF) **S** £115-£145; **D** £115-£345 **Facilities** STV FTV Wi-fi **Conf** Class 18 Board 12 Thtr 18 Del from £199 to £240 **Services** Air con **Parking** 15 **Notes** ⊗ Civ Wed 45

Holiday Inn Brighton - Seafront

Holiday Inn

★★★★ 70% HOTEL

☎ 01273 828250
137 Kings Rd BN1 2JF
e-mail: reservations@hibrighton.com
web: www.holidayinn.co.uk
dir: M25 junct 7 to M23 S'bound, A23 to town centre, follow signs to seafront, hotel on A259 opposite West Pier

Overlooking the seafront and within walking distance to the town centre, restaurants and pier, this spacious hotel offers modern amenities for leisure and business guests. The bedrooms are spacious and well equipped, and the executive rooms have additional facilities. Public areas include spacious lounges, sports bar and a modern restaurant with an outdoor terrace. A range of meeting rooms is also available.

Rooms 131 (23 fmly) **Facilities** STV Wi-fi Xmas New Year **Conf** Class 200 Board 50 Thtr 450 **Services** Lift Air con **Parking** 64 **Notes** Civ Wed 400

Best Western Brighton Hotel

Best Western

★★★ 75% METRO HOTEL

☎ 01273 820555
143/145 King's Rd BN1 2PQ
e-mail: info@thebrightonhotel.com
web: www.thebrightonhotel.co.uk
dir: M23 onto A23 to pier. Right at rdbt, hotel just past West Pier

This friendly hotel is well placed in a prime seafront location close to the historic West Pier. The contemporary bedrooms are spaciously appointed and well equipped. The lounge, bar and restaurant are sunny, bright and comfortable with great sea views. Dinner is not available in the restaurant but a 24-hour room service menu is in place, and restaurants are within easy walking distance. Parking facilities, though limited, are a real bonus in this area of town.

Rooms 55 (6 fmly) **Facilities** FTV Wi-fi ⊹ Xmas New Year **Conf** Class 30 Board 40 Thtr 70 **Services** Lift **Parking** 10 **Notes** ⊗ Civ Wed 140

Best Western Princes Marine

Best Western

★★★ 75% HOTEL

☎ 01273 207660
153 Kingsway BN3 4GR
e-mail: princesmarine@bestwestern.co.uk
dir: Right at Brighton Pier, follow seafront for 2m. Hotel 200yds from King Alfred leisure centre

This friendly hotel enjoys a seafront location and offers spacious, comfortable bedrooms equipped with a good range of facilities including free Wi-fi. There is a stylish restaurant, modern bar and selection of roof-top meeting rooms with sea views. Limited parking is available at the rear.

Rooms 48 (4 fmly) ✿ **S** £59-£130; **D** £89-£150*
Facilities STV FTV Wi-fi ▷ **Conf** Class 40 Board 40
Thtr 70 Del from £121 to £180* **Services** Lift
Parking 30 **Notes** LB ⊗

The Kings Hotel

★★★ 70% METRO HOTEL

☎ 01273 820854
139-141 Kings Rd BN1 2NA
dir: Follow signs to seafront. At Brighton Pier rdbt take 3rd exit & drive west (seafront on left). Hotel adjacent to West Pier

Located on the seafront adjacent to West Pier, this Grade II listed, Regency building has been restored to offer contemporary accommodation. Although the hotel does not provide a full dinner service, light snacks are available throughout the day and evening in the public areas and also in the guests' bedrooms. There is limited parking space which is a bonus in Brighton.

Rooms 90 (3 fmly) (6 GF) **Conf** Class 25 Board 30
Thtr 70 **Notes** ⊗

Queens Hotel

★★★ 70% HOTEL

☎ 01273 321222 & 0800 970 7570
1-3 King's Rd BN1 1NS
e-mail: info@queenshotelbrighton.com
dir: A23 to Brighton town centre, follow signs for seafront. At Brighton Pier right onto seafront, hotel 500mtrs

This hotel has a fantastic location with views of the beach and pier. The modern bedrooms and bathrooms

are spacious, and many benefit from uninterrupted sea views. All bedrooms have LCD TVs and free Wi-fi. There is a spacious bar and restaurant area plus fully equipped spa, gym and swimming pool.

B

Queens Hotel

Rooms 94 (24 fmly) **S** £69-£200; **D** £69-£300 (incl. bkfst) **Facilities** Spa FTV Wi-fi ▷ HL ⊛ supervised Gym Beauty salon **Conf** Class 50 Board 50 Thtr 150 Del from £100 to £175 **Services** Lift **Notes** LB ⊗ Civ Wed 120

See advert on this page

B

BRIGHTON & HOVE *continued*

The Courtlands Hotel & Conference Centre

★★★ 63% HOTEL

☎ 01273 731055

15-27 The Drive BN3 3JE

e-mail: info@courtlandshotel.com

web: www.courtlandshotel.com

dir: At junct of A23 & A27. Take 1st exit to Hove, 2nd exit at rdbt, right at 1st junct. Left at shops. Straight on at junct. Hotel on left

This hotel is located on a tree-lined avenue within walking distance of the seafront and has its own small car park. The bedrooms come in a variety of styles and include executive rooms and suites. Guests have the use of a comfortable lounge, and a light and spacious restaurant. Service is both friendly and attentive.

Rooms 64 (4 fmly) 🐾 **Facilities** STV FTV Wi-fi ⌔ Xmas New Year **Conf** Class 100 Board 80 Thtr 100 Del from £94 to £130* **Services** Lift **Parking** 30 **Notes** ⊗

Preston Park Hotel

★★ 67% HOTEL

☎ 01273 507853

216 Preston Rd BN1 6UU

e-mail: manager@prestonparkhotel.co.uk

dir: On A23 towards town centre. 5 mins from Preston Park train station

This hotel enjoys a convenient roadside location on the outskirts of Brighton. Bedrooms are modern in style and well provisioned for both the leisure and business guest. Freshly prepared meals are offered in the spacious Sussex Bar (open 24 hours to residents) and in the more intimate and relaxing restaurant. Guests can enjoy a drink on the patio in summer.

Rooms 33 (4 fmly) **S** £39-£92; **D** £49-£110 (incl. bkfst) **Facilities** Gym Xmas New Year **Conf** Class 80 Board 80 Thtr 200 Del from £130 to £160 **Parking** 60 **Notes** LB Civ Wed 150

The De Vere Grand, Brighton

DE VERE
Hotels & Resorts

[U]

☎ 01273 224300

King's Rd BN1 2FW

e-mail: reservations@grandbrighton.co.uk

web: www.devere.co.uk

dir: On A259 adjacent to Brighton Centre

Currently the rating for this establishment is not confirmed. This may be due to a change of ownership or because it has only recently joined the AA rating scheme. For further details please see the AA website: theAA.com

Rooms 200 (60 fmly) **Facilities** STV Wi-fi Gym In room therapies 🎵 Xmas New Year **Conf** Class 420 Board 50 Thtr 700 **Services** Lift **Parking** 50 **Notes** Civ Wed 800

Umi Brighton Hotel

Premier Inn

[U]

☎ 01273 323221

64 King's Rd BN1 1NA

e-mail: reservations@umibrighton.co.uk

dir: On A259 adjacent to Brighton Centre

Currently the rating for this establishment is not confirmed. This may be due to a change of ownership or because it has only recently joined the AA rating scheme. For further details please see the AA website: theAA.com

Rooms 77 (20 fmly) **S** £50-£150; **D** £50-£250 (incl. bkfst)* **Facilities** FTV Wi-fi ⌔ Free use of leisure centre in Queens Hotel **Conf** Class 20 Board 30 Thtr 50 Del from £99 to £180* **Services** Lift **Notes** ⊗

Premier Inn Brighton City Centre

BUDGET HOTEL

☎ 0871 527 8150

144 North St BN1 1RE

web: www.premierinn.com

dir: From A23 follow signs for city centre. Right at lights near Royal Pavilion, take road ahead on left (runs adjacent to Pavilion) into Church St, 1st left into New Rd leading North St

High quality, budget accommodation ideal for both families and business travellers. Spacious, en suite bedrooms feature tea and coffee making facilities, and Freeview TV in most hotels. Internet access and Wi-fi are available for a small fee. The adjacent family restaurant features a wide and varied menu. See also the Hotel Groups pages.

Rooms 160

BRISTOL
Bristol

Map 4 ST57

Aztec Hotel & Spa

shire
hotels & spas

★★★★ 80% ☺ HOTEL

☎ 01454 201090

Aztec West Business Park, Almondsbury BS32 4TS

e-mail: aztec@shirehotels.com

web: www.aztechotelbristol.com

dir: Access via M5 junct 16 & M4

Situated close to Cribbs Causeway shopping centre and major motorway links, this stylish hotel offers comfortable, very well-equipped bedrooms and suites. Built in a Nordic style, public rooms boast log fires and vaulted ceilings. Leisure facilities include a popular gym and good size pool. The Quarter Jacks Restaurant Bar & Lounge offers relaxed informal dining with a focus on simply prepared, quality regional foods. The hotel has a spa with a gym, pool, children's pool, whirlpool, sauna, steam room and a range of treatments.

Rooms 128 (8 fmly) (29 GF) **S** £80-£150; **D** £80-£150* **Facilities** Spa STV Wi-fi ⌔ Gym Steam room Sauna Children's splash pool Activity studio New Year **Conf** Class 120 Board 36 Thtr 200 Del from £125 to £175* **Services** Lift **Parking** 240 **Notes** ⊗ Civ Wed 120

Bristol Marriott Royal Hotel

Marriott
HOTELS & RESORTS

★★★★ 80% ☺ HOTEL

☎ 0117 925 5100

College Green BS1 5TA

web: www.bristolmarriottroyal.co.uk

dir: Adjacent to cathedral

A truly stunning hotel located in the centre of the city, next to the cathedral. Public areas are particularly impressive with luxurious lounges and a leisure club. Dining options include the informal Terrace and the really spectacular, restaurant adjacent to the champagne bar. The spacious bedrooms have the benefit of air conditioning, comfortable armchairs and marble bathrooms.

Rooms 242 (23 GF) (6 smoking) 🐾 **Facilities** Wi-fi ⌔ HL ☺ Gym Hair & beauty salon & treatment rooms **Conf** Class 180 Board 60 Thtr 300 **Services** Lift Air con **Parking** 200 **Notes** ⊗ Civ Wed 200

B

Bristol Marriott City Centre

Marriott HOTELS & RESORTS

★★★★ 76% HOTEL

☎ 0117 929 4281
Lower Castle St BS1 3AD
web: www.bristolmarriottcitycentre.co.uk
dir: M32 follow signs to Broadmead, take slip road to large rdbt, take 3rd exit. Hotel on right

Situated at the foot of the picturesque Castle Park, this mainly business-orientated hotel is well placed for the city centre. Executive and deluxe bedrooms have high speed internet access. In addition to a coffee bar and lounge menu, the Mediterrano Restaurant offers an interesting selection of well-prepared dishes.

Rooms 300 (135 fmly) **Facilities** STV FTV Wi-fi ♦ ⊗ Gym Steam room Sauna Spa pool Xmas New Year **Conf** Class 280 Board 40 Thtr 600 **Services** Lift Air con **Notes** ⊗ Civ Wed 700

The Grand, Bristol

thistle

★★★★ 75% HOTEL

☎ 0871 376 9042
Broad St BS1 2EL
e-mail: thegrand@thistle.co.uk
web: www.thistle.com/thegrand
dir: In city centre pass The Galleries. 3rd right into Broad St

This large hotel is situated in the heart of the city, and benefits from its own secure parking. Bedrooms are well equipped and comfortably appointed, and include a number of Premium Executive rooms. The public areas include leisure and therapy treatment rooms and there is an impressive range of conference and banqueting facilities.

Rooms 182 (10 fmly) ⚮ **S** £59-£169; **D** £89-£199 (incl. bkfst)* **Facilities** Spa STV Wi-fi ⊗ supervised Gym Steam room Sauna Solarium Xmas New Year **Conf** Class 250 Board 40 Thtr 600 Del from £129 to £200* **Services** Lift Air con **Parking** 150 **Notes** LB ⊗ Civ Wed 500

Hotel du Vin Bristol

Hotel du Vin & Bistro

★★★★ 74% ⊚
TOWN HOUSE HOTEL

☎ 0117 925 5577
The Sugar House, Narrow Lewins Mead BS1 2NU
e-mail: info.bristol@hotelduvin.com
web: www.hotelduvin.com
dir: From A4 follow city centre signs. After 400yds pass Rupert St NCP on right. Hotel on opposite carriageway

This hotel is part of one of Britain's most innovative hotel groups that offer high standards of hospitality and accommodation. Housed in a Grade II listed, converted 18th-century sugar refinery, it provides great facilities with a modern, minimalist design. The bedrooms are exceptionally well designed and the bistro offers an excellent menu and wine list.

Rooms 40 (10 fmly) ⚮ **S** £125-£160; **D** £160-£375* **Facilities** STV FTV Wi-fi ⊗ ♫ New Year **Conf** Class 36 Board 34 Thtr 72 Del from £175 to £225* **Services** Lift **Parking** 12 **Notes** LB Civ Wed 65

Holiday Inn Bristol Filton

Holiday Inn

★★★★ 74% HOTEL

☎ 0871 942 9014
Filton Rd, Hambrook BS16 1QX
e-mail: bristol@ihg.com
web: www.hibristolfiltonhotel.co.uk
dir: M4 junct 19/M32 junct 1/A4174 towards Filton & Bristol. Hotel 800yds on left

With easy access of both the M4 and M5 this is, understandably, a popular hotel in particular with business guests. Public areas are spacious and relaxing with a wide choice of comfortable seating options. There are two restaurants - Sampans with a selection of dishes from the Far East, and the more traditional Junction Restaurant. Bedrooms vary in size, but all are well furnished and well equipped. A large car park, leisure facilities and range of conference rooms are all available.

Rooms 211 (40 fmly) (70 GF) (2 smoking)
S £65-£152; **D** £75-£162 (incl. bkfst)* **Facilities** STV FTV Wi-fi ♦ ⊗ supervised Fishing Gym Beauty treatment room Sauna Xmas New Year **Conf** Class 180 Board 75 Thtr 250 Del from £99 to £195* **Services** Lift Air con **Parking** 250 **Notes** LB ⊗ Civ Wed 250

Mercure Bristol North The Grange

Mercure

★★★★ 74% COUNTRY HOUSE HOTEL

☎ 0844 815 9063
Northwoods, Winterbourne BS36 1RP
e-mail: gm.mercurebristolnorthgrange@jupiterhotels.co.uk
web: www.jupiterhotels.co.uk
dir: A38 towards Filton/Bristol. At rdbt 1st exit into Bradley Stoke Way, at lights 1st left into Woodlands Ln, at 2nd rdbt left into Tench Ln. In 1m left at T-junct, hotel 200yds on left

Built in the 19th century and surrounded by 18 acres of attractive grounds, this is a pleasant hotel situated only a short drive from the city centre. The bedrooms are spacious and well equipped; there is a leisure centre with a pool plus a range of meeting facilities. The conservatory bar has a terrace which makes a delightful place to enjoy a drink under the shade of a 200-year-old cedar tree. The hotel is popular as a wedding venue.

Rooms 68 (20 fmly) (22 GF) **Facilities** Spa STV FTV Wi-fi ⊗ supervised ⤵ Gym Sauna Xmas New Year **Conf** Class 120 Board 134 Thtr 150 **Parking** 150 **Notes** Civ Wed 150

Radisson Blu Hotel Bristol

Radisson BLU HOTELS & RESORTS

★★★★ 73% HOTEL

☎ 01179 349500
Broad Qauy BS1 4BY
dir: Telephone for directions (NB use BS1 4AQ for Sat Nav)

This city centre hotel has a great location and impressive facilities. There are a range of meeting rooms, a spa and a ground-floor bar which specialises in cocktails and opens out to Bristol's main shopping and business area. The bedrooms are spacious and very well equipped, so too are the stylish bathrooms. The Italian themed Filini Restaurant enjoys views across the city.

Rooms 176 (1 fmly) (4 smoking) ⚮ **S** fr £89; **D** fr £99 **Facilities** STV FTV Wi-fi ♦ Gym ♫ Xmas New Year **Conf** Class 60 Board 40 Thtr 120 Del from £129 to £199 **Services** Lift Air con **Notes** LB ⊗ Civ Wed 100

BRISTOL *continued*

Mercure Brigstow Bristol

★★★★ 72% HOTEL

☎ 0117 929 1030
5-7 Welsh Back BS1 4SP
e-mail: H6548@accor.com
web: www.mercure.com
dir: From the centre follow Baldwin St then right into Queen Charlotte St

In a prime position on the river this handsome purpose-built hotel is designed and finished with care. The shopping centre and theatres are within easy walking distance. The stylish bedrooms are extremely well equipped, including plasma TV screens in the bathrooms. There is an integrated state-of-the-art conference and meeting centre, and a smart restaurant and bar overlooking the harbour. Guests have complimentary use of a squash and health club, plus free internet access.

Rooms 116 ❧ S £70-£165; D £70-£165*
Facilities STV FTV Wi-fi ❧ Gym Free access to nearby gym & squash courts New Year **Conf** Class 40 Board 30 Thtr 85 Del from £130 to £180*
Services Lift Air con **Notes** LB Civ Wed 80

Mercure Bristol Holland House Hotel & Spa

★★★★ 72% HOTEL

☎ 0117 968 9900
Redcliffe Hill BS1 6SQ
e-mail: h6698@accor.com
web: www.mercure.com
dir: M4 junct 19 towards city centre, follow signs A4 then A370, take A38 Redcliffe Hill. Hotel opposite St Mary Redcliffe Church

This modern hotel, just a ten-minute walk from Bristol Temple Meads, has striking, contemporary style throughout, and offers some impressive facilities including a spa, a fitness suite and meeting rooms. The hotel has a green-bicycle service for guests. Bedrooms are stylishly designed with large plasma screen TVs, comfortable beds and free internet access. Dining is offered in the Phoenix Restaurant and bar.

Rooms 275 (59 fmly) (44 GF) ❧ **Facilities** Spa FTV Wi-fi ❧ HL ⊕ Gym Free bike rental & laptop use **Conf** Class 150 Board 80 Thtr 220 Del from £130 to £160 **Services** Lift Air con **Parking** 140 **Notes** ⊗ Civ Wed 220

Ramada Bristol City

★★★★ 72% HOTEL

☎ 0117 926 0041
Redcliffe Way BS1 6NJ
e-mail: sales@focusbristol.co.uk
web: www.ramada-bristol.co.uk
dir: 1m from M32. 400yds from Temple Meads BR station, before church

This large modern hotel is situated in the heart of the city centre and offers spacious public areas and ample parking. Bedrooms are well equipped for both business and leisure guests. Dining options include a relaxed bar and a unique kiln restaurant where a good selection of freshly prepared dishes is available.

Rooms 201 (4 fmly) (18 smoking) ❧ S £69-£150; D £69-£150 **Facilities** FTV Wi-fi ❧ ⊕ supervised Gym Sauna Steam room New Year **Conf** Class 120 Board 75 Thtr 300 Del from £99 to £170 **Services** Lift Air con **Parking** 150 **Notes** LB ⊗ Civ Wed 250

Novotel Bristol Centre

★★★★ 70% HOTEL

☎ 0117 976 9988
Victoria St BS1 6HY
e-mail: H5622@accor.com
web: www.novotel.com
dir: At end of M32 follow signs for Temple Meads station to rdbt. Final exit, hotel immediately on right

This city centre hotel provides smart, contemporary style accommodation. Most of the bedrooms demonstrate the Novotel 'Novation' style with unique swivel desk, internet access, air-conditioning and a host of extras. The hotel is convenient for the mainline railway station and also has its own car park.

Rooms 131 (20 fmly) **Facilities** STV Wi-fi ❧ Gym **Conf** Class 70 Board 35 Thtr 210 **Services** Lift **Parking** 120 **Notes** Civ Wed 100

Best Western Henbury Lodge Hotel

★★★ 80% ◉◉ HOTEL

☎ 0117 950 2615
Station Rd, Henbury BS10 7QQ
e-mail: info@henburyhotel.com
web: www.henburyhotel.com
dir: M5 junct 17/A4018 towards city centre, 3rd rdbt right into Crow Ln. At end turn right, hotel 200mtrs on right

This quietly located hotel is popular with both business and leisure guests. Bedrooms, in a wide range of shapes and sizes, are divided between the main house and a converted stable block; all are comfortable furnished and equipped. The small and friendly team offer a very personal welcome and many guests here are regulars. Dinner and breakfast are taken in the stylish restaurant where high quality local produce is used.

Rooms 20 (9 annexe) (4 fmly) (6 GF) S £89-£109; D £99-£129 (incl. bkfst)* **Facilities** FTV Wi-fi ❧ **Conf** Class 15 Board 20 Thtr 20 Del from £149 to £179* **Parking** 20 **Notes** LB ⊗ Closed 22 Dec-9 Jan

The Berkeley Square

★★★ 78% ◉ HOTEL

☎ 0117 925 4000
15 Berkeley Square, Clifton BS8 1HB
e-mail: berkeley@cliftonhotels.com
web: www.cliftonhotels.com/chg.html
dir: M32 follow Clifton signs. 1st left at lights by Wills Memorial Tower (University) into Berkeley Sq

Set in a pleasant square close to the university, art gallery and Clifton village, this smart, elegant Georgian hotel has modern, stylishly decorated bedrooms that feature many welcome extras. There are a cosy lounge and stylish restaurant on the ground floor and a smart, contemporary bar in the basement. A small garden is also available at the rear of the hotel.

Rooms 42 (4 GF) ❧ S £58-£110; D £76-£148 **Facilities** STV FTV Wi-fi ❧ Use of local gym & swimming pool **Services** Lift **Parking** 20 **Notes** Civ Wed

B

The Avon Gorge Hotel

★★★　75%　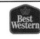　HOTEL

☎ 0117 973 8955
Sion Hill, Clifton BS8 4LD
e-mail: rooms@theavongorge.com
dir: From S: M5 junct 19, A369 to Clifton Toll, over
suspension bridge, 1st right into Clifton Toll. From N: M5
junct 18A, A4 to Bristol, under suspension bridge,
follow signs to bridge, exit Sion Hill

This is a delightful terraced property, overlooking the
Clifton Suspension Bridge, that offers bedrooms of
varying shapes and sizes with either views across the
river or of Clifton Village. For eating there is the
contemporary Bridge Café restaurant where a range
of carefully prepared, tempting dishes is available.
There is a limited amount of free parking space at the
rear of the hotel or on-street (no restrictions) in the
vicinity.

Rooms 75 (8 fmly) **Facilities** STV Wi-fi 🏊 Xmas New
Year **Conf** Class 40 Board 30 Thtr 100 **Services** Lift
Parking 25 **Notes** Civ Wed 100

Holiday Inn Bristol Airport

★★★　74% HOTEL　

☎ 01934 861123
**A38 Bridgwater Rd, Cowslip Garden, Wrington
BS40 5RB**
e-mail: reservations@hibristolairport.co.uk
web: www.hibristolairport.co.uk
dir: From Bristol, W on A38. Hotel 3m from Bristol
International Airport on right

While ideally located for Bristol Airport, this modern
hotel is also an ideal base for exploring the areas
surrounding Bath, Bristol and Wells; many attractions
are within easy reach. The bedrooms and bathrooms
are generally spacious and well equipped. Guests can
dine throughout the day on a range of lounge meals,
including room service, while in the evening an
additional selection of tempting dishes is offered in
the restaurant.

Rooms 80 (4 fmly) (12 GF) (12 smoking) 🐾
S £40-£100; D £60-£120 **Facilities** FTV Wi-fi 🏊 HL
Gym **Conf** Class 20 Board 24 Thtr 60 Del from £115 to
£165 **Services** Lift Air con **Parking** 100 **Notes** LB ⊗

Rodney Hotel

★★★　68%　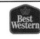　HOTEL

☎ 0117 973 5422
4 Rodney Place, Clifton BS8 4HY
e-mail: rodney@cliftonhotels.com
dir: Off Clifton Down Rd

With easy access from the M5, this attractive, listed
building in Clifton is conveniently close to the city

centre. The individually decorated bedrooms provide a
useful range of extra facilities for the business
traveller; the public areas include a smart bar and
small restaurant offering enjoyable and carefully
prepared dishes. A pleasant rear garden provides
additional seating in the summer months.

Rooms 31 (1 fmly) (2 GF) **S** £52-£94; **D** £65-£112
Facilities FTV Wi-fi **Conf** Class 20 Board 20 Thtr 30
Parking 10 **Notes** LB Closed 22 Dec-3 Jan RS Sun
Civ Wed 40

Best Western Victoria Square Hotel

★★　79% HOTEL

☎ 0117 973 9058
Victoria Square, Clifton BS8 4EW
e-mail: info@victoriasquarehotel.co.uk
dir: M5 junct 19, follow Clifton signs. Over
suspension/toll bridge, right into Clifton Down Rd.
Left into Merchants Rd then into Victoria Square

This welcoming hotel offers high quality, individual
bedrooms and bathrooms in a variety of shapes and
sizes. Well located, the hotel is just one mile from the
city centre and a two-minute stroll from the heart of
Clifton village. The atmosphere is relaxed, and guests
have a choice of dining options - from lighter meals
in the bar to a range of imaginative dishes in the
main restaurant.

Rooms 41 (20 annexe) (3 fmly) (3 GF) 🐾 **S** £61-£85;
D £69-£110 (incl. bkfst)* **Facilities** FTV Wi-fi
Conf Class 15 Board 20 Thtr 30 **Parking** 25 **Notes** ⊗

Clifton Hotel

★★　76% HOTEL

☎ 0117 973 6882
St Pauls Rd, Clifton BS8 1LX
e-mail: clifton@cliftonhotels.com
web: www.cliftonhotels.com/clifton
dir: M32 follow Bristol/Clifton signs, along Park St.
Left at lights into St Pauls Rd

This popular hotel offers very well equipped bedrooms
and relaxed, friendly service. There is a welcoming
lounge by the reception, and in summer months
drinks and meals can be enjoyed on the terrace.
Racks Bar and Restaurant offers an interesting
selection of modern dishes in informal surroundings.
There is some street parking, but for a small charge,
secure garage parking is available.

Rooms 59 (2 fmly) (12 GF) (8 smoking) **S** £43-£75;
D £53-£91* **Facilities** STV FTV Wi-fi **Services** Lift
Parking 12 **Notes** LB

Holiday Inn Express Bristol City Centre

BUDGET HOTEL

☎ 0117 930 4800
South End, Temple Gate House BS1 6PL
e-mail: gsa@hiexpressbristol.co.uk
web: www.hiexpressbristol.co.uk
dir: M4 junct 19/M32 into Bristol. Keep left, follow
Temple Meads train station signs. Hotel opposite
station

A modern hotel ideal for families and business
travellers. Fresh and uncomplicated, the spacious
rooms include Sky TV, power shower and tea and
coffee-making facilities. Continental buffet breakfast
is included in the room rate; other meals may be
taken at the nearby family pub or restaurant. See also
the Hotel Groups pages.

Rooms 96 (11 fmly) (8 smoking) 🐾

Holiday Inn Express Bristol - North

BUDGET HOTEL

☎ 0117 317 2700
New Rd, Bristol Parkway Business Park BS34 8SJ
e-mail: managerbristolnorth@expressholidayinn.co.
uk
web: www.hiexpress.com/bristolnorth
dir: M4 junct 19 or M32 junct 1. Follow Bristol
Parkway Station signs, right at main rdbt, hotel on
left. For access, left at next 2 rdbts onto New Rd,
hotel entrance 100yds past Bristol & West building

Rooms 133 (106 fmly) **Conf** Class 20 Board 24
Thtr 30

Ibis Bristol Centre (AKA Harbourside)

BUDGET HOTEL

☎ 0117 9897200
Explore Ln BS1 5TY
e-mail: H5547-GM@accor.com
dir: Off A4 in harbourside district

Modern, budget hotel offering comfortable
accommodation in bright and practical bedrooms.
Breakfast is self-service and dinner is available in
the restaurant. See also the Hotel Groups pages.

Rooms 182 (2 fmly)

B

BRISTOL *continued*

Ibis Bristol Temple Meads

BUDGET HOTEL

☎ 0117 954 3600
Avon St BS2 0PS
e-mail: H6593@accor.com
dir: M4 junct 19, M32, follow Temple Meads train station signs. Left after underpass

Rooms 141 (7 fmly) **Conf** Class 12 Board 12 Thtr 12

Premier Inn Bristol Airport (Sidcot)

BUDGET HOTEL

☎ 0871 527 8154
Bridgwater Rd, Winscombe BS25 1NN
web: www.premierinn.com
dir: Between M5 junct 21 & 22 (9m from Bristol Airport), onto A371 towards Banwell, Winscombe to A38. Right at lights, Hotel 300yds on left

High quality, budget accommodation ideal for both families and business travellers. Spacious, en suite bedrooms feature tea and coffee making facilities, and Freeview TV in most hotels. Internet access and Wi-fi are available for a small fee. The adjacent family restaurant features a wide and varied menu. See also the Hotel Groups pages.

Rooms 31

Premier Inn Bristol (Alveston)

BUDGET HOTEL

☎ 0871 527 8152
Thornbury Rd, Alveston BS35 3LL
web: www.premierinn.com
dir: Just off M5. From N: exit at junct 14 onto A38 towards Bristol. From S: exit at junct 16 onto A38 towards Gloucester

Rooms 75

Premier Inn Bristol City Centre (Haymarket)

BUDGET HOTEL

☎ 0871 527 8156
The Haymarket BS1 3LR
web: www.premierinn.com
dir: M4 junct 19, M32 towards city centre. Through 2 sets of lights, at 3rd lights turn right, to rdbt, take 2nd exit. Hotel on left

Rooms 224

Premier Inn Bristol City Centre King Street

BUDGET HOTEL

☎ 0871 527 8158
Llandoger Trow, King St BS1 4ER
web: www.premierinn.com
dir: A38 into city centre. Left onto B4053 Baldwin St. Right into Queen Charlotte St, follow one-way system, bear right at river. Hotel on right

Rooms 60

Premier Inn Bristol Cribbs Causeway

BUDGET HOTEL

☎ 0871 527 8160
Cribbs Causeway, Catbrain Ln BS10 7TQ
web: www.premierinn.com
dir: M5 junct 17, A4018. 1st left at rdbt into Lysander Rd. Right into Catbrain Hill, leads to Catbrain Lane

Rooms 106

Premier Inn Bristol East (Emersons Green)

BUDGET HOTEL

☎ 0871 527 8162
200/202 Westerleigh Rd, Emersons Green BS16 7AN
web: www.premierinn.com
dir: M4 junct 19 onto M32 junct 1, left onto A4174 (Avon Ring Rd). Hotel at 3rd rdbt

Rooms 67

Premier Inn Bristol Filton

BUDGET HOTEL

☎ 0871 527 8164
Shield Retail Park, Gloucester Road North, Filton BS34 7BR
web: www.premierinn.com
dir: M5 junct 16, A38 signed Filton/Patchway. Pass airport & Royal Mail on right. Left at 2nd rdbt, 1st left into retail park

Rooms 62

Premier Inn Bristol South

BUDGET HOTEL

☎ 0871 527 8166
Hengrove Leisure Park, Hengrove Way BS14 0HR
web: www.premierinn.com
dir: From city centre take A37 towards Wells & Shepton Mallet. Right onto A4174. Hotel at 3rd lights

Rooms 56

Quayside Hotel

★★★ 75% ◉ HOTEL

☎ 01803 855751
41-49 King St TQ5 9TJ
e-mail: reservations@quaysidehotel.co.uk
web: www.quaysidehotel.co.uk
dir: A380, at 2nd rdbt at Kinkerswell towards Brixham on A3022

With views over the harbour and bay, this hotel was formerly six cottages, and the public rooms retain a certain cosiness and intimacy, and include the lounge, residents' bar and Ernie Lister's public bar. Freshly landed fish features on the menus, alongside a number of creative and skilfully prepared dishes, served in the well-appointed restaurant. Good food is also available in the public bar. The owners and their team of local staff provide friendly and attentive service.

Rooms 29 (2 fmly) **Facilities** FTV Wi-fi ♫ Xmas New Year **Conf** Class 18 Board 18 Thtr 25 **Parking** 30

Berry Head Hotel

THE INDEPENDENTS
HOTEL ASSOCIATION

★★★ 75% HOTEL

☎ 01803 853225
Berry Head Rd TQ5 9AJ
e-mail: stay@berryheadhotel.com
dir: From marina, 1m, hotel on left

From its stunning cliff-top location, this imposing property that dates back to 1809, has spectacular views across Torbay. Public areas include two comfortable lounges, an outdoor terrace, a swimming pool, together with a bar serving a range of popular dishes. Many of the bedrooms have the benefit of the splendid sea views.

Rooms 32 (7 fmly) **S** £52-£72; **D** £104-£144 (incl. bkfst)* **Facilities** FTV Wi-fi ☺ ♨ Petanque Sailing Deep sea fishing Yacht charter ♫ Xmas New Year **Conf** Class 250 Board 40 Thtr 300 Del from £85 to £125* **Services** Lift **Parking** 200 **Notes** LB Civ Wed 200

Save on hotels. Book at **theAA.com/hotel**

BRI – BRO 101 ENGLAND

B

BROADWAY
Worcestershire

Map 10 SP03

The Lygon Arms

★★★★ 81% ◉ ◉ HOTEL

PUMA HOTELS COLLECTION

☎ 01386 852255
High St WR12 7DU
e-mail: thelygonarms@pumahotels.co.uk
web: www.pumahotels.co.uk
dir: From Evesham take A44 signed Oxford, 5m.
Follow Broadway signs. Hotel on left

A hotel with a wealth of historic charm and character, the Lygon Arms dates back to the 16th century. There is a choice of restaurants, a stylish cosy bar, an array of lounges and a smart spa and leisure club. Bedrooms vary in size and style, but all are thoughtfully equipped and include a number of stylish contemporary rooms as well as a cottage in the grounds.

Rooms 78 (16 fmly) (17 GF) **Facilities** Spa STV FTV Wi-fi ⌒ ⊙ supervised ⊛ ⊰ Gym Beauty treatments Billiard table ♫ Xmas New Year **Conf** Class 42 Board 30 Thtr 100 **Parking** 200 **Notes** Civ Wed 100

Dormy House Hotel

★★★★ 80% ◉ ◉ HOTEL

☎ 01386 852711
Willersey Hill WR12 7LF
e-mail: reservations@dormyhouse.co.uk.
web: www.dormyhouse.co.uk
dir: 2m E of Broadway off A44, at top of Fish Hill turn for Saintbury/Picnic area. In 0.5m turn left, hotel on left

A converted 17th-century farmhouse set in extensive grounds and with stunning views over Broadway. Some rooms are in an annexe at ground-floor level, some have a contemporary style. The best traditions are retained - customer care, real fires, comfortable sofas and afternoon teas. Dinner features an interesting choice of dishes created by a skilled kitchen brigade.

Rooms 45 (20 annexe) (8 fmly) (21 GF) ⬔
S £175-£230; **D** £195-£250 (incl. bkfst)*
Facilities STV FTV Wi-fi Putt green ⊰ Gym Nature &

jogging trail Sauna Steam room Xmas New Year **Conf** Class 100 Board 25 Thtr 170 Del from £180 to £198* **Parking** 90 **Notes** LB ⊗ Civ Wed 170

The Broadway Hotel

★★★ 78% HOTEL

COTSWOLD INNS & HOTELS

☎ 01386 852401
The Green, High St WR12 7AA
e-mail: info@broadwayhotel.info
web: www.cotswold-inns-hotels.co.uk/broadway
dir: Follow signs to Evesham, then Broadway

A half-timbered Cotswold stone property, built in the 15th century as a retreat for the Abbots of Pershore. The hotel combines modern, attractive decor with original charm and character. Bedrooms are tastefully furnished and well equipped while public rooms include a relaxing lounge, cosy bar and charming restaurant; alfresco all-day dining in summer months proves popular. Cotswold Inns & Hotels – AA Small Hotel Group of the Year 2012-13.

Rooms 19 (1 fmly) (3 GF) **S** £120-£160; **D** £160-£220 (incl. bkfst)* **Facilities** Wi-fi Xmas New Year **Parking** 20 **Notes** LB

Russell's

◉ ◉ RESTAURANT WITH ROOMS

☎ 01386 853555
20 High St WR12 7DT
e-mail: info@russellsofbroadway.co.uk
dir: Opposite village green

Situated in the centre of a picturesque Cotswold village this restaurant with rooms makes a great base for exploring local attractions. The superbly appointed bedrooms, each with its own character, have air conditioning and a wide range of extras for guests. The cuisine is a real draw here with freshly-prepared, local produce skilfully utilised.

Rooms 7 (3 annexe) (4 fmly)

BROCKENHURST
Hampshire

Map 5 SU30

INSPECTORS' CHOICE

Rhinefield House Hotel

Hand PICKED HOTELS

★★★★ ◉ ◉ HOTEL

☎ 01590 622922 & 0845 072 7516
Rhinefield Rd SO42 7QB
e-mail: rhinefieldhouse@handpicked.co.uk
web: www.handpickedhotels.co.uk/rhinefieldhouse
dir: A35 towards Christchurch. 3m from Lyndhurst turn left to Rhinefield, 1.5m to hotel

This stunning 19th-century, mock-Elizabethan mansion is set in 40 acres of beautifully landscaped gardens and forest. Bedrooms are spacious and great consideration is given to guest comfort. The elegant and award-winning Armada Restaurant is richly furnished, and features a fireplace carving (nine years in the making) that is worth taking time to admire. If the weather permits, the delightful terrace is just the place for enjoying alfresco eating. Hand Picked Hotels – AA Hotel Group of the Year 2012-13.

Rooms 50 (10 fmly) (18 GF) **S** £117-£415; **D** £127-£425 (incl. bkfst)* **Facilities** Spa STV Wi-fi ⌒ HL ⊙ ⌇ ⊛ ⊰ Gym Hydrotherapy pool Plunge pool Steam room Sauna Beauty treatment rooms Xmas New Year **Conf** Class 72 Board 56 Thtr 160 Del from £155 to £220 **Services** Lift **Parking** 100 **Notes** LB ⊗ Civ Wed 130

B

BROCKENHURST *continued*

Careys Manor Hotel

★★★★ 84% ◎◎ HOTEL

☎ 01590 624467

SO42 7RH

e-mail: stay@careysmanor.com

web: www.careysmanor.com

dir: M27 junct 3, M271, A35 to Lyndhurst. A337 towards Brockenhurst. Hotel on left after Beaulieu sign

This smart property offers a host of facilities that include an Oriental-style spa and leisure suite with an excellent range of unusual treatments, and three very contrasting restaurants that offer a choice of Thai, French or modern British cuisine. Many of the spacious and well appointed bedrooms have balconies overlooking the gardens. Extensive function and conference facilities are also available.

Rooms 79 (61 annexe) (31 GF) **S** £154-£358; **D** £208-£358 (incl. bkfst)* **Facilities** Spa FTV Wi-fi ↻ ⓧ ⌣ Gym Steam room Beauty therapists Hydrotherapy pool Xmas New Year **Conf** Class 70 Board 40 Thtr 120 Del £195* **Services** Lift **Parking** 180 **Notes** ⊗ No children 16yrs Civ Wed 100

The Balmer Lawn Hotel

★★★★ 80% ◎ HOTEL

☎ 01590 623116

Lyndhurst Rd SO42 7ZB

e-mail: info@balmerlawnhotel.com

dir: Just off A337 from Brockenhurst towards Lymington

Situated in the heart of the New Forest, this peacefully located hotel provides comfortable public rooms and a wide range of bedrooms. A selection of carefully prepared and enjoyable dishes is offered in the spacious restaurant. The extensive function and leisure facilities make this popular with both families and conference delegates.

Rooms 50 (10 fmly) ↻ **S** £79-£149; **D** £89-£189 (incl. bkfst) **Facilities** FTV Wi-fi ⓧ ⌁ ⌣ Gym Squash Indoor leisure suite Treatment room Sauna ♫ Xmas New Year **Conf** Class 76 Board 48 Thtr 150 Del from £109 to £175 **Services** Lift **Parking** 100 **Notes** LB Civ Wed 120

The Pig

★★★ ◎◎ COUNTRY HOUSE HOTEL

☎ 01590 622354

Beaulieu Rd SO42 7QL

e-mail: info@thepighotel.com

dir: At Brockenhurst onto B3055 (Beaulieu Road). 1m on left up private road

A delightful country house where the focus is very much on the food, with the chef, gardener and forager working as a team to create menus of seasonal, locally sourced produce; all ingredients are found within a 15-mile radius. The result of such a policy is that menus change daily, and sometimes even more frequently! The stylish dining room is an authentically reproduced Victorian greenhouse, and alfresco eating is possible as there is a wood-fired oven in the courtyard. The bedrooms have eclectic furnishings, good beds and views of either the forest or the garden; two suites with private courtyards are available.

Rooms 26 (10 annexe) (2 fmly) (10 GF) **D** £125-£250* **Facilities** STV FTV Wi-fi ↻ ⌣ ⌣ Treatment room Xmas New Year **Conf** Board 14 Del from £195 to £250* **Parking** 20

Cloud Hotel

★★ SMALL HOTEL

☎ 01590 622165 & 622354

Meerut Rd SO42 7TD

e-mail: enquiries@cloudhotel.co.uk

web: www.cloudhotel.co.uk

dir: M27 junct 1 signed New Forest, A337 through Lyndhurst to Brockenhurst. On entering Brockenhurst 1st right. Hotel 300mtrs

This charming hotel enjoys a peaceful location on the edge of the village. The bedrooms are bright and comfortable with pine furnishings and smart en suite facilities. Public rooms include a selection of cosy lounges, a delightful rear garden with outdoor seating and a restaurant specialising in home-cooked, wholesome English food.

Rooms 18 (1 fmly) (2 GF) ↻ **S** £110-£116; **D** £196-£232 (incl. bkfst & dinner)* **Facilities** FTV Wi-fi Xmas **Conf** Class 12 Board 12 Thtr 40 **Parking** 20 **Notes** LB ⊗ No children 12yrs Closed 27 Dec-12 Jan

Save on hotels. Book at **theAA.com/hotel**

BRO 103 **ENGLAND**

B

Watersplash Hotel

★★ 64% HOTEL

☎ 01590 622344
The Rise SO42 7ZP
e-mail: bookings@watersplash.co.uk
web: www.watersplash.co.uk
dir: M3 junct 13/M27 junct 1/A337 S through
Lyndhurst & Brockenhurst. The Rise on left, hotel on
left

This popular, welcoming hotel that dates from
Victorian times has been in the same family for over
40 years. Bedrooms have co-ordinated decor and
good facilities. The restaurant overlooks the neatly
tended garden and there is also a comfortably
furnished lounge, separate bar and an outdoor pool.

Rooms 23 (6 fmly) (3 GF) 🐾 **S** £75-£85; **D** £110-£116
(incl. bkfst)* **Facilities** FTV Wi-fi ⚐ Beauty &
massage therapist Xmas New Year **Conf** Class 20
Board 20 Thtr 80 Del from £105 to £125* **Parking** 29
Notes LB

BROMBOROUGH   Map 15 SJ38
Merseyside

Premier Inn Wirral (Bromborough)

BUDGET HOTEL

☎ 0871 527 9172
High St, Bromborough Cross CH62 7EZ
web: www.premierinn.com
dir: On A41 (New Chester Rd), 2m from M53 junct 5

High quality, budget accommodation ideal for both
families and business travellers. Spacious, en suite
bedrooms feature tea and coffee making facilities,
and Freeview TV in most hotels. Internet access and
Wi-fi are available for a small fee. The adjacent
family restaurant features a wide and varied menu.
See also the Hotel Groups pages.

Rooms 32

BROMLEY
Greater London

See London plan 1 H1

Best Western Bromley Court Hotel

★★★ 77% HOTEL

☎ 020 8461 8600
Bromley Hill BR1 4JD
e-mail: enquiries@bromleycourthotel.co.uk
web: www.bromleycourthotel.co.uk
dir: N of town centre, off A21. Private drive opposite
Volkswagen garage on Bromley Hill

Set amid three acres of grounds, this smart hotel
enjoys a peaceful location, in a residential area on
the outskirts of town. Well maintained bedrooms are
smartly appointed and thoughtfully equipped. The
contemporary-style restaurant offers a good choice of
meals in comfortable surroundings. Extensive
facilities include a leisure club and a good range of
meeting rooms.

Rooms 115 (4 fmly) 🐾 **Facilities** STV FTV Wi-fi ⚐ Gym
Steam room Spa pool **Conf** Class 70 Board 40
Thtr 150 Del from £135 to £155* **Services** Lift Air con
Parking 100 **Notes** ⊗ Civ Wed 65

BROMSGROVE   Map 10 SO97
Worcestershire

Holiday Inn Birmingham - Bromsgrove

★★★★ 73% HOTEL

☎ 01527 576600 & 0871 942 9142
Kidderminster Rd B61 9AB
e-mail: info@hi-birminghambromsgrove.co.uk
dir: From S: M5 junct 5, A38 to Bromsgrove 2m. At
rdbt left, B4091,1.5m. Left at 2nd rdbt A448. Hotel
0.5m on left. From N: M5 junct 4, A38/Bromsgrove for
2m. Through lights, straight on at rdbt. Filter right at
lights. Right at 2nd rdbt onto A448. Hotel 0.5m on left

Public areas in this striking building are comfortable
and spacious. A selection of meeting rooms is
available, along with function suites, a courtyard
garden and plenty of natural light. Bedrooms come in
a variety of styles - some are more compact than
others but all offer an excellent working environment
for the business guest. Leisure facilities include a
steam room, sauna, pool and gym. There is an
extensive car park.

Rooms 110 (11 fmly) (31 GF) **Facilities** Spa STV FTV
Wi-fi ⚐ HL ⚙ Gym Sauna Steam room Xmas
Conf Class 120 Board 50 Thtr 220 Del from £99 to
£139 **Services** Lift Air con **Parking** 220 **Notes** ⊗
Civ Wed 180

Premier Inn Bromsgrove Central

BUDGET HOTEL

☎ 0871 527 8168
Birmingham Rd B61 0BA
web: www.premierinn.com
dir: M42 junct 1 (S'bound access only) or M5 junct 4
S'bound or M5 junct 5 N'bound onto A38 towards
Bromsgrove. Hotel adjacent to Guild Brewers Fayre.
(NB for Sat Nav use B60 1GJ)

High quality, budget accommodation ideal for both
families and business travellers. Spacious, en suite
bedrooms feature tea and coffee making facilities,
and Freeview TV in most hotels. Internet access and
Wi-fi are available for a small fee. The adjacent
family restaurant features a wide and varied menu.
See also the Hotel Groups pages.

Rooms 78

Premier Inn Bromsgrove South (Worcester Road)

BUDGET HOTEL

☎ 0871 527 8170
Worcester Rd, Upton Warren B61 7ET
web: www.premierinn.com
dir: M5 junct 5, A38 towards Bromsgrove, 1.2m. Or
M42 junct 1, A38 S, cross over A448

Rooms 27

BROOK (NEAR CADNAM)   Map 5 SU21
Hampshire

Bell Inn

★★★ 82% ◉ HOTEL

☎ 023 8081 2214
SO43 7HE
e-mail: bell@bramshaw.co.uk
web: www.bellinnbramshaw.co.uk
dir: M27 junct 1 onto B3079, hotel 1.5m on right

The inn is part of the Bramshaw Golf Club and has
tailored its style to suit this market, but it is also an
ideal base for visiting the New Forest. Bedrooms are

continued

B

BROOK (NEAR CADNAM) *continued*

comfortable and attractively furnished, and the public areas, particularly the welcoming bar, have a cosy and friendly atmosphere.

Rooms 27 (2 annexe) (1 fmly) (8 GF) **S** £45-£70; **D** £90-£140 (incl. bkfst & dinner)* **Facilities** FTV Wi-fi ⅃ 54 Putt green Xmas New Year **Conf** Class 20 Board 30 Thtr 50 Del from £90 to £120* **Parking** 150 **Notes** LB ⊗ Civ Wed 50

BROXTON
Cheshire   Map 15 SJ45

De Vere Carden Park
★★★★ 82% ◉ HOTEL   DE VERE
                              Hotels & Resorts

☎ 01829 731000
Carden Park CH3 9DQ
e-mail: reservations.carden@devere-hotels.com
web: www.cardenpark.co.uk
dir: M56 junct 15, M53 Chester. Take A41 signed Whitchurch. 8m. At Broxton rdbt right onto A534 (signed Wrexham). Hotel 1.5m on left

This impressive Cheshire estate dates back to the 17th century and consists of 1000 acres of mature parkland. The hotel offers a choice of dining options along with superb leisure facilities that include golf courses, a fully equipped gym, a swimming pool and popular spa. Spacious, thoughtfully equipped bedrooms have excellent business and in-room entertainment facilities.

Rooms 196 (83 annexe) (24 fmly) (68 GF) **Facilities** Spa STV Wi-fi ⓢ supervised ⅃ 36 ⌁ Putt green Gym Archery Quad bikes Off-roading Bike & walking trails Laser clay shooting Xmas New Year **Conf** Class 240 Board 125 Thtr 400 **Services** Lift **Parking** 700 **Notes** Civ Wed 375

BRYHER
Cornwall (Isles of Scilly)   Map 2 SV81

Hell Bay Hotel
★★★★ 80% ◉◉◉ HOTEL

☎ 01720 422947
TR23 0PR
e-mail: contactus@hellbay.co.uk
web: www.hellbay.co.uk
dir: Access by helicopter or boat from Penzance, plane from Bristol, Exeter, Newquay, Southampton or Land's End

Located on the smallest of the inhabited islands of the Scilly Isles on the edge of the Atlantic, this hotel makes a really special destination. The owners have filled the hotel with original works of art by artists who have connections with the islands, and the interior is decorated in cool blues and greens creating an extremely restful environment. The contemporary bedrooms are equally stylish and many have garden access and stunning sea views. Eating here is a delight, and naturally, seafood features strongly on the award-winning, daily-changing menus.

Rooms 25 (25 annexe) (3 fmly) (15 GF) ⌑ **S** £168.75-£400; **D** £270-£640 (incl. bkfst & dinner)* **Facilities** STV FTV Wi-fi ⓠ ⌁ ⅃ 7 ⌁ Gym **Conf** Class 36 Board 36 Thtr 36 **Notes** LB Closed Nov-Feb

---

BUCKHURST HILL
Essex   Map 6 TQ49

Premier Inn Loughton/ Buckhurst Hill

BUDGET HOTEL

☎ 0871 527 8686
High Rd IG9 5HT
web: www.premierinn.com
dir: M25 junct 26 towards Loughton. A121 into Buckhurst Hill (approx 5m), hotel on left

High quality, budget accommodation ideal for both families and business travellers. Spacious, en suite bedrooms feature tea and coffee making facilities, and Freeview TV in most hotels. Internet access and Wi-fi are available for a small fee. The adjacent family restaurant features a wide and varied menu. See also the Hotel Groups pages.

Rooms 49

BUCKINGHAM
Buckinghamshire   Map 11 SP63

Villiers Hotel
★★★★ 72% ◉◉ HOTEL

☎ 01280 822444
3 Castle St MK18 1BS
e-mail: villiers@oxfordshire-hotels.co.uk
web: www.oxfordshire-hotels.co.uk
dir: M1 junct 13 (N) or junct 15 (S) follow signs to Buckingham. Castle St by Old Town Hall

Guests can enjoy a town centre location with a high degree of comfort at this 400-year-old former coaching inn. Relaxing public areas feature flagstone floors, oak panelling and real fires whilst bedrooms are modern, spacious and equipped to a high level. Diners can unwind in the atmospheric bar before taking dinner in the award-winning restaurant.

Rooms 49 (4 fmly) (3 GF) **S** £85-£140; **D** £110-£160 (incl. bkfst)* **Facilities** STV FTV Wi-fi Xmas New Year **Conf** Class 120 Board 80 Thtr 250 Del from £130 to £160* **Services** Lift **Parking** 52 **Notes** ⊗ Civ Wed 180

Best Western Buckingham Hotel

★★★ 77% HOTEL

☎ 01280 822622
Buckingham Ring Rd MK18 1RY
e-mail: info@thebuckinghamhotel.co.uk
dir: A421 to Buckingham, take ring road S towards Brackley & Bicester. Hotel on left

A purpose-built hotel, which offers comfortable and spacious rooms with well designed working spaces for business travellers. There are also extensive conference facilities. The open-plan restaurant and bar offer a good range of dishes, and the well-equipped leisure suite is popular with guests.

Rooms 70 (6 fmly) (31 GF) **S** £65-£130; **D** £65-£130* **Facilities** STV FTV Wi-fi ⓠ ⓢ supervised Gym Sauna Steam room Xmas New Year **Conf** Class 60 Board 60 Thtr 200 **Parking** 200 **Notes** LB Civ Wed 120

Save on hotels. Book at **theAA.com/hotel**

BRO – BUR 105 ENGLAND

B

BUDE
Cornwall

Map 2 SS20

Falcon Hotel

★★★ 79% HOTEL

☎ 01288 352005
Breakwater Rd EX23 8SD
e-mail: reception@falconhotel.com
web: www.falconhotel.com
dir: Exit A39 to Bude, then Widemouth Bay. Hotel on right over canal bridge

Dating back to 1798, this long-established hotel boasts delightful walled gardens, ideal for afternoon teas. Bedrooms offer high standards of comfort and quality; there is also a four-poster room complete with spa bath. A choice of menus is offered in the elegant restaurant and the friendly bar. The hotel has an impressive function room.

Rooms 29 (7 fmly) ⚓ **S** £57-£62; **D** £114-£124 (incl. bkfst)* **Facilities** STV FTV Wi-fi ⚓ 🎵 New Year **Conf** Class 50 Board 50 Thtr 200 **Services** Lift **Parking** 40 **Notes** LB ⊗ RS 25 Dec Civ Wed 160

Hartland Hotel

★★★ 78% HOTEL

☎ 01288 355661
Hartland Ter EX23 8JY
e-mail: hartlandhotel@aol.com
dir: Exit A39 to Bude, follow town centre signs. Left into Hartland Terrace opposite Boots the Chemist. Hotel at seaward end of road

This long established hotel has an enduring and timeless elegance with a reassuring sense of tradition. Its location is a wonderful asset, overlooking Summerleaze Beach with panoramic views of the town and coast. The comfortable bedrooms are individually styled and a number have four-poster beds and wonderful sea views. The spacious public areas include the convivial bar, lounges and attractive dining room where a varied menu is on offer. An outdoor pool is available for lazing away the summer days.

Rooms 28 (2 fmly) **Facilities** FTV 🎣 🎵 Xmas New Year **Services** Lift **Parking** 30 **Notes** Closed mid Nov-Etr (ex Xmas & New Year)

The Cliff Hotel at Bude

★★ 76% HOTEL

☎ 01288 353110
Maer Down, Crooklets Beach EX23 8NG
e-mail: cliff_hotel@btconnect.com
web: www.cliffhotel.co.uk
dir: A39 through Bude, left at top of High St, pass Sainsburys, 1st right between golf course, over x-rds, premises at end on right

Overlooking the sea from a clifftop location, this friendly and efficient establishment provides spacious, well-equipped bedrooms. The various public areas include a bar and lounge and an impressive range of leisure facilities. Delicious dinners and tasty breakfasts are available in the attractive dining room.

Rooms 15 (15 fmly) (8 GF) **S** £47.95-£53.95; **D** £79.90-£89.90 (incl. bkfst)* **Facilities** FTV Wi-fi ⊗ 🏊 Putt green Gym **Parking** 25 **Notes** LB Closed Nov-Mar

Hotel Penarvor

★★ 74% SMALL HOTEL

☎ 01288 352036
Crooklets Beach EX23 8NE
e-mail: stay@hotelpenarvor.co.uk
dir: A39 towards Bude for 1.5m. At 2nd rdbt turn right, pass shops. Top of hill, left signed Crooklets Beach

Adjacent to the golf course and overlooking Crooklets Beach, this family owned hotel has a relaxed and friendly atmosphere. Bedrooms vary in size but are all equipped to a similar standard. An interesting selection of dishes, using fresh local produce, is available in the restaurant; bar meals are also provided.

Rooms 16 (6 fmly) (3 GF) **S** £37-£43; **D** £74-£86 (incl. bkfst)* **Facilities** FTV Wi-fi **Parking** 20 **Notes** LB Closed 24-28 Dec

BURFORD
Oxfordshire

Map 5 SP21

The Bay Tree Hotel

★★★★ 73% ◉ HOTEL

Cotswold Inns & Hotels

☎ 01993 822791
Sheep St OX18 4LW
e-mail: info@baytreehotel.info
web: www.cotswold-inns-hotels.co.uk/bay-tree
dir: A40 or A361 to Burford. From High St turn into Sheep St, next to old market square. Hotel on right

The modern decorative style combines seamlessly with features from this delightful inn's long history. Bedrooms are tastefully furnished and some have four-poster and half-tester beds. Public areas consist of a character bar, a sophisticated airy restaurant, a selection of meeting rooms and an attractive walled garden. Cotswold Inns & Hotels – AA Small Hotel Group of the Year 2012-13.

Rooms 21 (13 annexe) (2 fmly) (3 GF) **Facilities** Wi-fi 🎣 Xmas New Year **Conf** Class 12 Board 25 Thtr 40 **Parking** 50 **Notes** Civ Wed 60

B

BURFORD *continued*

The Lamb Inn

★★★ 83% ◉ ◉ SMALL HOTEL

☎ 01993 823155

Sheep St OX18 4LR

e-mail: info@lambinn-burford.co.uk

web: www.cotswold-inns-hotels.co.uk/lamb

dir: A40 into Burford, downhill, 1st left into Sheep St, hotel last on right

This enchanting old inn is just a short walk from the centre of this delightful Cotswold village. Inside an abundance of character and charm is found in the cosy lounge with log fire, and intimate bar with flagged floors. An elegant restaurant offers locally sourced produce in carefully prepared dishes. Bedrooms, some with original features, are comfortable and well appointed. Cotswold Inns & Hotels – AA Small Hotel Group of the Year 2012-13.

Rooms 17 (1 fmly) (4 GF) **S** £120-£155; **D** £160-£290 (incl. bkfst)* **Facilities** Wi-fi Xmas New Year **Notes** LB

Cotswold Gateway Hotel

★★★ 75% HOTEL

☎ 01993 822695

Cheltenham Rd OX18 4HX

e-mail: cotswoldgateway@btconnect.com

dir: From A40 at rdbt in Burford take A361 (High St) towards town centre. Hotel on left

Ideally located for both business and leisure guests, this hotel prominently situated on the A40 and yet only a short walk away from Burford. Bedrooms are comfortable and well appointed with many guest comforts. Dinner menus offer an extensive choice of popular dishes, and guests have the option to eat in the character bar, the coffee shop or brasserie-style restaurant.

Rooms 20 (5 annexe) (2 fmly) (4 GF) **Facilities** FTV Wi-fi New Year **Parking** 30 **Notes** Closed 25-26 Dec

The Bull at Burford

◉ ◉ RESTAURANT WITH ROOMS

☎ 01993 822220

105 High St OX18 4RG

e-mail: info@bullatburford.co.uk

dir: In town centre

Situated in the heart of a pretty Cotswold town, The Bull was originally built in 1475 as a rest house for the local priory. It now has stylish, attractively presented bedrooms that still reflect charm and character. Dinner is a must and the award-winning restaurant has an imaginative menu along with an excellent choice of wines. Lunch is served daily and afternoon tea is popular. There is a residents' lounge, and free Wi-fi is available.

Rooms 12 (1 fmly)

The Inn For All Seasons

RESTAURANT WITH ROOMS

☎ 01451 844324

The Barringtons OX18 4TN

e-mail: sharp@innforallseasons.com

web: www.innforallseasons.com

dir: 3m W of Burford on A40 towards Cheltenham

This charming 16th-century coaching inn is close to the pretty village of Burford. The individually styled bedrooms are comfortable, and include a four-poster room, as well as a family room that sleeps four. The public areas include a cosy bar with oak beams and real fires. There is a good choice on the bar menu, and evening meals feature the best of local Cotswold produce. The inn is a dog-friendly establishment and there are ground-floor bedrooms with direct access to the garden and an exercise area.

Rooms 10 (1 fmly)

Premier Inn Burgess Hill

BUDGET HOTEL

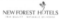

☎ 0871 527 8172

Charles Av RH15 9AG

web: www.premierinn.com

dir: M25 junct 7, M23, A23. Left at Burgess Hill follow A2300 signs. At rdbt 2nd exit onto A2300. At next rdbt 4th exit onto A273, straight on at next 2 rdbts, at 3rd rdbt (Tesco) 1st left. Hotel 2nd left

High quality, budget accommodation ideal for both families and business travellers. Spacious, en suite bedrooms feature tea and coffee making facilities, and Freeview TV in most hotels. Internet access and Wi-fi are available for a small fee. The adjacent family restaurant features a wide and varied menu. See also the Hotel Groups pages.

Rooms 60

Moorhill House Hotel

★★★ 78% ◉   NEW FOREST HOTELS

COUNTRY HOUSE HOTEL

☎ 01425 403285

BH24 4AH

e-mail: moorhill@newforesthotels.co.uk

web: www.newforesthotels.co.uk

dir: M27, A31, follow signs to Burley, through village, up hill, right opposite school & cricket grounds

Situated deep in the heart of the New Forest and formerly a grand gentleman's residence, this charming hotel offers a relaxed and friendly environment. Bedrooms, of varying sizes, are smartly decorated. A range of facilities is provided and guests can relax by walking around the extensive grounds. Both dinner and breakfast offer a choice of interesting and freshly prepared dishes.

Rooms 31 (13 fmly) (3 GF) ➘ **S** £61-£106; **D** £122-£172 (incl. bkfst)* **Facilities** FTV Wi-fi ➘ HL ⊗ ⤵ Badminton (Apr-Sep) Sauna Xmas New Year **Conf** Class 60 Board 65 Thtr 120 **Parking** 50 **Notes** LB Civ Wed 80

Save on hotels. Book at **theAA.com/hotel**

BUR 107 ENGLAND

B

BURNHAM
Buckinghamshire

Map 6 SU98

The Grovefield House Hotel

★★★★ 76% ◎◎ HOTEL

☎ 01628 603131
Taplow Common Rd SL1 8LP
e-mail: info.grovefield@classiclodges.co.uk
web: www.classiclodges.co.uk
dir: M4 junct 7, A4 towards Maidenhead. Next rdbt
right under rail bridge. Straight over mini rdbt,
garage on right. 1.5m, hotel on right

Set in its own spacious grounds, the Grovefield is
conveniently located for Heathrow Airport as well as
Slough and Maidenhead. Accommodation is spacious
and well presented and most rooms have views over
the attractive gardens. Public areas include a range
of meeting rooms, comfortable bar/lounge area and
Hamilton's restaurant.

Rooms 40 (5 fmly) (7 GF) **Facilities** Putt green
Fishing ⅃ Xmas New Year **Conf** Class 80 Board 80
Thtr 180 **Services** Lift **Parking** 155
Notes Civ Wed 200

Burnham Beeches Hotel

★★★★ 75% ◎ HOTEL

☎ 0844 736 8603
Grove Rd SL1 8DP
e-mail: sales.burnhambeeches@corushotels.com
web: www.corushotels.com/burnham-beeches
dir: M40 junct 2, A355 towards Slough, right at 2nd
rdbt, 1st right to Grove Rd

Set in attractive mature grounds on the fringes of
woodland, this extended Georgian manor house has
spacious, comfortable and well-equipped bedrooms.
Public rooms include a cosy lounge/bar offering all-
day snacks and an elegant wood-panelled restaurant
that serves interesting cuisine; there are also
conference facilities, a fitness centre and pool.

Rooms 82 (22 fmly) (12 GF) **Facilities** FTV Wi-fi ⓈⒷ
ⴽ Gym Xmas New Year **Conf** Class 80 Board 60
Thtr 150 Del from £160 to £265* **Services** Lift
Parking 150 **Notes** ⊗ Civ Wed 120

BURNHAM MARKET
Norfolk

Map 13 TF84

The Hoste Arms

★★★ 88% ◎◎ HOTEL

☎ 01328 738777
The Green PE31 8HD
e-mail: reception@hostearms.co.uk
web: www.hostearms.co.uk
dir: Signed on B1155, 5m W of Wells-next-the-Sea

A stylish, privately-owned inn situated in the heart of
a bustling village close to the north Norfolk coast. The
extensive public rooms feature a range of dining
areas that include a conservatory with plush
furniture, a sunny patio and a traditional pub. The
tastefully furnished and thoughtfully equipped
bedrooms are generally very spacious and offer a high
degree of comfort.

The Hoste Arms

Rooms 34 (7 GF) **Facilities** Spa STV Wi-fi Beauty
treatment rooms Xmas New Year **Conf** Class 40
Board 16 Thtr 25 **Services** Air con **Parking** 45

See advert on this page

BURNLEY
Lancashire

Map 18 SD83

Holiday Inn Express Burnley

BUDGET HOTEL

☎ 01282 855955 & 855963
M65 Jct 10, 55 Pendle Way BB12 0TJ
e-mail: cathy@starboardhotels.com
dir: M65 junct 10, 3rd exit at rdbt, Pendle Way, hotel
on right

A modern hotel ideal for families and business
travellers. Fresh and uncomplicated, the spacious
rooms include Sky TV, power shower and tea and
coffee-making facilities. Continental buffet breakfast
is included in the room rate; other meals may be
taken at the nearby family pub or restaurant. See also
the Hotel Groups pages.

Rooms 102 (67 fmly) (4 GF) ⵏ **S** £49.95-£74.95;
D £49.95-£74.95 (incl. bkfst) **Conf** Class 28 Board 28
Thtr 80

B

BURNLEY *continued*

Premier Inn Burnley
BUDGET HOTEL

☎ 0871 527 8174
Queen Victoria Rd BB10 3EF
web: www.premierinn.com
dir: M65 junct 12, 5th exit at rdbt, 1st exit at rdbt, keep in right lane at lights, 2nd exit at next rdbt, 3rd at next rdbt, under bridge, left before football ground

High quality, budget accommodation ideal for both families and business travellers. Spacious, en suite bedrooms feature tea and coffee making facilities, and Freeview TV in most hotels. Internet access and Wi-fi are available for a small fee. The adjacent family restaurant features a wide and varied menu. See also the Hotel Groups pages.

Rooms 43

BURNSALL	Map 19 SE06
North Yorkshire	

Red Lion Hotel & Manor House
★★ 77% HOTEL

☎ 01756 720204
By the Bridge BD23 6BU
e-mail: redlion@daelnet.co.uk
web: www.redlion.co.uk
dir: On B6160 between Grassington & Bolton Abbey

This delightful 16th-century Dales' inn stands adjacent to a five-arch bridge over the scenic River Wharfe. Stylish, comfortable bedrooms are individually decorated, and well equipped. Public areas include a tasteful lounge traditional oak-panelled bar and impressive function rooms. The elegant restaurant makes good use of fresh local ingredients. Additional bed and breakfast based accommodation is available in the Manor House.

Red Lion Hotel & Manor House

Rooms 25 (15 annexe) (5 fmly) (4 GF) **Facilities** FTV Wi-fi Fishing Xmas New Year **Conf** Class 50 Board 25 Thtr 60 **Parking** 80 **Notes** Civ Wed 125

The Devonshire Fell
◎ ◎ RESTAURANT WITH ROOMS

☎ 01756 729000 & 718111
BD23 6BT
e-mail: manager@devonshirefell.co.uk
web: www.devonshirefell.co.uk
dir: On B6160, 6m from Bolton Abbey rdbt, A59 junct

Located on the edge of the attractive village of Burnsall, this establishment offers comfortable, well-equipped accommodation in a relaxing atmosphere. There is an extensive menu featuring local produce, and meals can be taken either in the bar area or the more formal restaurant. A function room with views over the valley is also available.

Rooms 12 (2 fmly)

BURRINGTON	Map 3 SS61
(NEAR PORTSMOUTH ARMS STATION)	
Devon	

INSPECTORS' CHOICE

Northcote Manor
★★★ ◎◎ COUNTRY HOUSE HOTEL

☎ 01769 560501
EX37 9LZ
e-mail: rest@northcotemanor.co.uk
web: www.northcotemanor.co.uk
dir: From A377 opposite Portsmouth Arms, into hotel drive. (NB do not enter Burrington village)

A warm and friendly welcome is assured at this beautiful country-house hotel, built in 1716 and surrounded by 20 acres of grounds and woodlands. Guests can enjoy wonderful views over the Taw River Valley whilst relaxing in the delightful environment created by the attentive staff. A meal in either the intimate, more formal Manor House Restaurant or the Walled Garden Restaurant will prove a highlight; each offers menus of the finest local produce used in well-prepared dishes. Bedrooms, including some suites, are individually styled, spacious and well appointed.

Rooms 16 (2 fmly) (3 GF) ✿ **S** £90-£170; **D** £160-£260 (incl. bkfst)* **Facilities** FTV Wi-fi ◡ ◡ Xmas New Year **Conf** Class 50 Board 30 Thtr 80 Del from £150 to £170* **Parking** 50 **Notes** LB Civ Wed 100

BURTON UPON TRENT	Map 10 SK22
Staffordshire	

Three Queens Hotel
★★★ 78% ◎ HOTEL

☎ 01283 523800 & 0845 230 1332
One Bridge St DE14 1SY
e-mail: hotel@threequeenshotel.co.uk
web: www.threequeenshotel.co.uk
dir: On A511 in Burton upon Trent at junct of Bridge St & High St. Town side of Old River Bridge

Located in the centre of the town close to the river, this smartly presented hotel provides an appealing, high quality base from which to tour the area.

B

Bedrooms come in a mix of styles that include spacious duplex suites and executive rooms located in the original Jacobean heart of the building. Smart day rooms include the medieval styled Grill Restaurant, a modern bar and a contemporary breakfast room. A warm welcome is assured from the professional staff.

Rooms 38 (7 smoking) **S** £45-£73; **D** £50-£125 (incl. bkfst)* **Facilities** STV FTV Wi-fi ⌂ Xmas New Year **Conf** Class 40 Board 30 Thtr 60 Del from £75 to £125* **Services** Lift Air con **Parking** 55 **Notes** LB ⊗

Holiday Inn Express Burton upon Trent

BUDGET HOTEL

☎ 01283 504300
2nd Av, Centrum 100 DE14 2WF
e-mail: reservations@exhiburton.co.uk
web: www.exhiburton.co.uk
dir: From A38 Branston exit take A5121 signed Town Centre. At McDonalds rdbt, turn left into 2nd Avenue. Hotel on left

A modern hotel ideal for families and business travellers. Fresh and uncomplicated, the spacious rooms include Sky TV, power shower and tea and coffee-making facilities. Continental buffet breakfast is included in the room rate; other meals may be taken at the nearby family pub or restaurant. See also the Hotel Groups pages.

Rooms 82 (47 fmly) (14 GF) (3 smoking) ⌂
S £55-£95; **D** £55-£95 (incl. bkfst)* **Conf** Class 30 Board 25 Thtr 60 Del from £80 to £120*

Premier Inn Burton upon Trent East

BUDGET HOTEL

☎ 0871 527 8176
Ashby Road East DE15 0PU
web: www.premierinn.com
dir: 2m E of Burton upon Trent on A50

High quality, budget accommodation ideal for both families and business travellers. Spacious, en suite bedrooms feature tea and coffee making facilities, and Freeview TV in most hotels. Internet access and Wi-fi are available for a small fee. The adjacent family restaurant features a wide and varied menu. See also the Hotel Groups pages.

Rooms 34

BURY	**Map 15 SD81**
Greater Manchester	

Red Hall Hotel

★★★ 80% HOTEL

☎ 01706 822476
Manchester Rd, Walmersley BL9 5NA
e-mail: info@red-hall.co.uk
dir: M66 junct 1, A56. Over motorway bridge, hotel approx 300mtrs on right

Originally a farmhouse this hotel, located in the picturesque village of Warmersley on the outskirts of Ramsbottom, is just off the M66 making it ideal for business and leisure guests alike. Bedrooms are contemporary and well equipped. There is a restaurant and lounge bar, plus meeting and event facilities.

Rooms 37 (2 fmly) (18 GF) **Facilities** STV Wi-fi Xmas New Year **Conf** Class 60 Board 30 Thtr 140 **Services** Lift **Parking** 100 **Notes** Civ Wed

Premier Inn Bury

BUDGET HOTEL

☎ 0871 527 9294
5 Knowsley Place, Duke St BL9 0EJ
web: www.premierinn.com
dir: M66 junct 2, A58 towards Bolton & Bury. At rdbt in Bury centre follow A58 (Angouleme Way). Left in Knowsley St, hotel on left

High quality, budget accommodation ideal for both families and business travellers. Spacious, en suite bedrooms feature tea and coffee making facilities, and Freeview TV in most hotels. Internet access and Wi-fi are available for a small fee. The adjacent family restaurant features a wide and varied menu. See also the Hotel Groups pages.

BURY ST EDMUNDS	**Map 13 TL86**
Suffolk	

Angel Hotel

★★★★ 88% ◉ ◉ TOWN HOUSE HOTEL

☎ 01284 714000
Angel Hill IP33 1LT
e-mail: staying@theangel.co.uk
web: www.theangel.co.uk
dir: From A134, left at rdbt into Northgate St. Continue to lights, right into Mustow St, left into Angel Hill. Hotel on right

An impressive building situated just a short walk from the town centre. One of the Angel's more notable guests over the last 400 years was Charles Dickens who is reputed to have written part of *The Pickwick Papers* whilst in residence. The hotel offers a range of individually designed bedrooms that includes a selection of four-poster rooms and a suite.

Rooms 80 (5 fmly) (22 GF) ⌂ **Facilities** FTV Wi-fi Xmas **Conf** Board 16 **Services** Lift **Parking** 20

Boars Head Hotel

Lichfield Road Sudbury Derbyshire DE6 5GX
AA ★★★
75%
Tel: (01283) 820344
Fax: (01283) 820075

A country hotel of warmth and character dating back to the 17th century. The family run hotel has 22 en suite bedrooms all tastefully decorated and well equipped. The elegant à la carte restaurant – The Royal Boar and the less formal Hunter's Table Carvery and Bistro both provide a good selection of dishes along with an extensive bar snack menu available in the public bar. The hotel is the perfect setting for weddings, family parties or a weekend break. Ideally situated for visiting the numerous local and sporting attractions and many places of interest.

BURY ST EDMUNDS *continued*

Ravenwood Hall Hotel

★★★ 88% ◉◉ COUNTRY HOUSE HOTEL

☎ 01359 270345
Rougham IP30 9JA
e-mail: enquiries@ravenwoodhall.co.uk
web: www.ravenwoodhall.co.uk
dir: 3m E from A14 junct 45. Hotel on left

Delightful 15th-century property set in seven acres of woodland and landscaped gardens. The building has many original features including carved timbers and inglenook fireplaces. The spacious bedrooms are attractively decorated, tastefully furnished with well-chosen pieces and equipped with many thoughtful touches. Public rooms include an elegant restaurant and a smart lounge bar with an open fire.

Rooms 14 (7 annexe) (5 GF) ✆ **S** £102-£136; **D** £125-£175 (incl. bkfst)* **Facilities** Wi-fi ⚘ ⛳ Shooting, fishing & horse riding can be arranged Xmas New Year Child facilities **Conf** Class 80 Board 40 Thtr 130 Del £194.25* **Parking** 150 **Notes** LB Civ Wed 130

Best Western Priory Hotel

★★★ 83% ◉◉ HOTEL

☎ 01284 766181
Mildenhall Rd IP32 6EH
e-mail: reservations@prioryhotel.co.uk
web: www.prioryhotel.co.uk
dir: From A14 take Bury St Edmunds W slip road. Follow signs to Brandon. At mini-rdbt turn right. Hotel 0.5m on left

An 18th-century Grade II listed building set in landscaped grounds on the outskirts of town. The attractively decorated, tastefully furnished and thoughtfully equipped bedrooms are split between the main house and garden wings, which have their own sun terraces. Public rooms feature a smart restaurant, a conservatory dining room and a lounge bar.

Rooms 36 (29 annexe) (1 fmly) (30 GF) ✆ **S** £76-£84; **D** £88-£102 (incl. bkfst)* **Facilities** FTV Wi-fi Xmas New Year **Conf** Class 35 Board 35 Thtr 75 Del from £138 to £147 **Parking** 60 **Notes** LB Civ Wed 75

The Grange Hotel

★★★ 75% COUNTRY HOUSE HOTEL

☎ 01359 231260
Barton Rd, Thurston IP31 3PQ
e-mail: info@grangecountryhousehotel.com
web: www.grangecountryhousehotel.com
dir: A14 junct 45 towards Gt Barton, right at T-junct. At x-rds left into Barton Rd to Thurston. At rdbt, left after 0.5m, hotel on right

A Tudor-style country-house hotel situated on the outskirts of town. The individually decorated bedrooms have co-ordinated fabrics and many thoughtful touches; some rooms have nice views of the gardens. Public areas include a smart lounge bar, two private dining rooms, the Garden Restaurant and banqueting facilities.

Rooms 18 (5 annexe) (1 fmly) (3 GF) **Facilities** FTV Wi-fi Xmas New Year **Conf** Class 40 Board 30 Thtr 135 **Parking** 100 **Notes** Civ Wed 150

Suffolk Hotel Golf & Leisure Club

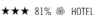
OXFORD HOTELS & INNS

★★★ 70% HOTEL

☎ 01284 706777
Fornham St Genevieve IP28 6JQ
e-mail: reservations.suffolkgolf@ohiml.com
web: www.oxfordhotelsandinns.com
dir: A14 junct 42, B1106, through Fornham All Saints towards Thetford. Hotel 0.75m on right

Situated on the outskirts of this historic town just a few minutes from the A14. The modern, well equipped bedrooms are suitable for both business and leisure guests alike; some rooms have superb countryside views. Public rooms include a smart lounge bar and an intimate restaurant. The hotel has an 18-hole golf course, gym, heated indoor pool and spa facilities.

Rooms 40 (3 fmly) (15 GF) **Facilities** Spa FTV Wi-fi ⊗ ⛳ 18 Putt green Gym Xmas New Year **Conf** Class 60 Board 60 Thtr 100 **Services** Lift **Parking** 100 **Notes** ⊗ Civ Wed 70

The Palace Hotel

PUMA HOTELS COLLECTION

★★★★ 73% HOTEL

☎ 01298 22001
Palace Rd SK17 6AG
e-mail: palace@pumahotels.co.uk
web: www.pumahotels.co.uk
dir: M6 junct 20, follow M56/M60 signs to Stockport then A6 to Buxton, hotel adjacent to railway station

This impressive Victorian hotel is located on the hill overlooking the town. Public areas are traditional and elegant in style, and include chandeliers and decorative ceilings. The bedrooms are spacious and equipped with modern facilities, and The Dovedale Restaurant provides modern British cuisine. Good leisure facilities are available.

Rooms 122 (18 fmly) **Facilities** Spa Wi-fi ⊗ supervised Gym Beauty facilities Xmas New Year **Conf** Class 125 Board 80 Thtr 350 **Services** Lift **Parking** 180 **Notes** Civ Wed 100

Best Western Lee Wood Hotel

★★★ 81% ◉ HOTEL

☎ 01298 23002
The Park SK17 6TQ
e-mail: reservations@leewoodhotel.co.uk
web: www.leewoodhotel.co.uk
dir: From town centre take A5004 NE, hotel 300mtrs beyond Devonshire Royal Hospital

This elegant Georgian hotel offers high standards of comfort and hospitality. The individually furnished bedrooms are generally spacious, with all of the expected modern conveniences. There is a choice of two comfortable lounges and a conservatory restaurant. The quality cooking, good service and fine hospitality are noteworthy.

Rooms 39 (5 annexe) (4 fmly) **Facilities** STV FTV Wi-fi ⊗ New Year **Conf** Class 65 Board 40 Thtr 120 **Services** Lift **Parking** 50 **Notes** Civ Wed 120

Save on hotels. Book at **theAA.com/hotel**

BUR – CAM 111 **ENGLAND**

C

CADNAM
Hampshire
Map 5 SU31

Bartley Lodge Hotel
★★★ 82% ⊛ HOTEL

NEW FOREST HOTELS

☎ 023 8081 2248
Lyndhurst Rd SO40 2NR
e-mail: bartley@newforesthotels.co.uk
web: www.newforesthotels.co.uk
dir: M27 junct 1 at 1st rdbt 1st exit, at 2nd rdbt 3rd exit onto A337. Hotel sign on left

This 18th-century former hunting lodge is very quietly situated, yet is just minutes from the M27. Bedrooms vary in size but all are well equipped. There is a selection of small lounge areas, a cosy bar and an indoor pool, together with a small fitness suite. The Crystal dining room offers a tempting choice of well prepared dishes.

Rooms 40 (15 fmly) (4 GF) ☏ **S** £71-£116;
D £142-£192* **Facilities** FTV Wi-fi ⌕ ⓣ ⤴ Sauna
Xmas New Year **Conf** Class 60 Board 60 Thtr 120
Parking 60 **Notes** Civ Wed 80

CALNE
Wiltshire
Map 4 ST97

Bowood Hotel, Spa and Golf Resort
★★★★ 82% ⊛⊛ COUNTRY HOUSE HOTEL

☎ 01249 822228
Derry Hill SN11 9PQ
e-mail: resort@bowood.org
web: www.bowood-hotel.co.uk
dir: M4 junct 17, 2.5m W of Calne off A4

Located within the Bowood Estate this hotel is furnished to a luxury standard, very much with guest comfort in mind. Bedrooms and bathrooms are very well appointed, with contemporary artwork adorning the walls and quality linen on the deeply comfortable beds. The stylish Shelburne Restaurant, with views overlooking the beautiful 'Capability' Brown designed parkland, offers award-winning cuisine, and the Spa Bar offers more casual dining. The spa features an infinity pool and crystal steam room, and there is a championship golf course within the grounds.

Rooms 43 (2 fmly) (10 GF) **Facilities** Spa FTV Wi-fi ⓣ
⌕ 18 Putt green ⤴ Gym Adventure playground Stately home & gardens New Year **Conf** Class 140 Board 85
Thtr 240 **Services** Lift Air con **Parking** 200 **Notes** ⊗
Civ Wed 60

The Lansdowne Hotel
★★★ 64% HOTEL

☎ 01249 812488
The Strand SN11 0EH
e-mail: reservations@lansdownestrand.co.uk
dir: From Chippenham take A4 signed Calne. Straight on at 2 rdbts, hotel in town centre

Situated in a picturesque market town, The Lansdowne was built in the 16th century as a coaching inn, and it still retains much of the charm and character of that era. Bedrooms are spacious and furnished in a traditional style. Guests can enjoy dinner in the pleasant bistro, in either of the bar areas, or choose from a varied room-service menu. An outdoor courtyard seating area is also available.

Rooms 26 (2 fmly) **S** £45-£55; **D** £55-£75 (incl. bkfst)
Facilities STV FTV Wi-fi **Conf** Class 60 Board 50
Thtr 60 Del £100 **Parking** 15 **Notes** LB ⊗ RS 25 Dec

CAMBERLEY
Surrey
Map 6 SU86

See also Yateley

Macdonald Frimley Hall Hotel & Spa
★★★★ 76% ⊛⊛ HOTEL

MACDONALD HOTELS & RESORTS

☎ 0844 879 9110
Lime Av GU15 2BG
e-mail: sales.frimleyhall@macdonald-hotels.co.uk
web: www.macdonaldhotels.co.uk/frimleyhall
dir: M3 junct 3, A321 follow Bagshot signs. Through lights, left onto A30 signed Camberley & Basingstoke. To rdbt, 2nd exit onto A325, take 5th right

The epitome of classic English elegance, this ivy-clad Victorian manor house is set in two acres of immaculate grounds in the heart of Surrey. The bedrooms and public areas are smart and have a modern decorative theme. The hotel boasts an impressive health club and spa with treatment rooms, a fully equipped gym and heated indoor swimming pool.

Rooms 98 (15 fmly) ☏ **Facilities** Spa FTV Wi-fi ⌕ HL
ⓣ Gym Beauty treatment rooms Technogym Sauna
Steam room Relaxation room Xmas New Year
Conf Class 100 Board 60 Thtr 250 **Parking** 150
Notes Civ Wed 220

Lakeside International
★★★ 75% HOTEL

☎ 01252 838000
Wharf Rd, Frimley Green GU16 6JR
e-mail: info@lakesideinthotel.com
dir: Exit A321 at mini-rdbt turn into Wharf Rd. Lakeside complex on right

This hotel, geared towards the business market, enjoys a lakeside location with noteworthy views. Bedrooms are modern, comfortable and with a range of facilities. Public areas are spacious and include a residents' lounge, bar and games room, a smart restaurant and an established health and leisure club.

Rooms 98 (1 fmly) (31 GF) ☏ **S** £120; **D** £140*
Facilities Wi-fi ⓣ Gym Squash Sauna Steam room
Conf Class 100 Board 40 Thtr 120 Del £165*
Services Lift **Parking** 250 **Notes** ⊗ Civ Wed 100

The Ely
★★★ 70% HOTEL

OldEnglish

☎ 01252 860444
London Road (A30), Blackwater GU17 9LJ
e-mail: ely.yateley@newbridgeinns.co.uk
dir: M3 junct 4A, A327 towards Yateley. Right onto A30

This establishment benefits from being conveniently located close to Camberley and the M3. Bedrooms are particularly spacious and families are well catered for. A variety of enjoyable, substantial dishes is available throughout the day with the addition of a specials board in the evening. The range of options at breakfast is impressive. There is ample free parking on site and free Wi-fi throughout the hotel.

Rooms 35

Premier Inn Sandhurst
BUDGET HOTEL

Premier Inn

☎ 0871 527 8958
221 Yorktown Rd, College Town, Sandurst GU47 0RT
web: www.premierinn.com
dir: M3 junct 4, A331 to Camberley. At large rdbt take A321 towards Bracknell. At 3rd lights, hotel on left

High quality, budget accommodation ideal for both families and business travellers. Spacious, en suite bedrooms feature tea and coffee making facilities, and Freeview TV in most hotels. Internet access and Wi-fi are available for a small fee. The adjacent family restaurant features a wide and varied menu. See also the Hotel Groups pages.

Rooms 40

C

CAMBOURNE
Cambridgeshire   **Map 12 TL35**

The Cambridge Belfry
★★★★ 80% HOTEL

☎ 01954 714600
Back St CB3 6BW
e-mail: cambridgebelfry@qhotels.co.uk
web: www.qhotels.co.uk
dir: M11 junct 13, A428 towards Bedford, follow signs to Cambourne. Exit at Cambourne, keep left. Left at rdbt, hotel on left

This exciting hotel, built beside the water, is located at the gateway to Cambourne Village and Business Park. Contemporary in style throughout, the hotel boasts state-of-the-art leisure facilities, including Reflections Spa offering a range of therapies and treatments, and extensive conference and banqueting rooms. There are two eating options - the Bridge Restaurant and the Brooks Brasserie. Original artwork is displayed throughout the hotel.

Rooms 120 (30 GF) ➤ **S** £85-£190; **D** £95-£200 (incl. bkfst)* **Facilities** Spa FTV Wi-fi 🕭 🖎 Gym Beauty treatments Xmas New Year **Conf** Class 70 Board 70 Thtr 250 Del from £130 to £155* **Services** Lift **Parking** 200 **Notes** ⊗ Civ Wed 200

CAMBRIDGE
Cambridgeshire   **Map 12 TL45**

Hotel Felix
★★★★ 80% ⍟⍟ HOTEL

☎ 01223 277977
Whitehouse Ln CB3 0LX
e-mail: help@hotelfelix.co.uk
web: www.hotelfelix.co.uk
dir: M11 junct 13. From A1 N, take A14 onto A1307. At 'City of Cambridge' sign left into Whitehouse Ln

A beautiful Victorian mansion set amidst three acres of landscaped gardens, this property was originally built in 1852 for a surgeon from the famous Addenbrookes Hospital. The contemporary-style bedrooms have carefully chosen furniture and many

thoughtful touches, whilst public rooms feature an open-plan bar, the adjacent Graffiti restaurant and a small quiet lounge.

Rooms 52 (5 fmly) (26 GF) ➤ **S** £165-£210; **D** £200-£320 (incl. bkfst)* **Facilities** STV Wi-fi ☖ Xmas New Year **Conf** Class 36 Board 34 Thtr 60 Del from £195 to £215* **Services** Lift **Parking** 90 **Notes** LB Civ Wed 60

Menzies Cambridge Hotel & Golf Club
★★★★ 77% ⍟ HOTEL

☎ 01954 249988
Bar Hill CB23 8EU
e-mail: cambridge@menzieshotels.co.uk
web: www.menzieshotels.co.uk
dir: M11 junct 13, A14, follow signs for Huntingdon. Take B1050 (Bar Hill), hotel 1st exit on rdbt

Ideally situated amidst 200 acres of open countryside, just five miles from the university city of Cambridge. Public rooms include a brasserie restaurant and the popular Gallery Bar. The contemporary-style bedrooms are smartly decorated and equipped with a good range of useful facilities. The hotel also has a leisure club, swimming pool and golf course.

Rooms 136 (35 fmly) (68 GF) (12 smoking) **Facilities** STV Wi-fi 🕭 🖎 ♿ 18 🎯 Putt green Gym Hair & beauty salon Steam room Sauna Xmas New Year **Conf** Class 90 Board 60 Thtr 200 **Services** Lift **Parking** 200 **Notes** Civ Wed 200

The Varsity Hotel & Spa
★★★★ 76% HOTEL

☎ 01223 306030
Thompson's Ln CB5 8AQ
e-mail: info@thevarsityhotel.co.uk
dir: M11 junct 13, pass Park & Ride, next rdbt 1st left, right at next junct into Bridge St, right into Thompou's Lane

Situated close to the River Cam and occupying a central location, this hotel is a stylish property. The bedrooms are smartly decorated and have all the expected facilities including power showers, CD players and free internet access. The River Bar, to the side of the hotel, has a buzzing atmosphere and offers a range of popular dishes. The hotel has a health club and spa and a roof top bar.

Rooms 48 (2 fmly) ➤ **D** £129-£640 (incl. bkfst) **Facilities** Spa FTV Wi-fi ☖ Gym Sauna Steam room New Year **Conf** Class 40 Board 30 Thtr 60 **Services** Lift Air con **Notes** LB Civ Wed 60

Hotel du Vin Cambridge
★★★★ 75% ⍟
TOWN HOUSE HOTEL

☎ 01223 227330
15-19 Trumpington St CB2 1QA
e-mail: info.cambridge@hotelduvin.com
web: www.hotelduvin.com
dir: M11 junct 11 Cambridge S, pass Trumpington Park & Ride on left. Hotel 2m on right after double rdbt

This beautiful building, which dates back in part to medieval times, has been transformed to enhance its many quirky architectural features. The bedrooms and suites, some with private terraces, have the company's trademark monsoon showers and Egyptian linen. The French-style bistro has an open-style kitchen and the bar is set in the unusual labyrinth of vaulted cellar rooms. There is also a library, specialist wine tasting room and private dining room.

Rooms 41 (3 annexe) (6 GF) **Facilities** STV Wi-fi Xmas New Year **Conf** Class 18 Board 18 Thtr 30 **Services** Lift Air con **Parking** 24

Crowne Plaza Cambridge
★★★★ 75% HOTEL

☎ 01223 556554 & 0871 942 9180
20 Downing St CB2 3DT
e-mail: chris.darcy@ihg.com
web: www.cpcambridgehotel.co.uk
dir: From M11 (either junct 11, 12 or 13). Follow signs to city centre then Grand Arcade car park. Hotel adjacent. Or from A14 take Cambridge exit, onto Huntingdon Rd, follow one-way system

Located in the heart of the city, this hotel enjoys an enviable position, with many of the universities and the town centre within easy walking distance. It is located adjacent to the Grand Arcade shopping centre: on site parking, although limited, is a plus. The hotel offers modern accommodation and large open-plan public areas; a fitness room and several conference rooms are also available.

Rooms 198 **S** £130-£350; **D** £140-£360 (incl. bkfst)* **Facilities** STV Wi-fi ☖ HL Gym Sauna New Year **Conf** Class 70 Board 50 Thtr 250 Del from £180 to £350* **Services** Lift Air con **Parking** 50 **Notes** LB ⊗ Civ Wed 250

De Vere University Arms Hotel

DE VERE
Hotels & Resorts

★★★★ 73% HOTEL

☎ 01223 273000
Regent St CB2 1AD
e-mail: dua.sales@devere-hotels.com
web: www.devere.co.uk
dir: M11 junct 11, follow city centre signs for 3m.
Right at 2nd mini rdbt, left at lights into Regent St.
Hotel 600yds on right

Built in 1834, the University Arms has an enviable
position in the very heart of the city, overlooking
Parker's Piece. Public rooms include an elegant
domed lounge, a smart restaurant, a bar and lounge
overlooking the park. Conference and banqueting
rooms are extensive, many with oak panelling. Given
the hotel's central location parking for guests is a
bonus.

Rooms 119 (2 fmly) 🐾 **S** £95-£275; **D** £105-£285
(incl. bkfst) **Facilities** STV FTV Wi-fi ♨ Xmas New Year
Conf Class 150 Board 80 Thtr 300 **Services** Lift
Parking 56 **Notes** ⊗ Civ Wed 250

Arundel House Hotel

★★★ 81% HOTEL

☎ 01223 367701
Chesterton Rd CB4 3AN
e-mail: info@arundelhousehotels.co.uk
web: www.arundelhousehotels.co.uk
dir: In city centre on A1303

Overlooking the River Cam and enjoying views over
open parkland, this popular and smart hotel was
originally a row of townhouses dating from Victorian
times. Bedrooms are attractive and have a special
character. The smart public areas feature a
conservatory for informal snacks, a spacious bar and
an elegant restaurant for more serious dining.

Rooms 103 (22 annexe) (7 fmly) (14 GF)
Facilities FTV Wi-fi ♨ New Year **Conf** Class 24
Board 22 Thtr 50 **Parking** 70 **Notes** ⊗ Closed 25-26
Dec

Best Western Cambridge Quy Mill Hotel

Best Western

★★★ 80% ⚜ ⚜ HOTEL

☎ 01223 293383 & 378118
Church Rd, Stow Cum Quy CB25 9AF
e-mail: info@cambridgequymill.co.uk
web: www.bw-cambridgequymill.co.uk
dir: Exit A14 at junct 35, E of Cambridge, onto B1102
for 50yds. Entrance opposite church

Set in open countryside, this 19th-century former
watermill is conveniently situated for access to
Cambridge. Bedroom styles differ, yet each room is
smartly appointed and brightly decorated; superior,
spacious courtyard rooms are noteworthy. Well-
designed public areas include several spacious bar/
lounges, with a choice of casual and formal eating
areas; service is both friendly and helpful. There is a
smart leisure club with state-of-the-art equipment.

Rooms 51 (30 annexe) (1 fmly) (24 GF) 🐾
S £55-£145; **D** £55-£205* **Facilities** Spa FTV Wi-fi ♨
🏊 Gym New Year **Conf** Class 30 Board 24 Thtr 80
Del from £145 to £195* **Parking** 90 **Notes** LB Closed
24-25 Dec RS 26 Dec Civ Wed 80

Holiday Inn Cambridge

Holiday Inn

★★★ 79% HOTEL

☎ 0871 942 9015
Lakeview, Bridge Rd, Impington CB24 9PH
e-mail: reservations-cambridge@ihg.com
web: www.hicambridgehotel.co.uk
dir: 2.5m N, on N side of rdbt junct A14 & B1049

A modern, purpose-built hotel conveniently situated
just off the A14 junction, a short drive from the city
centre. Public areas include a popular bar, the
Junction Restaurant and a large open-plan lounge.
Bedrooms come in a variety of styles and are suited to
both business and leisure guests alike.

Rooms 161 (14 fmly) (75 GF) **D** £70-£135 (incl.
bkfst)* **Facilities** Spa STV Wi-fi ♨ HL 🏊 supervised
Gym **Conf** Class 40 Board 45 Thtr 120 Del from £90 to
£155* **Services** Air con **Parking** 175 **Notes** LB ⊗
Civ Wed 100

Best Western Plus Gonville Hotel

Best Western PLUS

★★★ 78% HOTEL

C

☎ 01223 366611 & 221111
Gonville Place CB1 1LY
e-mail: all@gonvillehotel.co.uk
web: www.gonvillehotel.co.uk
dir: M11 junct 11, on A1309 follow city centre signs.
At 2nd mini rdbt right into Lensfield Rd, over
junct with lights. Hotel 25yds on right

A well established hotel situated on the inner ring
road, a short walk across the green from the city
centre. The air-conditioned public areas are cheerfully
furnished, and include a lounge bar and brasserie;
bedrooms are well appointed and appealing, offering
a good range of facilities for both corporate and
leisure guests.

Rooms 80 (2 fmly) (8 GF) 🐾 **S** £69.65-£199;
D £69.65-£199* **Facilities** FTV Wi-fi ♨ HL New Year
Conf Class 100 Board 50 Thtr 200 Del from £125 to
£180.50* **Services** Lift Air con **Parking** 80 **Notes** LB
RS 24-29 Dec Civ Wed 100

The Lensfield Hotel

★★★ 77% METRO HOTEL

☎ 01223 355017
53-57 Lensfield Rd CB2 1EN
e-mail: reservations@lensfieldhotel.co.uk
web: www.lensfieldhotel.co.uk
dir: M11 juncts 11, 12 or 13, follow signs to city
centre. Access via Silver St, Trumpington St, left into
Lensfield Rd

Located close to all the city's attractions, this
constantly improving hotel provides a range of
attractive bedrooms, equipped with thoughtful extras.
Comprehensive breakfasts are taken in an elegant
dining room and a comfortable bar and cosy foyer
lounge are also available.

Rooms 28 (3 fmly) (4 GF) **S** £72-£120; **D** £110-£132
(incl. bkfst)* **Facilities** STV FTV Wi-fi ♨ HL **Parking** 5
Notes LB ⊗ Closed last 2 wks in Dec-4 Jan

C

CAMBRIDGE *continued*

Centennial Hotel

★★★ 70% HOTEL

☎ 01223 314652
63-71 Hills Rd CB2 1PG
e-mail: reception@centennialhotel.co.uk
dir: M11 junct 11, A1309 to Cambridge. Right Into
Brooklands Ave to end. Left, hotel 100yds on right

This friendly hotel is convenient for the railway
station and town centre. Well-presented public areas
include a welcoming lounge, a relaxing bar and
restaurant on the lower-ground level. Bedrooms are
generally spacious, well maintained and thoughtfully
equipped with a good range of facilities; several
rooms are available on the ground floor.

Rooms 39 (1 fmly) (7 GF) 🐾 🛎 **S** £80-£90; **D** £100-£120
(incl. bkfst)* **Facilities** FTV Wi-fi 🐾 **Conf** Class 25
Board 25 Thtr 25 **Parking** 28 **Notes** ⊗ Closed 23
Dec-1 Jan

Ashley Hotel

★★ 81% METRO HOTEL

☎ 01223 350059 & 367701
74-76 Chesterton Rd CB4 1ER
e-mail: info@arundelhousehotels.co.uk
dir: On city centre ring road

Expect a warm welcome at this delightful Victorian
property situated just a short walk from the River
Cam. The smartly decorated bedrooms are generally
quite spacious and equipped with a good range of
useful extras. Breakfast is served at individual tables
in the smart lower ground floor dining room.

Rooms 16 (5 fmly) (5 GF) **Facilities** FTV Wi-fi
Parking 12 **Notes** ⊗ Closed 24-26 Dec

Helen Hotel

★★ 80% METRO HOTEL

☎ 01223 246465
167-169 Hills Rd CB2 2RJ
e-mail: enquiries@helenhotel.co.uk
dir: On A1307, 1.25m from city centre (south side). At
Cherry-Hinton Rd junct, opposite Homerton College

This extremely well maintained, privately owned hotel
is situated close to the city centre and a range of
popular eateries. Public areas include a smart lounge
bar with plush sofas and a cosy breakfast room.
Bedrooms are pleasantly decorated with co-ordinated
fabrics and have many thoughtful touches.

Rooms 19 (2 fmly) (2 GF) **Facilities** STV Wi-fi
Parking 12 **Notes** ⊗ Closed Xmas & New Year

Holiday Inn Express Cambridge

BUDGET HOTEL

☎ 01223 866800
15/17 Coldhams Park, Norman Way CB1 3LH
e-mail: info@expresscambridge.co.uk
web: www.expresscambridge.co.uk
dir: B1047 Fen Ditton. 1m to T-junct, right, at rdbt
left onto Barnwell Rd, to rdbt. Left, to Toyota garage,
right into Business Park

A modern hotel ideal for families and business
travellers. Fresh and uncomplicated, the spacious
rooms include Sky TV, power shower and tea and
coffee-making facilities. Continental buffet breakfast
is included in the room rate; and a choice of light
meals are served in the smart restaurant. See also
the Hotel Groups pages.

Rooms 100 🐾 **Conf** Class 20 Board 24 Thtr 50

Holiday Inn Express Cambridge - Duxford

BUDGET HOTEL

☎ 01223 497070
**Duxford M11 Jct 10, 42 Station Rd, East Whittlesford
Bridge CB22 4NL**
e-mail: reception@hiexpresscambridgeduxford.co.uk
dir: 1m from Imperial War Museum Duxford

Rooms 73 (40 fmly) (6 GF) **S** £49-£159; **D** £49-£159
(incl. bkfst)* **Conf** Class 10 Board 16 Thtr 25
Del from £99 to £159*

Premier Inn Cambridge (A14 Jct 32)

BUDGET HOTEL

☎ 0871 527 8186
Ring Fort Rd CB4 2GW
web: www.premierinn.com
dir: A14 junct 32, follow B1049/city centre signs. At
1st lights left into Kings Hedges Rd, 2nd left into
Ring Fort Rd

High quality, budget accommodation ideal for both
families and business travellers. Spacious, en suite
bedrooms feature tea and coffee making facilities,
and Freeview TV in most hotels. Internet access and
Wi-fi are available for a small fee. The adjacent
family restaurant features a wide and varied menu.
See also the Hotel Groups pages.

Rooms 154

Roman Way Hotel

★★★ 68% HOTEL

☎ 01543 572121
Watling St WS11 1SH
e-mail: reservations@romanwayhotel.co.uk
dir: M6 junct 11, A5 towards Telford. Hotel on left next
to Vauxhall Show room

A warm welcome and friendly service are guaranteed
at this hotel, which has a Roman theme due to its
position on the old Roman road, Watling Street. The
accommodation is fresh and modern; the bedrooms
are comfortable the bathrooms smart. Gilpins Bar
and Bistro is the relaxed and informal eating option.
Meetings and weddings can be held here. It is ideally
located for access to the M6 and M6 Toll, and it is
close to tourist locations such as Cannock Chase,
historic Lichfield and the National Memorial
Arboretum at Alrewas.

Rooms 55 (10 fmly) (23 GF) **S** £29-£80; **D** £29-£80*
Facilities FTV Wi-fi New Year **Conf** Class 60 Board 40
Thtr 100 Del from £85 to £110* **Parking** 100
Notes LB ⊗ Civ Wed 100

Premier Inn Cannock (Orbital)

BUDGET HOTEL

☎ 0871 527 8190
Eastern Way WS11 8XR
web: www.premierinn.com
dir: N'bound: M6 (Toll) junct 7, A5. At rdbt 1st exit
(A5), 4th exit onto A460, 1st exit. S'bound: (no access
from M6 Toll). M6 junct 11, A460 signed Cannock. At
next 2 rdbts take 3rd exit. At next rdbt 1st exit onto
service road. Hotel adjacent to Orbital Brewers Fayre

High quality, budget accommodation ideal for both
families and business travellers. Spacious, en suite
bedrooms feature tea and coffee making facilities,
and Freeview TV in most hotels. Internet access and
Wi-fi are available for a small fee. The adjacent
family restaurant features a wide and varied menu.
See also the Hotel Groups pages.

Rooms 21

Premier Inn Cannock South

BUDGET HOTEL

☎ 0871 527 8192
Watling St WS11 1SJ
web: www.premierinn.com
dir: At junct of A5 & A460, 2m from M6 juncts 11 &
12

Rooms 60

Save on hotels. Book at **theAA.com/hotel**

CAM – CAR 115 ENGLAND

C

CANTERBURY
Kent
Map 7 TR15

Holiday Inn Express Canterbury

BUDGET HOTEL

☎ 01227 865000
A2 Dover Rd, Upper Harbledown CT2 9HX
e-mail: canterbury@exbhi.co.uk
web: www.hiexpresscanterbury.co.uk
dir: M2 junct 7, take A2 towards Dover. 4m. Hotel access via Texaco service area

A modern hotel ideal for families and business travellers. Fresh and uncomplicated, the spacious rooms include Sky TV, power shower and tea and coffee-making facilities. Continental buffet breakfast is included in the room rate; other meals may be taken at the nearby family pub or restaurant. See also the Hotel Groups pages.

Rooms 89 (38 GF) **Conf** Class 20 Board 10 Thtr 36 Del £175*

CARBIS BAY

See St Ives (Cornwall)

CARLISLE
Cumbria
Map 18 NY35

Hallmark Hotel Carlisle
★★★★ 71% HOTEL

☎ 01228 531951 & 633503
Court Square CA1 1QY
e-mail: carlisle.reservations@hallmarkhotels.co.uk
dir: M6 junct 43, to city centre, then follow road to left & railway station

This hotel is at the heart of the town, opposite the railway station. Most of the bedrooms have benefited from an investment programme, and the smart ground-floor areas include a popular bar and restaurant. A number of meeting rooms are available and at the rear of the hotel is a small car park.

Rooms 70 (3 fmly) 🐾 **Facilities** FTV Wi-fi Xmas New Year **Conf** Class 100 Board 30 Thtr 240 Del from £110 to £130* **Services** Lift **Parking** 26 **Notes** ⊗ Civ Wed 200

Crown Hotel
★★★ 81% ⚫ HOTEL

☎ 01228 561888
Station Rd, Wetheral CA4 8ES
e-mail: info@crownhotelwetheral.co.uk
web: www.crownhotelwetheral.co.uk
dir: M6 junct 42, B6263 to Wetheral, right at village shop, car park at rear of hotel

Set in the attractive village of Wetheral and with landscaped gardens to the rear, this hotel is well suited to both business and leisure guests. Bedrooms vary in size and style and include two apartments in an adjacent house ideal for long stays. A choice of dining options is available, with the popular Waltons Bar an informal alternative to the main restaurant.

Rooms 51 (2 annexe) (10 fmly) (3 GF) 🐾 **S** £65-£85; **D** £110-£135 (incl. bkfst)* **Facilities** Spa STV Wi-fi HL ⚡ supervised Gym Squash Children's splash pool Steam room Beauty room Sauna Dance studio Xmas New Year **Conf** Class 90 Board 50 Thtr 175 Del from £125 to £145 **Parking** 55 **Notes** Civ Wed 120

The Crown & Mitre
★★★ 68% HOTEL

☎ 01228 525491
4 English St CA3 8HZ
e-mail: info@crownandmitre-hotel-carlisle.com
web: www.crownandmitre-hotel-carlisle.com
dir: A6 to city centre, pass station on left. Right into Blackfriars St. Rear entrance at end

Located in the heart of the city, this Edwardian hotel is close to the cathedral and a few minutes' walk from the castle. Bedrooms vary in size and style, from smart executive rooms to more functional standard rooms. Public rooms include a comfortable lounge area and the lovely bar with its feature stained-glass windows.

Rooms 95 (20 annexe) (4 fmly) (11 smoking) 🐾 **Facilities** STV FTV Wi-fi ⚡ Xmas New Year **Conf** Class 250 Board 50 Thtr 400 Del from £130 to £150* **Services** Lift **Parking** 42 **Notes** Civ Wed 200

Ibis Carlisle
BUDGET HOTEL

☎ 01228 518000
Portlands, Botchergate CA1 1RP
e-mail: H3443@accor.com
web: www.ibishotels.com
dir: M6 junct 42/43 follow signs for city centre. Hotel on Botchergate

Modern, budget hotel offering comfortable accommodation in bright and practical bedrooms. Breakfast is self-service and dinner is available in the restaurant See also the Hotel Groups pages.

Rooms 102 (17 fmly)

Premier Inn Carlisle Central

BUDGET HOTEL

☎ 0871 527 8210
Warwick Rd CA1 2WF
web: www.premierinn.com
dir: M6 junct 43, on A69

High quality, budget accommodation ideal for both families and business travellers. Spacious, en suite bedrooms feature tea and coffee making facilities, and Freeview TV in most hotels. Internet access and Wi-fi are available for a small fee. The adjacent family restaurant features a wide and varied menu. See also the Hotel Groups pages.

Rooms 44

C

CARLISLE *continued*

Premier Inn Carlisle Central North

BUDGET HOTEL

☎ 0871 527 8212
Kingstown Rd CA3 0AT
web: www.premierinn.com
dir: M6 junct 44, A7 towards Carlisle, hotel 1m on left

Rooms 49

Premier Inn Carlisle (M6 Jct 42)

BUDGET HOTEL

☎ 0871 527 8206
Carleton CA4 0AD
web: www.premierinn.com
dir: Just off M6 junct 42, S of Carlisle

Rooms 61

Premier Inn Carlisle (M6 Jct 44)

BUDGET HOTEL

☎ 0871 527 8208
Parkhouse Rd CA3 0HR
web: www.premierinn.com
dir: M6 junct 44, A7 signed Carlisle. Hotel on right at
1st set of lights

Rooms 127

CARTMEL	**Map 18 SD37**
Cumbria	

Aynsome Manor Hotel

★★★ 78% ◉ COUNTRY HOUSE HOTEL

☎ 015395 36653
LA11 6HH
e-mail: aynsomemanor@btconnect.com
dir: M6 junct 36, A590 signed Barrow-in-Furness
towards Cartmel. Left at end of road, hotel before
village

Dating back, in part, to the early 16th century, this
manor house overlooks the fells and the nearby priory.
Spacious bedrooms, including some courtyard rooms,
are comfortably furnished. Dinner in the elegant
restaurant features local produce whenever possible,
and there is a choice of lounges to relax in.

Rooms 12 (2 annexe) (2 fmly) 🐾 **S** £80-£105;
D £85-£130 (incl. bkfst) **Facilities** FTV Wi-fi New Year
Parking 20 **Notes** LB Closed 2-31 Jan RS Sun

L'enclume

◉ ◉ ◉ ◉ RESTAURANT WITH ROOMS

☎ 015395 36362
Cavendish St LA11 6PZ
e-mail: info@lenclume.co.uk
dir: From A590 turn left for Cartmel before Newby
Bridge

A delightful 13th-century property in the heart of
this lovely village offering 21st-century cooking
that is more than worth travelling some distance
for. Simon Rogan cooks imaginative and
adventurous food in this stylish restaurant.
Individually designed, modern, en suite rooms vary
in size and style, and are either in the main
property or dotted about the village only a few
moments' walk from the restaurant.

Rooms 12 (5 annexe) (3 fmly)

CASTLE CARY	**Map 4 ST63**
Somerset	

The George Hotel

★★ 65% HOTEL

☎ 01963 350761
Market Place BA7 7AH
e-mail: castlecarygeorge@aol.co.uk
dir: A303 onto A371. Signed Castle Cary, 2m on left

This 15th-century coaching inn provides well-
equipped bedrooms that are, in general, spacious.
Most rooms are at the back of the house and therefore
enjoy a quiet aspect; some are on the ground floor
and one is suitable for less able guests. Diners can
choose to eat in the more formal dining room, or in
one of the two cosy bars.

Rooms 17 (5 annexe) (1 fmly) (5 GF) 🐾 **S** £65;
D £85-£115 (incl. bkfst) **Facilities** Wi-fi ♨ Xmas New
Year **Conf** Class 40 Board 20 Thtr 50 Del from £100 to
£140 **Parking** 7 **Notes** LB

CASTLE COMBE	**Map 4 ST87**
Wiltshire	

Manor House Hotel and Golf Club

★★★★ ◉ ◉ ◉ COUNTRY HOUSE HOTEL

☎ 01249 782206
SN14 7HR
e-mail: enquiries@manorhouse.co.uk
web: www.manorhouse.co.uk
dir: M4 junct 17 follow Chippenham signs onto
A420 Bristol, then right onto B4039. Through
village, right after bridge. Useful to follow brown
tourism signs to Castle Combe Racing Circuit

This delightful hotel is situated in a secluded valley
adjacent to a picturesque village, where there have
been no new buildings for 300 years. There are 365
acres of grounds to enjoy, complete with an Italian
garden and an 18-hole golf course. Bedrooms,
some in the main house and some in a row of stone
cottages, have been superbly furnished, and public
rooms include a number of cosy lounges with
roaring fires. Service is a pleasing blend of
professionalism and friendliness. The award-
winning food utilises top quality local produce.

Rooms 48 (26 annexe) (8 fmly) (12 GF) 🐾
D £205-£650 (incl. bkfst)* **Facilities** STV Wi-fi ⅃ 18
♨ Putt green Fishing 🚶 Jogging track Hot air
ballooning Giant games on lawns Xmas New Year
Conf Class 50 Board 30 Thtr 100 Del from £200 to
£260* **Parking** 100 **Notes** LB Civ Wed 110

See East Midlands Airport

Save on hotels. Book at **theAA.com/hotel**

CAR – CHA 117 ENGLAND

C

CASTLEFORD
West Yorkshire — Map 16 SE42

Premier Inn Castleford M62 Jct 31

BUDGET HOTEL

☎ 0871 527 8216
Pioneer Way WF10 5TG
web: www.premierinn.com
dir: M62 junct 31, A655 towards Castleford, right at
1st lights, then left

High quality, budget accommodation ideal for both
families and business travellers. Spacious, en suite
bedrooms feature tea and coffee making facilities,
and Freeview TV in most hotels. Internet access and
Wi-fi are available for a small fee. The adjacent
family restaurant features a wide and varied menu.
See also the Hotel Groups pages.

Rooms 62

Premier Inn Castleford M62 Jct 32

BUDGET HOTEL

☎ 0871 527 8218
Colarado Way WF10 4TA
web: www.premierinn.com
dir: M62 junct 32, follow signs for Xscape. Hotel
adjacent to Xscape complex

Rooms 119

CAVENDISH
Suffolk — Map 13 TL84

The George

◉ RESTAURANT WITH ROOMS

☎ 01787 280248
The Green CO10 8BA
e-mail: thegeorgecavendish@gmail.com
web: www.thecavendishgeorge.co.uk
dir: A1092 into Cavendish, The George next to village
green

The George is situated in the heart of the pretty
village of Cavendish and has four very stylish
bedrooms. The front-facing rooms overlook the
village; the comfortable, spacious bedrooms retain
many of their original features. The award-winning
restaurant is very well appointed and dinner should
not be missed. Guests are guaranteed to receive a
warm welcome, attentive friendly service and great
food.

Rooms 5 (1 fmly)

CHADDESLEY CORBETT
Worcestershire — Map 10 SO87

Brockencote Hall Country House Hotel

★★★ ◉◉ HOTEL

☎ 01562 777876
DY10 4PY
e-mail: info@brockencotehall.com
web: www.brockencotehall.com
dir: A38 to Bromsgrove, off A448 towards
Kidderminster

Glorious countryside extends all around this
magnificent mansion, and grazing sheep can be
seen from the conservatory. Not surprisingly,
relaxation comes high on the list of priorities here.
Despite its very English location the hotel's owner
actually hails from Alsace and the atmosphere is
very much that of a provincial French château. The
spacious, chandeliered dining room is a popular
venue for accomplished classical French cuisine
which has modern British influences.

Rooms 21 (4 fmly) (5 GF) ⸙ **S** £95-£245;
D £120-£300 (incl. bkfst) **Facilities** FTV Wi-fi ⬙ ⬚
Fishing ⬙ Xmas New Year **Conf** Class 35 Board 35
Thtr 80 Del from £170 to £190 **Parking** 60 **Notes** LB
⊗ Civ Wed 80

CHAGFORD
Devon — Map 3 SX78

Gidleigh Park

★★★★★ ◉◉◉◉
COUNTRY HOUSE HOTEL

☎ 01647 432367
TQ13 8HH
e-mail: gidleighpark@gidleigh.co.uk
web: www.gidleigh.com
dir: From Chagford, right at Lloyds Bank into Mill
St. After 150yds fork right. 2m to end

Built in 1928 as a private residence for an
Australian shipping magnate and set in 107 acres
of lovingly tended grounds, this world-renowned
hotel retains a timeless charm and a very
endearing, homely atmosphere. The individually
styled bedrooms are sumptuously furnished; some
with separate seating areas, some with balconies
and many enjoying panoramic views. There are spa
suites, a loft suite, ideal for families, and the
stunning thatched Pavilion in the grounds, which
has two bedrooms, two bathrooms, a lounge and
kitchen diner. The spacious public areas feature
antique furniture, beautiful flower arrangements
and magnificent artwork. The award-winning
cuisine created by Michael Caines, together with
the top quality wine list, will make a stay here a
truly memorable experience.

Rooms 24 (4 fmly) (4 GF) ⸙ **S** £305-£1155;
D £325-£1175 (incl. bkfst)* **Facilities** STV FTV Wi-fi
⬚ Putt green Fishing ⬙ Bowls Xmas New Year
Conf Class 22 Board 18 Thtr 22 Del from £395 to
£595* **Parking** 45 **Notes** LB

C

CHARD
Somerset

Map 4 ST30

Cricket St Thomas Hotel

Warner Leisure Hotels
JUST FOR GROWN-UPS

★★★★ 73% ® COUNTRY HOUSE HOTEL

☎ 01460 30111
TA20 4DD
e-mail: cricket.sales@bourne-leisure.co.uk
dir: M5 junct 25, A358 towards Chard, A30 to
Crewkerne. Hotel 3m from Chard

This Grade II listed house has an interesting history
including the fact that Lord Nelson and Lady
Hamilton were frequent visitors. The hotel is set in
splendid parkland, with colourful gardens, lakes, and
a unique woodland area. Various holiday packages
are available, and there are extensive leisure
facilities, as well as live entertainment and various
dining venues, including Fenocchi's, with an Italian-
themed menu. The bedrooms are spacious and well
appointed. Please note that this is an adults-only
(over 21 years old) hotel.

Rooms 239 (84 GF) ↙ **S** £90-£240; **D** £120-£240
(incl. bkfst & dinner)* **Facilities** Spa FTV Wi-fi HL ⊗
↙ Putt green ↙ Gym Rifle shooting Archery Clay
pigeon Short mat bowls ♫ Xmas New Year
Conf Class 50 Board 25 Thtr 80 **Services** Lift
Parking 351 **Notes** LB ⊗ No children 18yrs
Civ Wed 60

Lordleaze Hotel

THE INDEPENDENTS
HOTEL ASSOCIATION

★★★ 77% HOTEL

☎ 01460 61066
Henderson Dr, Forton Rd TA20 2HW
e-mail: info@lordleazehotel.com
web: www.lordleazehotel.com
dir: A358 from Chard, left at St Mary's Church to
Forton & Winsham on B3162. Follow signs to hotel

Conveniently and quietly located, this hotel is close to
the Devon, Dorset and Somerset borders, and only
minutes from Chard. All bedrooms are well equipped
and comfortable. The friendly lounge bar has a wood-
burning stove and serves tempting bar meals. The
conservatory restaurant offers more formal dining.

Rooms 25 (2 fmly) (7 GF) ↙ **S** £77-£79; **D** £120-£125
(incl. bkfst)* **Facilities** FTV Wi-fi Xmas New Year
Conf Class 60 Board 40 Thtr 180 Del from £120 to
£125* **Parking** 55 **Notes** LB Civ Wed 100

CHARINGWORTH
Gloucestershire

Map 10 SP13

Charingworth Manor Hotel

CLASSIC LODGES
the sign of a great hotel

★★★★ 73% ®
COUNTRY HOUSE HOTEL

☎ 01386 593555
Charingworth Manor GL55 6NS
e-mail: gm.charingworthmanor@classiclodges.co.uk
web: www.classiclodges.co.uk/charingworthmanor

This 14th-century manor house retains many original
features including flagstone floors, exposed beams
and open fireplaces. The house has a beautiful
setting in 50 acres of grounds and has been carefully
extended to provide high quality accommodation and
a delightful, small leisure facility. Spacious bedrooms
are furnished with period pieces and modern
amenities.

Rooms 26 (18 annexe) (2 fmly) (12 GF) **Facilities** ⊗
↙ ↙ Gym Sauna Steam room Solarium Xmas New
Year **Conf** Class 30 Board 40 Thtr 80 **Parking** 50
Notes Civ Wed 60

CHARMOUTH
Dorset

Map 4 SY39

Fernhill Hotel

★★★ 80% HOTEL

☎ 01297 560492
Fernhill DT6 6BX
e-mail: mail@fernhill-hotel.co.uk
dir: A35 onto A3052 to Lyme Regis. Hotel 0.25m on
left

A small, friendly hotel on top of the hill in well tended
grounds. It boasts an outside pool and treatment
rooms, together with comfortable rooms and pleasant
public areas. Each bedroom is individually styled and
many have views of the Char Valley and beyond. The
menus are based on seasonal, locally sourced
produce.

Rooms 10 (1 fmly) **Facilities** Wi-fi ↘ Fishing Holistic
treatment centre Air/Massage baths Xmas New Year
Conf Class 20 Board 24 Thtr 60 **Parking** 30 **Notes** ⊗

CHARNOCK RICHARD
MOTORWAY SERVICE AREA (M6)
Lancashire

Map 15 SD51

Days Inn Charnock Richard - M6

Welcome Break

BUDGET HOTEL

☎ 01257 791746
Welcome Break Service Area PR7 5LR
e-mail: charnockhotel@welcomebreak.co.uk
web: www.welcomebreak.co.uk
dir: Between junct 27 & 28 of M6 N'bound. 500yds
from Camelot Theme Park via Mill Lane

This modern building offers accommodation in smart,
spacious and well-equipped bedrooms, suitable for
families and business travellers, and all with en suite
bathrooms. Continental breakfast is available and
other refreshments may be taken at the nearby family
restaurant. See also the Hotel Groups pages.

Rooms 100 (68 fmly) (32 GF) (20 smoking)
Conf Class 16 Board 24 Thtr 40 Del from £60.95 to
£100*

CHATHAM
Kent

Map 7 TQ76

Bridgewood Manor

QHOTELS

★★★★ 79% HOTEL

☎ 01634 201333
**Bridgewood Roundabout, Walderslade Woods
ME5 9AX**
e-mail: bridgewoodmanor@qhotels.co.uk
web: www.qhotels.co.uk
dir: Adjacent to Bridgewood rdbt on A229. Take 3rd
exit signed Walderslade & Lordswood. Hotel 50mtrs
on left

A modern, purpose-built hotel situated on the
outskirts of Rochester. Bedrooms are pleasantly
decorated, comfortably furnished and equipped with
many thoughtful touches. The hotel has an excellent
range of leisure and conference facilities. Guests can
dine in the informal Terrace Bistro or experience fine
dining in the more formal Squires restaurant, where
the service is both attentive and friendly.

Rooms 100 (12 fmly) (26 GF) **Facilities** Spa STV Wi-fi
⊗ supervised ↙ Gym Beauty treatments Xmas New
Year **Conf** Class 110 Board 80 Thtr 200 **Services** Lift
Parking 170 **Notes** Civ Wed 130

Holiday Inn Rochester - Chatham

★★★ 80% HOTEL

☎ 0871 942 9069 & 07736 746421
Maidstone Rd ME5 9SF
e-mail: christopher.ross@ihg.com
web: www.hirochesterhotel.co.uk
dir: M2 junct 3 or M20 junct 6, then A229 for Chatham

A modern, well-equipped hotel close to Rochester, Canterbury and the historic Chatham Dockyards. Bedrooms, including family rooms, are comfortable and spacious; all have air conditioning and broadband access. Public facilities include a lounge, bar and modern restaurant. There is a gym, indoor pool, sauna, spa and an impressive self-contained conference centre.

Rooms 149 (29 fmly) (53 GF) (16 smoking) **Facilities** STV FTV Wi-fi ⌁ 🕑 supervised Gym Steam room Sauna Pilates & beauty evenings **Conf** Class 45 Board 45 Thtr 100 **Services** Lift Air con **Parking** 200 **Notes** ⊗ Civ Wed 100

Ramada Encore Chatham

★★★ 70% HOTEL

☎ 01634 891677
Western Av, Chatham Historic Dockyard ME4 4NT
e-mail: operations@encorechatham.co.uk
dir: Follow signs for Chatham Historic Dockyard

Located in the historic dockyard and just minutes from the town centre, this hotel offers stylish, comfortable accommodation. The smart open-plan bar and restaurant are modern in design and provide a choice of seating areas; a full menu is on offer all day and in the evening. Free Wi-fi is available throughout the public areas, and there is a meeting room.

Rooms 90 (14 fmly) (8 smoking) **Facilities** STV FTV Wi-fi **Conf** Class 12 Board 12 Thtr 20 **Services** Lift Air con **Parking** 60 **Notes** ⊗

CHATHILL   Map 21 NU12
Northumberland

Doxford Hall Hotel & Spa

★★★★ 80% ◉ COUNTRY HOUSE HOTEL

☎ 01665 589700 & 589713
NE67 5DN
e-mail: info@doxfordhall.com
dir: 8m N of Alnwick just off A1, signed Christon Bank & Seahouses. Take B6347 follow signs for hotel

A beautiful country-house hotel set in a private estate, surrounded by countryside and convenient for visiting nearby historic towns and attractions. Bedrooms are spacious and luxuriously furnished, each named after Northumbrian Castles. The dining room and lounges are very attractive. There is an impressive grand staircase and beautiful wood throughout the hotel. The spa adds to the range of facilities.

Rooms 31 (1 fmly) (11 GF) ⌁ **S** £102.50-£162.50; **D** £145-£280* **Facilities** Spa FTV Wi-fi ⌁ HL 🕑 supervised Gym Sauna Steam room Xmas New Year **Conf** Class 100 Board 22 Thtr 250 Del from £140 to £160* **Services** Lift **Parking** 100 **Notes** Civ Wed 250

CHEADLE   Map 16 SJ88
Greater Manchester

Premier Inn Manchester (Cheadle)

BUDGET HOTEL

☎ 0871 527 8728
Royal Crescent SK8 3FE
web: www.premierinn.com
dir: Exit A34 at Cheadle Royal rdbt behind TGI Friday's

High quality, budget accommodation ideal for both families and business travellers. Spacious, en suite bedrooms feature tea and coffee making facilities, and Freeview TV in most hotels. Internet access and Wi-fi are available for a small fee. The adjacent family restaurant features a wide and varied menu. See also the Hotel Groups pages.

Rooms 65

CHELMSFORD   Map 6 TL70
Essex

County Hotel

★★★ 80% ◉ HOTEL

☎ 01245 455700
29 Rainsford Rd CM1 2PZ
e-mail: kloftus@countyhotelgroup.co.uk
web: www.countyhotelgroup.co.uk
dir: From town centre, past rail & bus station. Hotel 300yds left beyond lights

This popular hotel is ideally situated within easy walking distance of the railway station, bus depot and town centre. Stylish bedrooms offer spacious comfort and plentiful extras including free Wi-fi. There is a smart restaurant, bar and lounge as well as sunny outdoor terraces for making the most of warm weather. The hotel also has a range of meeting rooms and banqueting facilities.

Rooms 50 (2 fmly) ⌁ **S** £55-£95; **D** £75-£170* **Facilities** FTV Wi-fi HL Xmas New Year **Conf** Class 84 Board 64 Thtr 160 Del from £140 to £170* **Services** Lift **Parking** 80 **Notes** LB ⊗ Closed 27-30 Dec Civ Wed 80

Best Western Ivy Hill

★★★ 79% HOTEL

☎ 01277 353040 & 355111
Writtle Rd, Margaretting CM4 0EH
e-mail: sales@ivyhillhotel.co.uk
web: www.heritageleisure.co.uk
dir: Just off A12 junct 14. Hotel on left at top of slip road

A smartly appointed hotel conveniently situated just off the A12. The spacious bedrooms are tastefully decorated, have co-ordinated fabrics and all the expected facilities. Public rooms include a choice of lounges, a cosy bar, a smart conservatory and restaurant, as well as a range of conference and banqueting facilities.

Rooms 33 (5 fmly) (11 GF) **Facilities** FTV Wi-fi ⌁ **Conf** Class 80 Board 40 Thtr 180 Del from £150 to £156* **Parking** 200 **Notes** ⊗ Closed 24-26 Dec Civ Wed 100

C

CHELMSFORD *continued*

Pontlands Park

★★★ 78% HOTEL

☎ 01245 476444

West Hanningfield Rd, Great Baddow CM2 8HR
e-mail: sales@pontlandsparkhotel.co.uk
web: www.heritageleisure.co.uk
dir: A12, A130 , A1114 to Chelmsford. 1st exit at rdbt,
1st slip road on left. Left towards Great Baddow, 1st
left into West Hanningfield Rd. Hotel 400yds on left

A Victorian country-house hotel situated in a peaceful
rural location amidst attractive landscaped grounds.
The stylishly furnished bedrooms are generally quite
spacious; each is individually decorated and
equipped with modern facilities. The elegant public
rooms include a tastefully furnished sitting room, a
cosy lounge bar, smart conservatory restaurant and
an intimate dining room.

Rooms 35 (10 fmly) (11 GF) **Facilities** FTV Wi-fi ⊗ ⊰
Gym Beauty room **Conf** Class 40 Board 40 Thtr 100
Parking 100 **Notes** ⊗ Closed 24-26 Dec Civ Wed 100

Best Western Atlantic Hotel

★★★ 77% HOTEL

☎ 01245 268168

New St CM1 1PP
e-mail: info@atlantichotel.co.uk
dir: From Chelmsford rail station, left into Victoria Rd,
left at lights into New St, hotel on right

Ideally situated just a short walk from the railway
station with its quick links to London, this modern,
purpose-built hotel has contemporary-style bedrooms
equipped with modern facilities. The open-plan public
areas include Sapori Ristorante, an Italian restaurant,
a lounge bar and a conservatory.

Rooms 59 (3 fmly) (27 GF) **S** £125; **D** £200 (incl.
bkfst) **Facilities** FTV Wi-fi Gym Complimentary use of
facilities at Fitness First ♬ **Conf** Class 40 Board 10
Thtr 15 **Services** Air con **Parking** 60 **Notes** ⊗ Closed
23 Dec-3 Jan

Premier Inn Chelmsford (Boreham)

BUDGET HOTEL

☎ 0871 527 8220

Main Rd, Boreham CM3 3HJ
web: www.premierinn.com
dir: M25 junct 28, A12 to Colchester, B1137 to
Boreham

High quality, budget accommodation ideal for both
families and business travellers. Spacious, en suite

bedrooms feature tea and coffee making facilities,
and Freeview TV in most hotels. Internet access and
Wi-fi are available for a small fee. The adjacent
family restaurant features a wide and varied menu.
See also the Hotel Groups pages.

Rooms 78

Premier Inn Chelmsford (Springfield)

BUDGET HOTEL

☎ 0871 527 8222

**Chelmsford Service Area, Colchester Rd, Springfield
CM2 5PY**
web: www.premierinn.com
dir: At A12 junct 19, Chelmsford bypass, signed
Chelmsford Service Area

Rooms 61

CHELTENHAM   Map 10 SO92
Gloucestershire

Ellenborough Park

★★★★★ ◉◉◉ 86%
COUNTRY HOUSE HOTEL

☎ 01242 807361

Southam Rd GL52 3NH
e-mail: info@ellenboroughpark.com
dir: A46 right after 3m onto B4079, merges with
A435, 4m, over 3 rdbts, left onto Southam Lane, right
onto Old Road, right onto B4632, hotel on right

Set on the original Cheltenham Racecourse estate,
this impressive hotel has been beautifully restored.
Nina Campbell designed bedrooms and suites are
individual in style and are spread across the main
house and adjacent buildings. All feature superb
beds with Egyptian cotton, great range of modern
amenties and luxurious bathrooms. Guests can enjoy
a small, stylish spa complete with gym and outdoor
heated pool. Afternoon tea can be enjoyed in the
grandeur of the great hall. Two dining options exist in
the modern Tudor Club Brasserie and the elegant, oak
panelled Beaufort dining room which offers a high
standard of classic cuisine.

Rooms 62 (44 annexe) (20 GF) ⌒ **S** £240-£410;
D £240-£410 (incl. bkfst)* **Facilities** Spa STV FTV
Wi-fi ⊱ ⊰ ⬏ Gym Xmas New Year **Conf** Class 70
Board 40 Thtr 120 Del from £285 to £365*
Services Lift Air con **Parking** 130 **Notes** LB
Civ Wed 120

Hotel du Vin Cheltenham

★★★★ 80% ◉ HOTEL

☎ 01242 588450

Parabola Rd GL50 3AQ
e-mail: info@cheltenham.hotelduvin.com
web: www.hotelduvin.com
dir: M5 junct 11, follow signs for city centre. At rdbt
opposite Morgan Estate Agents take 2nd left, 200mtrs
to Parabola Rd

This hotel, in the Montpellier area of the town, has
spacious public areas that are packed with stylish
features. The pewter-topped bar has comfortable
seating and the spacious restaurant has the Hotel du
Vin trademark design; alfresco dining is possible on
the extensive terrace area. Bedrooms are very
comfortable, with Egyptian linen, deep baths and
power showers. The spa is the ideal place to relax and
unwind. Although parking is limited, it is a definite
bonus. Service is friendly and attentive.

Rooms 49 (2 fmly) (5 GF) ⌒ **D** £99-£495*
Facilities Spa STV Wi-fi **Conf** Class 24 Board 24
Thtr 30 Del from £195 to £235* **Services** Lift Air con
Parking 26 **Notes** Civ Wed 60

The Cheltenham Chase Hotel

★★★★ 80% HOTEL

☎ 01452 519988

Shurdington Rd, Brockworth GL3 4PB
e-mail: cheltenhamreservations@qhotels.co.uk
web: www.qhotels.co.uk
dir: M5 junct 11a onto A417 Cirencester. 1st exit A46
to Stroud, hotel 500yds on left.

Conveniently positioned for Cheltenham, Gloucester,
and the M5, this hotel is set in landscaped grounds
with ample parking. Bedrooms are spacious with
attractive colour schemes and excellent facilities;
executive rooms and suites benefit from air
conditioning. Public areas include an open-plan bar/
lounge, Hardey's restaurant, extensive meeting and
functions rooms and a well-equipped leisure club.

Rooms 122 (19 fmly) (44 GF) **Facilities** Spa STV FTV
Wi-fi ⊗ Gym Steam room Sauna Xmas New Year
Conf Class 150 Board 70 Thtr 400 **Services** Lift
Air con **Parking** 240 **Notes** ⊗ Civ Wed 344

Mercure Cheltenham Queen's Hotel

★★★★ 77% HOTEL

☎ 01242 514754
The Promenade GL50 1NN
e-mail: h6632@accor.com
web: www.mercure.com
dir: Follow town centre signs. Left at Montpellier Walk rdbt. Entrance 500mtrs right

With its spectacular position at the top of the main promenade, this landmark hotel is an ideal base from which to explore the charms of this Regency spa town and also the Cotswolds. Bedrooms are very comfortable and include two beautiful four-poster rooms. Smart public rooms include the popular Gold Cup bar and a choice of dining options.

Rooms 84 (15 fmly) ☞ **Facilities** STV Wi-fi HL Xmas New Year **Conf** Class 60 Board 40 Thtr 100 Del from £130 to £160* **Services** Lift Air con **Parking** 70 **Notes** LB Civ Wed 100

Thistle Cheltenham Hotel   thistle

★★★★ 76% HOTEL

☎ 0871 376 9013
Gloucester Rd GL51 0TS
e-mail: cheltenham@thistle.co.uk
web: www.thistlehotels.com/cheltenham
dir: M5 junct 11, A40 signed Cheltenham, at 1st rdbt take 2nd exit. Hotel immediately on left

Conveniently located for easy access to the M5, this large hotel offers a good range of dining options in addition to extensive leisure facilities. Bedrooms and bathrooms are well equipped and provide good ease of use for both the business and leisure guest. Ample parking and a range of conference rooms are provided.

Rooms 122 (9 fmly) (40 GF) ☞ **Facilities** FTV Wi-fi HL ☜ ⌇ Gym Sauna Steam room Xmas New Year **Conf** Class 220 Board 45 Thtr 400 Del £155 **Services** Lift **Parking** 300 **Notes** ⊗ Civ Wed 300

Cheltenham Park Hotel

PUMA HOTELS
COLLECTION

★★★★ 72% HOTEL

☎ 01242 222021
Cirencester Rd, Charlton Kings GL53 8EA
e-mail: cheltenhampark@pumahotels.co.uk
web: www.pumahotels.co.uk
dir: On A435, 2m SE of Cheltenham near Lilley Brook Golf Course

Located south of Cheltenham, this attractive Georgian property is set in its own landscaped gardens, adjacent to Lilley Brook Golf Course. All the bedrooms, whether premium or standard, are spacious and well equipped for both business and leisure guests. The hotel has an impressive health and leisure club with the latest gym equipment plus a pool, steam room and beauty salon; extensive meeting facilities are available. The Lakeside Restaurant serves carefully prepared cuisine.

Rooms 152 (119 annexe) **Facilities** STV Wi-fi ☜ supervised Gym Beauty treatment rooms Xmas New Year **Conf** Class 180 Board 110 Thtr 320 **Parking** 170 **Notes** ⊗ Civ Wed 100

The Greenway Hotel & Spa

★★★ 86% ◉◉ COUNTRY HOUSE HOTEL

☎ 01242 862352
Shurdington GL51 4UG
e-mail: info@thegreenway.co.uk
web: www.thegreenwayhotelandspa.com
dir: From Cheltenham centre 2.5m S on A46

This hotel, with a wealth of history, is peacefully located in a delightful setting close within easy reach of the many attractions of the Cotswolds and also the M5. The Manor House bedrooms are luxuriously appointed - traditional in style yet with plasma TVs and internet access. The tranquil Coach House rooms, in the converted stable block, have direct access to the beautiful grounds. The attractive dining room overlooks the sunken garden and is the venue for excellent food, proudly served by dedicated and attentive staff.

Rooms 17 (6 annexe) (1 fmly) ☞ **Facilities** Spa FTV Wi-fi ☜ ⌇ Gym Xmas New Year **Notes** Civ Wed

George Hotel

★★★ 80% ◉◉ HOTEL

☎ 01242 235751
St Georges Rd GL50 3DZ
e-mail: hotel@stayatthegeorge.co.uk
web: www.stayatthegeorge.co.uk
dir: M5 junct 11 follow town centre signs. At 2nd lights left into Gloucester Rd, past rail station over mini-rdbt. At lights right into St Georges Rd. Hotel 0.75m on left

A genuinely friendly, privately-owned hotel occupying part of a Regency terrace, just two-minutes walk from the town centre. The contemporary interior is elegant and stylish, and the well-equipped, modern bedrooms offer a relaxing haven; individually designed junior suites and deluxe double rooms are available. Lunch or dinner can be enjoyed in a lively atmosphere of Monty's Brasserie, perhaps followed by an evening in the vibrant and sophisticated cocktail bar which hosts live entertainment on Friday and Saturday evenings.

Rooms 31 (1 GF) ☞ **Facilities** STV Wi-fi Complimentary membership to local health club Live music at wknds ♫ **Conf** Class 18 Board 24 Thtr 30 **Parking** 30 **Notes** LB RS 24-26 Dec

Best Western Cheltenham Regency Hotel

★★★ 79% HOTEL

☎ 01452 713226 & 0845 194 9867
Gloucester Rd, Staverton GL51 0ST
e-mail: info@cheltenhamregency.co.uk
dir: M5 junct 11 onto A40 to Cheltenham. Left at rdbt, hotel 1m on left

This hotel provides high standards of quality and comfort. The large bedrooms, including several suites, are very well equipped and ideal for both the business and leisure guest. A good selection of carefully prepared dishes is available from either the extensive lounge/bar menu or a more formal offering, utilising high quality produce, can be found in the main restaurant.

Rooms 47 (2 fmly) (16 GF) ☞ **S** £75-£95; **D** £85-£225 (incl. bkfst) **Facilities** FTV Wi-fi ☜ Xmas New Year **Conf** Class 90 Board 80 Thtr 170 Del from £125 to £145 **Services** Lift Air con **Parking** 120 **Notes** LB ⊗ Civ Wed 140

CHELTENHAM *continued*

The Royal George Hotel

★★★ 71% HOTEL

☎ 01452 862506
Birdlip GL4 8JH
e-mail: royalgeorge.birdlip@greeneking.co.uk
web: www.oldenglish.co.uk
dir: M5 junct 11A take A417 towards Cirencester. At Air Balloon rdbt take 2nd exit then 1st right into Birdlip, hotel on right

This attractive 18th-century Cotswold building has been sympathetically converted and extended into a pleasant hotel. Bedrooms are spacious and comfortably furnished with modern facilities. The public areas have been designed around a traditional English pub with the bar leading on to a terrace overlooking extensive lawns.

Rooms 34 (4 fmly) (12 GF) **Facilities** ♬ Xmas **Conf** Class 60 Board 40 Thtr 90 **Notes** ⊗ Civ Wed 80

Premier Inn Cheltenham Central

BUDGET HOTEL

☎ 0871 527 8224
374 Gloucester Rd GL51 7AY
web: www.premierinn.com
dir: M5 junct 11, A40 (Cheltenham). Follow dual carriageway to end, straight on at 1st rdbt, right at 2nd rdbt

High quality, budget accommodation ideal for both families and business travellers. Spacious, en suite bedrooms feature tea and coffee making facilities, and Freeview TV in most hotels. Internet access and Wi-fi are available for a small fee. The adjacent family restaurant features a wide and varied menu. See also the Hotel Groups pages.

Rooms 43

Premier Inn Cheltenham West

BUDGET HOTEL

☎ 0871 527 8226
Tewkesbury Rd, Uckington GL51 9SL
web: www.premierinn.com
dir: M5 junct 10 (S'bound exit only), A4019, hotel in 2m. Or M5 junct 11, A40 towards Cheltenham. At Benhall Rdbt left onto A4103 (Princess Elizabeth Way) follow racecourse signs. At rdbt left onto A4019 signed Tewkesbury/M5 North. Hotel opposite Sainsburys

Rooms 40

CHENIES	**Map 6 TQ09**
Buckinghamshire	

The Bedford Arms Hotel

★★★ 79% ⊛ COUNTRY HOUSE HOTEL

☎ 01923 283301
WD3 6EQ
e-mail: contact@bedfordarms.co.uk
web: www.bedfordarms.co.uk
dir: M25 junct 18, A404 towards Amersham, hotel signed after 2m on right

This attractive, 19th-century country inn enjoys a peaceful rural setting. Comfortable bedrooms are decorated in traditional style and feature a range of thoughtful extras. Each room is named after a relation of the Duke of Bedford, whose family has an historic association with the property. There are two bars, a lounge and a cosy, wood-panelled restaurant.

Rooms 18 (8 annexe) (2 fmly) (8 GF) ↖ **S** £60-£110; **D** £95-£140 (incl. bkfst) **Facilities** STV FTV Wi-fi ↳ **Conf** Class 16 Board 24 Thtr 50 Del from £130 to £170 **Parking** 60 **Notes** RS 27 Dec-4 Jan Civ Wed 55

CHESHUNT	**Map 6 TL30**
Hertfordshire	

Cheshunt Marriott Hotel

★★★★ 74% HOTEL

☎ 01992 451245
Halfhide Ln, Turnford, Broxbourne EN10 6NG
web: www.cheshuntmarriott.co.uk
dir: Exit A10 at Broxbourne, right & right again at rdbt, hotel on right at next rdbt

This popular suburban hotel has an attractive courtyard garden, overlooked by many of the guest bedrooms. All bedrooms are spacious and air conditioned. Public areas include a small, unsupervised leisure facility, along with the busy Washington Bar and Restaurant.

Rooms 143 (37 fmly) (39 GF) **Facilities** STV Wi-fi ↳ ⓢ Gym Xmas New Year **Conf** Class 72 Board 56 Thtr 150 **Services** Lift Air con **Parking** 200 **Notes** ⊗ Civ Wed 120

CHESSINGTON	**Map 6 TQ16**
Greater London	

Holiday Inn London - Chessington

★★★★ 71% HOTEL

☎ 01372 734600
Leatherhead Rd KT9 2NE
e-mail: enquiries@holidayinnchessington.co.uk
web: www.holidayinnchessington.co.uk
dir: Follow signs for Chessington World of Adventures. Hotel at North Car Park entrance

In a convenient location just off the M25 (junction 9), two miles from the A3 and just 12 miles from London, this hotel is, of course, ideal for those visiting Chessington World of Adventures and the zoo. The bedrooms are safari-themed and include family rooms with a separate sleeping area for children with their own TV. The Merula Bar and lounge is a great place to relax, and guests can eat in the Langata brasserie. The leisure facilities are extensive and there's ample parking.

Rooms 150 (56 fmly) (6 smoking) **Facilities** Spa STV FTV Wi-fi ⓢ Gym Sauna Steam room Xmas New Year **Conf** Class 150 Board 70 Thtr 300 **Services** Lift Air con **Parking** 120 **Notes** Civ Wed 100

Premier Inn Chessington

BUDGET HOTEL

☎ 0871 527 8228
Leatherhead Rd KT9 2NE
web: www.premierinn.com
dir: M25 junct 9, A243 towards Kingston-upon-Thames for approx 2m. Hotel adjacent to Chessington World of Adventures

High quality, budget accommodation ideal for both families and business travellers. Spacious, en suite bedrooms feature tea and coffee making facilities, and Freeview TV in most hotels. Internet access and Wi-fi are available for a small fee. The adjacent family restaurant features a wide and varied menu. See also the Hotel Groups pages.

Rooms 42

Save on hotels. Book at **theAA.com/hotel**

CHE 123 ENGLAND

CHESTER
Cheshire

Map 15 SJ46

See also Puddington

INSPECTORS' CHOICE

The Chester Grosvenor

★★★★★ ◉◉◉◉ HOTEL

☎ 01244 324024
Eastgate CH1 1LT
e-mail: hotel@chestergrosvenor.com
dir: A56 follow signs for city centre hotels. On
Eastgate St next to the Eastgate clock

Located within the Roman walls of the city, this
Grade II listed, half-timbered building is the
essence of Englishness. Furnished with fine fabrics
and queen or king-size beds, the suites and
bedrooms are of the highest standard, each
designed with guest comfort as a priority. The
eating options are the art deco La Brasserie, a
bustling venue awarded 2 AA Rosettes, the Arkle
Bar and Lounge for morning coffee, light lunches,
afternoon tea and drinks plus the fine dining
restaurant 'Simon Radley at The Chester Grosvenor'
which offers creative cuisine with flair and style,
and awarded 4 AA Rosettes. The hotel has a luxury
spa and small fitness centre, and complimentary
undercover parking is available to guests in an
adjacent car park.

Rooms 80 (7 fmly) ⟨ **S** £230-£276; **D** £230-£276*
Facilities Spa STV FTV Wi-fi ⟨ HL Gym New Year
Conf Class 120 Board 48 Thtr 250 Del from £265 to
£318* **Services** Lift Air con **Notes** LB ⊗ Closed 25
Dec RS Sun & Mon Civ Wed 250

Rowton Hall Country House Hotel & Spa

★★★★ 81% ◉ HOTEL

☎ 01244 335262
Whitchurch Rd, Rowton CH3 6AD
e-mail: reception@rowtonhallhotelandspa.co.uk
web: www.rowtonhallhotel.co.uk
dir: M56 junct 12, A56 to Chester. At rdbt left onto
A41 towards Whitchurch. Approx 1m, follow hotel
signs

This delightful Georgian manor house, set in mature
grounds, retains many original features such as a
superb carved staircase and several eye-catching
fireplaces. Bedrooms vary in size but all have been
stylishly fitted and have impressive en suites. Public
areas include a smart leisure centre, extensive
function facilities and a striking restaurant that
serves imaginative dishes.

Rooms 37 (4 fmly) (8 GF) ⟨ **S** £85-£185; **D** £85-£500
Facilities Spa STV FTV Wi-fi ⟨ Gym Sauna
Steam room Xmas New Year **Conf** Class 48 Board 50
Thtr 170 **Parking** 200 **Notes** LB Civ Wed 170

Grosvenor Pulford Hotel & Spa

★★★★ 77% ◉ HOTEL

☎ 01244 570560
Wrexham Rd, Pulford CH4 9DG
e-mail: reservations@grosvenorpulfordhotel.co.uk
web: www.grosvenorpulfordhotel.co.uk
dir: M53, A55 at junct signed A483 Chester/Wrexham
& North Wales. Left onto B5445, hotel 2m on right

Set in a rural location, this modern, stylish hotel
features a magnificent spa with a large Roman-style
swimming pool. Among the range of bedrooms are
several executive suites and others that have spiral
staircases leading to the bedroom sections. A smart
brasserie restaurant and bar provide a wide range of
imaginative dishes in a relaxed atmosphere.

Rooms 73 (10 fmly) (21 GF) (6 smoking) ⟨
S £95-£200; **D** £140-£210 (incl. bkfst)*
Facilities Spa STV FTV Wi-fi ⟨ HL ⟨ Gym Steam
room Sauna Xmas New Year **Conf** Class 100 Board 50
Thtr 200 Del from £120 to £145* **Services** Lift
Parking 200 **Notes** LB Civ Wed 200

Best Western Premier Queen Hotel

★★★★ 77% HOTEL

C

☎ 01244 305000
City Rd CH1 3AH
e-mail: queenhotel@feathers.uk.com
web: www.feathers.uk.com
dir: Follow signs for railway station, hotel opposite

This hotel is ideally located opposite the railway
station and just a couple minutes' walk from the city.
Public areas include a restaurant, small gym, waiting
room bar, separate lounge and Roman-themed
gardens. Bedrooms are generally spacious and reflect
the hotel's Victorian heritage.

Rooms 218 (11 fmly) (12 GF) ⟨ **S** £79-£159;
D £89-£179 **Facilities** STV FTV Wi-fi ⟨ HL Gym Beauty
treatment room Table tennis ♫ Xmas New Year
Conf Class 150 Board 60 Thtr 400 Del from £119 to
£189 **Services** Lift **Parking** 150 **Notes** LB ⊗
Civ Wed 400

Macdonald New Blossoms Hotel

★★★★ 74% HOTEL

☎ 01244 323186 & 0844 8799113
St John St CH1 1HL
e-mail: events.blossoms@macdonald-hotels.co.uk
web: www.macdonaldhotels.co.uk/blossoms
dir: M53 junct 12 follow city centre signs for
Eastgate, through pedestrian zone, hotel on left

Ideally located to explore the historic city of Chester
this is a modern and contemporary hotel. Bedrooms
range from executive to feature four-poster rooms,
with many retaining the charm of the original
Victorian building. A stylish brasserie restaurant and
bar offer an informal dining experience.

Rooms 67 (1 fmly) **Facilities** Wi-fi Xmas New Year
Conf Class 50 Board 40 Thtr 90 **Services** Lift
Notes ⊗

CHESTER *continued*

Mercure Chester East
★★★★ 74% HOTEL

☎ 0844 815 9001
Whitchurch Rd, Christleton CH3 5QL
e-mail: gm.mercurechestereast@jupiterhotels.co.uk
web: www.jupiterhotels.co.uk
dir: A41 (Whitchurch) hotel on right in 200mtrs

This smart, modern hotel is located just a short drive
from the city centre; with extensive meeting and
function facilities, a well-equipped leisure club and
ample parking, it is a popular conference venue.
Bedrooms vary in size and style but all are well
equipped for both business and leisure guests. Food
is served in the airy restaurant and also in the large
open-plan bar lounge.

Rooms 126 (6 fmly) (58 GF) **D** £55-£179*
Facilities STV Wi-fi ♨ ☜ Gym Xmas New Year
Conf Class 80 Board 60 Thtr 230 Del from £106 to
£145* **Services** Lift **Parking** 160 **Notes** LB ⊗
Civ Wed 180

Best Western Westminster Hotel
★★★ 81% HOTEL

☎ 01244 317341
City Rd CH1 3AF
e-mail: westminsterhotel@feathers.uk.com
web: www.feathers.uk.com
dir: A56, 3m to city centre, left signed rail station.
Hotel opposite station, on right

Situated close to the railway station and city centre,
the Westminster is an established hotel. It has an
attractive Tudor-style exterior, while bedrooms are
brightly decorated with a modern theme; family rooms
are available. There is a choice of bars and lounges,
and the dining room serves a good range of dishes.

Rooms 75 (8 fmly) (6 GF) **Facilities** STV FTV Wi-fi Free
gym facilities at sister hotel **Conf** Class 60 Board 40
Thtr 150 **Services** Lift **Notes** ⊗ Civ Wed 100

Mill Hotel & Spa Destination
★★★ 79% HOTEL

☎ 01244 350035
Milton St CH1 3NF
e-mail: reservations@millhotel.com
web: www.millhotel.com
dir: M53 junct 12, A56, left at 2nd rdbt (A5268), 1st
left, 2nd left

This hotel is a stylish conversion of an old corn mill,
and enjoys an idyllic canalside location near to the
inner ring road and close to the city centre. The
bedrooms come in a variety of styles, and public
rooms are spacious and comfortable. There are
several dining options, and meals are often served on
a broad-beam boat that cruises Chester's canal
system, to and from the hotel. A well-equipped leisure
centre is also provided.

Rooms 128 (49 annexe) (57 fmly) 🏋 **Facilities** Spa
STV FTV Wi-fi ☜ supervised Gym Aerobic studio
Hairdresser Sauna Steam room Kinesis studio 🎵
Xmas New Year **Conf** Class 27 Board 28 Thtr 40
Services Lift **Parking** 120 **Notes** ⊗

Holiday Inn Chester South
★★★ 75% HOTEL

☎ 0871 942 9019 & 01244 688770
Wrexham Rd CH4 9DL
e-mail: reservations-chester@ihg.com
web: www.holidayinn.co.uk
dir: Near Wrexham junct on A483

Located close to the A55 and opposite the Park & Ride
for the city centre, this hotel offers spacious and
comfortable accommodation. Meals can be taken in
the attractive bar or in the restaurant. There is also a
well-equipped leisure club for residents, and
extensive conference facilities are available.

Rooms 143 (21 fmly) (71 GF) **Facilities** STV FTV Wi-fi
☜ supervised Gym Xmas New Year **Conf** Class 70
Board 70 Thtr 80 **Services** Air con **Parking** 150
Notes ⊗ Civ Wed 50

Brookside Hotel
★★★ 72% HOTEL

☎ 01244 381943 & 390898
Brook Ln CH2 2AN
e-mail: info@brookside-hotel.co.uk
web: www.brookside-hotel.co.uk
dir: M53 junct 12, A56 towards Chester, A41. 0.5m
left signed Newton (Plas Newton Ln). 0.5m right into
Brook Ln. Hotel 0.5m. Or from Chester inner ring road
follow A5116/Ellesmere Port/Hospital signs (keep in
right lane to take right fork). Immediately left. At
mini-rdbt 2nd right

This hotel is conveniently located in a residential area
just north of the city centre. The attractive public
areas consist of a foyer lounge, a small bar and a
split-level restaurant. The homely bedrooms are
thoughtfully furnished and some feature four-poster
beds.

Rooms 26 (9 fmly) (4 GF) **Facilities** Wi-fi
Conf Class 20 Board 12 **Parking** 20 **Notes** ⊗ Closed
20 Dec-3 Jan

Save on hotels. Book at **theAA.com/hotel**

CHE 125 ENGLAND

Holiday Inn Express at Chester Racecourse

BUDGET HOTEL

☎ 0870 9904065 & 01244 327900
The Racecourse, New Crane St CH1 2LY
e-mail: hotel@chester-races.com
web: www.hiexpress.com/exchesterrac
dir: M53, A483 (Wrexham). Follow ring road & signs for A548. Right into New Crane St. Hotel 0.5m on left at racecourse

A modern hotel ideal for families and business travellers. Fresh and uncomplicated, the spacious rooms include Sky TV, power shower and tea and coffee-making facilities. Continental buffet breakfast is included in the room rate; other meals may be taken at the nearby family pub or restaurant. See also the Hotel Groups pages.

Rooms 97 (66 fmly) (4 GF) **S** £45-£185; **D** £45-£185 (incl. bkfst)* **Conf** Class 30 Board 25 Thtr 20 Del from £90 to £120*

Premier Inn Chester Central (North)

BUDGET HOTEL

☎ 0871 527 8230
76 Liverpool Rd CH2 1AU
web: www.premierinn.com
dir: M53 junct 12, A56. At 2nd rdbt right signed A41 to Chester Zoo. At 1st lights left into Heath Rd, leads into Mill Ln. Under small rail bridge. Hotel at end on right

High quality, budget accommodation ideal for both families and business travellers. Spacious, en suite bedrooms feature tea and coffee making facilities, and Freeview TV in most hotels. Internet access and Wi-fi are available for a small fee. The adjacent family restaurant features a wide and varied menu. See also the Hotel Groups pages.

Rooms 31

Premier Inn Chester Central (South East)

BUDGET HOTEL

☎ 0871 527 8232
Caldy Valley Rd, Boughton CH3 5PR
web: www.premierinn.com
dir: M53 junct 12, A56 to Chester. At 1st lights onto A41 (Whitchurch). At 2nd rdbt rd exit into Caldy Valley Rd (Huntington). Hotel on right

Rooms 94

Premier Inn Chester City Centre

BUDGET HOTEL

☎ 0871 527 8234
20-24 City Rd CH1 3AE
web: www.premierinn.com
dir: M53 junct 12, follow A56/Chester City Centre signs. At rdbt 1st exit onto A5268 (St Oswalds Way) follow railway station signs. At Bar's Rdbt 1st exit. Hotel on right

Rooms 120

Oddfellows

◉ RESTAURANT WITH ROOMS

☎ 01244 400001
20 Lower Bridge St CH1 1RS
e-mail: reception@oddfellows.biz

Surrounded by designer shops and only a few minutes' walk from the Chester Rows, old meets new at this stylish Georgian mansion. The upper ground floor comprises a walled garden with ornamental moat, Arabian tents, a roofed patio, a cocktail bar with an excellent wine selection, a bustling brasserie and an Alice in Wonderland tea room. Fine dining, featuring local produce, is skilfully prepared in the brasserie restaurant and a sumptuous 'members' lounge is also available to diners and resident guests. Bedrooms have the wow factor with super beds and every conceivable guest extra. Conference facilities are also available.

Rooms 4

Coach House Restaurant with Rooms

RESTAURANT WITH ROOMS

☎ 01244 251900
29 Northgate St CH1 2HQ
web: www.coachhousechester.co.uk
dir: Telephone for detailed directions

Ideally located in the centre of the city, this restaurant with rooms has been appointed to provide high standards of comfort and good facilities. Its sumptuous bedrooms have a wealth of thoughtful extras, and imaginative food is available in the bistro-style restaurant or in the cosy bar area. A warm welcome is assured.

Rooms 9 (3 fmly)

CHESTERFIELD Map 16 SK37
Derbyshire

Casa Hotel

★★★★ 81% ◉ HOTEL

☎ 01246 245999
Lockoford Ln S41 7JB
e-mail: enquiries@casahotels.co.uk
web: www.casahotels.co.uk
dir: M1 junct 29 to A617 Chesterfield/A61 Sheffield, 1st exit at rdbt, hotel on left

A luxurious hotel with a contemporary Spanish theme throughout. The stylish bedrooms feature air conditioning, Hypnos beds and bathrooms with rainshowers. Some also have jacuzzi baths and two have balconies with hot tubs. Cocina Restaurant offers appealing menus featuring ingredients from the hotel's own organic farm. The conference and events facilities are excellent and complimentary Wi-fi is offered.

Rooms 100 (6 fmly) 🛏 **S** £85-£140; **D** fr £85 (incl. bkfst)* **Facilities** STV FTV Wi-fi ♨ Gym Xmas New Year **Conf** Class 140 Board 50 Thtr 280 Del from £140 to £165* **Services** Lift Air con **Parking** 200 **Notes** LB ⊗ Civ Wed 280

Ringwood Hall Hotel

THE INDEPENDENTS
HOTEL ASSOCIATION

★★★ 86% HOTEL

☎ 01246 280077
Brimington S43 1DQ
e-mail: reception@ringwoodhallhotel.com
web: www.ringwoodhallhotel.com
dir: M1 junct 30, A619 to Chesterfield through Staveley. Hotel on left

A beautifully presented Georgian manor house set in 29 acres of peaceful grounds, between the M1 and Chesterfield. The stylish bedrooms include 'Feature Rooms' and three apartments within the grounds. Public areas include comfortable lounges, the Markham Bar and a Cocktail Lounge. The health and fitness club has a pool, sauna, steam room and gym.

Rooms 74 (10 annexe) (32 fmly) (32 GF) 🛏 **S** £70-£98; **D** £85-£128 (incl. bkfst) **Facilities** FTV Wi-fi ♨ Gym Steam room Sauna Xmas **Conf** Class 80 Board 60 Thtr 250 Del from £95 to £120.84 **Parking** 150 **Notes** LB Civ Wed 250

C

CHESTERFIELD *continued*

Sandpiper Hotel

THE INDEPENDENTS
HOTEL ASSOCIATION

★★★ 68% HOTEL

☎ 01246 450550
Sheffield Rd, Sheepbridge S41 9EH
e-mail: sue@sandpiperhotel.co.uk
web: www.sandpiperhotel.co.uk
dir: M1 junct 29, A617 to Chesterfield then A61 to
Sheffield. 1st exit take Dronfield/Unstone sign. Hotel
0.5m on left

Conveniently situated for both the A61 and M1 and
providing a good touring base, being just three miles
from Chesterfield, this modern hotel offers
comfortable and well-furnished bedrooms. Public
areas are situated in a separate building across the
car park, and include a cosy bar and open-plan
restaurant, serving a range of interesting and popular
dishes.

Rooms 46 (11 fmly) (16 GF) **S** £75-£90; (incl. bkfst &
dinner)* **Facilities** FTV Wi-fi ♨ New Year
Conf Class 35 Board 35 Thtr 100 Del from £95 to
£110* **Services** Lift **Parking** 120 **Notes** Civ Wed 90

The Chesterfield Hotel

Ⓤ

☎ 01246 832 9907271141
Malkin St S41 7UA
e-mail: res-chesterfield@metroinns.co.uk

Currently the rating for this establishment is not
confirmed. This may be due to a change of ownership
or because it has only recently joined the AA rating
scheme. For further details please see the AA website:
theAA.com

Rooms 73 **S** £25-£85; **D** £30-£105* **Conf** Class 100
Board 56 Thtr 200 Del from £0*

Ibis Chesterfield

ibis

BUDGET HOTEL

☎ 01246 221333
Lordsmill St S41 7RW
e-mail: h3160@accor.com
web: www.ibishotel.com
dir: M1 junct 29/A617 to Chesterfield. 2nd exit at 1st
rdbt. Hotel on right at 2nd rdbt

Modern, budget hotel offering comfortable
accommodation in bright and practical bedrooms.
Breakfast is self-service and dinner is available in
the restaurant. See also the Hotel Groups pages.

Rooms 86 (21 fmly) (8 GF) **Conf** Board 12 Thtr 25

Premier Inn Chesterfield North

Premier Inn

BUDGET HOTEL

☎ 0871 527 8238
Tapton Lock Hill, off Rotherway S41 7NJ
web: www.premierinn.com
dir: Adjacent to Tesco, at A61 & A619 rdbt, 1m N of
city centre

High quality, budget accommodation ideal for both
families and business travellers. Spacious, en suite
bedrooms feature tea and coffee making facilities,
and Freeview TV in most hotels. Internet access and
Wi-fi are available for a small fee. The adjacent
family restaurant features a wide and varied menu.
See also the Hotel Groups pages.

Rooms 60

Premier Inn Chesterfield West

BUDGET HOTEL

☎ 0871 527 8240
Baslow Rd, Eastmoor S42 7DA
web: www.premierinn.com
dir: M1 junct 29, A617. At next rdbt 2nd exit. At next
rdbt 1st exit into Markham Rd. At next rdbt 2nd exit
into Wheatbridge Rd, left into Chatsworth Rd. 2.5m to
hotel

Rooms 23

CHICHESTER   Map 5 SU80
West Sussex

The Goodwood Hotel

★★★★ 81% ◉◉ HOTEL

☎ 01243 775537
PO18 0QB
e-mail: reservations@goodwood.com
web: www.goodwood.com

(For full entry see Goodwood)

The Millstream Hotel & Restaurant

★★★ 85% ◉◉ HOTEL

☎ 01243 573234
Bosham Ln PO18 8HL
e-mail: info@millstreamhotel.com
web: www.millstreamhotel.com

(For full entry see Bosham)

Crouchers Country Hotel & Restaurant

★★★ 81% ◉◉ HOTEL

☎ 01243 784995
Birdham Rd PO20 7EH
e-mail: crouchers@btconnect.com
dir: From A27 (Chichester bypass) onto A286 towards
West Wittering, 2m, hotel on left between Chichester
Marina & Dell Quay

This friendly, family-run hotel, situated in open
countryside, is just a short drive from the harbour.
The stylish and well-equipped bedrooms are situated
in a separate barn, coach house and stable block,
and include four-poster rooms and rooms with patios
that overlook the fields. The modern oak-beamed
restaurant, with country views, serves award-winning
cuisine.

Rooms 26 (23 annexe) (2 fmly) (15 GF) **S** £90-£108;
D £114-£165 (incl. bkfst) **Facilities** STV FTV Wi-fi
Xmas New Year **Conf** Class 80 Board 50 Thtr 80
Del from £126.50 to £144 **Parking** 80 **Notes** LB
Civ Wed 70

The Ship Hotel

★★★ 74% HOTEL

☎ 01243 778000
57 North St PO19 1NH
e-mail: enquiries@theshiphotel.net
dir: From A27, onto inner ring road to Northgate. At
Northgate rdbt left into North St, hotel on left

This well-presented Grade II listed, Georgian property
occupies a prime position at the top of North Street.
The stylish bedrooms have flat-screen TVs, Egyptian
cotton linen and high-speed Wi-fi access. The bar and
restaurant are contemporary venues for enjoying
meals and refreshments which are served all day. The
hotel is just a few minutes' away is the famous
Festival Theatre, and Goodwood, for motorsport and
horse racing, is also close by.

Rooms 36 (2 fmly) **S** fr £87.50; **D** £110-£135 (incl.
bkfst)* **Facilities** FTV Wi-fi ♨ Xmas New Year

Save on hotels. Book at **theAA.com/hotel**

CHE – CHI 127 ENGLAND

C

Conf Class 50 Board 30 Thtr 50 **Del** from £145 to £175* **Services** Lift **Parking** 35 **Notes** LB ⊗ Civ Wed 70

Premier Inn Chichester

BUDGET HOTEL

☎ 0871 527 8242
Chichester Gate Leisure Park, Terminus Rd PO19 8EL
web: www.premierinn.com
dir: A27 towards city centre. Follow Terminus Road Industrial Estate signs. Left at 1st lights, left at next lights into Chichester Gate Leisure Park. Hotel on right

High quality, budget accommodation ideal for both families and business travellers. Spacious, en suite bedrooms feature tea and coffee making facilities, and Freeview TV in most hotels. Internet access and Wi-fi are available for a small fee. The adjacent family restaurant features a wide and varied menu. See also the Hotel Groups pages.

Rooms 83

CHILDER THORNTON Map 15 SJ37
Cheshire

Brook Meadow

★★★ 74% HOTEL

OXFORD
HOTELS & INNS

☎ 0151 339 9350
Health Ln CH66 7NS
e-mail: reservations.brookmeadow@ohiml.com
web: www.oxfordhotelsandinns.com
dir: M53 junct 5, A41, right onto A550, 2nd right into Heath Ln

This delightful country hotel, set in its own lovely gardens, is within easy reach of Liverpool, Chester, the M53 and M56. Bedrooms are tastefully decorated and well equipped; the bathrooms have spa baths, and there is a comfortable lounge. The dining room has a conservatory which overlooks the grounds. Two function suites are available.

Rooms 25 (7 fmly) (7 GF) **Facilities** FTV Wi-fi Xmas New Year **Conf** Class 60 Board 60 Thtr 180 **Services** Lift Air con **Parking** 80 **Notes** ⊗ Civ Wed 160

Premier Inn Wirral (Childer Thornton)

BUDGET HOTEL

☎ 0871 527 9174
New Chester Rd CH66 1QW
web: www.premierinn.com
dir: M53 junct 5, A41 towards Chester. Hotel on right (same entrance as Burleydam Garden Centre)

High quality, budget accommodation ideal for both families and business travellers. Spacious, en suite bedrooms feature tea and coffee making facilities, and Freeview TV in most hotels. Internet access and Wi-fi are available for a small fee. The adjacent family restaurant features a wide and varied menu. See also the Hotel Groups pages.

Rooms 31

CHIPPENHAM Map 4 ST97
Wiltshire

Best Western Plus Angel Hotel

★★★ 80% HOTEL

☎ 01249 652615
Market Place SN15 3HD
e-mail: reception@angelhotelchippenham.co.uk
web: www.angelhotelchippenham.co.uk
dir: Follow tourist signs for Bowood House. Under railway arch, follow 'Borough Parade Parking' signs. Hotel adjacent to car park

Several impressive buildings combine to make a smart and comfortable hotel. The well-equipped bedrooms vary from those in the main house where character is the key, to the smart executive-style, courtyard rooms. The lounge and restaurant are bright and modern, and offer an imaginative carte and an all-day menu.

Rooms 50 (35 annexe) (3 fmly) (12 GF) **Facilities** STV FTV Wi-fi 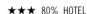 Gym **Conf** Class 50 Board 50 Thtr 100 **Parking** 50

Stanton Manor Hotel

★★★ 79% HOTEL

☎ 01666 837552
SN14 6DQ
e-mail: reception@stantonmanor.co.uk
web: www.stantonmanor.co.uk

(For full entry see Stanton St Quintin)

Premier Inn Chippenham

BUDGET HOTEL

☎ 0871 527 8244
Cepen Park, West Cepen Way SN14 6UZ
web: www.premierinn.com
dir: M4 junct 17, A350 towards Chippenham. Hotel at 1st main rdbt

High quality, budget accommodation ideal for both families and business travellers. Spacious, en suite bedrooms feature tea and coffee making facilities, and Freeview TV in most hotels. Internet access and Wi-fi are available for a small fee. The adjacent family restaurant features a wide and varied menu. See also the Hotel Groups pages.

Rooms 79

CHIPPING CAMPDEN Map 10 SP13
Gloucestershire

Three Ways House

★★★ 82% ⍟ HOTEL

☎ 01386 438429
Mickleton GL55 6SB
e-mail: reception@puddingclub.com
web: www.threewayshousehotel.com
dir: In Mickleton centre, on B4632 (Stratford-upon-Avon to Broadway road)

Built in 1870, this charming hotel has welcomed guests for over 100 years and is home to the world famous Pudding Club, formed in 1985 to promote traditional English puddings. Individuality is a hallmark here, as reflected in a number of the bedrooms that have been designed around to a pudding theme. Public areas are stylish and include the air-conditioned restaurant, lounges and meeting rooms.

Rooms 48 (7 fmly) (14 GF) ⍟ **S** £80-£120; **D** £145-£235 (incl. bkfst)* **Facilities** FTV Wi-fi ♫ Xmas New Year **Conf** Class 40 Board 35 Thtr 100 **Del** from £145 to £185* **Services** Lift **Parking** 37 **Notes** LB Civ Wed 100

CHIPPING CAMPDEN *continued*

Noel Arms Hotel

★★★ 78% HOTEL

☎ 01386 840317
High St GL55 6AT
e-mail: reception@noelarmshotel.com
web: www.noelarmshotel.com
dir: Exit A44 onto B4081 to Chipping Campden, 1st right down hill into town. Hotel on right

This historic 14th-century hotel has a wealth of character and charm, and retains some of its original features. Bedrooms are very individual in style, and all have high levels of comfort and interesting interior design. Such distinctiveness is also evident throughout the public areas, which include the popular bar, conservatory lounge and attractive restaurant.

Rooms 28 (1 fmly) (8 GF) **Facilities** Wi-fi Use of spa at sister hotel (charged) Xmas New Year
Conf Class 40 Board 40 Thtr 80 **Parking** 28
Notes Civ Wed 100

The Kings

◉◉ RESTAURANT WITH ROOMS

☎ 01386 840256 & 841056
The Square GL55 6AW
e-mail: info@kingscampden.co.uk
dir: In centre of town square

Located in the centre of this delightful Cotswold town, The Kings effortlessly blends a relaxed and friendly welcome with efficient service. Bedrooms and bathrooms come in a range of shapes and sizes but all are appointed to high levels of quality and comfort. Dining options, whether in the main restaurant or the comfortable bar area, include a tempting menu to suit all tastes, from light salads and pasta to meat and fish dishes.

Rooms 19 (5 annexe) (3 fmly)

CHIPPING NORTON   Map 10 SP32
Oxfordshire

Crowne Plaza Heythrop Park - Oxford

CROWNE PLAZA
HOTELS & RESORTS

[U]

☎ 01608 673333
Heythrop Park Resort, Enstone OX7 5UE
e-mail: info@heythroppark.co.uk
dir: From Woodstock take A44 towards Chipping Norton. Hotel on right. Telephone for detailed directions

Currently the rating for this establishment is not confirmed. This may be due to a change of ownership or because it has only recently joined the AA rating scheme. For further details please see the AA website: theAA.com

Rooms 197 (56 fmly) (9 GF) **Facilities** Spa STV Wi-fi ⓦ ⓦ ♪ 18 Putt green Fishing ⓦ Gym Xmas New Year **Conf** Class 280 Board 100 Thtr 450 **Services** Lift Air con **Parking** 350 **Notes** ⊗ Civ Wed 350

Wild Thyme Restaurant with Rooms

◉◉ RESTAURANT WITH ROOMS

☎ 01608 645060
10 New St OX7 5LJ
e-mail: enquiries@wildthymerestaurant.co.uk
dir: On A44 in town centre off market square

Located in the bustling Cotswold market town of Chipping Norton, this restaurant with rooms offers three en suite bedrooms that are individually designed, well equipped and have many thoughtful extras. The restaurant serves exciting modern British food along with relaxed and friendly service.

Rooms 3

CHORLEY   Map 15 SD51
Lancashire

Premier Inn Chorley North

BUDGET HOTEL

☎ 0871 527 8246
Malthouse Farm, Moss Ln, Whittle-le-Woods PR6 8AB
web: www.premierinn.com
dir: M61 junct 8 onto A674 (Wheelton), 400yds on left into Moss Ln

High quality, budget accommodation ideal for both families and business travellers. Spacious, en suite bedrooms feature tea and coffee making facilities, and Freeview TV in most hotels. Internet access and Wi-fi are available for a small fee. The adjacent family restaurant features a wide and varied menu. See also the Hotel Groups pages.

Rooms 81

Premier Inn Chorley South

BUDGET HOTEL

☎ 0871 527 8248
Bolton Rd PR7 4AB
web: www.premierinn.com
dir: From N: M61 junct 8, A6 to Chorley. From S: M6 junct 27 follow Standish signs. Left onto A5106 to Chorley, A6 towards Preston. Hotel 0.5m on right

Rooms 29

CHRISTCHURCH   Map 5 SZ19
Dorset

Captain's Club Hotel and Spa

★★★★ 81% ◉◉ HOTEL

☎ 01202 475111
Wick Ferry, Wick Ln BH23 1HU
e-mail: enquiries@captainsclubhotel.com
web: www.captainsclubhotel.com
dir: B3073 to Christchurch. On Fountain rdbt take 5th exit (Sopers Ln) 2nd left (St Margarets Ave) 1st right onto Wick Ln

Situated in the heart of the town on the banks of the River Stour at Christchurch Quay, and only ten minutes from Bournemouth. All bedrooms, including the suites and apartments have views overlooking the river. Guests can relax in the hydrotherapy pool, enjoy a spa treatment or enjoy the cuisine in Tides Restaurant.

Rooms 29 (12 fmly) ⓦ **Facilities** Spa STV FTV Wi-fi ⓦ Hydrotherapy pool Sauna Dry flotation ♪ Xmas New Year **Conf** Class 72 Board 64 Thtr 140 **Del** £195 **Services** Lift Air con **Parking** 41 **Notes** Civ Wed 100

Christchurch Harbour Hotel

★★★★ 78% ◉◉ HOTEL

☎ 01202 483434
95 Mudeford BH23 3NT
e-mail: christchurch@harbourhotels.co.uk
web: www.christchurch-harbour-hotel.co.uk
dir: On A35 to Christchurch onto A337 to Highcliffe. Right at rdbt, hotel 1.5m on left

Delightfully situated on the side of Mudeford Quay close to sandy beaches and conveniently located for Bournemouth Airport and the BIC, this hotel boasts an impressive spa and leisure facility. The bedrooms are particularly well appointed and stylishly finished; many have excellent views and some have balconies. Guests can eat in the award-winning Harbour Restaurant, or the waterside Rhodes South.

Rooms 64 (2 fmly) (14 GF) ⓦ **S** £155-£180; **D** £170-£195 (incl. bkfst)* **Facilities** Spa FTV Wi-fi ⓦ ⓦ Gym Steam room Sauna Exercise classes

Hydrotherapy pool ♫ Xmas New Year **Conf** Class 20 Board 30 Thtr 100 Del from £165 to £210* **Services** Lift **Parking** 55 **Notes** ⊗ Civ Wed 100

Premier Inn Christchurch East

BUDGET HOTEL

☎ 0871 527 8250
Somerford Rd BH23 3QG
web: www.premierinn.com
dir: In Christchurch from A35 & B3059 rdbt junct take B3059 (Somerford Rd)

High quality, budget accommodation ideal for both families and business travellers. Spacious, en suite bedrooms feature tea and coffee making facilities, and Freeview TV in most hotels. Internet access and Wi-fi are available for a small fee. The adjacent family restaurant features a wide and varied menu. See also the Hotel Groups pages.

Rooms 102

Premier Inn Christchurch West

BUDGET HOTEL

☎ 0871 527 8252
Barrack Rd BH23 2BN
web: www.premierinn.com
dir: From A338 take A3060 towards Christchurch. Left onto A35. Hotel on right

Rooms 41

CHURT　　　　　Map 5 SU83
Surrey

Best Western Frensham Pond Hotel

★★★ 79% HOTEL

☎ 01252 795161
Bacon Ln GU10 2QB
e-mail: info@frenshampondhotel.co.uk
web: www.frenshampondhotel.co.uk
dir: A3 onto A287. 4m left at 'Beware Horses' sign. Hotel 0.25m

This 15th-century house occupies a superb location on the edge of Frensham Pond. The bedrooms are mainly spacious, and the superior, garden annexe rooms have their own patio and air conditioning. The contemporary bar and lounge offers a range of snacks, and the leisure club has good facilities.

Rooms 51 (12 annexe) (14 fmly) (27 GF) **S** £75-£150; **D** £75-£250* **Facilities** STV FTV Wi-fi ⓣ supervised Gym Squash Steam room Sauna Xmas New Year **Conf** Class 45 Board 40 Thtr 120 Del from £110 to £175* **Parking** 120 **Notes** LB ⊗ Civ Wed 130

CIRENCESTER　　　　　Map 5 SP00
Gloucestershire

INSPECTORS' CHOICE

Barnsley House

★★★★ ◉◉ COUNTRY HOUSE HOTEL

☎ 01285 740000
Barnsley GL7 5EE
e-mail: info@barnsleyhouse.com
dir: 4m NE of Cirencester on B4425

This delightful Cotswold country house has been appointed to provide the highest levels of quality, comfort and relaxation. Individually styled bedrooms come in a range of shapes and sizes, from the large character rooms in the main house to the more contemporary-style stable rooms; all rooms have garden views and are packed with guest extras and little luxuries, including plasma TVs in the bathrooms. The delightful gardens, originally designed in the late 1950s by previous owner and award-winning gardener Rosemary Verey and her husband, include a fruit and vegetable area from where much produce is used in the delicious cuisine on offer in Potager Restaurant at lunch and dinner. In the grounds is the Garden Spa with treatment rooms, sauna, steam room and an outdoor hydrotherapy pool. The hotel also has a cinema.

Rooms 18 (12 annexe) (10 GF) **Facilities** Spa STV FTV Wi-fi ⓣ ⓢ ⓦ Cinema Bicycles Hydrotherapy pool Relaxation rooms Xmas New Year **Conf** Class 20 Board 18 Thtr 30 **Parking** 30 **Notes** ⊗ Civ Wed 100

The Crown of Crucis

★★★ 77% HOTEL

☎ 01285 851806
Ampney Crucis GL7 5RS
e-mail: reception@thecrownofcrucis.co.uk
web: www.thecrownofcrucis.co.uk
dir: A417 to Fairford, hotel 2.5m on left

This delightful hotel consists of two buildings; one a 16th-century coaching inn, which houses the bar and restaurant, and a more modern bedroom block which surrounds a courtyard. Rooms are attractively appointed and offer modern facilities; the restaurant serves a range of imaginative dishes.

Rooms 25 (2 fmly) (13 GF) (4 smoking) **Facilities** FTV Wi-fi ⓠ **Conf** Class 50 Board 40 Thtr 100 **Parking** 82 **Notes** RS 25-26 Dec Civ Wed 90

Corinium Hotel & Restaurant

★★★ 🅰 SMALL HOTEL

☎ 01285 659711
12 Gloucester St GL7 2DG
e-mail: info@coriniumhotel.co.uk
web: www.coriniumhotel.co.uk
dir: From A417/A419/A429 towards Cirencester. A435 at rdbt. After 500mtrs turn left at lights, then 1st right, car park on left

Rooms 15 (2 fmly) (2 GF) **S** £55-£75; **D** £65-£130 (incl. bkfst) **Facilities** FTV Wi-fi **Conf** Class 30 Board 34 Thtr 70 **Parking** 30 **Notes** LB

CLACTON-ON-SEA　　　　　Map 7 TM11
Essex

Premier Inn Clacton-on-Sea

BUDGET HOTEL

☎ 0871 527 8254
Crown Green Roundabout, Colchester Rd, Trending CO16 9AA
web: www.premierinn.com
dir: A12, A120 towards Harwich. In 4m take A133 to Clacton-on-Sea. Hotel off Weeley Rdbt

High quality, budget accommodation ideal for both families and business travellers. Spacious, en suite bedrooms feature tea and coffee making facilities, and Freeview TV in most hotels. Internet access and Wi-fi are available for a small fee. The adjacent family restaurant features a wide and varied menu. See also the Hotel Groups pages.

Rooms 40

C

C

Ardencote Manor Hotel, Country Club & Spa

★★★★ 74% ◉ HOTEL

☎ 01926 843111
The Cumsey, Lye Green Rd, Claverdon CV35 8LT
e-mail: hotel@ardencote.com
web: www.ardencote.com
dir: Telephone for directions

Originally built as a gentleman's residence around 1860, this hotel is set in 83 acres of landscaped grounds. Public rooms include a choice of lounge areas, a cocktail bar and conservatory breakfast room. Main meals are served in the Lodge Restaurant, a separate building with a light contemporary style, which sits beside a small lake. An extensive range of leisure and conference facilities is provided and bedrooms are smartly decorated and tastefully furnished.

Rooms 110 (10 fmly) (30 GF) ⊁ **S** £80-£110; **D** £100-£165 (incl. bkfst) **Facilities** Spa STV Wi-fi ◈ ⌇ ♣ 9 ⚑ Putt green ⚐ Gym Squash Sauna Steam room Dance studio Xmas New Year **Conf** Class 70 Board 50 Thtr 175 Del from £135 to £180 **Services** Lift Air con **Parking** 350 **Notes** ⊗ Civ Wed 150

Tudor Farmhouse Hotel & Restaurant

★★★ 79% ◉◉ HOTEL

☎ 01594 833046
High St GL16 8JS
e-mail: info@tudorfarmhousehotel.co.uk
web: www.tudorfarmhousehotel.co.uk
dir: A4136 onto B4228, through Coleford, right into Clearwell, hotel on right just before War Memorial Cross

Dating from the 13th century, this idyllic former farmhouse retains a host of original features including exposed stonework, oak beams, wall panelling and wonderful inglenook fireplaces. Bedrooms have great individuality and style and are located either in the main house or in converted buildings in the grounds. Creative menus offer quality cuisine, served in the intimate, candlelit restaurant.

Rooms 20 (15 annexe) (3 fmly) (8 GF) **Facilities** STV FTV Wi-fi New Year **Conf** Class 20 Board 12 Thtr 30 **Parking** 30 **Notes** Closed 24-27 Dec

The Wyndham Arms Hotel

★★★ 68% ◉ HOTEL

☎ 01594 833666
GL16 8JT
e-mail: nigel@thewyndhamhotel.co.uk
dir: Exit B4228, in village centre on B4231

The history of this charming village inn can be traced back over 600 years. It has exposed stone walls, original beams and an impressive inglenook fireplace in the friendly bar. Most bedrooms are in a modern extension, whilst the other rooms, in the main house, are more traditional in style. A range of dishes is offered in the bar or restaurant.

Rooms 18 (12 annexe) (3 fmly) (6 GF) **Facilities** FTV Wi-fi Xmas **Conf** Class 30 Board 22 Thtr 56 **Parking** 52 **Notes** Closed 1st week Jan Civ Wed 80

Ennerdale Country House Hotel

OXFORD
HOTELS & INNS

★★★ 73% HOTEL

☎ 01946 813907
CA23 3DT
e-mail: reservations.ennerdale@ohiml.com
web: www.oxfordhotelsandinns.com
dir: M6 junct 40 to A66, A5086 for 12m, hotel on left

This fine Grade II listed building lies on the edge of the village and has landscaped gardens. Impressive bedrooms, including split-level suites and four-poster rooms, are richly furnished, smartly decorated and offer a range of facilities. Attractive public areas include a stylish restaurant and an American themed bar which offers a good range of bar meals.

Rooms 30 (2 fmly) (2 GF) **S** £50-£110; **D** £60-£180 (incl. bkfst) **Facilities** FTV Wi-fi Xmas New Year **Conf** Class 60 Board 60 Thtr 120 Del from £110 to £160 **Parking** 40 **Notes** LB Civ Wed 120

The Whitcliffe Hotel

★★★ 70% HOTEL

☎ 0845 833 5362
Prospect Rd BD19 3HD
e-mail: info@thewhitcliffehotel.co.uk
web: www.thewhitcliffehotel.co.uk
dir: M62 junct 26, A638 to Dewsbury, over 1st lights, right into Mount St, to T-junct, right then 1st left

This popular and conveniently located commercial hotel offers comfortably equipped bedrooms. Spacious public areas provide a variety of amenities, including several meeting rooms, The Sportsman's Bar and The Blue Bar.

Rooms 41 (6 annexe) (3 fmly) (7 GF) **Facilities** FTV Wi-fi ♫ **Conf** Class 60 Board 40 Thtr 120 **Parking** 150 **Notes** ⊗ Civ Wed 80

Save on hotels. Book at **theAA.com/hotel**

CLA – CLO 131 ENGLAND

Premier Inn Bradford South

BUDGET HOTEL

☎ 0871 527 8136
Whitehall Rd, Dye House Dr BD19 6HG
web: www.premierinn.com
dir: On A58 at intersection with M62 & M606

High quality, budget accommodation ideal for both families and business travellers. Spacious, en suite bedrooms feature tea and coffee making facilities, and Freeview TV in most hotels. Internet access and Wi-fi are available for a small fee. The adjacent family restaurant features a wide and varied menu. See also the Hotel Groups pages.

Rooms 40

CLEETHORPES	Map 17 TA30
Lincolnshire	

Kingsway Hotel

★★★ 77% HOTEL

☎ 01472 601122
Kingsway DN35 0AE
e-mail: reception@kingsway-hotel.com
web: www.kingsway-hotel.com
dir: Exit A180 at Grimsby, to Cleethorpes seafront. Hotel at Kingsway & Queen Parade junct (A1098)

This seafront hotel has been in the same family for four generations and continues to provide traditional comfort and friendly service. The lounges are comfortable and good food is served in the pleasant dining room. The bedrooms are bright and nicely furnished - most are comfortably proportioned.

Rooms 49 ☝ **S** £79-£92; **D** £83-£107 (incl. bkfst)*
Facilities STV FTV Wi-fi **Conf** Board 18 Thtr 22
Del from £115* **Services** Lift **Parking** 50 **Notes** ⊗ No children 5yrs Closed 25-26 Dec

---

CLIMPING	Map 6 SU90
West Sussex	

Bailiffscourt Hotel & Spa

★★★ ◉◉ HOTEL

☎ 01903 723511
Climping St BN17 5RW
e-mail: bailiffscourt@hshotels.co.uk
web: www.hshotels.co.uk
dir: A259, follow Climping Beach signs. Hotel 0.5m on right

This delightful moated 'medieval manor' dating back only to the 1920s has the appearance of having been in existence for centuries. In fact it was built for Lord Moyne, a member of the Guinness family, who wanted to create an ancient manor house. It became a hotel just over 60 years ago and sits in 30 acres of delightful parkland that leads to the beach. Bedrooms vary from atmospheric feature rooms with log fires, oak beams and four-poster beds to spacious, stylish and contemporary rooms located in the grounds. The Tapestry Restaurant serves award-winning classic European cuisine, and in summer the Courtyard is the place for informal light lunches and afternoon tea. Superb facilities are to be found in the hotel's health spa.

Rooms 39 (30 annexe) (25 fmly) (12 GF) ☝
S £158-£446; **D** £210-£715 (incl. bkfst)*
Facilities Spa STV FTV Wi-fi ⌂ ⊗ ⌁ ☺ ⤿ Gym Sauna Steam room Dance/Fitness studio Yoga/Pilates/Gym inductions Xmas New Year
Conf Class 20 Board 26 Thtr 40 Del from £160 to £260* **Parking** 80 **Notes** LB Civ Wed 75

CLOVELLY	Map 3 SS32
Devon	

Red Lion Hotel

★★ 76% HOTEL

C

☎ 01237 431237
The Quay EX39 5TF
e-mail: redlion@clovelly.co.uk
web: www.clovelly.co.uk
dir: Exit A39 at Clovelly Cross onto B3237. Pass visitor centre, 1st left by white rails to harbour

'Idyllic' is the only word to describe the harbour-side setting of this charming 18th-century inn, with the famous fishing village forming a spectacular backdrop. Bedrooms are stylish and enjoy delightful views. The inn's relaxed atmosphere is conducive to switching off from the pressures of modern life, even when the harbour comes alive with the activities of the local fishermen during the day.

Rooms 17 (6 annexe) (5 fmly) (2 GF) ☝ **S** £85-£90.50;
D £134-£145 (incl. bkfst)* **Facilities** FTV Wi-fi Sea fishing Diving Tennis can be arranged Xmas New Year **Parking** 11 **Notes** LB Civ Wed 70

CLOVELLY continued

New Inn

★★ 72% HOTEL

☎ 01237 431303
High St EX39 5TQ
e-mail: newinn@clovelly.co.uk
web: www.clovelly.co.uk
dir: At Clovelly Cross, exit A39 onto B3237. Follow
down hill for 1.5m. Right at sign 'All vehicles for
Clovelly'

Famed for its cobbled descent to the harbour, this
fascinating fishing village is a traffic-free zone.
Consequently, luggage is conveyed by sledge or
donkey to this much-photographed hotel. Carefully
renovated bedrooms and public areas are smartly
presented with quality, locally-made furnishings.
Meals may be taken in the elegant restaurant or the
popular Upalong bar.

Rooms 8 (2 fmly) **Facilities** FTV Wi-fi Sea fishing
Diving Tennis can be arranged Xmas New Year
Notes Civ Wed 50

CLOWNE
Derbyshire   Map 16 SK47

Hotel Van Dyk

★★★★ 79% SMALL HOTEL

☎ 01246 810219
Worksop Rd S43 4TD
e-mail: marcus@hotelvandyk.co.uk
dir: M1 junct 30, 2nd right towards Worksop, 2nd rdbt
1st exit, 3rd rdbt straight over. Through lights, hotel
100yds on right

A sympathetic renovation has resulted in a small
vibrant boutique-style hotel where staff are always on
hand to offer friendly and welcoming service.
Accommodation is luxurious and equipped with many
thoughtful extras. Bowdens Restaurant offers fine
dining and makes the ideal setting for a memorable
evening; alternatively there's Southgate Grill for those
looking for a more casual eating option.

Rooms 15 (4 fmly) **Facilities** FTV Wi-fi ♫ Xmas New
Year **Conf** Class 50 Board 60 Thtr 200 **Parking** 78
Notes ⊗ Civ Wed 250

COALVILLE
Leicestershire   Map 11 SK41

Hermitage Park Hotel

★★★ 73% HOTEL

☎ 01530 814814
Whitwick Rd LE67 3FA
e-mail: hotel@hermitageparkhotel.co.uk
dir: A511 to outskirts of Coalville. Follow brown
tourist signs around bypass. Into Coalville at
Morrisons supermarket. Hotel on left

There's a relaxed and friendly environment throughout
this modern building which sits within easy access of
major road networks. Bedrooms are contemporary and
well equipped; ground-floor rooms are available.
Open-plan public areas include a lounge bar and
informal dining area.

Rooms 28 (5 fmly) (14 GF) **Facilities** STV Wi-fi ♫
Xmas New Year **Conf** Class 30 Board 30 Thtr 50
Parking 40 **Notes** ⊗ Civ Wed 100

COBHAM
Surrey   Map 6 TQ16

Premier Inn Cobham

BUDGET HOTEL

☎ 0871 527 8256
Portsmouth Rd, Fairmile KT11 1BW
web: www.premierinn.com
dir: M25 junct 10, A3 towards London, A245 towards
Cobham. In Cobham town centre left onto A307
(Portsmouth Rd). Hotel on left

High quality, budget accommodation ideal for both
families and business travellers. Spacious, en suite
bedrooms feature tea and coffee making facilities,
and Freeview TV in most hotels. Internet access and
Wi-fi are available for a small fee. The adjacent
family restaurant features a wide and varied menu.
See also the Hotel Groups pages.

Rooms 48

COCKERMOUTH
Cumbria   Map 18 NY13

The Trout Hotel

★★★★ 78% HOTEL

☎ 01900 823591
Crown St CA13 0EJ
e-mail: enquiries@trouthotel.co.uk
web: www.trouthotel.co.uk
dir: Adjacent to Wordsworth House

Dating back to 1670, this privately owned hotel has
an enviable setting on the banks of the River
Derwent. The well-equipped bedrooms, some
contained in a wing overlooking the river, are
comfortable and mostly spacious. The Terrace Bar &
Bistro, serving food all day, has a sheltered patio
area. There is also a cosy bar, a choice of lounge
areas and an attractive, traditional-style dining room
that offers a good choice of set-price dishes.

Rooms 49 (4 fmly) (15 GF) **Facilities** STV Wi-fi ⊗
Fishing Xmas New Year **Conf** Class 20 Board 20
Thtr 25 Del from £119 to £160* **Parking** 40
Notes Civ Wed 60

Shepherds Hotel

★★★ 75% HOTEL

☎ 0845 459 9770
**Lakeland Sheep & Wool Centre, Egremont Rd
CA13 0QX**
e-mail: info@argyllholidays.com
web: www.shepherdshotel.co.uk
dir: At junct of A66 & A5086 S of Cockermouth,
entrance off A5086, 200mtrs from rdbt

This hotel is modern in style and offers thoughtfully
equipped accommodation. It is well situated for the
northern lakes area and has good road links. The
restaurant, open all day, serves a wide variety of
meals and snacks; the Black Rock dishes are
recommended. Free Wi-fi is available in the
bedrooms.

Rooms 26 (4 fmly) (13 GF) **S** £58-£100; **D** £69-£120
(incl. bkfst)* **Facilities** STV FTV Wi-fi ⊗ Pool table
Small children's play area **Conf** Class 30 Board 30
Thtr 40 Del from £85 to £120* **Services** Lift
Parking 100 **Notes** LB Closed 25-26 Dec & 6-20 Jan

COGGESHALL
Essex   Map 7 TL82

White Hart Hotel

OldEnglish

★★★ 74% HOTEL

☎ 01376 561654
Market End CO6 1NH
e-mail: 6529@greeneking.co.uk
web: www.oldenglish.co.uk
dir: From A12 through Kelvedon & onto B1024 to
Coggeshall

A delightful inn situated in the centre of this bustling
market town. Bedrooms vary in size and style; each
one offers good quality and comfort with extras such
as CD players, fruit and mineral water. The heavily
beamed public areas include a popular bar serving a
varied menu, a large restaurant offering European
style cuisine and a cosy residents' lounge.

Rooms 18 (1 fmly) (18 smoking) **S** £45-£65;
D £55-£85 (incl. bkfst) **Facilities** STV FTV ♫ Xmas
Conf Class 10 Board 22 Thtr 30 **Parking** 47 **Notes** LB

Save on hotels. Book at **theAA.com/hotel**

CLO – COL 133 ENGLAND

COLCHESTER
Essex
Map 13 TL92

Crowne Plaza Resort Colchester - Five Lakes

★★★★ 75% HOTEL

☎ 01621 868888
Colchester Rd CM9 8HX
e-mail: enquiries@cpcolchester.co.uk
web: www.cpcolchester.co.uk

(For full entry see Tolleshunt Knights)

Best Western Marks Tey Hotel

★★★★ 70% HOTEL

☎ 01206 210001
London Rd, Marks Tey CO6 1DU
e-mail: info@marksteyhotel.co.uk
web: www.marksteyhotel.co.uk
dir: Off A12/A120 junct signed Marks Tey/Stansted. At rdbt follow Stanway signs. Follow over A12, at next rdbt take 1st exit. Hotel on left

A purpose-built hotel situated just off the A12 on the outskirts of Colchester. Public rooms include a brasserie restaurant, a choice of lounges, a bar and a conservatory. Bedrooms come in a variety of styles; each one is smartly furnished and equipped with modern facilities. The hotel also has conference and leisure facilities.

Rooms 110 (57 GF) Facilities FTV Wi-fi ✇ ⓢ supervised ⌇ Gym Steam room Beauty treatments Sauna Xmas New Year Conf Class 100 Board 60 Thtr 200 Services Lift Parking 200 Notes ⊗ Civ Wed 160

Stoke by Nayland Hotel, Golf & Spa

★★★ 82% HOTEL

☎ 01206 262836
Keepers Ln, Leavenheath CO6 4PZ
e-mail: sales@stokebynayland.com
web: www.stokebynaylandclub.co.uk
dir: Exit A134 at Leavenheath onto B1068, hotel 0.75m on right

This hotel is situated on the edge of Dedham Vale, an Area of Outstanding Natural Beauty, in 300 acres of undulating countryside with lakes and two golf courses. The spacious bedrooms are attractively decorated and equipped with modern facilities,

including ISDN lines. Free Wi-fi is available throughout. Public rooms include the Spikes bar, a conservatory, a lounge, a smart restaurant, conference and banqueting suites. The superb Peake Spa and Fitness Centre offers extensive facilities including health and beauty treatments.

Rooms 80 (4 fmly) (26 GF) S £50-£130; D £60-£140* Facilities Spa STV FTV Wi-fi ⓢ supervised ⌇ 36 Putt green Fishing Gym Squash Driving range Snooker tables ♫ New Year Conf Class 300 Board 60 Thtr 450 Services Lift Parking 335 Notes ⊗ Civ Wed 200

The North Hill Hotel

★★★ 81% HOTEL

☎ 01206 574001
51 North Hill CO1 1PY
e-mail: info@northhillhotel.com
dir: Follow signs for town centre. Up North Hill, hotel on right

This hotel is situated in the centre of this historic town. The contemporary open-plan public areas include a small lounge bar and the Green Room restaurant. The smartly appointed bedrooms are modern and well equipped with large flat-screen TVs and many thoughtful touches.

Rooms 17 (3 fmly) (1 GF) ⟋ S fr £64.50; D fr £89.50 (incl. bkfst) Facilities FTV Wi-fi Xmas New Year Conf Class 25 Board 20 Thtr 30 Del from £130 Notes ⊗

Holiday Inn Colchester

★★★ 81% HOTEL

☎ 0871 942 9020
Abbotts Ln, Eight Ash Green CO6 3QL
web: www.hicolchester.co.uk
dir: Exit A12 at junct with A1124, follow Halstead signs. 0.25m, hotel at rdbt on left

This hotel is situated three miles from Colchester and is ideally located just off the A12 in a quiet village setting. All bedrooms are air conditioned and have high-speed internet access. Trader's bar and grill offers a relaxed and informal environment; a range of conference rooms can cater for meetings and weddings.

Rooms 109 (25 fmly) (54 GF) Facilities Spa STV Wi-fi ✇ ⓢ supervised Gym Health club Xmas New Year Conf Class 60 Board 50 Thtr 120 Services Air con Parking 130 Notes ⊗ Civ Wed 100

Best Western The Rose & Crown Hotel

★★★ 80% HOTEL

☎ 01206 866677
East St CO1 2TZ
e-mail: info@rose-and-crown.com
web: www.rose-and-crown.com
dir: From A12 follow Rollerworld signs, hotel by level crossing

This delightful 14th-century coaching inn is situated close to the shops and is full of charm and character. Public areas feature a wealth of exposed beams and timbered walls, and includes the contemporary East St Grill. Although the bedrooms vary in size, all are stylishly decorated and equipped with many thoughtful extras suitable for both business and leisure guests; luxury executive rooms are available.

Rooms 39 (3 fmly) (12 GF) Facilities Wi-fi Conf Class 50 Board 45 Thtr 100 Services Lift Parking 50 Notes ⊗ Civ Wed 80

The George Hotel

OXFORD
HOTELS & INNS

★★★ 75% HOTEL

☎ 01206 578494
116 High St CO1 1TD
e-mail: reservations.thegeorgehotel@ohiml.com
web: www.oxfordhotelsandinns.com
dir: In town centre, 200yds from Town Hall

Ideally situated in the centre of town, this 500-year-old establishment has much to offer. The medieval cellar has, preserved behind glass, evidence of the Roman road than once ran through this town. The individually decorated bedrooms are equipped with a range of amenities. There's a popular lounge in which to relax and enjoy good food and real ales. The Bubbles Wine Bar offers an alternative to the traditional lounge.

Rooms 47 (7 fmly) Facilities FTV Wi-fi Conf Class 40 Board 34 Thtr 70 Parking 50 Notes ⊗

COLCHESTER continued

Holiday Inn Express Colchester

BUDGET HOTEL

☎ 01206 321510
Birchwood Rd CO7 6HX
dir: Exit A12 just after Shell garage, take exit signed Langham & Dedham

A modern hotel ideal for families and business travellers. Fresh and uncomplicated, the spacious rooms include Sky TV, power shower and tea and coffee-making facilities. Continental buffet breakfast is included in the room rate; other meals may be taken at the nearby family pub or restaurant. See also the Hotel Groups pages.

Rooms 101 (93 fmly) (46 GF) (6 smoking) 🐾
S £39-£139; **D** £39-£139 (incl. bkfst)* **Conf** Class 10 Board 10 Thtr 10

Premier Inn Colchester (A12)

BUDGET HOTEL

☎ 0871 527 8260
Ipswich Rd CO4 9WP
web: www.premierinn.com
dir: From A12 exit at Colchester Nrth/A1232 junct off towards Colchester. Hotel on right, 200yds from rdbt. (NB for Sat Nav use CO4 9TD)

High quality, budget accommodation ideal for both families and business travellers. Spacious, en suite bedrooms feature tea and coffee making facilities, and Freeview TV in most hotels. Internet access and Wi-fi are available for a small fee. The adjacent family restaurant features a wide and varied menu. See also the Hotel Groups pages.

Rooms 60

Premier Inn Colchester Central

BUDGET HOTEL

☎ 0871 527 8258
Cowdray Av CO1 1UT
web: www.premierinn.com
dir: From Ipswich A12 junct 29. At rdbt onto A1232 (Ipswich road). At 2nd rdbt 2nd exit onto A133 (Cowdray Ave). Hotel approx 0.5m on right

Rooms 20

Bells Hotel & The Forest of Dean Golf Club

★★ 72% HOTEL

☎ 01594 832583
Lords Hill GL16 8BE
e-mail: enquiries@bells-hotel.co.uk
dir: 0.25m from Coleford. Off B4228

Set in its own grounds, with an 18-hole golf course, this purpose-built establishment offers a range of facilities. Bedrooms vary in style and space, and a number are on the ground floor. There is a small gym, and a comfortable bar and lounge which is available until late. The hotel's club house, just yards away, has a bar with all-day meals and snacks, a restaurant, a games/TV room and conference and function rooms.

Rooms 53 (12 fmly) (36 GF) (5 smoking) 🐾
D £69-£89 (incl. bkfst) **Facilities** FTV Wi-fi ⅃ 18 Putt green Bowling green Short mat bowling room 🎵 Xmas New Year **Conf** Class 250 Board 100 Thtr 350 Del from £75 to £110 **Parking** 100 **Notes** LB ⊗ Civ Wed 150

Lucknam Park Hotel & Spa

★★★★★ ◉◉◉

COUNTRY HOUSE HOTEL

☎ 01225 742777
SN14 8AZ
e-mail: reservations@lucknampark.co.uk
web: www.lucknampark.co.uk
dir: M4 junct 17, A350 towards Chippenham, then A420 towards Bristol for 3m. At Ford left to Colerne, 3m, right at x-rds, entrance on right

Guests on arrival at this Palladian mansion may well experience a sense of the theatrical as they drive along a magnificent mile-long avenue of beech and lime trees. Surrounded by 500 acres of parkland and beautiful gardens, this fine hotel

---

offers a wealth of choices ranging from enjoying pampering treatments to taking vigorous exercise. Elegant bedrooms and suites are split between the main building and adjacent courtyard. Dining options range from the informal Pavilion Restaurant, to the formal, and very accomplished, main restaurant.

Lucknam Park Hotel & Spa

Rooms 42 (18 annexe) (16 GF) **S** £330-£1115;
D £330-£1115* **Facilities** Spa STV FTV Wi-fi ⅄ ☒ ☺ ⅃ Gym Cross country course Mountain bikes Equestrian centre Five-a-side football Xmas New Year **Conf** Class 24 Board 24 Thtr 60 **Parking** 70 **Notes** ⊗ Civ Wed 110

See advert on opposite page

Grimstock Country House Hotel

★★★ 71% COUNTRY HOUSE HOTEL

☎ 01675 462121
Gilson Rd, Gilson B46 1LJ
e-mail: enquiries@grimstockhotel.co.uk
web: www.grimstockhotel.co.uk
dir: Exit A446 at rdbt onto B4117 to Gilson, hotel 100yds on right

This privately owned hotel is convenient for Birmingham International Airport and the NEC, and benefits from a peaceful rural setting. Bedrooms are spacious and comfortable. Public rooms include two restaurants, a wood-panelled bar, good conference facilities and a gym featuring the latest cardiovascular equipment.

Rooms 44 (1 fmly) (13 GF) **S** £60-£95; **D** £70-£125 (incl. bkfst)* **Facilities** STV FTV Wi-fi ⅄ Gym Xmas New Year **Conf** Class 60 Board 50 Thtr 100 Del from £125 to £150* **Parking** 100 **Notes** LB Civ Wed 100

C

COLYFORD
Devon   Map 4 SY29

Swallows Eaves Hotel

★★ 85% SMALL HOTEL

☎ 01297 553184
Swan Hill Rd EX24 6QJ
e-mail: info@swallowseaves.co.uk
web: www.swallowseaves.co.uk
dir: On A3052 between Lyme Regis & Sidmouth, in village centre, opposite post office store

Close to the Devon and Dorset border, this intimate and welcoming hotel is ideally located for exploring this beautiful area. The relaxed atmosphere is matched with attentive service. Comfortable bedrooms come complete with Egyptian cotton bedding and large fluffy towels. Local produce features on the menu which is offered in the stylish Reeds restaurant.

Rooms 7 (1 GF) ❀ **S** £68-£80; **D** £76-£116 (incl. bkfst)* **Facilities** FTV Wi-fi Xmas **Conf** Thtr 20 **Parking** 18 **Notes** LB ⊗ No children 14yrs

---

CONSETT
Co Durham   Map 19 NZ15

Best Western Derwent Manor

OXFORD
HOTELS & INNS

★★★ 75% HOTEL

☎ 01207 592000
Allensford DH8 9BB
e-mail: reservations.derwentmanor@ohiml.com
web: www.oxfordhotelsandinns.com
dir: On A68

This hotel, built in the style of a manor house, is set in open grounds overlooking the River Derwent. Spacious bedrooms, including a number of suites, are comfortably equipped. A popular wedding venue, there are also extensive conference facilities and an impressive leisure suite. The Grouse & Claret bar serves a wide range of drinks and light meals, and Guinevere's restaurant offers the fine dining option.

Rooms 48 (29 fmly) (26 GF) **Facilities** STV FTV Wi-fi ⑧ supervised Gym Xmas New Year **Conf** Class 200 Board 60 Thtr 300 **Services** Lift **Parking** 100 **Notes** Civ Wed 300

COPTHORNE

See Gatwick Airport

CORBY
Northamptonshire   Map 11 SP88

Holiday Inn Corby - Kettering A43

Holiday Inn

★★★ 74% HOTEL

☎ 01536 401020
Geddington Rd NN18 8ET
e-mail: paulnoble@hicorby.com
web: www.hicorby.com
dir: M1 junct 19, A14 towards Kettering. Exit at junct 7 towards Corby. Follow Stamford & Corby East, A43. At end of road left through Geddington. After Eurohub rdbt turn left at next lights

Situated just one hour from three major airports and close to major motorway networks this establishment proves a good destination for both the business and leisure traveller. The comfortable bedrooms are well equipped and include free Wi-fi. The facilities include a 15-metre pool, steam room, sauna and fully equipped gym.

Rooms 105 (4 fmly) (9 GF) **Facilities** Spa STV FTV Wi-fi ⊗ ⑧ Gym Sauna Steam room Xmas New Year **Conf** Class 70 Board 44 Thtr 250 **Services** Lift Air con **Parking** 250 **Notes** Civ Wed 200

Premier Inn Corby

Premier Inn

BUDGET HOTEL

☎ 0871 527 8264
1 Little Colliers Field NN18 8TJ
web: www.premierinn.com
dir: M1 junct 19, A14 E'bound. Exit at junct 7, left at rdbt onto A43. At next rdbt left onto A6003. Hotel at next rdbt (NB for Sat Nav use NN18 9EX)

High quality, budget accommodation ideal for both families and business travellers. Spacious, en suite bedrooms feature tea and coffee making facilities, and Freeview TV in most hotels. Internet access and Wi-fi are available for a small fee. The adjacent family restaurant features a wide and varied menu. See also the Hotel Groups pages.

Rooms 56

CORFE CASTLE
Dorset   Map 4 SY98

Mortons House Hotel

★★★ 86% ◉◉ HOTEL

☎ 01929 480988
49 East St BH20 5EE
e-mail: stay@mortonshouse.co.uk
web: www.mortonshouse.co.uk
dir: On A351 between Wareham & Swanage

Set in delightful gardens and grounds with excellent views of Corfe Castle, this impressive building dates back to Tudor times. The oak-panelled drawing room has a roaring log fire in cooler months and an interesting range of enjoyable cuisine is available in the well-appointed dining room. Bedrooms, many with views of the castle, are comfortable and well equipped.

Rooms 21 (7 annexe) (2 fmly) (7 GF) ❀ **S** £80-£120; **D** £135-£160 (incl. bkfst)* **Facilities** FTV Wi-fi HL Xmas New Year **Conf** Class 45 Board 20 Thtr 45 Del from £130 to £160* **Parking** 40 **Notes** LB ⊗ Civ Wed 60

CORLEY MOTORWAY SERVICE AREA (M6)
Warwickshire   Map 10 SP38

Days Inn Corley - NEC - M6

Welcome Break

BUDGET HOTEL

☎ 01676 543800 & 540111
Junction 3-4, M6 North, Corley CV7 8NR
e-mail: corley.hotel@welcomebreak.co.uk
dir: On M6 between juncts 3 & 4 N'bound

This modern building offers accommodation in smart, spacious and well-equipped bedrooms, suitable for families and business travellers, and all with en suite bathrooms. Continental breakfast is available and other refreshments may be taken at the nearby family restaurant. See also the Hotel Groups pages.

Rooms 50 (13 fmly) (24 GF) (8 smoking)

Save on hotels. Book at **theAA.com/hotel**

COL – COV 137 ENGLAND

Tillmouth Park Country House Hotel

★★★ 86% ◉ COUNTRY HOUSE HOTEL

☎ 01890 882255
TD12 4UU
e-mail: reception@tillmouthpark.f9.co.uk
web: www.tillmouthpark.co.uk
dir: Exit A1(M) at East Ord rdbt at Berwick-upon-Tweed. Take A698 signed Cornhill & Coldstream. Hotel 9m on left

An imposing mansion set in landscaped grounds by the River Till. Gracious public rooms include a stunning galleried lounge with a drawing room adjacent. The quiet, elegant dining room overlooks the gardens, whilst lunches and early dinners are available in the bistro. Bedrooms retain much traditional character and include several magnificent master rooms.

Rooms 14 (2 annexe) (2 fmly) (2 GF) (4 smoking)
S £79; **D** £160-£235 (incl. bkfst)* **Facilities** FTV Wi-fi Game shooting Fishing New Year **Conf** Class 20 Board 20 Thtr 50 Del from £195* **Parking** 50 **Notes** LB Closed 3 Jan-1 Apr Civ Wed 50

INSPECTORS' CHOICE

Corse Lawn House Hotel

★★★ ◉◉ HOTEL

☎ 01452 780771
GL19 4LZ
e-mail: enquiries@corselawn.com
web: www.corselawn.com
dir: On B4211 5m SW of Tewkesbury

This gracious Grade II listed Queen Anne house, in 12-acre grounds, has been home to the Hine family for 34 years. Aided by an enthusiastic and committed team, the family continues to preside over all aspects of the hotel, creating a wonderfully relaxed environment. Bedrooms offer a reassuring mix of comfort and quality, and include four-poster rooms. In both The Restaurant and The Bistro the

impressive cuisine is based on excellent produce, much of it locally sourced.

Rooms 19 (2 fmly) (5 GF) ⟡ **S** £65-£100; **D** £120-£160 (incl. bkfst)* **Facilities** STV FTV Wi-fi ⟡ ⟡ ⟡ ⟡ Badminton Table tennis New Year **Conf** Class 30 Board 25 Thtr 50 Del from £140 to £160* **Parking** 62 **Notes** LB Closed 24-26 Dec Civ Wed 70

Guyers House Hotel

★★★ 82% ◉◉ HOTEL

☎ 01249 713399
Pickwick SN13 0PS
dir: A4 between Pickwick & Corsham

This privately owned hotel retains the charm and ambiance of a country house. The bedrooms are well appointed in keeping with the style of the house, and equipped with all modern amenities. The award-winning restaurant is the ideal place for an intimate dinner or a family gathering; alfresco dining is possible when the weather is favourable. The gardens are a feature and are open to the public on certain days under the National Garden Scheme. The hotel is conveniently located for easy access to Bath.

Rooms 37 (13 GF) ⟡ **S** £80-£95; **D** £116-£130 (incl. bkfst)* **Facilities** FTV Wi-fi ⟡ ⟡ ⟡ Gym **Conf** Class 34 Board 24 Thtr 75 Del from £135 to £148* **Parking** 60 **Notes** ⊗ Closed 30 Dec-3 Jan Civ Wed

The Methuen Arms

◉◉ RESTAURANT WITH ROOMS

☎ 01249 717060
2 High St SN13 0HB
e-mail: info@themethuenarms.com
web: www.themethuenarms.com
dir: M4 junct 17, A350 towards Chippenham, at rdbt take A4 towards Bath. 1m after lights, at next rdbt sharp left into Pickwick Rd, establishment 0.5m on left

This well-established restaurant with rooms in the centre of the thriving town of Corsham has undergone a complete refurb to provide high levels of quality and comfort. The bedrooms are modern and stylish with large comfortable beds and spacious, well-equipped bathrooms. Guests can enjoy a drink in the relaxing bar, a light snack in the day or evening, and should not miss the award-winning, high quality, carefully prepared dishes at dinner.

Rooms 12 (3 fmly)

See also Meriden & Nuneaton

Windmill Village Hotel, Golf & Leisure Club

★★★★ 79% HOTEL

☎ 02476 404040
Birmingham Rd, Allesley CV5 9AL
e-mail: reservations@windmillvillagehotel.co.uk
dir: A45, close to Coventry City Centre

This modern hotel is conveniently located on the outskirts of Coventry and is a short drive from Birmingham and the NEC. Bedrooms are all very attractively presented and most rooms have views over the hotel's challenging golf course. The leisure facilities are first rate and include a very well-equipped gym and a swimming pool. Guests are well catered for with a range of conference facilities including business suites, and free Wi-fi is available throughout the hotel.

Rooms 105 (39 GF) ⟡ **S** £70-£155; **D** £76-£161 (incl. bkfst)* **Facilities** FTV Wi-fi ⟡ ⟡ supervised ℒ 18 Putt green Gym Beauty Treatment Room Xmas New Year **Conf** Class 140 Board 60 Thtr 400 Del from £125 to £165* **Services** Lift **Parking** 400 **Notes** LB Civ Wed 100

Holiday Inn Coventry

★★★ 78% HOTEL

☎ 0871 942 9021 & 024 7658 7420
Hinckley Rd CV2 2HP
e-mail: reservations-coventrym6@ihg.com
web: www.holidayinn.co.uk
dir: M6 junct 2. Hotel on A4600

Situated close to the city centre and major motorway networks, this hotel offers comfortable and modern accommodation. Facilities include the Spirit Leisure Suite, Traders Restaurant, spacious lounges where food is served all day and extensive conference services.

Rooms 158 (11 fmly) (64 GF) (16 smoking)
S £69-£139; **D** £89-£159 **Facilities** STV Wi-fi HL ⟡ supervised Gym Steam room Sauna Aqua aerobic classes New Year **Conf** Class 120 Board 105 Thtr 250 **Services** Lift Air con **Parking** 246 **Notes** LB Civ Wed 200

C

COVENTRY *continued*

Novotel Coventry

★★★ 77% HOTEL

☎ 024 7636 5000
Wilsons Ln CV6 6HL
e-mail: h0506@accor-hotels.com
web: www.novotel.com
dir: M6 junct 3. Follow signs for B4113 towards
Longford & Bedworth. 3rd exit on large rdbt

A modern hotel convenient for Birmingham, Coventry
and the motorway network, offering spacious, well-
equipped accommodation. The bright brasserie has
extended dining hours, and alternatively there is an
extensive room-service menu. Family rooms and a
play area make this a child-friendly hotel, and there
is also a selection of meeting rooms.

Rooms 98 (25 GF) ⚬ Facilities STV Wi-fi
Conf Class 100 Board 40 Thtr 200 Services Lift
Parking 120 Notes Civ Wed 50

Quality Hotel

★★★ 64% HOTEL

☎ 024 7640 3835
Birmingham Rd, Allesley CV5 9BA
e-mail: enquiries@qualityhotelcoventry.co.uk
dir: A45 onto A4114 towards Allesley. Follow brown
signs for hotel

Conveniently situated on the A45 close to Birmingham
Airport and the National Exhibition Centre. The
bedrooms offer good comfort and space for both the
business traveller or leisure guest. There is a sauna
and steam room on site.

Rooms 80 (1 fmly) (21 GF) (27 smoking)
Facilities STV FTV Wi-fi ↻ Sauna Steam room Xmas
New Year Conf Class 40 Board 30 Thtr 120
Parking 150 Notes Civ Wed 75

Ibis Coventry Centre

BUDGET HOTEL

☎ 024 7625 0500
Mile Ln, St John's Ringway CV1 2LN
e-mail: H2793@accor.com
web: www.ibishotel.com
dir: A45, A4114 signed Jaguar Assembly Plant. At
inner ring road towards ring road S. Exit junct 5 for
Mile Lane

Modern, budget hotel offering comfortable
accommodation in bright and practical bedrooms.
Breakfast is self-service and dinner is available in
the restaurant. See also the Hotel Groups pages.

Rooms 89 (5 fmly) (25 GF) S £29-£125; D £29-£125*

Ibis Coventry South

BUDGET HOTEL

☎ 024 7663 9922
Abbey Rd, Whitley CV3 4BJ
e-mail: H2094@accor.com
web: www.ibishotel.com
dir: Signed from A46/A423 rdbt. Take A423 towards
A45. Follow signs for Racquets Health Club & Jaguar
Engineering Plant. 1st exit from Jaguar rdbt, hotel at
end of lane by The Racquets

Rooms 51 (51 annexe) (25 GF) Conf Class 20
Board 16 Thtr 20

Premier Inn Coventry
(Binley/A46)

BUDGET HOTEL

☎ 0871 527 8268
Rugby Rd, Binley Woods CV3 2TA
web: www.premierinn.com
dir: M6 junct 2 follow Warwick, A46 & M40 signs.
Follow 'All traffic' signs, under bridge onto A46. Left
at 1st rdbt to Binley. Hotel on right at next rdbt

High quality, budget accommodation ideal for both
families and business travellers. Spacious, en suite
bedrooms feature tea and coffee making facilities,
and Freeview TV in most hotels. Internet access and
Wi-fi are available for a small fee. The adjacent
family restaurant features a wide and varied menu.
See also the Hotel Groups pages.

Rooms 76

Premier Inn Coventry City Centre

BUDGET HOTEL

☎ 0871 527 8272
Belgrade Plaza, Bond St CV1 4AH
web: www.premierinn.com
dir: A4053 (ring road) junct 9, follow Belgrade Plaza
car park signs. Hotel in same complex

Rooms 119

Premier Inn Coventry East (Ansty)

BUDGET HOTEL

☎ 0871 527 8274
Coombe Fields Rd, Ansty CV7 9JP
web: www.premierinn.com
dir: M6 junct 2, B4065 towards Ansty. After village
right onto B4029 signed Brinklow. Right into Coombe
Fields Rd, hotel on right

Rooms 27

Premier Inn Coventry (M6 Jct 2)

BUDGET HOTEL

☎ 0871 527 8266
Gielgud Way, Cross Point Business Park CV2 2SZ
web: www.premierinn.com
dir: M6 junct 2 towards Coventry onto A4600
(Hinckley road). At rdbt 1st exit into Parkway, left at
next rdbt into Olivier Way. At next rdbt straight on into
retail park towards cinema, hotel on right

Rooms 48

Premier Inn Coventry South (A45)

BUDGET HOTEL

☎ 0871 527 8270
Kenpas Highway CV3 6PB
web: www.premierinn.com
dir: M6 junct 2, A46. Follow A45 towards Birmingham

Rooms 37

COWES Map 5 SZ49
Isle of Wight

Best Western New Holmwood Hotel

★★★ 77% HOTEL

☎ 01983 292508
Queens Rd, Egypt Point PO31 8BW
e-mail: reception@newholmwoodhotel.co.uk
dir: From A3020 at Northwood Garage lights, left &
follow to rdbt. 1st left then sharp right into Baring
Rd, 4th left into Egypt Hill. At bottom turn right

Just by the Esplanade, this hotel has an enviable
outlook. Bedrooms are comfortable and very well
equipped, and the light and airy, glass-fronted
restaurant looks out to sea and serves a range of
interesting meals. The sun terrace is delightful in the
summer and there is a small pool area.

Rooms 26 (1 fmly) (9 GF) ⚬ Facilities STV FTV Wi-fi
↻ Xmas New Year Conf Class 60 Board 50 Thtr 100
Del from £112 to £175 Parking 20 Notes Civ Wed 50

CRAMLINGTON Map 21 NZ27
Northumberland

Premier Inn Newcastle Gosforth/Cramlington

BUDGET HOTEL

☎ 0871 527 8788
**Moor Farm Roundabout, Off Front St, Annitsford
NE23 7QA**
web: www.premierinn.com
dir: At rdbt junct of A19 & A189, S of Cramlington

High quality, budget accommodation ideal for both families and business travellers. Spacious, en suite bedrooms feature tea and coffee making facilities, and Freeview TV in most hotels. Internet access and Wi-fi are available for a small fee. The adjacent family restaurant features a wide and varied menu. See also the Hotel Groups pages.

Rooms 40

CRATHORNE
North Yorkshire   Map 19 NZ40

INSPECTORS' CHOICE

Crathorne Hall Hotel   Hand PICKED
HOTELS
BUILT FOR PLEASURE

★★★★ ◉◉ HOTEL

☎ 01642 700398
TS15 0AR
e-mail: crathornehall@handpicked.co.uk
web: www.handpickedhotels.co.uk/crathorne-hall
dir: From A19 take slip road signed Teesside Airport & Kirklevington, right signed Crathorne to hotel

This splendid Edwardian hall sits in its own landscaped grounds and enjoys fine views of the Leven Valley and rolling Cleveland Hills. The impressively equipped bedrooms and the delightful public areas offer sumptuous levels of comfort, with elegant antique furnishings that complement the hotel's architectural style. All bedrooms and suites offer oversize flat-screen TVs and free broadband among their many facilities. The elegant Leven Restaurant is a traditional setting for fine dining; there's also the Drawing Room for lighter food options. Weather permitting, alfresco eating is available on the terrace, and afternoon tea is always popular. Conference and banqueting facilities are available. Hand Picked Hotels – AA Hotel Group of the Year 2012-13.

Rooms 37 (4 fmly) 🐾 **Facilities** STV FTV Wi-fi ↳ ⬆ Jogging track Clay pigeon shooting Xmas **Conf** Class 75 Board 60 Thtr 120 **Services** Lift **Parking** 88 **Notes** ⊗ Civ Wed 90

CRAWLEY
See Gatwick Airport

CREWE
Cheshire   Map 15 SJ75

Crewe Hall   QHOTELS
★★★★ 79% ◉ HOTEL

☎ 01270 253333
Weston Rd CW1 6UZ
e-mail: crewehall@qhotels.co.uk
web: www.qhotels.co.uk
dir: M6 junct 16, A500 to Crewe. Take A5020. 1st exit at next rdbt to Crewe. Hotel 150yds on right

Standing in 500 acres of mature grounds, this historic hall dates back to the 17th century. It retains an elaborate interior with Victorian-style architecture. Bedrooms are spacious, well equipped and comfortable with traditionally styled suites in the main hall and modern rooms in the west wing. Afternoon tea is served in The Sheridan Lounge and The Brasserie Restaurant and Bar is contemporary and has a relaxed atmosphere. The health and beauty spa ensure that the hotel is a popular choice with both corporate and leisure guests.

Rooms 117 (91 annexe) (5 fmly) (35 GF) **Facilities** Spa STV Wi-fi ↳ ⬚ ⬆ Gym Enclosed events field **Conf** Class 172 Board 96 Thtr 364 **Services** Lift **Parking** 500 **Notes** ⊗ Civ Wed 180

Hunters Lodge Hotel
★★★ 78% HOTEL

☎ 01270 539100
Sydney Rd, Sydney CW1 5LU
e-mail: info@hunterslodge.co.uk
web: www.hunterslodge.co.uk
dir: M6 junct 16. 1m from Crewe station, off A534

Dating back to the 18th century, the hotel has been extended and modernised. Accommodation, mainly located in adjacent well-equipped bedroom wings, includes family and four-poster rooms. Imaginative dishes are served in the spacious restaurant, and the popular bar also offers a choice of tempting meals. Service throughout is friendly and efficient.

Rooms 57 (4 fmly) (31 GF) (2 smoking) **Facilities** STV FTV Wi-fi ↳ Gym **Conf** Class 100 Board 80 Thtr 160 **Parking** 240 **Notes** ⊗ RS Sun Civ Wed 130

Premier Inn Crewe Central
BUDGET HOTEL

☎ 0871 527 8276
Weston Rd CW1 6FX
web: www.premierinn.com
dir: M6 junct 16, A500, at rdbt 3rd exit onto A5020 (Old Park Rd). At next rdbt 2nd exit into Western Rd, at next rdbt 3rd exit, hotel on left

High quality, budget accommodation ideal for both families and business travellers. Spacious, en suite bedrooms feature tea and coffee making facilities, and Freeview TV in most hotels. Internet access and Wi-fi are available for a small fee. The adjacent family restaurant features a wide and varied menu. See also the Hotel Groups pages.

Rooms 20

Premier Inn Crewe West
BUDGET HOTEL

☎ 0871 527 8278
Coppenhall Ln, Woolstanwood CW2 8SD
web: www.premierinn.com
dir: At junct of A530 & A532, 9m from M6 junct 16 N'bound

Rooms 42

CRICK
Northamptonshire   Map 11 SP57

Holiday Inn Rugby - Northampton
Holiday Inn

★★★ 72% HOTEL

☎ 0871 942 9059 & 01788 824800
M1 Junction 18 NN6 7XR
e-mail: rugbyhi@ihg.com
web: www.hirugbyhotel.co.uk
dir: 0.5m from M1 junct 18

Situated in pleasant surroundings, located just off the M1, this modern hotel offers well-equipped and comfortable bedrooms. Public areas include the popular Traders restaurant and a comfortable lounge where an all-day menu is available. The Spirit Health Club provides indoor swimming and a good fitness facility.

Rooms 90 (19 fmly) (42 GF) (12 smoking) **Facilities** STV Wi-fi ⬚ Gym New Year **Conf** Class 90 Board 64 Thtr 170 **Services** Lift Air con **Parking** 250 **Notes** Civ Wed

CRICK *continued*

Ibis Rugby

BUDGET HOTEL

☎ 01788 824331
Parklands NN6 7EX
e-mail: H3588@accor.com
web: www.ibishotel.com
dir: M1 junct 18, follow Daventry/Rugby A5 signs. At rdbt 3rd exit signed DIRFT East. Hotel on right

Modern, budget hotel offering comfortable accommodation in bright and practical bedrooms. Breakfast is self-service and dinner is available in the restaurant. See also the Hotel Groups pages.

Rooms 111 (47 fmly) (12 GF) **Conf** Class 25 Board 25 Thtr 30

CRICKLADE   **Map 5 SU09**
Wiltshire

Cricklade House

★★★ 78% HOTEL

☎ 01793 750751
Common Hill SN6 6HA
e-mail: reception@crickladehotel.co.uk
web: www.crickladehotel.co.uk
dir: A419 onto B4040. Left at clock tower. Right at rdbt. Hotel 0.5m up hill on left

A haven of peace and tranquillity with spectacular views, this hotel is set in over 30 acres of beautiful countryside. Bedrooms vary in size and style; there are main building rooms and courtyard rooms - all offer high levels of comfort and quality. Public areas include an elegant lounge, dining room and a Victorian-style conservatory that runs the full length of the building. The extensive leisure facilities include a 9-hole golf course, an indoor pool and a gym.

Cricklade House

Rooms 46 (21 annexe) (2 fmly) (5 GF) **Facilities** STV FTV Wi-fi 🕲 ♪ 9 ♨ 🌳 Gym Aromatherapy Beautician Xmas New Year **Conf** Class 60 Board 30 Thtr 80 **Parking** 100 **Notes** ⊗ Civ Wed 120

See advert on opposite page

CROMER   **Map 13 TG24**
Norfolk

Sea Marge Hotel

★★★ 87% ◉◉ HOTEL

☎ 01263 579579
16 High St, Overstrand NR27 0AB
e-mail: info@mackenziehotels.com
dir: A140 from Norwich then A149 to Cromer, B1159 to Overstrand. Hotel in village centre

An elegant Grade II listed Edwardian mansion perched on the clifftop amidst pretty landscaped gardens which lead down to the beach. Bedrooms are tastefully decorated and thoughtfully equipped; many have superb sea views. Public rooms offer a wide choice of areas in which to relax, including Frazer's restaurant and a smart lounge bar.

Rooms 25 (6 annexe) (6 fmly) (2 GF) 🐾 **S** £95-£150; **D** £150-£182 (incl. bkfst)* **Facilities** FTV Wi-fi 🌱 Xmas New Year **Conf** Class 55 Board 30 Thtr 70 Del from £115 to £140* **Services** Lift **Parking** 50 **Notes** LB

The Cliftonville Hotel

★★★ 77% HOTEL

☎ 01263 512543
Seafront NR27 9AS
e-mail: reservations@cliftonvillehotel.co.uk
web: www.cliftonvillehotel.co.uk
dir: From A149 (coast road), 500yds from town centre, N'bound on clifftop by sunken gardens

An imposing Edwardian hotel situated on the main coast road with stunning views of the sea. Public rooms feature a magnificent staircase, minstrels' gallery, coffee shop, lounge bar, a further residents' lounge, Boltons Bistro and an additional restaurant. The pleasantly decorated bedrooms are generally quite spacious and have lovely sea views.

Rooms 30 (2 fmly) **S** £65-£95; **D** £130-£190 (incl. bkfst)* **Facilities** Wi-fi Xmas New Year **Conf** Class 100 Board 60 Thtr 150 **Services** Lift **Parking** 20

Hotel de Paris

★★ 72% HOTEL

☎ 01263 513141
High St NR27 9HG
e-mail: deparis.cromer@alfatravel.co.uk
dir: Enter Cromer on A140 (Norwich road). Left at lights onto Mount St. At 2nd lights right into Prince of Wales Rd. 2nd right into New St leading into High St

An imposing, traditional-style resort hotel, situated in a prominent position overlooking the pier and beach. The bedrooms are pleasantly decorated and equipped with a good range of useful extras; many rooms have lovely sea views. The spacious public areas include a large lounge bar, restaurant, games room and a further lounge.

Rooms 63 (8 fmly) 🐾 **S** £38-£50; **D** £62-£86 (incl. bkfst)* **Facilities** FTV Games room 🎵 Xmas New Year **Services** Lift **Parking** 14 **Notes** ⊗ Closed Jan-Feb RS Mar, Nov & Dec

C

Cricklade House, Common Hill, Cricklade, Wiltshire, SN6 6HA
Tel: 01793 750751 Fax: 01793 751767
www.crickladehotel.co.uk Email: reception@crickladehotel.co.uk

Cricklade House, formally Cricklade Hotel & Country Club was purchased by Ambienza Hotels in August 2010. This is the latest hotel to hit the portfolio which includes the ultra chic Cotswolds88 Hotel in Painswick, just a 30 minute drive from Cricklade House.

Standing in over 30 acres of peaceful, secluded grounds on the edge of the Cotswolds, Cricklade House offers a traditional, warm and friendly welcome for those in search of tranquility, comfort, good food and wine, with extensive recreational facilities.

This beautiful and dignified country house, built at the turn of the last century, has been tastefully restored and carefully extended. Perhaps the most impressive addition is the magnificent Victorian-style glass conservatory which runs the full length of the original building, making the most of the hotel's elevated position, with wonderful panoramic views over Wiltshire countryside.

CROOKLANDS
Cumbria   Map 18 SD58

Crooklands Hotel

★★★ 78% HOTEL

☎ 015395 67432
LA7 7NW
e-mail: reception@crooklands.com
web: www.crooklands.com
dir: M6 junct 36 onto A65. Left at rdbt. Hotel 1.5m on right past garage

Although only a stone's throw from the M6, this hotel enjoys a peaceful rural location. Housed in a converted 200-year-old farmhouse, the restaurant retains many original features such as the beams and stone walls. Bedrooms are a mix of modern and traditional and vary in size. The hotel is a popular stop-over for both leisure and corporate guests travelling between England and Scotland.

Rooms 30 (3 fmly) (14 GF) **Facilities** FTV Wi-fi New Year **Conf** Class 50 Board 40 Thtr 80 **Services** Lift **Parking** 80 **Notes** ⊗ Closed 24-28 Dec

CROSTHWAITE
Cumbria   Map 18 SD49

Damson Dene Hotel

★★★ 72% HOTEL

☎ 015395 68676
LA8 8JE
e-mail: info@damsondene.co.uk
web: www.bestlakesbreaks.co.uk
dir: M6 junct 36, A590 signed Barrow-in-Furness, 5m right onto A5074. Hotel on right in 5m

A short drive from Lake Windermere, this hotel enjoys a tranquil and scenic setting. Bedrooms include a number with four-poster beds and jacuzzi baths. The spacious restaurant serves a daily-changing menu, with some of the produce coming from the hotel's own kitchen garden. Real fires warm the lounge in the cooler months, and leisure facilities are available.

Rooms 40 (3 annexe) (7 fmly) (9 GF) **S** £79-£100; **D** £118-£160 (incl. bkfst)* **Facilities** Spa Wi-fi ⓒ Gym Beauty salon Xmas New Year **Conf** Class 60 Board 40 Thtr 140 Del from £105 to £145* **Parking** 45 **Notes** LB Civ Wed 120

CROYDON
Greater London   Map 6 TQ36

Croydon Park Hotel

★★★★ 73% HOTEL

☎ 020 8680 9200
7 Altyre Rd CR9 5AA
e-mail: info@croydonparkhotel.com
dir: 3-min walk from East Croydon Station

This hotel is located in the heart of the town centre, a 3-minute walk to East Croydon train station and with easy access to both Gatwick Airport and central London. Bedrooms vary in style, but all are comfortably appointed. The two dining options are Whistlers Bar with a menu available throughout the day, and Oscars Brasserie with a daily buffet and carte menu. Conference and leisure facilities are available.

Rooms 211 (36 fmly) (6 GF) (15 smoking) **Facilities** FTV Wi-fi ⓘ ⓒ supervised Gym Squash Sauna Solarium Xmas New Year **Conf** Class 100 Board 30 Thtr 220 Del from £130 to £160* **Services** Lift Air con **Parking** 91 **Notes** ⊗ Civ Wed 220

Hallmark Hotel Croydon

★★★★ 73% HOTEL

☎ 020 8680 1999
Purley Way CR9 4LT
e-mail:
croydon.reservations@hallmarkhotels.co.uk
dir: Follow A23 & Central London signs. Hotel on left adjacent to Airport House

This hotel (formerly the Aerodrome Hotel) sits in a prime location and offers comfortably appointed bedrooms all with LCD TVs and free Wi-fi throughout. Following a refurbishment programme, public areas are stylish and modern in their design and include a spacious open-plan bar and brasserie. Ideal for both the leisure and corporate market, there are a number of fully-equipped meeting and conference facilities.

Rooms 110 **Conf** Class 60 Board 36 Thtr 170

Selsdon Park Hotel & Golf Club
PH | principal hayley

★★★★ 72% HOTEL

☎ 020 8657 8811
Addington Rd, Sanderstead CR2 8YA
e-mail:
selsdonpark.reception@principal-hayley.com
dir: 3m SE of Croydon, off A2022

Surrounded by 200 acres of mature parkland with it's own 18-hole golf course, this imposing Jacobean mansion is less than 20 minutes from central London. The hotel's impressive range of conference rooms along with the spectacular views of the North Downs countryside, make this a popular venue for both weddings and meetings. The leisure facilities are impressive.

Rooms 199 (19 fmly) (33 GF) **Facilities** Spa STV Wi-fi ⓒ supervised ⓘ supervised ♨ 18 ⓢ Putt green ⛳ Gym Squash Xmas **Conf** Class 250 Board 100 Thtr 350 **Services** Lift **Parking** 300 **Notes** ⊗ Civ Wed 350

Coulsdon Manor Hotel
OXFORD HOTELS & INNS

★★★★ 70% HOTEL

☎ 020 8668 0414
Coulsdon Court Rd, Coulsdon CR5 2LL
e-mail: reservations.coulsdon@ohiml.com
web: www.oxfordhotelsandinns.com
dir: M23/25 junct 7, A23 for 2.5m, B2030 for 1m, left onto Coulsdon Rd, then 0.5m to hotel

This delightful Victorian manor house is peacefully set amidst 140 acres of landscaped parkland, complete with its own professional 18-hole golf course. Bedrooms are spacious and comfortable, whilst public areas include a choice of lounges and an elegant restaurant serving carefully prepared, imaginative food.

Rooms 37 (4 fmly) **S** £55-£130; **D** £65-£150 (incl. bkfst)* **Facilities** STV FTV Wi-fi ♨ 18 ⓢ Putt green Gym Squash Aerobic studio Steam room Sauna Xmas New Year **Conf** Class 90 Board 70 Thtr 180 Del from £95 to £168 **Services** Lift **Parking** 200 **Notes** LB Civ Wed 100

Save on hotels. Book at **theAA.com/hotel**

CRO – CUL 143 ENGLAND

South Park Hotel

★★★ 73% HOTEL

☎ 020 8688 5644
3-5 South Park Hill Rd, South Croydon CR2 7DY
e-mail: reception@southparkhotel.co.uk
web: www.southparkhotel.co.uk
dir: Follow A235 to town centre. At Coombe Rd lights
turn right (A212) towards Addington, 0.5m to rdbt
take 3rd exit into South Park Hill Rd, hotel on left

This intimate hotel has easy access to rail and road
networks and some off-street parking is available.
Attractively decorated bedrooms vary in size and offer
a good range of in-room facilities. Public areas
consist of a bar and lounge with large sofas and an
informal dining area where meals are served.

Rooms 30 (2 fmly) (9 GF) **Facilities** FTV Wi-fi
Conf Class 50 Board 30 Thtr 60 **Parking** 15 **Notes** ⊗

Holiday Inn Express London - Croydon

BUDGET HOTEL

☎ 0208 2531200
1 Priddys Yard, Off Frith Rd CR0 1TS
e-mail: admin@exhicroydon.com
web: www.hiexpress.com/london-croydon
dir: From A235 into Lower Coombe St, at rdbt 1st exit,
at next rdbt 2nd exit onto dual carriageway, right to
Centrale Shopping Centre, under car park, follow to
right, 1st left

A modern hotel ideal for families and business
travellers. Fresh and uncomplicated, the spacious
rooms include Sky TV, power shower and tea and
coffee-making facilities. Continental buffet breakfast
is included in the room rate; other meals may be
taken at the nearby family pub or restaurant. See also
the Hotel Groups pages.

Rooms 156 (62 fmly) (16 smoking) **Conf** Class 30
Board 30 Thtr 60

Premier Inn Croydon South

BUDGET HOTEL

☎ 0871 527 8280
104 Coombe Rd CR0 5RB
web: www.premierinn.com
dir: M25 junct 7, A23 to Purley, A235 to Croydon. Pass
Tree House pub on left. Right at lights onto A212

High quality, budget accommodation ideal for both
families and business travellers. Spacious, en suite
bedrooms feature tea and coffee making facilities,
and Freeview TV in most hotels. Internet access and
Wi-fi are available for a small fee. The adjacent
family restaurant features a wide and varied menu.
See also the Hotel Groups pages.

Rooms 39

Premier Inn Croydon West

BUDGET HOTEL

☎ 0871 527 8282
**The Colonnades Leisure Park, 619 Purley Way
CR0 4RQ**
web: www.premierinn.com
dir: From N: M1, M25, A23 towards Croydon. From S:
M25 junct 7, A23 towards Purley Way, 8m, hotel close
to junct with Waddon Way

Rooms 84

CUCKFIELD Map 6 TQ32
West Sussex

INSPECTORS' CHOICE

Ockenden Manor Hotel & Spa

★★★ ◉◉◉ HOTEL

☎ 01444 416111
Ockenden Ln RH17 5LD
e-mail: reservations@ockenden-manor.com
web: www.hshotels.co.uk
dir: A23 towards Brighton. 4.5m left onto B2115
towards Haywards Heath. Cuckfield 3m. Ockenden
Lane off High St. Hotel at end

This charming 16th-century property enjoys fine
views of the South Downs. The individually
designed bedrooms and suites offer high standards
of accommodation, some with unique historic
features. Public rooms, retaining much original
character, include an elegant sitting room with all
the elements for a relaxing afternoon in front of the
fire. Imaginative, noteworthy cuisine is the
highlight to any stay. The beautiful rooms and
lovely garden make Ockenden a popular wedding
venue. The hotel has a spa, situated in a walled
garden, that offers a pool, hot tub, spa bath, rain
shower, floatation room, gym, sauna, steam room
plus health and beauty treatments.

Rooms 28 (6 annexe) (4 fmly) (4 GF) ⚫
S £113-£205; **D** £190-£395 (incl. bkfst)*
Facilities Spa STV FTV Wi-fi ⓢ ↗ ♨ Gym
Floatation tank Xmas New Year **Conf** Class 20
Board 26 Thtr 50 Del from £240 to £290*
Services Lift **Parking** 98 **Notes** LB ⊗ Civ Wed 150

CULLOMPTON Map 3 ST00
Devon

Padbrook Park

★★★ 78% HOTEL

C

☎ 01884 836100
EX15 1RU
e-mail: info@padbrookpark.co.uk
dir: 1m from M5 junct 28, follow brown signs

This purpose-built hotel is part of a golf and leisure
complex located in the Culm Valley, just one mile
from the M5. Set in 100 acres of parkland with an 18-
hole golf course, Padbrook Park has a friendly, relaxed
atmosphere and a contemporary feel. A variety of
room types is available, including family, interconnecting, superior and deluxe rooms.

Rooms 40 (4 fmly) (11 GF) **S** fr £60; **D** fr £90 (incl.
bkfst)* **Facilities** STV FTV Wi-fi ♨ HL ⌟ 18 Putt green
Fishing Gym 3 rink bowling centre Crazy golf ♫ Xmas
New Year **Conf** Class 150 Board 50 Thtr 200
Del from £95 to £110* **Services** Lift **Parking** 250
Notes LB ⊗ Civ Wed 200

DARLINGTON
Co Durham
Map 19 NZ21

Rockliffe Hall

★★★★★ 86% ◉ ◉ ◉ HOTEL

☎ 01325 729999
Rockliffe Park, Hurworth-on-Tees DL2 2DU
e-mail: enquiries@rockliffehall.com
web: www.rockliffehall.com
dir: A66 towards Darlington, A167, through Hurworth-on-Tees. In Croft-on-Tees left into Hurworth Rd

This impressive hotel enjoys a peaceful setting on a restored 18th-century estate on the banks of the River Tees. Luxurious, spacious bedrooms, contemporary in style, are split between the original old hall, the new hall and Tiplady Lodge. All the eating options are led by award-winning chef Kenny Atkinson - the fine-dining experience in The Orangery, The Clubhouse and The Brasserie. A state-of-the-art spa and championship golf course, with a first-class club house, complete the picture.

Rooms 61 (5 fmly) (17 GF) **S** £140-£460;
D £165-£485 (incl. bkfst)* **Facilities** Spa STV FTV Wi-fi ⓢ ♨ ♪ 18 Putt green Fishing Gym ♫ Xmas New Year **Conf** Class 100 Board 30 Thtr 180 Del from £175 to £195* **Services** Lift **Parking** 200 **Notes** ⊗ Civ Wed 180

See advert on opposite page

Headlam Hall

★★★★ 77% ◉ HOTEL

☎ 01325 730238
Headlam, Gainford DL2 3HA
e-mail: admin@headlamhall.co.uk
web: www.headlamhall.co.uk
dir: 2m N of A67 between Piercebridge & Gainford

This impressive Jacobean hall lies in farmland north-east of Piercebridge and has its own 9-hole golf course. The main house retains many historical features, including flagstone floors and a pillared hall. Bedrooms are well proportioned and traditionally styled; a converted coach house contains the more modern rooms. There are extensive conference facilities, and the hotel is popular as a wedding venue. There is a stunning spa complex with a 14-metre pool, an outdoor hot spa, drench shower, sauna and steam room. There is also a gym with the latest cardio and resistance equipment, and five treatment rooms offering a range of therapies and beauty treatments.

Rooms 39 (22 annexe) (4 fmly) (9 GF) ♠ **S** £95-£130; **D** £120-£155 (incl. bkfst)* **Facilities** Spa STV FTV Wi-fi ⓢ ♨ 9 ♨ Putt green Fishing ♪ Gym New Year **Conf** Class 40 Board 40 Thtr 120 Del from £140* **Services** Lift **Parking** 80 **Notes** LB Closed 24-26 Dec Civ Wed 150

Bannatyne Hotel Darlington

★★★★ 75% HOTEL

☎ 01325 365858
Southend Av DL3 7HZ
e-mail: enquiries.darlingtonhotel@bannatyne.co.uk
dir: From S: A1(M) junct 57, A66(M) signed Darlington. 2nd rdbt 2nd exit into Grange Rd. 3rd left into Southend Ave. From N: A1(M) junct 58, A68 signed Darlington, left at 1st rdbt, 2nd rdbt 2nd exit into Carmel Rd N, into Carmel Rd S. Left at 4th rdbt into Grange Rd, 3rd left

This hotel, with excellent parking, is close to the town centre and provides well-equipped accommodation with Wi-fi in all areas. Public areas include the brasserie-style bar and restaurant, Maxine's, plus good function, conference and wedding facilities. Free use of Bannatyne's Spa and gym (just five minutes away) is also available to guests. Very friendly hospitality is assured from the young and enthusiastic team at this hotel.

Rooms 60 (4 fmly) (11 GF) ♠ **S** £85-£115; **D** £95-£115 (incl. bkfst)* **Facilities** FTV Wi-fi ♨ Xmas New Year **Conf** Class 60 Board 60 Thtr 120 Del from £130 to £150* **Services** Lift **Parking** 50 **Notes** LB ⊗ Civ Wed 120

Best Western Walworth Castle Hotel

★★★ 77% ◉ HOTEL

☎ 01325 485470
Walworth DL2 2LY
e-mail: enquiries@walworthcastle.co.uk
web: www.walworthcastle.co.uk
dir: A1(M) junct 58 follow signs to Corbridge. Left at The Dog pub. Hotel on left after 2m

This 12th-century castle is privately owned and has been tastefully converted. Accommodation is offered in a range of styles, including an impressive suite and more compact rooms in an adjoining wing. Dinner can be taken in the fine dining Hansards Restaurant or the more relaxed Farmer's Bar. This is a popular venue for conferences and weddings.

Rooms 32 (14 annexe) (4 fmly) (8 GF) ♠ **S** £72-£82; **D** £86-£91 (incl. bkfst)* **Facilities** Spa FTV Wi-fi ♨ ♪ Beauty rooms Hair salon Xmas New Year **Conf** Class 60 Board 40 Thtr 120 Del from £125 to £150* **Parking** 100 **Notes** LB ⊗ Civ Wed 100

Save on hotels. Book at **theAA.com/hotel**

DAR 145 **ENGLAND**

Hall Garth Hotel, Golf and Country Club

★★★ 75% HOTEL

☎ 0844 855 9110
Coatham Mundeville DL1 3LU
e-mail: gm@hallgarthdarlignton.co.uk
web: www.hallgarthdarlington.co.uk
dir: A1(M) junct 59, A167 towards Darlington. After 600yds left at top of hill, hotel on right

Peacefully situated in grounds that feature a golf course, this hotel is just a few minutes from the motorway network. The well-equipped bedrooms come in various styles - it's worth asking for one of the trendy, modern rooms. Public rooms include relaxing lounges, a fine-dining restaurant and a separate pub. The extensive leisure and conference facilities are an important focus here.

Rooms 56 (16 annexe) (3 fmly) (1 GF) 🐾
Facilities Spa STV FTV Wi-fi 🚫 supervised ♨ 9 Putt green Gym Steam room Beauty salon Xmas New Year **Conf** Class 160 Board 80 Thtr 250 **Parking** 150 **Notes** Civ Wed 170

Premier Inn Darlington

BUDGET HOTEL

☎ 0871 527 8286
Morton Park Way, Morton Park DL1 4PJ
web: www.premierinn.com
dir: A1(M) junct 57, A66(M), A66 towards Teeside. At 3rd rdbt left onto B6280. Hotel on right. From N: A1(M) junct 57 onto A167, A1150, A66 towards Darlington, right onto B6280. Hotel on right

High quality, budget accommodation ideal for both families and business travellers. Spacious, en suite bedrooms feature tea and coffee making facilities, and Freeview TV in most hotels. Internet access and Wi-fi are available for a small fee. The adjacent family restaurant features a wide and varied menu. See also the Hotel Groups pages.

Rooms 58

Raby Hunt Inn and Restaurant with Rooms

RESTAURANT WITH ROOMS

☎ 01325 374237
Summerhouse DL2 3UD
e-mail: enquiries@rabyhuntrestaurant.co.uk
web: www.rabyhuntrestaurant.co.uk
dir: A1(M) junct 58 onto A68 N, B6275 & B6279

This Grade II listed building, situated in the quiet village of Summerhouse, is a family-owned restaurant with rooms providing well-equipped, stylish and comfortable accommodation. Both bedrooms are en suite and have many thoughtful extras. The comfortable and contemporary restaurant serves modern British and European dishes prepared with flair and creativity.

Rooms 2

DARTFORD
Kent

Map 6 TQ57

D

Rowhill Grange Hotel & Utopia Spa

★★★★ 81% ◉◉ HOTEL

☎ 01322 615136
Wilmington DA2 7QH
e-mail: admin@rowhillgrange.co.uk
web: www.rowhillgrange.co.uk
dir: M25 junct 3 take B2173 to Swanley, then B258 to Hextable

Set in nine acres of mature woodland this hotel enjoys a tranquil setting, yet is accessible to road networks. Bedrooms are stylishly and individually decorated; many have four-poster or sleigh beds. The elegant lounge is popular for afternoon teas, and the leisure and conference facilities are impressive. There is a smart, conservatory restaurant and also a more informal brasserie.

Rooms 38 (8 annexe) (4 fmly) (3 GF) **Facilities** Spa STV FTV Wi-fi 🚫 🏊 Gym Beauty treatment Hair salon Aerobic studio Japanese therapy pool Xmas New Year **Conf** Class 64 Board 34 Thtr 160 **Services** Lift **Parking** 150 **Notes** 🚫 Civ Wed 150

D

DARTFORD *continued*

Campanile Dartford

Campanile

BUDGET HOTEL

☎ 01322 278925
1 Clipper Boulevard West, Crossways Business Park DA2 6QN
e-mail: dartford@campanile.com
web: www.campanile.com
dir: Follow signs for Ferry Terminal from Dartford Bridge

This modern building offers accommodation in smart, well-equipped bedrooms, all with en suite bathrooms. Refreshments may be taken at the informal bistro. See also the Hotel Groups pages.

Rooms 125 (14 fmly) **Conf** Class 30 Board 30 Thtr 40

Holiday Inn Express Dartford Bridge

BUDGET HOTEL

☎ 01322 290333
Dartford Bridge, University Way DA1 5PA
e-mail: gm.dartford@expressholidayinn.co.uk
web: www.hiexpress.com/dartfordbridge
dir: A206 to Erith. Hotel off University Way via signed slip road

A modern hotel ideal for families and business travellers. Fresh and uncomplicated, the spacious rooms include Sky TV, power shower and tea and coffee-making facilities. Continental buffet breakfast is included in the room rate; other meals may be taken at the nearby family pub or restaurant. See also the Hotel Groups pages.

Rooms 126 (34 fmly) **Conf** Board 25 Thtr 35

DARTMOUTH   Map 3 SX85
Devon

The Dart Marina Hotel

★★★★ 80% ◉◉ HOTEL

☎ 01803 832580 & 837120
Sandquay Rd TQ6 9PH
e-mail: reservations@dartmarina.com
web: www.dartmarina.com
dir: A3122 from Totnes to Dartmouth. Follow road which becomes College Way, before Higher Ferry. Hotel sharp left in Sandquay Rd

Boasting a stunning riverside location with its own marina, this is a special place to stay. Bedrooms vary in style, and all have wonderful views; some have private balconies to sit and soak up the atmosphere. The stylish public areas take full advantage of the waterside setting with opportunities to dine alfresco. In addition to the Wildfire Bar & Bistro, the River Restaurant is the venue for accomplished cooking.

Rooms 49 (4 annexe) (4 fmly) (4 GF) ☜ **S** £95-£155; **D** £140-£200 (incl. bkfst)* **Facilities** Spa Wi-fi ◉ Gym Canoeing Sailing Xmas New Year **Services** Lift **Parking** 50 **Notes** LB Civ Wed 40

Royal Castle Hotel

★★★ 81% HOTEL

☎ 01803 833033
11 The Quay TQ6 9PS
e-mail: enquiry@royalcastle.co.uk
web: www.royalcastle.co.uk
dir: In centre of town, overlooking Inner Harbour

At the edge of the harbour, this imposing 17th-century former coaching inn is filled with charm and character. Bedrooms are well equipped and comfortable; many have harbour views. A choice of quiet seating areas is offered in addition to both the traditional and contemporary bars. A variety of eating options is available, including the main restaurant which has lovely views.

Rooms 25 (3 fmly) ☜ **S** £100-£120; **D** £149-£220 (incl. bkfst)* **Facilities** FTV Wi-fi 🎵 Xmas New Year **Conf** Class 30 Board 20 Thtr 50 **Parking** 15 **Notes** LB Civ Wed 80

Stoke Lodge Hotel

★★★ 74% HOTEL

☎ 01803 770523
Stoke Fleming TQ6 0RA
e-mail: mail@stokelodge.co.uk
web: www.stokelodge.co.uk
dir: 2m S A379

This family-run hotel continues to attract returning guests and is set in three acres of gardens and

---

grounds with lovely views across to the sea. A range of leisure facilities is offered including both indoor and outdoor pools, along with a choice of comfortable lounges. Bedrooms are pleasantly appointed. The restaurant offers a choice of menus and an impressive wine list.

Rooms 25 (5 fmly) (7 GF) ☜ **S** £71-£75.50; **D** £99-£129 (incl. bkfst)* **Facilities** FTV Wi-fi ◉ ⚲ ♨ Putt green Table tennis Pool & Snooker tables Sauna Xmas New Year **Conf** Class 60 Board 30 Thtr 80 Del from £100 to £125* **Parking** 50 **Notes** LB

Angélique Rooms

RESTAURANT WITH ROOMS

☎ 01803 839425
51 Victoria Rd TQ6 9RT
e-mail: info@angeliquedartmouth.co.uk
dir: In Dartmouth take one-way system, 1st left at NatWest Bank

This terrace property offers very comfortable, contemporary, stylish accommodation, equipped with numerous extra facilities. Breakfast is a feature, and includes freshly squeezed orange juice; specials such as eggs Benedict and scrambled eggs with smoked salmon should not be missed.

Rooms 7 (2 fmly)

DARWEN   Map 15 SD62
Lancashire

The Whitehall Hotel

★★★ 77% HOTEL

☎ 01254 701595
off Ross St BB3 2JU
e-mail: info@whitehallhotel.uk.com
dir: M61, A666 (Bolton Road) through Egerton. Turn right at Whitehall Park. From N: M65 junct 4 past Darwen town

This privately owned hotel is nestled at the base of the West Pennine Moor close to Bolton and Blackburn. Bedrooms are spacious and are equipped for both business and leisure guests. Public areas include a traditional lounge alongside a very modern dining room where a good range of dishes to suit all tastes is offered. Secure parking available to the front of the hotel.

Rooms 17 (3 fmly) (8 GF) ☜ **S** £40-£55; **D** £70-£140 (incl. bkfst) **Facilities** FTV Wi-fi Xmas New Year **Conf** Class 80 Board 40 Thtr 110 **Parking** 70 **Notes** LB ⊗ Civ Wed 120

Save on hotels. Book at **theAA.com/hotel**

DAR – DEA 147 ENGLAND

D

DAVENTRY
Northamptonshire   Map 11 SP56

INSPECTORS' CHOICE

Fawsley Hall
★★★★ ◎◎ HOTEL

☎ 01327 892000
Fawsley NN11 3BA
e-mail: reservations@fawsleyhall.com
web: www.fawsleyhall.com
dir: A361 S of Daventry, between Badby &
Charwelton, hotel signed (single track lane)

Dating back to the 15th century, this delightful
hotel is peacefully located in beautiful gardens
designed by 'Capability' Brown. Spacious,
individually designed bedrooms and stylish public
areas are beautifully furnished with antique and
period pieces. The different wings of the house -
Tudor, Georgian and Victorian - all have their
distinct identity. For a true sense of the past, why
not stay in the Queen's Suite, where Elizabeth I is
documented to have slept in 1575? Afternoon tea is
served in the impressive Great Hall, and dinner is
available in the award-winning fine-dining
Equilibrium Restaurant. Seating just 16 people, the
intimate restaurant has huge original beams and
stonework, an impressive inglenook fireplace and
candlelit tables dressed in fine white linen. The
other eating option is the more relaxed Bess's
Brasserie. The hotel has its own cinema and The
Grayshot Spa features an ozone pool, treatment
rooms and fitness studio.

Rooms 58 (14 annexe) (2 GF) **S** £185–£190;
D £185–£495 (incl. bkfst)* **Facilities** Spa STV Wi-fi
◎ ♨ ⚘ Gym Health & beauty treatment rooms
Fitness studio 29-seat cinema Xmas New Year
Conf Class 64 Board 40 Thtr 120 **Parking** 140
Notes LB Civ Wed 120

Daventry Court Hotel
★★★★ 72% HOTEL

PUMA HOTELS
COLLECTION

☎ 01327 307000
Sedgemoor Way NN11 0SG
e-mail: daventry@pumahotels.co.uk
web: www.pumahotels.co.uk
dir: M1 junct 16, A45 to Daventry, at 1st rdbt turn
right signed Kilsby/M1(N). Hotel on right in 1m

This modern, striking hotel overlooking Drayton Water
boasts spacious public areas that include a good
range of banqueting, meeting and leisure facilities. It
is a popular venue for conferences. Bedrooms are
suitable for both business and leisure guests.

Rooms 155 (17 fmly) **Facilities** STV Wi-fi ◎
supervised Gym Steam room Health & beauty salon
Xmas New Year **Conf** Class 200 Board 100 Thtr 600
Services Lift **Parking** 350 **Notes** Civ Wed 280

Premier Inn Daventry
BUDGET HOTEL

Premier Inn

☎ 0871 527 8288
High St, Weedon NN7 4PX
web: www.premierinn.com
dir: M1 junct 16, A45 towards Daventry. Through
Upper Heyford & Flore. Hotel on left before Weedon &
A5 junct

High quality, budget accommodation ideal for both
families and business travellers. Spacious, en suite
bedrooms feature tea and coffee making facilities,
and Freeview TV in most hotels. Internet access and
Wi-fi are available for a small fee. The adjacent
family restaurant features a wide and varied menu.
See also the Hotel Groups pages.

Rooms 47

DAWLISH
Devon   Map 3 SX97

Langstone Cliff Hotel
★★★ 78% HOTEL

THE INDEPENDENTS
HOTEL ASSOCIATION

☎ 01626 868000
Dawlish Warren EX7 0NA
e-mail: reception@langstone-hotel.co.uk
web: www.langstone-hotel.co.uk
dir: 1.5m NE off A379 (Exeter road) to Dawlish Warren

A family owned and run hotel, this hotel offers a
range of leisure, conference and function facilities.
Bedrooms, many with sea views and balconies, are
spacious, comfortable and well equipped. The hotel
has a number of attractive lounges and a well-
stocked bar. Dinner is served, often carvery style, in
the restaurant.

Rooms 66 (4 annexe) (52 fmly) (10 GF) ✒
S £81–£118; **D** £136–£228 (incl. bkfst)* **Facilities** STV
FTV Wi-fi ◎ ⚘ ♨ ⚘ Gym Table tennis Golf practice
area Hair & beauty salon Therapy room Ballroom ♫
Xmas New Year **Conf** Class 200 Board 80 Thtr 400
Del £112.50* **Services** Lift **Parking** 200 **Notes** LB
Civ Wed 400

DEAL
Kent   Map 7 TR35

Dunkerleys Hotel & Restaurant
★★★ 80% ◎◎ HOTEL

☎ 01304 375016
19 Beach St CT14 7AH
e-mail: info@dunkerleys.co.uk
web: www.dunkerleys.co.uk
dir: From M20 or M2 follow signs for A258 Deal. Hotel
close to Pier

This hotel is centrally located and on the seafront.
Bedrooms are furnished to a high standard with a
good range of amenities. The restaurant and bar offer
a comfortable and attractive environment in which to
relax and to enjoy the cuisine that makes the best use
of local ingredients. Service throughout is friendly
and attentive.

Rooms 16 (2 fmly) **S** £80–£110; **D** £120–£160 (incl.
bkfst)* **Facilities** FTV Wi-fi Xmas New Year **Notes** LB
⊗ RS Sun eve & Mon

D

DEDDINGTON
Oxfordshire
Map 11 SP43

Deddington Arms

★★★ 77% ⊛ HOTEL

☎ 01869 338364
Horsefair OX15 0SH
e-mail: deddarms@oxfordshire-hotels.co.uk
web: www.oxfordshire-hotels.co.uk
dir: From S: M40 junct 10/A43. 1st rdbt left to Aynho
(B4100) & left to Deddington (B4031). From N: M40
junct 11 to hospital & Adderbury on A4260, then to
Deddington

This charming and friendly old inn is conveniently
located off the market square. The well-equipped
bedrooms are comfortably appointed and situated
either in the main building or a purpose-built
courtyard wing. The bar is full of character, and the
delightful restaurant enjoys a well-deserved
reputation locally.

Rooms 27 (4 fmly) (10 GF) (2 smoking) **S** £59-£150;
D £69-£150 (incl. bkfst) **Facilities** STV Wi-fi Xmas
New Year **Conf** Class 20 Board 25 Thtr 40 **Parking** 36
Notes LB ⊗

DEDHAM
Essex
Map 13 TM03

INSPECTORS' CHOICE

Maison Talbooth

★★★ ⊛⊛
COUNTRY HOUSE HOTEL

☎ 01206 322367
Stratford Rd CO7 6HN
e-mail: maison@milsomhotels.co.uk
dir: A12 towards Ipswich, 1st turn signed Dedham,
follow to left bend, turn right. Hotel 1m on right

Warm hospitality and quality service are to be
expected at this Victorian country-house hotel,
which is situated in a peaceful rural location
amidst pretty landscaped grounds overlooking the
Stour River Valley. Public areas include a
comfortable drawing room where guests may take
afternoon tea or snacks. Residents are chauffeured
to the popular Le Talbooth Restaurant just a mile

away for dinner. The spacious bedrooms are
individually decorated and tastefully furnished with
lovely co-ordinated fabrics and many thoughtful
touches.

Maison Talbooth

Rooms 12 (1 fmly) (5 GF) **S** £170-£295;
D £210-£420 (incl. bkfst)* **Facilities** Spa STV Wi-fi
⤳ ⊛ ⤳ Xmas **Conf** Class 20 Board 16 Thtr 30
Parking 40 **Notes** LB Civ Wed 50

milsoms

★★★ 81% ⊛ SMALL HOTEL

☎ 01206 322795
Stratford Rd CO7 6HW
e-mail: milsoms@milsomhotels.com
web: www.milsomhotels.com
dir: 6m N of Colchester off A12, follow Stratford St
Mary/Dedham signs. Turn right over A12, hotel on left

Situated in the Dedham Vale, an Area of Outstanding
Natural Beauty, this is the perfect base to explore the
countryside on the Essex/Suffolk border. This
establishment is styled along the lines of a
contemporary 'gastro bar' combining good food
served in an informal atmosphere, with stylish and
well-appointed accommodation.

Rooms 15 (3 fmly) (4 GF) **S** £100-£185;
D £120-£185* **Facilities** STV Wi-fi Use of spa at
nearby sister hotel ⤳ Xmas **Conf** Board 24
Del from £186 to £192* **Parking** 90 **Notes** LB

DELPH
Greater Manchester
Map 16 SD90

The Saddleworth Hotel

★★★★ 83% ⊛⊛⊛
COUNTRY HOUSE HOTEL

☎ 01457 871888
Huddersfield Rd OL3 5LX
e-mail: enquiries@thesaddleworthhotel.co.uk
web: www.thesaddleworthhotel.co.uk
dir: M62 junct 21, A640 towards Huddersfield. At
Junction Inn take A6052 towards Delph; at White Lion
left onto unclassified road; in 0.5m left on A62
towards Huddersfield. Hotel 0.5m on right

Situated in nine acres of landscaped gardens and
woodlands in the Castleshaw Valley, this lovingly
restored 17th-century building, once a coaching
station, has stunning views. The hotel offers comfort
and opulence together with a team of staff who
provide delightful customer care. Antique pieces have
been acquired from far and wide, and no expense has
been spared to provide guests with the latest up-to-
date facilities. The restaurant, with black table linen
and crystal glassware, offers an award-winning,
fashionably understated, modern European menu.

Rooms 16 (8 annexe) (4 fmly) (4 GF) **S** £90-£110;
D £170-£350 (incl. bkfst)* **Facilities** FTV Wi-fi ⤳ ⤳
Xmas New Year **Conf** Class 40 Board 40 Thtr 150
Parking 140 **Notes** LB ⊗ Civ Wed 250

DERBY
Derbyshire
Map 11 SK33

See also Morley

Hallmark Derby

★★★★ 79% HOTEL

☎ 01332 345894
Midland Rd DE1 2SQ
e-mail: derby.reservations@hallmarkhotels.co.uk
web: www.hallmarkhotels.co.uk
dir: Opposite rail station

This early Victorian hotel situated opposite Derby
Midland Station provides very comfortable
accommodation. The executive rooms are ideal for
business travellers as they are equipped with writing
desks and high speed internet access. Public rooms
include a comfortable lounge and a popular
restaurant. Service is skilled, attentive and friendly.
There is also a walled garden and private parking.

Rooms 100 **S** £69-£145; **D** £79-£155* **Facilities** Wi-fi
⤳ ⤳ **Conf** Class 50 Board 35 Thtr 150
Del from £129* **Services** Lift **Parking** 70 **Notes** LB ⊗
Civ Wed 150

Save on hotels. Book at theAA.com/hotel

DED – DER 149 ENGLAND

Menzies Mickleover Court

★★★★ 77% HOTEL

☎ 01332 521234
Etwall Rd, Mickleover DE3 0XX
e-mail: mickleovercourt@menzieshotels.co.uk
web: www.menzieshotels.co.uk
dir: A50 towards Derby, exit at junct 5. A516 towards Derby, take exit signed Mickleover

Located close to Derby, this modern hotel is well suited to both the conference and leisure markets. Bedrooms are spacious, air conditioned, well equipped and include some smart executive rooms and suites. The well presented leisure facilities are amongst the best in the region.

Rooms 99 (20 fmly) (5 smoking) **Facilities** STV FTV Wi-fi ⓢ Gym Beauty salon Steam room Xmas New Year **Conf** Class 80 Board 40 Thtr 225 **Services** Lift Air con **Parking** 270 **Notes** Civ Wed 150

Breadsall Priory, A Marriott Hotel & Country Club

Marriott
HOTELS & RESORTS

★★★★ 75% ® COUNTRY HOUSE HOTEL

☎ 01332 832235
Moor Rd, Morley DE7 6DL
web: www.marriottbreadsallpriory.co.uk

(For full entry see Breadsall)

Holiday Inn Derby Riverlights

Holiday Inn

★★★★ 73% HOTEL

☎ 01332 412644 & 412533
Derby Riverlights, Mortledge DE1 2AY
e-mail: reservations@hiderby.co.uk
dir: M1 junct 25, A52 to Derby. Follow signs to City Centre/Westfield Shopping Centre. Hotel on Morledge on right by bus station

With a central location adjacent to the Westfield Shopping Centre, this hotel is ideal for both business and leisure guests. The lobby area is a four storey atrium. The stylish bedrooms are well equipped, and there is air conditioning throughout. The contemporary restaurant, Stresa, offers Italian cooking in a relaxed environment; complimentary Wi-fi is available in the bar. Discounted rates for guests are offered at the Riverside car park.

Rooms 105 (11 smoking) ⓡ **D** £69-£179*
Facilities FTV Wi-fi ⓢ HL Gym **Conf** Class 60 Board 50 Thtr 130 Del from £120 to £150* **Services** Lift Air con **Notes** LB Civ Wed 120

Ramada Encore Derby

★★★ 75% HOTEL

☎ 0844 801 3680
Locomotive Way, Pride Park DE24 8PU
e-mail: admin@encorederby.co.uk
dir: M1 junct 25, A52 towards Derby. Telephone for detailed directions

This hotel offers stylish and comfortable accommodation. The Hub is a smart, modern, open-plan bar and restaurant with a choice of seating areas - it offers an extensive menu throughout the day. Secure on-site parking is available, and the hotel is within walking distance of Derby railway station.

Rooms 112 (16 fmly) ⓡ **Facilities** STV Wi-fi HL Gym Sauna **Conf** Class 40 Board 20 Thtr 60 **Services** Lift Air con **Parking** 110 **Notes** ⊗

Hallmark Inn

★★★ 72% METRO HOTEL

☎ 01332 292000
Midland Rd DE1 2SL
e-mail: europeanreception@hallmarkhotels.co.uk
web: www.hallmarkhotels.co.uk
dir: City centre, 200yds from railway station

This is a contemporary hotel, offering quality accommodation plus a lounge bar, free Wi-fi and free parking. Situated just a 100 metres from the railway station and a not far from the city centre where there is an abundance of shops and restaurants.

Rooms 87 (18 fmly) **Facilities** FTV Wi-fi **Conf** Class 20 Board 30 Thtr 60 **Services** Lift **Parking** 90 **Notes** ⊗

Littleover Lodge Hotel

★★★ 72% HOTEL

☎ 01332 510161
222 Rykneld Rd, Littleover DE23 4AN
e-mail: enquiries@littleoverlodge.co.uk
web: www.littleoverlodge.co.uk
dir: A38 towards Derby approx 1m on left slip lane signed Littleover/Mickleover/Findon, take 2nd exit off island marked Littleover 0.25m on right

Situated in a rural location this friendly hotel offers modern bedrooms with direct access from the car park. Two styles of dining are available - an informal carvery operation which is very popular locally, and a more formal restaurant which is open for lunch and dinner each day. Service is excellent with the long serving staff being particularly friendly.

Rooms 16 (3 fmly) (6 GF) **Facilities** STV Wi-fi ♫ Xmas New Year **Parking** 75 **Notes** Civ Wed 100

Holiday Inn Express Derby Pride Park

BUDGET HOTEL

☎ 01332 388000
Wheelwright Way, Pride Park DE24 8HX
e-mail: info@expressderby.co.uk
web: www.expressderby.co.uk
dir: A52 towards Derby, after 7m follow Pride Park signs. Over 1st 3 rdbts. Right at 4th, left at next. Take 1st left, hotel on right

A modern hotel ideal for families and business travellers. Fresh and uncomplicated, the spacious rooms include Sky TV, power shower and tea and coffee-making facilities. Continental buffet breakfast is included in the room rate; other meals may be taken at the nearby family pub or restaurant. See also the Hotel Groups pages.

Rooms 103 (64 fmly) (25 GF) **Conf** Class 28 Thtr 20

Premier Inn Derby East

BUDGET HOTEL

☎ 0871 527 8292
The Wyvern, Stanier Way DE21 6BF
web: www.premierinn.com
dir: M1 junct 25, A52 towards Derby. After 6.5m exit for Wyvern/Pride Park. 1st exit at rdbt (A52 Nottingham), straight on at next rdbt. Hotel on left

High quality, budget accommodation ideal for both families and business travellers. Spacious, en suite bedrooms feature tea and coffee making facilities, and Freeview TV in most hotels. Internet access and Wi-fi are available for a small fee. The adjacent family restaurant features a wide and varied menu. See also the Hotel Groups pages.

Rooms 83

Premier Inn Derby North West

BUDGET HOTEL

☎ 0871 527 8294
95 Ashbourne Rd, Mackworth DE22 4LZ
web: www.premierinn.com
dir: Exit M1 junct 25 onto A52 towards Derby. At Pentagon Island straight ahead towards city centre. Follow A52/Ashbourne signs into Mackworth

Rooms 22

D

D

DERBY *continued*

Premier Inn Derby South

BUDGET HOTEL

☎ 0871 527 8296
**Foresters Leisure Park, Osmaston Park Rd
DE23 8AG**
web: www.premierinn.com
dir: M1 junct 24, A6 towards Derby. Left onto A5111
(ring road), hotel in 2m

Rooms 27

Premier Inn Derby West

BUDGET HOTEL

☎ 0871 527 8298
Manor Park Way, Uttoxeter New Rd DE22 3HN
web: www.premierinn.com
dir: M1 junct 25, A38 W towards Burton upon Trent
(approx 15m). Left at island (city hospital), right at
lights, 3rd exit at city hospital island

Rooms 66

Days Inn Donington - A50

BUDGET HOTEL

☎ 01332 799666
Welcome Break Services, A50 Westbound DE72 2WA
e-mail: derby.hotel@welcomebreak.co.uk
web: www.welcomebreak.co.uk
dir: M1 junct 24/24a, onto A50 towards Stoke/Derby.
Hotel between juncts 1 & 2

This modern building offers accommodation in smart,
spacious and well-equipped bedrooms, suitable for
families and business travellers, and all with en suite
bathrooms. Continental breakfast is available and
other refreshments may be taken at the nearby family
restaurant. See also the Hotel Groups pages.

Rooms 47 (39 fmly) (17 GF) (8 smoking)
Conf Class 20 Board 40 Thtr 40

Bear Hotel

★★★ 80% ◉◉ HOTEL

☎ 01380 722444
Market Place SN10 1HS
e-mail: info@thebearhotel.net
web: www.thebearhotel.net
dir: In town centre, follow Market Place signs

Tracing its history back over three centuries, this
friendly establishment occupies a prominent position
in a bustling town. Staff and management are keen
to please and offer friendly and hospitable service.
The bedrooms are pleasantly appointed and have flat-
screen TVs and broadband connection. The hotel has
two restaurants - Lambtons Restaurant for fine
dining, and the Lawrence Room Bistro open for lunch;
in summer there is a courtyard for alfresco dining.
The hotel is a popular venue for conferences and
weddings. Please note that there is restricted service
on Christmas Day and Boxing Day - accommodation
is not available.

Rooms 25 (5 fmly) ♟ **Facilities** Wi-fi ♫
Conf Class 55 Board 48 Thtr 110 Del from £159 to
£173 **Services** Lift **Parking** 14 **Notes** ⊗ RS 25-26
Dec Civ Wed 100

Heath Cottage Hotel & Restaurant

★★★ 72% HOTEL

☎ 01924 465399
Wakefield Rd WF12 8ET
e-mail: info@heathcottage.co.uk
dir: M1 junct 40/A638 for 2.5m towards Dewsbury.
Hotel before lights, opposite Earlsheaton Cemetery

Standing in an acre of grounds, Heath Cottage is just
two and a half miles from the M1. The service is
friendly and professional. All the bedrooms are
modern and well appointed, and some are in a
converted stable building. The lounge bar and
restaurant are air conditioned. Extensive parking is
available.

Rooms 28 (6 annexe) (3 fmly) (3 GF) **Facilities** Wi-fi
Conf Class 56 Board 32 Thtr 100 **Parking** 60
Notes RS 23-27 Dec Civ Wed 100

Premier Inn Oxford South (Didcot)

BUDGET HOTEL

☎ 0871 527 8868
Milton Heights, Milton OX14 4TX
web: www.premierinn.com
dir: On A4130. Just off A34 at Milton interchange,
between Oxford & Newbury

High quality, budget accommodation ideal for both
families and business travellers. Spacious, en suite
bedrooms feature tea and coffee making facilities,
and Freeview TV in most hotels. Internet access and
Wi-fi are available for a small fee. The adjacent
family restaurant features a wide and varied menu.
See also the Hotel Groups pages.

Rooms 83

Save on hotels. Book at **theAA.com/hotel**

DER – DON 151 ENGLAND

DISLEY
Cheshire   Map 16 SJ98

Best Western Moorside Grange Hotel & Spa

★★★ 74% HOTEL

☎ 01663 764151
Mudhurst Ln, Higher Disley SK12 2AP
e-mail: sales@moorsidegrangehotel.com
web: www.moorsidegrangehotel.com
dir: Exit A6 at Rams Head in Disley, onto Buxton Old Rd for 1m, right onto Mudhurst Ln, hotel on left

Situated on the edge of the Peak District National Park, and with spectacular views of the moors above Higher Disley, this large complex is in an area considered a walkers' paradise. The hotel has excellent conference and function facilities, a well-equipped leisure centre and two tennis courts in the extensive grounds. Suites, and bedrooms with four-poster beds, are available.

Rooms 98 (3 fmly) **Facilities** Spa Wi-fi ⊗ supervised ⊰ Putt green Gym Squash Xmas New Year **Conf** Class 140 Board 100 Thtr 280 **Services** Lift **Parking** 250 **Notes** Civ Wed 280

DISS
Norfolk   Map 13 TM18

The Scole Inn
OXFORD HOTELS & INNS

★★★ 67% HOTEL

☎ 01379 740481
Ipswich Rd, Scole IP21 4DR
e-mail: manager.scoleinn@ohiml.com
web: www.oxfordhotelsandinns.com
dir: A140, Diss rdbt signed Scole, left at T-junct, hotel on left

A charming 17th-century inn situated in the heart of the village where King Charles II and highwayman John Belcher are said to have stayed. Bedrooms come in a variety of styles; each one is pleasantly decorated

and well equipped. The hotel retains a wealth of original features such as exposed brickwork, huge open fires and a superb carved wooden staircase. The public areas include a bar, restaurant and lounge bar.

Rooms 23 (12 annexe) (1 fmly) (7 GF) **Facilities** Wi-fi ♫ Xmas New Year **Conf** Class 26 Board 35 Thtr 45 **Parking** 60 **Notes** Civ Wed 50

DOGMERSFIELD
Hampshire   Map 5 SU75

INSPECTORS' CHOICE

Four Seasons Hotel Hampshire
★★★★★ ◎◎ COUNTRY HOUSE HOTEL

☎ 01252 853000
Dogmersfield Park, Chalky Ln RG27 8TD
e-mail: reservations.ham@fourseasons.com
dir: M3 junct 5 onto A287 Farnham. After 1.5m left for Dogmersfield, hotel 0.6m on left

This Georgian manor house, set in 500 acres of rolling grounds and English Heritage listed gardens, offers the upmost in luxury and relaxation, just an hour from London. The spacious and stylish bedrooms are particularly well appointed and offer up-to-date technology. Fitness and spa facilities include nearly every conceivable indoor and outdoor activity, in addition to luxurious pampering. An elegant restaurant, a healthy eating spa café and a trendy bar are popular venues.

Rooms 133 (23 GF) **Facilities** Spa STV Wi-fi ⊗ ⊰ Fishing ⊰ Gym Clay pigeon shooting Bikes Canal boat Falconry Horse riding Jogging trails ♫ Xmas New Year **Conf** Class 110 Board 60 Thtr 260 **Services** Lift Air con **Parking** 165 **Notes** Civ Wed 200

DONCASTER
South Yorkshire   Map 16 SE50

Best Western Premier Mount Pleasant

★★★★ 80% ◎ HOTEL

☎ 01302 868696 & 868219
Great North Rd DN11 0HW
e-mail: reception@mountpleasant.co.uk
web: www.mountpleasant.co.uk

(For full entry see Rossington)

Ramada Encore Doncaster Airport

★★★ 73% HOTEL

☎ 01302 718520
Robin Hood Airport DN9 3RH
e-mail: reception@encoredoncaster.co.uk
dir: M180 junct 1, follow signs for airport

Conveniently situated only a few minutes' walk from the main terminal at Robin Hood Airport, this purpose-built hotel is an good base for both the business and the leisure traveller. The air-conditioned bedrooms are spacious and bright, with power shower rooms. Public areas include the Hub Bar and Lounge. Secure parking is available on site.

Rooms 102 (36 fmly) (3 GF) (8 smoking) ⋔ S £49-£79; D £49-£79* **Facilities** STV FTV Wi-fi ⊰ HL **Conf** Class 20 Board 20 Thtr 40 Del from £89 to £129* **Services** Lift Air con **Parking** 144 **Notes** LB ⊗

Grand St Leger

★★★ 68% HOTEL

☎ 01302 364111
Bennetthorpe DN2 6AX
e-mail: sales@grandstleger.com
web: www.grandstleger.com
dir: Follow Doncaster Racecourse signs. At racecourse rdbt hotel on corner

This friendly hotel is located next to the racecourse and is only ten minutes' walk from the town centre. There is a cheerful bar-lounge and a pleasant restaurant offering an extensive choice of dishes. The bedrooms are comfortable and thoughtfully equipped, including Wi-fi access.

Rooms 20 ⋔ S £34.95-£89.95; D £39.95-£124.95 (incl. bkfst) **Facilities** FTV Wi-fi **Conf** Class 50 Board 30 Thtr 80 Del from £77.95 to £122.95 **Parking** 28 **Notes** ⊗ RS 25 Dec Civ Wed 65

DONCASTER *continued*

Park Inn by Radisson Doncaster

★★★ 67% HOTEL

☎ 01302 760710
Decoy Bank S DN4 5PD
e-mail: info.doncaster@rezidorparkinn.com
dir: Telephone for directions

Situated in a thriving business park close to the city centre, this modern, contemporary hotel offers comfortable, spacious accommodation with individual climate control and complimentary Wi-fi, and is convenient for the A1 (north and south) and M18. A. An air-conditioned meeting room is available, and on-site parking is a real plus.

Rooms 85 (12 fmly) (21 GF) ♥ **Facilities** FTV Wi-fi Xmas New Year **Conf** Class 50 Board 50 Thtr 144 **Services** Lift Air con **Parking** 92

Danum Hotel

★★★ 66% HOTEL

☎ 01302 342261
High St DN1 1DN
e-mail: info@danumhotel.com
dir: M18 junct 3, A6182 to Doncaster. Over rdbt, right at next. Right at 'give way' sign, left at mini rdbt, hotel ahead

Situated in the centre of the town, this Edwardian hotel offers well equipped conference rooms together with comfortable bedrooms. A contemporary lounge area provides modern dining and specially negotiated rates at a local leisure centre are offered.

Rooms 64 (5 fmly) **Facilities** STV FTV Wi-fi Special rates at Cannons Health Club ♫ Xmas New Year **Conf** Class 160 Board 100 Thtr 350 **Services** Lift **Parking** 36 **Notes** RS 26-30 Dec Civ Wed 250

Campanile Doncaster

Campanile

BUDGET HOTEL

☎ 01302 370770
Doncaster Leisure Park, Bawtry Rd DN4 7PD
e-mail: doncaster@campanile.com
web: www.campanile.com
dir: Follow signs to Doncaster Leisure Centre, left at rdbt before Dome complex

This modern building offers accommodation in smart, well-equipped bedrooms, all with en suite bathrooms. Refreshments may be taken at the informal bistro. See also the Hotel Groups pages.

Rooms 50 (25 GF) **Conf** Class 15 Board 15 Thtr 25

Holiday Inn Express Doncaster

BUDGET HOTEL

☎ 01302 314100
Catesby Business Park, Bullrush Grove DN4 8SJ
e-mail: doncaster@holidayinnexpress.org.uk
web: www.hiexpress.com/doncaster
dir: M18 junct 3, A6182, left at 1st rdbt into Woodfield Way, straight over next rdbt, hotel on left

A modern hotel ideal for families and business travellers. Fresh and uncomplicated, the spacious rooms include Sky TV, power shower and tea and coffee-making facilities. Continental buffet breakfast is included in the room rate; other meals may be taken at the nearby family pub or restaurant. See also the Hotel Groups pages.

Rooms 94 (63 fmly) (16 GF) (14 smoking) **Conf** Class 16 Board 20 Thtr 40

Premier Inn Doncaster Central

BUDGET HOTEL

☎ 0871 527 8302
High Fishergate DN1 1QZ
web: www.premierinn.com
dir: Off A630 (Church Way)

High quality, budget accommodation ideal for both families and business travellers. Spacious, en suite bedrooms feature tea and coffee making facilities, and Freeview TV in most hotels. Internet access and Wi-fi are available for a small fee. The adjacent family restaurant features a wide and varied menu. See also the Hotel Groups pages.

Rooms 140

Premier Inn Doncaster Central East

BUDGET HOTEL

☎ 0871 527 8304
Doncaster Leisure Park, Herten Way DN4 7NW
web: www.premierinn.com
dir: M18 junct 3, signed Doncaster racecourse. Left into Whiterose Way (B&Q on left). Straight on at rdbt into Wilmington Dr, right at next rdbt into Lakeside Boulevard. At next rdbt 2nd exit. Straight on at next rdbt, hotel ahead

Rooms 47

Premier Inn Doncaster (Lakeside)

BUDGET HOTEL

☎ 0871 527 8300
Wilmington Dr, Doncaster Carr DN4 5PJ
web: www.premierinn.com
dir: M18 junct 3, A6182. Hotel near junct with access road

Rooms 42

DORCHESTER   Map 4 SY69
Dorset

Best Western King's Arms Hotel

★★★ 75% HOTEL

☎ 01305 265353
30 High East St DT1 1HF
e-mail: info@kingsarmsdorchester.com
web: www.kingsarmsdorchester.com
dir: In town centre

Previous guests at this 18th-century hotel, set in the very heart of Dorchester, have included Queen Victoria and John Lennon. Built in 1720, many Georgian features still remain, including beams in the cosy bar. Guests can dine in the bar, or in the restaurant which offers a traditional English menu. Bedrooms have suitable facilities, including a number with four-posters.

Rooms 37 (2 fmly) (3 GF) **Facilities** FTV Wi-fi **Conf** Class 40 Board 30 Thtr 80 **Services** Lift **Parking** 37 **Notes** ⊗ Civ Wed 80

The Wessex Royale Hotel THE INDEPENDENTS

★★★ 73% HOTEL

☎ 01305 262660
High West St DT1 1UP
e-mail: info@wessexroyalehotel.co.uk
web: www.wessexroyaledorchester.com
dir: From A35 follow town centre signs. Straight on, hotel at top of hill on left

This centrally situated Georgian townhouse dates from 1756 and successfully combines historic charm with modern comforts. The restaurant is a relaxed location for enjoying innovative food, and the hotel offers the benefit of a smart conservatory, ideal for functions. Limited courtyard parking is available.

Rooms 27 (2 annexe) (2 fmly) (2 GF) **Facilities** STV FTV Wi-fi ⟲ **Conf** Class 40 Board 40 Thtr 80 **Parking** 11 **Notes** ⊗ Closed 23-30 Dec

D

DORCHESTER (ON THAMES)   Map 5 SU59
Oxfordshire

White Hart Hotel

★★★ 74% HOTEL

☎ 01865 340074
High St OX10 7HN
e-mail: whitehart@oxfordshire-hotels.co.uk
web: www.oxfordshire-hotels.co.uk
dir: M40 junct 6, take B4009 through Watlington &
Benson to A4074. Follow signs to Dorchester. Hotel on
right

Period charm and character are plentiful throughout
this 17th-century coaching inn, which is situated in
the heart of a picturesque village. The spacious
bedrooms are individually decorated and thoughtfully
equipped. Public rooms include a cosy bar, a choice
of lounges and an atmospheric restaurant, complete
with vaulted timber ceiling.

Rooms 28 (4 annexe) (2 fmly) (9 GF) ₪ **S** £65-£110;
D £75-£150 (incl. bkfst) **Facilities** FTV Wi-fi ⅄ Xmas
New Year **Conf** Class 20 Board 18 Thtr 30
Del from £125 to £175 **Parking** 36 **Notes** LB ⊗

George Hotel

★★ 65% HOTEL

☎ 01865 340404
25 High St OX10 7HH
e-mail: thegeorgehotel@fsmail.net
dir: M40 junct 6 onto B4009 through Watlington &
Benson. Take A4074 at BP petrol station, follow
Dorchester signs. Hotel on left

Located on the quaint High Street The George is
directly opposite the stunning abbey. Once a coaching
inn, this historic property provides comfortable
accommodation in the main house and also in a
separate building which was once the stable. The
food is freshly prepared and can be enjoyed in the
formal beamed restaurant, in the more relaxed
Potboys Bar with open fires, or in the garden in
warmer months. Complimentary Wi-fi is available
throughout.

Rooms 17 (8 annexe) (1 fmly) (6 GF) ₪ **S** £65-£75;
D £65-£85 (incl. bkfst)* **Facilities** FTV Wi-fi Beauty
treatment room Xmas New Year **Conf** Class 20
Board 24 Thtr 40 Del from £120* **Parking** 50
Notes LB ⊗

DORKING   Map 6 TQ14
Surrey

Mercure Boxhill Burford Bridge Hotel

★★★★ 74% ◉ HOTEL

☎ 01306 884561
Burford Bridge, Box Hill RH5 6BX
e-mail: h6635@accor.com
web: www.mercure.com
dir: M25 junct 9, A245 towards Dorking. Hotel approx
5m on A24

Steeped in history, this hotel was reputedly where
Lord Nelson and Lady Hamilton met for the last time,
and it is said that the landscape around the hotel has
inspired many poets. The hotel has a contemporary
feel throughout. The grounds, running down to the
River Mole, are extensive, and there are good
transport links to major centres, including London.
The elegant Emlyn Restaurant offers a modern
award-winning menu.

Rooms 57 (22 fmly) (3 GF) **Facilities** Wi-fi ⅄ ♫
Xmas New Year **Conf** Class 80 Board 60 Thtr 120
Parking 130 **Notes** ⊗ Civ Wed 200

Gatton Manor Hotel & Golf Club

★★★ 80% HOTEL

☎ 01306 627555
Standon Ln RH5 5PQ
e-mail: info@gattonmanor.co.uk
web: www.gattonmanor.co.uk

(For full entry see Ockley)

Mercure Dorking White Horse Hotel

★★★ 70% HOTEL

☎ 01306 881138
High St RH4 1BE
e-mail: h6637@accor.com
web: www.mercure.com
dir: M25 junct 9, A24 S towards Dorking. Hotel in
town centre

The hotel was first established as an inn in 1750,
although parts of the building date back as far as the
15th century. Its town centre location and Dickensian
charm have long made this a popular destination for
travellers. There's beamed ceilings, open fires and
four-poster beds; more contemporary rooms can be
found in the garden wing.

Rooms 78 (41 annexe) (2 fmly) (5 GF) **Facilities** FTV
Wi-fi Discount at local leisure centre Xmas New Year
Conf Class 30 Board 30 Thtr 50 **Parking** 73

DORRIDGE   Map 10 SP17
West Midlands

The Forest

◉ ◉ RESTAURANT WITH ROOMS

☎ 01564 772120
25 Station Rd B93 8JA
e-mail: info@forest-hotel.com
web: www.forest-hotel.com
dir: In town centre near station

This very individual and stylish restaurant with rooms
is well placed for routes to Birmingham, Stratford-
upon-Avon and Warwick. The individually designed
bedrooms are very well equipped with modern
facilities, and imaginative food is served in the bars
and intimate restaurant. A warm welcome is assured.

Rooms 12

D

DOVER
Kent

Map 7 TR34

Best Western Dover Marina Hotel

★★★★ 75% HOTEL

☎ 01304 203633
Dover Waterfront CT17 9BP
e-mail: reservations@dovermarinahotel.co.uk
web: www.dovermarinahotel.co.uk
dir: M20 junct 13, A20 to Dover, straight on at 2
rdbts, at 3rd take 2nd exit into Union St. Cross swing
bridge, next left into Marine Pde/Waterloo Cres. Hotel
200yds on left

An attractive terraced waterfront hotel overlooking the
harbour that offers a wide range of facilities
including meeting rooms and a Spa. Some of the
tastefully decorated bedrooms have balconies and
many of the rooms have superb sea views. Each room
offers a range of amenities to meet the needs of the
modern traveller. The public rooms include an open-
plan lounge bar and a smart restaurant.

Rooms 81 (5 fmly) ⚘ **Facilities** STV Wi-fi Gym Xmas
New Year **Conf** Class 60 Board 50 Thtr 110
Services Lift **Notes** ⊗ Civ Wed 100

Ramada Hotel Dover

⊛RAMADA

★★★★ 75% HOTEL

☎ 01304 821230
Singledge Ln, Whitfield CT16 3EL
e-mail: reservations@ramadadover.co.uk
web: www.ramadadover.co.uk
dir: From M20 follow signs to A2 towards Canterbury.
Turn right after Whitfield rdbt. From A2 towards
Dover, turn left before Whitfield rdbt

A modern purpose-built hotel situated in a quiet
location between Dover and Canterbury, close to the
ferry port and seaside. The open-plan public areas
are contemporary in style and include a lounge, a bar
and The Olive Tree Restaurant. The stylish bedrooms
are simply decorated with co-ordinated soft
furnishings and many thoughtful extras.

Rooms 68 (68 GF) **Facilities** STV Wi-fi Gym Xmas New
Year **Conf** Class 25 Board 20 Thtr 400 **Parking** 110
Notes ⊗ Civ Wed

Wallett's Court Country House Hotel & Spa

★★★★ 72% ⊛ ⊛ HOTEL

☎ 01304 852424 & 0800 035 1628
West Cliffe, St Margarets-at-Cliffe CT15 6EW
e-mail: wc@wallettscourt.com
web: www.wallettscourt.com
dir: From Dover take A258 towards Deal. 1st right to
St Margarets-at-Cliffe & West Cliffe, 1m on right
opposite West Cliffe church

A lovely Jacobean manor situated in a peaceful
location on the outskirts of town. Bedrooms in the
original house are traditionally furnished whereas the
rooms in the courtyard buildings are more modern; all
are equipped to a high standard. Public rooms
include a smart bar, a lounge and a restaurant that
utilises local organic produce. An impressive spa
facility is housed in converted barn buildings in the
grounds.

Rooms 16 (13 annexe) (2 fmly) (7 GF) **Facilities** Spa
FTV Wi-fi ⊛ ⊛ Putt green ⊛ Gym Treatment
suite Aromatherapy massage Beauty therapy Golf pitching
range New Year **Conf** Class 25 Board 16 Thtr 25
Parking 30 **Notes** Closed 24-26 Dec Civ Wed

The White Cliffs Hotel

★★★ 75% ⊛ HOTEL

☎ 01304 852229 & 852400
High St, St Margaret's-at-Cliffe CT15 6AT
e-mail: mail@thewhitecliffs.com
dir: Opposite church in village centre

This fresh-looking traditional weather boarded inn
has a contemporary feel although it still retains much
traditional character. Comfortably appointed
bedrooms, divided between the main house and The
Mews, boast luxurious beds and well co-ordinated
furnishings. Public areas are styled to create a
relaxed beachside atmosphere. The Bay Restaurant is
open for lunch and dinner all week.

Rooms 15 (9 annexe) (2 fmly) (4 GF) **Facilities** FTV
Wi-fi Xmas New Year **Conf** Class 20 Board 14 Thtr 20
Parking 20

Premier Inn Dover (A20)

BUDGET HOTEL

☎ 0871 527 8310
Folkestone Rd CT15 7AB
web: www.premierinn.com
dir: A20 to Dover. Through tunnel, take 2nd exit onto
B2011. 1st left at rdbt. In 1m hotel on left

High quality, budget accommodation ideal for both
families and business travellers. Spacious, en suite
bedrooms feature tea and coffee making facilities,
and Freeview TV in most hotels. Internet access and
Wi-fi are available for a small fee. The adjacent
family restaurant features a wide and varied menu.
See also the Hotel Groups pages.

Rooms 64

Premier Inn Dover East

BUDGET HOTEL

☎ 0871 527 8308
Jubilee Way, Guston Wood CT15 5FD
web: www.premierinn.com
dir: At rdbt junct of A2 & A258

Rooms 40

Premier Inn Dover (Eastern Ferry Terminal)

BUDGET HOTEL

☎ 0871 527 8306
Marine Court, Marine Pde CT16 1LW
web: www.premierinn.com
dir: In town centre adjacent to ferry terminal. M20
junct 13 onto A20 for 8.2m

Rooms 100

The Marquis at Alkham

◉◉ RESTAURANT WITH ROOMS

☎ 01304 873410 & 822945
Alkham Valley Rd, Alkham CT15 7DF
e-mail: info@themarquisatalkham.co.uk
web: www.themarquisatalkham.co.uk
dir: A256 from Dover, at rdbt 1st exit into London Rd,
left into Alkham Rd, Alkham Valley Rd. Establishment
1.5m after sharp bend

Located between Dover and Folkestone, this modern,
contemporary restaurant with rooms offers luxury
accommodation with modern features - flat-screen
TVs, Wi-fi, power showers and bathrobes to name but
a few. All the stylish bedrooms are individually
designed and have fantastic views of the Kent Downs.
The award-winning restaurant, open for lunch and

dinner, serves modern British cuisine. Both
continental and a choice of cooked breakfasts are
offered.

Rooms 10 (3 fmly)

DOWNHAM MARKET   Map 12 TF60
Norfolk

Castle Hotel

★★★ 77% HOTEL

☎ 01366 384311
High St PE38 9HF
e-mail: howards@castle-hotel.com
dir: M11 take A10 for Ely into Downham Market. Hotel
opposite lights on corner of High St

This popular coaching inn is situated close to the
centre of town and has been welcoming guests for
over 300 years. Well maintained public areas include
a cosy lounge bar and two smartly appointed
restaurants. Inviting bedrooms, some with four-poster
beds, are attractively decorated, thoughtfully
equipped, and have bright, modern decor.

Rooms 12 (2 fmly) **S** £85-£120; **D** £105-£145 (incl.
bkfst) **Facilities** Wi-fi ⬚ New Year **Conf** Class 30
Board 40 Thtr 60 Del from £125 to £175 **Parking** 26
Notes LB

DRIFFIELD (GREAT)   Map 17 TA05
East Riding of Yorkshire

Best Western Bell Hotel

★★★ 78% HOTEL

☎ 01377 256661
46 Market Place YO25 6AN
e-mail: bell@bestwestern.co.uk
web: www.bw-bellhotel.co.uk
dir: From A164, right at lights. Car park 50yds on left
behind black railings

This 250-year-old hotel incorporates the old corn
exchange and the old town hall. It is furnished with
antique and period pieces, and contains many items
of local historical interest. The bedrooms vary in size,
but all offer modern facilities and some have their
own sitting rooms. The hotel has a relaxed and very
friendly atmosphere. There is a spa and gym
providing a very good range of facilities and
treatments.

Rooms 16 (3 GF) ⬚ **S** £81-£96; **D** £98-£122 (incl.
bkfst)* **Facilities** Spa FTV Wi-fi ⬚ ⬚ Gym Squash
Masseur Snooker ♫ New Year **Conf** Class 100
Board 40 Thtr 150 **Services** Lift **Parking** 18 **Notes** LB
⊗ No children 16yrs Closed 25 Dec & 1 Jan RS 24 &
26 Dec Civ Wed 120

DROITWICH   Map 10 SO86
Worcestershire

Holiday Inn Express Droitwich M5 Jct 5

BUDGET HOTEL

☎ 0870 442 5658
Worcester Rd, Wychbold WR9 7PA
e-mail: dgmdroitwich@expressholidayinn.co.uk
web: www.hiexpress.com/droitwichm5j
dir: M5 junct 5, at rdbt take A38 towards Bromsgrove.
Hotel 300yds on left next to MacDonalds

A modern hotel ideal for families and business
travellers. Fresh and uncomplicated, the spacious
rooms include Sky TV, power shower and tea and
coffee-making facilities. Continental buffet breakfast
is included in the room rate; other meals may be
taken at the nearby family pub or restaurant. See also
the Hotel Groups pages.

Rooms 94 (44 fmly) **Conf** Class 18 Board 20 Thtr 40

DUDLEY   Map 10 SO99
West Midlands

Copthorne Hotel Merry Hill - Dudley

MILLENNIUM

★★★★ 73% HOTEL

☎ 01384 482882
The Waterfront, Level St, Brierley Hill DY5 1UR
e-mail: reservations.merryhill@millenniumhotels.
co.uk
web: www.millenniumhotels.co.uk/copthornedudley
dir: Follow signs for Merry Hill Centre

This hotel enjoys a waterfront location and is close to
the Merry Hill Shopping Mall. Polished marble floors,
rich fabrics and striking interior design are all in
evidence in the stylish public areas. Bedrooms are
spacious and some have Connoisseur status, which
includes the use of a private lounge. A modern leisure
centre with pool occupies the lower level.

Rooms 138 (14 fmly) **S** £47-£198; **D** £47-£198*
Facilities Spa STV Wi-fi ⬚ HL ⬚ supervised Gym
Aerobics Beauty/massage therapists Steam room
Sauna Dance studio ♫ Xmas New Year
Conf Class 240 Board 60 Thtr 570 Del from £120 to
£160* **Services** Lift **Parking** 100 **Notes** LB ⊗
Civ Wed 400

D

DUMBLETON — Map 10 SP03
Gloucestershire

Dumbleton Hall Hotel

★★★ 79% COUNTRY HOUSE HOTEL

☎ 01386 881240
WR11 7TS
e-mail: dh@pofr.co.uk
web: www.dumbletonhall.co.uk
dir: M5 junct 9/A46. 2nd exit at rdbt signed Evesham. Through Beckford for 1m, turn right signed Dumbleton. Hotel at S end of village

Standing on the site of a 16th-century building also known as Dumbleton Hall, the current mansion, surrounded by 19 acres of landscaped gardens and parkland, was built in the mid-18th century. Panoramic views of the Vale of Evesham can be seen from every window, and the spacious public rooms make this an ideal venue for weddings, conferences or just as a hideaway retreat. The individually designed bedrooms vary in size and layout; one room is adapted for less able guests.

Rooms 34 (9 fmly) **Facilities** Wi-fi ⏀ Xmas New Year
Conf Class 60 Board 60 Thtr 100 **Services** Lift
Parking 60 **Notes** Civ Wed 100

DUNSTABLE — Map 11 TL02
Bedfordshire

Premier Inn Dunstable/Luton

BUDGET HOTEL

☎ 0871 527 8330
350 Luton Rd LU5 4LL
web: www.premierinn.com
dir: M1 junct 11, follow Dunstable signs. At 1st rdbt turn right. Hotel on left on A505

High quality, budget accommodation ideal for both families and business travellers. Spacious, en suite bedrooms feature tea and coffee making facilities, and Freeview TV in most hotels. Internet access and Wi-fi are available for a small fee. The adjacent family restaurant features a wide and varied menu. See also the Hotel Groups pages.

Rooms 42

Premier Inn Dunstable South (A5)

BUDGET HOTEL

☎ 0871 527 8332
Watling St, Kensworth LU6 3QP
web: www.premierinn.com
dir: M1 junct 9 towards Dunstable on A5, hotel on right after Packhorse pub

Rooms 40

DUNWICH — Map 13 TM47
Suffolk

The Ship at Dunwich

★★ 81% ⑳ SMALL HOTEL

☎ 01728 648219 & 07921 061060
St James St IP17 3DT
e-mail: info@shipatdunwich.co.uk
dir: From N: A12, exit at Blythburgh onto B1125, then left to village. Inn at end of road. From S: A12, turn right to Westleton. Follow signs for Dunwich

A delightful inn situated in the heart of this quiet village, surrounded by nature reserves and heathland, and just a short walk from the beach. Public rooms feature a smart lounge bar with an open fire and real ales on tap. The comfortable bedrooms are traditionally furnished; some rooms have lovely views across the sea or marshes.

Rooms 15 (4 annexe) (4 fmly) (4 GF) **Facilities** FTV
Xmas New Year **Parking** 15

DURHAM — Map 19 NZ24
Co Durham

Durham Marriott Hotel, Royal County

★★★★ 78% HOTEL

☎ 0191 386 6821
Old Elvet DH1 3JN
e-mail: mhrs.xvudm.frontdesk@marriotthotels.com
web: www.durhammarriottroyalcounty.co.uk
dir: From A1(M) junct 62, A690 to Durham, over 1st rdbt, left at 2nd rdbt left at lights, hotel on left

In a wonderful position on the banks of the River Wear, the hotel's central location makes it ideal for visiting the attractions of this historic city. The building was developed from a series of Jacobean town houses. The bedrooms are tastefully styled. Eating options include the County Restaurant, for formal dining, and the Cruz Restaurant.

Rooms 150 (8 annexe) (10 fmly) (15 GF) (2 smoking)
🏋 **Facilities** Spa STV FTV Wi-fi ↕ HL ⑳ supervised Gym Turkish steam room Plunge pool Sanarium Tropical fun shower **Conf** Class 50 Board 50 Thtr 120
Services Lift **Parking** 76 **Notes** Civ Wed 120

Radisson Blu Durham

★★★★ 77% HOTEL

☎ 0191 372 7200
Framwellgate Waterside DH1 5TL
e-mail: info.durham@radissonblu.com

Situated on the River Wear this smart hotel is a short walk from the city centre and the castle. The stylish accommodation includes business class rooms and a range of suites; most rooms have views of the cathedral and the old part of the city. Filini Restaurant serves Italian cuisine, and the PACE Health Club has an indoor pool, steam room, sauna, gym and five treatment rooms. The impressive conference facilities include a business centre.

Rooms 207 (8 fmly) 🏋 **Facilities** Spa STV Wi-fi ↕ ⑳
Gym New Year **Conf** Class 200 Board 120 Thtr 450
Services Lift Air con **Parking** 130 **Notes** ⊗
Civ Wed 80

Save on hotels. Book at **theAA.com/hotel**

DUM – EAS 157 **ENGLAND**

Ramside Hall Hotel

★★★★ 75% HOTEL

☎ 0191 386 5282
Carrville DH1 1TD
e-mail: mail@ramsidehallhotel.co.uk
web: www.ramsidehallhotel.co.uk
dir: A1(M) junct 62, A690 to Sunderland. Straight on at lights. 200mtrs after rail bridge turn right

With its proximity to the motorway and delightful parkland setting, this establishment combines the best of both worlds - convenience and tranquillity. The hotel boasts 27 holes of golf, a choice of lounges, two eating options and two bars. Bedrooms are furnished and decorated to a very high standard and include two very impressive presidential suites.

Rooms 80 (10 fmly) (28 GF) **Facilities** STV Wi-fi ⚡ 27 Putt green Steam room Sauna Golf academy Driving range ♫ Xmas New Year **Conf** Class 160 Board 40 Thtr 500 **Services** Lift **Parking** 500 **Notes** Civ Wed 500

Best Western Honest Lawyer Hotel

★★★ 82% ◉ HOTEL

☎ 0191 378 3780
Croxdale Bridge, Croxdale DH1 3SP
e-mail: enquiries@honestlawyerhotel.com
dir: A1(M) junct 61, A688 towards Bishops Auckland. Right at rdbt (continue on A688), right at next rdbt onto A167 towards Durham. In 2.5m hotel on right

This hotel offers a mixture of smart motel-style bedrooms along with six junior suites in the main building that have four-poster beds. 40" LCD TVs, power showers and complimentary Wi-fi are provided as standard. Bailey's Bar & Restaurant, with its open kitchen, offers a seasonally changing menu and friendly service. There are good transportation links to Durham and the motorway.

Rooms 46 (40 annexe) (6 fmly) (40 GF) **Facilities** FTV Wi-fi ⚡ ♫ Xmas New Year **Conf** Class 27 Board 24 Thtr 50 **Services** Air con **Parking** 150 **Notes** Civ Wed 40

Best Western Whitworth Hall Hotel

★★★ 79% HOTEL

☎ 01388 811772
Whitworth Hall Country Park DL16 7QX
e-mail: enquiries@whitworthhall.co.uk
web: www.whitworthhall.co.uk

(For full entry see Spennymoor)

Premier Inn Durham City Centre

BUDGET HOTEL

☎ 0871 527 8338
Freemans Place, Walkergate DH1 1SQ
web: www.premierinn.com
dir: A1(M) junct 62, A690 (Leazes Rd) towards city centre. In Durham follow Watergate signs, under bridge immediately left into Walkergate (one way). Back under A690, hotel on right

High quality, budget accommodation ideal for both families and business travellers. Spacious, en suite bedrooms feature tea and coffee making facilities, and Freeview TV in most hotels. Internet access and Wi-fi are available for a small fee. The adjacent family restaurant features a wide and varied menu. See also the Hotel Groups pages.

Premier Inn Durham East

BUDGET HOTEL

☎ 0871 527 8340
Broomside Park, Belmont Industrial Estate DH1 1GG
web: www.premierinn.com
dir: A1(M) junct 62, A690 W towards Durham. In 1m left. Hotel on left

Rooms 40

Premier Inn Durham North

BUDGET HOTEL

☎ 0871 527 8342
adj. Arnison Retail Centre, Pity Me DH1 5GB
web: www.premierinn.com
dir: A1 junct 63, A167 to Durham. Straight on at 5 rbts, left at 6th rbt. Hotel on right after 200yds

Rooms 60

DUXFORD   Map 12 TL44
Cambridgeshire

Duxford Lodge Hotel

THE INDEPENDENTS
HOTEL ASSOCIATION

★★★ 77% ◉ HOTEL

☎ 01223 836444
Ickleton Rd CB22 4RT
e-mail: admin@duxfordlodgehotel.co.uk
web: www.duxfordlodgehotel.co.uk
dir: M11 junct 10, onto A505 to Duxford. 1st right at rdbt, hotel 0.75m on left

A warm welcome is assured at this attractive red-brick hotel in the hart of a delightful village. Public areas include a cosy relaxing bar, separate lounge, and an attractive restaurant, where an excellent and imaginative menu is offered. The bedrooms are well appointed, comfortable and smartly furnished.

Rooms 15 (4 annexe) (2 fmly) (4 GF) **Facilities** FTV Wi-fi **Conf** Class 20 Board 26 Thtr 45 Del from £140* **Parking** 34 **Notes** Closed 25 Dec-2 Jan Civ Wed 50

EAST GRINSTEAD   Map 6 TQ33
West Sussex

The Felbridge Hotel & Spa

★★★★ 86% ◉◉ HOTEL

☎ 01342 337700
London Rd RH19 2BH
e-mail: sales@felbridgehotel.co.uk
dir: From W: M23 junct 10, follow signs to A22. From N: M25 junct 6. Hotel on A22 at Felbridge

This hotel is within easy of the M25 and Gatwick as well as Eastbourne and the glorious south coast. All bedrooms are beautifully styled and offer a wealth of amenities. Diners can choose from the Bay Tree Brasserie, Anise Fine Dining Restaurant or contemporary QUBE Bar. Facilities include a selection of modern meeting rooms, the luxurious Chakra Spa and swimming pool.

Rooms 120 (16 fmly) (53 GF) ⚡ **S** £79-£219; **D** £79-£219* **Facilities** Spa STV FTV Wi-fi ⚡ ⊙ ⊛ Gym Sauna Steam room Hairdresser Xmas New Year **Conf** Class 120 Board 100 Thtr 500 Del from £150 to £250 **Services** Air con **Parking** 300 **Notes** LB ⊗ Civ Wed 150

EAST GRINSTEAD *continued*

Gravetye Manor Hotel

★★★★ 85% ◎ ◎ ◎
COUNTRY HOUSE HOTEL

☎ 01342 810567
Vowels Ln, West Hoathly RH19 4LJ
e-mail: info@gravetyemanor.co.uk
web: www.gravetyemanor.co.uk
dir: B2028 to Haywards Heath. 1m after Turners Hill
fork left towards Sharpthorne, 1st left into Vowels
Lane

A beautiful Elizabethan mansion, built in 1598 and
enjoying a tranquil setting. One of the first country
house hotels in Britain, Gravetye Manor remains an
excellent example of its type. Bedrooms and
bathrooms have been sympathetically refurbished
with style and luxurious finishing touches. The day
rooms, each with oak panelling, fresh flower
arrangements and open fires, create a relaxing
atmosphere. Cuisine is excellent and makes use of
local suppliers and producers. Guests should take
time to explore the impressive gardens and grounds;
a perfect spot for afternoon tea.

Rooms 17 ☞ **D** £200–£430 (incl. bkfst)*
Facilities FTV Wi-fi ⓠ Fishing ⚓ Deer stalking Xmas
New Year **Conf** Board 15 Del from £295 to £350*
Parking 20 **Notes** ⊗ No children 7yrs Civ Wed 60

Premier Inn East Grinstead

BUDGET HOTEL

☎ 0871 527 8348
London Rd, Felbridge RH19 2QR
web: www.premierinn.com
dir: M25 junct 6. Hotel at junction of A22 & A264

High quality, budget accommodation ideal for both
families and business travellers. Spacious, en suite
bedrooms feature tea and coffee making facilities,
and Freeview TV in most hotels. Internet access and
Wi-fi are available for a small fee. The adjacent
family restaurant features a wide and varied menu.
See also the Hotel Groups pages.

Rooms 41

EAST HORSLEY Map 6 TQ05
Surrey

Ramada Guildford/Leatherhead

U

☎ 01483 280500 & 280503
Guildford Rd KT24 6TB
e-mail: reception@ramadaguildfordhotel.co.uk
web: www.ramadaguildfordhotel.co.uk
dir: M25 junct 10, A3. Follow Guildford signs, B2039
(Ockham & Ripley) 1st left into Ockham Road North.
4.5m left at T-junct onto A246. Hotel 50yds on left

Currently the rating for this establishment is not
confirmed. This may be due to a change of ownership
or because it has only recently joined the AA rating
scheme. For further details please see the AA website:
theAA.com

Rooms 87 (5 annexe) (13 fmly) (23 GF) **Facilities** STV
FTV Wi-fi ⓠ Xmas New Year **Conf** Class 70 Board 75
Thtr 170 **Services** Lift **Parking** 120 **Notes** ⊗
Civ Wed 170

EAST MIDLANDS AIRPORT Map 11 SK42
Leicestershire

The Priest House Hotel

★★★★ 80% ◎ ◎ HOTEL

☎ 01332 810649
Kings Mills DE74 2RR
e-mail: enquiries.priesthouse@handpicked.co.uk
web: www.handpickedhotels.co.uk/thepriesthouse
dir: M1 junct 24, A50, take 1st slip road signed
Castle Donington. Right at lights, hotel in 2m

A historic hotel peacefully situated in a picturesque
riverside setting. Public areas include a fine dining
restaurant, a modern brasserie and conference
rooms. Bedrooms are situated in both the main
building and converted cottages, and the executive
rooms feature state-of-the-art technology. Hand
Picked Hotels – AA Hotel Group of the Year 2012-13.

Rooms 42 (18 annexe) (5 fmly) (16 GF) ☞
S £85–£135; **D** £99–£160 (incl. bkfst)* **Facilities** STV
FTV Wi-fi ⓠ HL Fishing Xmas New Year **Conf** Class 40
Board 40 Thtr 120 Del from £135 to £165*
Parking 200 **Notes** LB ⊗ Civ Wed 120

Best Western Premier Yew Lodge Hotel & Spa

★★★★ 78% ◎ ◎ HOTEL

☎ 01509 672518
Packington Hill DE74 2DF
e-mail: info@yewlodgehotel.co.uk
web: www.yewlodgehotel.co.uk
dir: M1 junct 24. Follow signs to Loughborough &
Kegworth on A6. On entering village, 1st right, after
400yds hotel on right

This smart, family-owned hotel is close to both the
motorway and airport, yet is peacefully located.
Modern, stylish bedrooms and public areas are
thoughtfully appointed and smartly presented. The
restaurant serves interesting dishes, while lounge
service and extensive conference facilities are
available. A very well equipped spa and leisure centre
complete the picture.

Rooms 103 (22 fmly) ☞ **Facilities** Spa STV FTV Wi-fi
ⓠ HL ⓣ Gym Beauty therapy suite Steam room Sauna
Power plate Xmas New Year **Conf** Class 150 Board 84
Thtr 330 **Services** Lift **Parking** 180
Notes Civ Wed 260

Thistle East Midlands Airport thistle

★★★★ 77% HOTEL

☎ 0871 376 9015
DE74 2SH
e-mail: eastmidlandsairport@thistle.co.uk
web: www.thistle.com/eastmidlandsairport
dir: On A453, at entrance to East Midlands Airport

This large, two-storey purpose-built hotel is
conveniently located next to East Midlands Airport
with easy access to the M1 and M42. Bedrooms are
quite and generally spacious. Substantial public
areas include the popular Lord Byron bar, a
comprehensive range of meeting rooms and an Otium
health and leisure club.

Rooms 164 (11 fmly) (82 GF) (6 smoking)
S £35–£180; **D** £35–£180* **Facilities** STV FTV Wi-fi ⓣ
supervised Gym Sauna Steam room Spa bath Xmas
New Year **Conf** Class 150 Board 54 Thtr 250
Del from £125 to £165* **Services** Air con **Parking** 350
Notes Civ Wed 250

Save on hotels. Book at **theAA.com/hotel**

EAS 159 ENGLAND

E

Radisson Blu Hotel East Midlands Airport

U

☎ 01509 670575
Herald Way, Pegasus Business Park DE74 2TZ
e-mail: sales.eastmidlandsairport@radissonblu.com
web: www.radissonblu.co.uk/hotel-eastmidlandsairport
dir: S'bound: M1 junct 24/A453 exit to East Midlands Airport. N'bound: M1 junct 23A/A453 exit to East Midlands Airport

Currently the rating for this establishment is not confirmed. This may be due to a change of ownership or because it has only recently joined the AA rating scheme. For further details please see the AA website: theAA.com

Rooms 218 (9 fmly) 🐾 **D** £69-£159* **Facilities** Spa STV FTV Wi-fi ☙ HL ☀ Gym **Conf** Class 148 Board 50 Thtr 350 Del from £139 to £209* **Services** Lift Air con **Parking** 350 **Notes** Civ Wed 350

Holiday Inn Express East Midlands Airport

BUDGET HOTEL

☎ 01509 678000
Hunter Rd, Pegasus Business Park DE74 2TQ
e-mail: info@expresseastmidlandsairport.co.uk
web: www.expresseastmidsairport.co.uk
dir: Follow East Midlands Airport signs, right into Pegasus Business Park, hotel on left

A modern hotel ideal for families and business travellers. Fresh and uncomplicated, the spacious rooms include Sky TV, power shower and tea and coffee-making facilities. Continental buffet breakfast is included in the room rate; other meals may be taken at the nearby family pub or restaurant. See also the Hotel Groups pages.

Rooms 90 (55 fmly) (14 GF) (7 smoking) 🐾
Conf Class 26 Board 20 Thtr 40

Premier Inn East Midlands Airport

BUDGET HOTEL

☎ 0871 527 8350
Pegasus Business Park, Herald Way DE74 2TQ
web: www.premierinn.com
dir: From S: M1 junct 23a, A453 signed to airport. From N: M1 junct 24, A456 signed to airport. Hotel on Pegasus Business Park

High quality, budget accommodation ideal for both families and business travellers. Spacious, en suite

bedrooms feature tea and coffee making facilities, and Freeview TV in most hotels. Internet access and Wi-fi are available for a small fee. The adjacent family restaurant features a wide and varied menu. See also the Hotel Groups pages.

Rooms 80

The Grinkle Park Hotel

★★★★ 74%
COUNTRY HOUSE HOTEL

☎ 01287 640515
TS13 4UB
e-mail: info.grinklepark@classiclodges.co.uk
web: www.classiclodges.co.uk
dir: Take A171 from Guisborough towards Whitby. Hotel signed on left

A baronial hall built in 1880 situated between the North Yorkshire Moors and the coast, and surrounded by 35 acres of parkland and gardens where peacocks roam. It retains many original features including fine wood panelling, and the bedrooms are individually designed. The comfortable lounge and bar have welcoming log fires. The Camelia Room is ideal for smaller weddings and private dining.

Rooms 20 (1 fmly) **Facilities** Wi-fi ☙ ☙ Xmas New Year **Conf** Class 80 Board 40 Thtr 120 **Parking** 150 **Notes** ☙ Civ Wed 150

George Hotel

★★ 76% SMALL HOTEL

☎ 01347 821698
Market Place YO61 3AD
e-mail: info@the-george-hotel.co.uk
web: www.the-george-hotel.co.uk
dir: From A19 midway between York & Thirsk, into Easingwold

A friendly welcome awaits at this former coaching inn that faces the Georgian market square. Bedrooms are very comfortably furnished and well equipped, and the mews rooms have their own external access. An extensive range of well-produced food is available both in the bar and restaurant. There are two comfortable lounges and complimentary use of a local fitness centre.

Rooms 15 (2 fmly) (6 GF) **S** £80-£85; **D** £90-£110 (incl. bkfst)* **Facilities** FTV Wi-fi Complimentry use of local fitness centre New Year **Conf** Board 12 Del from £115 to £150* **Parking** 10 **Notes** LB ☙

The Grand Hotel

★★★★★ 84% ◉◉ HOTEL

☎ 01323 412345
King Edward's Pde BN21 4EQ
e-mail: reservations@grandeastbourne.com
web: www.grandeastbourne.com
dir: On seafront W of Eastbourne, 1m from railway station

This famous Victorian hotel offers high standards of service and hospitality, and is in close proximity to both the beach and the South Downs National Park. The extensive public rooms feature a magnificent Great Hall, with marble columns and high ceilings, where guests can relax and enjoy afternoon tea. The spacious bedrooms provide high levels of comfort; many with stunning sea views and a number with private balconies. Guests can choose to eat in the fine dining The Mirabelle or the Garden Restaurant and there are bars as well as superb spa and leisure facilities.

Rooms 152 (20 fmly) (4 GF) **Facilities** Spa STV HL ☀ supervised ☙ Putt green Gym Hairdressing Beauty therapy ♫ Xmas New Year Child facilities **Conf** Class 200 Board 40 Thtr 350 Del from £190 to £300* **Services** Lift **Parking** 80 **Notes** LB Civ Wed 300

EASTBOURNE *continued*

Langham Hotel

★★★ 82% ⊛ HOTEL

☎ 01323 731451
Royal Pde BN22 7AH
web: www.langhamhotel.co.uk
dir: Follow seafront signs. Hotel 0.5m E of pier

This popular hotel is situated in a prominent position with superb views of the sea and pier. Bedrooms are pleasantly decorated and equipped with modern facilities. Superior rooms, some with four-poster beds are stylish and offer sea views. The spacious public rooms include the Grand Parade bar, a lounge and a fine dining conservatory restaurant.

Rooms 81 (2 fmly) **♠ S** £35-£65; **D** £65-£130 (incl. bkfst)* **Facilities** STV FTV Wi-fi ↘ ♫ Xmas New Year **Conf** Class 40 Board 30 Thtr 80 Del from £95 to £120* **Services** Lift **Parking** 43 **Notes** LB ⊗ Civ Wed 140

Hydro Hotel

★★★ 82% HOTEL

☎ 01323 720643
Mount Rd BN20 7HZ
e-mail: sales@hydrohotel.com
dir: From pier/seafront, right along Grand Parade. At Grand Hotel follow Hydro Hotel sign. Into South Cliff, 200mtrs

This well-managed and popular hotel enjoys an elevated position with views of attractive gardens and the sea beyond. The spacious bedrooms are attractive and well equipped. In addition to the comfortable lounges, guests also have access to fitness facilities and a hairdressing salon. Service is both professional and efficient throughout.

Rooms 84 (3 fmly) (3 GF) **Facilities** FTV Wi-fi ↘ Putt green ⛳ Beauty room Hair salon 3/4 size snooker table Xmas New Year **Conf** Class 90 Board 40 Thtr 140 **Services** Lift **Parking** 40 **Notes** RS 24-28 & 30-31 Dec Civ Wed 120

Best Western Lansdowne Hotel

★★★ 79% HOTEL

☎ 01323 725174 & 745483
King Edward's Pde BN21 4EE
e-mail: reception@lansdowne-hotel.co.uk
web: www.bw-lansdownehotel.co.uk
dir: At W end of seafront opposite Western Lawns

Enjoying an enviable position at the quieter end of the parade, this hotel overlooks the Western Lawns and Wish Tower, and is just a few minutes' walk from many of the town's attractions. Public rooms include a variety of lounges, a range of meeting rooms and games rooms. Bedrooms are attractively decorated and many offer sea views. The hotel has a wheelchair lift near the front entrance that operates between the pavement and one of the ground-floor public rooms.

Rooms 102 (10 fmly) (7 smoking) **S** £59-£85; **D** £109-£189 (incl. bkfst) **Facilities** STV FTV Wi-fi ↘ Table tennis Pool table 2 Snooker tables Xmas New Year **Conf** Class 40 Board 40 Thtr 80 Del from £99 to £135 **Services** Lift **Parking** 22 **Notes** LB Civ Wed 60

The Devonshire Park Hotel

★★★ 79% HOTEL

☎ 01323 728144
27-29 Carlisle Rd BN21 4JR
e-mail: info@devonshire-park-hotel.co.uk
web: www.devonshire-park-hotel.co.uk
dir: Follow signs to seafront, exit at Wish Tower. Hotel opposite Congress Theatre

A handsome family-run hotel handily placed for the seafront and theatres. Attractively furnished rooms are spacious and comfortable; many boast king-sized beds and all are equipped with Wi-fi and satellite TV. Guests can relax in the well presented lounges, the cosy bar or, when the weather's fine, on the garden terrace.

Rooms 35 (8 GF) **♠ S** £50-£80; **D** £100-£160 (incl. bkfst) **Facilities** STV Wi-fi Xmas New Year **Services** Lift **Parking** 25 **Notes** LB ⊗ No children 12yrs

New Wilmington Hotel

★★★ 75% HOTEL

☎ 01323 721219
25-27 Compton St BN21 4DU
e-mail: info@new-wilmington-hotel.co.uk
web: www.new-wilmington-hotel.co.uk
dir: A22 to Eastbourne seafront. Right along promenade to Wish Tower. Right, then left at end of road, hotel 2nd on left

This friendly, family-run hotel is conveniently located close to the seafront, the Congress Theatre and Winter Gardens. Public rooms are well presented and include a cosy bar, a small comfortable lounge and a spacious restaurant. Bedrooms are comfortably appointed and tastefully decorated; family and superior bedrooms are available.

Rooms 40 (14 fmly) (3 GF) **♠ S** £48-£61; **D** £71-£133 (incl. bkfst)* **Facilities** STV FTV Wi-fi ↘ ♫ Xmas New Year **Conf** Class 20 Board 20 Thtr 40 **Services** Lift **Parking** 3 **Notes** LB Closed 3 Jan-mid Feb

Chatsworth Hotel

★★★ 74% HOTEL

☎ 01323 411016 & 748700
Grand Pde BN21 3YR
e-mail: chatsworth@lionhotelsltd.com
web: www.lionhotelsltd.com
dir: M23 then A27 to Polegate. A2270 into Eastbourne, follow seafront signs. Hotel near pier

Within minutes of the town centre and pier, this attractive Edwardian hotel is located on the seafront. The public areas consist of the Chatsworth Bar, a cosy lounge and the Devonshire Restaurant. Bedrooms, many with sea views, are traditional in style and have a range of facilities. Service is friendly and helpful throughout.

Rooms 45 (2 fmly) **♠ S** £45-£60; **D** £90-£120 (incl. bkfst) **Facilities** Spa STV FTV Wi-fi Gym Hairdresser Sauna Massage Beauty treatments ♫ Xmas New Year **Conf** Class 60 Board 40 Thtr 100 Del from £125 to £145 **Services** Lift **Notes** LB ⊗ Civ Wed 140

Albany Lions Hotel

★★★ 73% HOTEL

☎ 01323 722788 & 748700
Grand Pde BN21 4DJ
e-mail: albany@lionhotelsltd.com
dir: From town centre follow Seafront/Pier signs

This hotel, close to the bandstand, has a seafront location that is within walking distance of the main town shopping. A carvery dinner is served in the restaurant, which has great sea views from most tables, and a relaxing drink or afternoon tea can be enjoyed in the sun lounge.

Rooms 61 (5 fmly) **♠ S** £45-£60; **D** £90-£120 (incl. bkfst) **Facilities** STV FTV Wi-fi Hairdresser Massage ♫ Xmas New Year **Conf** Class 60 Board 40 Thtr 120 Del from £110 to £130 **Services** Lift **Notes** LB ⊗

Mansion Lions Hotel

★★★ 73% HOTEL

☎ 01323 727411 & 748700
Grand Pde BN21 3YS
e-mail: mansion@lionhotelsltd.com
dir: From town centre follow Seafront/Pier signs. Hotel on seafront

Directly overlooking the beach, this Victorian hotel is only two minutes' walk from the magnificent pier, the shopping centre and bandstand. The well-equipped bedrooms are spacious, comfortably furnished and some have sea views. An enjoyable four-course evening meal and a filling breakfast are served in the stylish Hartington Restaurant. There is an attractive lounge, and a pretty garden can be found at the back of the hotel.

Rooms 108 (6 fmly) (4 GF) 🐾 **S** £45–£60; **D** £90–£120 (incl. bkfst) **Facilities** STV Wi-fi 🎵 Xmas New Year **Conf** Class 80 Board 40 Thtr 150 Del from £110 to £130 **Services** Lift **Notes** LB ⊗ Closed 2-31 Jan Civ Wed 150

Claremont Lions Hotel

★★★ 72% HOTEL

☎ 01323 731417
Grand Pde BN21 3YL
e-mail: claremont@lionhotelsltd.com
dir: A27 E to Eastbourne. Follow seafront signs, hotel opposite pier

Located directly opposite the beautiful Carpet Gardens, the seafront and pier this majestic hotel offers spacious bedrooms that are comfortably furnished; all have fridges and many have sea views. Public areas including the elegant dining room are attractively presented and comfortable. Ground floor rooms are well equipped for less able guests.

Rooms 67 (2 fmly) (4 GF) 🐾 **S** £45–£60; **D** £90–£120 (incl. bkfst) **Facilities** STV FTV Wi-fi HL 🎵 Xmas New Year **Conf** Class 50 Board 40 Thtr 100 Del from £110 to £130 **Services** Lift **Parking** 6 **Notes** LB ⊗ Closed 2 Jan-28 Feb

Courtlands Hotel

★★★ 70% HOTEL

☎ 01323 723737
3-5 Wilmington Gardens BN21 4JN
e-mail: bookings@courtlandseastbourne.com
dir: Exit Grand Parade at Carlisle Rd

Situated opposite the Congress Theatre, this hotel is just a short walk from both the seafront and Devonshire Park. Bedrooms are comfortably furnished and pleasantly decorated. Public areas are smartly appointed and include a cosy bar, a separate lounge and an attractive dining room.

Rooms 45 (4 fmly) (3 GF) **S** £49–£59; **D** £98–£120 (incl. bkfst)* **Facilities** STV FTV 🏊 🎵 Xmas New Year **Conf** Class 60 Board 60 Thtr 60 **Services** Lift **Parking** 36 **Notes** LB Civ Wed 100

Queens Hotel

★★ 76% HOTEL   Leisureplex

☎ 01323 722822
Marine Pde BN21 3DY
e-mail: queens.eastbourne@alfatravel.co.uk
web: www.leisureplex.co.uk
dir: Follow signs for seafront, hotel opposite pier

Popular with tour groups, this long-established hotel enjoys a central, prominent seafront location overlooking the pier. Spacious public areas include a choice of lounges, and regular entertainment is also provided. Bedrooms are suitably appointed and equipped.

Rooms 122 (5 fmly) 🐾 **S** £38–£50; **D** £62–£86 (incl. bkfst)* **Facilities** Wi-fi Snooker 🎵 Xmas New Year **Services** Lift **Parking** 50 **Notes** LB ⊗ Closed Jan (ex New Year) RS Nov, Feb-Mar

Alexandra Hotel

★★ 75% HOTEL

☎ 01323 720131
King Edwards Pde BN21 4DR
e-mail: alexandrahotel@mistral.co.uk
web: http://alexandrahotel.eastbourne.biz/
dir: On seafront at junct of Carlisle Road & King Edward Parade

Located at the west end of the town, opposite the Wishing Tower, this hotel boasts panoramic views of the sea from many rooms. Bedrooms vary in size but are comfortable with good facilities for guests. A warm welcome is guaranteed at this long-standing, family run establishment.

Rooms 38 (2 fmly) (3 GF) **S** £35–£48; **D** £70–£96 (incl. bkfst)* **Facilities** FTV Wi-fi 🎵 Xmas New Year **Services** Lift **Notes** LB ⊗ Closed Jan & Feb RS Mar

Congress Hotel

★★ 75% HOTEL

☎ 01323 732118
31-41 Carlisle Rd BN21 4JS
e-mail: reservations@congresshotel.co.uk
web: www.congresshotel.co.uk
dir: From Eastbourne seafront W towards Beachy Head. Right at Wishtower into Wilmington Sq, cross Compton St, hotel on left

An attractive Victorian property ideally located close to the seafront, Wish Tower and Congress Theatre. The bedrooms are bright and spacious. Family rooms are available plus there are facilities for less mobile guests. Entertainment is provided in a large dining room that has a dance floor and bar.

Rooms 62 (6 fmly) (8 GF) 🐾 **S** £33–£48; **D** £66–£96 **Facilities** FTV Wi-fi Games room 🎵 Xmas New Year **Services** Lift **Parking** 12 **Notes** RS Jan-Feb

The Palm Court

★★ 74% HOTEL

☎ 01323 725811
15 Burlington Place BN21 4AR
e-mail: thepalmcourt@btconnect.com
web: www.thepalmcourthotel.co.uk
dir: From pier, W along seafront, Burlington Place 5th right

This family-run hotel is ideally situated close to the seafront and local theatres. The well appointed public areas include the lounge, spacious bar and stylish restaurant. Bedrooms vary in size but all offer plenty of handy accessories, comfortable furnishings and bright modern bathrooms. Good mobility facilities are provided.

Rooms 38 (5 GF) 🐾 **S** £38–£48; **D** £76–£96 (incl. bkfst) **Facilities** FTV Wi-fi Xmas New Year **Services** Lift **Notes** LB ⊗

E

EASTBOURNE *continued*

The Afton Hotel

★★ 68% HOTEL

☎ 01323 733162
2-8 Cavendish Place BN21 3EJ
e-mail: info@aftonhotel.com
dir: From A22, A27 or A259, follow seafront signs. Hotel by pier

This friendly family run hotel is ideally located in the centre of town, opposite the pier and close to the shopping centre. Bedrooms vary in size but are all comfortable and well co-ordinated. The spacious restaurant serves traditional home cooking. A full programme of entertainment is provided.

Rooms 56 (4 fmly) (4 GF) 🐾 **S** £25-£40; **D** £50-£80 (incl. bkfst)* **Facilities** Wi-fi ♨ ♫ Xmas New Year **Conf** Class 50 Board 50 Thtr 100 **Services** Lift **Notes** LB

Savoy Court Hotel

★★ 68% HOTEL

☎ 01323 723132
11-15 Cavendish Place BN21 3EJ
e-mail: info@savoycourthotel.co.uk
web: www.savoycourthotel.co.uk
dir: M25 junct 6, A22 to Eastbourne. Hotel 50mtrs from pier

Located close to the pier and within easy walking distance of the beaches and open-air bandstand this hotel offers bedrooms that are pleasantly decorated and furnished. The public areas include a cosy lounge and spacious bar/lounge for relaxing at the end of the day.

Rooms 29 (3 fmly) (5 GF) **Facilities** FTV Wi-fi ♨ Xmas New Year **Conf** Class 40 Board 30 Thtr 60 **Services** Lift **Notes** ⊗

West Rocks Hotel

★★ 61% HOTEL

☎ 01323 725217
Grand Pde BN21 4DL
e-mail: westrockshotel@btinternet.com
dir: West end of seafront

Ideally located near to the pier and bandstand, this hotel is only a short walk from the town centre. Bedrooms vary in size, with many offering stunning sea views. Guests have the choice of two comfortable lounges and a bar.

Rooms 47 (8 fmly) (6 GF) **Facilities** ♫ Xmas **Conf** Class 12 Board 12 Thtr 20 Del from £65 to £85* **Services** Lift **Notes** ⊗ Closed 3 Jan-20 Feb

Premier Inn Eastbourne

BUDGET HOTEL

☎ 0871 527 8352
Willingdon Dr BN23 8AL
web: www.premierinn.com
dir: From A22 or A27 at Polegate, take bypass signed Eastbourne (A22). Continue to Shinewater rdbt. Left towards Langney. Hotel 0.25m on left

High quality, budget accommodation ideal for both families and business travellers. Spacious, en suite bedrooms feature tea and coffee making facilities, and Freeview TV in most hotels. Internet access and Wi-fi are available for a small fee. The adjacent family restaurant features a wide and varied menu. See also the Hotel Groups pages.

Rooms 47

Premier Inn Eastbourne (Polegate)

BUDGET HOTEL

☎ 0871 527 8354
Hailsham Rd, Polegate BN26 6QL
web: www.premierinn.com
dir: At rdbt junct of A22 & A27

Rooms 40

Holiday Inn Southampton - Eastleigh M3 Jct 13

★★★ 81% HOTEL

☎ 0871 942 9075
Leigh Rd SO50 9PG
e-mail: reservations-eastleigh@ihg.com
web: www.hisouthamptoneastleighhotel.co.uk
dir: M3 junct 13, right at lights, follow signs to Eastleigh, hotel on right

Located close to the M3 and convenient for Southampton Airport and the New Forest, this hotel is suitable for both the business and leisure traveller. All bedrooms have air conditioning and work desks as standard, but there are also executive rooms and suites with extra facilities. Junction Restaurant serves international dishes and there is a cocktail lounge. The popular leisure area includes a swimming pool, jacuzzi, aerobics studio, steam room, sauna and beauty treatments.

Rooms 129 (3 fmly) (27 GF) (12 smoking) **Facilities** FTV Wi-fi ♨ ⊗ supervised Gym Beauty treatment rooms Whirlpool spa Steam room Sauna Personal trainer Studio **Conf** Class 60 Board 50 Thtr 120 **Services** Lift Air con **Parking** 175 **Notes** ⊗ Civ Wed 100

Ellington Lodge Hotel

★★★ 🅰 HOTEL

☎ 023 8065 1478 & 8061 3989
The Concorde Club SO50 9HQ
e-mail: hotel@theconcordeclub.com
web: www.theconcordeclub.com
dir: M27 junct 5, at rdbt follow Chandlers Ford signs, hotel 500yds on right

Rooms 35 (18 GF) **S** £50-£120; **D** £60-£140 (incl. bkfst)* **Facilities** FTV Wi-fi Fishing ♫ **Conf** Class 50 Board 40 Thtr 200 **Services** Lift Air con **Parking** 250 **Notes** LB No children 18yrs Closed 24-26 Dec

Premier Inn Southampton (Eastleigh)

BUDGET HOTEL

☎ 0871 527 8994
Leigh Rd SO50 9YX
web: www.premierinn.com
dir: M3 junct 13, A335 towards Eastleigh. Hotel on right

High quality, budget accommodation ideal for both families and business travellers. Spacious, en suite bedrooms feature tea and coffee making facilities, and Freeview TV in most hotels. Internet access and Wi-fi are available for a small fee. The adjacent family restaurant features a wide and varied menu. See also the Hotel Groups pages.

Rooms 60

Premier Inn London Edgware

BUDGET HOTEL

☎ 0871 527 8652
435 Burnt Oak Broadway HA8 5AQ
web: www.premierinn.com
dir: M1 junct 4, A41, A5 towards Edgware. 3m to hotel

High quality, budget accommodation ideal for both families and business travellers. Spacious, en suite bedrooms feature tea and coffee making facilities, and Freeview TV in most hotels. Internet access and Wi-fi are available for a small fee. The adjacent family restaurant features a wide and varied menu. See also the Hotel Groups pages.

Rooms 111

Save on hotels. Book at **theAA.com/hotel**

EAS – ELT 163 ENGLAND

EGGESFORD
Devon

Map 3 SS61

Fox & Hounds Country Hotel

★★★ 75% ⊛ HOTEL

☎ 01769 580345
EX18 7JZ
e-mail: relax@foxandhoundshotel.co.uk
web: www.foxandhoundshotel.co.uk
dir: M5 junct 27, A361 towards Tiverton. Take B3137
signed Witheridge. After Nomans Land follow signs
for Eggesford Station. Hotel 50mtrs up hill from
station

Situated midway between Exeter and Barnstaple, in
the beautiful Taw Valley, this extensively developed
hotel was originally a coaching inn dating back to the
1800s. Many of the comfortable, elegant bedrooms
have lovely countryside views. Good cooking utilises
excellent local produce and can be enjoyed in either
restaurant or the convivial bar. For fishing
enthusiasts, the hotel has direct access to the River
Taw, and equipment and tuition can be provided if
required.

Rooms 19 (6 fmly) (3 GF) ⟆ **S** £62.50-£75;
D £125-£145 (incl. bkfst)* **Facilities** FTV Wi-fi ⟆
Fishing Health & beauty suite Xmas New Year
Conf Class 60 Board 60 Thtr 100 **Parking** 100
Notes LB Civ Wed 130

EGHAM
Surrey

Map 6 TQ07

Great Fosters

★★★★ 83% ⊛⊛⊛ HOTEL

☎ 01784 433822
Stroude Rd TW20 9UR
e-mail: reception@greatfosters.co.uk
web: www.greatfosters.co.uk
dir: From A30 (Bagshot to Staines), right at lights by
Wheatsheaf pub into Christchurch Rd. Straight on at
rdbt (pass 2 shop parades on right). Left at lights
into Stroude Rd. Hotel 0.75m on right

This Grade I listed mansion dates back to the 16th
century. The main house rooms are very much in
keeping with the house's original style but are, of
course, up-to-date with modern amenities. The
stables and cloisters provide particularly stylish and
luxurious accommodation. Public areas include a cosy
bar and the award-winning Oak Room Restaurant, as
well as a host of meeting and event facilities.
Alfresco dining, overlooking the well manicured
grounds, in the summer months is a must.

Rooms 43 (22 annexe) (1 fmly) (13 GF) ⟆ **S** £135;
D £175-£445* **Facilities** STV Wi-fi ⟆ ⟆ ⟆ ⟆ Xmas
New Year **Conf** Class 72 Board 50 Thtr 150
Del from £275 to £325* **Parking** 200 **Notes** LB ⊗
Civ Wed 180

the runnymede-on-thames

★★★★ 81% HOTEL

☎ 01784 220600
Windsor Rd TW20 0AG
e-mail: info@therunnymede.co.uk
web: www.therunnymede.co.uk
dir: M25 junct 13, onto A308 towards Windsor

Enjoying a peaceful location beside the River Thames,
this large modern hotel, with its excellent range of
facilities, balances both leisure and corporate
business well. The extensive function suites, together
with spacious lounges and stylish, well laid out
bedrooms are impressive. Superb spa facilities are
available, and the good food and beverage venues
offer wonderful river views.

Rooms 181 (19 fmly) ⟆ **S** £132-£328; **D** £169-£350
(incl. bkfst)* **Facilities** Spa STV Wi-fi ⟆ HL ⟆
supervised ⟆ supervised ⟆ ⟆ Gym Dance studio
Children's play area River boat hire Group treatment
suite ♫ Xmas New Year Child facilities
Conf Class 250 Board 76 Thtr 300 Del from £249 to
£326* **Services** Lift Air con **Parking** 300 **Notes** LB ⊗
Civ Wed 140

ELLESMERE PORT
Cheshire

Holiday Inn Ellesmere Port/Chester

★★★ 75% HOTEL

☎ 0151 356 8111
Waterways, Lower Mersey St CH65 2AL
e-mail: reservations@hiellesmereport.com
web: www.hiellesmereport.com
dir: At M53 junct 9

This smart, modern hotel enjoys a waterside location
on the canal docks. The well equipped bedrooms are
spacious and comfortable. Extensive meeting
facilities, a well-equipped gym and swimming pool,
and its proximity to local tourist attractions make it
popular with business travellers and families alike.
Meals are served in the restaurant overlooking the
water.

Rooms 83

Mercure Chester North Woodhey House Hotel

★★★ 71% HOTEL

☎ 0151 339 5121
**Berwick Road West / Welsh Rd, Little Sutton
CH66 4PS**
e-mail: enquiries@woodheyhouse-hotel-chester.com
web: www.woodheyhouse-hotel-chester.com
dir: A41 S, right at 2nd set of lights onto A550
towards Queensferry. Hotel 1m on left

Located in a quiet rural setting, yet in easy reach of
the M53, the hotel is an ideal stop-off for both
business and leisure guests. All bedrooms are well
equipped. The day rooms are stylishly appointed and
include a bar, restaurant and a very good range of
meeting and conference facilities. The hotel also has
an indoor pool, gym and steam room.

Rooms 75 (8 fmly) (23 GF) **Facilities** FTV Wi-fi ⟆
Gym Sauna Steam room Xmas New Year
Conf Class 120 Board 80 Thtr 250 **Services** Lift
Parking 150 **Notes** Civ Wed 100

ELTERWATER
Cumbria

Map 18 NY30

Langdale Hotel & Spa

★★★★ 77% ⊛⊛ COUNTRY HOUSE HOTEL

☎ 015394 38014 & 38012
LA22 9JD
e-mail: info@langdale.co.uk
web: www.langdale.co.uk
dir: In Langdale Valley W of Ambleside

Founded on the site of an abandoned 19th-century
gunpowder works, this modern hotel is set in 35 acres
of woodland and waterways. Comfortable bedrooms,
many with spa baths, vary in size. Extensive public
areas include a choice of stylish restaurants,
conference and leisure facilities and an elegant bar
with an interesting selection of snuff. There is also a
traditional pub run by the hotel just along the main
road.

Rooms 56 (51 annexe) (4 fmly) (25 GF) ⟆
S £82-£139; **D** £109-£185 (incl. bkfst)*
Facilities Spa STV FTV Wi-fi ⟆ supervised ⟆ Fishing
Gym Steam room Solarium Aerobics studio Health &
beauty salon Cycle hire Xmas New Year Child
facilities **Conf** Class 40 Board 35 Thtr 80 **Parking** 65
Notes ⊗ Civ Wed 65

E

ELTERWATER *continued*

New Dungeon Ghyll Hotel

★★★ 74% HOTEL

☎ 015394 37213
Great Langdale, Ambleside LA22 9JX
e-mail: enquiries@dungeon-ghyll.com
web: www.dungeon-ghyll.com
dir: From Ambleside follow A593 towards Coniston for 3m, at Skelwith Bridge right onto B5343 towards 'The Langdales'

This friendly hotel enjoys a tranquil, idyllic position at the head of the valley, set among the impressive peaks of Langdale. Bedrooms vary in size and style; the rooms are brightly decorated and smartly furnished. Bar meals are served all day, and dinner can be enjoyed in the restaurant overlooking the landscaped gardens; there is also a cosy lounge/bar.

Rooms 22 (1 fmly) (4 GF) **Facilities** FTV Wi-fi
Xmas New Year **Conf** Class 30 Board 20 Thtr 20
Del from £110 to £150 **Parking** 30 **Notes** ⊗

ELY	Map 12 TL58
Cambridgeshire	

Lamb Hotel

★★★ Ⓐ HOTEL · OldEnglish

☎ 01353 663574
2 Lynn Rd CB7 4EJ
e-mail: lamb.ely@oldenglishinns.co.uk
web: www.oldenglish.co.uk
dir: From A10 into Ely, hotel in town centre

Rooms 31 (6 fmly) **Facilities** Xmas **Conf** Class 40
Board 70 Thtr 100 **Parking** 20

The Anchor Inn

⊛ RESTAURANT WITH ROOMS

☎ 01353 778537
Sutton Gault CB6 2BD
e-mail: anchorinn@popmail.bta.com
dir: W of Ely. Sutton Gault signed from B1381 at S end of Sutton

Located beside the New Bedford River with stunning country views, this 17th-century inn has a wealth of original features enhanced by period furniture. The spacious bedrooms are tastefully appointed and equipped with many thoughtful touches. The friendly team of staff offer helpful and attentive service.

Rooms 4 (2 fmly)

EMBLETON	Map 21 NU22
Northumberland	

Dunstanburgh Castle Hotel

★★ 85% HOTEL

☎ 01665 576111
NE66 3UN
e-mail: stay@dunstanburghcastlehotel.co.uk
web: www.dunstanburghcastlehotel.co.uk
dir: From A1 take B1340 to Denwick past Rennington & Masons Arms. Right signed Embleton

The focal point of the village, this friendly, family-run hotel has a dining room and grill room that offer different menus, plus a cosy bar and two lounges. In addition to the main bedrooms, a barn conversion houses three stunning suites, each with a lounge and gallery bedroom above.

Rooms 32 (12 annexe) (6 fmly) **S** £40-£61.50;
D £80-£123 (incl. bkfst)* **Facilities** Wi-fi **Parking** 33
Notes Closed Dec-Jan

EMSWORTH	Map 5 SU70
Hampshire	

Brookfield Hotel

★★★ 80% HOTEL · CLASSIC BRITISH HOTELS

☎ 01243 373363
Havant Rd PO10 7LF
e-mail: bookings@brookfieldhotel.co.uk
dir: From A27 onto A259 towards Emsworth. Hotel 0.5m on left

This well-established family-run hotel has spacious public areas with popular conference and banqueting facilities. Bedrooms are in a modern style, and comfortably furnished. The popular Hermitage Restaurant offers a seasonally changing menu and an interesting wine list.

Rooms 39 (6 fmly) (12 GF) **Facilities** STV FTV Wi-fi
Free pass to local leisure club New Year
Conf Class 50 Board 50 Thtr 100 Del from £154.95
Parking 80 **Notes** ⊗ Civ Wed 100

---

36 on the Quay

⊛⊛⊛ RESTAURANT WITH ROOMS

☎ 01243 375592 & 372257
47 South St PO10 7EG

Occupying a prime position with far reaching views over the estuary, this 16th-century house is the scene for some accomplished and exciting cuisine. The elegant restaurant occupies centre stage with peaceful pastel shades, local art and crisp napery together with glimpses of the bustling harbour outside. The contemporary bedrooms offer style, comfort and thoughtful extras.

Rooms 5

ENFIELD	Map 6 TQ39
Greater London	

Royal Chace Hotel

★★★★ 77% ⊛ HOTEL

☎ 020 8884 8181
The Ridgeway EN2 8AR
e-mail: reservations@royalchacehotel.co.uk
dir: M25 junct 24, A1005 towards Enfield. Hotel 3m on right

This professionally run, privately owned hotel enjoys a peaceful location with open fields to the rear. Public rooms are smartly appointed; the ground-floor Kings Restaurant is particularly appealing with its warm colour schemes and friendly service. Bedrooms are well presented and thoughtfully equipped.

Rooms 92 (5 fmly) (32 GF) **S** £85-£170;
D £95-£230 (incl. bkfst)* **Facilities** FTV Wi-fi Gym
New Year **Conf** Class 100 Board 40 Thtr 250 Del £150
Parking 200 **Notes** LB ⊗ RS Sun eve Civ Wed 220

Save on hotels. Book at **theAA.com/hotel**

ELT – ESC 165 ENGLAND

E

Comfort Hotel Enfield

BUDGET HOTEL

☎ 020 8366 3511
52 Rowantree Rd EN2 8PW
e-mail: admin@comfortenfield.co.uk
web: www.comfortenfield.co.uk
dir: M25 junct 24 follow signs for A1005 towards
Enfield. Hospital on left, across mini-rdbt, 3rd left
onto Bycullah Rd, 2nd left into Rowantree Rd

This hotel is situated in a quiet residential area, close
to the centre of Enfield. Comfortable accommodation
is provided in the thoughtfully equipped bedrooms,
which include ground floor and family rooms. Public
areas include a cosy bar and lounge, conference and
function rooms and the smart Etruscan Restaurant.
See also the Hotel Groups pages.

Rooms 34 (34 annexe) (3 fmly) **Conf** Class 25
Board 25 Thtr 65

Premier Inn Enfield

BUDGET HOTEL

☎ 0871 527 8374
Innova Park, Corner of Solar Way EN3 7XY
web: www.premierinn.com
dir: M25 junct 25, A10 towards London, left into
Bullsmoor Lane & Mollison Ave. Over rdbt, right at
lights into Innova Science Park

High quality, budget accommodation ideal for both
families and business travellers. Spacious, en suite
bedrooms feature tea and coffee making facilities,
and Freeview TV in most hotels. Internet access and
Wi-fi are available for a small fee. The adjacent
family restaurant features a wide and varied menu.
See also the Hotel Groups pages.

Rooms 160

EPPING
Essex

Map 6 TL40

Best Western The Bell Hotel

★★★ 75% HOTEL

☎ 01992 573138
High Rd, Bell Common CM16 4DG
e-mail: reservations@bellhotelepping.com
web: www.bellhotelepping.com
dir: M11 junct 7, B1393 to Epping. Hotel on right past
town centre

This hotel enjoys a convenient location on the
outskirts of the town centre, close to the M25 and M1
and the nearby tube station allows for quick access to
London. There is a range of bedroom styles and all
bedrooms are attractively presented and feature LCD
TVs and free Wi-fi. Public areas include a cosy bar, a
popular restaurant along with well-equipped
conference facilities.

Rooms 79 (79 annexe) (5 fmly) (38 GF) (10 smoking)
S £59-£195; **D** £59-£195 **Facilities** FTV Wi-fi ₺ Xmas
New Year **Conf** Class 50 Board 50 Thtr 85
Del from £130 to £180 **Parking** 80 **Notes** ⊗
Civ Wed 60

EPSOM
Surrey

Map 6 TQ26

Holiday Inn Express London - Epsom Downs

BUDGET HOTEL

☎ 01372 755200
Langley Vale Rd KT18 5LG
e-mail: epsom@holidayinnexpress.org.uk
dir: Just off M25 junct 9

A modern hotel ideal for families and business
travellers. Fresh and uncomplicated, the spacious
rooms include Sky TV, power shower and tea and
coffee-making facilities. Continental buffet breakfast
is included in the room rate; other meals may be
taken at the nearby family pub or restaurant. See also
the Hotel Groups pages.

Rooms 120 **Conf** Class 20 Board 12 Thtr 20

Premier Inn Epsom Central

BUDGET HOTEL

☎ 0871 527 8376
2-4 St Margarets Dr, off Dorking Rd KT18 7LB
web: www.premierinn.com
dir: M25 junct 9, A24 towards Epsom, hotel on left,
just before town centre

High quality, budget accommodation ideal for both
families and business travellers. Spacious, en suite
bedrooms feature tea and coffee making facilities,
and Freeview TV in most hotels. Internet access and
Wi-fi are available for a small fee. The adjacent
family restaurant features a wide and varied menu.
See also the Hotel Groups pages.

Rooms 58

Premier Inn Epsom North

BUDGET HOTEL

☎ 0871 527 8380
272 Kingston Rd, Ewell KT19 0SH
web: www.premierinn.com
dir: M25 junct 8, A217 towards Sutton. A240 towards
Ewell. At Beggars Hill rdbt 2nd exit into Kingston Rd

Rooms 29

ESCRICK
North Yorkshire

Map 16 SE64

The Parsonage Country House Hotel

★★★ 79% ◉ COUNTRY HOUSE HOTEL

☎ 01904 728111
York Rd YO19 6LF
e-mail: reservations@parsonagehotel.co.uk
web: www.parsonagehotel.co.uk
dir: A64 onto A19 (Selby). Follow to Escrick. Hotel by
St Helens Church

This 19th-century, former parsonage has been
carefully restored and extended to provide delightful
accommodation, set in well-tended gardens.
Bedrooms are smartly appointed and well equipped
both for business and leisure guests. Spacious public
areas include an elegant restaurant, excellent
meeting and conference facilities and a choice of
attractive lounges.

Rooms 50 (13 annexe) (4 fmly) (9 GF) (8 smoking)
S £65-£120; **D** £80-£140 (incl. bkfst)* **Facilities** Spa
STV Wi-fi ⊙ Putt green Gym Sauna Steam room
Solarium Xmas New Year **Conf** Class 80 Board 50
Thtr 240 Del from £135 to £180* **Services** Lift
Parking 120 **Notes** LB ⊗ Civ Wed 150

EVERSHOT
Dorset
Map 4 ST50

INSPECTORS' CHOICE

Summer Lodge Country House Hotel, Restaurant & Spa

★★★★ ◉◉◉ COUNTRY HOUSE HOTEL

☎ 01935 482000
DT2 0JR
e-mail: summer@relaischateaux.com
dir: 1m W of A37 halfway between Dorchester & Yeovil

This picturesque hotel is situated in the heart of Dorset and is the ideal retreat for getting 'away from it all', and it's worth arriving in time for the excellent afternoon tea. Bedrooms are appointed to a very high standard; each is individually designed with upholstered walls and come with a wealth of luxurious facilities. Expect plasma screen TVs, DVD players, radios, air conditioning and Wi-fi access, plus little touches such as homemade shortbread, fresh fruit and scented candles. The delightful public areas include a sumptuous lounge complete with an open fire, and the elegant restaurant where the cuisine continues to be the high point of any stay.

Rooms 24 (14 annexe) (6 fmly) (1 GF) 🐾 S £204-£589; D £231-£616 (incl. bkfst)* Facilities Spa STV FTV Wi-fi ⚲ 🕲 🏊 🏄 Gym Sauna Xmas New Year Conf Class 16 Board 16 Thtr 24 Del from £325 to £365* Services Air con Parking 41 Notes LB Civ Wed 30

George Albert Hotel

★★★ 77% HOTEL

☎ 01935 483430
Wardon Hill DT2 9PW
e-mail: enquiries@gahotel.co.uk
dir: On A37 (between Yeovil & Dorchester). Adjacent to Southern Counties Shooting Ground

Situated mid-way between Dorchester and Yeovil, this hotel has much to offer for both business and leisure guests. The bedrooms offer impressive levels of comfort and many also having wonderful views across the Dorset countryside. Stylish public areas include extensive function rooms, a relaxing lounge, and a choice of dining options. Additional facilities include a karting track and clay pigeon shooting.

Rooms 39 (3 fmly) 🐾 S £50-£140; D £60-£160 (incl. bkfst)* Facilities FTV Wi-fi 🏌 Shooting Clay pigeon Kart track Xmas New Year Conf Class 60 Board 90 Thtr 250 Del from £120 to £140 Services Lift Air con Parking 200 Notes ⊗ Civ Wed 405

EVESHAM
Worcestershire
Map 10 SP04

Northwick Hotel

★★★ 82% HOTEL

☎ 01386 40322
Waterside WR11 1BT
e-mail: enquiries@northwickhotel.co.uk
dir: A46 onto A44, over lights, right at next lights onto B4035. Past hospital, hotel on right

Located close to the centre of the town, this hotel benefits a good position overlooking the River Avon and adjacent park. The bedrooms are traditional in style and have broadband access; one room has been adapted to provide disabled access. Public areas offer a choice of drinking options, a restaurant and function and meeting rooms.

Rooms 29 (4 fmly) (1 GF) 🐾 S £76-£83; D £87-£120 (incl. bkfst)* Facilities STV FTV Wi-fi 🏌 New Year Conf Class 150 Board 80 Thtr 240 Del from £120 to £140* Parking 110 Notes LB ⊗ Closed 25-28 Dec Civ Wed 70

Dumbleton Hall Hotel

★★★ 79% COUNTRY HOUSE HOTEL

☎ 01386 881240
WR11 7TS
e-mail: dh@pofr.co.uk
web: www.dumbletonhall.co.uk

(For full entry see Dumbleton)

The Evesham Hotel

★★★ 77% HOTEL

☎ 01386 765566 & 0800 716969 (Res)
Coopers Ln, Off Waterside WR11 1DA
e-mail: reception@eveshamhotel.com
web: www.eveshamhotel.com
dir: M5 junct 9, A46 to Evesham. At rdbt on entering Evesham, take B4184 towards town, right at new bridge lights, 800yds, right into Coopers Ln

Dating from 1540 and set in extensive grounds, this delightful hotel has well-equipped accommodation that includes a selection of quirkily themed rooms - Alice in Wonderland, Egyptian, and Aquarium (which has a tropical fish tank in the bathroom). A reputation for food is well deserved, with a particularly strong choice for vegetarians. Children are welcome and toys are always available.

Rooms 39 (2 fmly) (11 GF) 🐾 S £80-£89.50; D fr £129 (incl. bkfst)* Facilities FTV Wi-fi 🕲 Putt green 🏄 New Year Child facilities Conf Class 12 Board 12 Thtr 12 Del from £144* Parking 50 Notes LB Closed 25-26 Dec

Premier Inn Evesham

BUDGET HOTEL

☎ 0871 527 8384
Evesham Country Park, A46 Trunk Rd, Twyford WR11 4TP
web: www.premierinn.com
dir: At rdbt junct of A46(T) & A4184 at N end of Evesham bypass. Adjacent to Evesham Country Park

High quality, budget accommodation ideal for both families and business travellers. Spacious, en suite bedrooms feature tea and coffee making facilities, and Freeview TV in most hotels. Internet access and Wi-fi are available for a small fee. The adjacent family restaurant features a wide and varied menu. See also the Hotel Groups pages.

Rooms 40

Save on hotels. Book at theAA.com/hotel

EVE – EXE 167 ENGLAND

E

Mercure Exeter Southgate Hotel & Spa

★★★★ 73% HOTEL

☎ 01392 412812
Southernhay East EX1 1QF
e-mail: h6624@accor.com
web: www.mercure.com
dir: M5 junct 30, 3rd exit (Exeter), 2nd left towards
city centre, 3rd exit at next rdbt, hotel 2m on right

Centrally located and with excellent parking, The
Southgate offers a diverse range of leisure and
business facilities. Public areas are pleasantly
spacious with comfortable seating in the bar and
lounge; there is also a pleasant terrace. The
bedrooms, in differing sizes, are well equipped and
have modern facilities.

Rooms 154 (6 fmly) (23 GF) ☀ **Facilities** FTV Wi-fi ☕
🕘 supervised Gym Sauna Spa bath New Year
Conf Class 70 Board 50 Thtr 150 **Services** Lift
Parking 101 **Notes** ⊗ Civ Wed 80

The Rougemont Hotel, Exeter   thistle

★★★★ 72% HOTEL

☎ 0871 376 9018
Queen St EX4 3SP
e-mail: exeter@thistle.co.uk
web: www.thistlehotels.com/exeter
dir: M5 junct 30 follow signs to services at 1st rdbt,
1st left towards city centre. In city centre follow
Museum/Central Station signs. Hotel opposite

Centrally located, this elegant hotel is well situated
for those visiting the city for business or leisure.

There is a charming, old-fashioned atmosphere here,
with traditional hospitality to the fore. All bedrooms
offer high levels of comfort and a number of suites
are available. A choice of bars is provided - the
convivial Drakes Bar and the smart and more formal
cocktail bar.

Rooms 98 (4 fmly) ☀ **Facilities** STV Wi-fi
Conf Class 110 Board 70 Thtr 250 **Services** Lift
Parking 24 **Notes** ⊗ Civ Wed 200

Best Western Lord Haldon Country Hotel

★★★ 77% HOTEL

☎ 01392 832483
Dunchideock EX6 7YF
e-mail: enquiries@lordhaldonhotel.co.uk
web: www.lordhaldonhotel.co.uk
dir: M5 junct 31, A30, 1st exit, follow signs through
Ide to Dunchideock

Set amid rural tranquillity, this is an attractive
country house where guests are assured of a warm
welcome from the professional team of staff, and the
well-equipped bedrooms are comfortable; many have
stunning views. The daily-changing menu features
skilfully cooked dishes with most of the produce
sourced locally.

Rooms 25 (3 fmly) ☀ **Facilities** FTV Wi-fi ☕ Xmas
New Year **Conf** Class 100 Board 40 Thtr 250
Parking 120 **Notes** Civ Wed 120

Devon Hotel

★★★ 77% HOTEL

☎ 01392 259268
Exeter Bypass, Matford EX2 8XU
e-mail: reservations@devonhotel.co.uk
web: www.devonhotel.co.uk
dir: M5 junct 30 follow Marsh Barton Ind Est signs on
A379. Hotel on Marsh Barton rdbt

Within easy access of the city centre, the M5 and the
city's business parks, this smart Georgian hotel offers
modern, comfortable accommodation. The Carriages
Bar and Brasserie is popular with guests and locals
alike, offering a wide range of dishes as well as a
carvery at both lunch and dinner. Service is friendly
and attentive, and extensive meeting and business
facilities are available.

Rooms 40 (40 annexe) (2 fmly) (11 GF) ☀ **S** £69-£89;
D £89-£99* **Facilities** FTV Wi-fi ☕ Xmas New Year
Conf Class 80 Board 40 Thtr 150 **Parking** 250
Notes LB ⊗ Civ Wed 100

E

EXETER continued

Queens Court Hotel

★★★ 75% ◉◉ HOTEL

☎ 01392 272709
6-8 Bystock Ter EX4 4HY
e-mail: enquiries@queenscourt-hotel.co.uk
web: www.queenscourt-hotel.co.uk
dir: Exit dual carriageway at junct 30 onto B5132
(Topsham Rd) towards city centre. Hotel 200yds from
Central Station

Quietly located within walking distance of the city
centre, this privately owned hotel is a listed, early
Victorian property that provides friendly hospitality.
The smart public areas and contemporary bedrooms
are tastefully furnished, and the stylish and
attractive Olive Tree restaurant offers an award-
winning selection of dishes. Rooms are available for
conferences, meetings, weddings and parties.
Complimentary parking is available in a public car
park directly opposite the hotel entrance.

Rooms 18 (1 fmly) **Facilities** FTV Wi-fi **Conf** Class 30
Board 30 Thtr 60 **Services** Lift **Notes** ✆ Closed Xmas
& New Year RS 25-30 Dec Civ Wed 60

Barton Cross Hotel & Restaurant

★★★ 71% ◉ HOTEL

☎ 01392 841245
Huxham, Stoke Canon EX5 4EJ
e-mail: bartonxhuxham@aol.com
web: www.thebartoncrosshotel.co.uk
dir: From A396, 0.5m to Stoke Canon, 3m N of Exeter

17th-century charm combined with 21st-century
luxury perfectly sums up the appeal of this lovely
country hotel. The bedrooms are spacious, tastefully

decorated and well maintained. Public areas include
the cosy first-floor lounge and the lounge/bar with its
warming log fire. The restaurant offers a seasonally
changing menu of consistently enjoyable cuisine.

Barton Cross Hotel & Restaurant

Rooms 9 (2 fmly) (2 GF) (2 smoking) **S** £80-£90;
D £110-£120 (incl. bkfst) **Facilities** STV FTV Wi-fi ⌨
Xmas New Year **Conf** Class 20 Board 20 Thtr 20
Parking 35 **Notes** LB

See advert on page 167

Gipsy Hill Hotel

THE INDEPENDENTS
HOTEL ASSOCIATION

★★★ 71% HOTEL

☎ 01392 465252
Gipsy Hill Ln, Monkerton EX1 3RN
e-mail: stay@gipsyhillhotel.co.uk
web: www.gipsyhillhotel.co.uk
dir: M5 junct 29 towards Exeter. Right at 1st rdbt,
right again at next rdbt. Hotel 0.5m on right

Located on the edge of the city, with easy access to
the M5 and the airport, this popular hotel is set in
attractive, well-tended gardens and boasts far-
reaching country views. The hotel offers a range of
conference and function rooms, comfortable
bedrooms and modern facilities. An intimate bar and
lounge are adjacent to the elegant restaurant.

Rooms 37 (17 annexe) (4 fmly) (12 GF) (1 smoking)
🏌 **S** £49-£79; **D** £49-£120* **Facilities** STV FTV Wi-fi ⌨
Xmas New Year **Conf** Class 80 Board 80 Thtr 300
Del from £124* **Parking** 60 **Notes** ✆ Civ Wed 160

Great Western Hotel

★★ 64% HOTEL

☎ 01392 274039
St David's Station Approach EX4 4NU
e-mail: bookings@greatwesternhotel.co.uk
dir: M5 junct 30, follow City Centre signs then St
Davids Station signs. Hotel on A377 W of city

This long-established railway hotel has been
providing rest and refreshment for weary travellers for
many years. Its long tradition of hospitality is still
very much in evidence in the convivial bar which is a
popular venue with both visitors and locals alike.
Bedrooms, in a variety of sizes, are soundly

appointed. In addition to the bar menu, guests also
have the option of eating in the attractive restaurant.

Rooms 35 (1 fmly) **Facilities** FTV Wi-fi **Conf** Class 12
Board 20 Thtr 35

Holiday Inn Express Exeter M5 Jct 29

BUDGET HOTEL

☎ 01392 261000
Guardian Rd EX1 3PE
e-mail: managerexeter@expressholidayinn.co.uk
web: www.expressexeter.com
dir: M5 junct 29, follow signs for Exeter city centre.
Hotel on 1st rdbt

A modern hotel ideal for families and business
travellers. Fresh and uncomplicated, the spacious
rooms include Sky TV, power shower and tea and
coffee-making facilities. Continental buffet breakfast
is included in the room rate; other meals may be
taken at the nearby family pub or restaurant. See also
the Hotel Groups pages.

Rooms 149 (94 fmly) (41 GF) (6 smoking)
Conf Class 20 Board 20 Thtr 30

Premier Inn Exeter Central St Davids

BUDGET HOTEL

☎ 0871 527 9278
Bonhay Rd EX4 4BG
web: www.premierinn.com
dir: M5 junct 31, A30 towards Bodmin &
Oakehampton. Exit onto A377 towards Exeter &
Crediton. Hotel on left

High quality, budget accommodation ideal for both
families and business travellers. Spacious, en suite
bedrooms feature tea and coffee making facilities,
and Freeview TV in most hotels. Internet access and
Wi-fi are available for a small fee. The adjacent
family restaurant features a wide and varied menu.
See also the Hotel Groups pages.

Rooms 102

Premier Inn Exeter (Countess Wear)

BUDGET HOTEL

☎ 0871 527 8386
398 Topsham Rd EX2 6HE
web: www.premierinn.com
dir: 2m from M5 junct 30/A30 junct 29. Follow signs
for Exeter & Dawlish (A379). On dual carriageway
take 2nd slip road on left at Countess Wear rdbt.
Hotel adjacent to Beefeater

Rooms 44

Save on hotels. Book at **theAA.com/hotel**

EXE – EYE 169 ENGLAND

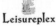

Chi Restaurant & Bar with Accommodation

RESTAURANT WITH ROOMS

☎ 01626 890213
Fore St, Kenton EX6 8LD
e-mail: enquiries@chi-restaurant.co.uk
web: www.chi-restaurant.co.uk
dir: 5m S of Exeter. M5 junct 30, A379 towards Dawlish, in village centre

This former pub has been spectacularly transformed into a chic and contemporary bar, allied with a stylish Chinese restaurant. Dishes are beautifully presented with an emphasis on quality produce and authenticity, resulting in a memorable dining experience. Bedrooms are well equipped and all provide good levels of space and comfort, along with modern bathrooms.

Rooms 5 (2 fmly)

EXFORD
Somerset   Map 3 SS83

Crown Hotel

★★★ 79% ⚫ HOTEL

☎ 01643 831554
TA24 7PP
e-mail: info@crownhotelexmoor.co.uk
web: www.crownhotelexmoor.co.uk
dir: M5 junct 25, follow Taunton signs. Take A358 from Taunton, then B3224 via Wheddon Cross to Exford

Guest comfort is certainly the hallmark here. Afternoon tea is served in the lounge beside a roaring fire, and tempting menus in the bar and restaurant are all part of the charm of this delightful old coaching inn that specialises in breaks for shooting and other country sports. Bedrooms retain a traditional style yet offer a range of modern comforts and facilities, many have views of this pretty moorland village.

Rooms 16 (3 fmly) ⌅ **S** £69-£79; **D** £119-£159 (incl. bkfst)* **Facilities** FTV Wi-fi ⌘ Xmas New Year **Conf** Board 15 **Parking** 30 **Notes** LB

EXMOUTH
Devon   Map 3 SY08

Royal Beacon Hotel

★★★ 79% HOTEL

☎ 01395 264886
The Beacon EX8 2AF
e-mail: info@royalbeacon.co.uk
web: www.royalbeaconhotel.co.uk
dir: From M5 onto A376 & Marine Way. Follow seafront signs. On Imperial Rd left at T-junct then 1st right. Hotel 100yds on left

This elegant Georgian property sits in an elevated position overlooking the town and has fine views of the estuary towards the sea. Bedrooms are individually styled and many have sea views. Public areas include a well stocked bar, a cosy lounge, an impressive function suite, and a choice of restaurants where freshly prepared and enjoyable cuisine is offered.

Rooms 52 (17 annexe) (2 fmly) (8 GF) ⌅
Facilities FTV Wi-fi ⌘ Xmas New Year **Conf** Class 100 Board 60 Thtr 160 Del from £115 to £155
Services Lift **Parking** 28 **Notes** ⊗ Civ Wed 160

Manor Hotel

★★ 72% HOTEL

☎ 01395 272549
The Beacon EX8 2AG
e-mail: post@manorexmouth.co.uk
dir: M5 junct 30, A376 to Exmouth. Hotel 300yds from seafront overlooking Manor Gardens

Conveniently located for easy access to the town centre and with views overlooking the sea, this friendly hotel offers traditional values of hospitality and service, drawing guests back year after year. The well-equipped bedrooms vary in style and size; many have far-reaching views. The fixed price menu offers a varied selection of dishes.

Rooms 39 (3 fmly) ⌅ **S** £40-£48; **D** £70-£96 (incl. bkfst) **Facilities** FTV Wi-fi Xmas New Year **Conf** Class 60 Board 60 Thtr 100 Del from £50 to £65
Services Lift **Parking** 12 **Notes** LB ⊗

Cavendish Hotel

★★ 71% HOTEL

☎ 01395 272528
11 Morton Crescent, The Esplanade EX8 1BE
e-mail: cavendish.exmouth@alfatravel.co.uk
web: www.leisureplex.co.uk
dir: Follow seafront signs, hotel in centre of large crescent

Situated on the seafront, this terraced hotel attracts many groups from around the country. With fine views out to sea, the hotel is within walking distance of the town centre. The bedrooms are neatly presented; front-facing rooms are always popular. Entertainment is provided on most evenings during the summer.

Rooms 78 (3 fmly) (21 GF) ⌅ **Facilities** FTV Snooker ♫ Xmas New Year **Services** Lift **Parking** 25 **Notes** ⊗ Closed Dec-Jan (ex Xmas) RS Nov & Mar

EYE
Suffolk   Map 13 TM17

The Cornwallis Hotel

★★★★ 73% ⚫ HOTEL

OXFORD
HOTELS & INNS

☎ 01379 870326 & 08444 146524
Rectory Rd, Brome IP23 8AJ
e-mail: reservations.cornwallis@ohiml.com
web: www.oxfordhotelsandinns.com
dir: 50yds from A140 (Norwich to Ipswich road)

Peacefully situated just off the A140 at the end of a tree lined lane in 23 acres of wooded grounds, this charming Grade II listed property has a wealth of original character such as exposed beams, open fireplaces and wood carvings. Public rooms include a 15th-century Tudor bar, a lounge, a conservatory and a fine-dining restaurant. The individually designed bedrooms are tastefully appointed and have lovely views of the gardens.

Rooms 16 (5 annexe) (1 fmly) (3 GF) **S** £49-£115; **D** £55-£125 (incl. bkfst)* **Facilities** FTV Wi-fi Xmas New Year **Conf** Class 50 Board 30 Thtr 70 Del from £92 to £108* **Parking** 100 **Notes** LB ⊗ Civ Wed 80

E

FALFIELD
Gloucestershire
Map 4 ST69

Best Western The Gables Hotel

★★★ 73% HOTEL

☎ 01454 260502
Bristol Rd GL12 8DL
e-mail: mail@thegablesbristol.co.uk
web: www.thegablesbristol.co.uk
dir: M5 junct 14 N'bound. Left at end of sliproad.
Right onto A38, hotel 300yds on right

Conveniently located, just a few minutes from the
motorway this establishment is ideally suited to both
business and leisure guests, with easy access to
Cheltenham, Gloucester, Bristol and Bath. Bedrooms
are spacious and well equipped. Relaxing public
areas consist of a light and airy bar and restaurant
where meals and all-day snacks are available; a more
formal restaurant is open for dinner. There is also a
range of meeting rooms.

Rooms 46 (4 fmly) (18 GF) **S** £60-£130; **D** £60-£130
(incl. bkfst)* **Facilities** FTV Wi-fi ⓘ **Conf** Class 90
Board 50 Thtr 200 Del from £135 to £150*
Parking 104 **Notes** LB ⊗ Civ Wed 150

FALMOUTH
Cornwall
Map 2 SW83

See also **Mawnan Smith**

Royal Duchy Hotel

★★★★ 79% ❀❀ HOTEL

☎ 01326 313042
Cliff Rd TR11 4NX
e-mail: reservations@royalduchy.com
web: www.royalduchy.com
dir: On Cliff Rd, along Falmouth seafront

Looking out over the sea and towards Pendennis
Castle, this hotel provides a friendly environment. The
comfortable lounge and cocktail bar are well
appointed, and leisure facilities and meeting rooms
are also available. The award-winning restaurant
serves carefully prepared dishes, and bedrooms vary
in size and aspect, with many rooms having sea
views.

Royal Duchy Hotel

Rooms 43 (6 fmly) (1 GF) **S** £80-£100; **D** £140-£290
(incl. bkfst)* **Facilities** FTV Wi-fi ⓘ Games room
Sauna Beauty treatment room ♫ Xmas New Year
Child facilities **Conf** Thtr 50 **Services** Lift **Parking** 50
Notes LB ⊗ Civ Wed 100

See advert on this page

St Michael's Hotel and Spa

★★★★ 75% HOTEL

☎ 01326 312707
Gyllyngvase Beach, Seafront TR11 4NB
e-mail: info@stmichaelshotel.co.uk
dir: A39 into Falmouth, follow beach signs, at 2nd
mini-rdbt into Pennance Rd. Take 2nd left & 2nd left
again

Overlooking the bay this hotel is in an excellent
position and commands lovely views. It is appointed
in a fresh, contemporary style that reflects its location
by the sea. The Flying Fish restaurant has a great
atmosphere and a buzz. The light and bright
bedrooms, some with balconies, are well equipped.
There are excellent leisure facilities including a
fitness and health club together with the spa offering
many treatments; the attractive gardens also provide
a place to relax and unwind.

Save on hotels. Book at **theAA.com/hotel**

FAL 171 ENGLAND

Rooms 61 (8 annexe) (7 fmly) (12 GF) ⚫ **D** £115–£220 (incl. bkfst)* **Facilities** Spa FTV Wi-fi ⌖ Gym Sauna Steam room Aqua aerobics Fitness classes Xmas New Year **Conf** Class 150 Board 50 Thtr 200 **Parking** 30 **Notes** LB ⊗ Civ Wed 80

The Greenbank Hotel

★★★★ 74% ☺ HOTEL

☎ 01326 312440
Harbourside TR11 2SR
e-mail: reception@greenbank-hotel.co.uk
web: www.greenbank-hotel.co.uk
dir: 500yds past Falmouth Marina on Penryn River

Located by the marina, and with its own private quay dating from the 17th century, this smart hotel has a strong marine theme throughout. Set at the water's edge, the lounge, restaurant and many bedrooms all benefit from harbour views. The restaurant provides a choice of interesting and enjoyable dishes.

Rooms 60 (6 fmly) **Facilities** FTV Wi-fi Private beach & quay Xmas New Year **Conf** Class 90 Board 25 Thtr 90 **Services** Lift **Parking** 68 **Notes** ⊗ Civ Wed 90

Best Western Penmere Manor Hotel

★★★ 79% HOTEL

☎ 01326 211411
Mongleath Rd TR11 4PN
e-mail: reservations@penmere.co.uk
web: www.penmere.co.uk
dir: Exit A39 at Hillhead rdbt, over double mini rdbt. After 0.75m left into Mongleath Rd

Set in five acres on the outskirts of town, this Georgian manor house was originally built for a ship's captain. Now a family owned hotel it provides friendly service and a good range of facilities. Bedrooms vary in size and are located in the manor house and the garden wing. Various menus are available in the bar and the smart restaurant. There is a health and beauty centre offering a wide range of treatments and the water in the indoor pool is UV filtered.

Rooms 37 (12 fmly) (13 GF) ⚫ **S** £68–£79; **D** £136–£156 (incl. bkfst)* **Facilities** FTV Wi-fi ⌖ ⚲ Gym Sauna New Year **Conf** Class 20 Board 30 Thtr 60 Del from £144.50 to £173* **Parking** 50 **Notes** LB Closed 22–27 Dec

Best Western Falmouth Beach Hotel

★★★ 78% HOTEL

☎ 01326 310500
Gyllyngvase Beach, Seafront TR11 4NA
e-mail: info@falmouthbeachhotel.co.uk
web: www.bw-falmouthbeachhotel.co.uk
dir: A39 to Falmouth, follow seafront signs

At the time of going to press this hotel was closed due to a serious fire in April 2012. We understand that repairs are already underway. For current details please see The AA website: www.theAA.com

Enjoying wonderful views, this popular hotel is situated opposite the beach and within easy walking distance of Falmouth's attractions and port. A friendly atmosphere is maintained and guests have a good choice of leisure, fitness, entertainment and dining options. Bedrooms, many with balconies and sea views, are well equipped and comfortable.

Best Western Falmouth Beach Hotel

Rooms 120 (20 fmly) (4 GF) ⚫ **S** £55–£77; **D** £110–£154 (incl. bkfst)* **Facilities** Spa FTV Wi-fi ⌖ supervised ⚲ Gym Sauna Steam room Hair & beauty salon ♫ Xmas New Year **Conf** Class 200 Board 250 Thtr 300 Del from £115* **Services** Lift **Parking** 88 **Notes** LB Civ Wed 220

See advert on this page

F

FALMOUTH *continued*

Green Lawns Hotel

★★★ 78% HOTEL

☎ 01326 312734
Western Ter TR11 4QJ
e-mail: info@greenlawnshotel.com
web: www.greenlawnshotel.com
dir: On A39

This attractive property enjoys a convenient location close to the town centre and is within easy reach of the sea. Spacious public areas include inviting lounges, an elegant restaurant, conference and meeting facilities and a leisure centre. Bedrooms vary in size and style but all are well equipped and comfortable. The friendly service is particularly noteworthy.

Rooms 39 (8 fmly) (11 GF) ⚘ **S** £60-£70;
D £109-£189 (incl. bkfst) **Facilities** FTV Wi-fi 🕸 ♨
Gym Squash Sauna Steam room Spa bath New Year
Conf Class 80 Board 80 Thtr 200 Del from £95 to
£115 **Parking** 69 **Notes** Closed 24-30 Dec
Civ Wed 150

Falmouth Hotel

R
RICHARDSON HOTELS
Where Memories are Made

★★★ 77% ⚜ HOTEL

☎ 01326 312671 & 0800 019 3121
Castle Beach TR11 4NZ
e-mail: reservations@falmouthhotel.com
web: www.falmouthhotel.com
dir: A30 to Truro then A390 to Falmouth. Follow signs for beaches, hotel on seafront near Pendennis Castle

This spectacular beach-front Victorian property affords wonderful sea views from many of its comfortable bedrooms, some of which have their own balconies. Spacious public areas include a number of inviting lounges, a choice of dining options and an impressive range of leisure facilities.

Rooms 70 (16 fmly) ⚘ **S** £60-£90; **D** £60-£210 (incl.
bkfst)* **Facilities** Spa FTV Wi-fi 🕸 Putt green Gym
Beauty salon & Therapeutic rooms Xmas New Year
Conf Class 150 Board 100 Thtr 250 **Services** Lift
Parking 120 **Notes** LB Civ Wed 250

Penmorvah Manor

★★★ 73% HOTEL

☎ 01326 250277
Budock Water TR11 5ED
e-mail: reception@penmorvah.co.uk
web: www.penmorvah.co.uk
dir: A39 to Hillhead rdbt, take 2nd exit. Right at Falmouth Football Club, through Budock. Hotel opposite Penjerrick Gardens

Situated within two miles of central Falmouth, this extended Victorian manor house is a peaceful hideaway, set in six acres of private woodland and gardens. Penmorvah is well positioned for visiting the local gardens, and offers many garden-tour breaks. Dinner features locally sourced, quality ingredients such as Cornish cheeses, meat, fish and game.

Rooms 27 (1 fmly) (10 GF) ⚘ **S** £60-£70;
D £105-£130 (incl. bkfst)* **Facilities** FTV Wi-fi
Conf Class 100 Board 56 Thtr 250 Del from £100*
Parking 100 **Notes** LB Closed 31 Dec-Jan
Civ Wed 120

Madeira Hotel

Leisureplex

★★ 69% HOTEL

☎ 01326 313531
Cliff Rd TR11 4NY
e-mail: madeira.falmouth@alfatravel.co.uk
web: www.leisureplex.co.uk
dir: A39 (Truro to Falmouth), follow tourist 'Hotels' signs to seafront

This popular hotel offers splendid sea views and a pleasant, convenient location, which is close to the town. Extensive sun lounges are popular haunts from which to enjoy the views, while additional facilities include an oak-panelled cocktail bar. Bedrooms, many with sea views, are available in a range of sizes.

Rooms 50 (8 fmly) (7 GF) **Facilities** FTV 🎵 Xmas New
Year **Services** Lift **Parking** 11 **Notes** ⊗ Closed Dec-
Feb (ex Xmas) RS Nov & Mar

Rosslyn Hotel

★★ 69% HOTEL

☎ 01326 312699 & 315373
110 Kimberley Park Rd TR11 2JJ
e-mail: mail@rosslynhotel.co.uk
web: www.rosslynhotel.co.uk
dir: On A39 towards Falmouth, to Hilend rdbt, turn right, straight on at next mini rdbt. At 2nd mini rdbt left into Trescobeas Rd. Hotel on left past hospital

A relaxed and friendly atmosphere is maintained at this family-run hotel. Situated on the northern edge of Falmouth, the Rosslyn is easily located and is suitable for both business and leisure guests. A comfortable lounge overlooks the well-tended garden, and enjoyable freshly prepared dinners are offered in the restaurant.

Rooms 25 (3 fmly) (6 GF) **Facilities** FTV New Year
Conf Class 60 Board 20 **Parking** 22

Membly Hall Hotel

★★ 68% HOTEL

☎ 01326 312869
Sea Front, Cliff Rd TR11 4NT
e-mail: memblyhallhotel@tiscali.co.uk
dir: A39 to Falmouth. Follow seafront & beaches signs

Located conveniently on the seafront and enjoying splendid views, this family-run hotel offers friendly service. Bedrooms are pleasantly spacious and well equipped. Carefully prepared and enjoyable meals are served in the spacious dining room. Live entertainment is provided on some evenings and there is also a sauna and spa pool.

Rooms 35 (3 fmly) (6 GF) ⚘ **S** £30-£47; (incl. bkfst)*
Facilities FTV Wi-fi 🏊 Gym Indoor short bowls Table
tennis Pool table Sauna Spa pool 🎵 New Year
Conf Class 130 Board 60 Thtr 150 Del from £35 to
£70* **Services** Lift **Parking** 30 **Notes** LB ⊗ Closed
Xmas week RS Dec-Jan

FAREHAM
Hampshire Map 5 SU50

Solent Hotel & Spa

★★★★ 80% ⊛ HOTEL

☎ 01489 880000
Rookery Av, Whiteley PO15 7AJ
e-mail: solent@shirehotels.com
web: www.solenthotel.com
dir: M27 junct 9, hotel on Solent Business Park

Close to the M27 with easy access to Portsmouth, the New Forest and other attractions, this smart, purpose-built hotel enjoys a peaceful location. Bedrooms are spacious and very well appointed and there is a well-equipped spa with health and beauty facilities.

Rooms 111 (9 fmly) (39 GF) **S** £80–£150;
D £80–£150* **Facilities** Spa STV Wi-fi ⓥ ⓩ ⚱ Gym Steam room Sauna Children's splash pool Activity studio Xmas New Year **Conf** Class 100 Board 80 Thtr 200 Del from £125 to £175* **Services** Lift **Parking** 200 **Notes** ⊗ Civ Wed 160

Holiday Inn Fareham - Solent

★★★ 79% HOTEL

☎ 0871 942 9028
Cartwright Dr, Titchfield PO15 5RJ
e-mail: fareham@ihg.com
web: www.holidayinn.co.uk
dir: M27 junct 9, follow signs for A27. Over Segensworth rdbt 1.5m, left at next rdbt

This hotel is well positioned and attracts both the business and leisure markets. Bedrooms are spacious and smart, and stylish public areas include a number of conference rooms. Beauty treatments are available in the leisure area which has a swimming pool, aerobics studio and gym.

Rooms 124 (4 fmly) (72 GF) (2 smoking) **Facilities** FTV Wi-fi ⓥ HL ⓩ supervised Gym Sauna Beauty treatment rooms **Conf** Class 64 Board 45 Thtr 140 **Services** Air con **Parking** 160 **Notes** ⊗ Civ Wed 100

Lysses House Hotel

★★★ 73% HOTEL

☎ 01329 822622
51 High St PO16 7BQ
e-mail: lysses@lysses.co.uk
web: www.lysses.co.uk
dir: M27 junct 11 follow Fareham signs, stay in left lane to Delme rdbt. At rdbt 3rd exit into East St, follow into High St. Hotel at top on right

This attractive Georgian hotel is situated on the edge of the town in a quiet location and provides spacious and well-equipped accommodation. There are conference facilities, and a lounge bar serving a range of snacks together with the Richmond Restaurant that offers imaginative cuisine.

Rooms 21 (2 fmly) (7 GF) **S** £63.50–£89.95;
D £92.50–£112.50 (incl. bkfst)* **Facilities** FTV Wi-fi Free entry to nearby LA Fitness **Conf** Class 42 Board 28 Thtr 95 Del from £138 to £158.50* **Services** Lift **Parking** 30 **Notes** ⊗ Closed 25 Dec-1 Jan RS 24 Dec & BHs Civ Wed 100

Red Lion Hotel

★★★ 70% HOTEL

☎ 01329 822640
East St PO16 0BP
e-mail: redlion.fareham@oldenglishinns.co.uk

This hotel, which was formerly a coaching inn, is conveniently located within a few moments' walk of the market town of Fareham. An array of substantial hot and cold meals is served throughout the day in the bright informal restaurant and bar area. Bedrooms provide good comfort levels, and the hotel has pretty gardens and benefits from barrier operated parking.

Rooms 46 **Conf** Class 60 Board 40 Thtr 100

Premier Inn Fareham

BUDGET HOTEL

☎ 0871 527 8396
Southampton Rd, Park Gate SO31 6AF
web: www.premierinn.com
dir: M27 junct 9, follow Fareham West, A27 signs. (NB for Sat Nav use SO31 6BZ)

High quality, budget accommodation ideal for both families and business travellers. Spacious, en suite bedrooms feature tea and coffee making facilities, and Freeview TV in most hotels. Internet access and Wi-fi are available for a small fee. The adjacent family restaurant features a wide and varied menu. See also the Hotel Groups pages.

Rooms 41

FARINGDON
Oxfordshire Map 5 SU29

Best Western Sudbury House Hotel & Conference Centre

Best Western

★★★ 74% ⊛ HOTEL

☎ 01367 241272
London St SN7 8AA
e-mail: events@sudburyhouse.co.uk
web: www.sudburyhouse.co.uk
dir: From A420, follow Folly Hill signs

Situated on the edge of the Cotswolds and in nine acres of pleasant grounds, this hotel offers spacious and well-equipped bedrooms that are attractively decorated in warm colours. Dining options include the comfortable restaurant for a good selection of carefully presented dishes, and the bar for lighter options; a comprehensive room-service menu is also available.

Rooms 49 (2 fmly) (10 GF) ⓡ **S** £68–£110;
D £78–£120 (incl. bkfst)* **Facilities** STV Wi-fi ⓥ ⚱ Gym Boules New Year **Conf** Class 40 Board 34 Thtr 100 Del from £99 to £159* **Services** Lift **Parking** 100 **Notes** LB Civ Wed 160

FARNBOROUGH
Hampshire Map 5 SU85

Aviator

★★★★ 80% ⊛ HOTEL

☎ 01252 555890
Farnborough Rd GU14 6EL
e-mail: enquiries@aviatorfarnborough.co.uk
web: www.aviatorfarnborough.co.uk
dir: A325 to Aldershot, 3m, hotel on right

A striking property with a modern, sleek interior overlooking Farnborough airfield and located close to the main transport networks. This hotel is suitable for both the business and leisure travellers. The bedrooms have are well designed and provide complimentary Wi-fi. Both the Brasserie and the Deli source local ingredients for their menus.

Rooms 169 ⓡ **S** £140–£305; **D** £140–£305* **Facilities** STV Wi-fi ⓥ Gym Exercise studio Xmas New Year **Conf** Class 30 Board 40 Thtr 110 **Services** Lift Air con **Parking** 169 **Notes** ⊗ Civ Wed 120

F

FARNBOROUGH *continued*

Holiday Inn Farnborough

★★★ 80% HOTEL

Holiday Inn

☎ 0871 942 9029 & 01252 894300
Lynchford Rd GU14 6AZ
e-mail: reservations-farnborough@ihg.com
web: www.holidayinn.co.uk
dir: M3 junct 4, A325 through Farnborough towards
Aldershot. Hotel on left at The Queen's rdbt

This hotel occupies a perfect location for events in
Aldershot and Farnborough with ample parking on
site and easy access to the M3. Modern bedrooms
provide good comfort levels, and internet access is
provided throughout. Leisure facilities comprise a
swimming pool, gym and beauty treatment rooms.
Smart meeting rooms are also available.

Rooms 142 (31 fmly) (35 GF) **Facilities** Spa STV Wi-fi
♌ ⊕ supervised Gym Sauna Steam room Beauty room
♫ Xmas New Year **Conf** Class 80 Board 60 Thtr 180
Services Air con **Parking** 170 **Notes** Civ Wed 180

Premier Inn Farnborough

BUDGET HOTEL

☎ 0871 527 8398
Ively Rd, Southwood GU14 0JP
web: www.premierinn.com
dir: M3 junct 4a, A327 to Farnborough. Hotel on left
at 5th rdbt (Monkey Puzzle Rdbt)

High quality, budget accommodation ideal for both
families and business travellers. Spacious, en suite
bedrooms feature tea and coffee making facilities,
and Freeview TV in most hotels. Internet access and
Wi-fi are available for a small fee. The adjacent
family restaurant features a wide and varied menu.
See also the Hotel Groups pages.

Rooms 62

FARNHAM
Surrey
Map 5 SU84

Best Western Frensham Pond Hotel

★★★ 79% HOTEL

☎ 01252 795161
Bacon Ln GU10 2QB
e-mail: info@frenshampondhotel.co.uk
web: www.frenshampondhotel.co.uk

(For full entry see Churt)

Mercure Farnham Bush Hotel

★★★ 77% HOTEL

☎ 01252 715237
The Borough GU9 7NN
e-mail: H6621@accor.com
web: www.mercure.com
dir: M3 junct 4, A31, follow town centre signs. At East
Street lights turn left, hotel on right

Dating back to the 17th century, this extended former
coaching inn is attractively presented and has a
courtyard and a lawned garden. The bedrooms are
well appointed, with quality fabrics and good
facilities. The public areas include the panelled Oak
Lounge, a smart cocktail bar and a conference facility
in an adjoining building.

Rooms 94 (3 fmly) (27 GF) **Facilities** FTV Wi-fi Xmas
Conf Class 80 Board 30 Thtr 140 **Parking** 70
Notes Civ Wed 90

Ramada Farnham

★★★ 75% HOTEL

☎ 01252 784800
Hog's Back GU10 1EX
e-mail: enquiries@ramadafarnhamhotel.co.uk
web: www.ramadafarnhamhotel.co.uk
dir: M3 junct 4, A331 towards Farnborough &
Farnham. At rdbt take A31 (Hog's Back) towards
Guildford. Exit at next slip road signed Tongham/
Seale/Runfold, straight on, pass Esso petrol station.
Hotel 200yds on left

This hotel is conveniently located for Guildford and
Thorpe Park. There is a range of bedroom styles and
all include modern amenities; most rooms have
wonderful views of the Surrey Downs. The leisure
facilities include an indoor pool, gym and spa
treatments. The restaurant serves international
cuisine; guests can also sit on the terrace with a
drink or a snack and enjoy the view.

Rooms 96 (7 fmly) (21 GF) **Facilities** Spa STV FTV
Wi-fi ♌ ⊕ Gym Sauna Steam room New Year
Conf Class 70 Board 50 Thtr 150 **Parking** 150
Notes Civ Wed 150

FELIXSTOWE
Suffolk
Map 13 TM33

The Brook Hotel

★★★ 77% HOTEL

☎ 01394 278441
Orwell Rd IP11 7PF
e-mail: welcome@brookhotel.com

A modern, well furnished hotel ideally situated in a
residential area close to the town centre and the sea.
Public areas include a lounge bar, a large open-plan
restaurant with a bar area and a residents' lounge.
Bedrooms are generally quite spacious; each one is
pleasantly decorated and equipped with modern
facilities.

Rooms 25 (5 fmly) (3 GF) ♞ **S** £40-£120; **D** £45-£120
(incl. bkfst) **Facilities** FTV Wi-fi ♫ Xmas New Year
Conf Class 60 Board 60 Thtr 100 Del from £65 to
£165 **Parking** 20 **Notes** LB ⊗ Civ Wed 150

Marlborough Hotel

★★ 72% HOTEL

☎ 01394 285621
Sea Front IP11 2BJ
e-mail: hsm@marlborough-hotel-felix.com
web: www.marlborough-hotel-felix.com
dir: From A14 follow 'Docks' signs. Over Dock rdbt,
rail crossing & lights. Left at T-junct. Hotel 400mtrs
on left

Situated on the seafront, overlooking the beach and
just a short stroll from the pier and town centre. This
traditional resort hotel offers a good range of
facilities including the smart Rattan Restaurant,
Flying Boat Bar and L'Aperitif lounge. The pleasantly
decorated bedrooms come in a variety of styles; some
have lovely sea views.

Rooms 48 (1 fmly) ♞ **Facilities** STV Wi-fi ♌ Pool
table Xmas New Year **Conf** Class 60 Board 40 Thtr 80
Services Lift **Parking** 16 **Notes** ⊗

Save on hotels. Book at **theAA.com/hotel**

FAR – FOL 175 ENGLAND

FERNDOWN Map 5 SU00
Dorset

Premier Inn Bournemouth/ Ferndown

BUDGET HOTEL

☎ 0871 527 8122
Ringwood Rd, Tricketts Cross BH22 9BB
web: www.premierinn.com
dir: Off A348 just before Tricketts Cross rdbt

High quality, budget accommodation ideal for both families and business travellers. Spacious, en suite bedrooms feature tea and coffee making facilities, and Freeview TV in most hotels. Internet access and Wi-fi are available for a small fee. The adjacent family restaurant features a wide and varied menu. See also the Hotel Groups pages.

Rooms 32

FLAMBOROUGH Map 17 TA27
East Riding of Yorkshire

North Star Hotel
★★ 79% SMALL HOTEL

☎ 01262 850379
North Marine Dr YO15 1BL
e-mail: info@thenorthstarhotel.co.uk
web: www.thenorthstarhotel.co.uk
dir: B1229 or B1255 to Flamborough. Follow signs for North Landing along North Marine Dr. Hotel 100yds from sea

Standing close to the North Landing of Flamborough Head, this family-run hotel overlooks delightful countryside. It provides excellent accommodation and caring hospitality. A good range of fresh local food, especially fish, is available in both the bar and the dining room.

Rooms 7 🕯 **S** £55; **D** £90 (incl. bkfst)* **Parking** 60
Notes LB ⊗ Closed Xmas RS Nov-Etr

FLEET MOTORWAY SERVICE AREA (M3) Map 5 SU75
Hampshire

Days Inn Fleet - M3
BUDGET HOTEL

☎ 01252 815587
Fleet Services GU51 1AA
e-mail: fleet.hotel@welcomebreak.co.uk
web: www.welcomebreak.co.uk
dir: Between junct 4a & 5 southbound on M3

This modern building offers accommodation in smart, spacious and well-equipped bedrooms, suitable for families and business travellers, and all with en suite bathrooms. Continental breakfast is available and other refreshments may be taken at the nearby family restaurant. See also the Hotel Groups pages.

Rooms 59 (46 fmly) (5 smoking)

FLITWICK Map 11 TL03
Bedfordshire

Menzies Flitwick Manor
★★★★ 73% ⊚
COUNTRY HOUSE HOTEL

☎ 01525 712242
Church Rd MK45 1AE
e-mail: flitwick@menzieshotels.co.uk
web: www.menzieshotels.co.uk
dir: M1 junct 12, follow signs for Flitwick, turn left into Church Rd, hotel on left

With its picturesque setting in acres of gardens and parkland, yet only minutes by car from the motorway, this lovely Georgian house combines the best of both worlds, being both accessible and peaceful. Bedrooms are individually decorated and furnished with period pieces; some are air conditioned. Cosy and intimate, the lounge and restaurant give the hotel a home-from-home feel.

Rooms 18 (1 fmly) (5 GF) (1 smoking) **Facilities** STV FTV Wi-fi ⌔ 🜁 Putt green 🜄 Xmas New Year
Conf Class 45 Board 24 Thtr 55 **Parking** 18
Notes Civ Wed 50

FOLKESTONE Map 7 TR23
Kent

Best Western Clifton Hotel
★★★ 77% HOTEL

☎ 01303 851231
The Leas CT20 2EB
e-mail: reservations@thecliftonhotel.com
dir: M20 junct 13, 0.25m W of town centre on A259

This privately-owned Victorian-style hotel occupies a prime location, looking out across the English Channel. The bedrooms are comfortably appointed and most have views of the sea. Public areas include a traditionally furnished lounge, a popular bar serving a good range of beers and several well-appointed conference rooms.

Rooms 80 (5 fmly) 🕯 **S** £50-£75; **D** £80-£110*
Facilities FTV Wi-fi Games room Xmas New Year
Conf Class 36 Board 32 Thtr 80 Del from £85 to £135* **Services** Lift

The Southcliff Hotel
★★ 72% HOTEL

☎ 01303 850075
22-26 The Leas CT20 2DY
e-mail: sales@thesouthcliff.co.uk
web: www.thesouthcliff.co.uk
dir: M20 junct 13, follow signs for The Leas. Left at rdbt onto Sandgate Rd, right at Blockbusters, right at end of road, hotel on right

Located on the town's panoramic promenade with a bird's eye view of the sea, this historical Victorian hotel is perfectly located for cross channel connections and is only minutes from the town centre. The bedrooms are spacious and airy with some boasting balconies and sea views. Enjoy dinner in the spacious restaurant or relax in the contemporary bar. Parking is available by arrangement.

Rooms 68 (2 fmly) 🕯 **S** £35-£42; **D** £49.50-£59.50 (incl. bkfst)* **Facilities** STV Wi-fi 🎜 Xmas New Year
Conf Class 120 Board 50 Thtr 200 Del from £42 to £75* **Services** Lift **Parking** 24 **Notes** ⊗

F

FOLKESTONE *continued*

Premier Inn Folkestone (Channel Tunnel)

BUDGET HOTEL

☎ 0871 527 8400
Cherry Garden Ln CT19 4AP
web: www.premierinn.com
dir: M20 junct 13. Follow Folkestone, A20 signs. At lights turn right, hotel on right

High quality, budget accommodation ideal for both families and business travellers. Spacious, en suite bedrooms feature tea and coffee making facilities, and Freeview TV in most hotels. Internet access and Wi-fi are available for a small fee. The adjacent family restaurant features a wide and varied menu. See also the Hotel Groups pages.

Rooms 79

Rocksalt Rooms

◎◎ RESTAURANT WITH ROOMS

☎ 01303 212070
2 Back St CT19 6NN
e-mail: info@rocksaltfolkestone.co.uk
dir: M20 junct 13 follow signs to harbour (A259). At harbour left onto Fish Market

Overlooking the busy harbour, that is crowded with small leisure boats, and having wonderful sea views, Rocksalt enjoys a great location in Folkestone. Bedrooms are stylish, well appointed and they all have an original antique beds and are equipped a host of thoughtful little extras. Continental breakfasts are delivered promptly to the guests' rooms each morning, and dinner is served in the award-winning restaurant that has panoramic views.

Rooms 4 (1 fmly)

FOREST ROW Map 6 TQ43
East Sussex

INSPECTORS' CHOICE

Ashdown Park Hotel & Country Club

★★★★ ◎◎ HOTEL

☎ 01342 824988
Wych Cross RH18 5JR
e-mail: reservations@ashdownpark.com
web: www.ashdownpark.com
dir: A264 to East Grinstead, then A22 to Eastbourne. 2m S of Forest Row at Wych Cross lights. Left to Hartfield, hotel on right 0.75m

Situated in 186 acres of landscaped gardens and parkland, this impressive country house enjoys a peaceful countryside setting in the heart of the Ashdown Forest. Bedrooms are individually styled and decorated. Public rooms include a restored 18th-century chapel, ideal for exclusive meetings and wedding parties, plus three drawing rooms, a cocktail bar and the award-winning Anderida Restaurant. The extensive indoor and outdoor leisure facilities include the Country Club and Spa plus an 18-hole, par 3 golf course and driving range.

Rooms 106 (16 GF) **Facilities** Spa FTV Wi-fi ⬧ HL ⬧ ⬧ 18 ⬧ Putt green ⬧ Gym Beauty salon & treatment rooms Aerobics studio Steam room Jogging trails Xmas New Year **Conf** Class 70 Board 40 Thtr 160 Del £270 **Parking** 200 **Notes** LB Civ Wed 150°

FORMBY Map 15 SD30
Merseyside

Formby Hall Golf Resort & Spa

★★★★ 76% HOTEL

☎ 01704 875699
Southport Old Rd L37 0AB
e-mail: gm@formbyhallgolfresort.co.uk
web: www.formbyhallgolfresort.co.uk
dir: A565 to 2nd rdbt, follow brown signs

This hotel offers modern, boutique-style bedrooms with state-of-the-art facilities, some with excellent views over the championship golf course. The lavish spa offers peace and tranquillity along with a superbly equipped gym. Two golf courses and a driving range also add to the hotel's outstanding facilities. The Brasserie is an informal eating option and guests can enjoy a relaxing drink in the 19th Hole bar.

Rooms 62 (10 fmly) (29 GF) ⬧ S £89-£139; D £99-£189 (incl. bkfst)* **Facilities** Spa STV FTV Wi-fi ⬧ HL ⬧ ⬧ 18 Putt green Gym Kinesis studio Driving range Short ball area ⬧ Xmas New Year **Conf** Class 60 Board 40 Thtr 300 Del from £115 to £145* **Services** Lift Air con **Parking** 457 **Notes** LB ⬧ Civ Wed 100

FOWEY Map 2 SX15
Cornwall

The Fowey Hotel

★★★★ 73% ◎ HOTEL

R RICHARDSON HOTELS
Where Memories are Made

☎ 01726 832551
The Esplanade PL23 1HX
e-mail: reservations@thefoweyhotel.co.uk
web: www.thefoweyhotel.co.uk
dir: A30 to Okehampton, continue to Bodmin. Then B3269 to Fowey for 1m, on right bend left junct then right into Dagands Rd. Hotel 200mtrs

This attractive hotel stands proudly above the estuary, with marvellous views of the river from the public areas and the majority of the bedrooms. High standards are evident throughout, augmented by a relaxed and welcoming atmosphere. There is a spacious bar, elegant restaurant and smart drawing room. Imaginative dinners make good use of quality local ingredients.

Rooms 37 (2 fmly) **Facilities** Wi-fi ⬧ Xmas New Year **Conf** Class 60 Board 20 Thtr 100 Del from £115 to £255* **Services** Lift **Parking** 20 **Notes** Civ Wed 120

Save on hotels. Book at **theAA.com/hotel**

FOL – GAR 177 **ENGLAND**

FRADDON
Cornwall   Map 2 SW95

Premier Inn Newquay (A30/Fraddon)

BUDGET HOTEL

☎ 0871 527 8816
Penhale Round TR9 6NA
web: www.premierinn.com
dir: On A30, 2m S of Indian Queens

High quality, budget accommodation ideal for both families and business travellers. Spacious, en suite bedrooms feature tea and coffee making facilities, and Freeview TV in most hotels. Internet access and Wi-fi are available for a small fee. The adjacent family restaurant features a wide and varied menu. See also the Hotel Groups pages.

Rooms 40

FRANKBY
Merseyside   Map 15 SJ28

Hillbark Hotel and Spa
★★★★★ 85% ◉◉◉ HOTEL

☎ 0151 625 2400
Royden Park CH48 1NP
e-mail: enquiries@hillbarkhotel.co.uk
web: www.hillbarkhotel.co.uk
dir: M53 junct 3, A552 (Upton), right onto A551 (Arrowe Park Rd). 0.6m at lights left into Arrowe Brook Rd. 0.5m on left

Originally built in 1891 on Bidston Hill, this striking black and white timbered Elizabethan-style mansion was actually moved, brick by brick, to its current site in 1931. The house now sits in a 250-acre woodland estate and enjoys delightful views towards the River Dee and to hills in north Wales. The bedrooms are luxuriously furnished and well equipped, whilst the elegant day rooms are richly styled. There is a choice of eating options - Stewart Warner at Hillbark (3 AA Rosettes), the Cellar Restaurant and the Hillbark Grill. The new spa offers a range of holistic treatments and has a fitness studio.

Rooms 18 (1 fmly) ⚑ **S** £114-£680; **D** £160-£700 (incl. bkfst)* **Facilities** Spa STV FTV Wi-fi ⚄ ⚲ Gym Cinema Library, games room and children's play area Xmas New Year Child facilities **Conf** Class 300 Board 60 Thtr 750 Del from £205 to £350* **Services** Lift **Parking** 160 **Notes** LB ⊗ Civ Wed 500

FRESHWATER
Isle of Wight   Map 5 SZ38

Albion Hotel
★★★ 70% HOTEL

☎ 01983 755755
PO40 9RA
e-mail: info@albion-hotel.net

In an idyllic location on the island's southern heritage coast, the hotel is right on the seafront with stunning views of Freshwater Bay. The bedrooms and bathrooms are spacious and offer guests modern, comfortable accommodation; many rooms have balconies. Breakfast and dinner are served in the traditionally styled restaurant that also enjoys the lovely views.

Rooms 41 **Facilities** ⚄ **Conf** Class 30 Board 40 Thtr 60 **Notes** Closed Nov-Apr

FROME
Somerset   Map 4 ST74

Premier Inn Frome

BUDGET HOTEL

☎ 9871 527 8404
Commerce Park, Jenson Av BA11 2LD
web: www.premierinn.com
dir: M4 junct 18, A46 follow Warminster & Frome signs. Hotel off A361 (Frome bypass) in Commerce Park

High quality, budget accommodation ideal for both families and business travellers. Spacious, en suite bedrooms feature tea and coffee making facilities, and Freeview TV in most hotels. Internet access and Wi-fi are available for a small fee. The adjacent family restaurant features a wide and varied menu. See also the Hotel Groups pages.

Rooms 40

GARFORTH
West Yorkshire   Map 16 SE43

Best Western Plus Milford Hotel

★★★ 83% HOTEL

☎ 01977 681800
A1 Great North Rd, Peckfield LS25 5LQ
e-mail: enquiries@mlh.co.uk
web: www.mlh.co.uk
dir: On A63, 1.5m W of A1(M) junct 42 & 4.5m E of M1 junct 46

This friendly, family owned and run hotel is conveniently situated, and provides very comfortable, modern accommodation. The air-conditioned bedrooms are particularly spacious and well equipped, and ten boutique-style superior rooms are available. Public areas include a relaxing lounge area, the contemporary Watermill Restaurant and lounge bar which has a working waterwheel.

Rooms 46 (13 GF) **S** £45-£89; **D** £45-£89* **Facilities** FTV Wi-fi ⚄ Xmas New Year **Conf** Class 35 Board 30 Thtr 60 **Services** Air con **Parking** 80 **Notes** LB

GARSTANG
Lancashire   Map 18 SD44

Best Western Garstang Country Hotel & Golf Centre

★★★ 78% HOTEL

☎ 01995 600100
Garstang Rd, Bowgreave PR3 1YE
e-mail: reception@ghgc.co.uk
web: www.garstanghotelandgolf.com
dir: M6 junct 32 take 1st right after Rogers Esso garage on A6 onto B6430. 1m, hotel on left

This smart, purpose-built hotel enjoys a peaceful location alongside its own 18-hole golf course. Comfortable and spacious bedrooms are well equipped for both business and leisure guests, whilst inviting public areas include a restaurant and a choice of bars - one serving food.

Rooms 32 (16 GF) **Facilities** STV FTV Wi-fi ⚄ 18 Putt green Golf driving range Xmas New Year **Conf** Class 150 Board 80 Thtr 250 **Services** Lift **Parking** 172 **Notes** ⊗ Civ Wed 200

Pickerings Country House Hotel
★★★ 77% HOTEL

☎ 01995 600999
Garstang Rd, Catterall PR3 0HD
e-mail: info@pickerings-hotel.co.uk
dir: On B6430, S of Garstang in Catterall opposite Cock Robin lane junct

An 18th-century country house, in large immaculately kept gardens, that has been sympathetically renovated to provide good standards of comfort and extensive facilities. Some bedrooms are very spacious, and all are equipped with a range of practical and thoughtful extras. Public areas include a choice of lounges, and well-equipped function rooms are also available.

Rooms 12 (1 fmly) **S** £55-£65; **D** £90-£140 (incl. bkfst)* **Facilities** FTV Wi-fi Children's play area Xmas New Year **Conf** Class 90 Board 40 Thtr 150 Del from £115* **Parking** 51 **Notes** LB ⊗ Civ Wed 150

G

GATESHEAD
Tyne & Wear　　　　　　　Map 21 NZ26

See also Whickham

Newcastle Gateshead Marriott Hotel MetroCentre

★★★★ 77% HOTEL

☎ 0191 493 2233
MetroCentre NE11 9XF
e-mail: reservations.newcastle.england.
metrocentre@marriotthotels.co.uk
web: www.newcastlemarriottmetrocentre.co.uk
dir: From N exit A1 at MetroCentre exit, take 'Other
Routes'. From S exit A1 at MetroCentre exit, turn right

Set just off the A1 and on the doorstep of the popular
Metro shopping centre, this stylish purpose-built
hotel provides modern amenities including a leisure
centre, conference facilities and an informal stylish
restaurant offering a range of dining styles. All
bedrooms are smartly laid out and thoughtfully
equipped to suit both the business traveller and the
leisure guest.

Rooms 150 (147 fmly) (5 smoking) **Facilities** Spa STV
Wi-fi ⌨ ⏳ Gym Health & beauty clinic Dance studio
Hairdresser Spinning studio Sauna Steam room
Conf Class 172 Board 48 Thtr 400 **Services** Lift
Air con **Parking** 300 **Notes** ⊗ Civ Wed 100

Eslington Villa Hotel

★★★ 79% ◉ HOTEL

☎ 0191 487 6017 & 420 0666
8 Station Rd, Low Fell NE9 6DR
e-mail: home@eslingtonvilla.co.uk
dir: From A1(M) exit for Team Valley Trading Estate.
Right at 2nd rdbt along Eastern Av. Left at car show
room, hotel 100yds on left

Set in a residential area, this smart hotel combines a
bright, contemporary atmosphere with the period style
of a fine Victorian villa. The overall ambience is
relaxed and inviting. Chunky sofas grace the cocktail
lounge, while tempting dishes can be enjoyed in
either the classical dining room or modern
conservatory overlooking the Team Valley.

Rooms 17 (2 fmly) (3 GF) **S** £79.50-£84.50;
D £94.50-£99.50 (incl. bkfst)* **Facilities** FTV Wi-fi
Conf Class 30 Board 25 Thtr 36 Del from £115 to
£125* **Parking** 28 **Notes** ⊗ Closed 25-26 Dec
RS BHs

Holiday Inn Express Newcastle Metro Centre

BUDGET HOTEL

☎ 01207 541100
Clasper Way, Riverside Way NE16 3BE
e-mail:
reservations@hiexpressnewcastlemetro.co.uk
web: www.hiexpress.com/gatesheaduk
dir: Follow signs for Metro Centre. Hotel on A1114
next to TGI Friday's & opposite Shell/Honda garage

A modern hotel ideal for families and business
travellers. Fresh and uncomplicated, the spacious
rooms include Sky TV, power shower and tea and
coffee-making facilities. Continental buffet breakfast
is included in the room rate; other meals may be
taken at the nearby family pub or restaurant. See also
the Hotel Groups pages.

Rooms 134 (92 fmly) (7 smoking) ⌨ **S** £65; (incl.
bkfst)* **Conf** Class 20 Board 20 Thtr 30

Premier Inn Newcastle (Metro Centre)

BUDGET HOTEL

☎ 0871 527 8792
Derwent Haugh Rd, Swalwell NE16 3BL
web: www.premierinn.com
dir: From A1 & A694 junct into Derwent Haugh Rd. 1m
N of Metro Centre

High quality, budget accommodation ideal for both
families and business travellers. Spacious, en suite
bedrooms feature tea and coffee making facilities,
and Freeview TV in most hotels. Internet access and
Wi-fi are available for a small fee. The adjacent
family restaurant features a wide and varied menu.
See also the Hotel Groups pages.

Rooms 69

Premier Inn Newcastle South

BUDGET HOTEL

☎ 0871 527 8806
Lobley Hill Rd NE11 9NA
web: www.premierinn.com
dir: A1 onto A692

Rooms 42

Premier Inn Newcastle (Team Valley)

BUDGET HOTEL

☎ 0871 527 8794
Maingate, Kingsway North, Team Valley NE11 0BE
web: www.premierinn.com
dir: A1 onto B1426 signed Team Valley (S'bound) or
Teams/Consett (N'bound). Take Gateshead exit at
rdbt. At bottom of hill straight on at rdbt. Hotel
opposite

Rooms 115

GATWICK AIRPORT (LONDON)　Map 6 TQ24
West Sussex

See also Dorking, East Grinstead & Reigate

INSPECTORS' CHOICE

Langshott Manor

★★★★ ◉ ◉
COUNTRY HOUSE HOTEL

☎ 01293 786680
Langshott Ln RH6 9LN
e-mail: admin@langshottmanor.com
dir: From A23 take Ladbroke Rd, off Chequers rdbt
to Langshott, after 0.75m hotel on right

On the outskirts of town this charming timber-
framed Tudor manor house is set amidst beautifully
landscaped grounds with an ancient moat. The
stylish public areas feature a choice of inviting
lounges with polished oak panelling, exposed
beams and crackling log fires. Each bedroom,
whether in the manor itself or in one of three mews
buildings in the grounds, has been designed with
flair and imagination. Expect sumptuous
furnishings, Egyptians linens, flat-screen TVs and
bathrooms with deep baths and powers showers.
The Mulberry restaurant overlooks a picturesque
pond and offers an imaginative menu.

Rooms 22 (15 annexe) (2 fmly) (8 GF) **D** £99-£399*
Facilities STV FTV Wi-fi ⌨ Xmas New Year
Conf Class 20 Board 22 Thtr 40 **Parking** 25
Notes LB ⊗ Civ Wed 60

Sofitel London Gatwick

★★★★ 77% ◉ HOTEL

☎ 01293 567070 & 555000
North Terminal RH6 0PH
e-mail: h6204-re@accor.com
dir: M23 junct 9, follow to 2nd rdbt. Hotel straight ahead

One of the closest hotels to the airport, this modern, purpose-built hotel is located only minutes from the terminals. Bedrooms are contemporary and all are air conditioned. Guests have a choice of eating options including a French-style café, a brasserie and an oriental restaurant.

Rooms 518 (19 fmly) **S** £89-£199; **D** £89-£199 **Facilities** Wi-fi Gym **Conf** Class 150 Board 90 Thtr 300 Del from £150 to £190 **Services** Lift Air con **Parking** 400 **Notes** ⊗

Ramada Plaza London Gatwick

★★★★ 74% HOTEL

☎ 01293 561186
Tinsley Ln, Three Bridges RH10 8XH
e-mail: gm@ramadahotelgatwick.co.uk
web: www.ramadaplazalondongatwick.co.uk
dir: M25 junct 7, M23 signed Brighton, exit junct 10 signed Crawley, then A2011 to 1st rdbt. Hotel on left

This modern purpose-built hotel is just four miles from the airport with easy access to the M23. The spacious bedrooms are comfortably appointed and well equipped; some family rooms are available. Air-conditioned public areas include a brightly appointed Arts Restaurant, first-floor conference centre and Sebastian Coe health club.

Rooms 151 (31 fmly) ⊀ **Facilities** STV Wi-fi ⌕ Gym New Year **Conf** Class 120 Board 90 Thtr 200 Del from £99 to £150 **Services** Lift Air con **Parking** 160 **Notes** ⊗ Civ Wed 100

Copthorne Hotel London Gatwick

★★★★ 72% HOTEL

☎ 01342 348800 & 348888
Copthorne Way RH10 3PG
e-mail: sales.gatwick@millenniumhotels.co.uk
web: www.millenniumhotels.co.uk
dir: On A264, 2m E of A264/B2036 rdbt

Situated in a tranquil position, the Copthorne is set in 100 acres of wooded, landscaped gardens containing jogging tracks, a putting green and a petanque pit. The sprawling building is built around a 16th-century farmhouse and has comfortable bedrooms; many are air conditioned. There are three dining options, ranging from the informal bar and carvery to the more formal Lion d'Or.

Rooms 227 (10 fmly) (122 GF) **S** £60-£135; **D** £60-£135* **Facilities** STV Wi-fi ⌕ HL ⏱ ☀ ⥾ Gym Squash Aerobic studio Jogging trail Xmas New Year **Conf** Class 60 Board 48 Thtr 155 Del from £115 to £185 **Parking** 300 **Notes** LB ⊗ Civ Wed 100

Crowne Plaza London - Gatwick Airport

★★★★ 72% HOTEL

☎ 01293 608608
Langley Dr RH11 7SX
e-mail: info@cpgatwick.co.uk
web: www.cpgatwick.co.uk
dir: M23 junct 10, 3rd exit at rdbt & 3rd exit at next rdbt. At lights take 3rd exit at rdbt

Ideally located for Gatwick Airport, this contemporary hotel offers comfortable and well-furnished rooms suitable for both the leisure and business travellers. Elite Health and Fitness Centre is the leisure centre which houses a stunning indoor swimming pool. Cube Restaurant & Bar offers a relaxed dining experience and the Gallery Sports Bar, an informal alternative. The hotel also has extensive conference facilities.

Rooms 294 (15 fmly) (6 GF) ⊀ **S** £200-£300; **D** £200-£300* **Facilities** STV FTV Wi-fi ⌕ ⏱ supervised Gym Saunas Steam room Xmas New Year **Conf** Class 110 Board 40 Thtr 230 **Services** Lift Air con **Parking** 200 **Notes** LB ⊗ Civ Wed 150

Copthorne Hotel Effingham Gatwick

★★★★ 71% HOTEL

☎ 01342 714994
West Park Rd RH10 3EU
e-mail: sales.effingham@millenniumhotels.co.uk
web: www.millenniumhotels.co.uk
dir: M23 junct 10, A264 towards East Grinstead. Over rdbt, at 2nd rdbt left onto B2028. Effingham Park on right

A former stately home, set in 40 acres of grounds, this hotel is popular for conference and weekend functions. The main restaurant is an open-plan brasserie serving modern continental cuisine, and snacks are also available in the bar. Bedrooms are spacious and well equipped. Facilities include a golf course and a leisure club.

Rooms 122 (9 fmly) (20 GF) ⊀ **S** £55-£135; **D** £55-£135* **Facilities** Spa STV Wi-fi HL ⏱ ♪ 9 ☀ Putt green ⥾ Gym Aerobic & Dance studios Xmas New Year **Conf** Class 450 Board 250 Thtr 800 Del from £115 to £185 **Services** Lift **Parking** 500 **Notes** LB ⊗ Civ Wed 600

Menzies Chequers

★★★★ 70% HOTEL

☎ 01293 766750
Brighton Rd RH6 8PH
e-mail: chequers@menzieshotels.co.uk
web: www.menzieshotels.co.uk
dir: M23 junct 9, A23 towards Redhill. At 'Longbridge' rdbt take 3rd exit signed Horley/A23. 1m to Sainsburys/Shell rdbt. Take 1st exit, hotel on right

A popular hotel located close to the town centre and also convenient for Gatwick Airport; original parts of the building date back to the 1750s. Bedrooms are comfortable and well equipped with good facilities. Dining areas include the contemporary restaurant and the traditional Chequers pub. Secure parking is available.

Rooms 104 (10 fmly) (46 GF) (6 smoking) **Facilities** FTV Wi-fi ⌕ Xmas New Year **Conf** Class 30 Board 32 Thtr 80 **Services** Lift **Parking** 140 **Notes** ⊗

G

Holiday Inn London - Gatwick Airport

★★★ 78% HOTEL

☎ 0871 942 9030 & 01293 787648
Povey Cross Rd RH6 0BA
web: www.holidayinn.co.uk
dir: M23 junct 9, follow Gatwick, then Reigate signs. Hotel on left after 3rd rdbt

Situated close to the airport, this modern hotel provides air conditioned, smart accommodation with facilities suiting both the business and leisure guest. There is a restaurant and bar, and a variety of conference rooms plus a supporting business centre. Park and Fly stays are popular.

Rooms 216 (13 fmly) (37 GF) (22 smoking)
Facilities STV Wi-fi ⌨ **Conf** Class 100 Board 70 Thtr 210 **Services** Lift Air con **Parking** 600

Holiday Inn Express Gatwick - Crawley

BUDGET HOTEL

☎ 01293 529991
Haslett Av, The Squareabout RH10 1UA
e-mail: ebhi-crawley@btconnect.com
web: www.hiexpress.com/crawleyuk

A modern hotel ideal for families and business travellers. Fresh and uncomplicated, the spacious rooms include Sky TV, power shower and tea and coffee-making facilities. Continental buffet breakfast is included in the room rate; other meals may be taken at the nearby family pub or restaurant. See also the Hotel Groups pages.

Rooms 74 (55 fmly) **Conf** Class 12 Board 16 Thtr 35

Ibis London Gatwick Airport

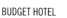

BUDGET HOTEL

☎ 01293 590300
London Rd, County Oak RH10 9GY
e-mail: H1889@accor.com
web: www.ibishotel.com
dir: M23 junct 10, A2011 towards Crawley. Onto A23 left towards Crawley/Brighton. Hotel on left

Modern, budget hotel offering comfortable accommodation in bright and practical bedrooms. Breakfast is self-service and dinner is available in the restaurant. See also the Hotel Groups pages.

Rooms 141

Premier Inn Crawley East

BUDGET HOTEL

☎ 0871 527 8412
Crawley Av, Gossops Green RH10 8BA
web: www.premierinn.com
dir: M23 junct 11, A23 towards Crawley & Gatwick Airport

High quality, budget accommodation ideal for both families and business travellers. Spacious, en suite bedrooms feature tea and coffee making facilities, and Freeview TV in most hotels. Internet access and Wi-fi are available for a small fee. The adjacent family restaurant features a wide and varied menu. See also the Hotel Groups pages.

Rooms 83

Premier Inn Crawley (Pound Hill)

BUDGET HOTEL

☎ 0871 527 8410
Balcombe Rd, Worth RH10 3NL
web: www.premierinn.com
dir: M23 junct 10, B2036 S towards Crawley

Rooms 41

Premier Inn Crawley South (Goffs Park)

BUDGET HOTEL

☎ 0871 527 8414
45 Goffs Park Rd RH11 8AX
web: www.premierinn.com
dir: M23 junct 11, A23 towards Crawley. At 2nd rdbt take 3rd exit for town centre, then 2nd right into Goffs Park Rd

Rooms 49

Premier Inn Gatwick Airport Central

BUDGET HOTEL

☎ 0871 527 8406
Longbridge Way, North Terminal RH6 0NX
web: www.premierinn.com
dir: M23 junct 9/9A towards North Terminal, at rdbt take 3rd exit, hotel on right

Rooms 219

Premier Inn Gatwick Airport South

BUDGET HOTEL

☎ 0871 527 8408
London Rd, Lowfield Heath RH10 9ST
web: www.premierinn.com
dir: M23 junct 9a towards North Terminal rdbt. Follow A23 & Crawley signs. Hotel in 2m

Rooms 102

Premier Inn Gatwick Manor Royal

BUDGET HOTEL

☎ 0871 527 9214
Crawley Business Quarter, Fleming Way RH10 9DF
web: www.premierinn.com
dir: M23 junct 10, A2011 (Crawley Ave). At rdbt 4th exit onto A23 (London Rd), at rdbt right into Fleming Way. Hotel 300yds on left

Rooms 180

GERRARDS CROSS   Map 6 TQ08
Buckinghamshire

The Bull Hotel

★★★★ 76% ◉ HOTEL

☎ 01753 885995
Oxford Rd SL9 7PA
e-mail: bull@sarova.co.uk
dir: M40 junct 2 follow Beaconsfield on A355. After 0.5m 2nd exit at rdbt signed A40 Gerrards Cross for 2m. The Bull on right

Dating from the 17th-century, this former inn has been extensively refurbished to provide smart, well-equipped bedrooms. Public areas include the popular bar and Beeches Restaurant, serving a wide variety of dishes to suit all tastes. In addition there is the informal Jack Shrimpton bar offering snacks and bar meals. Attractive gardens and a good range of function rooms make this a popular wedding and events venue.

Rooms 150 (15 fmly) (19 GF) **S** £105-£225;
D £105-£225 (incl. bkfst)* **Facilities** FTV Wi-fi Use of private leisure facilities Xmas New Year
Conf Class 108 Board 40 Thtr 180 Del £240*
Services Lift **Parking** 150 **Notes** LB Civ Wed 114

Save on hotels. Book at **theAA.com/hotel**

GAT – GLE 181 **ENGLAND**

GILLINGHAM
Kent   Map 7 TQ76

Premier Inn Gillingham Business Park

BUDGET HOTEL

☎ 0871 527 8416
Will Adams Way ME8 6BY
web: www.premierinn.com
dir: M2 junct 44, A278 to A2. Left at Tesco. Hotel at next rdbt

High quality, budget accommodation ideal for both families and business travellers. Spacious, en suite bedrooms feature tea and coffee making facilities, and Freeview TV in most hotels. Internet access and Wi-fi are available for a small fee. The adjacent family restaurant features a wide and varied menu. See also the Hotel Groups pages.

Rooms 46

Premier Inn Gillingham/Rainham

BUDGET HOTEL

☎ 0871 527 9268
High St, Rainham ME8 7JE
web: www.premierinn.com
dir: M25 junct 2 (Canterbury/Dover/A2), A2 to M2 (Dover). Exit at junct 4 (Rainham/Medway Tunnel), straight on at 2 rdbts. At 3rd rdbt take 3rd exit (Rainham High St). Hotel on right at 3rd lights

Rooms 26

GIRTON
Cambridgeshire   Map 12 TL46

Premier Inn Cambridge North (Girton)

BUDGET HOTEL

☎ 0871 527 8188
Huntingdon Rd CB3 0DR
web: www.premierinn.com
dir: A14 junct 31 follow signs towards Cambridge. Pass BP garage, next right. Hotel adjacent to Traveller's Rest Beefeater

High quality, budget accommodation ideal for both families and business travellers. Spacious, en suite bedrooms feature tea and coffee making facilities, and Freeview TV in most hotels. Internet access and Wi-fi are available for a small fee. The adjacent family restaurant features a wide and varied menu. See also the Hotel Groups pages.

Rooms 20

GISBURN
Lancashire   Map 18 SD84

Stirk House Hotel
★★★ 80% ⊛ HOTEL

☎ 01200 445581
BB7 4LJ
e-mail: reservations@stirkhouse.co.uk
dir: W of village, on A59. Hotel 0.5m on left

This delightful historic hotel enjoys a peaceful location in its own grounds, amid rolling countryside. Extensive public areas include excellent conference and banqueting facilities, a leisure centre and an elegant restaurant. The stylish bedrooms and suites vary in size and style but all are comfortable and well equipped. Hospitality is warm and friendly, and service attentive.

Rooms 30 (10 annexe) (2 fmly) (12 GF) ✆ **S** £55-£85; **D** £130-£216 (incl. bkfst)* **Facilities** STV Wi-fi 🔅 supervised 🏊 Gym Beauty treatment room Aromatherapy Personal training Kick boxing Xmas New Year **Conf** Class 150 Board 45 Thtr 200 **Parking** 400 **Notes** LB Civ Wed 200

GLAZEBROOK
Cheshire   Map 15 SJ69

The Rhinewood Country House Hotel
★★★ 77% HOTEL

☎ 0161 775 5555
Glazebrook Ln WA3 5BB
e-mail: info@therhinewoodhotel.co.uk
dir: M6 junct 21, A57 towards Irlam. Left at Glazebrook sign, hotel 0.25m on left

This privately owned hotel stands in spacious landscaped gardens is a short drive from Manchester and Warrington. The attractively presented bedrooms are well equipped. There is a popular restaurant and the stylish bar is ideal for more informal dining. Facilities include conference and function rooms and the hotel is a popular wedding venue.

Rooms 32 (4 fmly) (16 GF) (8 smoking) **Facilities** STV Wi-fi Complimentary membership at nearby health spa Xmas **Conf** Class 70 Board 40 Thtr 100 **Parking** 120 **Notes** Civ Wed 100

GLENRIDDING
Cumbria   Map 18 NY31

The Inn on the Lake
LAKE DISTRICT HOTELS
★★★ 83% ⊛ HOTEL

☎ 017684 82444
Lake Ullswater CA11 0PE
e-mail: innonthelake@lakedistricthotels.net
web: www.lakedistricthotels.net
dir: M6 junct 40, A66 to Keswick. At rdbt take A592 to Ullswater Lake. Along lake to Glenridding. Hotel on left on entering village

In a picturesque lakeside setting, this restored Victorian hotel is a popular leisure destination as well as catering for weddings and conferences. Superb views can be enjoyed from the bedrooms and from the garden terrace where afternoon teas are served during warmer months. There is a popular pub in the grounds, and moorings for yachts are available to guests. Sailing tuition can be arranged.

Rooms 47 (6 fmly) (1 GF) ✆ **S** fr £102; **D** fr £170 (incl. bkfst)* **Facilities** FTV Wi-fi ⏀ ♪ 9 Putt green Fishing 🏊 Gym 9 hole pitch & putt course Xmas New Year **Conf** Class 30 Board 24 Thtr 60 Del from £140* **Services** Lift **Parking** 200 **Notes** LB Civ Wed 100

Best Western Glenridding Hotel

★★★ 77% HOTEL

☎ 017684 82228 & 82289
CA11 0PB
e-mail: glenridding@bestwestern.co.uk
dir: N'bound M6 junct 36, A591 Windermere then A592, for 14m. S'bound M6 junct 40, A592 for 13m

This friendly hotel benefits from a picturesque location in the village centre, and many rooms have fine views of the lake and fells. Public areas are extensive and include a choice of dining options including Ratchers Restaurant and a café. Leisure facilities are available along with a conference room and a garden function room.

Rooms 36 (7 fmly) (8 GF) **Facilities** STV Wi-fi ⏀ Sauna Snooker Table tennis Xmas New Year **Conf** Class 30 Board 24 Thtr 30 **Services** Lift **Parking** 30 **Notes** Civ Wed 120

G

GLOSSOP
Derbyshire — Map 16 SK09

Wind in the Willows Hotel

★★ 83% COUNTRY HOUSE HOTEL

☎ 01457 868001
Derbyshire Level SK13 7PT
e-mail: info@windinthewillows.co.uk
dir: 1m E of Glossop on A57, turn right opposite Royal Oak, hotel 400yds on right

This impressive house sits in peaceful grounds with lovely views of the Peak District National Park. Individually furnished bedrooms are in keeping with the Victorian style of the house. Beautiful original oak panelling and crackling log fires add to the charm of the lounges and dining room. There is also a conference suite that is perfect for meetings, private dining or special occasions.

Rooms 12 🐾 **S** £95-£125; **D** £149-£179 (incl. bkfst) **Facilities** FTV Wi-fi ♭ Xmas New Year **Conf** Class 12 Board 16 Thtr 40 **Parking** 16 **Notes** LB ⊗ No children 10yrs

GLOUCESTER
Gloucestershire — Map 10 SO81

Hallmark Hotel Gloucester

★★★★ 73% HOTEL

☎ 01452 525653
Matson Ln, Robinswood Hill GL4 6EA
e-mail: gloucester.reservations@hallmarkhotels.co.uk
web: www.hallmarkhotels.co.uk/gloucester
dir: A40 towards Gloucester onto A38. 1st exit at 4th rdbt (Painswick Rd). Right onto Matson Lane

Ideally located for exploring the Cotswolds and Gloucester, this hotel offers well-appointed bedrooms and relaxing public areas. A large leisure club has a well-equipped gym, squash courts and pool. Complimentary Wi-fi is available throughout.

Rooms 95 🐾 **Facilities** FTV Wi-fi ♭ ⊛ supervised ⍒ Gym Squash Beauty salon Xmas New Year **Conf** Class 150 Board 18 Thtr 220 **Parking** 150 **Notes** Civ Wed 120

Hatherley Manor

★★★ 78% HOTEL

☎ 01452 730217
Down Hatherley Ln GL2 9QA
e-mail: reservations@hatherleymanor.com
web: www.hatherleymanor.com
dir: A38 into Down Hatherley Lane, signed. Hotel 600yds on left

Within easy striking distance of the M5, Gloucester, Cheltenham and the Cotswolds, this stylish 17th-century manor, set in attractive grounds, remains popular with both business and leisure guests. Bedrooms are well appointed and offer contemporary comforts. A particularly impressive range of meeting and function rooms is available.

Rooms 50 (5 fmly) (18 GF) **Facilities** FTV Wi-fi Xmas New Year **Conf** Class 90 Board 75 Thtr 400 **Parking** 250 **Notes** Civ Wed 300

Holiday Inn Gloucester - Cheltenham

★★★ 77% HOTEL

☎ 0871 942 9034
Crest Way, Barnwood GL4 3RX
e-mail: reservations-gloucester@ihg.com
web: www.holidayinn.co.uk
dir: A40 to Gloucester. At rdbt take 2nd exit signed A417/Cirencester. At next rdbt take 2nd exit then 1st left

This hotel is conveniently located close to the M5, and within easy driving distance of both Gloucester and Cheltenham. Bedrooms vary in size from the larger, well-equipped executive rooms to smaller style standard doubles. A good selection of dining options is available in either the lounge/bar, the relaxing restaurant or via room service. Guests can also enjoy the well-equipped leisure facilities.

Rooms 125 (25 fmly) (62 GF) (6 smoking) **S** £39-£235; **D** £39-£235 (incl. bkfst)* **Facilities** Spa STV FTV Wi-fi ♭ ⊛ Gym Dance studio New Year **Conf** Class 50 Board 60 Thtr 140 Del from £105 to £174* **Services** Air con **Parking** 200 **Notes** LB ⊗ Civ Wed 120

Hatton Court

★★★ 75% HOTEL

☎ 01452 617412
Upton Hill, Upton St Leonards GL4 8DE
e-mail: res@hatton-court.co.uk
web: www.hatton-court.co.uk
dir: From Gloucester on B4073 (Painswick road). Hotel at top of hill on right

Built in the style of a 17th-century Cotswold manor house, and set in seven acres of well-kept gardens this hotel is popular with both business and leisure guests. It stands at the top of Upton Hill and commands truly spectacular views of the Severn Valley. Bedrooms are comfortable and tastefully furnished with many extra facilities. The elegant Tara Restaurant offers a varied choice of menus, and there is also a bar and foyer lounge.

Rooms 45 (28 annexe) (6 fmly) 🐾 **S** £69-£129; **D** £75-£145 (incl. bkfst) **Facilities** FTV Wi-fi HL ⍒ Gym Xmas New Year **Conf** Class 100 Board 60 Thtr 200 Del from £105 to £160 **Parking** 80 **Notes** LB Civ Wed 80

Holiday Inn Express Gloucester - South M5

BUDGET HOTEL

☎ 01452 726400
Waterwells Business Park, Quedgeley GL2 2AB
e-mail: gloucester@morethanhotels.com
web: www.hiexpress.com/exgloucesterso

A modern hotel ideal for families and business travellers. Fresh and uncomplicated, the spacious rooms include Sky TV, power shower and tea and coffee-making facilities. Continental buffet breakfast is included in the room rate; other meals may be taken at the nearby family pub or restaurant. See also the Hotel Groups pages.

Rooms 106 **Conf** Class 20 Board 20 Thtr 35

Premier Inn Gloucester (Barnwood)

BUDGET HOTEL

☎ 0871 527 8456
Barnwood GL4 3HR
web: www.premierinn.com
dir: M5 junct 11, A40 towards Gloucester. At 1st rdbt A417 towards Cirencester, at next rdbt take 4th exit

High quality, budget accommodation ideal for both families and business travellers. Spacious, en suite bedrooms feature tea and coffee making facilities, and Freeview TV in most hotels. Internet access and Wi-fi are available for a small fee. The adjacent family restaurant features a wide and varied menu. See also the Hotel Groups pages.

Rooms 83

Premier Inn Gloucester Business Park

BUDGET HOTEL

☎ 0871 527 8462
Gloucester Business Park, Brockworth GL3 4AJ
web: www.premierinn.com
dir: M5 junct 11a, A417 towards Cirencester. At Brockworth Rdbt follow Gloucester Business Park signs, onto dual carriageway (Valiant Way). At next rdbt left into Delta Way. Hotel adjacent to Tesco

Rooms 48

Premier Inn Gloucester (Little Witcombe)

BUDGET HOTEL

☎ 0871 527 8458
Witcombe GL3 4SS
web: www.premierinn.com
dir: M5 junct 11a, A417 signed Cirencester. At 1st exit turn right onto A46 towards Stroud & Witcombe. Left at next rdbt by Crosshands pub

Rooms 39

Premier Inn Gloucester (Longford)

BUDGET HOTEL

☎ 0871 527 8460
Tewkesbury Rd, Longford GL2 9BE
web: www.premierinn.com
dir: M5 junct 11, A40 towards Gloucester & Ross-on-Wye. Hotel on A38 towards Gloucester

Rooms 60

Premier Inn Gloucester North

BUDGET HOTEL

☎ 0871 527 8464
Tewkesbury Rd, Twigworth GL2 9PG
web: www.premierinn.com
dir: On A38, 1m N from junct with A40

Rooms 50

The Wharf House Restaurant with Rooms

◉ RESTAURANT WITH ROOMS

☎ 01452 332900
Over GL2 8DB
e-mail: thewharfhouse@yahoo.co.uk
dir: From A40 between Gloucester & Highnam exit at lights for Over. Establishment signed

The Wharf House was built to replace the old lock cottage and, as the name suggests, it is located at the very edge of the river; it has pleasant views and an outdoor terrace. The bedrooms and bathrooms have been decorated and appointed to high levels of quality and comfort, and there are plenty of guest extras. Seasonal, local produce can be enjoyed both at breakfast and dinner in the delightfully relaxing restaurant.

Rooms 7 (1 fmly)

GODALMING
Surrey   Map 6 SU94

Premier Inn Godalming

BUDGET HOTEL

☎ 0871 527 8466
Guildford Rd GU7 3BX
web: www.premierinn.com
dir: Exit A3 onto A3000 signed Godalming. 1m to rdbt, turn right into Guildford Rd towards Godalming. Hotel on left in 500yds

High quality, budget accommodation ideal for both families and business travellers. Spacious, en suite bedrooms feature tea and coffee making facilities, and Freeview TV in most hotels. Internet access and Wi-fi are available for a small fee. The adjacent family restaurant features a wide and varied menu. See also the Hotel Groups pages.

Rooms 17

GOLANT
Cornwall   Map 2 SX15

Cormorant Hotel & Restaurant

★★★ 79% ◉◉ HOTEL

☎ 01726 833426
PL23 1LL
e-mail: relax@cormoranthotel.co.uk
web: www.cormoranthotel.co.uk
dir: A390 onto B3269 signed Fowey. In 3m left to Golant, through village to end of road, hotel on right

This hotel focuses on traditional hospitality, attentive service and good food. All the bedrooms enjoy the river views and guests can expect goose and down duvets, flat-screen digital TVs and free Wi-fi access. Breakfast and lunch may be taken on the terrace which overlooks the river.

Rooms 14 (4 GF) ⟲ D £90-£250* **Facilities** FTV Wi-fi ⟲ ⟳ Xmas New Year **Parking** 20 **Notes** LB ⊗ No children 16yrs

G

GOMERSAL
West Yorkshire   Map 19 SE22

Gomersal Park Hotel

★★★ 79% HOTEL

☎ 01274 869386
Moor Ln BD19 4LJ
e-mail: enquiries@gomersalparkhotel.com
web: www.gomersalparkhotel.com
dir: A62 to Huddersfield. At junct with A65, by Greyhound Pub right, after 1m take 1st right after Oakwell Hall

Constructed around a 19th-century house, this stylish, modern hotel enjoys a peaceful location and pleasant grounds. Deep sofas ensure comfort in the open-plan lounge and imaginative meals are served in the popular Brasserie 101. The well-equipped bedrooms provide high quality and comfort. Extensive public areas include a well-equipped leisure complex and pool, and a wide variety of air-conditioned conference rooms.

Rooms 100 (3 fmly) (32 GF) **Facilities** FTV Wi-fi ⟳ supervised Gym **Conf** Class 130 Board 60 Thtr 250 **Services** Lift **Parking** 150 **Notes** Civ Wed 200

See Paignton

GOODWOOD
West Sussex   Map 6 SU81

The Goodwood Hotel

★★★★ 81% ◉◉ HOTEL

☎ 01243 775537
PO18 0QB
e-mail: reservations@goodwood.com
web: www.goodwood.com
dir: Off A285, 3m NE of Chichester

Set at the centre of the 12,000-acre Goodwood Estate, this attractive hotel boasts extensive indoor and outdoor leisure facilities, along with a range of meeting rooms plus conference and banqueting facilities. Bedrooms are furnished to a consistently high standard, including a luxury suite located in the old coaching inn, and Executive rooms, each with a patio. Eating options are varied - the Richmond Arms which sources produce extensively from the estate farm, The Richmond Arms Bar, and the Goodwood Bar and Grill. Overnight guests can also choose to dine in The Kennels, a private members' clubhouse.

Rooms 91 (48 GF) ➧ **Facilities** Spa STV FTV Wi-fi ⓢ ⌁ 18 ◉ Putt green Gym Golf driving range Sauna Steam room Fitness studio Xmas New Year **Conf** Class 60 Board 50 Thtr 150 Del from £140 to £200* **Parking** 150 **Notes** Civ Wed 120

GOOLE
East Riding of Yorkshire   Map 17 SE72

Lowther Hotel

★★★ 80% HOTEL

☎ 01405 767999
Aire St DN14 5QW
web: www.lowtherhotel.co.uk
dir: M62 junct 36, A614, follow town centre signs. At clock tower rdbt right into Aire St. Hotel at end on left

A beautifully restored Georgian Grade II* listed building that combines historic features with contemporary design. Set in a unique location, its overlooks the port yet is within easy reach of motorway links. The bedrooms are stylish, well equipped and have free Wi-fi. Public areas include the New Bridge Lounge and The Burlington Restaurant, and the impressive Mural Rooms are perfect for weddings, conferences and meetings.

Lowther Hotel

Rooms 14 (1 fmly) **Facilities** FTV Wi-fi ♫ Xmas New Year **Conf** Class 90 Board 50 Thtr 90 **Parking** 30 **Notes** ⊗ Civ Wed 90

Premier Inn Goole

BUDGET HOTEL

☎ 0871 527 8468
Rawcliffe Rd, Airmyn DN14 8JS
web: www.premierinn.com
dir: M62 junct 36, A614 signed Rawcliffe. Hotel immediately on left

High quality, budget accommodation ideal for both families and business travellers. Spacious, en suite bedrooms feature tea and coffee making facilities, and Freeview TV in most hotels. Internet access and Wi-fi are available for a small fee. The adjacent family restaurant features a wide and varied menu. See also the Hotel Groups pages.

Rooms 41

GORDANO SERVICE AREA (M5)   Map 4 ST57
Somerset

Days Inn Bristol West - M5

BUDGET HOTEL

☎ 01275 373709 & 373624
BS20 7XG
e-mail: gordano.hotel@welcomebreak.co.uk
web: www.welcomebreak.co.uk
dir: M5 junct 19, follow signs for Gordano Services

This modern building offers accommodation in smart, spacious and well-equipped bedrooms, suitable for families and business travellers, and all with en suite bathrooms. Continental breakfast is available and other refreshments may be taken at the nearby family restaurant. See also the Hotel Groups pages.

Rooms 60 (52 fmly) (29 GF) (10 smoking)
Conf Board 10

GORLESTON ON SEA   Map 13 TG50
Norfolk

The Pier Hotel

★★★ 85% HOTEL

☎ 01493 662631
Harbourmouth, South Pier NR31 6PL
e-mail: bookings@pierhotelgorleston.co.uk
dir: From A47 W of Great Yarmouth take A12 signed Lowestoft. At 3rd rdbt 1st left (Beccles Rd) signed Gorleston. At rdbt 2nd left (Church Rd). Next rdbt 1st left (Baker St). Right into Pier Plain, then Pier Walk to Pier Gdns

Ideally situated on the seafront this hotel offers smartly appointed bedrooms that are thoughtfully equipped and have a good range of useful extras; some rooms have superb sea views. The public areas include a large restaurant and a conservatory, which leads to a terrace and bar.

Rooms 19 (1 fmly) ➧ **S** £65-£75; **D** £80-£125 (incl. bkfst)* **Facilities** STV FTV Wi-fi ⓠ ♫ New Year **Parking** 14 **Notes** ⊗

GOSFORTH   Map 18 NY00
Cumbria

Westlakes Hotel

★★★ 81% HOTEL

☎ 019467 25221
CA20 1HP
e-mail: info@westlakeshotel.co.uk
web: www.westlakeshotel.co.uk
dir: From A595 take B5344 signed Seascale. Hotel entrance 1st right

Located amid the stunning scenery of the western lakes and within easy striking distance of a whole array of visitor attractions, the hotel offers accommodation of a high standard, with many thoughtful extras provided. High quality food is served in the restaurant with relaxed and friendly service led by the hands-on owners and their team. There are excellent walking opportunities from this hotel.

Rooms 10 (4 annexe) (1 GF) ➧ **Facilities** FTV Wi-fi **Parking** 15 **Notes** ⊗

GRANGE-OVER-SANDS
Cumbria   Map 18 SD47

Netherwood Hotel
★★★ 80% HOTEL

☎ 015395 32552
Lindale Rd LA11 6ET
e-mail: enquiries@netherwood-hotel.co.uk
web: www.netherwood-hotel.co.uk
dir: On B5277 before station

This imposing hotel stands in terraced grounds and enjoys fine views of Morecambe Bay. Though a popular conference and wedding venue, good levels of hospitality and service ensure all guests are well looked after. Bedrooms vary in size but all are well furnished and have smart modern bathrooms. Magnificent woodwork is a feature of the public areas.

Rooms 34 (5 fmly) ♒ **S** £70-£100; **D** £160-£180 (incl. bkfst) **Facilities** Spa FTV Wi-fi ☺ supervised ⛳ Gym Beauty salon Steam room Sunbed New Year **Conf** Class 150 Board 60 Thtr 150 Del from £120 to £160 **Services** Lift **Parking** 100 **Notes** LB Civ Wed 200

Cumbria Grand Hotel
★★★ 68% HOTEL

☎ 015395 32331
LA11 6EN
e-mail: salescumbria@strathmorehotels.com
dir: M6 junct 36, A590 & follow Grange-over-Sands signs

Set within extensive grounds, this large hotel offers fine views over Morecambe Bay and caters well for a mixed market. Public areas are pure nostalgia, and include a grand dining room and fine ballroom. Bedrooms are comfortably equipped and some have views of the bay.

Rooms 122 (10 fmly) (25 GF) **Facilities** STV Wi-fi ☺ Putt green Snooker & pool table Table tennis Darts ♫ Xmas New Year **Services** Lift **Parking** 75

See advert on page 524

Graythwaite Manor Hotel
★★★ 68% HOTEL

☎ 015395 32001 & 33755
Fernhill Rd LA11 7JE
e-mail: enquiries@graythwaitemanor.co.uk
dir: B5277 through Grange, Fernhill Rd opposite fire station, hotel 1st left

This well established hotel is set in beautiful gardens complete with sub-tropical plants, and affords delightful views out over Morecambe Bay. Public areas include an Orangery, a number of comfortable lounges and an elegant restaurant. The bedrooms, which vary in size, are traditional in style.

Rooms 24 (2 fmly) (4 GF) **Facilities** FTV Wi-fi Xmas New Year **Parking** 34 **Notes** Civ Wed 100

Clare House
★★ ☺ HOTEL

☎ 015395 33026 & 34253
Park Rd LA11 7HQ
e-mail: info@clarehousehotel.co.uk
web: www.clarehousehotel.co.uk
dir: A590 onto B5277, through Lindale into Grange, keep left, hotel 0.5m on left past Crown Hill & St Paul's Church

A warm, genuine welcome awaits guests at this delightful hotel, proudly run by the Read family for over 40 years. Situated in its own secluded gardens, it provides a relaxed haven in which to enjoy the panoramic views across Morecambe Bay. The stylish bedrooms and public areas are comfortable and attractively furnished. Skilfully prepared dinners and hearty breakfasts are served in the elegant dining room.

Rooms 18 (4 GF) ♒ **S** £87-£92; **D** £172-£184 (incl. bkfst & dinner)* **Facilities** FTV Wi-fi Putt green ⛳ **Parking** 18 **Notes** LB ⊗ Closed mid Dec-late Mar

Hampsfell House Hotel
★★ 81% HOTEL

☎ 015395 32567
Hampsfell Rd LA11 6BG
e-mail: enquiries@hampsfellhouse.co.uk
web: www.hampsfellhouse.co.uk
dir: A590 at junct with B5277, signed to Grange-over-Sands. Left at rdbt into Main St, right at 2nd rdbt & right at x-rds. Hotel on left

Dating back to 1800, this owner managed hotel is peacefully set in two acres of private grounds yet is just a comfortable walk from the town centre. Bedrooms are smartly decorated and well maintained. There is a cosy bar where guests can relax and enjoy pre-dinner drinks. Comprehensive and imaginative dinners are taken in an attractive dining room.

Rooms 8 (1 fmly) ♒ **S** £45-£65; **D** £60-£95 (incl. bkfst)* **Facilities** FTV Wi-fi **Parking** 20

G

G

Ramada Grantham ®RAMADA.

★★★★ 72% HOTEL

☎ 01476 593000
Swingbridge Rd NG31 7XT
e-mail: info@ramadagrantham.co.uk
web: www.ramadagrantham.co.uk
dir: Exit A1 at Grantham/Melton Mowbray junct onto A607. From N: 1st exit at mini rdbt, hotel on right. From S: at rdbt 2nd exit. Next left at T-junct. At mini rdbt 2nd exit. Hotel on right

A modern, purpose-built hotel ideally placed for touring the area. Bedrooms are spacious, smartly decorated and equipped with modern facilities. Public rooms include a large open-plan lounge/bar area with comfortable seating and an intimate restaurant as well as conference and banqueting facilities. The property also has smart leisure facilities.

Rooms 89 (44 GF) (2 smoking) **S** £55-£99; **D** £55-£99* **Facilities** STV FTV Wi-fi ⓢ Gym Steam room Sauna Xmas New Year **Conf** Class 90 Board 60 Thtr 200 Del from £99 to £145* **Parking** 102 **Notes** ⊗ Civ Wed 200

Premier Inn Grantham

BUDGET HOTEL

☎ 0871 527 8470
A1/607 Junction, Harlaxton Rd NG31 7UA
web: www.premierinn.com
dir: A1 onto A607

High quality, budget accommodation ideal for both families and business travellers. Spacious, en suite bedrooms feature tea and coffee making facilities, and Freeview TV in most hotels. Internet access and Wi-fi are available for a small fee. The adjacent family restaurant features a wide and varied menu.

Rooms 59

Rothay Garden Hotel

★★★★ 84% ◉ ◉ HOTEL

☎ 015394 35334
Broadgate LA22 9RJ
e-mail: stay@rothaygarden.com
web: www.rothaygarden.com
dir: A591, opposite Swan Hotel, into Grasmere, 300yds on left

On the edge of the village, and sitting in two acres of riverside gardens, Rothay Garden offers an impressive combination of stylish design and luxurious comfort. Bedrooms include five Loft Suites, each named after one of the fells they overlook; newly added sun lounges and balconies to upper floor rooms are a real feature. The garden spa is the perfect way to relax with steam, sauna, heated relaxing beds and a hydrotherapy pool. There is a chic lounge bar and an elegant dining room. The friendly staff provide attentive service.

Rothay Garden Hotel

Rooms 30 (3 fmly) (8 GF) ↿ **Facilities** FTV Wi-fi ↾ Hydro spa pool Sauna Aromatherapy room Infra red loungers Reflexology Xmas New Year **Parking** 38 **Notes** No children 5yrs

See advert on this page

Wordsworth Hotel & Spa

★★★★ 80% ◎◎ HOTEL

☎ 015394 35592
LA22 9SW
e-mail: enquiry@thewordsworthhotel.co.uk
web: www.thewordsworthhotel.co.uk
dir: Off A591. In centre of village adjacent to St Oswald's Church

This historic hotel, ideally situated in the heart of Grasmere, has undergone a complete refurbishment and now provides high levels of style and luxury. The bedrooms are equipped with smart furnishings, comfortable beds with Egyptian cotton linens, and quality accessories. Guests can enjoy fine dining in the modernised Signature Restaurant which now boasts stylish and elegant decor, and for a less formal dining experience, light meals and fine ales are offered in the Dove Bistro. The hotel has a heated swimming pool, and the new sauna and spa make the ideal place for relaxation.

Wordsworth Hotel

Rooms 39 (2 fmly) (2 GF) ♥ **S** £50-£195; **D** £127-£350 (incl. bkfst) **Facilities** Spa FTV Wi-fi ♫ ☜ ⤸ Gym Beauty treatment room Mixed sauna Nail bar Xmas New Year **Conf** Class 50 Board 40 Thtr 100 Del from £150 to £250 **Services** Lift **Parking** 60 **Notes** LB Civ Wed 100

See advert on this page

Oak Bank Hotel

★★★ 81% ◎◎ HOTEL

☎ 015394 35217
Broadgate LA22 9TA
e-mail: info@lakedistricthotel.co.uk
web: www.lakedistricthotel.co.uk
dir: N'bound: M6 junct 36 onto A591 to Windermere, Ambleside, then Grasmere. S'bound: M6 junct 40 onto A66 to Keswick, A591 to Grasmere

Privately owned and personally run by the friendly proprietors, Oak Bank is a Victorian house in the charming village of Grasmere. Bedrooms are well-equipped and include one with a four-poster bed, as well as a suite with jacuzzi bath. In colder weather, welcoming log fires burn in the comfortable lounges. The restaurant has a conservatory extension overlooking the garden, and there is also a pleasant bar.

Rooms 14 (1 GF) ♥ **S** £96.50-£127.50; **D** £133-£192 (incl. bkfst & dinner) **Facilities** FTV Wi-fi Use of nearby leisure facilities New Year **Parking** 14 **Notes** LB Closed 2-26 Jan

G

GRASMERE *continued*

Best Western Grasmere Red Lion Hotel

★★★ 80% HOTEL

☎ 015394 35456
Red Lion Square LA22 9SS
e-mail: reservations@grasmereredlionhotel.co.uk
dir: From A591, signed Grasmere Village. Hotel in village centre

This modernised and extended 18th-century coaching inn, located in the heart of the village, offers spacious well-equipped rooms and a number of meeting and conference facilities. A range of pub meals complement the more formal Courtyard Restaurant. The comfortable lounge area is ideal for relaxing, and for the more energetic guest there is a pool and gym.

Rooms 49 (10 fmly) ⁂ **S** £45-£95; **D** £80-£175 (incl. bkfst)* **Facilities** STV Wi-fi ⓢ Gym Sauna Steam room Spa bath Xmas New Year **Conf** Class 24 Board 28 Thtr 60 Del from £122 to £162* **Services** Lift **Parking** 35 **Notes** LB

Macdonald Swan Hotel

★★★ 79% ⊛ HOTEL

☎ 0844 879 9120
LA22 9RF
e-mail: sales/oldengland@macdonald-hotels.co.uk
web: www.macdonaldhotels.co.uk
dir: M6 junct 36, A591 towards Kendal, A590 to Keswick through Ambleside. Hotel on right on entering village

Close to Dove Cottage and occupying a prominent position on the edge of the village, this 300-year-old inn is mentioned in Wordsworth's poem *The Waggoner*. Attractive public areas are spacious and comfortable, and bedrooms are equally stylish, some have CD players. A good range of bar meals is available, while the elegant restaurant offers more formal dining.

Rooms 38 (2 fmly) (28 GF) **D** £105-£185 (incl. bkfst) **Facilities** FTV Wi-fi Xmas New Year **Conf** Class 20 Board 30 Thtr 40 Del from £125 to £175* **Parking** 45 **Notes** LB Civ Wed 60

Gold Rill Country House Hotel

★★★ 78% HOTEL

☎ 015394 35486
Red Bank Rd LA22 9PU
e-mail: reception@goldrill.co.uk
web: www.goldrill.co.uk
dir: A591 into village centre, turn into road opposite St Oswald's Church. Hotel 300yds on left

This popular hotel enjoys a fine location on the edge of the village with spectacular views of the lake and surrounding fells. Attractive bedrooms, some with balconies, are tastefully decorated and many have separate, comfortable seating areas. The hotel boasts a private pier, an outdoor heated pool and a putting green. Public areas include a well-appointed restaurant and choice of lounges.

Rooms 32 (7 annexe) (2 fmly) (11 GF) ⁂ **S** £78-£91; **D** £156-£182 (incl. bkfst & dinner)* **Facilities** STV FTV Wi-fi ⁂ Putt green New Year **Parking** 35 **Notes** LB ⊗ Closed mid Dec-mid Jan (ex New Year)

GRASSINGTON   Map 19 SE06
North Yorkshire

Grassington House

◉◉ RESTAURANT WITH ROOMS

☎ 01756 752406
5 The Square BD23 5AQ
e-mail: bookings@grassingtonhousehotel.co.uk
web: www.grassingtonhousehotel.co.uk
dir: A59 into Grassington

Located in the square of the popular village of Grassington this beautifully converted Georgian house is personally run by owners John and Sue. Delicious food, individually designed bedrooms and warm hospitality ensure an enjoyable stay. There is a stylish lounge bar looking out to the square and the restaurant is split between two rooms; here guests will find the emphasis is on fresh, local ingredients and attentive, yet friendly service.

Rooms 9 (2 fmly)

GRAVESEND   Map 6 TQ67
Kent

Premier Inn Gravesend (A2/Singlewell)

BUDGET HOTEL

☎ 0871 527 8472
Hevercourt Rd, Singlewell DA12 5UQ
web: www.premierinn.com
dir: At Gravesend East exit on A2

High quality, budget accommodation ideal for both families and business travellers. Spacious, en suite

bedrooms feature tea and coffee making facilities, and Freeview TV in most hotels. Internet access and Wi-fi are available for a small fee. The adjacent family restaurant features a wide and varied menu. See also the Hotel Groups pages.

Rooms 31

Premier Inn Gravesend Central

BUDGET HOTEL

☎ 0871 527 8474
Wrotham Rd DA11 7LF
web: www.premierinn.com
dir: A2 onto A227 towards town centre, 1m to hotel

Rooms 36

GRAYS   Map 6 TQ67
Essex

Park Inn by Radisson Thurrock

★★★ 74% HOTEL

☎ 01708 719988
High Rd, North Stifford RM16 5UE
e-mail: info.thurrock@rezidorparkinn.com
dir: M25 junct 30/31, follow A13 towards Brentwood/Southend, A1012 (Grays), hotel is 1st exit on rdbt

This hotel is conveniently located just 20 minutes from London, and is within close proximity of the Lakeside Shopping Centre and Dartford. It is a Georgian manor house set in landscaped gardens that offers comfortable bedrooms with satellite TV; Wi-fi is available. There is a range of modern meeting rooms, a sport-themed bar and a large Regency restaurant which is open for lunch and dinner daily; hot dishes and a continental buffet are on offer at breakfast. The hotel is a popular wedding venue.

Rooms 97 (18 fmly) (48 GF) (2 smoking) ⁂ **Facilities** STV FTV Wi-fi ⁂ Xmas New Year **Conf** Class 134 Board 185 Thtr 445 Del from £135 to £175* **Services** Air con **Parking** 60 **Notes** ⊗ Civ Wed 150

GREAT BIRCHAM   Map 13 TF73
Norfolk

The Kings Head Hotel

★★★ 86% ⊛ HOTEL

☎ 01485 578265 & 572846
PE31 6RJ
e-mail: info@thekingsheadhotel.co.uk
web: www.thekingsheadhotel.co.uk

A delightful family-run hotel situated in the heart of this north Norfolk village close to Royal Sandringham. The property is very contemporary, yet still retains

Save on hotels. Book at **theAA.com/hotel**

GRA – GRE **189** ENGLAND

much of its original character. The spacious bedrooms are tastefully appointed and equipped with modern facilities. Public rooms inlude a lounge, bar, restaurant and further dining room.

Rooms 12 **S** £75-£130; **D** £75-£130* **Facilities** FTV Wi-fi ♨ Xmas **Conf** Class 30 Board 20 Thtr 40 Del from £125 to £140* **Parking** 30 **Notes** Civ Wed 80

GREAT CHESTERFORD
Essex   Map 12 TL54

The Crown House

★★★ 72% HOTEL

☎ 01799 530515
CB10 1NY
e-mail: reservations@crownhousehotel.com
web: www.crownhousehotel.com
dir: From N: M11 at junct 9 (from S junct 10) follow signs for Saffron Walden, then Great Chesterford (B1383)

This Georgian coaching inn, situated in a peaceful village close to the M11, has been sympathetically restored and retains much original character. The bedrooms are well equipped and individually decorated; some rooms have delightful four-poster beds. Public rooms include an attractive lounge bar, an elegant oak-panelled restaurant and an airy conservatory.

Rooms 18 (10 annexe) (1 fmly) (5 GF) **Facilities** FTV Wi-fi ♨ New Year **Conf** Class 14 Board 12 Thtr 30 **Parking** 30 **Notes** Closed 27-30 Dec Civ Wed 50

GREAT MILTON
Oxfordshire   Map 5 SP60

INSPECTORS' CHOICE

Le Manoir Aux Quat' Saisons

★★★★★ ◉◉◉◉◉ HOTEL

☎ 01844 278881
Church Rd OX44 7PD
e-mail: lemanoir@blanc.co.uk
web: www.manoir.com
dir: From A329 2nd right to Great Milton Manor, hotel 200yds on right

Even though Le Manoir is now very much part of the British scene, its iconic chef patron, Raymond Blanc, still fizzes with new ideas and projects. His first loves are his kitchen and his garden and the vital link between them. The fascinating grounds feature a Japanese tea garden and two acres of vegetables and herbs that supply the kitchen with an almost never ending supply of top notch produce. Even the car park has a stunning artichoke sculpture. The kitchen is the epicentre, with outstanding cooking highlighting freshness and seasonality. Bedrooms in this idyllic 'grand house on a small scale' are either in the main house or around an outside courtyard; all offer the highest levels of comfort and quality, have magnificent marble bathrooms and are equipped with a host of thoughtful extra touches. For something really special there is the 15th-century dovecot with a stunning upper-floor bedroom and a bathroom below. La Belle Epoque is the private dining room, ideal for weddings, celebrations and corporate events.

Rooms 32 (23 annexe) (13 GF) **S** £515-£1315; **D** £515-£1315 (incl. bkfst)* **Facilities** STV FTV Wi-fi ♨ Cookery school Water gardens Bikes Spa treatment Xmas New Year **Conf** Board 20 Thtr 24 **Parking** 60 **Notes** ❀ Civ Wed 50

GREAT TOTHAM
Essex   Map 7 TL81

The Bull at Great Totham

◉◉ RESTAURANT WITH ROOMS

☎ 01621 893385 & 894020
2 Maldon Rd CM9 8NH
e-mail: reservations@thebullatgreattotham.co.uk
dir: Exit A12 at Witham junct to Great Totham

A 16th-century coaching inn located in the village of Great Totham, The Bull is now a very stylish restaurant with rooms that offers en suite bedrooms with satellite TVs with Freeview; Wi-fi is available throughout. Guests can enjoy dinner in the gastro-pub or in the award-winning, fine dining restaurant, The Willow Room.

Rooms 4

GREAT YARMOUTH
Norfolk   Map 13 TG50

Imperial Hotel

THE INDEPENDENTS
HOTEL ASSOCIATION

★★★★ 75% ◉ HOTEL

☎ 01493 842000
North Dr NR30 1EQ
e-mail: reservations@imperialhotel.co.uk
web: www.imperialhotel.co.uk
dir: Follow signs to seafront, turn left. Hotel opposite Waterways

This friendly, family-run hotel is situated at the quieter end of the seafront within easy walking distance of the town centre. Bedrooms are attractively decorated with co-ordinated soft furnishings and many thoughtful touches; most rooms have superb sea views. Public areas include the smart Savoie Lounge Bar and the Rambouillet Restaurant.

Rooms 39 (4 fmly) ☎ **D** £80-£130 (incl. bkfst) **Facilities** FTV Wi-fi New Year **Conf** Class 40 Board 30 Thtr 140 **Services** Lift **Parking** 50 **Notes** Civ Wed 140

G

GREAT YARMOUTH *continued*

Furzedown Hotel

★★★ 78% HOTEL

☎ 01493 844138
19-20 North Dr NR30 4EW
e-mail: paul@furzedownhotel.co.uk
web: www.furzedownhotel.co.uk
dir: At end of A47 or A12, towards seafront, left, hotel opposite Waterways

Expect a warm welcome at this family-run hotel situated at the northern end of the seafront overlooking the town's Venetian Waterways. Bedrooms are pleasantly decorated and thoughtfully equipped; many rooms have superb sea views. The stylish public areas include a comfortable lounge bar, a smartly appointed restaurant and a cosy TV room.

Rooms 20 (11 fmly) **Facilities** FTV Wi-fi New Year **Conf** Class 80 Board 40 Thtr 75 **Parking** 30

Comfort Hotel Great Yarmouth

★★★ 75% HOTEL

☎ 01493 855070 & 850044
Albert Square NR30 3JH
e-mail: sales@comfortgreatyarmouth.co.uk
web: www.comfortgreatyarmouth.co.uk
dir: From seafront left at Wellington Pier into Kimberley Terr. Left into Albert Sq, hotel on left

A large hotel situated in the quieter end of town, just off the seafront and within easy walking distance of the town centre. The pleasantly decorated, well-equipped bedrooms are generally quite spacious and include Wi-fi. Public rooms include a comfortable lounge, a bar and smart brasserie-style restaurant.

Rooms 50 (6 fmly) (3 GF) **S** £39-£69; **D** £59-£99* **Facilities** FTV Wi-fi ↳ Xmas New Year **Conf** Class 50 Board 30 Thtr 120 Del from £89 to £109 **Parking** 15 **Notes** LB ⊗ Civ Wed 120

The Prom Hotel

★★★ 75% HOTEL

☎ 01493 842308
77 Marine Pde NR30 2DH
e-mail: info@promhotel.co.uk

Ideally situated on the seafront close to the bright lights and attractions of Marine Parade. The open-plan public areas include a smart lounge bar with views of the sea, and a relaxed restaurant; guests also have the use of a further quieter lounge bar with plush seating. The modern contemporary bedrooms are smartly appointed and have many thoughtful touches; many rooms have lovely sea views.

Rooms 25 (1 fmly) **S** £65-£85; **D** £85-£110 (incl. bkfst)* **Facilities** STV FTV Wi-fi ↳ Xmas

Knights Court Hotel

★★★ 72% HOTEL

☎ 01493 843089 & 07748 501009
22 North Dr NR30 4EW
e-mail: enquiries@knights-court.co.uk
dir: From A12 & A47 rdbt, A149 to seafront

Small privately-owned hotel situated on the seafront overlooking the beach. The smartly appointed bedrooms are comfortable and well equipped; many of the rooms have lovely sea views. Breakfast and dinner are served in the stylish dining room and there is a cosy lounge bar with views of the beach.

Rooms 20 (5 fmly) **S** £49-£63; **D** £49-£85 (incl. bkfst)* **Facilities** STV FTV Wi-fi ↳ **Conf** Class 40 Board 20 Thtr 40 Del from £92* **Parking** 22 **Notes** LB ⊗

Burlington Palm Hotel

★★★ 71% HOTEL

☎ 01493 844568
11 North Dr NR30 1EG
e-mail: enquiries@burlington-hotel.co.uk
web: www.burlington-hotel.co.uk
dir: A12 to seafront, left at Britannia Pier. Hotel near tennis courts

This privately owned hotel is situated at the quiet end of the resort, overlooking the sea. Bedrooms come in a variety of sizes and styles; they are pleasantly decorated and well equipped, and many have lovely sea views. The spacious public rooms include a range of seating areas, a choice of dining rooms, two bars and a heated indoor swimming pool.

Rooms 69 (9 fmly) (1 GF) ✎ **S** £60-£120; **D** £110-£150 (incl. bkfst)* **Facilities** FTV Wi-fi ⊗ Turkish steam room Xmas **Conf** Class 60 Board 30 Thtr 120 Del from £95 to £120 **Services** Lift **Parking** 70 **Notes** LB ⊗ Closed 28 Dec RS Dec-Feb

See advert on opposite page

Save on hotels. Book at **theAA.com/hotel**

GRE 191 ENGLAND

The Waverley Hotel

★★★ 70% HOTEL

☎ 01493 853388
32-34 Princes Rd NR30 2DG
e-mail: info@thewaverleyhotel.com

Situated in a side road adjacent to the seafront and close to the local amenities. The property has been totally refurbished by the current owner to a very good standard. Public rooms include a large lounge bar, foyer and spacious restaurant. Bedrooms are contemporary in style and have a good range of extra facilities.

Rooms 47 **Conf** Class 60 Board 60 Thtr 60

The Nelson Hotel

★★★ 66% HOTEL

☎ 01493 855551
1 Marine Pde NR30 3AG
e-mail: johnrushworth@theukholidaygroup.com
dir: On right of Marine Parade, opposite Sealife Centre

Ideally situated overlooking the sea, close to the pier and just a short stroll from the town centre and local amenities. The property is ideally suited to both business and leisure guests, and all of the bedrooms are well equipped, some rooms have lovely sea views. Public areas include a lounge with plush sofas, a bar and a separate dining room.

Rooms 50 (10 fmly) **S** £45-£90; **D** £60-£130 (incl. bkfst)* **Facilities** FTV Wi-fi ♫ Xmas New Year **Conf** Class 60 Board 60 Thtr 100 Del £75* **Services** Lift **Notes** ⊗ Closed 2 Jan-end Feb

New Beach Hotel

★★ 69% HOTEL

 Leisureplex

☎ 01493 332300
67 Marine Pde NR30 2EJ
e-mail: newbeach.gtyarmouth@alfatravel.co.uk
web: www.leisureplex.co.uk
dir: Follow signs to seafront. Hotel facing Britannia Pier

This Victorian building is centrally located on the seafront, overlooking Britannia Pier and the sandy beach. Bedrooms are pleasantly decorated and equipped with modern facilities; many have lovely sea views. Dinner is taken in the restaurant which doubles as the ballroom, and guests can also relax in the bar or sunny lounge.

Rooms 76 (3 fmly) **S** £35-£45; **D** £56-£76 (incl. bkfst)* **Facilities** FTV ♫ Xmas New Year **Services** Lift **Notes** LB ⊗ Closed Dec-Feb (ex Xmas) RS Nov & Mar

Andover House

◉ ◉ RESTAURANT WITH ROOMS

☎ 01493 843490
28-30 Camperdown NR30 3JB
e-mail: info@andoverhouse.co.uk
web: www.andoverhouse.co.uk
dir: Opposite Wellington Pier turn into Shadingfield Close, right into Kimberley Terrace, follow into Camperdown. Property on left

A lovely three-storey Victorian town house which was totally transformed by the current owners a few years ago. The property features a series of contemporary spaces that include a large open-plan lounge bar, a brasserie-style restaurant serving modern British cuisine, a cosy lounge and a smart sun terrace. Bedrooms are tastefully appointed with co-ordinated soft furnishings and have many thoughtful touches.

Rooms 20

GREAT YELDHAM	Map 13 TL73
Essex	

The White Hart

◉ ◉ RESTAURANT WITH ROOMS

☎ 01787 237250
Poole St CO9 4HJ
e-mail: mjwmason@yahoo.co.uk
dir: On A1017 in village

A large timber-framed character building houses the main restaurant and bar areas whilst the bedrooms are located in the converted coach house; all are smartly appointed and well equipped with many thoughtful extras. A comfortable lounge-bar area and beautifully landscaped gardens provide areas for relaxation. Locally sourced produce is used in the main house restaurant, popular with local residents and guests alike.

Rooms 11 (2 fmly)

G

GREENFORD
Greater London

See London plan 1 C4

Premier Inn London Greenford

BUDGET HOTEL

☎ 0871 527 8658
Western Av UB6 8TE
web: www.premierinn.com
dir: From A40 (Western Avenue) E'bound, exit at Perivale. Right, left at 2nd lights. Hotel opposite Hoover Building

High quality, budget accommodation ideal for both families and business travellers. Spacious, en suite bedrooms feature tea and coffee making facilities, and Freeview TV in most hotels. Internet access and Wi-fi are available for a small fee. The adjacent family restaurant features a wide and varied menu. See also the Hotel Groups pages.

Rooms 39

GREETHAM
Rutland
Map 11 SK91

Greetham Valley

★★★ 75% HOTEL

☎ 01780 460444
Wood Ln LE15 7SN
e-mail: info@greethamvalley.co.uk
web: www.greethamvalley.co.uk
dir: A1/B668. Left towards Greetham, Cottesmore & Oakham. Left at x-rds after 0.5m, follow brown signs to golf club entrance

Spacious bedrooms with storage facilities designed for golfers, offer high levels of comfort and many have superb views over the two golf courses. Meals are taken in the clubhouse restaurants with a choice of informal or more formal styles. A beauty suite and extensive conference facilities are ideal for both large and small groups.

Rooms 35 (17 GF) ↺ **S** £55-£86; **D** £64-£95 (incl. bkfst)* **Facilities** FTV Wi-fi ♨ 45 Putt green Fishing Gym 4x4 off-road course Archery centre Bowls green Driving range Petanque New Year **Conf** Class 150 Board 80 Thtr 280 Del from £117* **Services** Lift **Parking** 300 **Notes** LB ⊗ Civ Wed 200

GRIMSBY
Lincolnshire
Map 17 TA21

Millfields Hotel

★★★ Ⓐ HOTEL

☎ 01472 356068
53 Bargate DN34 5AD
e-mail: info@millfieldshotel.co.uk
web: www.millfieldshotel.co.uk
dir: A180, right at KFC rdbt then left at next rdbt. Right at 2nd lights & right onto Bargate, hotel 0.5m on left after Wheatsheaf pub

Rooms 27 (4 annexe) (7 fmly) (13 GF) ↺ **S** £75-£175; **D** £75-£175 (incl. bkfst)* **Facilities** FTV Wi-fi Gym Squash Sauna Steam room Hairdresser Beauty salon Aromatherapist **Conf** Class 25 Board 25 Thtr 50 Del from £125 **Parking** 75 **Notes** LB Civ Wed 50

Premier Inn Grimsby

BUDGET HOTEL

☎ 0871 527 8478
Europa Park, Appian Way, off Gilbey Rd DN31 2UT
web: www.premierinn.com
dir: M180 junct 5, A180 towards town centre. At 1st rdbt take 2nd exit. 1st left, left at mini rdbt into Appian Way

High quality, budget accommodation ideal for both families and business travellers. Spacious, en suite bedrooms feature tea and coffee making facilities, and Freeview TV in most hotels. Internet access and Wi-fi are available for a small fee. The adjacent family restaurant features a wide and varied menu. See also the Hotel Groups pages.

Rooms 40

GRIMSTON
Norfolk
Map 12 TF72

INSPECTORS' CHOICE

Congham Hall Country House Hotel

★★★ ◉◉ COUNTRY HOUSE HOTEL

☎ 01485 600250
Lynn Rd PE32 1AH
dir: At A149/A148 junct, NE of King's Lynn, take A148 towards Fakenham for 100yds. Right to Grimston, hotel 2.5m on left

An elegant 18th-century Georgian manor set amid 30 acres of mature landscaped grounds and surrounded by parkland. The inviting public rooms provide a range of tastefully furnished areas in which to sit and relax. Imaginative cuisine is served in the Orangery Restaurant which has an intimate atmosphere and panoramic views of the gardens. The bedrooms, tastefully furnished with period pieces, have modern facilities and many thoughtful touches.

Rooms 14 (1 GF) **Facilities** Wi-fi ♨ Putt green ⚑ Xmas New Year **Conf** Class 12 Board 28 Thtr 50 **Parking** 50 **Notes** ⊗ Civ Wed 100

GRINDLEFORD
Derbyshire
Map 16 SK27

The Maynard

★★★ 81% ◉◉ HOTEL

☎ 01433 630321
Main Rd S32 2HE
e-mail: info@themaynard.co.uk
dir: A625 from Sheffield to Castleton. Left into Grindleford on B6521. Hotel on left after Fox House Hotel

This building, dating back over 100 years, is situated in a beautiful and tranquil location yet is within easy reach of Sheffield and the M1. The bedrooms are contemporary in style and offer a wealth of accessories. The Peak District views from the restaurant and garden are stunning.

Rooms 10 (1 fmly) **Facilities** FTV Wi-fi
Conf Class 60 Board 40 Thtr 120 **Parking** 70
Notes Civ Wed 130

GUILDFORD   Map 6 SU94
Surrey

Holiday Inn Guildford

★★★ 80% HOTEL   Holiday Inn

☎ 0871 942 9036
Egerton Rd GU2 7XZ
e-mail: reservations-guildford@ihg.com
web: www.higuildfordhotel.co.uk
dir: A3 to Guildford. Exit at sign for Research Park/
Onslow Village. 3rd exit at 1st rdbt, 2nd exit at 2nd
rdbt

This hotel is in a convenient location just off the A3
and within a 25 minute-drive of the M25. Public
areas are stylish, and on-site facilities include a
swimming pool and gym. The accommodation is
spacious and comfortable and caters well for both the
business and leisure markets. A number of well-
equipped meeting rooms is available. There is ample
free parking.

Rooms 168 (89 fmly) (66 GF) 🐾 S £89-£285;
D £89-£285 (incl. bkfst) **Facilities** Spa STV FTV Wi-fi
 HL 🕲 Gym Fitness studio Beauty treatments
Conf Class 100 Board 60 Thtr 180 Del from £145 to
£315 **Services** Air con **Parking** 230 **Notes** LB ⊗
Civ Wed 180

Premier Inn Guildford Central

BUDGET HOTEL

☎ 0871 527 8482
Parkway GU1 1UP
web: www.premierinn.com
dir: M25 junct 10, follow Portsmouth (A3) signs. Exit
for Guildford Centre/Leisure Complex (A322/A320/
A25). Turn left, hotel on left

High quality, budget accommodation ideal for both
families and business travellers. Spacious, en suite
bedrooms feature tea and coffee making facilities,
and Freeview TV in most hotels. Internet access and
Wi-fi are available for a small fee. The adjacent
family restaurant features a wide and varied menu.
See also the Hotel Groups pages.

Rooms 87

Premier Inn Guildford (Worplesdon)

BUDGET HOTEL

☎ 0871 527 8480
Perry Hill GU3 3RY
web: www.premierinn.com
dir: A3 onto A322 towards Bagshot. In Wolpesdon,
hotel on right. Or from M3 junct 3, A322 S towards
Guildford. In Worplesdon hotel on left

Rooms 19

GUISBOROUGH   Map 19 NZ61
North Yorkshire

Macdonald Gisborough Hall

★★★★ 79% ⚜⚜ HOTEL   MACDONALD HOTELS & RESORTS

☎ 0844 879 9149
Whitby Ln TS14 6PT
e-mail: general.gisboroughhall@macdonald-hotels.
co.uk
web: www.macdonald-hotels.co.uk
dir: A171, follow signs for Whitby to Waterfall rdbt,
3rd exit into Whitby Ln, hotel 500yds on right

Dating back to the mid-19th century, this elegant
establishment provides a pleasing combination of
original features and modern facilities. Bedrooms,
including four-poster and family rooms, are richly
furnished, and there is a choice of welcoming lounges
with log fires. Imaginative food is served in Tockett's
restaurant.

Rooms 71 (2 fmly) (12 GF) **Facilities** Spa STV FTV
Wi-fi 🏊 Xmas New Year **Conf** Class 150 Board 32
Thtr 400 **Services** Lift **Parking** 180 **Notes** Closed 2-6
Jan Civ Wed 250

Premier Inn Middlesborough South (Guisborough)

BUDGET HOTEL

☎ 0871 527 8772
Middlesbrough Rd, Upsall TS14 6RW
web: www.premierinn.com
dir: Off A171 towards Whitby

High quality, budget accommodation ideal for both
families and business travellers. Spacious, en suite
bedrooms feature tea and coffee making facilities,
and Freeview TV in most hotels. Internet access and
Wi-fi are available for a small fee. The adjacent
family restaurant features a wide and varied menu.
See also the Hotel Groups pages.

Rooms 20

HADLEY WOOD   Map 6 TQ29
Greater London

West Lodge Park Hotel

★★★★ 81% ⚜ HOTEL

☎ 020 8216 3900   & 8216 3903
Cockfosters Rd EN4 0PY
e-mail: westlodgepark@bealeshotels.co.uk
web: www.bealeshotels.co.uk
dir: On A111, 1m S of M25 junct 24

A stylish country house set in stunning parkland and
gardens, yet only 12 miles from central London and a
few miles from the M25. Bedrooms are individually
decorated in traditional style and offer excellent in-
room facilities. Annexe rooms feature air-conditioning
and have access to an outdoor patio area. Public
rooms include the award-winning Cedar Restaurant,
cosy bar area and separate lounge.

Rooms 59 (13 annexe) (1 fmly) (11 GF) **S** £110;
D £160-£270* **Facilities** STV FTV Wi-fi Putt green ⛳
Free use of nearby leisure club 🎵 New Year
Conf Class 30 Board 30 Thtr 64 Del from £205 to
£225* **Services** Lift **Parking** 200 **Notes** LB ⊗
Civ Wed 72

HADLOW   Map 6 TQ65
Kent

Hadlow Manor Hotel

★★★ 77% HOTEL

☎ 01732 851442
Goose Green TN11 0JH
e-mail: gt@hadlowmanor.co.uk
dir: On A26 (Maidstone to Tonbridge road). 1m E of
Hadlow

This is a friendly, independently owned country-house
hotel, ideally situated between Maidstone and
Tonbridge. Traditionally styled bedrooms are spacious
and attractively furnished with many amenities.
Public areas include a sunny restaurant, bar and
lounge. The gardens are delightful and there's a
seated area ideal for relaxation in warmer weather.
Meeting and banqueting facilities are available.

Rooms 29 (2 fmly) (8 GF) **Facilities** STV FTV Wi-fi New
Year **Conf** Class 90 Board 103 Thtr 200
Del from £125* **Parking** 120 **Notes** ⊗ Civ Wed 200

H

HADNALL
Shropshire
Map 15 SJ52

Saracens at Hadnall

◎◎ RESTAURANT WITH ROOMS

☎ 01939 210877
Shrewsbury Rd SY4 4AG
e-mail: reception@saracensathadnall.co.uk
web: www.saracensathadnall.co.uk
dir: M54 onto A5 towards Shrewsbury, take A49
towards Whitchurch. In Hadnall, property diagonally
opposite church

This Georgian Grade II listed former farmhouse and
village pub has been tastefully converted into a very
smart restaurant with rooms, without any loss of
original charm and character. The bedrooms are
thoughtfully equipped and include a family room.
Skilfully prepared meals are served in either the
elegant dining room or the adjacent conservatory
where there is a glass-topped well.

Rooms 5

HAGLEY
Worcestershire
Map 10 SO98

Premier Inn Hagley

BUDGET HOTEL

☎ 0871 527 8484
Birmingham Rd DY9 9JS
web: www.premierinn.com
dir: M5 junct 3, A456 towards Kidderminster (dual
carriageway). Hotel visible on opposite side of road.
At next rdbt double back follow A456 Birmingham
signs. Hotel on left

High quality, budget accommodation ideal for both
families and business travellers. Spacious, en suite
bedrooms feature tea and coffee making facilities,
and Freeview TV in most hotels. Internet access and
Wi-fi are available for a small fee. The adjacent
family restaurant features a wide and varied menu.
See also the Hotel Groups pages.

Rooms 40

HALIFAX
West Yorkshire
Map 19 SE02

Holdsworth House Hotel

★★★★ 75% ◎◎ HOTEL

☎ 01422 240024
Holdsworth HX2 9TG
e-mail: info@holdsworthhouse.co.uk
web: www.holdsworthhouse.co.uk
dir: From town centre take A629 towards Keighley.
1.5m right at garage, into Shay Ln. Hotel on right
after 1m

This delightful 17th-century Jacobean manor house,
set in well tended gardens, offers individually
decorated, thoughtfully equipped bedrooms. Public
rooms, adorned with beautiful paintings and antique
pieces, include a choice of inviting lounges and
superb conference and function facilities. Dinner
provides the highlight of any stay and is served in the
elegant restaurant by friendly, attentive staff.

Rooms 40 (2 fmly) (15 GF) ⬦ **S** fr £65; **D** fr £85 (incl.
bkfst)* **Facilities** FTV Wi-fi New Year **Conf** Class 75
Board 50 Thtr 150 Del from £120* **Parking** 60
Notes LB Civ Wed 120

The Rock Hotel

★★★ 75% ◎◎ HOTEL

☎ 01422 379721
Holywell Green HX4 9BS
e-mail: info@rockhotelwestyorkshire.co.uk
web: www.rockhotelwestyorkshire.co.uk

Set in the heart of the scenic and rural valley of
Holywell Green, this hotel offers executive rooms,
standard rooms, a family room, as well as one room
which is fully equipped for disabled guests. All rooms
are well equipped with modern amenities including
free Wi-fi. Spacious public areas include Churchill's
Restaurant which is the fine dining option. There are
always friendly staff with a warm welcome at this
unique hotel.

Rooms 27 (3 fmly) (1 GF) ⬦ **S** £54-£75; **D** £65-£85
(incl. bkfst)* **Facilities** STV FTV Wi-fi ⬦ **Conf** Class 50
Board 40 Thtr 150 Del from £100 to £140*
Services Lift **Parking** 100 **Notes** LB Civ Wed

The White Swan Hotel

★★★ 74% HOTEL

☎ 01422 355541
Princess St HX1 1TS
e-mail: info@whiteswanhalifax.com
dir: Adjacent to Town Hall

A well established hotel noted for its friendly staff.
Located in the heart of the town it offers comfortable,
well-equipped bedrooms plus conference and
function facilities. The lounge area is ideal for
relaxing, and for the more energetic guest there is a
small fitness room.

Rooms 40 (2 fmly) ⬦ **D** £59-£99 (incl. bkfst)*
Facilities STV FTV Wi-fi Gym New Year **Conf** Class 35
Board 35 Thtr 80 **Services** Lift **Parking** 9 **Notes** LB

Premier Inn Halifax

BUDGET HOTEL

☎ 0871 527 8486
Salterhebble Hill, Huddersfield Rd HX3 0QT
web: www.premierinn.com
dir: Just off M62 junct 24 on A629 towards Halifax

High quality, budget accommodation ideal for both
families and business travellers. Spacious, en suite
bedrooms feature tea and coffee making facilities,
and Freeview TV in most hotels. Internet access and
Wi-fi are available for a small fee. The adjacent
family restaurant features a wide and varied menu.
See also the Hotel Groups pages.

Rooms 31

Save on hotels. Book at **theAA.com/hotel**

HAD – HAR 195 **ENGLAND**

HALLAND
East Sussex   Map 6 TQ41

The Halland Forge Hotel

★★ 71% HOTEL

☎ 01825 840456
BN8 6PW
e-mail: info@hallandforgehotel.co.uk
web: www.hallandforgehotel.co.uk
dir: On A22 at junct with B2192, 4.5m S of Uckfield

Conveniently located, this hotel offers comfortable annexed accommodation with parking spaces directly outside the bedrooms. Public areas include a spacious lounge bar, attractive outdoor seating (weather permitting) and an informal restaurant serving generous portions at dinner. An attractively presented room is available for private dining, special occasions or for meetings by prior arrangement.

Rooms 20 (20 annexe) (2 fmly) (8 GF) **Conf** Class 20 Board 26 Thtr 45 **Parking** 70 **Notes** ⊗

HAMPTON COURT
Greater London

See London plan 1 B1

The Carlton Mitre Hotel

★★★★ 73% HOTEL

☎ 020 8979 9988 & 8783 3505
Hampton Court Rd KT8 9BN
e-mail: info@carltonhotels.co.uk
dir: M3 junct 1 follow signs to Sunbury & Hampton Court Palace. At Hampton Court Palace rdbt right, hotel on right

This hotel, dating back in parts to 1655, enjoys an enviable setting on the banks of the River Thames opposite Hampton Court Palace. The riverside restaurant and Edge bar/brasserie command wonderful views as well as spacious terraces for alfresco dining. Bedrooms are spacious and elegant with excellent facilities. Parking is limited.

Rooms 36 (2 fmly) (12 GF) **S** £145-£200;
D £145-£200* **Facilities** STV FTV Wi-fi Xmas New Year **Conf** Class 60 Board 40 Thtr 120 Del from £197 to £225* **Services** Lift Air con **Parking** 13 **Notes** LB ⊗ Civ Wed 100

HANDFORTH

See Manchester Airport

HARLOW
Essex   Map 6 TL41

Park Inn by Radisson Harlow

★★★ 67% HOTEL

☎ 01279 829988
Southern Way CM18 7BA
e-mail: info.harlow@rezidorparkinn.com
web: www.parkinn.co.uk/hotel-harlow
dir: M11 junct 7, A414 towards Harlow, 1st exit at 1st rdbt then 1st left

This hotel provides a convenient and comfortable place to stay. Bedrooms are comfortably appointed with flat-screen TVs, Wi-fi and safes included. The RBG Restaurant dining concept offers a versatile format and service is attentive and unfussy. Conference facilities and convenient parking complete the picture.

Rooms 119 (2 fmly) (60 GF) **S** £45-£125;
D £45-£125* **Facilities** FTV Wi-fi ☉ Gym Beauty treatment room Dance studio & classes Xmas New Year **Conf** Class 110 Board 80 Thtr 200 Del from £105 to £145* **Services** Air con **Parking** 100 **Notes** LB ⊗ Civ Wed 180

HARPENDEN
Hertfordshire   Map 6 TL11

Harpenden House Hotel   CLASSIC BRITISH HOTELS

★★★★ 73% HOTEL

☎ 01582 855 9113
18 Southdown Rd AL5 1PE
e-mail: reservations@harpendenhouse.co.uk
web: www.harpendenhouse.co.uk
dir: M1 junct 10 left at rdbt. Next rdbt right onto A1081 to Harpenden. Over 2 mini rdbts, through town centre. Next rdbt left, hotel 200yds on left

This attractive Grade II listed Georgian building overlooks East Common. The hotel gardens are particularly attractive and the public areas are stylishly decorated, including the restaurant that has an impressive ceiling. Some of the bedrooms and a large suite are located in the original house but most of the accommodation is in the annexe.

Rooms 76 (59 annexe) (13 fmly) (2 GF)
Facilities Wi-fi Complimentary use of local leisure centre **Conf** Class 60 Board 60 Thtr 150 **Parking** 80 **Notes** ⊗ RS wknds & BHs Civ Wed 120

HARROGATE
North Yorkshire   Map 19 SE35

See also Knaresborough

INSPECTORS' CHOICE

Rudding Park Hotel, Spa & Golf

★★★★ ◎◎ HOTEL

☎ 01423 871350
Rudding Park, Follifoot HG3 1JH
e-mail: reservations@ruddingpark.com
web: www.ruddingpark.co.uk
dir: From A61 at rdbt with A658 take York exit, follow signs to Rudding Park

Set in beautiful parkland, Rudding Park dates from the early 19th century. Interiors are stylishly contemporary and elegant, with luxurious bedrooms; the new Follifoot wing features stunning suites and bedrooms with spas. Carefully prepared meals and Yorkshire tapas are served in the contemporary Clocktower, which has a striking pink chandelier. The stylish bar and conservatory lead to a generous terrace which is perfect for eating alfresco. The grandeur of the mansion house and grounds make this a popular wedding venue. The hotel has an impressive spa, gym, private cinema and extensive conference facilities, plus an adjoining 18-hole, par 72 golf course and driving range.

Rooms 90 (15 fmly) (31 GF) ⟨ **S** fr £112; **D** fr £133 (incl. bkfst)* **Facilities** Spa STV FTV Wi-fi ⟨ ⟨ supervised ⟨ 18 Putt green Gym Driving range Jogging trail Sauna Hammam ♫ Xmas New Year **Conf** Class 150 Board 40 Thtr 300 Del from £172* **Services** Lift **Parking** 250 **Notes** ⊗ Civ Wed 300

H

HARROGATE *continued*

Hotel du Vin Harrogate

★★★★ 80% ◉ ◉
TOWN HOUSE HOTEL

☎ 01423 856800
Prospect Place HG1 1LB
e-mail: info@harrogate.hotelduvin.com
web: www.hotelduvin.com
dir: A1(M) junct 47, A59 to Harrogate, follow town centre signs to Prince of Wales rdbt, 3rd exit, remain in right lane. Right at lights into Albert St, right into Prospect Place

This town house was created from eight Georgian-style properties and overlooks The Stray. The spacious, open-plan lobby has seating, a bar and the reception desk. Hidden downstairs is a cosy snug cellar. The French-influenced bistro offers high quality cooking and a great choice of wines. Bedrooms face front and back, and are smart and modern, with excellent 'deluge' showers.

Rooms 48 (4 GF) ✎ **Facilities** Spa STV FTV Wi-fi ⓑ New Year **Conf** Class 20 Board 30 Thtr 60 Del from £135* **Services** Lift **Parking** 30 **Notes** Civ Wed 90

Nidd Hall Hotel

Warner Leisure Hotels
JUST FOR GROWN-UPS

★★★★ 77% ◉ ◉ COUNTRY HOUSE HOTEL

☎ 01423 771598
Nidd HG3 3BN
dir: A59 through Knaresborough, follow signs for Ripley. Hotel on right

This fine hotel is set in 45 acres of Victorian and Edwardian gardens. The bedrooms are spacious and appointed to a high standard. Public areas are delightful and retain many original features. Leisure and spa facilities are available along with a variety of outdoor activities. This is an adults-only (above 21 years old) hotel.

Rooms 183 (47 GF) **Facilities** Spa FTV ⓢ supervised Putt green Fishing ⛳ Gym ♬ Xmas New Year **Conf** Class 40 Board 30 Thtr 60 **Services** Lift **Notes** ⊗ No children 21yrs

The Balmoral Hotel

★★★★ 77% HOTEL

☎ 01423 508208
16/18 Franklin Mount HG1 5EJ
e-mail: info@balmoralhotel.co.uk
web: www.balmoralhotel.co.uk
dir: A1, A59, A661 to Harrogate. In town centre at 1st rdbt into Skipton Rd. 4th left into Kings Rd (Nat West bank on corner). Or from A61 follow signs to Harrogate. Into West Park St, Parliament St (Betty's Tea Rooms on left). Right into Kings Rd. Keep in left lane, 0.25m to hotel on right

Set in a peaceful residential area of Harrogate, the property has been tastefully converted into very stylish hotel. The individually designed bedrooms, including suites, are beautifully furnished with luxury touches such as handmade quilts and designer wallpaper. The staff are well informed and help to create a memorable stay.

Rooms 23 (2 fmly) (2 GF) **S** £65-£105; **D** £79-£119 (incl. bkfst)* **Facilities** FTV Wi-fi ⓑ Xmas New Year **Conf** Class 20 Board 16 Thtr 20 Del from £75 to £150* **Parking** 14

Studley Hotel

★★★★ 76% ◉ ◉ HOTEL

☎ 01423 560425
Swan Rd HG1 2SE
e-mail: info@studleyhotel.co.uk
web: www.studleyhotel.co.uk
dir: Adjacent to Valley Gardens, opposite Mercer Gallery

This friendly, well-established hotel, close to the town centre and Valley Gardens, is well known for its

Orchid Restaurant, which provides a dynamic and authentic approach to Pacific Rim and Asian cuisine. Bedrooms are modern and come in a variety of styles and sizes, while the stylish bar lounge provides an excellent place for relaxing. A PC is available for guests' use.

Rooms 28 (1 fmly) ✎ **S** £70-£100; **D** £80-£200 (incl. bkfst)* **Facilities** STV Wi-fi ⓑ Free use of facilities at local Health Club **Conf** Class 15 Board 12 Thtr 15 Del from £90 to £120* **Services** Lift **Parking** 15 **Notes** LB ⊗ Closed 23-30 Dec

The Majestic Hotel

PUMA HOTELS
COLLECTION

★★★★ 76% HOTEL

☎ 01423 700300
Ripon Rd HG1 2HU
e-mail: majestic@pumahotels.co.uk
web: www.pumahotels.co.uk
dir: M1 onto A1(M) at Wetherby. Take A661 to Harrogate. Hotel in town centre adjacent to Royal Hall

Popular for conferences and functions, this grand Victorian hotel is set in 12 acres of landscaped grounds that is within walking distance of the town centre. It benefits from spacious public areas, and the comfortable bedrooms, including some spacious suites, come in a variety of sizes.

Rooms 174 (8 fmly) **Facilities** Spa STV Wi-fi ⓢ supervised ⓢ Gym Golf practice net Xmas New Year **Conf** Class 260 Board 70 Thtr 500 **Services** Lift **Parking** 250 **Notes** Civ Wed 200

Old Swan Hotel

CLASSIC
LODGES
the sign of a great hotel

★★★★ 76% HOTEL

☎ 01423 500055
Swan Rd HG1 2SR
e-mail: info.theoldswan@classiclodges.co.uk
dir: From A1, A59 Ripon, left Empress rdbt, keep left, right at Prince of Wales rdbt. Straight across lights, left into Swan Rd

In the heart of Harrogate and within walking distance of the Harrogate International Centre and Valley Gardens, this hotel is famed as being Agatha Christie's hiding place during her disappearance in 1926. The bedrooms are stylishly furnished, and the public areas include the Library Restaurant, the Wedgwood Room and the lounge bar. Extensive conference and banqueting facilities are available.

Rooms 136 **Facilities** STV Wi-fi ⛳ Xmas New Year **Conf** Class 130 Board 100 Thtr 450 **Services** Lift **Parking** 175 **Notes** ⊗ Civ Wed 300

Save on hotels. Book at **theAA.com/hotel**

HAR 197 ENGLAND

The White Hart Hotel

★★★★ 74% ◉◉ HOTEL

☎ 01423 505681
2 Cold Bath Rd HG2 0NF
e-mail: reception@whitehart.net
web: www.whitehart.net
dir: A59 to Harrogate. A661 3rd exit on rdbt to
Harrogate. Left at rdbt onto A6040 for 1m. Right onto
A61. Bear left down Montpellier Hill

This hotel has an excellent location in Harrogate and
has been welcoming guests for over 200 years. The
bedrooms, including executive rooms with four-
posters and views over the Montpellier Quarter, are
attractively designed. The Tea Rooms serve from early
morning until late afternoon, and the hotel has
introduced a pub concept called the Fat Badger, with
real ales, an extensive wine list and high quality food.
Alfresco eating and drinking are possible in good
weather. Secure parking is available and there is
Wi-fi throughout.

Rooms 53 (1 fmly) ☏ **S** £50-£80; **D** £60-£110 (incl.
bkfst)* **Facilities** FTV Wi-fi ☘ Gym Xmas New Year
Conf Class 40 Board 30 Thtr 80 Del from £115 to
£140* **Services** Lift **Parking** 80 **Notes** LB ⊗
Civ Wed 80

The Kimberley Hotel

★★★★ 74% HOTEL

☎ 01423 505613 & 0800 783 7642
11-19 Kings Rd HG1 5JY
e-mail: info@thekimberley.co.uk
dir: A661 Wetherby Road into town centre. Over 1st
rdbt onto Skipton Rd. 4th left at NatWest bank into
Kings Rd

This independently owned hotel is located close to the
centre of the town and only a short walk from the
Harrogate International Centre. Bedrooms are well
equipped for both business and leisure guests and
have a thoughtful range of extras including Wi-
fi. There is a stylish lounge-bar and a contemporary
bistro offering an extensive choice of dishes.

Rooms 93 (21 annexe) (3 fmly) (18 GF) ☏
Facilities STV FTV Wi-fi ☘ Xmas New Year
Conf Class 12 Board 16 Thtr 30 **Services** Lift
Parking 42

Best Western Cedar Court Hotel

★★★★ 71% HOTEL

☎ 01423 858585 & 858595 (Res)
Queens Buildings, Park Pde HG1 5AH
e-mail: cedarcourt@bestwestern.co.uk
web: www.cedarcourthotels.co.uk
dir: From A1(M) follow signs to Harrogate on A661
past Sainsburys. At rdbt left onto A6040. Hotel right
after church

This Grade II listed building was Harrogate's first
hotel and enjoys a peaceful location in landscaped
grounds, close to the town centre. It provides
spacious, well-equipped accommodation. Public
areas include a brasserie-style restaurant, a small
gym and an open-plan lounge and bar. Functions and
conferences are particularly well catered for.

Rooms 100 (8 fmly) (7 GF) **S** £72-£142; **D** £82-£152
(incl. bkfst)* **Facilities** FTV Wi-fi ☘ Gym Xmas New
Year **Conf** Class 80 Board 70 Thtr 320 Del from £125
to £150* **Services** Lift **Parking** 150 **Notes** LB ⊗
Civ Wed 320

Cairn Hotel

★★★ Ⓐ HOTEL

☎ 01423 504005
Ripon Rd HG1 2JD
e-mail: salescairn@strathmorehotels.com

Rooms 135 (7 fmly) **Facilities** Wi-fi Gym Xmas New
Year **Conf** Class 170 Board 100 Thtr 500 **Services** Lift
Parking 150 **Notes** Civ Wed

See advert on page 524

Premier Inn Harrogate

BUDGET HOTEL

☎ 0871 527 8490
Hornbeam Park Av HG2 8RA
web: www.premierinn.com
dir: A1(M) junct 46 W, A661 to Harrogate. In 2m left
at The Woodlands lights. 1.5m left into Hornbeam
Park Ave

High quality, budget accommodation ideal for both
families and business travellers. Spacious, en suite
bedrooms feature tea and coffee making facilities,
and Freeview TV in most hotels. Internet access and
Wi-fi are available for a small fee. The adjacent
family restaurant features a wide and varied menu.
See also the Hotel Groups pages.

Rooms 50

H

HARROW
Greater London

See London plan 1 C5

Best Western Cumberland Hotel

★★★ 72% METRO HOTEL

☎ 020 8863 4111
1 St Johns Rd HA1 2EF
e-mail: reservations@cumberlandhotel.co.uk
web: www.cumberlandhotel.co.uk
dir: Into Harrow via Station or Sheepcote Rd, into Gayton Rd, then Lyon Rd which becomes St Johns Rd

Situated within walking distance of the town centre, this hotel is ideally located for all local attractions and amenities. Bedrooms provide good levels of comfort and are practically equipped to meet the requirements of all travellers. The public areas comprise a well-stocked pub-style bar, which serves homemade food. Parking is located at the rear of the building.

Rooms 85 (54 annexe) (6 fmly) (15 GF) S £44-£102; D £59-£124* Facilities FTV Wi-fi Xmas New Year Conf Class 70 Board 62 Thtr 130 Del from £100 to £160* Parking 67 Notes ⊗ Civ Wed 150

HARROW WEALD
Greater London

See London plan 1 B5

Grim's Dyke Hotel

★★★ 82% ◉◉ HOTEL

☎ 020 8385 3100 & 8954 4227
Old Redding HA3 6SH
e-mail: reservations@grimsdyke.com
web: www.grimsdyke.com
dir: A410 onto A409 north towards Bushey, at top of hill at lights turn left into Old Redding, opposite 'The Viewpoint'

Once home to Sir William Gilbert, this Grade II mansion contains many references to well-known Gilbert and Sullivan productions. The house is set in over 40 acres of beautiful parkland and gardens. Bedrooms in the main house are elegant and traditional, while those in the adjacent lodge are aimed more at the business guest.

Rooms 46 (37 annexe) (4 fmly) (17 GF) ↖ S £50-£243; D £50-£243* Facilities STV FTV Wi-fi ↘ ↘ Gilbert & Sullivan opera dinner Murder mystery & Sabrage evenings ♫ Xmas New Year Conf Class 49 Board 32 Thtr 90 Del from £140 to £220 Parking 97 Notes LB RS 24-31 Dec Civ Wed 90

HARTINGTON
Derbyshire
Map 16 SK16

Biggin Hall Hotel

★★ ⒶHOTEL

☎ 01298 84451
SK17 0DH
e-mail: enquiries@bigginhall.co.uk
web: www.bigginhall.co.uk
dir: 0.5m from A515 midway between Ashbourne & Buxton

Rooms 20 (12 annexe) (2 fmly) (4 GF) S £70-£110; D £86-£126 (incl. bkfst)* Facilities STV FTV Wi-fi ↘ Xmas New Year Conf Class 20 Board 20 Thtr 20 Del from £125 to £150 Parking 25 Notes LB No children 12yrs Civ Wed 60

HARTLEPOOL
Co Durham
Map 19 NZ53

Best Western Grand Hotel

★★★ 77% HOTEL

☎ 01429 266345
Swainson St TS24 8AA
e-mail: grandhotel@tavistockleisure.com
dir: A689 into town centre. Left onto Victoria Rd, hotel on right

This hotel retains many original features and the public areas include a grand ballroom, an open-plan lounge bar and the basement restaurant, Italia. The bedrooms are modern in design and have high spec fixtures and fittings. The staff provide attentive and friendly service.

Rooms 48 (1 fmly) Facilities STV FTV Wi-fi Affiliation with local gym ♫ New Year Conf Class 200 Board 60 Thtr 250 Services Lift Parking 50 Notes ⊗ Civ Wed 200

Premier Inn Hartlepool Marina

BUDGET HOTEL

☎ 0871 527 8492
Maritime Av, Hartlepool Marina TS24 0XZ
web: www.premierinn.com
dir: Approx 1m from A689/A179 junct. On marina

High quality, budget accommodation ideal for both families and business travellers. Spacious, en suite bedrooms feature tea and coffee making facilities, and Freeview TV in most hotels. Internet access and Wi-fi are available for a small fee. The adjacent family restaurant features a wide and varied menu. See also the Hotel Groups pages.

Rooms 60

HARTLEY WINTNEY
Hampshire
Map 5 SU75

The Elvetham Hotel

★★★ 80% HOTEL

☎ 01252 844871
RG27 8AR
e-mail: enq@elvethamhotel.co.uk
web: www.elvethamhotel.co.uk
dir: M3 junct 4A W, junct 5 E (or M4 junct 11, A33, B3011). Hotel signed from A323 between Hartley Wintney & Fleet

A spectacular 19th-century mansion set in 35 acres of grounds with an arboretum. All bedrooms are individually styled and many have views of the manicured gardens. A popular venue for weddings and conferences, the hotel lends itself to team building events and outdoor pursuits.

Rooms 72 (29 annexe) (10 fmly) (7 GF) ↖ S £98-£200; D £140-£200 (incl. bkfst) Facilities STV FTV Wi-fi ↘ ⚲ Putt green ↘ Gym Badminton Boules Volleyball New Year Conf Class 80 Board 48 Thtr 110 Del from £180 to £235 Parking 200 Notes Closed 24-27 Dec Civ Wed 200

HARTSHEAD MOOR MOTORWAY SERVICE AREA (M62)
West Yorkshire
Map 19 SE12

Days Inn Bradford - M62

BUDGET HOTEL

☎ 01274 851706
Hartshead Moor Service Area, Clifton HD6 4JX
e-mail: hartshead.hotel@welcomebreak.co.uk
web: www.welcomebreak.co.uk
dir: M62 between junct 25 & 26

This modern building offers accommodation in smart, spacious and well-equipped bedrooms, suitable for families and business travellers, and all with en suite bathrooms. Continental breakfast is available and other refreshments may be taken at the nearby family restaurant. See also the Hotel Groups pages.

Rooms 38 (33 fmly) (16 GF) Conf Board 10

HARWICH   Map 13 TM23
Essex

The Pier at Harwich
★★★ 87% ⍟ ⍟ HOTEL

☎ 01255 241212
The Quay CO12 3HH
e-mail: pier@milsomhotels.com
web: www.milsomhotels.com
dir: From A12 take A120 to Quay. Hotel opposite
lifeboat station

Situated on the quay, overlooking the ports of Harwich
and Felixstowe. The bedrooms are tastefully
decorated, thoughtfully equipped, and furnished in a
contemporary style; many rooms have superb sea
views. The public rooms include the informal
Ha'Penny Bistro, the first-floor Harbourside
Restaurant, a smart lounge bar and a plush
residents' lounge.

Rooms 14 (7 annexe) (5 fmly) (1 GF) ✆ **S** £92-£160;
D £117-£215 (incl. bkfst)* **Facilities** STV Wi-fi Day
cruises on yachts Golf breaks arranged with nearby
course Sea bass fishing Xmas **Conf** Board 16
Del £155* **Parking** 10 **Notes** LB ⊗ Civ Wed 50

Tower Hotel
★★★ 77% HOTEL

☎ 01255 504952
Dovercourt CO12 3PJ
e-mail: reception@tower-hotel-harwich.co.uk
web: www.tower-hotel-harwich.co.uk
dir: Follow main road into Harwich. Past BP garage on
left

This hotel is an impressive late 17th-century Italian-
style building. There is a wealth of ornamental ceiling
cornices, beautiful architraves and an impressive
balustrade. Bedrooms, many named after prominent
people from Harwich's past, are spacious and
furnished to a very high standard. Evening meals and
breakfast are served in the decorative dining rooms,
and Rigby's bar offers tempting meals and a wide
range of refreshments.

Rooms 13 (2 fmly) (2 GF) **S** £48-£68; **D** £63-£95*
Facilities Wi-fi **Conf** Class 30 Board 30 Thtr 30
Parking 30 **Notes** ⊗ Civ Wed 40

Cliff Hotel
★★ 67% HOTEL

☎ 01255 503345 & 507373
Marine Pde, Dovercourt CO12 3RE
e-mail: reception@cliffhotelharwich.fsnet.co.uk
web: www.thecliffhotelharwich.co.uk
dir: From A120 at rdbt into Parkeston Rd. At mini rdbt
left onto B1325 signed Harwich. At lights in
Dovercourt right into Kingsway, to seafront. Right into
Marine Parade

Conveniently situated on the seafront close to the
railway station and ferry terminal. Public rooms are
smartly appointed and include the Shade Bar, a
comfortable lounge, a restaurant and the Marine Bar
with views of Dovercourt Bay. The pleasantly
decorated bedrooms have co-ordinated soft
furnishings and modern facilities; many have sea
views.

Rooms 26 (3 fmly) **Facilities** STV Wi-fi New Year
Conf Class 150 Board 40 Thtr 200 Del from £95.50*
Parking 50 **Notes** ⊗ RS Xmas & New Year

Premier Inn Harwich

BUDGET HOTEL

☎ 0871 527 8494
Parkstone Rd, Dovercourt CO12 4NX
web: www.premierinn.com
dir: A120 to Harwich, hotel opposite Morrisons. Right
at rdbt. Hotel entrance through Lidl car park

High quality, budget accommodation ideal for both
families and business travellers. Spacious, en suite
bedrooms feature tea and coffee making facilities,
and Freeview TV in most hotels. Internet access and
Wi-fi are available for a small fee. The adjacent
family restaurant features a wide and varied menu.
See also the Hotel Groups pages.

Rooms 45

HASLEMERE   Map 6 SU93
Surrey

Lythe Hill Hotel & Spa
★★★★ 74% ⍟ HOTEL   CLASSIC
                             BRITISH HOTELS

☎ 01428 651251
Petworth Rd GU27 3BQ
e-mail: lythe@lythehill.co.uk
web: www.lythehill.co.uk
dir: From High St onto B2131. Hotel 1.25m on right

This privately owned hotel sits in 30 acres of
attractive parkland with lakes, complete with
roaming geese. The hotel has been described as a
hamlet of character buildings, each furnished in a
style that complements the age of the property; the
oldest one dating back to 1475. Cuisine in the
adjacent 'Auberge de France' offers interesting,
quality dishes, whilst breakfast is served in the hotel
dining room. The bedrooms are split between a
number of 15th-century buildings and vary in size.
The stylish spa includes a 16-metre swimming pool.

Rooms 41 (8 fmly) (18 GF) **Facilities** Spa FTV Wi-fi ⊗
⌖ Fishing ⌖ Gym Boules Giant chess ♫ Xmas New
Year **Conf** Class 40 Board 30 Thtr 128 **Parking** 200
Notes Civ Wed 128

H

HASTINGS & ST LEONARDS
East Sussex   Map 7 TQ80

Bannatyne Spa Hotel Hastings

★★★★ 80% HOTEL

☎ 01424 851222
Battle Rd TN38 8EA
e-mail: enquiries.hastingshotel@bannatyne.co.uk
dir: M25 junct 5, A21 (Hastings). At 5th rdbt 2nd exit
(Hastings/Filmwell). After 2 rdbts right (Folkestone/
A259/Battle/A2100). Left at A2100/The Ridge Way. At
2nd rdbt right to hotel

This hotel offers a range of facilities that will appeal
both leisure and business travellers. The well-
appointed accommodation is available in a range of
types and sizes from small doubles to superior rooms,
while the public areas are a tasteful blend of
contemporary design and period features. The
Conservatory Restaurant has attractive views over the
formal garden. There is a spa and health club plus
meeting facilities. Free Wi-fi is available.

Rooms 38 (7 fmly) (4 GF) ⚡ **S** £90-£190;
D £100-£200 (incl. bkfst)* **Facilities** Spa FTV Wi-fi ⓣ
🕙 supervised 🏋 Gym Xmas New Year
Conf Class 300 Board 50 Thtr 500 Del from £135 to
£195* **Services** Lift **Parking** 150 **Notes** LB ⊗
Civ Wed 300

Best Western Royal Victoria Hotel

★★★ 74% HOTEL

☎ 01424 445544
Marina, St Leonards-on-Sea TN38 0BD
e-mail: reception@royalvichotel.co.uk
web: www.royalvichotel.co.uk
dir: On A259 (seafront road) 1m W of Hastings pier

This imposing 18th-century property is situated in a
prominent position overlooking the sea. A superb
marble staircase leads up from the lobby to the main
public areas on the first floor which has panoramic
views of the sea. The spacious bedrooms are
pleasantly decorated and well equipped, and include
duplex and family suites.

Rooms 50 (15 fmly) **Facilities** STV Wi-fi ⓣ Xmas New
Year **Conf** Class 40 Board 40 Thtr 100 **Services** Lift
Parking 6 **Notes** Civ Wed 50

The Chatsworth Hotel

★★★ 72% ⊛ HOTEL

☎ 01424 720188
Carlisle Pde TN34 1JG
e-mail: info@chatsworthhotel.com
dir: A21 to town centre. At seafront turn right before
next lights

Enjoying a central position on the seafront, close to
the pier, this hotel is a short walk from the old town
and within easy reach of the county's many
attractions. Bedrooms are smartly decorated,
equipped with a range of extras and many rooms
enjoy splendid sea views. Guests can also enjoy an
exciting Indian meal in the contemporary restaurant.

Rooms 52 (5 fmly) **Facilities** Wi-fi Xmas New Year
Conf Class 20 Board 20 Thtr 40 **Services** Lift
Parking 8 **Notes** ⊗

Premier Inn Hastings

BUDGET HOTEL

☎ 0871 527 8496
1 John Macadam Way, St Leonards on Sea TN37 7DB
web: www.premierinn.com
dir: A21 into Hastings. Hotel on right after junct with
A2100 (Battle road)

High quality, budget accommodation ideal for both
families and business travellers. Spacious, en suite
bedrooms feature tea and coffee making facilities,
and Freeview TV in most hotels. Internet access and
Wi-fi are available for a small fee. The adjacent
family restaurant features a wide and varied menu.
See also the Hotel Groups pages.

Rooms 44

HATFIELD
Hertfordshire   Map 6 TL20

Beales Hotel

★★★★ 79% ⊛⊛ HOTEL

☎ 01707 288500
Comet Way AL10 9NG
e-mail: hatfield@bealeshotels.co.uk
web: www.bealeshotels.co.uk
dir: On A1001 opposite Galleria Shopping Mall -
follow signs for Galleria

This hotel is a stunning contemporary property. Within
easy access of the M25, its striking exterior
incorporates giant glass panels and cedar wood
slats. Bedrooms have luxurious beds, flat-screen TVs

and smart bathrooms. Public areas include a small
bar and attractive restaurant, which opens
throughout the day. The hotel is fully air-conditioned
and free wired broadband is available in bedrooms,
conference and banqueting rooms.

Rooms 53 (3 fmly) (21 GF) ⚡ **Facilities** STV Wi-fi Free
use of nearby leisure club Xmas New Year
Conf Class 124 Board 64 Thtr 300 **Services** Lift
Air con **Parking** 126 **Notes** ⊗ RS 27-30 Dec
Civ Wed 300

Ramada Hatfield

★★★ 75% HOTEL

☎ 01707 252400
St Albans Road West AL10 9RH
e-mail: enquiries@ramadahatfieldhotel.co.uk
web: www.ramadahatfieldhotel.co.uk
dir: A1(M) junct 3, take 2nd exit at rdbt signed
Hatfield. Hotel on left

Conveniently located close to the business and
shopping districts and only a short drive from the
M25, this Ramada is perfectly situated for both
business and leisure guests. The bedrooms are
spacious and well equipped, and complimentary Wi-fi
is available throughout the hotel. The open-plan, art
deco inspired public areas include a stylish bar.

Rooms 128 (5 fmly) (53 GF) ⚡ **Facilities** STV FTV
Wi-fi ⓣ **Conf** Class 40 Board 45 Thtr 120 **Parking** 165
Notes ⊗ Civ Wed 100

Mercure Hatfield Oak Hotel

★★★ 73% HOTEL

☎ 01707 275701
Roehyde Way AL10 9AF
e-mail: enquiries@hotels-hatfield.com
web: www.hotels-hatfield.com
dir: M25 junct 23 between juncts 2 & 3 of A1(M).
Roehyde Way runs parallel to A1(M)

The hotel enjoys an enviable location for both leisure
and business guests, it is within easy reach of major
roads and central London. In addition, the University
of Hertfordshire is situated nearby. The
accommodation has been appointed to a good
standard with flat-screen TVs and Wi-fi to name but a
few facilities. The hotel also caters for conference and
banqueting.

Rooms 76 (5 fmly) (36 GF) ⚡ **Facilities** FTV Wi-fi
Conf Class 50 Board 50 Thtr 100 **Parking** 85
Notes ⊗ Civ Wed 120

Save on hotels. Book at **theAA.com/hotel**

HAS – HAY 201 ENGLAND

Premier Inn Hatfield

BUDGET HOTEL

☎ 0871 527 8498
Lemsford Rd AL10 0DZ
web: www.premierinn.com
dir: From A1(M) junct 4, A1001 towards Hatfield. At rbt take 2nd exit, 1st right

High quality, budget accommodation ideal for both families and business travellers. Spacious, en suite bedrooms feature tea and coffee making facilities, and Freeview TV in most hotels. Internet access and Wi-fi are available for a small fee. The adjacent family restaurant features a wide and varied menu. See also the Hotel Groups pages.

Rooms 40

HATHERSAGE   Map 16 SK28
Derbyshire

George Hotel

★★★ 83% ❀ ❀ HOTEL

☎ 01433 650436
Main Rd S32 1BB
e-mail: info@george-hotel.net
web: www.george-hotel.net
dir: In village centre on A6187, SW of Sheffield

The George is a relaxing 500-year-old hostelry in the heart of this picturesque town. The beamed bar lounge has great character and traditional comfort, and the restaurant is light, modern and spacious with original artworks. Upstairs the decor is simpler with lots of light hues; the split-level and four-poster rooms are especially appealing. The quality cooking is a key feature of the hotel.

Rooms 24 (2 fmly) (5 GF) ⚡ **S** £105-£115; **D** £198 (incl. bkfst)* **Facilities** FTV Wi-fi Xmas New Year **Conf** Class 20 Board 36 Thtr 80 Del £148* **Parking** 40 **Notes** LB ⊗ Civ Wed 70

HAVANT   Map 5 SU70
Hampshire

Premier Inn Portsmouth (Havant)

BUDGET HOTEL

☎ 0871 527 8900
65 Bedhampton Hill, Bedhampton PO9 3JN
web: www.premierinn.com
dir: At rdbt just off A3(M) junct 5 towards Bedhampton

High quality, budget accommodation ideal for both families and business travellers. Spacious, en suite bedrooms feature tea and coffee making facilities, and Freeview TV in most hotels. Internet access and Wi-fi are available for a small fee. The adjacent family restaurant features a wide and varied menu. See also the Hotel Groups pages.

Rooms 37

HAVERHILL   Map 12 TL64
Suffolk

Days Inn Haverhill

BUDGET HOTEL

☎ 01440 716950
Phoenix Road & Bumpstead Rd, Haverhill Business Park CB9 7AE
e-mail: reservations@daysinnhaverhill.co.uk
web: www.haverhilldaysinn.co.uk
dir: A1017 (Haverhill bypass). Hotel on 5th rdbt

This modern building offers accommodation in smart, spacious and well-equipped bedrooms, suitable for families and business travellers, and all with en suite bathrooms. Continental breakfast is available and other refreshments may be taken at the nearby family restaurant. See also the Hotel Groups pages.

Rooms 80 (8 fmly) (14 GF) **Conf** Class 28 Board 24 Thtr 60

HAWES   Map 18 SD88
North Yorkshire

Simonstone Hall Hotel

★★★ 77% HOTEL

☎ 01969 667255
Simonstone DL8 3LY
e-mail: email@simonstonehall.demon.co.uk
web: www.simonstonehall.co.uk
dir: 1.5m N of Hawes on road signed Muker & Buttertubs

This former hunting lodge provides professional, friendly service and a relaxed atmosphere. There is an inviting drawing room, stylish fine dining restaurant, a bar and conservatory. The generally spacious bedrooms are elegantly designed to reflect the style of the house, and many offer spectacular views of the countryside.

Rooms 18 (10 fmly) (2 GF) **Facilities** Wi-fi Xmas **Conf** Class 20 Board 20 Thtr 50 **Parking** 40 **Notes** Civ Wed 72

HAWORTH   Map 19 SE03
West Yorkshire

Weavers Restaurant with Rooms

◉ RESTAURANT WITH ROOMS

☎ 01535 643822
15 West Ln BD22 8DU
e-mail: weaversltd@btconnect.com
dir: In village centre. Pass Brontë Weaving Shed on right, 100yds left to Parsonage Museum car park

Centrally located on the cobbled main street, this family-owned restaurant with rooms provides well-equipped, stylish and comfortable accommodation. Each of the three en suite bedrooms has many thoughtful extras. The kitchen serves both modern and traditional dishes with flair and creativity.

Rooms 3

HAYDOCK   Map 15 SJ59
Merseyside

Thistle Haydock   thistle

★★★★ 75% HOTEL

☎ 0871 376 9044
Penny Ln WA11 9SG
e-mail: haydock@thistle.co.uk
web: www.thistle.com/haydock
dir: M6 junct 23, follow Haydock Racecourse signs (A49) N towards Ashton-in-Makerfield, 1st left, after bridge 1st turn left

A smart, purpose-built hotel which offers an excellent standard of thoughtfully equipped accommodation. It is conveniently situated between Liverpool and Manchester, just off the M6. The wide range of leisure and meeting facilities prove popular with guests.

Rooms 137 (10 fmly) (65 GF) **Facilities** STV FTV Wi-fi HL ⊗ supervised Gym Children's play area Sauna Steam room **Conf** Class 140 Board 40 Thtr 300 **Parking** 210 **Notes** Civ Wed 220

H

HAYDOCK *continued*

Premier Inn Haydock

BUDGET HOTEL

☎ 0871 527 8500
Yew Tree Way, Golbourne WA3 3JD
web: www.premierinn.com
dir: M6 junct 23, A580 towards Manchester. Approx 2m. Straight on at major rdbt. Hotel on left

High quality, budget accommodation ideal for both families and business travellers. Spacious, en suite bedrooms feature tea and coffee making facilities, and Freeview TV in most hotels. Internet access and Wi-fi are available for a small fee. The adjacent family restaurant features a wide and varied menu. See also the Hotel Groups pages.

Rooms 60

Premier Inn Hayle

BUDGET HOTEL

☎ 0871 527 8506
Carwin Rise, Loggans TR27 4PN
web: www.premierinn.com
dir: On A30 at Loggans Moor rdbt exit into Carwin Rise. Hotel on right

High quality, budget accommodation ideal for both families and business travellers. Spacious, en suite bedrooms feature tea and coffee making facilities, and Freeview TV in most hotels. Internet access and Wi-fi are available for a small fee. The adjacent family restaurant features a wide and varied menu. See also the Hotel Groups pages.

Rooms 56

Langstone Hotel

★★★★ 75% ◉◉ HOTEL

☎ 023 9246 5011
Northney Rd PO11 0NQ
e-mail: info@langstonehotel.co.uk
dir: From A27 take A3023 signed Havant/Hayling Island. Over bridge onto Hayling Island, sharp left after bridge

This hotel is located on the north shore of Hayling Island, yet is only minutes from the M27 and has easy access to Fareham, Havant and Chichester. All the smartly designed, air-conditioned bedrooms,

including 45 superior rooms, have views over Langstone harbour. The Brasserie offers a good choice of dishes and overlooks the harbour. There's a gym, indoor pool, sauna, steam, beauty salon and a fitness club.

Rooms 148 (40 fmly) (60 GF) (5 smoking) 🐾
S £69-£199; **D** £69-£199* **Facilities** Spa STV FTV Wi-fi HL supervised Gym Xmas New Year **Conf** Class 80 Board 50 Thtr 180 Del from £115 to £175* **Services** Lift Air con **Parking** 150 **Notes** LB Civ Wed 150

Sinah Warren Hotel

★★★ 79% HOTEL

☎ 023 9246 6421
Ferry Rd PO11 0BZ
e-mail: sinahwarren2@bourne-leisure.co.uk
dir: A27 at Havant junct, take A3023 to Hayling Island, 2nd exit at rdbt towards Manor Rd, 3rd exit at next rdbt into Ferry Rd. Hotel 1.5m on right

Located in a beautiful part of Hampshire, this hotel offers a great range of leisure facilities and numerous daily in-house and external activities catering for all. The accommodation is spacious, and some rooms have sea views. The packages range from a minimum two-night, half board stay. Please note that this is an adults-only (over 21 years) hotel.

Rooms 246 (116 GF) 🐾 **Facilities** Spa FTV Wi-fi HL supervised Gym Xmas New Year **Conf** Class 300 Board 250 Thtr 500 **Services** Lift **Parking** 260 **Notes** ⊗ No children 21yrs

Best Western The Birch Hotel

★★★ 77% HOTEL

☎ 01444 451565
Lewes Rd RH17 7SF
e-mail: info@birchhotel.co.uk
dir: On A272 opposite Princess Royal Hospital & behind Shell Garage

Originally the home of an eminent Harley Street surgeon, this attractive Victorian property has been extended to combine modern facilities with the charm of its original period. Public rooms include the conservatory-style Pavilion Restaurant, along with an open-plan lounge and brasserie-style bar serving a range of light meals.

Rooms 51 (3 fmly) (12 GF) **S** £60-£90; **D** £70-£110 **Facilities** STV Wi-fi **Conf** Class 30 Board 26 Thtr 60 **Parking** 60 **Notes** Civ Wed 60

Heacham Manor Hotel

★★★ 86% HOTEL

☎ 01485 536030 & 579800
Hunstanton Rd PE31 7JX
e-mail: info@heacham-manor.co.uk
dir: On A149 between Heacham & Hunstanton. Near Hunstanton rdbt with water tower

This delightful 16th-century, Grade II listed house has been beautifully restored. The property is approached via a winding driveway through landscaped grounds to the front of the hotel. Public areas include a smart dining room, a sunny conservatory and a cosy bar which leads out onto a terrace. The bedrooms are very stylish and have modern facilities.

Rooms 45 (32 annexe) (10 fmly) (12 GF) **Facilities** FTV Wi-fi 18 Swimming pools & leisure facilities available at sister resort Xmas New Year **Conf** Class 35 Board 20 Thtr 40 **Parking** 55 **Notes** ⊗

Save on hotels. Book at **theAA.com/hotel**

HAY – HEA 203 ENGLAND

HEATHROW AIRPORT (LONDON)
Greater London

**See also Slough & Staines-upon-Thames
See LONDON SECTION plan 1 A2**

Sheraton Skyline Hotel

★★★★ 82% HOTEL

☎ 020 8759 2535 & 8759 2535
Bath Rd UB3 5BP
e-mail: res268_skyline@sheraton.com
dir: M4 junct 4 for Heathrow, follow Terminal 1, 2 & 3 signs. Before airport entrance take slip road to left for 0.25m signed A4/Central London

Within easy reach of all terminals this hotel offers well appointed bedrooms featuring air conditioning. Bedrooms provide excellent levels of quality and comfort. The extensive, contemporary public areas are light and spacious, and include a wide range of eating and drinking options, function rooms, club lounge and a gym.

Rooms 350 (59 fmly) (27 smoking) ♠ **Facilities** STV FTV Wi-fi ♨ ⒮ supervised Gym Fitness centre Xmas New Year **Conf** Class 320 Board 100 Thtr 500 **Services** Lift Air con **Parking** 336 **Notes** Civ Wed 100

London Heathrow Marriott Hotel
Marriott HOTELS & RESORTS

★★★★ 77% ⊛ HOTEL

☎ 020 8990 1100 & 8990 1119
Bath Rd UB3 5AN
e-mail: mhrs.lhrhr.ays@marriott.com
web: www.londonheathrowmarriott.co.uk
dir: M4 junct 4, follow signs for Heathrow Terminals 1, 2 & 3. Left at rdbt onto A4 towards central London. Hotel 0.5m on left

This smart, modern hotel, with its striking design, meets all the expectations of a successful airport hotel. The light and airy atrium offers several eating and drinking options, each with a different theme. Spacious bedrooms are appointed to a good standard with an excellent range of facilities, and there is a leisure club and business centre.

Rooms 393 (139 fmly) (30 smoking) ♠ **S** £149-£198; **D** £149-£198* **Facilities** STV Wi-fi ♨ ⒮ supervised Gym Steam room Sauna Spa pool Xmas **Conf** Class 300 Board 65 Thtr 550 Del from £183 to £283* **Services** Lift Air con **Parking** 280 **Notes** LB ⊗ Civ Wed 414

Crowne Plaza London - Heathrow
CROWNE PLAZA HOTELS & RESORTS

★★★★ 76% HOTEL

☎ 0871 942 9140
Stockley Rd UB7 9NA
e-mail: lonha.reservations@ihg.com
web: www.cpheathrowairporthotel.co.uk
dir: M4 junct 4 follow signs to Uxbridge on A408, hotel 400yds on left

This smart hotel is conveniently located for access to Heathrow Airport and the motorway network. Excellent facilities include versatile conference and meeting rooms, a spa and leisure complex. Guests have the choice of two bars, both serving food plus two restaurants. Air-conditioned bedrooms are furnished and decorated to a high standard and feature a comprehensive range of extra facilities.

Rooms 465 (204 fmly) (37 GF) ♠ **Facilities** STV Wi-fi ♨ HL ⒮ supervised ♨ 9 Putt green Gym Steam room Sauna Physiotherapy **Conf** Class 120 Board 75 Thtr 200 Del from £190 to £320* **Services** Lift Air con **Parking** 800 **Notes** ⊗

Heathrow/Windsor Marriott
Marriott HOTELS & RESORTS

★★★★ 76% HOTEL

☎ 01753 544244
Ditton Rd SL3 8PT
e-mail: mhrs.lhrsl.ays@marriotthotels.com
web: www.heathrowwindsormarriott.co.uk
dir: M4 junct 5, follow 'Langley' signs, left at lights into Ditton Rd

Ideally located for access to Heathrow and the M4, this smart hotel offers a wide range of facilities. There is a well-appointed leisure centre, extensive conference facilities, a bar offering 24-hour snacks and light meals, and a restaurant with a wide ranging cuisine. Spacious bedrooms are well equipped for both leisure and business guests.

Rooms 382 (120 fmly) (96 GF) (20 smoking) **S** £142.80-£202.80; **D** £142.80-£202.80* **Facilities** STV FTV Wi-fi ♨ ⒮ supervised ♨ Gym Sauna Steam room **Conf** Class 220 Board 42 Thtr 400 Del from £162 to £234* **Services** Lift Air con **Parking** 550 **Notes** LB ⊗ Civ Wed 300

Renaissance London Heathrow Hotel
R RENAISSANCE LONDON HEATHROW HOTEL

★★★★ 75% HOTEL

☎ 020 8897 6363
Bath Rd TW6 2AQ
e-mail: rhi.lhrbr.reservations@renaissancehotels.com
web: www.renaissancelondonheathrow.co.uk
dir: M4 junct 4 take spur road towards airport, then 2nd left. At rdbt, 2nd exit signed 'Renaissance Hotel'. Hotel adjacent to Customs House

Located right on the perimeter of the airport, this hotel commands superb views over the runways. The smart bedrooms are fully soundproofed and equipped with air conditioning - each is well suited to meet the needs of today's business travellers. The hotel boasts extensive conference facilities, and is a very popular venue for air travellers and conference organisers.

Rooms 649 (56 GF) (30 smoking) ♠ **S** £93-£239; **D** £93-£239 **Facilities** STV Wi-fi ♨ Gym Steam room Solarium Fitness studio Beauty & massage treatment Personal trainer Xmas **Conf** Class 300 Board 80 Thtr 450 Del from £149 to £209 **Services** Lift Air con **Parking** 700 **Notes** Civ Wed 150

The Continental Hotel

★★★★ 73% HOTEL

☎ 020 8572 3131 & 8538 5883
29-31 Lampton Rd TW3 1JA
e-mail: reservations@thecontinental-hotel.com
dir: A4, right onto A3006, left onto A3005 then left onto Lampton Rd

This hotel enjoys a prime location just a few minutes walk from Hounslow Central Line; central London can be reached in 40 minutes. The bedrooms are air conditioned, and complimentary broadband is available. The bedroom en suites are marble-clad wet rooms with power showers. The on-site Golds Gym has a 21-metre indoor pool, a state-of-the-art fitness centre and beauty treatment rooms.

Rooms 70 (8 fmly) ♠ **S** £159-£199; **D** £159-£199 **Facilities** Spa STV FTV Wi-fi ⒮ Gym ♫ Xmas New Year **Conf** Del from £230 to £270 **Services** Lift Air con **Parking** 70 **Notes** LB ⊗

H

H

Holiday Inn London - Heathrow

★★★★ 73% HOTEL

☎ 020 8990 0000
Bath Rd, Corner Sipson Way UB7 0DP
e-mail: enquiries@hiheathrow.co.uk
web: www.holidayinnheathrow.co.uk
dir: Exit airport via main tunnel, at end left towards A4/Other Routes, follow signs for A4. At main lights (hotel visable) turn right, 1st left into Sipson Way

A property close to the terminals and with a frequent bus service to the airport. Public areas include a large brasserie-style restaurant and bar plus shop, mini gym and parking. Bedrooms are spacious and air conditioned, with facilities to suit the business traveller; there are a number of executive rooms available.

Rooms 230 (15 fmly) (58 GF) (23 smoking) **Facilities** Wi-fi ▷ HL Gym New Year **Conf** Class 50 Board 50 Thtr 130 **Services** Lift Air con **Parking** 60 **Notes** ⊗ Civ Wed 80

Ramada London Heathrow

★★★★ 73% HOTEL

☎ 0844 815 9041
Bath Rd, Cranford TW5 9QE
e-mail: fo.lhr@ramadajarvis.co.uk
dir: M4 junct 3 follow signs to Heathrow Terminals 1, 2 & 3. Hotel on right of A4 Bath Rd

This well presented hotel is conveniently situated just three miles from Heathrow Airport. Bedrooms are located in a smart block and all are well appointed for both business and leisure guests; each has a flat-screen TV with multi-channel choice, climate control and good lighting. Arts Bar and Brasserie lead from a contemporary open-plan reception area. Chargeable car park on site.

Rooms 200 (18 fmly) (37 GF) **Facilities** FTV Wi-fi ▷ **Conf** Class 45 Board 40 Thtr 70 **Services** Lift Air con **Parking** 60 **Notes** ⊗ Civ Wed 65

Novotel London Heathrow

★★★★ 72% HOTEL

☎ 01895 431431
Cherry Ln UB7 9HB
e-mail: H1551-gm@accor.com
web: www.novotel.com
dir: M4 junct 4, follow Uxbridge signs on A408. Keep left, take 2nd exit off traffic island into Cherry Ln signed West Drayton. Hotel on left

Conveniently located for Heathrow Airport and the motorway network, this modern hotel provides comfortable accommodation. The large, airy indoor atrium creates a sense of space to the public areas, which include an all-day restaurant and bar, meeting rooms, fitness centre and swimming pool. Ample secure parking is available.

Rooms 178 (178 fmly) (10 GF) **S** £65-£199; **D** £85-£250* **Facilities** STV Wi-fi ▷ ⊗ Gym **Conf** Class 100 Board 90 Thtr 250 **Services** Lift Air con **Parking** 100 **Notes** LB Civ Wed 160

Park Inn Heathrow

★★★★ 72% HOTEL

☎ 020 8759 6611
Bath Rd UB7 0DU
e-mail: info.heathrow@rezidorparkinn.com
dir: M4 junct 4, follow signs for T1, 2 & 3. Hotel on left, take exit on left up ramp

Ideally located for Heathrow Airports and central London. This hotel is spacious, purpose-built and offers a range of well-appointed bedrooms, conference rooms, a choice of bars and a fully-equipped health club. The restaurant offers varied dining ideal for a transient market, and there is plenty of parking available.

Rooms 895 (121 fmly) (95 GF) (95 smoking) ⋔ **S** £75-£295; **D** £75-£295* **Facilities** STV Wi-fi ▷ ⊗ supervised Gym Beauty treatment room Sauna Xmas New Year **Conf** Class 360 Board 120 Thtr 700 **Services** Lift Air con **Parking** 475 **Notes** LB Civ Wed 500

Holiday Inn London Heathrow M4 Jct 4

★★★★ 70% HOTEL

☎ 0871 942 9095
Sipson Rd UB7 0JU
e-mail: reservations-heathrowm4@ihg.com
web: www.holidayinn.co.uk
dir: M4 junct 4, keep left, 1st left into Holloway Lane, left at mini rdbt then left. For detailed directions contact hotel

This landmark hotel can be seen from for miles when travelling on the M4 and is situated close to Heathrow Airport; it is an ideal base for the airport and for families visiting local attractions. The bedrooms are air conditioned and well equipped. There are two restaurants, a small gym and ample parking.

Rooms 616 (120 fmly) (25 smoking) ⋔ **Facilities** STV Wi-fi ▷ Gym Xmas New Year **Conf** Class 80 Board 80 Thtr 180 Del from £99 to £225* **Services** Lift Air con **Parking** 450 **Notes** ⊗

Holiday Inn London Heathrow Ariel

★★★ 77% HOTEL

☎ 0871 942 9040
118 Bath Rd UB3 5AJ
e-mail: reservations-heathrow@ihg.com
web: www.holidayinn.co.uk
dir: M4 junct 4, take spur road to Heathrow Airport, 1st left onto A4 Bath Rd, through 3 sets of lights. Hotel on left

Located close to Heathrow Airport with good public transport links to all terminals, this well sited hotel is suitable for both the business and leisure traveller. Public areas benefit from a spacious lounge bar area, brasserie-style restaurant and extensive conference facilities. Ample secure parking is an additional plus.

Rooms 184 (18 smoking) **Facilities** STV Wi-fi Xmas **Conf** Class 35 Board 25 Thtr 50 **Services** Lift Air con **Parking** 100 **Notes** ⊗ Civ Wed 50

Save on hotels. Book at **theAA.com/hotel**

HEA 205 ENGLAND

Thistle London Heathrow

thistle

★★★ 73% HOTEL

☎ 0871 376 9021
Bath Rd, Longford UB7 0EQ
e-mail: londonheathrow@thistle.co.uk
web: www.thistlehotels.com/londonheathrow
dir: M25 junct 14 signed Terminal 4 & Cargo Area.
Right at 1st rdbt signed Heathrow. Left at lights onto
A3044 signed Colnbrook & Longford

Located adjacent to the airport and with the benefit of
secure parking and regular coach transfers, this long
established hotel provides a range of well equipped
bedrooms for both the business and leisure guest.
Imaginative food is available in an attractive
restaurant and comprehensive breakfasts are served
in a separate first-floor dining room.

Rooms 264 (3 fmly) (132 GF) **D** £49-£179*
Facilities FTV Wi-fi HL Use of nearby health club
Xmas New Year **Conf** Class 300 Board 25 Thtr 700
Del from £99 to £289* **Services** Air con **Parking** 450
Notes ⊗ Civ Wed 540

Days Hotel Hounslow

★★★ 72% HOTEL

☎ 020 8538 1230
8-10 Lampton Rd TW3 1JL
e-mail: gm@dhhounslow.com
dir: A4 (Bath Rd), A3006, into Lampton Rd (A3005)

A purpose-built hotel situated in the centre of
Hounslow and within walking distance of the tube
station and with easy access to the motorway
network. The accommodation is comfortable and
offers a range of amenities that the modern traveller
expects. The public areas are light and airy, and
parking is available.

Rooms 96 (11 fmly) (4 GF) **Facilities** FTV Wi-fi ♫
Xmas New Year **Conf** Class 50 Board 60 Thtr 100
Del from £129 to £149 **Services** Lift Air con
Parking 20 **Notes** ⊗ Civ Wed 120

Comfort Hotel Heathrow

Comfort INN

★★★ 71% HOTEL

☎ 020 8573 6162
Shepiston Ln UB3 1LP
e-mail: info@comfortheathrow.com
web: www.comfortheathrow.com
dir: M4 junct 4, follow signs to Hayes & Shepiston
Lane, hotel approx 1m, adjacent to fire station

This hotel is a short drive from the airport, and guests
may prefer its quieter location. There is a frequent
bus service, which runs to and from the hotel
throughout the day. Bedrooms are thoughtfully
equipped and many benefit from air conditioning.

Rooms 184 (7 fmly) (50 GF) (6 smoking)
S £39-£139; **D** £39-£149* **Facilities** STV FTV Wi-fi
Gym **Conf** Class 72 Board 90 Thtr 150 Del from £99 to
£149 **Services** Lift **Parking** 120 **Notes** LB ⊗
Civ Wed 90

Best Western Plus Park Grand London Heathrow

Best Western PLUS

Ⓤ

☎ 020 7479 2255
449 Great West Rd TW5 0BY
e-mail: john@montcalm.co.uk

Currently the rating for this establishment is not
confirmed. This may be due to a change of ownership
or because it has only recently joined the AA rating
scheme. For further details please see the AA website:
theAA.com

Rooms 112 (14 fmly) **S** £59-£250; **D** £69-£275
Facilities STV Wi-fi ♫ HL Gym **Conf** Class 200
Board 65 Thtr 65 Del £150 **Services** Lift Air con
Parking 30 **Notes** ⊗ Civ Wed 200

Ibis London Heathrow Airport

ibis

BUDGET HOTEL

☎ 020 8759 4888
112/114 Bath Rd UB3 5AL
e-mail: H0794@accor.com
web: www.ibishotel.com/heathrow
dir: Follow Heathrow Terminals 1, 2 & 3 signs, then
onto spur road, exit at sign for A4/Central London.
Hotel 0.5m on left

Modern, budget hotel offering comfortable
accommodation in bright and practical bedrooms.
Breakfast is self-service and dinner is available in
the restaurant. See also the Hotel Groups pages.

Rooms 351 (24 fmly) (39 GF) **Conf** Class 16 Board 16
Thtr 20

Premier Inn Hayes Heathrow

Premier Inn

BUDGET HOTEL

☎ 0871 527 8504
362 Uxbridge Rd UB4 0HF
web: www.premierinn.com
dir: M4 junct 3, A312 N straight across next rdbt onto
dual carriageway, at A4020 junct turn left, hotel
100yds on right

High quality, budget accommodation ideal for both
families and business travellers. Spacious, en suite
bedrooms feature tea and coffee making facilities,
and Freeview TV in most hotels. Internet access and
Wi-fi are available for a small fee. The adjacent
family restaurant features a wide and varied menu.
See also the Hotel Groups pages.

Rooms 62

H

Premier Inn Heathrow Airport (Bath Road)

BUDGET HOTEL

☎ 0871 527 8508
15 Bath Rd TW6 2AB
web: www.premierinn.com
dir: M4 junct 4, follow signs for Heathrow Terminals
1, 2 & 3. Left onto Bath Rd signed A4/London. Hotel
on right after 0.5m

Rooms 590

Premier Inn Heathrow Airport (M4 Jct 4)

BUDGET HOTEL

☎ 0871 527 8510
Shepiston Ln, Heathrow Airport UB3 1RW
web: www.premierinn.com
dir: M4 junct 4 take 3rd exit off rdbt. Hotel on right

Rooms 134

HEBDEN BRIDGE
West Yorkshire   **Map 19 SD92**

Moyles

⊛ RESTAURANT WITH ROOMS

☎ 01422 845272
6-10 New Rd HX7 8AD
e-mail: enquire@moyles.com
dir: A646 to Hebden Bridge, opposite marina

Centrally located in the charming town of Hebden Bridge, this Victorian building as been modernised to offer a high standard of contemporary accommodation. Fresh, local produce features on the imaginative menus served in the bar and in the restaurant. There's a relaxing ambience throughout.

Rooms 12 (6 fmly)

HEDDON-ON-THE-WALL
Northumberland   **Map 21 NZ16**

Close House

★★★★ 80% ⊛⊛ HOTEL

☎ 01661 852255
NE15 0HT
e-mail: reservations@closehouse.co.uk
web: www.closehouse.co.uk
dir: A1 N, A69 W. Follow B6528 at junct turn left, hotel signed

Dating back to 1779, this is a magnificent country house set in 300 acres of woodland and parkland in the secluded and beautiful Tyne Valley. It is just 20 minutes from Newcastle city centre which has good national and international transport links. The hotel provides accommodation designed to make a stay relaxing and special. All the bedrooms are equipped with high-tech mod cons. There is a magnificent restaurant and bar, and 24-hour room service is also available. There is a golf course in the grounds.

Rooms 31 (12 annexe) (6 GF) ↟ **S** £195-£300; **D** £195-£300 **Facilities** STV FTV Wi-fi ↻ ⅃ 36 Putt green Driving range Xmas New Year **Conf** Class 30 Board 30 Thtr 140 Del £310 **Services** Air con **Parking** 87 **Notes** LB Civ Wed 100

HELLIDON
Northamptonshire   **Map 11 SP55**

Hellidon Lakes Golf & Spa Hotel

★★★★ 75% HOTEL

☎ 01327 262550
NN11 6GG
e-mail: hellidonlakes@qhotels.co.uk
web: www.qhotels.co.uk
dir: Off A361 between Daventry & Banbury, signed

Some 220 acres of beautiful countryside, which include 27 holes of golf and 12 lakes, combine to form a rather spectacular backdrop to this impressive hotel. Bedroom styles vary, from ultra smart, modern rooms through to those in the original wing that offer superb views. There is an extensive range of facilities available from meeting rooms to a swimming pool, gym and ten-pin bowling. Golfers of all levels can try some of the world's most challenging courses on the indoor golf simulator.

Rooms 110 (5 fmly) **Facilities** Spa FTV Wi-fi ↻ ⊗ ⅃ 27 ☺ Putt green Fishing ⅃ Gym Beauty therapist Indoor smart golf 10-pin bowling Steam room Coarse fishing lake Xmas New Year **Conf** Class 150 Board 80 Thtr 300 Del from £115 to £189 **Services** Lift **Parking** 200 **Notes** Civ Wed 220

HELMSLEY
North Yorkshire   **Map 19 SE68**

INSPECTORS' CHOICE

Feversham Arms Hotel & Verbena Spa

★★★★ ⊛⊛⊛ HOTEL

☎ 01439 770766
1 High St YO62 5AG
e-mail: info@fevershamarmshotel.com
web: www.fevershamarmshotel.com
dir: A168 (signed Thirsk) A1, A170 or A64 (signed York) from A1 to York North, B1363 to Helmsley. Hotel 125mtrs from Market Place

This long established hotel lies just round the corner from the main square, and under its caring ownership proves to be a refined operation, yet without airs and graces. There are several lounge areas and a high-ceilinged conservatory restaurant where menus are created with skill and minimal fuss from good local ingredients. The bedrooms, including four air-conditioned poolside suites (some with wood-burners) and spa suites with balconies or French balconies, all have their own individual character and decor. Expect Egyptian cotton sheets, duck down duvets and Bang and Olufsen TVs with DVD and CD player. The spa offers a comprehensive range of pampering treatments.

Rooms 33 (9 fmly) (8 GF) **Facilities** Spa STV FTV Wi-fi ↻ Sauna Saunarium Xmas New Year **Conf** Class 20 Board 24 Thtr 35 **Services** Lift **Parking** 50 **Notes** Civ Wed 50

See advert in preliminary section

Save on hotels. Book at **theAA.com/hotel**

HEB – HEM 207 ENGLAND

Black Swan Hotel

★★★★ 77% ◉◉ ⊛ HOTEL

☎ 01439 770466
Market Place YO62 5BJ
e-mail: enquiries@blackswan-helmsley.co.uk
web: www.blackswan-helmsley.co.uk
dir: A1 junct 49, A168, A170 east, hotel 14m from
Thirsk

People have been visiting this establishment for over
200 years and it has become a landmark that
dominates the market square. The hotel is renowned
for its hospitality and friendliness; many of the staff
are long-serving and dedicated. The bedrooms are
stylish and include a junior suite and feature rooms.
Dinner in the award-winning restaurant is the
highlight of any stay. The hotel has a Tearoom and
Patisserie that is open daily.

Rooms 45 (4 fmly) ⊹ **S** £112-£206; **D** £142-£217
(incl. bkfst)* **Facilities** STV FTV Wi-fi Xmas New Year
Conf Class 30 Board 26 Thtr 50 Del from £165 to
£200* **Parking** 50 **Notes** LB Civ Wed 130

HELSTON   Map 2 SW62
Cornwall

Premier Inn Helston

BUDGET HOTEL

☎ 0871 527 8512
Clodgey Ln TR13 8FZ
web: www.premierinn.com
dir: A39 towards Falmouth. Right onto A394 towards
Helston, 8m. At rdbt 1st exit (Helston bypass) signed
Penzance (A394)/Lizard. Hotel at next rdbt on left (NB
for Sat Nav use TR13 0QD)

High quality, budget accommodation ideal for both
families and business travellers. Spacious, en suite
bedrooms feature tea and coffee making facilities,
and Freeview TV in most hotels. Internet access and
Wi-fi are available for a small fee. The adjacent
family restaurant features a wide and varied menu.
See also the Hotel Groups pages.

Rooms 50

HEMEL HEMPSTEAD   Map 6 TL00
Hertfordshire

Holiday Inn Hemel Hempstead

★★★ 77% HOTEL

☎ 0871 942 9041
Breakspear Way HP2 4UA
e-mail: reservations-hemelhempsteadm1@ihg.com
web: www.holidayinn.co.uk/hemelhempstead
dir: M1 junct 8, over rdbt, 1st left after BP garage

A modern, purpose-built hotel that is convenient for
the motorway networks. Bedrooms are spacious and
well suited to the business traveller. Executive rooms
and public areas are particularly well styled. Other
facilities include a leisure club and a range of
meeting rooms.

Rooms 144 (38 fmly) (42 GF) (12 smoking)
Facilities Spa STV Wi-fi ⌖ ⌖ supervised Gym Beauty
treaments & physiotherapy by appointment
Conf Class 22 Board 30 Thtr 80 **Services** Lift Air con
Parking 200 **Notes** ⊗ Civ Wed 60

Ramada Hemel Hempstead

★★★ 77% HOTEL

☎ 01582 791500 & 791511
Hemel Hempstead Rd, Redbourn AL3 7AF
e-mail: enquiries@ramadahemelhotel.co.uk
web: www.ramadahemelhotel.co.uk
dir: M1 junct 9 follow Hemel Hempstead & St Albans
signs for 3m, straight across 2 rdbts onto B487
signed Hemel Hempstead. Hotel on right

The hotel is conveniently located a short drive from
the historic Roman city of St Albans, close to the M1
and the M25, and is an ideal venue for both corporate
and leisure guests. Set in its own extensive grounds
the hotel offers a range of very comfortable, spacious
bedrooms. Free Wi-fi is available throughout.

Rooms 137 (10 fmly) (69 GF) **Facilities** STV Wi-fi ⌖
Xmas New Year **Conf** Class 30 Board 30 Thtr 75
Del from £126 to £150* **Services** Lift **Parking** 150
Notes ⊗ Civ Wed 100

The Bobsleigh Hotel

★★★ 75% ◉ HOTEL

MACDONALD
HOTELS & RESORTS

☎ 0844 879 9033
Hempstead Rd, Bovingdon HP3 0DS
e-mail: bobsleigh@macdonald-hotels.co.uk
web: www.macdonald-hotels.co.uk
dir: M1 junct 8, A414 signed Hemel Hempstead. At
Plough Rdbt follow railway station signs. Pass rail
station on left, straight on at rdbt, under 2 bridges.
Left onto B4505 (Box Lane) signed Chesham. Hotel
1.5m on left

Located just outside the town, the hotel enjoys a
pleasant rural setting, yet is within easy reach of
local transport links and the motorway network.
Bedrooms vary in size; all are modern in style. There
is an open-plan lobby, a bar area and an attractive
dining room with views over the garden.

Rooms 46 (14 annexe) (6 fmly) (30 GF) ⊹
Facilities STV Wi-fi New Year **Conf** Class 50 Board 40
Thtr 150 **Parking** 60 **Notes** Civ Wed 100

Best Western The Watermill

★★★ 74% HOTEL

Best Western

☎ 01442 349955
London Rd, Bourne End HP1 2RJ
e-mail: info@hotelwatermill.co.uk
web: www.hotelwatermill.co.uk
dir: From M25 & M1 follow signs to Aylesbury on A41,
A4251 to Bourne End. Hotel 0.25m on right

In the heart of the county this modern hotel has been
built around an old flour mill on the banks of the
River Bulbourne with water meadows adjacent. The
thoughtfully equipped, contemporary bedrooms are
located in three annexes situated around the complex.
A good range of air-conditioned conference and
meeting rooms complement the lounge bar and
restaurant.

Rooms 71 (67 annexe) (9 fmly) (35 GF) (8 smoking)
Facilities STV Wi-fi Fishing Xmas New Year
Conf Class 150 Board 125 Thtr 200 **Parking** 100
Notes ⊗ Civ Wed 180

H

H

HEMEL HEMPSTEAD *continued*

Holiday Inn Express Hemel Hempstead

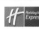

BUDGET HOTEL

☎ 01442 206600
Stationers Place, Apsley Lock HP3 9RH
e-mail: info@expresshemel.co.uk
web: www.hiexpress.com/hemelhempstead
dir: M25 junct 20, Kings Langley, hotel on right after 3rd rdbt

A modern hotel ideal for families and business travellers. Fresh and uncomplicated, the spacious rooms include Sky TV, power shower and tea and coffee-making facilities. Continental buffet breakfast is included in the room rate; other meals may be taken at the nearby family pub or restaurant. See also the Hotel Groups pages.

Rooms 116 (82 fmly) (28 smoking) **Conf** Class 18 Board 18 Thtr 40

Premier Inn Hemel Hempstead Central

BUDGET HOTEL

☎ 0871 527 8514
Moor End Rd HP1 1DL
web: www.premierinn.com
dir: M1 junct 8, A414, follow town centre signs. Right at 1st mini rdbt, right at 2nd mini rdbt into Seldon Hill Rd, follow Riverside car park sings (footbridge to hotel from floor 3). (NB for Sat Nav use HP1 1BT)

High quality, budget accommodation ideal for both families and business travellers. Spacious, en suite bedrooms feature tea and coffee making facilities, and Freeview TV in most hotels. Internet access and Wi-fi are available for a small fee. The adjacent family restaurant features a wide and varied menu. See also the Hotel Groups pages.

Rooms 113

Premier Inn Hemel Hempstead West

BUDGET HOTEL

☎ 0871 527 8516
A41 Service Area, Bourne End HP1 2SB
web: www.premierinn.com
dir: M25 junct 20, A41 exit at services. Or from M1 junct 8, A414, A41, exit at services

Rooms 61

Hotel du Vin Henley-on-Thames

★★★★ 76% ⓪⓪ TOWN HOUSE HOTEL

☎ 01491 848400
New St RG9 2BP
e-mail: info.henley@hotelduvin.com
web: www.hotelduvin.com
dir: M4 junct 8/9 signed High Wycombe, 2nd exit onto A404 in 2m. A4130 to Henley, over bridge, through lights, into Hart St, right into Bell St, right into New St, hotel on right

Situated just 50 yards from the water's edge, this hotel retains the character and much of the architecture of the former brewery. Food, and naturally wine, take on a strong focus here and guests will find an interesting mix of dishes to choose from; there are three private dining rooms where the fermentation room and old malt house once were; alfresco dining is popular when the weather permits. Bedrooms provide comfort, style and a good range of facilities including power showers. Parking is available and there is a drop-off point in the courtyard.

Rooms 43 (4 fmly) (4 GF) ↖ **S** £99-£405; D £99-£405* **Facilities** STV FTV Wi-fi ↕ Xmas New Year **Conf** Class 20 Board 36 Thtr 56 Del from £180 to £260* **Services** Air con **Parking** 42 **Notes** LB Civ Wed 60

Milsoms Henley-on-Thames

RESTAURANT WITH ROOMS

☎ 01491 845780 & 845789
20 Market Place RG9 2AH
e-mail: henley@milsomshotel.co.uk
dir: In centre of town, close to town hall

The seven en suite bedrooms are located in a listed building above the Loch Fyne Restaurant in Henley's Market Place. Each bedroom is individually appointed and equipped to meet the needs of the modern traveller; particular care has been taken to incorporate original features into the contemporary design. The restaurant has a commitment to offer ethically sourced seafood.

Rooms 7 (2 fmly)

See also Leominster

Holme Lacy House Hotel   Warner Leisure Hotels
JUST FOR GROWN-UPS

★★★★ 73% ⓪⓪ COUNTRY HOUSE HOTEL

☎ 01432 870870
Holme Lacy HR2 6LP
web: www.holmelacyhouse.co.uk
dir: B4399 at Holme Lacy, take lane opposite college. Hotel 500mtrs on right

This is a grand Grade I listed mansion with a rich history, just a short drive from Hereford and in a peaceful location, set in twenty acres of superb parkland in the heart of the Wye Valley. The well-appointed bedrooms are comfortable and vary in size and style. Exclusively for adults (above 21 years old), there is much to do here, with a full daily entertainment programmes, an indoor pool, and health and beauty treatments. The three restaurants provide carefully selected menus of quality cuisine.

Rooms 180 (150 annexe) (53 GF) **Facilities** Spa FTV Wi-fi ⓢ ⌣ Putt green Fishing ⌣ Gym Archery Rifle shooting Aquafit Salsa-cise classes Yoga Fencing ♫ Xmas New Year **Services** Lift **Parking** 200 **Notes** ⊗ No children 21yrs

---

Castle House

★★★ 86% ⓪⓪ HOTEL

☎ 01432 356321
Castle St HR1 2NW
e-mail: info@castlehse.co.uk
web: www.castlehse.co.uk
dir: Follow signs to City Centre East. At junct of Commercial Rd & Union St follow hotel signs

Enjoying a prime city centre location and with a terraced garden leading to the castle moat, this

Save on hotels. Book at **theAA.com/hotel**

HEM – HER 209 ENGLAND

delightful Grade II listed Georgian mansion is the epitome of elegance and sophistication. The character bedrooms are equipped with every luxury to ensure a memorable stay and are complemented perfectly by the well-proportioned and restful lounge and bar, together with the elegant topiary-themed restaurant where award-winning modern British cuisine is served.

Castle House

Rooms 24 (8 annexe) (2 GF) 🕯 **S** £130; **D** £150–£230 (incl. bkfst)* **Facilities** STV FTV Wi-fi ⏃ Free membership at local spa Xmas New Year **Services** Lift **Parking** 12 **Notes** LB ⊗ Civ Wed 50

See advert on this page

Three Counties Hotel
★★★ 78% HOTEL

☎ 01432 299955
Belmont Rd HR2 7BP
e-mail: enquiries@threecountieshotel.co.uk
web: www.threecountieshotel.co.uk
dir: On A465 (Abergavenny road)

Just a mile west of the city centre, this large, privately owned, modern complex has well-equipped, spacious bedrooms; many are located in separate single-storey buildings around the extensive car park. There is a

spacious, comfortable lounge, a traditional bar and an attractive restaurant.

Three Counties Hotel

Rooms 60 (32 annexe) (4 fmly) (46 GF) **S** £60; **D** £60* **Facilities** STV FTV Wi-fi **Conf** Class 200 Board 120 Thtr 450 Del from £95 to £105* **Parking** 250 **Notes** LB Civ Wed 350

See advert on page 210

H

HEREFORD *continued*

Premier Inn Hereford

BUDGET HOTEL

☎ 0871 527 8518
Holmer Rd, Holmer HR4 9RS
web: www.premierinn.com
dir: From N: M5 junct 7, A4103 to Worcester. M50 junct 4, A49 (Leominster road). Hotel 800yds on left

High quality, budget accommodation ideal for both families and business travellers. Spacious, en suite bedrooms feature tea and coffee making facilities, and Freeview TV in most hotels. Internet access and Wi-fi are available for a small fee. The adjacent family restaurant features a wide and varied menu. See also the Hotel Groups pages.

Rooms 81

HERNE BAY   Map 7 TR16
Kent

Premier Inn Canterbury North/Herne Bay

BUDGET HOTEL

☎ 0871 527 8520
Blacksole Farm, Margate Rd CT6 6LA
web: www.premierinn.com
dir: From M2 junct 7 follow Canterbury signs, A299 signed Ramsgate/Margate. Exit at Broomfield & Beltinge. Hotel just off rdbt

High quality, budget accommodation ideal for both families and business travellers. Spacious, en suite

---

bedrooms feature tea and coffee making facilities, and Freeview TV in most hotels. Internet access and Wi-fi are available for a small fee. The adjacent family restaurant features a wide and varied menu. See also the Hotel Groups pages.

Rooms 50

HERTFORD   Map 6 TL31
Hertfordshire

White Horse Hotel

★★★ 71% HOTEL

☎ 01992 586791
Hertingfordbury Rd, Hertingfordbury SG14 2LB
e-mail: bgray@aquariushotels.co.uk
dir: From A10 follow A414 signs. From Hertford under rail bridge, over rdbt, left at next rdbt, hotel 300yds on right

The Georgian façade of this former coaching inn belies a much older interior with oak beams dating back 400 years. Many of the spacious bedrooms overlook the picturesque gardens. Public rooms include a beamed bar with its open fireplace and a spacious conservatory restaurant.

Rooms 42 (4 fmly) **Facilities** FTV Wi-fi Xmas New Year **Conf** Class 30 Board 26 Thtr 60 **Services** Air con **Parking** 50 **Notes** ⊗ Civ Wed 75

HESWALL   Map 15 SJ28
Merseyside

Premier Inn Wirral (Heswall)

BUDGET HOTEL

☎ 0871 527 9178
Chester Rd, Gayton CH60 3SD
web: www.premierinn.com
dir: M53 junct 4, A5137 signed Heswall. In 3m left at next rdbt, hotel on left

High quality, budget accommodation ideal for both families and business travellers. Spacious, en suite bedrooms feature tea and coffee making facilities, and Freeview TV in most hotels. Internet access and Wi-fi are available for a small fee. The adjacent family restaurant features a wide and varied menu. See also the Hotel Groups pages.

Rooms 37

Save on hotels. Book at **theAA.com/hotel**

HER – HEX 211 ENGLAND

HETHERSETT
Norfolk

Map 13 TG10

Park Farm Hotel
★★★★ 77% ◉ HOTEL

☎ 01603 810264
NR9 3DL
e-mail: enq@parkfarm-hotel.co.uk
web: www.parkfarm-hotel.co.uk
dir: 5m S of Norwich, exit A11 onto B1172

An elegant Georgian farmhouse set in landscaped grounds surrounded by open countryside. The property has been owned and run by the Gowing family since 1958. Bedrooms are pleasantly decorated and tastefully furnished; some rooms have patio doors with a sun terrace. Public rooms include a stylish conservatory, a lounge bar, a smart restaurant and superb leisure facilities.

Rooms 53 (16 annexe) (15 fmly) (26 GF) ☞
S £99-£140; **D** £120-£190 (incl. bkfst) **Facilities** Spa
FTV Wi-fi ◔ supervised Gym Beauty salon
Hairdressing Xmas New Year **Conf** Class 50 Board 50
Thtr 120 Del from £130 to £160 **Parking** 150
Notes LB ⊗ Civ Wed 100

See advert on page 355

HETTON
North Yorkshire

Map 18 SD95

The Angel Inn
◉ ◉ RESTAURANT WITH ROOMS

☎ 01756 730263
BD23 6LT
e-mail: info@angelhetton.co.uk
dir: B6265 from Skipton towards Grassington. At Rylstone turn left by pond, follow signs to Hetton

This roadside inn is steeped in history; parts of the building go back over 500 years. The restaurant and bar are in the main building which has ivy and green canopies at the front. The large and stylish bedrooms are across the road in a converted barn which has great views of the Dales, its own wine cave and private parking.

Rooms 9

HEXHAM
Northumberland

Map 21 NY96

Langley Castle Hotel
★★★★ 81% ◉ ◉ HOTEL

☎ 01434 688888
Langley NE47 5LU
e-mail: manager@langleycastle.com
web: www.langleycastle.com
dir: From A69 S on A686 for 2m. Hotel on right

Langley is a magnificent 14th-century fortified castle, with its own chapel, set in ten acres of parkland. There is an award-winning restaurant, a comfortable drawing room and a cosy bar. Bedrooms are furnished with period pieces and most feature window seats.

Restored buildings in the grounds have been converted into very stylish Castle View bedrooms.

Langley Castle Hotel

Rooms 27 (18 annexe) (8 fmly) (9 GF) **S** £119-£209;
D £149-£275 (incl. bkfst)* **Facilities** STV Wi-fi Xmas
Conf Class 60 Board 40 Thtr 120 Del from £160 to
£245* **Services** Air con **Parking** 70 **Notes** LB ⊗
Civ Wed 120

De Vere Slaley Hall
DE VERE
Hotels & Resorts

★★★★ 80% ◉ HOTEL

☎ 01434 673350
Slaley NE47 0BX
e-mail: slaley.hall@devere-hotels.com
web: www.devere.co.uk
dir: A1 from S to A68 (link road) follow signs for Slaley Hall

One thousand acres of Northumbrian forest and parkland, two championship golf courses and indoor leisure facilities can all be found here. The spacious bedrooms are fully air conditioned, equipped with a range of extras, and the deluxe rooms offer excellent standards. Public rooms include a number of lounges and the fine-dining Dukes Grill, informal Claret Jug and an impressive main restaurant overlooking the golf course.

Rooms 142 (18 fmly) (37 GF) **Facilities** Spa Wi-fi ◔
supervised ⌁ 36 Putt green Gym Quad bikes Archery
Clay pigeon shooting 4x4 driving Xmas New Year
Conf Class 220 Board 150 Thtr 300 **Services** Lift
Air con **Parking** 500 **Notes** Civ Wed 250

H

HEXHAM continued

Best Western Beaumont Hotel

★★★ 80% HOTEL

☎ 01434 602331
Beaumont St NE46 3LT
e-mail:
reservations@beaumonthotel.eclipse.co.uk
dir: A69 towards town centre

In a region steeped in history, this family-run hotel is located in the centre of Hexham, a popular town, overlooking the park and 7th-century abbey. The hotel has two bars, a comfortable reception lounge and a first-floor restaurant. Bedrooms are a mix of traditional and contemporary; the South Wing rooms are spacious with a more contemporary feel and have 37" flat-screen TVs.

Rooms 34 (3 fmly) **Facilities** FTV Wi-fi
Conf Class 60 Board 40 Thtr 100 **Services** Lift
Parking 16 **Notes** ⊗ Closed 25-26 Dec Civ Wed 50

HICKSTEAD	Map 6 TQ22
West Sussex	

The Hickstead Hotel

★★★ 78% COUNTRY HOUSE HOTEL

☎ 01444 248023
Jobs Ln, Bolney RH17 5NZ
e-mail: info.hickstead@classiclodges.co.uk
web: www.classiclodges.co.uk
dir: M23, A23, becomes A2300. Follow Burgess Hill/Hickstead signs. Left at top of slip road. Follow brown hotel sign on left

This hotel is located in seven acres of grounds not far from the main London to Brighton road. The smart bedrooms have satellite TV, free Wi-fi and power showers. Guests can choose to eat in the Oak Tree Bistro or in the Grange Bar. The indoor leisure centre is very popular. The hotel is close to a business park and within easy striking distance of the south coast.

Rooms 52 (5 fmly) (26 GF) **Facilities** STV FTV Wi-fi Xmas New Year **Conf** Class 60 Board 55 Thtr 150 Del from £135 to £150 **Parking** 100 **Notes** ⊗ Civ Wed 80

HIGHAM	Map 16 SK35
Derbyshire	

Santo's Higham Farm Hotel

★★★ 79% ◉ HOTEL

☎ 01773 833812
Main Rd DE55 6EH
e-mail: reception@santoshighamfarm.co.uk
web: www.santoshighamfarm.co.uk
dir: M1 junct 28, A38 towards Derby, then A61 towards Chesterfield. Onto B6013 towards Belper, hotel 300yds on right

With panoramic views across the rolling Amber Valley, this 15th-century crook barn and farmhouse has been expertly restored and extended. There's an Italian wing and an international wing of themed bedrooms and mini suites. Freshly prepared dishes, especially fish, are available in Guiseppe's restaurant. This hotel makes an ideal romantic hideaway.

Rooms 29 (2 fmly) (7 GF) ⚡ **S** £80-£220; **D** £120-£260 (incl. bkfst)* **Facilities** FTV Wi-fi Xmas New Year **Conf** Class 40 Board 34 Thtr 100 Del from £102* **Parking** 100 **Notes** LB ⊗ Civ Wed 100

HIGHBRIDGE	Map 4 ST34
Somerset	

Laburnum House Hotel

★★ 65% HOTEL

☎ 01278 781830
Sloway Ln, West Huntspill TA9 3RJ
e-mail: laburnumhh@aol.com
dir: M5 junct 22. W on A38 approx 5m, right at Crossways Inn. 300yds & left into Sloway Ln, 300yds to hotel

This hotel is in an excellent rural location, set in its own grounds, and offers an impressive range of facilities. Bedrooms (all individual lodge accommodation with their own access) are spacious, and many are suitable for families. The hotel also offers a range of meeting rooms and leisure facilities. Dogs are welcome here.

Rooms 68 **Conf** Class 60 Board 40 Thtr 100

HIGHCLIFFE	Map 5 SZ29
Dorset	

Premier Inn Christchurch/ Highcliffe

BUDGET HOTEL

☎ 0871 527 9276
266 Lymington Rd BH23 5ET
web: www.premierinn.com
dir: From A35 (Christchurch rdbt) onto A337 towards New Milton & Lymington. Approx 2m hotel on left

High quality, budget accommodation ideal for both families and business travellers. Spacious, en suite bedrooms feature tea and coffee making facilities, and Freeview TV in most hotels. Internet access and Wi-fi are available for a small fee. The adjacent family restaurant features a wide and varied menu. See also the Hotel Groups pages.

Rooms 62

HIGH WYCOMBE	Map 5 SU89
Buckinghamshire	

Kings Hotel

★★★ 77% HOTEL

☎ 01494 609090
Oxford Rd HP14 3TA
e-mail: jo@dhillonhotels.co.uk

This historic hotel, once visited by Charles II, is conveniently located just off M40, only half an hour from Heathrow and is near Marlow, Aylesbury and Henley-on-Thames. It offers attractive and modern accommodation with comfortable beds, attractive soft furnishings, free Wi-fi and en suite Italian marble bathrooms. The restaurant, which has been refurbished, serves excellent dishes. The Kings Sports Bar is ideal for an informal drink or for watching major sporting events on the large-screen TV. Guests are made to feel very welcome.

Rooms 43 **S** £89-£139; **D** £99-£149 (incl. bkfst)* **Notes** Civ Wed 120

Holiday Inn High Wycombe

★★★ 75% HOTEL

☎ 0871 942 9042
Handy Cross HP11 1TL
e-mail: reception-highwycombe@ihg.com
web: www.hihighwycombehotel.co.uk
dir: M40 junct 4, take A4010 towards Aylesbury

A modern, purpose-built hotel, convenient for the motorway networks. Bedrooms are spacious and well-equipped for the business traveller and feature a comprehensive range of extra facilities. Public rooms

Save on hotels. Book at **theAA.com/hotel**

HEX – HIN 213 **ENGLAND**

are particularly stylish, while the Academy offers a full range of meeting and conference services.

Rooms 112 (7 fmly) (57 GF) **S** £49-£199; **D** £59-£209 **Facilities** FTV Wi-fi HL **Conf** Class 72 Board 50 Thtr 140 **Services** Air con **Parking** 200 **Notes** LB ⊗ Civ Wed 120

Fox Country Inn

★★★ 67% HOTEL

☎ 0845 643 9933
Ibstone HP14 3XT
e-mail: info@foxcountryinn.co.uk
dir: M40 junct 5 follow signs to Ibstone, hotel 1.5m

This stylish modern hotel enjoys a peaceful rural location on the outskirts of High Wycombe. The modern bedrooms are all attractively presented and have a host of thoughtful little extras. Free Wi-fi is available throughout the hotel. The bar and restaurant have a contemporary open-plan style and food is served throughout the day in the bar and on the terrace.

Rooms 18 (2 fmly) (10 GF) **S** £54-£77; **D** £63-£87* **Facilities** FTV Wi-fi ♫ Xmas New Year **Conf** Class 40 Board 35 Thtr 45 Del from £130 to £150 **Parking** 45 **Notes** LB Civ Wed 200

Premier Inn High Wycombe

BUDGET HOTEL

☎ 0871 527 8522
Thanstead Farm, London Rd, Loudwater HP10 9YL
web: www.premierinn.com
dir: M40 junct 3, A40 towards High Wycombe

High quality, budget accommodation ideal for both families and business travellers. Spacious, en suite bedrooms feature tea and coffee making facilities, and Freeview TV in most hotels. Internet access and Wi-fi are available for a small fee. The adjacent family restaurant features a wide and varied menu. See also the Hotel Groups pages.

Rooms 108

HINCKLEY Map 11 SP49
Leicestershire

Sketchley Grange Hotel

★★★★ 81% ◉◉ HOTEL

☎ 01455 251133
Sketchley Ln, Burbage LE10 3HU
e-mail: info@sketchleygrange.co.uk
web: www.sketchleygrange.co.uk
dir: M69 junct 1, B4109 towards Hinkley. Left at 2nd rdbt. Into Sketchley Ln, 1st right (also Sketchley Ln)

Close to motorway connections, this hotel is peacefully set in its own grounds, and enjoys open

country views. Extensive leisure facilities include a stylish health and leisure spa. Modern meeting facilities, a choice of bars, and two dining options, together with comfortable bedrooms furnished with many extras, make this a special hotel.

Rooms 94 (9 fmly) (6 GF) ♠ **S** £59-£130; **D** £84-£190 **Facilities** Spa STV FTV Wi-fi ⊘ ⊛ Gym Steam room Sauna Xmas New Year **Conf** Class 150 Board 30 Thtr 300 Del from £110 to £165 **Services** Lift **Parking** 270 **Notes** Civ Wed 120

Hinckley Island Hotel

★★★★ 76% HOTEL

☎ 01455 631122
Watling Street (A5) LE10 3JA
e-mail: hinckleyisland@pumahotels.co.uk
web: www.pumahotels.co.uk
dir: On A5, S of junct 1 on M69

A large, constantly improving hotel offering good facilities for both leisure and business guests. Bedrooms are well equipped, with the Club Floors providing high levels of comfort and workspace. A choice of dining styles is available in the Brasserie or Conservatory restaurants and the Triumph Bar is a must for motor cycle enthusiasts. The modern leisure club also offers a range of spa treatments.

Rooms 362 (14 GF) **Facilities** STV Wi-fi ⊛ supervised Gym Steam room **Conf** Class 240 Board 40 Thtr 400 **Services** Lift Air con **Parking** 600 **Notes** ⊗ Civ Wed 350

Premier Inn Hinckley

BUDGET HOTEL

☎ 0871 527 8524
Coventry Rd LE10 0NB
web: www.premierinn.com
dir: M69 junct 1, A5 towards Nuneaton. In 2.5m right at rdbt onto B4666 signed Hinckley Town Centre. Hotel on right (entrance via Total petrol station)

High quality, budget accommodation ideal for both families and business travellers. Spacious, en suite bedrooms feature tea and coffee making facilities, and Freeview TV in most hotels. Internet access and Wi-fi are available for a small fee. The adjacent family restaurant features a wide and varied menu. See also the Hotel Groups pages.

Rooms 53

HINTLESHAM Map 13 TM04
Suffolk

INSPECTORS' CHOICE

Hintlesham Hall Hotel

★★★★ ◉◉ HOTEL

☎ 01473 652334
George St IP8 3NS
e-mail: reservations@hintleshamhall.com
web: www.hintleshamhall.com
dir: 4m W of Ipswich on A1071 to Hadleigh & Sudbury

Hospitality and service are key features at this imposing Grade I listed country-house hotel, situated in 175 acres of grounds and landscaped gardens. Originally a manor house dating from the Elizabethan era, the building was extended in the 17th and 18th centuries. It was a Red Cross hospital in World War II and has been a hotel for nearly forty years. Individually decorated bedrooms offer a high degree of comfort; each one is tastefully furnished and equipped with many thoughtful touches. The spacious public rooms include a series of comfortable lounges, and an elegant restaurant which serves fine classical cuisine based on top-notch ingredients. Wi-fi is available throughout.

Rooms 33 (10 GF) **Facilities** FTV Wi-fi ⊰ ⅃ 18 ⊱ Putt green ⊴ Gym Health & Beauty services Clay pigeon shooting ♫ Xmas New Year **Conf** Class 50 Board 32 Thtr 80 **Parking** 60 **Notes** RS Sat Civ Wed 110

H

H

HINTON CHARTERHOUSE
Somerset   Map 4 ST75

Homewood Park Hotel & Spa
★★★★ 81% ◉◉ HOTEL

☎ 01225 723731
BA2 7TB
e-mail: info@homewoodpark.co.uk
web: www.homewoodpark.co.uk
dir: 6m SE of Bath on A36, left at 2nd sign for
Freshford

This hotel enjoys a delightful location in attractive
parkland, close to Bath and the Longleat estate; it
offers a friendly and very comfortable place to stay.
Bedrooms are stylishly and comfortably appointed,
many with countryside views. The spa and leisure
facilities are notable and cuisine should not be
missed.

Rooms 21 (2 annexe) (3 fmly) (2 GF) **S** £120; **D** £140
(incl. bkfst)* **Facilities** Spa FTV Wi-fi Sauna Steam
room Xmas New Year **Conf** Class 30 Board 25 Thtr 40
Parking 30 **Notes** Civ Wed 50

HITCHIN
Hertfordshire   Map 12 TL12

Redcoats Farmhouse Hotel
★★★ 73% ◉ SMALL HOTEL

☎ 01438 729500
Redcoats Green SG4 7JR
e-mail: sales@redcoats.co.uk
web: www.redcoats.co.uk
dir: A602 to Wymondley. Turn left to Redcoats Green.
At top of hill straight over at junct

This delightful 15th-century property is situated in
four acres of landscaped grounds only a short drive
from the A1(M). Bedrooms in the main house and
courtyard annexe are well appointed and spacious.
Breakfast and dinner are served in the conservatory
which overlooks the garden, and a series of intimate
dining rooms is also available.

Rooms 13 (9 annexe) (1 fmly) (9 GF) 🐾 **S** £75-£155;
D £95-£165 (incl. bkfst)* **Facilities** FTV Wi-fi 😊 New
Year **Conf** Board 15 Thtr 30 Del from £125 to £175*
Parking 50 **Notes** LB Closed BH & Xmas-7 Jan
Civ Wed 75

HOCKLEY HEATH
West Midlands   Map 10 SP17

Nuthurst Grange Country House & Restaurant
★★★ 87% ◉◉ HOTEL

☎ 01564 783972
Nuthurst Grange Ln B94 5NL
e-mail: info@nuthurst-grange.co.uk
web: www.nuthurst-grange.co.uk
dir: Off A3400, 0.5m south of Hockley Heath. Turn at
sign into Nuthurst Grange Lane

A stunning avenue is the approach to this country-
house hotel, set amid several acres of well-tended
gardens and mature grounds with views over rolling
countryside. The spacious bedrooms and bathrooms
offer considerable luxury and comfort, and public
areas include restful lounges, meeting rooms and a
sunny restaurant. The kitchen brigade produces
highly imaginative British and French cuisine,
complemented by very attentive, professional
restaurant service.

Rooms 19 (19 fmly) (2 GF) **Facilities** STV FTV Wi-fi 😊
Conf Class 50 Board 45 Thtr 100 **Parking** 80
Notes ⊗ Civ Wed 100

HOLKHAM
Norfolk   Map 13 TF84

The Victoria at Holkham
★★ 85% ◉◉ SMALL HOTEL

☎ 01328 711008
Park Rd NR23 1RG
e-mail: victoria@holkham.co.uk
web: www.victoriaatholkham.co.uk
dir: A149, 2m W of Wells-next-the-Sea

A Grade II listed property, built from local flint, is
ideally situated on the north Norfolk coast road and
forms part of the Holkham Estate. Decor is very much
influenced by the local landscape: the stylish
bedrooms are individually decorated and tastefully
furnished with pieces specially made for the hotel in
India. The brasserie-style restaurant serves an
interesting choice of dishes.

Rooms 10 (1 annexe) (2 fmly) (1 GF) 🐾 **D** £90-£205
(incl. bkfst)* **Facilities** FTV Fishing Shooting on
Holkham Estate Xmas New Year **Conf** Class 40
Board 30 Thtr 12 **Parking** 30 **Notes** LB ⊗ Civ Wed 70

HOLT
Norfolk   Map 13 TG03

The Lawns Wine Bar
◉ RESTAURANT WITH ROOMS

☎ 01263 713390
26 Station Rd NR25 6BS
e-mail: mail@lawnsatholt.co.uk
dir: A148 (Cromer road). 0.25m from Holt rdbt, turn
left, 400yds along Station Rd

A superb Georgian house situated in the centre of this
delightful north Norfolk market town. The open-plan
public areas include a large wine bar, a conservatory
and a smart restaurant. The spacious bedrooms are
tastefully appointed with co-ordinated soft
furnishings and have many thoughtful touches.

Rooms 10 (2 annexe)

Save on hotels. Book at theAA.com/hotel

HIN – HOR 215 ENGLAND

HONITON
Devon — Map 4 ST10

Monkton Court
◎ ◎ RESTAURANT WITH ROOMS

☎ 01404 42309
Monkton EX14 9QH
e-mail: enquiries@monktoncourthotel.co.uk
dir: 2m E A30 from Honiton

Located on the A30 near Honiton and on the edge of the ancient Blackdown Hills, Monkton Court is a former vicarage steeped in history. There is a range of well-equipped and comfortably furnished bedrooms and bathrooms in addition to a relaxing lounge and spacious restaurant. Dinner should not be missed with a range of skilful and flavoursome dishes showcasing local produce and creativity.

Rooms 7 (1 fmly)

HOOK
Hampshire — Map 5 SU75

Raven Hotel
★★★ 67% HOTEL   OldEnglish

☎ 01256 762541
Station Rd RG27 9HS
e-mail: raven.hook@greeneking.co.uk

This former coaching inn, conveniently located close to Hook railway station and a short distance from the M3, has been tastefully converted into a hotel. Bedrooms are comfortable and well appointed and have free Wi-fi. The popular restaurant offers an inviting menu of freshly prepared dishes plus daily-changing specials. Function rooms are available as is parking.

Rooms 41 (2 fmly) (5 GF) **Facilities** FTV Wi-fi ↳ New Year **Conf** Class 60 Board 70 Thtr 100 Del from £99 to £120 **Parking** 60 **Notes** ⊗ Civ Wed 120

HOPE
Derbyshire — Map 16 SK18

Losehill House Hotel & Spa
★★★★ 78% ◎ ◎ HOTEL

☎ 01433 621219
Lose Hill Ln, Edale Rd S33 6AF
e-mail: info@losehillhouse.co.uk
web: www.losehillhouse.co.uk
dir: A6187 into Hope. Into Edale Rd opposite church. 1m, left & follow signs to hotel

Situated down a quiet leafy lane, this hotel occupies a secluded spot in the Peak District National Park. Bedrooms are comfortable and beautifully appointed. The outdoor hot tub, with stunning views over the valley, is a real indulgence; a heated swimming pool, sauna and spa treatments are also on offer. The views from the Orangery Restaurant are a real delight.

Rooms 24 (3 annexe) (4 fmly) (3 GF) ♠ **S** £145-£175; **D** £190-£265 (incl. bkfst) **Facilities** Spa FTV Wi-fi ☜ Sauna Cross trainer ♫ Xmas New Year **Conf** Class 20 Board 15 Thtr 30 Del from £150 to £165 **Services** Lift **Parking** 25 **Notes** LB ⊗ Civ Wed 100

HOPE COVE
Devon — Map 3 SX63

Lantern Lodge Hotel
★★ 78% HOTEL

☎ 01548 561280
TQ7 3HE
e-mail: lantern.lodge@btinternet.com
web: www.lantern-lodge.co.uk
dir: From Kingsbridge on A381 towards Salcombe turn right. 1st right after passing Hope Cove sign then 1st left along Grand View Rd

This attractive hotel, close to the South Devon coastal path, benefits from a friendly team of loyal staff. Bedrooms are well furnished and some have balconies. An imaginative range of home cooked meals is available. There is a choice of lounges and a pretty garden with putting green. The indoor pool has large doors opening directly on to the garden.

Rooms 14 (1 fmly) (1 GF) ♠ **D** £116-£180 (incl. bkfst & dinner)* **Facilities** FTV Wi-fi ☜ Putt green Running machine Sauna **Parking** 15 **Notes** ⊗ No children 12yrs Closed Dec-Feb

HORLEY

Hotels are listed under Gatwick Airport

HORSHAM
West Sussex — Map 6 TQ13

Premier Inn Horsham
BUDGET HOTEL

☎ 0871 527 8526
57 North St RH12 1RB
web: www.premierinn.com
dir: Opposite railway station, 5m from M23 junct 11

High quality, budget accommodation ideal for both families and business travellers. Spacious, en suite bedrooms feature tea and coffee making facilities, and Freeview TV in most hotels. Internet access and Wi-fi are available for a small fee. The adjacent family restaurant features a wide and varied menu. See also the Hotel Groups pages.

Rooms 40

HORSLEY
Derbyshire — Map 11 SK34

Horsley Lodge Hotel & Golf Club
★★★ 79% HOTEL

☎ 01332 780838
Smalley Mill Rd DE21 5BL
e-mail: reception@horsleylodge.co.uk
web: www.horsleylodge.co.uk
dir: A61 N, A38 signed 'Ripley'. Right at Coxbench. Follow to end, turn right, hotel 1m on left

This family-run hotel is full of character. Situated equidistant from Derby and Nottingham, it is ideal for exploring the Peak District. Bedrooms and bathrooms have stylish decor, beautiful fabrics and quality furnishings. Barn Cottage offers even greater luxury and is tucked away not far from the main building. The Brasserie overlooks the 18-hole golf course.

Rooms 11 (1 annexe) (2 fmly) **S** £90; **D** £140 (incl. bkfst) **Facilities** STV FTV Wi-fi ↳ ♿ 18 Putt green Fishing Golf driving range Xmas New Year **Conf** Class 70 Board 50 Thtr 100 **Parking** 100 **Notes** LB Civ Wed 100

H

H

HOUGHTON-LE-SPRING
Tyne & Wear
Map 19 NZ34

Chilton Country Pub & Hotel

★★ 76% HOTEL

☎ 0191 385 2694
Black Boy Rd, Chilton Moor, Fencehouses DH4 6PY
e-mail: reception@chiltoncountrypub.co.uk
web: www.chiltoncountrypubandhotel.co.uk
dir: A1(M) junct 62, onto A690 towards Sunderland.
Left at Rainton Bridge & Fencehouses sign, right at
rdbt, next rdbt straight over, next left. At next
junct left, hotel on right

This country pub and hotel has been extended from
the original farm cottages. Bedrooms are modern and
comfortable and some rooms are particularly
spacious. This hotel is popular for weddings and
functions; there is also a well stocked bar, and a wide
range of dishes is served in the Orangery and
restaurant.

Chilton Country Pub & Hotel

Rooms 25 (7 fmly) (11 GF) **Facilities** STV Wi-fi 🎵
Xmas **Conf** Class 50 Board 30 Thtr 150 **Parking** 100
Notes ⊗

See advert on this page

HOVE

See Brighton & Hove

HOWTOWN
(NEAR POOLEY BRIDGE)
Cumbria
Map 18 NY41

INSPECTORS' CHOICE

Sharrow Bay Country House Hotel

★★★ ⊛⊛ COUNTRY HOUSE HOTEL

☎ 017684 86301
Sharrow Bay CA10 2LZ
e-mail: info@sharrowbay.co.uk
dir: From Pooley Bridge follow Howtown then hotel
signs

Enjoying breathtaking views and an idyllic location
on the shores of Lake Ullswater, Sharrow Bay is
often described as the first country-house hotel.
Individually styled bedrooms, all with a host of
thoughtful extras, are situated either in the main
house, in delightful buildings in the grounds or at
Bank House - an Elizabethan farmhouse complete
with lounges and breakfast room. Opulently
furnished public areas include a choice of inviting
lounges and two elegant dining rooms.

Rooms 24 (14 annexe) (5 GF) **Facilities** FTV Wi-fi
Xmas New Year **Conf** Class 15 Board 20 Thtr 30
Parking 35 **Notes** ⊗ No children 10yrs Civ Wed 30

HUCKNALL
Nottinghamshire   Map 16 SK54

Premier Inn Nottingham North West (Hucknall)

BUDGET HOTEL

☎ 0871 527 8852
Nottingham Rd NG15 7PY
web: www.premierinn.com
dir: A611, A6002, straight on at 2 rdbts. Hotel 500yds on right

High quality, budget accommodation ideal for both families and business travellers. Spacious, en suite bedrooms feature tea and coffee making facilities, and Freeview TV in most hotels. Internet access and Wi-fi are available for a small fee. The adjacent family restaurant features a wide and varied menu. See also the Hotel Groups pages.

Rooms 35

HUDDERSFIELD
West Yorkshire   Map 16 SE11

Cedar Court Hotel
★★★★ 71% HOTEL

☎ 01422 375431
Ainley Top HD3 3RH
e-mail: sales@cedarcourthotels.co.uk
web: www.cedarcourthotels.co.uk
dir: 500yds from M62 junct 24

Sitting adjacent to the M62, this hotel is an ideal location for business travellers and for those touring the West Yorkshire area. Bedrooms are comfortably appointed; there is a busy lounge with snacks available all day, as well as a modern restaurant and a fully equipped leisure centre. In addition, the hotel has extensive meeting and banqueting facilities.

Rooms 113 (6 fmly) (9 GF) **S** £55-£85; **D** £65-£120 (incl. bkfst)* **Facilities** STV FTV Wi-fi ⌕ ⌖ supervised Gym Steam room Sauna Xmas New Year **Conf** Class 150 Board 100 Thtr 500 Del from £99 to £145* **Services** Lift **Parking** 250 **Notes** LB Civ Wed 400

Bagden Hall
★★★ 76% HOTEL

☎ 01484 865330
Wakefield Rd, Scissett HD8 9LE
e-mail: info@bagdenhallhotel.co.uk
web: www.bagdenhallhotel.co.uk
dir: On A636, between Scissett & Denby Dale

This elegant mansion house with wonderful views over the valley boasts its own 9-hole golf course. Comfortable bedrooms include classical feature rooms in the main house and contemporary rooms in a separate building. Guests can dine in the all-day Mediterranean bistro or the more formal elegant restaurant. The airy, stylish conference suite and beautiful grounds make this a popular wedding destination.

Rooms 36 (3 fmly) (15 GF) **Facilities** STV Wi-fi ⌕ 9 Putt green **Conf** Class 120 Board 50 Thtr 180 **Parking** 96 **Notes** ⊗ RS 25-26 Dec Civ Wed 150

Premier Inn Huddersfield Central

BUDGET HOTEL

☎ 0871 527 8528
St Andrews Way HD1 3AQ
web: www.premierinn.com
dir: Telephone or see website for detailed directions

High quality, budget accommodation ideal for both families and business travellers. Spacious, en suite bedrooms feature tea and coffee making facilities, and Freeview TV in most hotels. Internet access and Wi-fi are available for a small fee. The adjacent family restaurant features a wide and varied menu. See also the Hotel Groups pages.

Rooms 52

Premier Inn Huddersfield West

BUDGET HOTEL

☎ 0871 527 8532
New Hey Rd, Ainley Top HD2 2EA
web: www.premierinn.com
dir: Just off M62 junct 24. From M62 take Brighouse exit from rdbt (A643). 1st left into Grimescar Rd, right into New Hey Rd

Rooms 42

315 Bar and Restaurant
◉ RESTAURANT WITH ROOMS

☎ 01484 602613
315 Wakefield Rd HD8 0LX
e-mail: info@315barandrestaurant.co.uk
dir: M1 junct 38, A637 towards Huddersfield. At rdbt take A642 towards Huddersfield. Establishment on right in Lepton

In a wonderful setting 315 Bar and Restaurant is very well presented and benefits from countryside views from the well-appointed dining room and conservatory areas. The interior is modern with open fires to add character and ambiance, while the chef's table gives a real insight into the working of the kitchen. Bedrooms are well appointed and modern, and most have feature bathrooms. Staff are friendly and attentive, and there are excellent parking facilities.

Rooms 8 (3 fmly)

HUNGERFORD
Berkshire   Map 5 SU36

Littlecote House Hotel   Warner Leisure Hotels
JUST FOR GROWN-UPS
★★★★ 74% ◉ COUNTRY HOUSE HOTEL

☎ 01488 682509
RG17 0SU
e-mail: marie.jones@bourne-leisure.co.uk
dir: M4 junct 14, A338, right onto A4, right onto B4192, left into Littlecote Road, hotel 0.5m on right at top of hill

This hotel provides comfortable, spacious accommodation and is located in stunning grounds close to the Cotswolds and only a 10-minute drive from Hungerford. There are traditional-style bedrooms in the ornate Grade I listed Tudor building and more contemporary rooms in the main building. Facilities include a regular programme of entertainment, beauty treatments and a choice of dining locations in either Oliver's Bistro or Pophams Restaurant. This is an adults-only (over 21 years) hotel.

Rooms 201 (12 annexe) (55 GF) **S** £95-£120; **D** £190-£240 (incl. dinner)* **Facilities** Spa FTV Wi-fi HL ⌖ ⌕ Putt green ⌕ Gym ♫ Xmas New Year **Services** Lift **Parking** 520 **Notes** No children 21yrs Civ Wed 120

H

HUNGERFORD *continued*

The Bear Hotel

★★★ 80% ⊛ HOTEL

☎ 01488 682512
41 Charnham St RG17 OEL
e-mail: info@thebearhotelhungerford.co.uk
web: www.thebearhotelhungerford.co.uk
dir: M4 junct 14, A338 to Hungerford for 3m, left at
T-junct onto A4, hotel on left

Situated five miles south of the M4 this hotel dates
back as far as early 13th century and was once
owned by King Henry VIII. It now has a contemporary
feel throughout. Bedrooms are split between the main
house, the courtyard and Bear Island. The award-
winning restaurant is open for lunch and dinner, and
lighter snacks are available in the bar and lounge.
Guests can enjoy the sun terrace in the summer and
log fires in the winter.

Rooms 39 (26 annexe) (2 fmly) (24 GF) **S** £69-£105;
D £72-£145 **Facilities** FTV Wi-fi Xmas New Year
Conf Class 35 Board 34 Thtr 80 Del from £135 to
£175* **Parking** 68 **Notes** LB Civ Wed 80

Three Swans Hotel

★★★ 68% HOTEL

☎ 01488 682721
117 High St RG17 OLZ
e-mail: info@threeswans.net
web: www.threeswans.net
dir: M4 junct 14 follow signs to Hungerford. Hotel in
High St on left

Centrally located in the bustling market town of
Hungerford this charming former inn, dating back
some 700 years, has been renovated in a fresh and
airy style. Visitors will still see the original arch under
which the horse-drawn carriages once passed. There
is a wood panelled bar, a spacious lounge and
attractive rear garden to relax in. The informal
restaurant is decorated with artwork by local artists.
Bedrooms are well appointed and comfortable.

Rooms 26 (10 annexe) (2 fmly) (5 GF) (3 smoking) ⁅
Facilities FTV Wi-fi Access to local private gym Xmas
New Year **Conf** Class 40 Board 30 Thtr 55 **Parking** 30
Notes LB

HUNSTANTON   Map 12 TF64
Norfolk

Best Western Le Strange Arms Hotel

★★★★ 75% HOTEL

☎ 01485 534411
Golf Course Rd, Old Hunstanton PE36 6JJ
e-mail: reception@lestrangearms.co.uk
web: www.abacushotels.co.uk
dir: Off A149 1m N of Hunstanton. Left at sharp right
bend by pitch & putt course

An impressive hotel with superb views from the wide
lawns down to the sandy beach and across The Wash.
Bedrooms in the main house have period furnishings
whereas the rooms in the wing are more contemporary
in style. Public rooms include a comfortable lounge
bar and a conference and banqueting suite, plus a
choice of dining options - Le Strange Restaurant and
the Ancient Mariner.

Rooms 43 (7 annexe) (2 fmly) ⁅ **S** £60-£120;
D £90-£160 (incl. bkfst)* **Facilities** STV Wi-fi ⌇ Xmas
New Year **Conf** Class 150 Board 50 Thtr 180
Del from £137.90* **Services** Lift **Parking** 80 **Notes** ⊗
Civ Wed 70

Caley Hall Hotel

★★★ 85% ⊛ HOTEL

☎ 01485 533486
Old Hunstanton Rd PE36 6HH
e-mail: mail@caleyhallhotel.co.uk
web: www.caleyhallhotel.co.uk
dir: 1m from Hunstanton, on A149

Situated within easy walking distance of the seafront.
The tastefully decorated bedrooms are in a series of
converted outbuildings; each is smartly furnished and
thoughtfully equipped. Public rooms feature a large
open-plan lounge/bar with plush leather seating, and
a restaurant offering an interesting choice of dishes.

Rooms 39 (20 fmly) (30 GF) ⁅ **S** £50-£70;
D £80-£160 (incl. bkfst)* **Facilities** STV FTV Wi-fi New
Year **Parking** 50 **Notes** Closed 17-28 Dec & 3-16 Jan

The Neptune Restaurant with Rooms

⊛ ⊛ ⊛ RESTAURANT WITH ROOMS

☎ 01485 532122
85 Old Hunstanton Rd, Old Hunstanton PE36 6HZ
e-mail: reservations@theneptune.co.uk
web: www.theneptune.co.uk
dir: On A149, past Hunstanton, 200mtrs on left after
post office

This charming 18th-century coaching inn, now a
restaurant with rooms, is ideally situated for touring
the Norfolk coastline. The smartly appointed
bedrooms are brightly finished with co-ordinated
fabrics and hand-made New England furniture.
Public rooms feature white clapboard walls, polished
dark wood floors, fresh flowers and Lloyd Loom
furniture. The food is very much a draw here with the
carefully prepared, award-winning cuisine utilising
excellent local produce, from oysters and mussels
from Thornham to quinces grown on a neighbouring
farm.

Rooms 6

Save on hotels. Book at theAA.com/hotel

HUN – HYT 219 ENGLAND

HUNTINGDON
Cambridgeshire   Map 12 TL27

Huntingdon Marriott Hotel

Marriott
HOTELS & RESORTS

★★★★ 78% HOTEL

☎ 01480 446000
Kingfisher Way, Hinchingbrooke Business Park PE29 6FL
e-mail: mhrs.cbghd.front.office@marriotthotels.com
web: www.huntingdonmarriott.co.uk
dir: On A14, 1m from Huntington centre near Brampton racecourse

With its excellent road links, this modern, purpose-built hotel is a popular venue for conferences and business meetings, and is convenient for Huntingdon, Cambridge and racing at Brampton and Newmarket. Bedrooms are spacious and offer every modern comfort, including air conditioning. The leisure facilities are also impressive.

Rooms 150 (5 fmly) (45 GF) (2 smoking) **S** fr £69;
Facilities FTV Wi-fi ⤢ ☜ supervised Gym Sauna
Steam room Xmas New Year **Conf** Class 150
Board 100 Thtr 300 Del from £125 to £150*
Services Lift Air con **Parking** 300 **Notes** LB ⊗
Civ Wed 300

The Old Bridge Hotel

★★★ 87% ◉◉ HOTEL

☎ 01480 424300
1 High St PE29 3TQ
e-mail: oldbridge@huntsbridge.co.uk
web: www.huntsbridge.com
dir: From A14 or A1 follow Huntingdon signs. Hotel visible from inner ring road

An imposing 18th-century building situated close to shops and amenities. This charming hotel offers superb accommodation in stylish and individually decorated bedrooms that include many useful extras. Guests can choose from the same menu whether dining in the open-plan terrace, or the more formal restaurant with its bold colour scheme. There is also an excellent business centre.

Rooms 24 (2 fmly) (2 GF) ⤢ **S** £99-£140;
D £150-£230 (incl. bkfst) **Facilities** STV FTV Wi-fi ⤢
Fishing Private mooring for boats Xmas New Year
Conf Class 50 Board 30 Thtr 60 Del £190
Services Air con **Parking** 50 **Notes** LB Civ Wed 100

The George

★★★ 74% HOTEL

OldEnglish

☎ 01480 432444
George St PE29 3AB
e-mail: george.huntingdon@oldenglishinns.co.uk
web: www.oldenglish.co.uk
dir: Exit A14 for Huntingdon racecourse. 3m to junct with ring road. Hotel opposite

This former coaching inn is ideally situated in the centre of town and was once the home of Oliver Cromwell's grandfather. The public rooms include a spacious lounge bar with plush seating and a smart brasserie offering an interesting choice of dishes. Bedrooms are pleasantly decorated and equipped with modern facilities.

Rooms 24 (3 fmly) **Facilities** Wi-fi ♫ Xmas
Conf Class 60 Board 60 Thtr 80 **Parking** 55
Notes Civ Wed 120

Premier Inn Huntingdon (A1/A14)

Premier Inn

BUDGET HOTEL

☎ 0871 527 8540
Great North Rd, Brampton PE28 4NQ
web: www.premierinn.com
dir: At junct of A1 & A14. (NB from N do not use junct 14. Take exit for Huntingdon & Brampton). Access to hotel via Services

High quality, budget accommodation ideal for families and business travellers. Spacious, en suite bedrooms feature tea and coffee making facilities, and Freeview TV in most hotels. Internet access and Wi-fi are available for a small fee. The adjacent family restaurant features a wide and varied menu. See also the Hotel Groups pages.

Rooms 80

HURLEY
Berkshire   Map 5 SU88

Black Boys Inn

◉◉ RESTAURANT WITH ROOMS

☎ 01628 824212
Henley Rd SL6 5NQ
e-mail: info@blackboysinn.co.uk
web: www.blackboysinn.co.uk
dir: 1m W of Hurley on A4130

Just a short drive from Henley, the traditional exterior of this friendly establishment is a contrast to the smart modernity within. Popular with locals, the

restaurant is the stage for Simon Bonwick's imaginative cuisine, and has a buzzing atmosphere. The well-appointed bedrooms are situated in converted barns close by.

Rooms 8 (8 annexe)

HYDE
Greater Manchester   Map 16 SJ99

Premier Inn Manchester (Hyde)

Premier Inn

BUDGET HOTEL

☎ 0871 527 8712
Stockport Rd, Mottram SK14 3AU
web: www.premierinn.com
dir: At end of M67 between A57 & A560

High quality, budget accommodation ideal for both families and business travellers. Spacious, en suite bedrooms feature tea and coffee making facilities, and Freeview TV in most hotels. Internet access and Wi-fi are available for a small fee. The adjacent family restaurant features a wide and varied menu. See also the Hotel Groups pages.

Rooms 83

HYTHE
Kent   Map 7 TR13

Mercure Hythe Imperial

★★★★ 68% HOTEL

Mercure

☎ 01303 267441
Princes Pde CT21 6AE
e-mail: h6862@accor.com
web: www.mercure.com
dir: M20, junct 11 onto A261. In Hythe follow Folkestone signs. Right into Twiss Rd to hotel

This imposing seafront hotel is enhanced by impressive grounds including a 13-hole golf course, tennis court and extensive gardens. Bedrooms are varied in style but all offer modern facilities, and many enjoy stunning sea views. The elegant restaurant, bar and lounges are traditional in style and retain many original features. The leisure club includes a gym, a squash court, an indoor pool, and the spa offers a range of luxury treatments.

Rooms 100 (11 fmly) (6 GF) ⤢ **Facilities** Spa FTV
Wi-fi ⤢ ☜ ⊿ 13 ☺ Putt green Gym Squash Snooker &
pool table Aerobic studio Table tennis Sauna Steam
room ♫ Xmas New Year **Conf** Class 120 Board 80
Thtr 220 **Services** Lift **Parking** 207
Notes Civ Wed 120

HYTHE *continued*

Best Western Stade Court

★★★ 75% HOTEL

☎ 01303 268263

Stade St, West Pde CT21 6DT
e-mail: stadecourt@bestwestern.co.uk
dir: M20 junct 11 follow signs for Hythe town centre. Follow brown tourist sign for hotel

This hotel is situated right on the seafront with many bedrooms having the benefit of uninterrupted views of the English Channel. The comfortable bedrooms are tastefully decorated and provide free Wi-fi and in-room beverage-making facilities. Guests can enjoy traditional English or Indian cuisine in the sea facing restaurant.

Rooms 42 (5 fmly) ☜ **S** £50-£85; **D** £60-£95*
Facilities FTV Wi-fi Fishing ♫ Xmas New Year
Conf Class 20 Board 30 Thtr 40 Del from £110 to £130* **Services** Lift **Parking** 11 **Notes** Civ Wed 60

ILFORD
Greater London

See London plan 1 H5

Holiday Inn Express Newbury Park

BUDGET HOTEL

☎ 020 8709 2200

713 Eastern Av IG2 7RH
web: www.hiexpress.com/londongantshil
dir: On A12 hotel on left between Gants Hill & Newbury Park station

A modern hotel ideal for families and business travellers. Fresh and uncomplicated, the spacious rooms include Sky TV, power shower and tea and coffee-making facilities. Continental buffet breakfast is included in the room rate; other meals may be taken at the nearby family pub or restaurant. See also the Hotel Groups pages.

Rooms 126 **Conf** Class 50 Board 50 Thtr 200

Premier Inn Ilford

BUDGET HOTEL

☎ 0871 527 8542

Redbridge Lane East IG4 5BG
web: www.premierinn.com
dir: At end of M11 follow London East, A12 & Chelmsford signs onto A12, hotel on left at bottom of slip road

High quality, budget accommodation ideal for both families and business travellers. Spacious, en suite bedrooms feature tea and coffee making facilities, and Freeview TV in most hotels. Internet access and Wi-fi are available for a small fee. The adjacent family restaurant features a wide and varied menu. See also the Hotel Groups pages.

Rooms 44

ILFRACOMBE
Devon   Map 3 SS54

Sandy Cove Hotel

★★★ 75% ◉ HOTEL

☎ 01271 882 243

Old Coast Rd, Combe Martin Bay, Berrynarbor EX34 9SR
e-mail: info@sandycove-hotel.co.uk
dir: A339 to Combe Martin, through village towards Ilfracombe for approx 1m. Turn right just over brow of hill marked Sandy Cove

This hotel enjoys a truly spectacular position, with front-facing bedrooms benefiting from uninterrupted views of the north Devon coastline. In addition, guests can relax on the sea decks or in the terraced garden and really appreciate the peace and tranquillity. Locally sourced produce create the menus offered in the dining room, which makes the perfect setting for a romantic dinner or a family gathering.

Rooms 37 (15 fmly) (7 GF) ☜ **S** £45-£105;
D £90-£210 (incl. bkfst & dinner)* **Facilities** Wi-fi ☇ ☒ ⊰ Sauna Steam room Xmas New Year
Conf Class 20 Board 30 Thtr 30 Del from £65 to £95*
Parking 45 **Notes** LB Civ Wed 150

Darnley Hotel

★★ 78% HOTEL

☎ 01271 863955

3 Belmont Rd EX34 8DR
e-mail: darnleyhotel@yahoo.co.uk
web: www.darnleyhotel.co.uk
dir: A361 to Barnstaple & Ilfracombe. Left at Church Hill, 1st left into Belmont Rd. 3rd entrance on left under walled arch

Standing in award-winning, mature gardens, with a wooded path to the High Street and the beach (about a five minute stroll away), this former Victorian gentleman's residence offers friendly, informal service. The individually furnished and decorated bedrooms vary in size. Dinners feature honest home cooking, with 'old fashioned puddings' always proving popular.

Rooms 10 (2 fmly) (2 GF) ☜ **S** £40-£45; **D** £62-£83 (incl. bkfst)* **Facilities** FTV Wi-fi Xmas New Year **Parking** 10 **Notes** No children 3yrs

Imperial Hotel

★★ 69% HOTEL

☎ 01271 862536

Wilder Rd EX34 9AL
e-mail: imperial.ilfracombe@alfatravel.co.uk
web: www.leisureplex.co.uk
dir: Opposite Landmark Theatre

This popular hotel is just a short walk from the shops and harbour, overlooking gardens and the sea. Public areas include the spacious sun lounge, where guests can relax and enjoy the excellent views. Comfortable bedrooms are well equipped, with several having the added bonus of sea views.

Rooms 104 (6 fmly) ☜ **Facilities** FTV ♫ Xmas New Year **Services** Lift **Parking** 10 **Notes** ⊗ Closed Dec-Feb (ex Xmas) RS Mar & Nov

ILKLEY
West Yorkshire Map 19 SE14

Best Western Rombalds Hotel & Restaurant

★★★ 83% ◉ HOTEL

☎ 01943 603201
11 West View, Wells Rd LS29 9JG
e-mail: reception@rombalds.demon.co.uk
web: www.rombalds.co.uk
dir: A65 from Leeds. Left at 3rd main lights, follow Ilkley Moor signs. Right at HSBC Bank onto Wells Rd. Hotel 600yds on left

This elegantly furnished Georgian townhouse is located in a peaceful terrace between the town and the moors. Delightful day rooms include a choice of comfortable lounges and an attractive restaurant that provides a relaxed venue in which to sample the skilfully prepared, imaginative meals. The bedrooms are tastefully furnished, well equipped and include several spacious suites.

Rooms 15 (2 fmly) **S** £57.50-£110; **D** £65-£128 **Facilities** STV FTV Wi-fi ❧ Xmas **Conf** Class 40 Board 25 Thtr 70 **Parking** 28 **Notes** LB Closed 28 Dec-2 Jan Civ Wed 70

The Craiglands Hotel

★★★ 68% HOTEL

☎ 01943 430001 & 886450
Cowpasture Rd LS29 8RQ
e-mail: reservations@craiglands.co.uk
web: www.craiglands.co.uk
dir: A65 into Ilkley. Left at T-junct. Past rail station, fork right into Cowpasture Rd. Hotel opposite school

This grand Victorian hotel is ideally situated close to the town centre. Spacious public areas and a good range of services are ideal for business or leisure. Extensive conference facilities are available along with an elegant restaurant and traditionally styled bar and lounge. Bedrooms, varying in size and style, are comfortably furnished and well equipped.

Rooms 62 (4 fmly) **S** £64-£109; **D** £69-£129* **Facilities** FTV Wi-fi ❧ Xmas New Year **Conf** Class 200 Board 100 Thtr 500 Del from £119.95 to £134.95 **Services** Lift **Parking** 200 **Notes** ⊗ Civ Wed 500

ILSINGTON
Devon Map 3 SX77

Ilsington Country House Hotel

★★★ 86% ◉◉ COUNTRY HOUSE HOTEL

☎ 01364 661452
Ilsington Village TQ13 9RR
e-mail: hotel@ilsington.co.uk
web: www.ilsington.co.uk
dir: M5 onto A38 to Plymouth. Exit at Bovey Tracey. 3rd exit from rdbt to 'Ilsington', then 1st right. Hotel in 5m by Post Office

This friendly, family owned hotel, offers tranquillity and far-reaching views from its elevated position on the southern slopes of Dartmoor. The stylish suites and bedrooms, some on the ground floor, are individually furnished. The restaurant provides a stunning backdrop for the innovative, daily changing menus which feature local fish, meat and game. Additional facilities include an indoor pool and the Blue Tiger Inn, where a pint, a bite to eat and convivial banter can all be enjoyed.

Rooms 25 (4 fmly) (6 GF) **S** £85-£125; **D** £95-£210 (incl. bkfst)* **Facilities** FTV Wi-fi ⊛ supervised ➴ Gym Steam room Sauna Beauty treatments Xmas New Year **Conf** Class 60 Board 40 Thtr 100 Del from £135 to £175 **Services** Lift **Parking** 100 **Notes** LB Civ Wed 120

INSTOW
Devon Map 3 SS43

Commodore Hotel

★★★ 81% HOTEL

☎ 01271 860347
Marine Pde EX39 4JN
e-mail: admin@commodore-instow.co.uk
web: www.commodore-instow.co.uk
dir: M5 junct 27 follow N Devon link road to Bideford. Right before bridge, hotel in 3m

Maintaining its links with the local maritime and rural communities, The Commodore provides an interesting place to stay. Situated at the mouth of the Taw and Torridge rivers and overlooking a sandy beach, it offers well-equipped bedrooms, many with balconies. There are five ground-floor suites. Eating options include the restaurant, the Quarterdeck bar, or the terrace in the warmer months.

Rooms 25 (1 fmly) (5 GF) **Facilities** FTV Wi-fi Xmas New Year **Parking** 200 **Notes** ⊗ No children 3yrs

IPSWICH
Suffolk Map 13 TM14

INSPECTORS' CHOICE

Hintlesham Hall Hotel

★★★★ ◉◉ HOTEL

☎ 01473 652334
George St IP8 3NS
e-mail: reservations@hintleshamhall.com
web: www.hintleshamhall.com

(For full entry see Hintlesham)

INSPECTORS' CHOICE

Salthouse Harbour Hotel

★★★★ ◉◉ TOWN HOUSE HOTEL

☎ 01473 226789
No 1 Neptune Quay IP4 1AX
e-mail: staying@salthouseharbour.co.uk
dir: From A14 junct 56 follow signs for town centre, then Salthouse signs

Situated just a short walk from the town centre, this waterfront warehouse conversion is a clever mix of contemporary styles and original features. The hotel is stylish designed throughout with modern art, sculptures, interesting artefacts and striking colours. The spacious bedrooms provide luxurious comfort; some have feature bathrooms and some have balconies. Two air-conditioned penthouse suites, with stunning views, have extras such as state-of-the-art sound systems and telescopes. Award-winning food is served in the busy, ground-floor brasserie, and alfresco eating is possible in warmer weather.

Rooms 70 (6 fmly) **Facilities** FTV Wi-fi **Services** Lift **Parking** 30

IPSWICH *continued*

milsoms Kesgrave Hall

★★★★ 77% ⑧ HOTEL

☎ 01473 333741
Hall Rd, Kesgrave IP5 2PU
e-mail: reception@kesgravehall.com
web: www.milsomshotels.com
dir: A12 N of Ipswich, left at Ipswich/Woodbridge rdbt
onto A1214. Right after 0.5m into Hall Rd. Hotel
200yds on left

A superb 18th-century, Grade II listed Georgian
mansion set amidst 38 acres of mature grounds.
Appointed in a contemporary style, the large open-
plan public areas include a smart bar, a lounge with
plush sofas, and a restaurant where guests can
watch the chefs in action. Bedrooms are tastefully
appointed and thoughtfully equipped.

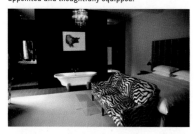

Rooms 23 (8 annexe) (3 fmly) (8 GF) ⁕ **S** £115-£275;
D £125-£275* **Facilities** STV FTV Wi-fi ⌔ ⌣ Xmas
Conf Class 200 Board 24 Thtr 300 Del £198*
Parking 100

Novotel Ipswich Centre

★★★★ 72% HOTEL

☎ 01473 232400
Greyfriars Rd IP1 1UP
e-mail: h0995@accor.com
web: www.novotel.com
dir: From A14 towards Felixstowe. Left onto A137, 2m
into town centre. Hotel on double rdbt by Stoke Bridge

A modern, red brick hotel perfectly placed in the
centre of town close to shops, bars and restaurants.
The open-plan public areas include a Mediterranean-
style restaurant and a bar with a small games area.
The bedrooms are smartly appointed and have many
thoughtful touches; three rooms are suitable for less
mobile guests.

Rooms 101 (8 fmly) ⁕ **S** £60-£145; **D** £60-£145*
Facilities STV Wi-fi ⌔ HL Gym Xmas New Year
Conf Class 75 Board 45 Thtr 180 Del from £120 to
£225* **Services** Lift Air con **Parking** 53 **Notes** LB
Civ Wed 75

Best Western Claydon Country House Hotel

★★★ 83% ⑧ HOTEL

☎ 01473 830382
16-18 Ipswich Rd, Claydon IP6 0AR
e-mail: reception@hotelsipswich.com
dir: From A14, NW of Ipswich. After 4m take Great
Blakenham Rd (B1113) to Claydon, hotel on left

A delightful hotel situated just off the A14, within
easy driving distance of the town centre. The
pleasantly decorated bedrooms are thoughtfully
equipped and one room has a lovely four-poster bed.
An interesting choice of freshly prepared dishes is
available in the smart restaurant, and guests have
the use of a relaxing lounge bar.

Rooms 36 (5 fmly) (13 GF) ⁕ **Facilities** STV Wi-fi ⌔
Xmas New Year **Conf** Class 60 Board 55 Thtr 120
Del from £120 to £145* **Services** Air con **Parking** 85
Notes ⊗ Civ Wed 100

Best Western The Gatehouse Hotel

★★★ 80% ⑧ HOTEL

☎ 01473 741897
799 Old Norwich Rd IP1 6LH
dir: A14 junct 53, A1156 signed Ipswich, left at lights
into Norwich Rd, hotel on left

A Regency-style property set amidst three acres of
landscaped grounds, on the outskirts of town in a
quiet road just a short drive from the A14. The
spacious bedrooms have co-ordinated soft
furnishings and many thoughtful touches. Public
rooms include a smart lounge bar, an intimate
restaurant and a cosy drawing room with plush
leather sofas.

Rooms 15 (4 annexe) (3 fmly) (6 GF) ⁕ **S** £59-£79;
D £69-£99* **Facilities** STV FTV Wi-fi ⌔ Xmas
Parking 25 **Notes** ⊗

Ramada Encore Ipswich

★★★ 78% HOTEL

☎ 01473 694600
Ranelagh Rd IP2 0AD
e-mail: reservations@encoreipswich.co.uk
dir: A14/A1214. Hotel 0.3m from Ipswich rail station

A modern purpose-built hotel situated close to the
railway station and within easy walking distance of
Ipswich Town FC. The contemporary open-plan public
areas feature a smart lounge bar which leads through
to the bright and airy restaurant. The smart bedrooms
are very well equipped and have interactive flat-
screen TVs with internet access. The hotel also has a
small gym.

Rooms 126 (9 fmly) (16 GF) ⁕ **Facilities** Wi-fi HL Gym
Conf Class 16 Board 20 Thtr 35 Del from £105*
Services Lift Air con **Parking** 24 **Notes** ⊗

Save on hotels. Book at **theAA.com/hotel**

IPS – KEI 223 ENGLAND

Holiday Inn Ipswich

★★★ 77% HOTEL

☎ 0871 942 9045
London Rd IP2 0UA
e-mail: reservations-ipswich@ihg.com
web: www.hiipswichhotel.co.uk
dir: From A14 & A12 junct take A1214 to West
Ipswich. Over 1st rdbt. Hotel on left on A1071

A modern, purpose built hotel conveniently situated
just off the A12/A14 junction to the west of the town
centre. Public areas include a popular bar, the
Junction Restaurant and a large open-plan lounge.
Bedrooms come in a variety of styles and are suited to
the needs of both the business and leisure guest
alike.

Rooms 108 (40 fmly) (48 GF) **Facilities** STV FTV Wi-fi
🕸 supervised Gym Sauna **Conf** Class 50 Board 40
Thtr 120 **Services** Lift Air con **Parking** 200 **Notes** ⊗
Civ Wed 80

Premier Inn Ipswich (Chantry Park)

BUDGET HOTEL

☎ 0871 527 8548
Old Hadleigh Rd IP8 3AR
web: www.premierinn.com
dir: From A12/A14 junct take A1214 to Ipswich town
centre. Left at lights by Holiday Inn, left onto A1071.
At mini rdbt turn right. Hotel on right

High quality, budget accommodation ideal for both
families and business travellers. Spacious, en suite
bedrooms feature tea and coffee making facilities,
and Freeview TV in most hotels. Internet access and
Wi-fi are available for a small fee. The adjacent
family restaurant features a wide and varied menu.
See also the Hotel Groups pages.

Rooms 49

Premier Inn Ipswich North

BUDGET HOTEL

☎ 0871 527 8550
Paper Mill Ln, Claydon IP6 0BE
web: www.premierinn.com
dir: A14 junct 52. At rdbt exit onto Paper Mill Lane.
Hotel 1st left

Rooms 59

Premier Inn Ipswich South

BUDGET HOTEL

☎ 0871 527 8552
Bourne Hill, Wherstead IP2 8ND
web: www.premierinn.com
dir: From A14 follow Ipswich Central A137 signs, then
Ipswich Central & Docks signs. At bottom of hill at
rdbt 2nd exit. Hotel on right

Rooms 40

Premier Inn Ipswich South East

BUDGET HOTEL

☎ 0871 527 8554
Augusta Close, Ransomes Euro Park IP3 9SS
web: www.premierinn.com
dir: A14 junct 57, stay in right lane. At rdbt 2nd exit,
then 1st left. Hotel adjacent to Swallow Restaurant

Rooms 20

IREBY
Cumbria   Map 18 NY23

Overwater Hall

★★★ 86% ◉◉ COUNTRY HOUSE HOTEL

☎ 017687 76566
CA7 1HH
e-mail: welcome@overwaterhall.co.uk
dir: From A591 take turn to Ireby at Castle Inn. Hotel
signed after 2m on right

This privately owned country house dates back to
1811 and is set in lovely gardens surrounded by
woodland. The owners have lovingly restored this
Georgian property over the years paying great
attention to the authenticity of the original design;
guests will receive warm hospitality and attentive
service in a relaxed manner. The elegant and well
appointed bedrooms include the more spacious
Superior Rooms and the Garden Room; all bedrooms
have Wi-fi. Creative dishes are served in the
traditional-style dining room.

Rooms 11 (2 fmly) (1 GF) **Facilities** FTV Wi-fi 🐾 Xmas
New Year **Parking** 20 **Notes** Civ Wed 30

KEGWORTH

See East Midlands Airport

KEIGHLEY   Map 19 SE04
West Yorkshire

Dalesgate Hotel

★★ 70% HOTEL

☎ 01535 664930
406 Skipton Rd, Utley BD20 6HP
e-mail: stephen.e.atha@btinternet.com
dir: In town centre follow A629 over rdbt onto B6265.
Right after 0.75m into St. John's Rd. 1st right into
hotel car park

Originally the residence of a local chapel minister,
this modern, well-established hotel provides well-
equipped, comfortable bedrooms. It also boasts a
cosy bar and pleasant restaurant, serving an
imaginative range of dishes. A large car park is
provided to the rear.

Rooms 20 (2 fmly) (3 GF) **Parking** 25 **Notes** RS 22
Dec-4 Jan

K

Premier Inn Bradford North (Bingley)

BUDGET HOTEL

☎ 0871 527 8134
502 Bradford Rd, Sandbeds BD20 5NG
web: www.premierinn.com
dir: M62 juncts 26 or 27 follow A650/Keighley &
Skipton signs. From Bingley Bypass (A650 Cottingley)
right at 1st rdbt signed Crossflatts & Micklethwaite.
Hotel 50yds on left. (NB for Sat Nav use BD20 5NH)

High quality, budget accommodation ideal for both
families and business travellers. Spacious, en suite
bedrooms feature tea and coffee making facilities,
and Freeview TV in most hotels. Internet access and
Wi-fi are available for a small fee. The adjacent
family restaurant features a wide and varied menu.
See also the Hotel Groups pages.

Rooms 40

KENDAL
Cumbria — Map 18 SD59

See also Crooklands

Best Western Castle Green Hotel in Kendal

★★★ 83% ◉◉ HOTEL

☎ 01539 734000
LA9 6RG
e-mail: reception@castlegreen.co.uk
web: www.castlegreen.co.uk
dir: M6 junct 37, A684 towards Kendal. Hotel on right in 5m

This smart, modern hotel enjoys a peaceful location and is conveniently situated for access to both the town centre and the M6. Stylish bedrooms are thoughtfully equipped for both the business and leisure guest. The Greenhouse Restaurant provides imaginative dishes and boasts a theatre kitchen; alternatively Alexander's pub serves food all day. The hotel has a fully equipped business centre and leisure club.

Rooms 99 (3 fmly) (25 GF) ✆ **S** £79-£113; **D** £77-£154 (incl. bkfst)* **Facilities** Spa FTV Wi-fi ⬧ ⊛ Gym Steam room Aerobics Yoga Beauty salon Xmas New Year **Conf** Class 120 Board 100 Thtr 300 Del from £120 to £150* **Services** Lift **Parking** 200 **Notes** LB ⊗ Civ Wed 250

Riverside Hotel Kendal

★★★ 77% HOTEL

☎ 01539 734861
Beezon Rd, Stramongate Bridge LA9 6EL
e-mail: info@riversidekendal.co.uk
web: www.bestlakesbreaks.co.uk
dir: M6 junct 36 Sedburgh, Kendal 7m, left at end of Ann St, 1st right onto Beezon Rd, hotel on left

Centrally located in this market town, and enjoying a peaceful riverside location, this 17th-century former tannery provides a suitable base for both business travellers and tourists. The comfortable bedrooms are well equipped, and open-plan day rooms include the attractive restaurant and bar. Conference facilities are available, and the state-of-the-art leisure club has a heated pool, sauna, steam room, solarium and gym.

Rooms 50 (18 fmly) (10 GF) ✆ **S** £79-£100; **D** £118-£180 (incl. bkfst)* **Facilities** STV Wi-fi ⬧ ⊛ supervised Gym Sauna Steam room Spa bath Xmas New Year **Conf** Class 200 Board 90 Thtr 200 Del from £105 to £165* **Services** Lift **Parking** 60 **Notes** LB Civ Wed 250

Stonecross Manor Hotel

★★★ 75% HOTEL

☎ 01539 733559
Milnthorpe Rd LA9 5HP
e-mail: info@stonecrossmanor.co.uk
web: www.stonecrossmanor.co.uk
dir: M6 junct 36, A590, follow signs to Windermere, take exit for Kendal South. Hotel just past 30mph sign on left

Located on the edge of Kendal, this smart hotel offers a good combination of traditional style and modern facilities. Bedrooms are comfortable, well equipped and some feature four-poster beds. Guests can relax in the lounges or bar and enjoy an extensive choice of home cooked meals in the pleasant restaurant. Facilities also include a swimming pool.

Rooms 30 (4 fmly) **S** £92-£153; **D** £103-£164 (incl. bkfst)* **Facilities** FTV Wi-fi ⬧ HL ⊛ Xmas New Year **Conf** Class 80 Board 40 Thtr 140 Del from £110 to £120* **Services** Lift **Parking** 55 **Notes** Civ Wed 130

Premier Inn Kendal Central

BUDGET HOTEL

☎ 0871 527 8562
Maude St LA9 4QD
web: www.premierinn.com
dir: M6 junct 36, A591 to Kendal. (NB ignore exit for Kendal South). At Plumbgarm Rdbt take 3rd exit, 0.5m to Kendal. Hotel on right

High quality, budget accommodation ideal for both families and business travellers. Spacious, en suite bedrooms feature tea and coffee making facilities, and Freeview TV in most hotels. Internet access and Wi-fi are available for a small fee. The adjacent family restaurant features a wide and varied menu. See also the Hotel Groups pages.

Rooms 55

KENILWORTH
Warwickshire — Map 10 SP27

Chesford Grange

★★★★ 78% HOTEL

☎ 01926 859331
Chesford Bridge CV8 2LD
e-mail: chesfordreservations@qhotels.co.uk
web: www.qhotels.co.uk
dir: 0.5m SE of junct A46/A452. At rdbt turn right signed Leamington Spa, follow signs to hotel

This much-extended hotel set in 17 acres of private grounds is well situated for Birmingham International Airport, the NEC and major routes. Bedrooms range from traditional style to contemporary rooms featuring state-of-the-art technology. Public areas include a leisure club and extensive conference and banqueting facilities.

Rooms 205 (20 fmly) (43 GF) **Facilities** Spa STV Wi-fi ⬧ ⊛ supervised Gym Steam room Solarium Xmas New Year **Conf** Class 350 Board 50 Thtr 710 **Services** Lift **Parking** 650 **Notes** Civ Wed 700

Best Western Peacock Hotel

★★★ 78% HOTEL

☎ 01926 851156 & 864500
149 Warwick Rd CV8 1HY
e-mail: reservations@peacockhotel.com
dir: A46/A452 signed Kenilworth. Hotel 0.25m on right after St John's Church

Conveniently located for the town centre, the Peacock offers a peaceful retreat, and service is delivered in a very professional manner by friendly staff. The accommodation is attractive, and vibrant colour schemes run throughout the pleasant public rooms; there are two dining options: the Malabar Room offering modern European dining, and the Coconut Lagoon serving southern Indian dishes.

Rooms 29 (6 annexe) (5 fmly) (10 GF) **Facilities** FTV Wi-fi Xmas **Conf** Class 24 Board 28 Thtr 60 **Parking** 30 **Notes** ⊗ Civ Wed 70

Save on hotels. Book at **theAA.com/hotel**

KEN – KET 225 ENGLAND

KENTON
Greater London

See London plan 1 C5

Premier Inn London Harrow

BUDGET HOTEL

☎ 0871 527 8664
Kenton Rd HA3 8AT
web: www.premierinn.com
dir: M1 junct 5, follow Harrow & Kenton signs. Hotel between Harrow & Wembley on A4006 opposite Kenton railway station

High quality, budget accommodation ideal for both families and business travellers. Spacious, en suite bedrooms feature tea and coffee making facilities, and Freeview TV in most hotels. Internet access and Wi-fi are available for a small fee. The adjacent family restaurant features a wide and varied menu. See also the Hotel Groups pages.

Rooms 101

KESWICK
Cumbria
Map 18 NY22

Highfield Hotel
★★★ 79% ◉◉ SMALL HOTEL

☎ 017687 72508
The Heads CA12 5ER
e-mail: info@highfieldkeswick.co.uk
web: www.highfieldkeswick.co.uk
dir: M6 junct 40, A66, 2nd exit at rdbt. Left to T-junct, left again. Right at mini-rdbt. Take 4th right

This friendly hotel, close to the centre of town, offers stunning views of Skiddaw, Cats Bells and Derwentwater. Attractively furnished bedrooms, many of them spacious, are thoughtfully equipped. Public areas include a choice of comfortable lounges and an elegant restaurant, where imaginative, modern cuisine is served.

Rooms 18 (1 fmly) (2 GF) 🐾 **S** £95; **D** £170-£220 (incl. bkfst & dinner)* **Facilities** FTV Wi-fi ↘ **Parking** 20 **Notes** LB ⊗ Closed Jan

Dale Head Hall Lakeside Hotel
★★★ 79% ◉ COUNTRY HOUSE HOTEL

☎ 017687 72478
Lake Thirlmere CA12 4TN
e-mail: onthelakeside@daleheadhall.co.uk
web: www.daleheadhall.co.uk
dir: Between Keswick & Grasmere. Exit A591 onto private drive

Set in attractive, tranquil grounds on the shores of Lake Thirlmere, this historic lakeside residence dates from the 16th century. Comfortable and inviting public areas include a choice of lounges and a traditionally furnished restaurant featuring a daily-changing menu. Most bedrooms are spacious and have views of the lake or surrounding mountains.

Rooms 12 (1 fmly) (2 GF) **Facilities** STV Wi-fi ♨ Fishing ↘ Fishing permits Boating Xmas New Year **Conf** Class 20 Board 20 Thtr 20 **Parking** 34 **Notes** ⊗ Closed 3-30 Jan Civ Wed 50

Skiddaw Hotel
LAKE DISTRICT ▄▄▄▄▄ HOTELS
★★★ 78% HOTEL

☎ 017687 72071
Main St CA12 5BN
e-mail: info@skiddawhotel.co.uk
web: www.skiddawhotel.co.uk
dir: A66 to Keswick, follow town centre signs. Hotel in market square

Occupying a central position overlooking the market square, this hotel provides smartly furnished bedrooms that include several family suites and a room with a four-poster bed. In addition to the restaurant, food is served all day in the bar and in the conservatory bar. There is also a quiet residents' lounge and two conference rooms.

Rooms 43 (7 fmly) 🐾 **S** £81-£109; **D** £162-£218 (incl. bkfst)* **Facilities** STV Wi-fi Use of leisure facilities at sister hotels (3m) Xmas New Year **Conf** Class 60 Board 40 Thtr 70 Del from £110* **Services** Lift **Parking** 35 **Notes** Civ Wed 90

Keswick Country House Hotel
★★★ 74% HOTEL

☎ 0844 811 5580
Station Rd CA12 4NQ
e-mail: reservations@choice-hotels.co.uk
web: www.thekeswickhotel.co.uk
dir: M6 junct 40, A66, 1st slip road into Keswick, then follow signs for leisure pool

This impressive Victorian hotel is set amid attractive gardens close to the town centre. Eight superior bedrooms are available in the Station Wing, which is accessed through a conservatory. The attractively appointed main house rooms are modern in style and offer a good range of amenities. Public areas include a well-stocked bar, a spacious and relaxing lounge, and a restaurant serving interesting dinners.

Rooms 74 (6 fmly) (4 GF) **S** £39-£109; **D** £78-£178 (incl. bkfst) **Facilities** Wi-fi Putt green ↘ Xmas New Year **Conf** Class 70 Board 60 Thtr 110 Del from £85 to £160 **Services** Lift **Parking** 70 **Notes** LB ⊗ Civ Wed 100

Swinside Lodge Country House Hotel
★★ 85% ◉◉ COUNTRY HOUSE HOTEL

☎ 017687 72948
Grange Rd, Newlands CA12 5UE
e-mail: info@swinsidelodge-hotel.co.uk
web: www.swinsidelodge-hotel.co.uk
dir: A66, left at Portinscale to Grange, 2m (NB ignore signs to Swinside). Hotel on right

Surrounded by fells, this beautifully maintained Georgian property is situated at the foot of Cat Bells and is only a five-minute stroll from the shores of Derwentwater. Guests are made to feel genuinely welcome with the friendly proprietors on hand to provide attentive service. The elegantly furnished lounges are an ideal place to relax before dinner. The four-course set dinner menu is creative, featuring high quality ingredients and beautifully presented dishes.

Rooms 7 (7 fmly) 🐾 **S** £138-£174; **D** £196-£304 (incl. bkfst & dinner)* **Facilities** Wi-fi **Parking** 12 **Notes** LB ⊗ No children 12yrs Closed 9 Dec-1 Feb

KETTERING
Northamptonshire
Map 11 SP87

Rushton Hall Hotel and Spa
★★★★ 87% ◉◉ COUNTRY HOUSE HOTEL

☎ 01536 713001
NN14 1RR
e-mail: enquiries@rushtonhall.com
web: www.rushtonhall.com
dir: A14 junct 7, A43 to Corby then A6003 to Rushton, turn after bridge

An elegant country house hotel set amidst 30 acres of parkland and surrounded by open countryside. The stylish public rooms include a library, a superb open-plan lounge bar with a magnificent vaulted ceiling and plush sofas, and an oak-panelled dining hall. The tastefully appointed bedrooms have co-ordinated fabrics and many thoughtful touches.

Rooms 45 (5 fmly) (3 GF) 🐾 **S** £150-£350; **D** £150-£350 (incl. bkfst)* **Facilities** Spa FTV Wi-fi ♨ ♨ ↘ Gym Billiard table Sauna Steam room Xmas New Year **Conf** Class 100 Board 40 Thtr 200 Del from £195* **Services** Lift **Parking** 140 **Notes** ⊗ Civ Wed 160

K

KETTERING *continued*

Kettering Park Hotel & Spa

★★★★ 80% ® HOTEL

☎ 01536 416666
Kettering Parkway NN15 6XT
e-mail: kpark@shirehotels.com
web: www.ketteringparkhotel.com
dir: Exit A14 junct 9 (M1 to A1 link road), hotel in Kettering Venture Park

Expect a warm welcome at this stylish hotel situated just off the A14. The spacious, smartly decorated bedrooms are well equipped and meticulously maintained. Guests can choose from classical or contemporary dishes in the restaurant and lighter meals that are served in the bar. The extensive leisure facilities are impressive.

Rooms 119 (29 fmly) (35 GF) **S** £80-£150; **D** £80-£150* **Facilities** STV FTV Wi-fi ⌖ HL ⌕ Gym Steam room Sauna Beauty treatment room Children's splash pool Activity studio New Year **Conf** Class 120 Board 40 Thtr 260 Del from £125 to £175* **Services** Lift Air con **Parking** 200 **Notes** ⊗ Civ Wed 120

Best Western Naseby Hotel

★★★ 73% HOTEL

☎ 01536 734736
Sheep St NN16 0AN
e-mail: reservations@thenasebyhotel.co.uk
dir: A14 junct 8, left at rdbt, follow road to set of lights. At rdbt take middle lane, straight over & left at lights. Hotel on left

Situated in the heart of Kettering, and originally built in the 16th century, this hotel has undergone major refurbishment and now has a sleek modern interior along with some lovely original features. There is a good range of stylish, modern bedrooms. Secure parking is available, as is free Wi-fi.

Rooms 41 (1 fmly) (3 GF) **Facilities** FTV Wi-fi Xmas New Year **Conf** Class 100 Board 80 Thtr 200 **Services** Air con **Parking** 15 **Notes** ⊗

Premier Inn Kettering

BUDGET HOTEL

☎ 0871 527 8564
Rothwell Rd NN16 8XF
web: www.premierinn.com
dir: Off A14 junct 7

High quality, budget accommodation ideal for both families and business travellers. Spacious, en suite bedrooms feature tea and coffee making facilities, and Freeview TV in most hotels. Internet access and Wi-fi are available for a small fee. The adjacent family restaurant features a wide and varied menu. See also the Hotel Groups pages.

Rooms 59

KIDDERMINSTER	Map 10 SO87
Worcestershire	

Stone Manor Hotel

★★★★ 76% ® HOTEL

☎ 01562 777555
Stone DY10 4PJ
e-mail: enquiries@stonemanorhotel.co.uk
web: www.stonemanorhotel.co.uk
dir: 2.5m from Kidderminster on A448, on right

This converted, much extended former manor house stands in 25 acres of impressive grounds and gardens. The well-equipped accommodation includes rooms with four-poster beds and luxuriously appointed annexe bedrooms. Quality furnishing and decor styles throughout the public areas highlight the intrinsic charm of the interior; the hotel is a popular venue for wedding receptions.

Rooms 57 (5 annexe) (7 GF) **Facilities** STV ⌕ ⌖ ⌕ ⌕ Pool table Complimentary use of local leisure centre **Conf** Class 48 Board 60 Thtr 150 **Parking** 400 **Notes** ⊗ Civ Wed 150

The Granary Hotel & Restaurant

★★★ 80% ®® HOTEL

☎ 01562 777535
Heath Ln, Shenstone DY10 4BS
e-mail: info@granary-hotel.co.uk
web: www.granary-hotel.co.uk
dir: On A450 between Stourbridge & Worcester, 1m from Kidderminster

This modern hotel offers spacious, well-equipped accommodation with many rooms enjoying views towards Great Witley and the Amberley Hills. Public areas include a new bar and a residents' lounge. The attractive, modern restaurant serves dishes created

from locally sourced produce, and cooked with flair and imagination. There are also extensive conference facilities, and the hotel is popular as a wedding venue.

Rooms 18 (1 fmly) (18 GF) **Facilities** FTV Wi-fi **Conf** Class 80 Board 70 Thtr 200 Del from £144 to £160* **Parking** 96 **Notes** Civ Wed 120

Gainsborough House Hotel

THE INDEPENDENTS
HOTEL ASSOCIATION

★★★ 78% HOTEL

☎ 01562 820041
Bewdley Hill DY11 6BS
e-mail: reservations@gainsboroughhousehotel.com
web: www.gainsboroughhousehotel.com
dir: Follow A456 to Kidderminster (West Midlands Safari Park), pass hospital, hotel 500yds on left

This listed Georgian hotel provides a wide range of thoughtfully furnished bedrooms that have smart modern bathrooms. The contemporary decor and furnishing throughout the public areas highlights the many retained period features. A large function suite and several meeting rooms are available.

Rooms 42 (16 fmly) (12 GF) **S** £68-£93; **D** £74-£99 (incl. bkfst)* **Facilities** STV FTV Wi-fi Xmas New Year **Conf** Board 60 Thtr 250 Del from £95 to £120* **Services** Air con **Parking** 90 **Notes** ⊗ Civ Wed 250

KINGHAM	Map 10 SP22
Oxfordshire	

The Mill House Hotel & Restaurant

★★★ 77% ® HOTEL

☎ 01608 658188
OX7 6UH
e-mail: stay@millhousehotel.co.uk
web: www.millhousehotel.co.uk
dir: Exit A44 onto B4450. Hotel signed

This Cotswold-stone, former mill house is a stylish and peaceful hotel, set in well-kept grounds bordered by its own trout stream. The individually designed bedrooms are very comfortable and provide thoughtfully equipped facilities; most rooms have lovely views out over the extensive lawned gardens to the Cotswold Hills beyond. There is a peaceful lounge and bar, plus an atmospheric restaurant. The hotel is a popular venue for weddings.

Rooms 23 (2 annexe) (1 fmly) (7 GF) **S** fr £87.50; **D** fr £100 (incl. bkfst) **Facilities** STV FTV Wi-fi ⌖ Fishing ⌕ Xmas New Year **Conf** Class 24 Board 24 Thtr 70 **Parking** 62 **Notes** Civ Wed 100

Save on hotels. Book at **theAA.com/hotel**

KET – KIN 227 ENGLAND

| KING'S LANGLEY | Map 6 TL00 |
Hertfordshire

Premier Inn King's Langley

BUDGET HOTEL

☎ 0871 527 8568
Hempstead Rd WD4 8BR
web: www.premierinn.com
dir: 1m from M25 junct 20 on A4251 after King's Langley

High quality, budget accommodation ideal for both families and business travellers. Spacious, en suite bedrooms feature tea and coffee making facilities, and Freeview TV in most hotels. Internet access and Wi-fi are available for a small fee. The adjacent family restaurant features a wide and varied menu. See also the Hotel Groups pages.

Rooms 60

| KING'S LYNN | Map 12 TF62 |
Norfolk

The Duke's Head Hotel

★★★★ 76% HOTEL

☎ 01553 774996
5-6 Tuesday Market Place PE30 1JS
e-mail: reception@dukesheadhotel.com

Occupying a central location and overlooking the market square, this hotel is a beautiful property, which has now undergone a multi-million pound refurbishment. The bedrooms are smartly decorated, and include wide-screen TVs, free Wi-fi and bathrooms with walk-in showers. Parking is also available.

Rooms 81

Best Western Knights Hill Hotel and Spa

★★★★ 72% HOTEL

☎ 01553 675566
Knights Hill Village, South Wootton PE30 3HQ
e-mail: reception@knightshill.co.uk
web: www.abacushotels.co.uk
dir: At junct A148 & A149

This hotel village complex is set on a 16th-century site on the outskirts of town. The smartly decorated, well-equipped bedrooms are situated in extensions of the original hunting lodge. Public areas have a wealth of historic charm including the Garden Restaurant and the Farmers Arms pub. The hotel also has conference and leisure facilities, including Imagine Spa.

Rooms 79 (12 annexe) (1 fmly) (38 GF) **S** £50-£130; **D** £55-£136* **Facilities** Spa STV Wi-fi ⓣ ⓢ ⤢ Gym Xmas New Year **Conf** Class 150 Board 30 Thtr 200 **Parking** 350 **Notes** LB ⊗ Civ Wed 90

INSPECTORS' CHOICE

Congham Hall Country House Hotel

★★★ ◉◉ COUNTRY HOUSE HOTEL

☎ 01485 600250
Lynn Rd PE32 1AH

(For full entry see Grimston)

Bank House Hotel

★★★ 83% ◉ HOTEL

☎ 01553 660492
King's Staithe Square PE30 1RD
e-mail: info@thebankhouse.co.uk
dir: In King's Lynn Old Town follow quay, through floodgates, hotel on right opposite Custom House

This Grade II listed, 18th-century town house is situated on the quay side in the heart of King's Lynn's historical quarter. Bedrooms are individually decorated and have high quality fabrics and furnishings along with a range of useful facilities. Public rooms include the Counting House coffee shop, a wine bar and brasserie restaurant, as well as a residents' lounge.

Rooms 11 (5 fmly) **S** £80-£110; **D** £100-£140 (incl. bkfst)* **Facilities** FTV Wi-fi ⓠ Xmas New Year **Conf** Class 20 Board 15 Thtr 30 **Notes** LB ⊗

Stuart House Hotel

★★★ 74% HOTEL

☎ 01553 772169
35 Goodwins Rd PE30 5QX
e-mail: reception@stuarthousehotel.co.uk
web: www.stuarthousehotel.co.uk
dir: At A47/A10/A149 rdbt follow signs to town centre. Under Southgate Arch, right into Guanock Terrace, right into Goodwins Rd

Small privately-owned hotel situated in a peaceful residential area just a short walk from the town centre. Bedrooms come in a variety of styles and sizes; all are pleasantly decorated and thoughtfully equipped. There is a choice of eating options with informal dining in the bar and a daily-changing menu in the elegant restaurant.

Rooms 18 (2 fmly) (3 GF) ⓕ **S** £70-£90; **D** £90-£180 (incl. bkfst) **Facilities** FTV Wi-fi ⓠ **Conf** Class 30 Board 20 Thtr 50 Del from £100 to £200 **Parking** 30 **Notes** LB ⊗ RS 25-26 Dec & 1 Jan Civ Wed 60

K

KING'S LYNN *continued*

Grange Hotel

★★ 72% HOTEL

☎ 01553 673777 & 671222
Willow Park, South Wootton Ln PE30 3BP
e-mail: info@thegrangehotelkingslynn.co.uk
dir: A148 towards King's Lynn for 1.5m. At lights left into Wootton Rd, 400yds, on right into South Wootton Ln. Hotel 1st on left

Expect a warm welcome at this Edwardian house which is situated in a quiet residential area in its own grounds. Public rooms include a smart lounge bar and a cosy restaurant. The spacious bedrooms are pleasantly decorated and equipped with many thoughtful touches; some are located in an adjacent wing.

Rooms 9 (4 annexe) (2 fmly) (4 GF) **Facilities** Xmas **Conf** Class 15 Board 12 Thtr 20 **Parking** 15

Premier Inn King's Lynn

BUDGET HOTEL

☎ 0871 527 8570
Clenchwarton Rd, West Lynn PE34 3LJ
web: www.premierinn.com
dir: At junct of A47 & A17

High quality, budget accommodation ideal for both families and business travellers. Spacious, en suite bedrooms feature tea and coffee making facilities, and Freeview TV in most hotels. Internet access and Wi-fi are available for a small fee. The adjacent family restaurant features a wide and varied menu. See also the Hotel Groups pages.

Rooms 61

KINGSTON BAGPUIZE   Map 5 SU49
Oxfordshire

Fallowfields Hotel and Restaurant

★★★ 75% ◉◉ HOTEL

☎ 01865 820416
Faringdon Rd OX13 5BH
e-mail: stay@fallowfields.com
web: www.fallowfields.com
dir: A34 (Oxford Ring Rd) take A420 towards Swindon. At junct with A415 left, 100yds, exit at mini rdbt. Hotel on left after 1m

Located in rural Oxfordshire just ten miles from Oxford city centre, this small family-run hotel offers the personal touch. The bedrooms are generous in size and some have delightful views over the croquet lawn. The grounds are home to several breeds of cattle, pigs and chickens along with the kitchen garden where much of the produce for the menus is sourced.

Rooms 10 (2 fmly) 🐾 **S** £90-£120; **D** £99-£185 (incl. bkfst) **Facilities** FTV Wi-fi 🏌 Falconry Archery Xmas New Year **Conf** Class 25 Board 20 Thtr 60 Del from £160 to £195 **Parking** 50 **Notes** LB Civ Wed 100

KINGSTON UPON HULL   Map 17 TA02
East Riding of Yorkshire

Best Western Willerby Manor Hotel

★★★ 83% ◉ HOTEL

☎ 01482 652616
Well Ln HU10 6ER
e-mail: willerbymanor@bestwestern.co.uk
web: www.willerbymanor.co.uk

(For full entry see Willerby)

Holiday Inn Hull Marina

★★★ 81% HOTEL

☎ 0871 942 9043 & 01482 386300
The Marina, Castle St HU1 2BX
e-mail: reservations-hull@ihg.com
web: www.holidayinn.co.uk
dir: M62 junct 38, A63 to Hull. Follow Marina & Ice Arena signs. Hotel on left adjacent to Ice Arena

Situated overlooking the marina just off the A63. The well-equipped accommodation includes executive rooms. Public areas are attractively designed and include meeting rooms and a leisure club. The Junction Restaurant serves contemporary cuisine, and guests can eat alfresco on the patio if the weather permits.

Rooms 100 (10 fmly) **Facilities** STV Wi-fi 🕊 🔅 supervised Gym New Year **Conf** Class 70 Board 50 Thtr 120 **Services** Lift Air con **Parking** 151 **Notes** ⊗ Civ Wed 120

Mercure Hull Royal Hotel

★★★ 75% HOTEL

☎ 01482 325087
170 Ferensway HU1 3UF
e-mail: reservations@hotels-hull.co.uk
web: www.hotels-hull.com
dir: A63 to city centre. Follow signs to railway station, hotel adjacent

A 'railway hotel' in Victorian times, this impressive building, has been modernised in recent years. The stunning central lounge area is the focal point and there are extensive conference and banqueting facilities, with complimentary parking and Wi-fi access also provided. The contemporary bedrooms have bold colour schemes with good facilities

including flat-screen TVs; many have air conditioning. There is a leisure club adjacent to the hotel.

Rooms 155 (29 fmly) (20 smoking) **Facilities** FTV Wi-fi Xmas New Year **Conf** Class 150 Board 70 Thtr 400 **Services** Lift **Parking** 84 **Notes** Civ Wed 400

Campanile Hull

Campanile

BUDGET HOTEL

☎ 01482 325530
Beverley Rd, Freetown Way (City Centre) HU2 9AN
e-mail: hull@campanile.com
web: www.campanile.com
dir: M62 junct 38, A63 to Hull, pass Humber Bridge on right. Over flyover, follow railway station signs onto A1079. Hotel at bottom of Ferensway

This modern building offers accommodation in smart, well-equipped bedrooms, all with en suite bathrooms. Refreshments may be taken at the informal bistro. See also the Hotel Groups pages.

Rooms 48 (48 annexe) (24 GF) **S** £29-£59; **D** £35-£59* **Conf** Class 15 Board 15 Thtr 25

Ibis Hull

ibis

BUDGET HOTEL

☎ 01482 387500
Osborne St HU1 2NL
e-mail: h3479-gm@accor-hotels.com
web: www.ibishotel.com
dir: M62/A63 straight across at rdbt, follow signs for Princes Quay onto Myton St. Hotel on corner of Osborne St & Ferensway

Modern, budget hotel offering comfortable accommodation in bright and practical bedrooms. Breakfast is self-service and dinner is available in the restaurant. See also the Hotel Groups pages.

Rooms 106 (19 GF)

K

Premier Inn Hull City Centre

BUDGET HOTEL

☎ 0871 527 8534
Tower St HU9 1TQ
web: www.premierinn.com
dir: M62, A63 into Hull city centre. At rdbt left onto A1165 (Great Union St), left into Citadel Way. Hotel at end on right

High quality, budget accommodation ideal for both families and business travellers. Spacious, en suite bedrooms feature tea and coffee making facilities, and Freeview TV in most hotels. Internet access and Wi-fi are available for a small fee. The adjacent family restaurant features a wide and varied menu. See also the Hotel Groups pages.

Rooms 136

Premier Inn Hull North

BUDGET HOTEL

☎ 0871 527 8536
Ashcombe Rd, Kingswood Park HU7 3DD
web: www.premierinn.com
dir: A63 to town centre, take A1079 N for approx 5m. Right at rdbt onto A1033. Hotel at 2nd rdbt in New Kingswood Park

Rooms 42

Premier Inn Hull West

BUDGET HOTEL

☎ 0871 527 8538
Ferriby Rd, Hessle HU13 0JA
web: www.premierinn.com
dir: A63 onto A15 to Humber Bridge (Beverley & Hessle Viewpoint). Hotel at 1st rdbt

Rooms 61

KINGSWINFORD Map 10 SO88
West Midlands

Premier Inn Dudley (Kingswinford)

BUDGET HOTEL

☎ 0871 527 8314
Dudley Rd DY6 8WT
web: www.premierinn.com
dir: A4123 to Dudley, A461 follow signs for Russell's Hall Hospital. On A4101 to Kingswinford, hotel opposite Pensnett Trading Estate

High quality, budget accommodation ideal for both families and business travellers. Spacious, en suite bedrooms feature tea and coffee making facilities, and Freeview TV in most hotels. Internet access and Wi-fi are available for a small fee. The adjacent family restaurant features a wide and varied menu. See also the Hotel Groups pages.

Rooms 45

KINGTON Map 9 SO25
Herefordshire

Burton Hotel

★★★ 78% HOTEL

☎ 01544 230323
Mill St HR5 3BQ
e-mail: info@burtonhotel.co.uk
web: www.burtonhotel.co.uk
dir: At A44 & A411 rdbt junct follow Town Centre signs

Situated in the town centre, this friendly, privately-owned hotel offers spacious, pleasantly proportioned and well-equipped bedrooms. Smartly presented public areas include a lounge bar, leisure facilities including a well equipped gym, spa and swimming pool. Outside there is a small golf putting area layed to astral turf with flood lighting. There is an attractive restaurant where carefully prepared cuisine can be enjoyed, and function and meeting facilities are available in a purpose-built, modern wing. Good spaced parking is to the rear of the hotel.

Rooms 16 (5 fmly) ☞ **S** £56-£80; **D** £96-£130 (incl. bkfst) **Facilities** Spa FTV Wi-fi ⮑ ⊛ supervised Putt green Gym Steam room Therapy rooms Xmas New Year **Conf** Class 100 Board 20 Thtr 150 Del £110 **Services** Lift **Parking** 50 **Notes** LB Civ Wed 120

KIRKBY FLEETHAM Map 19 SE29
North Yorkshire

The Black Horse

◉◉ RESTAURANT WITH ROOMS

☎ 01609 749010 & 749011
Lumley Ln DL7 0SH
e-mail: gm@blackhorsekirkbyfleetham.com
web: www.blackhorsekirkbyfleetham.com
dir: A1 onto A648 towards Northallerton. Left into Ham Hall Ln, through Scruton. At T-junct left into Fleetham Ln. Through Great Fencote to Kirkby Fleetham, into Lumley Ln, inn on left past post office

Set in a small village, the Black Horse provides everything needed for a getaway break including award-winning food. The spacious bedrooms, named after famous racehorses, are beautifully designed in New England/French style with pastel colours, co-ordinating fabrics and excellent beds; many of the superb bathrooms feature slipper or roll-top baths. There is a large dining room and bar that attracts locals as well as visitors from further afield.

Rooms 7 (1 fmly)

KIRKBY LONSDALE Map 18 SD67
Cumbria

The Whoop Hall

★★ 76% HOTEL

☎ 015242 71284
Burrow with Burrow LA6 2HP
e-mail: info@whoophall.co.uk
dir: On A65, 1m SE of Kirkby Lonsdale

This popular inn combines traditional charm with modern facilities, that include a very well-equipped leisure complex. Bedrooms, some with four-poster beds, and some housed in converted barns, are appointed to a smart, stylish standard. A fire warms the bar on chillier days, and an interesting choice of dishes is available in both the bar and galleried restaurant throughout the day and evening.

Rooms 24 (4 fmly) (2 GF) **Facilities** ⊛ supervised Gym ♫ Xmas **Conf** Class 72 Board 56 Thtr 169 **Parking** 100 **Notes** ⊗ Civ Wed 120

K

KIRKBY LONSDALE *continued*

Hipping Hall

◉ ◉ ◉ RESTAURANT WITH ROOMS

☎ 015242 71187
Cowan Bridge LA6 2JJ
e-mail: info@hippinghall.com
dir: M6 junct 36, A65 through Kirkby Lonsdale
towards Skipton. On right after Cowan Bridge

Close to the market town of Kirkby Lonsdale, Hipping
Hall offers spacious, feature bedrooms, designed in
soft shades with sumptuous textures and fabrics; the
bathrooms use natural stone, slate and limestone to
great effect. There are also three spacious cottage
suites that create a real hideaway experience. The
sitting room, with large, comfortable sofas has a
traditional feel. The restaurant is a 15th-century hall
with tapestries and a minstrels' gallery that is as
impressive as it is intimate.

Rooms 9 (3 annexe)

Plato's

RESTAURANT WITH ROOMS

☎ 01524 274180
2 Mill Brow LA6 2AT
e-mail: sally@platoskirkby.co.uk
dir: M6 junct 36, A65 Kirkby Lonsdale, after 5m at
rdbt take 1st exit, onto one-way system

Tucked away in the heart of the popular market town,
Plato's is steeped in history. Sumptuous bedrooms
have a wealth of thoughtful extras, and imaginative
food is available in the elegant restaurant with its
open-plan kitchen. The lounge bar is more rustic in
style with fires to relax by. A warm welcome and
professional service is assured.

Rooms 8

| **KIRKHAM** | Map 18 SD43 |
| Lancashire | |

Premier Inn Blackpool Kirkham M55 Jct 3

BUDGET HOTEL

☎ 0871 527 8104
Fleetwood Rd, Greenhalgh PR4 3HE
web: www.premierinn.com
dir: M6 junct 32, M55 towards Blackpool. Hotel just
off junct 3 towards Kirkham

High quality, budget accommodation ideal for both
families and business travellers. Spacious, en suite
bedrooms feature tea and coffee making facilities,
and Freeview TV in most hotels. Internet access and
Wi-fi are available for a small fee. The adjacent
family restaurant features a wide and varied menu.
See also the Hotel Groups pages.

Rooms 28

| **KNARESBOROUGH** | Map 19 SE35 |
| North Yorkshire | |

General Tarleton Inn

◉ ◉ RESTAURANT WITH ROOMS

☎ 01423 340284
Boroughbridge Rd, Ferrensby HG5 0PZ
e-mail: gti@generaltarleton.co.uk
dir: A1(M) junct 48 at Boroughbridge, take A6055 to
Knaresborough. 4m on right

This beautiful 18th-century coaching inn has been
stylishly renovated. Though the physical aspects are
impressive, the emphasis here is on food with high
quality, skilfully prepared dishes served in the smart
bar/brasserie and in the Orangery. There is also a
richly furnished cocktail lounge with a galleried
private dining room above it. Bedrooms are very
comfortable and business guests are also well
catered for.

Rooms 13

| **KNIPTON** | Map 11 SK83 |
| Leicestershire | |

The Manners Arms

RESTAURANT WITH ROOMS

☎ 01476 879222
Croxton Rd NG32 1RH
e-mail: info@mannersarms.com
web: www.mannersarms.com
dir: From A607 follow signs to Knipton

Part of the Rutland Estate and built as a hunting
lodge for the 6th Duke, the Manners Arms offers

---

thoughtfully furnished bedrooms designed by the
present Duchess. Public areas include the intimate
Beater's Bar and attractive Red Coats Restaurant,
popular for its imaginative menus.

Rooms 10 (1 fmly)

| **KNOWSLEY** | Map 15 SJ49 |
| Merseyside | |

Suites Hotel Knowsley

THE INDEPENDENTS
HOTEL ASSOCIATION

★★★★ 73% HOTEL

☎ 0151 549 2222
Ribblers Ln L34 9HA
e-mail: enquiries@suiteshotelgroup.com
web: www.suiteshotelgroup.com
dir: M57 junct 4. Telephone for detailed directions

Located close to the M57, this hotel is just a
10-minute drive from Liverpool's city centre. It offers
superior, well-equipped accommodation and there is
a choice of lounges plus Handley's Restaurant.
Guests have the use of the impressive leisure centre,
and there are extensive conference facilities.

Rooms 101 (39 fmly) (20 GF) (6 smoking) 🐾
S £69-£94; **D** £69-£104 (incl. bkfst) **Facilities** STV
Wi-fi 🏃 HL 🏊 supervised Gym Xmas New Year
Conf Class 60 Board 50 Thtr 240 Del £96
Services Lift Air con **Parking** 200 **Notes** LB ⊗
Civ Wed 140

Save on hotels. Book at **theAA.com/hotel**

KIR – KNU 231 ENGLAND

KNUTSFORD
Cheshire
Map 15 SJ77

The Mere Golf Resort & Spa
★★★★ 82% ◉ HOTEL

☎ 01565 830155
WA16 6LJ

This hotel sits alongside Mere Lake and is close to the picturesque town of Knutsford; there are excellent transport links with Manchester International Airport being only ten minutes away. The resort's historic main Victorian building conveys the classic charm of that era, and offers stylish, luxury accommodation. The championship golf course designed by James Braid is both beautiful and challenging. The spa features an extensive range of treatments and facilities including a Thermal Zone. The staff are professional and very friendly, offering personal service.

Rooms 81 **S** £100-£180; **D** £100-£180 (incl. bkfst)*
Conf Class 350 Board 40 Thtr 700

Cottons Hotel & Spa
★★★★ 79% ◉ HOTEL

shire
hotels & spas

☎ 01565 650333
Manchester Rd WA16 0SU
e-mail: cottons@shirehotels.com
web: www.cottonshotel.com
dir: On A50, 1m from M6 junct 19

The superb leisure facilities and quiet location are great attractions at this hotel, which is just a short distance from Manchester Airport. Bedrooms are smartly appointed in various styles, and executive rooms have very good working areas. The hotel has spacious lounge areas and an excellent leisure centre.

Rooms 109 (14 fmly) (38 GF) **S** £80-£150;
D £80-£150* **Facilities** Spa STV Wi-fi ⌨ ⟳ ♨ Gym
Steam room Activity studio for exercise classes Sauna
Children's splash pool Xmas New Year
Conf Class 100 Board 36 Thtr 200 Del from £125 to
£175* **Services** Lift Air con **Parking** 180 **Notes** ⊗
Civ Wed 120

Mere Court Hotel & Conference Centre
★★★★ 77% ◉ HOTEL

☎ 01565 831000
Warrington Rd, Mere WA16 0RW
e-mail: sales@merecourt.co.uk
web: www.merecourt.co.uk
dir: A50, 1m W of junct with A556, on right

This is a smart and attractive hotel, set in extensive, well-tended gardens. The elegant and spacious bedrooms are individually styled and offer a host of thoughtful extras. Conference facilities are particularly impressive and there is a large, self contained, conservatory function suite. Dining is available in the fine dining Arboreum Restaurant.

Mere Court Hotel & Conference Centre
Rooms 34 (24 fmly) (12 GF) **S** £85-£145;
D £105-£185 (incl. bkfst) **Facilities** STV Wi-fi Xmas
Conf Class 75 Board 50 Thtr 200 Del from £132 to
£155 **Services** Lift **Parking** 150 **Notes** LB ⊗
Civ Wed 120

See advert on this page

K

KNUTSFORD *continued*

The Longview Hotel & Stuffed Olive Restaurant

★★ 81% HOTEL

☎ 01565 632119
55 Manchester Rd WA16 0LX
e-mail: enquiries@longviewhotel.com
web: www.longviewhotel.com
dir: M6 junct 19 take A556 W towards Chester. Left at lights onto A5033, 1.5m to rdbt then left. Hotel 200yds on right

This friendly Victorian hotel offers high standards of hospitality and service. Attractive public areas include a cellar bar and foyer lounge area. The restaurant has a traditional feel and offers an imaginative selection of dishes. Bedrooms, some located in a superb renovation of nearby houses, are individually styled and offer a good range of thoughtful amenities, including broadband internet access.

Rooms 32 (19 annexe) (1 fmly) (5 GF) **S** £92-£140; **D** £110-£165 (incl. bkfst)* **Facilities** FTV Wi-fi **Conf** Class 20 Board 20 Del from £112 to £185* **Parking** 20 **Notes** RS 21 Dec-6 Jan

Premier Inn Knutsford (Bucklow Hill)

BUDGET HOTEL

☎ 0871 527 8572
Bucklow Hill WA16 6RD
web: www.premierinn.com
dir: M6 junct 19, A556 towards Manchester Airport & Stockport

High quality, budget accommodation ideal for both families and business travellers. Spacious, en suite bedrooms feature tea and coffee making facilities, and Freeview TV in most hotels. Internet access and Wi-fi are available for a small fee. The adjacent family restaurant features a wide and varied menu. See also the Hotel Groups pages.

Rooms 69

Premier Inn Knutsford (Mere)

BUDGET HOTEL

☎ 0871 527 8574
Warrington Rd, Hoo Green, Mere WA16 0PZ
web: www.premierinn.com
dir: M6 junct 19, A556, follow Manchester signs. At 1st lights left onto A50 towards Warrington. Hotel 1m on right

Rooms 28

LACEBY   Map 17 TA20
Lincolnshire

Best Western Oaklands Hall Hotel

★★★ 72% HOTEL

☎ 01472 872248
Barton St DN37 7LF
e-mail: reception@oaklandshallhotel.co.uk
dir: At junct of A46 & A18 at Laceby, on edge of Grimsby

Built in the 19th century and set in five acres of parkland and lawns, the main house still retains a great deal of elegance. The garden restaurant serves traditional English cuisine. Modern, comfortable bedrooms complement the traditional, spacious lounges now used for conferences, meetings and other special occasions.

Rooms 45 (4 fmly) (9 GF) 🐾 **S** £75-£85; **D** £80-£100* **Facilities** FTV Wi-fi Xmas New Year **Conf** Class 150 Board 50 Thtr 180 Del £120* **Parking** 80 **Notes** LB Civ Wed 200

LANCASTER   Map 18 SD46
Lancashire

Lancaster House

English Lakes
Hotels Resorts & Venues

★★★★ 77% HOTEL

☎ 01524 844822
Green Ln, Ellel LA1 4GJ
e-mail: lancasterhouse@englishlakes.co.uk
web: www.elh.co.uk/hotels/lancaster
dir: M6 junct 33 N towards Lancaster. Through Galgate into Green Ln. Hotel before university on right

This modern hotel enjoys a rural setting south of the city and close to the university. The attractive open-plan reception and lounge boast a roaring log fire in colder months. Bedrooms are spacious, and include 19 rooms that are particularly well equipped for business guests. There are leisure facilities with a hot tub and a function suite.

Rooms 99 (29 fmly) (44 GF) 🐾 **S** £74-£118; **D** £88-£176 (incl. bkfst)* **Facilities** Spa STV Wi-fi 🐾 HL 🐾 supervised Gym Beauty salon Xmas New Year **Conf** Class 60 Board 48 Thtr 250 Del from £99 to £145* **Parking** 120 **Notes** LB Civ Wed 140

Holiday Inn Lancaster

Holiday Inn

★★★ 79% HOTEL

☎ 01524 840066 & 0871 942 9047
Waterside Park, Caton Rd LA1 3RA
e-mail: reservations-lancaster@ihg.com
web: www.hilancasterhotel.co.uk
dir: M6 junct 34 towards Lancaster. Hotel 1st on right

Close to the M6 and Lancaster, this modern hotel caters well for business and leisure guests, including families. The ground floor is open plan, with an informal atmosphere in the lounge-bar and Traders restaurant. The Spirit Health Club features a 15-metre pool, sauna, steam room, beauty treatment rooms and a well-equipped gym.

Rooms 156 (72 fmly) (25 GF) (8 smoking) **Facilities** STV Wi-fi 🐾 supervised Gym Fitness classes Xmas New Year **Conf** Class 60 Board 60 Thtr 120 **Services** Lift Air con **Parking** 200 **Notes** Civ Wed 110

Penny Street Bridge

THWAITES
Inns
of Character

★★★ 74% TOWN HOUSE HOTEL

☎ 01524 599900
Penny St LA1 1XT
e-mail: relax@pennystreetbridge.co.uk
dir: In city centre

Ideally situated in the heart of the city, Penny Street Bridge has been transformed from a typical Victorian property to one that is fresh and contemporary, yet retains all the elegance of its original era. Bedrooms are modern and very well equipped. The stylish Bar & Brasserie are popular with both guests and local residents, serving meals and light bites throughout the day.

Rooms 28 (2 fmly) **Facilities** FTV Wi-fi 🐾 **Conf** Board 20 Thtr 20 **Services** Lift Air con **Parking** 4 **Notes** ⊗

Save on hotels. Book at **theAA.com/hotel**

KNU – LAN 233 **ENGLAND**

Royal Kings Arms

★★★ 67% METRO HOTEL

☎ 01524 32451
Market St LA1 1HP
e-mail: reservations.lancaster@ohiml.com
web: www.oxfordhotelsandinns.com
dir: M6 junct 33, A6 to city centre, 1st left, after
Market Hotel. Hotel at lights before Lancaster Castle

A distinctive period building located in the town
centre, close to the castle. Bedrooms are comfortable
and suitable for both business and leisure guests.
Public areas include a small lounge on the ground
floor and The Castle Bar and Brasserie Restaurant on
the first floor. The hotel also has a private car park.

Rooms 55 (14 fmly) **S** £35-£50; **D** £45-£85 (incl.
bkfst)* **Facilities** FTV Wi-fi ⬮ Xmas **Conf** Class 60
Board 40 Thtr 100 **Services** Lift **Parking** 26 **Notes** LB
Civ Wed 100

Premier Inn Lancaster

BUDGET HOTEL

☎ 0871 527 8576
Lancaster Business Park, Caton Rd LA1 3PE
web: www.premierinn.com
dir: M6 junct 34, A683 towards Lancaster. Hotel
0.25m on left at entrance to Business Park

High quality, budget accommodation ideal for both
families and business travellers. Spacious, en suite
bedrooms feature tea and coffee making facilities,
and Freeview TV in most hotels. Internet access and
Wi-fi are available for a small fee. The adjacent
family restaurant features a wide and varied menu.
See also the Hotel Groups pages.

Rooms 85

LAND'S END Map 2 SW32
Cornwall

The Land's End Hotel

★★★ 71% HOTEL

☎ 01736 871844
TR19 7AA
e-mail: reservations@landsendhotel.co.uk
web: www.landsendhotel.co.uk
dir: From Penzance take A30, follow Land's End signs

This famous location provides a memorable setting
for this well-established hotel. Bedrooms, many with
stunning views of the Atlantic, are pleasantly
decorated and comfortable. Public areas provide
plenty of style and comfort with the relaxing lounge
and convivial bar. The restaurant is equally
impressive with accomplished cuisine complementing
the amazing views out to sea.

Rooms 32 (2 fmly) **S** £60-£90; **D** £80-£100 (incl.
bkfst)* **Facilities** FTV Wi-fi Free entry to Land's End
Visitor Centre & Attractions Xmas New Year
Conf Class 100 Board 50 Thtr 200 **Parking** 1000
Notes Civ Wed 110

LANGAR Map 11 SK73
Nottinghamshire

Langar Hall

★★★ 81% ◉◉ HOTEL

☎ 01949 860559
NG13 9HG
e-mail: info@langarhall.co.uk
web: www.langarhall.com
dir: Via Bingham from A52 or Cropwell Bishop from
A46, both signed. Hotel behind church

This delightful hotel enjoys a picturesque rural
location, yet is only a short drive from Nottingham.
Individually styled bedrooms are furnished with fine
period pieces and benefit from some thoughtful
extras. There is a choice of lounges, warmed by real
fires, and a snug little bar. Imaginative food is served
in a dining room and the garden conservatory
provides a lighter menu.

Rooms 12 (1 fmly) (1 GF) **Facilities** FTV Wi-fi Fishing
⬮ Xmas New Year **Conf** Class 16 Board 12 Thtr 16
Parking 20 **Notes** Civ Wed 50

LANGHO Map 18 SD73
Lancashire

INSPECTORS' CHOICE

Northcote

★★★★ ◉◉◉◉ SMALL HOTEL

☎ 01254 240555
Northcote Rd BB6 8BE
e-mail: reception@northcote.com
web: www.northcote.com
dir: M6 junct 31, 9m to Northcote. Follow Clitheroe
(A59) signs, Hotel on left before rdbt

This is a gastronomic haven where guests return to
sample the delights of its famous kitchen. The
outstanding cooking includes Lancashire's finest
fare, and fruit and herbs from the hotel's own
beautifully laid out organic gardens. Drinks can be
enjoyed in the comfortable, elegantly furnished
lounges and bar. Each of the luxury bedrooms has
its own identity with sumptuous fabrics and soft
furnishings, sophisticated lighting and ultra
modern bathrooms; some have a garden patio.

Rooms 14 (2 fmly) (4 GF) ⬮ **S** £195-£245;
D £230-£280 (incl. bkfst)* **Facilities** STV FTV Wi-fi
⬮ **Conf** Class 10 Board 22 Thtr 36 **Parking** 50
Notes LB ⊗ Closed 25 Dec Civ Wed 40

Best Western Mytton Fold Hotel and Golf Complex

★★★ 🅰 HOTEL

☎ 01254 240662 & 245392
Whalley Rd BB6 8AB
e-mail: reception@myttonfold.co.uk
web: www.bw-myttonfoldhotel.co.uk
dir: At large rdbt on A59, follow signs for Whalley, exit
into Whalley Road. Hotel on right

Rooms 43 (12 fmly) (10 GF) ⬮ **S** £64-£76.50;
D £77.50-£113 (incl. bkfst)* **Facilities** STV Wi-fi ⬮ 18
Putt green Xmas **Conf** Class 60 Board 40 Thtr 290
Del from £87 to £99* **Services** Lift **Parking** 300
Notes LB ⊗ Closed 1 Jan Civ Wed 250

L

LASTINGHAM
North Yorkshire   Map 19 SE79

Lastingham Grange Hotel
★★★ 80% HOTEL

☎ 01751 417345 & 417402
Y062 6TH
e-mail: reservations@lastinghamgrange.com
web: www.lastinghamgrange.com
dir: From A170 follow signs for Appleton-le-Moors, continue into Lastingham, pass church on left, right, then left up hill. Hotel on right

A warm welcome and sincere hospitality have been the hallmarks of this hotel for over 50 years. Antique furniture is plentiful, and the lounge and the dining room both look out onto the terrace and sunken rose garden below. There is a large play area for older children and the moorland views are breathtaking.

Rooms 12 (2 fmly) **S** £110-£135; **D** £160-£199 (incl. bkfst)* **Facilities** FTV Wi-fi ⬥ Large adventure playground **Parking** 30 **Notes** LB Closed Dec-Feb

LAUNCESTON
Cornwall   Map 3 SX38

See also Lifton

Eagle House Hotel
★★ 74% SMALL HOTEL

☎ 01566 772036 & 774488
Castle St PL15 8BA
e-mail: eaglehousehotel@aol.com
dir: From Launceston on Holsworthy Rd follow brown hotel signs

Next to the castle, this elegant Georgian house dates back to 1767 and is within walking distance of all the local amenities. Many of the bedrooms have wonderful views over the Cornish countryside. A short carte is served each evening in the restaurant.

Rooms 14 (1 fmly) **Facilities** Wi-fi **Conf** Class 170 Board 170 Thtr 170 **Parking** 80 **Notes** ⊗ Civ Wed 170

LAVENHAM
Suffolk   Map 13 TL94

The Swan
★★★★ 86% ⊛⊛ HOTEL   T|A|HOTEL COLLECTION

☎ 01787 247477
High St C010 9QA
e-mail: info@theswanatlavenham.co.uk
web: www.theswanatlavenham.co.uk
dir: From Bury St Edmunds take A134 (S), then A1141 to Lavenham

A delightful collection of listed buildings dating back to the 14th century, lovingly restored to retain their original charm. Public rooms include comfortable lounge areas, a charming rustic bar, an informal brasserie and a fine-dining restaurant. Bedrooms are tastefully furnished and equipped with many thoughtful touches. The friendly staff are helpful, attentive and offer professional service.

Rooms 45 (7 fmly) (9 GF) ⌁ **S** £105; **D** £195-£350 (incl. bkfst)* **Facilities** FTV Wi-fi ⬥ Xmas New Year **Conf** Class 36 Board 30 Thtr 50 Del from £198* **Parking** 14 **Notes** LB Civ Wed 100

Lavenham Great House 'Restaurant With Rooms'
⊛⊛ RESTAURANT WITH ROOMS

☎ 01787 247431
Market Place C010 9QZ
e-mail: info@greathouse.co.uk
web: www.greathouse.co.uk
dir: Exit A1141 into Market Ln, behind cross on Market Place

The 18th-century frontage on Market Place conceals a 15th-century timber-framed building that is now a restaurant with rooms. The Great House remains a pocket of France offering high-quality rural cuisine served by French staff. The spacious bedrooms are individually decorated and thoughtfully equipped with many useful extras; some rooms have a separate lounge area.

Rooms 5 (1 fmly)

LEA MARSTON
Warwickshire   Map 10 SP29

Lea Marston Hotel & Spa
★★★★ 76% ⊛⊛ HOTEL   CLASSIC BRITISH HOTELS

☎ 01675 470468
Haunch Ln B76 0BY
e-mail: info@leamarstonhotel.co.uk
web: www.leamarstonhotel.co.uk
dir: M42 junct 9, A4097 to Kingsbury. Hotel signed 1.5m on right

Excellent access to the motorway network and a good range of sports facilities make this hotel a popular choice for conferences and leisure breaks. Bedrooms are mostly set around an attractive quadrangle and are generously equipped. Diners can choose between the popular Sportsman's Lounge Bar and the elegant Adderley Restaurant.

Rooms 88 (18 fmly) (49 GF) ⌁ **Facilities** Spa FTV Wi-fi ⊗ ♨ 9 ⬥ Putt green Gym Golf driving range Golf simulator Sauna Steam room Rasul Hydrotherapy bath Xmas New Year **Conf** Class 50 Board 30 Thtr 140 Del from £129 to £170* **Services** Lift **Parking** 200 **Notes** ⊗ Civ Wed 100

INSPECTORS' CHOICE

Mallory Court Hotel

★★★ ◉◉◉ HOTEL

☎ 01926 330214
Harbury Ln, Bishop's Tachbrook CV33 9QB
e-mail: reception@mallory.co.uk
web: www.mallory.co.uk
dir: M40 junct 13 N'bound left, left again towards Bishops Tachbrook, right into Harbury Ln after 0.5m. M40 junct 14 S'bound A452 to Leamington, at 2nd rdbt left into Harbury Ln

With its tranquil rural setting, this elegant Lutyens-style country house is an idyllic retreat. Set in ten acres of landscaped gardens with immaculate lawns and an orchard. Relaxation is easy in the two sumptuous lounges, drawing room or conservatory. Dining is a treat in either the elegant restaurant or the brasserie. Simon Haigh heads up a team of expert chefs producing dishes that continue to delight. Bedrooms in the main house are luxuriously decorated and most have wonderful views. Those in the Knights Suite are more contemporary and have their own access via a smart conference and banqueting facility.

Mallory Court Hotel

Rooms 30 (11 annexe) (2 fmly) (4 GF) **Facilities** FTV Wi-fi 🏊 🏖 Use of nearby club facilities Xmas New Year **Conf** Class 160 Board 50 Thtr 200 **Services** Lift **Parking** 100 **Notes** ⊗ Civ Wed 160

See advert on this page

Angel Hotel

★★★ 77% HOTEL

☎ 01926 881296
143 Regent St CV32 4NZ
e-mail: angelhotel143@hotmail.com
web: www.angelhotelleamington.co.uk
dir: In town centre at junct of Regent St & Holly Walk

This centrally located hotel is divided in two parts - the original inn and a more modern extension. Public rooms include a comfortable foyer lounge area, a smart restaurant and an informal bar. Bedrooms are individual in style, and, whether modern or traditional, all have the expected facilities.

Rooms 48 (3 fmly) (3 GF) **S** £59-£85; **D** £85-£95 (incl. bkfst)* **Facilities** STV FTV Wi-fi **Conf** Class 40 Board 40 Thtr 70 Del from £95 to £150* **Services** Lift **Parking** 38 **Notes** LB ⊗

L

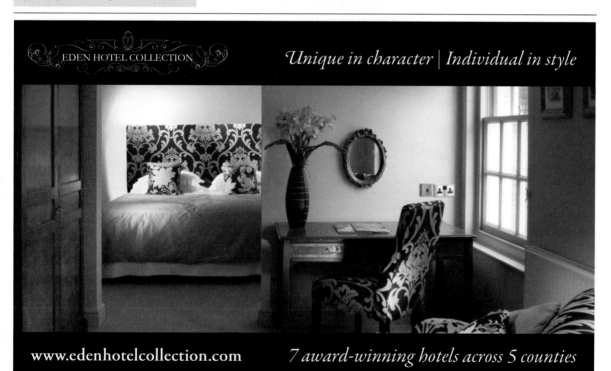

LEAMINGTON SPA (ROYAL) *continued*

Best Western Falstaff Hotel

★★★ 72% HOTEL

☎ 01926 312044

16-20 Warwick New Rd CV32 5JQ
e-mail: sales@falstaffhotel.com
web: www.falstaffhotel.com
dir: M40 junct 13 or 14, follow Leamington Spa signs.
Over 4 rdbts, under bridge. Left into Princes Dr, right
at mini-rdbt

Bedrooms at this hotel come in a variety of sizes and
styles and are well equipped, with many thoughtful
extras. Snacks can be taken in the relaxing lounge
bar, and an interesting selection of English and
continental dishes is offered in the restaurant; 24-
hour room service is also available. Conference and
banqueting facilities are extensive.

Rooms 59 (3 fmly) (16 GF) ✆ **S** £45-£95; **D** £65-£115
(incl. bkfst) **Facilities** FTV Wi-fi ⌨ Arrangement with
local health club Xmas New Year **Conf** Class 30
Board 30 Thtr 70 Del from £95 to £145 **Parking** 40
Notes LB Civ Wed 60

LEDBURY
Herefordshire   Map 10 SO73

Feathers Hotel

★★★ 81% ◉ HOTEL

☎ 01531 635266 & 638950

High St HR8 1DS
e-mail: mary@feathers-ledbury.co.uk
web: www.feathers-ledbury.co.uk
dir: S from Worcester on A449, E from Hereford on
A438, N from Gloucester on A417. Hotel in town centre

A wealth of authentic features can be found at this
historic timber-framed hotel, set in the middle of
town. The comfortably equipped bedrooms are
tastefully decorated; there is also Eve's Cottage, in
the grounds, and also Lanark House, a two-bedroom
apartment that is ideal for families and self catering
use. Well-prepared meals can be taken in Fuggles
Brasserie with its adjoining bar, and breakfast is
served in Quills Restaurant.

Rooms 22 (3 annexe) (2 fmly) ✆ **S** £95-£127.50;
D £140-£245 (incl. bkfst)* **Facilities** STV Wi-fi ⌨
Gym Steam room New Year **Conf** Class 80 Board 40
Thtr 140 **Parking** 30 **Notes** Civ Wed 100

LEEDS
West Yorkshire   Map 19 SE23

See also Gomersal, Shipley & Wakefield

The New Ellington

"bespoke"

★★★★ 85% ◉◉

TOWN HOUSE HOTEL

☎ 0113 204 2150

23-25 York Place LS1 2EY
e-mail: info@thenewellington.com

Near the central railway station and the civic and
business quarters, this new hotel, with an art deco
and a musical theme in part, offers guests modern
requirements and amenities. Bedrooms are air-
conditioned, offer free Wi-fi, high quality bed linen
and Nespresso coffee machines; some have quiet
balconies too. The ground floor atrium Gin Bar lounge
leads to the lower ground floor restaurant that serves
a range of interesting dishes. Limited on-site
chargeable parking is available on a first come first
served basis.

Rooms 34 (3 GF) ✆ **S** £85-£295; **D** £85-£295
Facilities FTV Wi-fi ⌨ **Conf** Class 15 Board 16 Thtr 30
Del from £135 to £195 **Services** Lift Air con **Parking** 7
Notes LB ⊗ Closed 24-27 Dec

Thorpe Park Hotel & Spa

shire
hotels & spas

★★★★ 84% ◉ HOTEL

☎ 0113 264 1000

Century Way, Thorpe Park LS15 8ZB
e-mail: thorpepark@shirehotels.com
web: www.thorpeparkhotel.com
dir: M1 junct 46, follow signs for Thorpe Park

Conveniently close to the M1, this hotel offers
bedrooms that are modern in both style and facilities.
The terrace and courtyard offer all-day casual dining
and refreshments, and the restaurant features a
Mediterranean-themed menu. There is also a state-
of-the-art spa and leisure facility.

Rooms 111 (3 fmly) (25 GF) ✆ **S** £80-£150;
D £80-£150* **Facilities** Spa STV Wi-fi ⌨ HL ⌨ Gym
Activity studio Steam room Sauna New Year
Conf Class 100 Board 50 Thtr 200 Del from £125 to
£175* **Services** Lift Air con **Parking** 200 **Notes** ⊗
Civ Wed 150

De Vere Oulton Hall

★★★★ 83% ◉◉ HOTEL

☎ 0113 282 1000

Rothwell Ln, Oulton LS26 8HN
e-mail: oulton.hall@devere-hotels.com
web: www.devere-hotels.co.uk
dir: 2m from M62 junct 30, follow Rothwell signs,
then 'Oulton 1m' sign. 1st exit at next 2 rdbts. Hotel
on left. Or 1m from M1 junct 44, follow Castleford &
Pontefract sign on A639

Surrounded by the beautiful Yorkshire Dales, yet only
15 minutes from the city centre, this elegant 19th-
century house offers the best of both worlds.
Impressive features include stylish, opulent day
rooms and delightful formal gardens, which have
been restored to their original design. The hotel
boasts a choice of dining options, extensive leisure
facilities and golfers can book preferential tee times
at the adjacent golf club.

Rooms 152 **S** £75-£195; **D** fr £75 (incl. bkfst)*
Facilities Spa STV FTV Wi-fi HL ⌨ ♨ 27 ⛳ Gym
Beauty therapy Aerobics Xmas New Year
Conf Class 150 Board 40 Thtr 350 Del from £130 to
£175 **Services** Lift Air con **Parking** 260 **Notes** LB ⊗
Civ Wed 200

The Queens

QHOTELS

★★★★ 80% HOTEL

☎ 0113 243 1323

City Square LS1 1PJ
e-mail: queensreservations@qhotels.co.uk
web: www.qhotels.co.uk
dir: M621, M1 & M62 follow signs for city centre &
rail station, along Neville St towards City Square.
Under rail bridge, at lights left into slip road in front
of hotel

A legacy from the golden age of railways and located
in the heart of the city, overlooking City Square, this
grand Victorian hotel retains much of its original
splendour. Public rooms include the spacious lounge
bar, a range of conference and function rooms along
with the grand Ballroom. Bedrooms vary in size but
all are very well equipped, and there is a choice of
suites available.

Rooms 215 (16 fmly) ✆ **S** £49-£155; **D** £59-£165*
Facilities STV Wi-fi ⌨ Xmas New Year **Conf** Class 255
Board 80 Thtr 600 Del from £129 to £175*
Services Lift Air con **Parking** 80 **Notes** LB ⊗
Civ Wed 600

Leeds Marriott Hotel

Marriott
HOTELS & RESORTS

★★★★ 74% HOTEL

☎ 0113 236 6366
4 Trevelyan Square, Boar Ln LS1 6ET
e-mail: london.regional.reservations@marriott.com
web: www.leedsmarriott.co.uk
dir: M621, M1 junct 3. Follow signs for city centre on A653. Stay in right lane. Energis building on left, turn right, follow signs to hotel

With a charming courtyard setting in the heart of the city, this modern, elegant hotel provides the perfect base for shopping and sightseeing. Air-conditioned bedrooms are tastefully decorated and offer good workspace. Public areas include a leisure club, an informal bar, lobby lounge area and a choice of restaurants including Georgetown which offers Colonial Malaysian cuisine. Valet parking is available.

Rooms 244 (29 fmly) (10 smoking) **Facilities** STV Wi-fi ♨ HL ⊠ supervised Gym Sauna Steam Room **Conf** Class 144 Board 80 Thtr 300 **Services** Lift Air con **Notes** ⊗ Civ Wed 300

Radisson Blu Hotel Leeds *Radisson* BLU
HOTELS & RESORTS

★★★★ 74% HOTEL

☎ 0113 236 6000
No 1 The Light, The Headrow LS1 8TL
e-mail: sales.leeds@radissonblu.com
web: www.radissonblu.co.uk
dir: Follow city centre 'loop' towards The Headrow/Light Complex. Hotel access on Cockeridge St off The Headrow

Situated in the shopping complex known as 'The Light', the hotel occupies a converted building that was formerly the headquarters of the Leeds Permanent Building Society. Three styles of bedrooms are available but all have air conditioning and excellent business facilities. The lobby bar area serves substantial meals and is ideal for relaxation. Public parking is available, contact the hotel for details.

Rooms 147 (9 smoking) **Facilities** STV FTV Wi-fi ⊠ Gym Access to Esporta Health Club Xmas New Year **Conf** Class 30 Board 28 Thtr 60 **Services** Lift Air con **Notes** ⊗ Civ Wed

Crowne Plaza Hotel Leeds

CROWNE PLAZA
HOTELS & RESORTS

★★★★ 73% HOTEL

☎ 0871 942 9170
Wellington St LS1 4DL
e-mail: sales.cpleeds@ihg.com
web: www.crowneplaza.co.uk
dir: From M1 follow signs to city centre. Left at City Sq into Wellington St

With easy access to the motorway and city centre, this modern hotel is an ideal choice for the business traveller. Bedrooms are of a good size with excellent facilities including air conditioning. There's a good sized pool and large gym - both are well worth a visit.

Rooms 135 (38 fmly) **Facilities** Spa STV Wi-fi ♨ HL ⊠ Gym Xmas New Year **Conf** Class 80 Board 60 Thtr 180 **Services** Lift Air con **Parking** 120 **Notes** ⊗ Civ Wed 180

The Met

P*H* principal hayley

★★★★ 71% HOTEL

☎ 0113 245 0841
King St LS1 2HQ
e-mail: metropole.sales@principal-hotels.com
web: www.principal-hotels.com
dir: From M1, M62 & M621 follow city centre signs. A65 into Wellington St. At 1st traffic island right into King St, hotel on right

Said to be the best example of this type of building in the city, this splendid terracotta-fronted hotel is centrally located and convenient for the railway station. All bedrooms are appointed to suit the business traveller, with hi-speed internet access and a working area. The Restaurant and the Tempest Bar make convenient dining options. There are impressive conference and banqueting facilities. Some parking space is available.

Rooms 120 **Facilities** STV FTV Wi-fi ♨ **Conf** Class 100 Board 80 Thtr 250 **Services** Lift **Parking** 40 **Notes** ⊗ RS 24 Dec-1 Jan Civ Wed 200

Park Plaza Leeds

Park Plaza
Hotels & Resorts

★★★★ 71% HOTEL

☎ 0113 380 4000
Boar Ln LS1 5NS
e-mail: pplinfo@pphe.com
web: www.parkplaza.com
dir: Follow signs for city centre

Chic, stylish, ultra modern, city-centre hotel located just opposite City Square. Chino Latino, located on the first floor, is a fusion Far East and modern Japanese restaurant with a Latino bar. Stylish, air-conditioned bedrooms are spacious and have a range of modern facilities, including high-speed internet connection.

Rooms 187 ✿ **Facilities** STV Wi-fi ♨ Gym Xmas New Year **Conf** Class 70 Board 40 Thtr 160 **Services** Lift Air con **Parking** 6 **Notes** Civ Wed 120

Malmaison Leeds

Malmaison
hotels that dare to be different

★★★ 85% ⊛ HOTEL

☎ 0113 398 1000
1 Swinegate LS1 4AG
e-mail: leeds@malmaison.com
web: www.malmaison.com
dir: M621/M1 junct 3, follow city centre signs. At KPMG building, right into Sovereign Street. Hotel at end on right

Close to the waterfront, this stylish property offers striking bedrooms with CD players and air conditioning. The popular bar and brasserie feature vaulted ceilings, intimate lighting and offer a choice of a full three-course meal or a substantial snack. Service is both willing and friendly. A small fitness centre and impressive meeting rooms complete the package.

Rooms 100 (4 fmly) ✿ **D** £79-£175* **Facilities** STV Wi-fi ♨ Gym Xmas New Year **Conf** Class 30 Board 30 Thtr 80 Del from £160 to £210* **Services** Lift Air con **Notes** LB Civ Wed 70

Best Western Plus Milford Hotel

Best Western PLUS

★★★ 83% HOTEL

☎ 01977 681800
A1 Great North Rd, Peckfield LS25 5LQ
e-mail: enquiries@mlh.co.uk
web: www.mlh.co.uk

(For full entry see Garforth)

L

LEEDS *continued*

Novotel Leeds Centre

★★★ 80% HOTEL

☎ 0113 242 6446
4 Whitehall, Whitehall Quay LS1 4HR
e-mail: H3270@accor.com
web: www.novotel.com
dir: M621 junct 3, follow signs to rail station. Into
Aire St & left at lights

With a minimalist style, this contemporary hotel
provides a quality, value-for-money experience close
to the city centre. Spacious, climate-controlled
bedrooms are provided, whilst public areas offer deep
leather sofas and an eye-catching water feature in
reception. Light snacks are provided in the airy bar,
and the restaurant doubles as a bistro. Staff are
committed to guest care and nothing is too much
trouble.

Rooms 195 (50 fmly) 🐾 **S** £49-£169; **D** £49-£169
Facilities STV FTV Wi-fi HL Gym Steam room Xmas
Conf Class 50 Board 50 Thtr 100 Del from £99 to
£179* **Services** Lift **Parking** 80 **Notes** LB

The Cosmopolitan

★★★ 78% HOTEL

☎ 0113 243 6454
2 Lower Briggate LS1 4AE
e-mail: info@cosmopolitan-hotel-leeds.com
web: www.cosmopolitan-hotel-leeds.com
dir: M621 junct 3. Keep in right lane. Follow until road
splits into 4 lanes. Keep right, right at lights. (ASDA
House on left). Left at lights. Over bridge, left, hotel
opposite. Parking in 150mtrs

This smartly presented, Victorian building is located
on the south side of the city. The well-equipped
bedrooms offer a choice of standard or executive
grades. Staff are friendly and helpful ensuring a
warm and welcoming atmosphere. Discounted
overnight parking is provided in the adjacent 24-hour
car park.

Rooms 89 (5 fmly) (14 smoking) 🐾 **Facilities** STV FTV
Wi-fi ⟐ Xmas New Year **Conf** Class 45 Board 40
Thtr 120 **Services** Lift

Bewleys Hotel Leeds

★★★ 77% HOTEL

☎ 0113 234 2340
City Walk, Sweet St LS11 9AT
e-mail: leeds@bewleyshotels.com
web: www.bewleyshotels.com
dir: M621 junct 3, at 2nd lights left into Sweet St,
right & right again

Located on the edge of the city centre, this hotel has
the added advantage of secure underground parking.
Bedrooms are spacious and comfortable with an
extensive room service menu. Downstairs, the light
and airy bar lounge leads into a brasserie where a
wide selection of popular dishes is offered. High
quality meeting rooms are also available.

Rooms 334 (99 fmly) (27 smoking) **S** fr £50;
D fr £50* **Facilities** Wi-fi New Year **Conf** Class 44
Board 18 Thtr 60 Del from £139* **Services** Lift
Parking 160 **Notes** ⊗ Closed 24-29 Dec Civ Wed

Chevin Country Park Hotel & Spa

★★★ 75% ⊛ HOTEL

☎ 01943 467818
Yorkgate LS21 3NU
e-mail: chevin@crerarhotels.com

(For full entry see Otley)

Holiday Inn Express Leeds City Centre

BUDGET HOTEL

☎ 0113 242 6200
Cavendish St LS3 1LY
e-mail: reservations@expressleeds.co.uk
web: www.hiexpress.com/leedscityctr
dir: M621 junct 2, A643 to city centre. At large rdbt
3rd exit signed A58(M). 1st left onto A65. Right after
pedestrian crossing & right again

A modern hotel ideal for families and business
travellers. Fresh and uncomplicated, the spacious
rooms include Sky TV, power shower and tea and
coffee-making facilities. Continental buffet breakfast
is included in the room rate; other meals may be
taken at the nearby family pub or restaurant. See also
the Hotel Groups pages.

Rooms 112 (44 fmly) **Conf** Class 15 Board 20 Thtr 35

Holiday Inn Express Leeds City Centre Armouries

BUDGET HOTEL

☎ 0113 380 4400
Armouries Dr LS10 1LT
e-mail: leeds@holidayinnexpress.org.uk
web: www.hiexpress.com/leeds
dir: M1 junct 43, follow brown Royal Armouries signs,
M621 junct 4 follow Leeds City Centre signs to A61

Rooms 130 (72 fmly) (19 smoking) **D** £40-£139 (incl.
bkfst) **Conf** Class 18 Board 20 Thtr 30

Holiday Inn Express Leeds - East

BUDGET HOTEL

☎ 0845 112 6039 & 0113 288 0574
Aberford Rd, Oulton LS26 8EJ
e-mail: reservations@hiexpressleedseast.co.uk
web: www.hiexpressleedseast.co.uk
dir: M62 junct 29, E towards Pontefract. Exit at
junct 30, A642 signed Rothwell. Hotel opposite at 1st
rdbt

Rooms 77 (50 fmly) (32 GF) 🐾 **S** £39-£69; **D** £39-£69
(incl. bkfst)* **Conf** Class 20 Board 20 Thtr 25

Ibis Leeds Centre

BUDGET HOTEL

☎ 0113 220 4100
Marlborough St LS1 4PB
e-mail: H3652@accor.com
web: www.ibishotel.com
dir: M1 junct 43 or M62 junct 2 take A643 & follow
city centre signs. Left on slip road opposite Yorkshire
Post. Hotel opposite

Modern, budget hotel offering comfortable
accommodation in bright and practical bedrooms.
Breakfast is self-service and dinner is available in
the restaurant See also the Hotel Groups pages.

Rooms 168 (14 fmly) 🐾 **S** £51-£85; **D** £51-£85*

Premier Inn Leeds/ Bradford Airport

BUDGET HOTEL

☎ 0871 527 8578
Victoria Av, Yeadon LS19 7AW
web: www.premierinn.com
dir: On A658, near Leeds/Bradford Airport

High quality, budget accommodation ideal for both families and business travellers. Spacious, en suite bedrooms feature tea and coffee making facilities, and Freeview TV in most hotels. Internet access and Wi-fi are available for a small fee. The adjacent family restaurant features a wide and varied menu. See also the Hotel Groups pages.

Rooms 60

Premier Inn Leeds/Bradford (South)

BUDGET HOTEL

☎ 0871 527 8580
Wakefield Rd, Drighlington BD11 1EA
web: www.premierinn.com
dir: On Drighlington bypass, adjacent to M62 junct 27. Take A650, right to Drighlington, right, hotel on left

Rooms 42

Premier Inn Leeds City Centre

BUDGET HOTEL

☎ 0871 527 8582
Citygate, Wellington St LS3 1LW
web: www.premierinn.com
dir: At A65 & A58 junct

Rooms 140

Premier Inn Leeds City West

BUDGET HOTEL

☎ 0871 527 8584
City West One Office Park, Gelderd Rd LS12 6LX
web: www.premierinn.com
dir: M621 junct 1 take ring road towards Leeds. At 1st lights right into Gelderd Rd, right at rdbt

Rooms 126

Premier Inn Leeds East

BUDGET HOTEL

☎ 0871 527 8586
Selby Rd, Whitkirk LS15 7AY
web: www.premierinn.com
dir: M1 junct 46 towards Leeds. At 2nd rdbt follow Temple Newsam signs. Hotel 500mtrs on right

Rooms 87

LEEK   Map 16 SJ95
Staffordshire

Three Horseshoes Inn & Country Hotel

★★★ 79% ◉◉ HOTEL

☎ 01538 300296
Buxton Rd, Blackshaw Moor ST13 8TW
e-mail: enquires@threeshoesinn.co.uk
web: www.threeshoesinn.co.uk
dir: 2m N of Leek on A53

This traditional, family-owned hostelry provides stylish, individually designed, modern bedrooms, including several four-poster rooms. The smart brasserie, with an open kitchen and countryside views, offers modern English and Thai dishes, and there is also a pub and carvery; the award-winning gardens and grounds are ideal for alfresco dining. The staff are attentive and friendly.

Rooms 26 (2 fmly) (10 GF) **Facilities** FTV **Conf** Class 50 Board 25 Thtr 60 **Services** Lift **Parking** 80 **Notes** ⊗ Closed 24 Dec-1 Jan Civ Wed 120

LEICESTER   Map 11 SK50
Leicestershire

See also Rothley

Leicester Marriott

★★★★ 79% HOTEL

☎ 0116 282 0100
Smith Way, Grove Park, Enderby LE19 1SW
e-mail: mhrs.emalm.frontoffice@marriotthotels.com
web: www.leicestermarriott.co.uk
dir: M1 junct 21/A563 signed Leicester. At rdbt take 1st left onto A563. Into right lane, at 2nd slip road turn right. At rdbt take last exit, hotel straight ahead

This purpose-built hotel offers stylish bedrooms, some of which are executive rooms with access to the executive lounge. There is a popular brasserie, cocktail bar, atrium lounge, indoor heated pool, gym, sauna and steam room. 18 meeting rooms provide conference facilities for up to 500 delegates and parking is extensive.

Rooms 227 (91 fmly) ⚑ **Facilities** STV Wi-fi ⊰ ⊛ supervised Gym **Conf** Class 180 Board 52 Thtr 500 **Services** Lift Air con **Parking** 280 **Notes** ⊗ Civ Wed 300

Hotel Maiyango

★★★★ 73% ◉ SMALL HOTEL

☎ 0116 251 8898
13-21 St Nicholas Place LE1 4LD
e-mail: reservations@maiyango.com
dir: B4114 (Narborough Rd) to city centre, right onto A47 (Hinkley Rd), keep right into St Nicholas Place

A boutique hotel offering a warm welcome and professional service. Access to the public areas is via a discreet foyer adjacent to a Middle Eastern themed restaurant (under the same ownership), where imaginative food is sure to be a memorable experience. Spacious bedrooms, decorated in minimalist style are enhanced by quality modern art, fine furnishings and superb bathrooms. Parking is available close by.

Rooms 14 **Facilities** FTV Wi-fi ⊰ ♫ Xmas New Year **Conf** Class 50 Board 30 Thtr 70 **Services** Lift Air con **Notes** ⊗

L

LEICESTER *continued*

Belmont Hotel

★★★ 81% HOTEL

☎ 0116 254 4773
De Montfort St LE1 7GR
e-mail: info@belmonthotel.co.uk
web: www.belmonthotel.co.uk
dir: From A6 take 1st right after rail station. Hotel
200yds on left

This well established hotel, under the same family
ownership, has been welcoming guests for over 70
years. It is conveniently situated within easy walking
distance of the railway station and city centre though
it sits in a quiet leafy residential area. Extensive
public rooms are smartly appointed and include the
informal Bowie's Bistro, Jamie's Bar with its relaxed
atmosphere, and the more formal Cherry Restaurant.

Rooms 75 (7 fmly) (9 GF) (2 smoking) **Facilities** FTV
Wi-fi ♫ Gym **Conf** Class 75 Board 65 Thtr 175
Services Lift **Parking** 70 **Notes** Closed 25-26 Dec
Civ Wed 150

Holiday Inn Leicester

★★★ 79% HOTEL

☎ 0871 942 9048
St Nicholas Circle LE1 5LX
web: www.holidayinn.co.uk
dir: From S: M1 junct 21, A5460 towards city centre.
Approx 3m follow Castle Gardens signs. Hotel at next
rdbt. From N: M1 junct 22, A50 to city centre. Into
Vaughan Way follow signs for A47 (avoid underpass).
Hotel at rdbt

This purpose-built city centre hotel offers impressive
accommodation suitable for both business and
leisure guests. The smartly appointed bar and
restaurant are open throughout the day and there is a
well-equipped leisure club. Overnight guests are
offered free parking at the adjacent multi-storey car
park.

Rooms 188 **S** £65-£225; **D** £75-£225* **Facilities** FTV
Wi-fi HL ♫ supervised Gym **Conf** Class 140 Board 90
Thtr 260 Del from £119 to £175* **Services** Lift Air con
Notes LB Civ Wed 200

Campanile Leicester

BUDGET HOTEL

☎ 0116 261 6600
St Matthew's Way, 1 Bedford Street North LE1 3JE
e-mail: leicester@campanile.com
web: www.campanile.com
dir: A5460. Right at end of road, left at rdbt on A594.
Follow Vaughan Way, Burleys Way then St. Matthew's
Way. Hotel on left

This modern building offers accommodation in smart,
well-equipped bedrooms, all with en suite bathrooms.
Refreshments may be taken at the informal bistro.
See also the Hotel Groups pages.

Rooms 93 **Conf** Class 30 Board 30 Thtr 40

Holiday Inn Express - Walkers Stadium

BUDGET HOTEL

☎ 0116 249 4590
Filbert Way, Raw Dykes Rd LE2 7FQ
e-mail: info@exhileicester.co.uk
web: www.hiexpress.com/leicesterwalke
dir: From A5460 follow signs to Walkers Stadium

A modern hotel ideal for families and business
travellers. Fresh and uncomplicated, the spacious
rooms include Sky TV, power shower and tea and
coffee-making facilities. Continental buffet breakfast
is included in the room rate; other meals may be
taken at the nearby family pub or restaurant. See also
the Hotel Groups pages.

Rooms 110 (56 fmly) (12 smoking) ♟ **S** £39-£119;
D £39-£119 (incl. bkfst) **Conf** Class 100 Board 60
Thtr 160

Ibis Leicester

BUDGET HOTEL

☎ 0116 248 7200
St Georges Way, Constitution Hill LE1 1PL
e-mail: H3061@accor.com
web: www.ibishotel.com
dir: From M1/M69 junct 21, follow town centre signs,
central ring road (A594)/railway station, hotel
opposite Leicester Mercury

Modern, budget hotel offering comfortable
accommodation in bright and practical bedrooms.
Breakfast is self-service and dinner is available in
the restaurant. See also the Hotel Groups pages.

Rooms 94 (15 fmly) **S** £39-£65; **D** £39-£65*

Premier Inn Leicester (Braunstone)

BUDGET HOTEL

☎ 0871 527 8590
**Meridian Business Park, Thorpe Astley, Braunstone
LE19 1LU**
web: www.premierinn.com
dir: M1 junct 21, follow A563 (outer ring road) signs
W to Thorpe Astley. At slip road after Texaco garage.
Hotel on left

High quality, budget accommodation ideal for both
families and business travellers. Spacious, en suite
bedrooms feature tea and coffee making facilities,
and Freeview TV in most hotels. Internet access and
Wi-fi are available for a small fee. The adjacent
family restaurant features a wide and varied menu.
See also the Hotel Groups pages.

Rooms 51

Premier Inn Leicester (Braunstone South)

BUDGET HOTEL

☎ 0871 527 8588
Braunstone Lane East LE3 2FW
web: www.premierinn.com
dir: M1 junct 21, at M69 junct take A5460 towards
city. After 1m right at lights to hotel

Rooms 170

Premier Inn Leicester Central (A50)

BUDGET HOTEL

☎ 0871 527 8594
Heathley Park, Groby Rd LE3 9QE
web: www.premierinn.com
dir: Off A50, city centre side of County Hall &
Glenfield General Hospital

Rooms 76

Premier Inn Leicester City Centre

BUDGET HOTEL

☎ 0871 527 8596
1 St Georges Way LE1 1AA
web: www.premierinn.com
dir: Telephone for detailed directions

Rooms 135

Premier Inn Leicester (Forest East)

BUDGET HOTEL

☎ 0871 527 8592
Hinckley Rd, Leicester Forest East LE3 3GD
web: www.premierinn.com
dir: M1 junct 21, A5460. At major junct (Holiday Inn on right), left into Braunstone Lane. In 2m left onto A47 towards Hinkley. Hotel 400yds on left

Rooms 40

Premier Inn Leicester North West

BUDGET HOTEL

☎ 0871 527 8598
Leicester Rd, Glenfield LE3 8HB
web: www.premierinn.com
dir: M1 junct 21a N'bound, A46. Onto A50 for Glenfield & County Hall. Or M1 junct 22 S'bound onto A50 towards Glenfield. Into County Hall. Hotel on left adjacent to Gynsills

Rooms 43

Premier Inn Leicester South (Oadby)

BUDGET HOTEL

☎ 0871 527 8600
Glen Rise, Oadby LE2 4RG
web: www.premierinn.com
dir: M1 junct 21, A563 signed South. Right at Leicester racecourse. Follow Market Harborough signs. Dual carriageway, straight on at rdbt. Into single lane, hotel on right

Rooms 30

Days Inn Leicester Forest East - M1

BUDGET HOTEL

☎ 0116 239 0534
Leicester Forest East, M1 Junct 21 LE3 3GB
e-mail: leicester.hotel@welcomebreak.co.uk
web: www.welcomebreak.co.uk
dir: On M1 N'bound between junct 21 & 21A

This modern building offers accommodation in smart, spacious and well-equipped bedrooms, suitable for families and business travellers, and all with en suite bathrooms. Continental breakfast is available, and other refreshments may be taken at the nearby family restaurant. See also the Hotel Groups pages.

Rooms 92 (71 fmly) (10 smoking) Conf Board 10

Park Inn by Radisson Leigh

★★★ 75% HOTEL

☎ 01942 366334 & 687111
Altherleigh Way WN7 4JZ
e-mail: info.leigh@rezidorparkinn.com
dir: M6 junct 23, A580, 3.1m follow signs to Leigh Sports Village

A stylish modern hotel that is conveniently located close to the motorway network and a short drive from Manchester Airport and Warrington. The hotel is adjacent to Leigh Sports Village and the contemporary bedrooms are equipped with the latest in facilities including air conditioning, flat-screen TVs and Wi-fi. The hotel has a fitness suite, sauna and steam room along with modern meeting rooms and a business centre.

Rooms 135 (10 fmly) 🐾 Facilities FTV Wi-fi Gym Sauna Steam room Xmas New Year Conf Class 72 Board 40 Thtr 150 Del from £99 to £109* Services Lift Air con Parking 50 Notes Civ Wed 100

The Lion

◉ RESTAURANT WITH ROOMS

☎ 01547 540203 & 540747
High St SY7 0JZ
e-mail: enquiries@thelionleintwardine.co.uk
web: www.thelionleintwardine.co.uk
dir: Beside bridge on A4113 (Ludlow to Knighton road) in Leintwardine

This quiet country inn in the picturesque village of Leintwardine, and set beside the River Teme, is just a short distance from Ludlow and Craven Arms. The interior has been totally renovated and all the contemporary bedrooms are en suite. Dining is taken seriously here and the modern, imaginative food uses the freshest local ingredients. The well-stocked bar offers a selection of real ales and lagers and there is a separate drinkers' bar too. The inn is particularly popular with families as the garden has a secure children's play area, and in warmer months guests can eat alfresco. The friendly staff help to make any visit memorable.

Rooms 8 (1 fmly)

INSPECTORS' CHOICE

Chilston Park Hotel

★★★★ ◉◉ HOTEL

☎ 01622 859803
Sandway ME17 2BE
e-mail: chilstonpark@handpicked.co.uk
web: www.handpickedhotels.co.uk/chilstonpark
dir: Exit A20 to Lenham, right into High St, pass station on right, 1st left, over x-roads, hotel 0.25m on left

This elegant Grade I listed country house is set in 23 acres of immaculately landscaped gardens and parkland. An impressive collection of original paintings and antiques creates a unique environment. The sunken Venetian-style restaurant serves modern British food with French influences. Bedrooms are individual in design, some have four-poster beds and many have garden views. Hand Picked Hotels – AA Hotel Group of the Year 2012-13.

Rooms 53 (23 annexe) (2 fmly) (3 GF) S £89-£179; D £89-£179 (incl. bkfst) Facilities STV FTV Wi-fi ⅋ Fishing 🛶 Xmas New Year Conf Class 60 Board 50 Thtr 100 Services Lift Parking 100 Notes LB ⊗ Civ Wed 90

L

LEOMINSTER — Map 10 SO45
Herefordshire

Best Western Talbot Hotel
★★★ 75% HOTEL

☎ 01568 616347
West St HR6 8EP
e-mail: talbot@bestwestern.co.uk
dir: From A49, A44 or A4112, hotel in town centre

This charming former coaching inn is located in the town centre and makes an ideal base for exploring this delightful area. Public areas feature original beams and antique furniture, and include an atmospheric bar and elegant restaurant. The bedrooms vary in size, but all are comfortably furnished and equipped. Facilities are available for private functions and conferences.

Rooms 28 (3 fmly) (2 GF) **S** £70.25-£86.75;
D £91.25-£107 (incl. bkfst)* **Facilities** FTV Wi-fi
Conf Class 60 Board 30 Thtr 130 Del £95 **Parking** 26
Notes LB ⊗

LEWDOWN — Map 3 SX48
Devon

INSPECTORS' CHOICE

Lewtrenchard Manor
★★★ HOTEL

☎ 01566 783256 & 783222
EX20 4PN
e-mail: info@lewtrenchard.co.uk
dir: A30 from Exeter to Plymouth/Tavistock road. At T-junct turn right, then left onto old A30 (Lewdown road). Left in 6m signed Lewtrenchard

This Jacobean mansion was built in the 1600s, with many interesting architectural features, and is surrounded by its own idyllic grounds in a quiet valley close to the northern edge of Dartmoor. Public rooms include a fine gallery, as well as magnificent carvings and oak panelling. Meals can be taken in the dining room where bright, modern dishes are served using the best Devon produce. Bedrooms are comfortably furnished and spacious. The Rosette award is suspended due to a change of chef. The new award will be in place once our

inspectors have assessed the food cooked by the new chef.

Rooms 16 (2 fmly) (3 GF) **Facilities** FTV Wi-fi Fishing ⌁ Clay pigeon shooting Falconry Beauty therapies Xmas New Year **Conf** Class 40 Board 20 Thtr 50 **Parking** 50 **Notes** Civ Wed 100

LEWES — Map 6 TQ41
East Sussex

Shelleys Hotel
★★★★ 74% HOTEL

☎ 01273 472361 & 483403
136 High St BN7 1XS
e-mail: reservations@theshelleys.co.uk
web: www.the-shelleys.co.uk
dir: A23 to Brighton onto A27 to Lewes. At 1st rdbt left for town centre, after x-rds hotel on left

Originally a coaching inn dating from the 16th century, this charming establishment is the perfect base for exploring the South Downs and for the shops in nearby Brighton. All bedrooms are comfortably furnished in a traditional style and equipped with modern amenities such as Wi-fi. As well as a cosy bar and lounge, a fine dining restaurant is available, and home-made cream teas in the stunning garden are a speciality.

Rooms 19 **Conf** Class 20 Board 25 Thtr 60

LEYLAND — Map 15 SD52
Lancashire

Best Western Premier Leyland Hotel
★★★★ 76% HOTEL

☎ 01772 422922
Leyland Way PR25 4JX
e-mail: leylandhotel@feathers.uk.com
web: www.feathers.uk.com
dir: M6 junct 28, left at end of slip road, hotel 100mtrs on left

This purpose-built hotel enjoys a convenient location, just off the M6, within easy reach of Preston and Blackpool. Spacious public areas include extensive conference and banqueting facilities as well as a smart leisure club.

Rooms 93 (4 fmly) (31 GF) ⌁ **S** £49-£275;
D £49-£275 **Facilities** FTV Wi-fi ⌁ HL ⌁ supervised Gym Xmas New Year **Conf** Class 250 Board 250 Thtr 500 Del from £125 to £175* **Parking** 150 **Notes** LB ⊗ Civ Wed 200

Farington Lodge Hotel
★★★★ 73% HOTEL

☎ 01772 421321
Stanifield Ln, Farington PR25 4QR
e-mail: info.farington@classiclodges.co.uk
web: www.classiclodges.co.uk
dir: Left at rdbt at end of M65, left at next rdbt. Entrance 1m on right after lights

This Grade II listed Georgian house, ideally located close to the M6, M61 and M65, is set in three acres of quiet, mature gardens and offers a romantic getaway. The choice of bedroom styles range from classic and traditional rooms in the original house to the contemporary, purpose-built executive rooms; all are stylishly decorated to a very high standard. This hotel is a popular venue for weddings, private dining and other special occasions.

Rooms 27 (3 fmly) (6 GF) **S** £79-£115; **D** £89-£145 (incl. bkfst)* **Facilities** FTV Wi-fi ⌁ Xmas New Year **Conf** Class 80 Board 60 Thtr 180 **Parking** 90 **Notes** LB ⊗ Civ Wed 150

LICHFIELD — Map 10 SK10
Staffordshire

INSPECTORS' CHOICE

Swinfen Hall Hotel
★★★★ ❀❀ HOTEL

☎ 01543 481494
Swinfen WS14 9RE
e-mail: info@swinfenhallhotel.co.uk
web: www.swinfenhallhotel.co.uk
dir: Set back from A38, 2.5m outside Lichfield, towards Birmingham

Dating from 1757, this lavishly decorated mansion has been painstakingly restored by the present owners. It is set in 100 acres of parkland which includes a deer park. Public rooms are particularly stylish, with intricately carved ceilings and impressive oil portraits. Bedrooms on the first floor boast period features and tall sash windows; those on the second floor (the former servants' quarters) are smaller and more contemporary by comparison.

Service in the award-winning restaurant is both professional and attentive.

Rooms 17 (5 fmly) ⟰ **S** £145-£295; **D** £180-£335 (incl. bkfst)* **Facilities** STV FTV Wi-fi ⟳ ⚓ Fishing ⚓ Jogging trail 100 acre park New Year **Conf** Class 50 Board 120 Thtr 96 Del from £180* **Parking** 80 **Notes** LB ⊗ Civ Wed 120

Best Western The George Hotel

★★★ 79% HOTEL

☎ 01543 414822
12-14 Bird St WS13 6PR
e-mail: mail@thegeorgelichfield.co.uk
web: www.thegeorgelichfield.co.uk
dir: From Bowling Green Island on A461 take Lichfield exit. Left at next island into Swan Rd, as road bears left, turn right into Bird St for hotel car park

Situated in the city centre, this privately owned hotel provides good quality, well-equipped accommodation which includes a room with a four-poster bed. Facilities here include a large ballroom, plus several other rooms for meetings and functions.

Rooms 45 (5 fmly) **S** £45-£126; **D** £45-£156 (incl. bkfst) **Facilities** FTV Wi-fi ⟳ HL Gym **Conf** Class 60 Board 40 Thtr 110 Del from £135 to £150* **Services** Lift **Parking** 45 **Notes** LB ⊗ Civ Wed 110

Cathedral Lodge Hotel

★★★ 67% HOTEL

☎ 01543 414500
62 Beacon St WS13 7AR
e-mail: enquiries@cathedrallodgehotel.com
dir: From Birmingham, A38 to Lichfield. Hotel in city centre

This hotel is within easy walking distance of the famous cathedral and just a short drive to the NEC, Belfry Golf Course and many other attractions. The accommodation is modern, spacious and comfortable, and each room has a large, flat-screen TV with Sky Sports. There is a large function suite together with conference facilities.

Rooms 36 (2 fmly) (6 smoking) **Facilities** STV FTV Wi-fi Xmas New Year **Conf** Class 80 Board 70 Thtr 80 **Notes** ⊗

Holiday Inn Express Lichfield

BUDGET HOTEL

☎ 01543 482700
Wall Island, Birmingham Rd, Shenstone WS14 0QP
e-mail: lichfield@morethanhotels.com
web: www.hiexpress.com/lichfielduk
dir: M6 junct 12/A5 towards Lichfield/Tamworth, to junct with A5127. Hotel on left on Wall Island

A modern hotel ideal for families and business travellers. Fresh and uncomplicated, the spacious rooms include Sky TV, power shower and tea and coffee-making facilities. Continental buffet breakfast is included in the room rate; other meals may be taken at the nearby family pub or restaurant. See also the Hotel Groups pages.

Rooms 102 (60 fmly) (25 GF) (7 smoking) **Conf** Class 16 Board 20 Thtr 30

Premier Inn Lichfield

BUDGET HOTEL

☎ 0871 527 8602
Fine Ln, Fradley WS13 8RD
web: www.premierinn.com
dir: On A38, 3 NE of Lichfield

High quality, budget accommodation ideal for both families and business travellers. Spacious, en suite bedrooms feature tea and coffee making facilities, and Freeview TV in most hotels. Internet access and Wi-fi are available for a small fee. The adjacent family restaurant features a wide and varied menu. See also the Hotel Groups pages.

Rooms 30

LIFTON **Map 3 SX38**
Devon

Arundell Arms

★★★ 80% ◉◉ HOTEL

☎ 01566 784666
PL16 0AA
e-mail: reservations@arundellarms.co.uk
dir: 1m off A30, 3m E of Launceston

This former coaching inn, boasting a long history, sits in the heart of a quiet Devon village. It is internationally famous for its country pursuits such as winter shooting and angling. The bedrooms offer individual style and comfort. Public areas are full of character with a relaxed atmosphere, particularly around the open log fire during colder evenings. Award-winning cuisine is a celebration of local produce.

Rooms 21 (3 fmly) (4 GF) **S** £98; **D** £175-£199 (incl. bkfst)* **Facilities** STV Wi-fi Fishing Skittle alley Game shooting (in winter) Fly fishing school New Year **Conf** Class 30 Board 40 Thtr 100 Del from £120 to £177* **Parking** 70 **Notes** LB Civ Wed 80

Tinhay Mill Guest House and Restaurant

◉ RESTAURANT WITH ROOMS

☎ 01566 784201
Tinhay PL16 0AJ
e-mail: tinhay.mill@talk21.com
web: www.tinhaymillrestaurant.co.uk
dir: A30/A388 approach Lifton, establishment at bottom of village on right

These former mill cottages are now a delightful restaurant with charming rooms. Beams and open fireplaces set the scene, and everything is geared to ensure a relaxed and comfortable stay. Bedrooms are spacious and well equipped, with many thoughtful extras. Cuisine is taken seriously here, using the best of local produce.

Rooms 6

LINCOLN
Lincolnshire
Map 17 SK97

Best Western Plus Bentley Hotel & Spa

★★★★ 85% HOTEL

☎ 01522 878000
Newark Rd, South Hykeham LN6 9NH
e-mail: info@bentleyhotellincoln.co.uk
web: www.bentleyhotellincoln.co.uk
dir: A1 onto A46 E towards Lincoln for 10m. Over 1st rdbt on Lincoln Bypass to hotel 50yds on left

This modern hotel is on a ring road, so it is conveniently located for all local attractions. Attractive bedrooms, most with air conditioning are well equipped and spacious. The hotel has a leisure suite with gym and large pool (with a hoist for the less able). New spa facilities are now available with a hairdresser, treatment rooms and thermal suite. Extensive conference facilities are available.

Rooms 80 (5 fmly) (26 GF) 🐾 **S** £94-£143; **D** £109-£143 (incl. bkfst)* **Facilities** Spa STV FTV Wi-fi ⓘ HL ⓣ Gym Steam room Sauna New Year **Conf** Class 150 Board 30 Thtr 300 Del £118* **Services** Lift Air con **Parking** 170 **Notes** LB ⊗ Civ Wed 120

Washingborough Hall Hotel

★★★ 79% ⓢ COUNTRY HOUSE HOTEL

☎ 01522 790340
Church Hill, Washingborough LN4 1BE
e-mail: enquiries@washingboroughhall.com
dir: B1190 into Washingborough. Right at rdbt, hotel 500yds on left

This Georgian manor stands on the edge of the quiet village of Washingborough and is set in attractive gardens. Public rooms are pleasantly furnished and comfortable, while the restaurant offers interesting menus. Bedrooms are individually designed and most have views out over the grounds to the countryside beyond.

Rooms 12 (3 fmly) 🐾 **S** £55-£85; **D** £70-£135 (incl. bkfst)* **Facilities** FTV Wi-fi ⓘ 🛶 Bicycles for hire New Year **Conf** Class 30 Board 26 Thtr 50 Del £165* **Parking** 40 **Notes** Civ Wed 70

The Lincoln Hotel

★★★ 78% ⓢ HOTEL

☎ 01522 520348
Eastgate LN2 1PN
e-mail: reservations@thelincolnhotel.com
web: www.thelincolnhotel.com
dir: Adjacent to cathedral

This privately owned modern hotel enjoys superb uninterrupted views of Lincoln Cathedral. There are ruins of the Roman wall and Eastgate in the grounds. Bedrooms are contemporary with up-to-the-minute facilities. An airy restaurant and bar, a cellar bar, plus a comfortable lounge are provided. There are substantial conference and meeting facilities.

Rooms 71 (4 fmly) (8 GF) **Facilities** FTV Wi-fi Gym **Conf** Class 50 Board 40 Thtr 120 **Services** Lift **Parking** 120 **Notes** ⊗ Civ Wed 150

The White Hart

★★★ 75% HOTEL

☎ 01522 526222 & 563293
Bailgate LN1 3AR
e-mail: info@whitehart-lincoln.co.uk
web: www.whitehart-lincoln.co.uk
dir: A46 onto B1226, through Newport Arch. Hotel 0.5m on left as road bends left

Lying in the shadow of Lincoln's magnificent cathedral, this hotel is perfectly positioned for exploring the shops and sights of this medieval city. The attractive bedrooms are furnished and decorated in a traditional style and many have views of the cathedral. Given the hotel's central location, parking is a real benefit.

Rooms 50 (3 fmly) **S** £79-£99; **D** £99-£150 (incl. bkfst) **Facilities** FTV Wi-fi ⓘ **Conf** Class 80 Board 103 Thtr 160 Del from £130 to £150 **Services** Lift **Parking** 50 **Notes** LB Civ Wed 120

Branston Hall Hotel

★★★ 74% ⓢⓢ COUNTRY HOUSE HOTEL

☎ 01522 793305
Branston Park, Branston LN4 1PD
e-mail: info@branstonhall.com
web: www.branstonhall.com
dir: On B1188

Dating back to 1885 this country house sits in 88 acres of beautiful grounds complete with a lake. There is an elegant restaurant, a spacious bar and a beautiful lounge in addition to impressive conference and leisure facilities. Individually styled bedrooms vary in size and include several with four-poster beds. The hotel is a popular wedding venue.

Rooms 50 (7 annexe) (3 fmly) (4 GF) **Facilities** Spa STV Wi-fi ⓣ Gym Jogging circuit Xmas New Year **Conf** Class 54 Board 40 Thtr 200 **Services** Lift **Parking** 100 **Notes** ⊗ Civ Wed 160

L

Save on hotels. Book at **theAA.com/hotel**

LIN – LIP 245 **ENGLAND**

Tower Hotel
★★★ 71% ⊛ HOTEL

☎ 01522 529999
38 Westgate LN1 3BD
e-mail: tower.hotel@btclick.com
web: www.lincolntowerhotel.com
dir: From A46 follow signs to Lincoln N then to
Bailgate area. Through arch, 2nd right

This hotel faces the Norman castle wall and is in a
very convenient location for the city. The relaxed and
friendly atmosphere is very noticeable here. There's a
modern conservatory bar and a stylish restaurant
where contemporary dishes are available throughout
the day.

Rooms 15 (1 fmly) **Facilities** STV FTV Wi-fi
Conf Class 24 Board 16 Thtr 24 **Notes** Closed 24-27
Dec & 1 Jan

Holiday Inn Express Lincoln City Centre

BUDGET HOTEL

☎ 01522 504200
Ruston Way, Brayford Park LN6 7DB
e-mail: gm@expresslincoln.co.uk
dir: M180 junct 4, A15 signed Lincoln, A46 (Lincoln
bypass). Take exit signed A57/Lincoln Central. Over
bridge. At rdbt 3rd exit. Hotel on left

A modern hotel ideal for families and business
travellers. Fresh and uncomplicated, the spacious
rooms include Sky TV, power shower and tea and
coffee-making facilities. Continental buffet breakfast
is included in the room rate; other meals may be
taken at the nearby family pub or restaurant. See also
the Hotel Groups pages.

Rooms 118 (96 fmly) 🐾 **Conf** Class 20 Board 20
Thtr 40

Ibis Lincoln

BUDGET HOTEL

☎ 01522 698333
Runcorn Rd (A46), off Whisby Rd LN6 3QZ
e-mail: H3161@accor-hotels.com
web: www.ibishotel.com
dir: Exit A46 (ring road) into Whisby Rd. 1st left

Modern, budget hotel offering comfortable
accommodation in bright and practical bedrooms.
Breakfast is self-service and dinner is available in
the restaurant See also the Hotel Groups pages.

Rooms 86 (19 fmly) (8 GF) **Conf** Class 12 Board 20
Thtr 35

Premier Inn Lincoln
BUDGET HOTEL

☎ 0871 527 8604
Lincoln Rd, Canwick Hill LN4 2RF
web: www.premierinn.com
dir: Approx 1m S of city centre at junction of B1188 &
B1131

High quality, budget accommodation ideal for both
families and business travellers. Spacious, en suite
bedrooms feature tea and coffee making facilities,
and Freeview TV in most hotels. Internet access and
Wi-fi are available for a small fee. The adjacent
family restaurant features a wide and varied menu.
See also the Hotel Groups pages.

Rooms 60

The Old Bakery
⊛ ⊛ RESTAURANT WITH ROOMS

☎ 01522 576057 & 07949 035554
26/28 Burton Rd LN1 3LB
e-mail: enquiries@theold-bakery.co.uk
dir: Exit A46 at Lincoln North follow signs for
cathedral. 3rd exit at 1st rdbt, 1st exit at next rdbt

Situated close to the castle at the top of the town,
this converted bakery offers well-equipped bedrooms
and a delightful dining operation. The cooking is
international and uses much local produce. Expect
good friendly service from the dedicated staff.

Rooms 4 (1 fmly)

LIPHOOK Map 5 SU83
Hampshire

Old Thorns Hotel Golf & Country Estate
★★★★ 74% HOTEL

☎ 01428 724555 & 725883
Griggs Green GU30 7PE
e-mail: halliss@oldthorns.com
web: www.oldthorns.com
dir: At Griggs Green exit A3, hotel 0.5m

This hotel, with easy access to the A3, is peacefully
located in 400 acres of rolling countryside that
includes a championship golf course. The spacious
bedrooms are stylish in design and offer high levels
of comfort. The leisure facilities are extensive and
include a health club and spa; in addition there is a
sports bar, and the Kings Carvery Brasserie offers all-
day dining.

Rooms 86 (2 fmly) (39 GF) 🐾 **Facilities** Spa STV FTV
Wi-fi 🕸 🕐 supervised ⚓ 18 Putt green Gym Xmas
New Year **Conf** Class 100 Board 30 Thtr 300
Del £129* **Services** Lift **Parking** 278 **Notes** ⊗
Civ Wed 250

L

LISKEARD
Cornwall   Map 2 SX26

Premier Inn Liskeard

BUDGET HOTEL

☎ 0871 527 8608
Liskeard Retail Park, Haviland Rd PL14 3FG
web: www.premierinn.com
dir: Off A38, on A390 SW of Liskeard

High quality, budget accommodation ideal for both families and business travellers. Spacious, en suite bedrooms feature tea and coffee making facilities, and Freeview TV in most hotels. Internet access and Wi-fi are available for a small fee. The adjacent family restaurant features a wide and varied menu. See also the Hotel Groups pages.

Rooms 51

LITTLEHAMPTON
West Sussex   Map 6 TQ00

Premier Inn Littlehampton

BUDGET HOTEL

☎ 0871 527 8610
Roundstone Ln, East Preston BN16 1EB
web: www.premierinn.com
dir: A27 onto A280 signed Littlehampton/Rustington & Angmering. At next rdbt follow Littlehampton, Rustington/A259 signs. At next rdbt 1st exit signed East Preston. Hotel on left

High quality, budget accommodation ideal for both families and business travellers. Spacious, en suite bedrooms feature tea and coffee making facilities, and Freeview TV in most hotels. Internet access and Wi-fi are available for a small fee. The adjacent family restaurant features a wide and varied menu. See also the Hotel Groups pages.

Rooms 20

LIVERPOOL
Merseyside   Map 15 SJ39

Thornton Hall Hotel and Spa
★★★★ 81% ◉◉◉ HOTEL

☎ 0151 336 3938 & 353 3717
Neston Rd CH63 1JF
e-mail: reservations@thorntonhallhotel.com
web: www.thorntonhallhotel.com

(For full entry see Thornton Hough)

Hope Street Hotel
★★★★ 78% ◉◉ HOTEL

☎ 0151 709 3000
40 Hope St L1 9DA
e-mail: sleep@hopestreethotel.co.uk
dir: Follow Cathedral & University signs on entering city. Telephone for detailed directions

This stylish property is located within easy walking distance of the city's cathedrals, theatres, major shops and attractions. Stylish bedrooms and suites are appointed with flat-screen TVs, DVD players, internet access and comfy beds with Egyptian cotton sheets; the bathrooms have rain showers and deep tubs. The London Carriage Works Restaurant specialises in local, seasonal produce and the adjacent lounge bar offers lighter all-day dining and wonderful cocktails.

Rooms 89 (16 fmly) (5 GF) ✆ **S** £89-£680; **D** £89-£680* **Facilities** STV FTV Wi-fi Gym Massage & beauty rooms Xmas New Year **Conf** Class 40 Board 30 Thtr 60 Del from £180 to £220* **Services** Lift Air con **Parking** 14 **Notes** Civ Wed 70

Crowne Plaza Liverpool
★★★★ 78% HOTEL

CROWNE PLAZA
HOTELS & RESORTS

☎ 0151 243 8000
St Nicholas Place, Princes Dock, Pier Head L3 1QW
e-mail: enquiries@cpliverpool.com
web: www.crowneplaza.co.uk

Situated right on the waterfront, yet still within striking distance of the city centre this hotel offers comprehensive leisure and meeting facilities, whether taking a snack in the spacious lounge or using the business centre. Contemporary in style with superb quality, this hotel offers a welcome to business or leisure guests alike.

Rooms 159 (57 fmly) **D** fr £75* **Facilities** Spa STV FTV Wi-fi ⊗ Gym Sauna Steam room New Year **Conf** Class 340 Board 30 Thtr 500 Del from £129 to £179* **Services** Lift Air con **Parking** 150 **Notes** ⊗ Civ Wed 500

Crowne Plaza Liverpool - John Lennon Airport
CROWNE PLAZA
HOTELS & RESORTS

★★★★ 78% HOTEL

☎ 0151 494 5000
Speke Aerodrome, Speke L24 8QD
e-mail: reservations@liverpool.kewgreen.co.uk
web: www.crowne-plaza-liverpool.co.uk
dir: M62 junct 6, take Knowsley Expressway towards Speke. At end of Expressway right onto A561 towards Liverpool. Approx 4m, hotel on left just after Estuary Commerce Park

This stylish art decor hotel was originally part of the airport buildings and is just a few minutes' drive from the Liverpool John Lennon Airport. The bedrooms are comfortable, and all have air conditioning. The day rooms are striking with furnishing inspired by the 1930s. Ample on-site parking is provided.

Rooms 164 (50 fmly) (46 GF) **Facilities** STV Wi-fi ⊗ HL ⊗ ᚷ supervised ⊚ Gym Squash Xmas New Year **Conf** Class 120 Board 80 Thtr 280 **Services** Lift Air con **Parking** 300 **Notes** ⊗ Civ Wed 280

Liverpool Marriott Hotel City Centre
Marriott
HOTELS & RESORTS

★★★★ 75% HOTEL

☎ 0151 476 8000
1 Queen Square L1 1RH
e-mail: liverpool.city@marriotthotels.com
web: www.liverpoolmarriottcitycentre.co.uk
dir: End of M62 follow city centre signs, A5047, Edge Lane. From city centre follow signs for Queens Square parking

An impressive modern hotel located in the heart of the city. The elegant public rooms include a ground-floor café bar, a cocktail bar and stylish Oliver's Restaurant on the first floor. The hotel also boasts a well-equipped, indoor leisure health club with pool. Bedrooms are stylishly appointed and benefit from a host of extra facilities.

Rooms 146 (29 fmly) (12 smoking) **Facilities** STV Wi-fi ⊗ Gym Xmas New Year **Conf** Class 90 Board 30 Thtr 300 **Services** Lift Air con **Parking** 137 **Notes** ⊗ Civ Wed 300

Save on hotels. Book at **theAA.com/hotel**

LIS – LIV 247 ENGLAND

Novotel Liverpool

★★★★ 73% HOTEL

☎ 0151 702 5100
40 Hanover St L1 4LY
e-mail: h6495@accor.com

This attractive and stylish city centre hotel is convenient for Liverpool Echo Arena, Liverpool One shopping centre and the Albert Dock; it is adjacent to a town centre car park. The hotel has a range of conference and leisure facilities which include an indoor heated pool and fitness suite. The restaurant offers a contemporary style menu. The bedrooms are comfortable and stylishly designed.

Rooms 209 (127 fmly) ↖ **S** £75-£305; **D** £75-£305*
Facilities STV Wi-fi ↴ ℞ Gym Steam room
Conf Class 60 Board 50 Thtr 90 Del from £105 to £210* **Services** Lift **Notes** LB

Atlantic Tower, Liverpool   thistle

★★★★ 72% HOTEL

☎ 0871 376 9025
Chapel St L3 9RE
e-mail: atlantictower@thistle.co.uk
web: www.thistle.com/atlantictower
dir: M6 onto M62, follow signs for Albert Dock, right at Liver Building. Stay in lane marked Chapel St, hotel on left

Designed to include the shape of a ship's prow, this notable hotel commands a prominent position overlooking Pier Head and the Liver Building. There's a choice of junior suites, executive and standard rooms, and although many are compact, all are of good quality and benefit from full air conditioning. Public areas include a choice of lounges and The Vu Bar which adjoins an attractive patio garden with superb river views.

Rooms 225 (24 smoking) **S** £50-£195; **D** £60-£195*
Facilities STV FTV Wi-fi HL **Conf** Class 40 Board 30 Thtr 120 Del from £115* **Services** Lift Air con
Parking 50 **Notes** LB ⊗ Civ Wed 120

Radisson Blu Hotel Liverpool

★★★★ 72% HOTEL

☎ 0151 966 1500
107 Old Hall St L3 9LQ
e-mail: info.liverpool@radissonblu.com
dir: M62 W to end, follow signs to Albert Dock. Left onto Old Hall St from main Leeds St dual carriageway

This smart hotel is centrally located. Spacious public areas include the White Bar, an airy restaurant and an impressive lobby. Bedrooms are well equipped and include a number of business class rooms and suites. A range of conference and meeting rooms is available, as well as a good choice of leisure facilities.

Rooms 194 **Facilities** STV FTV Wi-fi ↴ ℞ Gym Steam room Sauna **Conf** Class 120 Board 44 Thtr 180
Services Lift Air con **Parking** 25 **Notes** Civ Wed 180

Malmaison Liverpool

★★★ 82% ⊛ HOTEL

☎ 0151 229 5000
7 William Jessop Way, Princes Dock L3 1QZ
e-mail: liverpool@malmaison.com
dir: A5080 follow signs for Pier Head/Southport/Bootle. Into Baln St to rdbt, 1st exit at rdbt, immediately left onto William Jessop Way

This is a purpose-built hotel with cutting edge and contemporary style. 'Mal' Liverpool, as its known, has a stunning location, alongside the river and docks, and in the heart of the city's regeneration. Bedrooms are stylish and comfortable and are provided with lots of extra facilities. The public areas are packed with fun and style, and there is a number of meeting rooms as well as private dining, including a chef's table.

Rooms 130 ↖ **Facilities** STV Wi-fi Gym **Conf** Class 28 Board 22 Thtr 50 **Services** Lift Air con

Best Western Alicia Hotel

★★★ 78% HOTEL

☎ 0151 727 4411
3 Aigburth Dr, Sefton Park L17 3AA
e-mail: aliciahotel@feathers.uk.com
web: www.feathers.uk.com
dir: From end of M62 take A5058 to Sefton Park, then left, follow park around

This stylish and friendly hotel overlooks Sefton Park and is just a few minutes' drive from both the city centre and John Lennon Airport. Bedrooms are well equipped and comfortable. Day rooms include a striking modern restaurant and bar. Extensive, stylish function facilities make this a popular wedding venue.

Rooms 41 (8 fmly) ↖ **Facilities** STV Wi-fi HL Xmas New Year **Conf** Class 80 Board 40 Thtr 120
Services Lift **Parking** 40 **Notes** ⊗ Civ Wed 120

Days Inn Liverpool City Centre

★★★ 75% HOTEL

☎ 0151 203 1910
James St L2 7PQ
e-mail: reservations@daysinnliverpool.com
dir: Telephone for detailed directions

A stylish, contemporary hotel, within walking distance of the Albert Dock, the newly developed ACC (the BT Convention Centre and Echo Arena) and Liverpool One. The bedrooms are spacious and feature LCD TVs, air conditioning and high quality bathrooms. The first-floor, open-plan bar and restaurant, with views of the River Mersey, is where residents can enjoy their complimentary breakfasts. Free Wi-fi is available.

Rooms 154 (30 fmly) **Facilities** FTV Wi-fi ↴
Services Lift Air con **Notes** ⊗

L

LIVERPOOL *continued*

Jurys Inn Liverpool

★★★ 75% HOTEL

☎ 0151 244 3777
No 31 Keel Wharf L3 4FN
e-mail: jurysinnliverpool@jurysinns.com
dir: Follow City Centre & Albert Dock signs. Hotel at
Kings Waterfront adjacent to Albert Dock, opposite BT
Convention Centre & Echo Arena

Located on the Kings Waterfront adjacent to the BT
Convention Centre, Echo Arena, Albert Dock complex
and a short walk from the very popular shopping
district of Liverpool One, this hotel offers
contemporary and spacious bedrooms. Guests have a
choice of dining options - the Innfusion restaurant
and the Inntro bar. There are ten dedicated meeting
rooms and Wi-fi is available throughout. There is
ample secure parking nearby.

Rooms 310 (58 fmly) **S** £52-£249; **D** £52-£249*
Facilities FTV Wi-fi ♪ **Conf** Class 50 Board 40
Thtr 100 Del from £120 to £145* **Services** Lift Air con
Notes ⊗ Civ Wed 100

Holiday Inn Liverpool City Centre

★★★ 74% HOTEL

☎ 0151 709 7090
Lime St L1 1NQ
e-mail: enquiries@hiliverpool.com
web: www.hiliverpool.com
dir: M62 junct 4, follow edge lane A5047, left to
Coppers Hill Lane (signed Post Lime St Station). Right
onto Skelhorne St to hotel

Centrally located opposite Lime Street Train Station
and within easy reach of all attractions. Bedrooms
feature air-conditioning, flat-screen TVs, high speed
internet access and en suites with both bath and
shower. The Lime Lounge on the second floor
comprises a modern bar and restaurant with informal
dining and fantastic views of the city. There is also a
mini gym, and discounted rates at the adjacent car
park are available.

Rooms 139 (20 smoking) **Facilities** STV Wi-fi ♪ Gym
New Year **Conf** Class 250 Board 60 Thtr 400
Services Lift Air con **Notes** ⊗ Closed 25 Dec
Civ Wed 270

Campanile Liverpool

BUDGET HOTEL

☎ 0151 709 8104
Chaloner St, Queens Dock L3 4AJ
e-mail: liverpool@campanile.com
web: www.campanile.com
dir: Follow tourist signs marked Albert Dock. Hotel on
waterfront

This modern building offers accommodation in smart,
well-equipped bedrooms, all with en suite bathrooms.
Refreshments may be taken at the informal bistro.
See also the Hotel Groups pages.

Rooms 100 (4 fmly) (33 GF) **S** £49-£125;
D £49-£125* **Conf** Class 18 Board 24 Thtr 35

Holiday Inn Express Liverpool - Albert Dock

BUDGET HOTEL

☎ 0151 7026369
Britannia Building, Albert Dock L3 4AD
e-mail: reservations@exliverpool.com
web: www.exliverpool.com
dir: Follow signs for Liverpool City Centre and Albert
Dock

A modern hotel ideal for families and business
travellers. Fresh and uncomplicated, the spacious
rooms include Sky TV, power shower and tea and
coffee-making facilities. Continental buffet breakfast
is included in the room rate; other meals may be
taken at the nearby family pub or restaurant. See also
the Hotel Groups pages.

Rooms 135

Holiday Inn Express Liverpool Knowsley

BUDGET HOTEL

☎ 0151 549 2700
Ribblers Ln, Knowsley L34 9HA
e-mail: liverpool@exhi.co.uk
web: www.hiexpress.com/lpool-knowsley
dir: M57 junct 4, last exit off rdbt, then 1st left. Hotel
on left

Rooms 86 (62 fmly) (8 GF) (8 smoking) **D** fr £49.95
(incl. bkfst)* **Conf** Class 24 Board 25 Thtr 40

Ibis Liverpool City Centre

BUDGET HOTEL

☎ 0151 706 9800
27 Wapping L1 8LY
e-mail: H3140@accor.com
web: www.ibishotel.com
dir: From M62 follow Albert Dock signs. Opposite Dock
entrance

Modern, budget hotel offering comfortable
accommodation in bright and practical bedrooms.
Breakfast is self-service and dinner is available in
the restaurant. See also the Hotel Groups pages.

Rooms 127 (15 fmly) (23 GF) ⚘

Premier Inn Liverpool (Aintree)

BUDGET HOTEL

☎ 0871 527 8612
Ormskirk Rd, Aintree L9 5AS
web: www.premierinn.com
dir: M58, A57, A59 towards Liverpool. Pass Aintree
Retail Park, left at lights into Aintree Racecourse.
Hotel on left

High quality, budget accommodation ideal for both
families and business travellers. Spacious, en suite
bedrooms feature tea and coffee making facilities,
and Freeview TV in most hotels. Internet access and
Wi-fi are available for a small fee. The adjacent
family restaurant features a wide and varied menu.
See also the Hotel Groups pages.

Rooms 40

Premier Inn Liverpool Airport

BUDGET HOTEL

☎ 0871 527 8626
57 Speke Hall Av L24 1YQ
web: www.premierinn.com
dir: A561 towards Liverpool follow 'Liverpool John Lennon Airport' signs into Seake Hall Ave, at 1st rdbt take 2nd left. Hotel 300mtrs on left

Rooms 10

Premier Inn Liverpool Albert Dock

BUDGET HOTEL

☎ 0871 527 8622
East Britannia Building, Albert Dock L3 4AD
web: www.premierinn.com
dir: Follow signs for Liverpool City Centre & Albert Dock

Rooms 130

Premier Inn Liverpool City Centre

BUDGET HOTEL

☎ 0871 527 8624
Vernon St L2 2AY
web: www.premierinn.com
dir: From M62 follow Liverpool City Centre & Birkenhead Tunnel signs. At rdbt 3rd exit into Dale St, right into Vernon St. Hotel on left

Rooms 165

Premier Inn Liverpool North

BUDGET HOTEL

☎ 0871 527 8628
Northern Perimeter Rd L30 7PT
web: www.premierinn.com
dir: 0.25m from end of M58/M5, on A5207

Rooms 63

Premier Inn Liverpool (Roby)

BUDGET HOTEL

☎ 0871 527 8616
Roby Rd, Huyton L36 4HD
web: www.premierinn.com
dir: Just off M62 junct 5 on A5080

Rooms 53

Premier Inn Liverpool (Tarbock)

BUDGET HOTEL

☎ 0871 527 8618
Wilson Rd, Tarbock L36 6AD
web: www.premierinn.com
dir: At M62 & M57 junct. M62 junct 6, take A5080 (Huyton).1st right into Wilson Rd

Rooms 41

Premier Inn Liverpool (West Derby)

BUDGET HOTEL

☎ 0871 527 8620
Queens Dr, West Derby L13 0DL
web: www.premierinn.com
dir: At end of M62 right under flyover onto A5058 (follow football stadium signs). Hotel 1.5m on left, just past Esso garage

Rooms 84

LIVERSEDGE Map 16 SE12
West Yorkshire

Healds Hall Hotel & Restaurant

THE INDEPENDENTS
HOTEL ASSOCIATION

★★★ 77% ◉ HOTEL

☎ 01924 409112
Leeds Rd WF15 6JA
e-mail: enquire@healdshall.co.uk
web: www.healdshall.co.uk
dir: On A62 between Leeds & Huddersfield. 50yds on left after lights at Swan Pub

This 18th-century house, in the heart of West Yorkshire, provides comfortable and well-equipped accommodation and excellent hospitality. The hotel has earned a good local reputation for the quality of its food and offers a choice of casual or more formal dining styles, from a wide range of dishes on the various menus.

Rooms 24 (3 fmly) (3 GF) ⌔ S £50-£95; D £65-£110 (incl. bkfst) **Facilities** FTV Wi-fi ⌔ **Conf** Class 60 Board 45 Thtr 100 Del from £90 to £125 **Parking** 90 **Notes** LB Closed 1 Jan & BH Mon RS Sun eve Civ Wed 100

LIZARD Map 2 SW71
Cornwall

Housel Bay Hotel

★★★ 71% ◉ HOTEL

☎ 01326 290417 & 290917
Housel Cove TR12 7PG
e-mail: info@houselbay.com
dir: A39 or A394 to Helston, then A3083. At Lizard sign turn left, left at school, down lane to hotel

This long-established hotel has stunning views across the Western Approaches, equally enjoyable from the lounge and many of the bedrooms. Good cuisine is available in the stylish dining room, from where guests might enjoy a stroll to the end of the garden, which leads directly onto the Cornwall coastal path.

Rooms 20 (1 fmly) ⌔ S £65-£70; D £85-£170 (incl. bkfst)* **Facilities** FTV Wi-fi ⌔ Xmas New Year **Services** Lift **Parking** 35 **Notes** ⊗

L

London

The London Eye

Index of London Hotels

London Plan 7

Holiday Inn Express London - Royal Docks
Crowne Plaza London - Docklands
Ibis London ExCeL Docklands
Novotel London ExCeL
Custom House Hotel
ExCeL London (London 2012 venue)
Premier Inn London Docklands (ExCeL)
Ramada Hotel & Suites London Docklands
Custom House
Canning Town
Royal Victoria Dock

London Plan 8

Ibis London Greenwich
Novotel London Greenwich
Premier Inn London Greenwich
Cutty Sark
Trinity College of Music
University of Greenwich
National Maritime
GREENWICH
Greenwich Park
Royal Observatory
Peter Harrison Planetarium
Ranger's House (Wernher Collection)
Blackheath

London Plan 9

Save on hotels. Book at **theAA.com/hotel**

E1 – E4 269 ENGLAND

LONDON

Greater London Plans 1-9, pages 256-264. (Small scale maps 6 & 7 at back of book.) Hotels are listed below in postal district order, commencing East, then North, South and West, with a brief indication of the area covered. Detailed plans 2-9 show the locations of AA-appointed hotels within the Central London postal districts. If you do not know the postal district of the hotel you want, refer to the index preceding the street plans for the entry and map pages. The plan reference for each AA-appointed hotel also appears within its directory entry.

E1 STEPNEY AND EAST OF THE TOWER OF LONDON

Crowne Plaza Hotel London - Shoreditch

CROWNE PLAZA
HOTELS & RESORTS

★★★★ 74% HOTEL PLAN 3 H5

☎ 020 7613 9800
100 Shoreditch High St E1 6JQ
e-mail: info@cplondon.com
web: www.crowneplaza.com
dir: Nearest station: Liverpool St

This hotel is located in London's fashionable east end, close to the financial district and many attractions. It is contemporary in style and rooms are well appointed and tastefully decorated: air conditioning and mini bar are just two of the many amenities available. Dinner and breakfast are served in the rooftop restaurant which commands fantastic views.

Rooms 196 (10 fmly) 🐾 **Facilities** STV FTV Wi-fi ↘ HL **Conf** Class 40 Board 40 Thtr 90 Del from £189 to £350* **Services** Lift Air con **Parking** 8 **Notes** ⊗

The Tower

GUOMAN
HOTELS

★★★★ 73% HOTEL PLAN 5 J6

☎ 0870 333 9106
St Katherine's Way E1W 1LD
e-mail: tower@guoman.com
dir: Follow signs for Tower Bridge, left into St Katherine's Way. Car park (via control barrier)

This extensive modern hotel enjoys superb views over the Thames, Tower Bridge and St Katherine's Docks. Public areas include several lounges, a modern, contemporary bar and a choice of restaurants. Bedrooms are traditionally furnished and include a selection of impressive suites.

Rooms 801 (34 fmly) **Facilities** Wi-fi HL Gym Xmas New Year **Conf** Class 350 Board 65 Thtr 500 Del from £220 to £340* **Services** Lift Air con **Parking** 120 **Notes** ⊗ Civ Wed 500

Holiday Inn Express London - Limehouse

Holiday Inn Express

BUDGET HOTEL PLAN 1 G3

☎ 020 7791 3850
469-475 The Highway E1W 3HN
e-mail: jcniclas@exhi-limehouse.co.uk
web: www.hiexpress.com/limehouse

A modern hotel ideal for families and business travellers. Fresh and uncomplicated, the spacious rooms include Sky TV, power shower and tea and coffee-making facilities. Continental buffet breakfast is included in the room rate; other meals may be taken at the nearby family pub or restaurant. See also the Hotel Groups pages.

Rooms 150 **Conf** Class 26 Board 25 Thtr 60

Ibis London City

ibis

BUDGET HOTEL PLAN 3 J2

☎ 020 7422 8400
5 Commercial St E1 6BF
e-mail: H5011@accor.com
dir: M25 junct 30, A13, follow The City signs, then Aldgate signs

Modern, budget hotel offering comfortable accommodation in bright and practical bedrooms. Breakfast is self-service and dinner is available in the restaurant. See also the Hotel Groups pages.

Rooms 348

Premier Inn London City (Tower Hill)

Premier Inn

BUDGET HOTEL PLAN 3 J1

☎ 0871 527 8646
22-24 Prescott St, Tower Hill E1 8BB
web: www.premierinn.com
dir: Nearest tube: Tower Hill. 3 mins walk from Docklands Light Rail (DLR)

High quality, budget accommodation ideal for both families and business travellers. Spacious, en suite bedrooms feature tea and coffee making facilities, and Freeview TV in most hotels. Internet access and Wi-fi are available for a small fee. The adjacent family restaurant features a wide and varied menu. See also the Hotel Groups pages.

E2 BETHNAL GREEN

The RE London Shoreditch

★★★ 72% HOTEL PLAN 3 K6

☎ 020 7613 6501
419-437 Hackney Rd E2 8PP
e-mail: reservations@hotelshoreditch.com
web: www.hotelshoreditch.com
dir: Off A1208, 400mtrs from junct with Cambridge Heath Rd

A purpose-built hotel conveniently located for the financial district and the City Airport. The hotel offers comfortable and contemporary bedrooms with air-conditioning, Wi-fi and flat-screen TVs. The Executive Rooms have been designed to accommodate the needs of the business traveller. A secure car park is available.

Rooms 178 (53 fmly) (11 GF) **Facilities** STV FTV Wi-fi Xmas New Year **Conf** Class 30 Board 16 Thtr 50 **Services** Lift Air con **Parking** 23 **Notes** ⊗ Civ Wed 100

E4 CHINGFORD   Map 6 TQ39

Holiday Inn Express London Chingford

Holiday Inn Express

BUDGET HOTEL

☎ 0870 444 2789
5 Walthamstow Av, Chingford E4 8ST
e-mail: dgmchingford@expressholidayinn.co.uk
web: www.hiexpress.com/lonchingford
dir: On A406 (North Circular) at Crooked Billet rdbt, adjacent to A112 (Chingford-Walthamstow)

A modern hotel ideal for families and business travellers. Fresh and uncomplicated, the spacious rooms include Sky TV, power shower and tea and coffee-making facilities. Continental buffet breakfast is included in the room rate; other meals may be taken at the nearby family pub or restaurant. See also the Hotel Groups pages.

Rooms 102 (65 fmly) **Conf** Class 10 Board 16 Thtr 20

LONDON

E6 EAST HAM

Premier Inn London Beckton

BUDGET HOTEL PLAN 1 H4

☎ 0871 527 8644
1 Woolwich Manor Way, Beckton E6 5NT
web: www.premierinn.com
dir: A13 onto A117 (Woolwich Manor Way) towards City Airport, hotel on left after 1st rdbt

High quality, budget accommodation ideal for both families and business travellers. Spacious, en suite bedrooms feature tea and coffee making facilities, and Freeview TV in most hotels. Internet access and Wi-fi are available for a small fee. The adjacent family restaurant features a wide and varied menu. See also the Hotel Groups pages.

Rooms 90

E14 CANARY WHARF & LIMEHOUSE

INSPECTORS' CHOICE

Four Seasons Hotel London at Canary Wharf

★★★★★ ❀ HOTEL PLAN 6 A3

☎ 020 7510 1999
Westferry Circus, Canary Wharf E14 8RS
e-mail: reservations.caw@fourseasons.com
web: www.fourseasons.com/canarywharf
dir: From A13 follow Canary Wharf, Isle of Dogs & Westferry Circus signs. Hotel off 3rd exit of Westferry Circus rdbt

With superb views over the London skyline and the Thames, this stylish modern hotel enjoys a delightful riverside location. Spacious contemporary bedrooms are particularly thoughtfully equipped. Public areas include the Italian Quadrato Bar and Restaurant, an impressive business centre and a gym. Guests also have complimentary use of the impressive Virgin Active Health Club adjacent to the hotel. Welcoming staff provide exemplary levels of service and hospitality.

Rooms 142 🐾 **Facilities** STV FTV Wi-fi ⅃ ⊙ supervised ⊛ Gym Fitness centre Beauty treatment room Xmas New Year **Conf** Class 120 Board 56 Thtr 200 **Services** Lift Air con **Parking** 26 **Notes** Civ Wed 200

London Marriott West India Quay

★★★★★ 80% HOTEL PLAN 6 B4

☎ 020 7093 1000
22 Hertsmere Rd, Canary Wharf E14 4ED
web: www.londonmarriottwestindiaquay.co.uk
dir: Exit Aspen Way at Hertsmere Rd. Hotel opposite, adjacent to Canary Wharf

This spectacular skyscraper with curved glass façade is located at the heart of the docklands, adjacent to Canary Wharf and overlooking the water. The hotel is modern, but not pretentiously trendy; eye-catching floral displays add warmth to the public areas. Bedrooms, many of which overlook the quay, provide every modern convenience, including broadband and air conditioning. Curve Restaurant offers good quality cooking focusing on fresh fish.

Rooms 301 (22 fmly) 🐾 **Facilities** STV Wi-fi ⅃ Gym Xmas New Year **Conf** Class 132 Board 27 Thtr 290 **Services** Lift Air con **Notes** ⊗ Civ Wed 290

Ibis London Docklands

BUDGET HOTEL PLAN 6 D4

☎ 020 7517 1100
1 Baffin Way E14 9PE
e-mail: H2177@accor.com
web: www.ibishotel.com
dir: From Tower Bridge follow City Airport and Royal Docks signs, exit for 'Isle of Dogs'. Hotel on 1st left opposite McDonalds

Modern, budget hotel offering comfortable accommodation in bright and practical bedrooms. Breakfast is self-service and dinner is available in the restaurant. See also the Hotel Groups pages.

Rooms 87 (15 GF)

E15 STRATFORD

Ibis London Stratford

BUDGET HOTEL PLAN 9 D3

☎ 020 8536 3700
1A Romford Rd, Stratford E15 4LJ
e-mail: h3099@accor.com
web: www.ibishotel.com

Modern, budget hotel offering comfortable accommodation in bright and practical bedrooms. Breakfast is self-service and dinner is available in the restaurant. See also the Hotel Groups pages.

Rooms 108 **S** £67-£200; **D** £67-£200

Premier Inn London - Stratford

BUDGET HOTEL PLAN 9 B3

☎ 0871 527 9286
International Square, Westfield Stratfield City, Montfichet Road, Olympic Park E15 1AZ
web: www.premierinn.com
dir: From A11 or A12 follow signs for Westfield Shopping City & Stratford International & Car Park A

High quality, budget accommodation ideal for both families and business travellers. Spacious, en suite bedrooms feature tea and coffee making facilities, and Freeview TV in most hotels. Internet access and Wi-fi are available for a small fee. The adjacent family restaurant features a wide and varied menu. See also the Hotel Groups pages.

Rooms 267

LONDON

LONDON

E16 SILVERTOWN

Crowne Plaza London - Docklands

★★★★ 78%   HOTEL PLAN 7 B1

☎ 020 7055 2000
Royal Victoria Dock, Western Gateway E16 1AL
e-mail: sales@crowneplazadocklands.co.uk
web: www.cpdocklands.co.uk
dir: A1020 towards ExCeL. Follow signs for ExCeL
West. Hotel on left 400mtrs before ExCeL

Ideally located for the ExCel exhibition centre, Canary
Wharf and London City airport, this unique,
contemporary hotel overlooking Royal Victoria Dock,
offers accommodation suitable for both the leisure
and business travellers. Rooms are spacious and
equipped with all modern facilities. The hotel has a
busy bar, a contemporary restaurant and health and
fitness facilities with an indoor pool, jacuzzi and
sauna.

Rooms 210 (10 fmly) (4 smoking) **Facilities** STV
Wi-fi HL supervised Gym Beauty treatments
Sauna Steam room Xmas New Year **Conf** Class 140
Board 62 Thtr 250 **Services** Lift Air con **Parking** 75
Notes Civ Wed 275

Novotel London ExCeL

★★★★ 75% HOTEL PLAN 7 C1

☎ 020 7540 9700 & 0870 850 4560
7 Western Gateway, Royal Victoria Docks E16 1AA
e-mail: H3656@accor.com
web: www.novotel.com/3656
dir: M25 junct 30, A13 follow City signs, exit at
Canning Town. Follow ExCeL West signs. Hotel
adjacent

This hotel is situated adjacent to the ExCeL exhibition
centre and overlooks the Royal Victoria Dock. Design
throughout the hotel is contemporary and stylish.
Public rooms include a range of meeting rooms, a
modern coffee station, indoor leisure facilities and a
smart bar and restaurant, both with a terrace
overlooking the dock. Bedrooms feature modern decor,
a bathroom with separate bath and shower, and an
extensive range of extras.

Rooms 257 (211 fmly) **Facilities** STV FTV Wi-fi Gym
Sauna Steam room Relaxation room with massage
bed **Conf** Class 55 Board 30 Thtr 70 **Services** Lift
Air con **Parking** 160 **Notes** Civ Wed 50

Ramada Hotel & Suites London Docklands

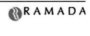

★★★★ 71% HOTEL PLAN 7 E1

☎ 020 7540 4820 & 7540 4820
Excel 2 Festoon Way, Royal Victoria Dock E16 1RH
e-mail: reservations@ramadadocklands.co.uk
dir: Follow signs for ExCeL East & London City Airport.
Over Connaught Bridge then immediately left at rdbt

This hotel benefits from a stunning waterfront
location and is close to the events venue, ExCeL, the
O2 Arena, Canary Wharf and London City Airport. The
accommodation comprises a mix of spacious
bedrooms and suites. The relaxed public areas
consist of a modern restaurant and informal lounge
area. Parking, a fitness room and meeting rooms are
available on site.

Rooms 224 (71 fmly) (50 smoking) **Facilities** FTV
Wi-fi Gym Xmas **Conf** Class 20 Board 25 Thtr 30
Services Lift Air con **Parking** 60 **Notes** Civ Wed 120

Custom House Hotel

★★★ 64% HOTEL PLAN 7 C1

☎ 020 7474 0011 & 7474 7472
272-283 Victoria Dock Rd E16 3BY
e-mail: reservations@customhouse-hotel.co.uk
dir: Nearest station: DLR. Custom House Station
opposite hotel

Conveniently located for the ExCeL Centre, the
financial district and City Airport, the hotel offers
comfortable accommodation to meet the requirements
of the modern traveller. Superior bedrooms are air
conditioned. There is a choice of dining options and a
secure car park on a first-come-first-served basis.

Rooms 282 (12 smoking) **Facilities** STV FTV Wi-fi
Xmas New Year **Conf** Class 50 Board 44 Thtr 110
Services Lift Air con **Parking** 70 **Notes**

Holiday Inn Express London Royal Docks

BUDGET HOTEL PLAN 7 A2

☎ 020 7540 4040
1 Silvertown Way, Silvertown E16 1EA
e-mail: info@exhi-royaldocks.co.uk
web: www.hiexpress.com/londonroyal
dir: A13 onto A1011 towards Silvertown, City Airport &
ExCeL. Hotel on left

A modern hotel ideal for families and business
travellers. Fresh and uncomplicated, the spacious
rooms include Sky TV, power shower and tea and
coffee-making facilities. Continental buffet breakfast
is included in the room rate; other meals may be
taken at the nearby family pub or restaurant. See also
the Hotel Groups pages.

Rooms 136 (48 fmly) **Conf** Class 30 Board 30 Thtr 80

Ibis London ExCeL Docklands

BUDGET HOTEL PLAN 7 B1

☎ 020 7055 2300
9 Western Gateway, Royal Victoria Docks E16 1AB
e-mail: H3655@accor.com
web: www.ibishotel.com
dir: M25, A13 to London, City Airport, ExCeL East

Modern, budget hotel offering comfortable
accommodation in bright and practical bedrooms.
Breakfast is self-service and dinner is available in
the restaurant See also the Hotel Groups pages.

Rooms 278 (33 fmly)

Premier Inn London Docklands (ExCeL)

BUDGET HOTEL PLAN 7 D1

☎ 0871 527 8650
Excel East, Royal Victoria Dock E16 1SL
web: www.premierinn.com
dir: A13 onto A1020. At Connaught rdbt take 2nd exit
into Connaught Rd. Hotel on right

High quality, budget accommodation ideal for both
families and business travellers. Spacious, en suite
bedrooms feature tea and coffee making facilities,
and Freeview TV in most hotels. Internet access and
Wi-fi are available for a small fee. The adjacent
family restaurant features a wide and varied menu.
See also the Hotel Groups pages.

Rooms 202

EC1 CITY OF LONDON

The Zetter Hotel

★★★★ 81% ◉◉ HOTEL PLAN 3 E3

☎ 020 7324 4444

St John's Square, 86-88 Clerkenwell Rd EC1M 5RJ
e-mail: info@thezetter.com
dir: From West A401, Clerkenwell Rd A5201. Hotel 200mtrs on left

This iconic hotel offers individually styled bedrooms with an impressive array of amenities, including the latest in-room entertainment. The Roof Top Studio rooms, some with a private patio, have amazing views over London's historic Clerkenwell and beyond. The Bistrot Bruno Loubet offers award-winning, imaginative and modern French cuisine, and the Atrium Bar and Lounge is the place to meet for coffee, have a light lunch or enjoy a drink. Two stylish rooms are available for private events.

Rooms 59 D £185-£365* **Facilities** STV Wi-fi **Conf** Class 28 Board 32 Thtr 50 **Services** Lift Air con **Parking** 1 **Notes** ⊗

Malmaison Charterhouse Square

★★★ 88% ◉◉ HOTEL PLAN 3 E3

☎ 020 7012 3700

18-21 Charterhouse Square, Clerkenwell EC1M 6AH
e-mail: london@malmaison.com
web: www.malmaison.com
dir: Exit Barbican Station turn left, take 1st left. Hotel on far left corner of Charterhouse Square

Situated in a leafy and peaceful square, Malmaison Charterhouse maintains the same focus on quality service and food as the other hotels in the group. The bedrooms, stylishly decorated in calming tones, have all the expected facilities including power showers, CD players and free internet access. The brasserie and bar at the hotel's centre has a buzzing atmosphere and offers traditional French cuisine.

Rooms 97 (5 GF) **Facilities** STV Wi-fi ♘ Gym **Conf** Class 18 Board 16 Thtr 30 **Services** Lift Air con

Thistle City Barbican

thistle

★★★ 75% HOTEL PLAN 3 F5

☎ 0871 376 9004

Central St, Clerkenwell EC1V 8DS
e-mail: citybarbican@thistle.co.uk
web: www.thistlehotels.com/citybarbican
dir: From Kings Cross E, follow Pentonville Rd, right into Goswell Rd. At lights left into Lever St. Hotel at junct of Lever St & Central St

Situated on the edge of The City, this modern hotel offers a complimentary shuttle bus to Barbican, Liverpool Street and Moorgate tube stations at peak times. Bedrooms are well equipped and include some smart executive and superior rooms; public areas include a bar, a coffee shop and restaurant along with a smart Otium leisure club.

Rooms 463 (166 annexe) (13 fmly) **Facilities** Spa STV FTV Wi-fi ⊛ supervised Gym Sauna Steam room Xmas New Year **Conf** Class 75 Board 35 Thtr 175 **Services** Lift **Parking** 10 **Notes** ⊗

The Montcalm London City at The Brewery

Ⓤ PLAN 3 F3

☎ 020 7614 0100

52 Chiswell St EC1Y 4SB

Currently the rating for this establishment is not confirmed. This may be due to a change of ownership or because it has only recently joined the AA rating scheme. For further details please see the AA website: theAA.com

Rooms 235 S £190-£210; D £210-£260* **Conf** Class 40 Board 40 Thtr 60

Holiday Inn Express London City

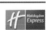

BUDGET HOTEL PLAN 3 H5

☎ 020 7300 4300

275 Old St EC1V 9LN
e-mail: rescity@holidayinnlondon.com
web: www.hiexpress.com/londoncityex
dir: At City Rd rdbt turn left, hotel on left, next to fire station

A modern hotel ideal for families and business travellers. Fresh and uncomplicated, the spacious rooms include Sky TV, power shower and tea and coffee-making facilities. Continental buffet breakfast is included in the room rate; other meals may be taken at the nearby family pub or restaurant. See also the Hotel Groups pages.

Rooms 224 (132 fmly) (20 smoking) **Conf** Class 32 Board 32 Thtr 70

EC2

ANdAZ Liverpool Street

★★★★★ 84% ◉◉◉ HOTEL PLAN 3 H3

☎ 020 7961 1234

40 Liverpool St EC2M 7QN
e-mail: guestservices.londonliv@andaz.com
dir: On corner of Liverpool St & Bishopsgate, attached to Liverpool St station

ANdAZ is an exciting and contemporary place to stay - no reception desk here so guests are checked-in by staff with laptops. Bedrooms are stylish, and designed very much with the executive in mind, with iPods and Wi-fi as well as a mini bar stocked with healthy choices. The dining options are varied and many - Miyako restaurant (1 AA Rosette) for Japanese cuisine, 1901 Restaurant and Wine Bar (3 AA Rosettes), St Georges pub, Catch and Champagne bar (1 AA Rosette), and the Eastway brasserie. There are also rooms for private dining and other events.

Rooms 267 ♠ **Facilities** STV FTV Wi-fi ♘ Gym Steam room Beauty treatment rooms New Year **Conf** Class 120 Board 60 Thtr 250 **Services** Lift Air con **Notes** ⊗ Civ Wed 230

Apex London Wall Hotel

★★★★ 80%
HOTEL PLAN 3 G2

☎ 0845 365 0000 & 020 7562 3030

7-9 Copthall Av EC2R 7NJ
e-mail: london.reservations@apexhotels.co.uk
dir: Near Moorgate & Bank stations

A sister property to the nearby City of London Hotel. This hotel is situated in the heart of London's financial district and is close to many places of interest. This 'boutique' property offers contemporary accommodation for both the business and leisure travellers. Bedrooms and bathrooms have been fitted to a very high standard and feature some great guest comforts. Off the Wall restaurant offers informal dining with a modern British menu.

Rooms 89 ♠ **Facilities** FTV Wi-fi ♘ Gym Xmas New Year **Services** Lift Air con **Notes** ⊗ No children

Save on hotels. Book at theAA.com/hotel

EC1 – N3 273 ENGLAND

EC3 CHEAPSIDE

Apex City of London Hotel

★★★★ 81% ⊛ HOTEL PLAN 3 H1

☎ 0845 365 0000 & 020 7702 2020
No 1 Seething Ln EC3N 4AX
e-mail: london.reservations@apexhotels.co.uk
web: www.apexhotels.co.uk
dir: Opposite Tower of London

Situated close to Tower Bridge, this hotel is in the heart of the business district. Bedrooms are appointed to a high standard and have walk-in power showers in the en suites. The gym has the most up-to-date equipment, and there is a sauna room. The Addendum Restaurant offers a good dining option.

Rooms 179 (5 GF) (6 smoking) ✆ **Facilities** STV Wi-fi ↕ Gym Xmas **Conf** Class 36 Board 30 Thtr 80 **Services** Lift Air con **Notes** ⊗

The Chamberlain Hotel

★★★★ 75% HOTEL PLAN 3 J2

☎ 020 7680 1500
130-135 Minories EC3N 1NU
e-mail: thechamberlain@fullers.co.uk
web: www.thechamberlainhotel.com
dir: M25 junct 30, A13 W towards London. Follow into Aldgate, left after bus station. Hotel halfway down Minories

This smart hotel is ideally situated for the City, Tower Bridge, plus both Aldgate and Tower underground stations. The impressive bedrooms are stylish, well equipped and comfortable, and the modern bathrooms are fitted with TVs to watch from the bath. Informal day rooms include a popular pub, a lounge and an attractive restaurant.

Rooms 64 ✆ **S** £335; **D** £335* **Facilities** STV Wi-fi ↕ **Conf** Class 20 Board 22 Thtr 40 **Del** £285*
Services Lift Air con **Notes** LB ⊗ Closed 24-28 Dec

Novotel London Tower Bridge

★★★★ 74% HOTEL PLAN 3 J1

☎ 020 7265 6000 & 7265 6002
10 Pepys St EC3N 2NR
e-mail: H3107@accor.com
web: www.novotel.com

Located near the Tower of London, this smart hotel is convenient for Docklands, the City, Heathrow and London City airports. Air-conditioned bedrooms are spacious, modern, and offer a great range of facilities. There is a smart bar and restaurant, a small gym, children's play area and extensive meeting and conference facilities.

Rooms 203 (130 fmly) ✆ **Facilities** STV FTV Wi-fi ↕ Gym Steam room Sauna Fitness room Xmas New Year **Conf** Class 56 Board 25 Thtr 100 **Services** Lift

EC4

Crowne Plaza London - The City

★★★★ 80% ⊛ HOTEL PLAN 3 E1

☎ 0871 942 9190
19 New Bridge St EC4V 6DB
e-mail: loncy.info@ihg.com
web: www.cplondoncityhotel.co.uk
dir: Opposite Blackfriars station

This hotel has a 1919 façade, but is modern and bright inside; it is situated close to the north bank of the River Thames and also to Blackfriars station. Bedrooms are modern and well equipped. There is a small gym and valet parking is available. Booking for dinner is required.

Rooms 203 (60 fmly) (7 smoking) **Facilities** STV Wi-fi ↕ HL Gym Sauna Xmas New Year **Conf** Class 100 Board 50 Thtr 160 **Del** from £360* **Services** Lift Air con **Notes** ⊗ Civ Wed 160

Apex Temple Court Hotel

★★★★ 78% HOTEL PLAN 3 D2

☎ 0845 365 0000 & 020 7353 4113
1-2 Serjeant's Inn, Fleet St EC4Y 1LL
dir: Within Inner Temple, off Fleet St

This property, located just off Fleet Street and a moment's walk from the Inner Temple, has undergone a complete transformation - the interior is now contemporary yet from the outside its appearance remains traditional. Bedrooms, incorporating up-to-date technology, are stylish and furnished with guest comfort in mind; some benefit from city skyline views. The cuisine is a highlight with brasserie-style dining in Chambers Restaurant and Bar, plus there are excellent breakfasts to look forward to. The hotel has a gym.

Rooms 184 ✆ **Facilities** STV FTV Wi-fi ↕ HL Gym Xmas New Year **Services** Lift Air con **Notes** ⊗

N1 ISLINGTON

Premier Inn London King's Cross St Pancras

BUDGET HOTEL PLAN 3 B6

☎ 0871 527 8672
26-30 York Way, Kings Cross N1 9AA
web: www.premierinn.com
dir: M25 junct 16 onto M40 (becomes A40). Follow City signs, exit at Euston Rd, follow one-way system to York Way

High quality, budget accommodation ideal for both families and business travellers. Spacious, en suite bedrooms feature tea and coffee making facilities, and Freeview TV in most hotels. Internet access and Wi-fi are available for a small fee. The adjacent family restaurant features a wide and varied menu. See also the Hotel Groups pages.

Rooms 276

N3 FINCHLEY, GOLDERS GREEN

Holiday Inn Express London Golders Green North

BUDGET HOTEL PLAN 1 E5

☎ 0870 770 4059
58 Regents Park Rd N3 3JN
web: www.hiexpress.co.uk
dir: M1 junct 1, A404 (North Circular Rd) E to junct with A41. At lights left then 1st right into Tillingbourne Gdns. Hotel entrance on right

A modern hotel ideal for families and business travellers. Fresh and uncomplicated, the spacious rooms include Sky TV, power shower and tea and coffee-making facilities. Continental buffet breakfast is included in the room rate; other meals may be taken at the nearby family pub or restaurant. See also the Hotel Groups pages.

Rooms 83

LONDON

NW1 REGENT'S PARK & CAMDEN TOWN

INSPECTORS' CHOICE

The Landmark London

★★★★★ ◉◉ HOTEL PLAN 2 F4

☎ 020 7631 8000
222 Marylebone Rd NW1 6JQ
e-mail: reservations@thelandmark.co.uk
web: www.landmarklondon.co.uk
dir: Adjacent to Marylebone Station. Hotel on Marylebone Rd

Once one of the last truly grand railway hotels, The Landmark boasts a number of stunning features, the most spectacular being the naturally lit central atrium forming the hotel's focal point. When it comes to eating and drinking there are a number of choices, including the Cellars bar for cocktails and upmarket bar meals, the Mirror Bar, and The Gazebo - ideal for a business meeting or a quick snack. The Winter Garden Restaurant has the centre stage in the atrium and is a great place to watch the world go by; and the twotwentytwo restaurant and bar is a relaxing place to meet, eat and drink. The air-conditioned bedrooms are luxurious and have large, stylish bathrooms. The health club offers a complete wellbeing experience.

Rooms 300 (71 fmly) (52 smoking) ⚑
S £179-£850; **D** £179-£850* **Facilities** Spa STV FTV Wi-fi ↕ ⊗ Gym Beauty treatments & massages 🎵 Xmas **Conf** Class 364 Board 50 Thtr 568 Del from £255 to £360* **Services** Lift Air con **Parking** 80 **Notes** ⊗ Civ Wed 300

Meliá White House

★★★★ 80% ◉◉ HOTEL PLAN 2 H4

☎ 020 7391 3000
Albany St, Regents Park NW1 3UP
e-mail: melia.white.house@solmelia.com
dir: Opposite Gt Portland St underground station & next to Regents Park/Warren Street underground

Owned by the Spanish Solmelia company, this impressive art deco property is located opposite Great Portland Street tube station. Spacious public areas offer a high degree of comfort and include an elegant cocktail bar, a fine dining restaurant and a more informal brasserie. Stylish bedrooms come in a variety of sizes, but all offer high levels of comfort and are thoughtfully equipped.

Rooms 581 (7 fmly) ⚑ **Facilities** STV FTV Wi-fi ↕ HL Gym Beauty treatment room 🎵 Xmas New Year **Conf** Class 80 Board 60 Thtr 140 **Services** Lift Air con **Notes** ⊗ Civ Wed 140

Thistle Euston   thistle

★★★★ 80% HOTEL PLAN 2 J5

☎ 0871 376 9017
Cardington St NW1 2LP
e-mail: euston@thistle.co.uk
web: www.thistlehotels.com/euston
dir: From M40 continue to end of A40, follow Marylebone Rd, take Euston Rd to Melton St & into Cardington St

This smart, modern hotel is ideally located a short walk from Euston Station. Spacious public areas include a spacious bar/lounge, extensive meeting and function rooms and a bright basement restaurant. Bedrooms include a large number of deluxe and executive rooms that are spacious, comfortable and well equipped. The hotel also has limited on-site parking.

Rooms 362 (18 fmly) (42 GF) **Facilities** STV FTV Wi-fi **Conf** Class 45 Board 35 Thtr 90 **Services** Lift Air con **Parking** 21 **Notes** ⊗

Pullman London St Pancras

★★★★ 75% HOTEL PLAN 3 A5

☎ 020 7666 9000 & 7666 9010
100-110 Euston Rd NW1 2AJ
e-mail: H5309@accor.com
web: www.pullmanhotels.com
dir: Between St Pancras & Euston stations, entrance opposite British Library

This hotel enjoys a central location adjacent to the British Library and close to some of London's main transport hubs. The style is modern and contemporary throughout. Bedrooms vary in size but are all very well equipped and many have views over the city. Open-plan public areas include a leisure suite and extensive conference facilities including the Shaw Theatre.

Rooms 312 ⚑ **Facilities** Wi-fi ↕ Gym Steam room Sauna Xmas **Conf** Class 220 Board 80 Thtr 446 **Services** Lift Air con **Notes** ⊗

St Pancras Renaissance London Hotel

RENAISSANCE. HOTELS & RESORTS

Ⓤ PLAN 3 B5

☎ 020 7841 3540
Euston Rd NW1 2AR
e-mail: stpancras.hotel@renaissancehotels.com
dir: Euston Rd towards Kings Cross, hotel on left just after British Library

Refurbished to the highest standards, the St Pancras Renaissance is truly an iconic building, designed by Sir Gilbert Scott as the Midland Grand Hotel at the height of railway travel. Victorian splendour is evident inside the impressive entrance hall and lounge. Suites have been restored and updated to their former glory, and new rooms offer the latest in comfort and quality. All-day dining is offered in what was once the former booking hall (adjoining St Pancras station), whilst Marcus Wareing oversees the cuisine in the hotel's main dining room. The hotel also features a spa and traditional men's barbers. At the time of going to press the rating for this establishment was not confirmed. For up-to-date details please see the AA website: theAA.com

Rooms 245 (207 annexe) (40 fmly) **D** £228-£12,000 (incl. bkfst)* **Facilities** Spa STV FTV Wi-fi ↕ ⊗ Gym Barber 🎵 Xmas New Year **Conf** Class 225 Board 50 Thtr 450 **Services** Lift Air con **Parking** 15 **Notes** LB Civ Wed 400

LONDON

Save on hotels. Book at **theAA.com/hotel**

NW1 – NW4 275 ENGLAND

Ibis London Euston St Pancras

BUDGET HOTEL PLAN 2 J5

☎ 020 7388 7777
3 Cardington St NW1 2LW
e-mail: H0921@accor-hotels.com
web: www.ibishotel.com
dir: From Euston Rd or station, right to Melton St & into Cardington St

Modern, budget hotel offering comfortable accommodation in bright and practical bedrooms. Breakfast is self-service and dinner is available in the restaurant. See also the Hotel Groups pages.

Rooms 380 ☍ **S** £85-£195; **D** £85-£195*
Conf Class 40 Board 40 Thtr 100

NW2 BRENT CROSS & CRICKLEWOOD

Crown Moran Hotel

★★★★ 77% HOTEL PLAN 1 D5

☎ 020 8452 4175
142-152 Cricklewood Broadway, Cricklewood NW2 3ED
e-mail: crownres@moranhotels.com
web: www.moranhotels.com
dir: M1 junct 1 follow signs onto North Circular (W) A406. Junct with A5 (Staples Corner). At rdbt take 1st exit onto A5 to Cricklewood

This striking hotel is connected by an impressive glass atrium to the popular Crown Pub. Features include excellent function and conference facilities, a leisure club, a choice of stylish lounges and bars and a contemporary restaurant. The air-conditioned bedrooms are appointed to a high standard and include a number of trendy suites.

Rooms 152 (82 fmly) (35 GF) ☍ **S** £105-£250; **D** £115-£295* **Facilities** STV Wi-fi ↕ HL ☺ Gym ♫ **Conf** Class 200 Board 80 Thtr 300 Del from £175 to £250* **Services** Lift Air con **Parking** 41 **Notes** ⊗ Closed 24-30 Dec Civ Wed 300

Holiday Inn London - Brent Cross

★★★ 78% HOTEL PLAN 1 D5

☎ 0871 942 9112 & 020 8967 6359
Tilling Rd, Brent Cross NW2 1LP
web: www.holidayinn.co.uk
dir: At M1 junct 1. At rdbt after bridge turn left into Tilling Rd

Ideally located beside the M1 on the A406 North Circular, just a few minutes' walk from Brent Cross Shopping Centre and four miles from Wembley Stadium. The hotel offers well-appointed bedrooms with air conditioning and high-speed internet access; Wi-fi is available in the public areas. Conference rooms and a contemporary restaurant are available, plus there is ample parking.

Rooms 154 (87 fmly) (16 smoking) **Facilities** STV FTV Wi-fi ↕ New Year **Conf** Class 40 Board 32 Thtr 80 **Services** Lift Air con **Parking** 150 **Notes** ⊗

NW3 HAMPSTEAD AND SWISS COTTAGE

London Marriott Hotel Regents Park

★★★★ 76% HOTEL PLAN 1 E4

☎ 020 7722 7711 & 0800 221222
128 King Henry's Rd NW3 3ST
e-mail: london.regional.reservations@marriott.com
web: www.londonmarriottregentspark.co.uk
dir: 200yds off Finchley Rd on A41

Situated in a quieter part of town and close to the tube station, this hotel offers guests comfortably appointed, air-conditioned accommodation; all rooms boast balconies and are particularly well equipped to meet the needs of today's business traveller. The open-plan ground floor is spacious and airy and includes a well-equipped leisure centre with indoor pool. Secure parking is a bonus.

Rooms 304 (148 fmly) **Facilities** STV Wi-fi ↕ ☺ supervised Gym Hair & beauty salon Steam room Sauna **Conf** Class 150 Board 120 Thtr 300 **Services** Lift Air con **Parking** 110 **Notes** ⊗ Civ Wed 300

Premier Inn London Hampstead

BUDGET HOTEL PLAN 1 E4

☎ 0871 527 8662
215 Haverstock Hill, Hampstead NW3 4RB
web: www.premierinn.com
dir: A41 to Swiss Cottage. Before junct take feeder road left into Buckland Cresent into Belsize Ave. Left into Haverstock Hill

High quality, budget accommodation ideal for both families and business travellers. Spacious, en suite bedrooms feature tea and coffee making facilities, and Freeview TV in most hotels. Internet access and Wi-fi are available for a small fee. The adjacent family restaurant features a wide and varied menu. See also the Hotel Groups pages.

Rooms 143

NW4 HENDON

Hendon Hall Hotel

★★★★ 76% ◉◉ HOTEL
PLAN 1 D5

☎ 020 8203 3341
Ashley Ln, Hendon NW4 1HF
e-mail: reception.hendon@handpicked.co.uk
web: www.handpickedhotels.co.uk/hendonhall
dir: M1 junct 2 follow A406. Right at lights into Parson St, right into Ashley Ln. Hotel on right

This impressive property was originally built in the 16th century when it was known as Hendon Manor, and is now a stylish hotel boasting smart, well-equipped, comfortable bedrooms with luxury toiletries, free Wi-fi and well-appointed en suites. Public areas include meeting and conference facilities, a contemporary cocktail bar and a richly decorated restaurant that opens onto a garden terrace. Staff are friendly and attentive. Hand Picked Hotels – AA Hotel Group of the Year 2012-13.

Rooms 57 ☍ **S** £99-£119; **D** £109-£149 (incl. bkfst)*
Facilities STV FTV Wi-fi ↕ Xmas New Year
Conf Class 130 Board 76 Thtr 350 Del from £151 to £200* **Services** Lift Air con **Parking** 70 **Notes** LB ⊗ Civ Wed 120

LONDON

NW6 MAIDA VALE

London Marriott Maida Vale

★★★★ 75% HOTEL PLAN 1 E4

☎ 020 7543 6000
Plaza Pde, Maida Vale NW6 5RP
e-mail: reservations.london.england.maidavale@
marriotthotels.com
web: www.londonmarriottmaidavale.co.uk
dir: From M1 take A5 S'bound for 3m. Hotel on left.
From Marble Arch take A5 N'bound. Hotel on right

This smart, modern hotel is conveniently located just
north of central London. Air-conditioned bedrooms are
tastefully decorated and provide a range of extras.
The hotel also boasts extensive function facilities as
well as an indoor leisure centre which has a
swimming pool, gym and health and beauty salon.

Rooms 237 (40 fmly) **Facilities** STV Wi-fi ॐ ⓦ Gym
Hair & beauty salon Beauty treatment rooms Exercise
studio & classes Xmas **Conf** Class 70 Board 30
Thtr 200 **Services** Lift Air con **Parking** 28 **Notes** ⊗
Civ Wed 100

SE1 SOUTHWARK AND WATERLOO

London Marriott Hotel County Hall

★★★★★ 82% HOTEL PLAN 5 C5

☎ 020 7928 5200
Westminster Bridge Rd, County Hall SE1 7PB
e-mail: sales.countyhall@marriott.com
web: www.londonmarriottcountyhall.co.uk
dir: On Thames South Bank, between Westminster
Bridge & London Eye

This impressive building, appointed to a very high
standard, enjoys an enviable position on the south
bank of the Thames, adjacent to the London Eye.
Public areas have a traditional elegance and the
crescent-shaped restaurant offers fine views of
Westminster. All bedrooms are smartly laid out and
thoughtfully equipped especially with the business
traveller in mind.

Rooms 200 (58 fmly) **S** £210-£720; **D** £220-£730*
Facilities Spa STV Wi-fi ॐ HL ⓦ Gym Sauna Steam
room Pilates classes Dance studio Xmas New Year
Conf Class 40 Board 30 Thtr 80 Del from £299 to
£549* **Services** Lift Air con **Parking** 70 **Notes** ⊗
Civ Wed 80

Plaza on the River - Club & Residence

★★★★★ 81% TOWN HOUSE HOTEL
PLAN 5 B2

☎ 020 7769 2525
18 Albert Embankment SE1 7TJ
e-mail: guestrelations@plazaontheriver.co.uk
dir: From Houses of Parliament turn into Millbank, at
rdbt left into Lambeth Bridge. At rdbt 3rd exit into
Albert Embankment

This is a superb modern townhouse overlooking
London from the south bank of the Thames, with
outstanding views of the capital's landmarks. The
bedrooms are large and many are full suites with
state-of-the-art technology and kitchen facilities; all
are decorated in an elegant modern style. Service
includes a full range of in-room dining options;
additionally, the bar and restaurant in the adjacent
Park Plaza are available to guests.

Rooms 65 (65 fmly) (65 smoking) ⚑ **Facilities** STV
FTV Wi-fi ॐ HL Gym ♫ Xmas New Year
Conf Class 450 Board 40 Thtr 650 **Services** Lift
Air con **Parking** 64 **Notes** Civ Wed 600

London Bridge Hotel

★★★★ 79% HOTEL PLAN 5 G6

☎ 020 7855 2200
8-18 London Bridge St SE1 9SG
e-mail: sales@londonbridgehotel.com
web: www.londonbridgehotel.com
dir: Access through London Bridge Station (bus/taxi
yard), into London Bridge St (one-way). Hotel on left,
50yds from station

This elegant, independently owned hotel enjoys a
prime location on the edge of the city, adjacent to
London Bridge station. Smartly appointed, well-
equipped bedrooms include a number of spacious
deluxe rooms and suites. Free Wi-fi is available
throughout. The Quarter Bar & Lounge is the ideal

place for light bites, old favourites and cocktails. The
Londinium restaurant offers a seasonal British menu.

London Bridge Hotel

Rooms 138 (10 fmly) (5 smoking) **Facilities** STV FTV
Wi-fi ॐ Gym **Conf** Class 36 Board 36 Thtr 80
Services Lift Air con **Notes** ⊗

Park Plaza County Hall

★★★★ 78% ⊛ HOTEL PLAN 5 C5

☎ 020 7021 1800
1 Addington St SE1 7RY
e-mail: ppchsales@pphe.com
web: www.parkplazacountyhall.com
dir: From Houses of Parliament cross Westminster
Bridge (A302). At rdbt turn left. 1st right into
Addington St. Hotel on left

This hotel is located just south of Westminster Bridge
near Waterloo international rail station. This
contemporary design-led, air-conditioned
establishment features studios and suites, most with
kitchenettes and seating areas with a flat-screen TV.
There are six meeting rooms, an executive lounge, a
restaurant and bar plus a fully-equipped gym with
sauna and steam room. Wi-fi is available.

Rooms 398 (303 fmly) ⚑ **Facilities** STV FTV Wi-fi ॐ
Gym Sauna Steam room Beauty therapy room ♫
Xmas New Year **Conf** Class 60 Board 40 Thtr 100
Services Lift Air con **Parking** 3 **Notes** ⊗

Mercure London City Bankside

Mercure

★★★★ 78% HOTEL PLAN 5 E6

☎ 020 7902 0800
71-79 Southwark St SE1 0JA
e-mail: H2814@accor.com
web: www.mercure.com
dir: A200 to London Bridge. Left into Southwark St

This smart, contemporary hotel forms part of the
rejuvenation of the South Bank. With the City of
London just over the river and a number of tourist
attractions within easy reach, the hotel is well located
for business and leisure visitors alike. Facilities
include spacious air-cooled bedrooms, a modern bar
and the stylish Loft Restaurant.

Save on hotels. Book at **theAA.com/hotel**

NW6 – SE1 277 ENGLAND

Rooms 144 (15 fmly) (5 GF) **Facilities** STV Wi-fi Gym 🎵 **Conf** Class 40 Board 30 Thtr 60 **Services** Lift Air con

Park Plaza Riverbank London

★★★★ 77% ◉◉ HOTEL

PLAN 5 C3

☎ 020 7958 8000
18 Albert Embankment SE1 7SP
e-mail: rppres@pphe.com
web: www.parkplazariverbank.com
dir: From Houses of Parliament turn onto Millbank, at rdbt left onto Lambeth Bridge. At rdbt take 3rd exit onto Albert Embankment

Situated on the south side of the River Thames, this hotel offers guests the convenience of a central London location and high levels of comfort. Contemporary design coupled with a host of up-to-date facilities, the hotel is home to the Chino Latino brasserie. The air-conditioned bedrooms have flat-screen TVs and large work desks; some rooms and suites have stunning views of the Houses of Parliament. Other facilities include Wi-fi throughout, high-tech conference rooms, a business centre, and a fitness centre with cardiovascular equipment.

Rooms 394 🐾 **Facilities** FTV Wi-fi ৬ HL Gym **Conf** Class 405 Board 40 Thtr 700 **Services** Lift Air con **Parking** 90 **Notes** ⊗ Civ Wed 150

H10 London Waterloo Hotel

★★★★ 75% HOTEL PLAN 5 E5

☎ 020 7928 4062
284-302 Waterloo Rd SE1 8RQ
e-mail: h10.london.waterloo@h10hotels.com
dir: 450mtrs from Waterloo Station

This hotel, conveniently situated for the South Bank and Waterloo Station, has a host of features. Bedrooms are stylish and designed with the international traveller in mind. The bar provides a useful internet facility and the stylish restaurant offers fresh and interesting dishes. The staff are friendly and efficient.

Rooms 177 **S** £129-£249; **D** £149-£269* **Facilities** STV FTV Wi-fi ৬ Gym Beauty treatment room Xmas New Year **Conf** Class 45 Board 24 Thtr 70 **Services** Lift Air con **Notes** LB ⊗

Novotel London City South

★★★★ 74% HOTEL PLAN 5 F6

☎ 020 7089 0400
Southwark Bridge Rd SE1 9HH
e-mail: H3269@accor.com
web: www.novotel.com
dir: At junct at Thrale St, off Southwark St

Conveniently located for both business and leisure guests, with The City just across the Thames; other major attractions are also easily accessible. The hotel is contemporary in design with smart, modern bedrooms and spacious public rooms. There is a gym, sauna and steam room on the 6th floor, and limited parking is available at the rear of the hotel.

Rooms 182 (139 fmly) 🐾 **Facilities** STV FTV Wi-fi ৬ Gym Steam room Sauna **Conf** Class 45 Board 40 Thtr 100 **Services** Lift Air con **Parking** 50

Novotel London Waterloo

★★★★ 74% HOTEL PLAN 5 C3

☎ 020 7793 1010
113 Lambeth Rd SE1 7LS
e-mail: h1785@accor.com
web: www.novotel.com/1785
dir: Opposite Houses of Parliament on S bank of River Thames

This hotel is in an excellent location, with Lambeth Palace, the Houses of Parliament and Waterloo Station all within a short walk. The bedrooms are spacious and benefit from air conditioning. The open-plan public areas include the Elements bar and restaurant, and also a children's play area. There's also a fitness room, well-equipped conference facilities and secure parking.

Rooms 187 (80 fmly) **S** £109-£325; **D** £109-£325* **Facilities** STV Wi-fi ৬ HL Gym Steam room Sauna **Conf** Class 24 Board 24 Thtr 40 Del from £220 to £436* **Services** Lift Air con **Parking** 40 **Notes** LB

Bermondsey Square Hotel

★★★★ 73% ◉ HOTEL PLAN 5 H4

☎ 020 7378 2465 & 7378 2450
Bermondsey Square, Tower Bridge Rd, Southward SE1 3UN
e-mail: gm@bermondseysquarehotel.co.uk
dir: From London Bridge Station exit towards Guys Hospital, left into Saint Thomas St, 200mtrs then right into Bermondsey St, 400mtrs cross Abbey St into Bermondsey Square

This establishment offers a perfect haven for a variety of visitors including local residents, leisure and business guests. Alfie's provides a buzzing environment and a great range of freshly prepared food. A members and residents' club is available on the first floor providing a more exclusive area in which to relax and unwind. Accommodation is extremely stylish and comfortable with a range of individually designed, luxurious, rooftop rooms that have stunning views of London. Health and beauty treatments are available.

Rooms 79 (10 fmly) **Facilities** Spa STV FTV Wi-fi Access to local gym Xmas New Year **Conf** Class 48 Board 40 Thtr 77 **Services** Lift Air con **Notes** Civ Wed 80

All Seasons London Southwark Rose Hotel

BUDGET HOTEL PLAN 5 F6

☎ 020 7015 1480 & 7015 1491
Southwark Rose, 47 Southwark Bridge Rd SE1 9HH
e-mail: h7465@accor.com
dir: From Westminster Bridge, into Stamford Rd, continue to Southwark St, left into Southwark Bridge Rd

Conveniently located just south of the River Thames on Southwark Bridge, this modern hotel offers well equipped air-conditioned bedrooms, internet and ample work space. There is a pleasant restaurant, bar lounge and business area on the 6th floor offering breakfast and dinner. The staff are friendly and welcoming. A limited amount of parking is available at the rear of the hotel.

Rooms 84 (6 fmly) **Conf** Class 35 Board 26 Thtr 60

LONDON

LONDON

SE1 SOUTHWARK AND WATERLOO *continued*

Days Hotel London Waterloo

BUDGET HOTEL PLAN 5 D4

☎ 020 7922 1331
54 Kennington Rd SE1 7BJ
e-mail: book@hotelwaterloo.com
web: www.daysinn.com
dir: On corner of Kennington Rd & Lambeth Rd. Opposite Imperial War Museum

This modern building offers accommodation in smart, spacious and well-equipped bedrooms, suitable for families and business travellers, and all with en suite bathrooms. Continental breakfast is available and other refreshments may be taken at the nearby family restaurant. See also the Hotel Groups pages.

Rooms 162 (15 fmly) (13 GF) **S** £79-£169; **D** £89-£169*

Holiday Inn Express London - Southwark

BUDGET HOTEL PLAN 5 E6

☎ 020 7401 2525
103-109 Southwark St SE1 0JQ
e-mail: stay@expresssouthwark.co.uk
web: www.hiexpress.com/lon-southwark
dir: A20 onto A2 to city centre towards Elephant & Castle. Right before Blackfriars Bridge at 1st large lights junct

A modern hotel ideal for families and business travellers. Fresh and uncomplicated, the spacious rooms include Sky TV, power shower and tea and coffee-making facilities. Continental buffet breakfast is included in the room rate; other meals may be taken at the nearby family pub or restaurant. See also the Hotel Groups pages.

Rooms 88 (10 fmly) **Conf** Board 12

Premier Inn London County Hall

BUDGET HOTEL PLAN 5 C5

☎ 0871 527 8648
Belvedere Rd, Westminster SE1 7PB
web: www.premierinn.com
dir: In County Hall building. Nearest tube: Waterloo

High quality, budget accommodation ideal for both families and business travellers. Spacious, en suite bedrooms feature tea and coffee making facilities, and Freeview TV in most hotels. Internet access and Wi-fi are available for a small fee. The adjacent family restaurant features a wide and varied menu. See also the Hotel Groups pages.

Rooms 313

Premier Inn London Greenwich

BUDGET HOTEL PLAN 8 A1

☎ 0871 527 9208
43-81 Greenwich High Rd, Greenwich SE10 8JL
web: www.premierinn.com
dir: Telephone for detailed directions

Rooms 150

Premier Inn London Southwark

BUDGET HOTEL PLAN 5 F6

☎ 0871 527 8676
Bankside, 34 Park St SE1 9EF
web: www.premierinn.com
dir: A3200 onto A300 (Southwark Bridge Rd), 1st left into Sumner St, right into Park St. From S: M3, A3 follow Central London signs

Rooms 59

Premier Inn London Tower Bridge

BUDGET HOTEL PLAN 5 H5

☎ 0871 527 8678
159 Tower Bridge Rd SE1 3LP
web: www.premierinn.com
dir: S of Tower Bridge on A100

Rooms 196

SE10 GREENWICH

Novotel London Greenwich

★★★★ 74% HOTEL PLAN 8 A2

☎ 020 8312 6800
173-185 Greenwich High Rd, Greenwich SE10 8JA
e-mail: H3476@accor.com
web: www.novotel.com
dir: Adjacent to Greenwich Station

This purpose-built hotel is conveniently located for rail and DLR stations, as well as major attractions such as the Royal Maritime Museum and the Royal Observatory. Air-conditioned bedrooms are spacious and equipped with a host of extras, and public areas include a small gym, contemporary lounge bar and restaurant.

Rooms 151 (34 fmly) **S** £79-£359; **D** £79-£359*
Facilities STV FTV Wi-fi Gym Steam room
Conf Class 40 Board 32 Thtr 92 Del from £179 to £205* **Services** Lift Air con **Parking** 30 **Notes** LB

Holiday Inn Express London - Greenwich

BUDGET HOTEL PLAN 1 H3

☎ 020 8269 5000
162 Bugsby Park, Greenwich SE10 0DQ
e-mail: greenwich@expressholidayinn.co.uk
web: www.hiexpress.com/greenwicha102m
dir: From A102 follow Woolwich A206 signs onto A1020 (Peartree Way). Left at rdbt into Bugby's Way (signed A102 Blackwall Tunnel), pass Odeon, hotel on left

A modern hotel ideal for families and business travellers. Fresh and uncomplicated, the spacious rooms include Sky TV, power shower and tea and coffee-making facilities. Continental buffet breakfast is included in the room rate; other meals may be taken at the nearby family pub or restaurant. See also the Hotel Groups pages.

Rooms 162 **Conf** Class 55 Board 35 Thtr 80

Save on hotels. Book at **theAA.com/hotel**

SE1 – SW1 279 **ENGLAND**

Ibis London Greenwich

BUDGET HOTEL PLAN 8 B3

☎ 020 8305 1177
30 Stockwell St, Greenwich SE10 9JN
e-mail: H0975@accor.com
web: www.ibishotel.com
dir: From Waterloo Bridge, Elephant & Castle, A2 to
Greenwich

Modern, budget hotel offering comfortable
accommodation in bright and practical bedrooms.
Breakfast is self-service and dinner is available in
the restaurant. See also the Hotel Groups pages.

Rooms 82 (10 fmly) (12 GF)

SW1 WESTMINSTER

INSPECTORS' CHOICE

The Berkeley

MAYBOURNE
HOTEL GROUP

★★★★★ 🌸🌸🌸🌸🌸 HOTEL PLAN 4 G5

☎ 020 7235 6000
Wilton Place, Knightsbridge SW1X 7RL
e-mail: info@the-berkeley.co.uk
dir: 300mtrs from Hyde Park Corner along
Knightsbridge

This stylish hotel, just off Knightsbridge, boasts an
excellent range of bedrooms; each furnished with
care and a host of thoughtful extras. Newer rooms
feature trendy, spacious glass and marble
bathrooms and some of the private suites have
their own roof terrace. The striking Blue Bar
enhances the reception rooms, all adorned with
magnificent flower arrangements. Various eating
options include the Caramel Room for breakfast, an
all-day menu from 11am and afternoon tea. Marcus
Wareing at The Berkeley is awarded 5 AA Rosettes
for stunning French cuisine, and here guests can
also book the chef's table. The health spa offers a
range of treatment rooms and includes a stunning
open-air, roof-top pool.

Rooms 214 🕊 **Facilities** Spa STV FTV Wi-fi ⌗ ☒
Gym Beauty/therapy treatments Xmas
Conf Class 80 Board 52 Thtr 180 **Services** Lift
Air con **Notes** ⊗ Civ Wed 160

INSPECTORS' CHOICE

St James's Hotel and Club

★★★★★ 🌸🌸🌸🌸 TOWN HOUSE HOTEL

PLAN 4 J6

☎ 020 7316 1600
7-8 Park Place SW1A 1LP
e-mail: info@stjameshotelandclub.com
web: www.stjameshotelandclub.com
dir: On A4 near Picadilly Circus & St James's St

Dating back to 1857 this elegant property with its
distinctive neo-Gothic exterior is discreetly set in
the heart of St James. Inside there is impressive
decor created by interior designer Anne Maria
Jagdfeld. Air-conditioned bedrooms are appointed
to a very high standard and feature luxurious beds
and a range of modern facilities. Stylish open-plan
public areas offer a smart bar/lounge and the fine
dining restaurant, Seven Park Place by William
Drabble, which serves outstanding modern French
dishes based on the best seasonal British
ingredients.

Rooms 60 (8 fmly) (15 GF) 🕊 **D** £250-£2750*
Facilities STV FTV Wi-fi **Conf** Class 30 Board 25
Thtr 40 **Services** Lift Air con **Notes** ⊗ Civ Wed

INSPECTORS' CHOICE

Dukes London

★★★★★ 🌸🌸🌸 HOTEL PLAN 4 J6

☎ 020 7491 4840
35 St James's Place SW1A 1NY
e-mail: bookings@dukeshotel.com
web: www.dukeshotel.com
dir: From Pall Mall into St James's St. 2nd left into
St James's Place. Hotel in courtyard on left

Discreetly tucked away in St James's, Dukes is over
100 years old. Its style is understated with smart,
well-equipped bedrooms and public areas. The
Penthouse Suite has its own balcony with views
over Green Park. Facilities include a gym, marble
steam room and body-care treatments. The award-
winning restaurant, Thirty Six by Nigel Mendham,
offers British cuisine based on the very best
ingredients. A smart lounge and a sophisticated
and buzzing cocktail bar add to guests' enjoyment,
and Martinis are a must!

Rooms 90 (40 fmly) (4 GF) 🕊 **Facilities** STV FTV
Wi-fi ⌗ Gym Steam room Health club Personal
training Xmas New Year **Conf** Class 30 Board 30
Thtr 70 **Services** Lift Air con **Notes** ⊗ Civ Wed 60

See advert on page 281

LONDON

SW1 WESTMINSTER *continued*

INSPECTORS' CHOICE

The Halkin Hotel

★★★★★ ⊛⊛⊛

TOWN HOUSE HOTEL PLAN 4 G5

☎ 020 7333 1000
Halkin St, Belgravia SW1X 7DJ
e-mail: res@halkin.como.bz
dir: Between Belgrave Sq & Grosvenor Place. Via
Chapel St into Headfort Place, left into Halkin St

This smart, contemporary hotel has an enviable
and peaceful position just a short stroll from both
Hyde Park and the designer shops of Knightsbridge.
Service is attentive, friendly and very personalised.
The stylish bedrooms and suites are equipped to
the highest standard with white marble bathrooms
and every conceivable extra. Each floor is discreetly
designed following the themes of water, air, fire,
earth and sky. There is the airy Halkin Bar that
offers all day eating including an afternoon tea
menu, and the famous, award-winning Thai
restaurant, Nahm.

Rooms 41 **Facilities** STV FTV Wi-fi Complimentary
use of gym & spa at sister hotel **Conf** Class 20
Board 26 Thtr 40 **Services** Lift Air con **Notes** ⊗

INSPECTORS' CHOICE

The Lanesborough

★★★★★ ⊛⊛⊛ HOTEL PLAN 4 G5

☎ 020 7259 5599
Hyde Park Corner SW1X 7TA
e-mail: pmccolgan@lanesborough.com
dir: At Hyde Park corner

Occupying an enviable position on Hyde Park
Corner, this elegant hotel offers the highest
international standards of comfort, quality and
security, much appreciated by a loyal clientele. The
stylish bedrooms and suites reflect the historic
nature of the property, offering high levels of
comfort and a superb range of complimentary
facilities including laptops and high speed internet
access. Services are equally impressive with
personal butlers ensuring individual attention.
Apsleys offers award-winning, modern Italian
cuisine and afternoon tea is offered.

Rooms 93 (7 fmly) (6 GF) (38 smoking) ⌇
S £395-£455; **D** £525-£2700* **Facilities** Spa STV
FTV Wi-fi ⌇ Gym ♫ **Conf** Class 48 Board 52
Thtr 100 **Services** Lift Air con **Parking** 48 **Notes** LB
Civ Wed 100

INSPECTORS' CHOICE

Mandarin Oriental Hyde Park, London

★★★★★ ⊛⊛⊛ HOTEL PLAN 4 F5

☎ 020 7235 2000
66 Knightsbridge SW1X 7LA
e-mail: molon-reservations@mohg.com
web: www.mandarinoriental.com/london
dir: Harrods 400mtrs on right & Harvey Nichols
directly opposite hotel

Situated in fashionable Knightsbridge and
overlooking Hyde Park, this iconic venue is a
popular destination for highfliers, celebrities and
the young and fashionable. Bedrooms, many with
park views, are appointed to the highest standards
with luxurious features such as the finest Irish linen
and goose down pillows. Guests have a choice of
dining options - Bar Boulud (with 2 AA Rosettes)
offering a contemporary bistro menu of seasonal,
rustic French dishes; and Dinner by Heston
Blumenthal (awarded AA Restaurant of the Year for
London 2012-2013) where the dishes are based on
recipes dating as far back as the 14th century but
have Heston's legendary modern twist. The
Mandarin Bar serves light snacks and cocktails.
The stylish spa is a destination in its own right and
offers a range of innovative treatments.

Rooms 198 ⌇ **Facilities** Spa STV FTV Wi-fi ⌇ Gym
Sanarium Steam room Vitality pool Zen colour
therapy Relaxation area ♫ Xmas New Year
Conf Class 120 Board 60 Thtr 250 **Services** Lift
Air con **Notes** ⊗ Civ Wed 250

DUKES
ST. JAMES, LONDON

**St. James's Place, London
SW1A 1NY**

**Tel: +44 (0)20 7491 4840
Fax: +44 (0)20 7493 1264**

**www.dukeshotel.com
bookings@dukeshotel.com**

Located in the heart of St James's, DUKES LONDON is a discreet boutique hotel which has been welcoming guests for over 100 years. DUKES has a fresh look which is entirely English in spirit with warm, charming service.

Each of the 90 bedrooms and suites are enhanced with complementary Wi-Fi, handmade chocolates, flat screen televisions, and top of the range bath products from REN, just a few perks to indulge ones self.

The legendary DUKES Bar has a cozy, clubby charm enhanced by the original marble fireplace, mahogany bar and walls hung with portraits and prints from the DUKES collection.

THIRTY SIX by Nigel Mendham is a very British affair. The restaurant offers Nigel's refined and feel-good cuisine using the freshest seasonal ingredients, coupled with an emphasis on first-

class service and elegant surroundings, which means that breakfast, lunch and dinner is always something to look forward to with anticipation.

The Drawing Room and Conservatory overlook a peaceful courtyard garden, the perfect spot for morning coffee, light lunches, traditional afternoon tea or cigars and cognacs in the garden during the evening.

The Perrier Jouet Lounge at DUKES is a relaxation Champagne lounge and is the perfect venue for a pre-dinner glass of champagne.

SW1 WESTMINSTER *continued*

The Goring

★★★★★ ◉ ◉ HOTEL PLAN 4 H4

☎ 020 7396 9000
Beeston Place SW1W 0JW
e-mail: reception@thegoring.com
web: www.thegoring.com
dir: Off Lower Grosvenor Place, just prior to Royal Mews

This icon of British hospitality for over 100 years is centrally located and within walking distance of the Royal Parks and principal shopping areas. Spacious bedrooms and suites, some contemporary in style with state-of-the-art technology and others more classically furnished; all boast high levels of comfort and quality. The Duchess of Cambridge stayed in the Royal Suite on the night before her wedding. Elegant day rooms include the Garden Bar and the drawing room, both popular for afternoon tea and cocktails. The stylish airy restaurant offers a popular menu of contemporary British cuisine and delightful private dining rooms are available. Guests will experience a personalised service from the attentive and friendly team.

Rooms 69 (9 fmly) 🐾 **S** £286.80-£504;
D £269-£582* **Facilities** STV Wi-fi ⬦ Free membership of nearby health club Xmas New Year **Conf** Class 30 Board 25 Thtr 50 **Services** Lift Air con **Parking** 16 **Notes** ⊗ Civ Wed 50

Jumeirah Carlton Tower

★★★★★ ◉ ◉ ◉ HOTEL PLAN 4 F4

☎ 020 7235 1234
Cadogan Place SW1X 9PY
e-mail: jctinfo@jumeirah.com
web: www.jumeirahcarltontower.com
dir: A4 towards Knightsbridge, right onto Sloane St. Hotel on left before Cadogan Place

This impressive hotel enjoys an enviable position in the heart of Knightsbridge, overlooking Cadogan Gardens. The stunningly designed bedrooms, including a number of suites, vary in size and style, and many have wonderful city views. Leisure facilities include a glass-roofed swimming pool, a well-equipped gym and a number of treatment rooms. The renowned Rib Room provides excellent dining, together with the other options of the Club Room, the Chinoiserie and the GILT Cocktail Lounge.

Rooms 220 (59 fmly) (70 smoking) **Facilities** Spa STV FTV Wi-fi ⬦ supervised 🏊 Gym Golf simulator (50 courses) 🎵 Xmas New Year **Conf** Class 250 Board 30 Thtr 400 **Services** Lift Air con **Parking** 170 **Notes** ⊗ Civ Wed 320

The Stafford London by Kempinski

★★★★★ ◉ HOTEL PLAN 4 J6

☎ 020 7493 0111
16-18 St James's Place SW1A 1NJ
e-mail: reservation.london@kempinski.com
web: www.kempinski.com/en/london
dir: Exit Pall Mall into St James's St. 2nd left into St James's Place

Tucked away in a quiet corner of St James's, this classically styled boutique hotel retains an air of understated luxury. The American Bar is a fabulous venue in its own right, festooned with an eccentric array of celebrity photos, caps and ties. Afternoon tea is a long established tradition here. From the pristine, tastefully decorated and air-conditioned bedrooms, to the highly professional, yet friendly service, this exclusive hotel maintains the highest standards. 26 stunning mews suites are available.

Rooms 105 (38 annexe) (8 GF) (5 smoking) 🐾 **S** £378-£564; **D** £402-£600* **Facilities** STV Wi-fi ⬦ Gym Use of fitness club nearby Xmas New Year **Conf** Class 20 Board 24 Thtr 60 Del £645* **Services** Lift Air con **Notes** ⊗ Civ Wed 44

LONDON

Save on hotels. Book at **theAA.com/hotel**

SW1 283 ENGLAND

INSPECTORS' CHOICE

51 Buckingham Gate, Taj Suites and Residences

★★★★★ TOWN HOUSE HOTEL PLAN 4 J4

☎ 020 7769 7766
SW1E 6AF
e-mail: info@51-buckinghamgate.co.uk
dir: From Buckingham Palace onto Buckingham Gate, 100mtrs, hotel on right

This all-suites hotel is a favourite with those who desire a quiet, sophisticated environment. Each of the suites has its own butler on hand plus a kitchen, and most have large lounge areas furnished in a contemporary style with modern accessories. There are one, two, three and four bedroom suites to choose from. The hotel has a spa and a well-equipped gym.

Rooms 86 (86 fmly) (4 GF) ↻ **S** £306-£665; **D** £306-£665 **Facilities** Spa STV Wi-fi ↻ HL Gym Sauna Steam room Xmas New Year **Conf** Class 90 Board 60 Thtr 180 **Services** Lift Air con **Notes** LB ⊗ Civ Wed 150

INSPECTORS' CHOICE

No 41

THE RED CARNATION HOTEL COLLECTION

★★★★★

TOWN HOUSE HOTEL PLAN 4 H4

☎ 020 7300 0041
41 Buckingham Palace Rd SW1W 0PS
e-mail: book41@rchmail.com
web: www.41hotel.com
dir: Opposite Buckingham Palace Mews entrance

Small, intimate and very private, this stunning town house is located opposite the Royal Mews. Decorated in stylish black and white, bedrooms successfully combine comfort with state-of-the-art technology such as iPod docking stations, interactive TV and free high speed internet access. Thoughtful touches such as fresh fruit, flowers and scented candles add to the very welcoming atmosphere. The large lounge is the focal point; food and drinks are available as are magazines and newspapers from around the world plus internet access. Attentive personal service and a host of thoughtful extra touches make No 41 really special.

Rooms 30 (2 fmly) ↻ **D** £299-£443* **Facilities** STV Wi-fi ↻ Local health club Beauty treatments In-room spa Xmas New Year **Conf** Board 10 **Services** Lift Air con **Notes** LB

Sofitel London St James

SOFITEL LUXURY HOTELS

★★★★★ 87% ⚜ HOTEL
PLAN 4 K6

☎ 020 7747 2200
6 Waterloo Place SW1Y 4AN
e-mail: H3144@sofitel.com
dir: 3 mins' walk from Piccadilly Circus & Trafalgar Square

Located in the exclusive area of St James's, this Grade II listed, former bank is convenient for most of the city's attractions, theatres and the financial district. The modern bedrooms are equipped to a high standard and feature luxurious beds, whilst more traditional public areas, including the French restaurant, provide a taste of classical charm.

Rooms 184 (98 fmly) ↻ **S** £450-£1062; **D** £450-£1062* **Facilities** Spa STV Wi-fi ↻ Gym So spa So fit ♫ Xmas New Year **Conf** Class 125 Board 44 Thtr 170 **Services** Lift Air con **Notes** Civ Wed 140

Sheraton Park Tower

★★★★★ 86% ⚜⚜⚜ HOTEL
PLAN 4 F5

☎ 020 7235 8050
101 Knightsbridge SW1X 7RN
e-mail: sheratonparktower@reservestarwood.com
web: www.luxurycollection.com/parktowerlondon
dir: Adjacent to Harvey Nichols

Superbly located for some of London's most fashionable stores, the Park Tower offers stunning views over the city. Bedrooms combine a high degree of comfort with up-to-date decor and a super range of extras; the suites are particularly impressive. The hotel offers the intimate Knightsbridge lounge, the more formal Piano Bar and extensive conference and banqueting facilities. Restaurant One-O-One is renowned for its seafood.

Rooms 280 (280 fmly) (62 smoking) ↻ **Facilities** STV Wi-fi ↻ Gym Fitness room ♫ **Conf** Class 60 Board 26 Thtr 120 **Services** Lift Air con **Notes** Civ Wed 100

SW1 WESTMINSTER *continued*

Corinthia Hotel London

★★★★★ 86% ◉◉ HOTEL PLAN 5 B6

☎ 020 7930 8181
Whitehall Place SW1A 2BD
e-mail: london@corinthia.com
dir: M4 onto A4, follow Central London signs. Pass
Green Park, right into Coventry St, 1st right into
Haymarket, left into Pall Mall East, right into
Trafalgar Sq, 3rd exit into Whitehall Place

This refurbished hotel is steeped in history and is
reputed to be one of London's earliest hotels having
opened in 1885. Now after a very high quality
refurbishment, hotel has emerged with exceptional
style. The team are welcoming and friendly and all
requests are met with aplomb. Bedrooms, including
suites and penthouses, are equipped to very high
standards and offer all the modern amenities. The
eating options are The Northall with British cuisine
and The Massimo Restaurant offering Mediterranean
seafood. The Bassoon Bar is the place for cocktails
and its worth noting the counter which is actually an
elongated piano. The Espa Spa offers world class
facilities. Valet parking available.

Rooms 294 (10 fmly) (46 smoking) **Facilities** Spa STV
Wi-fi ⑤ Gym Vitality pool Nail studio Hair salon
Relaxation sleep pod Xmas New Year **Conf** Class 120
Board 50 Thtr 250 **Services** Lift Air con **Notes** ⊗
Civ Wed 250

The Royal Horseguards

★★★★★ 82% ◉◉ HOTEL

PLAN 5 B6

☎ 0871 376 9033
2 Whitehall Court SW1A 2EJ
e-mail: royalhorseguards@guoman.co.uk
web: www.theroyalhorseguards.com
dir: Trafalgar Sq to Whitehall, left to Whitehall Pl,
turn right

This majestic looking hotel in the heart of Whitehall
sits beside the Thames and enjoys unrivalled views of
the London Eye and the city skyline. Bedrooms,
appointed to a high standard, are well equipped and
some of the luxurious bathrooms are finished in
marble. Impressive public areas and outstanding
meeting facilities are also available.

Rooms 282 (7 fmly) ✆ **S** fr £540; **D** fr £600
Facilities STV Wi-fi Gym ♫ Xmas New Year
Conf Class 180 Board 84 Thtr 240 **Services** Lift
Air con **Notes** LB ⊗ Civ Wed 228

The Rubens at the Palace

THE
RED CARNATION
HOTEL COLLECTION

★★★★ 83% ◉◉ HOTEL PLAN 4 H4

☎ 020 7834 6600
39 Buckingham Palace Rd SW1W 0PS
e-mail: bookrb@rchmail.com
web: www.rubenshotel.com
dir: Opposite Royal Mews, 100mtrs from Buckingham
Palace

This hotel enjoys an enviable location close to
Buckingham Palace. Stylish, air-conditioned
bedrooms include the pinstripe-walled Savile Row
rooms, which follow a tailoring theme, and the
opulent Royal rooms, named after different monarchs.
Public rooms include The Library fine dining
restaurant and a comfortable stylish cocktail bar and
lounge. The team here pride themselves on their
warmth and friendliness.

Rooms 161 (13 fmly) ✆ **S** £190-£323; **D** £203-£335*
Facilities STV Wi-fi ↻ Health club & beauty treatment
available nearby ♫ Xmas New Year **Conf** Class 40
Board 30 Thtr 90 Del from £280 to £400*
Services Lift Air con **Notes** LB Civ Wed 80

St Ermins Hotel

★★★★ 82% ◉ HOTEL PLAN 4 K4

☎ 020 7222 7888 & 0800 635 0438
2 Caxton St, St James Park, Westminster SW1H 0QW
e-mail: reservations@sterminshotel.co.uk
dir: Just off Victoria St, directly opposite New
Scotland Yard

Located in an enviable London location, the delightful
courtyard offers a sanctuary from the hustle and
bustle of the city. Following an impressive
refurbishment the property boasts day rooms with
quality finishes - no detail has been overlooked. The
results are fresh, modern and innovative, with a
respectful nod to the hotel's former character. Award-
winning cuisine is served in the popular Caxton Grill.
Limited valet parking is available by arrangement.

Rooms 331 (18 fmly) (12 GF) ✆ **S** £250.80-£826.80;
D £250.80-£826.80* **Facilities** STV FTV Wi-fi ↻ Gym
Xmas New Year **Conf** Class 80 Board 60 Thtr 160
Services Lift Air con **Notes** LB Civ Wed 160

Cavendish London

★★★★ 80% ◉ HOTEL PLAN 4 J6

☎ 020 7930 2111
81 Jermyn St SW1Y 6JF
e-mail: info@thecavendishlondon.com
web: www.thecavendishlondon.com
dir: From Piccadilly, pass The Ritz, 1st right into
Dukes St before Fortnum & Mason

This smart, stylish hotel enjoys an enviable location
in the prestigious St James's area, just a short walk
from Green Park and Piccadilly. Bedrooms have a
fresh, contemporary feel, and there are a number of
spacious executive rooms, studios and suites. Elegant
public areas include a spacious first-floor lounge and
well-appointed conference and function facilities. The
popular Petrichor restaurant is committed to sourcing
sustainable ingredients, especially from British
producers. A good value, pre-theatre menu is
available.

Rooms 230 (12 fmly) **Facilities** STV Wi-fi
Conf Class 50 Board 40 Thtr 80 **Services** Lift Air con
Parking 50 **Notes** ⊗

Park Plaza Victoria London

Park Plaza
Hotels & Resorts

★★★★ 76% ◉ HOTEL PLAN 4 J3

☎ 020 7769 9999 & 7769 9800
239 Vauxhall Bridge Rd SW1V 1EQ
e-mail: info@victoriaparkplaza.com
web: www.parkplaza.com
dir: Turn right from Victoria Station

This smart modern hotel close to Victoria station is
well located for all of central London's major
attractions. Air-conditioned bedrooms are tastefully
appointed and thoughtfully equipped for both
business and leisure guests. Airy, stylish public areas
include an elegant bar and restaurant, a popular
coffee bar and extensive conference facilities
complete with a business centre.

Rooms 299 ✆ **D** £179-£270* **Facilities** Spa STV FTV
Wi-fi ↻ Gym Sauna Steam room Xmas **Conf** Class 240
Board 45 Thtr 550 **Services** Lift Air con **Parking** 36
Notes ⊗ Civ Wed 500

Crowne Plaza London - St James

★★★★ 76% HOTEL PLAN 4 J4

☎ 020 7834 6655 & 7963 8308
Buckingham Gate SW1E 6AF
e-mail: reservations@cplonsj.co.uk
web: www.london.crowneplaza.com
dir: With Buckingham Palace facing, turn left to Buckingham Gate. After 100mtrs hotel on right

Enjoying a prestigious location, this elegant Victorian hotel is a few minutes' walk from Buckingham Palace. Air-conditioned bedrooms are smartly appointed and superbly equipped. Public areas include a choice of three restaurants - Bank, Bistro 51 and Quilon, two bars, conference and business facilities and a fitness club with Sodashi Spa. Service is attentive and friendly.

Rooms 340 (36 fmly) (26 smoking) 🐾
S £160.80-£426; D £160.80-£426* **Facilities** Spa STV FTV Wi-fi ⬇ Gym Steam room Sauna ♫ Xmas New Year **Conf** Class 90 Board 60 Thtr 180 **Services** Lift Air con **Notes** LB ⊗ Civ Wed 180

Millennium Hotel London Knightsbridge

★★★★ 75% ⬤ HOTEL PLAN 4 F4

☎ 020 7235 4377
17 Sloane St, Knightsbridge SW1X 9NU
e-mail: reservations.knightsbridge@ millenniumhotels.co.uk
web: www.millenniumhotels.co.uk
dir: From Knightsbridge tube station towards Sloane St. Hotel 70mtrs on right

This fashionable hotel boasts an enviable location in Knightsbridge's chic shopping district. Air-conditioned, thoughtfully equipped bedrooms are complemented by a popular lobby lounge and MU Restaurant and Lounge where the cuisine is French with Asian influences. Valet parking is available if pre-booked.

Rooms 222 (41 fmly) (38 smoking) **Facilities** STV FTV Wi-fi ⬇ HL Xmas New Year **Conf** Class 80 Board 50 Thtr 120 Del from £215* **Services** Lift Air con **Parking** 11 **Notes** ⊗

The Grosvenor

★★★★ 74% HOTEL PLAN 4 H4

☎ 0871 376 9038 & 020 7834 9494
101 Buckingham Palace Rd SW1W 0SJ
e-mail: grosvenor@guoman.co.uk
web: www.guoman.com
dir: Part of Victoria Station complex

Following a multi-million pound refurbishment The Grosvenor, a listed building, has been sympathetically restored to its former Victorian splendour. It now offers guests all the comforts of a 21st-century hotel. Just a short stroll from Buckingham Palace, it is well positioned for Victoria station. The quiet, air-conditioned bedrooms have Bose iPod docking stations, plasma-screen TVs, surround sound and Wi-fi, plus bathrooms with rainfall showers. The bar and brasserie is open all day, Cantonese cuisine is available in the Grand Imperial London, champagne and cocktails can be found in Reunion, and afternoon tea is served in the traditional lounge. A gym is located on the 7th floor.

Rooms 345 S £120-£180; D £210-£550 **Facilities** STV FTV Wi-fi ⬇ HL Gym ♫ Xmas New Year **Conf** Class 80 Board 50 Thtr 110 **Services** Lift Air con **Notes** LB ⊗ Civ Wed 80

Thistle Westminster

thistle

★★★★ 71% HOTEL PLAN 4 H4

☎ 0871 376 9039
49 Buckingham Palace Rd SW1W 0QT
e-mail: westminster@thistle.co.uk
web: www.thistlehotels.com/westminster
dir: Opposite Buckingham Palace Mews

A purpose built hotel situated in the heart of London's political landmarks and close to Buckingham Palace. The spacious bedrooms come in a variety of styles; each one is smartly decorated and well equipped. Public rooms include a large lounge, a bar, a brasserie and a range of meeting rooms.

Rooms 134 (66 fmly) **Facilities** FTV Wi-fi **Conf** Class 70 Board 45 Thtr 170 **Services** Lift **Parking** 7 **Notes** ⊗

Jumeirah Lowndes Hotel

Ⓤ PLAN 4 F4

☎ 020 7823 1234
21 Lowndes St SW1X 9ES
e-mail: jlhinfo@jumeirah.com
web: www.jumeirahlowndeshotel.com
dir: M4 onto A4 into London. Left from Brompton Rd into Sloane St. Left into Pont St, Lowndes St next left. Hotel on right

This hotel is a smart modern townhouse set in the Belgravia area of Knightsbridge. Public areas are limited in scale but an all-day bar and restaurant with an outside terrace overlooking the leafy side street. The bedrooms vary in size, but all have a very modern style and have high spec facilities such as air-conditioning and iPod speakers. Guests can also enjoy the extensive facilities at the nearby Jumeirah Carlton Hotel.

Rooms 87 (14 fmly) 🐾 **Facilities** Spa STV FTV Wi-fi ⬇ **Conf** Class 12 Board 18 Thtr 25 **Services** Lift Air con **Notes** ⊗

Holiday Inn Express London - Victoria

BUDGET HOTEL PLAN 4 J2

☎ 020 7630 8888
106-110 Belgrave Rd, Victoria SW1V 2BJ
e-mail: info@hiexpressvictoria.co.uk
web: www.hiexpress.com/londonvictoria
dir: 600mtrs from Pimlico underground station

A modern hotel ideal for families and business travellers. Fresh and uncomplicated, the spacious rooms include Sky TV, power shower and tea and coffee-making facilities. Continental buffet breakfast is included in the room rate; other meals may be taken at the nearby family pub or restaurant. See also the Hotel Groups pages.

Rooms 52 (9 fmly) (4 GF) (15 smoking)

LONDON

SW1 WESTMINSTER *continued*

Premier Inn London Victoria

BUDGET HOTEL PLAN 4 J3

☎ 0871 527 8680
82-83 Eccleston Square, Victoria SW1V 1PS
web: www.premierinn.com
dir: From Victoria Station, right into Wilton Rd, 3rd right into Gillingham St, hotel 150mtrs

High quality, budget accommodation ideal for both families and business travellers. Spacious, en suite bedrooms feature tea and coffee making facilities, and Freeview TV in most hotels. Internet access and Wi-fi are available for a small fee. The adjacent family restaurant features a wide and varied menu. See also the Hotel Groups pages.

Rooms 110

SW3 CHELSEA, BROMPTON

INSPECTORS' CHOICE

The Capital

★★★★★ TOWN HOUSE HOTEL

PLAN 4 F5

☎ 020 7589 5171
Basil St, Knightsbridge SW3 1AT
e-mail: reservations@capitalhotel.co.uk
web: www.capitalhotel.co.uk
dir: 20yds from Harrods, & Knightsbridge tube station

Personal service is assured at this small, family-owned hotel set in the heart of Knightsbridge. Beautifully designed bedrooms come in a number of styles, but all rooms feature antique furniture, a marble bathroom and a thoughtful range of extras. Cocktails are a speciality in the delightful, stylish bar, whilst afternoon tea in the elegant, bijou lounge is a must. The AA Rosette award for the cuisine is temporarily suspended as there has been a change of chef. A new award will be in place, once our inspectors have completed their

assessments of meals cooked by the new kitchen team.

Rooms 49 **S** £200-£320; **D** £300-£600*
Facilities STV FTV Wi-fi ↻ Xmas New Year
Conf Class 24 Board 24 Thtr 30 **Services** Lift
Air con **Parking** 12 **Notes** LB ⊗

The Egerton House Hotel   RED CARNATION
THE HOTEL COLLECTION

★★★★★ 84%
TOWN HOUSE HOTEL PLAN 4 E4

☎ 020 7589 2412
17 Egerton Ter, Knightsbridge SW3 2BX
e-mail: bookeg@rchmail.com
web: www.egertonhousehotel.com
dir: Just off Brompton Rd, between Harrods & Victoria & Albert Museum, opposite Brompton Oratory

This delightful town house enjoys a prestigious Knightsbridge location, a short walk from Harrods and close to the Victoria & Albert Museum. Air-conditioned bedrooms and public rooms are appointed to the highest standards, with luxurious furnishings and quality antique pieces; an exceptional range of facilities include iPods, safes, mini bars and flat-screen TVs. Staff offer the highest levels of personalised, attentive service.

Rooms 28 (5 fmly) (2 GF) **Facilities** STV Wi-fi Xmas
New Year **Conf** Class 12 Board 10 Thtr 14
Services Lift Air con

The Draycott Hotel

★★★★★ 81% TOWN HOUSE HOTEL PLAN 4 F3

☎ 020 7730 6466
26 Cadogan Gardens SW3 2RP
e-mail: reservations@draycotthotel.com
web: www.draycotthotel.com
dir: From Sloane Sq station towards Peter Jones, keep to left. At Kings Rd take 1st right into Cadogan Gdns, 2nd right, hotel on left corner

Enjoying a prime location just yards from Sloane Square, this town house provides an ideal base in one of the most fashionable areas of London. Many regular guests regard this as their London residence and staff pride themselves on their hospitality. Beautifully appointed bedrooms include a number of very spacious suites and all are equipped to a high standard. Attractive day rooms, furnished with antique and period pieces, include a choice of lounges, one with access to a lovely sheltered garden.

Rooms 35 (9 fmly) (2 GF) ✎ **S** £174-£198;
D £306-£342 **Facilities** STV FTV Wi-fi Beauty
treatments Massage **Conf** Class 12 Board 12 Thtr 20
Del from £294 to £310* **Services** Lift Air con

LONDON

Save on hotels. Book at **theAA.com/hotel**

SW1 – SW3 287 ENGLAND

LONDON

Twenty Nevern Square

hotel@twentynevernsquare.co.uk
www.mayflowercollection.com

A distinctive, unique and elegantly stylish hotel that
overlooks a tranquil garden square, providing a
luxurious haven for travellers on business or pleasure...

'Unrivalled attention to detail...'

SW3 CHELSEA, BROMPTON *continued*

INSPECTORS' CHOICE

The Levin

★★★★ TOWN HOUSE HOTEL

PLAN 4 F4

☎ 020 7589 6286
28 Basil St, Knightsbridge SW3 1AS
e-mail: reservations@thelevinhotel.co.uk
web: www.thelevinhotel.co.uk
dir: 20yds from Harrods, & Knightsbridge tube
station

This sophisticated town house is the sister property
to the adjacent Capital Hotel and enjoys a prime
location on the doorstep of Knightsbridge's stylish
department and designer stores. Bedrooms and en
suites offer stylish elegance alongside a host of up-
to-date modern comforts; extra touches include
champagne bars and state-of-the-art audio-visual
systems. Guests can enjoy all-day dining in the
stylish, popular, lower ground floor Metro
Restaurant.

Rooms 12 (1 GF) **D** £265-£540 (incl. bkfst)
Facilities STV FTV Wi-fi ✎ Xmas New Year
Services Lift Air con **Parking** 8 **Notes** ⊗

The Beaufort

★★★★ 77% TOWN HOUSE HOTEL PLAN 4 F4

☎ 020 7584 5252
33 Beaufort Gardens SW3 1PP
e-mail: reservations@thebeaufort.co.uk
web: www.thebeaufort.co.uk
dir: 100yds past Harrods on left of Brompton Rd

This friendly, attractive town house enjoys a peaceful
location in a tree-lined cul-de-sac just a few minutes'
walk from Knightsbridge. Air-conditioned bedrooms
are thoughtfully furnished and equipped with CD
players, movie channel access, safe and free Wi-fi.
Guests are offered complimentary drinks and
afternoon cream tea with home-made scones and
clotted cream. A good continental breakfast is served
in bedrooms.

Rooms 29 (3 GF) **Facilities** STV Wi-fi **Conf** Thtr 10
Services Lift Air con **Notes** ⊗

SW5 EARL'S COURT

London Marriott Kensington

Marriott
HOTELS & RESORTS

★★★★ 82% HOTEL PLAN 4 B3

☎ 020 7973 1000
Cromwell Rd SW5 0TH
e-mail: kensington.marriott@marriotthotels.com
web: www.londonmarriottkensington.co.uk
dir: On A4, opposite Cromwell Rd Hospital

This stylish contemporary hotel features a stunning
glass exterior and a seven-storey atrium lobby. Fully
air conditioned throughout, the hotel has elegant
design combined with a great range of facilities,
including indoor leisure, a range of conference rooms
and parking. Smart bedrooms offer a host of extras
including the very latest communications technology.

Rooms 216 (39 fmly) **Facilities** STV FTV Wi-fi Gym
Conf Class 80 Board 60 Thtr 150 **Services** Lift Air con
Parking 20 **Notes** ⊗

Twenty Nevern Square Hotel

★★★★ 71% TOWN HOUSE HOTEL PLAN 4 A3

☎ 020 7565 9555 & 7370 4934
20 Nevern Square, Earls Court SW5 9PD
e-mail: hotel@twentynevernsquare.co.uk
web: www.twentynevernsquare.co.uk
dir: From station take Warwick Rd exit, right, 2nd
right into Nevern Sq. Hotel 30yds on right

This smart boutique-style town house hotel is
discreetly located in Nevern Square and is ideally
situated for both Earls Court and Olympia. The
stylish, individually furnished bedrooms, which vary
in shape and size, are appointed to a high standard
and are well equipped. Public areas include a
delightful lounge and Café Twenty where breakfast
and light meals are served.

Rooms 20 (3 GF) **Facilities** FTV Wi-fi **Conf** Class 20
Board 20 Thtr 20 **Services** Lift **Parking** 4 **Notes** ⊗

See advert on page 287

Save on hotels. Book at **theAA.com/hotel**

SW3 – SW6 289 ENGLAND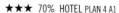

K + K Hotel George

★★★ 83% HOTEL PLAN 4 A3

☎ 020 7598 8700 & 7598 8707
1-15 Templeton Place, Earl's Court SW5 9NB
e-mail: hotelgeorge@kkhotels.co.uk
web: www.kkhotels.com/george
dir: Earls Court Rd (A3220), right into Trebovir Rd,
right into Templeton Place

This smart hotel enjoys a central location, just a few
minutes' walk from Earls Court and with easy access
to London's central attractions. Stylish public areas
include a bar/bistro, an executive lounge and meeting
facilities and a restaurant that overlooks the
attractive rear garden. Bedrooms are particularly well
equipped with a host of useful extras including free,
high-speed internet access.

Rooms 154 (38 fmly) (8 GF) (14 smoking)
S £130-£264; **D** £150-£300 (incl. bkfst)*
Facilities STV FTV Wi-fi Gym Wellness area with
exercise machines Sauna **Conf** Class 14 Board 18
Thtr 35 Del from £216 to £280 **Services** Lift Air con
Parking 20 **Notes** LB

Best Western Burns Hotel

★★★ 70% METRO HOTEL PLAN 4 B3

☎ 020 7373 3151
18-26 Barkston Gardens, Kensington SW5 0EN
e-mail: burnshotel@vienna-group.co.uk
dir: From A4, right to Earls Court Rd (A3220), 2nd left

This friendly Victorian hotel overlooks a leafy garden
in a quiet residential area not far from the Earls Court
exhibition centre and tube station. Bedrooms are
attractively appointed, with modern facilities. Public
areas, although not extensive, are stylish.

Rooms 105 (10 fmly) **Services** Lift **Notes** ⊗

Premier Inn London Kensington

BUDGET HOTEL PLAN 4 B3

☎ 0871 527 8666
11 Knaresborough Place, Kensington SW5 0TJ
web: www.premierinn.com
dir: Just off A4 (Cromwell Rd). Nearest tube: Earls
Court

High quality, budget accommodation ideal for both
families and business travellers. Spacious, en suite
bedrooms feature tea and coffee making facilities,
and Freeview TV in most hotels. Internet access and
Wi-fi are available for a small fee. The adjacent
family restaurant features a wide and varied menu.
See also the Hotel Groups pages.

Rooms 184

Premier Inn London Kensington (Olympia)

BUDGET HOTEL PLAN 4 A3

☎ 0871 527 8668
22-32 West Cromwell Rd, Kensington SW5 9QJ
web: www.premierinn.com
dir: On N side of West Cromwell Rd, between juncts of
Cromwell Rd, Earls Court Rd & Warwick Rd

Rooms 86

SW6 FULHAM

Millennium & Copthorne Hotels at Chelsea FC

★★★★ 76% HOTEL PLAN 1 E3

☎ 020 7565 1400
Stamford Bridge, Fulham Rd SW6 1HS
e-mail: reservations@chelseafc.com
web: www.millenniumhotels.co.uk
dir: 4 mins walk from Fulham Broadway tube station

A unique destination in a fashionable area of the city.
Situated at Chelsea's famous Stamford Bridge
football club the accommodation offered here is very
up-to-the-minute. Bedroom facilities include flat-
screen LCD TVs, video on demand, broadband, Wi-fi
and good sized desk space; larger Club rooms have
additional features. For eating there's a brasserie, the
Bridge Bar and sports bar, and for corporate guests a
flexible arrangement of meeting and event rooms is
available.

Rooms 281 (64 fmly) **Facilities** STV Wi-fi Gym
Health club Treatments Stadium tours Football
packages **Conf** Class 600 Board 30 Thtr 950
Services Lift Air con **Parking** 360 **Notes** ⊗
Civ Wed 50

Ibis London Earls Court

★★★ 70% HOTEL PLAN 4 A1

☎ 020 7610 0880
47 Lillie Rd SW6 1UD
e-mail: h5623@accor.com
web: www.ibishotel.com
dir: From Hammersmith flyover towards London, keep
in right lane, right at Kings pub on Talgarth Rd to join
North End Rd. At mini-rdbt turn right. Hotel on left

Situated opposite the Earls Court Exhibition Centre,
this large, modern hotel is popular with business and
leisure guests. Bedrooms are comfortable and well
equipped. There is a café bar open all day and a
restaurant that serves evening meals. There are also
extensive conference facilities and an underground
car park.

Rooms 504 (20 fmly) **Facilities** FTV Wi-fi
Conf Class 750 Board 25 Thtr 1200 **Services** Lift
Parking 130

Premier Inn London Putney Bridge

BUDGET HOTEL PLAN 1 D3

☎ 0871 527 8674
3 Putney Bridge Approach SW6 3JD
web: www.premierinn.com
dir: Nearest tube: Putney Bridge. Hotel on A219, N of
River Thames

High quality, budget accommodation ideal for both
families and business travellers. Spacious, en suite
bedrooms feature tea and coffee making facilities,
and Freeview TV in most hotels. Internet access and
Wi-fi are available for a small fee. The adjacent
family restaurant features a wide and varied menu.
See also the Hotel Groups pages.

Rooms 154

LONDON

SW7 SOUTH KENSINGTON

INSPECTORS' CHOICE

Baglioni Hotel

★★★★★ @ HOTEL PLAN 4 C5

☎ 020 7368 5700
60 Hyde Park Gate, Kensington Rd, Kensington SW7 5BB
e-mail: baglioni.london.@baglionihotels.com
dir: On corner of Hyde Park Gate & De Vere Gardens

Located in the heart of Kensington and overlooking Hyde Park, this small hotel buzzes with Italian style and chic. Bedrooms, mostly suites, are generously sized and designed in bold dark colours; they have espresso machines, interactive plasma-screen TVs and a host of other excellent touches. Service is both professional and friendly, with personal butlers for the bedrooms. Public areas include the main open-plan space with bar, lounge and Brunello Restaurant, all merging together with great elan; there is a spa with four treatment rooms and a techno-gym, and a fashionable private club bar downstairs.

Rooms 67 (7 fmly) (30 smoking) 🐾 **S** £220-£550; **D** £220-£550* **Facilities** Spa STV FTV Wi-fi ✈ Gym Xmas New Year **Conf** Class 33 Board 34 Thtr 60 **Services** Lift Air con **Parking** 2 **Notes** Civ Wed 60

Crowne Plaza London-Kensington

★★★★ 77% HOTEL PLAN 4 C3

☎ 020 7373 2222
100 Cromwell Rd SW7 4ER
e-mail: info@cpkensington.co.uk
dir: Opposite Gloucester Road tube station. From M4 follow Central London signs. At Cromwell Rd hotel is visible on left

A boutique hotel with a grand Victorian townhouse façade and a one-acre landscaped garden, offering contemporary accommodation. Facilities include a state-of-the-art fitness suite, and sauna. The ground-floor Streetside Restaurant offers a relaxed atmosphere.

Rooms 162

Millennium Bailey's Hotel London Kensington

MILLENNIUM
MILLENNIUM • COPTHORNE

★★★★ 76% @ HOTEL PLAN 4 C3

☎ 020 7373 6000
140 Gloucester Rd SW7 4QH
e-mail: reservations.baileys@millenniumhotels.co.uk
web: www.millenniumhotels.co.uk
dir: From A4, at Cromwell Hospital, into Knaresborough Place, to Courtfield Rd to corner of Gloucester Rd, hotel opposite tube station

This elegant hotel has a town house feel and enjoys a prime location. Air-conditioned bedrooms are smartly appointed and thoughtfully equipped, particularly the club rooms which benefit from DVD players. Public areas include a stylish contemporary restaurant and bar. Guests may also use the facilities at the larger sister hotel which is adjacent.

Rooms 211 (3 smoking) **Facilities** STV Wi-fi Gym **Conf** Class 12 Board 12 Thtr 12 **Services** Lift Air con **Parking** 110 **Notes** ⊗

Millennium Gloucester Hotel London Kensington

MILLENNIUM
MILLENNIUM • COPTHORNE

★★★★ 74% HOTEL PLAN 4 C3

☎ 020 7373 6030
4-18 Harrington Gardens SW7 4LH
e-mail: reservations.gloucester@millenniumhotels.co.uk
web: www.millenniumhotels.co.uk
dir: Opposite Gloucester Rd tube station

This spacious, stylish hotel is centrally located, close to The Victoria & Albert Museum and Gloucester Road tube station. Air-conditioned bedrooms are furnished in a variety of contemporary styles and Clubrooms benefit from a dedicated club lounge with complimentary breakfast and snacks. A wide range of eating options includes Singaporean and Mediterranean cuisine.

Rooms 610 (8 fmly) (37 smoking) **S** £546; **D** £546* **Facilities** STV Wi-fi Gym **Conf** Class 300 Board 100 Thtr 500 **Services** Lift Air con **Parking** 110 **Notes** LB ⊗ Civ Wed 500

The Rembrandt Hotel

SAROVA HOTELS

★★★★ 74% HOTEL PLAN 4 E4

☎ 020 7589 8100
11 Thurloe Place, Knightsbridge SW7 2RS
e-mail: rembrandt@sarova.co.uk
dir: M4 onto A4 (Cromwell Rd) into central London. Hotel opposite Victoria & Albert Museum

This attractive hotel is conveniently situated opposite the Victoria and Albert Museum, a stone's throw from Harrods. Smart, well-appointed bedrooms are thoughtfully equipped and public areas include a restaurant and an attractive bar lounge and conservatory. Guests also benefit from concessions at the adjacent Roman-styled health and leisure suite.

Rooms 193 **S** £440; **D** £510 (incl. bkfst)* **Facilities** Spa STV FTV Wi-fi ✈ 🎾 Gym **Conf** Class 84 Board 80 Thtr 200 Del from £195 to £280* **Services** Lift **Notes** LB ⊗ Civ Wed 200

Save on hotels. Book at theAA.com/hotel

SW7 – SW19 291 ENGLAND

Harrington Hall Hotel

★★★★ 73% HOTEL PLAN 4 C3

☎ 020 7396 9696
5-25 Harrington Gardens SW7 4JW
e-mail: nhharringtonhall@nh-hotels.com
web: www.nh-hotels.com
dir: 2 mins walk from Gloucester Road tube station

This splendid period property is centrally located just
a stone's throw from Gloucester Road tube station
and is convenient for visiting the museums and for
shopping in Knightsbridge. Spacious bedrooms are
smartly appointed and boast a host of extra touches.
The public areas include extensive meeting facilities,
a lounge bar and a restaurant.

Rooms 200 (4 fmly) **Facilities** STV FTV Wi-fi HL Gym
Sauna Xmas New Year **Conf** Class 100 Board 50
Thtr 240 **Services** Lift Air con **Notes** ⊗ Civ Wed 200

Holiday Inn London -
Kensington Forum

★★★★ 72% HOTEL PLAN 4 C3

☎ 0871 942 9100
97 Cromwell Rd SW7 4DN
e-mail: hikensingtonforum@ihg.com
web: www.holidayinn.co.uk
dir: From S Circular onto N Circular at Chiswick
Flyover. Onto A4 (Cromwell Rd) to Gloucester Rd

This hotel is ideally situated within a few minutes'
walk from the Gloucester Road underground station
and close to many of London's attractions such as the
Natural History Museum, Science Museum,
Kensington High Street and the West End. The
bedrooms and bathrooms are well appointed and vary
in size. The ground-floor areas including a gym and a
stylish business lounge.

Rooms 906 (26 fmly) (46 smoking) **Facilities** STV FTV
Wi-fi ⇘ Gym Fitness room Xmas New Year
Conf Class 150 Board 50 Thtr 300 Del from £140 to
£320 **Services** Lift Air con **Parking** 76 **Notes** ⊗
Civ Wed 250

Park International Hotel

⊍ PLAN 4 D3

☎ 207 370 5711
117 - 129 Cromwell Rd SW7 4DT

Currently the rating for this establishment is not
confirmed. This may be due to a change of ownership
or because it has only recently joined the AA rating
scheme. For further details please see the AA
website: theAA.com

Rooms 172 **S** £130-£160; **D** £160-£190 (incl. bkfst)*
Conf Class 20 Board 18 Thtr 30

SW10 WEST BROMPTON

Wyndham Grand London Chelsea Harbour

★★★★★ 83% ◉ HOTEL PLAN 1 E3

☎ 020 7823 3000
Chelsea Harbour SW10 0XG
e-mail: wyndhamlondon@wyndham.com
web: www.wyndhamgrandlondon.co.uk
dir: A4 to Earls Court Rd S towards river. Right into
Kings Rd, left into Lots Rd

Against the picturesque backdrop of Chelsea
Harbour's small marina, this modern hotel offers
spacious, comfortable accommodation. All rooms are
suites, which are superbly equipped; many enjoy
splendid views of the marina. In addition, there are
also several luxurious penthouse suites. Public areas
include a modern bar and restaurant, excellent
leisure facilities (including a spa) and extensive
meeting and function rooms.

Rooms 158 (36 fmly) **Facilities** Spa STV FTV Wi-fi ⇘
⊛ Gym Sauna Steam room ♫ Xmas New Year
Conf Class 115 Board 40 Thtr 600 **Services** Lift
Air con **Parking** 2000 **Notes** Civ Wed 450

SW18 WANDSWORTH

Holiday Inn Express Wandsworth - Battersea

BUDGET HOTEL PLAN 1 E2

☎ 020 8877 5950
Smugglers Way, Wandsworth SW18 1EG
e-mail: wandsworth@morethanhotels.com
web: www.hiexpress.com/londonwandswth
dir: From S side of Wandsworth Bridge, take A3205 W.
0.5m to Smugglers Way on right

A modern hotel ideal for families and business
travellers. Fresh and uncomplicated, the spacious
rooms include Sky TV, power shower and tea and
coffee-making facilities. Continental buffet breakfast
is included in the room rate; other meals may be
taken at the nearby family pub or restaurant. See also
the Hotel Groups pages.

Rooms 148 (60 fmly) **Conf** Class 16 Board 15 Thtr 35

SW19 WIMBLEDON

Cannizaro House

★★★★ 80% ◉◉ COUNTRY HOUSE HOTEL
PLAN 1 D2

☎ 020 8879 1464
West Side, Wimbledon Common SW19 4UE
e-mail: info@cannizarohouse.com
web: www.cannizarohouse.com
dir: From A3 follow A219 signed Wimbledon into
Parkside, right into Cannizaro Rd, sharp right into
West Side

This unique, elegant 18th-century house has a long
tradition of hosting the rich and famous of London
society. A few miles from the city centre, the
landscaped grounds provide a peaceful escape and a
country-house ambience; fine art, murals and
stunning fireplaces feature throughout. Spacious
bedrooms are individually furnished and equipped to
a high standard. The award-winning restaurant
menus proudly herald locally sourced, organic
ingredients.

Rooms 46 (10 fmly) (5 GF) ➠ **D** £150-£500 (incl.
bkfst)* **Facilities** STV FTV Wi-fi ⤵ **Conf** Class 50
Board 40 Thtr 120 Del from £199 to £350*
Services Lift **Parking** 95 **Notes** LB Civ Wed 100

SW19 WIMBLEDON *continued*

Holiday Inn Express Wimbledon South

BUDGET HOTEL PLAN 1 E1

☎ 020 8545 7300
Miller's Meadhouse, 200 High St, Colliers Wood SW19 2BH
e-mail: reservations@exhiwimbledon.co.uk
web: www.exhiwimbledon.co.uk
dir: A238 Kingston Road, at lights into Merton High St, signed Colliers Wood. Hotel directly opposite Colliers Wood underground station

A modern hotel ideal for families and business travellers. Fresh and uncomplicated, the spacious rooms include Sky TV, power shower and tea and coffee-making facilities. Continental buffet breakfast is included in the room rate; other meals may be taken at the nearby family pub or restaurant. See also the Hotel Groups pages.

Rooms 83 (57 fmly) (7 GF) **S** £130-£280; **D** £130-£280 (incl. bkfst)* **Conf** Class 16 Board 25 Thtr 45 Del from £150*

Premier Inn London Wimbledon South

BUDGET HOTEL PLAN 1 E1

☎ 0871 527 8684
27 Chapter Way, Off Merantun Way, Wimbledon SW19 2RF
web: www.premierinn.com
dir: M25 junct 10, A3 towards London. Exit A298 (Wimbledon) onto A238. Right onto A219, left onto A24 (Merantun Way). At rdbt 3rd exit signed Merton Abbey Mills

High quality, budget accommodation ideal for both families and business travellers. Spacious, en suite bedrooms feature tea and coffee making facilities, and Freeview TV in most hotels. Internet access and Wi-fi are available for a small fee. The adjacent family restaurant features a wide and varied menu. See also the Hotel Groups pages.

Rooms 132

W1 WEST END

INSPECTORS' CHOICE

The Connaught

MAYBOURNE HOTEL GROUP

★★★★★ ◉◉◉◉ HOTEL PLAN 2 G1

☎ 020 7499 7070
Carlos Place W1K 2AL
e-mail: info@the-connaught.co.uk
dir: Between Grosvenor Sq & Berkeley Sq

This iconic hotel is truly spectacular with stunning interior design. There are sumptuous day rooms and stylish bedrooms with state-of-the-art facilities and marble en suites with deep tubs, TV screens and power showers. Butlers are available at the touch of a button and guests are pampered by friendly, attentive staff offering intuitive service. There is a choice of bars and restaurants including the Espelette bistro, and the award-winning cuisine of Hélène Darroze which is imaginative, inspired and truly memorable. The excellent Aman Spa at the hotel offers health and beauty treatments, a swimming pool and fitness centre.

Rooms 123 (17 smoking) 🐾 **Facilities** Spa STV FTV Wi-fi 🗘 Gym **Conf** Class 70 Board 60 Thtr 120 **Services** Lift Air con **Notes** ⊗ Civ Wed 200

INSPECTORS' CHOICE

45 Park Lane

★★★★★ ◉◉◉ HOTEL PLAN 4 G6

☎ 0207 493 4545
45 Park Ln W1K 1BJ
e-mail: info45parklane@dorchestercollection.com

This hotel offers luxurious and contemporary interiors. The bedrooms, including ten suites, all have a view of Hyde Park; the Penthouse Suite has its own roof terrace. A striking central staircase leads to a mezzanine featuring Bar 45, a library and a private media room. Other public areas include a lounge area and the award-winning restaurant CUT at 45 Park Lane, a modern American steak restaurant, overseen by chef Wolfgang Puck.

Rooms 45

LONDON

Save on hotels. Book at **theAA.com/hotel**

SW19 – W1 293 ENGLAND

INSPECTORS' CHOICE

Claridge's

MAYBOURNE HOTEL GROUP

★★★★★ 🏵🏵🏵 HOTEL PLAN 2 H1

☎ 020 7629 8860
Brook St W1A 2JQ
e-mail: info@claridges.co.uk
dir: 1st turn after Green Park tube station to Berkeley Sq & 4th exit into Davies St. 3rd right into Brook St

Once renowned as the resort of kings and princes, Claridge's today continues to set the standards by which other hotels are judged. The sumptuous, air-conditioned bedrooms are elegantly themed to reflect the Victorian or art deco architecture of the building. Gordon Ramsay at Claridge's is now established as one of London's most popular dining venues, while the stylish cocktail bar is a hit with residents and non-residents alike. Service throughout is punctilious and thoroughly professional.

Rooms 203 (144 fmly) **Facilities** Spa STV Wi-fi Gym Beauty & health treatments Use of sister hotel's swimming pool 🎵 Xmas New Year **Conf** Class 130 Board 60 Thtr 250 **Services** Lift Air con **Notes** ⊗ Civ Wed 200

INSPECTORS' CHOICE

The Ritz London

★★★★★ 🏵🏵🏵 HOTEL PLAN 4 J6

☎ 020 7493 8181
150 Piccadilly W1J 9BR
e-mail: enquire@theritzlondon.com
web: www.theritzlondon.com
dir: From Hyde Park Corner E on Piccadilly. Hotel on right after Green Park

This renowned, stylish hotel offers guests the ultimate in sophistication whilst still managing to retain all its former historical glory. Bedrooms and suites are exquisitely furnished in Louis XVI style, with fine marble bathrooms and every imaginable comfort. Elegant reception rooms include the Palm Court with its legendary afternoon teas, the beautiful fashionable Rivoli Bar and the sumptuous Ritz Restaurant, complete with gold chandeliers and extraordinary trompe-l'oeil decoration.

Rooms 134 (44 fmly) (24 smoking) 🐾
S £255-£7000; **D** £255-£7000* **Facilities** STV Wi-fi ᗡ HL Gym Beauty treatment room Fitness centre The Ritz Club & Casino 🎵 Xmas New Year **Conf** Class 40 Board 30 Thtr 60 **Services** Lift Air con **Parking** 10 **Notes** LB ⊗ Civ Wed 60

INSPECTORS' CHOICE

Athenaeum Hotel & Apartments

★★★★★ 🏵🏵 HOTEL PLAN 4 H6

☎ 020 7499 3464
116 Piccadilly W1J 7BJ
e-mail: info@athenaeumhotel.com
web: www.athenaeumhotel.com
dir: On Piccadilly, overlooking Green Park

With a discreet address in Mayfair, this well-loved hotel offers bedrooms appointed to the highest levels of comfort; all include Bose iPod speakers, a pillow menu and Wi-fi, and several boast views over Green Park. The hotel also has suites, and for the ultimate luxury there's a roof-top suite with a private balcony. The hotel has a whisky bar, the Garden Lounge for award-winning afternoon teas, and even a pudding parlour open in the evenings. The stylish restaurant serves British cuisine which will appeals to all ages. A range of spacious and well-appointed apartments can be found in a row of Edwardian townhouses adjacent to the hotel. There is an extensive range of beauty treatments available along with conference and meeting facilities.

Rooms 156 (8 smoking) **Facilities** STV Wi-fi Gym Steam rooms Sauna Hairdressing salon Xmas New Year **Conf** Class 35 Board 36 Thtr 55 **Services** Lift Air con **Notes** ⊗ Civ Wed 80

LONDON

W1 WEST END *continued*

INSPECTORS' CHOICE

Brown's Hotel

★★★★★ ◎ ◎ HOTEL PLAN 2 J1

☎ 020 7493 6020
Albemarle St, Mayfair W1S 4BP
e-mail: reservations.browns@roccofortehotels.com
web: www.roccofortehotels.com
dir: A short walk from Green Park, Bond St, Piccadilly & Buckingham Palace

Brown's is a London hospitality icon that retains much charm by the successful balance of the traditional and the contemporary. Bedrooms are luxurious, furnished to the highest standard and come with all the modern comforts expected of such a grand Mayfair hotel. The hotel has 29 suites including two Royal Suites and two Presidential Suites. The elegant, yet informal, HIX at the Albemarle serves a traditional selection of popular British dishes that are created with great skill; it is home to a collection of works by leading British artists; the English Tea Room proves a great meeting place for afternoon tea.

Rooms 117 (12 smoking) **Facilities** Spa STV Wi-fi Gym ♫ Xmas New Year **Conf** Class 30 Board 30 Thtr 70 **Services** Lift Air con **Notes** ⊗ Civ Wed 70

INSPECTORS' CHOICE

The Dorchester

★★★★★ ◎ ◎ HOTEL PLAN 4 G6

☎ 020 7629 8888
Park Ln W1K 1QA
e-mail: info@thedorchester.com
dir: Halfway along Park Ln between Hyde Park Corner & Marble Arch

One of London's finest. The Dorchester remains one of the best-loved hotels in the country and always delivers. The spacious bedrooms and suites are beautifully appointed and feature fabulous marble bathrooms. Leading off from the foyer, The Promenade is the perfect setting for afternoon tea or drinks. In the evening guests can relax to the sound of live jazz, whilst enjoying a cocktail in the stylish bar. Dining options include the sophisticated Chinese restaurant, China Tang (2 AA Rosettes); Alain Ducasse at The Dorchester from the world renowned French chef of the same name (3 AA Rosettes), and of course, The Grill (2 AA Rosettes).

Rooms 250 ☛ **S** £282-£618; **D** £318-£834*
Facilities Spa STV FTV Wi-fi ♀ Gym Steam rooms Fitness suite ♫ Xmas New Year **Conf** Class 300 Board 42 Thtr 500 **Services** Lift Air con **Parking** 13 **Notes** ⊗ Civ Wed 500

HOTEL OF THE YEAR

INSPECTORS' CHOICE

Four Seasons Hotel London at Park Lane

★★★★★ ◎ ◎ HOTEL PLAN 4 G6

☎ 020 7499 0888
Hamilton Place, Park Ln W1J 7DR
e-mail: reservations@fourseasons.com
dir: From Piccadilly into Old Park Ln, into Hamilton Place

This long-established popular hotel is discreetly located near Hyde Park Corner, in the heart of Mayfair. It successfully combines modern efficiencies with traditional luxury. Guest care is consistently of the highest order, even down to the smallest detail of the personalised wake-up call. The bedrooms are elegant and spacious, and the unique conservatory rooms are particularly special. Spacious public areas include extensive conference and banqueting facilities, Lane's bar and fine-dining restaurant and an elegant lounge where wonderful afternoon teas are served. AA Hotel of the Year for London 2012-13.

Rooms 193 (67 smoking) ☛ **S** fr £495; **D** fr £495*
Facilities Spa STV FTV Wi-fi ♀ Gym Fitness Centre ♫ Xmas New Year **Conf** Class 180 Board 100 Thtr 400 **Services** Lift Air con **Parking** 10 **Notes** Civ Wed 350

Save on hotels. Book at **theAA.com/hotel**

W1 295 ENGLAND

The Langham, London

★★★★★ 86% ⓢ ⓢ HOTEL PLAN 2 H3

☎ 020 7636 1000
Portland Place W1B 1JA
e-mail: lon.info@langhamhotels.com
dir: N of Regent St, left opposite All Soul's Church

This hotel has a grand entrance which leads into restored interior elegance. Dating back to 1865 the building displays a contemporary, luxurious style. Situated near Regent Street it is ideally located for both theatreland and the principal shopping areas. Bedrooms are delightfully appointed and many have excellent views. The Landau restaurant and Artesian bar offer high standards of service, delivered by a friendly team. Palm Court is a great place for afternoon tea or a glass of champagne. There is also an extensive health club complete with a 16-metre pool.

Rooms 378 (9 fmly) (15 smoking) **S** £200-£9000; **D** £200-£9000* **Facilities** Spa STV Wi-fi ♀ ⓧ supervised Gym Health club Sauna Steam room ♫ Xmas New Year Child facilities **Conf** Class 148 Board 80 Thtr 300 **Services** Lift Air con **Notes** ⊗ Civ Wed 280

Metropolitan London

★★★★★ 85% ⓢ ⓢ HOTEL PLAN 4 G6

☎ 020 7447 1000
Old Park Ln W1K 1LB
e-mail: res.lon@metropolitan.como.bz
dir: On corner of Old Park Ln & Hertford St

Overlooking Hyde Park this hotel is located within easy reach of the fashionable stores of Knightsbridge and Mayfair. The hotel's contemporary style allows freedom and space to relax. Understated luxury is the key here with bedrooms enjoying great natural light. There is also a Shambhala Spa, steam room and fully equipped gym. For those seeking a culinary experience, Nobu offers innovative Japanese cuisine with an upbeat atmosphere.

Rooms 144 (23 smoking) ♪ **Facilities** Spa STV FTV Wi-fi ♀ Gym Steam rooms ♫ **Conf** Class 25 Board 30 Thtr 40 **Services** Lift Air con **Parking** 12 **Notes** Civ Wed 30

London Marriott Hotel Park Lane

Marriott.
HOTELS & RESORTS

★★★★★ 84% ⓢ ⓢ HOTEL PLAN 2 F1

☎ 020 7493 7000
140 Park Ln W1K 7AA
e-mail: mhrs.parklane@marriotthotels.com
web: www.londonmarriottparklane.co.uk
dir: From Hyde Park Corner left on Park Ln onto A4202, 0.8m. At Marble Arch onto Park Ln. Take 1st left into North Row. Hotel on left

This modern and stylish hotel is situated in a prominent position in the heart of central London. Bedrooms are superbly appointed and air conditioned. Public rooms include a popular lounge/bar, and there are excellent leisure facilities and an executive lounge.

Rooms 157 (11 smoking) ♪ **S** £229-£950; **D** £229-£950* **Facilities** STV Wi-fi ♀ ⓧ Gym Steam room Xmas New Year **Conf** Class 33 Board 42 Thtr 72 **Services** Lift Air con **Notes** LB ⊗

Hyatt Regency London - The Churchill

★★★★★ 82% ⓢ ⓢ ⓢ HOTEL PLAN 2 F2

☎ 020 7486 5800
30 Portman Square W1H 7BH
e-mail: london.churchill@hyatt.com
dir: From Marble Arch rdbt, follow signs for Oxford Circus into Oxford St. Left after 2nd lights into Portman St. Hotel on left

This smart hotel enjoys a central location overlooking Portman Square. Excellent conference and in-room facilities, plus a fitness room make this the ideal choice for both corporate and leisure guests. To set the style guests are greeted by stunning floral displays in the sophisticated lobby. The Montagu restaurant (with 2 AA Rosettes) offers contemporary dining, plus the option to sit at the Chef's Table for a front row seat to watch all the action in the kitchen.

Rooms 434 (87 smoking) ♪ **S** £200-£500; **D** £200-£500* **Facilities** STV FTV Wi-fi ♀ ♨ Gym Jogging track ♫ Xmas New Year **Conf** Class 160 Board 68 Thtr 250 **Services** Lift Air con **Parking** 48 **Notes** ⊗ Civ Wed 250

Grosvenor House, A JW Marriott Hotel

GROSVENOR HOUSE
A JW MARRIOTT HOTEL
LONDON

★★★★★ 82% ⓢ HOTEL PLAN 2 G1

☎ 020 7499 6363 & 7399 8400
Park Ln W1K 7TN
e-mail: grosvenor.house@marriotthotels.com
web: www.londongrosvenorhouse.co.uk
dir: Centrally located on Park Ln, between Hyde Park Corner & Oxford St

This quintessentially British hotel, overlooking Hyde Park offers luxurious accommodation, warm hospitality and exemplary service that epitomises the fine hotel culture of London. The property boasts the largest ballroom in Europe, and there is a steakhouse and a cocktail bar. The Park Room and The Library make perfect settings for afternoon tea.

Rooms 494 (111 smoking) **Facilities** STV Wi-fi ♀ Gym Fitness centre Xmas New Year **Conf** Class 800 Board 140 Thtr 1500 **Services** Lift Air con **Parking** 48 **Notes** ⊗ Civ Wed 1500

The Westbury Hotel

★★★★★ 81% ⓢ ⓢ ⓢ HOTEL PLAN 2 H1

☎ 020 7629 7755
Bond St W1S 2YF
e-mail: reservations@westburymayfair.com
dir: From Oxford Circus S down Regent St, right onto Conduit St, hotel at junct of Conduit St & Bond St

A well-known favourite with an international clientele, The Westbury is located at the heart of London's finest shopping district and provides a calm atmosphere away from the hubbub. The standards of accommodation are high throughout and bedrooms have panoramic views; the options include a variety of suites and a two-bedroom penthouse suite. Reception rooms offer a good choice for both relaxing and eating and include the stylish Polo Bar, The Westbury lounge, the Tsukiji Sushi Restaurant and the fine-dining option in award-winning Alyn Williams at the Westbury. Private dining is also available.

Rooms 246 (80 fmly) **Facilities** STV FTV Wi-fi ♀ Gym Fitness centre Steam room Sauna Xmas New Year **Conf** Class 100 Board 40 Thtr 200 **Services** Lift Air con **Notes** ⊗ Civ Wed 80

LONDON

W1 WEST END *continued*

London Hilton on Park Lane

★★★★★ 81% HOTEL PLAN 4 G6

☎ 020 7493 8000
22 Park Ln W1K 1BE
e-mail: reservations.parklane@hilton.com
dir: From N: M1/A41 towards central London & West
End. W along Oxford St, into Park Lane. From S: A23
for central London & West End, cross Vauxhall Bridge
(A202) & into Park Lane

Located in the heart of Park Lane, this landmark hotel
offers a luxury environment overlooking Hyde Park and
the city. A dedicated team of staff is available to
meet their guests' every need. Having undergone a
full refurbishment, the bedrooms are designed with
quality appointments and luxury fabrics. Several
eating options are available - from the renowned
Galvin at Windows to the all-day dining of Podium,
which also serves a splendid afternoon tea. For
guests arriving by car, valet parking is offered.

Rooms 453 (52 smoking) **Facilities** Spa STV FTV Wi-fi
⊘ Gym ♫ Xmas New Year **Conf** Class 600 Board 60
Thtr 1100 **Services** Lift Air con **Parking** 242 **Notes** ⊗
Civ Wed 1000

Le Meridien Piccadilly

★★★★★ 81% HOTEL PLAN 2 J1

☎ 0207 734 8000
21 Piccadilly W1J 0BH
e-mail: reservations.piccadilly@lemeridien.com
dir: 100mtrs from Piccadilly Circus

Situated in heart of Piccadilly, this well established
hotel is ideally located for both the west end and
Theatreland. The well-equipped, air-conditioned
bedrooms, varying in shape and size, are modern and
contemporary in style. Public areas include extensive
leisure facilities, with a state-of-the-art gym, pool
and sauna, the trendy Longitude 0° 8' cocktail bar,
and the popular Terrace Restaurant which overlooks
Piccadilly.

Rooms 280 ⌖ **S** £250-£1007; **D** £250-£1007*
Facilities Spa STV Wi-fi ⊘ ⊗ supervised Gym Squash
Conf Class 160 Board 80 Thtr 250 **Services** Lift
Air con **Notes** ⊗ Civ Wed 200

The Chesterfield Mayfair

THE RED CARNATION HOTEL COLLECTION

★★★★ ◉◉ HOTEL PLAN 4 H6

☎ 020 7491 2622
35 Charles St, Mayfair W1J 5EB
e-mail: bookch@rchmail.com
web: www.chesterfieldmayfair.com
dir: Hyde Park Corner along Piccadilly, left into Half
Moon St. At end left & 1st right into Queens St, then
right into Charles St

Quiet elegance and an atmosphere of exclusivity
characterise this stylish Mayfair hotel where
attentive, friendly service is paramount. The
bedrooms, each with a marble-clad bathroom, have
contemporary styles - perhaps with floral fabric
walls, an African theme or with Savile Row stripes.
In addition to these deluxe bedrooms there are 13
individually designed suites; some with four-poster
beds and some with jacuzzis. The Butler's
Restaurant is the fine dining option, and The
Conservatory, with views over the garden, is just
the place for cocktails, light lunches and afternoon
teas. The hotel is air conditioned throughout.

Rooms 107 ⌖ **Facilities** STV Wi-fi ⊘ ♫ Xmas
Conf Class 45 Board 45 Thtr 100 **Services** Lift
Air con **Notes** Civ Wed 120

London Marriott Hotel Grosvenor Square

Marriott HOTELS & RESORTS

★★★★ 84% ◉◉ HOTEL PLAN 2 G1

☎ 020 7493 1232
Grosvenor Square W1K 6JP
e-mail: dann.davies@marriotthotels.com
web: www.londonmarriottgrosvenorsquare.co.uk
dir: M4 E to Cromwell Rd through Knightsbridge to
Hyde Park Corner. Into Park Lane, right at Brook Gate
into Upper Brook St to Grosvenor Sq

Situated adjacent to Grosvenor Square in the heart of
Mayfair, this hotel boasts convenient access to the
city, West End and some of London's most exclusive
shops. Bedrooms and public areas are furnished and
decorated to a high standard and retain the

---

traditional elegance for which the area is known. The
hotel's eating options include Maze Grill with 2 AA
Rosettes.

Rooms 237 (26 fmly) **S** £150-£195; **D** £175-£559*
Facilities Wi-fi Gym Exercise & fitness centre Xmas
Conf Class 500 Board 120 Thtr 900 **Services** Lift
Air con **Notes** ⊗ Civ Wed 600

London Marriott Hotel Marble Arch

Marriott HOTELS & RESORTS

★★★★ 84% HOTEL PLAN 2 F2

☎ 020 7723 1277
134 George St W1H 5DN
e-mail: mhrs.lonma.sales.mkt.cood@marriotthotels.
com
web: www.londonmarriottmarblearch.co.uk
dir: From Marble Arch turn into Edgware Rd, then 4th
right into George St. Left into Dorset St for entrance

Situated just off the Edgware Road and close to the
Oxford Street shops, this friendly hotel offers smart,
well-equipped, air-conditioned bedrooms. Public
areas are stylish, and include a smart indoor leisure
club and an Italian themed restaurant. Secure
underground parking is available.

Rooms 240 (100 fmly) (20 smoking) **Facilities** STV
FTV Wi-fi HL ⊗ supervised Gym Xmas New Year
Conf Class 75 Board 80 Thtr 150 **Services** Lift Air con
Parking 83 **Notes** ⊗ Civ Wed 150

The Mandeville Hotel

★★★★ 80% ◉◉ HOTEL PLAN 2 G2

☎ 020 7935 5599
Mandeville Place W1U 2BE
e-mail: sales@mandeville.co.uk
web: www.mandeville.co.uk
dir: 3 mins walk from Bond St tube station

This is a stylish and attractive boutique-style hotel
with a very contemporary feel. Bedrooms have state-
of-the-art TVs, air conditioning and large, very
comfortable beds. One of the suites, The Penthouse,
has a patio with views over London. The deVille
Restaurant offers award-winning modern British
cuisine, and the deVigne cocktail bar is always
popular.

Rooms 142 (6 fmly) ⌖ **S** £140-£300; **D** £160-£350*
Facilities STV FTV Wi-fi ⊘ Xmas New Year
Conf Class 20 Board 20 Thtr 40 **Services** Lift Air con
Notes ⊗

Save on hotels. Book at **theAA.com/hotel**

W1 297 ENGLAND

Millennium Hotel London Mayfair

★★★★ 79% ◉◉ HOTEL PLAN 2 G1

☎ 020 7629 9400
Grosvenor Square W1K 2HP
e-mail: reservations@millenniumhotels.co.uk
web: www.millenniumhotels.co.uk
dir: S side of Grosvenor Square, 5 mins walk from Oxford St & Bond St stations

This hotel benefits from a prestigious location in the heart of Mayfair, close to Bond Street. Smart bedrooms are generally spacious and club-floor rooms have exclusive use of their own lounge with complimentary refreshments. A choice of bars and dining options is available along with conference facilities and a fitness room.

Rooms 336 ☞ **S** £199-£540; **D** £210-£575 **Facilities** STV FTV Wi-fi ↻ HL Gym Fitness suite ♬ Xmas New Year **Conf** Class 250 Board 70 Thtr 500 Del from £305 to £730 **Services** Lift Air con **Notes** LB ⊗ Civ Wed 250

Best Western Premier Mostyn Hotel

★★★★ 77% ◉◉◉ HOTEL PLAN 2 F2

☎ 020 7935 2361
4 Bryanston St W1H 7BY
e-mail: info@mostynhotel.co.uk
web: www.bw-mostynhotel.co.uk
dir: Nearest tube stations: Marble Arch & Bond St

This hotel is a well located, historic property. The bedrooms, including executive and deluxe club floor rooms, vary in size but all are smartly equipped, boast bright trendy soft furnishings and are air conditioned; the en suites are equally modern and stylish. The public areas include a cocktail bar/lounge, Fire & Spice all-day dining concept, and the acclaimed Texture Restaurant which delivers impressive, modern cooking. The hotel offers free Wi-fi throughout.

Rooms 121 (15 fmly) (9 GF) **Facilities** Spa STV FTV Wi-fi ↻ ⌣ Gym ♬ Xmas **Conf** Class 70 Board 50 Thtr 130 **Services** Lift Air con **Notes** ⊗

Park Plaza Sherlock Holmes

★★★★ 76% ◉ HOTEL PLAN 2 F3

☎ 020 7486 6161
108 Baker St W1U 6LJ
e-mail: info@sherlockholmeshotel.com
web: www.sherlockholmeshotel.com
dir: From Marylebone Flyover into Marylebone Rd. At Baker St turn right for hotel on left

Chic and modern, this boutique-style hotel is near a number of London underground and rail stations. Public rooms include a popular bar, sited just inside the main entrance, and Sherlock's Grill, where the mesquite-wood burning stove is a feature of the cooking. The hotel also features an indoor health suite and a relaxing lounge.

Rooms 119 (20 fmly) **S** £116-£387; **D** £116-£387* **Facilities** STV Wi-fi Gym Beauty treatment room ♬ Xmas **Conf** Class 35 Board 30 Thtr 80 Del from £200 to £359* **Services** Lift Air con **Notes** LB ⊗ Civ Wed 80

Thistle Marble Arch

thistle

★★★★ 75% HOTEL PLAN 2 G2

☎ 0871 971 1753 & 020 7629 8040
Bryanston St W1A 4UR
e-mail: marblearch@thistle.co.uk
web: www.thistlehotels.com/marblearch
dir: From Marble Arch monument into Oxford St. 1st left into Portman St, 1st left into Bryanston St. Hotel entrance on left

This centrally located hotel, adjacent to a car park, is ideal for the attractions of Oxford Street and Knightsbridge. The spacious bedrooms come in a range of size and price options, but all are very well equipped and have air conditioning. The public areas include a fast food service, Co-Motion, and a more leisurely carvery restaurant, which also offers a carte menu. There is also a gym, a range of meeting rooms and an executive lounge.

Rooms 692 (60 fmly) (97 smoking) ☞ **Facilities** STV FTV Wi-fi Gym ↻ Xmas New Year **Conf** Class 180 Board 94 Thtr 380 Del from £250 to £310* **Services** Lift Air con **Notes** ⊗ Civ Wed 300

The Cumberland

★★★★ 73% ◉ HOTEL PLAN 2 F2

☎ 0871 376 9014
Great Cumberland Place W1A 4RF
e-mail: enquiries@thecumberland.co.uk
dir: Behind Marble Arch monument, at top of Park Lane & Oxford St

This landmark hotel, occupying a prime position at Marble Arch, has a striking, airy lobby that is the

focal point. A choice of bars, two Gary Rhodes restaurants (one with 3 AA Rosettes and the other with 1 Rosette) and extensive conference and meeting facilities are just some of what's on offer here. Bedrooms have a stylish contemporary feel and boast an excellent range of facilities.

Rooms 1019 (119 annexe) (8 fmly) (9 GF) **Facilities** Wi-fi Gym ♬ Xmas New Year **Conf** Class 170 Board 85 Thtr 350 **Services** Lift Air con **Notes** ⊗ Civ Wed 300

Holiday Inn London - Mayfair

Holiday Inn

★★★★ 73% HOTEL PLAN 2 H1

☎ 0871 942 9110
3 Berkeley St W1J 8NE
e-mail: himayfair-reservations@ihg.com
web: www.hilondonmayfairhotel.co.uk
dir: At corner of Berkeley St & Piccadilly

Located in the heart of Mayfair and just minutes from Green Park tube station, this busy hotel has the benefit of well-proportioned, attractive bedrooms and elegant public areas. Options for dining include the graceful Nightingales Restaurant or choices from a substantial snack menu in the lounge bar.

Rooms 195 (63 fmly) **Facilities** STV Wi-fi ↻ Xmas New Year **Conf** Class 32 Board 32 Thtr 65 **Services** Lift Air con **Parking** 18 **Notes** ⊗

The Washington Mayfair Hotel

★★★★ 73% HOTEL PLAN 4 H6

☎ 020 7499 7000
5-7 Curzon St, Mayfair W1J 5HE
e-mail: sales@washington-mayfair.co.uk
web: www.washington-mayfair.co.uk
dir: From Green Park station take Piccadilly exit & turn right. 4th right into Curzon St

Situated in the heart of Mayfair, this stylish independently owned hotel offers a very high standard of accommodation. Personalised, friendly service is noteworthy. Bedrooms are attractively furnished and provide high levels of comfort. The hotel is also a popular venue for afternoon tea and refreshments, served in the marbled and wood-panelled lounge.

Rooms 171 (32 smoking) ☞ **S** £160-£445; **D** £160-£7000* **Facilities** Wi-fi ↻ Gym Xmas New Year **Conf** Class 40 Board 36 Thtr 110 Del from £260 to £500* **Services** Lift Air con **Notes** LB ⊗

LONDON

W1 WEST END *continued*

Holiday Inn London - Regents Park

★★★★ 72% HOTEL PLAN 2 H4

☎ 0871 942 9111 & 020 7388 2302
Carburton St, Regents Park W1W 5EE
e-mail: reservations-londonregentspark@ihg.com
web: www.hilondonregentsparkhotel.co.uk
dir: From E: from King's Cross, A50, left into Bolsover St. From W: A40 onto A501 (Regent's Park Station on right). Left into Albany St, 1st right to cross Euston Rd. Pass Gt Portland St tube station to Bolsover St. Hotel on left

Well located and with the benefit of an adjacent public car park, this popular modern hotel provides a range of comfortable bedrooms equipped for both business and leisure guests. The attractive Junction Restaurant is the setting for brasserie-style eating and a comprehensive buffet breakfast provides a good start to the day. The hotel also provides excellent conference facilities within The Academy Centre.

Rooms 332 (28 smoking) **S** £90-£384; **D** £90-£384* **Facilities** STV FTV Wi-fi ⤵ HL **Conf** Class 200 Board 50 Thtr 350 Del from £130 to £400* **Services** Lift Air con **Notes** LB ⊗

Radisson Blu Portman Hotel

★★★★ 72% HOTEL PLAN 2 F2

☎ 020 7208 6000
22 Portman Square W1H 7BG
e-mail: reservations.london@radissonblu.com
web: www.radissonblu.co.uk
dir: 100mtrs N of Oxford St; 300mtrs E of Edgware Rd

This smart, popular hotel enjoys a prime location a short stroll from Oxford Street and close to all the city's major attractions. The spacious, well-equipped bedrooms are themed, ranging from Oriental through to classical and contemporary Italian decor. Public areas include extensive conference facilities, a bar and the modern European Portman Restaurant.

Rooms 272 (93 fmly) (14 smoking) **Facilities** FTV Wi-fi ⤵ Gym Xmas **Conf** Class 280 Board 65 Thtr 600 **Services** Lift Air con **Parking** 400 **Notes** ⊗ Civ Wed 500

Thistle Piccadilly

thistle

★★★ 77% METRO HOTEL PLAN 3 A1

☎ 0871 376 9031
39 Coventry St W1D 6BZ
e-mail: piccadilly@thistle.co.uk
web: www.thistlehotels.com/piccadilly
dir: From Kings Cross follow signs for West End & Piccadilly

This popular hotel is centrally located between Leicester Square and Piccadilly Circus, ideal for all of the West End's attractions. Bedrooms vary in size and style but all are well equipped; deluxe and stylish executive rooms have air conditioning. Public areas include a cosy bar/lounge, where snacks are available, and a smart breakfast room. Numerous restaurants are located within walking distance.

Rooms 92 (2 fmly) **Facilities** STV FTV Wi-fi **Services** Lift Air con **Notes** ⊗

Holiday Inn London - Oxford Circus

★★★ 75% HOTEL PLAN 2 H2

☎ 020 7935 4442
57-59 Welbeck St W1M 8HS
e-mail: dmelrose@holidayinnoxfordcircus.com
web: www.holidayinn.co.uk
dir: From M1, North Circular Rd, A41. Into Finchley Rd & Baker St to Portman Sq. Left into Wigmore St, left into Queen Anne St. Left into Wellbeck St

This Edwardian property enjoys a prime location only a few minutes' walk from Oxford Street and close to all of London's major theatres, shops and attractions. Bedrooms are particularly well equipped and include a number of spacious executive and junior suites. Public areas include a split-level bar, restaurant and mini-gym.

Rooms 164 (18 fmly) (18 smoking) **S** £110-£310; **D** £120-£420* **Facilities** STV Wi-fi ⤵ Gym **Conf** Class 45 Board 32 Thtr 75 Del from £210* **Services** Lift Air con **Notes** ⊗

The Montcalm

Ⓤ PLAN 2 F2

☎ 020 7402 4288
Great Cumberland Place W1H 7TW
e-mail: reservations@montcalm.co.uk
dir: 2 mins' walk N from Marble Arch station

Currently the rating for this establishment is not confirmed. This may be due to a change of ownership or because it has only recently joined the AA rating scheme For further details please see the AA website: theAA.com

Rooms 143 (17 fmly) (7 GF) 🐾 **D** £350-£3500* **Facilities** Spa STV Wi-fi ⊗ supervised Gym **Conf** Class 250 Board 250 Thtr 500 Del from £300 to £1000* **Services** Lift Air con **Notes** LB ⊗

W2 BAYSWATER, PADDINGTON

Lancaster London

★★★★ 85% ◉◉ HOTEL PLAN 2 D1

☎ 020 7262 6737
Lancaster Ter W2 2TY
e-mail: book@lancasterlondon.com
web: www.lancasterlondon.com
dir: Adjacent to Lancaster Gate tube station

Located adjacent to Hyde Park, this large hotel offers a wide range of facilities. There are many room types; higher floors have excellent panoramic views of the city and park, and the suites are truly impressive. The hotel also offers two contrasting award-winning restaurants - the contemporary Island Restaurant & Bar, and Nipa restaurant with authentic Thai cuisine. There are spacious state-of-the-art, flexible conference and banqueting facilities, a 24-hour business centre and secure parking. This is an environmentally conscious hotel which has instigated many initiatives including a honey farm on the roof.

Rooms 416 (11 fmly) **Facilities** STV Wi-fi Xmas New Year **Conf** Class 600 Board 40 Thtr 1400 **Services** Lift Air con **Parking** 65 **Notes** ⊗ Civ Wed 1000

LONDON

Save on hotels. Book at **theAA.com/hotel**

W1 – W3 299 ENGLAND

Novotel London Paddington

★★★★ 78% HOTEL PLAN 2 C3

☎ 020 7266 6000
3 Kingdom St, Paddington W2 6BD
e-mail: h6455@accor.com
dir: Easy access from Westway (A40) & Bishops
Bridge Rd (A4206)

Located in the Paddington Central area, this hotel is
easily accessible by road, and is only a few minutes
walk from Paddington Station. Ideal for business or
leisure guests. The facilities include the Elements
Restaurant, a bar, conference facilities, a swimming
pool, sauna, plus steam and fitness rooms. An NCP
car park is a 5-minute walk away.

Rooms 206 (24 fmly) **Facilities** STV Wi-fi ⌕ ⌕ Gym
Steam room Sauna **Conf** Class 70 Board 40 Thtr 150
Services Lift

Thistle Hyde Park

thistle

★★★★ 74% HOTEL PLAN 2 C1

☎ 0871 376 9022
90-92 Lancaster Gate W2 3NR
e-mail: hydepark@thistle.co.uk
web: www.thistlehotels.com/hydepark
dir: From Marble Arch rdbt take A404
(Bayswater Rd)

Delightful building ideally situated overlooking Hyde
Park and just a short walk from Kensington Gardens.
The stylish public areas include a piano bar, a lounge
and a smart restaurant. Bedrooms are tastefully
appointed and equipped with many thoughtful
touches; some rooms have views of the park.

Rooms 54 (12 fmly) **Facilities** STV FTV Wi-fi
Conf Class 20 Board 20 Thtr 35 **Services** Lift Air con
Parking 20 **Notes** ⊗

Hotel Indigo

★★★★ 72% HOTEL PLAN 2 D2

☎ 020 7706 4444
16 London St, Paddington W2 1HL
e-mail: malcolm@lth-hotels.com

This smart hotel is located within a stone's throw of
Paddington Station. Contemporary and stylish,
bedrooms are equipped with all modern extras; they
boast high quality comfy beds ensuring a great
night's sleep and en suites with power showers and
quality toiletries. Delightful public areas include a
restaurant, bar and a coffee shop offering tempting
cakes.

Rooms 64 ⌕ **S** £180-£300; **D** £250-£400*
Facilities STV FTV Wi-fi Gym **Services** Lift Air con
Notes ⊗

Thistle Kensington Gardens

thistle

★★★★ 72% HOTEL PLAN 2 C1

☎ 0871 376 9024
104 Bayswater Rd W2 3HL
e-mail: kensingtongardens@thistle.co.uk
web: www.thistle.com/kensingtongardens

Located alongside Hyde Park, this modern hotel
provides contemporary comforts in comfortable
surroundings. The bedrooms and bathrooms are of a
high standard and are suitable for both the leisure
and business traveller. The informal Brasserie and
Bar provide a good range of dishes served. Parking is
available on site, and the property is convenient for
several tube stations.

Rooms 175 (13 fmly) (11 smoking) **Facilities** FTV
Wi-fi **Conf** Class 30 Board 30 Thtr 45 **Services** Lift
Air con **Parking** 62 **Notes** ⊗

Ramada Hyde Park

★★★★ 70% HOTEL PLAN 2 B1

☎ 020 7229 1212 & 792 7004
150 Bayswater Rd W2 4RT
e-mail: enquiries@ramadahydepark.co.uk
web: www.ramadahydepark.co.uk
dir: From Hammersmith flyover left into Warwick Rd.
At Kensington High St right, into Kensington Church
St, left to T-junct, right into Bayswater Rd. Hotel
0.25m on left

This large hotel overlooks Kensington Gardens and
Hyde Park and is ideal for the West End, Oxford Street
and Paddington. Modern air conditioned bedrooms
are comfortably appointed for both business and
leisure guests. Public areas include the Brasserie and
Bar and a range of meeting rooms. Limited parking is
available.

Rooms 213 (6 fmly) (10 GF) (14 smoking)
Facilities STV FTV Wi-fi ⌕ Xmas New Year
Conf Class 50 Board 30 Thtr 100 **Services** Lift Air con
Notes ⊗

Lancaster Gate Hotel

★★★ 70% HOTEL PLAN 2 C1

☎ 020 7479 2500 & 7262 5090
66 Lancaster Gate W2 3NA
e-mail: info@lghhydepark.co.uk
dir: Just off Bayswater Rd

This hotel offers a convenient location between Oxford
Street and Knightsbridge and is also close to Hyde
Park and Kensington Gardens. Bedrooms are well
equipped with broadband and safes, as well as a
range of TV channels. There is a comfortable bar and
stylish restaurant, and the hotel also has a range of
meeting rooms.

Rooms 188 (3 fmly) (13 GF) (4 smoking) **S** £64-£300;
D £79-£360 **Facilities** STV FTV Wi-fi Off site leisure
facilities available **Conf** Class 18 Board 18 Thtr 35
Del from £179 to £229 **Services** Lift Air con **Notes** LB

Mitre House Hotel

★★ 69% METRO HOTEL PLAN 2 D2

☎ 020 7723 8040 & 7402 5695
178-184 Sussex Gardens, Hyde Park W2 1TU
e-mail: reservations@mitrehousehotel.com
web: www.mitrehousehotel.com
dir: Parallel to Bayswater Rd & one block from
Paddington Station

This family-run hotel continues to offers a warm
welcome and attentive service. It is ideally located,
close to Paddington station and near the West End
and major attractions. Bedrooms include a number of
family suites and there is a lounge bar. Limited
parking is available.

Rooms 69 (7 fmly) (7 GF) (69 smoking) **S** £80;
D £95-£100 (incl. bkfst)* **Facilities** STV Wi-fi
Services Lift **Parking** 20 **Notes** ⊗

W3 ACTON

Ramada Encore London West

★★★ 75% HOTEL PLAN 1 D4

☎ 020 8753 0800
4 Portal Way, Gypsy Corner, A40 Western Av W3 6RT
e-mail: reservations@encorelondonwest.co.uk
web: www.encorelondonwest.co.uk

Conveniently situated on the A40, this modern,
purpose-built glass-fronted hotel offers smartly
appointed accommodation with en suite power
shower rooms and air conditioning. Open-plan public
areas include a popular Asian and European
restaurant, Wok Around the World, and a 2go café and
sandwich bar. Secure parking and a range of meeting
rooms complete the picture.

Rooms 150 (35 fmly) (15 smoking) ⌕ **Facilities** STV
FTV Wi-fi ⌕ Gym **Conf** Class 28 Board 26 Thtr 50
Services Lift Air con **Parking** 72 **Notes** ⊗

LONDON

W3 ACTON *continued*

Holiday Inn Express London - Park Royal

BUDGET HOTEL PLAN 1 D4

☎ 020 8896 4460
Victoria Rd, Acton W3 6UB
e-mail: info@hiexparkroyal.co.uk
web: www.hiexpress.co.uk
dir: A40 towards North Acton. 1st right onto Portal Way. Left Wales Farm Rd, left Victoria Rd, hotel 100mtrs on right

A modern hotel ideal for families and business travellers. Fresh and uncomplicated, the spacious rooms include Sky TV, power shower and tea and coffee-making facilities. Continental buffet breakfast is included in the room rate; other meals may be taken at the nearby family pub or restaurant. See also the Hotel Groups pages.

Rooms 108 (35 fmly) **Conf** Class 30 Board 30 Thtr 50

W4 CHISWICK

Chiswick Moran Hotel

★★★★ 75% HOTEL PLAN 1 C3

☎ 020 8996 5200
626 Chiswick High Rd W4 5RY
e-mail: chiswickres@moranhotels.com
web: www.moranhotels.com
dir: 200yds from M4 junct 2

This stylish, modern hotel is conveniently located for Heathrow and central London, with Gunnersby tube station just a few minutes' walk away. Airy, spacious public areas include a modern restaurant, a popular bar and excellent meeting facilities. Fully air-conditioned bedrooms are stylish and extremely well appointed with broadband, laptop safes and flat-screen TVs. All boast spacious, modern bathrooms, many with walk-in rain showers.

Rooms 123 (6 fmly) ⟋ **Facilities** STV FTV Wi-fi ⟳ Gym Xmas New Year **Conf** Class 45 Board 40 Thtr 90 **Services** Lift Air con **Parking** 40 **Notes** ⊗ Civ Wed 80

W5 EALING

Crowne Plaza London-Ealing

★★★★ 77% ⊛ HOTEL PLAN 1 C4

☎ 0871 942 9114 & 020 8233 3200
Western Av, Hanger Ln, Ealing W5 1HG
e-mail: info@cp-londonealing.co.uk
web: www.cp-londonealing.co.uk
dir: A40 from central London towards M40. Exit at Ealing & North Circular A406 sign. At rdbt take 2nd exit signed A40. Hotel on left

Appointed to a high standard, this hotel occupies a prime position on the A40 and North Circular at Hangar Lane; Wembley Stadium is easily accessible. Modern, well-equipped, air-conditioned and sound-proofed bedrooms offer good facilities. There is a smart gym, a steam room together with meeting facilities and the West 5 Brasserie. On-site parking is available.

Rooms 131 (17 GF) (15 smoking) **Facilities** FTV Wi-fi Gym Steam room Xmas New Year **Conf** Class 48 Board 35 Thtr 80 **Services** Lift Air con **Parking** 85 **Notes** ⊗

The London Ealing Hotel

★★★ 74% HOTEL PLAN 1 C3

☎ 020 8896 8499 & 8896 8400
Ealing Common W5 3HN
e-mail: reception@londonealinghotel.co.uk
web: www.londonealinghotel.co.uk
dir: At junct of North Circular (A406) & Uxbridge Road (A4020)

This large, comfortable hotel is conveniently located a few minutes' walk from Ealing Common underground station and has easy access to the A40, M40 and the North Circular. The bedrooms, which vary in size, are well appointed for both business and leisure guests. There is a spacious brasserie and bar, a range of meeting rooms and a substantial amount of parking.

Rooms 189 (6 fmly) ⟋ **Facilities** STV FTV Wi-fi ⟳ ♫ Xmas New Year **Conf** Class 110 Board 80 Thtr 200 **Services** Lift Air con **Parking** 150 **Notes** ⊗ Civ Wed 80

Premier Inn London Hanger Lane

BUDGET HOTEL PLAN 1 C4

☎ 0871 527 8346
1-6 Ritz Pde, Ealing W5 3RA
web: www.premierinn.com
dir: M4 junct 2, A4 follow North Circular/A406 signs, for 0.5m. Take A406 for approx 2.5m. Right into Ashbourne Rd, immediately left into Ashbourne Parade, right into Ritz Parade. Hotel on right

High quality, budget accommodation ideal for both families and business travellers. Spacious, en suite bedrooms feature tea and coffee making facilities, and Freeview TV in most hotels. Internet access and Wi-fi are available for a small fee. The adjacent family restaurant features a wide and varied menu. See also the Hotel Groups pages.

Rooms 59

W6 HAMMERSMITH

Novotel London West

★★★★ 71% ⊛ HOTEL PLAN 1 D3

☎ 020 8741 1555
1 Shortlands W6 8DR
e-mail: H0737@accor.com
web: www.novotellondonwest.co.uk
dir: M4 (A4) & A316 junct at Hogarth rdbt. Along Great West Rd, left for Hammersmith before flyover. On Hammersmith Bridge Rd to rdbt, take 5th exit. 1st left into Shortlands, 1st left to hotel main entrance

A Hammersmith landmark, this substantial hotel is a popular base for both business and leisure travellers. Spacious, air-conditioned bedrooms have a good range of extras and many have additional beds, making them suitable for families. The hotel also has its own car park, business centre and shop, and boasts one of the largest convention centres in Europe.

Rooms 630 (148 fmly) **Facilities** STV Wi-fi Gym **Conf** Class 700 Board 200 Thtr 1700 **Services** Lift Air con **Parking** 240 **Notes** Civ Wed 1400

LONDON

Save on hotels. Book at **theAA.com/hotel**

W3 – W8 301 ENGLAND

Holiday Inn Express London - Hammersmith

BUDGET HOTEL PLAN 1 D3

☎ 020 8746 5100
120 -124 King St W6 0QU
e-mail: info@expresshammersmith.co.uk
web: www.expresshammersmith.co.uk
dir: M4/A4 junct 1 to Hammersmith Broadway. 2nd
left to A315 towards Chiswick (King St). Hotel on right

A modern hotel ideal for families and business
travellers. Fresh and uncomplicated, the spacious
rooms include Sky TV, power shower and tea and
coffee-making facilities. Continental buffet breakfast
is included in the room rate; other meals may be
taken at the nearby family pub or restaurant. See also
the Hotel Groups pages.

Rooms 135 (49 fmly) **Conf** Class 18 Board 20 Thtr 35

Premier Inn London Hammersmith

BUDGET HOTEL PLAN 1 D3

☎ 0871 527 8660
255 King St, Hammersmith W6 9LU
web: www.premierinn.com
dir: From central London on A4 to Hammersmith,
follow A315 towards Chiswick

High quality, budget accommodation ideal for both
families and business travellers. Spacious, en suite
bedrooms feature tea and coffee making facilities,
and Freeview TV in most hotels. Internet access and
Wi-fi are available for a small fee. The adjacent
family restaurant features a wide and varied menu.
See also the Hotel Groups pages.

Rooms 106

W8 KENSINGTON

INSPECTORS' CHOICE

Royal Garden Hotel

★★★★★ ◎◎◎ HOTEL PLAN 4 B5

☎ 020 7937 8000
2-24 Kensington High St W8 4PT
e-mail: reservations@royalgardenhotel.co.uk
web: www.royalgardenhotel.co.uk
dir: Adjacent to Kensington Palace

This landmark hotel, just a short walk from the
Royal Albert Hall, has airy, stylish public rooms that
include the Park Terrace Restaurant, Lounge and
Bar, Bertie's cocktail bar and the contemporary
10th-floor Min Jiang Restaurant, an exciting
elegant restaurant offering authentic Chinese
cuisine and enjoying breathtaking views of the city.
The stylish and contemporary bedrooms are
equipped with up-to-date facilities and include a
number of spacious, air-conditioned rooms and
suites with super views over Kensington Gardens.
All rooms have iPod docking stations, flat-screen
TVs and triple glazed windows as standard. Guests
have complimentary use of the Soma Spa gym,
sauna and steam room.

Rooms 394 (41 fmly) (45 smoking) ✎ **S** £359;
D £399* **Facilities** Spa STV FTV Wi-fi ⬇ HL Gym
Health & fitness centre ♪ Xmas New Year
Conf Class 320 Board 100 Thtr 550 Del £450
Services Lift Air con **Parking** 130 **Notes** LB ⊗
Civ Wed 400

INSPECTORS' CHOICE

The Milestone Hotel

★★★★★ ◎◎

HOTEL PLAN 4 B5

☎ 020 7917 1000
1 Kensington Court W8 5DL
e-mail: bookms@rchmail.com
web: www.milestonehotel.com
dir: From Warwick Rd right into Kensington High St.
Hotel 400yds past Kensington tube station

This delightful town house enjoys a wonderful
location opposite Kensington Palace and is near the
elegant shops. The individually themed bedrooms
include a selection of stunning suites that are
equipped with every conceivable extra - fruit,
cookies, chocolates, complimentary newspapers
and even the next day's weather forecast. Up-to-
the-minute technology includes high speed Wi-fi
and interactive TV. Public areas include the
luxurious Park Lounge where afternoon tea is
served, the delightful split-level Stables Bar, a
conservatory, the sumptuous Cheneston's
restaurant and a fully equipped small gym,
resistance pool and a spa treatment room.

Rooms 62 (3 fmly) (1 GF) (5 smoking)
S £324-£456; **D** £360-£516* **Facilities** STV FTV
Wi-fi ⬇ ⓢ Gym Health club ♪ Xmas New Year
Conf Class 20 Board 20 Thtr 50 **Services** Lift
Air con **Parking** 1 **Notes** LB Civ Wed 30

LONDON

W8 KENSINGTON *continued*

Copthorne Tara Hotel London Kensington

MILLENNIUM
HOTELS AND RESORTS
MILLENNIUM • COPTHORNE

★★★★ 75% HOTEL PLAN 4 B4

☎ 020 7937 7211 & 7872 2000
Scarsdale Place, Wrights Ln W8 5SR
e-mail: reservations.tara@millenniumhotels.co.uk
web: www.millenniumhotels.co.uk
dir: From Kensington High St into Wrights Ln (NB for Sat Nav use W8 5SY)

This expansive hotel that is ideally placed for the stylish shops and also the tube station. Smart public areas include a trendy coffee shop, a gym, a stylish brasserie and bar plus extensive conference facilities. Bedrooms include several well-equipped rooms for less mobile guests, in addition to a number of Connoisseur rooms that have the use of a club lounge with its many complimentary facilities.

Rooms 833 (3 fmly) **S** £96-£450; **D** £96-£450*
Facilities FTV Wi-fi ॐ HL Gym Xmas New Year
Conf Class 160 Board 90 Thtr 280 **Services** Lift
Air con **Parking** 91 **Notes** ⊗ Civ Wed 280

W13 BARNES

Best Western Maitrise Suites

⊍ PLAN 1 C3

☎ 020 8799 3850
50-54 The Broadway, West Ealing W13 0SY

Currently the rating for this establishment is not confirmed. This may be due to a change of ownership or because it has only recently joined the AA rating scheme. For further details please see the AA website: theAA.com

Rooms 17 **S** £99-£129; **D** £119-£199*

W14 WEST KENSINGTON

K West Hotel & Spa

★★★★ 80% HOTEL PLAN 1 D3

☎ 020 8008 6600
Richmond Way W14 0AX
e-mail: info@k-west.co.uk
web: www.k-west.co.uk
dir: From A40(M) take Shepherd's Bush exit. At Holland Park rdbt 3rd exit. 1st left & left again. Hotel straight ahead

This stylish, contemporary hotel is conveniently located for Notting Hill, the exhibition halls and the BBC; Bond Street is only a 10-minute tube journey away. Funky, minimalist public areas include a trendy lobby bar and mezzanine-style restaurant. Spacious bedrooms and suites are extremely well appointed and offer luxurious bedding and a host of thoughtful extras such as CD and DVD players. Wi-fi is available throughout. The spa offers a comprehensive range of health, beauty and relaxation treatments.

Rooms 220 (31 GF) (44 smoking) ॏ **Facilities** Spa
STV FTV Wi-fi ॐ Gym Hydrotherapy pool Sauna Steam room Snow room Solarium ♫ New Year **Conf** Class 20
Board 25 Thtr 55 **Services** Lift Air con **Parking** 100
Notes ⊗

Holiday Inn Express London-Earl's Court

Holiday Inn
Express

BUDGET HOTEL PLAN 4 A1

☎ 020 7384 5151
295 North End Rd W14 9NS
e-mail: info@exhiearlscourt.co.uk
web: www.hiexpress.com/lonearlscourt
dir: From Heathrow Airport, A4 to central London. At 2nd lights, after crossing Hammersmith Flyover, right into North End Rd. Hotel on left

A modern hotel ideal for families and business travellers. Fresh and uncomplicated, the spacious rooms include Sky TV, power shower and tea and coffee-making facilities. Continental buffet breakfast is included in the room rate; other meals may be taken at the nearby family pub or restaurant. See also the Hotel Groups pages.

Rooms 100 (65 fmly) **Conf** Class 12 Board 12 Thtr 50

WC1 BLOOMSBURY, HOLBORN

Chancery Court Hotel, London

CHANCERY
·COURT·
LONDON

★★★★★ 83% ⊚⊚⊚ HOTEL PLAN 3 C3

☎ 020 7829 9888
252 High Holborn WC1V 7EN
e-mail: sales@chancerycourthotel.com
web: www.chancerycourthotel.com
dir: From Shaftesbury Ave into High Holborn, hotel on right

This is a grand place with splendid public areas, decorated from top to bottom in rare marble. Craftsmen meticulously restored the sweeping staircases, archways and stately rooms of this 1914 building. The result is a spacious, relaxed hotel offering everything from stylish, luxuriously appointed bedrooms to a health club and state-of-the-art meeting rooms. The sophisticated Pearl Restaurant & Bar offers an impressive standard of cooking.

Rooms 305 ॏ **S** £240-£2400; **D** £240-£2400*
Facilities Spa Gym **Conf** Class 234 Board 40 Thtr 435
Services Lift Air con **Notes** LB ⊗ Civ Wed 280

The Montague on the Gardens

THE
RED CARNATION
HOTEL COLLECTION

★★★★ 85% ⊚ HOTEL PLAN 3 B3

☎ 020 7637 1001
15 Montague St, Bloomsbury WC1B 5BJ
e-mail: bookmt@rchmail.com
web: www.montaguehotel.com
dir: Just off Russell Square, adjacent to British Museum

This stylish hotel is situated right next to the British Museum. A special feature is the alfresco terrace overlooking a delightful garden. Other public rooms include the Blue Door Bistro and Chef's Table, a bar, a lounge and a conservatory where traditional afternoon teas are served. The bedrooms are beautifully appointed and range from split-level suites to more compact rooms.

Rooms 100 (10 fmly) (19 GF) ॏ **S** £145-£265;
D £170-£290* **Facilities** STV Wi-fi ॐ HL Gym ♫ Xmas
New Year **Conf** Class 50 Board 50 Thtr 120
Del from £243 to £383* **Services** Lift Air con
Notes LB Civ Wed 90

Hotel Russell

★★★★ 73% HOTEL PLAN 3 B4

☎ 020 7837 6470
Russell Square WC1B 5BE
e-mail: russell.reservations@principal-hayley.com
web: www.principal-hayley.com
dir: From A501 into Woburn Place. Hotel 500mtrs on left

This landmark Grade II, Victorian hotel is located on Russell Square, within walking distance of the West End and theatre district. Many bedrooms are stylish and state-of-the-art in design, and others are more traditional. Spacious public areas include the impressive foyer with a restored mosaic floor, a choice of lounges and an elegant restaurant.

Rooms 373 (2 fmly) **Facilities** STV FTV Wi-fi **Conf** Class 200 Board 75 Thtr 450 **Services** Lift Air con **Notes** ⊗ Civ Wed 300

The Kingsley by Thistle

thistle

★★★★ 71% HOTEL PLAN 3 B3

☎ 0871 376 9006
Bloomsbury Way WC1A 2SD
e-mail: thekingsley@thistle.co.uk
web: www.thistlehotels.com/thekingsley
dir: A40(M) to A501 (Marylebone Rd), take sliproad before underpass to Holburn. Into Gower St, Bloomsbury St (A400). Left into Oxford St, then Bloomsbury Way

Well situated for theatregoers, this hotel enjoys a convenient central location. The well-equipped rooms are generally spacious with good quality fabrics and furnishings, with both family rooms and executive suites available. The ground-floor bar and lounge areas are well appointed. There is a public car park nearby.

Rooms 129 **Facilities** STV FTV Wi-fi HL **Conf** Class 50 Board 30 Thtr 100 **Services** Lift Air con **Notes** ⊗

Holiday Inn London Kings Cross/Bloomsbury

★★★★ 69% HOTEL PLAN 3 C5

☎ 020 7833 3900
1 Kings Cross Rd WC1X 9HX
e-mail: sales@holidayinnlondon.com
web: www.holidayinn.co.uk
dir: On corner of King Cross Rd & Calthorpe St

Conveniently located for Kings Cross station and The City, this modern hotel offers smart, spacious air-conditioned accommodation with a wide range of facilities. There are versatile meeting rooms, a bar, a well-equipped fitness centre and a choice of restaurants including one serving Indian cuisine.

Rooms 405 (163 fmly) (126 smoking) **Facilities** STV FTV Wi-fi 🏊 Gym Beauty treatment room **Conf** Class 120 Board 30 Thtr 220 **Services** Lift Air con **Parking** 15 **Notes** ⊗

Holiday Inn London Bloomsbury

HolidayInn

★★★ 80% HOTEL PLAN 3 B4

☎ 0871 942 9222
Coram St WC1N 1HT
e-mail: bloomsbury@ihg.com
web: www.holidayinn.co.uk
dir: Off Upper Woburn Place

Centrally located, this modern and stylish hotel is within easy reach of many of London's tourist attractions and close to St Pancras International Rail Station. The bedrooms boast a pillow menu, air-conditioning and high-speed internet access. The Junction restaurant offers a modern menu whilst Callaghans is a traditional Irish pub featuring the best Irish beers. The meeting rooms can cater for many different events.

Rooms 313 (30 fmly) (14 smoking) **Facilities** STV Wi-fi 🏊 **Conf** Class 180 Board 80 Thtr 350 **Services** Lift Air con **Notes** ⊗

Bedford Hotel

★★★ 73% HOTEL PLAN 3 B3

☎ 020 7636 7822 & 7692 3620
83-93 Southampton Row WC1B 4HD
e-mail: info@imperialhotels.co.uk
web: www.imperialhotels.co.uk

Just off Russell Square, this intimate hotel is ideal for visits to the British Museum and Covent Garden. The bedrooms are well equipped with all the expected facilities including modem points if requested. The ground floor has a lounge, a bar and restaurant plus there's a delightful secret rear garden. The underground car park is a bonus.

Rooms 184 (1 fmly) **S** £87; **D** £116 (incl. bkfst)*
Facilities FTV Wi-fi Xmas New Year **Conf** Board 12 **Services** Lift **Parking** 50 **Notes** ⊗

Ambassadors Bloomsbury Hotel

Ⓤ PLAN 3 A5

☎ 020 7693 5400 & 693 5410
12 Upper Woburn Place WC1H 0HX
e-mail: dutymanager@ambassadors.co.uk

Currently the rating for this establishment is not confirmed. This may be due to a change of ownership or because it has only recently joined the AA rating scheme. For further details please see the AA website: theAA.com

Rooms 100 **Facilities** STV Wi-fi 🏊 Gym **Conf** Class 110 Board 50 Thtr 250 **Services** Lift Air con **Notes** ⊗

Premier Inn London Euston

BUDGET HOTEL PLAN 3 A5

☎ 0871 527 8656
1 Duke's Rd, Euston WC1H 9PJ
web: www.premierinn.com
dir: On corner of Euston Road & Duke's Road, between Kings Cross/St Pancras & Euston stations

High quality, budget accommodation ideal for both families and business travellers. Spacious, en suite bedrooms feature tea and coffee making facilities, and Freeview TV in most hotels. Internet access and Wi-fi are available for a small fee. The adjacent family restaurant features a wide and varied menu. See also the Hotel Groups pages.

Rooms 220

WC2 SOHO, STRAND

INSPECTORS' CHOICE

The Savoy

★★★★★ ◉◉ HOTEL PLAN 3 C1

☎ 020 7836 4343
Strand WC2R 0EU
e-mail: savoy@fairmont.com
dir: Halfway along The Strand between Trafalgar Sq & Aldwych

The Savoy Hotel has been at the fore of the London hotel scene since it opened in 1889. The hotel been lovingly restored in recent years, with much of its art deco and Edwardian heritage kept intact. The bedrooms, including an extensive range of stunning suites, vary in style and size, and many overlook the Thames. The famous River Restaurant, Savoy Grill and American Bar remain as well loved favourites, the Thames Foyer is well known for its afternoon teas and the Beaufort Bar offers a comprehensive range of champagnes. Immaculately presented staff offer excellent standards of hospitality and service.

Rooms 268 (5 fmly) (10 smoking) ⬥ **Facilities** Spa STV FTV Wi-fi ⬥ ⬥ supervised Gym Fitness gallery Health & beauty treatments Personal training ♫ Xmas New Year **Conf** Class 200 Board 32 Thtr 500 **Services** Lift Air con **Parking** 65 **Notes** Civ Wed 400

Charing Cross Hotel

★★★★ 80% HOTEL PLAN 3 B1   GUOMAN HOTELS

☎ 0871 376 9012
The Strand WC2N 5HX
e-mail: charingcross@guoman.co.uk
web: www.guoman.com
dir: E on The Strand towards Trafalgar Square, right into station forecourt

This centrally located and historic landmark hotel provides a friendly welcome. Spacious in design, the

original grand architecture blends nicely with the modern style of interior appointments, particularly in the bedrooms and bathrooms. There is a choice of dining options including the relaxed Brasserie, which has splendid views of London especially at night. The gym is exclusively for guests.

Rooms 239 (83 annexe) (12 fmly) **Facilities** STV Wi-fi Gym Xmas New Year **Conf** Class 96 Board 46 Thtr 140 **Services** Lift Air con **Notes** Civ Wed 140

The Royal Trafalgar, London   thistle

★★★★ 75% HOTEL PLAN 3 A1

☎ 0871 376 9037
Whitcomb St WC2H 7HG
e-mail: theroyaltrafalgar@thistle.co.uk
web: www.thistle.com/theroyaltrafalgar
dir: 100mtrs from Trafalgar Sq adjacent to Sainsbury Wing of National Gallery

Quietly located, this handily placed hotel is just a short walk from Trafalgar Square and theatreland. This property has undergone refurbishment with bedrooms and bathrooms, in a variety of sizes, offering very good levels of comfort and modern amenities. Dining options include Squares Restaurant serving a wide selection, and Gravity Lounge and Bar where light meals can be taken.

Rooms 108 (12 fmly) **Facilities** STV FTV Wi-fi **Conf** Class 20 Board 18 Thtr 30 **Services** Lift Air con **Notes** ⊗

LONDON GATEWAY MOTORWAY   Map 6 TQ19
SERVICE AREA (M1)

Days Hotel London North - M1

★★★ 67% HOTEL

☎ 020 8906 7000
Welcome Break Service Area NW7 3HU
e-mail: lgw.hotel@welcomebreak.co.uk
web: www.welcomebreak.co.uk
dir: On M1 between junct 2/4 N'bound & S'bound

This modern building offers accommodation in smart, spacious and well-equipped bedrooms, suitable for families and business travellers, and all with en suite bathrooms. Continental breakfast is available and other refreshments may be taken at the nearby family restaurant.

Rooms 200 (190 fmly) (80 GF) (20 smoking) **Facilities** FTV Wi-fi ⬥ **Conf** Class 30 Board 50 Thtr 70 **Services** Lift Air con **Parking** 160 **Notes** Civ Wed 80

LONG EATON   Map 11 SK43
Derbyshire

Novotel Nottingham East Midlands

★★★ 67% HOTEL

☎ 0115 946 5111
Bostock Ln NG10 4EP
e-mail: H0507@accor.com
web: www.novotel.com
dir: M1 junct 25 onto B6002 to Long Eaton. Hotel 400yds on left

In close proximity to the M1, this purpose-built hotel has much to offer. All bedrooms are spacious, have sofa beds and provide exceptional desk space. Public rooms include a bright brasserie, which is open all day and provides extended dining until midnight. There is a comprehensive range of meeting rooms.

Rooms 108 (40 fmly) (20 GF) **S** £45-£95; **D** £45-£95* **Facilities** Wi-fi ⬥ **Conf** Class 100 Board 100 Thtr 250 Del from £105 to £135* **Services** Lift **Parking** 220

LONGHORSLEY   Map 21 NZ19
Northumberland

Macdonald Linden Hall, Golf & Country Club

★★★★ 80% ◉◉ HOTEL

☎ 01670 500000 & 0844 879 9084
NE65 8XF
e-mail: lindenhall@macdonald.hotels.co.uk
web: www.macdonaldhotels.co.uk
dir: N'bound on A1 take A697 towards Coldstream. Hotel 1m N of Longhorsley

This impressive Georgian mansion lies in 400 acres of parkland and offers extensive indoor and outdoor leisure facilities including a golf course. The Dobson Restaurant provides a fine dining experience, or guests can eat in the more informal Linden Tree pub. The good-sized bedrooms have a restrained modern style. The team of staff are enthusiastic and professional.

Rooms 50 (3 fmly) (16 GF) **Facilities** Spa STV FTV Wi-fi ⬥ ⬥ supervised ⬥ 18 ⬥ Putt green ⬥ Gym Steam room Sauna Xmas New Year **Conf** Class 120 Board 50 Thtr 300 **Services** Lift **Parking** 300 **Notes** Civ Wed 120

Save on hotels. Book at **theAA.com/hotel**

WC2 – LOU 305 **ENGLAND**

LONG MELFORD
Suffolk   Map 13 TL84

The Black Lion Hotel
★★★ 83% ◉◉ HOTEL

☎ 01787 312356
Church Walk, The Green CO10 9DN
e-mail: enquiries@blacklionhotel.net
web: www.blacklionhotel.net
dir: At junct of A134 & A1092

This charming 15th-century hotel is situated on the edge of this bustling town overlooking the green. Bedrooms are generally spacious and each is attractively decorated, tastefully furnished and equipped with useful extras. An interesting range of dishes is served in the lounge bar or guests may choose to dine from the same innovative menu in the more formal restaurant.

Rooms 10 (1 fmly) **S** £102-£136; **D** £125-£175 (incl. bkfst)* **Facilities** Wi-fi Xmas New Year Child facilities **Conf** Class 28 Board 28 Thtr 50 Del from £117* **Parking** 10 **Notes** LB Civ Wed 50

The Bull
★★★ 73% HOTEL

OldEnglsh

☎ 01787 378494
Hall St CO10 9JG
e-mail: bull.longmelford@greeneking.co.uk
web: www.bull-hotel.com
dir: 3m N of Sudbury on A134

The public areas of this delightful 14th-century property feature a wealth of charm and character, including exposed beams, carvings, heraldic markings and huge open fireplaces. Bedrooms are smartly decorated, thoughtfully equipped and retain many original features. Snacks or light lunches are served in the bar, or guests can choose to dine in the more formal restaurant.

Rooms 25 (4 fmly) ✆ **S** £69-£80; **D** £99-£120 (incl. bkfst)* **Facilities** FTV Wi-fi Xmas New Year **Conf** Class 40 Board 30 Thtr 100 Del £135 **Parking** 35 **Notes** ⊗ Civ Wed 100

LOOE
Cornwall   Map 2 SX25

Trelaske Hotel & Restaurant
★★★ 79% ◉◉ HOTEL

☎ 01503 262159
Polperro Rd PL13 2JS
e-mail: info@trelaske.co.uk
dir: B252 signed Looe. Over Looe bridge signed Polperro. 1.9m, hotel signed on left, turn right

This small and welcoming hotel offers comfortable accommodation, professional, and friendly service plus award-winning food. Set in its own very well-tended and pretty grounds, it is only two miles from Polperro and Looe.

Rooms 7 (4 annexe) (2 fmly) (2 GF) ✆ **S** £85-£105; **D** £98-£105 (incl. bkfst)* **Facilities** FTV Wi-fi **Conf** Class 30 Board 40 Thtr 100 Del from £120 to £140* **Parking** 50 **Notes** LB

Hannafore Point Hotel
THE INDEPENDENTS
HOTEL ASSOCIATION

★★★ 71% HOTEL

☎ 01503 263273
Marine Dr, West Looe PL13 2DG
e-mail: stay@hannaforepointhotel.com
dir: A38, left onto A385 to Looe. Over bridge turn left. Hotel 0.5m on left

With panoramic coastal views of St George's Island around to Rame Head, this popular hotel provides a warm welcome. The wonderful view is certainly a feature of the spacious restaurant and bar, creating a scenic backdrop for both dinners and breakfasts. Additional facilities include a heated indoor pool and a gym.

Rooms 37 (5 fmly) **S** £52-£78; **D** £104-£156 (incl. bkfst)* **Facilities** STV Wi-fi ⊗ Gym Spa pool Steam room Sauna ♫ Xmas New Year **Conf** Class 80 Board 40 Thtr 120 Del from £80 to £130* **Services** Lift **Parking** 32 **Notes** LB Civ Wed 150

LOSTWITHIEL
Cornwall   Map 2 SX15

Best Western Restormel Lodge

★★★ 75% HOTEL

☎ 01208 872223
Castle Hill PL22 0DD
e-mail: bookings@restormellodgehotel.co.uk
web: www.restormellodgehotel.co.uk
dir: On A390 in Lostwithiel

A short drive from the Eden Project, this popular hotel offers a friendly welcome to all visitors and is ideally situated for exploring the area. The older building houses the bar, restaurant and lounges, with original features adding to the character. Bedrooms are comfortably furnished, with a number overlooking the secluded outdoor pool.

Rooms 36 (12 annexe) (2 fmly) (9 GF) ✆ **S** £29-£69; **D** £49-£119 (incl. bkfst)* **Facilities** FTV Wi-fi ⋌ ⊰ Xmas New Year **Conf** Class 12 Board 12 Thtr 12 **Parking** 40 **Notes** LB

LOUGHBOROUGH
Leicestershire   Map 11 SK51

Quorn Country Hotel
PRIMA
HOTEL GROUP

★★★★ 76% HOTEL

☎ 01509 415050 & 415061
Charnwood House, 66 Leicester Rd LE12 8BB
e-mail: reservations@quorncountryhotel.co.uk
web: www.quorncountryhotel.co.uk

(For full entry see Quorn)

LOUTH
Lincolnshire   Map 17 TF38

L

Brackenborough Hotel
★★★ 87% ◉ HOTEL

☎ 01507 609169
Cordeaux Corner, Brackenborough LN11 0SZ
e-mail: reception@brackenborough.co.uk
web: www.oakridgehotels.co.uk
dir: On A16 (Louth to Grimsby road), 1m from Louth

In an idyllic setting amid well-tended gardens, this hotel offers attractive bedrooms, each individually decorated with co-ordinated furnishings and many extras. The award-winning bistro offers informal dining and the menu is based on locally sourced produce. The hotel specialises in weddings, events and private functions and has excellent conference facilities. Free Wi-fi is available. Guests have free access to state-of-the-art leisure facilities (less than half a mile away) that includes a swimming pool, tennis courts and a gym.

Rooms 24 (2 fmly) (6 GF) ✆ **S** £86.50-£124.50; **D** £101.50-£159.50 (incl. bkfst) **Facilities** FTV Wi-fi ⊰ ♫ Xmas New Year **Conf** Class 150 Board 50 Thtr 300 Del £119.95* **Services** Air con **Parking** 90 **Notes** LB ⊗ Civ Wed 220

LOUTH continued

Best Western Kenwick Park Hotel

★★★ 77% HOTEL

☎ 01507 608806
Kenwick Park Estate LN11 8NR
e-mail: enquiries@kenwick-park.co.uk
web: www.kenwick-park.co.uk
dir: A16 from Grimsby, then A157 Mablethorpe/Manby
Rd. Hotel 400mtrs down hill on right

This elegant Georgian house is situated on the 320-acre Kenwick Park estate, overlooking its own golf course. Bedrooms are spacious, comfortable and provide modern facilities. Public areas include a restaurant and a conservatory bar that overlook the grounds. There is also an extensive leisure centre and state-of-the-art conference and banqueting facilities.

Rooms 34 (5 annexe) (10 fmly) **Facilities** Spa Wi-fi ⓧ supervised ⚘ 18 ♗ Putt green Gym Squash Health & beauty centre Xmas New Year **Conf** Class 40 Board 90 Thtr 250 **Parking** 100 **Notes** Civ Wed 200

Bartle Hall Hotel

★★★★ 71% HOTEL

☎ 01772 690506
Lea Ln PR4 0HA
e-mail: recp@bartlehall.co.uk
dir: M6 junct 32 onto Tom Benson Way, follow signs
for Woodplumpton

Ideally situated between Preston and Blackpool, Bartle Hall is within easy access of the M6 and the Lake District. Set in its own extensive grounds the hotel offers comfortable, well-equipped and renovated accommodation. The restaurant cuisine uses local produce and there is a large comfortable bar and lounge. There are also extensive conference facilities, and this hotel is a popular wedding venue.

Rooms 15 (2 annexe) (2 fmly) (2 GF) ⚑ **S** £65-£150; **D** £80-£200 **Facilities** FTV Wi-fi ⚘ HL New Year **Conf** Class 50 Board 40 Thtr 200 Del from £120 to £160 **Parking** 150 **Notes** Closed 25-26 Dec Civ Wed 130

South Lodge Hotel

★★★★★ 87% ◉◉◉◉
COUNTRY HOUSE HOTEL

☎ 01403 891711
Brighton Rd RH13 6PS
e-mail: enquiries@southlodgehotel.co.uk
web: www.southlodgehotel.co.uk
dir: A23, onto B2110. Right, through Handcross to
A281 junct. Left, hotel on right

This impeccably presented 19th-century lodge with stunning views of the rolling South Downs is an ideal retreat. There is the traditional and elegant Camellia Restaurant, with 2 AA rosettes, offering memorable, seasonal dishes, and The Pass Restaurant, with 4 AA Rosettes, which is an innovative take on the chef's table concept - a mini-restaurant within the kitchen itself. Guests can take a tour of the restored Victorian wine cellar, either with a sommelier or on their own. The elegant lounge is popular for afternoon teas. Bedrooms are individually designed with character and quality throughout. The conference facilities are impressive.

Rooms 89 (11 fmly) (19 GF) ⚑ **S** £195-£275; **D** £195-£679 (incl. bkfst)* **Facilities** STV Wi-fi ⚘ ⚘ 36 ♗ Putt green Fishing ⚘ Gym Mountain biking Archery Clay pigeon shooting Xmas New Year **Conf** Class 60 Board 50 Thtr 160 Del from £280 to £360* **Services** Lift **Parking** 200 **Notes** LB Civ Wed 130

INSPECTOR'S CHOICE

Lower Slaughter Manor

★★★ ◉◉ COUNTRY HOUSE HOTEL

☎ 01451 820456
GL54 2HP
e-mail: info@lowerslaughterter.co.uk
web: www.lowerslaughter.co.uk
dir: Exit A429 signed 'The Slaughters'. Manor 0.5m
on right on entering village

There is a timeless elegance about this wonderful manor, which dates back to the 17th century. Its imposing presence makes it very much the centrepiece of this famous Cotswold village. Inside, the levels of comfort and quality are immediately evident, with crackling log fires warming the many sumptuous lounges. Spacious and tastefully furnished bedrooms are either in the main building or in the adjacent coach house. Fine dining at the hotel is in the award-winning Sixteen58 Restaurant where the menus are based on local, seasonal produce; special dietary needs can be catered for.

Rooms 19 (8 annexe) (5 fmly) (4 GF) **S** £175-£905; **D** £195-£925 (incl. bkfst)* **Conf** Class 40 Board 30 Thtr 70

Ivy House Country Hotel

★★★ 85% ◉◉ HOTEL

☎ 01502 501353 & 588144
Ivy Ln, Beccles Rd, Oulton Broad NR33 8HY
e-mail: aa@ivyhousecountryhotel.co.uk
web: www.ivyhousecountryhotel.co.uk
dir: On A146 SW of Oulton Broad turn into Ivy Ln
beside Esso petrol station. Over railway bridge, follow
private drive

A peacefully located, family-run hotel set in three acres of mature landscaped grounds and just a short walk from Oulton Broad. Public rooms include an 18th-century thatched barn restaurant where an interesting choice of dishes is served. The attractively decorated bedrooms are housed in garden wings, and many have lovely views of the grounds to the countryside beyond.

Rooms 20 (20 annexe) (1 fmly) (17 GF)
S £99-£135; **D** £135-£250 (incl. bkfst)* **Facilities** FTV Wi-fi **Conf** Board 22 Thtr 55 **Parking** 50 **Notes** LB Closed 15 Dec-4 Jan Civ Wed 80

Premier Inn Lowestoft

BUDGET HOTEL

☎ 0871 527 8688
249 Yarmouth Rd NR32 4AA
web: www.premierinn.com
dir: On A12, 2m N of Lowestoft

High quality, budget accommodation ideal for both families and business travellers. Spacious, en suite bedrooms feature tea and coffee making facilities, and Freeview TV in most hotels. Internet access and Wi-fi are available for a small fee. The adjacent family restaurant features a wide and varied menu. See also the Hotel Groups pages.

Rooms 60

LOWESWATER   **Map 18 NY12**
Cumbria

Grange Country House Hotel

★★ 74% SMALL HOTEL

☎ 01946 861211 & 861570
CA13 0SU
e-mail: info@thegrange-loweswater.co.uk
dir: Exit A5086 for Mockerkin, through village. After 2m left signed Loweswater Lake. Hotel at bottom of hill on left

This delightful country hotel is set in extensive grounds in a quiet valley at the north-western end of Loweswater, and continues to prove popular with guests seeking peace and quiet. It has a friendly and relaxed atmosphere, and the cosy public areas include a small bar, a residents' lounge and an attractive dining room. The bedrooms are well equipped and comfortable, and include four-poster rooms.

Rooms 8 (2 fmly) (1 GF) **Facilities** FTV National Trust boats & fishing Xmas **Conf** Class 25 Board 25 Thtr 25 **Parking** 22 **Notes** RS Jan-Feb

---

LUDLOW   **Map 10 SO57**
Shropshire

INSPECTORS' CHOICE

Fishmore Hall

★★★ ◉◉◉ SMALL HOTEL

☎ 01584 875148
Fishmore Rd SY8 3DP
e-mail: reception@fishmorehall.co.uk
web: www.fishmorehall.co.uk
dir: A49 into Henley Rd. 1st right, Weyman Rd, at bottom of hill right into Fishmore Rd

Located in a rural area within easy reach of town centre, this Palladian-style Georgian house has been sympathetically renovated and extended to provide high standards of comfort and facilities. The contemporary interior highlights many period features, and public areas include a comfortable lounge and restaurant, the setting for award-winning imaginative cooking.

Rooms 15 (1 GF) **S** £110-£210; **D** £150-£250 (incl. bkfst) **Facilities** FTV Wi-fi ⌂ In room beauty treatments & massage Xmas New Year **Conf** Class 60 Board 40 Thtr 130 Del from £165* **Services** Lift **Parking** 48 **Notes** LB Civ Wed 130

Overton Grange Hotel and Restaurant

★★★ 86% ◉◉ HOTEL

☎ 01584 873500 & 0845 476 1000
Old Hereford Rd SY8 4AD
e-mail: info@overtongrangehotel.com
dir: A49, B4361 to Ludlow. Hotel 200yds on left

This is a traditional country-house hotel with stylish, comfortable bedrooms, and high standards of guest care. Food is an important part of what the hotel has to offer and the restaurant serves classically based, French-style cuisine using locally sourced produce whenever possible. Meeting and conference rooms are available.

Rooms 14 **Facilities** Spa FTV Wi-fi ⊛ Xmas New Year **Conf** Class 50 Board 30 Thtr 100 **Parking** 45 **Notes** ⊗ No children 7yrs Civ Wed 100

Dinham Hall Hotel

★★★ 80% ◉◉ HOTEL

☎ 01584 876464
By The Castle SY8 1EJ
e-mail: info@dinhamhall.com
dir: In town centre, opposite castle

Built in 1792, this lovely house stands in attractive gardens immediately opposite Ludlow Castle; it has a well-deserved reputation for warm hospitality. The well-equipped bedrooms include two in a converted cottage, and some rooms have four-poster beds. The comfortable public rooms are elegantly appointed. Dishes served in the brasserie-style restaurant are based on good, seasonal produce.

Rooms 13 (2 annexe) (2 fmly) (2 GF) **Facilities** FTV Wi-fi Xmas New Year **Conf** Class 20 Board 26 Thtr 40 **Parking** 16 **Notes** No children 7yrs

---

The Feathers Hotel

★★★ 80% ◉ HOTEL

☎ 01584 875261
The Bull Ring SY8 1AA
e-mail: feathers.ludlow@btconnect.com
web: www.feathersatludlow.co.uk
dir: From A49 follow town centre signs to centre. Hotel on left

Famous for the carved woodwork outside and in, this picture-postcard 17th-century hotel is one of the town's best-known landmarks and is in an excellent location. Bedrooms are traditional both in style and decor. The public areas have retained much of the traditional charm, and the first-floor lounge is particularly stunning. Modern British menus are offered in the smart restaurant which has wooden beams and exposed brickwork.

Rooms 40 (3 fmly) **S** £85-£95; **D** £105-£205 (incl. bkfst)* **Facilities** STV FTV Wi-fi Xmas New Year **Conf** Class 40 Board 40 Thtr 80 Del from £120 to £139* **Services** Lift **Parking** 33 **Notes** LB Civ Wed 80

LUDLOW *continued*

Cliffe Hotel

★★ 81% SMALL HOTEL

☎ 01584 872063
Dinham SY8 2JE
e-mail: thecliffehotel@hotmail.com
web: www.thecliffehotel.co.uk
dir: From town centre, left at castle gates to Dinham, over bridge. Right fork, hotel 200yds on left

Built in the 19th century and standing in extensive grounds and gardens, this privately owned and personally run hotel is quietly located close to the castle and the river. It provides well-equipped accommodation, and facilities include a lounge bar, a pleasant restaurant and a patio overlooking the garden.

Rooms 9 (2 fmly) **S** £50-£65; **D** £65-£100 (incl. bkfst)* **Facilities** FTV Wi-fi **Parking** 22
Notes RS 24-26 Dec

The Clive Bar & Restaurant with Rooms

◎◎ RESTAURANT WITH ROOMS

☎ 01584 856565 & 856665
Bromfield SY8 2JR
e-mail: info@theclive.co.uk
web: www.theclive.co.uk
dir: 2m N of Ludlow on A49 in Bromfield

The Clive is just two miles from the busy town of Ludlow and is a convenient base for visiting the local attractions or for business. The bedrooms, located outside the main restaurant area, are spacious and very well equipped; some are suitable for families and many are on the ground-floor level. Meals are available in the well-known Clive Restaurant or in the bar areas. The property also has a small meeting room.

Rooms 15 (15 annexe) (9 fmly)

Luton Hoo Hotel, Golf and Spa

★★★★★ 86% ◎◎ HOTEL

☎ 01582 734437 & 698888
The Mansion House LU1 3TQ
e-mail: reservations@lutonhoo.com
dir: M1 junct 10a, 3rd exit onto A1081 towards Harpenden & St Albans. Hotel approx 1m on left

A luxury hotel in more than 1,000 acres of 'Capability' Brown designed parkland and formal gardens, with an 18-hole, par 73 golf course and the River Lea meandering through. The centrepiece is the Grade I listed Mansion House that has architectural influences by many famous architects including Robert Adams. There are three sumptuous lounges where guests can enjoy afternoon tea and pre-dinner drinks, and two eating options - The Wernher Restaurant and the Adams Brasserie. The spacious bedrooms and impressive suites combine historic character with modern amenities. The Robert Adams Club House is the perfect place for relaxation, with the brasserie, a spa, golf, pool and gym together with two bars, and Warren Weir, at the foot of the estate, on the river bank is an exclusive retreat for weddings and meetings.

Rooms 228 (50 fmly) (65 GF) 🐾 **Facilities** Spa FTV Wi-fi ⌕ ♨ 18 🏌 Putt green Fishing 🏊 Gym Bird watching Cycling Snooker Jogging trails 🎵 Xmas New Year **Conf** Class 220 Board 60 Thtr 388 **Services** Lift **Parking** 316 **Notes** Civ Wed 380

Best Western Menzies Strathmore Hotel

MenziesHotels

★★★★ 77% ◎ HOTEL

☎ 01582 734199
Arndale Centre LU1 2TR
e-mail: strathmore@menzieshotels.co.uk
web: www.menzieshotels.co.uk
dir: Exit M1 junct 10a towards town centre, hotel adjacent to Arndale Centre car park

Situated in the centre of town with adjacent parking, this hotel is convenient for the shopping areas and many guests stay here prior to catching flights at the nearby airport. The bedrooms are comfortable and well equipped with good facilities. Public areas include a spacious lounge bar and a contemporary brasserie-style restaurant. Waves health and leisure club offers guests beauty and message therapies plus a pool, sauna and steam room.

Rooms 152 (6 fmly) (21 smoking) 🐾 **S** £44-£114; **D** £64-£144 (incl. bkfst)* **Facilities** Spa FTV Wi-fi ⌕ HL ⌕ supervised Gym Beauty salon Xmas New Year **Conf** Class 120 Board 90 Thtr 250 **Services** Lift **Parking** 5 **Notes** LB ⊗ Civ Wed 200

Icon Hotel

★★★ 81% HOTEL

☎ 01582 722123
15 Stuart St LU1 2SA
e-mail: reservations@iconhotelluton.com
dir: M1 junct 10 & 10A, A1081 signed Luton, left follow Luton Retail Park & station signs. Left at next rdbt, left at next rdbt onto A505 (Park Viaduct). Straight on at next rdbt, left into Hastings St

This modern, purpose-built hotel occupies a prominent position close to the town centre and is a short drive from the international airport. The contemporary, open-plan bar is very comfortable and Capello's Restaurant offers a modern Mediterranean menu. The bedrooms are attractively presented and feature the latest technology along with large LCD TVs and complimentary Wi-fi. There is a range of business suites and a well-equipped gym.

Rooms 60 (7 fmly) (5 GF) 🐾 **S** £49-£169; **D** £49-£209* **Facilities** FTV Wi-fi ⌕ Gym Therapy treatments by prior arrangement 🎵 Xmas New Year **Conf** Class 30 Board 25 Thtr 50 Del from £125 to £165* **Services** Lift Air con **Parking** 18 **Notes** ⊗

Save on hotels. Book at **theAA.com/hotel**

LUD – LYM 309 ENGLAND

LUTON AIRPORT
Bedfordshire   Map 6 TL12

Holiday Inn Express London - Luton Airport

BUDGET HOTEL

☎ 0870 444 8920
2 Percival Way LU2 9GP
e-mail: lutonairport@expressbyholidayinn.net
web: www.hiexpress.com/lutonairport
dir: M1 junct 10, follow signs for airport (hotel easily visable), right into Percival Way, hotel car park on right

A modern hotel ideal for families and business travellers. Fresh and uncomplicated, the spacious rooms include Sky TV, power shower and tea and coffee-making facilities. Continental buffet breakfast is included in the room rate; other meals may be taken at the nearby family pub or restaurant. See also the Hotel Groups pages.

Rooms 147 (87 fmly) **Conf** Class 30 Board 20 Thtr 60

Ibis London Luton Airport
ibis

BUDGET HOTEL

☎ 01582 424488
Spittlesea Rd LU2 9NH
e-mail: H1040@accor.com
web: www.ibishotel.com
dir: M1 junct 10, follow signs to Luton Airport. Hotel 600mtrs from airport

Modern, budget hotel offering comfortable accommodation in bright and practical bedrooms. Breakfast is self-service and dinner is available in the restaurant. See also the Hotel Groups pages.

Rooms 162 (8 fmly) (4 GF) **Conf** Class 64 Board 80 Thtr 114

Premier Inn Luton Airport

BUDGET HOTEL

☎ 0871 527 8690
Osborne Rd LU1 3HJ
web: www.premierinn.com
dir: M1 junct 10, A1081 follow signs for Luton, at 3rd rdbt left into Gypsy Lane, left at next rdbt

High quality, budget accommodation ideal for both families and business travellers. Spacious, en suite bedrooms feature tea and coffee making facilities, and Freeview TV in most hotels. Internet access and Wi-fi are available for a small fee. The adjacent family restaurant features a wide and varied menu. See also the Hotel Groups pages.

Rooms 129

LYME REGIS
Dorset   Map 4 SY39

Royal Lion Hotel
★★★ 72% HOTEL

☎ 01297 445622
Broad St DT7 3QF
e-mail: enquiries@royallionhotel.com
web: www.royallionhotel.com
dir: From W on A35 take A3052, or from E take B3165 to Lyme Regis. Hotel in town centre, opposite The Fossil Shop

This 17th-century, former coaching inn is full of character and charm, and is situated a short walk from the seafront. Bedrooms vary in size; those in the newer wing are more spacious and some have balconies, sea views or a private terrace. In addition to the elegant dining room and guest lounges, a heated pool, jacuzzi, sauna and small gym are available. A good selection of enjoyable, well prepared dishes is offered in either the bar or main restaurant. There is a car park at the rear.

Rooms 33 (8 fmly) (4 GF) **S** £70-£80; **D** £105-£115 (incl. bkfst)* **Facilities** FTV Wi-fi 🕑 Sauna Games room Snooker tables Table tennis Xmas New Year **Conf** Class 20 Board 20 Thtr 50 **Parking** 33 **Notes** LB

Swallows Eaves Hotel
★★ 85% SMALL HOTEL

☎ 01297 553184
Swan Hill Rd EX24 6QJ
e-mail: info@swallowseaves.co.uk
web: www.swallowseaves.co.uk

(For full entry see Colyford, Devon)

LYMINGTON
Hampshire   Map 5 SZ39

Stanwell House Hotel
★★★ 88% ◉◉ HOTEL

☎ 01590 677123
14-15 High St SO41 9AA
e-mail: enquiries@stanwellhouse.com
dir: M27 junct 1, follow signs to Lyndhurst then Lymington

A privately owned Georgian house situated on the wide high street only a few minutes from the marina, and a short drive from the New Forest. Styling itself as a boutique hotel, the bedrooms are individually designed; there are Terrace rooms with garden access, four-poster rooms, and Georgian rooms in the older part of the building. The four suites include two with their own roof terrace. Dining options include the informal bistro and the intimate Seafood Restaurant.

Service is friendly and attentive. A meeting room is available.

Rooms 30 (6 fmly) (5 GF) **S** £89-£99; **D** £119-£140 (incl. bkfst)* **Facilities** FTV Wi-fi Xmas New Year **Conf** Class 25 Board 20 Thtr 70 Del from £120 to £140* **Parking** 12 **Notes** LB Civ Wed 100

Passford House Hotel
★★★ 83% HOTEL

☎ 01590 682398
Mount Pleasant Ln SO41 8LS
e-mail: sales@passfordhousehotel.co.uk
web: www.passfordhousehotel.co.uk
dir: From A337 Lymington over 2 mini rdbts. 1st right at Tollhouse pub, 1m right into Mount Pleasant Lane

A peaceful hotel set in attractive grounds on the edge of town. Bedrooms vary in size but all are comfortably furnished and well equipped. Extensive public areas include lounges, a smartly appointed restaurant and bar plus leisure facilities. The friendly and well motivated staff provide attentive service.

Rooms 51 (2 annexe) (5 fmly) (10 GF) ⟳ **S** £99-£110; **D** £140-£160 (incl. bkfst)* **Facilities** FTV Wi-fi 🕑 ⚐ Putt green ⚑ Gym Petanque Table tennis Pool table Xmas New Year **Conf** Class 30 Board 30 Thtr 80 **Parking** 100 **Notes** LB Civ Wed 80

Macdonald Elmers Court Hotel & Resort

★★★ 82% HOTEL

☎ 0844 879 9060
South Baddesley Rd SO41 5ZB
e-mail: elmerscourt@macdonald-hotels.co.uk
web: www.macdonaldhotels.co.uk
dir: M27 junct 1, through Lyndhurst, Brockenhurst to Lymington, hotel 200yds right after Lymington ferry terminal

Originally known as The Elms, this Tudor manor house dates back to the 1820s. Ideally located at the edge of the New Forest and overlooking The Solent with views towards the Isle of Wight, the hotel offers suites and self-catering accommodation in the grounds, along with a host of leisure facilities.

Rooms 42 (42 annexe) (8 fmly) (22 GF) ⟳ **Facilities** Spa FTV Wi-fi 🕑 ⚐ supervised ⚑ Putt green ⚑ Gym Squash Steam room Aerobics classes Sauna Table tennis Xmas New Year **Conf** Class 70 Board 40 Thtr 120 Del from £150 to £200* **Parking** 100 **Notes** ⊗ Civ Wed 120

L

LYMINGTON *continued*

Premier Inn Lymington (New Forest Hordle)

BUDGET HOTEL

☎ 0871 527 8692
Silver St, Hordle SO41 0FN
web: www.premierinn.com
dir: M27 junct 1, A337. 3.5m, left into High St (A35) right into Gosport Ln. Left into Clay Hill (A337). Right into Grigg Ln (B3055). Approx 8m, left into Barrows Ln, right into Silver St

High quality, budget accommodation ideal for both families and business travellers. Spacious, en suite bedrooms feature tea and coffee making facilities, and Freeview TV in most hotels. Internet access and Wi-fi are available for a small fee. The adjacent family restaurant features a wide and varied menu. See also the Hotel Groups pages.

Rooms 20

LYMM	Map 15 SJ68
Cheshire	

The Lymm Hotel

MACDONALD HOTELS & RESORTS

★★★ 74% HOTEL

☎ 01925 752233
Whitbarrow Rd WA13 9AQ
e-mail: general.lymm@macdonald-hotels.co.uk
web: www.macdonaldhotels.co.uk/lymm
dir: M6 junct 20, B5158 to Lymm. Left at junct, 1st right, left at mini-rdbt, into Brookfield Rd, 3rd left into Whitbarrow Rd

In a peaceful residential area, this hotel benefits from both a quiet setting and convenient access to local motorway networks. It offers comfortable bedrooms equipped for both the business and leisure guest. Public areas include an attractive bar and an elegant restaurant. There is also extensive parking.

Rooms 62 (38 annexe) (5 fmly) (11 GF) **S** £59-£89; **D** £59-£89* **Facilities** STV Wi-fi Xmas New Year **Conf** Class 60 Board 40 Thtr 120 Del from £99 to £139* **Parking** 75 **Notes** LB Civ Wed 100

LYNDHURST	Map 5 SU30
Hampshire	

INSPECTORS' CHOICE

Lime Wood

RELAIS & CHATEAUX

★★★★★ ◉◉◉
COUNTRY HOUSE HOTEL

☎ 023 8028 7177
Beaulieu Rd SO43 7FZ
e-mail: info@limewood.co.uk
dir: Exit A35 onto B3056 towards Beaulieu, hotel 1m on right

This meticulously restored country house situated deep in the New Forest, provides a wealth of facilities and much opulence. The hotel prides itself on its relaxed, friendly and attentive service, and has lots to interest and captivate. The luxurious bedrooms are notable; some are in the pavilion and some in the main house. There are choices for eating - the Scullery, styled on an 18th-century country kitchen which has a relaxed atmosphere, and the more formal Dining Room, overlooking the botanical gardens, that serves interesting cuisine. The Herb House spa offers a hydro therapy pool and many other excellent facilities along with a gym and steam room. AA Hotel of the Year for England 2012-13.

Rooms 29 (13 annexe) (5 fmly) (4 GF) ☛
S £245-£775; **D** £245-£775* **Facilities** Spa STV FTV Wi-fi ⌨ ⓒ Gym Xmas New Year **Conf** Board 18 Thtr 20 Del from £345 to £445* **Services** Lift **Parking** 60 **Notes** Civ Wed 80

Best Western Forest Lodge Hotel

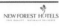
NEW FOREST HOTELS

★★★ 83% ◉◉ HOTEL

☎ 023 8028 3677
Pikes Hill, Romsey Rd SO43 7AS
e-mail: forest@newforesthotels.co.uk
web: www.newforesthotels.co.uk
dir: M27 junct 1, A337 towards Lyndhurst. In village, with police station & courts on right, take 1st right into Pikes Hill

Situated on the edge of Lyndhurst, this hotel is set well back from the main road. The smart, contemporary bedrooms include four-poster rooms and family rooms; children are very welcome here. The eating options are the Forest Restaurant and the fine-dining Glasshouse Restaurant. There is an indoor swimming pool and Nordic sauna.

Rooms 36 (11 fmly) (10 GF) ☛ **S** £102-£116; **D** £142-£192* **Facilities** FTV Wi-fi ⌨ ⓒ Xmas New Year **Conf** Class 70 Board 60 Thtr 120 **Parking** 50 **Notes** Civ Wed 60

Bell Inn

★★★ 82% ◉ HOTEL

☎ 023 8081 2214
SO43 7HE
e-mail: bell@bramshaw.co.uk
web: www.bellinnbramshaw.co.uk

(For full entry see Brook (Near Cadnam))

Penny Farthing Hotel

★★ 81% METRO HOTEL

☎ 023 8028 4422
Romsey Rd SO43 7AA
e-mail: stay@pennyfarthinghotel.co.uk
dir: M27 junct 1, A337 to Lyndhurst. Hotel on left after White Rabbit Inn

This friendly, well-appointed establishment on the edge of town is suitable for business or for exploring the New Forest area. The attractive bedrooms are well-equipped, and some are located in an adjacent cottage. There is a spacious breakfast room, a comfortable lounge bar and a cycle store.

Rooms 20 (4 annexe) (1 fmly) (1 GF) ☛
S £52.50-£78; **D** £78-£118 (incl. bkfst)*
Facilities FTV Wi-fi ⌨ **Parking** 26 **Notes** LB ⊗ Closed Xmas week & New Year

LYNMOUTH
Devon   Map 3 SS74

See also **Lynton**

Tors Hotel

★★★ 78% HOTEL

☎ 01598 753236
EX35 6NA
e-mail: info@torshotellynmouth.co.uk
dir: Adjacent to A39 on Countisbury Hill just before entering Lynmouth from Minehead

In an elevated position overlooking Lynmouth Bay, this friendly hotel is set in five acres of woodland. The majority of the bedrooms benefit from the superb views, as do the public areas which are generously proportioned and well presented. A fixed-price menu is offered with local, seasonal produce to the fore.

Rooms 31 (3 fmly) **S** £80-£90; **D** £100-£120 (incl. bkfst)* **Facilities** STV FTV Wi-fi ↝ Xmas New Year **Conf** Class 40 Board 25 Thtr 60 Del from £130 to £150* **Services** Lift **Parking** 40 **Notes** LB Closed 7 Nov-7 Dec Civ Wed 70

Rising Sun Hotel

★★ 76% ⊛ HOTEL

☎ 01598 753223
Harbourside EX35 6EG
e-mail: reception@risingsunlynmouth.co.uk
web: www.risingsunlynmouth.co.uk
dir: M5 junct 23, A39 to Minehead. Hotel on harbour

This delightful thatched establishment, once a smugglers' inn, sits on the harbour front. Popular with locals and guests alike, there is the option of eating in either the convivial bar or the restaurant; a comfortable, quiet lounge is also available. Bedrooms, located in the inn and adjoining cottages, are individually designed and have modern facilities.

Rooms 14 (1 fmly) (1 GF) **Facilities** Xmas

Bath Hotel

★★ 71% HOTEL

☎ 01598 752238
Sea Front EX35 6EL
e-mail: info@bathhotellynmouth.co.uk
dir: M5 junct 25, A39 to Lynmouth

This well established, friendly hotel, situated near the harbour offers lovely views from the attractive, sea-facing bedrooms and is an excellent starting point for scenic walks. There are two lounges and a sun lounge. The restaurant menu is extensive and features daily-changing specials that make good use of fresh produce and local fish.

Rooms 22 (9 fmly) **S** £45-£55; **D** £75-£115 (incl. bkfst)* **Facilities** FTV Wi-fi **Parking** 12 **Notes** Closed Dec & Jan RS Nov & Feb

LYNTON
Devon   Map 3 SS74

See also **Lynmouth**

Lynton Cottage Hotel

★★★ 77% ⊛⊛ HOTEL

☎ 01598 752342
Northwalk EX35 6ED
e-mail: enquiries@lynton-cottage.co.uk
dir: M5 junct 23 to Bridgwater, A39 to Minehead, follow signs to Lynton. 1st right after church, right

Boasting breathtaking views, this wonderfully relaxing and friendly hotel stands some 500 feet above the sea and makes a peaceful hideaway. Bedrooms are individual in style and size, with the added bonus of the wonderful views; public areas have charm and character in equal measure. Accomplished cuisine is on offer with dishes created with care and skill.

Rooms 16 (1 fmly) (1 GF) **S** £63; **D** £90-£164 (incl. bkfst) **Facilities** FTV Wi-fi **Parking** 20 **Notes** LB Closed 2 Dec-12 Jan

LYTHAM ST ANNES
Lancashire   Map 18 SD32

Clifton Arms Hotel

★★★★ 75% ⊛ HOTEL

☎ 01253 739898
West Beach, Lytham FY8 5QJ
e-mail: welcome@cliftonarms-lytham.com
web: www.cliftonarms-lytham.com
dir: On A584 along seafront

This well established hotel occupies a prime position overlooking Lytham Green and the Ribble estuary

beyond. Bedrooms vary in size and are appointed to a high standard; front-facing rooms are particularly spacious and enjoy splendid views. There is an elegant restaurant, a stylish open-plan lounge and cocktail bar as well as function and conference facilities.

Rooms 48 (2 fmly) **S** £70-£115; **D** £120-£180 (incl. bkfst)* **Facilities** STV FTV Wi-fi Xmas New Year **Conf** Class 100 Board 60 Thtr 200 Del from £155 to £185* **Services** Lift **Parking** 50 **Notes** LB ⊗ Civ Wed 100

Bedford Hotel

★★★ 80% HOTEL

☎ 01253 724636
307-313 Clifton Drive South FY8 1HN
e-mail: reservations@bedford-hotel.com
web: www.bedford-hotel.com
dir: From M55 follow signs for airport to last lights. Left through 2 sets of lights. Hotel 300yds on left

This popular family-run hotel is close to the town centre and the seafront. Bedrooms vary in size and style and include superior and club class rooms. The newer bedrooms are particularly elegant and tastefully appointed. Spacious public areas include a choice of lounges, a coffee shop, fitness facilities and an impressive function suite.

Rooms 45 (6 GF) **Facilities** FTV Wi-fi Gym Hydrotherapy spa bath Xmas New Year **Conf** Class 140 Board 60 Thtr 200 Del from £97.50* **Services** Lift **Parking** 25 **Notes** LB ⊗ Civ Wed 150

Best Western Glendower Promenade Hotel

★★★ 77% HOTEL

☎ 01253 723241
North Promenade FY8 2NQ
e-mail: recp@theglendowerhotel.co.uk
web: www.theglendowerhotel.co.uk
dir: M55 follow airport signs. Left at Promenade to St Annes. Hotel 500yds from pier

Located on the seafront and with easy access to the town centre, this popular, friendly hotel offers comfortably furnished, well-equipped accommodation. Bedrooms vary in size and style, and include four-poster rooms and very popular family suites. Public areas feature a choice of smart, comfortable lounges, a bright, modern leisure club and function facilities.

Rooms 60 (17 fmly) **S** £55-£95; **D** £75-£125 (incl. bkfst) **Facilities** FTV Wi-fi Gym Nintendo Wii play area Snooker table ♫ Xmas New Year **Conf** Class 120 Board 50 Thtr 150 Del from £86 to £120 **Services** Lift **Parking** 45 **Notes** LB Civ Wed 150

L

LYTHAM ST ANNES *continued*

Chadwick Hotel

THE INDEPENDENTS
HOTEL ASSOCIATION

★★★ 74% HOTEL

☎ 01253 720061
South Promenade FY8 1NP
e-mail: info@thechadwickhotel.com
web: www.thechadwickhotel.com
dir: M6 junct 32, M55 to Blackpool, A5230 to South
Shore. Follow signs for St Annes, hotel on
Promenade's south end

This popular, comfortable and traditional hotel enjoys
a seafront location. Bedrooms vary in size and style,
but all are very thoughtfully equipped; those at the
front boast panoramic sea views. Public rooms are
spacious and comfortably furnished and the smart
bar is stocked with some 200 malt whiskies. The hotel
has a well-equipped, air-conditioned gym and indoor
pool.

Rooms 73 (28 fmly) (13 GF) ✿ **S** fr £68; **D** fr £110
(incl. bkfst)* **Facilities** FTV Wi-fi ⓢ Gym Turkish bath
Games room Soft play adventure area Wii room Sauna
♫ Xmas New Year Child facilities **Conf** Class 24
Board 28 Thtr 70 Del from £130* **Services** Lift
Parking 40 **Notes** LB ⊗

MACCLESFIELD	Map 16 SJ97
Cheshire	

Shrigley Hall Hotel, Golf
& Country Club

PUMA HOTELS
COLLECTION

★★★★ 74% HOTEL

☎ 01625 575757
Shrigley Park, Pott Shrigley SK10 5SB
e-mail: shrigleyhall@pumahotels.co.uk
web: www.pumahotels.co.uk
dir: Exit A523 at Legh Arms towards Pott Shrigley.
Hotel 2m on left before village

Originally built in 1825, Shrigley Hall is an impressive
hotel set in 262 acres of mature parkland and
commands stunning views of the countryside.
Features include a championship golf course. There is
a wide choice of bedroom sizes and styles. The public
areas are spacious, combining traditional and
contemporary decor, and include a well-equipped
gym.

Rooms 148 (11 fmly) **Facilities** Spa STV Wi-fi ⓢ
supervised ♨ 18 ⛳ Putt green Fishing Gym Beauty
salon Hydro centre ♫ Xmas New Year **Conf** Class 110
Board 42 Thtr 180 **Services** Lift **Parking** 300
Notes Civ Wed 150

The Legacy Hollin Hall
Country House Hotel

LEGACY HOTELS

★★★ 75% HOTEL

☎ 08444 119072 & 0330 333 2872
Jackson Ln, Kerridge, Bollington SK10 5BG
e-mail: res-hollinhall@legacy-hotels.co.uk
dir: From Macclesfield A523 (The Silk Road) towards
Bollington, at rdbt right onto B5090 signed
Bollington. 1st right signed Kerridge. 2.5m, hotel
entrance on left

Within easy reach of the Peak District and visitor
attractions, this elegant Victorian hotel offers a
combination of traditional and contemporary design.
Beautifully maintained period features are
complemented by stylish, smartly presented decor
and furnishings. Bedrooms are well equipped and
cater well for both leisure and business guests;
complimentary Wi-fi is provided.

Rooms 58 (5 fmly) (16 GF) ✿ **Facilities** FTV Wi-fi ⓑ
Gym Xmas New Year **Conf** Class 50 Board 50 Thtr 120
Services Lift **Parking** 75 **Notes** Civ Wed 120

Premier Inn Macclesfield North

Premier Inn

BUDGET HOTEL

☎ 0871 527 8694
**Tytherington Business Park, Springwood Way,
Tytherington SK10 2XA**
web: www.premierinn.com
dir: On A523 in Tytherington Business Park

High quality, budget accommodation ideal for both
families and business travellers. Spacious, en suite
bedrooms feature tea and coffee making facilities,
and Freeview TV in most hotels. Internet access and
Wi-fi are available for a small fee. The adjacent
family restaurant features a wide and varied menu.
See also the Hotel Groups pages.

Rooms 41

Premier Inn Macclesfield South West

BUDGET HOTEL

☎ 0871 527 8696
Congleton Rd, Gawsworth SK11 7XD
web: www.premierinn.com
dir: M6 junct 17, A534 towards Congleton, A536
towards Macclesfield to Gawsworth. Hotel on left

Rooms 28

MAIDENCOMBE	

See Torquay

MAIDENHEAD	Map 6 SU88
Berkshire	

INSPECTORS' CHOICE

Fredrick's Hotel
Restaurant Spa

"bespoke" HOTELS

★★★★ ⍟⍟ HOTEL

☎ 01628 581000
Shoppenhangers Rd SL6 2PZ
e-mail: reservations@fredricks-hotel.co.uk
web: www.fredricks-hotel.co.uk
dir: M4 junct 8/9 onto A404(M) to Maidenhead West
& Henley. 1st exit 9a to White Waltham. Left into
Shoppenhangers Rd to Maidenhead, hotel on right

Just 30 minutes from London, this delightful hotel
enjoys a peaceful location yet is within easy reach
of the M4 and only 20 minutes' drive from
Wentworth and Sunningdale golf courses. The
spacious bedrooms are comfortably furnished and
very well equipped. An enthusiastic team of staff
ensure friendly and efficient service. The
imaginative cuisine is a highlight, as is the
luxurious spa that offers the ultimate in relaxation
and wellbeing.

Rooms 34 (11 GF) **S** £125-£270; **D** £135-£320 (incl.
bkfst) **Facilities** Spa Wi-fi ⓑ supervised ⍩
supervised Gym Rasul suite Oriental steam Dead
Sea floatation room **Conf** Class 80 Board 60
Thtr 120 Del from £220 to £320 **Services** Air con
Parking 90 **Notes** LB ⊗ Closed 24 Dec-3 Jan
Civ Wed 120

Holiday Inn Maidenhead/ Windsor

Holiday Inn

★★★★ 73% HOTEL

☎ 0871 942 9053 & 01628 506000
Manor Ln SL6 2RA
e-mail: reservations-maidenhead@ihg.com
web: www.himaidenheadhotel.co.uk
dir: A404 towards High Wycombe. Exit at junct 9A.
Left at mini rdbt. Hotel on right

Located close to Maidenhead town centre with transport links to Windsor and the M4, this well sited hotel is suitable for both the business and leisure traveller. Public areas benefit from a spacious lounge bar, brasserie-style restaurant and extensive conference facilities. The popular leisure club includes swimming pool and full gym facilities.

Rooms 197 (23 fmly) (56 GF) ➔ **Facilities** STV Wi-fi ⓑ HL ⓑ supervised Gym Steam room Sauna New Year **Conf** Class 200 Board 100 Thtr 400 Del from £89 to £175 **Services** Lift Air con **Parking** 250 **Notes** ⓧ Civ Wed 400

Walton Cottage Hotel

★★★ 78% METRO HOTEL

☎ 01628 624394
Marlow Rd SL6 7LT
e-mail: res@waltoncottagehotel.co.uk
dir: A308 towards Marlow, hotel on right after passing town centre

Conveniently located close to the town centre, this hotel offers an extensive choice of very attractively presented bedrooms. Heathrow Airport is just a 20-minute drive away, with Windsor, Henley and Ascot also close by. The hotel has well-equipped conference and business suites, ample parking, and Wi-fi is available for guests.

Rooms 72 (8 fmly) (20 GF) **S** £70-£150; **D** £85-£170 (incl. bkfst) **Facilities** FTV Wi-fi ⓑ Discounted day membership at nearby David Lloyd Gym & Spa **Conf** Class 30 Board 25 Thtr 70 Del from £150 to £200 **Services** Lift **Parking** 65 **Notes** ⓧ Closed 22 Dec-4 Jan

---

MAIDSTONE　　　　　　　**Map 7 TQ75**
Kent

Tudor Park, A Marriott Hotel & Country Club

TUDOR PARK

★★★★ 78% HOTEL

☎ 01622 734334 & 632004
Ashford Rd, Bearsted ME14 4NQ
e-mail: mhrs.tdmgs.salesadmin@marriotthotels.com
web: www.marriotttudorpark.co.uk
dir: M20 junct 8 to Lenham. At rdbt follow Bearsted & Maidstone signs on A20. Hotel 1m on left

Located on the outskirts of Maidstone in a wooded valley below Leeds Castle, this fine country hotel is set in 220 acres of parkland. Spacious bedrooms provide good levels of comfort and a comprehensive range of extras. Facilities include a championship golf course, a fully equipped gym and two dining options.

Rooms 120 (48 fmly) (60 GF) **Facilities** Spa Wi-fi ⓑ ↧ 18 ♣ Putt green Gym Driving range Beauty salon Steam room Xmas New Year **Conf** Class 100 Board 60 Thtr 250 **Services** Lift **Parking** 250 **Notes** ⓧ Civ Wed 160

Grange Moor Hotel

★★★ Ⓐ

☎ 01622 677623
4-8 St Michael's Rd ME16 8BS
e-mail: reservations@grangemoor.co.uk
dir: From town centre towards A26 (Tonbridge road). Hotel 0.25m on left, just after church

Rooms 50 (11 annexe) (5 fmly) (7 GF) ➔ **Facilities** FTV Wi-fi **Conf** Class 60 Board 40 Thtr 100 **Parking** 60 **Notes** ⓧ Closed 23-30 Dec Civ Wed

---

Premier Inn Maidstone (A26/Wateringbury)

Premier Inn

BUDGET HOTEL

☎ 0871 527 8706
103 Tonbridge Rd, Wateringbury ME18 5NS
web: www.premierinn.com
dir: M25 junct 3 onto M20. Exit at junct 4 onto A228 towards West Malling. A26 towards Maidstone, approx 3m

High quality, budget accommodation ideal for both families and business travellers. Spacious, en suite bedrooms feature tea and coffee making facilities, and Freeview TV in most hotels. Internet access and Wi-fi are available for a small fee. The adjacent family restaurant features a wide and varied menu. See also the Hotel Groups pages.

Rooms 40

Premier Inn Maidstone (Allington)

BUDGET HOTEL

☎ 0871 527 8698
London Rd ME16 0HG
web: www.premierinn.com
dir: M20 junct 5, 0.5m on London Rd towards Maidstone

Rooms 40

Premier Inn Maidstone (Leybourne)

BUDGET HOTEL

☎ 0871 527 8702
Castle Way, Leybourne, West Malling ME19 5TR
web: www.premierinn.com
dir: M20 junct 4, A228, hotel on left

Rooms 40

Premier Inn Maidstone (Sandling)

BUDGET HOTEL

☎ 0871 527 8704
Allington Lock, Sandling ME14 3AS
web: www.premierinn.com
dir: M20 junct 6, follow Museum of Kent Life signs

Rooms 40

M

MALMESBURY
Wiltshire   Map 4 ST98

Whatley Manor Hotel and Spa

★★★★★ ◉◉◉◉ HOTEL

☎ 01666 822888
Easton Grey SN16 0RB
e-mail: reservations@whatleymanor.com
web: www.whatleymanor.com
dir: M4 junct 17, follow signs to Malmesbury, continue over 2 rdbts. Follow B4040 & signs for Sherston, hotel 2m on left

Sitting in 12 acres of beautiful countryside, this impressive country house provides the most luxurious surroundings. Spacious bedrooms, most with views over the attractive gardens, are individually decorated with splendid features such as Bang & Olufsen sound and vision systems and unique works of art. Several eating options are available: Le Mazot, a Swiss-style brasserie, The Dining Room that serves classical French cuisine with a contemporary twist via carte and tasting menus, plus the Kitchen Garden Terrace for alfresco breakfasts, lunches and dinners. Guests might even like to take a hamper and a picnic rug and find a quiet spot in the grounds. The old Loggia Barn is ideal for wedding ceremonies, and the Aquarius Spa is magnificent.

Rooms 23 (4 GF) ✿ **S** £305-£865; **D** £305-£865 (incl. bkfst) **Facilities** Spa STV Wi-fi ⌇ Fishing Gym Cinema Hydro pool (indoor/outdoor) Xmas New Year **Conf** Class 20 Board 24 Thtr 60 Del £335 **Services** Lift **Parking** 100 **Notes** LB No children 12yrs Civ Wed 120

Old Bell Hotel

★★★ 81% ◉◉ HOTEL

☎ 01666 822344
Abbey Row SN16 0BW
e-mail: info@oldbellhotel.com
web: www.oldbellhotel.com
dir: M4 junct 17, A429 N. Left at 1st rdbt. Left at T-junct. Hotel adjacent to Abbey

Dating back to 1220, the wisteria-clad Old Bell is reputed to be the oldest purpose-built hotel in England. Bedrooms vary in size and style; those in the main house tend to be more spacious and are traditionally furnished with antiques, while the newer bedrooms in the coach house have a contemporary feel. Guests have a choice of comfortable sitting areas and dining options, including the main restaurant where the award-winning cuisine is based on high quality ingredients.

Rooms 33 (15 annexe) (7 GF) ✿ **S** £89.50; **D** £115-£275 (incl. bkfst) **Facilities** FTV Wi-fi Xmas New Year **Conf** Class 32 Board 32 Thtr 60 Del £175* **Parking** 33 **Notes** LB Civ Wed 90

Best Western Mayfield House Hotel

★★★ 74% ◉ HOTEL

☎ 01666 577409
Crudwell SN16 9EW
e-mail: reception@mayfieldhousehotel.co.uk
web: www.mayfieldhousehotel.co.uk
dir: M4 junct 17, A429 to Cirencester. 2m N of Malmesbury on left in Crudwell

This popular hotel is in an ideal location for exploring the many attractions that Wiltshire and The Cotswolds have to offer. Bedrooms come in a range of shapes and sizes, and include some on the ground-floor level in a cottage adjacent to the main building. In addition to outdoor seating, guests can relax with a drink in the comfortable lounge area where orders are taken for the carefully prepared dinner to follow.

Rooms 28 (8 annexe) (4 fmly) (8 GF) ✿ **S** £60-£75; **D** £83-£103 (incl. bkfst)* **Facilities** FTV Wi-fi ⌇ ♨ Xmas New Year **Conf** Class 30 Board 25 Thtr 40 Del from £85 to £125* **Parking** 50 **Notes** LB

MALTON
North Yorkshire   Map 19 SE77

The Talbot Hotel

★★★★ 85% ◉◉ HOTEL

☎ 01653 639096
Yorkersgate YO17 7AJ
e-mail: info@talbotmalton.co.uk
dir: From York take A64, exit at Malton sign. Hotel on right

This hotel is owned by the Fitzwilliam Estate and is set in its own beautifully landscaped grounds close to the historic market town. The newly designed interior features individually decorated bedrooms, including two luxurious suites. Each of the guest rooms has been given a distinct personality. The restaurant has elegant furniture, crisp white linen and fine silver cutlery, and with James Martin as executive chef the best of Yorkshire produce is sure to be sourced. Elegant public areas can be found throughout this stunning hotel.

Rooms 26 (3 GF) ✿ **D** £145-£295 (incl. bkfst)* **Facilities** FTV Wi-fi HL Xmas New Year **Conf** Class 30 Board 24 Thtr 60 Del from £195* **Parking** 35 **Notes** LB

MALVERN
Worcestershire   Map 10 SO74

The Malvern

★★★★ 74% ◉ HOTEL

☎ 01684 898290
Grovewood Rd WR14 1GD
e-mail: enquiries@themalvernspa.com
dir: A4440 to Malvern. Over 2 rdbts, at 3rd rdbt turn left. 6m, left at rdbt, over 1st rdbt, hotel on right

This modern, friendly hotel is set on the outskirts of the famous spa town. The bedrooms are contemporary with sumptuous beds, and many guest extras are provided; the bathrooms have quality fixtures and fittings. There is a brasserie restaurant which offers quality seasonal menus that include healthy options and vegetarian dishes. The Malvern Spa, designed exclusively for adults, includes a hydrotherapy pool which goes from inside to outside, heat experiences, a range of saunas, crystal steam room, salt grotto, adventure showers along with a host of treatments. There is also a 50-station gym with state-of-the-art equipment. There is ample parking around the hotel.

Rooms 32 ✿ **S** £85-£129; **D** £99-£169 (incl. bkfst)* **Facilities** Spa FTV Wi-fi ⌖ ⌘ Gym Exercise classes Xmas New Year **Conf** Class 40 Board 20 Thtr 80 Del from £160 to £180* **Services** Lift Air con **Parking** 82 **Notes** LB ⊗ No children 18yrs

M

The Abbey Hotel

★★★★ 74% HOTEL

☎ 01684 892332 & 897897
Abbey Rd WR14 3ET
e-mail: abbey@sarova.co.uk
dir: In Great Malvern town centre, opposite theatres

This large, impressive, ivy-clad hotel stands in the centre of Great Malvern, at the foot of the Malvern Hills, next to the Abbey and close to the theatre. It provides well-equipped modern accommodation equally suitable for business guests and tourists. Facilities include a good range of function rooms making the hotel a popular venue for meetings and events.

Rooms 103 (11 fmly) (23 GF) **S** £70-£170;
D £80-£180 (incl. bkfst)* **Facilities** STV FTV Wi-fi Ⓡ
Xmas New Year **Conf** Class 120 Board 40 Thtr 300
Del from £110 to £140* **Services** Lift **Parking** 85
Notes LB Civ Wed 300

The Cottage in the Wood Hotel

★★★ 86% ◉◉ HOTEL

☎ 01684 588860
Holywell Rd, Malvern Wells WR14 4LG
e-mail: reception@cottageinthewood.co.uk
web: www.cottageinthewood.co.uk
dir: 3m S of Great Malvern off A449, 500yds N of B4209, on opposite side of road

Sitting high up on a wooded hillside, this delightful, family-run hotel boasts stunning views over the Severn Valley. The bedrooms are divided between the main house, Beech Cottage and the Pinnacles. The public areas are very stylishly decorated, and imaginative food is served in an elegant dining room, overlooking the immaculate grounds.

The Cottage in the Wood Hotel

Rooms 30 (23 annexe) (9 GF) ⓇⓈ £79-£121;
D £99-£198 (incl. bkfst)* **Facilities** FTV Wi-fi Ⓡ Xmas
New Year **Conf** Board 14 Thtr 20 Del £159*
Parking 40

Colwall Park Hotel, Bar & Restaurant

★★★ 82% ◉◉ HOTEL

☎ 01684 540000
Walwyn Rd, Colwall WR13 6QG
e-mail: hotel@colwall.com
web: www.colwall.co.uk
dir: Between Malvern & Ledbury in centre of Colwall on B4218

Standing in extensive gardens, this hotel was purpose built in the early 20th century to serve the local racetrack. Today the proprietors and loyal staff provide high levels of hospitality and service. The Seasons Restaurant has a well-deserved reputation for its cuisine. Bedrooms are tastefully appointed and public areas help to create a fine country-house atmosphere.

Rooms 22 (1 fmly) Ⓡ **S** fr £65; **D** fr £130 (incl. bkfst)* **Facilities** FTV Wi-fi Ⓡ Ⓢ Boules Xmas New Year **Conf** Class 80 Board 50 Thtr 150 Del from £160*
Parking 40 **Notes** LB ⊗

M

MALVERN *continued*

The Malvern Hills Hotel

★★★ 80% HOTEL

☎ 01684 540690
Wynds Point WR13 6DW
web: www.malvernhillshotel.co.uk
dir: 4m S, at junct of A449 & B4232

This 19th-century hostelry is situated to the west of Malvern, opposite the British Camp, which was fortified and occupied by the Ancient Britons. The bedrooms are well equipped and benefit from smart modern bathrooms. Public areas include a choice of bars, retaining original features, modern conference facilities and an attractive restaurant.

Rooms 14 (1 fmly) (2 GF) ✆ **S** £75-£85; **D** £120-£140 (incl. bkfst)* **Facilities** STV FTV Wi-fi Xmas New Year **Conf** Class 24 Board 30 Thtr 40 **Parking** 45 **Notes** LB

The Cotford Hotel & L'Amuse Bouche Restaurant

★★★ 79% ◉◉ HOTEL

☎ 01684 572427
51 Graham Rd WR14 2HU
e-mail: reservations@cotfordhotel.co.uk
web: www.cotfordhotel.co.uk
dir: From Worcester follow signs to Malvern on A449. Left into Graham Rd signed town centre, hotel on right

This delightful house, built in 1851, reputedly for the Bishop of Worcester, stands in attractive gardens with stunning views of The Malverns. Bedrooms have been authentically renovated, retaining many of the original features and with a good selection of welcome extras. Food, service and hospitality are all major strengths.

The Cotford Hotel & L'Amuse Bouche Restaurant

Rooms 15 (3 fmly) (1 GF) ✆ **S** £65-£85; **D** £125-£145 (incl. bkfst) **Facilities** STV FTV Wi-fi ⌂ ☕ **Conf** Class 26 Board 12 Thtr 26 **Parking** 15 **Notes** LB

See advert on page 315

Mount Pleasant Hotel

★★★ 68% HOTEL

☎ 01684 561837
Belle Vue Ter WR14 4PZ
e-mail: reception@mountpleasanthotel.co.uk
web: www.mountpleasanthotel.co.uk
dir: On A449, in town centre opposite Priory Church

An attractive Georgian house in the town centre that occupies an elevated position, and overlooks Priory Church and the picturesque Severn Plain; it sits at the gateway to the Malvern Hills. This family-run hotel, with a relaxed atmosphere, offers spacious, fully equipped bedrooms, and the Spring Bar and Restaurant serves home-made classic British cuisine as well as tea, coffee, cakes and biscuits. In winter guests can sit beside real log fires, and in warmer months the garden makes a delightful place to relax.

Rooms 14 (1 fmly) **S** £74-£84; **D** £105-£125 (incl. bkfst) **Facilities** FTV Wi-fi ⌂ Hair salon Xmas New Year **Conf** Class 40 Board 50 Thtr 90 **Parking** 20 **Notes** ⊗

The Great Malvern Hotel

★★ 71% HOTEL

☎ 01684 563411
Graham Rd WR14 2HN
e-mail: sutton@great-malvern-hotel.co.uk
dir: From Worcester on A449, left after fire station into Graham Rd. Hotel at end on right

Close to the town centre this privately owned and managed hotel is ideally situated for many of Malvern's attractions. The accommodation is spacious and well equipped. Public areas include quiet lounge areas, and a cosy bar which is popular with locals.

Rooms 13 (1 fmly) **S** £55-£65; **D** £79.50 (incl. bkfst) **Facilities** STV FTV Wi-fi ⌂ ♫ **Conf** Class 20 Board 20 Thtr 20 **Services** Lift **Parking** 9 **Notes** LB

MANCHESTER
Greater Manchester
Map 16 SJ89

See also Manchester Airport & Sale

The Lowry Hotel

★★★★★ 84% ◉◉ HOTEL

☎ 0161 827 4000
50 Dearmans Place, Chapel Wharf, Salford M3 5LH
e-mail: enquiries.lowry@roccofortehotels.com
web: www.roccofortehotels.com
dir: M6 junct 19, A556/M56/A5103 for 4.5m. At rdbt take A57(M) to lights, right onto Water St. Left to New Quay St/Trinity Way. At 1st lights right into Chapel St for hotel

This modern, contemporary hotel, set beside the River Irwell in the centre of the city, offers spacious bedrooms equipped to meet the needs of business and leisure visitors alike. Many of the rooms look out over the river, as do the sumptuous suites. The River Room restaurant produces good brasserie cooking. Extensive business and function facilities are available, together with a spa to provide extra pampering.

Rooms 165 (7 fmly) ✆ **S** £129-£2500; **D** £129-£2500* **Facilities** Spa STV FTV Wi-fi ⌂ HL Gym Swimming facilities available nearby ♫ Xmas New Year **Conf** Class 250 Board 60 Thtr 400 Del from £210 to £559* **Services** Lift Air con **Parking** 100 **Notes** LB Civ Wed 400

The Midland

★★★★ 85% ◉◉ HOTEL

☎ 0161 236 3333
Peter St M60 2DS
e-mail: midlandsales@qhotels.co.uk
web: www.qhotels.co.uk
dir: M602 junct 3, follow Manchester Central Convention Complex signs, hotel opposite

This much loved, centrally located, well-established Edwardian-style hotel (Grade II listed) offers stylish, thoughtfully equipped bedrooms that have a contemporary feel. Elegant public areas are equally impressive and facilities include extensive function and meeting rooms. Eating options include the award-winning classical French Restaurant, the Colony Restaurant and the Octogan Lounge.

Rooms 312 (13 fmly) ✆ **D** £95-£359* **Facilities** STV Wi-fi ⌂ HL ⏲ Gym Squash Hair & beauty salon ♫ **Conf** Class 300 Board 120 Thtr 600 Del from £129 to £239* **Services** Lift Air con **Notes** LB ⊗ Civ Wed 600

Worsley Park, A Marriott Hotel & Country Club

★★★★ 80% ◉ HOTEL

☎ 0161 975 2000
Worsley Park, Worsley M28 2QT
e-mail: uk.pennines.sales.office@marriotthotels.com
web: www.marriottworsleypark.co.uk
dir: M60 junct 13, over 1st rdbt take A575. Hotel 400yds on left

This smart, modern hotel is set in impressive grounds with a championship golf course. Bedrooms are comfortably appointed and well equipped for both leisure and business guests. Public areas include extensive leisure and conference facilities, and an elegant restaurant offering imaginative cuisine.

Rooms 158 (33 fmly) (49 GF) **Facilities** Spa STV Wi-fi ⓘ ⓘ ⓛ 18 Putt green Gym Fitness suite Sauna Steam room Health & beauty salon Aerobics studio **Conf** Class 150 Board 100 Thtr 250 **Services** Lift **Parking** 400 **Notes** ⊗ Civ Wed 200

Marriott Manchester Victoria & Albert Hotel
Marriott HOTELS & RESORTS

★★★★ 79% HOTEL

☎ 0161 832 1188
Water St M3 4JQ
e-mail: london.regional.reservations@marriott.com
web: www.manchestermarriottvictoriaandalbert.co.uk
dir: M602 to A57 through lights on Regent Rd. Pass Sainsbury's, left at lights onto ring road, right at lights into Water St

This uniquely converted warehouse, with an interior featuring exposed brickwork and iron pillars, is located on the banks of the River Irwell, just a short stroll from the city centre. There are stylish, comfortable and well-equipped bedrooms together with attractive public areas. A large bar lounge leads onto an intimate restaurant, and extensive conference facilities are available.

Rooms 148 (30 fmly) (7 smoking) **S** £99-£179; **D** £99-£179* **Facilities** FTV Wi-fi ⓘ HL Complimentary use of Bannatyne's Health Club New Year **Conf** Class 120 Board 72 Thtr 250 Del from £140 to £189* **Services** Lift Air con **Parking** 100 **Notes** LB ⊗ Civ Wed 200

Macdonald Manchester Hotel

★★★★ 78% ◉ HOTEL

☎ 0844 879 9088   & 0161 272 3200
London Rd M1 2PG
e-mail: general.manchester@macdonald-hotels.co.uk
web: www.macdonald-hotels.co.uk
dir: Opposite Piccadilly Station

Ideally situated just a short walk from Piccadilly Station, this hotel provides a handy location for both business and leisure travellers. Stylish, modern rooms have plasma TVs and iPod docking stations and the bathrooms offer walk-in power showers and luxury baths. The first-floor restaurant serves skilfully prepared dinners and hearty breakfasts. Staff throughout are cheerful and keen to please.

Rooms 338 (14 fmly) ⓡ **Facilities** Spa FTV Wi-fi ⓘ HL Gym Sauna New Year **Conf** Class 150 Board 80 Thtr 250 Del from £135* **Services** Lift Air con **Parking** 85 **Notes** ⊗ Civ Wed 200

Holiday Inn Manchester - MediaCityUK

★★★★ 77% HOTEL

☎ 0845 250 8458
Media City UK, Salford M50 2HT
dir: M602 junct 2 onto A576 to Salford Quays

Located in the heart of the exciting media district on Salford Quays, this hotel is adjacent to the main production studios and only minutes from Old Trafford and The Lowry Centre. The stylish Hub Bar features TV-themed murals and the attractive Green Room Restaurant is on the mezzanine floor. Bedrooms are well equipped with safes, mini-bars and many have views of the Manchester Shipping Canal. There's complimentary Wi-fi throughout, and a mini-gym is available to guests.

Rooms 218 (10 fmly) ⓡ **S** £69-£179; **D** £69-£259* **Facilities** STV FTV Wi-fi ⓘ HL Gym Xmas New Year **Conf** Class 25 Board 30 Thtr 44 Del from £139 to £199* **Services** Lift Air con **Parking** 5000 **Notes** LB ⊗

Copthorne Hotel Manchester

★★★★ 76% HOTEL

☎ 0161 873 7321
Clippers Quay, Salford Quays M50 3SN
e-mail: reservations.manchester@millenniumhotels.co.uk
web: www.millenniumhotels.co.uk
dir: From M602 follow signs for Salford Quays & Trafford Park on A5063. Hotel 0.75m on right

This smart hotel enjoys a convenient location on the redeveloped Salford Quays close to Old Trafford, The Lowry Centre and The Imperial War Museum. Bedrooms are comfortably appointed and well equipped for both business and leisure guests. The informal Clippers Restaurant serves a wide range of modern dishes.

Rooms 166 (6 fmly) (23 GF) ⓡ **Facilities** STV Wi-fi ⓘ HL **Conf** Class 80 Board 70 Thtr 160 Del from £95 to £115* **Services** Lift **Parking** 120 **Notes** ⊗ Civ Wed 160

Crowne Plaza Manchester City Centre

★★★★ 76% HOTEL

☎ 0161 828 8660
70 Shudehill M4 4AF
e-mail: reception@cpmanchester.com
web: www.cpmanchester.com
dir: In city centre, Northern Quarter

A stylish hotel located in the heart of Manchester in the trendy Northern Quarter, with Victoria and Piccadilly Stations and Shudehill Tram and Bus Interchange all within walking distance. Bedrooms, including Club Rooms with a Club Lounge, have one or two queen or king sized beds. The contemporary bathrooms feature separate bath and shower. Complimentary internet access is provided and a mini gym is available 24 hours a day.

Rooms 228 **Facilities** STV FTV Wi-fi ⓘ Gym Xmas New Year **Conf** Class 160 Board 60 Thtr 200 **Services** Lift Air con **Notes** ⊗ Civ Wed 200

MANCHESTER *continued*

Macdonald Townhouse Manchester

★★★★ 74% TOWN HOUSE HOTEL

☎ 0161 236 5122
101 Portland St M1 6DF
e-mail: gm.townhouse@macdonald-hotels.co.uk
dir: From Piccadilly Station, along Piccadilly. Left into Portland St, hotel at junct with Princess St

This hotel, a former cotton warehouse and now a Grade II listed building, is ideally located for exploring the City of Manchester. There are comfortable and well-appointed bedrooms, a stylish bar and a lounge with the restaurant that is open for pre-theatre meals.

Rooms 85 (24 fmly) **Facilities** FTV Wi-fi ♫ **Conf** Class 26 Board 30 Thtr 48 **Services** Lift Air con

Novotel Manchester Centre

★★★★ 74% HOTEL

☎ 0161 235 2200
21 Dickinson St M1 4LX
e-mail: H3145@accor.com
web: www.novotel.com
dir: From Oxford St into Portland St, left into Dickinson St. Hotel on right

This smart, modern property enjoys a central location convenient for theatres, shops, China Town and Manchester's business district. Spacious bedrooms are thoughtfully equipped and brightly decorated. Open-plan, contemporary public areas include an all-day restaurant and a stylish bar. Extensive conference and meeting facilities are available.

Rooms 164 (15 fmly) ♠ **S** £69-£179; **D** £69-£179* **Facilities** STV FTV Wi-fi ♭ HL Gym Steam room Sauna Aromatherapy **Conf** Class 50 Board 36 Thtr 90 **Services** Lift Air con **Notes** LB

The Palace Hotel

★★★★ 74% HOTEL

☎ 0161 288 1111
Oxford St M60 7HA
e-mail: richard.grove@principal-hayley.com
web: www.principal-hayley.com
dir: Opposite Manchester Oxford Road rail station

Formerly the offices of the Refuge Life Assurance Company, this impressive neo-Gothic building occupies a central location. There is a vast lobby, spacious open-plan bar lounge and restaurant, and extensive conference and function facilities. Bedrooms vary in size and style but are all spacious and well equipped.

Rooms 275 (59 fmly) ♠ **S** fr £69; **D** £225* **Facilities** STV Wi-fi **Conf** Class 650 Board 200 Thtr 1000 Del from £135 to £189* **Services** Lift **Notes** ⊗ Civ Wed 600

Malmaison Manchester

★★★ 86% ⊛ HOTEL

☎ 0161 278 1000
Piccadilly M1 3AQ
e-mail: manchester@malmaison.com
web: www.malmaison.com
dir: Follow city centre signs, then signs to Piccadilly station. Hotel at bottom of station approach

Stylish and chic, Malmaison Manchester offers the best of contemporary hotel keeping in a relaxed and comfortable environment. Converted from a former warehouse it offers a range of bright meeting rooms, a gym and treatment rooms. The new Smoak Bar & Grill is impressive and understandably popular. Air-conditioned suites combine comfort with stunning design. Expect the unusual in some of the rooms, for instance the Cinema Suites have a private screening room with 52" screen and surround-sound.

Rooms 167 ♠ **D** £79-£185* **Facilities** STV Wi-fi ♭ HL Gym Xmas New Year **Conf** Class 48 Board 30 Thtr 100 Del from £140 to £225* **Services** Lift Air con **Notes** LB Civ Wed 100

The Portland by Thistle, Manchester

thistle

★★★ 81% HOTEL

☎ 0871 376 9026
3/5 Portland St, Piccadilly Gardens M1 6DP
e-mail: reservations.manchester@thistle.co.uk
web: www.thistlehotels.com/manchester
dir: M6 junct 19 onto M56, A5103 signed city centre, straight on at rdbt, right at 2nd lights, straight at next lights into Portland St, hotel on right

The hotel is located close to the Piccadilly Gardens and five minutes' walk from the central and financial districts. Bedrooms are compact and well equipped, and the Portland Bar and Restaurant offers a wide selection of meals, drinks and wines. There is also an Otium Leisure Centre, and conference facilities are available.

Rooms 204 (1 fmly) **Facilities** STV Wi-fi ⊛ supervised Gym Steam room Sauna Plunge pool Xmas New Year **Conf** Class 140 Board 40 Thtr 300 **Services** Lift Air con **Notes** ⊗ Civ Wed 220

Best Western Willow Bank Hotel

★★★ 79% HOTEL

☎ 0161 224 0461
340-342 Wilmslow Rd, Fallowfield M14 6AF
e-mail: gm-willowbank@feathers.uk.com
web: www.feathers.uk.com
dir: M60 junct 5, A5103, left onto B5093. Hotel 2.5m on left

This popular hotel is conveniently located three miles from the city centre, close to the universities. Bedrooms vary in size and style but all are appointed to impressively high standards; they are well equipped and many rooms benefit from CD players and PlayStations. Spacious, elegant public areas include a bar, a restaurant and meeting rooms.

Rooms 116 (4 fmly) **Facilities** STV Wi-fi Xmas New Year **Conf** Class 60 Board 70 Thtr 125 Del from £105 to £145* **Parking** 100 **Notes** Civ Wed 125

Jurys Inn Manchester

★★★ 78% HOTEL

☎ 0161 953 8888
56 Great Bridgewater St M1 5LE
e-mail: manchester_inn@jurysinns.com
web: www.jurysinns.com
dir: In city centre adjacent to Manchester Central & Bridgewater Hall

Enjoying a prime city centre location, this hotel offers good value, air-conditioned accommodation, ideal for both business travellers and families. Public areas include a smart, spacious lobby, the Inn Pub and the Infusion Restaurant. There are several conveniently located car parks with special rates available.

Rooms 265 (11 fmly) (16 GF) **Facilities** FTV Wi-fi ♭ **Conf** Class 25 Board 25 Thtr 50 **Services** Lift Air con **Notes** ⊗

Chancellors Hotel & Conference Centre

★★★ 72% HOTEL

☎ 0161 907 7414
Moseley Rd, Fallowfield M14 6NN
e-mail: chancellors@manchester.ac.uk
dir: Telephone for detailed directions

A Grade II listed manor house set in five acres of landscaped gardens hidden in the heart of Fallowfield, well located for the city's shopping, business and commercial centres. Bedrooms offer modern facilities and the cuisine is enjoyable. Wi-fi and secure parking are available.

Rooms 70 **Parking** 70

Save on hotels. Book at **theAA.com/hotel**

MAN 319 ENGLAND

Novotel Manchester West

★★★ 72% HOTEL

☎ 0161 799 3535
Worsley Brow M28 2YA
e-mail: H0907@accor.com
web: www.novotel.com

(For full entry see Worsley)

Diamond Lodge

★★ 71% HOTEL

☎ 0161 231 0770
Hyde Rd, Belle Vue M18 7BA
web: www.diamondlodge.co.uk
dir: On A57, 2.5m W of M60 junct 24 (Manchester Orbital) into city

Offering very good value, this modern lodge, near the city centre, motorway networks and football stadiums, provides comfortable accommodation. The ground floor features a bright open-plan lounge and informal dining room where complimentary tea and coffee are provided; a wide choice of evening meals are served. Wi-fi is available throughout the hotel.

Diamond Lodge

Rooms 85 (13 fmly) (16 GF) (13 smoking) ♪ **S** £44; **D** £44 (incl. bkfst)* **Facilities** FTV Wi-fi ♫ **Parking** 90 **Notes** ⊗ Closed 24-26 Dec RS 31 Dec

See advert on this page

Campanile Manchester
Campanile
HOTEL RESTAURANT

BUDGET HOTEL

☎ 0161 833 1845
55 Ordsall Ln, Regent Rd, Salford M5 4RS
e-mail: manchester@campanile.com
web: www.campanile.com
dir: M602 to Manchester, then A57. After large rdbt with Sainsbury's on left, left at next lights. Hotel on right

This modern building offers accommodation in smart, well-equipped bedrooms, all with en suite bathrooms.

Refreshments may be taken at the informal bistro. See also the Hotel Groups pages.

Rooms 104 (25 GF) **Conf** Class 40 Board 30 Thtr 50

Holiday Inn Express Manchester East

BUDGET HOTEL

☎ 0161 231 9900
Hyde Rd M18 7LJ
e-mail: manchester@morethanhotels.com
web: www.hiexpress.co.uk
dir: 1m from M60 junct 24 (Manchester Orbital)

A modern hotel ideal for families and business travellers. Fresh and uncomplicated, the spacious rooms include Sky TV, power shower and tea and coffee-making facilities. Continental buffet breakfast is included in the room rate; other meals may be taken at the nearby family pub or restaurant. See also the Hotel Groups pages.

Rooms 97 (58 fmly) (27 GF) (14 smoking) **Conf** Class 18 Board 18 Thtr 35

Holiday Inn Express Manchester - Oxford Road

BUDGET HOTEL

☎ 0843 208 3005
Oxford Road 2 M1 5QA
e-mail: info@hiemanchester.co.uk
dir: From A57(M) follow signs for Peters Fields & A5103, into Cambridge St. 1st right into Chester St. NCP car park on left at end (NB for Sat Nav use M1 5GE)

Rooms 147 (80 fmly) ♪ **Conf** Class 20 Board 20 Thtr 20

M

MANCHESTER *continued*

Holiday Inn Express Manchester Salford Quays

BUDGET HOTEL

☎ 0161 868 1000
Waterfront Quay, Salford Quays M50 3XW
e-mail: info@expressmanchester.co.uk
web: www.hiexpress.com/salfordquays

Rooms 120 (72 fmly) ✎ Conf Class 10 Board 12
Thtr 25 Del from £50 to £170

Ibis Manchester Charles Street

BUDGET HOTEL

☎ 0161 272 5000
Charles St, Princess St M1 7DL
e-mail: H3143@accor.com
web: www.ibishotel.com
dir: M62, M602 towards Manchester Centre, follow signs for UMIST(A34)

Modern, budget hotel offering comfortable accommodation in bright and practical bedrooms. Breakfast is self-service and dinner is available in the restaurant. See also the Hotel Groups pages.

Rooms 126 ✎ S £49-£115; D £49-£115*

Ibis Manchester City Centre

BUDGET HOTEL

☎ 0161 234 0600
96 Portland St M1 4GY
e-mail: H3142@accor.com
web: www.ibishotel.com
dir: In city centre, between Princess St & Oxford St

Rooms 127 (16 fmly) S £45-£115; D £45-£115*

Premier Inn Manchester Central

BUDGET HOTEL

☎ 0871 527 8742
Bishopsgate, 7-11 Lower Mosley St M2 3DW
web: www.premierinn.com
dir: M56 to end, A5103 towards city. Right at 2nd lights. At next lights left into Oxford Rd, left at junct of St Peters Sq. Hotel on left

High quality, budget accommodation ideal for both families and business travellers. Spacious, en suite

bedrooms feature tea and coffee making facilities, and Freeview TV in most hotels. Internet access and Wi-fi are available for a small fee. The adjacent family restaurant features a wide and varied menu. See also the Hotel Groups pages.

Rooms 147

Premier Inn Manchester City Centre (Deansgate)

BUDGET HOTEL

☎ 0871 527 8740
Medlock St M15 5FJ
web: www.premierinn.com
dir: M60 junct 24, A57(M) (Mancunian Way) towards city centre. Hotel adjacent, on A5103 (Medlock St)

Rooms 200

Premier Inn Manchester City Centre (Portland Street)

BUDGET HOTEL

☎ 0871 527 8746
The Circus, 112-114 Portland St M1 4WB
web: www.premierinn.com
dir: M6 junct 19, A556. M56, exit junct 3 onto A5103 to Medlock St, right into Whitworth St, left into Oxford St, right into Portland St

Rooms 225

Premier Inn Manchester City MEN/Printworks

BUDGET HOTEL

☎ 0871 527 8744
North Tower, Victoria Bridge St, Salford M3 5AS
web: www.premierinn.com
dir: M602 to city centre, A57(M) towards GMEX. 2nd exit follow A56 city centre signs. Left before MEN arena onto A6, 1st left

Rooms 170

Premier Inn Manchester (Denton)

BUDGET HOTEL

☎ 0871 527 8708
Alphagate Dr, Manchester Rd South, Denton M34 3SH
web: www.premierinn.com
dir: M60 junct 24, A57 signed Denton. 1st right at lights, right at next lights, hotel on left

Rooms 40

Premier Inn Manchester (Heaton Park)

BUDGET HOTEL

☎ 0871 527 8710
Middleton Rd, Crumpsall M8 4NB
web: www.premierinn.com
dir: M60 junct 19, A576 towards Manchester, through 2 sets of lights. Hotel on left

Rooms 45

Premier Inn Manchester North (Middleton)

BUDGET HOTEL

☎ 0871 527 8748
818 Manchester Old Rd, Rhodes, Middleton M24 4RF
web: www.premierinn.com
dir: M60/M62 junct 18 follow Manchester/Middleton signs. M60 junct 19 take A576 towards Middleton

Rooms 42

Premier Inn Manchester Old Trafford

BUDGET HOTEL

☎ 0871 527 8750
Waters Reach, Trafford Park M17 1WS
web: www.premierinn.com
dir: M6 junct 19, A556 towards Altrincham. Follow Stretford & Manchester City Centre signs (road becomes A56). Follow Manchester United Football Stadium signs. At stadium left at lights. Into Sir Matt Busby Way, after 1st lights hotel on right

Rooms 160

Premier Inn Manchester (Salford Quays)

BUDGET HOTEL

☎ 0871 527 8718
11 The Quays, Salford Quays, Salford M50 3SQ
web: www.premierinn.com
dir: M602 junct 3, A5063, on Salford Quays

Rooms 52

Premier Inn Manchester Trafford Centre North

BUDGET HOTEL

☎ 0871 527 8752
18-20 Trafford Boulevard,, Urmston M41 7JE
web: www.premierinn.com
dir: M6, onto M62 at junct 21a, towards Manchester.
M62 junct 1, M60 towards south. M60 junct 10, take
B5214. Hotel on left just before Ellesmere Circle

Rooms 42

Premier Inn Manchester Trafford Centre South

BUDGET HOTEL

☎ 0871 527 8754
Wilderspool Wood, Trafford Centre M17 8WW
web: www.premierinn.com
dir: M6 onto M62 junct 21a towards Manchester. Or
M62 junct 1 onto M60 S. Or M60 junct 10, B5124
towards Trafford Park. At 1st rdbt take last exit for
Trafford Centre parking. At 2nd rdbt straight on. Hotel
on left

Rooms 59

Premier Inn Manchester Trafford Centre West

BUDGET HOTEL

☎ 0871 527 8756
Old Park Ln M17 8PG
web: www.premierinn.com
dir: M60 junct 10 towards The Trafford Centre

Rooms 161

Premier Inn Manchester (West Didsbury)

BUDGET HOTEL

☎ 0871 527 8722
**Christies Field Office Park, Derwent Ave, Didsbury
M21 7QS**
web: www.premierinn.com
dir: M60 junct 5, A5103 (Princess Parkway) towards
Manchester on A5103. Hotel approx 1m

Rooms 80

MANCHESTER AIRPORT   Map 15 SJ88
Greater Manchester

See also Altrincham

Manchester Airport Marriott Hotel

★★★★ 80% HOTEL

☎ 0161 904 0301
Hale Rd, Hale Barns WA15 8XW
e-mail: london.regional.reservations@marriott.com
web: www.manchesterairportmarriott.co.uk
dir: M56 junct 6, in left lane (Hale, Altrincham). Left
at lights, on approach to bridge into right lane. At
rdbt 3rd exit into hotel car park

With good airport links and convenient access to the
city, this sprawling modern hotel is a popular
destination. The hotel offers extensive leisure and
business facilities, a choice of eating and drinking
options and ample parking. Bedrooms are situated
around courtyards and have a comprehensive range
of facilities.

Rooms 215 (22 fmly) (43 GF) (16 smoking)
Facilities Spa STV Wi-fi ⓦ supervised Gym
Conf Class 70 Board 50 Thtr 160 Services Lift Air con
Parking 400 Notes ⊗ Civ Wed 110

Stanneylands Hotel

PRIMA

★★★★ 79% ◉◉ HOTEL

☎ 01625 525225
Stanneylands Rd SK9 4EY
e-mail: reservations@stanneylandshotel.co.uk
web: www.stanneylandshotel.co.uk
dir: From M56 at airport exit, follow signs to
Wilmslow. Left towards Handforth. Left at lights into
Stanneylands Rd, hotel on left

This traditional hotel offers well-equipped bedrooms
and delightful, comfortable day rooms. The cuisine in
the restaurant is of a high standard and ranges from
traditional favourites to more imaginative
contemporary dishes. Staff throughout are friendly
and obliging.

Rooms 56 (2 fmly) (10 GF) ⓦ S £60-£250;
D £70-£250* Facilities STV FTV Wi-fi ♫ Xmas New

Year Conf Class 50 Board 40 Thtr 120 Del from £110
to £160 Services Lift Parking 108 Notes ⊗
Civ Wed 100

Radisson Blu Hotel Manchester Airport

★★★★ 78% HOTEL

☎ 0161 490 5000
Chicago Av M90 3RA
e-mail: sales.manchester@radissonblu.com
web: www.radissonblu.co.uk/hotel-manchesterairport
dir: M56 junct 5, follow signs for Terminal 2. At rdbt
2nd left & follow signs for railway station. Hotel next
to station

All the airport terminals are quickly accessed by
covered, moving walkways from this modern hotel.
There is an excellent and well-equipped leisure club
complete with indoor pool, and extensive conference
and banqueting facilities are available. Air-
conditioned bedrooms are thoughtfully equipped and
come in a variety of decorative themes. Super views
of the runway can be enjoyed in the Phileas Fogg
Restaurant that offers international cuisine; there's
also an all-day brasserie.

Rooms 360 (2 fmly) (25 smoking) ⓦ S £89-£159;
D £89-£159 Facilities Spa STV Wi-fi ⓦ Gym Sauna
Steam room Xmas New Year Child facilities
Conf Class 150 Board 60 Thtr 350 Del from £135 to
£155 Services Lift Air con Parking 222 Notes LB ⊗
Civ Wed 350

Crowne Plaza Manchester Airport

CROWNE PLAZA
HOTELS & RESORTS

★★★★ 76% HOTEL

☎ 0871 942 9055
Ringway Rd M90 3NS
e-mail: reservations-manchesterairport@ihg.com
web: www.crowneplaza.co.uk
dir: M56 junct 5 signed Manchester Airport. At
airport, follow signs to Terminal 1 & 3. Hotel adjacent
to Terminal 3. Long stay car park on left

Located by Terminal 3 this smart, modern hotel offers
well-equipped, comfortable bedrooms, all with air
conditioning and effective double glazing. A choice of
dining options and bars is available, and the hotel
has spacious leisure facilities and ample on-site
parking. The hospitality is friendly, with several long-
serving staff members who greet regular customers
as friends.

Rooms 294 (100 fmly) (51 GF) (25 smoking)
Facilities STV Wi-fi Gym Saunas Conf Class 25
Board 20 Thtr 30 Services Lift Air con Parking 300

M

MANCHESTER *continued*

Hallmark Hotel Manchester

★★★★ 76% HOTEL

☎ 0161 437 0511
Stanley Rd SK9 3LD
e-mail: linda.gregory@hallmarkhotels.co.uk
dir: M60 junct 3/A34 signed Cheadle/Wilmslow. Right
at 3rd rdbt onto Stanley Rd (B5094). Hotel on left

Ideally located for Manchester Airport and just a few
miles from both the Trafford Centre and the city's
many shops, the hotel offers well appointed
bedrooms. Guests can relax and unwind in the hotel's
20-metre pool, jacuzzi and steam rooms. The
brasserie is open for both lunch and dinner and offers
a range of international dishes.

Rooms 88 (12 fmly) (12 GF) **Facilities** Spa FTV Wi-fi
Gym Steam room Sauna Hair salon New Year
Conf Class 300 Board 150 Thtr 500 **Services** Lift
Notes Civ Wed

Etrop Grange Hotel

★★★★ 71% HOTEL

M

☎ 0844 855 9118
Thorley Ln M90 4EG
e-mail: gm@etrophotel.co.uk
dir: M56 junct 5 follow signs for Terminal 2, on slip
road to rdbt take 1st exit. Immediately left, hotel
400yds

This Georgian country-house style hotel is close to
Terminal 2 but one would never know once inside.
Stylish, comfortable bedrooms provide modern
comforts and good business facilities. Elegant day
rooms include the Coach House Restaurant that
serves creative dishes. Complimentary chauffeured
transport to the airport is available for guests using
the airport.

Rooms 64 (4 fmly) (9 GF) **Facilities** STV Wi-fi New
Year **Conf** Class 35 Board 35 Thtr 80 **Parking** 80
Notes Civ Wed 90

Bewleys Hotel Manchester Airport

★★★ 78% HOTEL

☎ 0161 498 0333 & 498 1390
Outwood Ln M90 4HL
e-mail: man@bewleyshotels.com
web: www.bewleyshotels.com
dir: At Manchester Airport. Follow signs to Manchester
Airport Terminal 3. Hotel on left on Terminal 3 rdbt

Located adjacent to the airport this modern, stylish
hotel provides an ideal stop-off for air travellers and
business guests alike. All bedrooms are spacious and
well equipped and include a wing of superior rooms.
Spacious, open-plan day rooms are stylishly
appointed and include a large bar and restaurant
along with a good range of meeting and conference
facilities.

Rooms 365 (111 fmly) (30 GF) (19 smoking)
S £56-£150; D £56-£150 **Facilities** Wi-fi Gym
Conf Class 35 Board 18 Thtr 90 Del from £130 to
£150 **Services** Lift **Parking** 300 **Notes**

Best Western Pinewood on Wilmslow

U

☎ 01625 529211
180 Wilmslow Rd, Handforth SK9 3LG
e-mail: pinewood.res@pinewood-hotel.co.uk
dir: Telephone for detailed directions

Currently the rating for this establishment is not
confirmed. This may be due to a change of ownership
or because it has only recently joined the AA rating
scheme. For further details please see the AA website:
theAA.com

Rooms 58 (2 fmly) **Facilities** FTV Wi-fi Use of nearby
Total Fitness Club Xmas New Year **Conf** Class 60
Board 60 Thtr 120 Del from £110 to £120*
Services Lift **Parking** 120 **Notes** Civ Wed 120

Premier Inn Manchester Airport

BUDGET HOTEL

☎ 0871 527 8726
Runger Ln, Wilmslow Rd M90 5DL
web: www.premierinn.com
dir: M56 junct 6, follow Wilmslow & Hale signs. Merge
onto M56 signed Warrington, Macclesfield & Hale.
Left into Runger Ln (signed Freight Terminal)

High quality, budget accommodation ideal for both
families and business travellers. Spacious, en suite
bedrooms feature tea and coffee making facilities,
and Freeview TV in most hotels. Internet access and
Wi-fi are available for a small fee. The adjacent
family restaurant features a wide and varied menu.
See also the Hotel Groups pages.

Rooms 195

Premier Inn Manchester Airport (FT)

BUDGET HOTEL

☎ 0871 527 8730
Runger Ln, Wilmslow Rd M90 5DL
web: www.premierinn.com
dir: M56 junct 6, follow Airport signs. 2nd exit at rdbt.
Hotel on left. Through Travelodge car park. Hotel on
right

Rooms 166

Premier Inn Manchester (Handforth)

BUDGET HOTEL

☎ 0871 527 8732
30 Wilmslow Rd SK9 3EW
web: www.premierinn.com
dir: M56 junct 6, A538 towards Wilmslow. At main
junct into town centre bear left. In 2m hotel at top of
hill on right just after Wilmslow Garden Centre

Rooms 35

Premier Inn Manchester (Wilmslow)

BUDGET HOTEL

☎ 0871 527 8736
Racecourse Rd, Wilmslow SK9 5LR
web: www.premierinn.com
dir: M6 junct 19 to Knutsford, follow Wilmslow signs.
Left at 1st & 2nd lights towards Wilmslow. Through
Mobberley, left just before Bird in Hand pub. At
T-junct, right. Hotel 150yds on right

Rooms 37

MARAZION
Cornwall   Map 2 SW53

Mount Haven Hotel & St Michaels Restaurant

★★★ 84% ◉◉ HOTEL

☎ 01736 710249
Turnpike Rd TR17 0DQ
e-mail: reception@mounthaven.co.uk
web: www.mounthaven.co.uk
dir: From A30 towards Penzance. At rdbt take exit for Helston onto A394. Next rdbt right into Marazion, hotel on left

This hotel enjoys spectacular views across the sea towards St Michael's Mount; all rooms have spacious balconies from where the views can be enjoyed - sunrises and sunsets can be spectacular. Bedrooms are contemporarily styled and have comfortable beds and exotic fabrics. Dining is a highlight with the freshest local seafood and fish used to create interesting menus. A range of holistic therapies is available. The attentive and friendly service helps make a relaxing and enchanting environment throughout.

Rooms 18 (1 fmly) (6 GF) ↖ **S** £90-£150; **D** £130-£290 (incl. bkfst)* **Facilities** FTV Wi-fi Aromatherapy Reflexology Massage Reiki Hot rocks Beauty treatment room **Parking** 30 **Notes** ⊗ Closed 20 Dec-5 Feb

Marazion Hotel

★★ 74% SMALL HOTEL

☎ 01736 710334
The Square TR17 0AP
e-mail: enquiries@marazionhotel.co.uk
web: www.marazionhotel.co.uk
dir: A30 to Penzance, at rdbt follow St Michael's Mount signs. Hotel on left

Within 50 yards of one of Cornwall's safest beaches, this family run hotel, offers a relaxed atmosphere

with friendly service. The individually furnished and decorated bedrooms are comfortable, many with the benefit of stunning views across to St Michael's Mount. The hotel incorporates the Cutty Sark public bar and restaurant, where a wide range of meals is offered to suit all palates and budgets.

Rooms 10 (3 fmly) ↖ **S** £72-£109; **D** £88-£134 (incl. bkfst)* **Facilities** FTV Wi-fi ☷ Xmas **Parking** 20 **Notes** LB ⊗

MARCH
Cambridgeshire   Map 12 TL49

Oliver Cromwell Hotel

★★★ 70% HOTEL

☎ 01354 602890
High St PE15 9LH
e-mail: reception@olivercromwellhotel.co.uk
dir: In village centre

This purpose built hotel is ideally situated for touring the Cambridgeshire countryside, and within easy reach of Ely and Wisbech. The spacious bedrooms are pleasantly decorated and thoughtfully equipped. Public rooms include a smart lounge bar and a dining room as well as conference and banqueting facilities.

Rooms 42 (2 fmly) (8 GF) **Facilities** FTV Wi-fi ☷ Gym Sauna Steam room **Conf** Class 80 Board 40 Thtr 120 **Services** Lift Air con **Parking** 60 **Notes** ⊗ Civ Wed 100

MARGATE
Kent   Map 7 TR37

Smiths Court Hotel

★★★ ⊠ HOTEL

☎ 01843 222310
Eastern Esplanade, Cliftonville CT9 2HL
e-mail: info@smithscourt.co.uk
dir: From clocktower on seafront, left onto A28 approx 1m. Hotel on right

Rooms 43 (10 fmly) (4 GF) **Facilities** FTV Wi-fi Gym ♪ New Year **Conf** Class 50 Board 80 Thtr 80 **Services** Lift **Parking** 15 **Notes** Civ Wed 80

Premier Inn Margate

BUDGET HOTEL

☎ 0871 527 8762
Station Green, Station Rd CT9 5AF
web: www.premierinn.com
dir: M2, A299, A28 to Margate seafront. Hotel adjacent to Margate station

High quality, budget accommodation ideal for both families and business travellers. Spacious, en suite bedrooms feature tea and coffee making facilities, and Freeview TV in most hotels. Internet access and Wi-fi are available for a small fee. The adjacent family restaurant features a wide and varied menu. See also the Hotel Groups pages.

Rooms 44

MARKET DRAYTON
Shropshire   Map 15 SJ63

Goldstone Hall

★★★ 87% ◉◉ HOTEL

☎ 01630 661202
Goldstone TF9 2NA
e-mail: enquiries@goldstonehall.com
dir: 4m S of Market Drayton, 4m N of Newport. Hotel signed from A529 & A41

Situated in extensive grounds, this sympathetically refurbished period property is a family-run hotel. It provides traditionally furnished, well-equipped accommodation with outstanding en suite bathrooms and lots of thoughtful extras. Public rooms are extensive and include a choice of lounges, a snooker room and a conservatory. The hotel has a well deserved reputation for good food that utilises home-grown produce. A warm welcome is assured.

Rooms 12 (2 GF) **S** fr £81; (incl. bkfst)* **Facilities** STV FTV Wi-fi Snooker table New Year **Conf** Class 30 Board 30 Thtr 50 **Parking** 60 **Notes** LB ⊗ Civ Wed 100

M

MARKET DRAYTON *continued*

Ternhill Farm House & The Cottage Restaurant

 RESTAURANT WITH ROOMS

☎ 01630 638984
Ternhill TF9 3PX
e-mail: info@ternhillfarm.co.uk
web: www.ternhillfarm.co.uk
dir: On junct A53 & A41, archway off A53 to back of property

This elegant Grade II listed Georgian farmhouse stands in a large pleasant garden and has been modernised to provide quality accommodation. There is a choice of comfortable lounges, and the Cottage Restaurant features imaginative dishes using local produce. Secure parking is an additional benefit.

Rooms 7 (2 fmly)

MARKET HARBOROUGH   Map 11 SP78
Leicestershire

Best Western Three Swans Hotel

★★★ 77% HOTEL

☎ 01858 466644
21 High St LE16 7NJ
e-mail: sales@threeswans.co.uk
web: www.bw-threeswanshotel.co.uk
dir: M1 junct 20, A304 to Market Harborough. Through town centre on A6 from Leicester, hotel on right

Public areas in this former coaching inn include an elegant fine dining restaurant and cocktail bar, a smart foyer lounge and popular public bar areas. Bedroom styles and sizes vary, but are very well appointed and equipped. Those in the wing are particularly impressive, offering high quality and spacious accommodation.

Rooms 61 (48 annexe) (8 fmly) (20 GF) ⚡ **S** £48-£68; **D** £48-£125 (incl. bkfst) **Facilities** STV FTV Wi-fi ⌕ Xmas New Year **Conf** Class 90 Board 50 Thtr 250 Del from £110 to £145 **Services** Lift **Parking** 100 **Notes** LB Civ Wed 140

Premier Inn Market Harborough

BUDGET HOTEL

☎ 0871 527 8764
Melton Rd, East Langton LE16 7TG
web: www.premierinn.com
dir: On A6, N of Market Harborough. Hotel on rdbt junct of A6 & B6047

High quality, budget accommodation ideal for both families and business travellers. Spacious, en suite bedrooms feature tea and coffee making facilities, and Freeview TV in most hotels. Internet access and Wi-fi are available for a small fee. The adjacent family restaurant features a wide and varied menu. See also the Hotel Groups pages.

Rooms 40

MARKET RASEN   Map 17 TF18
Lincolnshire

The Advocate Arms

⊚ RESTAURANT WITH ROOMS

☎ 01673 842364
2 Queen St LN8 3EH
e-mail: info@advocatearms.co.uk
dir: In town centre

Appointed to a high standard this 18th-century property is located in the heart of Market Rasen and combines historic character and contemporary design. The operation centres around the stylish restaurant where service is friendly yet professional and the food is a highlight. The attractive bedrooms are very well equipped and feature luxury bathrooms.

Rooms 10 (2 fmly)

MARKFIELD   Map 11 SK40
Leicestershire

Field Head Hotel

★★★ 66% HOTEL   OldEnglish

☎ 01530 245454
Markfield Ln LE6 9PS
e-mail: 9160@greeneking.co.uk
web: www.oldenglish.co.uk
dir: M1 junct 22, towards Leicester. At rdbt turn left, then right

This conveniently situated hotel dates back to the 17th century when it was a farmhouse; it has been considerably extended over the years. Within the public areas, the bar and lounge are the focal point for residents and non-residents alike, whilst meals can be taken either in the bar or the dining room. Bedrooms are modern and well furnished and offer good all-round comforts and facilities. Four large feature bedrooms are available.

Rooms 28 (1 fmly) (13 GF) **S** £30-£65; **D** £30-£65 (incl. bkfst)* **Facilities** FTV Wi-fi ♫ Xmas New Year **Conf** Class 30 Board 36 Thtr 60 Del from £99 to £119* **Parking** 65 **Notes** Civ Wed 50

MARLBOROUGH   Map 5 SU16
Wiltshire

The Castle & Ball

★★★ 73% HOTEL   OldEnglish

☎ 01672 515201
High St SN8 1LZ
e-mail: castleandballmarlboroughreservations@greeneking.co.uk
web: www.oldenglish.co.uk
dir: From either A4 or A346 into town centre

This traditional coaching inn in the town centre offers contemporary and very well equipped bedrooms. Open-plan public areas include a comfortable bar/lounge area and a smartly appointed restaurant, which serves food all day. Meeting rooms are also available.

Rooms 37 (3 annexe) (5 fmly) (3 GF) ⚡ **S** £79-£99; **D** £89-£109 (incl. bkfst) **Facilities** Wi-fi Xmas New Year **Parking** 48

M

Save on hotels. Book at **theAA.com/hotel**

MAR 325 ENGLAND

INSPECTORS' CHOICE

Macdonald Compleat Angler

MACDONALD
HOTELS & RESORTS

★★★★ ◎◎◎ HOTEL

☎ 0844 879 9128
Marlow Bridge SL7 1RG
e-mail: compleatangler@macdonald-hotels.co.uk
web: www.macdonald-hotels.co.uk/compleatangler
dir: M4 junct 8/9 or M40 junct 4, A404(M) to rdbt,
Bisham exit, 1m to Marlow Bridge, hotel on right

This well-established hotel enjoys an idyllic location
overlooking the River Thames and the delightful
Marlow weir. The bedrooms, which differ in size and
style, are all individually decorated and are
equipped with flat-screen satellite TVs, high speed
internet and air conditioning; some rooms have
balconies with views of the weir and some have
four-posters. Aubergine has three AA rosettes and
offers modern French cuisine; Bowaters Restaurant
serves British dishes and has gained two AA

rosettes. In summer guests can use two boats that
the hotel has moored on the river and the fishing is,
of course, a popular activity - a ghillie can
accompany guests if prior arranged. Staff
throughout are keen to please and nothing is too
much trouble.

Rooms 64 (6 fmly) (6 GF) **D** £120-£270 (incl.
bkfst)* **Facilities** STV FTV Wi-fi ↻ HL Fly & coarse
fishing River trips (Apr-Sep) Xmas New Year
Conf Class 65 Board 36 Thtr 150 Del from £220 to
£300 **Services** Lift **Parking** 100 **Notes** LB
Civ Wed 120

Danesfield House Hotel & Spa

★★★★ 83% ◎◎◎◎ HOTEL

☎ 01628 891010
Henley Rd SL7 2EY
e-mail: reservations@danesfieldhouse.co.uk
web: www.danesfieldhouse.co.uk
dir: 2m from Marlow on A4155 towards Henley

Set in 65 acres of elevated grounds just 45 minutes
from central London and 30 minutes from Heathrow,
this hotel enjoys spectacular views across the River

Thames. Impressive public rooms include the
cathedral-like Great Hall, an impressive spa, and The
Orangery for informal dining. The beautiful
restaurant, Adam Simmonds at Danesfield House, is
an ideal setting to enjoy superb, imaginative fine
dining. Some bedrooms have balconies and stunning
views. Nothing is too much trouble for the team of
committed staff.

Danesfield House Hotel & Spa

Rooms 78 (3 fmly) (27 GF) ↻ **S** £135-£195;
D £150-£285 (incl. bkfst)* **Facilities** Spa STV Wi-fi ↻
⊛ ⚘ Putt green ⛳ Gym Jogging trail Steam room
Hydrotherapy room Sauna Xmas New Year
Conf Class 60 Board 50 Thtr 100 Del from £245 to
£345* **Services** Lift **Parking** 100 **Notes** LB ⊗
Civ Wed 100

See advert on this page

M

MARLOW *continued*

Crowne Plaza Marlow

★★★★ 82% ⊛ HOTEL

☎ 01628 496800
Field House Ln SL7 1GJ
e-mail: enquiries@cpmarlow.co.uk
web: www.cpmarlow.co.uk
dir: A404 exit to Marlow, left at mini rdbt, left into
Field House Lane

This hotel is in the Thames Valley not far from
Windsor, Henley-on-Thames and the motorway. The
public areas are air conditioned and include the Agua
Café and Bar and Glaze Restaurant. Leisure facilities
include an up-to-the-minute gym and large pool. The
bedrooms, including six contemporary suites, enjoy
plenty of natural light and have excellent
workstations; the Club Rooms have European and US
power points

Rooms 168 (47 fmly) (56 GF) (11 smoking) 🌊
Facilities Spa STV FTV Wi-fi HL 🕓 🏊 Gym Sauna
Steam room Dance studio Xmas New Year
Conf Class 180 Board 30 Thtr 450 Del from £150*
Services Lift Air con **Parking** 300 **Notes** ⊗
Civ Wed 400

Premier Inn Marlow

BUDGET HOTEL

☎ 0871 527 8767
The Causeway SL7 2AA
web: www.premierinn.com
dir: M40 junct 4, A404 signed Marlow/Maidenhead.
Left, follow A4155 signs to Marlow. At 3rd rdbt 1st
exit into High St, signed Bisham. Straight on at mini
rdbt. Hotel on left

High quality, budget accommodation ideal for both
families and business travellers. Spacious, en suite
bedrooms feature tea and coffee making facilities,
and Freeview TV in most hotels. Internet access and
Wi-fi are available for a small fee. The adjacent
family restaurant features a wide and varied menu.
See also the Hotel Groups pages.

MARSDEN
West Yorkshire   Map 16 SE01

The Olive Branch Restaurant with Rooms

⊛ RESTAURANT WITH ROOMS

☎ 01484 844487
Manchester Rd HD7 6LU
e-mail: eat@olivebranch.uk.com
web: www.olivebranch.uk.com
dir: 1m NE of Marsden on A62

The Olive Branch, once a roadside inn, was developed
into a popular restaurant with three comfortable
bedrooms. The menu features the best of seasonal
produce cooked with flair and enthusiasm. The
surrounding countryside has many historic attractions
and offers pleasant walking opportunities.

Rooms 3

MARSTON
Lincolnshire   Map 11 SK84

The Olde Barn Hotel

★★★ 73% HOTEL

☎ 01400 250909
Toll Bar Rd NG32 2HT
e-mail: reservations@theoldebarnhotel.co.uk
dir: From A1 N: left to Marston adjacent to petrol
station. From A1 S: 1st right after Allington/Belton
exit

Located in the countryside one mile from the A1, this
sympathetically renovated and extended former
period barn provides a range of thoughtfully
furnished bedrooms, ideal for both business and
leisure customers. Imaginative food is offered in the
attractive beamed restaurant, and extensive leisure
facilities include a swimming pool, sauna, steam
room and a well-equipped gym.

Rooms 103 (11 fmly) (51 GF) (6 smoking) **S** £50-£90;
D £50-£90* **Facilities** Spa STV FTV Wi-fi 🕓 🕓 Gym
Xmas New Year **Conf** Class 180 Board 100 Thtr 300
Del from £110 to £125 **Services** Lift **Parking** 280
Notes LB Civ Wed 250

MASHAM
North Yorkshire   Map 19 SE28

INSPECTORS' CHOICE

Swinton Park

★★★★ ⊛⊛⊛ HOTEL

☎ 01765 680900
HG4 4JH
e-mail: reservations@swintonpark.com
web: www.swintonpark.com
dir: A1 onto B6267/8 to Masham. Follow signs
through town centre & turn right into Swinton
Terrace. 1m past golf course, over bridge, up hill.
Hotel on right

Although extended during the Victorian and
Edwardian eras, the original part of this welcoming
castle dates from the 17th century. Bedrooms are
luxuriously furnished and come with a host of
thoughtful extras. Samuel's restaurant (built by the
current owner's great-great-great grandfather) is
very elegant and serves imaginative dishes using
local produce. The majority of the food is sourced
from the 20,000-acre Swinton Estate, as the hotel,
winner of several green awards, is committed to
keeping the 'food miles' to a minimum. The
gardens, including a four-acre walled garden, have
been gradually restored. The Deerhouse is the venue
for the hotel's alfresco food festivals, summer
BBQs and weddings.

Rooms 31 (6 fmly) 🌊 **D** £185-£380 (incl. bkfst)*
Facilities Spa FTV Wi-fi 🕓 ♣ 9 Putt green Fishing 🏊
Gym Shooting Falconry Pony trekking Cookery school
Off-road driving Xmas New Year **Conf** Class 60
Board 40 Thtr 120 Del from £165 to £185*
Services Lift **Parking** 50 **Notes** LB Civ Wed 120

Save on hotels. Book at **theAA.com/hotel**

MAR – MAW 327 ENGLAND

MATFEN
Northumberland   Map 21 NZ07

Matfen Hall
★★★★ 81% ◉◉ HOTEL

☎ 01661 886500 & 855708
NE20 0RH
e-mail: info@matfenhall.com
web: www.matfenhall.com
dir: A69 onto B6318. Hotel just before village

This fine mansion lies in landscaped parkland overlooking its own golf course. Bedrooms are a blend of contemporary and traditional, but all are very comfortable and well equipped. Impressive public rooms include a splendid drawing room and the elegant Library and Print Room Restaurant, as well as a conservatory bar and very stylish spa, leisure and conference facilities.

Rooms 53 (11 fmly) **S** £75-£205; **D** £79-£210 (incl. bkfst)* **Facilities** Spa STV FTV Wi-fi ᗡ ⊗ supervised ₰ 27 Putt green Gym Sauna Steam room Salt grotto Ice fountain Aerobics Driving range Golf academy Xmas **Conf** Class 46 Board 40 Thtr 120 Del from £150 to £180* **Services** Lift **Parking** 150 **Notes** LB Civ Wed 120

MATLOCK
Derbyshire   Map 16 SK35

The Red House Country Hotel
★★ 85% ◉ SMALL HOTEL

☎ 01629 734854
Old Rd, Darley Dale DE4 2ER
e-mail: enquiries@theredhousecountryhotel.co.uk
web: www.theredhousecountryhotel.co.uk
dir: A6 into Old Rd signed Carriage Museum, 2.5m N of Matlock

A peaceful country hotel set in delightful Victorian gardens. Rich colour schemes are used to excellent effect throughout. The well-equipped bedrooms include two ground-floor rooms in the adjacent coach house. A comfortable lounge with delightful rural views is available for refreshments and pre-dinner drinks; service is friendly and attentive.

Rooms 9 (2 annexe) (2 GF) **S** £55-£70; **D** £105-£120 (incl. bkfst)* **Facilities** FTV Wi-fi New Year **Conf** Class 10 Board 10 Thtr 10 Del £155* **Parking** 12 **Notes** LB ⊗ No children 12yrs Closed 1-14 Jan

MAWGAN PORTH
Cornwall   Map 2 SW86

The Scarlet Hotel
★★★★ 81% ◉◉ HOTEL

☎ 01637 861800
Tredragon Rd TR8 4DQ
e-mail: stay@scarlethotel.co.uk
dir: A39, A30 towards Truro. At Trekenning rdbt take A3059, follow Newquay Airport signs. Right after garage signed St Mawgan & Airport. Right after airport, right at T-junct signed Padstow (B3276). At Mawgan Porth left. Hotel 250yds

Built as an eco hotel, this strikingly modern property has a stunning cliff-top location with magnificent views and offers something a little different. The very stylish and well-equipped bedrooms are categorised in five types: Just Right, Generous, Unique, Spacious and Indulgent. The Ayurvedic spa is exceptional and encompasses the rejuvenation of the whole body and mind; relaxation is the key here. Cuisine is equally important, and in tune with the hotel's environment policies, daily-changing menus feature fresh, seasonal and local produce. The team of 'hosts' offer a high level of hospitality and service.

Rooms 37 (5 GF) ᐠ **S** £170-£430; **D** £190-£450 (incl. bkfst)* **Facilities** Spa FTV Wi-fi ⊗ ᗡ Yoga ⌂ Xmas New Year **Conf** Board 16 **Services** Lift **Parking** 37 **Notes** LB ⊗ No children 16yrs Closed 2 Jan-1 Feb Civ Wed 74

Bedruthan Steps Hotel
★★★★ 76% HOTEL

☎ 01637 860555 & 860860
TR8 4BU
e-mail: stay@bedruthan.com
dir: From A39 or A30 follow signs to Newquay Airport. Pass airport, right at T-junct to Mawgan Porth. Hotel at top of hill on left

With stunning views over Mawgan Porth Bay from the public rooms and the majority of the bedrooms, this is a child-friendly hotel. Children's clubs for various ages are provided in addition to children's dining areas and appropriate meals and times. A homage to architecture of the 1970s, with a modern, comfortable, contemporary feel, this hotel also has conference facilities. In the spacious restaurants, an imaginative fixed-price menu is offered; a short carte is available from Tuesdays to Saturdays.

Rooms 101 (60 fmly) (1 GF) **Facilities** Spa FTV Wi-fi ⊗ ᐠ ᗡ Gym Jungle tumble ball pool Sauna Steam room Hydro pool Pool table ⌂ Xmas New Year **Conf** Class 60 Board 40 Thtr 180 **Services** Lift **Parking** 100 **Notes** ⊗ Closed 21-28 Dec Civ Wed 150

MAWNAN SMITH
Cornwall   Map 2 SW72

Budock Vean-The Hotel on the River
★★★★ 79% ◉ COUNTRY HOUSE HOTEL

☎ 01326 252100 & 0800 833927
TR11 5LG
e-mail: relax@budockvean.co.uk
web: www.budockvean.co.uk
dir: From A39 follow tourist signs to Trebah Gardens. 0.5m to hotel

Set in 65 acres of attractive, well-tended grounds, this peaceful hotel offers an impressive range of facilities. Convenient for visiting the Helford River Estuary and the many local gardens, or simply as a tranquil venue for a leisure break. Bedrooms are spacious and come in a choice of styles; some overlook the grounds and golf course.

Rooms 57 (2 fmly) ᐠ **S** £72-£139; **D** £144-£278 (incl. bkfst & dinner)* **Facilities** Spa FTV Wi-fi ⊗ ₰ 9 ᗡ Putt green ᗡ Private river boat & foreshore ⌂ Xmas New Year **Conf** Class 40 Board 30 Thtr 60 Del from £119.50 to £174.50* **Services** Lift **Parking** 100 **Notes** LB Closed 3 wks Jan Civ Wed 65

M

MAWNAN SMITH *continued*

Meudon Hotel

★★★ 85% COUNTRY HOUSE HOTEL

☎ 01326 250541
TR11 5HT
e-mail: wecare@meudon.co.uk
web: www.meudon.co.uk
dir: From Truro A39 towards Falmouth at Hillhead (Anchor & Cannons) rdbt, follow signs to Maenporth Beach. Hotel on left in 1m

This charming late Victorian mansion is a relaxing place to stay, with friendly hospitality and attentive service. It sits in impressive nine-acre gardens that lead down to a private beach. The spacious and comfortable bedrooms are situated in a more modern building. The cuisine features the best of local Cornish produce and is served in the conservatory restaurant.

Rooms 29 (2 fmly) (15 GF) **Facilities** FTV Wi-fi ♨ Fishing Private beach Hair salon Yacht for skippered charter Xmas **Conf** Class 20 Board 15 Thtr 30 **Services** Lift **Parking** 50 **Notes** Closed 28 Dec-Jan

Trelawne Hotel

★★★ 77% HOTEL

☎ 01326 250226
TR11 5HS
e-mail: info@trelawnehotel.co.uk
web: www.trelawnehotel.co.uk
dir: A39 to Falmouth, right at Hillhead rdbt signed Maenporth. Past beach, up hill, hotel on left

This hotel is surrounded by attractive lawns and gardens, and enjoys superb coastal views. An informal atmosphere prevails, and many guests return year after year. Bedrooms, many with sea views, are of varying sizes, but all are well equipped. Dinner features quality local produce used in imaginative dishes.

Rooms 14 (2 fmly) (4 GF) **Parking** 20 **Notes** Closed end Nov-mid Feb

Beechfield House Hotel, Restaurant & Gardens

★★★ 79% ⊛ COUNTRY HOUSE HOTEL

☎ 01225 703700
Beanacre SN12 7PU
e-mail: reception@beechfieldhouse.co.uk
web: www.beechfieldhouse.co.uk
dir: M4 junct 17, A350 S, bypass Chippenham, towards Melksham. Hotel on left after Beanacre

This is a charming, privately owned hotel set within eight acres of beautiful grounds that has its own arboretum. Bedrooms are individually styled and include four-poster rooms, and ground-floor rooms in the coach house. Relaxing public areas are comfortably furnished and there is a beauty salon with a range of pampering treatments available. At dinner there is a very good selection of carefully prepared dishes with an emphasis on seasonal and local produce.

Rooms 24 (6 fmly) (4 GF) ♦ **D** £125-£175 (incl. bkfst)* **Facilities** FTV Wi-fi ⚗ ⚘ Beauty treatment room Xmas New Year **Conf** Class 60 Board 45 Thtr 100 **Parking** 70 **Notes** LB Civ Wed 70

Shaw Country Hotel

★★ 76% SMALL HOTEL

☎ 01225 702836 & 790321
Bath Rd, Shaw SN12 8EF
e-mail: info@shawcountryhotel.com
web: www.shawcountryhotel.com
dir: 1m from Melksham, 9m from Bath on A365

Located within easy reach of both Bath and the M4, this relaxed and friendly hotel sits in its own gardens and includes a patio area ideal for enjoying a drink during the summer months. The house boasts very well-appointed bedrooms, a comfortable lounge and bar, and the Mulberry Restaurant, where a wide selection of innovative dishes make up both carte and set menus. A spacious function room is a useful addition.

Rooms 13 (2 fmly) ♦ **S** £63-£88; **D** £88-£108 (incl. bkfst)* **Facilities** FTV Wi-fi **Conf** Class 40 Board 20 Thtr 60 **Parking** 30 **Notes** RS 26-27 Dec & 1 Jan Civ Wed 90

INSPECTORS' CHOICE

Stapleford Park

★★★★ ⊛⊛ COUNTRY HOUSE HOTEL

☎ 01572 787000
Stapleford LE14 2EF
e-mail: reservations@stapleford.co.uk
web: www.staplefordpark.com
dir: 1m SW of B676, 4m E of Melton Mowbray & 9m W of Colsterworth

This stunning mansion, dating back to the 14th century, sits in over 500 acres of beautiful grounds. Spacious, sumptuous public rooms include a choice of lounges and an elegant restaurant; an additional brasserie-style restaurant is located in the golf complex. The hotel also boasts a spa with health and beauty treatments and gym, plus horse riding and many other country pursuits. Bedrooms are individually styled and furnished to a high standard. Attentive service is delivered with a relaxed yet professional style. Dinner, in the impressive dining room, is a highlight of any stay.

Rooms 55 (7 annexe) (10 fmly) **Facilities** Spa STV FTV Wi-fi ⚗ ⅃ 18 ⅁ Putt green Fishing ⚘ Gym Archery Croquet Falconry Horse riding Petanque Shooting Billiards Xmas New Year **Conf** Class 140 Board 80 Thtr 200 **Services** Lift **Parking** 120 **Notes** Civ Wed 150

M

Save on hotels. Book at **theAA.com/hotel**

MAW – MER 329 ENGLAND

Sysonby Knoll Hotel

★★★ 78% HOTEL

☎ 01664 563563
Asfordby Rd LE13 0HP
e-mail: reception@sysonby.com
web: www.sysonby.com
dir: 0.5m from town centre on A6006

This well established hotel sits on the edge of Melton Mowbray and is set in attractive gardens with ample parking. The hotel has been run by the same family since 1965 and continues to provide friendly, attentive service. The lounges are comfortable and Wi-fi is available throughout. Freshly prepared dishes are served in the restaurant which overlooks the attractive gardens. The bedrooms are spacious and of a high quality and include four-poster rooms in the main building and executive rooms in an annexe.

Rooms 30 (7 annexe) (1 fmly) (7 GF) ☏ **S** £76-£106; **D** £98-£134 (incl. bkfst)* **Facilities** FTV Wi-fi ⌨ Fishing ⚓ **Conf** Class 25 Board 34 Thtr 50 **Parking** 48 **Notes** LB Closed 25 Dec-1 Jan

Scalford Hall

★★★ 75% HOTEL

☎ 01664 444654
Scalford Rd LE14 4UB
e-mail: sales@scalfordhall.co.uk
dir: A6006 towards Melton Mowbray. Left at 2nd lights into Scalford Rd, hotel 3m on left

Set in extensive grounds, Scalford Hall is just three miles north of Melton Mowbray. The bedrooms are tastefully furnished, and well equipped for both business and leisure guests; many have views over the gardens. Public rooms include a spacious lounge area and a small bar.

Rooms 88 (21 annexe) (6 fmly) (19 GF) ☏ **S** £59-£99; **D** £69-£120* **Facilities** FTV Wi-fi Putt green ⚓ Gym New Year **Conf** Class 36 Board 40 Thtr 150 Del from £130 to £150* **Parking** 120 **Notes** ⊗ Civ Wed 100

Quorn Lodge Hotel

★★★ 70% HOTEL

☎ 01664 566660
46 Asfordby Rd LE13 0HR
e-mail: quornlodge@aol.com
dir: From town centre take A6006. Hotel 300yds from junct of A606/A607 on right

Centrally located, this smart privately owned and managed hotel offers a comfortable and welcoming atmosphere. Bedrooms are individually decorated and thoughtfully designed. The public rooms consist of a bright restaurant overlooking the garden, a cosy lounge bar and a modern function suite. High standards are maintained throughout and parking is a bonus.

Rooms 21 (4 fmly) (3 GF) ☏ **S** £33-£69; **D** £45-£79 (incl. bkfst)* **Facilities** STV FTV Wi-fi ⌨ Gym **Conf** Class 70 Board 80 Thtr 100 Del from £105 to £125* **Parking** 38 **Notes** LB ⊗ Civ Wed 80

MEMBURY MOTORWAY
SERVICE AREA (M4)
Berkshire

Map 5 SU37

Days Inn Membury - M4

BUDGET HOTEL

☎ 01488 72336
Membury Service Area RG17 7TZ
e-mail: membury.hotel@welcomebreak.co.uk
web: www.welcomebreak.co.uk
dir: M4 between junct 14 & 15

This modern building offers accommodation in smart, spacious and well-equipped bedrooms, suitable for families and business travellers, and all with en suite bathrooms. Continental breakfast is available and other refreshments may be taken at the nearby family restaurant. See also the Hotel Groups pages.

Rooms 38 (32 fmly) (17 GF) (5 smoking) **Conf** Board 10

MERIDEN
West Midlands

Map 10 SP28

Forest of Arden, A Marriott Hotel & Country Club

Marriott HOTELS & RESORTS

★★★★ 81% ◉ HOTEL

☎ 01676 522335
Maxstoke Ln CV7 7HR
web: www.marriottforestofarden.co.uk
dir: M42 junct 6 onto A45 towards Coventry, over Stonebridge flyover. After 0.75m left into Shepherds Ln. Left at t-junct. Hotel 1.5m on left

The ancient oaks, rolling hills and natural lakes of the 10,000 acre Forest of Arden estate provide an idyllic backdrop for this modern hotel and country club. The hotel boasts an excellent range of leisure facilities and is regarded as one of the finest golfing destinations in the UK. Bedrooms provide every modern convenience and a full range of facilities.

Rooms 214 (65 GF) (5 smoking) ☏ **Facilities** Spa Wi-fi ⊛ ♨ 18 ⚲ Putt green Fishing ⚓ Gym Floodlit golf academy New Year **Conf** Class 180 Board 40 Thtr 300 **Services** Lift **Parking** 300 **Notes** ⊗ Civ Wed 250

M

MERIDEN *continued*

Best Western Plus Manor Hotel Meriden

★★★★ 75% ◉◉ HOTEL

☎ 01676 522735
Main Rd CV7 7NH
e-mail: reservations@manorhotelmeriden.co.uk
web: www.manorhotelmeriden.co.uk
dir: M42 junct 6, A45 towards Coventry then A452 signed Leamington. At rdbt take B4102 signed Meriden, hotel on left

A sympathetically extended Georgian manor in the heart of a sleepy village is just a few minutes away from the M6, M42 and National Exhibition Centre. The Regency Restaurant offers modern dishes, while Houston's serves lighter meals and snacks. The bedrooms are smart and well equipped.

Rooms 110 (20 GF) **Facilities** FTV Wi-fi ⇖ Xmas New Year **Conf** Class 150 Board 60 Thtr 250 **Services** Lift **Parking** 200 **Notes** Civ Wed 150

MEVAGISSEY	Map 2 SX04
Cornwall	

Trevalsa Court Hotel

★★★ 78% HOTEL

☎ 01726 842468
School Hill, Polstreath PL26 6TH
e-mail: stay@trevalsa-hotel.co.uk
web: www.trevalsa-hotel.co.uk
dir: From St Austell take B3273 to Mevagissey. Pass sign to Pentewan. At top of hill left at x-rds. Hotel signed

Very well located above the town of Mevagissey with easy access to nearby attractions this establishment is an Arts & Crafts style property appointed to a high standard throughout with lots of original features retained. Bedrooms, many with sea views, are comfortable and well presented; there is also a stylish guests' sitting room with views across the bay.

Rooms 13 (3 GF) ⋔ **S** £60-£100; **D** £85-£250 (incl. bkfst) **Facilities** FTV Wi-fi **Parking** 20 **Notes** LB Closed Dec & Jan

Tremarne Hotel

★★ 84% HOTEL

☎ 01726 842213
Polkirt PL26 6UY
e-mail: info@tremarne-hotel.co.uk
dir: From A390 at St Austell take B3273 to Mevagissey. Follow Portmellon signs through Mevagissey. At top of Polkirt Hill 1st right into Higherwell Park. Hotel drive facing

A very popular hotel, set in landscaped gardens with a swimming pool, that has superb views across to Mevagissey. The friendliness of Michael, Fitz and the team cannot be bettered. The hotel offers comfortable, individually styled bedrooms that either have views of the sea or the countryside. Guests can expect good service and freshly-cooked food on a daily-changing menu.

Rooms 13 (2 fmly) ⋔ **Facilities** FTV Wi-fi ⇖ New Year **Parking** 14 **Notes** ⊗ No children 6yrs Closed Jan

---

MEXBOROUGH	Map 16 SE40
South Yorkshire	

Best Western Pastures Hotel

★★★ 82% HOTEL

☎ 01709 577707
Pastures Rd S64 0JJ
e-mail: info@pastureshotel.co.uk
web: www.pastureshotel.co.uk
dir: 0.5m from town centre on A6023, left by CLS Mot, signed Denaby Ings & Cadeby. Hotel on right

This private hotel is in a rural setting beside a working canal with view of Conisbro Castle in the distance, and is convenient for Doncaster or the Dearne Valley with its nature reserves and leisure centre. Guests can dine in the Pastures Lodge pub and family restaurant situated opposite the hotel, or in Reeds fine dining restaurant in the hotel (open Tuesday-Saturday). Bedrooms, in a modern, purpose-built block, are quiet, comfortable and equipped with many modern facilities.

Rooms 60 (5 fmly) (28 GF) ⋔ **S** fr £60; **D** fr £70 (incl. bkfst)* **Facilities** STV Wi-fi ⇖ Xmas New Year **Conf** Class 170 Board 100 Thtr 250 Del £118.80* **Services** Lift **Parking** 179 **Notes** LB ⊗ Civ Wed 200

MICHAELWOOD MOTORWAY SERVICE AREA (M5)	Map 4 ST79
Gloucestershire	

Days Inn Michaelwood - M5

BUDGET HOTEL

☎ 01454 261513
Michaelwood Service Area, Lower Wick GL11 6DD
e-mail: michaelwood.hotel@welcomebreak.co.uk
web: www.welcomebreak.co.uk
dir: M5 N'bound between junct 13 & 14

This modern building offers accommodation in smart, spacious and well-equipped bedrooms, suitable for families and business travellers, and all with en suite bathrooms. Continental breakfast is available and other refreshments may be taken at the nearby family restaurant. See also the Hotel Groups pages.

Rooms 38 (34 fmly) (5 smoking) **Conf** Board 10

MIDDLESBROUGH	Map 19 NZ41
North Yorkshire	

Thistle Hotel Middlesbrough   thistle

★★★★ 73% HOTEL

☎ 0871 376 9028 & 01642 232000
Fry St TS1 1JH
e-mail: middlesbrough@thistle.co.uk
web: www.thistlehotels.com/middlesbrough
dir: A19 onto A66 signed Middlesbrough. A66 after Zetland car park. 3rd exit at 1st rdbt, 2nd exit at 2nd rdbt

The staff here are committed to guest care and nothing is too much trouble. Located close to the town centre and football ground this establishment offers bedrooms of varying sizes, that are well furnished and comfortably equipped. The contemporary first-floor CoMotion café bar leads into the open-plan Gengis restaurant featuring an interesting range of globally inspired dishes. Guests have full use of the hotel's Otium health club.

Rooms 132 (8 fmly) ⋔ **S** £59-£199; **D** £59-£199 **Facilities** Spa STV FTV Wi-fi ⇖ HL ⟳ Gym Steam room Sauna Hair & beauty salon New Year **Conf** Class 144 Board 100 Thtr 400 Del from £130 to £165 **Services** Lift **Parking** 66 **Notes** LB Civ Wed 400

M

Premier Inn Middlesbrough Central South

BUDGET HOTEL

☎ 0871 527 8770
Marton Way TS4 3BS
web: www.premierinn.com
dir: Off A172 opposite South Cleveland Hospital complex

High quality, budget accommodation ideal for both families and business travellers. Spacious, en suite bedrooms feature tea and coffee making facilities, and Freeview TV in most hotels. Internet access and Wi-fi are available for a small fee. The adjacent family restaurant features a wide and varied menu. See also the Hotel Groups pages.

Rooms 74

MIDDLETON-IN-TEESDALE   Map 18 NY92
Co Durham

The Teesdale Hotel

★★ 67% HOTEL

☎ 01833 640264
Market Place DL12 0QG
e-mail: enquiries@teesdalehotel.co.uk
web: www.teesdalehotel.co.uk
dir: From Barnard Castle take B6278, follow signs for Middleton-in-Teesdale & Highforce. Hotel in town centre

Located in the heart of the popular town, this family-run hotel offers a relaxed and friendly atmosphere. Bedrooms and bathrooms are well equipped and offer a good standard of quality and comfort. Public areas include a residents' lounge on the first floor, a spacious restaurant and a lounge bar which is popular with locals.

Rooms 14 (1 fmly) **S** £30-£45; **D** £65-£80 (incl. bkfst)* **Facilities** Wi-fi **Conf** Class 20 Board 20 Thtr 40 Del from £66 to £80* **Parking** 20

MIDDLETON STONEY   Map 11 SP52
Oxfordshire

Best Western The Jersey Arms

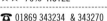

★★ 76% HOTEL

☎ 01869 343234 & 343270
OX25 4AD
e-mail: jerseyarms@bestwestern.co.uk
web: www.jerseyarms.co.uk
dir: 3m from A34, on B430, 10m N of Oxford, between junct 9 & 10 of M40

With a history dating back to the 13th century, the Jersey Arms combines old-fashioned charm with contemporary style and elegance. The individually designed bedrooms are well equipped and comfortable. The lounge has an open fire, and the smart and spacious restaurant provides a calm atmosphere in which to enjoy the popular cuisine.

Rooms 20 (14 annexe) (3 fmly) (9 GF) **S** £69-£79; **D** £89-£99 (incl. bkfst)* **Facilities** FTV Wi-fi ⌨ Xmas New Year **Conf** Class 20 Board 20 Thtr 20 Del from £125 to £150* **Parking** 55 **Notes** LB ⊗

MIDHURST   Map 6 SU82
West Sussex

Spread Eagle Hotel and Spa

★★★ 80% ◉ ◉ HOTEL

☎ 01730 816911
South St GU29 9NH
e-mail: spreadeagle@hshotels.co.uk
web: www.hshotels.co.uk/spread/spreadeagle-main.htm
dir: M25 junct 10, A3 to Milford, take A286 to Midhurst. Hotel adjacent to market square

Offering accommodation since 1430, this historic property is full of character, evident in its sloping floors and inglenook fireplaces. Individually styled bedrooms provide modern comforts; those in the main house have oak panelling and include some spacious feature rooms. The hotel also boasts a well-equipped spa and offers noteworthy food in the oak beamed restaurant.

Rooms 38 (4 annexe) (8 GF) ⌁ **S** £80-£190; **D** £95-£335 (incl. bkfst)* **Facilities** Spa STV FTV Wi-fi ⊛ Gym Health & beauty treatment rooms Steam room Sauna Fitness trainer Xmas New Year **Conf** Class 40 Board 34 Thtr 80 Del from £135 to £185* **Parking** 75 **Notes** LB Civ Wed 120

MIDSOMER NORTON   Map 4 ST65
Somerset

The Moody Goose at The Old Priory

◉ ◉ RESTAURANT WITH ROOMS

☎ 01761 416784
Church Square BA3 2HX
e-mail: info@theoldpriory.co.uk
dir: From E: on A362 at mini-rdbt left into High St signed town centre. Right at lights. Right by church. Old Priory signed

Dating back to the 12th century, this relaxing establishment, with plenty of historic charm and character has been sensitively restored to maintain original features. The bedrooms, including one with a four-poster, are individually styled with plenty of welcome extras. The intimate, open-plan restaurant serves innovative, carefully prepared dishes utilising local produce whenever possible. There are two cosy lounges with log fires blazing in the colder months.

Rooms 6 (1 fmly)

M

MILDENHALL
Suffolk

Map 12 TL77

The Olde Bull Inn
★★★ 85% ☺ HOTEL

☎ 01638 711001
The Street, Barton Mills IP28 6AA
e-mail: bookings@bullinn-bartonmills.com
dir: Exit A11 between Newmarket & Mildenhall,
signed Barton Mills. Hotel by Five Ways rdbt

This delightful 16th-century coaching inn is lovingly
care for by the owners. Public rooms offer a choice of
bars, a brasserie-style restaurant and a further
lounge area. The contemporary bedrooms are
tastefully appointed with co-ordinated soft
furnishings and many thoughtful touches.

The Olde Bull Inn

Rooms 14 (2 annexe) (2 fmly) (2 GF) ☏ **S** £79–£115;
D £89–£149 (incl. bkfst)* **Facilities** STV FTV Wi-fi
Conf Class 20 Board 20 Thtr 30 **Parking** 60 **Notes** LB
☒ RS 25 Dec

See advert on this page

MILFORD ON SEA
Hampshire

Map 5 SZ29

South Lawn Hotel
★★★ 68% HOTEL

OXFORD
HOTELS & INNS

☎ 01590 643911
Lymington Rd SO41 0RF
e-mail: reservations.southlawn@ohiml.com
web: www.oxfordhotelsandinns.com
dir: M27 junct 1, A337 to Lymington, follow signs for
Christchurch, in 3m left on B3058 signed Milford on
Sea, hotel 1m on right

Close to the coast and enjoying a quiet location, this
pleasant hotel is set in well tended and spacious
grounds this hotel is a comfortable place to stay.
Bedrooms are spacious and well appointed. Guests
can relax or take afternoon tea in the lounge; the
restaurant menu offers a good range of choice. Staff
are friendly and attentive.

Rooms 24 (3 fmly) (3 GF) **Facilities** FTV Xmas New
Year **Conf** Class 40 Board 30 Thtr 100 **Parking** 60
Notes LB Civ Wed 120

Save on hotels. Book at **theAA.com/hotel**

MIL 333 ENGLAND

The Oxfordshire

★★★★ 82% ◉ HOTEL

☎ 01844 278300
Rycote Ln OX9 2PU
e-mail: gm@theoxfordshire.com
dir: M40 junct 7 N'bound (junct 8 S'bound), A329
towards Thame

Located within easy reach of the M40, this hotel is at
the championship golf course, The Oxfordshire, in the
heart of the beautiful Chilterns. The accommodation
offers impressive levels of comfort and quality and all
rooms are air conditioned and have access onto a
balcony. The Tempus Spa includes a 15-metre pool,
modern gym and three treatment rooms. This resort
makes an ideal location for a relaxing break,
especially for golf enthusiasts.

Rooms 50 (18 GF) **Facilities** Spa FTV Wi-fi ⤷ ⓣ
⚑ 18 Putt green Gym Sauna Steam room New Year
Conf Class 66 Board 54 Thtr 180 **Services** Lift Air con
Parking 150 **Notes** ⊗ Civ Wed

The Oxford Belfry

★★★★ 79% HOTEL

QHOTELS

☎ 01844 279381
OX9 2JW
e-mail: oxfordbelfry@qhotels.co.uk
web: www.qhotels.co.uk
dir: M40 junct 7 onto A329 to Thame. Left onto A40,
hotel 300yds on right

This modern hotel has a relatively rural location and
enjoys lovely views of the countryside to the rear. The
hotel is built around two very attractive courtyards
and has a number of lounges and conference rooms,
as well as indoor leisure facilities and outdoor tennis
courts. Bedrooms are large and feature a range of
extras.

Rooms 154 (20 fmly) (66 GF) ⟋ **S** £79-£155;
D £89-£165 (incl. bkfst)* **Facilities** Spa FTV Wi-fi ⤷
HL ⓣ ⌣ ⚲ Gym Steam room Sauna Aerobics studio
Xmas New Year **Conf** Class 180 Board 100 Thtr 450
Del from £130 to £179* **Services** Lift **Parking** 350
Notes LB Civ Wed 300

See also Aspley Guise

Mercure Milton Keynes Parkside Hotel

★★★★ 73% ◉ HOTEL

☎ 01908 661919
Newport Rd, Woughton on the Green MK6 3LR
e-mail: H6627-gm@accor.com
web: www.mercure.com
dir: M1 junct 14, A509 towards Milton Keynes. 2nd
exit on H6 follow signs to Woughton on the Green

Situated in five acres of landscaped grounds in a
peaceful village setting, this hotel is only five
minutes' drive from the hustle and bustle of the town
centre. Bedrooms are divided between executive
rooms in the main house and standard rooms in the
adjacent coach house. Public rooms include a range
of meeting rooms, and Strollers bar. The Lanes
Restaurant provides a relaxing venue where eclectic
modern dishes are offered.

Rooms 49 (1 fmly) (19 GF) **Facilities** STV Wi-fi Free
entry to health & fitness club (approx 2m) Xmas New
Year **Conf** Class 60 Board 50 Thtr 150 **Parking** 75
Notes Civ Wed 120

Holiday Inn Milton Keynes

★★★★ 72% HOTEL

 Holiday Inn

☎ 01908 698541
500 Saxon Gate West MK9 2HQ
e-mail: reservations-miltonkeynes@ihg.com
web: www.holidayinn.co.uk/miltonkeynes
dir: M1 junct 14. Straight on at 7 rdbts. At 8th (Saxon
South) turn right. Hotel after lights on left

Ideally located to explore central England, with both
Oxford and Cambridge within an hour's drive, and
central London just 40 minutes away by train. The
hotel is a spacious, purpose-built, city-centre
property offering a range of well-appointed bedrooms,
conference rooms and a fully-equipped health club.
The Junction restaurant offers a contemporary dining
experience in a relaxing environment.

Rooms 166 (17 fmly) **Facilities** STV Wi-fi ⓣ
supervised Gym Sauna Beauty room Xmas New Year
Conf Class 50 Board 50 Thtr 130 **Services** Lift Air con
Parking 85 **Notes** ⊗ Civ Wed 70

Novotel Milton Keynes

★★★ 73% HOTEL

 NOVOTEL

☎ 01908 322212
Saxon St, Layburn Court, Heelands MK13 7RA
e-mail: H3272@accor.com
web: www.novotel.com
dir: M1 junct 14, follow Childsway signs towards city
centre. Right into Saxon Way, straight across all
rdbts, hotel on left

Contemporary in style, this purpose-built hotel is
situated on the outskirts of the town, just a few
minutes' drive from the centre and mainline railway
station. Bedrooms provide ample workspace and a
good range of facilities for the modern traveller, and
public rooms include a children's play area and
indoor leisure centre.

Rooms 124 (40 fmly) (40 GF) **Facilities** FTV Wi-fi ⤷ ⓣ
Gym Steam bath **Conf** Class 75 Board 40 Thtr 120
Services Lift **Parking** 130 **Notes** Civ Wed 100

Ramada Encore Milton Keynes

★★★ 72% HOTEL

☎ 01908 545500
312 Midsummer Boulevard MK9 2EA
e-mail: enquiries@encoremiltonkeynes.co.uk

This hotel is located in the heart of the town centre,
close to the central railway station. The
accommodation is stylish, contemporary and has all
the modern comforts such as air conditioning and Wi-
fi. There are two meeting rooms as well as an
attractive bar and restaurant. Limited on-site parking
is available, charged at a daily rate.

Rooms 159 (28 fmly) (16 smoking) **Facilities** STV
Wi-fi Xmas New Year **Conf** Class 30 Board 30 Thtr 64
Services Lift Air con **Parking** 50 **Notes** ⊗

Broughton Hotel

BUDGET HOTEL

☎ 01908 667726
Broughton MK10 9AA
e-mail: 6418@greeneking.co.uk
web: www.hungryhorse.co.uk
dir: M1 junct 14, at 1st rdbt A5130 signed Woburn,
600yds. Right for Broughton, hotel on left

This hotel is within easy reach of road networks and
offers modern accommodation. Day rooms are
dominated by an open-plan lounge bar and the
Hungry Horse food concept, which proves particularly
popular with young families.

Rooms 30 (2 fmly) (14 GF) **D** £40-£67 **Conf** Class 30
Board 30 Thtr 80

M

MILTON KEYNES *continued*

Campanile Milton Keynes

BUDGET HOTEL

☎ 01908 649819
40 Penn Road (off Watling St), Fenny Stratford, Bletchley MK2 2AU
e-mail: miltonkeynes@campanile.com
web: www.campanile.com
dir: M1 junct 14, A4146 to A5. S'bound on A5. 4th exit at 1st rdbt to Fenny Stratford. Hotel 500yds on left

This modern building offers accommodation in smart, well-equipped bedrooms, all with en suite bathrooms. Refreshments may be taken at the informal bistro. See also the Hotel Groups pages.

Rooms 80 (26 GF) **S** £45-£63; **D** £45-£63*
Conf Class 30 Board 30 Thtr 40 Del from £100 to £300*

Holiday Inn Express Milton Keynes

BUDGET HOTEL

☎ 01908 681000
Eastlake Park, Tongwell St MK15 0YA
e-mail: info@expressmiltonkeynes.co.uk
web: www.hiexpress.com/exmiltonkeynes
dir: M1 junct 14 follow sign for centre, at Northfields rdbt, straight across dual carriageway (H6) follow signs to Fox Milne 3rd exit V11

A modern hotel ideal for families and business travellers. Fresh and uncomplicated, the spacious rooms include Sky TV, power shower and tea and coffee-making facilities. Continental buffet breakfast is included in the room rate; other meals may be taken at the nearby family pub or restaurant. See also the Hotel Groups pages.

Rooms 178 (96 fmly) (47 GF) ♪ **S** £49-£180; (incl. bkfst) **Conf** Class 45 Board 45 Thtr 80 Del from £80 to £145

Premier Inn Milton Keynes Central

BUDGET HOTEL

☎ 0871 527 8774
Secklow Gate West MK9 3BZ
web: www.premierinn.com
dir: M1 junct 14 follow H6 route over 6 rdbts, at 7th (South Secklow) turn right, hotel on left

High quality, budget accommodation ideal for both families and business travellers. Spacious, en suite bedrooms feature tea and coffee making facilities, and Freeview TV in most hotels. Internet access and Wi-fi are available for a small fee. The adjacent

family restaurant features a wide and varied menu. See also the Hotel Groups pages.

Rooms 38

Premier Inn Milton Keynes East (Willen Lake)

BUDGET HOTEL

☎ 0871 527 8778
Brickhill St, Willen Lake MK15 9HQ
web: www.premierinn.com
dir: M1 junct 14 , H6 (Childsway). Right at 3rd rdbt into Brickhill St. Right at 1st mini rdbt, hotel 1st left

Rooms 41

Premier Inn Milton Keynes South

BUDGET HOTEL

☎ 0871 527 8780
Lakeside Grove, Bletcham Way, Caldecotte MK7 8HP
web: www.premierinn.com
dir: M1 junct 14, towards Milton Keynes on H6 (Childs Way). Straight on at 2 rdbts. Left at 3rd onto V10 (Brickhill St). Straight on at 5 rdbts, at 6th right onto H10 (Bletcham Way)

Rooms 41

Premier Inn Milton Keynes South West (Furzton Lake)

BUDGET HOTEL

☎ 0871 527 8776
Shirwell Crescent, Furzton MK4 1GA
web: www.premierinn.com
dir: M1 junct 14, A509 to Milton Keynes. Straight on at 8 rdbts, at 9th rdbt (North Grafton) left onto V6. Right at next onto H7. Over The Bowl rdbt, hotel on left

Rooms 120

MINEHEAD   Map 3 SS94
Somerset

Channel House Hotel

★★★ 78% SMALL HOTEL

☎ 01643 703229
Church Path TA24 5QG
e-mail: channelhouse@btconnect.com
dir: From A39 right at rdbt to seafront, left onto promenade. 1st right, 1st left into Blenheim Gdns,1st right into Northfield Rd

This family-run hotel offers relaxing surroundings, yet is only a short walk from the town centre. The South West Coastal Path starts from the hotel's two-acre

gardens. Many of the exceptionally well-equipped bedrooms benefit from wonderful views. Imaginative menus are created from the best local produce. The hotel is totally non-smoking.

Rooms 8 **S** £85-£95; **D** £170-£196 (incl. bkfst & dinner) **Facilities** FTV Wi-fi **Services** Air con **Parking** 10 **Notes** LB ⊗ No children 15yrs Closed Nov & 29 Dec-15 Mar

Best Western Northfield Hotel

★★★ 74% HOTEL

☎ 01643 705155 & 0845 1302678
Northfield Rd TA24 5PU
e-mail: reservations@northfield-hotel.co.uk
web: www.northfield-hotel.co.uk
dir: M5 junct 23, follow A38 to Bridgwater then A39 to Minehead

Located conveniently close to the town centre and the seafront, this hotel is set in delightfully maintained gardens and has a loyal following. A range of comfortable sitting rooms and leisure facilities, including an indoor, heated pool is provided. A fixed-price menu is served every evening in the oak-panelled dining room. The attractively co-ordinated bedrooms vary in size and are equipped to a good standard.

Rooms 31 (7 fmly) (4 GF) (6 smoking) ♪ **Facilities** STV FTV Wi-fi 🕙 Putt green Gym Steam room Xmas New Year **Conf** Class 45 Board 30 Thtr 70 **Services** Lift **Parking** 34

MONK FRYSTON   Map 16 SE52
North Yorkshire

Monk Fryston Hall Hotel

★★★ 81% COUNTRY HOUSE HOTEL

☎ 01977 682369
LS25 5DU
e-mail: reception@monkfrystonhallhotel.co.uk
web: www.monkfrystonhallhotel.co.uk
dir: A1(M) junct 42, A63 towards Selby. Monk Fryston 2m, hotel on left

This delightful 16th-century mansion house enjoys a peaceful location in 30 acres of grounds, yet is only minutes' drive from the A1. Many original features have been retained and the public rooms are furnished with antique and period pieces. Bedrooms are individually styled and thoughtfully equipped for both business and leisure guests.

Rooms 29 (2 fmly) (5 GF) ♪ **S** £65-£79; **D** £115-£135 (incl. bkfst)* **Facilities** STV FTV Wi-fi ♨ 🍽 Xmas New Year **Conf** Class 30 Board 25 Thtr 70 Del from £125 to £140* **Parking** 80 **Notes** LB Civ Wed 72

Save on hotels. Book at **theAA.com/hotel**

MIL – MOR 335 ENGLAND

MORECAMBE
Lancashire   Map 18 SD46

The Midland
English Lakes
Hotels Resorts & Venues

★★★★ 75% HOTEL

☎ 01524 424000
Marine Road West LA4 4BU
e-mail: themidland@englishlakes.co.uk
dir: A589 towards Morecambe, follow seafront signs, left on B5321 (Lancaster Rd) then Easton Rd, left into Central Drive. Right at rdbt on seafront. Left to hotel entrance

This art deco hotel sits on the seafront and commands stunning views across Morecambe Bay to the mountains of the Lake District. Stylish and modern accommodation is provided in the well-appointed bedrooms. Spa facilities are available on site, and guests can use the leisure club at the nearby sister hotel.

Rooms 44 ☁ **S** £77-£204; **D** £94-£348 (incl. bkfst)*
Facilities FTV Wi-fi ☈ Xmas New Year **Conf** Class 30 Board 48 Thtr 140 Del from £155* **Services** Lift **Parking** 70 **Notes** LB Civ Wed 140

Clarendon Hotel

★★★ 70% HOTEL

☎ 01524 410180
76 Marine Road West, West End Promenade LA4 4EP
e-mail: clarendon@mitchellshotels.co.uk
dir: M6 junct 34 follow Morecambe signs. At rdbt (with 'The Shrimp' on corner) 1st exit to Westgate, follow to seafront. Right at lights, hotel 3rd block

This traditional seafront hotel offers views over Morecambe Bay, modern facilities and convenient parking. An extensive fish and grill menu is offered in the contemporary Waterfront Restaurant and guests can relax in the comfortable lounge bar. Davy Jones Locker in the basement has a more traditional pub atmosphere and offers cask ales and regular live entertainment.

Rooms 29 (3 fmly) ☁ **S** £45-£60; **D** £65-£90 (incl. bkfst)* **Facilities** Wi-fi HL **Conf** Class 40 Board 40 Thtr 90 Del from £100 to £150* **Services** Lift **Parking** 22 **Notes** Civ Wed 60

MORETON-IN-MARSH
Gloucestershire   Map 10 SP23

Manor House Hotel

Cotswold
Inns & Hotels

★★★★ 79% ◉◉ HOTEL

☎ 01608 650501
High St GL56 0LJ
e-mail: info@manorhousehotel.info
web: www.cotswold-inns-hotels.co.uk/manor
dir: Off A429 at south end of town. Take East St off High St, hotel car park 3rd right

Dating back to the 16th century, this charming Cotswold coaching inn retains much of its original character with stone walls, impressive fireplaces and a relaxed, country-house atmosphere. Bedrooms vary in size and reflect the individuality of the building; all are well equipped and some are particularly opulent. Comfortable public areas include a popular bar, a brasserie and the stylish Mulberry Restaurant where the chance to enjoy an evening meal should not be missed. Cotswold Inns & Hotels – AA Small Hotel Group of the Year 2012-13.

Rooms 35 (1 annexe) (3 fmly) (1 GF) ☁ **Facilities** FTV Wi-fi Xmas New Year **Conf** Class 48 Board 54 Thtr 120 **Services** Lift **Parking** 24 **Notes** Civ Wed 120

White Hart Royal Hotel

★★★ 79% ◉ HOTEL

☎ 01608 650731
High St GL56 0BA
e-mail: whr@bpcmail.co.uk
web: www.whitehartroyal.co.uk
dir: On High St at junct with Oxford Rd

This historic hotel has been providing accommodation for hundreds of years and today offers high standards of quality and comfort. Public areas are full of character, and the bedrooms, in a wide range of shapes and sizes, include several very spacious and luxurious rooms situated adjacent to the main building. A varied range of well prepared dishes is available throughout the day and evening in the main bar and the relaxing restaurant.

Rooms 28 (8 annexe) (2 fmly) (9 GF) ☁ **S** £80-£105; **D** £110-£135 **Facilities** FTV Wi-fi ☈ HL Xmas New Year **Conf** Class 40 Board 20 Thtr 55 Del £150 **Parking** 6

Redesdale Arms

★★★ 77% ◉ HOTEL

☎ 01608 650308
High St GL56 0AW
e-mail: info@redesdalearms.com
dir: On A429, 0.5m from rail station

This fine old inn has played a central role in the town for centuries. Traditional features combine successfully with contemporary comforts; bedrooms are located in the main building and in an annexe. Guests can choose from an imaginative menu in either in the stylish restaurant or the conservatory.

Rooms 24 (16 annexe) (2 fmly) (11 GF) **Facilities** STV FTV Wi-fi ☈ Xmas New Year **Parking** 14 **Notes** ⊗

MORLEY
Derbyshire   Map 11 SK34

The Morley Hayes Hotel

★★★★ 77% ◉ HOTEL

☎ 01332 780480
Main Rd DE7 6DG
e-mail: hotel@morleyhayes.com
web: www.morleyhayes.com
dir: 4m N of Derby on A608

Located in rolling countryside this modern golfing destination provides extremely comfortable, stylish bedrooms with wide-ranging facilities, plasma TVs, and state-of-the-art bathrooms; the plush suites are particularly eye-catching. Creative cuisine is offered in the Dovecote Restaurant, and both Roosters and the Spikes sports bar provide informal eating options.

Rooms 32 (4 fmly) (15 GF) ☁ **S** £80-£255; **D** £120-£276 (incl. bkfst)* **Facilities** STV Wi-fi ☈ HL ☈ 27 Putt green Golf driving range **Conf** Class 50 Board 40 Thtr 120 Del from £147 to £169.95* **Services** Lift Air con **Parking** 245 **Notes** LB ⊗ Civ Wed 90

M

MOTTRAM ST ANDREW — Map 16 SJ87
Cheshire

De Vere Mottram Hall
★★★★ 79% HOTEL

DE VERE Hotels & Resorts

☎ 01625 828135
Wilmslow Rd SK10 4QT
e-mail: dmh.sales@devere-hotels.com
web: www.devere.co.uk
dir: M6 junct 18 from S, M6 junct 20 from N, M56 junct 6, A538 Prestbury

Set in 272 acres of some of Cheshire's most beautiful parkland, this 18th-century Georgian country house is certainly an idyllic retreat. The hotel boasts extensive leisure facilities, including a championship golf course, swimming pool, gym and spa. Bedrooms are well equipped and elegantly furnished, and include a number of four-poster rooms and suites.

Rooms 131 (44 GF) **Facilities** Spa STV Wi-fi ⓧ supervised ⚓ 18 ⚘ Putt green Fishing Gym Squash Children's playground Rugby & football pitch Xmas New Year **Conf** Class 120 Board 60 Thtr 180 **Services** Lift **Parking** 300 **Notes** ⊗ Civ Wed 160

MOUSEHOLE — Map 2 SW42
Cornwall

The Cornish Range Restaurant with Rooms
⊛ RESTAURANT WITH ROOMS

☎ 01736 731488
6 Chapel St TR19 6BD
e-mail: info@cornishrange.co.uk
dir: From Penzance take B3315, through Newlyn to Mousehole. Along harbour, past Ship Inn, sharp right, left, establishment on right

This is a memorable place to eat and stay. Stylish rooms, with delightful Cornish home-made furnishings, and attentive, friendly service create a relaxing environment. Interesting and accurate cuisine relies heavily on freshly-landed, local fish and shellfish, as well as local meat and poultry, and the freshest fruit and vegetables.

Rooms 3

MUCH WENLOCK — Map 10 SO69
Shropshire

Raven Hotel
★★★ 78% ⊛⊛ HOTEL

☎ 01952 727251
30 Barrow St TF13 6EN
e-mail: enquiry@ravenhotel.com
web: www.ravenhotel.com
dir: M54 junct 4 or 5, take A442 S, then A4169 to Much Wenlock

This town-centre hotel spreads across several historic buildings with a 17th-century coaching inn at its centre. The accommodation is well furnished and equipped to offer modern comfort; some ground-floor rooms are available. Public areas feature an interesting collection of prints and memorabilia connected with the modern-day Olympic Games - an idea which was, interestingly, born in Much Wenlock.

Rooms 20 (13 annexe) (5 GF) **S** £85-£95; **D** £105-£120 (incl. bkfst)* **Facilities** FTV Wi-fi ⇗ New Year **Conf** Board 16 Thtr 16 **Parking** 30 **Notes** LB ⊗

Gaskell Arms
★★★ 75% SMALL HOTEL

☎ 01952 727212
Bourton Rd TF13 6AQ
e-mail: maxine@gaskellarms.co.uk
web: www.gaskellarms.co.uk
dir: M6 junct 10A onto M54, exit at junct 4, follow signs for Ironbridge/Much Wenlock & A4169

This 17th-century former coaching inn has exposed beams and log fires in the public areas, and much original charm and character is retained throughout. In addition to the lounge bar and restaurant offering a wide range of meals and snacks, there is a small bar which is popular with locals. Well-equipped bedrooms, some located in stylishly renovated stables, provide good standards of comfort.

Rooms 16 (3 fmly) (5 GF) **Facilities** FTV Wi-fi **Conf** Class 30 Board 20 Thtr 30 **Parking** 40 **Notes** ⊗

MUDEFORD

See Christchurch

MULLION — Map 2 SW61
Cornwall

Mullion Cove Hotel
★★★ 80% ⊛ HOTEL

☎ 01326 240328
TR12 7EP
e-mail: enquiries@mullion-cove.co.uk
web: www.mullion-cove.co.uk
dir: A3083 towards The Lizard. Through Mullion towards Mullion Cove. Hotel in approx 1m

Built at the turn of the last century and set high above the working harbour of Mullion, this hotel has spectacular views of the rugged coastline; seaward facing rooms are always popular. The stylish restaurant offers some carefully prepared dishes using local produce; an alternative option is to eat less formally in the bar. After dinner guests might like to relax in one of the elegant lounges.

Rooms 30 (3 fmly) (3 GF) ⬯ **S** £60-£255; **D** £120-£340 (incl. bkfst)* **Facilities** FTV Wi-fi ⚲ Xmas New Year **Conf** Class 20 Board 30 Thtr 50 Del from £95 to £250* **Services** Lift **Parking** 60 **Notes** LB

See advert on opposite page

Save on hotels. Book at **theAA.com/hotel**

MOT – NAN 337 ENGLAND

Polurrian Bay Hotel

★★★ 77% HOTEL

☎ 01326 240421
TR12 7EN
e-mail: info@polurrianhotel.com
web: www.polurrianhotel.com
dir: A394 to Helston. Follow The Lizard & Mullion signs onto A3083. Approx 5m, right onto B3296 to Mullion. Follow one-way system to T-junct, left signed Mullion Cove. 0.5m right, follow hotel sign.

With spectacular views across St Mount's Bay, this is a well managed and relaxed hotel where guests are assured of a warm welcome from the friendly team of staff. In addition to the formal eating option, the High Point restaurant offers a more casual approach, open throughout the day and into the evening. The popular leisure club has a good range of equipment. Bedrooms vary in size, and the sea-view rooms are always in demand.

Rooms 41 (6 fmly) (8 GF) ➦ **S** £94-£226;
D £110-£265 (incl. bkfst)* **Facilities** Spa FTV Wi-fi ⊗
⌁ Gym Child facilities Children's games room & outdoor play area Crèche Xmas New Year
Conf Class 25 Board 26 Thtr 50 Del from £100 to £160* **Parking** 60 **Notes** Civ Wed 80

NAILSWORTH   Map 4 ST89
Gloucestershire

Wild Garlic Restaurant and Rooms

◉ ◉ RESTAURANT WITH ROOMS

☎ 01453 832615
3 Cossack Square GL6 0DB
e-mail: info@wild-garlic.co.uk
dir: M4 junct 18, A46 towards Stroud. Enter Nailsworth, left at rdbt, immediately left. Establishment opposite Britannia pub

Situated in a quiet corner of this charming Cotswold town, this restaurant with rooms offers a delightful combination of welcoming, relaxed hospitality and high quality cuisine. The spacious and well-equipped bedrooms are situated above the restaurant. The small and friendly team of staff ensure guests are very well looked after throughout their stay.

Rooms 3 (2 fmly)

NANTWICH   Map 15 SJ65
Cheshire

Rookery Hall Hotel & Spa

★★★★ 85% ◉ ◉ HOTEL

☎ 01270 610016 & 0845 072 7533
Main Rd, Worleston CW5 6DQ
e-mail: rookeryhall@handpicked.co.uk
web: www.handpickedhotels.co.uk/rookeryhall
dir: From A51 N of Nantwich take B5074 (Winsford) signed Rookery Hall. Hotel 1.5m on right

This fine 19th-century mansion is set in 38 acres of gardens, pasture and parkland. Bedrooms are spacious and appointed to a high standard with wide-screen plasma TVs and DVD players; many rooms have separate walk-in showers as well as deep tubs. Public areas are delightful and retain many original features. There is an extensive, state-of-the art spa and leisure complex. Hand Picked Hotels – AA Hotel Group of the Year 2012-13.

Rooms 70 (39 annexe) (6 fmly) (23 GF) ➦
S £95-£200; **D** £95-£400 (incl. bkfst)* **Facilities** Spa STV FTV Wi-fi ⊗ HL ⊗ ⌁ Gym Sauna Crystal steam room Hydrotherapy pool ♫ Xmas New Year
Conf Class 90 Board 46 Thtr 200 Del from £129 to £189* **Services** Lift **Parking** 120 **Notes** LB ⊗ Civ Wed 140

N

NANTWICH *continued*

Alvaston Hall Hotel

Warner Leisure Hotels
JUST FOR GROWN-UPS

★★★ 77% HOTEL

☎ 01270 624341
Middlewich Rd CW5 6PD

A Grade-II listed Victorian property located in the delightful Cheshire countryside and set in extensive grounds. Bedrooms vary in size and style; some have spacious seating areas and some have outdoor terraces.Outdoor and indoor leisure facilities include a 9-hole golf course, hair and beauty treatments, and a great range of entertainment and activities. Please note that this is an adults-only (over 21 years) hotel.

Rooms 168 (52 annexe) (96 GF) ✦ **Facilities** Spa FTV Wi-fi ⊙ supervised ⚐ 9 Putt green ⚑ Gym Archery Bowling green Floodlit driving range ♫ Xmas New Year **Conf** Class 24 Board 16 Thtr 30 **Services** Lift **Parking** 108 **Notes** ⊗ No children 21yrs

Crown Hotel & Casa Brasserie

★★ 74% HOTEL

☎ 01270 625283
High St CW5 5AS
e-mail: info@crownhotelnantwich.com
web: www.crownhotelnantwich.com
dir: A52 to Nantwich, hotel in town centre

Ideally set in the heart of this historic and delightful market town, The Crown has been offering hospitality for centuries. It has an abundance of original features and the well-equipped bedrooms retain an old world charm. The atmospheric bar offers real ales and the lively brasserie is an ideal venue for relaxed dining. Complimentary Wi-fi is available.

Rooms 18 (2 fmly) (1 smoking) **Facilities** FTV Wi-fi ♫ **Conf** Class 150 Board 70 Thtr 200 **Parking** 18 **Notes** Closed 25 Dec Civ Wed 140

Premier Inn Crewe/ Nantwich

BUDGET HOTEL

☎ 0871 527 8782
221 Crewe Rd CW5 6NE
web: www.premierinn.com
dir: M6 junct 16, A500 towards Chester, A534 towards Nantwich. Hotel approx 100yds on right

High quality, budget accommodation ideal for both families and business travellers. Spacious, en suite bedrooms feature tea and coffee making facilities, and Freeview TV in most hotels. Internet access and Wi-fi are available for a small fee. The adjacent family restaurant features a wide and varied menu. See also the Hotel Groups pages.

Rooms 37

NETHER STOWEY
Somerset

Map 4 ST13

Apple Tree Hotel

★★★ 70% HOTEL

☎ 01278 733238
Keenthorne TA5 1HZ
e-mail: reservations@appletreehotel.com
web: www.appletreehotel.com
dir: A39 from Bridgwater towards Minehead. Hotel on left, 2m past Cannington

Parts of this cottage-style property, conveniently located for the coast and the M5, date back some 340 years. Bedrooms, which vary in character and style, are suited to both leisure and corporate guests; some are in a single storey annexe adjacent to the main building. Public areas include an attractive conservatory restaurant, a bar and a library lounge. The friendly owners and their staff make every effort to guarantee an enjoyable stay.

Rooms 16 (2 fmly) (7 GF) ✦ **S** fr £72; **D** £95-£105 (incl. bkfst)* **Facilities** FTV Wi-fi **Conf** Class 12 Board 12 Thtr 20 **Parking** 30 **Notes** LB ⊗

Save on hotels. Book at **theAA.com/hotel**

NAN – NEW 339 ENGLAND

NEW ALRESFORD
Hampshire
Map 5 SU53

Swan Hotel
THE INDEPENDENTS
HOTEL ASSOCIATION

★★ 68% HOTEL

☎ 01962 732302 & 734427
11 West St SO24 9AD
e-mail: swanhotel@btinternet.com
web: www.swanhotelalresford.com
dir: Exit A31 onto B3047

This former coaching inn dates back to the 18th century and remains a busy and popular destination for travellers and locals alike. Bedrooms are situated in both the main building and the more modern wing. The lounge bar and adjacent restaurant are open all day; for more traditional dining there is another restaurant which overlooks the busy village street.

Rooms 23 (12 annexe) (3 fmly) (5 GF) **S** £50-£90;
D £80-£90 (incl. bkfst)* **Facilities** FTV Wi-fi New Year
Conf Class 60 Board 40 Thtr 90 **Parking** 25
Notes RS 25 Dec

See advert on opposite page

NEWARK-ON-TRENT
Nottinghamshire
Map 17 SK75

The Grange Hotel
★★★ 83% ◉ HOTEL

☎ 01636 703399
73 London Rd NG24 1RZ
e-mail: info@grangenewark.co.uk
web: www.grangenewark.co.uk
dir: From A1 follow signs to Balderton, hotel opposite Polish War Graves

Expect a warm welcome at this family-run hotel, situated just a short walk from the town. Bedrooms are attractively decorated with co-ordinated soft furnishings and equipped with many thoughtful extras. Public rooms include the Potters Bar, a residents' lounge and the Cutlers Restaurant, where enjoyable cuisine is presented. In the summer guests can enjoy the delightful terrace gardens.

Rooms 19 (9 annexe) (1 fmly) ☏ **S** £85-£120;
D £120-£165 (incl. bkfst)* **Facilities** FTV Wi-fi
Parking 17 **Notes** LB ⊗ Closed 23 Dec-4 Jan

Premier Inn Newark
BUDGET HOTEL

Premier Inn

☎ 0871 527 8784
Lincoln Rd NG24 2DB
web: www.premierinn.com
dir: At junct of A1 & A46 & A17, follow B6166 signs

High quality, budget accommodation ideal for both families and business travellers. Spacious, en suite bedrooms feature tea and coffee making facilities, and Freeview TV in most hotels. Internet access and Wi-fi are available for a small fee. The adjacent family restaurant features a wide and varied menu. See also the Hotel Groups pages.

Rooms 40

NEWBURY
Berkshire
Map 5 SU46

See also Andover

INSPECTORS' CHOICE

The Vineyard at Stockcross

RELAIS &
CHATEAUX

★★★★★ ◉◉◉ HOTEL

☎ 01635 528770
Stockcross RG20 8JU
e-mail: general@the-vineyard.co.uk
web: www.the-vineyard.co.uk
dir: From M4 junct 13, A34 towards Newbury, exit at 3rd junct for Speen. Right at rdbt then right again at 2nd rdbt

A haven of style in the Berkshire countryside, this hotel prides itself on a superb art collection, which can be seen throughout the building. Bedrooms come in a variety of styles - many split-level suites that are exceptionally well equipped. Comfortable lounges lead into the stylish restaurant, which serves the imaginative and precise cooking created by Daniel Galmiche, complemented by an equally impressive selection of wines from California and around the world. The welcome throughout the hotel is warm and sincere, the service professional yet relaxed.

N

Rooms 49 (18 GF) ☏ **S** £200-£645; **D** £220-£665
(incl. bkfst)* **Facilities** Spa STV Wi-fi �€ ⊗ Gym ♫
Xmas New Year **Conf** Class 70 Board 30 Thtr 140
Del from £295 to £395* **Services** Lift Air con
Parking 100 **Notes** LB ⊗ Civ Wed 100

N

NEWBURY *continued*

Donnington Valley Hotel & Spa

★★★★ 84% ◉◉ HOTEL

☎ 01635 551199

Old Oxford Rd, Donnington RG14 3AG
e-mail: general@donningtonvalley.co.uk
web: www.donningtonvalley.co.uk
dir: M4 junct 13, A34 signed Newbury. Take exit signed Donnington/Services, at rdbt 2nd exit signed Donnington. Left at next rdbt. Hotel 2m on right

In its own grounds complete with an 18-hole golf course, this stylish hotel boasts excellent facilities for both corporate and leisure guests; from the state-of-the-art spa offering excellent treatments, to an extensive range of meeting and function rooms. Air-conditioned bedrooms are stylish, spacious and particularly well equipped with fridges, lap-top safes and internet access. The Wine Press restaurant offers imaginative food complemented by a superb wine list.

Rooms 111 (3 fmly) (36 GF) ⚑ **S** £107-£227; **D** £115-£235 (incl. bkfst)* **Facilities** Spa STV Wi-fi ⓦ ⓧ ↧ 18 Putt green Gym Aromatherapy Sauna Steam room Studio Xmas New Year **Conf** Class 50 Board 65 Thtr 160 Del from £175 to £270* **Services** Lift Air con **Parking** 150 **Notes** LB ⊗ Civ Wed 85

Regency Park Hotel

★★★★ 75% HOTEL

☎ 01635 871555

Bowling Green Rd, Thatcham RG18 3RP
e-mail: info@regencyparkhotel.co.uk
web: www.regencyparkhotel.co.uk
dir: From Newbury take A4 signed Thatcham & Reading. 2nd rdbt exit signed Cold Ash. Hotel 1m on left

This smart, stylish hotel is ideal for both business and leisure guests. Spacious, well-equipped bedrooms include a number of contemporary, tasteful executive rooms. Smart, airy public areas include a state-of-the-art spa and leisure club, plus the Watermark Restaurant which offers appealing cuisine.

Rooms 108 (10 fmly) (9 GF) **Facilities** Spa STV FTV Wi-fi ⓦ ⓧ Gym Beauty treatments Sauna Steam room New Year **Conf** Class 80 Board 70 Thtr 200 **Services** Lift **Parking** 200 **Notes** ⊗ Civ Wed 100

Best Western West Grange Hotel

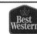

★★★★ 71% HOTEL

☎ 01635 273074

Cox's Ln, Bath Rd, Midgham RG7 5UP
e-mail: reservations@westgrangehotel.co.uk
dir: M4 junct 12, A4 (Bath Rd), follow Newbury signs. Through Woolhampton, hotel on right in approx 2m

Conveniently situated between Reading and Newbury this modern hotel has well-appointed, spacious bedrooms; executive rooms are beautifully presented and have a host of additional features. The contemporary open-plan lounge and restaurant area serves an extensive choice of British cuisine. There is a range of business suites along with a larger conference room. The gardens are a real feature and the central courtyard is popular with guests.

Rooms 62 **S** £50-£95; **D** £70-£140* **Conf** Class 25 Board 30 Thtr 50

Mercure Newbury Elcot Park

★★★★ 71% HOTEL

☎ 0845 815 9060

Elcot RG20 8NJ
e-mail: gm.mercurenewburyelcotpark@jupiterhotels. co.uk
web: www.jupiterhotels.co.uk
dir: M4 junct 13, A338 to Hungerford, A4 to Newbury. Hotel 4m from Hungerford

Enjoying a peaceful location yet within easy access to both the A4 and M4, this country-house hotel is set in 16 acres of gardens and woodland. Bedrooms are comfortably appointed and include some located in an adjacent mews. Public areas include the Orangery Restaurant, which enjoys views over the Kennet Valley, a leisure club and a range of conference rooms.

Rooms 73 (17 annexe) (4 fmly) (25 GF) (5 smoking) **Facilities** FTV Wi-fi ⓦ ⓧ supervised ⌇ ⚑ Gym Sauna Steam room Xmas New Year **Conf** Class 45 Board 35 Thtr 110 **Services** Lift **Parking** 130 **Notes** Civ Wed 120

Newbury Manor Hotel

★★★ 82% ◉◉ HOTEL

☎ 01635 528838

London Rd RG14 2BY
e-mail: enquiries@newbury-manor-hotel.co.uk
dir: On A4 between Newbury & Thatcham

This former Georgian watermill, which still features the original millrace, is situated beside the River Kennet in well tended grounds. The character bedrooms vary in style and size and offer many accessories. Guests can dine in the award-winning River Bar Restaurant.

Rooms 34 (4 fmly) (11 GF) ⚑ **S** £75-£120; **D** £85-£200 (incl. bkfst)* **Facilities** STV FTV Wi-fi ⓦ Fishing Xmas New Year **Conf** Class 140 Board 90 Thtr 190 Del from £125 to £185 **Parking** 100 **Notes** LB ⊗ Civ Wed 180

The Chequers Hotel

★★★ 70% HOTEL

☎ 01635 38000

6-8 Oxford St RG14 1JB
e-mail: info@chequershotelnewbury.co.uk
web: www.chequershotelnewbury.co.uk
dir: M4 junct 13, A34 S, A339 to Newbury. At 2nd rdbt right to town centre. At clock tower rdbt right, hotel on right

Situated just at the top of the main shopping street in Newbury and convenient for fast road connections, this 18th-century former coaching inn retains original features along with contemporary touches. The bedrooms come in a range of sizes and JP's Bistro is a popular eatery. The hotel has ample parking which is a definite advantage in this town.

Rooms 56 (2 fmly) (6 GF) **Facilities** FTV Wi-fi ⓦ **Conf** Class 36 Board 40 Thtr 160 **Parking** 60 **Notes** ⊗ Civ Wed 120

Save on hotels. Book at **theAA.com/hotel**

NEW 341 ENGLAND

Hare & Hounds Hotel

★★ 68% HOTEL

☎ 01635 521152
Bath Rd, Speen RG14 1QY
e-mail: reservations@hareandhoundshotel.net
web: www.hareandhoundshotel.net
dir: A34 (Newbury bypass) onto A4 towards Newbury signed Speen. Hotel 300yds on right

A privately owned, historic hotel just a few minutes from the centre of Newbury. The hotel offers bedrooms in the coach house and in the mews, and all are modern and tastefully decorated. There is a relaxed, informal restaurant offering regularly changing menus, and the bar is popular with locals and guests alike.

Rooms 30 (23 annexe) (3 fmly) (11 GF) (6 smoking)
S £49.50-£69.50; **D** £66.50-£89.50 (incl. bkfst)*
Facilities STV FTV Wi-fi New Year **Parking** 64
Notes LB

Premier Inn Newbury/ Thatcham

BUDGET HOTEL

☎ 0871 527 8786
Bath Rd, Midgham RG7 5UX
web: www.premierinn.com
dir: M4 junct 12, A4 towards Newbury. Hotel 7m on right

High quality, budget accommodation ideal for both families and business travellers. Spacious, en suite bedrooms feature tea and coffee making facilities, and Freeview TV in most hotels. Internet access and Wi-fi are available for a small fee. The adjacent family restaurant features a wide and varied menu. See also the Hotel Groups pages.

Rooms 49

NEWBY BRIDGE
Cumbria
Map 18 SD38

Lakeside Hotel Lake Windermere

★★★★ 87% ◉ ◉ HOTEL

☎ 015395 30001
Lakeside LA12 8AT
e-mail: sales@lakesidehotel.co.uk
web: www.lakesidehotel.co.uk
dir: M6 junct 36, A590 to Barrow, follow signs to Newby Bridge. Right over bridge, hotel 1m on right

This impressive hotel enjoys an enviable location on the southern edge of Lake Windermere and has easy access to the Lakeside & Haverthwaite Steam Railway and ferry terminal. Bedrooms are individually styled and many enjoy delightful lake views. Spacious lounges and a choice of restaurants are available. The state-of-the-art spa is exclusive to residents and provides a range of treatment suites. Staff throughout are friendly and nothing is too much trouble.

Rooms 75 (8 fmly) (8 GF) 🐾 **S** £125-£395;
D £149-£399 (incl. bkfst) **Facilities** Spa STV Wi-fi 🕲
Fishing Gym Private jetty Rowing boats ♫ Xmas New
Year **Conf** Class 50 Board 40 Thtr 100 Del from £140
to £220 **Services** Lift **Parking** 200 **Notes** LB ⊗
Civ Wed 70

The Swan Hotel & Spa

★★★★ 81% HOTEL

☎ 015395 31681
LA12 8NB
e-mail: enquiries@swanhotel.com
web: www.swanhotel.com
dir: M6 junct 36, A591, merge onto A590. At rdbts follow A590, left at Newby Bridge rdbt, 1st right for hotel

Set in idyllic surroundings, this hotel offers something to suit every taste, from a gym and spa therapies for adults to a dedicated children's lounge. The well-equipped bedrooms are thoroughly modern, each has a vintage touch. Good quality meals are served in the River Room; in good weather guests can eat on the riverside terrace.

Rooms 51 (8 fmly) (14 GF) **S** £119-£190;
D £119-£190 (incl. bkfst)* **Facilities** Spa FTV Wi-fi 🕲
Gym Sauna Steam room Xmas New Year Child
facilities **Conf** Class 60 Board 40 Thtr 100 Del £175*
Services Lift Air con **Parking** 100 **Notes** ⊗
Civ Wed 100

Whitewater Hotel

★★★★ 73% ◉ HOTEL

☎ 015395 31133
The Lakeland Village LA12 8PX
e-mail: enquiries@whitewater-hotel.co.uk
web: www.whitewater-hotel.co.uk
dir: M6 junct 36, follow signs for A590 (Barrow), 1m, through Newby Bridge. Right at sign for Lakeland Village, hotel on left

This tasteful conversion of an old mill on the River Leven is close to the southern end of Lake Windermere. Bedrooms, many with lovely river views, are spacious and comfortable. Public areas include a luxurious, well-equipped spa, squash courts, and a choice of comfortable lounges. The Dolly Blue bar overlooks the river and is a vibrant informal alternative to the fine dining restaurant.

Rooms 38 (10 fmly) (2 GF) 🐾 **Facilities** Spa STV FTV
Wi-fi 🕲 supervised ⌣ Gym Squash Table tennis
Xmas New Year **Conf** Class 32 Board 40 Thtr 80
Del from £99.50 to £129.50 **Services** Lift **Parking** 50
Notes ⊗ Civ Wed 110

N

NEWCASTLE-UNDER-LYME
Staffordshire   Map 10 SJ84

Holiday Inn Stoke-on-Trent
★★★ 75% HOTEL   *Holiday Inn*

☎ 01782 557000 & 557018
Clayton Rd, Clayton ST5 4DL
e-mail: reservations-stoke@ihg.com
web: www.holidayinn.co.uk
dir: M6 junct 15. Follow Clayton Rd signs towards
Newcastle-under-Lyme. Hotel 200yds on left

Stylish and contemporary, this modern hotel is well
located just minutes from the motorway junction.
Bedrooms are comfortable and boast an excellent
range of facilities. Guests have the use of the leisure
club.

Rooms 118 (38 fmly) **S** £49-£100; (incl. bkfst)*
Facilities STV Wi-fi ↻ HL ⊙ supervised Gym Beauty
treatment room New Year **Conf** Class 30 Board 22
Thtr 70 Del from £90 to £120* **Services** Air con
Parking 150 **Notes** LB ⊗

Premier Inn Newcastle-under-Lyme

BUDGET HOTEL

☎ 0871 527 8808
Talke Rd, Chesterton ST5 7AL
web: www.premierinn.com
dir: M6 junct 12, A500, A34 to Newcastle-under-
Lyme. Hotel 0.5m on right

High quality, budget accommodation ideal for both
families and business travellers. Spacious, en suite
bedrooms feature tea and coffee making facilities,
and Freeview TV in most hotels. Internet access and
Wi-fi are available for a small fee. The adjacent
family restaurant features a wide and varied menu.
See also the Hotel Groups pages.

Rooms 83

NEWCASTLE UPON TYNE
Tyne & Wear   Map 21 NZ26

INSPECTORS' CHOICE

Jesmond Dene House
★★★★ ⊛⊛⊛ HOTEL

☎ 0191 212 3000
Jesmond Dene Rd NE2 2EY
e-mail: info@jesmonddenehouse.co.uk
web: www.jesmonddenehouse.co.uk
dir: A167 N to A184. Right, right again into
Jesmond Dene Rd, hotel on left

This grand house, overlooking the wooded valley of
Jesmond Dene, yet just five minutes from the centre
of town, has been sympathetically converted into a
stylish, contemporary hotel destination. The
bedrooms are beautifully designed and boast flat-
screen TVs, sumptuous beds with Egyptian cotton
linen, digital radios, well-stocked mini bars, free
broadband, desk space and safes. Equally eye-
catching bathrooms with under floor heating are
equipped with high quality bespoke amenities. The
stylish restaurant is the venue for innovative
cooking which will prove a highlight of any stay.

Rooms 40 (8 annexe) (1 fmly) (4 GF) ⌂
S £115-£277; **D** £130-£450* **Facilities** STV Wi-fi ↻
Conf Class 80 Board 44 Thtr 125 Del from £185 to
£264* **Services** Lift **Parking** 64 **Notes** LB ⊗
Civ Wed 100

Hotel du Vin Newcastle
★★★★ 80% ⊛ ⊛   *Hotel du Vin & Bistro*

TOWN HOUSE HOTEL

☎ 0191 229 2200
Allan House, City Rd NE1 2BE
e-mail: lkelk@malmaison.com
dir: A1 junct 65 onto A184 Gateshead/Newcastle,
Quayside to City Rd

The former maintenance depot of the Tyne Tees
Shipping Company, this is a landmark building on the
Tyne. It has been transformed into a modern and
stylish hotel. Bedrooms are well equipped and deeply
comfortable with all the Hotel du Vin trademark items
such as Egyptian cotton sheets, plasma TVs, DVD
players and monsoon showers. Guests can dine in the
bistro or alfresco if the weather allows in the
courtyard.

Rooms 42 (6 GF) **Facilities** STV Wi-fi **Conf** Board 20
Thtr 26 **Services** Lift Air con **Parking** 10
Notes Civ Wed 40

Newcastle Gateshead Marriott Hotel MetroCentre
Marriott HOTELS & RESORTS

★★★★ 77% HOTEL

☎ 0191 493 2233
MetroCentre NE11 9XF
e-mail: reservations.newcastle.england.
metrocentre@marriotthotels.co.uk
web: www.newcastlemarriottmetrocentre.co.uk

(For full entry see Gateshead)

Newcastle Marriott Hotel Gosforth Park
Marriott HOTELS & RESORTS

★★★★ 76% HOTEL

☎ 0191 236 4111
High Gosforth Park, Gosforth NE3 5HN
web: www.newcastlemarriottgosforthpark.co.uk
dir: Onto A1056 to Killingworth & Wideopen. 3rd exit
to Gosforth Park, hotel ahead

Set within its own grounds, this modern hotel offers
extensive conference and banqueting facilities, along
with indoor and outdoor leisure. There is a choice of
dining in the more formal Plate Restaurant or the
relaxed Chat's lounge bar. Many of the air-
conditioned bedrooms have views over the park. The
hotel is conveniently located for the bypass, airport
and racecourse.

Rooms 178 (17 smoking) **Facilities** Spa STV Wi-fi ⊙
supervised ⌘ Gym Squash Jogging trail ♫ New Year
Conf Class 280 Board 60 Thtr 800 **Services** Lift
Air con **Parking** 340 **Notes** Civ Wed 300

N

Copthorne Hotel Newcastle

★★★★ 73% HOTEL

☎ 0191 222 0333
The Close, Quayside NE1 3RT
e-mail: sales.newcastle@millenniumhotels.co.uk
web: www.millenniumhotels.co.uk
dir: Follow signs to Newcastle city centre. Take B1600 Quayside exit, hotel on right

Set on the banks of the River Tyne close to the city centre, this stylish purpose-built hotel provides modern amenities including a leisure centre, conference facilities and a choice of restaurants for dinner. Bedrooms overlook the river, and there is a floor of 'Connoisseur' rooms that have their own dedicated exclusive lounge and business support services.

Rooms 156 (4 fmly) **Facilities** STV Wi-fi 🕃 supervised Gym Steam room Xmas New Year **Conf** Class 90 Board 60 Thtr 220 **Services** Lift **Parking** 180 **Notes** ⊗ Civ Wed 150

Malmaison Newcastle

★★★ 88% ⊛ HOTEL

☎ 0191 245 5000
Quayside NE1 3DX
e-mail: newcastle@malmaison.com
dir: Follow signs for city centre, then for Quayside/Law Courts. Hotel 100yds past Law Courts

Overlooking the river and the Millennium Bridge, the hotel has a prime position in the very popular quayside district. Bedrooms have striking decor, CD/DVD players, mini-bars and a number of individual touches. Food and drink are an integral part of the operation here, with a stylish brasserie-style restaurant and café bar, plus the Café Mal, a deli-style café next door to the main entrance.

Rooms 122 (10 fmly) **Facilities** Spa STV Wi-fi Gym **Conf** Board 18 Thtr 30 **Services** Lift Air con **Parking** 50

Mercure Newcastle George Washington Hotel

Mercure

★★★ 81% HOTEL

☎ 0191 402 9988
Stone Cellar Rd, High Usworth NE37 1PH
e-mail: reservations@georgewashington.co.uk
web: www.georgewashington.co.uk

(For full entry see Washington)

County Hotel, Newcastle

thistle

★★★ 80% HOTEL

☎ 0871 376 9029
Neville St NE1 5DF
e-mail: newcastle@thistle.co.uk
web: www.thistlehotels.com/newcastle
dir: A1 onto A184. Cross Redheugh Bridge, right at 2nd lights, right after cathedral, left at pedestrian zone

A 19th-century listed building, the hotel enjoys a central location opposite the city's Central Station, which also has links to the Metro system. Bedrooms are comfortably appointed for both business and leisure guests. Limited free parking is available.

Rooms 114 **Facilities** FTV Wi-fi Complimentary use of nearby gym New Year **Conf** Class 100 Board 100 Thtr 250 **Services** Lift **Parking** 19 **Notes** ⊗ Civ Wed 100

Horton Grange Country House Hotel

★★★ 80% HOTEL

☎ 01661 860686
Berwick Hill, Ponteland NE13 6BU
e-mail: info@hortongrange.co.uk
web: www.hortongrange.co.uk
dir: A1/A19 junct at Seaton Burn take 1st exit at 1st rdbt, after 1m, left signed Ponteland/Dinnington. Hotel on right approx 2m

A Grade II listed building set in its own grounds just a short distance from Newcastle Airport and Ponteland. The main house has traditionally styled executive bedrooms, and in addition there are four contemporary garden rooms that are elegant and spacious. All bedrooms have flat-screen TVs, digital radios and broadband access. Food is served in the light and airy restaurant and the lounge that both overlook the gardens.

Rooms 9 (4 annexe) (1 fmly) (4 GF) **S** £95-£115; **D** £105-£145 (incl. bkfst) **Facilities** FTV Wi-fi Xmas New Year **Conf** Class 40 Board 30 Thtr 120 Del from £125 to £165 **Parking** 50 **Notes** LB ⊗ Civ Wed 120

Eslington Villa Hotel

★★★ 79% ⊛ HOTEL

☎ 0191 487 6017 & 420 0666
8 Station Rd, Low Fell NE9 6DR
e-mail: home@eslingtonvilla.co.uk

(For full entry see Gateshead)

Best Western New Kent Hotel

★★★ 74% HOTEL

☎ 0191 281 7711
127 Osborne Rd NE2 2TB
e-mail: newkenthotel@hotmail.com
web: www.newkenthotel.com
dir: On B1600, opposite St Georges Church

This popular business hotel offers relaxed service and typical Geordie hospitality. The bright modern bedrooms are well equipped and the modern bar is an ideal meeting place. A range of generous, good value dishes is served in the restaurant, which doubles as a wedding venue.

Rooms 32 (4 fmly) **S** £71.50; **D** £91.50 (incl. bkfst)* **Facilities** STV FTV Wi-fi 🕃 Xmas New Year **Conf** Class 30 Board 40 Thtr 60 **Parking** 22 **Notes** LB Civ Wed 90

The Caledonian Hotel, Newcastle

PEEL HOTELS PLC

★★★ 71% HOTEL

☎ 0191 281 7881
64 Osborne Rd, Jesmond NE2 2AT
e-mail: info@caledonian-hotel-newcastle.com
web: www.peelhotels.co.uk
dir: From A1 follow signs to Newcastle City, cross Tyne Bridge to Tynemouth. Left at lights at Osborne Rd, hotel on right

This hotel is located in the Jesmond area of the city, and offers comfortable bedrooms that are well equipped. The public areas include the trendy Billabong Bar and Bistro which serves food all day, and the terrace where a cosmopolitan atmosphere prevails. Alfresco dining is available.

Rooms 90 (6 fmly) (7 GF) (15 smoking) **Facilities** Wi-fi Xmas New Year **Conf** Class 50 Board 50 Thtr 100 **Services** Lift **Parking** 35 **Notes** ⊗ Civ Wed 70

N

NEWCASTLE UPON TYNE *continued*

Newgate Hotel

★★★ 66% METRO HOTEL

☎ 0191 232 6570
Newgate St NE1 5SX
e-mail: enquiries@hotels-newcastle.com
dir: A184, A189 over bridge, right at 2nd lights, left
at lights into Clayton St. 1st right to Fenkle St, 1st
left to car park at end

Ideally located right in the heart of Newcastle, this
hotel makes the perfect base for exploring the city.
Bedrooms offer comfortable beds and free Wi-fi.
Breakfast is served in the sixth-floor restaurant that
has great views of the city.

Rooms 93 (8 fmly) **Facilities** STV Wi-fi **Conf** Board 12
Thtr 14 **Services** Lift **Parking** 120 **Notes** Closed
24-27 Dec

Holiday Inn Express Newcastle City Centre

BUDGET HOTEL

☎ 0870 4281488
Waterloo Square, St James Boulevard NE1 4DN
e-mail: gm.newcastle@expressholidayinn.co.uk
web: www.hiexpress.com/newcastlectyct

A modern hotel ideal for families and business
travellers. Fresh and uncomplicated, the spacious
rooms include Sky TV, power shower and tea and
coffee-making facilities. Continental buffet breakfast
is included in the room rate; other meals may be
taken at the nearby family pub or restaurant. See also
the Hotel Groups pages.

Rooms 130 (50 fmly) **Conf** Class 15 Board 16 Thtr 30

Premier Inn Newcastle Central

BUDGET HOTEL

☎ 0871 527 8802
New Bridge Street West NE1 8BS
web: www.premierinn.com
dir: Follow Gateshead & Newcastle signs on A167(M),
over Tyne Bridge. A193 signed Wallsend & city centre,
left to Carliol Square, hotel on corner

High quality, budget accommodation ideal for both
families and business travellers. Spacious, en suite
bedrooms feature tea and coffee making facilities,
and Freeview TV in most hotels. Internet access and
Wi-fi are available for a small fee. The adjacent
family restaurant features a wide and varied menu.
See also the Hotel Groups pages.

Rooms 172

Premier Inn Newcastle City Centre (Millennium Bridge)

BUDGET HOTEL

☎ 0871 527 8800
City Rd, Quayside NE1 2AN
web: www.premierinn.com
dir: At corner of City Rd (A186) & Crawhall Rd

Rooms 81

Premier Inn Newcastle (Holystone)

BUDGET HOTEL

☎ 0871 527 8790
The Stonebrook, Edmund Rd, Holystone NE27 0UN
web: www.premierinn.com
dir: 3m N of Tyne Tunnel. From A19 take A191 signed
Gosforth. Hotel on left

Rooms 40

Premier Inn Newcastle Quayside

BUDGET HOTEL

☎ 0871 527 8804
The Quayside NE1 3AE
web: www.premierinn.com
dir: S'bound: A1, A167(M), A186 signed Walker &
Wallsend follow B1600 Quayside signs. N'bound: A1,
A184, A189 (cross river). 1st exit, follow B1600
Quayside signs. Hotel at foot of Tyne Bridge in
Exchange building

Rooms 152

Novotel Newcastle Airport

★★★ 77% HOTEL

☎ 0191 214 0303
Ponteland Rd, Kenton NE3 3HZ
e-mail: H1118@accor-hotels.com
web: www.novotel.com
dir: A1(M) airport junct onto A696, take Kingston Park
exit

This modern, well-proportioned hotel lies just off the
bypass and is just a five minute drive from the airport
and has secure parking. The hotel has a scheduled
shuttle service and flight information screens for air
passengers. Bedrooms are spacious with a range of
extras. The Elements Restaurant offers a flexible
dining option and is open until late. There is a
contemporary lounge bar and also a small leisure
centre for the more energetic guests.

Rooms 126 (36 fmly) **Facilities** Wi-fi ⊗ Gym
Conf Class 90 Board 40 Thtr 200 **Services** Lift
Parking 260 **Notes** Civ Wed 200

Premier Inn Newcastle Airport

BUDGET HOTEL

☎ 0871 527 8796
**Newcastle Int Airport, Ponteland Rd, Prestwick
NE20 9DB**
web: www.premierinn.com
dir: A1 onto A696, follow Airport signs. At rdbt take
turn immediately after airport exit

High quality, budget accommodation ideal for both
families and business travellers. Spacious, en suite
bedrooms feature tea and coffee making facilities,
and Freeview TV in most hotels. Internet access and
Wi-fi are available for a small fee. The adjacent
family restaurant features a wide and varied menu.
See also the Hotel Groups pages.

Rooms 88

Save on hotels. Book at **theAA.com/hotel**

NEW 345 ENGLAND

Premier Inn Newcastle Airport (South)

BUDGET HOTEL

☎ 0871 527 8798
Callerton Lane Ends, Woolsington NE13 8DF
web: www.premierinn.com
dir: Just off A696 on B6918, 0.3m from airport

Rooms 53

NEWENT   Map 10 SO72
Gloucestershire

Three Choirs Vineyards

◉ ◉ RESTAURANT WITH ROOMS

☎ 01531 890223
GL18 1LS
e-mail: info@threechoirs.com
web: www.threechoirs.com
dir: On B4215 N of Newent, follow brown tourist signs

This thriving vineyard continues to go from strength to strength and provides a wonderfully different place to stay. The restaurant, which overlooks the 100-acre estate, enjoys a popular following thanks to well-executed dishes that make good use of local produce. Spacious, high quality bedrooms are equipped with many extras, and each opens onto a private patio area which has wonderful views.

Rooms 11 (11 annexe) (1 fmly)

NEWHAVEN   Map 6 TQ40
East Sussex

Premier Inn Newhaven

BUDGET HOTEL

☎ 0871 527 8810
Avis Rd BN9 0AG
web: www.premierinn.com
dir: From A26 (New Rd) through Drove Industrial Estate, left after underpass. Hotel in same complex as Sainsbury's

High quality, budget accommodation ideal for both families and business travellers. Spacious, en suite bedrooms feature tea and coffee making facilities, and Freeview TV in most hotels. Internet access and Wi-fi are available for a small fee. The adjacent family restaurant features a wide and varied menu. See also the Hotel Groups pages.

Rooms 70

NEWICK   Map 6 TQ42
East Sussex

Newick Park Hotel & Country Estate

★★★ ◉ ◉ HOTEL

☎ 01825 723633
BN8 4SB
e-mail: bookings@newickpark.co.uk
web: www.newickpark.co.uk
dir: Exit A272 at Newick Green, 1m, pass church & pub. Turn left, hotel 0.25m on right

Delightful Grade II listed Georgian country house set amid 250 acres of Sussex parkland and landscaped gardens. The spacious, individually decorated bedrooms are tastefully furnished, thoughtfully equipped and have superb views of the grounds; many rooms have huge American king-size beds. The comfortable public rooms include a study, a sitting room, lounge bar and an elegant restaurant.

Rooms 16 (3 annexe) (5 fmly) (1 GF) ☏
S £125-£245; **D** £165-£285 (incl. bkfst)
Facilities FTV Wi-fi ⌁ Fishing ⤛ Clay pigeon shooting Helicopter rides Quad biking Tank driving Laser quest Xmas **Conf** Class 40 Board 40 Thtr 80 Del from £185 to £210* **Parking** 52 **Notes** LB Closed 31 Dec & 1 Jan Civ Wed 100

NEWMARKET   Map 12 TL66
Suffolk

Tuddenham Mill

★★★★ 81% ◉◉◉ HOTEL

☎ 01438 713552
High St, Tuddenham St Mary IP28 6SQ
e-mail: info@tuddenhammill.co.uk

A beautifully converted old watermill set amidst landscaped grounds between Newmarket and Bury St Edmunds. The contemporary style bedrooms are situated in separate buildings adjacent to the main building, each one is tastefully appointed with co-ordinated fabrics and soft furnishings. The public areas have a wealth of original features such as the water wheel and exposed beams; they include a lounge bar, a smart, award-winning restaurant serving contemporary dishes that include many rarely seen ingredients, a meeting room and a choice of terraces.

Rooms 15 **Conf** Class 36 Board 16 Thtr 50
Notes Civ Wed

Bedford Lodge Hotel

★★★★ 80% ◉ ◉ HOTEL

☎ 01638 663175
Bury Rd CB8 7BX
e-mail: info@bedfordlodgehotel.co.uk
web: www.bedfordlodgehotel.co.uk
dir: From town centre take A1304 towards Bury St Edmunds, hotel 0.5m on left

Imposing 18th-century Georgian hunting lodge with more modern additions, set in three acres of secluded landscaped gardens. Public rooms feature the newly refurbished and re-named Squires restaurant, Roxana Bar and a small lounge. The hotel also features superb leisure facilities including the Eden Health and Fitness Club, and self-contained conference and banqueting suites. Contemporary bedrooms have a light, airy feel, and each is tastefully furnished and well equipped.

Rooms 55 (3 fmly) (16 GF) (3 smoking) ☏
Facilities FTV Wi-fi ⌁ ⌖ Gym Steam room Sauna Spa bath Xmas New Year **Conf** Class 80 Board 60 Thtr 200 Del from £150 to £195 **Services** Lift **Parking** 120 **Notes** ⊗ RS Sat lunch Civ Wed 150

N

NEWMARKET *continued*

The Rutland Arms Hotel

★★★ 79% ❀ HOTEL

☎ 01638 664251
High St CB8 8NB
e-mail: reservations.rutlandarms@ohiml.com
web: www.oxfordhotelsandinns.com
dir: A14 junct 37 onto A142, or M11 junct 9 onto A11 then A1304 - follow signs for town centre

Expect a warm welcome at this former coaching inn situated in the heart of town. The property is built around a 17th-century cobbled courtyard and still retains many original features. The public rooms include a large lounge bar and Carriages, a contemporary restaurant and wine bar. Bedrooms are smartly appointed and well equipped.

Rooms 46 (1 fmly) **S** £50-£130; **D** £60-£170 (incl. bkfst)* **Facilities** FTV Wi-fi ♫ **Conf** Class 40 Board 30 Thtr 70 Del from £95 to £130* **Parking** 40 **Notes** LB ⊗

Best Western Heath Court Hotel

★★★ 78% HOTEL

☎ 01638 667171
Moulton Rd CB8 8DY
e-mail: quality@heathcourthotel.com
dir: Exit A14 for Newmarket & Ely onto A142. Follow town centre signs over mini rdbt. At clocktower left into Moulton Rd

A modern red-brick hotel situated close to Newmarket Heath and perfectly placed for the town centre. Public rooms include a choice of dining options - informal meals can be taken in the lounge bar or a modern carte menu is offered in the restaurant. The smartly presented bedrooms are mostly spacious and some have air conditioning.

Rooms 41 (2 fmly) **S** £40-£100; **D** £60-£198 (incl. bkfst)* **Facilities** STV FTV Wi-fi New Year **Conf** Class 50 Board 40 Thtr 130 Del from £85 to £115* **Services** Lift **Parking** 70 **Notes** LB Civ Wed 100

Premier Inn Newmarket

BUDGET HOTEL

☎ 0871 527 9296
Fred Archer Way CB8 7XN
web: www.premierinn.com
dir: A14 junct 37, A142 (Fordham Rd). 2.3m, straight on at 2 rdbts. At end of Fordham Rd, into right lane, turn right. Hotel on right

High quality, budget accommodation ideal for both families and business travellers. Spacious, en suite bedrooms feature tea and coffee making facilities, and Freeview TV in most hotels. Internet access and Wi-fi are available for a small fee. The adjacent family restaurant features a wide and varied menu. See also the Hotel Groups pages.

Rooms 75

NEW MILTON Map 5 SZ29
Hampshire

INSPECTORS' CHOICE

Chewton Glen Hotel & Spa

★★★★★ ❀❀❀

COUNTRY HOUSE HOTEL

☎ 01425 275341
Christchurch Rd BH25 6QS
e-mail: reservations@chewtonglen.com
web: www.chewtonglen.com
dir: A35 from Lyndhurst for 10m, left at staggered junct. Follow tourist sign for hotel through Walkford, take 2nd left

This outstanding hotel has been at the forefront of British hotel-keeping for many years. Once past the wrought iron entrance gates, guests are transported into a world of luxury. Log fires and afternoon tea are part of the tradition here, and lounges enjoy fine views over sweeping croquet lawns. Most bedrooms are very spacious, with private patios or balconies. Dining is a treat, and the extensive wine lists are essential reading for

---

the enthusiast. The spa and leisure facilities are superb.

Rooms 58 (11 GF) ⁂ **S** £362-£1557; **D** £362-£1557 (incl. bkfst)* **Facilities** Spa STV FTV Wi-fi ⊠ ⛲ ⊰ ♨ 9 ⌘ Putt green ⛳ Gym Hydrotherapy spa Dance studio Cycling & jogging trail Clay shooting Archery ♫ Xmas New Year **Conf** Class 70 Board 40 Thtr 150 **Services** Air con **Parking** 150 **Notes** ⊗ Civ Wed 140

NEWPORT Map 15 SJ71
Shropshire

Premier Inn Newport / Telford

BUDGET HOTEL

☎ 0871 527 8808
Stafford Rd TF10 9BY
web: www.premierinn.com
dir: From A41 E of Newport take A518 towards Stafford. Hotel on right adjacent to Mere Park Garden Centre

High quality, budget accommodation ideal for both families and business travellers. Spacious, en suite bedrooms feature tea and coffee making facilities, and Freeview TV in most hotels. Internet access and Wi-fi are available for a small fee. The adjacent family restaurant features a wide and varied menu. See also the Hotel Groups pages.

Rooms 50

NEWPORT Map 5 SZ58
Isle of Wight

Premier Inn Isle of Wight (Newport)

BUDGET HOTEL

☎ 0871 527 8556
Seaclose, Fairlee Rd PO30 2DN
web: www.premierinn.com
dir: From Newport take A3054 signed Ryde. In 0.75m at Seaclose lights, turn left. Hotel adjacent to council offices

High quality, budget accommodation ideal for both families and business travellers. Spacious, en suite bedrooms feature tea and coffee making facilities, and Freeview TV in most hotels. Internet access and Wi-fi are available for a small fee. The adjacent family restaurant features a wide and varied menu. See also the Hotel Groups pages.

Rooms 68

Save on hotels. Book at **theAA.com/hotel**

NEW 347 ENGLAND

N

NEWQUAY
Cornwall

Map 2 SW86

Headland Hotel

★★★★ 79% HOTEL

☎ 01637 872211
Fistral Beach TR7 1EW
e-mail: reception@headlandhotel.co.uk
web: www.headlandhotel.co.uk
dir: A30 onto A392 at Indian Queens, approaching Newquay follow signs for Fistral Beach, hotel adjacent

This Victorian hotel enjoys a stunning location overlooking the sea on three sides - views can be enjoyed from most of the windows. Bedrooms are comfortable and spacious. The grand public areas, with impressive floral displays, include various lounges and in addition to the formal dining room, Sands Brasserie offers a relaxed alternative. Self-catering cottages are available, and guests staying in these can use the hotel facilities.

Rooms 96 (40 fmly) 🐾 **S** £79-£159; **D** £99-£379 (incl. bkfst) **Facilities** STV FTV Wi-fi ⌾ ⚘ ♨ 9 ♨ Putt green ♨ Boules Outdoor activities Xmas New Year Child facilities **Conf** Class 120 Board 40 Thtr 250 Del from £150 to £250 **Services** Lift **Parking** 300 **Notes** LB Closed 6 Jan-8 Feb Civ Wed 250

Atlantic Hotel

★★★★ 75% HOTEL

☎ 01637 872244
Dane Rd TR7 1EN
e-mail: info@atlantichotelnewquay.co.uk
web: www.atlantichotelnewquay.co.uk

Located on a cliff top with stunning views of Newquay and the Atlantic seascape, this imposing property dominates the skyline and offers traditional hotel keeping with modern comforts. All bedrooms are appointed to a high standard and offer ample modern comforts; balcony suites are available. Silks restaurant is popular with locals and residents alike.

Atlantic Hotel

Rooms 55 (10 fmly) 🐾 **Facilities** FTV Wi-fi ⌾ ⚘ Xmas New Year **Conf** Class 300 Board 150 Thtr 300 **Services** Lift **Parking** 55 **Notes** ⊗ Civ Wed 360

See advert on this page

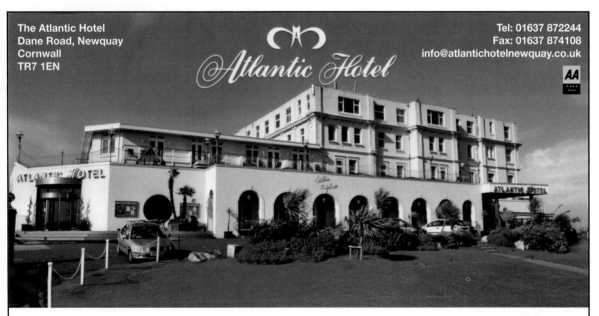

NEWQUAY *continued*

Porth Veor Manor

★★★ 78% HOTEL

☎ 01637 873274 & 839542
Porth Way, Porth TR7 3LW
e-mail: enquiries@porthveormanor.com
web: www.porthveormanor.com
dir: From A3058 at main rdbt onto B3276, hotel 0.5m
on left

Overlooking Porth Beach and in a quiet location, this
pleasant mid 19th-century manor house offers a
relaxed and friendly atmosphere. The spacious
bedrooms have satellite TVs, and many have views of
the beach; superior rooms are available. The hotel
has a fine dining restaurant, a lounge/bar, and an
outdoor heated pool. There is direct access via a
private path from the hotel grounds to the beach, and
the coastal paths are just a short walk away.

Rooms 18 (6 fmly) **D** £70-£148 (incl. bkfst)*
Facilities STV FTV Wi-fi ⊹ ⋎ Putt green ⋓ Xmas
New Year **Parking** 36 **Notes** LB ⊗ No children 5yrs
Civ Wed 80

Best Western Hotel Bristol

★★★ 77% HOTEL

☎ 01637 875181
Narrowcliff TR7 2PQ
e-mail: info@hotelbristol.co.uk
web: www.hotelbristol.co.uk
dir: A30 onto A392, then A3058. Hotel 2.5m on left

This hotel is conveniently situated and many of the
bedrooms enjoy fine sea views. Staff are friendly and
provide a professional and attentive service. There is
a range of comfortable lounges, ideal for relaxing
prior to eating in the elegant dining room. There are
also leisure and conference facilities.

Rooms 74 (23 fmly) **Facilities** FTV Wi-fi ⓧ Table
tennis New Year **Conf** Class 80 Board 30 Thtr 200
Services Lift **Parking** 105 **Notes** Closed 23-27 Dec &
4-18 Jan

Hotel Victoria

★★★ 75% HOTEL

☎ 01637 872255
East St TR7 1DB
e-mail: bookings@hotel-victoria.co.uk
web: www.hotel-victoria.co.uk
dir: A30 towards Bodmin following signs to Newquay.
Hotel next to Newquay's main post office

Standing on the cliffs, overlooking Newquay Bay, the
hotel is situated at the centre of this vibrant town.
The spacious lounges and bar areas all benefit from
glorious views. Varied menus, using the best of local
produce, are offered in the restaurant. Bedrooms vary
from spacious superior rooms and suites to standard
inland-facing rooms. Berties pub, a nightclub, and
indoor leisure facilities are also available.

Rooms 71 (23 fmly) (1 GF) (5 smoking) ⋔ **S** £45-£84;
D £75-£135 (incl. bkfst)* **Facilities** FTV Wi-fi ⓧ Gym
Beauty room New Year **Conf** Class 130 Board 50
Thtr 200 Del from £102.50* **Services** Lift **Parking** 50
Notes Civ Wed 90

See advert on opposite page

Trebarwith Hotel

★★★ 75% HOTEL

☎ 01637 872288 & 0800 387520
Trebarwith Crescent TR7 1BZ
e-mail: trebahotel@aol.com
web: www.trebarwith-hotel.co.uk
dir: From A3058 into Mount Wise Rd. 3rd right into
Marcus Hill, across East St into Trebarwith Cres. Hotel
at end

With breathtaking views of the rugged coastline and
a path leading to the beach, this friendly, family-run
hotel is set in its own grounds close to the town
centre. The public rooms include a lounge, ballroom,
restaurant and cinema. The comfortable bedrooms
include four-poster and family rooms, and many
benefit from the sea views.

Rooms 41 (8 fmly) (1 GF) ⋔ **Facilities** FTV Wi-fi ⊹ ⓧ
Fishing Video theatre Games room Surf school ♬
Conf Class 30 Board 18 Thtr 45 Del from £100 to
£500* **Parking** 41 **Notes** ⊗ Closed Nov-5 Apr

Kilbirnie Hotel

★★★ 68% HOTEL

☎ 01637 875155
Narrowcliff TR7 2RS
e-mail: info@kilbirniehotel.co.uk
web: www.kilbirniehotel.co.uk
dir: On A392

With delightful views over the open space known as
The Barrowfields and beyond to the sea, this
privately-run hotel offers an impressive range of
facilities. The reception rooms are spacious and
comfortable, and during summer months become the
venue for a programme of entertainment. Bedrooms
vary in size and style, and some enjoy fine sea views.

Rooms 66 (6 fmly) (8 GF) ⋔ **S** £35-£50; **D** £60-£100
(incl. bkfst)* **Facilities** Wi-fi ⓧ ⋎ Gym Fitness room
Hair salon Xmas New Year **Conf** Class 50 Board 25
Thtr 100 Del from £60 to £80* **Services** Lift Air con
Parking 58 **Notes** ⊗ Closed 2-31 Jan

Hotel California

★★★ 67% HOTEL

☎ 01637 879292 & 872798
Pentire Crescent TR7 1PU
e-mail: info@hotel-california.co.uk
web: www.hotel-california.co.uk
dir: A392 to Newquay, follow signs for Pentire Hotels
& Guest Houses

This hotel is tucked away in a delightful location,
close to Fistral Beach and adjacent to the River
Gannel. Many rooms have views across the river
towards the sea, and some have balconies. There is
an impressive range of leisure facilities, including
indoor and outdoor pools, and ten-pin bowling.
Cuisine is enjoyable and menus offer a range of
interesting dishes.

Rooms 70 (27 fmly) (13 GF) **S** £43-£68; **D** £86-£136
(incl. bkfst) **Facilities** FTV Wi-fi HL ⊕ ⌖ Squash
4-lane American bowling alley Hairdresser Snooker &
pool room Sauna Solarium ♫ Xmas New Year
Conf Class 100 Board 30 Thtr 100 Del from £66 to
£96* **Services** Lift **Parking** 66 **Notes** LB Civ Wed 150

Glendorgal Resort

★★★ Ⓐ HOTEL

☎ 01637 874937 & 859981
Lusty Glaze Rd, Porth TR7 3AD
e-mail: info@glendorgal.co.uk
dir: A30 onto A392, 2nd rdbt, right onto A3058, at
mini rdbt straight on, right into Lusty Glaze Rd, follow
signs for Glendorgal

Rooms 26 (8 fmly) ♙ **Facilities** FTV Wi-fi ⇘ ⊕ Gym
Cardiovascular room Sauna **Conf** Class 36 Board 30
Thtr 60 **Parking** 100 **Notes** Civ Wed 110

Priory Lodge Hotel

★★ 75% HOTEL

☎ 01637 874111
30 Mount Wise TR7 2BN
e-mail: fionapocklington@tiscali.co.uk
dir: From lights in town centre onto Berry Rd, right
onto B3282 (Mount Wise), 0.5m on right

This hotel enjoys a central location close to the town
centre, the harbour and the local beaches. Secure
parking is available at the hotel along with a range of
leisure facilities including a heated pool, sauna,
games room and hot tub. Attractively decorated
bedrooms vary in size and style - many have sea
views over Towan Beach.

Rooms 28 (6 annexe) (13 fmly) (1 GF) **S** £35-£45;
D £50-£95 (incl. bkfst)* **Facilities** FTV Wi-fi ⇘ ⌖ ♫
Xmas New Year **Parking** 30 **Notes** ⊗ Closed 18-22
Dec & 4 Jan-early Mar

Sandy Lodge Hotel

★★ 72% HOTEL

☎ 01637 872851
6-12 Hilgrove Rd TR7 2QY
e-mail: info@sandylodgehotel.co.uk
dir: Exit Hever Rd into Hilgrove Rd (by Tesco). Hotel
150yds on left

This friendly, family-run hotel is ideally located for
easy access to the seafront and surfing beaches, and
is within walking distance of the town centre.
Accommodation is comfortable with a choice of
family, twin and double rooms. There is a spacious
dining room and a choice of lounge areas; nightly
entertainment is provided.

Rooms 80 (8 fmly) (12 GF) ♙ **S** £27-£34; **D** £49-£61*
Facilities FTV Wi-fi ⊕ Gym Sauna Spa bath ♫ Xmas
New Year **Conf** Class 40 Board 30 Thtr 100
Services Lift **Parking** 50 **Notes** ⊗ Closed 5-23 Jan

N

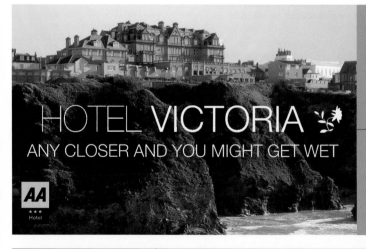

NEWQUAY continued

Eliot Hotel

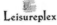 **Leisureplex**

★★ 71% HOTEL

☎ 01637 878177
Edgcumbe Av TR7 2NH
e-mail: eliot.newquay@alfatravel.co.uk
web: www.leisureplex.co.uk
dir: A30 onto A392 towards Quintrell Downs. Right at rdbt onto A3058. 4m to Newquay, left at amusements onto Edgcumbe Av. Hotel on left

Located in a quiet residential area just a short walk from the beaches and the varied attractions of the town, this long-established hotel offers comfortable accommodation. Entertainment is provided most nights throughout the season and guests can relax in the spacious public areas.

Rooms 76 (10 fmly) **S** £28-£45; **D** £56-£76 (incl. bkfst)* **Facilities** FTV ⚲ Pool table Table tennis ♫ Xmas New Year **Services** Lift **Parking** 20 **Notes** ⊗ Closed Dec-Jan (ex Xmas) RS Nov & Feb-Mar

Premier Inn Quintrell Downs

 Premier Inn

BUDGET HOTEL

☎ 0871 527 8818
Quintrell Downs TR8 4LE
web: www.premierinn.com
dir: From A30 take A39. At rdbt 2nd exit signed Newquay A392. 4m, in Quintrell Downs take 1st exit at rdbt. Hotel on left

High quality, budget accommodation ideal for both families and business travellers. Spacious, en suite bedrooms feature tea and coffee making facilities, and Freeview TV in most hotels. Internet access and Wi-fi are available for a small fee. The adjacent family restaurant features a wide and varied menu. See also the Hotel Groups pages.

Rooms 75

NEWTON ABBOT   Map 3 SX87
Devon

See also Ilsington

Best Western Passage House Hotel

 Best Western

★★★ 73% HOTEL

☎ 01626 355515
Hackney Ln, Kingsteignton TQ12 3QH
e-mail: hotel@passagehousegroup.co.uk
dir: A380 onto A381, follow racecourse signs

With memorable views of the Teign Estuary, this popular hotel provides spacious, well-equipped bedrooms. An impressive range of leisure and meeting facilities is offered and a conservatory provides a pleasant extension to the bar and lounge. A choice of eating options is available, either in the main restaurant, or the adjacent Passage House Inn for less formal dining.

Rooms 90 (52 annexe) (64 fmly) (26 GF)
Facilities Spa STV Wi-fi ⚲ ⓒ supervised Gym **Conf** Class 50 Board 40 Thtr 120 Del from £95 to £115 **Services** Lift **Parking** 300 **Notes** ⊗ RS 24-27 Dec Civ Wed 75

Best Western Queens Hotel

 Best Western

★★★ 70% METRO HOTEL

☎ 01626 363133
Queen St TQ12 2EZ
e-mail: reservations@queenshotel-southwest.co.uk
dir: A380. At Penn Inn turn right towards town, hotel opposite station

Pleasantly and conveniently located close to the railway station and racecourse, this hotel continues to be a popular venue for both business visitors and tourists. Bedrooms are comfortable and spacious. Light snacks and sandwiches are available in the café/bar and lounge.

Rooms 24 (3 fmly) ⚲ **Facilities** FTV Wi-fi **Conf** Class 20 Board 20 Thtr 40 **Parking** 6 **Notes** ⊗ RS 24 Dec-2 Jan

---

NEWTON AYCLIFFE   Map 19 NZ22
Co Durham

Premier Inn Durham (Newton Aycliffe)

 Premier Inn

BUDGET HOTEL

☎ 0871 527 8336
Ricknall Ln, Great North Rd DL5 6JG
web: www.premierinn.com
dir: On A167 E of Newton Aycliffe, 3m from A1(M)

High quality, budget accommodation ideal for both families and business travellers. Spacious, en suite bedrooms feature tea and coffee making facilities, and Freeview TV in most hotels. Internet access and Wi-fi are available for a small fee. The adjacent family restaurant features a wide and varied menu. See also the Hotel Groups pages.

Rooms 44

NEWTON-LE-WILLOWS   Map 15 SJ59
Merseyside

Holiday Inn Haydock M6 Jct 23

 Holiday Inn

★★★ 79% HOTEL

☎ 0871 942 9039
Lodge Ln WA12 0JG
e-mail: haydock@ihg.com
web: www.holidayinn.co.uk
dir: M6 junct 23, A49 to Ashton-in-Makerfield. Hotel 0.25m on right by racecourse

This hotel has an ideal location adjacent to Haydock Racecourse and within easy reach of most north-west cities and attractions. A variety of bedrooms is available and public areas include extensive meeting and conference facilities, a smart Spirit health and leisure club and a spacious bar and restaurant.

Rooms 136 (12 fmly) (23 GF) (38 smoking)
Facilities STV Wi-fi ⓒ Gym Xmas New Year **Conf** Class 70 Board 60 Thtr 180 **Services** Lift Air con **Parking** 204 **Notes** Civ Wed 120

Save on hotels. Book at **theAA.com/hotel**

NEW – NOR 351 ENGLAND

NEWTON POPPLEFORD
Devon   Map 3 SY08

Moores' Restaurant & Rooms

◉ ◉   RESTAURANT WITH ROOMS

☎ 01395 568100
6 Greenbank, High St EX10 0EB
e-mail: info.moores@btconnect.com
dir: On A3052 in village centre, 3m from Sidmouth

Centrally located in the village, this small restaurant offers very comfortable, practically furnished bedrooms. Guests are assured of a friendly welcome and relaxed, efficient service. Good quality, locally sourced ingredients are used to produce imaginative dishes full of natural flavours.

Rooms 3 (2 fmly)

NORMAN CROSS
Cambridgeshire   Map 12 TL19

Premier Inn Peterborough A1(M) Jct 16

BUDGET HOTEL

☎ 0871 527 8870
Norman Cross, A1(M) Junct 16 PE7 3TB
web: www.premierinn.com
dir: A1(M) junct 16, A15 towards Yaxley, hotel in 100yds

High quality, budget accommodation ideal for both families and business travellers. Spacious, en suite bedrooms feature tea and coffee making facilities, and Freeview TV in most hotels. Internet access and Wi-fi are available for a small fee. The adjacent family restaurant features a wide and varied menu. See also the Hotel Groups pages.

Rooms 95

NORMANTON
Rutland   Map 11 SK90

Best Western Normanton Park Hotel

★★★   69%   HOTEL

☎ 01780 720315
Oakham LE15 8RP
e-mail: info@normantonpark.co.uk
web: www.normantonpark.com
dir: From A1 follow A606 towards Oakham, 5m. Turn left, 1.5m. Hotel on right

This hotel offers some of Rutland Water's best views over the south shore. The comfortable bedrooms are located in the main house and the courtyard. Public rooms include a conservatory dining room overlooking the water, and a cosy lounge is available for guests to relax in.

Rooms 30 (7 annexe) (6 fmly) (11 GF) ⌇
Facilities FTV Wi-fi Xmas New Year **Conf** Class 60 Board 80 Thtr 200 **Parking** 100 **Notes** Civ Wed 100

NORTHAMPTON
Northamptonshire   Map 11 SP76

Northampton Marriott Hotel

Marriott
HOTELS & RESORTS

★★★★   75%   HOTEL

☎ 01604 768700
Eagle Dr NN4 7HW
e-mail: mhrs.ormnh.salesadmin@marriotthotels.com
web: www.northamptonmarriott.co.uk
dir: M1 junct 15, follow signs to Delapre Golf Course, hotel on right

Located on the outskirts of town, close to major road networks, this modern hotel caters to a cross section of guests. A self-contained management centre makes this a popular conference venue, and its spacious and well-designed bedrooms will suit business travellers particularly well. This makes a good base for exploring the attractions the area has to offer.

Rooms 120 (10 fmly) (52 GF) (5 smoking) ⌇
Facilities STV Wi-fi ⌇ ⌇ supervised Gym Steam room Beauty treatment room Sauna Xmas New Year **Conf** Class 72 Board 30 Thtr 250 **Services** Air con **Parking** 200 **Notes** ⊗ Civ Wed 180

Park Inn by Radisson Northampton

park inn by Radisson

★★★   73%   HOTEL

☎ 01604 739988
Silver St NN1 2TA
e-mail: reservations.northampton@rezidorparkinn.com
web: www.northampton.parkinn.co.uk
dir: In town centre

Ideally located within the city centre, the hotel is a spacious, purpose-built property offering a range of well-appointed bedrooms, conference rooms and a fully-equipped health club. The popular restaurant offers an open-plan contemporary dining experience in a relaxing environment.

Rooms 146 ⌇ S £50-£200; D £50-£200*
Facilities Spa FTV Wi-fi ⌇ ⌇ Gym New Year **Conf** Class 300 Board 100 Thtr 600 Del from £100 to £200* **Services** Lift Air con **Parking** 160 **Notes** ⊗ Civ Wed 600

Best Western Lime Trees Hotel

★★★   70%   HOTEL

☎ 01604 632188
8 Langham Place, Barrack Rd NN2 6AA
e-mail: info@limetreeshotel.co.uk
web: www.limetreeshotel.co.uk
dir: From city centre 0.5m N on A508 towards Market Harborough, near racecourse & cathedral

This well presented hotel is popular with business travellers during the week and leisure guests at the weekend. Service is both efficient and friendly. Bedrooms are comfortable and in addition to all the usual facilities, many offer air conditioning. Notable features include an internal courtyard and a row of charming mews houses that have been converted into bedrooms.

Rooms 28 (8 annexe) (4 fmly) (5 GF) ⌇ S £40-£60; D £55-£75* **Facilities** FTV Wi-fi Xmas New Year **Conf** Class 50 Board 45 Thtr 140 **Services** Air con **Parking** 25 **Notes** Civ Wed 140

N

NORTHAMPTON *continued*

Campanile Northampton

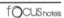

★★★ 70% HOTEL

☎ 01604 662599
Cheaney Dr, Grange Park NN4 5FB
e-mail: northampton@campanile.com
web: www.campanile.com
dir: M1 junct 15, A508 towards Northampton. 2nd exit at 1st rdbt, 2nd exit at 2nd rdbt into Grange Park

This modern building offers accommodation in smart, well-equipped bedrooms, all with en suite bathrooms. Refreshments may be taken at the informal bistro.

Rooms 87 (18 fmly) **Facilities** STV FTV Wi-fi Xmas New Year **Conf** Class 60 Board 60 Thtr 150 **Services** Lift Air con **Parking** 100

Westone Manor Hotel

*f*OCUShotels

★★★ 67% HOTEL

☎ 01604 739955
Ashley Way, Weston Favell NN3 3EA
e-mail: enquiries@hotels-northampton.com
dir: M1 junct 15 towards Wellingborough/Northampton. Follow Kettering signs for 0.5m. A4500 (Town Centre/Weston Favell). Take left A4500, 1st right over small rdbt, hotel on left

Ideally located with easy access to the motorway network and the city centre, this hotel, situated in peaceful gardens, offers a good range of accommodation to suit both business and leisure travellers. Built in 1924 for a shoe manufacturer, the house retains many original features. The bedrooms have free Wi-fi and TVs with Sky channels. There are banqueting facilities that cater for various functions from small business meetings to wedding receptions; the hotel holds a civil wedding licence.

Rooms 69 (30 annexe) (1 fmly) (15 GF) **Facilities** FTV Wi-fi **Conf** Class 50 Board 50 Thtr 140 **Services** Lift **Parking** 65 **Notes** Civ Wed 100

Holiday Inn Express Northampton M1 Jct 15

BUDGET HOTEL

☎ 01604 432800
Loake Close, Grange Park NN4 5EZ
e-mail: info@expressnorthampton.co.uk
web: www.hiexpress.com/exnorthampton
dir: Just off M1 junct 15, follow signs for Grange Park

A modern hotel ideal for families and business travellers. Fresh and uncomplicated, the spacious rooms include Sky TV, power shower and tea and coffee-making facilities. Continental buffet breakfast is included in the room rate; other meals may be taken at the nearby family pub or restaurant. See also the Hotel Groups pages.

Rooms 126 **Conf** Class 28 Board 28 Thtr 70

Ibis Northampton Centre

BUDGET HOTEL

☎ 01604 608900
Sol Central, Marefair NN1 1SR
e-mail: H3657@accor.com
web: www.ibishotel.com
dir: M1 junct 15/15a & city centre towards railway station

Modern, budget hotel offering comfortable accommodation in bright and practical bedrooms. Breakfast is self-service and dinner is available in the restaurant. See also the Hotel Groups pages.

Rooms 151 (14 fmly) **S** £45-£75; **D** £45-£75* **Conf** Board 10

Premier Inn Northampton Bedford Road/A428

BUDGET HOTEL

☎ 0871 527 8822
The Lakes, Bedford Rd NN4 7YD
web: www.premierinn.com
dir: M1 junct 15, follow A508 (A45) signs to Northampton. A428 at rdbt take 4th exit (signed Bedford). Left at next rdbt. Hotel on right

High quality, budget accommodation ideal for both families and business travellers. Spacious, en suite bedrooms feature tea and coffee making facilities, and Freeview TV in most hotels. Internet access and Wi-fi are available for a small fee. The adjacent family restaurant features a wide and varied menu. See also the Hotel Groups pages.

Rooms 44

Premier Inn Northampton Great Billing/A45

BUDGET HOTEL

☎ 0871 527 8824
Crow Ln, Great Billing NN3 9DA
web: www.premierinn.com
dir: M1 junct 15, A508, A45 follow Billing Aquadrome signs

Rooms 60

Premier Inn Northampton South (Wootton)

BUDGET HOTEL

☎ 0871 527 8826
Newport Pagnell Road West, Wootton NN4 7JJ
web: www.premierinn.com
dir: M1 junct 15, A508 towards Northampton, exit at junct with A45. At rdbt take B526. Hotel on right

Rooms 45

Premier Inn Northampton West (Harpole)

BUDGET HOTEL

☎ 0871 527 8828
Harpole Turn, Weedon Rd, Harpole NN7 4DD
web: www.premierinn.com
dir: M1 junct 16, A45 towards Northampton. In 1m left into Harpole Turn. Hotel on left

Rooms 51

NORTH FERRIBY   Map 17 SE92
East Riding of Yorkshire

Hallmark Hotel Hull

★★★★ 71% HOTEL

☎ 01482 645212
Ferriby High Rd HU14 3LG
dir: M62 onto A63 towards Hull. Exit at Humber Bridge signage. Follow North Ferriby signs, hotel 0.5m on left

This property is situated just outside Hull city centre, with breathtaking views of the Humber Bridge. Service is attentive with a friendly atmosphere. The comfortable bedrooms are tastefully appointed and are suitable for both business and leisure guests. The restaurant and bar serve a good choice of dishes. Conference facilities are available along with free Wi-fi and private parking.

Rooms 95 (3 fmly) (16 GF) **Facilities** STV FTV Wi-fi Xmas New Year **Conf** Class 85 Board 86 Thtr 200 Del from £95 to £125* **Parking** 150 **Notes** Civ Wed 200

Save on hotels. Book at **theAA.com/hotel**

NOR 353 ENGLAND

NORTH KILWORTH
Leicestershire   **Map 11 SP68**

INSPECTORS' CHOICE

Kilworth House Hotel & Theatre

★★★★ ◉◉ HOTEL

☎ 01858 880058
Lutterworth Rd LE17 6JE
e-mail: info@kilworthhouse.co.uk
web: www.kilworthhouse.co.uk
dir: A4304 towards Market Harborough, after Walcote, hotel 1.5m on right

A restored Victorian country house located in 38 acres of private grounds offering state-of-the-art conference rooms. The gracious public areas feature many period pieces and original art works. The bedrooms are very comfortable and well equipped, and the large Orangery is now used for informal dining, while the opulent Wordsworth Restaurant has a more formal air. Close to the lake an open-air theatre which seats 540 has been built; professional productions take place here and picnics can be arranged, or dinner back at the hotel is also an option.

Rooms 44 (2 fmly) (13 GF) ⌕ **S** £150-£240; **D** £180-£340 (incl. bkfst & dinner)* **Facilities** FTV Wi-fi ⌕ Fishing ⌣ Gym Beauty therapy rooms Xmas **Conf** Class 30 Board 30 Thtr 80 Del from £190 to £234* **Services** Lift **Parking** 140 **Notes** ⊗ Civ Wed 130

NORTH SHIELDS
Tyne & Wear   **Map 21 NZ36**

Premier Inn North Shields
BUDGET HOTEL

☎ 0871 527 8818
Coble Dene Rd NE29 6DL
web: www.premierinn.com
dir: From all directions follow signs for Royal Quays (Outlet Centre) & International Ferry Terminal. From A187 take Coble Dene Rd. At 3rd rdbt right, 1st right at mini rdbt

High quality, budget accommodation ideal for both families and business travellers. Spacious, en suite bedrooms feature tea and coffee making facilities, and Freeview TV in most hotels. Internet access and Wi-fi are available for a small fee. The adjacent family restaurant features a wide and varied menu. See also the Hotel Groups pages.

Rooms 50

NORTH WALSHAM
Norfolk   **Map 13 TG23**

INSPECTORS' CHOICE

Beechwood Hotel

★★★ ◉◉ HOTEL

☎ 01692 403231
Cromer Rd NR28 0HD
e-mail: info@beechwood-hotel.co.uk
web: www.beechwood-hotel.co.uk
dir: B1150 from Norwich. At North Walsham left at 1st lights, then right at next

Expect a warm welcome at this elegant 18th-century house, situated just a short walk from the town centre. The individually styled bedrooms are tastefully furnished with well chosen antique pieces, attractive co-ordinated soft fabrics and many thoughtful touches. The spacious public areas include a lounge bar with plush furnishings, a further lounge and a smartly appointed restaurant.

Beechwood Hotel

Rooms 17 (4 GF) ⌕ **S** fr £85; **D** £100-£160 (incl. bkfst) **Facilities** FTV Wi-fi ⌣ New Year **Conf** Class 20 Board 20 Thtr 20 Del from £140 **Parking** 20 **Notes** LB No children 10yrs

NORTH WALTHAM
Hampshire   **Map 5 SU54**

Premier Inn Basingstoke South
BUDGET HOTEL

☎ 0871 527 8064
RG25 2BB
web: www.premierinn.com
dir: M3 junct 7, A30 follow signs for Kingsworthy and crematorium. Hotel 2m on right, adjacent to Wheatsheaf

High quality, budget accommodation ideal for both families and business travellers. Spacious, en suite bedrooms feature tea and coffee making facilities, and Freeview TV in most hotels. Internet access and Wi-fi are available for a small fee. The adjacent family restaurant features a wide and varied menu. See also the Hotel Groups pages.

Rooms 28

N

NORTHWICH
Cheshire   Map 15 SJ67

Premier Inn Northwich (Sandiway)

BUDGET HOTEL

☎ 0871 527 8830
520 Chester Rd, Sandiway CW8 2DN
web: www.premierinn.com
dir: M6 junct 19, A556 towards Chester. Hotel in 11m

High quality, budget accommodation ideal for both families and business travellers. Spacious, en suite bedrooms feature tea and coffee making facilities, and Freeview TV in most hotels. Internet access and Wi-fi are available for a small fee. The adjacent family restaurant features a wide and varied menu. See also the Hotel Groups pages.

Rooms 42

Premier Inn Northwich South

BUDGET HOTEL

☎ 0871 527 8832
London Rd, Leftwich CW9 8EG
web: www.premierinn.com
dir: Just off M6 junct 19. Follow A556 towards Chester. Right at sign for Northwich & Davenham

Rooms 33

NORWICH
Norfolk   Map 13 TG20

See also **Hethersett**

Sprowston Manor, A Marriott Hotel & Country Club

★★★★ 82% ⊛ HOTEL

☎ 01603 410871
Sprowston Park, Wroxham Rd, Sprowston NR7 8RP
e-mail: mhrs.nwigs.frontdesk@marriotthotels.com
web: www.marriottsprowstonmanor.co.uk
dir: NE of Norwich take A1151 (Wroxham road). 2m, follow signs to Sprowston Park

Surrounded by open parkland, this imposing property is set in attractively landscaped grounds and is just a short drive from the city centre. Bedrooms are spacious and feature a variety of decorative styles. The hotel also has extensive conference, banqueting and leisure facilities. Other public rooms include an array of seating areas and the elegant Manor Restaurant.

Rooms 94 (31 fmly) (5 GF) (8 smoking) **S** £105-£135; **D** £145-£170 (incl. bkfst)* **Facilities** Spa FTV Wi-fi ⏱ ⅃ 18 Putt green Gym Steam room Sauna Xmas New Year **Conf** Class 100 Board 80 Thtr 500 **Services** Lift **Parking** 150 **Notes** LB ⊗ Civ Wed 300

St Giles House Hotel

★★★★ 81% ⊛⊛ HOTEL

☎ 01603 275180
41-45 St Giles St NR2 1JR
e-mail: reception@stgileshousehotel.com
web: www.stgileshousehotel.com
dir: A11 into central Norwich. Left at rdbt (Chapelfield Shopping Centre). 3rd exit at next rdbt. Left onto St Giles St. Hotel on left

A stylish 19th-century, Grade II listed building situated in the heart of the city. The property has a wealth of magnificent original features such as wood-panelling, ornamental plasterwork and marble floors. Public areas include an open-plan lounge bar/restaurant, a smart lounge with plush sofas and a Parisian-style terrace. The spacious, contemporary bedrooms are individually designed and have many thoughtful touches.

Rooms 24 **Facilities** Spa FTV Wi-fi Xmas New Year **Conf** Class 20 Board 24 Thtr 45 **Services** Lift **Parking** 30 **Notes** ⊗ Civ Wed 60

De Vere Dunston Hall

DE VERE
Hotels & Resorts

★★★★ 77% HOTEL

☎ 01508 470444
Ipswich Rd NR14 8PQ
e-mail: dhreception@devere-hotels.com
web: www.devere.co.uk
dir: From A47 take A140 (Ipswich road). 0.25m, hotel on left

An imposing Grade II listed building set amidst 170 acres of landscaped grounds just a short drive from the city centre. The spacious bedrooms are smartly decorated, tastefully furnished and equipped to a high standard. The attractively appointed public rooms offer a wide choice of areas in which to relax, and the hotel also boasts a superb range of leisure facilities including an 18-hole PGA golf course, floodlit tennis courts and a football pitch.

Rooms 169 (16 fmly) (16 GF) (2 smoking) **Facilities** Spa Wi-fi ⏱ ⅃ 18 Putt green Gym Floodlit driving range Xmas New Year **Conf** Class 140 Board 80 Thtr 300 **Services** Lift **Parking** 500 **Notes** Civ Wed 90

The Maids Head Hotel

CLASSIC BRITISH HOTELS

★★★★ 76% ⊛ HOTEL

☎ 0844 855 9120
Tombland NR3 1LB
e-mail: gm@maidsheadhotel.co.uk
web: www.maidsheadhotel.co.uk
dir: In city centre. Telephone or see website for detailed directions

An impressive 13th-century building situated close to the impressive Norman cathedral, the Anglian TV studios and within easy walking distance of the city centre. The bedrooms are pleasantly decorated and thoughtfully equipped; some rooms have original oak beams. The spacious public rooms include a Jacobean bar, a range of seating areas and the Courtyard Restaurant.

Rooms 84 (10 fmly) (10 GF) **S** £69-£149; **D** £69-£149* **Facilities** FTV Wi-fi ⏱ Beauty treatment room Use of nearby gym Xmas New Year **Conf** Class 30 Board 50 Thtr 100 Del from £110 to £159* **Services** Lift **Parking** 83 **Notes** ⊗ Civ Wed 100

Barnham Broom Hotel, Golf & Restaurant

★★★★ 74% ⊛⊛ HOTEL

☎ 01603 759393
NR9 4DD
e-mail: amortimer@barnham-broom.co.uk
web: www.barnham-broom.co.uk

(For full entry see Barnham Broom)

Holiday Inn Norwich - North
Holiday Inn

★★★★ 71% HOTEL

☎ 01603 410544
Cromer Rd NR6 6JA
e-mail: frontoffice@hinorwich.com
web: www.hinorwich.com
dir: A140, follow Cromer signs, right at lights signed 'Airport Passengers'. Hotel on right

A modern, purpose-built hotel situated to the north of Norwich at the airport. Bedrooms are smartly decorated, equipped with modern facilities and have a good range of useful extras. Public areas include a large open-plan lounge bar and restaurant, as well as meeting rooms, a banqueting suite and leisure facilities.

Rooms 121 (8 fmly) (33 GF) (5 smoking) **Facilities** Wi-fi ⏱ Gym ♫ **Conf** Class 200 Board 70 Thtr 600 **Services** Lift Air con **Parking** 200 **Notes** ⊗ Civ Wed 500

Best Western Annesley House Hotel

★★★ 87% ◉◉ HOTEL

☎ 01603 624553
6 Newmarket Rd NR2 2LA
e-mail: annesleyhouse@bestwestern.co.uk
dir: On A11, 0.5m before city centre

Delightful Georgian property set in three acres of landscaped gardens close to the city centre. Bedrooms are split between three separate houses, two of which are linked by a glass walkway. Each is attractively decorated, tastefully furnished and thoughtfully equipped. Public rooms include a comfortable lounge/bar and a smart conservatory restaurant which overlooks the gardens.

Rooms 30 (12 annexe) (1 fmly) (9 GF) ☙ **S** £65-£85; **D** £95-£105 (incl. bkfst)* **Facilities** FTV Wi-fi ☙ **Parking** 28 **Notes** LB ⊗ Closed 24 Dec-2 Jan

Holiday Inn Norwich

★★★ 79% HOTEL

☎ 0871 942 9060 & 0800 405060
Ipswich Rd NR4 6EP
e-mail: reservations-norwich@ihg.com
web: www.holidayinn.co.uk
dir: A47 (Great Yarmouth) then A140 (Norwich). 1m, hotel on right

A modern, purpose-built hotel situated just off the A140 which is a short drive from the city centre. Public areas include a popular bar, the Junction Restaurant and a large open-plan lounge. Bedrooms come in a variety of styles and are suited to the needs of both the business and leisure guest alike.

Rooms 119 (41 fmly) (39 GF) **Facilities** STV FTV Wi-fi ☙ HL ⊠ supervised Gym Sauna Steam room Xmas New Year **Conf** Class 48 Board 40 Thtr 150 Del from £79 to £145 **Services** Air con **Parking** 250 **Notes** ⊗ Civ Wed 120

Best Western George Hotel

★★★ 75% ◉ HOTEL

☎ 01603 617841
10 Arlington Ln, Newmarket Rd NR2 2DA
e-mail: reservations@georgehotel.co.uk
web: www.arlingtonhotelgroup.co.uk
dir: From A11 follow city centre signs, becomes Newmarket Rd. Hotel on left

Within just 10 minutes' walk of the town centre, this friendly, family-run hotel is well placed for guests wishing to explore the many sights of this historic city. The hotel occupies three adjacent buildings; the restaurant, bar and most bedrooms are located in the main building, while the adjacent cottages have been converted into comfortable and modern guest bedrooms.

Rooms 43 (5 annexe) (4 fmly) (19 GF) **S** £65-£75; **D** £85-£100 (incl. bkfst) **Facilities** FTV Wi-fi Beauty therapist Holistic treatments Xmas New Year **Conf** Class 30 Board 30 Thtr 70 Del from £110 to £150 **Parking** 40 **Notes** LB ⊗

Stracey Hotel

★★★ 75% SMALL HOTEL

☎ 01603 628093
2 Stracey Rd NR1 1EZ
e-mail: info@straceyhotel.co.uk
dir: Telephone for detailed directions

Ideally situated for the railway station, and within easy walking distance of the historic city centre, with its range of shops and amenities. The contemporary-style bedrooms are smartly decorated and well equipped. Public rooms include a smart open-plan lounge bar and an outside terrace.

Rooms 20 (2 fmly) (5 GF) ☙ **Facilities** FTV Wi-fi Xmas New Year **Notes** ⊗

The Brook Hotel Norwich

★★★ 71% HOTEL

☎ 01603 741161
2 Barnard Rd, Bowthorpe NR5 9JB
e-mail: welcome@brookhotelnorwich.com
dir: A47 towards Swaffham then A1074. Over double rdbt, to next rdbt, hotel on last exit

A modern, purpose-built hotel situated to the west of the city centre, just off the A47. The open-plan public areas include a lounge bar with TV, a foyer with plush sofas and a large dining room. The spacious bedrooms are equipped for both leisure and business guest alike.

Rooms 81 (13 fmly) (40 GF) **Facilities** FTV Wi-fi Gym Xmas New Year **Conf** Class 90 Board 60 Thtr 200 **Services** Air con **Parking** 100 **Notes** Civ Wed 200

N

NORWICH *continued*

The Old Rectory

★★ ◎◎ SMALL HOTEL

☎ 01603 700772
103 Yarmouth Rd, Thorpe St Andrew NR7 0HF
e-mail: enquiries@oldrectorynorwich.com
web: www.oldrectorynorwich.com
dir: From A47 southern bypass onto A1042 towards
Norwich N & E. Left at mini rdbt onto A1242. After
0.3m through lights. Hotel 100mtrs on right

This delightful Grade II listed Georgian property is
ideally located in a peaceful area overlooking the
River Yare, just a few minutes' drive from the city
centre. Spacious bedrooms are individually
designed with carefully chosen soft fabrics, plush
furniture and many thoughtful touches; many of the
rooms overlook the swimming pool and landscaped
gardens. Accomplished cooking is offered via an
interesting daily-changing menu, which features
skilfully prepared local produce.

Rooms 8 (3 annexe) ♠ **S** £99-£145; **D** £130-£166
(incl. bkfst)* **Facilities** FTV Wi-fi ⓠ ⚲
Conf Class 18 Board 16 Thtr 25 **Parking** 15
Notes LB ⊗ Closed 23 Dec-3 Jan

Stower Grange

★★ 85% ◎ HOTEL

☎ 01603 860210
School Rd, Drayton NR8 6EF
e-mail: enquiries@stowergrange.co.uk
web: www.stowergrange.co.uk
dir: Norwich ring road N to Asda supermarket. Take
A1067 (Fakenham road) at Drayton, right at lights
into School Rd. Hotel 150yds on right

Expect a warm welcome at this 17th-century,
ivy-clad property situated in a peaceful residential
area close to the city centre and airport. The
individually decorated bedrooms are generally quite
spacious; each is tastefully furnished and equipped
with many thoughtful touches. Public rooms include a
smart open-plan lounge bar and an elegant
restaurant.

Rooms 11 (1 fmly) ♠ **S** £80; **D** £100 (incl. bkfst)*
Facilities FTV Wi-fi ⓠ New Year **Conf** Class 45
Board 30 Thtr 100 Del from £125 to £140*
Parking 40 **Notes** Civ Wed 100

Holiday Inn Express Norwich

BUDGET HOTEL

☎ 01603 780010
Drayton High Rd, Hellesdon NR6 5DU
e-mail: gm@exhinorwich.co.uk
web: www.hiexpress.com/norwich
dir: At junct of A140 (ring road) & A1067 to
Fakenham, follow brown tourist signs

A modern hotel ideal for families and business
travellers. Fresh and uncomplicated, the spacious
rooms include Sky TV, power shower and tea and
coffee-making facilities. Continental buffet breakfast
is included in the room rate; other meals may be
taken at the nearby family pub or restaurant. See also
the Hotel Groups pages.

Rooms 78 (45 fmly) (14 GF) (14 smoking)
Conf Class 12 Board 12 Thtr 12

Premier Inn Norwich Airport

BUDGET HOTEL

☎ 0871 527 8836
Delft Way NR6 6BB
web: www.premierinn.com
dir: From Norwich take A140 signed Cromer & Airport.
Right at lights into Amsterdam Way. At mini-rdbt turn
right. Hotel on right

High quality, budget accommodation ideal for both
families and business travellers. Spacious, en suite
bedrooms feature tea and coffee making facilities,
and Freeview TV in most hotels. Internet access and
Wi-fi are available for a small fee. The adjacent
family restaurant features a wide and varied menu.
See also the Hotel Groups pages.

Rooms 40

Premier Inn Norwich Central South

BUDGET HOTEL

☎ 0871 527 8838
**Broadlands Business Park, Old Chapel Way
NR7 0WG**
web: www.premierinn.com
dir: A47 onto A1042, 3m E of city centre

Rooms 92

Premier Inn Norwich City Centre (Duke Street)

BUDGET HOTEL

☎ 0871 527 8840
Duke St NR3 3AP
web: www.premierinn.com
dir: From A1074, straight on at lights (Toys'R'Us) into
St Benedict's St (or from A147 (A140, A11) right at
lights. At next lights into Duke St (car park in St
Andrews multi-storey on right - free to guests)

Rooms 117

Premier Inn Norwich Nelson City Centre

BUDGET HOTEL

☎ 0871 527 8842
Prince of Wales Rd NR1 1DX
web: www.premierinn.com
dir: Follow city centre, football ground & railway
station signs. Hotel opposite station

Rooms 160

Save on hotels. Book at theAA.com/hotel

NOR – NOT 357 ENGLAND

Premier Inn Norwich (Showground A47)

BUDGET HOTEL

☎ 0871 527 8834

Longwater Interchange, Dereham Rd, New Costessey NR5 0TP
web: www.premierinn.com
dir: A47 towards Dereham, take A1074 to City Centre. At rdbt 2nd exit, hotel on right. From N: A47 through Dereham. Straight on at 1st rdbt, at 2nd rdbt take 3rd exit. Hotel on left

Rooms 40

Brasteds

◉ ◉ RESTAURANT WITH ROOMS

☎ 01508 491112

Manor Farm Barns, Framingham Pigot NR14 7PZ
e-mail: enquiries@brasteds.co.uk
web: www.brasteds.co.uk
dir: A11 onto A47 towards Great Yarmouth, then A146. 0.5m, right into Fox Rd, 0.5m on left

Brasteds is a lovely detached property set in 20 acres of mature, landscaped parkland on the outskirts of Norwich. The tastefully appointed bedrooms have beautiful soft furnishings and fabrics along with comfortable seating and many thoughtful touches. Public rooms include a cosy snug with plush sofas, and a smart dining room where breakfast is served. Dinner is available in Brasteds Restaurant, which can be found in an adjacent building.

Rooms 6 (1 fmly)

NOTTINGHAM   Map 11 SK53
Nottinghamshire

See also Langar

Hart's Hotel

★★★★ 82% ◉ ◉ HOTEL

☎ 0115 988 1900

Standard Hill, Park Row NG1 6FN
e-mail: reception@hartsnottingham.co.uk
web: www.hartsnottingham.co.uk
dir: At junct of Park Row & Ropewalk

This outstanding modern building stands on the site of the ramparts of the medieval castle, overlooking the city. Many of the bedrooms enjoy splendid views; all are well appointed and stylish. The Park Bar is the focal point of the public areas. Service is professional and caring and fine dining is offered at nearby Hart's Restaurant. Secure parking and private gardens are an added bonus.

Rooms 32 (1 fmly) (7 GF) ⊁ **D** £125-£265* **Facilities** STV FTV Wi-fi ↘ Small unsupervised exercise room Xmas New Year **Conf** Class 75 Board 30 Thtr 100 Del from £190* **Services** Lift **Parking** 16 **Notes** Civ Wed 100

The Nottingham Belfry

QHOTELS

★★★★ 79% HOTEL

☎ 0115 973 9393

Mellor's Way, Off Woodhouse Way NG8 6PY
e-mail: nottinghambelfry@qhotels.co.uk
web: www.qhotels.co.uk
dir: A610 towards Nottingham. A6002 to Stapleford/ Strelley. 0.75m, last exit at rdbt, hotel on right

Set conveniently close to the motorway links, yet not far from the city centre attractions, this modern hotel has a stylish and impressive interior. Bedrooms and bathrooms are spaciously appointed and very comfortable. There are two restaurants and two bars that offer interesting and satisfying cuisine. Staff are friendly and helpful.

Rooms 120 (20 fmly) (36 GF) ⊁ **Facilities** Spa STV FTV Wi-fi ↘ ☜ Gym Sauna Steam room Aerobic studio Xmas New Year **Conf** Class 360 Board 60 Thtr 700 **Services** Lift **Parking** 250 **Notes** Civ Wed 150

Park Plaza Nottingham

Park Plaza
Hotels & Resorts

★★★★ 73% HOTEL

☎ 0115 947 7200

41 Maid Marian Way NG1 6GD
e-mail: ppnsales@pphe.com
web: www.parkplaza.com/nottinghamuk
dir: A6200 (Derby Rd) into Wollaton St. 2nd exit into Maid Marian Way. Hotel on left

This ultra modern hotel is located in the centre of the city within walking distance of retail, commercial and tourist attractions. Bedrooms are spacious and comfortable, with many extras, including laptop safes, high-speed phone lines and air conditioning. Service is discreetly attentive in the foyer lounge and the Chino Latino restaurant, where Pan Asian cooking is a feature.

Rooms 178 (10 fmly) (16 smoking) **Facilities** STV FTV Wi-fi Gym Complimentary fitness suite **Conf** Class 100 Board 54 Thtr 200 **Services** Lift Air con **Notes** ⊗

Days Hotel

★★★ 74% HOTEL

☎ 0115 912 8000

19-21 Wollaton St NG1 5FW
e-mail: reception@dayshotelnottingham.co.uk
dir: M1 junct 25, A52 to Nottingham city centre, then follow signs to Royal Centre. Hotel on right in Wollaton St

This city centre hotel offers comfortable accommodation along with a good range of food and drinks in the conservatory restaurant. Conferencing is a strength, with a range of quality meeting rooms and an impressive 100-seater tiered lecture theatre. Bedrooms are spacious and light with an excellent range of facilities including air conditioning and free broadband access. There is limited on-site parking, but there is ample directly opposite.

Rooms 90 (27 fmly) **Facilities** STV FTV Wi-fi ↘ **Conf** Class 30 Board 30 Thtr 100 **Services** Lift Air con **Parking** 12 **Notes** ⊗

N

NOTTINGHAM *continued*

Park Inn by Radisson Nottingham

★★★ 72% HOTEL

☎ 0115 935 9988
Mansfield Rd NG5 2BT
e-mail: reservations.nottingham@rezidorparkinn.com
dir: Approx 1m from city centre on A60 (Mansfield Rd), at large rdbt, straight on at lights. Hotel on right

Ideally located to explore the city centre, the hotel is a spacious, purpose-built property offering a range of well-appointed bedrooms, conference rooms and a fully-equipped leisure club. The popular restaurant offers a contemporary dining experience in an airy environment.

Rooms 172 (8 fmly) **S** £45-£130; **D** £55-£140*
Facilities STV FTV Wi-fi ⊗ supervised Gym Beauty treatment room Sauna Steam room Spa bath New Year **Conf** Class 45 Board 40 Thtr 180 Del from £99 to £160 **Services** Lift Air con **Parking** 410 **Notes** LB ⊗ Civ Wed 200

Best Western Bestwood Lodge

★★★ 71% HOTEL

☎ 0115 920 3011
Bestwood Country Park, Arnold NG5 8NE
e-mail: enquiries@bestwoodlodgehotel.co.uk
web: www.bw-bestwoodlodge.co.uk
dir: From Nottingham take A60, left at lights into Oxclose Ln, right at next lights into Queens Bower Rd. 1st right. Keep right at fork in road

Set in 700 acres of parkland this Victorian building, once a hunting lodge, has stunning architecture that includes Gothic features and high vaulted ceilings. Bedrooms include all the modern comforts, suitable for both business and leisure guests, and the popular restaurant serves an extensive menu.

Best Western Bestwood Lodge

Rooms 39 (5 fmly) **Facilities** FTV Wi-fi ⊜ Guided walks Xmas **Conf** Class 65 Board 50 Thtr 200 **Parking** 120 **Notes** RS 25 Dec & 1 Jan Civ Wed 80

See advert on opposite page

The Strathdon

PEEL HOTELS PLC

★★ 69% HOTEL

☎ 0115 941 8501
Derby Rd NG1 5FT
e-mail: info@strathdon-hotel-nottingham.com
web: www.strathdon-hotel-nottingham.com
dir: From M1 follow city centre signs. At Canning Circus into one-way system into Wollaton St, keep right, next right to hotel

This city-centre hotel has modern facilities and is very convenient for all city attractions. A popular themed bar has a large-screen TV and serves an extensive range of popular fresh food, while more formal dining is available in Bobbins Restaurant on certain evenings.

Rooms 68 (4 fmly) (16 smoking) **Facilities** FTV Wi-fi ⌕ Xmas New Year **Conf** Class 60 Board 40 Thtr 150 **Services** Lift **Notes** Civ Wed 85

Ibis Nottingham Centre

ibis

BUDGET HOTEL

☎ 0115 985 3600
16 Fletcher Gate NG1 2FS
e-mail: h6160@accor.com
dir: In Lace Market area of city centre

Modern, budget hotel offering comfortable accommodation in bright and practical bedrooms. Breakfast is self-service and dinner is available in the restaurant. See also the Hotel Groups pages.

Rooms 142 (33 fmly) ✆ **S** £29-£129; **D** £29-£129*

Premier Inn Nottingham Arena (London Rd)

Premier Inn

BUDGET HOTEL

☎ 0871 527 8848
Island Site, London Rd NG2 4UU
web: www.premierinn.com
dir: M1 junct 25, A52 into city centre. Follow signs for A60 to Loughborough. Hotel adjacent to BBC building

High quality, budget accommodation ideal for both families and business travellers. Spacious, en suite bedrooms feature tea and coffee making facilities, and Freeview TV in most hotels. Internet access and Wi-fi are available for a small fee. The adjacent family restaurant features a wide and varied menu. See also the Hotel Groups pages.

Rooms 87

Premier Inn Nottingham Castle Marina

BUDGET HOTEL

☎ 0871 527 8844
Castle Marina Park, Castle Bridge Rd NG7 1GX
web: www.premierinn.com
dir: M1 junct 24, A453. Follow ring road & signs for Queen's Drive Industrial Estate. After Homebase left into Castle Bridge Rd, opposite Pizza Hut restaurant. Hotel adjacent to Boathouse Beefeater

Rooms 39

Premier Inn Nottingham City Centre (Goldsmith Street)

BUDGET HOTEL

☎ 0871 527 8846
Goldsmith St NG1 5LT
web: www.premierinn.com
dir: A610 to city centre. Follow signs for Nottingham Trent University into Talbot St. 1st left into Clarendon St. Right at lights. Hotel on right

Rooms 161

Premier Inn Nottingham North (Daybrook)

BUDGET HOTEL

☎ 0871 527 8850
101 Mansfield Rd, Daybrook NG5 6BH
web: www.premierinn.com
dir: M1 junct 26, A610 towards Nottingham. Left onto A6514. Left onto A60 towards Mansfield. Hotel 0.25m on left

Rooms 64

Save on hotels. Book at **theAA.com/hotel**

NOT – NUN 359 ENGLAND

Premier Inn Nottingham South

BUDGET HOTEL

☎ 0871 527 8854
Loughborough Rd, Ruddington NG11 6LS
web: www.premierinn.com
dir: M1 junct 24, follow A453 signs to Nottingham,
A52 to Grantham. Hotel at 1st rdbt on left

Rooms 42

Premier Inn Nottingham West

BUDGET HOTEL

☎ 0871 527 8856
The Phoenix Centre, Millennium Way West NG8 6AS
web: www.premierinn.com
dir: M1 junct 26, 1m on A610 towards Nottingham

Rooms 86

Restaurant Sat Bains with Rooms

@ @ @ @   RESTAURANT WITH ROOMS

☎ 0115 986 6566
Trentside, Lenton Ln NG7 2SA
e-mail: info@restaurantsatbains.net
dir: M1 junct 24, A453 Nottingham S. Over River
Trent into central lane to rdbt. Left, left again
towards river. Establishment on left after bend

This charming restaurant with rooms, a stylish
conversion of Victorian farm buildings, is situated
on the river and close to the industrial area of
Nottingham. The bedrooms create a warm
atmosphere by using quality soft furnishings
together with antique and period furniture; suites
and four-poster rooms are available. Public areas
are chic and cosy, and the delightful restaurant
complements the truly outstanding, much
acclaimed cuisine.

Rooms 8 (4 annexe)

Cockliffe Country House

@   RESTAURANT WITH ROOMS

☎ 0115 968 0179
Burntstump Country Park, Burntstump Hill, Arnold NG5 8PQ
e-mail: enquiries@cockliffehouse.co.uk

Expect a warm welcome at this delightful property
situated in a peaceful rural location amidst neat

landscaped grounds, close to Sherwood Forest. Public
areas include a smart breakfast room, a tastefully
appointed restaurant and a cosy lounge bar. The
individually decorated bedrooms have
co-ordinated soft furnishings and many thoughtful
touches.

Rooms 11 (4 annexe)

Best Western Weston Hall Hotel

★★★ 73% HOTEL

☎ 024 7631 2989
Weston Ln, Bulkington CV12 9RU
e-mail: info@westonhallhotel.co.uk
dir: M6 junct 2, B4065 through Ansty. Left in Shilton,
from Bulkington follow Nuneaton signs, into Weston
Ln at 30mph sign

This Grade II listed hotel, with origins dating back to
the reign of Elizabeth I, sits within seven acres of
peaceful grounds. The original three-gabled building
retains many original features, such as the carved
wooden fireplace in the library. Friendly service is
provided; and the bedrooms, that vary in size, are
thoughtfully equipped.

Rooms 40 (1 fmly) (14 GF) **Facilities** FTV Wi-fi ⌂
New Year **Conf** Class 100 Board 60 Thtr 200
Parking 300 **Notes** Civ Wed 200

N

NUNEATON continued

Premier Inn Nuneaton/Coventry

BUDGET HOTEL

☎ 0871 527 8858
Coventry Rd CV10 7PJ
web: www.premierinn.com
dir: M6 junct 3, A444 towards Nuneaton. Hotel on B4113 on right, just off Griff Rdbt towards Bedworth

High quality, budget accommodation ideal for both families and business travellers. Spacious, en suite bedrooms feature tea and coffee making facilities, and Freeview TV in most hotels. Internet access and Wi-fi are available for a small fee. The adjacent family restaurant features a wide and varied menu. See also the Hotel Groups pages.

Rooms 48

| OAKHAM | Map 11 SK80 |
Rutland

INSPECTORS' CHOICE

Hambleton Hall

★★★★ ◉◉◉◉
COUNTRY HOUSE HOTEL

☎ 01572 756991
Hambleton LE15 8TH
e-mail: hotel@hambletonhall.com
web: www.hambletonhall.com
dir: 3m E off A606

Established 30 years ago by Tim and Stefa Hart this delightful country house enjoys tranquil and spectacular views over Rutland Water. The beautifully manicured grounds are a delight to walk in. The bedrooms in the main house are stylish, individually decorated and equipped with a range of thoughtful extras. A two-bedroom folly, with its own sitting and breakfast room, is only a short walk away. Day rooms include a cosy bar and a sumptuous drawing room, both featuring open fires. The elegant restaurant serves very accomplished,

award-winning cuisine with menus highlighting locally sourced, seasonal produce - some grown in the hotel's own grounds.

Rooms 17 (2 annexe) ☞ **S** £195-£215; **D** £250-£400 (incl. bkfst) **Facilities** STV FTV Wi-fi ☚ ⚲ ⚒ ⚑ Private access to lake Xmas New Year **Conf** Board 24 Thtr 40 Del from £300 to £330 **Services** Lift **Parking** 40 **Notes** LB Civ Wed 64

Barnsdale Lodge Hotel

★★★ 77% ◉ HOTEL

☎ 01572 724678
The Avenue, Rutland Water, North Shore LE15 8AH
e-mail: enquiries@barnsdalelodge.co.uk
web: www.barnsdalelodge.co.uk
dir: A1 onto A606. Hotel 5m on right, 2m E of Oakham

A popular and interesting hotel converted from a farmstead overlooking Rutland Water. The public areas are dominated by a successful food operation with a good range of appealing meals on offer for either formal or informal dining. Bedrooms are comfortably appointed with excellent beds enhanced by contemporary soft furnishings and thoughtful extras.

Rooms 44 (2 fmly) (15 GF) **Facilities** FTV Wi-fi ☚ Fishing ⚒ Archery Beauty treatment room Golf Sailing Shooting Xmas New Year **Conf** Class 120 Board 76 Thtr 330 **Parking** 200 **Notes** Civ Wed 160

| OCKLEY | Map 6 TQ14 |
Surrey

Gatton Manor Hotel & Golf Club

★★★ 80% HOTEL

☎ 01306 627555
Standon Ln RH5 5PQ
e-mail: info@gattonmanor.co.uk
web: www.gattonmanor.co.uk
dir: Exit A29 at Ockley into Cat Hill Ln, left into Standon Ln, follow signs for approx 1m

Gatton Manor enjoys a peaceful setting in private grounds. It is a popular golf and country club, with an

18-hole professional course, that offers a range of comfortable, modern bedrooms. The public areas include the main club bar and restaurant. Conference facilities are also available.

Rooms 18 (2 fmly) ☞ **Facilities** FTV Wi-fi ⚲ 18 Putt green Gym Beauty treatments New Year **Conf** Class 22 Board 30 Thtr 80 Del from £135 to £150* **Parking** 250 **Notes** ⊗ Closed 25 Dec Civ Wed 90

| OKEHAMPTON | Map 3 SX59 |
Devon

Ashbury Hotel

★★ 74% HOTEL

☎ 01837 55453
Higher Maddaford, Southcott EX20 4NL
dir: Exit A30 at Sourton Cross onto A386. Left onto A3079 to Bude at Fowley Cross. After 1m right to Ashbury. Hotel 0.5m on right

With no less than five courses and a clubhouse with lounge, bar and dining facilities, The Ashbury is a golfers' paradise. The majority of the well-equipped bedrooms are located in the farmhouse and the courtyard-style development around the putting green. Guests can enjoy the many on-site leisure facilities or join the activities available at the nearby sister hotel.

Rooms 186 (79 fmly) (77 GF) ☞ **Facilities** Spa FTV Wi-fi ⚲ ⚒ 99 ⚲ Putt green Fishing Gym Badminton Shooting ranges Ten-pin bowling Indoor bowls 5-a-side New Year **Conf** Thtr 250 Del from £60 to £100* **Parking** 200 **Notes** ⊗

See advert on opposite page

Manor House Hotel

★★ 72% HOTEL

☎ 01837 53053
Fowley Cross EX20 4NA
e-mail: reception@manorhousehotel.co.uk
web: www.manorhousehotel.co.uk
dir: Exit A30 at Sourton Cross flyover, right onto A386. Hotel 1.5m on right

Enjoying views to Dartmoor in the distance, this hotel specialises in short breaks and is set in 17 acres of

Save on hotels. Book at **theAA.com/hotel**

NUN – OLD 361 ENGLAND

grounds, close to the A30. The superb range of sporting and craft facilities has been enhanced by an impressive swimming pool; golf is also offered at the adjacent sister hotel. Bedrooms, many located on the ground floor, are comfortable and well equipped.

Manor House Hotel

Rooms 200 (91 fmly) (90 GF) ✿ **Facilities** Spa FTV Wi-fi ⊙ ⅃ 99 ♨ Putt green Fishing ⏩ Gym Squash Craft centre Indoor bowls Shooting ranges Indoor tennis Exercise classes Xmas New Year **Parking** 200 **Notes** ⊗

See advert on this page

White Hart Hotel

★★ 72% HOTEL

☎ 01837 52730 & 54514
Fore St EX20 1HD
e-mail: enquiry@thewhitehart-hotel.com
web: www.thewhitehart-hotel.com
dir: In town centre, adjacent to lights, car park at rear of hotel

Dating back to the 17th century and situated on the edge of the Dartmoor National Park, the White Hart offers modern facilities. Bedrooms are well equipped and spacious. Locally sourced, home-cooked food is on offer in the bars and the Courtney Restaurant; or guests can choose to eat in Vines Pizzeria. Wi-fi is available in public areas.

Rooms 19 (2 fmly) **Facilities** FTV Wi-fi ⟳ Xmas **Conf** Class 30 Board 40 Thtr 100 **Parking** 20

Holiday Inn Express Birmingham Oldbury M5

BUDGET HOTEL

☎ 0121 511 0000
Birchley Park B69 2BD
e-mail: oldbury@expressholidayinn.co.uk
web: www.hiexpress.com/bhx-oldbury
dir: M5 junct 2, behind Total Garage on Wolverhampton Rd

A modern hotel ideal for families and business travellers. Fresh and uncomplicated, the spacious rooms include Sky TV, power shower and tea and coffee-making facilities. Continental buffet breakfast is included in the room rate; other meals may be taken at the nearby family pub or restaurant. See also the Hotel Groups pages.

Rooms 109 (55 fmly) (16 GF) **Conf** Class 20 Board 25 Thtr 30

O

OLDBURY *continued*

Premier Inn Birmingham Oldbury M5 Jct 2

BUDGET HOTEL

☎ 0871 527 8090
Wolverhampton Rd B69 2BH
web: www.premierinn.com
dir: M5 junct 2, A4123 (Wolverhampton Rd) N towards Dudley

High quality, budget accommodation ideal for both families and business travellers. Spacious, en suite bedrooms feature tea and coffee making facilities, and Freeview TV in most hotels. Internet access and Wi-fi are available for a small fee. The adjacent family restaurant features a wide and varied menu. See also the Hotel Groups pages.

Rooms 60

OLDHAM	**Map 16 SD90**
Greater Manchester	

Best Western Hotel Smokies Park

★★★ 80% HOTEL

☎ 0161 785 5000
Ashton Rd, Bardsley OL8 3HX
e-mail: sales@smokies.co.uk
web: www.smokies.co.uk
dir: On A627 between Oldham & Ashton-under-Lyne

This modern, stylish hotel offers smart, comfortable bedrooms and suites. A wide range of Italian and English dishes is offered in the Mediterranean-style restaurant and there is a welcoming lounge bar with live entertainment at weekends. There is a small yet well equipped, residents-only fitness centre and extensive function facilities are also available.

Rooms 73 (2 fmly) (22 GF) **Facilities** FTV Wi-fi ⓑ Xmas New Year **Conf** Class 100 Board 40 Thtr 400 **Services** Lift **Parking** 120 **Notes** ⊗ RS 25 Dec-3 Jan Civ Wed 400

Premier Inn Oldham (Broadway)

BUDGET HOTEL

☎ 0871 527 8860
Broadway/Hollinwood Av, Chadderton OL9 8DW
web: www.premierinn.com
dir: M60 (anti-clockwise) junct 21, signed Manchester city centre. Take A663, hotel 400yds on left

High quality, budget accommodation ideal for both families and business travellers. Spacious, en suite bedrooms feature tea and coffee making facilities, and Freeview TV in most hotels. Internet access and Wi-fi are available for a small fee. The adjacent family restaurant features a wide and varied menu. See also the Hotel Groups pages.

Rooms 40

Premier Inn Oldham Central

BUDGET HOTEL

☎ 0871 527 8862
Westwood Park, Chadderton Way, Chadderton OL1 2NA
web: www.premierinn.com
dir: M62 junct 20, A627(M) to Oldham. Take A627 (Chadderton Way). Hotel on left opposite B&Q Depot

Rooms 40

OLD HARLOW	**Map 6 TL41**
Essex	

Premier Inn Harlow

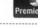

BUDGET HOTEL

☎ 0871 527 8488
Cambridge Rd CM20 2EP
web: www.premierinn.com
dir: M11 junct 7, A414, A1184 (Sawbridgeworth to Bishop's Stortford road)

High quality, budget accommodation ideal for both families and business travellers. Spacious, en suite bedrooms feature tea and coffee making facilities, and Freeview TV in most hotels. Internet access and Wi-fi are available for a small fee. The adjacent family restaurant features a wide and varied menu. See also the Hotel Groups pages.

Rooms 61

OLDSTEAD	**Map 19 SE57**
North Yorkshire	

INSPECTORS' CHOICE

The Black Swan at Oldstead

◉◉◉ RESTAURANT WITH ROOMS

☎ 01347 868387
YO61 4BL
e-mail: enquiries@blackswanoldstead.co.uk
dir: Exit A19, 3m S Thirsk for Coxwold, left in Coxwold, left at Byland Abbey for Oldstead

The Black Swan is set amidst the stunning scenery of the North Yorkshire National Park, and parts of the building date back to the 16th century. Well appointed, very comfortable bedrooms and bathrooms provide the perfect get-away-from-it-all. Open fires, a traditional bar and a restaurant, serving award-winning food, is the icing on the cake for this little gem of a property.

Rooms 4

OLLERTON	**Map 16 SK66**
Nottinghamshire	

Thoresby Hall Hotel

Warner Leisure Hotels
JUST FOR GROWN-UPS

★★★★ 81% ◉◉ COUNTRY HOUSE HOTEL

☎ 01623 821000 & 821033
Thoresby Park NG22 9WH
e-mail: reception.thoresbyhall@bourne-leisure.co.uk

This hotel is set in acres of rolling parklands on the edge of Sherwood Forest. Thoresby Hall is a magnificent Grade I Victorian country house. Guests can choose to relax in the spa, stroll around the beautiful gardens or just sit and relax in the Great Hall. Bedrooms vary in style and size. This is an adults only (over 21 years) hotel.

Rooms 221 (168 annexe) (72 GF) **Facilities** Spa Wi-fi HL ⓑ supervised ⏟ Putt green Fishing ⏟ Gym Rifle shooting Archery Outdoor bowls Fencing Laser clay Yoga Tai chi ♫ Xmas New Year **Conf** Class 200 Board 30 Thtr 400 **Services** Lift **Parking** 140 **Notes** ⊗ No children 21yrs Civ Wed 92

Save on hotels. Book at **theAA.com/hotel**

OLD – OSW 363 ENGLAND

ORFORD
Suffolk

Map 13 TM45

The Crown & Castle

★★★ 87% ◉◉ HOTEL

☎ 01394 450205
IP12 2LJ
e-mail: info@crownandcastle.co.uk
web: www.crownandcastle.co.uk
dir: Turn right from B1084 on entering village, towards castle

A delightful inn situated adjacent to the Norman castle keep. Contemporary style bedrooms are spilt between the main house and the garden wing; the latter are more spacious and have patios with access to the garden. The restaurant has an informal atmosphere with polished tables and local artwork; the menu features quality, locally sourced produce.

Rooms 19 (12 annexe) (2 fmly) (13 GF) 🐾
D £130-£190 (incl. bkfst)* **Facilities** FTV Wi-fi ♨ HL
Xmas New Year **Parking** 20 **Notes** LB No children 8yrs

ORMSKIRK
Lancashire

Map 15 SD40

Premier Inn Southport (Ormskirk)

BUDGET HOTEL

☎ 0871 527 9010
544 Southport Rd, Scarisbrick L40 9RG
web: www.premierinn.com
dir: From Southport follow Ormskirk/A570 signs. Hotel on right of A570 (Southport Rd) at 1st lights (entrance just after lights)

High quality, budget accommodation ideal for both families and business travellers. Spacious, en suite bedrooms feature tea and coffee making facilities, and Freeview TV in most hotels. Internet access and Wi-fi are available for a small fee. The adjacent family restaurant features a wide and varied menu. See also the Hotel Groups pages.

Rooms 20

ORSETT
Essex

Map 6 TQ68

Orsett Hall Banqueting & Conference Centre

★★★★ 77% ◉◉ COUNTRY HOUSE HOTEL

☎ 01375 89402
Prince Charles Av RM16 3HS

This beautiful country house hotel, conveniently located for the M25, is set in 12 acres of landscaped gardens, and has individually designed, luxurious bedrooms. The award-winning Garden Restaurant is a fabulous dining venue and the stylish modern bar is popular with guests for afternoon tea. Orsett Hall has a first rate spa, a very well equipped gym along with a range of business suites, and free Wi-fi is available throughout.

Rooms 36 **S** £119-£159; **D** £139-£199*

OSWESTRY
Shropshire

Map 15 SJ22

Wynnstay Hotel

★★★★ 77% ◉◉ HOTEL

☎ 01691 655261
Church St SY11 2SZ
e-mail: info@wynnstayhotel.com
web: www.wynnstayhotel.com
dir: B4083 to town, fork left at Honda Garage, right at lights. Hotel opposite church

This Georgian property was once a coaching inn and posting house and surrounds a unique 200-year-old Crown Bowling Green. Elegant public areas include a health, leisure and beauty centre, which is housed in a former coach house. Well-equipped bedrooms are individually styled and include several suites, four-poster rooms and a self-catering apartment. The Four

Seasons Restaurant has a well deserved reputation for its food, and the adjacent Wilsons café/bar is a stylish, informal alternative.

Rooms 34 (5 fmly) 🐾 **S** £50-£70; **D** £70-£120*
Facilities Spa FTV Wi-fi ♨ supervised Gym Crown bowling green Beauty suite ♫ New Year
Conf Class 150 Board 50 Thtr 290 **Parking** 80
Notes LB ⊗ Civ Wed 90

Lion Quays Waterside Resort

★★★★ 77% HOTEL

☎ 01691 684300
Moreton, Weston Rhyn SY11 3EN
e-mail: reservations@lionquays.com
dir: On A5, 3m N of Oswestry

This resort is situated beside the Llangollen Canal which is in a convenient location for visiting Chester to the north and the Snowdonia region to the west. The comfortable bedrooms have views over the countryside or the magnificent grounds and gardens. Guests can dine either in the Waterside Bar or the Country Club which has a stunning 25-metre swimming pool, a state-of-the-art gym plus spa facilities. Extensive conference and meeting facilities are also available.

Rooms 82 (3 fmly) (25 GF) 🐾 **Facilities** Spa FTV Wi-fi ♨ supervised ♨ Gym Sauna Steam room Xmas New Year **Conf** Class 200 Board 150 Thtr 600 **Services** Lift **Parking** 250 **Notes** ⊗ Civ Wed 600

Pen-y-Dyffryn Country Hotel

WELSH RAREBITS
Hotels of Distinction

★★★ 83% ◉◉
COUNTRY HOUSE HOTEL

☎ 01691 653700
Rhydycroesau SY10 7JD
e-mail: stay@peny.co.uk
web: www.peny.co.uk
dir: A5 into town centre. Follow signs to Llansilin on B4580, hotel 3m W of Oswestry before Rhydycroesau

Peacefully situated in five acres of grounds, this charming old house dates back to around 1840, when it was built as a rectory. The tastefully appointed public rooms have real fires, lit in colder weather, and the accommodation includes several mini-cottages, each with its own patio. Many guests are attracted to this hotel for the excellent food and attentive, friendly service.

Rooms 12 (4 annexe) (1 fmly) (1 GF) 🐾 **S** £75-£92;
D £120-£180 (incl. bkfst) **Facilities** STV FTV Wi-fi ♨
Guided walks **Parking** 18 **Notes** LB No children 3yrs
Closed 18 Dec-19 Jan

O

OSWESTRY continued

Premier Inn Oswestry

BUDGET HOTEL

☎ 0871 527 8864
SY10 8NN
web: www.premierinn.com
dir: From rdbt junct of A483 & A5 (SE of Oswestry)
take A5 signed Oswestry B4579. Hotel 500yds

High quality, budget accommodation ideal for both
families and business travellers. Spacious, en suite
bedrooms feature tea and coffee making facilities,
and Freeview TV in most hotels. Internet access and
Wi-fi are available for a small fee. The adjacent
family restaurant features a wide and varied menu.
See also the Hotel Groups pages.

Rooms 59

OTLEY	Map 19 SE24
West Yorkshire	

Chevin Country Park Hotel & Spa

★★★ 75% ◎ HOTEL

☎ 01943 467818
Yorkgate LS21 3NU
e-mail: chevin@crerarhotels.com
dir: From Leeds/Bradford Airport rdbt take A658 N
towards Harrogate, 0.75m to lights. Left, 2nd left into
Yorkgate. Hotel 0.5m on left

Peacefully located in its own woodland yet convenient
for major road links and the airport. Bedrooms are
split between the original main log building and
chalet-style accommodation in the extensive grounds.
Public areas include a bar and several lounges. The
Lakeside Restaurant provides views over the small
lake and good leisure facilities are available.

Rooms 49 (30 annexe) (7 fmly) (45 GF) **Facilities** Spa
FTV Wi-fi ⓢ ♨ Fishing Gym Steam room Xmas New
Year **Conf** Class 90 Board 50 Thtr 120 **Parking** 100
Notes Civ Wed 100

OTTERSHAW	Map 6 TQ06
Surrey	

Foxhills Club and Resort

★★★★ 80% HOTEL

☎ 01932 872050 & 704500
Stonehill Rd KT16 0EL
e-mail: reservations@foxhills.co.uk
web: www.foxhills.co.uk
dir: M25 junct 11, A320 to Woking. 2nd rdbt last exit
into Chobham Rd. Right into Foxhills Rd, left into
Stonehill Rd

This 19th-century mansion hotel enjoys a peaceful
setting in extensive grounds, not far from the M25

and Heathrow. Spacious well-appointed bedrooms are
provided in a choice of annexes situated a short walk
from the main house. Golf, tennis, three pools and
impressive indoor leisure facilities are available.
There is a superb spa offering a range of treatments
and therapies plus a health club with all the latest
fitness equipment. The eating options are the Manor
Restaurant, in the former music room, and the
Summerhouse Brasserie.

Rooms 70 (8 fmly) (39 GF) ⓢ **S** £100-£300;
D £100-£300 **Facilities** Spa STV FTV Wi-fi ⓢ ♨ ♿ 45
♨ Putt green ♨ Gym Squash Children's adventure
playground Country pursuits Off-road course
Hairdresser ♫ Xmas New Year **Conf** Class 52
Board 56 Thtr 100 Del from £200 to £290
Services Lift **Parking** 500 **Notes** LB ⊗ Civ Wed 75

OTTERY ST MARY	Map 3 SY19
Devon	

Tumbling Weir Hotel

★★ 78% SMALL HOTEL

☎ 01404 812752
Canaan Way EX11 1AQ
e-mail: reception@tumblingweirhotel.com
web: www.tumblingweirhotel.co.uk
dir: A30 onto B3177 into Ottery St Mary, hotel signed
from Mill St, access through old mill

Quietly located between the River Otter and its
millstream and set in well-tended gardens, this
family-run hotel offers friendly and attentive service.
Bedrooms are attractively presented and equipped
with modern comforts. In the dining room, where a
selection of carefully prepared dishes makes up the
carte menu, beams and subtle lighting help to create
an intimate atmosphere.

Rooms 10 (1 fmly) ⓢ **S** £55-£65; **D** £95-£110 (incl.
bkfst)* **Facilities** FTV Wi-fi ♨ ♨ **Conf** Class 60
Board 50 Thtr 90 Del from £90 to £100* **Parking** 10
Notes LB ⊗ Closed 22 Dec-7 Jan Civ Wed 80

OXFORD	Map 5 SP50
Oxfordshire	

Macdonald Randolph Hotel

★★★★★ 82% ◎◎ HOTEL

☎ 01865 256400
Beaumont St OX1 2LN
e-mail: randolph@macdonald-hotels.co.uk
web: www.macdonaldhotels.co.uk
dir: M40 junct 8, A40 signed Oxford/Cheltenham, 5m,
at lights to ring road rdbt. Right signed Kidlington/
North Oxford. At next rdbt left towards city centre
(A4165/ Banbury Rd). Through Summertown to lights
at end of St Giles. Hotel on right

Superbly located near the city centre, The Randolph
boasts impressive neo-Gothic architecture and
tasteful decor. The spacious and traditional
restaurant, complete with picture windows, is the
ideal place to watch the world go by while enjoying
freshly prepared, modern dishes. Bedrooms include a
mix of classical and contemporary wing rooms, which
have been appointed to a high standard. Parking is a
real bonus.

Rooms 151 **Facilities** Spa STV Wi-fi Gym Beauty
treatment rooms Thermal suite Mini gym ♫ Xmas
New Year **Conf** Class 130 Board 60 Thtr 300
Services Lift **Parking** 60 **Notes** Civ Wed 120

The Old Bank Hotel

★★★★ 77% TOWN HOUSE HOTEL

☎ 01865 799599
92-94 High St OX1 4BN
e-mail: reception@oldbank-hotel.co.uk
web: www.oldbank-hotel.co.uk
dir: From Magdalen Bridge onto High St, hotel 50yds
on left

Located close to the city centre and the colleges, this
former bank benefits from an excellent location. An
eclectic collection of modern pictures and
photographs, many by well-known artists, are on
display. Bedrooms are smart with excellent business
facilities plus the benefit of air conditioning. Public
areas include the vibrant all-day Quod Bar and
Restaurant. The hotel has its own car park - a definite
advantage in this busy city.

Rooms 42 (4 fmly) (1 GF) ⓢ **S** fr £134; **D** fr £134*
Facilities STV FTV Wi-fi ♨ Beauty treatment room
Bicycles Free use of nearby gym Walking tours ♫
Xmas **Conf** Board 30 Thtr 50 Del from £260 to £380*
Services Lift Air con **Parking** 40 **Notes** LB ⊗

Save on hotels. Book at **theAA.com/hotel**

OSW – OXF 365 **ENGLAND**

The Oxford Hotel

PUMA HOTELS COLLECTION

★★★★ 76% ⊛ HOTEL

☎ 01865 489988
Godstow Rd, Wolvercote Roundabout OX2 8AL
e-mail: oxford@pumahotels.co.uk
web: www.pumahotels.co.uk
dir: Adjacent to A34/A40, 2m from city centre

Conveniently located on the northern edge of the city centre, this purpose-built hotel offers bedrooms that are bright, modern and well equipped. Guests can eat in the Medio Restaurant or try the Cappuccino Lounge menu. There is the option to eat alfresco on the Patio Terrace when the weather is fine. The hotel offers impressive conference, business and leisure facilities.

Rooms 168 (11 fmly) (89 GF) **Facilities** Spa STV Wi-fi ⓑ supervised Gym Squash Steam room Beauty treatments New Year **Conf** Class 130 Board 110 Thtr 320 **Parking** 250 **Notes** Civ Wed 250

Oxford Thames Four Pillars Hotel

FOUR PILLARS HOTELS

★★★★ 76% HOTEL

☎ 0800 374 692 & 01865 334444
Henley Rd, Sandford-on-Thames OX4 4GX
e-mail: thames@four-pillars.co.uk
web: www.four-pillars.co.uk/thames
dir: M40 junct 8 towards Oxford, follow ring road. Left at rdbt towards Cowley. At rdbt with lights turn left to Littlemore, hotel approx 1m on right

Set in 30 acres of beautiful grounds beside the river, this mellow stone property provides a quiet retreat, yet is close to the city. The spacious and traditional River Room Restaurant has superb views of the hotel's own boat moored on the river. The gardens can be enjoyed from the patios or balconies in the newer bedroom wings. Public rooms include a beamed bar and lounge area with minstrels' gallery, and Jerome's Leisure Club. The hotel is popular as a wedding venue.

Rooms 62 (5 fmly) (30 GF) ⓡ **S** £105-£195; **D** £120-£210 (incl. bkfst) **Facilities** FTV Wi-fi ⓑ ⓒ ⓓ Gym Steam room Sauna Beauty treatment room Xmas New Year **Conf** Class 80 Board 40 Thtr 200 Del from £165 to £189 **Parking** 120 **Notes** LB ⊗ Civ Wed 100

Old Parsonage Hotel

★★★★ 75% ⊛ TOWN HOUSE HOTEL

☎ 01865 310210
1 Banbury Rd OX2 6NN
e-mail: reception@oldparsonage-hotel.co.uk
web: www.oldparsonage-hotel.co.uk
dir: From Oxford ring road to city centre via Summertown. Hotel last building on right before entering St Giles

Dating back in parts to the 16th century, this stylish hotel offers great character and charm and is conveniently located at the northern edge of the city centre. Having undergone a complete refurbishment throughout, this hotel now has five new bedrooms and two new suites. All the reappointed bedrooms are attractively styled and particularly well appointed. The focal point of the operation is the busy all-day bar and restaurant which has a clubby, bohemian atmosphere; the small garden areas and terraces prove popular in summer months. The Pike Room is available for private lunches and dinners, weddings and meetings.

Rooms 30 (4 fmly) (10 GF) **S** £134-£245; **D** £134-£245* **Facilities** STV FTV Wi-fi ⓑ In room beauty treatments Use of nearby fitness club House bikes Walking tours ♫ Xmas New Year **Conf** Class 8 Board 12 Thtr 20 Del £260* **Services** Air con **Parking** 14 **Notes** LB Civ Wed 60

Cotswold Lodge Hotel

CLASSIC BRITISH HOTELS

★★★★ 75% HOTEL

☎ 01865 512121
66a Banbury Rd OX2 6JP
e-mail: info@cotswoldlodgehotel.co.uk
web: www.cotswoldlodgehotel.co.uk
dir: A40 (Oxford ring road) onto A4165 (Banbury road) signed city centre/Summertown. Hotel 2m on left

This Victorian property is located close to the centre of Oxford and offers smart, comfortable accommodation. Stylish bedrooms and suites are attractively presented and some have balconies. The public areas have an elegant country-house feel. The hotel is popular with business guests and caters for conferences and banquets.

Rooms 49 (14 GF) ⓡ **S** £65-£165; **D** £115-£220 (incl. bkfst)* **Facilities** STV Wi-fi ⓑ Xmas New Year **Conf** Class 45 Board 40 Thtr 100 Del from £140 to £195* **Parking** 40 **Notes** LB ⊗ Civ Wed 100

Oxford Spires Four Pillars Hotel

FOUR PILLARS HOTELS

★★★★ 75% HOTEL

☎ 0800 374 692 & 01865 324324
Abingdon Rd OX1 4PS
e-mail: spires@four-pillars.co.uk
web: www.four-pillars.co.uk/spires
dir: M40 junct 8 towards Oxford. Left towards Cowley. At 3rd rdbt follow city centre signs. Hotel in 1m

This purpose-built hotel is surrounded by extensive parkland, yet is only a short walk from the city centre. Bedrooms are attractively furnished, well equipped and include several apartments. Public areas include a spacious restaurant, open-plan bar/lounge, leisure club and extensive conference facilities.

Rooms 170 (10 annexe) (1 fmly) (54 GF) ⓡ **S** £100-£260; **D** £120-£280 (incl. bkfst) **Facilities** FTV Wi-fi ⓑ ⓒ Gym Beauty Steam room Sauna Xmas New Year **Conf** Class 96 Board 76 Thtr 266 Del from £130 to £199 **Services** Lift **Parking** 95 **Notes** LB ⊗ Civ Wed 200

Malmaison Oxford

Malmaison
hotels that dare to be different

★★★ 85% ⊛ HOTEL

☎ 01865 268400
3 Oxford Castle, New Rd OX1 1AY
web: www.malmaison.com
dir: M40 junct 9, A34 N to Botley interchange. Follow city centre & rail station signs. At rail station straight ahead to 2nd lights. Turn right, at next lights left into Park End St. Straight on at next lights, hotel 2nd left

Once the city's prison, this is definitely a hotel with a difference. Many of the rooms are actually converted from the old cells. Not to worry though there have been many improvements since the prisoners left! Exceedingly comfortable beds and luxury bathrooms are just two of the changes. The hotel has a popular brasserie with quality and value much in evidence. Limited parking space is available.

Rooms 95 (5 GF) ⓡ **S** £125-£490; **D** £135-£500* **Facilities** STV Wi-fi Gym Xmas New Year **Conf** Class 40 Board 40 Thtr 80 Del from £200 to £260* **Services** Lift **Parking** 30 **Notes** Civ Wed 80

O

OXFORD *continued*

Mercure Oxford Eastgate Hotel

★★★ 81% ◉ HOTEL

☎ 01865 248332
73 High St OX1 4BE
e-mail: h6668@accor.com
web: www.mercure.com
dir: A40 follow signs to Headington & Oxford city centre, over Magdalen Bridge, stay in left lane, through lights, left into Merton St, entrance to car park on left

Just a short stroll from the city centre, this hotel, as its name suggests, occupies the site of the city's medieval East Gate and boasts its own car park. Bedrooms are appointed and equipped to a high standard. Stylish public areas include the all-day Town House Brasserie and Bar.

Rooms 64 (3 fmly) (4 GF) ↖ **S** £110-£150;
D £130-£180* **Facilities** Wi-fi Xmas New Year
Services Lift Air con **Parking** 40 **Notes** ⊗

Holiday Inn Oxford

★★★ 80% HOTEL

☎ 0870 942 9086 & 01865 888300
Peartree Roundabout, Woodstock Rd OX2 8JD
e-mail: oxford@ihg.com
web: www.hioxfordhotel.co.uk
dir: A34 at Peartree Interchange signed Oxford & Services. Hotel on left

Located at The Peartree Roundabout, this purpose-built, modern hotel is ideal for business and leisure guests visiting Oxford. Bedrooms are spacious, well equipped and have air cooling. There is a smart bar and restaurant plus as a well-equipped gym and large swimming pool. There are meeting facilities and ample free parking.

Rooms 154 (33 fmly) (23 GF) (6 smoking)
Facilities Spa STV FTV Wi-fi ↳ ⊕ supervised Gym
Sauna Steam room **Conf** Class 65 Board 40 Thtr 150
Services Lift Air con **Parking** 184 **Notes** ⊗
Civ Wed 100

Hawkwell House

★★★ 79% HOTEL

☎ 01865 749988
Church Way, Iffley Village OX4 4DZ
e-mail: reservations@hawkwellhouse.co.uk
web: www.hawkwellhouse.co.uk
dir: A34 follow signs to Cowley. At Littlemore rdbt A4158 exit into Iffley Rd. After lights left to Iffley

Set in a peaceful residential location, Hawkwell House is just a few minutes' drive from the Oxford ring road. The spacious rooms are modern, attractively decorated and well equipped. Public areas are tastefully appointed and the conservatory-style restaurant offers an interesting choice of dishes. The hotel also has a range of conference and function facilities.

Rooms 66 (10 fmly) (4 GF) ↖ **S** £69-£179;
D £79-£199 (incl. bkfst) **Facilities** FTV Wi-fi ↳ Xmas
New Year **Conf** Class 100 Board 80 Thtr 200
Del from £125 to £285 **Services** Lift **Parking** 120
Notes LB ⊗ Civ Wed 150

Manor House Hotel

★★ 69% METRO HOTEL

☎ 01865 727627
250 Iffley Rd OX4 1SE
e-mail: manorhousehotel@hotmail.com
dir: On A4158, 1m from city centre

This family run establishment is easily accessible from the city centre and all major road links. The hotel provides informal but friendly and attentive service. The comfortably furnished bedrooms are well equipped. The hotel has a bar but there is a selection of restaurants and popular pubs within easy walking distance. Limited private parking is available.

Rooms 8 (2 fmly) **S** £69-£99; **D** £69-£99 (incl. bkfst)*
Facilities STV FTV Wi-fi ↳ **Parking** 6 **Notes** ⊗ Closed
20 Dec-20 Jan

Bath Place Hotel

★★ 65% METRO HOTEL

☎ 01865 791812
4-5 Bath Place, Holywell St OX1 3SU
e-mail: info@bathplace.co.uk
dir: On S side of Holywell St (parallel to High St)

The hotel has been created from a group of 17th-century cottages originally built by Flemish weavers who were permitted to settle outside the city walls. This lovely hotel is very much at the heart of the city today and offers individually designed bedrooms, including some with four-posters.

Rooms 16 (3 fmly) (5 GF) ↖ **S** £95-£105;
D £120-£155 (incl. bkfst)* **Facilities** FTV Wi-fi
Parking 16

The Balkan Lodge Hotel

★★ 64% METRO HOTEL

☎ 01865 244524
315 Iffley Rd OX4 4AG
e-mail: info@balkanlodgeoxford.co.uk
web: www.balkanlodgeoxford.co.uk
dir: From M40, A40 take eastern bypass, into city on A4158

Conveniently located for the city centre and the ring road, this family operated metro hotel offers a comfortable stay. Bedrooms are attractive and well equipped. Public areas include a lounge and bar. A secure private car park is located to the rear of the building.

Rooms 12 **S** £70-£85; **D** £82-£92 (incl. bkfst)
Facilities Wi-fi **Parking** 12 **Notes** ⊗

Holiday Inn Express Oxford - Kassam Stadium

BUDGET HOTEL

☎ 01865 780888
Grenoble Rd OX4 4XP
e-mail: reservations@expressoxford.com
web: www.hiexpress.com/oxfrdkassam
dir: M40 junct 8 onto A40 for 4m. Left at McDonald's onto A4142. After 3.5m left onto A4074, take 1st exit signed Science Park & Kassam Stadium

A modern hotel ideal for families and business travellers. Fresh and uncomplicated, the spacious rooms include Sky TVs, power showers and tea and coffee-making facilities. A continental buffet breakfast is included in the room rate; other meals may be taken at the nearby family pub or restaurant. See also the Hotel Groups pages.

Rooms 162 (131 fmly) (31 GF) **Conf** Class 18
Board 28 Thtr 30

Premier Inn Oxford

BUDGET HOTEL

☎ 0871 527 8866
Oxford Business Park, Garsington Rd OX4 2JZ
web: www.premierinn.com
dir: On Oxford Business Park, just off A4142 & B480 junct

High quality, budget accommodation ideal for both families and business travellers. Spacious, en suite bedrooms feature tea and coffee making facilities, and Freeview TV in most hotels. Internet access and Wi-fi are available for a small fee. The adjacent family restaurant features a wide and varied menu. See also the Hotel Groups pages.

Rooms 121

OXFORD MOTORWAY SERVICE AREA (M40)   Map 5 SP60
Oxfordshire

Days Inn Oxford - M40

BUDGET HOTEL

☎ 01865 877000
M40 junction 8A, Waterstock OX33 1LJ
e-mail: oxford.hotel@welcomebreak.co.uk
web: www.welcomebreak.co.uk
dir: M40 junct 8a, at Welcome Break service area

This modern building offers accommodation in smart, spacious and well-equipped bedrooms, suitable for families and business travellers, and all with en suite bathrooms. Continental breakfast is available and other refreshments may be taken at the nearby family restaurant. See also the Hotel Groups pages.

Rooms 59 (56 fmly) (25 GF) (10 smoking)

PADSTOW   Map 2 SW97
Cornwall

The Metropole

★★★★ 74% ◉ HOTEL

☎ 01841 532486
Station Rd PL28 8DB
e-mail: info@the-metropole.co.uk
web: www.the-metropole.co.uk
dir: M5/A30 pass Launceston, follow Wadebridge & N Cornwall signs. Take A39, follow Padstow signs

This long-established hotel first opened its doors to guests back in 1904 and it still retains an air of the sophistication and elegance of a bygone age. Bedrooms are soundly appointed and well equipped; dining options include the informal Met Café Bar, and the main restaurant with its enjoyable cuisine and wonderful views over the Camel estuary.

Rooms 58 (3 fmly) (2 GF) **S** £59-£135; **D** £79-£180 (incl. bkfst)* **Facilities** Spa FTV Wi-fi ⚲ Swimming pool open Jul & Aug only Xmas New Year **Conf** Class 20 Board 20 Thtr 40 **Services** Lift **Parking** 36 **Notes** LB Civ Wed 110

St Petroc's Hotel and Bistro

★★ 85% ◉ SMALL HOTEL

☎ 01841 532700
4 New St PL28 8EA
e-mail: reservations@rickstein.com
dir: A39 onto A389, follow signs to town centre. Follow one-way system, hotel on right on leaving town

One of the oldest buildings in town, this charming establishment is just up the hill from the picturesque harbour. Style, comfort and individuality are all great strengths here, particularly so in the impressively equipped bedrooms. Breakfast, lunch and dinner all reflect a serious approach to cuisine, and the popular restaurant has a relaxed, bistro style. Comfortable lounges, a reading room and lovely gardens complete the picture.

Rooms 14 (4 annexe) (3 fmly) (3 GF) **D** £190-£235 (incl. bkfst)* **Facilities** FTV Wi-fi Cookery school New Year **Conf** Board 12 **Services** Lift **Parking** 12 **Notes** LB Closed 1 May & 25-26 Dec RS 24 Dec eve

---

The Old Ship Hotel

★★ 75% HOTEL

☎ 01841 532357
Mill Square PL28 8AE
e-mail: stay@oldshiphotel-padstow.co.uk
web: www.oldshiphotel-padstow.co.uk
dir: From M5 take A30 to Bodmin then A389 to Padstow, follow brown tourist signs to car park

This attractive inn is situated in the heart of the old town's quaint and winding streets, just a short walk from the harbour. A warm welcome is assured, accommodation is pleasant and comfortable, and public areas offer plenty of character. Freshly caught fish features on both the bar and restaurant menus. On site parking is a bonus.

Rooms 14 (4 fmly) **S** £30-£60; **D** £80-£120 (incl. bkfst)* **Facilities** STV Wi-fi ♬ Xmas New Year **Parking** 20 **Notes** LB

The Seafood Restaurant

◉ ◉ ◉ RESTAURANT WITH ROOMS

☎ 01841 532700
Riverside PL28 8BY
e-mail: reservations@rickstein.com
dir: Into town centre down hill, follow round sharp bend, restaurant on left

Food lovers continue to beat a well-trodden path to this legendary establishment. Situated on the edge of the harbour, just a stone's throw from the shops, the Seafood Restaurant offers stylish and comfortable bedrooms that boast numerous thoughtful extras; some have views of the estuary and a couple have stunning private balconies. Service is relaxed and friendly; booking is essential for both accommodation and a table in the restaurant.

Rooms 20 (6 annexe) (6 fmly)

P

PAIGNTON
Devon   Map 3 SX86

Redcliffe Hotel

★★★ 78% HOTEL

☎ 01803 526397
Marine Dr TQ3 2NL
e-mail: redclfe@aol.com
dir: On seafront at Torquay end of Paignton Green

Set at the water's edge in three acres of well-tended grounds, this popular hotel enjoys uninterrupted views across Tor Bay. Offering a diverse range of facilities including a leisure complex, beauty treatments and lots of outdoor family activities in the summer. Bedrooms are pleasantly appointed and comfortably furnished, while public areas offer ample space for rest and relaxation.

Rooms 68 (8 fmly) (3 GF) ➧ **S** £60-£65; **D** £120-£130 (incl. bkfst) **Facilities** Spa FTV Wi-fi ⓢ supervised ⤳ Putt green Fishing Gym Table tennis Carpet bowls Xmas New Year **Conf** Class 50 Board 50 Thtr 150 Del from £70 to £90 **Services** Lift **Parking** 80 **Notes** LB ⊗ Civ Wed 150

Premier Inn (Goodrington Sands)

BUDGET HOTEL

☎ 0871 527 9206
Tanners Rd, Goodrington TQ4 6LP
web: www.premierinn.com
dir: From Newton Abbot take A380 S. Left into A3022 (Totnes Rd), right at Hayes Rd into Penwill Way, right at B3199 into Dartmouth Rd, at lights left into Tanners Rd

High quality, budget accommodation ideal for both families and business travellers. Spacious, en suite bedrooms feature tea and coffee making facilities, and Freeview TV in most hotels. Internet access and Wi-fi are available for a small fee. The adjacent family restaurant features a wide and varied menu. See also the Hotel Groups pages.

Rooms 33

PAINSWICK
Gloucestershire   Map 4 SO80

INSPECTORS' CHOICE

Cotswolds88 Hotel

★★★★ ◉◉◉ SMALL HOTEL

☎ 01452 813688
Kemps Ln GL6 6YB
e-mail: reservations@cotswolds88hotel.com
web: www.cotswolds88hotel.com
dir: From Stroud towards Cheltenham on A46, in Painswick centre right at St Marys Church into Victoria St. Left into St Marys St, right into Tibbiwell St, right into Kemps Lane

In the heart of a pretty village, this 18th-century house has become a 'boutique' hotel. Step inside to find a strikingly designed interior of bold colours and textures. The individually styled bedrooms are beautifully presented and individually styled and have plasma TVs and bathrooms with power showers. Eight of the bedrooms have stunning countryside views. Residents have access to the private lounge with balcony and the cosy library. There is also a small bar where guests can enjoy cocktails or a pre- or post-dinner drink. The modern award-winning restaurant has a well deserved reputation for its excellent cuisine; the menus are created from the finest locally sourced and organic produce. The hotel runs a cookery school.

Rooms 17 (8 annexe) (2 fmly) **Facilities** FTV Wi-fi Beauty treatment room Xmas New Year **Conf** Class 34 Board 30 Thtr 60 **Parking** 17 **Notes** Civ Wed 120

St Michaels

RESTAURANT WITH ROOMS

☎ 01452 814555
Victoria St GL6 6QA
e-mail: info@stmickshouse.co.uk

This 17th-century Grade II listed building has a wealth of character and overlooks the famous Church of St Michaels with its 99 yew trees. Each stylish bedroom has its own theme and is equipped with a host of thoughtful extras. The award-winning restaurant has an imaginative menu based on the best local produce, and the delicious breakfasts should not be missed. Situated in the heart of the very pretty Cotswold village of Painswick this establishment makes an ideal base for exploring the beautiful Cotswolds. A warm welcome is guaranteed.

Rooms 3

PANGBOURNE
Berkshire   Map 5 SU67

The Elephant at Pangbourne

★★★ 79% ◉ HOTEL

☎ 0118 984 2244
Church Rd RG8 7AR
e-mail: dominic@elephanthotel.co.uk
web: www.elephanthotel.co.uk
dir: M4 junct 12, A4 signed Theale/Newbury, right at 2nd rdbt signed Pangbourne. Hotel in village centre on left

Centrally located in this bustling village, just a short drive from Reading. Bedrooms are individual in style but identical in the attention to detail, with handcrafted Indian furniture and rich oriental rugs. Guests can enjoy award-winning cuisine in the restaurant, or there is bistro-style dining in the bar area.

Rooms 22 (8 annexe) (2 fmly) (4 GF) **Facilities** FTV Wi-fi ➧ Xmas New Year **Conf** Class 40 Board 30 Thtr 60 Del from £145 to £175* **Parking** 10 **Notes** Civ Wed 70

P

Save on hotels. Book at **theAA.com/hotel**

PAI – PEN 369 ENGLAND

PATTERDALE
Cumbria
Map 18 NY31

Patterdale Hotel

★★ 69% HOTEL

☎ 0844 811 5580 & 017684 82231
CA11 0NN
e-mail: reservations@choice-hotels.co.uk
dir: M6 junct 40, A592 towards Ullswater. 10m to Patterdale

Patterdale is a real tourist destination and this hotel makes a good base for those taking part in the many activity pursuits available in this area. The hotel enjoys delightful views of the valley and fells, being located at the southern end of Ullswater. The modern bedrooms vary in style. In busier periods accommodation is let for a minimum period of two nights.

Rooms 57 (16 fmly) (6 GF) **S** £34-£60; **D** £68-£120 (incl. bkfst & dinner) **Facilities** FTV Wi-fi ➔ Free bike hire ♫ Xmas New Year **Services** Lift **Parking** 30 **Notes** LB ⊗

PATTINGHAM
Staffordshire
Map 10 SO89

Patshull Park Hotel Golf & Country Club

★★★ 80% HOTEL

☎ 01902 700100
Patshull Park WV6 7HR
e-mail: sales@patshull-park.co.uk
web: www.patshull-park.co.uk
dir: 1.5m W of Pattingham, at church into Patshull Rd, hotel 1.5m on right

Dating from the 1730s and sitting in 280 acres of parkland, with good golf and fishing, this comfortably appointed hotel has a range of modern leisure and conference facilities. Public rooms include a lounge bar, Earl's Brasserie and the Lakeside Restaurant with delightful views over the lake. Bedrooms are well appointed and thoughtfully equipped; most have good views of either the golf course or lake.

Rooms 49 (15 fmly) (16 GF) **S** £49-£114; **D** £59-£134 (incl. bkfst) **Facilities** STV FTV Wi-fi ⊗ ♿ 18 Putt green Fishing Gym Beauty therapist Cardio suite Weights room Steam rooms Saunas Xmas New Year **Conf** Class 75 Board 44 Thtr 160 Del from £111 to £136 **Parking** 200 **Notes** LB Civ Wed 120

PECKFORTON
Cheshire
Map 15 SJ55

Peckforton Castle

★★★★ 76% ⚜⚜ HOTEL

☎ 01829 260930
Stone House Ln CW6 9TN
e-mail: info@peckfortoncastle.co.uk
web: www.peckfortoncastle.co.uk
dir: A49. At Beeston Castle pub right signed Peckforton Castle. Approx 2m, entrance on right

Built in the mid 19th century by parliamentarian and landowner Lord John Tollemache and now lovingly cared for by The Naylor Family, this Grade I medieval-style castle has been sympathetically renovated to provide high standards of comfort without losing original charm and character. Bedrooms and public areas retain many period features, and dining in the 1851 Restaurant is a memorable experience. There is a falconry centre at the castle.

Rooms 48 (7 fmly) (2 GF) ⟋ **S** £80-£140; **D** £90-£160 (incl. bkfst)* **Facilities** FTV Wi-fi HL ➔ Falconry Outdoor pursuits Land Rover experience Abseiling Beauty salon Xmas New Year **Conf** Class 80 Board 40 Thtr 180 Del from £135 to £175* **Services** Lift **Parking** 400 **Notes** LB ⊗ Civ Wed 165

PENDLEBURY
Greater Manchester
Map 15 SD70

Premier Inn Manchester (Swinton)

BUDGET HOTEL

☎ 0871 527 8720
219 Bolton Rd M27 8TG
web: www.premierinn.com
dir: M60 junct 13 towards A572, at rdbt take 3rd exit towards Swinton. At next rdbt take A572. In 2m right onto A580. After 2nd lights A666 Kearsley, 1st left at rdbt. Pass fire station on right, 1st right

High quality, budget accommodation ideal for both families and business travellers. Spacious, en suite bedrooms feature tea and coffee making facilities, and Freeview TV in most hotels. Internet access and Wi-fi are available for a small fee. The adjacent family restaurant features a wide and varied menu. See also the Hotel Groups pages.

Rooms 31

PENKRIDGE
Staffordshire
Map 10 SJ91

Mercure Stafford South Hatherton House Hotel

★★★ 71% HOTEL

☎ 01785 712459
Pinfold Ln ST19 5QP
e-mail: enquiries@hotels-stafford.com
web: www.hotels-stafford.com
dir: A449 to Wolverhampton. In Penkridge turn right into Pinfold Ln. Hotel on left in 300yds

The hotel offers comfortable accommodation to both leisure and business guests. The leisure facilities consist of a pool, steam room and jacuzzi with a well-equipped gym and two squash courts. Conference facilities are also available. There is free parking and easy access to the city and countryside.

Rooms 51 (4 fmly) (18 GF) (4 smoking) **Facilities** FTV Wi-fi ⊗ Gym Squash Sauna Steam room Xmas New Year **Conf** Class 160 Board 120 Thtr 260 **Parking** 200 **Notes** Civ Wed 200

PENRITH
Cumbria
Map 18 NY53

See also Glenridding and Shap

North Lakes Hotel & Spa

shire
hotels & spas

★★★★ 77% ⚜ HOTEL

☎ 01768 868111
Ullswater Rd CA11 8QT
e-mail: nlakes@shirehotels.com
web: www.northlakeshotel.com
dir: M6 junct 40 at junct with A66

With a great location, it's no wonder that this modern hotel is perpetually busy. Amenities include a good range of meeting and function rooms and excellent health and leisure facilities including a full spa. Themed public areas have a contemporary, Scandinavian country style and offer plenty of space and comfort. High standards of service are provided by a friendly team of staff.

Rooms 84 (6 fmly) (22 GF) **S** £80-£150; **D** £80-£150* **Facilities** Spa STV Wi-fi ⊗ Gym Children's splash pool Steam room Activity & wellness studios Sauna Xmas New Year **Conf** Class 140 Board 30 Thtr 200 Del from £125 to £175* **Services** Lift **Parking** 150 **Notes** ⊗ Civ Wed 200

P

PENRITH *continued*

Temple Sowerby House Hotel & Restaurant

★★★ 87% ◉◉ COUNTRY HOUSE HOTEL

☎ 017683 61578
CA10 1RZ
e-mail: stay@templesowerby.com
web: www.templesowerby.com

(For full entry see Temple Sowerby)

Westmorland Hotel

★★★ 83% ◉ HOTEL

☎ 015396 24351
Westmorland Place, Orton CA10 3SB
e-mail: reservations@westmorlandhotel.com
web: www.westmorlandhotel.com

(For full entry see Tebay)

The George Hotel

LAKE DISTRICT
▪▪▪▪▪▪ HOTELS

★★★ 78% HOTEL

☎ 01768 862696 & 0800 840 1242
Devonshire St CA11 7SU
e-mail: georgehotel@lakedistricthotels.net
dir: M6 junct 40, 1m to town centre. From A6/A66 to Penrith

This inviting and popular hotel was once visited by 'Bonnie' Prince Charlie. Extended over the years, it currently offers well equipped bedrooms, and spacious public areas that retain a timeless charm. There is a choice of lounge areas that make ideal places for morning coffee and afternoon tea.

Rooms 35 (4 fmly) **S** £84; **D** £134 (incl. bkfst)
Facilities FTV Wi-fi ⌨ Xmas New Year Child facilities
Conf Class 80 Board 50 Thtr 120 **Parking** 40
Notes LB Civ Wed 120

PENZANCE Map 2 SW43
Cornwall

Hotel Penzance

★★★ 86% ◉◉ HOTEL

☎ 01736 363117
Britons Hill TR18 3AE
e-mail: reception@hotelpenzance.com
web: www.hotelpenzance.com
dir: From A30 pass heliport on right, left at next rdbt for town centre. 3rd right onto Britons Hill. Hotel on right

This Edwardian house has been tastefully redesigned, particularly in the contemporary Bay Restaurant. The focus on style is not only limited to the decor, but is also apparent in the award-winning cuisine that is based on fresh Cornish produce. Bedrooms have been appointed to modern standards and are particularly well equipped; many have views across Mounts Bay.

Rooms 25 (2 GF) ⌨ **S** £85-£89; **D** £135-£195 (incl. bkfst)* **Facilities** FTV Wi-fi ⌨ Xmas New Year **Conf** Class 50 Board 25 Thtr 80 **Parking** 12
Notes Civ Wed 80

Queens Hotel

★★★ 74% HOTEL

☎ 01736 362371
The Promenade TR18 4HG
e-mail: enquiries@queens-hotel.com
web: www.queens-hotel.com
dir: A30 to Penzance, follow signs for seafront pass harbour onto promenade, hotel on right

With views across Mount's Bay towards Newlyn, this impressive Victorian hotel has a long and distinguished history. Comfortable public areas are filled with interesting pictures and artefacts, and in the dining room guests can choose from the daily-changing menu. Bedrooms, many with sea views, vary in style and size.

Rooms 70 (10 fmly) ⌨ **S** £79-£91; **D** £158-£192 (incl. bkfst) **Facilities** FTV Wi-fi ⌨ Xmas New Year **Conf** Class 200 Board 120 Thtr 200 Del from £85 to £135 **Services** Lift **Parking** 50 **Notes** LB Civ Wed 250

PETERBOROUGH Map 12 TL19
Cambridgeshire

Peterborough Marriott Hotel

Marriott
HOTELS & RESORTS

★★★★ 77% HOTEL

☎ 01733 371111
Peterborough Business Park, Lynchwood PE2 6GB
e-mail: reservations.peterborough@marriotthotels.co.uk
web: www.peterboroughmarriott.co.uk
dir: From A1 exit at Alwalton Showground, Chesterton. Left at T-junct. Hotel on left at next rdbt

This modern hotel is opposite the East of England Showground, and a just few minutes' drive from the heart of the city. Alwalton is famous for being the birthplace of Sir Frederick Henry Royce, one of the founders of the Rolls-Royce company. Air-conditioned bedrooms are spacious and well designed for business use. Public rooms include the Garden Lounge, cocktail bar, Laurels Restaurant and a leisure club.

Rooms 163 (8 fmly) (74 GF) (6 smoking)
Facilities Spa STV Wi-fi ⌨ HL ⌨ Gym Beauty therapist Hairdressing New Year **Conf** Class 160 Board 45 Thtr 300 **Services** Air con **Parking** 165
Notes ⊗ Civ Wed 300

Bull Hotel

PEEL HOTELS PLC

★★★★ 75% ◉ HOTEL

☎ 01733 561364
Westgate PE1 1RB
e-mail: rooms@bull-hotel-peterborough.com
web: www.peelhotels.co.uk
dir: From A1 follow city centre signs. Hotel opposite Queensgate shopping centre. Car park on Broadway adjacent to library

This pleasant city-centre hotel offers well-equipped, modern accommodation, which includes several wings of deluxe bedrooms. Public rooms include a popular bar and a brasserie-style restaurant serving a flexible range of dishes, with further informal dining available in the lounge. There is a good range of meeting rooms and conference facilities.

Rooms 118 (2 fmly) (5 GF) (4 smoking) **Facilities** STV Wi-fi Xmas New Year **Conf** Class 120 Board 40 Thtr 200 **Parking** 100 **Notes** ⊗ Civ Wed 200

Save on hotels. Book at **theAA.com/hotel**

PEN – PET 371 ENGLAND

Best Western Plus Orton Hall Hotel

★★★★ 71% @ HOTEL

☎ 01733 391111
Orton Longueville PE2 7DN
e-mail: reception@ortonhall.co.uk
web: www.ortonhall.co.uk
dir: Off A605 E, opposite Orton Mere

An impressive country-house hotel set in 20 acres of woodland on the outskirts of town and with easy access to the A1. The spacious and relaxing public areas include the baronial Great Room and the Orton Suite for banqueting and for meetings, and the oak-panelled, award-winning Huntly Restaurant. The on-site pub, Ramblewood Inn, is an alternative, informal dining option.

Rooms 70 (2 fmly) (15 GF) ➤ **S** £30-£140;
D £40-£160* **Facilities** Spa FTV Wi-fi ➤ ➤ Gym
Sauna Steam room Xmas New Year **Conf** Class 70
Board 60 Thtr 160 Del from £110 to £147.50*
Parking 200 **Notes** LB Civ Wed 150

Bell Inn Hotel

★★★ 81% @ HOTEL

☎ 01733 241066
Great North Rd PE7 3RA
e-mail: reception@thebellstilton.co.uk
web: www.thebellstilton.co.uk

(For full entry see Stilton)

Queensgate Hotel

★★★ 81% HOTEL

☎ 01733 562572
5-7 Fletton Av PE2 8AX
e-mail: reservations@thequeensgatehotel.co.uk
dir: In town centre

This hotel is ideally situated close to the centre of town with its range of shops and amenities. Bedrooms are contemporary in style, and ideally equipped for both business and leisure guests. The modern public rooms include a lounge bar, two dining areas and a beauty therapy suite.

Rooms 40 (2 fmly) (10 GF) ➤ **Facilities** FTV Wi-fi
Beauty clinic Xmas New Year **Conf** Class 35 Board 26
Thtr 72 **Notes** ⊗

Park Inn by Radisson Peterborough

★★★ 79% HOTEL

☎ 01733 353750
Wentworth St PE1 1BA
e-mail: info.peterborough@rezidorparkinn.com
dir: Off A15, 4 mins walk from station

Situated adjacent to Queensgate Shopping Centre which has a range of stores and amenities, and within easy walking distance of the main train station. The spacious bedrooms are modern and equipped to a very good standard. Public rooms feature the open-plan Red Bar Grill, a cosy lounge and a range of meeting rooms.

Rooms 115 (9 fmly) ➤ **Facilities** FTV Wi-fi Beauty
treatment room Use of gym facilities (1m) &
swimming pool (0.5m) **Conf** Class 80 Board 40
Thtr 140 Del from £125 to £185 **Services** Lift Air con
Parking 45 **Notes** ⊗ Civ Wed 30

Days Inn Peterborough - A1

BUDGET HOTEL

☎ 01733 371540
**Peterborough Extra Services, A1 Junction 17, Great
North Road, Haddon PE7 3UQ**
e-mail: peterborough.hotel@welcomebreak.co.uk
dir: A1(M) junct 17

This modern, purpose-built accommodation offers smartly appointed, particularly well-equipped bedrooms with good power showers. There is a choice of adjacent food outlets where guests can enjoy breakfast, snacks and meals. See also the Hotel Groups pages.

Rooms 82 (16 fmly) (40 GF) (11 smoking) ➤
S fr £35.95; **D** fr £35.95*

Holiday Inn Express Peterborough

BUDGET HOTEL

☎ 01733 284450
East of England Way, Orton Northgate PE2 6HE
e-mail:
reservations@hiexpresspeterborough.co.uk
web: www.hiexpress.com/peterboroughex
dir: Follow signs on A1(M) for Peterborough
Showground, hotel adjacent to showground

A modern hotel ideal for families and business travellers. Fresh and uncomplicated, the spacious rooms include Sky TV, power shower and tea and coffee-making facilities. Continental buffet breakfast is included in the room rate; other meals may be taken at the nearby family pub or restaurant. See also the Hotel Groups pages.

Rooms 80 (44 fmly) (37 GF) ➤ **Conf** Class 20
Board 20 Thtr 30

Premier Inn Peterborough (Ferry Meadows)

Premier Inn

BUDGET HOTEL

☎ 0871 527 8872
Ham Ln, Orton Meadows, Nene Park PE2 5UU
web: www.premierinn.com
dir: A1(M) S junct 16, A15 through Yaxley, left at rdbt.
A1(M) N junct 17, A1139 junct 3 right to Yaxley, right
at 2nd rdbt

High quality, budget accommodation ideal for both families and business travellers. Spacious, en suite bedrooms feature tea and coffee making facilities, and Freeview TV in most hotels. Internet access and Wi-fi are available for a small fee. The adjacent family restaurant features a wide and varied menu. See also the Hotel Groups pages.

Rooms 40

Premier Inn Peterborough (Hampton)

BUDGET HOTEL

☎ 0871 527 8874
Ashbourne Rd, off London Rd, Hampton PE7 8BT
web: www.premierinn.com
dir: A1(M) S junct 16, A15 through Yaxley, hotel on
left at 1st rdbt. Or A1(M) N junct 17, A1139, 2nd exit
junct 3 follow Yaxley signs. Hotel on right at 2nd rdbt

Rooms 83

P

PETERBOROUGH *continued*

Premier Inn Peterborough North

BUDGET HOTEL

☎ 0871 527 8876
1023 Lincoln Rd, Walton PE4 6AH
web: www.premierinn.com
dir: A1, A47 towards Peterborough. In 7m exit at junct 17 signed city centre. At rdbt (bottom of slip road) straight on signed city centre. At next rdbt left onto dual carriageway. At next rdbt double back, follow signs for city centre. Hotel in 200mtrs

Rooms 40

PETERSFIELD	Map 5 SU72
Hampshire	

Langrish House

★★★ 78% ◉◉ HOTEL

☎ 01730 266941
Langrish GU32 1RN
e-mail: frontdesk@langrishhouse.co.uk
web: www.langrishhouse.co.uk
dir: A3 onto A272 towards Winchester. Hotel signed, 2.5m on left

Langrish House has been in the same family for seven generations. It is located in an extremely peaceful area just a few minutes' drive from Petersfield, halfway between Guildford and Portsmouth. Bedrooms are comfortable and well equipped with stunning views across the gardens to the hills. Guests can eat in the intimate Frederick's Restaurant with views over the lawn, or in the Old Vaults which have an interesting history dating back to 1644. The hotel is licensed for civil ceremonies and various themed events take place throughout the year.

Rooms 13 (1 fmly) (3 GF) 🐾 **S** £89-£109; **D** £119-£179 (incl. bkfst)* **Facilities** FTV Wi-fi 🏊 Xmas New Year **Conf** Class 18 Board 25 Thtr 60 **Parking** 80 **Notes** Closed 1-17 Jan Civ Wed 80

Premier Inn Petersfield

BUDGET HOTEL

☎ 0871 527 8878
Winchester Rd GU32 3BS
web: www.premierinn.com
dir: At junct of A3 & A272 W'bound signed Services

High quality, budget accommodation ideal for both families and business travellers. Spacious, en suite bedrooms feature tea and coffee making facilities, and Freeview TV in most hotels. Internet access and Wi-fi are available for a small fee. The adjacent family restaurant features a wide and varied menu. See also the Hotel Groups pages.

Rooms 51

PICKERING	Map 19 SE78
North Yorkshire	

The White Swan Inn

★★★ 80% ◉ HOTEL

☎ 01751 472288
Market Place YO18 7AA
e-mail: welcome@white-swan.co.uk
web: www.white-swan.co.uk
dir: In town, between church & steam railway station

This 16th-century coaching inn offers well-equipped, comfortable bedrooms, including suites, either of a more traditional style in the main building or modern in the annexe. Service is friendly and attentive. Good food is served in the attractive restaurant, in the cosy bar and the lounge, where a log fire burns in cooler months. A comprehensive wine list focuses on many fine vintages. A private dining room is also available.

Rooms 21 (9 annexe) (3 fmly) (8 GF) 🐾 **Facilities** FTV Wi-fi Xmas New Year **Conf** Class 18 Board 25 Thtr 35 Del from £150* **Parking** 45 **Notes** LB

Best Western Forest & Vale Hotel

★★★ 80% HOTEL

☎ 01751 472722
Malton Rd YO18 7DL
e-mail: forestvale@bestwestern.co.uk
dir: On A169 towards York at rdbt on outskirts of Pickering

This lovely 18th-century hotel is an excellent base from which to explore the North Yorkshire Moors, one of England's most beautiful areas. A dedicated approach to upgrading means that the hotel is particularly well maintained, inside and out. Bedrooms vary in size and include some spacious 'superior' rooms; one has a four-poster.

Rooms 22 (5 annexe) (7 fmly) (5 GF) **Facilities** FTV Wi-fi ◊ **Conf** Class 50 Board 30 Thtr 120 **Parking** 40 **Notes** ⊗ Closed 24-26 Dec Civ Wed 90

Fox & Hounds Country Inn

★★ 82% ◉ HOTEL

☎ 01751 431577
Main St, Sinnington YO62 6SQ
e-mail: fox.houndsinn@btconnect.com
web: www.thefoxandhoundsinn.co.uk
dir: 3m W of Pickering, off A170, between Pickering & Helmsley

This attractive inn lies in the quiet village of Sinnington just off the main road. The smartly maintained, yet traditional public areas are cosy and inviting. The menu offers a good selection of freshly cooked, modern British dishes and is available in the restaurant or informally in the bar. Bedrooms and bathrooms are well equipped and offer a good standard of quality and comfort. Service throughout is friendly and attentive.

Rooms 10 (4 GF) 🐾 **S** £59-£79; **D** £70-£170 (incl. bkfst) **Facilities** FTV Wi-fi ◊ New Year **Parking** 40 **Notes** No children 12yrs Closed 25-26 Dec

The Old Manse

★★ 76% HOTEL

☎ 01751 476484
19 Middleton Rd YO18 8AL
e-mail: info@oldmansepickering.com
web: www.oldmansepickering.co.uk
dir: A169, left at rdbt, through lights, 1st right into Potter Hill. Follow road to left. From A170 left at 'local traffic only' sign

A peacefully located house standing in mature grounds close to the town centre. It offers a combined dining room and lounge area, and comfortable bedrooms that are well equipped. Expect good hospitality from the resident owners.

Rooms 10 (2 fmly) (2 GF) **Facilities** Wi-fi New Year
Conf Class 12 Board 10 Thtr 20 **Parking** 12
Notes Closed 24-27 Dec

PLYMOUTH
Devon
Map 3 SX45

Duke of Cornwall Hotel

★★★ 78% ⑧ HOTEL

☎ 01752 275850 & 275855
Millbay Rd PL1 3LG
e-mail: enquiries@thedukeofcornwall.co.uk
web: www.thedukeofcornwall.co.uk
dir: Follow city centre, then Plymouth Pavilions Conference & Leisure Centre signs. Hotel opposite Plymouth Pavilions

A historic landmark, this city centre hotel is conveniently located. The spacious public areas

include a popular bar, comfortable lounge and multi-functional ballroom. Bedrooms, many with far reaching views, are individually styled and comfortably appointed. The range of dining options includes meals in the bar, or the elegant dining room for a more formal atmosphere.

Rooms 71 (4 fmly) (20 smoking) ✆ **S** £75-£109;
D £85-£140 (incl. bkfst)* **Facilities** STV FTV Wi-fi ⌨
Xmas New Year **Conf** Class 125 Board 84 Thtr 300
Services Lift **Parking** 25 **Notes** LB Civ Wed 300

Invicta Hotel

★★★ 78% HOTEL

☎ 01752 664997
11-12 Osborne Place, Lockyer St, The Hoe PL1 2PU
e-mail: info@invictahotel.co.uk
web: www.invictahotel.co.uk
dir: A38 to Plymouth, follow city centre signs, then signs to The Hoe & Barbican. Hotel opposite Hoe Park on Lockyer St at junct with Citadel Rd

Just a short stroll from the city centre, this elegant Victorian establishment stands opposite the famous bowling green. The atmosphere is relaxed and friendly and bedrooms are neatly presented, well-equipped and attractively decorated. Eating options include meals in the bar or in the more formal setting of the dining room.

Rooms 23 (4 fmly) (1 GF) **Facilities** FTV Wi-fi Xmas
Conf Class 30 Board 45 Thtr 45 **Parking** 14 **Notes** ⊗

New Continental Hotel

★★★ 77% HOTEL

☎ 01752 220782 & 276798
Millbay Rd PL1 3LD
e-mail: reservations@newcontinental.co.uk
web: www.newcontinental.co.uk
dir: A38, follow city centre signs for Continental Ferryport. Hotel before ferryport, adjacent to Plymouth Pavilions Conference Centre

Within easy reach of the city centre and The Hoe, this privately owned hotel continues to offer high standards of service and hospitality. A variety of bedroom sizes and styles is available, all with the same levels of equipment and comfort. The hotel is a popular choice for conferences and functions.

Rooms 99 (20 fmly) **S** £65-£110; **D** £75-£130 (incl. bkfst)* **Facilities** FTV Wi-fi ⌨ supervised Gym Sauna Steam room **Conf** Class 100 Board 70 Thtr 350
Del from £120 to £135* **Services** Lift **Parking** 100
Notes ⊗ Closed 24 Dec-2 Jan Civ Wed 140

Copthorne Hotel Plymouth

★★★ 74% HOTEL

MILLENNIUM
HOTELS AND RESORTS
MILLENNIUM · COPTHORNE

☎ 01752 224161
Armada Way PL1 1AR
e-mail: sales.plymouth@millenniumhotels.co.uk
web: www.millenniumhotels.co.uk
dir: From M5 follow A38 to Plymouth city centre. Follow ferryport signs over 2 rdbts. Hotel on 1st exit left before 4th rdbt

This hotel is conveniently located near the city's main attractions and the business area, and is also well situated for the theatre and The Hoe. The bedrooms offer good facilities and are available in a range of sizes. The restaurant provides enjoyable dining and there is an all-day lounge and bar service. The secure parking is an asset.

Rooms 135 **Facilities** STV Wi-fi Gym New Year
Conf Class 60 Board 60 Thtr 140 **Services** Lift
Parking 50 **Notes** ⊗ Civ Wed 100

Elfordleigh Hotel, Golf & Country Club

★★★ 74% HOTEL

☎ 01752 336428
Colebrook, Plympton PL7 5EB
e-mail: reception@elfordleigh.co.uk
dir: Exit A38 for city centre, at Marsh Mills/Sainsbury's rdbt take Plympton road. At 4th lights left into Larkham Ln, at end right then left into Crossway. At end left into The Moors, hotel 1m

Located in the beautiful Plym Valley, this well-established hotel is set in attractive wooded countryside. Bedrooms, many with lovely views, are spacious and comfortable. There is an excellent range of leisure facilities including an 18-hole golf course. A choice of dining options is available - a friendly brasserie and the more formal restaurant.

Rooms 34 (2 fmly) (7 GF) **S** £55-£65; **D** £65-£75*
Facilities Spa STV FTV Wi-fi ⓢ ⌨ 18 ⛳ Putt green Fishing ⚓ Gym Squash Hairdresser Beautician Dance & aerobics studio 5-a-side (hard) football pitch Xmas New Year **Conf** Class 120 Board 50 Thtr 200
Del £120* **Services** Lift **Parking** 200 **Notes** LB
Civ Wed 200

P

PLYMOUTH *continued*

The Legacy Plymouth International Hotel

★★★ 64% HOTEL

☎ 08444 119 097 & 0330 333 2897
Marsh Mills PL6 8NH
e-mail: res-plymouthinternational@legacy-hotels.co.uk
web: www.legacy-hotels.co.uk
dir: From N: exit A38 at Marsh Mills, follow Plympton signs, hotel on left. From S: exit A38 at Plympton, hotel on immediate left

Conveniently located on the outskirts of the city, close to Marsh Mills roundabout and Sainsbury's, this modern hotel offers good value accommodation. All bedrooms are spacious and designed with flexibility for family use. Public areas are open-plan, with meals available throughout the day in either the Garden Brasserie, the bar, or from room service.

Rooms 100 (17 fmly) (18 GF) **Facilities** STV FTV Wi-fi ⊃ ⚘ Xmas New Year **Conf** Class 120 Board 100 Thtr 300 **Services** Lift **Parking** 140
Notes Civ Wed 200

Ibis Hotel Plymouth

BUDGET HOTEL

☎ 01752 601087
Marsh Mills, Longbridge Rd, Forder Valley PL6 8LD
e-mail: H2093@accor.com
web: www.ibishotel.com
dir: A38 to Plymouth, 1st exit after flyover towards Estover, Leigham & Parkway Industrial Est. At rdbt, hotel at 4th exit

Modern, budget hotel offering comfortable accommodation in bright and practical bedrooms. Breakfast is self-service and dinner is available in the restaurant. See also the Hotel Groups pages.

Rooms 52 (1 fmly) (26 GF) 🐾

Premier Inn Plymouth Centre (Sutton Harbour)

BUDGET HOTEL

☎ 0871 527 8882
Sutton Rd, Shepherds Wharf PL4 0HX
web: www.premierinn.com
dir: A38, A374 towards Plymouth. Follow Coxside & National Marine Aquarium signs. Right at lights after leisure park. Hotel adjacent to Lockyers Quay (NB there are 2 Premier Inns on this site, this hotel is the larger)

High quality, budget accommodation ideal for both families and business travellers. Spacious, en suite

bedrooms feature tea and coffee making facilities, and Freeview TV in most hotels. Internet access and Wi-fi are available for a small fee. The adjacent family restaurant features a wide and varied menu. See also the Hotel Groups pages.

Rooms 107

Premier Inn Plymouth City Centre (Lockyers Quay)

BUDGET HOTEL

☎ 0871 527 8880
1 Lockyers Quay, Coxside PL4 0DX
web: www.premierinn.com
dir: From A38 (Marsh Mills rdbt) take A374 into Plymouth. Follow Coxside & National Marine Aquarium signs

Rooms 62

Premier Inn Plymouth East

BUDGET HOTEL

☎ 0871 527 8884
300 Plymouth Rd, Crabtree PL3 6RW
web: www.premierinn.com
dir: From E: Exit A38 at Marsh Mill junct. Straight on at rdbt, exit slip road 100mtrs on left. From W: Exit A38 at Plympton junct, at rdbt exit slip road adjacent to A38

Rooms 41

Feathers Hotel

★★ 71% HOTEL

☎ 01759 303155
56 Market Place YO42 2AH
e-mail: info@thefeathers-hotel.co.uk
dir: From York, B1246 signed Pocklington. Hotel just off A1079

This busy, traditional inn provides comfortable, well-equipped and spacious accommodation. Public areas are smartly presented. Enjoyable meals are served in the bar and the conservatory restaurant; the wide choice of dishes makes excellent use of local and seasonal produce.

Rooms 16 (10 annexe) (1 fmly) (10 GF) 🐾
Facilities FTV Wi-fi **Parking** 30 **Notes** ⊗

Talland Bay Hotel

★★★ 87% ⊛⊛ COUNTRY HOUSE HOTEL

☎ 01503 272667
Porthallow PL13 2JB
e-mail: info@tallandbayhotel.co.uk
web: www.tallandbayhotel.co.uk
dir: From Looe over bridge towards Polperro on A387, 2nd turn to hotel

This hotel has the benefit of a wonderful location with far reaching views, being situated in its own extensive gardens that run down almost to the cliff edge. A warm and friendly atmosphere prevails. The bedrooms come in a range of styles - classic twins and doubles, and rooms and suites with sea views. There is also cottage accommodation, and one is particularly suitable for families or those with dogs. The public areas of the hotel are impressive and stylish. Eating options include the Brasserie and Terrace Restaurant where guests will find accomplished cooking, with an emphasis on carefully prepared local produce, remains a key feature.

Rooms 20 (2 fmly) (5 GF) 🐾 **Facilities** FTV Wi-fi ⊃ ⚘ Xmas New Year **Conf** Class 20 Board 20 Thtr 20 **Parking** 20 **Notes** Civ Wed 65

Wentbridge House Hotel

★★★★ 77% ⊛⊛ HOTEL

☎ 01977 620444
Wentbridge WF8 3JJ
e-mail: info@wentbridgehouse.co.uk
web: www.wentbridgehouse.co.uk
dir: M62 junct 33 onto A1 S, hotel in 4m

This well-established hotel sits in 20 acres of landscaped gardens, offering spacious, well-equipped bedrooms and a choice of dining styles. Service in the Fleur de Lys restaurant is polished and friendly, and a varied menu offers a good choice of interesting dishes. The Brasserie has a more relaxed style of modern dining.

Rooms 41 (4 annexe) (4 fmly) (4 GF) ⌇ S £110-£190;
D £140-£220 (incl. bkfst)* **Facilities** FTV Wi-fi Xmas
New Year **Conf** Class 100 Board 60 Thtr 130
Del £150* **Services** Lift **Parking** 100 **Notes** LB ⊗
Civ Wed 130

Premier Inn Pontefract North

BUDGET HOTEL

☎ 0871 527 8886
Pontefract Rd, Knottingley WF11 0BU
web: www.premierinn.com
dir: M62 junct 33 onto A1 N. Exit at Pontefract
junct (A645) to T-junct, right towards Pontefract.
Hotel on right

High quality, budget accommodation ideal for both
families and business travellers. Spacious, en suite
bedrooms feature tea and coffee making facilities,
and Freeview TV in most hotels. Internet access and
Wi-fi are available for a small fee. The adjacent
family restaurant features a wide and varied menu.
See also the Hotel Groups pages.

Rooms 41

Premier Inn Pontefract South

BUDGET HOTEL

☎ 0871 527 8888
Great North Rd, Darrington WF8 3BL
web: www.premierinn.com
dir: Just off A1, 2m S of M62 junct 33

Rooms 28

POOLE
Dorset   **Map 4 SZ09**

Harbour Heights

★★★★ 80% ◉◉ HOTEL

☎ 01202 707272 & 0845 337 1550
73 Haven Rd, Sandbanks BH13 7LW
e-mail: reservations@fjbhotels.co.uk
web: www.fjbcollection.net
dir: Follow signs for Sandbanks, hotel on left after
Canford Cliffs

The unassuming appearance of this 'boutique' hotel
belies a wealth of innovation, quality and style. The
very stylish, contemporary bedrooms, many with sea
views, combine state-of-the-art facilities with
traditional comforts; all have spa baths. The smart
public areas include the award-winning Harbar
Bistro, popular bars and sitting areas where picture
windows accentuate panoramic views of Poole
Harbour. The south-facing sun deck is the perfect
setting for watching the cross-channel ferries come
and go.

Rooms 38 (2 fmly) **Facilities** STV Wi-fi Spa bath in all
rooms Xmas New Year **Conf** Class 36 Board 22
Thtr 70 **Services** Lift Air con **Parking** 50 **Notes** ⊗
Civ Wed 90

Hotel du Vin Poole

★★★★ 78% ◉ HOTEL

☎ 01202 785570
Thames St BH15 1JN
e-mail: info.poole@hotelduvin.com
web: www.hotelduvin.com
dir: A31 to Poole, follow channel ferry signs. Left at
Poole bridge onto Poole Quay, 1st left into Thames St.
Hotel opposite St James Church

Offering a fresh approach to the well established
company style, this property boasts some delightful

rooms packed with comfort and all the expected Hotel
du Vin features. Situated near the harbour the hotel
offers nautically-themed bedrooms and suites that
have plasma TVs, DVD players and bathrooms with
power showers. The public rooms are light, open
spaces, and as with the other hotels in this group, the
bar and restaurant form centre stage.

Rooms 38 (4 GF) ⌇ S £120-£400; D £120-£400*
Facilities STV Wi-fi Xmas New Year **Conf** Class 20
Board 20 Thtr 35 Del from £160 to £230*
Services Air con **Parking** 50 **Notes** LB Civ Wed 100

The Haven

★★★★ 76% ◉◉ HOTEL

☎ 01202 707333 & 0845 337 1550
Banks Rd, Sandbanks BH13 7QL
e-mail: reservations@fjbhotels.co.uk
web: www.fjbcollection.co.uk
dir: B3965 towards Poole Bay, left onto the Peninsula.
Hotel 1.5m on left adjacent to Swanage Toll Ferry

Enjoying an enviable location at the water's edge with
views of Poole Bay, this well established hotel was
once the home of radio pioneer, Guglielmo Marconi. A
friendly team of staff provide good levels of customer
care. Bedrooms vary in size and style; many have
balconies and wonderful sea or harbour views. The
leisure facilities are noteworthy - the refurbished
Harmony at the Haven is where guests can find spa
treatments, a fully equipped gym, indoor and outdoor
heated pools and an all-weather tennis court. The
hotel is a popular venue for conferences and
weddings.

Rooms 84 (4 fmly) **Facilities** Spa STV Wi-fi ⌇ ⊛
supervised ⌇ supervised ⌇ Gym Dance studio
Health & Beauty suite Sauna Steam room Xmas New
Year **Conf** Class 70 Board 50 Thtr 160 **Services** Lift
Parking 160 **Notes** ⊗ Civ Wed 100

POOLE *continued*

The Sandbanks

★★★★ 75% ⊛ HOTEL

☎ 01202 707377 & 0845 337 1550
15 Banks Rd, Sandbanks BH13 7PS
e-mail: reservations@fjbhotels.co.uk
web: www.fjbcollection.co.uk
dir: A338 from Bournemouth onto Wessex Way, to
Liverpool Victoria rdbt. Left, then 2nd exit onto B3965.
Follow beach signs. Hotel on left

Set on the delightful Sandbanks Peninsula, this well
loved hotel has direct access to the seven-mile blue
flag beach and has stunning views across Poole
Harbour and the sea. Most of the spacious bedrooms
have sea views; some are air conditioned. There is an
extensive range of leisure facilities, including an on-
site watersports academy. A family friendly hotel.

Rooms 108 (31 fmly) **Facilities** Spa STV FTV Wi-fi ⊙
supervised Gym Sailing Mountain bikes Children's
play area Massage room Watersports academy Xmas
New Year **Conf** Class 50 Board 80 Thtr 150
Services Lift **Parking** 120 **Notes** ⊗ Civ Wed 70

Thistle Poole

thistle

★★★ 80% HOTEL

☎ 0871 376 9032
The Quay BH15 1HD
e-mail: poole@thistle.co.uk
web: www.thistlehotels.com/poole
dir: On quay adjacent to Dolphin Marina

Situated on the quayside overlooking the harbour, this
modern hotel is situated close to the ferry terminal
and is also a good base for exploring the beautiful
Dorset countryside. Many of the bedrooms have views
of Poole harbour. There is a restaurant and two bars,
plus two meeting rooms are available.

Rooms 70 (22 GF) **Facilities** FTV Wi-fi ⌖ HL Xmas
New Year **Conf** Class 80 Board 60 Thtr 120
Services Lift **Parking** 120 **Notes** Civ Wed 120

Arndale Court Hotel

★★★ 70% HOTEL

☎ 01202 683746
62/66 Wimborne Rd BH15 2BY
e-mail: info@arndalecourthotel.com
web: www.arndalecourthotel.com
dir: On A349, opposite Poole Stadium

Ideally situated for the town centre and ferry terminal,
this is a small, privately owned hotel. Bedrooms are
well equipped, spacious and comfortable. Particularly
well suited to business guests, this hotel has a
pleasant range of stylish public areas and good
parking.

Rooms 39 (7 fmly) (14 GF) (8 smoking) **S** £45-£83;
D £80-£110 (incl. bkfst)* **Facilities** STV FTV Wi-fi
Conf Class 20 Board 30 Thtr 50 **Parking** 40 **Notes** LB

Holiday Inn Express Poole

BUDGET HOTEL

☎ 01202 649222
Walking Field Ln, Seldown Bridge Site BH15 1TJ
e-mail: reservations@exhipoole.co.uk
web: www.hiexpress.com/pooleuk
dir: A350 to town centre, pass bus station. Right at
next rdbt, take slip road to left. Hotel adjacent to
Dolphin Swimming Pool

A modern hotel ideal for families and business
travellers. Fresh and uncomplicated, the spacious
rooms include Sky TV, power shower and tea and
coffee-making facilities. Continental buffet breakfast
is included in the room rate; evening meals are
available in the spacious café/bar. See also the Hotel
Groups pages.

Rooms 85 (42 fmly) (10 GF) (7 smoking) ⌖
Conf Class 16 Board 18 Thtr 30

Premier Inn Poole Centre (Holes Bay)

BUDGET HOTEL

☎ 0871 527 8892
Holes Bay Rd BH15 2BD
web: www.premierinn.com
dir: S of A35 & A349 on A350 (dual carriageway).
Follow Poole Channel Ferry signs

High quality, budget accommodation ideal for both
families and business travellers. Spacious, en suite
bedrooms feature tea and coffee making facilities,
and Freeview TV in most hotels. Internet access and
Wi-fi are available for a small fee. The adjacent
family restaurant features a wide and varied menu.
See also the Hotel Groups pages.

Rooms 83

Premier Inn Poole North

BUDGET HOTEL

☎ 0871 527 8894
Cabot Ln BH17 7DA
web: www.premierinn.com
dir: Follow Poole/Channel Ferries signs. At Darby's
Corner rdbt take 2nd exit. At 2nd lights right into
Cabot Ln. Hotel on right

Rooms 126

Milsoms Poole

RESTAURANT WITH ROOMS

☎ 01202 609000
47 Haven Rd, Canford Cliffs BH13 7LH
e-mail: poole@milsomshotel.co.uk

Milsoms Poole is located in the Canford Cliffs area,
moments from some of the country's best beaches
and the picturesque Purbeck Hills. Comfortable and
stylish en suite accommodation is situated above the
popular seafood Loch Fyne Restaurant. The friendly
and helpful team provide a warm welcome. Limited
on-site parking is available.

Rooms 8

P

Save on hotels. Book at **theAA.com/hotel**

POO – POR 377 ENGLAND

PORLOCK
Somerset — Map 3 SS84

The Oaks Hotel

★★★ ◉ HOTEL

☎ 01643 862265
TA24 8ES
e-mail: info@oakshotel.co.uk
dir: From E of A39, enter village (road narrows to single track) then follow hotel sign. From W: down Porlock Hill, through village, hotel sign on right

A relaxing atmosphere is found at this charming Edwardian house, located near to the setting of R D Blackmore's novel *Lorna Doone*. Quietly located and set in attractive grounds, the hotel enjoys elevated views across the village towards the sea. Bedrooms are thoughtfully furnished and comfortable, and the public rooms include a charming bar and a peaceful drawing room. In the dining room, guests can choose from the daily-changing menu, which features fresh, quality local produce.

Rooms 8 🐾 **S** £165; **D** £235 (incl. bkfst & dinner)*
Facilities FTV Wi-fi ♨ Xmas New Year **Parking** 12
Notes ⊗ No children 8yrs Closed Nov-Mar (ex Xmas & New Year)

PORTHLEVEN
Cornwall — Map 2 SW62

Kota Restaurant with Rooms

◉ RESTAURANT WITH ROOMS

☎ 01326 562407
Harbour Head TR13 9JA
e-mail: kota@btconnect.com
dir: B3304 from Helston into Porthleven. Kota on harbour opposite slipway

Overlooking the water, this 300-year-old building is the home of Kota Restaurant (Kota being the Maori word for shellfish). The bedrooms are approached from a granite stairway to the side of the building. The family room is spacious and has the benefit of harbour views, while the smaller, double room is at the rear of the property. The enthusiastic young owners ensure guests enjoy their stay here, and a meal in the restaurant should not be missed. Breakfast features the best local produce.

Rooms 2 (2 annexe) (1 fmly)

PORT ISAAC
Cornwall — Map 2 SW98

The Longcross Hotel

★★ 78% HOTEL

☎ 01208 880243
Trelights PL29 3TF
e-mail: info@longcrosshotel.co.uk
dir: B3314 from Wadebridge towards Rock/Delabole, 5m, left signed Trelights, through village, follow hotel signs. Or B3266 from Camelford towards Delabole/ Tintagel. 1.5m, left onto B3314. Through Delabole & Pendoggett, right before church. Hotel in 1m

Located in a beautiful setting just minutes from Port Isaac, this hotel has a very friendly and relaxed atmosphere. The bedrooms are light and airy and there is a contemporary bar and separate lounge for guests. There are stunning views from the restaurant and many of the well-appointed bedrooms. Set in carefully tended gardens and grounds which are open to the public, it also offers a series of suites in a separate building. Food is locally sourced and menus offer a wide range of well cooked dishes.

Rooms 15 (5 annexe) (3 fmly) (6 GF) 🐾 **S** £70-£150;
D £100-£210 (incl. bkfst)* **Facilities** FTV Wi-fi
Conf Class 100 Board 40 Thtr 150 **Parking** 30
Notes Closed Jan RS Nov-Dec & Feb-Mar Civ Wed 150

PORTISHEAD
Somerset — Map 4 ST47

Premier Inn Portishead

BUDGET HOTEL

☎ 0871 527 8898
Wyndham Way BS20 7GA
web: www.premierinn.com
dir: M5 junct 19, A369 towards Portishead. Over 1st rdbt, hotel at next rdbt

High quality, budget accommodation ideal for both families and business travellers. Spacious, en suite bedrooms feature tea and coffee making facilities, and Freeview TV in most hotels. Internet access and Wi-fi are available for a small fee. The adjacent family restaurant features a wide and varied menu. See also the Hotel Groups pages.

Rooms 58

PORTLAND
Dorset — Map 4 SY67

The Venue Hotel & Conference Centre

Ⓤ

☎ 01305 826060
Southwell Park DT5 2NS
e-mail: info@thevenuehotel.co.uk
web: www.thevenuehotel.co.uk

Currently the rating for this establishment is not confirmed. This may be due to a change of ownership or because it has only recently joined the AA rating scheme. For further details please see the AA website: theAA.com

Rooms 77 (30 GF) 🐾 **S** £110-£140; **D** £110-£150 (incl. bkfst)* **Facilities** Spa FTV Wi-fi ♨ Gym Sauna Steam room Xmas New Year **Conf** Class 100 Board 70 Thtr 180 Del from £159.50 to £199.50* **Services** Lift Air con **Parking** 80 **Notes** ⊗ Civ Wed 300

P

PORTLOE
Cornwall   Map 2 SW93

The Lugger Hotel
★★★ 82% ⬡ HOTEL

OXFORD
HOTELS & INNS

☎ 01872 501322
TR2 5RD
e-mail: reservations.lugger@ohiml.com
web: www.oxfordhotelsandinns.com
dir: A390 to Truro, B3287 to Tregony, A3078 (St Mawes Rd), left for Veryan, left for Portloe

This delightful hotel enjoys a unique setting adjacent to the slipway of the harbour where fishing boats still come and go. Bedrooms, some in adjacent buildings and cottages, are contemporary in style and well equipped. The sitting room, which reflects the original building's character, has beams and open fireplaces that create a cosy atmosphere. The modern restaurant enjoys superb views, and in warmer months a sun terrace overlooking the harbour proves a popular place.

Rooms 22 (17 annexe) (1 GF) **Facilities** FTV Wi-fi Xmas New Year **Parking** 26 **Notes** Civ Wed 50

PORTSCATHO
Cornwall   Map 2 SW83

INSPECTORS' CHOICE

Driftwood
★★★ ⬡⬡⬡ HOTEL

☎ 01872 580644
Rosevine TR2 5EW
e-mail: info@driftwoodhotel.co.uk
dir: A390 towards St Mawes. On A3078 turn left to Rosevine at Trewithian

Poised on the cliff side with panoramic views, this contemporary hotel has a peaceful and secluded location. A warm welcome is guaranteed here, where professional standards of service are provided in an effortless and relaxed manner. Cuisine is at the heart of any stay, with quality local produce used in a sympathetic and highly skilled manner. The extremely comfortable and elegant bedrooms are decorated in soft shades reminiscent of the seashore. There is a sheltered terraced garden that has a large deck for sunbathing.

Rooms 15 (1 annexe) (3 fmly) (1 GF) **Facilities** FTV Wi-fi ⇘ Private beach Beauty treatments on request **Parking** 30 **Notes** ⊗ Closed 7 Dec-5 Feb RS Xmas & New Year

---

PORTSMOUTH & SOUTHSEA
Hampshire   Map 5 SU60

Portsmouth Marriott Hotel
★★★★ 79% ⬡ HOTEL

Marriott
HOTELS & RESORTS

☎ 0870 400 7285 & 023 9238 3151
Southampton Rd PO6 4SH
web: www.portsmouthmarriott.co.uk
dir: M27 junct 12, keep left off slip road, exit Cosham. Hotel on left at lights

Close to the motorway and ferry port, this hotel is well suited to the business trade. The comfortable and well laid-out bedrooms provide a comprehensive range of facilities including up-to-date workstations. The leisure club offers a pool, a gym, and a health and beauty salon.

Rooms 174 (77 fmly) (5 smoking) **S** £80-£260; **D** £80-£260 **Facilities** STV FTV Wi-fi ⇘ HL ⬡ supervised Gym Exercise studio Beauty salon & treatment room Xmas New Year **Conf** Class 180 Board 30 Thtr 350 Del from £145 to £190 **Services** Lift Air con **Parking** 196 **Notes** LB Civ Wed 350

Holiday Inn Portsmouth
★★★ 79% HOTEL

Holiday Inn

☎ 0871 942 9065
Pembroke Rd PO1 2TA
e-mail: portsmouth@ihg.com
web: www.holidayinn.co.uk
dir: M275 into city centre, follow signs for seafront. Hotel on right after Kings Rd rdbt

This hotel occupies a great location close to Portsmouth seafront and near the Gunwharf Quays Shopping Centre. Restricted, complimentary parking is available on a first-come-first-served basis at the hotel. Accommodation is comfortable and very well maintained; some rooms have magnificent sea views. On-site facilities include a swimming pool, fitness room, a stylish restaurant and meeting rooms.

Rooms 166 (12 fmly) (6 GF) (6 smoking) **Facilities** FTV Wi-fi HL ⬡ supervised Gym Health club Steam room Sauna Xmas New Year **Conf** Class 70 Board 60 Thtr 160 **Services** Lift Air con **Parking** 60 **Notes** ⊗ Civ Wed 120

P

Best Western Royal Beach Hotel

★★★ 78% HOTEL

☎ 023 9273 1281
South Pde, Southsea PO4 0RN
e-mail: enquiries@royalbeachhotel.co.uk
web: www.royalbeachhotel.co.uk
dir: M27 to M275, follow signs to seafront. Hotel on seafront

This former Victorian seafront hotel is a smart and comfortable venue suitable for leisure and business guests alike. Bedrooms and public areas are well presented and generally spacious, and the smart Coast Bar is an ideal venue for a relaxing drink.

Rooms 124 (12 fmly) 🐾 **Facilities** STV FTV Wi-fi 🏐 Xmas New Year **Conf** Class 180 Board 40 Thtr 280 Del from £112 to £132 **Services** Lift **Parking** 50 **Notes** Civ Wed 85

Seacrest Hotel

★★ 80% HOTEL

☎ 023 9273 3192
11/12 South Pde, Southsea PO5 2JB
e-mail: office@seacresthotel.co.uk
dir: From M27/M275 follow signs for seafront, Pyramids & Sea Life Centre. Hotel opposite Rock Gardens & Pyramids

In a premier seafront location, this smart hotel provides the ideal base for exploring the town. Bedrooms, many benefiting from sea views, are decorated to a high standard with good facilities. Guests can relax in either the south-facing lounge, furnished with large leather sofas, or the adjacent bar; there is also a cosy dining room popular with residents.

Rooms 28 (3 fmly) (3 GF) **Facilities** STV FTV Wi-fi **Services** Lift **Parking** 12 **Notes** Closed 24 Dec-2 Jan

The Farmhouse & Innlodge Hotel

OldEngl🏠sh

BUDGET HOTEL

☎ 023 9265 0510
Burrfields Rd PO3 5HH
e-mail: farmhouse.portsmouth@greeneking.co.uk
web: www.farmhouseinnlodge.com
dir: A3(M)/M27 onto A27. Take Southsea exit, follow A2030. 3rd lights right into Burrfields Rd. Hotel 2nd car park on left

Located on the eastern fringe of the city, this purpose-built hotel is conveniently located for all major routes. The spacious, modern bedrooms are well equipped and include ground floor and family

rooms. The Farmhouse Hungry Horse Pub offers a wide range of eating options, and there is an ActionZone adventure area.

Rooms 74 (6 fmly) (33 GF) **Conf** Class 64 Board 40 Thtr 150 Del from £95*

Ibis Portsmouth Centre

BUDGET HOTEL

☎ 023 9264 0000
Winston Churchill Av PO1 2LX
e-mail: h1461@accor.com
web: www.ibishotel.com
dir: M27 junct 12 onto M275. Follow signs for city centre, Sealife Centre & Guildhall. Right at rdbt into Winston Churchill Ave

Modern, budget hotel offering comfortable accommodation in bright and practical bedrooms. Breakfast is self-service and dinner is available in the restaurant. See also the Hotel Groups pages.

Rooms 144 **Conf** Class 20 Board 20 Thtr 30

Premier Inn Portsmouth (Horndean)

BUDGET HOTEL

☎ 0871 527 8902
2 Havant Rd PO8 0DT
web: www.premierinn.com
dir: A3(M) junct 2, take B2149 signed Emsworth, Horndean. At rdbt left onto B2149, follow Horndean signs. At next rdbt left onto A3 towards Waterlooville. Hotel on left (behind Red Lion)

High quality, budget accommodation ideal for both families and business travellers. Spacious, en suite bedrooms feature tea and coffee making facilities, and Freeview TV in most hotels. Internet access and Wi-fi are available for a small fee. The adjacent family restaurant features a wide and varied menu. See also the Hotel Groups pages.

Rooms 25

Premier Inn Portsmouth (Port Solent)

BUDGET HOTEL

☎ 0871 527 8906
Binnacle Way PO6 4FB
web: www.premierinn.com
dir: M27 junct 12, left at lights onto Southampton Rd. Left after 200mtrs at lights onto Compass Rd. At mini-rdbt right onto Binnacle Way, hotel on right

Rooms 108

Premier Inn Portsmouth (Port Solent East)

BUDGET HOTEL

☎ 0871 527 8904
1 Southampton Rd, North Harbour PO6 4SA
web: www.premierinn.com
dir: M27 junct 12, A3, left onto A27. Hotel on left

Rooms 64

Premier Inn Southsea

BUDGET HOTEL

☎ 0871 527 9014
Long Curtain Rd, Southsea PO5 3AA
web: www.premierinn.com
dir: M1 junct 24, A453. Follow ring road & Queen's Drive Industrial Estate signs. After Homebase left into Castle Bridge Rd, hotel opposite Pizza Hut restaurant

Rooms 40

PORT SUNLIGHT Map 15 SJ38
Merseyside

Leverhulme Hotel

★★★★ 83% ❀❀ HOTEL

☎ 0151 644 6655 & 644 5555
Central Rd CH62 5EZ
e-mail: enquiries@leverhulmehotel.co.uk
web: www.leverhulmehotel.co.uk
dir: From Chester: M53 junct 5, A41 (Birkenhead) in approx 4m left into Bolton Rd, on at rdbt, 0.1m right into Church Drive. 0.2m hotel on right. From Liverpool: A41 (Chester), 2.7m, 3rd exit at 3rd rdbt into Bolton Rd (follow directions as above)

Built in 1907, this Grade II listed, former cottage hospital is set in the picturesque garden village of Port Sunlight, which was created by Lord Leverhulme for his soap-factory workers in the late 19th century. Following an extensive restoration project, this art deco hotel has stylish bedrooms, appointed to a very high standard; all have impressive facilities including bathrooms with separate showers and LCD TVs; the suites have roof-top terraces and hot tubs. The hotel also features a range of day rooms and an ultra-modern, award-winning restaurant.

Rooms 19 (4 annexe) (1 fmly) (4 GF) 🐾 **S** £114-£490; **D** £150-£510 (incl. bkfst)* **Facilities** STV FTV Wi-fi 🏐 HL Putt green 🏌 Gym Games room Children's play area Xmas New Year Child facilities **Conf** Class 140 Board 30 Thtr 300 Del from £205 to £325* **Parking** 73 **Notes** LB ⊗ Civ Wed 240

P

PRESTON
Lancashire   Map 18 SD52

See also Garstang

Barton Grange Hotel

★★★★ 77% HOTEL

☎ 01772 862551
Garstang Rd PR3 5AA
e-mail: stay@bartongrangehotel.com
web: www.bartongrangehotel.co.uk

(For full entry see Barton)

Preston Marriott Hotel
Marriott
HOTELS & RESORTS
★★★★ 77% HOTEL

☎ 01772 864087
Garstang Rd, Broughton PR3 5JB
e-mail: reservations.preston@marriotthotels.co.uk
web: www.prestonmarriott.co.uk
dir: M6 junct 32 to M55 junct 1, follow A6 towards Garstang. Hotel 0.5m on right

Exuding a country-club atmosphere this stylish hotel enjoys good links to both the city centre and motorway network. There are two dining options and the extensive leisure facilities ensure that there is plenty to do. The bedrooms are smartly decorated and equipped with a comprehensive range of extras.

Rooms 149 (41 fmly) (63 GF) **Facilities** Spa STV Wi-fi ॐ ॐ supervised Gym Steam room Beauty salon Hairdresser Xmas New Year **Conf** Class 100 Board 70 Thtr 220 **Services** Lift Air con **Parking** 250 **Notes** ⊗ Civ Wed 180

Pines Hotel
★★★ 81% ◉ HOTEL

☎ 01772 338551
570 Preston Rd, Clayton-Le-Woods, Chorley PR6 7ED
e-mail: mail@thepineshotel.co.uk
dir: Exit M6 junct 28 N'bound towards Blackburn for 2.5m to hotel. M6 junct 2 S'bound towards Chorley for 1m. On A6

This unique and stylish hotel sits in four acres of mature grounds just a short drive from the motorway network. Elegant bedrooms are individually designed and offer high levels of comfort and facilities. Day rooms include a smart bar and the aptly named Rosette Restaurant, while extensive function rooms make this hotel a popular venue for weddings.

Rooms 35 (2 fmly) (14 GF) **S** £75-£175; **D** £85-£200 (incl. bkfst)* **Facilities** FTV Wi-fi ♫ Xmas New Year **Conf** Class 250 Board 100 Thtr 400 **Parking** 120 **Notes** ⊗ Civ Wed 250

See advert on opposite page

Holiday Inn Preston

Holiday Inn
★★★ 79% HOTEL

☎ 01772 567000 & 567020
The Ringway PR1 3AU
e-mail: reservations@hipreston.com
web: www.hipreston.com
dir: M6 junct 31, A59 follow signs for town centre. Right at T-junct, hotel on left

Ideally situated in the city centre, yet accessible from the M6 which is just two miles away. The bedrooms are comfortable, well equipped and have useful accessories. The hotel offers Wi-fi, a conference centre and seminar venue, plus a small gym with excellent views across the city. Meals are served in the Ringway Bar and Grill Restaurant, and a bar offers light meals and live TV sport channels. Room service is available 24 hours a day.

Rooms 133 **Facilities** STV FTV Wi-fi ☜ HL Gym **Conf** Class 25 Board 30 Thtr 60 **Services** Lift Air con **Parking** 30 **Notes** ⊗

Macdonald Tickled Trout

MACDONALD HOTELS & RESORTS
★★★ 75% HOTEL

☎ 0844 8799053
Preston New Rd, Samlesbury PR5 0UJ
e-mail: general.tickledtrout@macdonald-hotels.co.uk
web: www.macdonald-hotels.co.uk
dir: M6 junct 31. A59 towards Preston

On the banks of the River Ribble, this hotel is conveniently located for the motorway, making it a popular venue for both business and leisure guests. Smartly appointed bedrooms are all tastefully decorated and equipped with a thoughtful range of extras. The hotel boasts a stylish wing of meeting rooms.

Rooms 98 (6 fmly) (10 GF) ☜ **Facilities** FTV Wi-fi ☜ Fishing ♫ Xmas New Year **Conf** Class 60 Board 50 Thtr 120 **Services** Lift **Parking** 180 **Notes** Civ Wed 90

Ibis Preston North

BUDGET HOTEL

☎ 01772 861800
Garstang Rd, Broughton PR3 5JE
e-mail: H3162@accor.com
web: www.ibishotel.com
dir: M6 junct 32, then M55 junct 1. Left lane onto A6.
Left at slip road, left again at mini-rdbt. 2nd turn,
hotel on right past pub

Modern, budget hotel offering comfortable
accommodation in bright and practical bedrooms.
Breakfast is self-service and dinner is available in
the restaurant. See also the Hotel Groups pages.

Rooms 82 (27 fmly) (16 GF) (12 smoking)
Conf Class 20 Board 20 Thtr 30

Premier Inn Preston Central

BUDGET HOTEL

☎ 0871 527 8908
Fox St PR1 2AB
web: www.premierinn.com
dir: Off Ridgway (A59). Telephone for detailed
directions

High quality, budget accommodation ideal for both
families and business travellers. Spacious, en suite
bedrooms feature tea and coffee making facilities,
and Freeview TV in most hotels. Internet access and
Wi-fi are available for a small fee. The adjacent
family restaurant features a wide and varied menu.
See also the Hotel Groups pages.

Rooms 110

Premier Inn Preston East

BUDGET HOTEL

☎ 0871 527 8910
**Bluebell Way, Preston East Link Rd, Fulwood
PR2 5PZ**
web: www.premierinn.com
dir: M6 junct 31a, follow ring road under motorway,
hotel on left. (NB no exit for S'bound traffic - exit at
M6 junct 31, join M6 N'bound, exit at junct 31a)

Rooms 65

Premier Inn Preston South (Craven Drive)

BUDGET HOTEL

☎ 0871 527 8914
Lostock Ln, Bamber Bridge PR5 6BZ
web: www.premierinn.com
dir: M6 junct 29, A582 (Lostock Ln). Straight on at 1st
lights, into left lane, hotel on left adjacent to B&Q

Rooms 74

Premier Inn Preston South (Cuerden Way)

BUDGET HOTEL

☎ 0871 527 8916
Lostock Ln, Bamber Bridge PR5 6BA
web: www.premierinn.com
dir: Off M65 junct 1 (0.5m from M6 junct 29) close to
rdbt junct of A582 & A6

Rooms 42

Premier Inn Preston West

BUDGET HOTEL

☎ 0871 527 8918
Blackpool Rd, Lea PR4 0XB
web: www.premierinn.com
dir: Off A583, opposite Texaco garage

Rooms 38

PRESTWICH   Map 15 SD80
Greater Manchester

Premier Inn Manchester (Prestwich)

BUDGET HOTEL

☎ 0871 527 8714
Bury New Rd M25 3AJ
web: www.premierinn.com
dir: M60 junct 17, A56 signed Manchester City
Centre, Prestwich & Whitefield. Hotel on left

High quality, budget accommodation ideal for both
families and business travellers. Spacious, en suite
bedrooms feature tea and coffee making facilities,
and Freeview TV in most hotels. Internet access and
Wi-fi are available for a small fee. The adjacent
family restaurant features a wide and varied menu.
See also the Hotel Groups pages.

Rooms 60

P

PUDDINGTON
Cheshire — Map 15 SJ37

Macdonald Craxton Wood Hotel

★★★★ 77% ®® HOTEL

☎ 0844 879 9038
Parkgate Rd, Ledsham CH66 9PB
e-mail: craxton@macdonald-hotels.co.uk
web: www.macdonald-hotels.co.uk
dir: From M6 take M56 towards N Wales, then A5117/A540 to Hoylake. Hotel on left 200yds past lights

Set in extensive grounds, this hotel offers a variety of bedroom styles; the modern rooms are particularly comfortable. The Aiden Byrne British Grill is a highlight, featuring stylish decor and classic dishes on the menu. Full leisure facilities and a choice of function suites complete the package.

Rooms 72 (8 fmly) (30 GF) **S** £60-£149; **D** £60-£149*
Facilities Spa FTV Wi-fi Gym Sauna Steam room Xmas New Year **Conf** Class 200 Board 160 Thtr 300 **Services** Lift **Parking** 220 **Notes** LB Civ Wed 350

Premier Inn Wirral (Two Mills)

BUDGET HOTEL

☎ 0871 527 9180
Parkgate Rd, Two Mills CH66 9PD
web: www.premierinn.com
dir: 5m from M56 junct 16 & M53 junct 5. On x-rds of A550 & A540

High quality, budget accommodation ideal for both families and business travellers. Spacious, en suite bedrooms feature tea and coffee making facilities, and Freeview TV in most hotels. Internet access and Wi-fi are available for a small fee. The adjacent family restaurant features a wide and varied menu. See also the Hotel Groups pages.

Rooms 31

PURTON
Wiltshire — Map 5 SU08

The Pear Tree at Purton

★★★ 81% ®® HOTEL

☎ 01793 772100
Church End SN5 4ED
e-mail: stay@peartreepurton.co.uk
dir: M4 junct 16 follow signs to Purton, at Best One shop turn right. Hotel 0.25m on left

A charming 15th-century, former vicarage set amidst extensive landscaped gardens in a peaceful location in the Vale of the White Horse and near the Saxon village of Purton. The resident proprietors and staff provide efficient, dedicated service and friendly hospitality. The spacious bedrooms are individually decorated and have a good range of thoughtful extras such as fresh fruit, sherry and shortbread. Fresh ingredients feature on the award-winning menus.

Rooms 17 (2 fmly) (6 GF) **S** £120-£160; **D** £120-£200 (incl. bkfst) **Facilities** STV FTV Wi-fi Outdoor giant chess Vineyard **Conf** Class 30 Board 30 Thtr 70 Del from £159 to £180 **Parking** 60 **Notes** LB Civ Wed 50

QUORN
Leicestershire — Map 11 SK51

Quorn Country Hotel

★★★★ 76% HOTEL

☎ 01509 415050 & 415061
Charnwood House, 66 Leicester Rd LE12 8BB
e-mail: reservations@quorncountryhotel.co.uk
web: www.quorncountryhotel.co.uk
dir: M1 junct 23 onto A512 into Loughborough. Follow A6 signs. At 1st rdbt towards Quorn, through lights, hotel 500yds from 2nd rdbt

Professional service is one of the key strengths of this pleasing hotel, which sits beside the river in four acres of landscaped gardens and grounds. The smart modern conference centre and function suites are popular for both corporate functions and weddings. Public rooms include a smart comfortable lounge and bar, and guests have the choice of two dining options: the formal Shires restaurant and the informal conservatory-style Orangery.

Rooms 36 (2 fmly) (11 GF) **D** £79-£159 **Facilities** STV Wi-fi Fishing New Year **Conf** Class 162 Board 40 Thtr 300 Del from £109 to £172 **Services** Lift **Parking** 100 **Notes** LB Civ Wed 200

RADLETT
Hertfordshire — Map 6 TL10

Premier Inn St Albans/Bricket Wood

BUDGET HOTEL

☎ 0871 527 9016
Smug Oak Ln, Bricketwood AL2 3PN
web: www.premierinn.com
dir: M1 junct 6 (or M25 junct 21a) follow Watford signs, left at lights signed M1/Bricket Wood. 2nd left into Mount Pleasant Ln, straight on at 2 mini rdbts, right at The Gate pub. Hotel at end

High quality, budget accommodation ideal for both families and business travellers. Spacious, en suite bedrooms feature tea and coffee making facilities, and Freeview TV in most hotels. Internet access and Wi-fi are available for a small fee. The adjacent family restaurant features a wide and varied menu. See also the Hotel Groups pages.

Rooms 56

RAINHAM
Greater London — Map 6 TQ58

The Manor Hotel & Restaurant
★★★ 78% HOTEL

☎ 01708 555586
Berwick Pond Rd RM13 9EL
e-mail: info@themanoressex.co.uk
web: www.themanoressex.co.uk
dir: M25 junct 30/31, A13, 1st exit signed Wennington, right, at main lights right onto Upminster Rd North, left into Berwick Pond Rd

Located in the countryside the former Berwick Manor has been lovingly restored, and today offers well-appointed, contemporary accommodation. The rooms are equipped with a good range of amenities including complimentary Wi-fi. Lunch and dinner are served in the attractive restaurant whilst alfresco dining is possible on the terrace. Two function suites provide the ideal events venue.

Save on hotels. Book at **theAA.com/hotel**

PUD – RAM 383 ENGLAND

The Manor Hotel & Restaurant

Rooms 15 (1 fmly) **Facilities** STV Wi-fi Xmas New Year **Conf** Class 60 Board 40 Thtr 100 **Services** Lift **Parking** 60 **Notes** ⊗ Civ Wed 60

Premier Inn Rainham

BUDGET HOTEL

☎ 0871 527 8920
New Rd, Wennington RM13 9ED
web: www.premierinn.com
dir: M25 junct 30/31, A13 for Dagenham/Rainham, A1306 towards Wennington, Aveley, & Rainham. Hotel 0.5m on right

High quality, budget accommodation ideal for both families and business travellers. Spacious, en suite bedrooms feature tea and coffee making facilities, and Freeview TV in most hotels. Internet access and Wi-fi are available for a small fee. The adjacent family restaurant features a wide and varied menu. See also the Hotel Groups pages.

Rooms 61

RAINHILL Map 15 SJ49
Merseyside

Premier Inn Liverpool (Rainhill)

BUDGET HOTEL

☎ 0871 527 8614
804 Warrington Rd L35 6PE
web: www.premierinn.com
dir: Just off M62 junct 7, A57 towards Rainhill

High quality, budget accommodation ideal for both families and business travellers. Spacious, en suite bedrooms feature tea and coffee making facilities, and Freeview TV in most hotels. Internet access and Wi-fi are available for a small fee. The adjacent family restaurant features a wide and varied menu. See also the Hotel Groups pages.

Rooms 34

RAMSGATE Map 7 TR36
Kent

The Pegwell Bay Hotel

★★★ 78% HOTEL

☎ 01843 599590
81 Pegwell Rd, Pegwell CT11 0NJ
e-mail: reception@pegwellbayhotel.co.uk
dir: Telephone for detailed directions

Boasting stunning views over The Channel, this historic cliff-top hotel is suitable for guests staying either on business or for leisure. Spacious, comfortable bedrooms are well equipped and include Wi-fi. A modern lounge, majestic dining room and traditional pub offer a variety of options for eating and for relaxation.

Rooms 42 (1 fmly) (6 GF) **Facilities** FTV Wi-fi Xmas New Year **Conf** Class 65 Board 65 Thtr 100 **Services** Lift **Notes** ⊗ Civ Wed 70

Comfort Inn Ramsgate

★★★ 70% HOTEL

☎ 01843 592345
Victoria Pde, East Cliff CT11 8DT
e-mail: reservations@comfortinnramsgate.co.uk
dir: From M2 take A299 signed Ramsgate, B2054 to Victoria Parade, follow sign to harbour

This Victorian hotel stands on the seafront, close to the ferry terminal and the town. Bedrooms, some with balconies, are generously sized and well equipped. Guests can relax in the modern bar and lounge or be pampered in the beauty treatment room. The popular restaurant serves a particularly wide choice of dishes ranging from traditional British cuisine to Indian favourites.

Rooms 44 (8 fmly) ⌇ **S** £40-£60; **D** £60-£120 (incl. bkfst) **Facilities** STV FTV Wi-fi ⌇ Beauty salon Xmas New Year **Conf** Class 30 Board 30 Thtr 50 **Del** from £75 to £95 **Services** Lift Air con **Parking** 10 **Notes** LB ⊗

The Oak Hotel

★★ 84% HOTEL

☎ 01843 583686 & 581582
66 Harbour Pde CT11 8LN
e-mail: reception@oakhotel.co.uk
dir: Follow road around harbour, right into Harbour Parade

Located within easy reach of the railway station, ferry terminal and the town centre's shops, this stylish hotel enjoys spectacular views of the marina and harbour. The comfortable bedrooms are attractively presented and very well equipped. The Atlantis fish restaurant, Caffe Roma and the contemporary bar offer a variety of dining options.

Rooms 34 (9 fmly) (7 GF) **Facilities** STV FTV Wi-fi **Conf** Class 60 Board 50 Thtr 100 **Notes** ⊗

Royal Harbour Hotel

★★ 79% METRO HOTEL

☎ 01843 591514
10-11 Nelson Crescent CT11 9JF
e-mail: info@royalharbourhotel.co.uk
dir: A253 to Ramsgate. Follow signs to seafront. At Churchill Tavern, 1st left into Nelson Crescent

Dating back to 1799, this hotel is made up of adjoining Georgian Grade II listed townhouses, and occupies a prime position in the town's well known historic garden crescent. Many of the bedrooms boast magnificent views over the 'Royal Harbour', the yacht marina and the English Channel. The atmosphere is relaxed, the service is attentive and the breakfast is superb.

Rooms 19 (3 fmly) (1 GF) **Facilities** FTV Wi-fi **Conf** Class 30 Board 25 Thtr 30 **Parking** 4

R

Holiday Inn Express Ramsgate - Minster

BUDGET HOTEL

☎ 01843 820250
Tothill St CT12 4AU
e-mail: reservations@express-kia.co.uk
web: www.hiexpress.co.uk
dir: On A299, off rdbt junct with B2048

A modern hotel ideal for families and business travellers. Fresh and uncomplicated, the spacious rooms include Sky TV, power shower and tea and coffee-making facilities. Continental buffet breakfast is included in the room rate; other meals may be taken at the nearby family pub or restaurant. See also the Hotel Groups pages.

Rooms 105 (62 fmly) (33 GF) (17 smoking) **Conf** Class 30 Board 20 Thtr 40

RAVENGLASS
Cumbria   Map 18 SD09

The Pennington Hotel

★★★ 82% HOTEL

☎ 01229 717222 & 0845 450 6445
CA18 1SD
e-mail: info@penningtonhotels.com
dir: In village centre

This hotel has a very relaxed atmosphere throughout and the public areas are open plan with high quality fabrics and artwork. The bedrooms are modern in design and have high spec fixtures and fittings in the bathrooms. Honest cooking, based on local and fine quality ingredients, is offered on the seasonal menus. Staff show exceptional customer awareness by providing very attentive and friendly service.

Rooms 21 (3 annexe) (6 fmly) (5 GF) ❀ **S** £80–£120; **D** £90–£140 (incl. bkfst) **Facilities** FTV Wi-fi ⬥ Xmas New Year **Conf** Class 40 Board 40 Thtr 80 Del from £100 to £190 **Parking** 53 **Notes** LB

RAVENSCAR
North Yorkshire   Map 19 NZ90

Raven Hall Country House Hotel

★★★ 78% HOTEL

☎ 01723 870353
YO13 0ET
e-mail: enquiries@ravenhall.co.uk
web: www.ravenhall.co.uk
dir: A171 towards Whitby. At Cloughton turn right onto unclassified road to Ravenscar

This impressive cliff top mansion enjoys breathtaking views over Robin Hood's Bay. Extensive well-kept grounds include tennis courts, putting green, swimming pools and historic battlements. The bedrooms vary in size but all are comfortably equipped, many offer panoramic views. There are also eight environmentally-friendly Finnish lodges that have been furnished to a high standard.

Rooms 60 (8 annexe) (20 fmly) (5 GF) **Facilities** FTV Wi-fi ⬥ ♪ 9 ♨ Putt green ♨ Bowls Table tennis Xmas New Year **Conf** Class 80 Board 40 Thtr 100 Del from £95 to £140* **Services** Lift **Parking** 200 **Notes** LB Civ Wed 100

RAYLEIGH
Essex   Map 7 TQ89

Premier Inn Basildon (Rayleigh)

BUDGET HOTEL

☎ 0871 527 8058
Rayleigh Weir, Arterial Road (A127) SS6 7XJ
web: www.premierinn.com
dir: M25 junct 29, A127 towards Southend. Approx 13m exit at Rayleigh Weir junct onto A129 to Rayleigh. Straight on at 2 lights, 1st left (NB Sat Nav use code SS6 7XJ)

High quality, budget accommodation ideal for both families and business travellers. Spacious, en suite bedrooms feature tea and coffee making facilities, and Freeview TV in most hotels. Internet access and Wi-fi are available for a small fee. The adjacent family restaurant features a wide and varied menu. See also the Hotel Groups pages.

Rooms 49

READING
Berkshire   Map 5 SU77

See also Sonning

Forbury Hotel

★★★★★ 81% ◉◉ HOTEL

☎ 0118 952 7770
26 The Forbury RG1 3EJ
e-mail: reception@theforburyhotel.co.uk
dir: Telephone for detailed directions

The imposing exterior of this hotel belies the caring approach of the staff who provide helpful service with a smile. The up-to-the-minute bedrooms have very appealing designs and sensory appeal. For film buffs, a 30-seater cinema is also available, complete with refreshments! Cerise is the convivial and stylish venue for enjoying the award-winning cuisine.

Rooms 23 ❀ **S** £174–£372; **D** £174–£372 (incl. bkfst) **Facilities** FTV Wi-fi ⬥ ♪ Xmas New Year **Conf** Class 24 Board 24 Thtr 35 Del from £234 to £264 **Services** Lift **Parking** 20 **Notes** LB ⊗ Civ Wed 50

Crowne Plaza Reading

CROWNE PLAZA
HOTELS & RESORTS

★★★★ 80% ◉◉ HOTEL

☎ 0118 925 9988
Caversham Bridge, Richfield Av RG1 8BD
e-mail: info@cp-reading.co.uk
web: www.cp-reading.co.uk
dir: A33 to Reading. Follow signs for Caversham & Henley. Take 1st exit at rdbt onto Caversham Rd. Left at rdbt & entrance on right

Located on the banks of the River Thames, this hotel is well positioned for both business and leisure travellers. The air-conditioned bedrooms are smartly appointed and well equipped. Public areas include the stylish Acqua Restaurant, a lounge bar, extensive conference and business facilities and the Revive Health Club and Spa. Secure parking is a real bonus.

Rooms 122 (9 fmly) ❀ **S** £69–£155; **D** £69–£155* **Facilities** Spa STV FTV Wi-fi ⬥ HL ⬥ Gym Sauna Steam room **Conf** Class 110 Board 60 Thtr 200 Del from £175 to £225* **Services** Lift Air con **Parking** 200 **Notes** LB ⊗ Civ Wed 180

Millennium Madejski Hotel Reading

MILLENNIUM
HOTELS AND RESORTS
MILLENNIUM • COPTHORNE

★★★★ 79% ◉◉ HOTEL

☎ 0118 925 3500
Madejski Stadium RG2 0FL
e-mail: sales.reading@millenniumhotels.co.uk
web: www.millenniumhotels.co.uk
dir: M4 junct 11 onto A33, follow signs for Madejski Stadium Complex

A stylish hotel, that features an atrium lobby with specially commissioned water sculpture, is part of the Madejski stadium complex, home to both Reading Football and London Irish Rugby teams. Bedrooms are appointed with spacious workstations and plenty of amenities; there is also a choice of suites and a club floor with its own lounge. The hotel also has a fine dining restaurant.

Rooms 201 (39 fmly) (19 smoking) **Facilities** Spa STV Wi-fi ⬥ ⬥ supervised Gym **Conf** Class 36 Board 30 Thtr 66 **Services** Lift Air con **Parking** 250 **Notes** RS Xmas & New Year

Save on hotels. Book at **theAA.com/hotel**

RAV – REA 385 ENGLAND

Novotel Reading Centre

★★★★ 78% HOTEL

☎ 0118 952 2600
25b Friar St RG1 1DP
e-mail: h5432@accor.com
web: www.novotel.com
dir: M4 junct 11 or A33 towards Reading, left for Garrard St car park, at rdbt 3rd exit on Friar St

This attractive and stylish city centre hotel is convenient for Reading's business and shopping centre; it is adjacent to a town centre car park, and has a range of conference facilities and excellent leisure options. The restaurant offers a contemporary style menu and a good wine list too. Bedrooms are comfortable and stylishly designed.

Rooms 178 (15 fmly) **Facilities** STV FTV Wi-fi ⓢ Gym Steam room **Conf** Class 50 Board 36 Thtr 90 **Services** Lift Air con **Parking** 15

Holiday Inn Reading M4 Jct 10

★★★★ 77% HOTEL

☎ 0118 944 0444
Wharfedale Rd, Winnersh Triangle RG41 5TS
e-mail: reservations@hireadinghotel.com
web: www.meridianleisurehotels.com/reading
dir: M4 junct 10/A329(M) towards Reading (E), 1st exit signed Winnersh/Woodley/A329, left at lights into Wharfesale Rd. Hotel on left

Situated in the Winnersh Triangle within close proximity of the M4, Reading, Bracknell and Wokingham, this hotel offers a range of contemporary and stylish bedrooms, eight state-of-the-art meeting rooms and extensive leisure facilities including a 19-metre indoor pool. The Caprice Restaurant offers relaxed dining throughout the day.

Rooms 174 (25 fmly) (16 smoking) ☍ **D** £52-£199* **Facilities** FTV Wi-fi ⓢ HL ⓢ Gym Sauna Steam room Beauty treatment room ♫ Xmas New Year **Conf** Class 160 Board 64 Thtr 260 Del from £122.95 to £235* **Services** Lift Air con **Parking** 120 **Notes** LB Civ Wed 260

Malmaison Reading

★★★ 85% ⓐ HOTEL

☎ 0118 956 2300
Great Western House, 18-20 Station Rd RG1 1JX
e-mail: reading@malmaison.com
web: www.malmaison.com
dir: Opposite rail station

This historic hotel has been transformed to a funky, Malmaison style which reflects its proximity and long-standing relationship with the railway. Public areas feature rail memorabilia and excellent pictures, and include a Café Mal and a meeting room. Bedrooms here have all the amenities a modern executive would expect, plus comfort and quality in abundance. Dining is interesting too, with a menu that features home-grown and local produce accompanied by an impressive wine list.

Rooms 75 (6 fmly) **Facilities** Wi-fi Gym Xmas New Year **Conf** Board 16 **Services** Lift Air con

Holiday Inn Reading South M4 Jct 11

★★★ 78% HOTEL

☎ 0871 702 9067
Basingstoke Rd RG2 0SL
e-mail: reading@ihg.com
web: www.holidayinn.co.uk
dir: A33 to Reading. 1st rdbt right onto Imperial Way. Hotel on left

This bright hotel provides modern accommodation and the addition of leisure facilities is a bonus at the end of a busy day. Meals are served in Traders restaurant, or snacks are available in the lounge. Callaghans, an Irish-style pub, offers live sports coverage. The business centre has a good range of conference and meeting rooms.

Rooms 202 (60 fmly) (99 GF) (10 smoking) **S** £39-£179; **D** £44-£189* **Facilities** FTV Wi-fi ⓢ HL ⓢ supervised Gym Health & fitness centre Beauty treatment room New Year **Conf** Class 45 Board 50 Thtr 100 **Services** Air con **Parking** 300 **Notes** ⓧ Civ Wed 100

Best Western Calcot Hotel

★★★ 73% HOTEL

☎ 0118 941 6423
98 Bath Rd, Calcot RG31 7QN
e-mail: enquiries@calcothotel.net
web: www.calcothotel.co.uk
dir: M4 junct 12, A4 towards Reading, hotel in 0.5m

This hotel is conveniently located in a residential area just off the motorway. Bedrooms are well equipped with good business facilities, such as data ports and good workspace. There are attractive public rooms and function suites, and the informal restaurant offers enjoyable food in welcoming surroundings.

Rooms 80 (3 fmly) (6 GF) **Facilities** FTV Wi-fi ♫ New Year **Conf** Class 35 Board 35 Thtr 120 Del from £135 to £145 **Parking** 130 **Notes** Closed 25-27 Dec Civ Wed 200

Ibis Reading Centre

BUDGET HOTEL

☎ 0118 953 3500
25A Friar St RG1 1DP
e-mail: H5431@accor.com
web: www.ibishotel.com
dir: A329 into Friar St. Hotel near central railway station. Access by car in Garrard St

Modern, budget hotel offering comfortable accommodation in bright and practical bedrooms. Breakfast is self-service and dinner is available in the restaurant. See also the Hotel Groups pages.

Rooms 182 ☍

Premier Inn Reading (Caversham Bridge)

BUDGET HOTEL

R

☎ 0871 527 8922
Richfield Av RG1 8EQ
web: www.premierinn.com
dir: M4 junct 11, A33 to Reading. A329 towards Caversham. Left at TGI Friday's. Left at Crowne Plaza. Hotel 200yds on right

High quality, budget accommodation ideal for both families and business travellers. Spacious, en suite bedrooms feature tea and coffee making facilities, and Freeview TV in most hotels. Internet access and Wi-fi are available for a small fee. The adjacent family restaurant features a wide and varied menu. See also the Hotel Groups pages.

Rooms 74

READING continued

Premier Inn Reading Central

BUDGET HOTEL

☎ 0871 527 8924

Letcombe St RG1 2HN

web: www.premierinn.com

dir: M4 junct 11, A33 towards town centre, straight on at 3 rdbts (approx 3.5m). Right onto A329 signed The Oracle, Riverside Shopping Centre. Branch immediately left, hotel opposite The Oracle shopping centre

Rooms 151

Premier Inn Reading South

BUDGET HOTEL

☎ 0871 527 8926

Goring Ln, Grazeley Green RG7 1LS

web: www.premierinn.com

dir: M4 junct 11, A33 towards Basingstoke. At rdbt take exit towards Burghfield & Mortimer. 3rd right into Grazeley Green. Under rail bridge turn left. Hotel on left

Rooms 32

Abbey Hotel Golf & Spa

★★★★ 78% HOTEL

☎ 01527 406600

Hither Green Ln, Dagnell End Rd, Bordesley B98 9BE

e-mail: info@theabbeyhotel.co.uk

web: www.theabbeyhotel.co.uk

dir: M42 junct 2, A441 to Redditch. End of carriageway turn left (A441), Dagnell End Rd on left. Hotel 600yds on right

With convenient access to the motorway and a proximity to many attractions, this modern hotel is popular with both business and leisure travellers. Bedrooms are well equipped and attractively decorated; the executive corner rooms are especially spacious. Facilities include an 18-hole golf course, pro shop, large indoor pool and extensive conference facilities.

Rooms 100 (20 fmly) (23 GF) ⬥ **Facilities** Spa FTV Wi-fi ⬥ ⬥ 18 Putt green Fishing Gym Golf driving range Xmas New Year **Conf** Class 60 Board 30 Thtr 170 Del from £129 to £170* **Services** Lift **Parking** 200 **Notes** ⊗ Civ Wed 100

Holiday Inn Express Birmingham - Redditch

BUDGET HOTEL

☎ 01527 584658

2 Hewell Rd, Enfield B97 6AE

e-mail: reservations@express.gb.com

web: www.meridianleisurehotels.com/redditch

dir: M42 junct 2/A441 follow signs to rail station. Before station turn right into Hewell Rd, 1st left into Gloucester Close

A modern hotel ideal for families and business travellers. Fresh and uncomplicated, the spacious rooms include satellite channels, and bathrooms with power showers. Complimentary hot breakfast is included in the room rate; freshly prepared meals are served in the GR Restaurant daily from 6pm-10pm.

Rooms 100 (75 fmly) (10 GF) (14 smoking) ⬥ **S** £40-£74.95; **D** £40-£74.95 (incl. bkfst)* **Conf** Class 26 Board 20 Thtr 50 Del from £105 to £130*

Premier Inn Redditch

BUDGET HOTEL

☎ 0871 527 8928

Birchfield Rd B97 6PX

web: www.premierinn.com

dir: M5 junct 4, A38 towards Bromsgrove. At rdbt take A448 to Redditch. 1st exit for Webheath. At next rdbt 3rd exit, 1st right into Birchfield Rd

High quality, budget accommodation ideal for both families and business travellers. Spacious, en suite bedrooms feature tea and coffee making facilities, and Freeview TV in most hotels. Internet access and Wi-fi are available for a small fee. The adjacent family restaurant features a wide and varied menu. See also the Hotel Groups pages.

Rooms 33

Nutfield Priory Hotel & Spa

★★★★ 82% ◉◉ HOTEL

☎ 01737 824400 & 0845 072 7485

Nutfield RH1 4EL

e-mail: nutfieldpriory@handpicked.co.uk

web: www.handpickedhotels.co.uk/nutfieldpriory

dir: M25 junct 6, follow Redhill signs via Godstone on A25. Hotel 1m on left after Nutfield Village. Or M25 junct 8, A25 through Reigate & Redhill. Hotel on right 1.5m after rail bridge

This Victorian country house dates back to 1872 and is set in 40 acres of grounds with stunning views over the Surrey countryside. Bedrooms are individually decorated and equipped with an excellent range of facilities. Public areas include the impressive grand hall, Cloisters Restaurant, the library, and a cosy lounge bar area. Hand Picked Hotels – AA Hotel Group of the Year 2012-13.

Rooms 60 (4 fmly) ⬥ **Facilities** Spa STV FTV Wi-fi ⬥ HL ⬥ Gym Squash Steam room Beauty therapy Aerobic & Step classes Saunas Xmas New Year **Conf** Class 45 Board 40 Thtr 80 **Services** Lift Air con **Parking** 130 **Notes** ⊗ Civ Wed 80

Premier Inn Redhill

BUDGET HOTEL

☎ 0871 527 8930

Brighton Rd, Salfords RH1 5BT

web: www.premierinn.com

dir: On A23, 2m S of Redhill; 3m N of Gatwick Airport

High quality, budget accommodation ideal for both families and business travellers. Spacious, en suite bedrooms feature tea and coffee making facilities, and Freeview TV in most hotels. Internet access and Wi-fi are available for a small fee. The adjacent family restaurant features a wide and varied menu. See also the Hotel Groups pages.

Rooms 48

R

Save on hotels. Book at theAA.com/hotel

REA – RET 387   ENGLAND

REDRUTH   Map 2 SW64
Cornwall

Penventon Park Hotel
★★★ 79% HOTEL

☎ 01209 203000
TR15 1TE
e-mail: info@penventon.com
web: www.penventon.co.uk
dir: Exit A30 at Redruth. Follow signs for Redruth West, hotel 1m S

Set in attractive parkland, this Georgian mansion is ideal for either the business or leisure guest. Bedrooms include 20 Garden Suites. The restaurant offers a wide choice and specialises in British, Cornish, Italian and French dishes. Leisure facilities include a fitness suite and health spa as well as function rooms and bars.

Rooms 64 (3 fmly) (25 GF) ⌀ **Facilities** Spa FTV Wi-fi ⌀ ⌀ supervised Gym Masseuse Steam bath Pool table Beautician Solarium ♬ Xmas New Year **Conf** Class 100 Board 60 Thtr 200 **Parking** 100 **Notes** Civ Wed 150

REDWORTH   Map 19 NZ22
Co Durham

Redworth Hall Hotel

★★★★ 79% ◉
COUNTRY HOUSE HOTEL
PUMA HOTELS COLLECTION

☎ 01388 770600
DL5 6NL
e-mail: redworthhall@pumahotels.co.uk
web: www.pumahotels.co.uk
dir: From A1(M) junct 58, A68 signed Corbridge. Follow hotel signs

This imposing Georgian building includes a health club with state-of-the-art equipment and impressive conference facilities making this hotel a popular destination for business travellers. There are several spacious lounges to relax in along with the Conservatory Restaurant. Bedrooms are very comfortable and well equipped.

Rooms 143 (12 fmly) **Facilities** STV Wi-fi ⌀ ⌀ ⌀ Gym Bodysense Health & Leisure Club ♬ Xmas New Year **Conf** Class 144 Board 90 Thtr 300 **Services** Lift **Parking** 300 **Notes** Civ Wed 240

REEPHAM   Map 13 TG12
Norfolk

Old Brewery House
★★★ 68% HOTEL
OXFORD HOTELS & INNS

☎ 01603 870881
Market Place NR10 4JJ
e-mail: reservations.oldbreweryhouse@ohiml.com
web: www.oxfordhotelsandinns.com
dir: A1067, right at Bawdeswell onto B1145 into Reepham, hotel on left in Market Place

This Grade II listed Georgian building is situated in the heart of this bustling town centre. Public areas include a cosy lounge, a bar, a conservatory and a smart restaurant. Bedrooms come in a variety of styles; each one is pleasantly decorated and equipped with a good range of facilities.

Rooms 23 (2 fmly) (7 GF) **Facilities** ⌀ Gym Squash Xmas **Conf** Class 80 Board 30 Thtr 200 **Parking** 40 **Notes** Civ Wed 45

REIGATE   Map 6 TQ25
Surrey

Best Western Reigate Manor Hotel

★★★ 73% HOTEL

☎ 01737 240125
Reigate Hill RH2 9PF
e-mail: hotel@reigatemanor.co.uk
web: www.reigatemanor.co.uk
dir: On A217, 1m S of M25 junct 8

On the slopes of Reigate Hill, the hotel is ideally located for access to the town and for motorway links. A range of public rooms is provided along with a variety of function rooms. Bedrooms are either traditional in style in the old house or of contemporary design in the wing.

Rooms 50 (1 fmly) **Facilities** STV Wi-fi **Conf** Class 80 Board 50 Thtr 200 **Parking** 130 **Notes** ⊗ Civ Wed 200

RENISHAW   Map 16 SK47
Derbyshire

Sitwell Arms Hotel
★★★ 73% HOTEL

☎ 01246 435226
Station Rd S21 3WF
e-mail: info@sitwellarms.com
dir: On A6135 to Sheffield, W of M1 junct 30

Parts of this attractive stone building date from the 18th century when it was a coaching inn. It has been extended to provide spacious comfortable bedrooms with modern facilities. A wide range of meals is served in the Wild Boar Restaurant; there is also a cocktail bar, informal lounge bar and a smart beer garden with patio and children's play area. The hotel has a gym and a hair and beauty salon.

Rooms 31 (8 fmly) (9 GF) **Facilities** FTV Wi-fi Gym Fitness studio Hair & beauty salon Xmas New Year **Conf** Class 60 Board 60 Thtr 160 Del from £87 to £150* **Services** Lift **Parking** 150 **Notes** LB ⊗ Civ Wed 150

RETFORD   Map 17 SK78
Nottinghamshire

Ye Olde Bell Hotel & Restaurant
★★★★ 78% HOTEL

☎ 01777 705121
DN22 8QS
e-mail: enquiries@yeoldebell-hotel.co.uk
web: www.yeoldebell-hotel.co.uk

(For full entry see Barnby Moor)

R

RETFORD *continued*

Best Western Plus West Retford Hotel

★★★ 77% HOTEL

☎ 01777 706333
24 North Rd DN22 7XG
e-mail: reservations@westretfordhotel.co.uk
dir: From A1 take A620 to Ranby/Retford. Left at rdbt into North Rd (A638). Hotel on right

Stylishly appointed throughout, and set in very attractive gardens close to the town centre, this 18th-century manor house offers a good range of well-equipped meeting facilities. The spacious, well-laid out bedrooms and suites are located in separate buildings and all offer modern facilities and comforts.

Rooms 63 (15 fmly) (32 GF) ✔ **S** £57-£105; **D** £64-£125 (incl. bkfst) **Facilities** FTV Wi-fi Xmas New Year **Conf** Class 80 Board 40 Thtr 150 **Parking** 150 **Notes** Civ Wed 150

| RICHMOND | Map 19 NZ10 |
| North Yorkshire | |

The Frenchgate Restaurant and Hotel

★★★★ 73% ⊛⊛ TOWN HOUSE HOTEL

☎ 01748 822087 & 07921 136362
59-61 Frenchgate DL10 7AE
e-mail: info@thefrenchgate.co.uk
dir: From A1 (Scotch Corner) to Richmond on A6108. After lights, 1st left into Lile Close (leading to Flints Terr) for hotel car park. Or for front entrance continue to 1st rdbt, left into Dundas St. At T-junct left into Frenchgate

This sympathetic conversion of an 18th-century town house building offers an impressive level of contemporary, quality accommodation. Modern artworks by local artists adorn the walls of the house. The intimate dining room serves award-winning evening meals and memorable breakfasts. Personal, attentive and friendly staff are on hand to ensure a relaxing stay. Some off-road parking is available.

Rooms 9 (3 fmly) (1 GF) ✔ **S** £88-£138; **D** £118-£250 (incl. bkfst)* **Facilities** FTV Wi-fi Xmas New Year **Conf** Class 24 Board 20 Thtr 20 Del from £130 to £160* **Parking** 12 **Notes** LB ⊗ Civ Wed 150

| RICHMOND (UPON THAMES) |
| Greater London |

See London plan 1 C2

The Petersham Hotel

★★★★ 78% ⊛⊛ HOTEL

☎ 020 8940 7471 & 8939 1010
Nightingale Ln TW10 6UZ
e-mail: enq@petershamhotel.co.uk
web: www.petershamhotel.co.uk
dir: From Richmond Bridge rdbt A316 follow Ham & Petersham signs. Hotel in Nightingale Ln on left off Petersham Rd

Managed by the same family for over 25 years, this attractive hotel is located on a hill overlooking water meadows and a sweep of the River Thames. Bedrooms and suites are comfortably furnished, whilst public areas combine elegance and some fine architectural features. High quality produce features in dishes offered in the restaurant that looks out over the Thames below.

Rooms 60 (6 fmly) (3 GF) ✔ **S** £95-£140; **D** £165-£195* **Facilities** STV FTV Wi-fi Xmas New Year **Conf** Board 25 Thtr 35 Del from £255 to £299* **Services** Lift **Parking** 60 **Notes** LB ⊗ Civ Wed 40

The Richmond Hill Hotel

★★★★ 75% ⊛ HOTEL

☎ 0208 940 2247
Richmond Hill TW10 6RW
e-mail: info.richmond@kewgreen.co.uk
dir: A316 for Richmond, hotel at top of Richmond Hill

This attractive Georgian manor is situated on Richmond Hill, enjoying elevated views over the Thames, and the town and the park are within walking distance. Bedrooms vary in size and style but all are comfortable and contemporary in style. There is a well-designated heath club, and extensive conference and banqueting facilities.

Rooms 149 (1 fmly) (15 GF) ✔ **Facilities** Spa STV FTV Wi-fi ⊙ Gym Steam room Health & beauty suite Sauna Xmas New Year **Conf** Class 80 Board 50 Thtr 180 **Services** Lift Air con **Parking** 97 **Notes** LB ⊗ Civ Wed 182

Bingham

★★★ 86% ⊛⊛⊛ TOWN HOUSE HOTEL

☎ 020 8940 0902
61-63 Petersham Rd TW10 6UT
e-mail: info@thebingham.co.uk
web: www.thebingham.co.uk
dir: On A307

This Georgian building, dating back to 1740, overlooks the River Thames and is within easy reach of the town centre, Kew Gardens and Hampton Court. The contemporary bedrooms feature bespoke art deco style furniture and up-to-the-minute facilities such as Wi-fi, a digital music library, flat-screen TVs and 'rain dance' showers. Public rooms have views of the pretty garden and river. Guests can choose from a selection of meals that range from light snacks to two or three-course dinners.

Rooms 15 (2 fmly) ✔ **S** fr £170; **D** £190-£285* **Facilities** FTV Wi-fi In room beauty treatments Xmas New Year **Conf** Class 70 Board 40 Thtr 100 Del from £304 to £404* **Services** Lift Air con **Parking** 8 **Notes** LB ⊗ Civ Wed 100

R

Save on hotels. Book at theAA.com/hotel

RET – RIS 389 ENGLAND

See also Chenies

The Grove

★★★★★ 88% ◉◉◉ HOTEL

☎ 01923 807807
Chandler's Cross WD3 4TG
e-mail: info@thegrove.co.uk
web: www.thegrove.co.uk
dir: M25 junct 19, A411 towards Watford. Hotel on right

Set amid 300 acres of rolling countryside, much of which is golf course, the hotel combines historic features with cutting-edge, modern design. The spacious bedrooms have the latest in temperature control, lighting technology and flat-screen TVs; many have balconies. Suites in the original mansion are particularly stunning. Championship golf, a world-class spa and three dining options are just a few of the treasures to sample here. The hotel also has extensive crèche facilities. The hotel has three dining options - Collette's with 3 AA Rosettes that offers fine dining, and a more relaxed style in the Glasshouse and Stables restaurants. The walled garden is also well worth exploring.

Rooms 217 (69 fmly) (35 GF) ❦ **S** £285-£825; **D** £310-£850 (incl. bkfst)* **Facilities** Spa STV FTV Wi-fi ⓑ ⤳ supervised ♨ 18 ⚑ Putt green ✦ Gym Walking & cycling trails Giant chess Orchid house Golf driving range Xmas New Year Child facilities **Conf** Class 300 Board 78 Thtr 450 Del from £325 to £505* **Services** Lift Air con **Parking** 400 **Notes** LB ⊗ Civ Wed 450

Long Island Hotel

OldEngl sh

★★ Ⓐ HOTEL

☎ 01923 779466
2 Victoria Close WD3 4EQ
e-mail: office@longisland.fsbusiness.co.uk
web: www.oldenglish.co.uk
dir: M25 junct 18, A404, 1.5m. Left at rdbt into Nightingale Rd, 1st left

Rooms 50 (3 fmly) (12 GF) **Facilities** ♫ **Conf** Class 15 Board 8 Thtr 12 **Parking** 120 **Notes** ⊗

Tyrrells Ford Country House Hotel

★★★ 71% SMALL HOTEL

☎ 01425 672646
Avon BH23 7BH
e-mail: info@tyrrellsford.co.uk
web: www.tyrrellsford.co.uk
dir: From A31 to Ringwood take B3347. Hotel 3m S on left

Set in the New Forest, this delightful family-run hotel has much to offer. Most bedrooms have views over the open country. Diners may eat in the formal restaurant, or sample the wide range of bar meals; all dishes are prepared using fresh local produce. The Gallery Lounge offers guests a peaceful area in which to relax.

Rooms 14 **Conf** Class 20 Board 20 Thtr 40 **Parking** 100 **Notes** ⊗ Civ Wed 60

Premier Inn Ripley

BUDGET HOTEL

☎ 0871 527 8935
Nottingham Rd DE5 3QP
web: www.premierinn.com
dir: From S: M1 junct 26, A610 towards Ripley. Hotel off rdbt adjacent to Butterley Park. From N: M1 junct 28, A38, A610 towards Nottingham. Hotel on right at rdbt

High quality, budget accommodation ideal for both families and business travellers. Spacious, en suite bedrooms feature tea and coffee making facilities, and Freeview TV in most hotels. Internet access and Wi-fi are available for a small fee. The adjacent family restaurant features a wide and varied menu. See also the Hotel Groups pages.

Rooms 60

Risley Hall Hotel & Spa

OXFORD
HOTELS & INNS

★★★ 74% ◉ HOTEL

☎ 0115 939 9000 & 921 8523
Derby Rd DE72 3SS
e-mail: reservations.risleyhall@ohiml.com
web: www.oxfordhotelsandinns.com
dir: M1 junct 25, Sandiacre exit into Bostock Ln. Left at lights, hotel on left in 0.25m

Set in 17 acres of private landscaped grounds and attractive mature gardens, this 11th-century manor house offers a good range of comfortable accommodation and relaxing day rooms. The friendly and attentive service complements the imaginative cuisine in the fine dining restaurant. The spa and beauty treatment rooms prove particularly popular with members and leisure guests alike.

Rooms 35 (8 GF) **Facilities** Spa STV FTV ⓑ Xmas New Year **Conf** Class 22 Board 20 Thtr 100 **Services** Lift **Notes** ⊗ Civ Wed 100

R

ROCHDALE
Greater Manchester   Map 16 SD81

Mercure Manchester Norton Grange Hotel & Spa

★★★★ 76% HOTEL

☎ 0870 1942119 & 01706 630788
Manchester Rd, Castleton OL11 2XZ
e-mail: h6631@accor.com
web: www.mercure.com
dir: M62 junct 20, follow A664/Castleton signs. Right at next 2 rdbts. Hotel 0.5m on left. (NB for Sat Nav use M24 2UB)

Standing in nine acres of grounds and mature gardens, this Victorian house provides comfort in elegant surroundings. The well-equipped bedrooms provide a host of extras for both the business and leisure guest. Public areas include the Pickwick bistro and smart Grange Restaurant, both offering a good choice of dishes. There is also an impressive leisure centre.

Rooms 81 (17 fmly) (10 GF) **Facilities** Spa Wi-fi
Gym Leisure centre Indoor/Outdoor hydrotherapy pool Thermal suite Rock sauna Xmas New Year
Conf Class 120 Board 70 Thtr 220 **Services** Lift
Parking 150 **Notes** Civ Wed 150

Best Western Broadfield Park Hotel

★★★ 77% HOTEL

☎ 01706 639000
Sparrow Hill OL16 1AF
e-mail: reservations@broadfieldparkhotel.co.uk
web: www.broadfieldparkhotel.co.uk
dir: M60 junct 20, follow signs for Rochdale & town centre. A640 into Drake St, hotel signed 0.5m on left

Overlooking historic Broadfield Park and the town centre and only minutes away from the M60 and M62. Bedrooms are comfortably furnished and attractively decorated. The hotel offers a range of carefully prepared meals and snacks in either the formal restaurant, or the lounge bar. Service is friendly and attentive.

Rooms 29 (4 fmly) **Facilities** FTV Wi-fi Xmas New Year **Conf** Class 120 Board 80 Thtr 200 **Parking** 30
Notes RS 24-26 Dec Civ Wed 200

Premier Inn Rochdale

BUDGET HOTEL

☎ 0871 527 8936
Newhey Rd, Milnrow OL16 4JF
web: www.premierinn.com
dir: M62 junct 21, at rdbt right towards Shaw, under motorway bridge, & 1st left

High quality, budget accommodation ideal for both families and business travellers. Spacious, en suite bedrooms feature tea and coffee making facilities, and Freeview TV in most hotels. Internet access and Wi-fi are available for a small fee. The adjacent family restaurant features a wide and varied menu. See also the Hotel Groups pages.

Rooms 40

ROCHESTER
Kent   Map 6 TQ76

Premier Inn Rochester

BUDGET HOTEL

☎ 0871 527 8938
Medway Valley Leisure Park, Chariot Way, Strood ME2 2SS
web: www.premierinn.com
dir: M2 junct 2, follow Rochester & West Malling signs. At rdbt onto A228 signed Rochester & Strood. At next rdbt 2nd exit into Roman Way signed Medway Valley Park. At next rdbt 1st exit into Chariot Way, hotel in 100mtrs

High quality, budget accommodation ideal for both families and business travellers. Spacious, en suite bedrooms feature tea and coffee making facilities, and Freeview TV in most hotels. Internet access and Wi-fi are available for a small fee. The adjacent family restaurant features a wide and varied menu. See also the Hotel Groups pages.

Rooms 121

ROMALDKIRK
Co Durham   Map 19 NY92

INSPECTORS' CHOICE

Rose & Crown Hotel

★★ ◉◉ HOTEL

☎ 01833 650213
DL12 9EB
e-mail: hotel@rose-and-crown.co.uk
web: www.rose-and-crown.co.uk
dir: 6m NW from Barnard Castle on B6277

This charming 18th-century country inn is located in the heart of the village, overlooking fine dale scenery. The attractively furnished bedrooms, including suites, are split between the main house and the rear courtyard. Guests might like to have a drink in the cosy bar with its log fire, after returning from a long walk. Good local produce features extensively on the menus that can be enjoyed in the oak-panelled restaurant, or in the brasserie and bar. Service is both friendly and attentive.

Rooms 12 (5 annexe) (1 fmly) (5 GF) ❦ **S** £95;
D £150-£225 (incl. bkfst)* **Facilities** STV Wi-fi New Year **Parking** 20 **Notes** LB Closed 24-26 Dec

ROMFORD
Greater London   Map 6 TQ58

Premier Inn Romford Central

BUDGET HOTEL

☎ 0871 527 8940
Mercury Gardens RM1 3EN
web: www.premierinn.com
dir: M25 junct 28, A12 to Gallows Corner. Take A118 to next rdbt, turn left

High quality, budget accommodation ideal for both families and business travellers. Spacious, en suite bedrooms feature tea and coffee making facilities, and Freeview TV in most hotels. Internet access and Wi-fi are available for a small fee. The adjacent family restaurant features a wide and varied menu. See also the Hotel Groups pages.

Rooms 64

R

R

ROMFORD *continued*

Premier Inn Romford West

BUDGET HOTEL

☎ 0871 527 8942
Whalebone Lane North, Chadwell Heath RM6 6QU
web: www.premierinn.com
dir: 6m from M25 junct 28 on A12 at junct with A1112

Rooms 42

The White Horse Hotel & Brasserie

★★★★ 75% ◉◉ HOTEL

☎ 01794 512431
19 Market Place SO51 8ZJ
e-mail: reservations@silkshotels.com
web: www.silkshotels.com
dir: In town centre

This family friendly hotel is located overlooking the market square of this historic town. This traditional, former coaching inn provides very comfortable and very stylish, individually designed bedrooms, including Loft Suites and a Penthouse. Public areas boast relaxing day rooms and an elegant contemporary bar. The Brasserie offers award-winning cuisine, with alfresco dining a possibility during the warmer summer months. Public car parks can be found close by, although the property does operate a valet parking service.

The White Horse Hotel & Brasserie

Rooms 31 (4 fmly) ⟡ S £90–£110; D £110–£135*
Facilities FTV Wi-fi ↯ Xmas New Year Conf Class 40 Board 30 Thtr 30 Del from £175 to £245* Notes LB Civ Wed 65

See advert on page 391

Potters Heron Hotel

★★★ 77% HOTEL

☎ 023 8027 7800
Winchester Rd, Ampfield SO51 9ZF
e-mail: thepottersheron@pebblehotels.com
dir: M3 junct 12 follow Chandler's Ford signs. 2nd exit at 3rd rdbt follow Ampfield signs, over x-rds. Hotel on left in 1m

This distinctive thatched hotel retains many original features. In a convenient location with access to Winchester, Southampton and the M3, this establishment has modern accommodation and stylish, spacious public areas. Most of the bedrooms have their own balcony or terrace. The pub and restaurant both offer an interesting range of dishes that will suit a variety of tastes.

Rooms 54 (1 fmly) (29 GF) ⟡ S £60–£95; D £60–£95* Facilities Wi-fi ↯ Xmas New Year Conf Class 40 Board 30 Thtr 100 Del from £145 to £165* Services Lift Parking 120 Notes ⊗ Civ Wed 100

Premier Inn Southampton West

BUDGET HOTEL

☎ 0871 527 9004
Romsey Rd, Ower SO51 6ZJ
web: www.premierinn.com
dir: Just off M27 junct 2. Take A36 towards Salisbury. Follow brown tourist signs 'Vine Inn'

High quality, budget accommodation ideal for both families and business travellers. Spacious, en suite bedrooms feature tea and coffee making facilities, and Freeview TV in most hotels. Internet access and Wi-fi are available for a small fee. The adjacent family restaurant features a wide and varied menu. See also the Hotel Groups pages.

Rooms 67

Best Western Premier Mount Pleasant Hotel

★★★★ 80% ◉ HOTEL

☎ 01302 868696 & 868219
Great North Rd DN11 0HW
e-mail: reception@mountpleasant.co.uk
web: www.mountpleasant.co.uk
dir: On A638 (Great North Road) between Bawtry & Doncaster

This charming 18th-century house stands in 100 acres of wooded parkland between Doncaster and Bawtry near Robin Hood Airport. The spacious public areas that include cosy lounges and an elegant restaurant have been designed for maximum comfort. The spacious bedrooms are beautifully furnished and individual in design; some rooms have four-poster beds, half-tester beds or sledge beds - one even has a five poster!

Rooms 56 (18 fmly) (27 GF) ⟡ S £79–£149; D £99–£199 (incl. bkfst) Facilities Spa STV Wi-fi ↯ Beauty salon Conf Class 70 Board 70 Thtr 200 Services Lift Parking 140 Notes ⊗ Closed 25 Dec RS 24 Dec Civ Wed 180

Chase Hotel

CLASSIC
BRITISH HOTELS

★★★ 81% ◉ HOTEL

☎ 01989 763161 & 760644
Gloucester Rd HR9 5LH
e-mail: res@chasehotel.co.uk
web: www.chasehotel.co.uk
dir: M50 junct 4, 1st left exit towards rdbt, left at rdbt towards A40. Right at 2nd rdbt towards town centre, hotel 0.5m on left

This attractive Georgian mansion sits in its own landscaped grounds and is only a short walk from the town centre. Bedrooms, including two four-poster rooms, vary in size and character; all rooms are appointed to impressive standards. There is a light and spacious bar, and also Harry's restaurant which offers an excellent selection of enjoyable dishes.

Rooms 36 (1 fmly) ⟡ S £55–£205; D £85–£215 (incl. bkfst)* Facilities STV FTV Wi-fi ↯ New Year Conf Class 100 Board 80 Thtr 300 Parking 75 Notes LB ⊗ Closed 24-27 Dec Civ Wed 150

Save on hotels. Book at **theAA.com/hotel**

ROM – ROS 393 **ENGLAND**

Glewstone Court Hotel

★★★ 74% @ COUNTRY HOUSE HOTEL

☎ 01989 770367
Glewstone HR9 6AW
e-mail: glewstone@aol.com
web: www.glewstonecourt.com
dir: From Ross-on-Wye market place follow A40/A49 Monmouth/Hereford signs, over Wilton Bridge to rdbt, left onto A40 towards Monmouth, in 1m right for hotel

This charming hotel enjoys an elevated position with views over Ross-on-Wye, and is set in well-tended gardens. Informal service is delivered with great enthusiasm by Bill Reeve-Tucker, whilst the kitchen is the domain of Christine Reeve-Tucker who offers an extensive menu of well executed dishes. Bedrooms come in a variety of sizes and are tastefully furnished and well equipped.

Rooms 8 (2 fmly) (1 GF) **S** £70-£85; **D** £125-£150 (incl. bkfst)* **Facilities** FTV Wi-fi 🌙 New Year **Conf** Class 18 Board 12 Thtr 24 Del from £129 to £135* **Parking** 25 **Notes** LB Closed 25-27 Dec Civ Wed 72

The Royal Hotel

★★★ 72% HOTEL   OldEnglish

☎ 01989 565105
Palace Pound HR9 5HZ
e-mail: 6504@greeneking.co.uk
web: www.oldenglish.co.uk
dir: At end of M50 take A40 signed Monmouth. At 3rd rdbt, left to Ross-on-Wye, over bridge, follow The Royal Hotel sign

Close to the town centre, this imposing hotel enjoys panoramic views from its prominent hilltop position. Reputedly visited by Charles Dickens in 1867, the establishment has been sympathetically furnished to combine the ambience of a bygone era with the comforts of today. In addition to the bar and dining areas, there are function rooms, an elegant restaurant and an attractive garden.

Rooms 42 (1 fmly) 🐾 **S** £20-£60; **D** £40-£99 (incl. bkfst)* **Facilities** FTV Wi-fi ☕ Xmas New Year **Conf** Class 20 Board 28 Thtr 85 Del from £99 to £119* **Parking** 38 **Notes** LB Civ Wed 75

King's Head Hotel

★★★ 71% HOTEL

☎ 01989 763174
8 High St HR9 5HL
e-mail: enquiries@kingshead.co.uk
web: www.kingshead.co.uk
dir: In town centre, past market building on right

This establishment dates back to the 14th century and has a wealth of charm and character. Bedrooms are well equipped and comfortable with thoughtful guest extras provided; both four-poster and family rooms are available. The restaurant offers menus and a specials board that reflect a varied selection of local produce including fresh fish, free range beef and lamb. There is a also a well-stocked bar serving hand-pulled, real ales.

Rooms 15 (1 fmly) 🐾 **S** £56-£90; **D** £80-£110 (incl. bkfst)* **Facilities** FTV Wi-fi **Parking** 13

Chasedale Hotel

★★ 74% SMALL HOTEL

☎ 01989 562423 & 565801
Walford Rd HR9 5PQ
e-mail: chasedale@supanet.com
web: www.chasedale.co.uk
dir: From town centre, S on B4234, hotel 0.5m on left

This large, mid-Victorian property is situated on the south-west outskirts of the town. Privately owned and personally run, it provides spacious, well-proportioned public areas and extensive grounds. The accommodation is well equipped and includes ground floor and family rooms, whilst the restaurant offers a wide selection of wholesome food.

Rooms 10 (2 fmly) (1 GF) **Facilities** FTV Wi-fi Xmas **Conf** Class 30 Board 25 Thtr 40 **Parking** 14

Premier Inn Ross-on-Wye

BUDGET HOTEL

☎ 0871 527 8944
Ledbury Rd HR9 7QJ
web: www.premierinn.com
dir: M50 junct 4, 1m from town centre

High quality, budget accommodation ideal for both families and business travellers. Spacious, en suite bedrooms feature tea and coffee making facilities, and Freeview TV in most hotels. Internet access and Wi-fi are available for a small fee. The adjacent family restaurant features a wide and varied menu. See also the Hotel Groups pages.

Rooms 43

Wilton Court Restaurant with Rooms

@@ RESTAURANT WITH ROOMS

☎ 01989 562569
Wilton Ln HR9 6AQ
e-mail: info@wiltoncourthotel.com
dir: M50 junct 4, A40 towards Monmouth at 3rd rdbt left signed Ross-on-Wye, 1st right, on right

Dating back to the 16th century, this establishment has great charm and a wealth of character. Standing on the banks of the River Wye and just a short walk from the town centre, there is a genuinely relaxed, friendly and unhurried atmosphere created by hosts Roger and Helen Wynn and their reliable team. Bedrooms are tastefully furnished and well equipped, while public areas include a comfortable lounge, traditional bar and pleasant restaurant with a conservatory extension overlooking the garden. High standards of food, using fresh, locally sourced ingredients, are offered.

Rooms 10 (1 fmly)

Orles Barn

@@ RESTAURANT WITH ROOMS

☎ 01989 562155
Wilton HR9 6AE
e-mail: reservations@orles-barn.co.uk
web: www.orles-barn.co.uk
dir: A49/A40 rdbt outside Ross-on-Wye, take slip road between petrol station & A40 to Monmouth. 100yds on left

The proprietors of this character property offer a warm welcome to all their guests. Older sections of the property date back to the 14th and 17th centuries when it was a farmhouse with a barn. The property offers comfortable bedrooms, a smart cosy lounge with a bar and a spacious restaurant. Dinner and Sunday lunch are offered on a balanced menu of fresh local and seasonal ingredients. Breakfast also utilises quality local produce and makes a good start to the day.

Rooms 6 (1 fmly)

R

ROSTHWAITE
Cumbria   Map 18 NY21

See also Borrowdale

Scafell Hotel

★★★ 79% HOTEL

☎ 017687 77208
CA12 5XB
e-mail: info@scafell.co.uk
web: www.scafell.co.uk
dir: M6 junct 40 to Keswick on A66. Take B5289 to Rosthwaite

A friendly hotel, popular with walkers and enjoying a peaceful location. Bedrooms have been tastefully appointed in a warm country house style with a contemporary twist; some have traditional antique furniture. Public areas include a residents' cocktail bar, lounge and spacious restaurant as well as the popular Riverside Inn pub, offering all-day menus in summer months.

Rooms 23 (2 fmly) (8 GF) **S** £39-£70; **D** £78-£140 (incl. bkfst)* **Facilities** FTV Wi-fi Guided walks Xmas New Year **Parking** 50 **Notes** LB Civ Wed 75

ROTHERHAM
South Yorkshire   Map 16 SK49

Hellaby Hall Hotel

★★★★ 71% HOTEL   PRIMA

☎ 01709 702701
Old Hellaby Ln, Hellaby S66 8SN
e-mail: reservations@hellabyhallhotel.co.uk
web: www.hellabyhallhotel.co.uk
dir: 0.5m off M18 junct 1, onto A631 towards Maltby. Hotel in Hellaby. (NB do not use postcode for Sat Nav)

This 17th-century house was built to a Flemish design with high, beamed ceilings, staircases which lead off to private meeting rooms and a series of oak-panelled lounges. Bedrooms are elegant and well equipped, and guests can dine in the formal Attic Restaurant. There are extensive leisure facilities and conference areas, and the hotel holds a licence for civil weddings.

Rooms 90 (2 fmly) (17 GF) **Facilities** Spa STV FTV Wi-fi ⌨ supervised Gym Beauty salon Exercise studio Spinning bike studio Xmas New Year **Conf** Class 300 Board 150 Thtr 500 **Services** Lift **Parking** 250 **Notes** Civ Wed 200

Carlton Park Hotel

★★★ 78% HOTEL

☎ 01709 849955
102/104 Moorgate Rd S60 2BG
e-mail: reservations@carltonparkhotel.com
web: www.carltonparkhotel.com
dir: M1 junct 33, onto A631, then A618. Hotel 800yds past District General Hospital

This modern hotel is situated in a pleasant residential area of the town, close to the hospital, yet within minutes of the M1. Bedrooms and bathrooms offer very modern facilities; three have separate sitting rooms. The restaurant and bar provide a lively atmosphere and there is a pool and leisure centre.

Rooms 80 (19 fmly) (16 GF) (7 smoking) **S** £49-£71; **D** £54-£77 (incl. bkfst) **Facilities** STV FTV Wi-fi ⌨ Gym ♫ Xmas New Year **Conf** Class 120 Board 60 Thtr 300 Del from £90 to £140 **Services** Lift **Parking** 120 **Notes** LB ⊗ Civ Wed 150

Park Inn by Radisson Rotherham

★★★ 77% HOTEL

☎ 01709 760666
Express Park, Manvers Way, Wath-upon-Dearne S63 7EQ
e-mail: reservations.rotherham@rezidorparkinn.com
dir: M1 junct 36, A6195 towards Doncaster. Right onto A633 signed Rotherham & Manvers. Hotel on left

Convenient for the Manvers Business Estate and M1, this purpose-built hotel provides versatile and well-equipped contemporary accommodation with Wi-fi throughout. Facilities include a spacious restaurant, comfortable lounge area, bar, fitness centre, sauna and steam room as well as meeting rooms.

Rooms 130 (30 fmly) ⌨ **S** £39-£129; **D** £49-£139 (incl. bkfst) **Facilities** STV FTV Wi-fi ⌨ Gym Sauna Steam room Xmas New Year **Conf** Class 93 Board 60 Thtr 140 **Services** Lift Air con **Parking** 200 **Notes** LB Civ Wed 130

Ibis Rotherham East

BUDGET HOTEL

☎ 01709 730333
Moorhead Way, Bramley S66 1YY
e-mail: H3163@accor-hotels.com
web: www.ibishotel.com
dir: M18 junct 1, left at rdbt, left at 1st lights. Hotel adjacent to supermarket

Modern, budget hotel offering comfortable accommodation in bright and practical bedrooms. Breakfast is self-service and dinner is available in the restaurant. See also the Hotel Groups pages.

Rooms 86 (22 fmly) (8 GF) **Conf** Class 20 Board 20 Thtr 30 Del from £45 to £170*

Premier Inn Rotherham

BUDGET HOTEL

☎ 0871 527 8946
Bawtry Rd S65 3JB
web: www.premierinn.com
dir: On A631 towards Wickersley, between M18 junct 1 & M1 junct 33

High quality, budget accommodation ideal for both families and business travellers. Spacious, en suite bedrooms feature tea and coffee making facilities, and Freeview TV in most hotels. Internet access and Wi-fi are available for a small fee. The adjacent family restaurant features a wide and varied menu. See also the Hotel Groups pages.

Rooms 37

Save on hotels. Book at **theAA.com/hotel**

ROS – ROW 395 ENGLAND

ROTHERWICK
Hampshire — Map 5 SU75

Tylney Hall Hotel
★★★★ ◎◎ HOTEL

☎ 01256 764881
RG27 9AZ
e-mail: sales@tylneyhall.com
web: www.tylneyhall.com
dir: M3 junct 5, A287 to Basingstoke, over junct with A30, over rail bridge, towards Newnham. Right at Newnham Green. Hotel 1m on left

A grand Victorian country house set in 66 acres of beautiful parkland. The hotel offers high standards of comfort in relaxed yet elegant surroundings, featuring magnificently restored water gardens, originally laid out by the famous gardener, Gertrude Jekyll. Spacious public rooms include Italian and Wedgwood styled drawing rooms and the panelled Oak Room Restaurant, filled with stunning flower arrangements and warmed by log fires, that offers cuisine based on locally sourced ingredients. The spacious bedrooms are traditionally furnished and offer individual style and high degrees of comfort. The excellent leisure facilities include indoor and outdoor swimming pools, tennis courts, jogging trails, croquet lawns and a spa.

Rooms 112 (77 annexe) (1 fmly) (40 GF) 🐾
S £145-£470; **D** £155-£500 (incl. bkfst)*
Facilities Spa STV FTV Wi-fi 🕸 🏇 ⚲ 🏊 ⛳ Gym Clay pigeon shooting Archery Falconry Balloon rides Laser shooting Xmas New Year **Conf** Class 70 Board 40 Thtr 120 Del from £190 to £285*
Parking 120 **Notes** LB Civ Wed 120

ROTHLEY
Leicestershire — Map 11 SK51

Rothley Court
★★★ 73% HOTEL   OldEngl☘sh

☎ 0116 237 4141
Westfield Ln LE7 7LG
e-mail: 6501@greeneking.co.uk
web: www.oldenglish.co.uk
dir: On B5328

Mentioned in the Domesday Book, and complete with its own chapel, this historic property sits in seven acres of well-tended grounds. Public areas retain much of their original character and include an oak-panelled restaurant and a choice of function and meeting rooms. Bedrooms, some located in an adjacent stable block, are individually styled.

Rooms 30 (18 annexe) (3 fmly) (6 GF) **Facilities** Xmas **Conf** Class 35 Board 35 Thtr 100 **Parking** 100 **Notes** ⊗ Civ Wed 85

ROWDE
Wiltshire — Map 4 ST96

The George & Dragon
◎◎ RESTAURANT WITH ROOMS

☎ 01380 723053
High St SN10 2PN
e-mail: thegandd@tiscali.co.uk
dir: 1.5m from Devizes on A350 towards Chippenham

The George & Dragon dates back to the 14th century when it was a meeting house. Exposed beams, wooden floors, antique rugs and open fires create a warm atmosphere in the bar and restaurant. Bedrooms and bathrooms are very well decorated and equipped with some welcome extras. Dining in the bar or restaurant should not be missed, as local produce and fresh fish deliveries from Cornwall are offered on the daily-changing blackboard menu.

Rooms 3 (1 fmly)

ROWSLEY
Derbyshire — Map 16 SK26

East Lodge Country House Hotel
★★★ ◎◎◎ HOTEL

☎ 01629 734474
DE4 2EF
e-mail: info@eastlodge.com
web: www.eastlodge.com
dir: A6, 3m from Bakewell, 5m from Matlock

This hotel enjoys a romantic setting in ten acres of landscaped grounds and gardens. The stylish bedrooms are equipped with many extras such as TVs with DVD players, and most have lovely garden views. The popular restaurant serves much produce sourced from the area, and the conservatory lounge, overlooking the gardens, offers afternoon teas and light meals.

Rooms 12 (2 fmly) (1 GF) 🐾 **S** £120-£375; **D** £120-£375 (incl. bkfst)* **Facilities** STV FTV Wi-fi 🕸 HL Fishing ⛳ Xmas New Year **Conf** Class 50 Board 25 Thtr 100 Del £195* **Parking** 40 **Notes** LB ⊗ No children 12yrs Civ Wed 150

ROWSLEY *continued*

The Peacock at Rowsley

★★★ ◉◉◉ HOTEL

☎ 01629 733518
Bakewell Rd DE4 2EB
e-mail: reception@thepeacockatrowsley.com
web: www.thepeacockatrowsley.com
dir: A6, 3m before Bakewell, 6m from Matlock towards Bakewell

Owned by Lord Manners of Haddon Hall, this hotel combines stylish contemporary design by India Mahdavi with original period and antique features. Bedrooms are individually designed and boast DVD players, complimentary Wi-fi and smart marble bathrooms. Two rooms are particularly special - one with a four-poster and one with an antique bed originating from Belvoir Castle in Leicestershire. Imaginative cuisine, using local, seasonal produce, is a highlight. Guests are warmly welcomed and service is attentive. Fly fishing is popular in this area and the hotel has its own fishing rights on seven miles of the Rivers Wye and Derwent.

Rooms 16 (5 fmly) **S** £85-£117.50; **D** £155-£257.50 (incl. bkfst)* **Facilities** Wi-fi Fishing 🌂 Free use of Woodlands Fitness Centre Free membership to Bakewell Golf Club 🎵 New Year **Conf** Class 8 Board 16 Thtr 16 Del £200 **Parking** 25 **Notes** LB No children 10yrs

See Wootton Bassett (Royal)

Premier Inn Birmingham South (Rubery)

BUDGET HOTEL

☎ 0871 527 8094
Birmingham Great Park, Ashbrook Dr, Parkway B45 9FP
web: www.premierinn.com
dir: M5 junct 4, A38 towards Birmingham. Left at lights before Morrisons signed Great Park. Right at rdbt. Right at next rdbt, hotel on right

High quality, budget accommodation ideal for both families and business travellers. Spacious, en suite bedrooms feature tea and coffee making facilities, and Freeview TV in most hotels. Internet access and Wi-fi are available for a small fee. The adjacent family restaurant features a wide and varied menu. See also the Hotel Groups pages.

Rooms 62

Brownsover Hall Hotel

★★★ 78% HOTEL

CLASSIC BRITISH HOTELS

☎ 01788 546100 & 555362
Brownsover Ln, Old Brownsover CV21 1HU
e-mail: reservations@brownsoverhall.co.uk
web: www.brownsoverhall.co.uk
dir: M6 junct 1, A426 to Rugby. After 0.5m at rdbt follow Brownsover signs, right into Brownover Rd, right again into Brownsover Ln. Hotel 250yds on left

A Grade II listed, Victorian Gothic hall designed by Sir Gilbert Scott, set in seven acres of wooded parkland. Bedrooms vary in size and style, including spacious and contemporary rooms in the converted stable block. The former chapel makes a stylish restaurant, and for a less formal meal or a relaxing drink, the Whittle Bar is popular.

Rooms 47 (20 annexe) (3 fmly) (11 GF) **S** £69-£129; **D** £69-£129* **Facilities** STV FTV Wi-fi 🐾 Xmas New Year **Conf** Class 36 Board 40 Thtr 70 Del from £110 to £155* **Parking** 100 **Notes** LB ⊗ Civ Wed 56

The Golden Lion Hotel

★★★ 74% HOTEL

☎ 01788 833577 & 832265
Easenhall CV23 0JA
e-mail: reception@goldenlionhotel.org
web: www.goldenlionhotel.org
dir: From A426 at Avon Mill rdbt follow Newbold-upon-Avon B4112 signs, approx 2m left at Harborough Parva sign, follow brown tourist signs, opposite agricultural showroom, 1m to Easenhall

This friendly, family-run, 16th-century inn is situated between Rugby and Coventry, and is convenient for access to the M6. Bedrooms, some in a smart extension, are equipped with both practical and homely items; one features a stunning Chinese bed. The beamed bar and restaurant retain many original features and a warm welcome is assured.

Rooms 20 (2 fmly) (6 GF) **Facilities** FTV Wi-fi 🐾 Xmas New Year **Conf** Class 30 Board 24 Thtr 80 Del from £99* **Parking** 80 **Notes** ⊗ Civ Wed 100

Premier Inn Rugby North M6 Jct 1

BUDGET HOTEL

☎ 0871 527 8948
Central Park Dr, Central Park CV23 0WE
web: www.premierinn.com
dir: M6 junct 1, S'bound onto A426. Hotel approx 1m on left at rdbt

High quality, budget accommodation ideal for both families and business travellers. Spacious, en suite bedrooms feature tea and coffee making facilities, and Freeview TV in most hotels. Internet access and Wi-fi are available for a small fee. The adjacent family restaurant features a wide and varied menu. See also the Hotel Groups pages.

Rooms 58

Premier Inn Rugby North (Newbold)

BUDGET HOTEL

☎ 0871 527 8950
Brownsover Rd CV21 1HL
web: www.premierinn.com
dir: M6 junct 1, A426 follow Rugby signs. Straight on at 2 rdbts. At 3rd rdbt, hotel on right. (NB for Sat Nav use CV21 1NX)

Rooms 49

RUGELEY
Staffordshire — Map 10 SK01

Premier Inn Rugeley
BUDGET HOTEL

☎ 0871 527 9272
Tower Business Park WS15 2HJ
web: www.premierinn.com
dir: M6 junct 14, A5013 towards Stafford. At rdbt 2nd exit onto A34. Take A513 signed Rugeley. At rdbt take 2nd exit onto A51. Left into Wolsley Rd, left into Powerstation Rd. Hotel off rdbt. (NB for Sat Nav use WS15 1PR)

High quality, budget accommodation ideal for both families and business travellers. Spacious, en suite bedrooms feature tea and coffee making facilities, and Freeview TV in most hotels. Internet access and Wi-fi are available for a small fee. The adjacent family restaurant features a wide and varied menu. See also the Hotel Groups pages.

Rooms 50

RUISLIP
Greater London

See London plan 1 A5

Barn Hotel
★★★ 78% ◎◎ HOTEL

☎ 01895 636057
West End Rd HA4 6JB
e-mail: info@thebarnhotel.co.uk
web: www.thebarnhotel.co.uk
dir: A40 onto A4180 (Polish War Memorial) exit to Ruislip. 2m to hotel entrance at mini-rdbt before Ruislip tube station

A mix of old and new, with parts dating back to the 17th century, this impressive property sits in three acres of gardens. Bedrooms vary in style, from contemporary to traditional with oak-beams; all are comfortable and well appointed. The public areas provide a high level of quality and luxury.

Barn Hotel

Rooms 73 (3 fmly) (33 GF) (20 smoking) **Facilities** FTV Wi-fi ↻ Xmas New Year **Conf** Class 50 Board 30 Thtr 80 **Parking** 42 **Notes** ⊗ Civ Wed 74

See advert on this page

Premier Inn Ruislip
BUDGET HOTEL

☎ 0871 527 8952
Ickenham Rd HA4 7DR
web: www.premierinn.com
dir: From Ruislip High St into Ickenham Rd (B466). At mini rdbt 1st exit (The Orchard on left)

High quality, budget accommodation ideal for both families and business travellers. Spacious, en suite bedrooms feature tea and coffee making facilities, and Freeview TV in most hotels. Internet access and Wi-fi are available for a small fee. The adjacent family restaurant features a wide and varied menu. See also the Hotel Groups pages.

Rooms 20

RUNCORN
Cheshire   Map 15 SJ58

Holiday Inn Runcorn

★★★ 73% HOTEL

☎ 0871 942 9070
Wood Ln, Beechwood WA7 3HA
e-mail: vince.garrington@ihg.com
web: www.holidayinn.co.uk
dir: M56 junct 12, left at rdbt, 100yds on left into
Halton Station Rd under rail bridge, into Wood Ln

This modern hotel offers extensive conference,
meeting and leisure facilities. The bedrooms are well
equipped and the spacious restaurant is open for
lunch and dinner with an all-day menu provided in
the lounge and bar. There is also a well equipped
leisure centre and extensive conference facilities
available.

Rooms 153 (149 fmly) (31 GF) **Facilities** STV Wi-fi ⓢ
supervised Gym Xmas New Year **Conf** Class 250
Board 60 Thtr 500 **Services** Lift Air con **Parking** 250
Notes Civ Wed 500

Campanile Runcorn
Campanile

BUDGET HOTEL

☎ 01928 581771
Lowlands Rd WA7 5TP
e-mail: runcorn@campanile.com
web: www.campanile.com
dir: M56 junct 12, A557, follow signs for Runcorn rail
station/Runcorn College

This modern building offers accommodation in smart,
well-equipped bedrooms, all with en suite bathrooms.
Refreshments may be taken at the informal bistro.
See also the Hotel Groups pages.

Rooms 53 (18 GF) **S** £39-£70; **D** £39-£70*
Conf Class 24 Board 24 Thtr 35 Del from £50 to
£150*

Premier Inn Runcorn

BUDGET HOTEL

☎ 0871 527 8954
Chester Rd, Preston Brook WA7 3BB
web: www.premierinn.com
dir: 1m from M56 junct 11, at Preston Brook

High quality, budget accommodation ideal for both
families and business travellers. Spacious, en suite
bedrooms feature tea and coffee making facilities,
and Freeview TV in most hotels. Internet access and
Wi-fi are available for a small fee. The adjacent
family restaurant features a wide and varied menu.
See also the Hotel Groups pages.

Rooms 43

RUSPER
West Sussex   Map 6 TQ23

Ghyll Manor

★★★ 86% ◉ COUNTRY HOUSE HOTEL

☎ 0845 345 3426
High St RH12 4PX
e-mail: enquiries@ghyllmanor.co.uk
web: www.ghyllmanor.co.uk
dir: A24 onto A264. Exit at Faygate, follow signs for
Rusper, 2m to village

Located in the quiet village of Rusper, this traditional
mansion house is set in 45 acres of idyllic, peaceful
grounds. Accommodation is in either the main house
or a range of courtyard-style cottages. A pre-dinner
drink can be taken beside the fire, followed by an
imaginative meal in the charming restaurant.

Rooms 29 (20 annexe) (7 fmly) (18 GF) ⓡ
Facilities STV FTV Wi-fi ⓠ ⚑ Gym Xmas New Year
Conf Class 60 Board 40 Thtr 120 **Parking** 50
Notes Civ Wed 120

RYDE
Isle of Wight   Map 5 SZ59

Lakeside Park Hotel

★★★★ 79% ◉◉ HOTEL

☎ 01983 882266
High St PO33 4LJ
e-mail: reception@lakesideparkhotel.com
web: www.lakesideparkhotel.com
dir: A3054 towards Newport. Hotel on left after
crossing Wotton Bridge

This hotel has picturesque views of the tidal lake and
surrounding countryside. Bedrooms are well
appointed with modern amenities, stylish design with
guest comfort in mind. Public areas feature a
comfortable open-plan bar and lounge, and two
restaurants that showcase the best of island produce.
Sizable conference and banqueting facilities are
available whilst the leisure area includes an indoor
pool and spa therapy.

Rooms 44 (2 fmly) (16 GF) **Facilities** Spa FTV Wi-fi ⓢ
Sauna Steam room Relaxation room Xmas New Year
Conf Class 60 Board 40 Thtr 150 **Services** Lift Air con
Parking 140 **Notes** ⊗ Civ Wed 120

Yelf's Hotel

★★★ 73% HOTEL

☎ 01983 564062
Union St PO33 2LG
e-mail: manager@yelfshotel.com
web: www.yelfshotel.com
dir: From Esplanade into Union St. Hotel on right

This former coaching inn has smart public areas
including a busy bar, a separate lounge and an
attractive dining room. Bedrooms are comfortably
furnished and well equipped; some are located in an
adjoining wing and some in an annexe. A conservatory
lounge bar and stylish terrace are ideal for relaxing.

Rooms 40 (9 annexe) (5 fmly) (3 GF) (6 smoking) ⓡ
Facilities STV Wi-fi Spa & treatments at sister hotel
nearby **Conf** Class 30 Board 50 Thtr 100 Del £135
Services Lift **Parking** 23 **Notes** ⊗ Civ Wed 100

R

Save on hotels. Book at **theAA.com/hotel**

RUN – RYE 399 ENGLAND

Appley Manor Hotel

★★ 74% HOTEL

☎ 01983 564777
Appley Rd PO33 1PH
e-mail: appleymanor@live.co.uk
web: www.appley-manor.co.uk
dir: A3055 onto B3330. Hotel 0.25m on left

A Victorian manor house located only five minutes from the town and set in peaceful surroundings. The spacious bedrooms are well furnished and decorated. Dinner can be taken in the popular adjoining Manor Inn.

Rooms 12 (2 fmly) **S** £54; **D** £64* **Conf** Class 40 Board 30 Thtr 40 **Parking** 60 **Notes** ⊗

RYE	Map 7 TQ92
East Sussex	

The George in Rye

★★★★ 78% ⊛ HOTEL

☎ 01797 222114
98 High St TN31 7JT
e-mail: stay@thegeorgeinrye.com
dir: M20 junct 10, A2070 to Brenzett, A259 to Rye

This attractive 16th-century property, situated in the heart of historic Rye, has been sympathetically styled to retain many original features including a stunning Georgian ballroom complete with a minstrels' gallery. The bedrooms are stylishly appointed and filled with an abundance of thoughtful touches. Contemporary public areas include a bar, lounge and dining room plus an excellent alfresco area for summer dining.

Rooms 34 (3 GF) **Facilities** FTV Wi-fi Xmas New Year **Conf** Class 65 Board 40 Thtr 100 **Notes** ⊗ Civ Wed 100

Mermaid Inn

★★★ 81% ⊛ HOTEL

☎ 01797 223065 & 223788
Mermaid St TN31 7EY
e-mail: info@mermaidinn.com
web: www.mermaidinn.com
dir: A259, follow signs to town centre, then into Mermaid St

Situated near the top of a cobbled side street, this famous smugglers' inn is steeped in history, dating back to 1450 with 12th-century cellars. The charming interior has many architectural features such as attractive stone work. The bedrooms vary in size and style but all are tastefully furnished; there are no less than eight with four-posters, and the Elizabethan and Dr Syn's Bedchambers are particularly noteworthy. Delightful public rooms include a choice of lounges, cosy bar and smart restaurant.

Rooms 31 (5 fmly) **S** £70-£90; **D** £140-£260 (incl. bkfst)* **Facilities** Wi-fi Xmas New Year **Conf** Class 40 Board 30 Thtr 50 Del from £160* **Parking** 25 **Notes** LB ⊗

The Hope Anchor Hotel

★★★ 78% SMALL HOTEL

☎ 01797 222216
Watchbell St TN31 7HA
e-mail: info@thehopeanchor.co.uk
web: www.thehopeanchor.co.uk
dir: From A268, Quayside, right into Wish Ward, into Mermaid St, right into West St, right into Watchbell St, hotel at end

This historic inn sits high above the town with enviable views out over the harbour and Romney Marsh, and is accessible via delightful cobbled streets. A relaxed and friendly atmosphere prevails within the cosy public rooms, while the attractively furnished bedrooms are well equipped and many enjoy good views over the marshes.

Rooms 16 (23 fmly) (1 GF) ☍ **S** £75-£160; **D** £115-£190 (incl. bkfst) **Facilities** FTV Wi-fi Xmas New Year **Conf** Class 30 Board 20 Thtr 40 Del from £130 to £180 **Parking** 12 **Notes** LB Civ Wed 40

Rye Lodge Hotel

★★★ 75% HOTEL

☎ 01797 223838 & 226688
Hilders Cliff TN31 7LD
e-mail: info@ryelodge.co.uk
web: www.ryelodge.co.uk
dir: On one-way system follow town centre signs, through Landgate arch, hotel 100yds on right

Standing in an elevated position, Rye Lodge has panoramic views across Romney Marshes and the Rother Estuary. Traditionally styled bedrooms come in a variety of sizes; they are attractively decorated and thoughtfully equipped. Public rooms feature indoor leisure facilities and the Terrace Room Restaurant where home-made dishes are offered. Lunch and afternoon tea are served on the flower-filled outdoor terrace in warmer months.

Rooms 19 (5 GF) ☍ **S** £82.50-£140; **D** £105-£195* **Facilities** STV FTV Wi-fi ▷ HL ⊙ Aromatherapy Steam cabinet Sauna Exercise machines **Parking** 20 **Notes** LB

White Vine House

RESTAURANT WITH ROOMS

☎ 01797 224748
24 High St TN31 7JF
e-mail: info@whitevinehouse.co.uk
dir: In town centre

Situated in the heart of the ancient Cinque Port town of Rye, this property's origins go back to the 13th century. The cellar is the oldest part, but the current building dates from 1560 and boasts an impressive Georgian frontage. The original timber framework is visible in many areas, and certainly adds to the house's sense of history. The bedrooms have period furniture along with luxury bath or shower rooms; one bedroom has an antique four-poster.

Rooms 7 (1 fmly)

R

ST AGNES
Cornwall
Map 2 SW75

Rose-in-Vale Country House Hotel

★★★ 81% COUNTRY HOUSE HOTEL

☎ 01872 552202
Mithian TR5 0QD
e-mail: reception@rose-in-vale-hotel.co.uk
web: www.rose-in-vale-hotel.co.uk
dir: A30 S towards Redruth. At Chiverton Cross at
rdbt take B3277 signed St Agnes. In 500mtrs follow
tourist sign for Rose-in-Vale. Into Mithian, right at
Miners Arms, down hill. Hotel on left

Peacefully located in a wooded valley this Georgian
manor house has a wonderfully relaxed atmosphere
and abundant charm. Guests are assured of a warm
welcome. Accommodation varies in size and style;
several rooms are situated on the ground floor. An
imaginative fixed-price menu featuring local produce
is served in the spacious restaurant.

Rooms 23 (3 annexe) (1 fmly) (6 GF) ↟ **S** £90-£180;
D £100-£250 (incl. bkfst) **Facilities** FTV Wi-fi ↟ ↟ ↟
♫ Xmas New Year **Conf** Class 50 Board 40 Thtr 75
Services Lift **Parking** 50 **Notes** LB No children 12yrs
Civ Wed 80

Rosemundy House Hotel

★★★ 70% HOTEL

☎ 01872 552101
Rosemundy Hill TR5 0UF
e-mail: info@rosemundy.co.uk
dir: A30 to St Agnes, approx 3m. On entering village
1st right signed Rosemundy, hotel at foot of hill

This elegant Queen Anne house has been carefully
restored and extended to provide comfortable
bedrooms and spacious, inviting public areas. The
hotel is set in well-maintained gardens complete with
an outdoor pool which is available in warmer months.
There is a choice of relaxing lounges and a cosy bar.

Rooms 46 (3 fmly) (9 GF) ↟ **Facilities** FTV Wi-fi ↟
Putt green ↟ ♫ Xmas New Year **Conf** Board 80
Parking 50 **Notes** ⊗ No children 5yrs

Beacon Country House Hotel

★★ 82% HOTEL

☎ 01872 552318
Goonvrea Rd TR5 0NW
e-mail: info@beaconhotel.co.uk
dir: A30 onto B3277 to St Agnes. At rdbt left into
Goonvrea Rd. Hotel 0.75m on right

Set in a quiet and attractive area away from the busy
village, this family-run, relaxed hotel has splendid
views over the countryside and along the coast to St
Ives. Hospitality and customer care are great

strengths with guests assured of a very warm and
friendly stay. Bedrooms are comfortable and well
equipped, and many benefit from glorious views.

Rooms 11 (2 GF) ↟ **S** £65-£150; **D** £70-£170 (incl.
bkfst)* **Facilities** FTV Wi-fi ↟ Xmas New Year
Conf Class 20 Board 20 Del from £130 to £200*
Parking 12 **Notes** LB No children 8yrs Closed 4-31
Jan

ST ALBANS
Hertfordshire
Map 6 TL10

St Michael's Manor

★★★★ 77% HOTEL

☎ 01727 864444
Fishpool St AL3 4RY
e-mail: reservations@stmichaelsmanor.com
web: www.stmichaelsmanor.com
dir: From St Albans Abbey follow Fishpool Street
towards St Michael's village. Hotel 0.5m on left

Hidden from the street, adjacent to listed buildings,
mills and ancient inns, this hotel, with a history
dating back 500 years, is set in six acres of beautiful
landscaped grounds. Inside there is a real sense of
luxury, the high standard of decor and attentive
service is complemented by award-winning food; the
elegant restaurant overlooks the gardens and lake.
The bedrooms are individually styled and have
satellite TVs, DVDs and free internet access.

Rooms 30 (8 annexe) (3 fmly) (4 GF) (6 smoking) ↟
Facilities STV FTV Wi-fi ↟ ↟ Licenced fishing in
season Guided tours New Year **Conf** Class 20
Board 24 Thtr 30 **Services** Air con **Parking** 60
Notes ⊗ Civ Wed 140

Thistle St Albans
thistle

★★★★ 72% HOTEL

☎ 0871 376 9034
Watford Rd AL2 3DS
e-mail: stalbans@thistle.co.uk
web: www.thistlehotels.com/stalbans
dir: M1 junct 6/M25 junct 21a, follow St. Albans
signs, A405. Hotel 0.5m

Conveniently located for access to both the M1 and
M25, this Victorian hotel lies within its own grounds

and has secure parking. Bedrooms are neatly
appointed in a traditional style. Public areas include
a choice of restaurants, The Noke or the more
informal Oak and Avocado, and there is also a small
modern leisure club.

Rooms 110 (2 fmly) (56 GF) (4 smoking)
Facilities FTV Wi-fi ↟ supervised Gym Sauna Steam
room Beauty treatment room New Year **Conf** Class 30
Board 30 Thtr 300 **Parking** 150 **Notes** Civ Wed 100

Quality Hotel St Albans

★★★ 72% HOTEL

☎ 01727 857858
232-236 London Rd AL1 1JQ
e-mail: st.albans@quality-hotels.net
dir: M25 junct 22 follow A1081 to St Albans, after
2.5m hotel on left, before overhead bridge

This smartly presented property is conveniently
situated close to the major road networks and the
railway station. The contemporary style bedrooms
have co-ordinated fabrics and a good range of useful
facilities. Public rooms include an open-plan lounge
bar and brasserie restaurant. The hotel has a leisure
complex along with air-conditioned meeting rooms.

Rooms 81 (7 fmly) (14 GF) ↟ **S** £45-£90; **D** £65-£120
(incl. bkfst) **Facilities** STV FTV Wi-fi ↟ ↟ supervised
Gym Saunarium Sunbed Beauty treatments
Conf Class 40 Board 50 Thtr 200 Del from £90 to
£140 **Services** Lift **Parking** 80 **Notes** ⊗

Ardmore House Hotel
THE INDEPENDENTS
HOTEL ASSOCIATION

★★★ ⊡ HOTEL

☎ 01727 859313
54 Lemsford Rd AL1 3PR
e-mail: info@ardmorehousehotel.co.uk
web: www.ardmorehousehotel.co.uk
dir: A1081 signed St Albans, through 3 sets of lights
& 2 mini rdbts. Right at 3rd mini rdbt, through 2 sets
of lights. Hotel on right in 800yds

Rooms 40 (4 annexe) (5 fmly) (5 GF) **S** £65-£69.50;
D £75-£145 (incl. bkfst) **Facilities** STV FTV Wi-fi ↟
Conf Class 50 Board 50 Thtr 130 Del from £140 to
£150 **Parking** 40 **Notes** ⊗ Civ Wed 150

Premier Inn Luton South M1 Jct 9

BUDGET HOTEL

☎ 0871 527 8334
London Rd, Flamstead AL3 8HT
web: www.premierinn.com
dir: M1 junct 9, A5 towards Dunstable

High quality, budget accommodation ideal for both
families and business travellers. Spacious, en suite

Save on hotels. Book at **theAA.com/hotel**

ST 401 ENGLAND

bedrooms feature tea and coffee making facilities, and Freeview TV in most hotels. Internet access and Wi-fi are available for a small fee. The adjacent family restaurant features a wide and varied menu. See also the Hotel Groups pages.

Rooms 75

ST ANNES

See Lytham St Annes

ST AUSTELL
Cornwall

Map 2 SX05

The Carlyon Bay Hotel

Brend Hotels

★★★★ 76% HOTEL

☎ 01726 812304
Sea Rd, Carlyon Bay PL25 3RD
e-mail: reservations@carlyonbay.com
web: www.carlyonbay.com
dir: From St Austell, follow signs for Charlestown. Carlyon Bay signed on left, hotel at end of Sea Rd

Built in the 1920s, this long-established hotel sits on the cliff top in 250 acres of grounds which include indoor and outdoor pools, a golf course and a spa. Bedrooms are well maintained, and many have

marvellous views across St Austell Bay. A good choice of comfortable lounges is available, whilst facilities for families include kids' clubs and entertainment.

The Carlyon Bay Hotel

Rooms 86 (14 fmly) ✿ **S** £70-£140; **D** £120-£380*
Facilities Spa FTV Wi-fi ⌂ ☜ ☇ ⌁ 18 ⌁ Putt green Gym Hydrotherapy spa pool Hot stone beds ♫ Xmas New Year Child facilities **Conf** Thtr 150 **Services** Lift **Parking** 100 **Notes** LB ⊗ Civ Wed 100

See advert on this page

The Cornwall Hotel Spa & Estate

★★★★ 75% ◉ COUNTRY HOUSE HOTEL

☎ 01726 874050
Pentewan Rd, Tregorrick PL26 7AB
e-mail: enquiries@thecornwall.com
dir: A391 to St Austell then B3273 towards Mevagissey. Hotel approx 0.5m on right

Set in 43 acres of wooded parkland, this renovated manor house offers guests a real retreat. The restored White House has suites and traditionally styled bedrooms, and adjoining are the contemporary Woodland rooms ranging from standard, family, accessible, and also deluxe which have private balcony areas overlooking the Pentewan Valley. There

are superb leisure facilities including the spa with luxury treatments, an infinity pool and state-of-the-art fitness centre. There is a choice of eating options - The Arboretum and the more informal Acorns plus the Drawing Room and Parkland Terrace for afternoon tea and cocktails. This is an ideal base for visiting The Eden Project, The Lost Gardens of Heligan and south Cornwall fishing villages.

Rooms 65 (4 fmly) **S** £84-£189; **D** £99-£235 (incl. bkfst)* **Facilities** Spa STV FTV Wi-fi ⌂ ☜ ⌁ ☜ Gym Xmas New Year **Conf** Class 30 Board 14 Thtr 50 **Services** Lift **Parking** 200 **Notes** Civ Wed 60

Porth Avallen Hotel

★★★ 77% HOTEL

☎ 01726 812802
Sea Rd, Carlyon Bay PL25 3SG
e-mail: info@porthavallen.co.uk
web: www.porthavallen.co.uk
dir: A30 onto A391 to St Austell. Right onto A390. Left at lights, follow brown signs, left at rdbt, right into Sea Rd

This traditional hotel boasts panoramic views over the rugged Cornish coastline. It offers smartly appointed public areas and well-presented bedrooms, many with sea views. There is an oak-panelled lounge and conservatory; both are ideal for relaxation. Extensive dining options, including the stylish Reflections Restaurant, invite guests to choose from fixed-price, carte and all-day brasserie menus. The Olive Garden, inspired by the Mediterranean, is a lovely place to eat alfresco.

Rooms 28 (3 fmly) (3 GF) **Facilities** FTV Wi-fi Xmas New Year **Conf** Class 100 Board 80 Thtr 160 **Parking** 60 **Notes** ⊗ Civ Wed 160

S

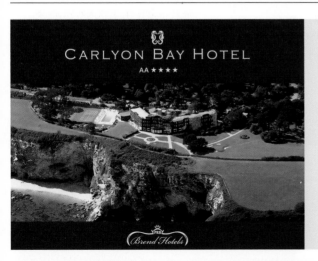

ST AUSTELL *continued*

Best Western Cliff Head Hotel

★★★ 75% HOTEL

☎ 01726 812345
Sea Rd, Carlyon Bay PL25 3RB
e-mail: info@cliffheadhotel.com
web: www.cliffheadhotel.com
dir: 2m E off A390

Set in extensive grounds and conveniently located for visiting the Eden Project, this hotel faces south and enjoys views over Carlyon Bay. A choice of lounges is provided, together with a swimming pool and solarium. Expressions restaurant offers a range of menus, which feature an interesting selection of dishes.

Rooms 57 (4 fmly) (11 GF) ✿ **S** £50-£90; **D** £90-£110 (incl. bkfst) **Facilities** FTV Wi-fi ✕ Xmas New Year **Conf** Class 90 Board 50 Thtr 150 Del from £95 to £125 **Parking** 60 **Notes** LB Civ Wed 70

The Pier House

★★★ 75% HOTEL

☎ 01726 67955
Harbour Front, Charlestown PL25 3NJ
e-mail: pierhouse@btconnect.com
dir: A390 to St Austell, at Mt Charles rdbt left into Charlestown Rd

This genuinely friendly hotel boasts a wonderful harbour location. The unspoilt working port has been the setting for many film and television productions. Most bedrooms have sea views, and the hotel's convivial Harbourside Inn is popular with locals and tourists alike. Locally caught fish features on the varied and interesting restaurant menu.

Rooms 28 (2 annexe) (3 fmly) (2 GF) **Facilities** STV Wi-fi **Parking** 50 **Notes** ⊗ Closed 24-25 Dec

Boscundle Manor Country House Hotel

★★ 82% ⊛ COUNTRY HOUSE HOTEL

☎ 01726 813557
Tregrehan PL25 3RL
e-mail: reservations@boscundlemanor.co.uk
dir: 2m E on A390, 200yds on road signed Tregrehan

Set in beautifully maintained gardens and grounds, this handsome 18th-century stone manor house is a short distance from the Eden Project. Quality and comfort are apparent in the public areas and spacious, well-equipped bedrooms. A choice of eating options is available, with both fine dining and brasserie alternatives. Equally suitable for both leisure and business travellers, this hotel boasts both indoor and outdoor pools.

Rooms 14 (4 annexe) (4 fmly) (4 GF) **Facilities** FTV Wi-fi ⌖ ✿ 🌿 Beauty treatment room Xmas New Year **Conf** Class 20 Board 20 Thtr 40 **Parking** 20 **Notes** ⊗ Civ Wed 60

Premier Inn St Austell

BUDGET HOTEL

☎ 0871 527 9018
St Austell Enterprise Park, Treverbyn Rd PL25 4EL
web: www.premierinn.com
dir: A30 onto A391 signed St Austell. Through Bugle. Continue on A391 at rdbt. Continue to follow St Austell signs. 1st exit at Carclaze rdbt. Hotel at St Austell Enterprise Park

High quality, budget accommodation ideal for both families and business travellers. Spacious, en suite bedrooms feature tea and coffee making facilities, and Freeview TV in most hotels. Internet access and Wi-fi are available for a small fee. The adjacent family restaurant features a wide and varied menu. See also the Hotel Groups pages.

Rooms 61

ST HELENS
Merseyside — Map 15 SJ59

Premier Inn St Helens (A580/East Lancs)

BUDGET HOTEL

☎ 0871 527 9020
Garswood Old Rd, East Lancs Rd WA11 7LX
web: www.premierinn.com
dir: 3m from M6 junct 23, on A580 towards Liverpool

High quality, budget accommodation ideal for both families and business travellers. Spacious, en suite bedrooms feature tea and coffee making facilities, and Freeview TV in most hotels. Internet access and Wi-fi are available for a small fee. The adjacent family restaurant features a wide and varied menu. See also the Hotel Groups pages.

Rooms 44

Premier Inn St Helens South

BUDGET HOTEL

☎ 0871 527 9022
Eurolink, Lea Green WA9 4TT
web: www.premierinn.com
dir: M62 junct 7, A570 towards St Helens

Rooms 40

ST IVES
Cambridgeshire — Map 12 TL37

Slepe Hall Hotel

★★★ 79% HOTEL

☎ 01480 463122
Ramsey Rd PE27 5RB
e-mail: reception@slepehallhotel.co.uk
dir: A14 junct 26 onto A1096, left at Toyota car showroom into Ramsey Rd

Ideally situated just a short walk from the town centre and only 20 minutes from Cambridge. The public areas have been appointed to a very high standard and are very smart; they include a brasserie, a lounge bar and a restaurant. The contemporary-style bedrooms are well equipped and have co-ordinated soft furnishings.

Rooms 16 (5 fmly) ✿ **S** £82-£92; **D** £92-£112 (incl. bkfst)* **Facilities** STV FTV Wi-fi ♫ Xmas New Year **Conf** Class 250 Board 250 Thtr 300 **Parking** 60 **Notes** LB ⊗ Civ Wed 250

S

Save on hotels. Book at **theAA.com/hotel**

ST 403 ENGLAND

ST IVES *continued*

Olivers Lodge Hotel

THE INDEPENDENTS
HOTEL ASSOCIATION

★★★ 74% HOTEL

☎ 01480 463252
Needingworth Rd PE27 5JP
e-mail: reception@oliverslodge.co.uk
web: www.oliverslodge.co.uk
dir: A14 towards Huntingdon/Cambridge, take B1040
to St Ives. Cross 1st rdbt, left at 2nd rdbt then 1st
right. Hotel 500mtrs on right

A privately owned hotel situated in a peaceful
residential area just a short walk from the town
centre. Public rooms include a smart air-conditioned
bar, a choice of lounges and a conservatory dining
room. The pleasantly decorated bedrooms are
equipped with modern facilities and have co-
ordinated fabrics.

Rooms 17 (5 annexe) (3 fmly) (5 GF) **Facilities** Wi-fi
Conf Class 30 Board 25 Thtr 65 **Notes** Civ Wed 65

The Dolphin Hotel

★★★ 70% HOTEL

☎ 01480 466966
London Rd PE27 5EP
e-mail: enquiries@dolphinhotelcambs.co.uk
dir: A14 between Huntingdon & Cambridge onto
A1096 towards St Ives. Left at 1st rdbt & immediately
right. Hotel on left after 0.5m

This modern hotel sits by delightful water meadows
on the banks of the River Ouse. Open-plan public
rooms include a choice of bars and a pleasant
restaurant offering fine river views. The bedrooms are
modern and varied in style; some are in the hotel
while others occupy an adjacent wing; all are
comfortable and spacious. Conference and function
suites are available.

Rooms 67 (37 annexe) (4 fmly) (22 GF) (2 smoking)
♦ **Facilities** FTV ♦ Fishing Gym **Conf** Class 50
Board 50 Thtr 150 **Parking** 400 **Notes** ⊗ RS 24
Dec-2 Jan Civ Wed 60

Carbis Bay Hotel

★★★ 81% ⚜ HOTEL

☎ 01736 795311
Carbis Bay TR26 2NP
e-mail: info@carbisbayhotel.co.uk
web: www.carbisbayhotel.co.uk
dir: A3074, through Lelant. 1m, at Carbis Bay 30yds
before lights, right into Porthrepta Rd to hotel

In a peaceful location with access to its own white-
sand beach, this hotel offers comfortable
accommodation. The attractive public areas feature a
smart bar and lounge, and a sun lounge overlooking
the sea. Bedrooms, many with fine views, are well
equipped. Interesting cuisine and particularly
enjoyable breakfasts are offered. A small complex of
luxury, self-catering apartments is available.

Rooms 47 (16 fmly) (3 GF) ♦ **S** £85-£150;
D £130-£300 (incl. bkfst & dinner) **Facilities** Wi-fi ♦
Fishing Private beach ♫ Xmas New Year Child
facilities **Conf** Class 80 Board 60 Thtr 120
Del from £130 to £150 **Parking** 200 **Notes** LB ⊗
Civ Wed 150

See advert on page 403

Garrack Hotel & Restaurant

★★★ 78% ⚜ HOTEL

☎ 01736 796199
Burthallan Ln, Higher Ayr TR26 3AA
e-mail: aa@garrack.com
dir: Exit A30 for St Ives. From B3311 follow brown
signs for Tate Gallery, then Garrack signs

Enjoying a peaceful, elevated position with splendid
views across the harbour and Porthmeor Beach, the
Garrack sits in its own delightful grounds and
gardens. Bedrooms are comfortable and many have
sea views. Public areas include a small leisure suite,
a choice of lounges and an attractive restaurant,
where locally sourced ingredients are used in the
enjoyable dishes.

Rooms 18 (2 annexe) (2 fmly) (3 GF) **Facilities** FTV
Wi-fi ⊛ Gym New Year **Conf** Class 10 Board 10
Thtr 20 **Parking** 30

St Ives Harbour Hotel

★★★ 78% HOTEL

☎ 01736 795221
The Terrace TR26 2BN
e-mail: stives@harbourhotels.co.uk
web: www.stives-harbour-hotel.co.uk
dir: On A3074

This friendly hotel enjoys an enviable location with
spectacular views of St Ives Bay. Extensive leisure
facilities, a versatile function suite and a number of
elegant and stylish lounges are available. The
majority of bedrooms are appointed to a very high
standard and many rooms have spectacular sea
views, likewise the restaurant which looks out over
the bay and golden sands below.

Rooms 46 (9 fmly) ♦ **S** £100-£140; **D** £145-£325
(incl. bkfst & dinner)* **Facilities** Spa FTV Wi-fi Gym
Steam room Xmas New Year **Conf** Class 20 Board 35
Thtr 130 **Services** Lift **Parking** 60 **Notes** Civ Wed 160

Tregenna Castle Hotel

★★★ 74% HOTEL

☎ 01736 795254
TR26 2DE
e-mail: hotel@tregenna-castle.co.uk
web: www.tregenna-castle.co.uk
dir: A30 from Exeter to Penzance, at Lelant take A3074 to St Ives, through Carbis Bay, main entrance signed on left

Sitting at the top of town in beautiful landscaped sub-tropical gardens with woodland walks, this popular hotel boasts spectacular views of St Ives. Many leisure facilities are available, including indoor and outdoor pools, a gym and a sauna. Families are particularly welcome. The individually designed bedrooms are in general, spacious. There are two restaurants, the Trelawny Room and the Godrevy Room, and a brasserie provides lighter options in a less formal atmosphere.

Rooms 81 (12 fmly) (16 GF) **Facilities** Spa ⊗ ⊰ supervised ⚎ 14 ♲ Putt green ⚐ Gym Squash Steam room Badminton court Xmas New Year **Conf** Class 150 Board 30 Thtr 250 **Services** Lift **Parking** 200 **Notes** ⊗ Civ Wed 160

Primrose Valley

★★★ 73% METRO HOTEL

☎ 01736 794939
Porthminster Beach TR26 2ED
e-mail: info@primroseonline.co.uk
web: www.primroseonline.co.uk
dir: A3074 to St Ives, 25yds after town sign right into Primrose Valley, left under bridge, along beach front, left back under bridge, property on left

St Ives is just a short walk from this stylish, friendly, family-run establishment close to Porthminster Beach. The property is light and airy, and modernisation has resulted in good levels of comfort; some bedrooms have balconies with stunning views. There is a lounge and bar area, and breakfast features local produce and home-made items.

Rooms 9 ⌇ **S** £75-£175; **D** £85-£240 (incl. bkfst)* **Facilities** FTV Wi-fi ♲ **Parking** 11 **Notes** LB ⊗ No children 8yrs Closed 23-27 Dec & 2-31 Jan

Chy-an-Albany Hotel

★★★ 71% HOTEL

☎ 01736 796759
Albany Ter TR26 2BS
e-mail: info@chyanalbanyhotel.com
dir: A30 onto A3074 signed St Ives, hotel on left just before junct

Conveniently located, this pleasant hotel enjoys splendid sea views. The comfortable bedrooms come in a variety of sizes; some featuring balconies and sea views. Friendly staff and the relaxing environment mean that guests return on a regular basis. Freshly prepared and appetising cuisine is served in the dining room and a bar menu is also available.

Rooms 39 (9 fmly) ⌇ **Facilities** FTV Wi-fi **Conf** Class 30 Board 30 Thtr 50 **Services** Lift **Parking** 33 **Notes** ⊗ Civ Wed 70

Cottage Hotel

Leisureplex

★★ 71% HOTEL

☎ 01736 795252
Boskerris Rd, Carbis Bay TR26 2PE
e-mail: cottage.stives@alfatravel.co.uk
web: www.leisureplex.co.uk
dir: From A30 take A3074 to Carbis Bay. Right into Porthreptor Rd. Just before rail bridge, left through railway car park into hotel car park

Set in quiet, lush gardens, this pleasant hotel offers friendly and attentive service. Smart bedrooms are pleasantly spacious and many rooms enjoy splendid views. Public areas are varied and include a snooker room, a comfortable lounge and a spacious dining room with sea views over the beach and Carbis Bay.

Rooms 80 (7 fmly) (2 GF) **Facilities** FTV ⊰ Snooker ♫ Xmas New Year **Services** Lift **Parking** 20 **Notes** ⊗ Closed Dec-Feb (ex Xmas) RS Nov & Mar

Hotel St Eia

★★ 69% HOTEL

☎ 01736 795531
Trelyon Av TR26 2AA
e-mail: info@hotelsteia.co.uk
dir: A30 onto A3074, follow signs to St Ives, approaching town, hotel on right

This smart hotel is conveniently located and enjoys spectacular views over St Ives, the harbour and Porthminster Beach. The friendly proprietors provide a relaxing environment. Bedrooms are comfortable and well equipped, and some have sea views. The spacious lounge bar has a well-stocked bar and views can be enjoyed from the rooftop terrace.

Rooms 18 (3 fmly) (1 GF) **S** £40-£60; **D** £80-£120 (incl. bkfst)* **Facilities** FTV Wi-fi **Parking** 16 **Notes** ⊗ Closed Nov-Mar

ST LEONARDS-ON-SEA

See Hastings & St Leonards

ST MARY CHURCH

See Torquay

ST MARY'S　　　　　　　Map 2 SV91
Cornwall (Isles of Scilly)

Tregarthen's Hotel

★★★ 78% HOTEL

☎ 01720 422540
Hugh Town TR21 0PP
e-mail: reception@tregarthens-hotel.co.uk
dir: 100yds from town & quay

Opened in 1848 by Captain Tregarthen this is a well-established hotel. The impressive public areas provide wonderful views overlooking St Mary's harbour and some of the many islands, including Tresco and Bryher. Bedrooms are well equipped and neatly furnished. Traditional cuisine is served in the restaurant.

Rooms 33 (1 annexe) (6 fmly) ⌇ **S** £148-£162; **D** £280-£346 (incl. bkfst & dinner)* **Facilities** FTV Wi-fi **Conf** Class 20 Board 15 Thtr 30 Del from £160 to £180* **Notes** LB ⊗ Closed late Oct-mid Mar

S

ST MAWES — Map 2 SW83
Cornwall

Idle Rocks Hotel
★★★ 81% ◉◉ HOTEL

RICHARDSON HOTELS
Where Memories are Made

☎ 01326 270771
Harbour Side TR2 5AN
e-mail: reception@idlerocks.co.uk
web: www.idlerocks.co.uk
dir: A390 onto A3078, 14m to St Mawes. Hotel on left

This hotel has splendid sea views overlooking the attractive fishing port. The lounge and bar also benefit from the views and in warmer months service is available on the terrace. Bedrooms are individually styled and tastefully furnished to a high standard. The daily-changing menu served in the restaurant features fresh, local produce in imaginative cuisine.

Rooms 27 (4 annexe) (6 fmly) (2 GF) **Facilities** FTV Wi-fi Xmas New Year **Parking** 4

ST MELLION — Map 3 SX36
Cornwall

St Mellion International Resort
★★★★ 80% ◉◉ HOTEL

☎ 01579 351351
PL12 6SD
e-mail: stmellion@crown-golf.co.uk
dir: From M5, A38 towards Plymouth & Saltash. St Mellion off A38 on A388 towards Callington & Launceston

Set amidst 450 acres of Cornish countryside, this impressive golfing and leisure complex has much to offer. A vast range of leisure facilities are provided, including three pools, spa facilities and a health club. In addition, the hotel also boasts a choice of championship golf courses with the Jack Nicklaus signature course having hosted many PGA tour events. The bedrooms provide contemporary comforts and many have views across the course. Public areas are equally stylish with a choice of dining options including An Boesti, a fine-dining restaurant overlooking the 18th green.

Rooms 80 (20 fmly) (18 GF) **Facilities** Spa FTV Wi-fi ⌖ ⊛ supervised ⌖ 36 ⛳ Putt green Gym Studio classes Lawn bowls Xmas New Year **Conf** Class 200 Board 80 Thtr 400 **Services** Lift Air con **Parking** 450 **Notes** ⊗ Civ Wed 300

ST NEOTS — Map 12 TL16
Cambridgeshire

The George Hotel & Brasserie
★★★ 88% ◉◉ HOTEL

☎ 01480 812300
High St, Buckden PE19 5XA
e-mail: mail@thegeorgebuckden.com
web: www.thegeorgebuckden.com
dir: 2m S of A1 & A14 junct at Buckden

Ideally situated in the heart of this historic town centre and just a short drive from the A1. Public rooms feature a bustling ground-floor brasserie, which offers casual dining throughout the day and evening; there is also an informal lounge bar with an open fire and comfy seating. Bedrooms are stylish, tastefully appointed and thoughtfully equipped.

Rooms 12 (1 fmly) ⌖ **S** £95; **D** £120-£150 (incl. bkfst)* **Facilities** STV Wi-fi ⌖ Xmas **Conf** Class 30 Board 30 Thtr 50 Del from £160* **Services** Lift **Parking** 25 **Notes** LB Civ Wed 60

Abbotsley Golf Hotel
★★★ 64% HOTEL

☎ 01480 474000
Potton Rd, Eynesbury Hardwicke PE19 6XN
e-mail: manager@abbotsley.com
web: www.abbotsley.com

Situated in a rural location on the outskirts of St Neots, this property is set in 250-acre grounds with two golf courses, a golf school and leisure complex. The well-equipped bedrooms are situated in a courtyard and another adjacent block; some rooms have views over the golf course. Public rooms include two bars, a conservatory dining room and a choice of lounges.

Rooms 42 (42 annexe) (2 fmly) (29 GF) **S** fr £59; **D** fr £85 (incl. bkfst)* **Facilities** FTV Wi-fi ⌖ 45 Putt green Gym Squash ⌖ Xmas New Year **Conf** Class 60 Board 60 Thtr 80 Del from £95* **Parking** 200 **Notes** LB Civ Wed 90

Premier Inn St Neots (A1/Wyboston)

BUDGET HOTEL

☎ 0871 527 9024
Great North Rd, Eaton Socon PE19 8EN
web: www.premierinn.com
dir: Just off A1 at rdbt of A428 & B1428 before St Neots. 1m from St Neots rail station

High quality, budget accommodation ideal for both families and business travellers. Spacious, en suite bedrooms feature tea and coffee making facilities, and Freeview TV in most hotels. Internet access and Wi-fi are available for a small fee. The adjacent family restaurant features a wide and varied menu. See also the Hotel Groups pages.

Rooms 65

Premier Inn St Neots (Colmworth Park)

BUDGET HOTEL

☎ 0871 527 9026
2 Marlborough Rd, Colmworth Business Park PE19 8YP
web: www.premierinn.com
dir: From A1 N'bound: A428 towards Cambridge. 2nd exit at rdbt onto A4128 signed St Neots. Hotel on right. From A1 S'bound: follow A428 Cambridge signs. At rdbt 1st exit onto A4128 signed St Neots, hotel on right

Rooms 41

SALCOMBE — Map 3 SX73
Devon

See also Hope Cove

Thurlestone Hotel
★★★★ 83% ◉ HOTEL

☎ 01548 560382
TQ7 3NN
e-mail: enquiries@thurlestone.co.uk
web: www.thurlestone.co.uk

(For full entry see Thurlestone)

Save on hotels. Book at **theAA.com/hotel**

ST – SAL **407** ENGLAND

Soar Mill Cove Hotel

★★★★ 79% ◉◉ HOTEL

☎ 01548 561566
Soar Mill Cove, Malborough TQ7 3DS
e-mail: info@soarmillcove.co.uk
web: www.soarmillcove.co.uk
dir: 3m W of town off A381 at Malborough. Follow Soar signs

Situated amid spectacular scenery with dramatic sea views, this hotel is ideal for a relaxing stay. Family-run, with a committed team, keen standards of hospitality and service are upheld. The bedrooms are well equipped and many have private terraces. There are different seating areas where, if guests wish, impressive cream teas can be enjoyed, and for the more active, there's a choice of swimming pools. Local produce and seafood are used to good effect in the restaurant.

Rooms 22 (5 fmly) (21 GF) ⌘ **S** £125-£155; **D** £150-£180 (incl. bkfst)* **Facilities** FTV Wi-fi ⊗ ⊣ 🌳 Putt green Table tennis Games room ♫ **Conf** Class 50 Board 50 Thtr 100 **Parking** 30 **Notes** Closed 2 Jan-8 Feb Civ Wed 150

Tides Reach Hotel

★★★ 83% ◉ HOTEL

☎ 01548 843466
South Sands TQ8 8LJ
e-mail: enquire@tidesreach.com
web: www.tidesreach.com
dir: Exit A38 at Buckfastleigh to Totnes. Then A381 to Salcombe, follow signs to South Sands

Superbly situated at the water's edge, this personally run, friendly hotel has splendid views of the estuary and beach. Bedrooms, many with balconies, are spacious and comfortable. In the bar and lounge, attentive service can be enjoyed along with the view, and the Garden Room restaurant serves appetising and accomplished cuisine.

Rooms 32 (5 fmly) ⌘ **S** £85-£150; **D** £146-£349 (incl. bkfst & dinner)* **Facilities** Spa STV FTV Wi-fi ⊗ supervised Gym Squash Windsurfing Sailing Kayaking Scuba diving Hair & beauty treatment **Services** Lift **Parking** 100 **Notes** LB No children 8yrs Closed Dec-early Feb

---

SALE
Greater Manchester   Map 15 SJ79

Premier Inn Manchester (Sale)

BUDGET HOTEL

☎ 0871 527 8716
Carrington Ln, Ashton-upon-Mersey M33 5BL
web: www.premierinn.com
dir: M60 junct 8, A6144(M) towards Carrington. Left at 1st lights, hotel on left

High quality, budget accommodation ideal for both families and business travellers. Spacious, en suite bedrooms feature tea and coffee making facilities, and Freeview TV in most hotels. Internet access and Wi-fi are available for a small fee. The adjacent family restaurant features a wide and varied menu. See also the Hotel Groups pages.

Rooms 43

SALISBURY
Wiltshire   Map 5 SU12

Milford Hall Hotel

★★★★ 73% ◉ HOTEL   CLASSIC BRITISH HOTELS

☎ 01722 417411 & 424116
206 Castle St SP1 3TE
e-mail: reception@milfordhallhotel.com
web: www.milfordhallhotel.com
dir: Near junct of Castle St, A36 (ring road) & A345 (Amesbury road)

This hotel offers high standards of accommodation and is within easy walking distance of the city centre. There are two categories of bedroom - traditional rooms in the original Georgian house, and spacious, modern rooms in a purpose-built extension; all are extremely well equipped. Meals are served in the smart brasserie where a varied choice of dishes is provided.

Rooms 45 (2 fmly) (22 GF) ⌘ **Facilities** STV FTV Wi-fi New Year **Conf** Class 90 Board 60 Thtr 160 **Parking** 60 **Notes** ⊗ Civ Wed 120

Mercure Salisbury White Hart Hotel

Mercure

★★★★ 73% HOTEL

☎ 0870 400 8125 & 01722 327476
St John St SP1 2SD
e-mail: H6616@accor.com
web: www.mercure.com
dir: M3 juncts 7/8, A303 to A343 for Salisbury then A30. Follow city centre signs on ring road, into Exeter St, leading into St John St. Car park at rear on Brown St

There has been a hotel on this site since the 16th century. Bedrooms vary - some are contemporary and some are decorated in more traditional style, but all boast a comprehensive range of facilities. The bar and lounge areas are popular with guests and locals alike for morning coffees and afternoon teas.

Rooms 68 (6 fmly) **Facilities** STV Wi-fi Xmas New Year **Conf** Class 40 Board 40 Thtr 100 **Parking** 60 **Notes** Civ Wed 100

The Legacy Rose & Crown Hotel

LEGACY HOTELS

★★★★ 71% HOTEL

☎ 08444 119046 & 0330 333 2846
Harnham Rd SP2 8JQ
e-mail: res-roseandcrown@legacy-hotels.co.uk
web: www.legacy-hotels.co.uk
dir: M3 junct 8, A303 & follow Salisbury Ring Road & A338 towards Harnham then Harnham Rd. Hotel on right

This 13th-century coaching inn, situated beside the river, enjoys picturesque views of Salisbury Cathedral, especially from the Pavilion Restaurant which provides a good range of dishes. Many original features are still retained in the heavy oak-beamed bars. All bedrooms and bathrooms are beautifully appointed. Excellent conference and banqueting facilities are available.

Rooms 29 (5 fmly) (3 GF) **Facilities** FTV Wi-fi Xmas New Year **Conf** Class 30 Board 26 Thtr 90 **Parking** 60 **Notes** ⊗ Civ Wed 120

S

SALISBURY continued

Best Western Red Lion Hotel

★★★ 77% ● HOTEL

☎ 01722 323334
Milford St SP1 2AN
e-mail: reception@the-redlion.co.uk
web: www.the-redlion.co.uk
dir: In city centre close to Guildhall Square

This 750-year-old hotel is full of character, with individually designed bedrooms that combine contemporary comforts with historic features; one room has a medieval fireplace dating back to 1220. The distinctive public areas include a bar, lounge and the elegant Vine Restaurant that serves an interesting mix of modern and traditional dishes.

Rooms 51 (1 fmly) **Facilities** Wi-fi Xmas New Year **Conf** Class 50 Board 40 Thtr 100 **Services** Lift **Notes** ⊗ Civ Wed 80

Grasmere House Hotel

THE INDEPENDENTS
HOTEL ASSOCIATION

★★★ 70% HOTEL

☎ 01722 338388
Harnham Rd SP2 8JN
e-mail: info@grasmerehotel.com
web: www.grasmerehotel.com
dir: On A3094 on S side of Salisbury adjacent to Harnham church

This popular hotel, dating from 1896, has gardens that overlook the water meadows and the cathedral. The attractive bedrooms vary in size, some offer excellent quality and comfort, and some rooms are specially equipped for less mobile guests. In summer there is the option of dining on the pleasant outdoor terrace.

Rooms 38 (31 annexe) (16 fmly) (9 GF) 🐾 **Facilities** STV FTV Wi-fi Fishing ⛵ Xmas New Year **Conf** Class 45 Board 45 Thtr 110 **Parking** 64 **Notes** Civ Wed 120

Premier Inn Salisbury

BUDGET HOTEL

☎ 0871 527 8956
Pearce Way, Bishopsdown SP1 3YU
web: www.premierinn.com
dir: From Salisbury take A30 towards Marlborough. 1m. Hotel off Hampton Park at rdbt

High quality, budget accommodation ideal for both families and business travellers. Spacious, en suite bedrooms feature tea and coffee making facilities, and Freeview TV in most hotels. Internet access and Wi-fi are available for a small fee. The adjacent family restaurant features a wide and varied menu. See also the Hotel Groups pages.

Rooms 62

SALTASH — Map 3 SX45
Cornwall

China Fleet Country Club

★★★ 78% ● HOTEL

☎ 01752 854664 & 854661
PL12 6LJ
e-mail: sales@china-fleet.co.uk
web: www.china-fleet.co.uk
dir: A38 towards Plymouth/Saltash. Cross Tamar Bridge, take slip road before tunnel. Right at lights, 1st right follow signs, 0.5m

Set in 180 acres of stunning Cornish countryside overlooking the beautiful Tamar estuary, this hotel has easy access to Plymouth and the countryside. It offers an extensive range of leisure facilities including an impressive golf course. The one and two-bedroom apartments are located in annexe buildings; each has a kitchen, lounge and flexible sleeping arrangements. There are dining options include the brasserie, coffee shop and award-winning Farm House Restaurant which offers interesting and imaginative choices.

Rooms 40 (39 fmly) (21 GF) 🐾 **S** £71-£101; **D** £71-£145 **Facilities** Spa FTV Wi-fi ⓑ ⓒ supervised ⛳ 18 ⛳ Putt green Gym Squash 28-bay floodlit driving range Health & beauty suite Hairdresser Xmas New Year Child facilities **Conf** Class 80 Board 60 Thtr 300 **Services** Lift **Parking** 400 **Notes** ⊗ Civ Wed 300

SALTBURN-BY-THE-SEA — Map 19 NZ62
North Yorkshire

Hunley Hotel & Golf Club

★★★ 75% HOTEL

☎ 01287 676216
Ings Ln, Brotton TS12 2QQ
e-mail: enquiries@hunleyhotel.co.uk
dir: From A174 bypass left at rdbt with monument, left at T-junct, pass church, turn right. 50yds right, through housing estate, hotel approx 0.5m

Spectacularly situated, this hotel overlooks the 27-hole golf course and beyond to the coastline. The members' bar is licensed and serves snacks all day, and the restaurant offers a wide choice of interesting dishes. The bedrooms are very comfortably equipped and some are particularly spacious.

Rooms 27 (2 fmly) (17 GF) **Facilities** STV FTV Wi-fi ⓑ ⛳ 27 Putt green Driving range Xmas New Year **Conf** Class 32 Board 28 Thtr 50 **Parking** 100 **Notes** Civ Wed 130

SANDBANKS

See Poole

SANDIACRE — Map 11 SK43
Derbyshire

Holiday Inn Derby/Nottingham

Holiday Inn

★★★ 73% HOTEL

☎ 0871 942 9062
Bostocks Ln NG10 5NJ
e-mail: reservations-derby-nottingham@ihg.com
web: www.hiderbyhotel.co.uk
dir: M1 junct 25 follow Sandiacre signs, hotel on right

This hotel is conveniently located by the M1, and ideal for exploring Derby and Nottingham. The bedrooms are modern and smart. The restaurant offers a wide range of dishes for breakfast, lunch and dinner. The lounge/bar area is a popular meeting place, with food served all day.

Rooms 92 (31 fmly) (53 GF) **S** £29-£99; **D** £39-£109* **Facilities** STV Wi-fi ⓑ Xmas New Year **Conf** Class 32 Board 32 Thtr 70 Del from £89 to £120* **Services** Air con **Parking** 200 **Notes** LB Civ Wed 50

Save on hotels. Book at **theAA.com/hotel**

SAL – SAN 409 ENGLAND

SANDIWAY
Cheshire
Map 15 SJ67

INSPECTORS' CHOICE

Nunsmere Hall Hotel

★★★★ ◎◎
COUNTRY HOUSE HOTEL

☎ 01606 889100
Tarporley Rd CW8 2ES
e-mail: reception@nunsmere.co.uk
web: www.nunsmere.co.uk
dir: M6 junct 18, A54 to Chester, at x-rds with A49
turn left towards Tarporley, hotel 2m on left

In an idyllic and peaceful setting of well-kept
grounds, including a 60-acre lake, this delightful
house dates back to 1900. Spacious bedrooms are
individually styled, tastefully appointed to a very
high standard and thoughtfully equipped. Guests
can relax in the elegant lounges, the library or the
oak-panelled bar. Dining in the Crystal Restaurant
is a highlight and both a traditional carte and a
gourmet menu are offered.

Rooms 36 (8 fmly) (2 GF) 🐾 **Facilities** FTV Wi-fi 🏊
🌳 Xmas New Year **Conf** Class 24 Board 30 Thtr 50
Del from £149 to £250* **Services** Lift **Parking** 80
Notes Civ Wed 120

SANDOWN
Isle of Wight
Map 5 SZ58

Melville Hall Hotel & Utopia Spa

★★★ 80% HOTEL

☎ 01983 400500 & 406526
Melville St PO36 9DH
e-mail: enquiries@melvillehall.co.uk
web: www.melvillehall.co.uk
dir: Exit A3055, hotel 30yds on left

Situated in the quiet semi-rural outskirts of Sandown,
a few minutes walk from the seafront, railway station,
cliff walks and shops. There is a leisure suite, with
both indoor and outdoor pool, and beauty treatment
rooms are available. Bedrooms offer a good range of
accessories and many have jacuzzi baths.

Rooms 30 (3 fmly) (4 GF) **Facilities** Spa STV Wi-fi 🕄
🏌 Putt green Xmas New Year **Parking** 20 **Notes** ⊗

The Wight Montrene Hotel

★★ 78% HOTEL

☎ 01983 403722
11 Avenue Rd PO36 8BN
e-mail: enquiries@wighthotel.co.uk
web: www.wighthotel.co.uk
dir: 100yds after mini-rdbt between High St & Avenue
Rd

A family hotel, set in secluded grounds, that is only a
short walk from Sandown's beach and high street
shops. Bedrooms provide comfort and are either on
the ground or first floor. Guests can relax in the
heated swimming pool and enjoy the spa facility;
there's also evening entertainment in the bar. The
dinner menu changes nightly, and a plentiful
breakfast is served in the colourful dining room.

Rooms 41 (18 fmly) (21 GF) **Facilities** Spa Wi-fi 🕄
Gym Steam room Sauna Solarium Table tennis Full
size snooker table 🎵 Xmas New Year **Conf** Thtr 80
Parking 40

Sandringham Hotel

★★ 74% HOTEL

☎ 01983 406655
Esplanade PO36 8AH
e-mail: info@sandringhamhotel.co.uk

With a prime seafront location and splendid views,
this is one of the largest hotels on the island.
Comfortable public areas include a spacious lounge
and a heated indoor swimming pool and jacuzzi.
Bedrooms vary in size and many sea-facing rooms
have a balcony. Regular entertainment is provided in
the ballroom.

Rooms 110 (39 fmly) (6 GF) **Facilities** 🕄 🎵 Xmas
Services Lift **Parking** 82 **Notes** ⊗

Bayshore Hotel

★★ 72% HOTEL

☎ 01983 403154
12-16 Pier St PO36 8JX
e-mail: bayshore.sandown@alfatravel.co.uk
web: www.leisureplex.co.uk
dir: From Broadway into Melville St, follow Tourist
Information Office signs. Across High St, right
opposite pier. Hotel on right

This large hotel is located on the seafront opposite
the pier and offers extensive public rooms where live
entertainment is provided in season. The bedrooms
are well equipped and staff very friendly and helpful.

Rooms 80 (18 fmly) (2 GF) **Facilities** FTV 🎵 Xmas
New Year **Services** Lift **Notes** ⊗ Closed Dec-Feb (ex
Xmas) RS Mar & Nov

Riviera Hotel

★★ 71% HOTEL

☎ 01983 402518
2 Royal St PO36 8LP
e-mail: enquiries@rivierahotel.org.uk
web: www.rivierahotel.org.uk
dir: At top of High St, beyond Post Office

Guests return year after year to this friendly and
welcoming family-run hotel. It is located near to the
High Street and just a short stroll from the beach,
pier and shops. Bedrooms, including several at
ground floor level, are very well furnished and
comfortably equipped. Enjoyable home-cooked meals
are served in the spacious dining room.

Rooms 43 (6 fmly) (11 GF) 🐾 **S** £40-£48; **D** £80-£96
(incl. bkfst) **Facilities** FTV 🎵 Xmas New Year
Parking 30 **Notes** LB

S

SANDOWN *continued*

Sandown Hotel

★★ 69% HOTEL

☎ 01983 402072
Culver Pde PO36 8AS
e-mail: info@sandown.co.uk
dir: In town centre

In a prime location on Sandown seafront and close to the town centre, convenient for bars and restaurants as well as the pier and promenade, the hotel offers traditional, comfortably appointed bedrooms. Guests can enjoy both breakfast and dinner in the restaurant, which is open daily.

Rooms 45

SANDWICH	Map 7 TR35
Kent	

The Lodge at Princes

U

☎ 01304 611118
Prince's Dr, Sandwich Bay CT13 9QB
e-mail: j.george@princesgolfclub.co.uk

Currently the rating for this establishment is not confirmed. This may be due to a change of ownership or because it has only recently joined the AA rating scheme. For further details please see the AA website: theAA.com

Rooms 12

SAUNTON	Map 3 SS43
Devon	

Saunton Sands Hotel

★★★★ 79% ◉ HOTEL

☎ 01271 890212
EX33 1LQ
e-mail: reservations@sauntonsands.com
web: www.sauntonsands.com
dir: Exit A361 at Braunton, signed Croyde B3231, hotel 2m on left

Stunning sea views and direct access to five miles of sandy beach are just two of the highlights at this popular hotel. The majority of sea-facing rooms have balconies, and splendid views can be enjoyed from all of the public areas, which include comfortable lounges. In addition to the dining room, in summer an outside grill has tables on the terrace overlooking the sea. Alternatively, The Sands café/bar, an informal eating option, is a successful innovation located on the beach.

Saunton Sands Hotel

Rooms 92 (39 fmly) ♦ **S** £105-£150; **D** £210-£460 (incl. bkfst)* **Facilities** STV FTV Wi-fi ⊗ ⊕ ↝ ⚓ Putt green Gym Squash Sauna Beauty treatment room ♫ Xmas New Year Child facilities **Conf** Class 180 Board 50 Thtr 200 **Services** Lift **Parking** 140 **Notes** LB ⊗ Civ Wed 200

See advert on this page

Save on hotels. Book at **theAA.com/hotel**

SAN – SCA 411 ENGLAND

Manor of Groves Hotel, Golf & Country Club

★★★ 77% HOTEL

☎ 01279 600777 & 0870 410 8833
High Wych CM21 0JU
e-mail: info@manorofgroves.co.uk
web: www.manorofgroves.com
dir: A1184 to Sawbridgeworth, left to High Wych, right at village green & hotel 200yds left

Delightful Georgian manor house set in 150 acres of secluded grounds and gardens, with its own 18-hole championship golf course and superb leisure facilities. Public rooms include an imposing open-plan glass atrium that features a bar, lounge area and modern restaurant. The spacious bedrooms are smartly decorated and equipped with modern facilities.

Rooms 80 (2 fmly) (17 GF) ⚲ **S** £70-£150;
D £99-£200* **Facilities** Spa FTV Wi-fi ⚲ ⚲ supervised ⚲ 18 Putt green Gym Dance studio Beauty salon Sauna Steam rooms Xmas New Year
Conf Class 250 Board 50 Thtr 500 Del from £140 to £190* **Services** Lift **Parking** 350 **Notes** ⊗ RS 24 Dec-2 Jan Civ Wed 300

Crown Spa Hotel

★★★★ 78% HOTEL

☎ 01723 357400
Esplanade YO11 2AG
e-mail: info@crownspahotel.com
web: www.crownspahotel.com
dir: On A64 follow town centre signs to lights opposite railway station, turn right over Valley Bridge, 1st left, right into Belmont Rd to cliff top

This well known hotel has an enviable position overlooking the harbour and South Bay and most of the front-facing bedrooms have excellent views. All the bedrooms, including suites, are contemporary and have the latest amenities including feature

bathrooms. An extensive range of treatments is available in the outstanding spa.

Crown Spa Hotel

Rooms 115 (20 fmly) **Facilities** Spa FTV Wi-fi ⚲ ⚲ Gym Fitness classes Massage Sauna Steam room Beauty treatments Xmas New Year **Conf** Class 100 Board 80 Thtr 260 **Services** Lift **Parking** 10 **Notes** ⊗ Civ Wed 260

See advert on this page

S

SCARBOROUGH *continued*

Best Western Ox Pasture Hall Country Hotel

★★★★ 75% ◉◉ COUNTRY HOUSE HOTEL

☎ 01723 365295
Lady Edith's Dr, Raincliffe Woods YO12 5TD
e-mail: oxpasture.hall@btconnect.com
web: www.oxpasturehall.com
dir: A171, left onto Lady Edith's Drive, 1.5m, hotel on right

This charming country hotel is set in the North Riding Forest Park and has a very friendly atmosphere. Bedrooms (split between the main house, townhouse and the delightful courtyard) are stylish, comfortable and well equipped. Public areas include a split-level bar, quiet lounge and an attractive restaurant. There is also an extensive banqueting area licensed for civil weddings.

Rooms 21 (1 fmly) (14 GF) **S** £79-£129; **D** £89-£195 (incl. bkfst)* **Facilities** FTV Wi-fi ↘ Xmas New Year **Conf** Class 75 Board 50 Thtr 150 **Parking** 100 **Notes** LB Civ Wed 150

Ambassador Spa Hotel

★★★ 80% HOTEL

☎ 01723 362841
Centre of the Esplanade YO11 2AY
e-mail: ask@ambassadorspahotel.co.uk
web: www.ambassadorspahotel.co.uk
dir: A64, right at mini rdbt opposite B&Q, right at next mini rdbt, immediately left into Avenue Victoria to cliff top

Standing on the South Cliff with excellent views over the bay, this friendly hotel offers well-equipped bedrooms; some are executive rooms, some have sea views. A spa with pool and many rejuvenating and pampering facilities is available. Entertainment is provided during the summer season.

Rooms 58 (10 fmly) (1 GF) **Facilities** FTV Wi-fi ↘ ⊗ Sauna Spa bath ♫ Xmas New Year **Conf** Class 60 Board 40 Thtr 100 **Services** Lift Air con **Notes** Civ Wed 120

Palm Court Hotel

★★★ 80% HOTEL

☎ 01723 368161
St Nicholas Cliff YO11 2ES
e-mail: info@palmcourt-scarborough.co.uk
dir: Follow signs for town centre & town hall, hotel before town hall on right

The public rooms are spacious and comfortable at this modern, town centre hotel. Traditional cooking is provided in the attractive restaurant and staff are friendly and helpful. Bedrooms are quite delightfully furnished and are also well equipped. Extra facilities include a swimming pool and free, covered parking.

Rooms 40 (11 fmly) ⟋ **S** £45-£70; **D** £79-£130 (incl. bkfst) **Facilities** FTV Wi-fi ⊗ Xmas New Year **Conf** Class 70 Board 60 Thtr 80 Del from £99 to £129.50 **Services** Lift **Parking** 40 **Notes** LB ⊗ Civ Wed

Save on hotels. Book at **theAA.com/hotel**

SCA 413 ENGLAND

Beiderbecke's Hotel

★★★ 75% ⊛ HOTEL

☎ 01723 365766
1-3 The Crescent YO11 2PW
e-mail: info@beiderbeckes.com
dir: In town centre, 200mtrs from railway station

Situated in a Georgian crescent this hotel is close to all the main attractions. Bedrooms are very smart, well equipped and offer plenty of space and comfort. Some rooms have views over the town to the sea. Marmalade's, the restaurant, offers international cuisine with a modern twist and hosts live music acts at weekends, including the resident jazz band.

Rooms 27 (4 fmly) **Facilities** STV FTV Wi-fi ♫ Xmas New Year **Conf** Class 40 Board 30 Thtr 80 **Services** Lift **Parking** 18 **Notes** ⊗

Esplanade Hotel

★★★ 68% HOTEL

☎ 01723 360382
Belmont Rd YO11 2AA
e-mail: enquiries@theesplanade.co.uk
dir: From town centre over Valley Bridge, left then immediately right into Belmont Rd, hotel 100mtrs on right

This large hotel enjoys a superb position overlooking South Bay and the harbour. Both the terrace, leading from the lounge bar, and the restaurant, with its striking oriel window, benefit from magnificent views. Bedrooms are comfortably furnished and are well equipped. Touring groups are also well catered for.

Rooms 70 (7 fmly) ⚓ **S** £45-£60; **D** £90-£120 (incl. bkfst)* **Facilities** Xmas New Year **Conf** Class 100 Board 30 Thtr 120 Del from £80 to £100* **Services** Lift **Parking** 15 **Notes** LB Closed 2 Jan-9 Feb

The Mount Hotel

★★ 75% HOTEL

☎ 01723 360961
Cliff Bridge Ter, Saint Nicholas Cliff YO11 2HA
e-mail: info@mounthotel.com
dir: On one-way system. From A165 (Valley Bridge Rd) left into Somerset Terrace, straight on at lights, straight on at rdbt (Palm Court Hotel on right). Next right into St Nicholas Cliff. Hotel at end on right

Standing in a superb, elevated position and enjoying magnificent views of the South Bay, this elegant Regency hotel is operated to high standards. The richly furnished and comfortable public rooms are inviting, and the well-equipped bedrooms have been attractively decorated. The spacious deluxe rooms are mini-suites.

Rooms 50 (5 fmly) **Facilities** Xmas **Services** Lift **Notes** Closed Jan-mid Mar

See advert on opposite page

S

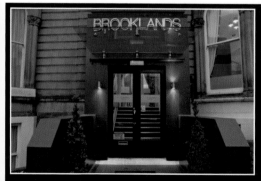

SCARBOROUGH *continued*

Red Lea Hotel

★★ 74% HOTEL

☎ 01723 362431
Prince of Wales Ter YO11 2AJ
e-mail: redlea@globalnet.co.uk
web: www.redleahotel.co.uk
dir: Follow South Cliff signs. Prince of Wales Terrace is off Esplanade opposite cliff lift

This friendly, family-run hotel is situated close to the cliff lift. Bedrooms are well equipped and comfortably furnished, and many at the front have picturesque views of the coast. There are two large lounges and a spacious dining room where good-value, traditional food is served.

Rooms 67 (7 fmly) (2 GF) **Facilities** FTV 🕲 Gym
Xmas New Year **Conf** Class 25 Board 25 Thtr 40
Services Lift **Notes** ⊗

Brooklands Hotel

★★ 72% HOTEL

☎ 01723 376576
Esplanade Gardens, South Cliff YO11 2AW
e-mail: info@brooklands-scarborough.co.uk
web: www.brooklands-scarborough.co.uk
dir: From A64 York, right at B&Q rdbt, right at lights, 1st left into Avenue Victoria, at end left, then 2nd left

Located on the South Cliff, overlooking the Esplanade Gardens and very close to the seafront, this is a contemporary hotel. There is a friendly team of staff and a range of stylish lounge areas, a games room and spacious restaurant. Entertainment is provided most evenings in the lower-ground floor bar.

Brooklands Hotel

Rooms 63 (13 fmly) (2 GF) **Facilities** FTV Wi-fi 🎵
Xmas New Year **Conf** Class 90 Board 40 **Services** Lift

See advert on page 413

The Cumberland

 Leisureplex

★★ 72% HOTEL

☎ 01723 361826
Belmont Rd YO11 2AB
e-mail: cumberland@alfatravel.co.uk
web: www.leisureplex.co.uk
dir: A64 onto B1437, left at A165 towards town centre. Right into Ramshill Rd, right into Belmont Rd

On the South Cliff, convenient for the spa complex, beach and town centre shops, this hotel offers comfortably appointed bedrooms; each floor can be accessed by lift. Entertainment is provided most evenings and the meals are carefully cooked.

Rooms 81 (6 fmly) 🐾 **S** £38-£47; **D** £62-£80 (incl. bkfst)* **Facilities** FTV Wi-fi 🎵 Xmas New Year
Services Lift **Notes** LB ⊗ Closed Jan RS Nov-Dec & Feb

Park Manor Hotel

★★ 72% HOTEL

☎ 01723 372090
Northstead Manor Dr YO12 6BB
e-mail: info@parkmanor.co.uk
web: www.parkmanor.co.uk
dir: Off A165, adjacent to Peasholm Park

Enjoying a peaceful residential setting with sea views, this smartly presented, friendly hotel provides the seaside tourist with a wide range of facilities. Bedrooms vary in size and style but all are smartly furnished and well equipped. There is a spacious lounge, smart restaurant, games room and indoor pool plus a steam room for relaxation.

Rooms 41 (6 fmly) 🐾 **S** £43-£53.25; **D** £86-£106.50 (incl. bkfst)* **Facilities** FTV Wi-fi 🕲 Pool table Spa bath Steam room Table tennis New Year
Conf Class 20 Board 20 Thtr 30 Del from £70 to £85*
Services Lift **Parking** 20 **Notes** LB ⊗ No children 3yrs

Forest Pines Hotel & Golf Resort

★★★★ 79% ⊛ HOTEL

☎ 01652 650770
Ermine St, Broughton DN20 0AQ
e-mail: forestpines@qhotels.co.uk
web: www.qhotels.co.uk
dir: 200yds from M180 junct 4, on Brigg-Scunthorpe rdbt

This smart hotel provides a comprehensive range of leisure facilities. Extensive conference rooms, a modern health and beauty spa, and a championship golf course ensure that it is a popular choice with both corporate and leisure guests. The well-equipped bedrooms are modern, spacious, and appointed to a good standard. Extensive public areas include a choice of dining options, with fine dining available in The Eighteen57 fish restaurant, and more informal eating in the Grill Bar.

Rooms 188 (66 fmly) (67 GF) **Facilities** Spa STV FTV
Wi-fi 🕲 supervised ⚓ 27 Putt green Gym Mountain bikes Jogging track Xmas New Year **Conf** Class 170 Board 96 Thtr 370 **Services** Lift **Parking** 400
Notes Civ Wed 250

Premier Inn Scunthorpe

BUDGET HOTEL

☎ 0871 527 8960
Lakeside Retail Park, Lakeside Parkway DN16 3UA
web: www.premierinn.com
dir: M180 junct 4, A18 towards Scunthorpe. At Morrisons rdbt left onto Lakeside Retail Park, hotel behind Morrisons petrol station

High quality, budget accommodation ideal for both families and business travellers. Spacious, en suite bedrooms feature tea and coffee making facilities, and Freeview TV in most hotels. Internet access and Wi-fi are available for a small fee. The adjacent family restaurant features a wide and varied menu. See also the Hotel Groups pages.

Rooms 60

S

Save on hotels. Book at **theAA.com/hotel**

SCA – SEA 415 ENGLAND

SEAHAM
Co Durham — Map 19 NZ44

Seaham Hall Hotel & Serenity Spa

U

☎ 0191 516 1400
Lord Byron's Walk SR7 7AG
e-mail: info@seaham-hall.co.uk
web: www.seaham-hall.co.uk
dir: From A19 take B1404 to Seaham. At lights straight over level crossing. Hotel approx 0.25m on right

At the time of going to press the rating for this establishment was not confirmed, due to a change of ownership. For further details please see the AA website: theAA.com

Rooms 20 (4 GF) **Facilities** Spa FTV Wi-fi ⓖ Gym Xmas New Year **Conf** Class 48 Board 40 Thtr 100 **Services** Lift Air con **Parking** 122 **Notes** ⊗ Civ Wed 100

SEASCALE
Cumbria — Map 18 NY00

Sella Park House Hotel

★★★ 85% COUNTRY HOUSE HOTEL

☎ 0845 450 6445 & 01946 841601
Calderbridge CA20 1DW
e-mail: info@penningtonhotels.com
dir: From A595 at Calderbridge, follow sign for North Gate. Hotel 0.5m on left

This property, which some believe dates back to the 13th century, is set in six acres of mature grounds which lead down to the River Calder. Inside the hotel, the massive refurbishment undertaken in recent years shows excellent results. The individually designed bedrooms are very well appointed and have many extras; public areas are comfortable and welcoming. Food in the Priory Restaurant is a highlight with local produce at the heart of each menu selection.

Rooms 16 (5 annexe) (2 GF) ⓕ **S** £90-£130; **D** £100-£145 (incl. bkfst) **Facilities** FTV Wi-fi ⓖ HL Fishing Xmas New Year **Conf** Class 80 Board 80 Thtr 300 Del from £120 to £160 **Parking** 30 **Notes** LB Civ Wed 150

Cumbrian Lodge

◉ RESTAURANT WITH ROOMS

☎ 019467 27309
Gosforth Rd CA20 1JG
e-mail: cumbrianlodge@btconnect.com
web: www.cumbrianlodge.com
dir: Exit A595 at Gosforth onto B5344 signed Seascale, 2m on left

This well-run restaurant with rooms enjoys a relaxed and friendly atmosphere, and tasty, well-prepared dinners prove popular locally. The decor and fixtures are modern throughout, and the bedrooms are well-equipped for both business and leisure guests. The thatched garden buildings provide a delightful opportunity for eating alfresco under canvas panels, for up to 12 diners.

Rooms 6 (1 fmly)

SEAVIEW
Isle of Wight — Map 5 SZ69

The Seaview Hotel & Restaurant

★★★ 83% ◉ HOTEL

☎ 01983 612711
High St PO34 5EX
e-mail: reception@seaviewhotel.co.uk
web: www.seaviewhotel.co.uk
dir: From B3330 (Ryde-Seaview road), turn left via Puckpool along seafront

Located in the quiet and tranquil area of Seaview, the hotel is just a short walk from the seafront, and there are views from the front terrace, especially enjoyable in the summer months. Bedrooms are split between three main areas yet all offer modern and stylish accommodation; all have free broadband, DVD TVs plus slippers and robes. There is a modern restaurant where guests can enjoy breakfast, lunch and dinner, and there is also The Pump Bar with very traditional decor which is popular with both residents and locals alike.

Rooms 28 (4 fmly) (5 GF) ⓕ **S** £105-£130; **D** £160-£188 (incl. bkfst) **Facilities** FTV Wi-fi ⓖ Use of nearby sports club New Year **Conf** Class 20 Board 20 Thtr 20 **Parking** 10 **Notes** Closed 22-26 Dec

Priory Bay Hotel

★★★ 78% ◉ HOTEL

☎ 01983 613146
Priory Dr PO34 5BU
e-mail: enquiries@priorybay.co.uk
web: www.priorybay.co.uk
dir: B3330 towards Seaview, through Nettlestone. (NB do not follow Seaview turn, but continue 0.5m to hotel sign)

This peacefully located hotel has much to offer and comes complete with its own stretch of private beach and 6-hole golf course. Bedrooms are a wonderful mix of styles, all of which provide much comfort and character. Public areas are equally impressive with a choice of enticing lounges to relax and unwind. The kitchen creates interesting and imaginative dishes, using the excellent island produce as much as possible.

Rooms 22 (4 annexe) (6 fmly) (2 GF) **Facilities** FTV Wi-fi ⓖ ⓖ 6 ⓖ ⓖ Private beach Xmas New Year **Conf** Class 60 Board 40 Thtr 80 **Parking** 100 **Notes** ⊗ Civ Wed 100

S

SEDGEFIELD
Co Durham — Map 19 NZ32

Best Western Hardwick Hall Hotel

★★★★ 79% ◉ HOTEL

☎ 01740 620253
TS21 2EH
e-mail: info@hardwickhallhotel.co.uk
dir: Exit A1(M) junct 60 towards Sedgefield, left at 1st rdbt, hotel 400mtrs on left

Set in extensive parkland, this 18th-century house suits both leisure and corporate guests. It is a top conference and function venue offering an impressive meeting and banqueting complex. Luxurious bedrooms include contemporary rooms and some with antique furnishings but all are appointed to the same high standard; many have feature bathrooms and some have stunning views over the lake. Both the modern lounge bar and cellar bistro have a relaxed atmosphere.

Rooms 51 (6 fmly) (12 GF) ★ **S** £75-£115; **D** £85-£140* **Facilities** STV FTV Wi-fi ⚲ **Conf** Class 100 Board 80 Thtr 700 Del from £115* **Services** Lift **Parking** 300 **Notes** LB ⊗ Civ Wed 450

SEDGEMOOR MOTORWAY SERVICE AREA (M5)
Somerset — Map 4 ST35

Days Inn Sedgemoor - M5

BUDGET HOTEL

☎ 01934 750831
Sedgemoor BS24 0JL
e-mail: sedgemoor.hotel@welcomebreak.co.uk
web: www.welcomebreak.co.uk
dir: M5 northbound junct 21/22

This modern building offers accommodation in smart, spacious and well-equipped bedrooms, suitable for families and business travellers, all with en suite bathrooms. Continental breakfast is available and other refreshments may be taken at the nearby family restaurant. See also the Hotel Groups pages.

Rooms 40 (39 fmly) (19 GF) (8 smoking)

SHAFTESBURY
Dorset — Map 4 ST82

Best Western Royal Chase Hotel

★★★ 70% ◉ HOTEL

☎ 01747 853355
Royal Chase Roundabout SP7 8DB
e-mail: reception@theroyalchasehotel.co.uk
web: www.theroyalchasehotel.co.uk
dir: A303 to A350 signed Blandford Forum. Avoid town centre, follow road to 3rd rdbt

Equally suitable for both leisure and business guests, this well-known local landmark is situated close to the famous Gold Hill. Both Standard and Crown bedrooms offer good levels of comfort and quality. In addition to the fixed-price menu in the Byzant Restaurant, guests have the option of eating more informally in the convivial bar.

Rooms 33 (13 fmly) (6 GF) **S** £55-£99; **D** £85-£125 (incl. bkfst)* **Facilities** FTV Wi-fi ⚲ ⊗ Turkish steam room Spa pool Xmas New Year **Conf** Class 90 Board 50 Thtr 180 Del from £95 to £120 **Parking** 100 **Notes** LB Civ Wed 76

La Fleur de Lys Restaurant with Rooms

◉◉ RESTAURANT WITH ROOMS

☎ 01747 853717
Bleke St SP7 8AW
e-mail: info@lafleurdelys.co.uk
web: www.lafleurdelys.co.uk
dir: From junct of A30 & A350, 0.25m towards town centre

Located just a few minutes' walk from the famous Gold Hill, this light and airy restaurant with rooms combines efficient service in a relaxed and friendly atmosphere. Bedrooms, which are suitable for both business and leisure guests, vary in size but all are well equipped, comfortable and tastefully furnished. A relaxing guest lounge and courtyard are available for afternoon tea or pre-dinner drinks.

Rooms 7 (2 fmly)

SHANKLIN
Isle of Wight — Map 5 SZ58

Channel View Hotel

★★★ 78% HOTEL

☎ 01983 862309
Hope Rd PO37 6EH
e-mail: enquiries@channelviewhotel.co.uk
web: www.channelviewhotel.co.uk
dir: Exit A3055 at Esplanade & Beach sign. Hotel 250mtrs on left

With an elevated cliff-top location overlooking Shanklin Bay, several rooms at this hotel enjoy pleasant views and all are very well decorated and furnished. The hotel is family run, and guests can enjoy efficient service, regular evening entertainment, a heated indoor swimming pool and holistic therapy.

Rooms 56 (15 fmly) ★ **S** £38-£56; **D** £76-£112 (incl. bkfst)* **Facilities** FTV Wi-fi ⚲ ⊗ Holistic therapies Aromatherapy ♫ **Services** Lift **Parking** 32 **Notes** Closed Jan-Feb

Luccombe Hall Hotel

★★★ 77% HOTEL

☎ 01983 869000
8 Luccombe Rd PO37 6RL
e-mail: enquiries@luccombehall.co.uk
dir: Take A3055 to Shanklin, through old village then 1st left into Priory Rd, left into Popham Rd, 1st right into Luccombe Rd. Hotel on left

Appropriately described as 'the view with the hotel', this property was originally built in 1870 as a summer home for the Bishop of Portsmouth. Enjoying an impressive cliff-top location, the hotel benefits from wonderful sea views, delightful gardens and direct access to the beach. Well-equipped bedrooms are comfortably furnished and there is a range of leisure facilities.

Rooms 29 (15 fmly) (7 GF) ★ **S** £59-£84; **D** £118-£208 (incl. bkfst)* **Facilities** STV Wi-fi ⚲ ⊗ ⚲ Putt green Gym Squash Games room Beauty treatment room Sauna Xmas New Year Child facilities **Parking** 20 **Notes** LB ⊗

Save on hotels. Book at **theAA.com/hotel**

SED – SHE 417 ENGLAND

Melbourne Ardenlea Hotel

★★ 78% HOTEL

☎ 01983 862596
4-6 Queens Rd PO37 6AP
e-mail: reservations@mahotel.co.uk
web: www.mahotel.co.uk
dir: A3055 to Shanklin. Then follow signs to Ventnor via A3055 (Queens Rd). Hotel just before end of road on right

This quietly located hotel is within easy walking distance of the town centre and the lift down to the promenade. Bedrooms are traditionally furnished and guests can enjoy the various spacious public areas including a welcoming bar and a large heated indoor swimming pool.

Rooms 54 (5 fmly) (6 GF) ⚓ **S** £40-£85; **D** £60-£110 (incl. bkfst)* **Facilities** FTV Wi-fi 🕸 Sauna 🎵 Xmas New Year **Conf** Class 24 Board 20 Thtr 80 Del from £45 to £85* **Services** Lift **Parking** 26 **Notes** LB Closed 1-15 Jan

Malton House Hotel

★★ 69% HOTEL

☎ 01983 865007
8 Park Rd PO37 6AY
e-mail: couvoussis@maltonhouse.freeserve.co.uk
web: www.maltonhouse.co.uk
dir: Up hill from Hope Rd lights then 3rd left

A well-kept Victorian hotel set in its own gardens in a quiet area, conveniently located for cliff-top walks and the public lift down to the promenade. The bedrooms are comfortable and public rooms include a small lounge, a separate bar and a dining room where traditional homemade meals are served.

Rooms 12 (3 fmly) (2 GF) **S** £34-£37; **D** £60-£66 (incl. bkfst)* **Facilities** Wi-fi **Parking** 12 **Notes** ⊗ No children 3yrs Closed Oct-Apr

SHAP	Map 18 NY51
Cumbria	

Best Western Shap Wells Hotel

★★★ 77% HOTEL

☎ 01931 716628
CA10 3QU
e-mail: manager@shapwells.com
dir: Between A6 & B6261, 4m S of Shap

This hotel occupies a wonderful secluded position amid trees and waterfalls. Extensive public areas include function and meeting rooms, a well-stocked bar, a choice of lounges and a spacious restaurant. Bedrooms vary in size and style but all are equipped with the expected facilities.

Rooms 98 (7 annexe) (10 fmly) (10 GF) **Facilities** FTV Wi-fi Games room Cardiovascular gym Xmas New Year **Conf** Class 80 Board 40 Thtr 170 **Services** Lift **Parking** 200 **Notes** Civ Wed 150

SHEDFIELD	Map 5 SU51
Hampshire	

Meon Valley, A Marriott Hotel & Country Club

★★★★ 78% ◉ HOTEL

☎ 01329 833455
Sandy Ln SO32 2HQ
web: www.marriottmeonvalley.co.uk
dir: M27 junct 7 take A334 towards Wickham & Botley. Sandy Ln on left 2m from Botley

This modern, smartly appointed hotel and country club has extensive indoor and outdoor leisure facilities, including two golf courses. Bedrooms are spacious and well equipped, and guests have a choice of eating and drinking options. It is ideally suited for easy access to both Portsmouth and Southampton.

Rooms 113 (43 fmly) (29 GF) (10 smoking) **Facilities** Spa FTV Wi-fi 🕸 🏊 27 🏌 Putt green Gym Cardiovascular aerobics Health & beauty salon Xmas New Year **Conf** Class 50 Board 32 Thtr 100 **Services** Lift **Parking** 360 **Notes** ⊗ Civ Wed 90

SHEFFIELD	Map 16 SK49
South Yorkshire	

Copthorne Hotel Sheffield

★★★★ 79% ◉ HOTEL

☎ 0114 252 5480
Sheffield United Football Club, Bramhall Ln S2 4SU
e-mail: orla.watt@millenniumhotels.co.uk
dir: M1 junct 33, A57. At Park Square rdbt follow A61 (Chesterfield Rd). Follow brown signs for Bramall Lane

This modern and stylish hotel is situated in the centre of Sheffield. Located next to the home of Sheffield United FC it offers contemporary public areas and its award-winning restaurant to the ground floor. A well-equipped gym is situated on the first floor. Bedrooms are spacious and comfortable. Ample parking is a plus in this central location.

Rooms 158 (23 fmly) ⚓ **S** £49-£200; **D** £49-£200* **Facilities** STV FTV Wi-fi Fitness room **Conf** Class 150 Board 40 Thtr 400 Del from £99 to £299* **Services** Lift Air con **Parking** 250 **Notes** LB ⊗

Whitley Hall Hotel

★★★★ 78% ◉◉ HOTEL

☎ 0114 245 4444 & 246 0456
Elliott Ln, Grenoside S35 8NR
e-mail: reservations@whitleyhall.com
web: www.whitleyhall.com
dir: A61 past football ground, 2m, right just before Norfolk Arms, left at bottom of hill. Hotel on left

This 16th-century house stands in 20 acres of landscaped grounds and gardens. Public rooms are full of character and interesting architectural features, and command the best views of the gardens. The individually styled bedrooms are furnished in keeping with the country house setting, as are the oak-panelled restaurant and bar. The hotel is a popular wedding venue.

Rooms 32 (3 annexe) (2 fmly) (8 GF) ⚓ **S** £72-£102; **D** £72-£102* **Facilities** STV FTV Wi-fi 🕸 **Conf** Class 50 Board 34 Thtr 70 Del £144* **Services** Lift **Parking** 100 **Notes** LB ⊗ Civ Wed 100

Mercure Sheffied St Paul's Hotel & Spa

★★★★ 77% HOTEL

☎ 0114 278 2000
119 Norfolk St S1 2JE
e-mail: h6628@accor.com
web: www.mercure.com
dir: M1 junct 33, 4th exit at rdbt, left at 1st lights, right at 2nd in front of Crucible Theatre

This modern, luxury hotel enjoys a central location close to key attractions in the city. Open-plan public areas are situated in a steel and glass atrium and include a popular Champagne bar, the Yard Restaurant and Zucca, an Italian Bistro. Bedrooms are superbly presented and richly furnished. The Vital health and beauty treatment centre provides a fabulous thermal suite.

Rooms 163 (40 fmly) **Facilities** Spa Wi-fi 🕸 Sauna Steam room Snail shower Ice fountain Fitness classes Xmas New Year **Conf** Class 400 Board 30 Thtr 600 **Services** Lift Air con **Notes** ⊗ Civ Wed 350

S

SHEFFIELD *continued*

Kenwood Hall

★★★★ 75% HOTEL

☎ 0114 258 3811
Kenwood Rd S7 1NQ
dir: A61 (Barnsley ring road) into St Mary's Rd.
Straight over rdbt, left into London Rd, right at lights.
2nd exit at 2nd rdbt, hotel ahead

A smart, modern hotel peacefully located in a
residential suburb a few miles from the city centre.
The stylishly decorated bedrooms are spacious, quiet
and well equipped. The hotel also has an extensive
range of leisure and meeting facilities, and secure
parking is located in extensive landscaped gardens.

Rooms 114 (8 fmly) **Facilities** STV Wi-fi ⓢ Fishing
Gym Steam room Sauna Solarium Beauty treatment
rooms New Year **Conf** Class 100 Board 60 Thtr 250
Services Lift **Parking** 150 **Notes** Civ Wed 260

Novotel Sheffield Centre

★★★★ 72% HOTEL

☎ 0114 278 1781
50 Arundel Gate S1 2PR
e-mail: h1348-re@accor.com
web: www.novotel.com
dir: Between Registry Office & Crucible/Lyceum
Theatres, follow signs to Town Hall/Theatres & Hallam
University

In the heart of the city centre, this hotel has stylish
public areas including a very modern restaurant,
indoor swimming pool and a range of meeting rooms.
Spacious bedrooms are suitable for family
occupation, and the Novation rooms are ideal for
business users.

Rooms 144 (136 fmly) **Facilities** STV FTV Wi-fi ⓢ
Gym Steam room Xmas New Year **Conf** Class 180
Board 100 Thtr 220 **Services** Lift Air con **Parking** 60
Notes Civ Wed 180

Staindrop Lodge Hotel

★★★ 80% ⓐ HOTEL

☎ 0114 284 3111
Lane End, Chapeltown S35 3UH
e-mail: info@staindroplodge.co.uk
dir: M1 junct 35, A629 for 1m, straight over 1st rdbt,
right at 2nd rdbt, hotel approx 0.5m on right

This hotel, bar and brasserie offers smart modern
public areas and accommodation. An art deco theme
continues throughout the open-plan public rooms and
the comfortably appointed, spacious bedrooms.
Service is relaxed and friendly, and all-day menus are
available.

Rooms 37 (5 annexe) (6 fmly) (3 GF) ⌒ **Facilities** STV
FTV Wi-fi ↘ **Conf** Class 60 Board 40 Thtr 80
Parking 80 **Notes** ⊗ Civ Wed 80

Best Western Plus Mosborough Hall Hotel

★★★ 80% HOTEL

☎ 0114 248 4353
High St, Mosborough S20 5EA
e-mail: hotel@mosboroughhall.co.uk
web: www.mosboroughhall.co.uk
dir: M1 junct 30, A6135 towards Sheffield. Follow
Eckington/Mosborough signs 2m. Sharp bend at top
of hill, hotel on right

This 16th-century, Grade II listed manor house is set
in gardens not far from the M1 and is convenient for
the city centre. The bedrooms offer very high quality
and good amenities; some are very spacious. There is
a galleried lounge and conservatory bar, and freshly
prepared dishes are served in the traditional style
dining room.

Rooms 44 (17 GF) ⌒ **Facilities** FTV Wi-fi ↘ Spa &
beauty treatments Xmas New Year **Conf** Class 125
Board 70 Thtr 220 Del from £90 to £175 **Parking** 100
Notes Civ Wed 250

Best Western Cutlers Hotel

★★★ 72% HOTEL

☎ 0114 273 9939
Theatreland George St S1 2PF
e-mail: enquiries@cutlershotel.co.uk
dir: M1 junct 33. At Park Sq follow signs to City
Centre & Theatres. At top of Commercial St, left into
Arundel Gate. Into tight lane, at lights right into
Norfolk St, 2nd right into George St. Hotel 50mtrs on
left

Situated in the heart of the city, near the theatres and
only minutes from the bus and railway stations. Each
of the bedrooms has a flat-screen TV; iPod docking
station, free Wi-fi and broadband access. Mariano's
Restaurant & Bar on the upper mezzanine level offers
a relaxed atmosphere. A function room is also
available. Discounted overnight parking is provided in
the nearby public car park.

Rooms 45 (2 fmly) **S** £55-£85; **D** £65-£95*
Facilities STV FTV Wi-fi Beauty treatment rooms Xmas
New Year **Conf** Class 20 Board 25 Thtr 80
Del from £120 to £175* **Services** Lift **Notes** LB ⊗
Civ Wed 60

Ibis Sheffield City Centre

BUDGET HOTEL

☎ 0114 241 9600
Shude Hill S1 2AR
e-mail: H2891@accor.com
web: www.ibishotel.com
dir: M1 junct 33, follow signs to Sheffield City Centre
(A630/A57), at rdbt take 5th exit, signed Ponds Forge,
for hotel

Modern, budget hotel offering comfortable
accommodation in bright and practical bedrooms.
Breakfast is self-service and dinner is available in
the restaurant. See also the Hotel Groups pages.

Rooms 95 (15 fmly) (3 GF) ⌒ **S** £38-£67; **D** £38-£67*

S

Premier Inn Sheffield (Arena)

BUDGET HOTEL

☎ 0871 527 8964
Attercliffe Common Rd S9 2LU
web: www.premierinn.com
dir: M1 junct 34, follow signs to city centre. Hotel opposite Arena

High quality, budget accommodation ideal for both families and business travellers. Spacious, en suite bedrooms feature tea and coffee making facilities, and Freeview TV in most hotels. Internet access and Wi-fi are available for a small fee. The adjacent family restaurant features a wide and varied menu. See also the Hotel Groups pages.

Rooms 61

Premier Inn Sheffield City Centre

BUDGET HOTEL

☎ 0871 527 8972
Young St, St Marys Gate S1 4LA
web: www.premierinn.com
dir: M1 junct 33, A630, A57 follow Sheffield City Centre signs. At Park Square rdbt 3rd exit signed A61/Chesterfield. At Granville Square right onto A61 signed Ring Rd. Keep in left lane. At rdbt 3rd exit signed A621. Left into Cumberland St. Left into South Lane. Right into Young St

Rooms 122

Premier Inn Sheffield City Centre Angel St

BUDGET HOTEL

☎ 0871 527 8970
Angel St, (Corner of Bank Street) S3 8LN
web: www.premierinn.com
dir: M1 junct 33, follow city centre, A630, A57 signs. At Park Square rdbt 4th exit (A61 Barnsley). Left at 4th lights into Snig Hill, right at lights into Bank St

Rooms 160

Premier Inn Sheffield (Meadowhall)

BUDGET HOTEL

☎ 0871 527 8966
Sheffield Rd, Meadowhall S9 2YL
web: www.premierinn.com
dir: On A6178 approx 6m from city centre

Rooms 103

SHEPPERTON
Surrey

See LONDON SECTION plan 1 A1

Harrisons Hotel

★★★ 64% HOTEL

☎ 01932 227320
Rusell Rd TW17 9HX
e-mail: apreston@martynleisure.co.uk

Being located on the banks of the Thames, close to a number of visitor attractions and major transport networks makes this hotel suitable for both the leisure and business traveller. The tastefully appointed bedrooms and bathrooms are appointed to a high standard and have guest comfort very much in mind. The Bar and Bistro offers contemporary dining with popular favourites available for all tastes. Parking with CCTV is located nearby.

Rooms 32 **Conf** Class 45 Board 30 Thtr 100

SHEPTON MALLET   Map 4 ST64
Somerset

Charlton House Spa Hotel

★★★★ 75% ⚜ HOTEL

☎ 01749 342008
Charlton Rd BA4 4PR
e-mail: gm.charltonhousehotel@bannatyne.co.uk
web: www.bannatyne.co.uk
dir: On A361 towards Frome, 1m from town centre

A peaceful location with grounds and relaxing spa facilities are just part of the charm of this interesting hotel. The individually designed bedrooms include larger suites and a luxurious lodge in the garden. Guests can relax in the 'shabby chic' lounges or bar area, or in the warmer months there's plenty of outdoor seating. Dinner in the stylish restaurant offers a selection of carefully prepared, high quality dishes. The spa offers a wide range of facilities including treatments rooms, hydrotherapy pool, crystal room, sauna and a fitness studio to name but a few. The hotel is a popular wedding venue.

Rooms 28 (6 annexe) (3 fmly) (12 GF) 🐾 **D** £95-£400 (incl. bkfst)* **Facilities** Spa FTV Wi-fi 🌀 ♨ ♨ Gym Sauna Steam room Laconium Xmas New Year **Conf** Class 50 Board 30 Thtr 90 Del from £165 to £179* **Parking** 70 **Notes** LB ⊗ Civ Wed 120

SHERBORNE   Map 4 ST61
Dorset

The Grange at Oborne

★★★ 80% ⚜⚜ HOTEL

☎ 01935 813463
Oborne DT9 4LA
e-mail: reception@thegrange.co.uk
web: www.thegrangeatoborne.co.uk
dir: Exit A30, follow signs through village

Set in beautiful gardens in a quiet hamlet, this 200-year-old, family run, country-house hotel has a wealth of charm and character. It offers friendly hospitality together with attentive service. Bedrooms are comfortable and tastefully appointed. Public areas are elegantly furnished and the popular restaurant offers a good selection of dishes.

Rooms 18 (3 fmly) (2 GF) **S** £90-£145; **D** £109-£175 (incl. bkfst) **Facilities** STV Wi-fi ♨ Xmas New Year **Conf** Class 40 Board 30 Thtr 80 Del from £146.95* **Parking** 45 **Notes** LB ⊗ Civ Wed 120

The Sherborne Hotel

★★★ 66% HOTEL

☎ 01935 813191
Horsecastles Ln DT9 6BB
e-mail: info@sherbornehotel.co.uk
dir: At junct of A30 & A352

This hotel is in a quiet location with attractive grounds yet is only just off the main road. The bedrooms are spacious and well equipped, and the open-plan lounge and bar area are comfortable, and satellite TV is provided. There's a good range of dishes to choose from and the dining room looks out to the garden.

Rooms 60 (24 GF) 🐾 **S** £39-£55; **D** £45-£75 (incl. bkfst) **Facilities** FTV Wi-fi HL ♨ Concessionary swimming rates at leisure centre opposite 🎵 Xmas New Year **Conf** Class 35 Board 30 Thtr 80 **Parking** 90 **Notes** LB ⊗

S

Dales Country House Hotel

★★★★ 83% ◉ ◉ HOTEL

☎ 01263 824555
Lodge Hill, Upper Sheringham NR26 8TJ
e-mail: dales@mackenziehotels.com
dir: From Sheringham take B1157 to Upper
Sheringham. Through village, hotel on left

Superb Grade II listed building situated in extensive
landscaped grounds on the edge of Sheringham Park.
The attractive public rooms are full of original
character; they include a choice of lounges as well as
an intimate restaurant and a cosy lounge bar. The
spacious bedrooms are individually decorated with
co-ordinated soft furnishings and many thoughtful
touches.

Rooms 21 (5 GF) ✆ **S** £101-£115; **D** £162-£184 (incl.
bkfst)* **Facilities** Wi-fi ☺ ⚒ Giant garden games
(chess & Jenga) Xmas New Year **Conf** Class 20
Board 27 Thtr 40 Del from £125 to £140*
Services Lift **Parking** 50 **Notes** LB No children 14yrs

Beaumaris Hotel

★★ 79% HOTEL

☎ 01263 822370
South St NR26 8LL
e-mail: beauhotel@aol.com
web: www.thebeaumarishotel.co.uk
dir: Exit A148, left at rdbt, 1st right over rail bridge,
1st left by church, 1st left into South St

Situated in a peaceful side road just a short walk
from the beach, town centre and golf course. This
friendly hotel has been owned and run by the same
family for over 60 years and continues to provide
comfortable, thoughtfully equipped accommodation
throughout. Public rooms feature a smart dining
room, a cosy bar and two quiet lounges.

Rooms 21 (5 fmly) (2 GF) ✆ **S** £55-£65; **D** £110-£130
(incl. bkfst)* **Facilities** FTV Wi-fi **Parking** 25 **Notes** LB
✪ Closed mid Dec-1 Mar

Park House Hotel

★★★★ 78% ◉ HOTEL

☎ 01952 460128
Park St TF11 9BA
e-mail: reception@parkhousehotel.net
dir: M54 junct 4, A464 (Wolverhampton road) for
approx 2m, under railway bridge, hotel 100yds on left

This hotel was created from what were originally two
country houses of very different architectural styles.
Located on the edge of the historic market town, it
offers guests easy access to motorway networks, a
choice of banqueting and meeting rooms, plus leisure
facilities. Butlers Bar and Restaurant is the setting
for imaginative food. Service is friendly and attentive.

Rooms 54 (16 annexe) (4 fmly) (8 GF) (4 smoking)
S £65-£120; **D** £90-£200 (incl. bkfst)* **Facilities** STV
FTV Wi-fi ⚓ ⚙ Gym Steam room Sauna Xmas New
Year **Conf** Class 80 Board 40 Thtr 160 **Services** Lift
Parking 90 **Notes** LB Civ Wed 200

Hollins Hall, A Marriott Hotel & Country Club

★★★★ 76% ◉ HOTEL

☎ 01274 530053
Hollins Hill, Baildon BD17 7QW
e-mail: mhrs.lbags.frontdesk@marriotthotels.com
web: www.marriotthollinshall.co.uk
dir: From A650 follow signs to Salt Mill. At lights in
Shipley take A6038. Hotel 3m on left

The hotel is located close to Leeds and Bradford and
is easily accessible from motorway networks. Built in
the 19th-century, this Elizabethan-style building is
set within 200 acres of grounds and offers extensive
leisure facilities, including a golf course and gym.
Bedrooms are attractively decorated and have a
range of additional facilities.

Rooms 122 (50 fmly) (25 GF) **S** £99; **D** £99
Facilities Spa STV FTV Wi-fi ⚓ HL ⚙ supervised
⚑ 18 Putt green Gym Dance studio Swimming lessons
Conf Class 90 Board 80 Thtr 200 Del from £130 to
£150 **Services** Lift **Parking** 260 **Notes** LB ✪
Civ Wed 70

Ibis Bradford Shipley

ibis

BUDGET HOTEL

☎ 01274 589333
Quayside, Salts Mill Rd BD18 3ST
e-mail: H3158@accor.com
web: www.ibishotel.com
dir: Follow tourist signs for Salts Mill. Follow A650
signs through Bradford for approx 5m to Shipley

Modern, budget hotel offering comfortable
accommodation in bright and practical bedrooms.
Breakfast is self-service and dinner is available in
the restaurant. See also the Hotel Groups pages.

Rooms 78 (20 fmly) (22 GF) **Conf** Class 16 Board 18
Thtr 20

Albright Hussey Manor Hotel & Restaurant

★★★★ 77% ◉ ◉ HOTEL

☎ 01939 290571 & 290523
Ellesmere Rd SY4 3AF
e-mail: info@albrighthussey.co.uk
web: www.albrighthussey.co.uk
dir: 2.5m N of Shrewsbury on A528, follow signs for
Ellesmere

First mentioned in the Domesday Book, this
enchanting medieval manor house is approached over
its Tudor moat. Dating from around 1524, this Grade
II listed, partly black and white timbered building
maintains an abundance of original features
including huge open fireplaces, oak-panelling and
beams. The bedrooms, including four-poster rooms,
are situated in either the sumptuously appointed
main house or in the more modern wing. There's an
intimate, award-winning restaurant and a
comfortable cocktail bar and lounge.

Rooms 26 (4 fmly) (8 GF) **S** £65-£130; **D** £95-£190
(incl. bkfst)* **Facilities** FTV Wi-fi ⚒ Xmas New Year
Conf Class 180 Board 80 Thtr 250 Del from £115 to
£135 **Parking** 100 **Notes** LB Civ Wed 180

Mercure Shrewsbury Albrighton Hall Hotel & Spa

★★★★ 75% COUNTRY HOUSE HOTEL

☎ 01939 291000
Albrighton SY4 3AG
e-mail: H6629@accor.com
web: www.mercure.com
dir: From S: M6 junct 10a to M54 to end. From N: M6 junct 12 to M5 then M54. Follow signs Harlescott & Ellesmere to A528

Dating back to 1630, this former ancestral home is set in 15 acres of attractive gardens. The bedrooms are generally spacious and the stable rooms are particularly popular. Elegant public rooms have rich oak panelling and there is a modern, well-equipped health and fitness centre.

Rooms 87 (16 annexe) (6 fmly) (21 GF) **Facilities** Spa STV Wi-fi Gym Squash Beauty treatment rooms Thermal suite Relax room Spray tan Aerobics Xmas New Year **Conf** Class 150 Board 80 Thtr 300 Del from £110 to £180 **Services** Lift **Parking** 200 **Notes** Civ Wed 250

Rowton Castle Hotel

★★★ 88% HOTEL

☎ 01743 884044
Halfway House SY5 9EP
e-mail: post@rowtoncastle.com
web: www.rowtoncastle.com
dir: From A5 near Shrewsbury take A458 to Welshpool. Hotel 4m on right

Standing in 17 acres of grounds where a castle has stood for nearly 800 years, this Grade II listed building dates in parts back to 1696. Many original features remain, including the oak panelling in the restaurant and a magnificent carved oak fireplace. Most bedrooms are spacious and all have modern facilities; some have four-poster beds. The hotel has a well deserved reputation for its food and is understandably a popular venue for weddings.

Rooms 19 (3 fmly) **Facilities** Wi-fi **Conf** Class 30 Board 30 Thtr 80 **Parking** 100 **Notes** Civ Wed 110

Prince Rupert Hotel

★★★ 85% HOTEL

☎ 01743 499955
Butcher Row SY1 1UQ
e-mail: reservations@prince-rupert-hotel.co.uk
web: www.prince-rupert-hotel.co.uk
dir: Follow town centre signs, over English Bridge & Wyle Cop Hill. Right into Fish St, hotel 200yds

Parts of this popular town centre hotel date back to medieval times and many bedrooms have exposed beams and other original features. Luxury suites, family rooms and rooms with four-poster beds are all available. As an alternative to the main Royalist Restaurant, diners have a less formal option in Chambers, a popular brasserie. The Camellias Tea Rooms are adjacent providing snacks and afternoon teas. The hotel's valet parking service is also commendable.

Rooms 70 (4 fmly) **S** £85; **D** £115-£185 (incl. bkfst) **Facilities** FTV Wi-fi Gym Weight training room Steam shower Sauna Snooker room Hair salon Xmas New Year **Conf** Class 80 Board 40 Thtr 120 Del from £140 to £160 **Services** Lift **Parking** 70 **Notes** LB

Lion & Pheasant Hotel

★★★ 78% TOWN HOUSE HOTEL

☎ 01743 770345
49-50 Wyle Cop SY1 1XJ
e-mail: info@lionandpheasant.co.uk
web: www.lionandpheasant.co.uk

This 16th-century property stands on Wyle Cop, part of the historic centre of Shrewsbury. The interior décor is minimalist and uses natural materials such as limed oak, linens and silks. The bedrooms are of a high standard and include twin, double and family rooms. Award-winning food is offered in the first-floor restaurant and also in the ground-floor bar area.

Rooms 22 (2 fmly) **Facilities** FTV Wi-fi **Conf** Class 30 Board 30 Thtr 30 **Parking** 15 **Notes**

Mytton & Mermaid Hotel

★★★ 77% HOTEL

☎ 01743 761220
Atcham SY5 6QG
e-mail: reception@myttonandmermaid.co.uk
web: www.myttonandmermaid.co.uk
dir: From Shrewsbury over old bridge in Atcham. Hotel opposite main entrance to Attingham Park on B4380

Convenient for Shrewsbury, this former coaching inn enjoys a pleasant location beside the River Severn. Some bedrooms, including family suites, are in a converted stable block adjacent to the hotel. There is a large lounge bar, a comfortable lounge, and a brasserie that has gained a well-deserved local reputation for the quality of its food.

Rooms 18 (7 annexe) (1 fmly) (6 GF) **S** £85-£95; **D** £110-£175 (incl. bkfst) **Facilities** Wi-fi Fishing New Year **Conf** Class 24 Board 28 Thtr 70 Del from £150 to £160 **Parking** 50 **Notes** LB Closed 25 Dec Civ Wed 80

Lord Hill Hotel

★★★ 75% HOTEL

☎ 01743 232601
Abbey Foregate SY2 6AX
e-mail: reception@thelordhill.co.uk
web: www.thelordhill.co.uk
dir: From M54 take A5, left at 1st rdbt , at 2nd rdbt 4th exit into London Rd. At next rdbt (Lord Hill Column) take 3rd exit, hotel 300yds on left

This pleasant, attractively appointed hotel is located close to the town centre. Most of the modern bedrooms are set in a separate purpose-built property, but those in the main building include one with a four-poster, as well as full suites. Public areas include a conservatory restaurant and spacious function suites.

Rooms 35 (24 annexe) (2 fmly) (8 GF) **Facilities** FTV Wi-fi **Conf** Class 180 Board 180 Thtr 250 **Parking** 110 **Notes** Civ Wed 250

S

SHREWSBURY *continued*

Abbots Mead Hotel

★★ 74% METRO HOTEL

☎ 01743 235281
9 St Julian's Friars SY1 1XL
e-mail: res@abbotsmeadhotel.co.uk
dir: From S into town, 2nd left after English Bridge

This well maintained Georgian town house is located in a quiet cul-de-sac, near the English Bridge and close to both the River Severn and town centre with its many restaurants. Bedrooms are compact, neatly decorated and well equipped. Two lounges are available in addition to an attractive dining room, the setting for breakfasts, and dinner parties by prior arrangement.

Rooms 16 (2 fmly) **S** £55-£59; **D** £70-£90 (incl. bkfst)* **Facilities** Wi-fi **Parking** 10 **Notes** Closed certain days at Xmas

Premier Inn Shrewsbury (Harmers Hill)

BUDGET HOTEL

☎ 0871 527 8974
Wem Rd, Harmer Hill SY4 3DS
web: www.premierinn.com
dir: M54 junct 7, A5 signed Telford for approx 7m, at rdbt take A49, approx 3m. At next 2 rdbts 2nd exit, at next rdbt 4th exit signed Ellesmere & A528. In approx 3m hotel on left

High quality, budget accommodation ideal for both families and business travellers. Spacious, en suite bedrooms feature tea and coffee making facilities, and Freeview TV in most hotels. Internet access and Wi-fi are available for a small fee. The adjacent family restaurant features a wide and varied menu. See also the Hotel Groups pages.

Rooms 20

Drapers Hall

◉ ◉ RESTAURANT WITH ROOMS

☎ 01743 344679
10 Saint Mary's Place SY1 1DZ
e-mail: goodfood@drapershallrestaurant.co.uk
dir: From A5191 (St Mary's St) on one-way system into St Mary's Place

This 16th-century timber-framed property is situated in the heart of the market town of Shrewsbury. It provides high quality accommodation, including two suites, with modern facilities. Careful renovation of the original beams and wood panels together with beautiful wooden furniture has created a harmony of the past and present. Accomplished dining, headed up by Nigel Huxley, can be enjoyed in the main restaurant, Huxleys at Drapers Hall.

Rooms 4 (2 fmly)

Mad Jack's Restaurant & Bar

◉ RESTAURANT WITH ROOMS

☎ 01743 358870 & 761220
15 Saint Mary's St SY1 1EQ
e-mail: info@madjacks.uk.com
dir: Follow one-way system around town, opposite St Mary's church

This fine property is located in the heart of the town. Its name comes from a eccentric squire in the 18th century who squandered a fortune and then landed in jail for his drunken and riotous behaviour. The four individually designed bedrooms, including a suite, are very comfortable and have spacious and contemporary bathrooms. Downstairs the award-winning, vibrant bar and restaurant specialises in British food with a classic twist. Breakfast offers a quality range of dishes. Secure parking is available in a nearby public car park.

Rooms 4 (1 fmly)

SIDLESHAM   **Map 5 SZ89**
West Sussex

The Crab & Lobster

◉ RESTAURANT WITH ROOMS

☎ 01243 641233
Mill Ln PO20 7NB
e-mail: enquiries@crab-lobster.co.uk
dir: A27 onto B2145 signed Selsey. 1st left after garage at Sidlesham into Rookery Ln to Crab & Lobster

Hidden away on the south coast near Pagham Harbour and only a short drive from Chichester is the stylish Crab & Lobster. Bedrooms are superbly appointed, and bathrooms are a feature with luxury toiletries and powerful 'raindrop' showers. Guests can enjoy lunch or dinner in the smart restaurant where the menu offers a range of locally caught fresh fish amongst other regionally-sourced, seasonal produce.

Rooms 4

SIDMOUTH   **Map 3 SY18**
Devon

Victoria Hotel

★★★★ 83% ◉ HOTEL   *Brend Hotels*

☎ 01395 512651
The Esplanade EX10 8RY
e-mail: reservations@victoriahotel.co.uk
web: www.victoriahotel.co.uk
dir: On seafront

This imposing building, with manicured gardens, is situated overlooking the town. Wonderful sea views can be enjoyed from many of the comfortable bedrooms and elegant lounges. With indoor and outdoor leisure facilities, the hotel caters to a year-round clientele. Carefully prepared meals are served in the refined atmosphere of the restaurant. The staff provide a professional and friendly service.

Rooms 62 (6 fmly) ⭘ **S** £135-£155; **D** £175-£360* **Facilities** FTV Wi-fi ⭘ ⭘ ⭘ ⭘ Putt green Hot stone relaxation beds Spa bath Sauna Beauty treatment room Games room ♫ Xmas New Year Child facilities **Conf** Thtr 60 **Services** Lift **Parking** 100 **Notes** LB ⭘

See advert on opposite page

Save on hotels. Book at **theAA.com/hotel**

SHR – SID 423 ENGLAND

S

SIDMOUTH *continued*

Riviera Hotel

★★★★ 82% HOTEL

☎ 01395 515201
The Esplanade EX10 8AY
e-mail: enquiries@hotelriviera.co.uk
web: www.hotelriviera.co.uk
dir: M5 junct 30 & follow A3052

Overlooking the sea and close to the town centre, the Riviera is a fine example of Regency architecture. The large number of guests that become regular visitors here are testament to the high standards of service and hospitality offered. The front-facing bedrooms benefit from wonderful sea views, and the daily-changing menu places an emphasis on fresh, local produce.

Rooms 26 (6 fmly) ⚘ **S** £125-£194; **D** £250-£368 (incl. bkfst & dinner)* **Facilities** FTV Wi-fi ❧ ♫ Xmas New Year **Conf** Class 60 Board 30 Thtr 85 **Services** Lift **Parking** 26 **Notes** LB

See advert on opposite page

Belmont Hotel

(Brend Hotels)

★★★★ 75% HOTEL

☎ 01395 512555
The Esplanade EX10 8RX
e-mail: reservations@belmont-hotel.co.uk
web: www.belmont-hotel.co.uk
dir: On seafront

Prominently positioned on the seafront just a few minutes' walk from the town centre, this traditional hotel has many returning guests. A choice of comfortable lounges provides ample space for relaxation, and the air-conditioned restaurant has a pianist playing most evenings. Bedrooms are attractively furnished and many have fine views over the esplanade. Leisure facilities are available at the adjacent sister hotel, The Victoria.

Rooms 50 (4 fmly) (2 GF) ⚘ **S** £120-£160; **D** £150-£235* **Facilities** STV Wi-fi ❧ Putt green Leisure facilities available at sister hotel ♫ Xmas New Year Child facilities **Conf** Thtr 50 **Services** Lift **Parking** 45 **Notes** LB ⊗ Civ Wed 110

See advert on page 423

Kingswood & Devoran Hotel

★★★ 85% HOTEL

☎ 01395 516367 & 08000 481731
The Esplanade EX10 8AX
e-mail: kingswoodanddevoran@hotels-sidmouth.co.uk
web: www.hotels-sidmouth.co.uk
dir: M5 junct 30, A3052 signed Sidmouth on right, follow Station Rd down to Esplanade

This seafront hotel continues to offer friendly hospitality and service. Many bedrooms enjoy the sea views; all are well appointed and have smart bathrooms. Cuisine is pleasant and offers enjoyable dining featuring freshly prepared dishes.

Rooms 49 (8 fmly) (1 GF) ⚘ **S** £61-£86; **D** £122-£172 (incl. bkfst & dinner)* **Facilities** FTV Wi-fi Xmas **Conf** Class 30 Board 40 Thtr 60 **Services** Lift **Parking** 23 **Notes** Closed 27 Dec-10 Feb

Westcliff Hotel

★★★ 79% HOTEL

☎ 01395 513252
Manor Rd EX10 8RU
e-mail: stay@westcliffhotel.co.uk
web: www.westcliffhotel.co.uk
dir: Exit A3052 to Sidmouth then to seafront & esplanade, turn right, hotel directly ahead

This charming hotel is ideally located within walking distance of Sidmouth's elegant promenade and beaches. The spacious lounges and the cocktail bar open onto a terrace which leads to the pool and croquet lawn. Bedrooms, several with balconies and glorious sea views, are spacious and comfortable, whilst the restaurant offers a choice of well-prepared dishes.

Rooms 40 (1 fmly) (5 GF) **Facilities** FTV Wi-fi ❧ Putt green Table tennis Pool table Xmas New Year **Conf** Class 20 Board 15 Thtr 30 **Services** Lift **Parking** 40 **Notes** Civ Wed 80

Hotel Elizabeth

★★★ 75% HOTEL

☎ 01395 513503 & 08000 481731
The Esplanade EX10 8AT
e-mail: elizabeth@hotels-sidmouth.co.uk
web: www.hotels-sidmouth.co.uk
dir: M5 junct 30, A3052 to Sidmouth. 1st exit on right to Sidmouth, left onto esplanade

Occupying a prime location on the Esplanade, this elegant hotel attracts many loyal guests who return to enjoy the relaxed atmosphere and attentive service.

Save on hotels. Book at **theAA.com/hotel**

SID 425 ENGLAND

Bedrooms are both comfortable and smartly appointed; all have sea views and some have balconies. The spacious lounge and sunny patio, with wonderful views across the bay, are perfect places to sit and just watch the world go by.

Rooms 28 (3 fmly) (1 GF) ❦ **S** £66-£82; **D** £126-£142 (incl. bkfst & dinner)* **Facilities** FTV Wi-fi Xmas **Services** Lift **Parking** 16 **Notes** ⊗ Closed 28 Dec-10 Feb

Royal Glen Hotel

★★★ 75% HOTEL

☎ 01395 513221 & 513456
Glen Rd EX10 8RW
e-mail: info@royalglenhotel.co.uk
dir: A303 to Honiton, A375 to Sidford, follow seafront signs, right onto esplanade, right at end into Glen Rd

This historic 17th-century, Grade I listed hotel has been owned by the same family for several generations. The comfortable bedrooms are furnished in period style. Guests may use the well-maintained gardens and a heated indoor pool, and can enjoy well-prepared food in the elegant dining room.

Rooms 32 (3 fmly) (3 GF) ❦ **S** £48-£75; **D** £96-£150 (incl. bkfst)* **Facilities** FTV Wi-fi ⊕ Gym **Services** Lift **Parking** 22 **Notes** LB Closed Dec-21 Feb

Bedford Hotel

★★★ 74% HOTEL

☎ 01395 513047 & 0797 394 0671
Esplanade EX10 8NR
e-mail: info@bedfordhotelsidmouth.co.uk
web: www.bedfordhotelsidmouth.co.uk
dir: M5 junct 30, A3052 & to Sidmouth. Hotel at centre of Esplanade

Situated on the seafront, this long established, family-run hotel provides a warm welcome and relaxing atmosphere. Bedrooms are well appointed and many have the added bonus of wonderful sea views. Public areas combine character and comfort with a choice of lounges in which to relax. In addition to the hotel dining room, Pyne's bar and restaurant offers an interesting range of dishes in a convivial environment.

Rooms 37 (1 GF) **Facilities** Xmas **Services** Lift **Parking** 6

Hunters Moon Hotel

★★ 82% HOTEL

☎ 01395 513380
Sid Rd EX10 9AA
e-mail: huntersmoon.hotel@virgin.net
dir: From Exeter on A3052 to Sidford, right at lights into Sidmouth, 1.5m, at cinema turn left. Hotel in 0.25m

Set amid three acres of attractive and well-tended grounds, this friendly, family-run hotel is peacefully located in a quiet area within walking distance of the town and esplanade. The light and airy bedrooms, some located at ground floor level, are comfortable and well equipped. There is a lounge and a cosy bar. The restaurant provides a choice of imaginative dishes, and, weather permitting tea may be taken on the lawn.

Rooms 33 (4 fmly) (11 GF) ❦ **S** £63-£66; **D** £120-£126 (incl. bkfst) **Facilities** FTV Wi-fi Putt green Xmas **Parking** 33 **Notes** LB No children 3yrs Closed Jan-9 Feb RS Dec & Feb

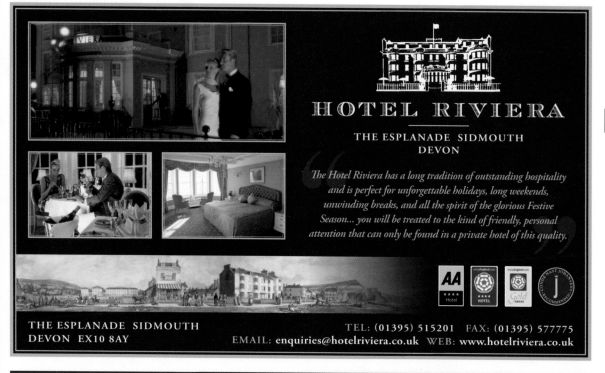

S

SIDMOUTH *continued*

The Royal York & Faulkner Hotel

★★ 80% HOTEL

☎ 01395 513043 & 0800 220714
The Esplanade EX10 8AZ
e-mail: stay@royalyorkhotel.co.uk
web: www.royalyorkhotel.co.uk
dir: M5 junct 30 take A3052, 10m to Sidmouth, hotel
in centre of Esplanade

This seafront hotel, owned and run by the same
family for over 60 years, maintains its Regency charm
and grandeur. The attractive bedrooms vary in size,
and many have balconies and sea views. Public
rooms are spacious and traditional dining is offered,
alongside Blinis Café-Bar, which is more
contemporary in style and offers coffees, lunch and
afternoon tea. The spa facilities include a
hydrotherapy pool, steam room, sauna and a variety
of treatments.

Rooms 70 (2 annexe) (8 fmly) (5 GF) 🐾
S £57.50-£88.50; **D** £115-£177 (incl. bkfst & dinner)*
Facilities Spa FTV Wi-fi ⬗ HL Steam cabin Snooker
table Sauna Complimentary use of pool (200yds from
hotel) 🎵 Xmas New Year **Services** Lift **Parking** 20
Notes LB Closed Jan

Mount Pleasant Hotel

★★ 78% HOTEL

☎ 01395 514694
Salcombe Rd EX10 8JA
dir: Exit A3052 at Sidford x-rds, in 1.25m turn left
into Salcombe Rd, opposite Radway Cinema. Hotel on
right after bridge

Quietly located within almost an acre of gardens, this
modernised Georgian hotel is minutes from the town
centre and seafront. Bedrooms and public areas
provide good levels of comfort and high quality
furnishings. Guests return on a regular basis,
especially to experience the friendly, relaxed
atmosphere. The light and airy restaurant overlooks
the pleasant garden and offers a daily-changing
menu of imaginative, yet traditional home-cooked
dishes.

Rooms 17 (1 fmly) (3 GF) **S** £59.50-£74.50;
D £107-£149 (incl. bkfst & dinner) **Facilities** Putt
green **Parking** 20 **Notes** ⊗ No children 8yrs Closed
Dec-Feb

The Woodlands Hotel

★★ 74% HOTEL

☎ 01395 513120
Cotmaton Cross EX10 8HG
e-mail: info@woodlands-hotel.com
web: www.woodlands-hotel.com
dir: Follow signs for Sidmouth

Located in the heart of the town and ideally situated
for exploring Devon and Dorset, this listed property
has numerous character features. There is a spacious
bar and a lounge where guests may relax. Freshly
prepared dinners can be enjoyed in the smart dining
room. Families with children are made very welcome
and may dine early.

Rooms 20 (4 fmly) (8 GF) 🐾 **S** £37-£73; **D** £74-£146
(incl. bkfst) **Facilities** FTV Wi-fi ⬗ **Parking** 20
Notes LB Closed 20 Dec-15 Jan

The Salty Monk

◉◉ RESTAURANT WITH ROOMS

☎ 01395 513174
Church St, Sidford EX10 9QP
e-mail: saltymonk@btconnect.com
web: www.saltymonk.co.uk
dir: On A3052 opposite church in Sidford

Set in the village of Sidford, this attractive property
dates from the 16th century. There's oodles of style
and appeal here and each bedroom has a unique
identity. Bathrooms are equally special with multi-jet
showers, spa baths and cosseting robes and towels.
The output from the kitchen is impressive with
excellent local produce very much in evidence.

Rooms 6 (1 annexe)

The Golf Hotel

★★ 75% HOTEL

☎ 016973 31438
Criffel St CA7 4AB
e-mail: info@golfhotelsilloth.co.uk

A friendly welcome waits at this hotel which occupies
a prime position in the centre of the historic market
town; it is a popular meeting place for the local
community. Bedrooms are mostly well proportioned
and are comfortably equipped. The lounge bar is a
popular venue for dining, with a wide range of dishes
on offer.

Rooms 22 (4 fmly) 🐾 **S** £50-£80; **D** £90-£140 (incl.
bkfst)* **Facilities** FTV Wi-fi ⬗ Xmas New Year
Conf Class 50 Board 30 Thtr 100 Del from £100 to
£120* **Notes** LB Civ Wed 100

Premier Inn Silverstone

BUDGET HOTEL

☎ 0871 527 8976
Brackley Hatch, Syresham NN13 5TX
web: www.premierinn.com
dir: On A43 near Silverstone

High quality, budget accommodation ideal for both
families and business travellers. Spacious, en suite
bedrooms feature tea and coffee making facilities,
and Freeview TV in most hotels. Internet access and
Wi-fi are available for a small fee. The adjacent
family restaurant features a wide and varied menu.
See also the Hotel Groups pages.

Rooms 41

Hempstead House Country Hotel

★★★ 86% ◉ HOTEL

☎ 01795 428020
London Rd, Bapchild ME9 9PP
e-mail: info@hempsteadhouse.co.uk
web: www.hempsteadhouse.co.uk
dir: 1.5m from town centre on A2 towards Canterbury

Expect a warm welcome at this charming detached
Victorian property, situated amidst four acres of
mature landscaped gardens. Bedrooms are
attractively decorated with lovely co-ordinated
fabrics, tastefully furnished and equipped with many
thoughtful touches. Public rooms feature a choice of
elegant lounges as well as a superb conservatory
dining room. In summer guests can eat on the
terraces. There is a spa and fitness studio.

Rooms 34 (7 fmly) (1 GF) **S** £85-£105; **D** £110-£160
(incl. bkfst) **Facilities** Spa STV FTV Wi-fi ❄ ⬗ Gym
Fitness studio Steam room Sauna Hydrotherapy pool
Xmas New Year **Conf** Class 150 Board 100 Thtr 150
Services Lift **Parking** 200 **Notes** LB Civ Wed 150

Premier Inn Sittingbourne
BUDGET HOTEL

☎ 9871 527 8978
Bobbing Corner, Sheppy Way, Bobbing ME9 8RZ
web: www.premierinn.com
dir: M2 junct 5, A249 towards Sheerness, approx 2m.
Take 1st slip road after A2 underpass. At rdbt take
1st exit, hotel on left

High quality, budget accommodation ideal for both
families and business travellers. Spacious, en suite
bedrooms feature tea and coffee making facilities,
and Freeview TV in most hotels. Internet access and
Wi-fi are available for a small fee. The adjacent
family restaurant features a wide and varied menu.
See also the Hotel Groups pages.

Rooms 40

SKEGNESS   Map 17 TF56
Lincolnshire

Best Western Vine Hotel
★★★ 71% HOTEL

☎ 01754 763018 & 610611
Vine Rd, Seacroft PE25 3DB
e-mail: info@thevinehotel.com
dir: A52 to Skegness, S towards Gibraltar Point, right
into Drummond Rd, 0.5m, right into Vine Rd

With its long history this traditional hotel is
something of a local landmark. The smartly decorated
bedrooms are well equipped and comfortably
appointed. Public areas include two character bars
that serve excellent local beers. Freshly prepared
dishes are offered in both the bar and the restaurant;
service is both friendly and helpful.

Rooms 25 (3 fmly) **Facilities** FTV Wi-fi Xmas New
Year **Conf** Class 25 Board 30 Thtr 100 **Parking** 50
Notes Civ Wed 100

Best Western North Shore Hotel & Golf Course
★★★ 70% HOTEL

☎ 01754 763298
North Shore Rd PE25 1DN
e-mail: info@northshorehotel.co.uk
web: www.northshorehotel.co.uk
dir: 1m N of town centre on A52, turn right into North
Shore Rd (opposite Fenland laundry)

This hotel enjoys an enviable position on the
beachfront, adjacent to its own championship golf
course and only ten minutes from the town centre.
Spacious public areas include a terrace bar serving
informal meals and real ales, a formal restaurant and
impressive function rooms. Bedrooms are smartly
decorated and thoughtfully equipped.

Rooms 34 (3 annexe) (4 fmly) (3 GF) ⌘ **S** £35-£50;
D £55-£75 **Facilities** FTV Wi-fi ⌘ 18 Putt green Xmas
New Year **Conf** Class 60 Board 60 Thtr 220
Del from £95 to £120 **Parking** 200 **Notes** LB ⊗
Civ Wed 180

SKIPTON   Map 18 SD95
North Yorkshire

The Coniston Hotel
★★★★ 77% HOTEL

☎ 01756 748080
Coniston Cold BD23 4EA
e-mail: info@theconistonhotel.com
web: www.theconistonhotel.com
dir: On A65, 6m NW of Skipton

This privately owned hotel set in 1,500 acres of prime
country estate is a haven for guests staying or just
visiting the hotel. All bedrooms and bathrooms are
appointed to a very high standard; the bedroom wing
offers large rooms with balconies. The reception, bar
and restaurant have style and elegance, and the
stunning spa adds to the impressive list of activities
for guests.

Rooms 71 (13 fmly) (25 GF) ⌘ **S** £75-£104;
D £75-£104 **Facilities** STV Wi-fi Fishing Clay pigeon
shooting Falconry Off-road Land Rover driving Archery
Target golf Xmas New Year **Conf** Class 80 Board 50
Thtr 200 Del from £139 to £189* **Services** Lift
Parking 170 **Notes** LB Civ Wed 120

SKIPTON continued

Herriots Hotel

★★★ 79% HOTEL

☎ 01756 792781
Broughton Rd BD23 1RT
e-mail: info@herriotsforleisure.co.uk
web: www.herriotsforleisure.co.uk
dir: 2m from A59 at entrance to town; 50yds from railway station

This friendly hotel is situated in the centre of the delightful market town of Skipton and is just a short walk from the canal; the nearby railway has links to Leeds and the Settle to Carlisle route with its breathtaking scenery. The well-equipped bedrooms are contemporary in style yet maintain the character of this Victorian listed building; some rooms have French doors that overlook the canal; the largest rooms have four-posters and spas, and can be converted for accommodate families. Rhubarb restaurant offers British cuisine with a Yorkshire 'twist' that is based on local, seasonal produce.

Rooms 23 (3 fmly) ↟ **S** £59-£79; **D** £85-£110 (incl. bkfst) **Facilities** FTV Wi-fi ↻ Private access onto Leeds Liverpool Canal Xmas New Year **Conf** Class 50 Board 52 Thtr 100 Del from £120 to £140 **Services** Lift **Parking** 26 **Notes** LB ⊗ Civ Wed 80

Rendezvous Hotel

★★★ 77% HOTEL

☎ 01756 700100
Keighley Rd BD23 2TA
e-mail: reservations@rendezvous-skipton.com
dir: On A6131 (Keighley road) S from town centre

Located beside the canal just outside the town, the hotel has the advantage of plenty of parking and a leisure club with pool and gym. Bedrooms are well equipped and spacious, and have delightful views over the rolling countryside. There are extensive conference facilities. This hotel makes an ideal base for touring The Dales.

Rooms 80 (10 fmly) (13 GF) ↟ **S** £65-£105; **D** £65-£105* **Facilities** STV Wi-fi ↻ supervised Gym Xmas New Year **Conf** Class 200 Board 120 Thtr 500 Del from £99 to £150* **Services** Lift **Parking** 120 **Notes** LB ⊗ Civ Wed 400

Premier Inn Skipton North (Gargrave)

BUDGET HOTEL

☎ 0871 527 8980
Hellifield Rd, Gargrave BD23 3NB
web: www.premierinn.com
dir: NW of Skipton at rdbt junct of A59 & A65, take A65 signed Kendal, Settle & Gargrave. 3.5m. Through Gargrave. Hotel on left

High quality, budget accommodation ideal for both families and business travellers. Spacious, en suite bedrooms feature tea and coffee making facilities, and Freeview TV in most hotels. Internet access and Wi-fi are available for a small fee. The adjacent family restaurant features a wide and varied menu. See also the Hotel Groups pages.

Rooms 21

SLEAFORD
Lincolnshire   Map 12 TF04

The Carre Arms Hotel & Conference Centre

★★★ 68% SMALL HOTEL

☎ 01529 303156
1 Mareham Ln NG34 7JP
e-mail: enquiries@carrearmshotel.co.uk
web: www.carrearmshotel.co.uk
dir: Take A153 to Sleaford, hotel on right at level crossing

This friendly, family run hotel is located close to the station and offers suitably appointed accommodation. Public areas include a smart brasserie and two spacious bars where a good selection of meals is offered. There is also a conservatory and a former stable that houses the spacious function room.

Rooms 13 (2 fmly) ↟ **S** £57-£67; **D** £87-£97 (incl. bkfst)* **Facilities** FTV Wi-fi **Conf** Class 70 Board 40 Thtr 120 **Parking** 80 **Notes** ⊗ Civ Wed 80

SLOUGH
Berkshire   Map 6 SU97

Copthorne Hotel Slough-Windsor

★★★★ 75% HOTEL

☎ 01753 516222
400 Cippenham Ln SL1 2YE
e-mail: sales.slough@millenniumhotels.co.uk
web: www.millenniumhotels.co.uk
dir: M4 junct 6, A355 towards Slough. At next rdbt left & left again for hotel entrance

Conveniently located for the motorway and for Heathrow Airport, this modern hotel of striking design offers visitors a wide range of indoor leisure facilities; Bugis Street Brasserie offers menus of Chinese, Malaysian and Singaporean dishes. Bedrooms provide a useful range of extras including climate control and satellite TV. The hotel offers a discounted entrance fee to some of the attractions in the area.

Rooms 219 (47 fmly) (8 smoking) ↟ **S** £61.20-£169.20; **D** £61.20-£169.20* **Facilities** STV FTV Wi-fi ↻ Gym Steam room Sauna **Conf** Class 160 Board 60 Thtr 280 **Services** Lift **Parking** 303 **Notes** LB ⊗ Civ Wed 280

The Pinewood Hotel

★★★★ 72% HOTEL

☎ 01753 896400
Wexham Park Ln, George Green SL3 6AP
e-mail: info@pinewoodhotel.co.uk
web: www.pinewoodhotel.co.uk
dir: A4 N from Slough, A412 towards Uxbridge. Hotel 3m on left

This is a small luxury hotel on the outskirts of Slough. Excellent design is at the forefront throughout, together with good levels of comfort. The Eden brasserie specialises in quality produce, carefully prepared, including dishes cooked on the wood-burning stove. Service is friendly and attentive.

Rooms 49 (16 annexe) (4 fmly) (12 GF) **S** £69-£149; **D** £79-£159* **Facilities** FTV Wi-fi ↻ Free use of nearby leisure facilities New Year **Conf** Class 46 Board 40 Thtr 120 Del from £145 to £210* **Services** Lift Air con **Parking** 40 **Notes** ⊗ Civ Wed 130

Save on hotels. Book at **theAA.com/hotel**

SKI – SOL 429 ENGLAND

Holiday Inn Express London Heathrow T5

BUDGET HOTEL

☎ 01753 684001
London Rd SL3 8QB
e-mail: info@hiexheathrowt5.co.uk
web: www.hiexheathrowt5.co.uk
dir: M4 junct 5, follow signs for Colnbrook. Hotel 0.5m on right

A modern hotel ideal for families and business travellers. Fresh and uncomplicated, the spacious rooms include Sky TV, power shower and tea and coffee-making facilities. Continental buffet breakfast is included in the room rate; other meals may be taken at the nearby family pub or restaurant. See also the Hotel Groups pages.

Rooms 300 (300 fmly) ⊷ **Conf** Class 50 Board 40 Thtr 120 Del from £90 to £150

Holiday Inn Express Slough

BUDGET HOTEL

☎ 0844 499 2890
Mill St SL2 5DD
e-mail: info@hiexslough.co.uk
web: www.hiexpress.co.uk
dir: Telephone for directions

Rooms 142 (110 fmly) ⊷ **D** £52-£250 (incl. bkfst)*
Conf Class 25 Board 20 Thtr 30

Premier Inn Slough

BUDGET HOTEL

☎ 0871 527 8982
76 Uxbridge Rd SL1 1SU
web: www.premierinn.com
dir: 2m from M4 junct 5, 3m from junct 6. Just off A4

High quality, budget accommodation ideal for both families and business travellers. Spacious, en suite bedrooms feature tea and coffee making facilities, and Freeview TV in most hotels. Internet access and Wi-fi are available for a small fee. The adjacent family restaurant features a wide and varied menu. See also the Hotel Groups pages.

Rooms 84

SNAINTON
North Yorkshire
Map 17 SE98

The Coachman Inn

◉ RESTAURANT WITH ROOMS

☎ 01723 859231
Pickering Road West YO13 9PL
e-mail: info@coachmaninn.co.uk
web: www.coachmaninn.co.uk
dir: From A170 between Pickering & Scarborough onto B1258 (High St) in Stainton

This Grade II listed property was built in 1776 as a coaching inn and stands just on the outskirts of Snainton. It now offers comfortable, double, en suite rooms, fine dining in a wonderful large dining room, a locals' bar, a quiet lounge for residents and ample parking.

Rooms 6 (1 fmly)

SNETTISHAM
Norfolk
Map 12 TF63

Rose & Crown

★★ 81% ◉ HOTEL

☎ 01485 541382
Old Church Rd PE31 7LX
e-mail: info@roseandcrownsnettisham.co.uk
dir: A149 towards Hunstanton. In village centre into Old Church Rd, hotel 100yds on left

This lovely village inn provides comfortable, well-equipped bedrooms. A range of quality meals is served in the many dining areas, complemented by a good variety of real ales and wines. Service is friendly and a delightful atmosphere prevails. A walled garden is available on sunny days, as is a children's play area.

Rooms 16 (5 fmly) (2 GF) ⊷ **S** £70-£85; **D** £90-£110 (incl. bkfst)* **Facilities** FTV Wi-fi ⊗ ☺ ⊱ Xmas New Year **Conf** Class 40 Board 40 Thtr 60 **Parking** 70 **Notes** LB

SOLIHULL
West Midlands
Map 10 SP17

See also Dorridge

The St Johns Hotel

_PH_ | principal hayley

★★★★ 75% HOTEL

☎ 0121 711 3000 & 712 7601
651 Warwick Rd B91 1AT
e-mail: enquiriesstjohns@principal-hayley.com
dir: M42 junct 5, A41 (Solihull Bypass) signed Solihull. At lights left into Load Ln (signed Solihull Town Centre). At next rdbt 3rd exit onto B425 (Warwick Rd). Hotel on right

With its town centre location, this modern hotel is conveniently situated for the NEC, Birmingham and many local attractions. Bedrooms are air conditioned, attractively decorated and equipped with a comprehensive range of extras. The hotel provides extensive conference facilities, an indoor leisure facility and extensive parking.

Rooms 180 (4 fmly) (9 GF) ⊷ **D** £65-£199*
Facilities STV FTV Wi-fi HL ⊗ Gym Sauna Steam room Xmas New Year **Conf** Class 350 Board 40 Thtr 700 Del from £95 to £180 **Services** Lift Air con **Parking** 300 **Notes** Civ Wed 350

Ramada Birmingham/Solihull

[U]

☎ 0121 711 2121 & 711 5400
The Square B91 3RF
e-mail: sales@ramadasolihullhotel.co.uk
dir: M42 junct 5, A41 towards Solihull. 1st left on slip road. Right at island, left at 2 sets of lights. Hotel 600yds on right

Currently the rating for this establishment is not confirmed. This may be due to a change of ownership or because it has only recently joined the AA rating scheme. For further details please see the AA website: theAA.com

Rooms 145 (14 fmly) (36 GF) **Facilities** STV FTV Wi-fi ⊗ Xmas New Year **Conf** Class 60 Board 40 Thtr 150 **Services** Lift **Parking** 200 **Notes** Civ Wed 200

S

SOLIHULL *continued*

Premier Inn Solihull (Hockley Heath)

BUDGET HOTEL

☎ 0871 527 8984
Stratford Rd, Hockley Heath B94 6NX
web: www.premierinn.com
dir: On A3400, 2m S of M42 junct 4

High quality, budget accommodation ideal for both families and business travellers. Spacious, en suite bedrooms feature tea and coffee making facilities, and Freeview TV in most hotels. Internet access and Wi-fi are available for a small fee. The adjacent family restaurant features a wide and varied menu. See also the Hotel Groups pages.

Rooms 55

Premier Inn Solihull North

BUDGET HOTEL

☎ 0871 527 8988
Stratford Rd, Shirley B90 3AG
web: www.premierinn.com
dir: M42 junct 4 follow signs for Birmingham. Hotel in Shirley town centre on A34

Rooms 43

Premier Inn Solihull (Shirley)

BUDGET HOTEL

☎ 0871 527 8986
Stratford Rd, Shirley B90 4EP
web: www.premierinn.com
dir: M42 junct 4, A34N. Hotel in 1m

Rooms 51

SONNING
Berkshire
Map 5 SU77

The French Horn

★★★ 85% ◉◉ HOTEL

☎ 0118 969 2204
RG4 6TN
e-mail: info@thefrenchhorn.co.uk
dir: From A4 into Sonning, follow B478 through village over bridge, hotel on right, car park on left

This long established Thames-side establishment has a lovely village setting and retains the traditions of classic hotel keeping. The restaurant is a particular attraction and provides attentive service. Bedrooms, including four cottage suites, are spacious and comfortable; many offer stunning views over the river. A private boardroom is available for corporate guests.

Rooms 22 (8 annexe) (4 GF) (4 smoking) 🐾
D £125–£170 (incl. bkfst)* **Facilities** FTV Wi-fi Fishing Affiliation with Nirvana Spa (15 mins by car) **Conf** Board 14 **Services** Air con **Parking** 40 **Notes** ⊗ Closed 26-29 Dec

SOURTON
Devon
Map 3 SX59

Collaven Manor Hotel

★★ 79% COUNTRY HOUSE HOTEL

☎ 01837 861522
EX20 4HH
e-mail: collavenmanor@supanet.com
dir: A30 onto A386 to Tavistock, hotel 2m on right

This delightful 15th-century manor house is quietly located in five acres of well-tended grounds. The friendly proprietors provide attentive service and ensure a relaxing environment. Charming public rooms have old oak beams and granite fireplaces, and provide a range of comfortable lounges and a well stocked bar. In the restaurant, a daily-changing menu offers interesting dishes.

Rooms 9 (1 fmly) **Facilities** FTV Wi-fi 🛥 Bowls **Conf** Class 20 Board 16 Thtr 30 **Parking** 50 **Notes** Closed Dec-Jan Civ Wed 50

SOUTHAMPTON
Hampshire
Map 5 SU41

See also Botley

De Vere Grand Harbour

★★★★ 78% HOTEL

☎ 023 8063 3033
West Quay Rd SO15 1AG
e-mail: grandharbour@devere-hotels.com
web: www.devere.co.uk
dir: M27 junct 3 follow Waterfront signs. Keep in left lane of dual carrriageway, then follow Heritage & Waterfront signs onto West Quay Rd

Enjoying views of the harbour, this hotel stands alongside the medieval town walls and close to the West Quay centre. The modern design is impressive, with leisure facilities located in the dramatic glass pyramid. The spacious bedrooms are well appointed and thoughtfully equipped. For dining, guests can choose between two bars as well as fine dining in Allertons Restaurant and a more informal style in No 5 Brasserie.

Rooms 173 (22 fmly) (6 smoking) 🐾 **Facilities** Spa STV Wi-fi 🛒 HL 🕭 Gym Beauty suite Sauna Steam room Xmas New Year **Conf** Class 200 Board 150 Thtr 500 **Services** Lift **Parking** 190 **Notes** ⊗ Civ Wed 310

The Legacy Botleigh Grange Hotel & Spa

★★★★ 75% ◉ HOTEL

☎ 08444 119050 & 0330 333 2850
Grange Rd, Hedge End SO30 2GA
e-mail: res-botleighgrange@legacy-hotels.co.uk
web: www.legacy-hotels.co.uk
dir: M27 junct 7, A334 to Botley, hotel 0.5m on left

This impressive mansion, situated close to the M27, displays good quality throughout. The bedrooms are spacious with a good range of facilities. Public areas include a large conference room and a pleasant terrace with views overlooking the gardens and lake. The restaurant offers interesting menus using fresh, local produce.

Rooms 56 (8 fmly) (9 GF) **Facilities** Spa STV FTV Wi-fi ⊱ 🕃 Putt green Fishing Gym Sauna Steam room Relaxation room Monsoon showers Xmas New Year **Conf** Class 175 Board 60 Thtr 500 **Services** Lift **Parking** 200 **Notes** Civ Wed 180

Novotel Southampton

★★★★ 72% HOTEL

☎ 023 8033 0550
1 West Quay Rd SO15 1RA
e-mail: H1073@accor.com
web: www.novotel.com
dir: M27 junct 3, follow city centre/A33 signs. In 1m take right lane for West Quay & Dock Gates 4-10. Hotel entrance on left. Turn at lights by McDonalds, left at rdbt, hotel straight ahead

A modern purpose-built hotel situated close to the city centre, railway station, ferry terminal and major road networks. The brightly decorated bedrooms are ideal for families and business guests; four rooms have facilities for the less mobile. The open-plan public areas include the Garden Brasserie, a bar and a leisure complex.

Rooms 121 (50 fmly) 🐾 **Facilities** STV FTV Wi-fi 🕭 Gym Sauna New Year **Conf** Class 300 Board 150 Thtr 450 **Services** Lift **Parking** 300 **Notes** Civ Wed 300

S

Save on hotels. Book at **theAA.com/hotel**

SOL – SOU 431 ENGLAND

Mercure Southampton Centre Dolphin Hotel

★★★★ 70% ⊛ HOTEL

☎ 023 8038 6460
34-35 High St SO14 2HN
e-mail: H7876@accor.com
web: www.mercure.com
dir: From A33 follow signs for Docks, Old Town & Isle of Wight ferry. At ferry terminal right into High Street, hotel 400yds on left

Originally a coaching inn, this hotel enjoys a central location set almost in the heart of the town, yet close to the ferry terminals. The bedrooms are appointed to a high standard, and public areas include a traditional bar, popular restaurant and two meeting rooms. Parking at the rear of the hotel is an added bonus.

Rooms 90 (4 fmly) (22 GF) ➧ **Facilities** FTV Wi-fi Xmas New Year **Conf** Class 50 Board 40 Thtr 120 Del from £115 to £145* **Services** Lift **Parking** 80 **Notes** Civ Wed 120

Best Western Chilworth Manor

★★★ 79% HOTEL

☎ 023 8076 7333
Chilworth SO16 7PT
e-mail: sales@chilworth-manor.co.uk
web: www.bw-chilworthmanor.co.uk
dir: 1m from M3/M27 junct on A27 (Romsey road) N from Southampton. Pass Chilworth Arms on left, in 200mtrs turn left at Southampton Science Park sign. Hotel immediately right

Set in 12 acres of delightful grounds, this attractive Edwardian manor house is conveniently located for Southampton and also the New Forest National Park. Bedrooms are located in both the main house and an adjoining wing. The hotel is particularly popular as both a conference and a wedding venue.

Best Western Chilworth Manor

Rooms 95 (6 fmly) (23 GF) **S** £69-£145; **D** £79-£155 **Facilities** Spa FTV Wi-fi ➧ ⊛ Gym Trail walking Giant chess Petanque New Year **Conf** Class 50 Board 50 Thtr 130 **Services** Lift **Parking** 200 **Notes** LB ⊛ Civ Wed 105

See advert on this page

Holiday Inn Southampton

★★★ 75% HOTEL

☎ 0871 942 9073
Herbert Walker Av SO15 1HJ
e-mail: southamptonhi@ihg.com
web: www.holidayinn.co.uk
dir: M27 junct 3 follow 'Dockgate 1-10 & Southampton Waterfront' signs. Hotel adjacent to Dock Gate 8

Convenient for both the port and town centre, this modern hotel is popular with both business and leisure guests. The well-equipped bedrooms are comfortably furnished. Public areas include an informal lounge bar and a contemporary restaurant offering an extensive range of popular dishes. Conference and leisure facilities are also available.

Rooms 130 (6 fmly) (15 smoking) **Facilities** STV Wi-fi ⊛ supervised Gym New Year **Conf** Class 75 Board 60 Thtr 180 **Services** Lift Air con **Parking** 140 **Notes** ⊛ Civ Wed

S

SOUTHAMPTON *continued*

The Elizabeth House Hotel

THE INDEPENDENTS

★★ 80% HOTEL

☎ 023 8022 4327
42-44 The Avenue SO17 1XP
e-mail: mail@elizabethhousehotel.com
web: www.elizabethhousehotel.com
dir: On A33, hotel on left after Southampton Common, before main lights

This hotel is conveniently situated close to the city centre, so provides an ideal base for both business and leisure guests. The bedrooms are well equipped and are attractively furnished with comfort in mind. There is also a cosy and atmospheric bistro in the cellar where evening meals are served.

Rooms 27 (7 annexe) (9 fmly) (8 GF)
S £60-£69.95; **D** £70-£81.95 (incl. bkfst)*
Facilities FTV Wi-fi **Conf** Class 24 Board 24 Thtr 40
Del £112.50* **Parking** 31

Holiday Inn Express Southampton M27 Jct 7

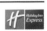

BUDGET HOTEL

☎ 023 8060 6060 & 8060 6040
Botley Rd, West End SO30 3XA
e-mail: reservations@expressbyholidayinn.uk.net
web: www.meridianleisurehotels.com/southampton
dir: M27 junct 7, follow brown Rose Bowl signs. Hotel 1m from junct 7 at entrance to The Rose Bowl on corner Marshall Drive & Botley Rd

This hotel, adjacent to the Rose Bowl, is conveniently located for Southampton Airport and Docks and has ample free parking. There is an air-conditioned restaurant serving conference lunches, evening meals and complimentary hot breakfast, a fully licensed bar and lounge area with a 42" plasma TV with Freeview channels. The hotel offers high speed Wi-fi throughout. Leisure facilities are available at the adjacent Esporta Leisure Centre for a nominal fee.

Rooms 176 (129 fmly) (38 GF) (18 smoking)
S £48-£109; **D** £48-£109 (incl. bkfst)* **Conf** Class 26 Board 20 Thtr 52 Del from £104.50 to £152.50*

Holiday Inn Express Southampton - West

BUDGET HOTEL

☎ 023 8074 3100
Adanac Park, Redbridge Ln SO16 0YP
e-mail: southampton@morethanhotels.com
web: www.hiexpress.com/southamptonuk
dir: M27 junct 3 to M271 junct 1 (Lordshill Interchange), hotel on left in Redbridge Lane

Rooms 105 (63 fmly) **Conf** Class 20 Board 20 Thtr 35

Ibis Southampton Centre

BUDGET HOTEL

☎ 023 8063 4463
West Quay Rd, Western Esplanade SO15 1RA
e-mail: H1039@accor.com
web: www.ibishotel.com
dir: M27 junct 3, M271, left to city centre (A35), follow Old Town Waterfront to 4th lights, left, left again, hotel opposite station

Modern, budget hotel offering comfortable accommodation in bright and practical bedrooms. Breakfast is self-service and dinner is available in the restaurant. See also the Hotel Groups pages.

Rooms 93 **S** £57-£130; **D** £57-£130* **Conf** Class 50 Board 40 Thtr 80 Del from £99 to £198*

Premier Inn Southampton Airport

BUDGET HOTEL

☎ 0871 527 8998
Mitchell Way SO18 2XU
web: www.premierinn.com
dir: M27 junct 5, A335 towards Eastleigh. Right at rdbt into Wide Lane. 1st exit at next rdbt into Mitchell Way

High quality, budget accommodation ideal for both families and business travellers. Spacious, en suite bedrooms feature tea and coffee making facilities, and Freeview TV in most hotels. Internet access and Wi-fi are available for a small fee. The adjacent family restaurant features a wide and varied menu. See also the Hotel Groups pages.

Rooms 121

Premier Inn Southampton City Centre

BUDGET HOTEL

☎ 0871 527 9266
6 Dials, New Rd SO14 0YN
web: www.premierinn.com
dir: M27 junct 3, A335 signed City Centre. At Charlotte Place rdbt take 3rd exit into East Park Terrace, 1st left into New Rd. Hotel on right

Rooms 172

Premier Inn Southampton North

BUDGET HOTEL

☎ 0871 527 9002
Romsey Rd, Nursling SO16 0XJ
web: www.premierinn.com
dir: M27 junct 3, M271 towards Romsey. At next rdbt take 3rd exit towards Southampton (A3057). Hotel 1.5m on right

Rooms 32

Premier Inn Southampton West Quay

BUDGET HOTEL

☎ 0871 527 9298
Harbour Pde SO15 1ST
web: www.premierinn.com
dir: M27 junct 3, follow M271(S)/Southampton/The Docks signs, onto M271, at Redbridge rdbt onto A35 follow Southampton/The Docks/A3024 signs. Merge onto A35 (Redbridge Rd), continue onto Millbrook Flyover/A3024, right at West Quay Rd/A3057, left after Ikea into Harbour Parade

Rooms 155

SOUTH CAVE
East Riding of Yorkshire   **Map 17 SE93**

Cave Castle Hotel & Country Club

★★★ 73% HOTEL

☎ 01430 422245
Church Hill HU15 2EU
e-mail: info@cavecastlehotel.com
web: www.cavecastlehotel.com
dir: In village, opposite school

This beautiful Victorian manor retains original turrets, stone features and much charm together with modern comforts and style. It stands in 150 acres of meadow and parkland that provide a peaceful setting. Bedrooms are a careful mix of traditional and contemporary styles. Public areas include a well-equipped leisure complex and pool.

Rooms 70 (14 GF) **Facilities** Spa Wi-fi ⓩ supervised ⌇ 18 Putt green Gym New Year **Conf** Class 150 Board 100 Thtr 250 **Services** Lift **Parking** 100 **Notes** ⊗ Civ Wed 150

SOUTH CERNEY
Gloucestershire   **Map 5 SU09**

Cotswold Water Park Four Pillars Hotel

★★★★ 79% HOTEL

☎ 0800 374692 & 01285 864000
Lake 6 Spine Road East GL7 5FP
e-mail: waterpark@four-pillars.co.uk
web: www.cotswoldwaterparkhotel.co.uk
dir: Off A419, 3m from Cirencester (NB for Sav Nav use GL7 5TL)

This impressive hotel has well-appointed bedrooms and suites, conference facilities for up to 800 delegates, a spa with an 11-metre pool, a gym, a hydro pool and treatment rooms. An excellent range of dining options is available. A large car park is provided.

Rooms 318 (57 fmly) (126 GF) ⏿ **S** £79-£129; **D** £99-£149 (incl. bkfst) **Facilities** Spa FTV Wi-fi ⓩ Fishing Gym Beauty treatment rooms & therapies

---

Steam room Sauna Xmas New Year **Conf** Class 204 Board 68 Thtr 370 Del from £125 to £175 **Services** Lift **Parking** 200 **Notes** LB ⊗ Civ Wed 370

SOUTHEND-ON-SEA
Essex   **Map 7 TQ88**

The Roslin Beach Hotel

★★★★ 77% ⊛ HOTEL

☎ 01702 586375
Thorpe Esplanade, Thorpe Bay SS1 3BG
e-mail: info@roslinhotel.com
web: www.roslinhotel.com
dir: A127, follow Southend-on-Sea signs. Hotel between Walton Rd & Clieveden Rd on seafront

This friendly hotel is situated at the quiet end of the esplanade, overlooking the beach and sea. The spacious bedrooms are pleasantly decorated and thoughtfully equipped; some rooms have superb sea views. Public rooms include a large lounge bar, the Mulberry Restaurant and a smart conservatory which overlooks the sea.

Rooms 57 (5 fmly) (7 GF) **Facilities** FTV Wi-fi Xmas New Year **Conf** Class 45 Board 39 Thtr 60 **Parking** 40 **Notes** ⊗ Civ Wed 25

Park Inn by Radisson Palace
park inn *by Radisson*

★★★ 78% HOTEL

☎ 01702 455100
Church Rd SS1 2AL
e-mail: info.southend-on-sea@rezidorparkinn.com
dir: From N: via A1, M11, M25, A27. Take M25 junct 29 for 32km, then follow signs for Southend. From S: via M25, Dartford Tunnel, A13. Take M25 junct 30 for 40km, then follow signs for Southend

This hotel, in the centre of the town's tourist area, offers comfortable and modern rooms to meet the needs of both leisure and business travellers; the front facing bedrooms have breathtaking sea views. The public areas include the all-day dining RBG Bar & Grill, both overlooking the mouth of the River Thames. There is a range of meeting rooms to cater for all occasions.

Rooms 137 (22 fmly) ⏿ **S** fr £89; **D** fr £89* **Facilities** STV FTV Wi-fi ⓩ Gym Xmas New Year **Conf** Class 90 Board 70 Thtr 280 Del from £145* **Services** Lift Air con **Notes** LB ⊗ Civ Wed 280

Westcliff Hotel

★★★ 75% HOTEL

☎ 01702 345247
Westcliff Pde, Westcliff-on-Sea SS0 7QW
e-mail: westcliff@zolahotels.com
dir: M25 junct 29, A127 towards Southend, follow signs for Cliffs Pavillion when approaching town centre

This impressive Grade II listed Victorian building is situated in an elevated position overlooking gardens and cliffs with views to the sea beyond. The spacious bedrooms are tastefully decorated and thoughtfully equipped; many have lovely sea views. Public rooms include a smart conservatory-style restaurant, a spacious lounge and a range of function rooms.

Rooms 55 (2 fmly) **Facilities** FTV Wi-fi ♫ Xmas New Year **Conf** Class 90 Board 64 Thtr 225 **Services** Lift **Notes** ⊗ Civ Wed 120

Camelia Hotel

★★★ Ⓐ HOTEL

☎ 01702 587917
176-178 Eastern Esplanade, Thorpe Bay SS1 3AA
e-mail: enquiries@cameliahotel.com
web: www.cameliahotel.com
dir: From A13 or A127 follow signs to Southend seafront; on seafront left, hotel 1m E of pier

Rooms 28 (8 annexe) (3 fmly) (8 GF) ⏿ **Facilities** FTV Wi-fi ⓩ New Year **Parking** 100 **Notes** ⊗

Premier Inn Southend Airport

BUDGET HOTEL

☎ 0871 527 9008
Thanet Grange SS2 6GB
web: www.premierinn.com
dir: At A127 & B1013 junct

High quality, budget accommodation ideal for both families and business travellers. Spacious, en suite bedrooms feature tea and coffee making facilities, and Freeview TV in most hotels. Internet access and Wi-fi are available for a small fee. The adjacent family restaurant features a wide and varied menu. See also the Hotel Groups pages.

Rooms 80

S

SOUTHEND-ON-SEA *continued*

Premier Inn Southend-on-Sea (Thorpe Bay)

BUDGET HOTEL

☎ 0871 527 9006
213 Eastern Esplanade SS1 3AD
web: www.premierinn.com
dir: Follow signs for A1159 (A13) Shoebury onto dual carriageway. At rdbt, follow signs for Thorpe Bay & seafront, at seafront turn right. Hotel on right

Rooms 43

SOUTH MIMMS SERVICE AREA (M25)
Hertfordshire
Map 6 TL20

Days Inn South Mimms - M25

BUDGET HOTEL

☎ 01707 665440
Bignells Corner, Potters Bar EN6 3QQ
e-mail: south.mimms@welcomebreak.co.uk
web: www.welcomebreak.co.uk
dir: M25 junct 23, at rdbt follow signs

This modern building offers accommodation in smart, spacious and well-equipped bedrooms, suitable for families and business travellers, and all with en suite bathrooms. Continental breakfast is available and other refreshments may be taken at the nearby family restaurant. See also the Hotel Groups pages.

Rooms 74 (56 fmly) (18 GF) (8 smoking)
S £39.95-£75.95; **D** £49.95-£75.95*

Premier Inn South Mimms/ Potters Bar

BUDGET HOTEL

☎ 0871 527 8990
Swanland Rd EN6 3NH
web: www.premierinn.com
dir: M25 junct 23 & A1 take services exit off main rdbt then 1st left & follow hotel signs

High quality, budget accommodation ideal for both families and business travellers. Spacious, en suite bedrooms feature tea and coffee making facilities, and Freeview TV in most hotels. Internet access and Wi-fi are available for a small fee. The adjacent family restaurant features a wide and varied menu. See also the Hotel Groups pages.

Rooms 142

SOUTH MOLTON
Devon
Map 3 SS72

The George Hotel

★★ 76% HOTEL

☎ 01769 572514
1 Broad St EX36 3AB
e-mail: info@georgehotelsouthmolton.co.uk
web: www.georgehotelsouthmolton.co.uk
dir: Exit A361 at rdbt signed South Molton, 1.5m to centre

Retaining many of its original features, this charming 17th-century hotel is situated in the centre of town. Providing comfortable accommodation, complemented by informal and friendly service to all guests including children, this hotel is an ideal base for touring the area. Regularly changing menus, featuring local produce, are offered in the both the restaurant and the bar, which also serves real ales.

Rooms 9 (1 fmly) ⚑ **S** £60-£65; **D** £85-£100 (incl. bkfst)* **Facilities** FTV Wi-fi ♬ **Conf** Class 30 Board 30 Thtr 100 Del from £90 to £110* **Parking** 12 **Notes** LB RS 1st wk Jan

---

SOUTH NORMANTON
Derbyshire
Map 16 SK45

The Derbyshire Hotel

★★★★ 73% HOTEL

PH principal hayley

☎ 01773 812000
Carter Lane East DE55 2EH
e-mail: reservations.derbyshire@principal-hayley.com
dir: M1 junct 28, E on A38 to Mansfield

Conveniently located by the motorway, this hotel offers comfortable accommodation and a relaxed informal atmosphere through the lounge bar and restaurant. The conference and meeting rooms are appointed to a smart modern standard; delegates also have use of on-site sauna, jacuzzi and steam room in the spa.

Rooms 157 (10 fmly) (61 GF) **Facilities** Spa STV Wi-fi ⬃ ⬃ Gym Steam room Sauna New Year **Conf** Class 120 Board 25 Thtr 250 **Parking** 220 **Notes** ⊗ Civ Wed 150

Premier Inn Mansfield

BUDGET HOTEL

☎ 0871 527 8758
Carter Lane East DE55 2EH
web: www.premierinn.com
dir: M1 junct 28, A38 signed Mansfield. Entrance 200yds on left

High quality, budget accommodation ideal for both families and business travellers. Spacious, en suite bedrooms feature tea and coffee making facilities, and Freeview TV in most hotels. Internet access and Wi-fi are available for a small fee. The adjacent family restaurant features a wide and varied menu. See also the Hotel Groups pages.

Rooms 82

SOUTHPORT
Merseyside
Map 15 SD31

Vincent Hotel

★★★★ 81% ⑧⑧ TOWN HOUSE HOTEL

☎ 01704 883800
98 Lord St PR8 1JR
e-mail: manager@thevincenthotel.com
dir: M58 junct 3, follow signs to Ormskirk & Southport

This stylish, boutique property occupies a prime location on Southport's famous boulevard. Bedrooms, some with views of the beach, are appointed to a high standard with oversized beds, extremely well stocked mini-bars and stylish en suites with deep tubs. Public areas include a trendy cocktail bar, an all-day dining concept. Friendly staff offer personalised service.

Rooms 59 (2 fmly) ⚑ **Facilities** Spa STV FTV Wi-fi ⬃ Gym **Conf** Class 96 Board 50 Thtr 196 Del from £135 to £175 **Services** Lift Air con **Parking** 50 **Notes** ⊗ Civ Wed 150

Best Western Royal Clifton Hotel & Spa

★★★ 74% HOTEL

☎ 01704 533771
Promenade PR8 1RB
e-mail: sales@royalclifton.co.uk
dir: Adjacent to Marine Lake

This grand, traditional hotel benefits from a prime location on the promenade. Bedrooms range in size and style, but all are comfortable and thoughtfully equipped. Public areas include the lively Bar C, the elegant Pavilion Restaurant and a modern, well-equipped leisure club. Extensive conference and banqueting facilities make this hotel a popular function venue.

Save on hotels. Book at **theAA.com/hotel**

SOU 435 **ENGLAND**

Rooms 120 (23 fmly) (6 GF) **Facilities** Spa STV Wi-fi ⌨ supervised Gym Hair & beauty Steam room Aromatherapy ♫ Xmas New Year **Conf** Class 100 Board 65 Thtr 250 **Services** Lift **Parking** 60 **Notes** ⊗ Civ Wed 150

Balmoral Lodge Hotel

★★ 74% HOTEL

☎ 01704 544298
41 Queens Rd PR9 9EX
e-mail: balmorallg@aol.com
dir: On edge of town on A565 (Preston road). E at rdbt at North Lord St, left at lights, hotel 200yds on left

Situated in a quiet residential area, this popular friendly hotel is ideally situated just 50 yards from Lord Street. Bedrooms are comfortably appointed and family rooms are available. In addition to the restaurant which offers freshly prepared dishes, there is a choice of lounges including a comfortable lounge bar.

Rooms 15 (4 annexe) (3 fmly) (4 GF) **S** £25-£45; **D** £40-£80 (incl. bkfst)* **Facilities** STV FTV Wi-fi ⌨ **Conf** Class 30 Board 30 Thtr 30 Del from £50 to £70* **Parking** 12 **Notes** LB

Premier Inn Southport Central

BUDGET HOTEL

☎ 0871 527 9012
Marine Dr PR8 1RY
web: www.premierinn.com
dir: From Southport follow Promenade & Marine Drive signs. Hotel at junct of Marine Parade & Marine Drive

High quality, budget accommodation ideal for both families and business travellers. Spacious, en suite bedrooms feature tea and coffee making facilities, and Freeview TV in most hotels. Internet access and Wi-fi are available for a small fee. The adjacent family restaurant features a wide and varied menu. See also the Hotel Groups pages.

Rooms 59

SOUTHSEA

See Portsmouth & Southsea

SOUTH SHIELDS
Tyne & Wear — Map 21 NZ36

Best Western Sea Hotel

★★★ 77% HOTEL

☎ 0191 427 0999
Sea Rd NE33 2LD
e-mail: info@seahotel.co.uk
dir: A1(M), past Washington Services onto A194. Then A183 through town centre along Ocean Rd. Hotel on seafront

Dating from the 1930s this long-established business hotel overlooks the boating lake and the Tyne estuary. Bedrooms are generally spacious and well equipped and include five annexe rooms with wheelchair access. A range of generously portioned meals is served in both the bar and restaurant.

Rooms 37 (5 annexe) (5 fmly) (5 GF) ⌨ **S** fr £71.50; **D** fr £82.50 (incl. bkfst)* **Facilities** STV Wi-fi ⌨ New Year **Conf** Class 100 Board 50 Thtr 200 **Parking** 70 **Notes** LB RS 26 Dec

Premier Inn South Shields (Port of Tyne)

BUDGET HOTEL

☎ 0871 527 8992
Hobson Av, Newcastle Rd NE34 9PQ
web: www.premierinn.com
dir: A1(M) onto A194(M). 2nd exit at rdbt into Leam Lane (A194). At next rdbt 2nd exit, next rdbt 3rd exit, next rdbt 2nd exit (A194), next rdbt 2nd exit. Hotel on left adjacent to Taybarns

High quality, budget accommodation ideal for both families and business travellers. Spacious, en suite bedrooms feature tea and coffee making facilities, and Freeview TV in most hotels. Internet access and Wi-fi are available for a small fee. The adjacent family restaurant features a wide and varied menu. See also the Hotel Groups pages.

Rooms 66

SOUTHWOLD
Suffolk — Map 13 TM57

Swan Hotel

★★★★ 78% ◉◉ HOTEL

☎ 01502 722186
Market Place IP18 6EG
e-mail: swan.hotel@adnams.co.uk
dir: A1095 to Southwold. Hotel in town centre. Parking via archway to left of building

A charming 17th-century coaching inn situated in the heart of this bustling town centre overlooking the market place. Public rooms feature an elegant restaurant, a comfortable drawing room, a cosy bar and a lounge where guests can enjoy afternoon tea. The spacious bedrooms are attractively decorated, tastefully furnished and thoughtfully equipped.

Rooms 42 (17 annexe) (11 fmly) (17 GF) ⌨ **Facilities** STV FTV Wi-fi HL Beauty treatment room Xmas New Year **Conf** Class 24 Board 12 Thtr 40 **Services** Lift **Parking** 42 **Notes** Civ Wed 60

The Blyth Hotel

★★ 85% ◉ SMALL HOTEL

☎ 01502 722632 & 0845 348 6867
Station Rd IP18 6AY
e-mail: reception@blythhotel.com
dir: A12 onto A1095 signed Southwold

Expect a warm welcome at this delightful family run hotel which is situated just a short walk from the town centre. The spacious public rooms include a smart residents' lounge, an open-plan bar and a large restaurant. Bedrooms are tastefully appointed with co-ordinated fabrics and have many thoughtful touches.

Rooms 13 ⌨ **S** £65-£85; **D** £95-£150 (incl. bkfst) **Facilities** FTV Wi-fi Xmas New Year **Conf** Class 20 Board 12 Thtr 20 Del from £95 to £150* **Parking** 8 **Notes** LB

S

SOUTHWOLD *continued*

The Crown

★★ 85% ⚙ HOTEL

☎ 01502 722275
90 High St IP18 6DP
e-mail: crown.hotel@adnams.co.uk
web: www.adnams.co.uk
dir: A12 onto A1095 to Southwold. Hotel on left in
High Street

A delightful old posting inn situated in the heart of
this bustling town. The property combines a pub, wine
bar and restaurant with superb accommodation. The
tastefully decorated bedrooms have attractive co-
ordinated soft furnishings and many thoughtful
touches. Public rooms feature an elegant lounge and
a back room bar serving traditional Adnams ales.

Rooms 14 (2 fmly) **Facilities** FTV Wi-fi Xmas New
Year **Conf** Board 8 **Parking** 23 **Notes** ⊗

Sutherland House

⚙ ⚙ RESTAURANT WITH ROOMS

☎ 01502 724544
56 High St IP18 6DN
e-mail: enquiries@sutherlandhouse.co.uk
web: www.sutherlandhouse.co.uk
dir: A1095 into Southwold, on High St on left after
Victoria St

A delightful 16th-century house situated in the heart
of the bustling town centre with a wealth of
character; there are oak beams, exposed brickwork,
open fireplaces and two superb ornate plasterwork
ceilings. The stylish bedrooms are tastefully
decorated, have co-ordinated fabrics and many
thoughtful touches. Public rooms feature a large
open-plan contemporary restaurant with plush
furniture.

Rooms 4 (1 fmly)

SPENNYMOOR   **Map 19 NZ23**
Co Durham

Best Western Whitworth Hall Hotel

★★★ 79% HOTEL

☎ 01388 811772
Whitworth Hall Country Park DL16 7QX
e-mail: enquiries@whitworthhall.co.uk
web: www.whitworthhall.co.uk
dir: A688 to Spennymoor, then Bishop Auckland. At
rdbt right to Middlestone Moor. Left at lights, hotel on
right

This hotel, peacefully situated in its own grounds in
the centre of the deer park, offers comfortable
accommodation. Spacious bedrooms, some with
excellent views, offer stylish and elegant decor. Public
areas include a choice of restaurants and bars, a
bright conservatory and well-equipped function and
conference rooms.

Rooms 29 (4 fmly) (17 GF) **S** £55-£85; **D** £55-£85*
Facilities FTV Wi-fi ⌦ Fishing **Conf** Class 40 Board 30
Thtr 100 Del from £120 to £145* **Parking** 100
Notes LB ⊗ Civ Wed 120

STAFFORD   **Map 10 SJ92**
Staffordshire

The Moat House

★★★★ 82% ⚙ ⚙ HOTEL

☎ 01785 712217
Lower Penkridge Rd, Acton Trussell ST17 0RJ
e-mail: info@moathouse.co.uk
web: www.moathouse.co.uk
dir: M6 junct 13 onto A449 through Acton Trussell.
Hotel on right on exiting village

This 17th-century timbered building, with an idyllic
canal-side setting, has been skilfully extended.
Bedrooms are stylishly furnished, well equipped and
comfortable. The bar offers a range of snacks and the
restaurant boasts a popular fine dining option where
the head chef displays his skills using top quality
produce.

Rooms 41 (4 fmly) (15 GF) **Facilities** Wi-fi New Year
Conf Class 60 Board 50 Thtr 200 **Services** Lift
Parking 200 **Notes** ⊗ Closed 25 Dec Civ Wed 150

Tillington Hall Hotel

★★★ 73% HOTEL

☎ 01785 253531
Eccleshall Rd ST16 1JJ
e-mail: reservations@tillingtonhall.co.uk
web: www.tillingtonhall.co.uk
dir: M6 junct 14, A5013 towards Stafford. Hotel 0.5m
on left

Located close to the M6, this modern hotel is ideal for
both business and leisure guests. There is a spacious
restaurant, relaxing coffee lounge and smart bar.
There is a range of function rooms for meetings and
events, including the new Garden Suite.
Complimentary Wi-fi access is available.

Rooms 91 **Facilities** STV Wi-fi **Conf** Class 150
Board 75 Thtr 300 **Services** Lift **Parking** 200
Notes ⊗ Civ Wed 300

Abbey Hotel

THE INDEPENDENTS
HOTEL ASSOCIATION

★★ 74% HOTEL

☎ 01785 258531
65-68 Lichfield Rd ST17 4LW
web: www.abbeyhotelstafford.co.uk
dir: M6 junct 13 towards Stafford. Right at Esso
garage, to mini-rdbt, follow Silkmore Lane to 2nd
rdbt. Hotel 0.25m on right

This friendly privately owned and personally run hotel
provides well-equipped accommodation and is
particularly popular with commercial visitors. Family
rooms are available. Facilities here include a choice
of lounges and the spacious car park proves a real
benefit to guests.

Rooms 17 (3 fmly) **Facilities** FTV Wi-fi **Parking** 21
Notes ⊗ Closed 22 Dec-7 Jan

Holiday Inn Express Stafford M6 Jct 13

BUDGET HOTEL

☎ 01785 212244
Acton Gate, Acton Court ST18 9AP
e-mail: stafford@morethanhotels.com
web: www.hiexpress.com/stafford
dir: M6 junct 13. Hotel on A449 towards Stafford

A modern hotel ideal for families and business
travellers. Fresh and uncomplicated, the spacious
rooms include Sky TV, power shower and tea and
coffee-making facilities. Continental buffet breakfast
is included in the room rate; other meals may be
taken at the nearby family pub or restaurant. See also
the Hotel Groups pages.

Rooms 103 ⌦ **Conf** Class 20 Board 20 Thtr 40

S

Save on hotels. Book at **theAA.com/hotel**

SOU – STA 437 ENGLAND

Premier Inn Stafford North (Hurricane)

BUDGET HOTEL

☎ 0871 527 9030
1 Hurrican Close ST16 1GZ
web: www.premierinn.com
dir: M6 junct 14, A34 towards Stafford. Hotel approx 2m NW of town centre

High quality, budget accommodation ideal for both families and business travellers. Spacious, en suite bedrooms feature tea and coffee making facilities, and Freeview TV in most hotels. Internet access and Wi-fi are available for a small fee. The adjacent family restaurant features a wide and varied menu. See also the Hotel Groups pages.

Rooms 96

Premier Inn Stafford North (Spitfire)

BUDGET HOTEL

☎ 0871 527 9032
1 Spitfire Close ST16 1GX
web: www.premierinn.com
dir: M6 junct 14, A34 N. Hotel approx 1m on left

Rooms 60

STAINES-UPON-THAMES Map 6 TQ07
Surrey

Mercure London Staines Thames Lodge

★★★ 75% HOTEL

☎ 01784 464433
Thames St TW18 4SJ
e-mail: h6620@accor.com
web: www.mercure.com
dir: M25 junct 13. Follow A30/town centre signs (bus station on right). Hotel straight ahead

Located on the banks of the River Thames in a bustling town, this hotel is well positioned for both business and leisure travellers. Meals are served in the Riverside Restaurant, and snacks are available in the spacious lounge/bar; weather permitting the terrace provides a good place for a drink on a summer evening. Onsite parking is an additional bonus.

Rooms 88 (17 fmly) (31 GF) **Facilities** STV FTV Wi-fi Moorings Xmas New Year **Conf** Class 40 Board 20 Thtr 40 **Parking** 40

STAMFORD Map 11 TF00
Lincolnshire

The William Cecil

★★★★ 81% ◉ HOTEL

☎ 01780 750070
High St PE9 2LG
e-mail: enquiries@thewilliamcecil.co.uk
dir: Exit A1 signed Stamford & Burghley Park. Hotel 1st building on right on entering town

This is a lovely refurbished property is situated on the edge of town within the Burghley Estate. The stylish bedrooms are spacious, individually decorated and have lots of extra little touches. The public rooms include a lounge bar with plush seating and a panelled restaurant; a smart terrace is available for alfresco dining when the weather permits.

Rooms 27 (2 fmly) (5 GF) ✱ **S** £110-£160; **D** £130-£170 (incl. bkfst)* **Facilities** FTV Wi-fi ♨ Xmas New Year **Conf** Class 60 Board 40 Thtr 120 Del from £130 to £150* **Parking** 80 **Notes** LB Civ Wed 120

The George of Stamford

★★★★ 77% ◉ HOTEL

☎ 01780 750750 & 750700 (res)
71 St Martins PE9 2LB
e-mail: reservations@georgehotelofstamford.com
web: www.georgehotelofstamford.com
dir: A1, 15m N of Peterborough onto B1081, hotel 1m on left

Steeped in hundreds of years of history, this delightful coaching inn provides spacious public areas that include a choice of dining options, inviting, lounges, a business centre and a range of quality shops. A highlight is afternoon tea, taken in the colourful courtyard when the weather permits. Bedrooms are stylishly appointed and range from traditional to contemporary in design.

Rooms 47 (24 fmly) **S** £95-£100; **D** £150-£280 (incl. bkfst)* **Facilities** STV Wi-fi ♨ ⚓ Complimentary membership to local gym Xmas New Year **Conf** Class 25 Board 25 Thtr 50 Del from £150 to £180* **Parking** 110 **Notes** LB Civ Wed 50

Crown Hotel

★★★ 82% HOTEL

☎ 01780 763136
All Saints Place PE9 2AG
e-mail: reservations@thecrownhotelstamford.co.uk
web: www.thecrownhotelstamford.co.uk
dir: A1 onto A43, through town to Red Lion Sq, hotel behind All Saints Church

This small, privately owned hotel where hospitality is spontaneous and sincere, is ideally situated in the town centre. Unpretentious British food is served in the modern dining areas and the spacious bar is popular with locals. Bedrooms are appointed to a very high standard being quite contemporary in style and very well equipped; some have four-poster beds. Additional 'superior' rooms are located in a renovated Georgian town house just a short walk up the street.

Rooms 28 (10 annexe) (1 fmly) (1 GF) ✱ **S** £95-£120; **D** £100-£160 (incl. bkfst)* **Facilities** FTV Wi-fi ♨ Use of local health/gym club Xmas New Year **Conf** Class 12 Board 12 Thtr 20 Del from £140 to £180* **Parking** 21 **Notes** LB ⊗

Candlesticks

RESTAURANT WITH ROOMS

☎ 01780 764033
1 Church Ln PE9 2JU
e-mail: info@candlestickshotel.co.uk
dir: B1081 into Stamford. Left onto A43. Right into Worthorpe Rd, right into Church Lane

Candlesticks is a 17th-century property situated in a quiet lane in the oldest part of Stamford just a short walk from the centre of town. The bedrooms are pleasantly decorated and equipped with a good range of useful extras. Public rooms feature Candlesticks restaurant, a small lounge and a cosy bar.

Rooms 8

S

STANDISH
Greater Manchester Map 15 SD51

Premier Inn Wigan North
BUDGET HOTEL

☎ 0871 527 9166
Almond Brook Rd WN6 0SS
web: www.premierinn.com
dir: M6 junct 27 follow signs for Standish. Left at T-junct, then 1st right

High quality, budget accommodation ideal for both families and business travellers. Spacious, en suite bedrooms feature tea and coffee making facilities, and Freeview TV in most hotels. Internet access and Wi-fi are available for a small fee. The adjacent family restaurant features a wide and varied menu. See also the Hotel Groups pages.

Rooms 36

STANLEY
Co Durham Map 19 NZ15

Best Western Beamish Hall Hotel
★★★★ 73% COUNTRY HOUSE HOTEL

☎ 01207 233733
Beamish DH9 0YB
e-mail: info@beamish-hall.co.uk
dir: A693 to Stanley. Follow signs for hotel & Beamish Museum. Left at museum entrance. Hotel on left 0.2m after golf club

This hotel is set in 24 acres of impeccably maintained grounds and can trace its history back many centuries. The public areas are elegant, with leather suites and wooden floors. The beautifully decorated dining room gives that real feel of grandeur with high ceilings and wonderful views of the gardens. All the bedrooms are stylishly designed and well equipped, and include larger rooms that have jacuzzi baths and separate showers; some of the premier rooms are interconnecting, and there is also a two bedroom apartment with its own kitchen and family room.

Rooms 42 (18 fmly) (4 GF) **Facilities** STV FTV Wi-fi ⌕ Xmas New Year **Conf** Class 160 Board 160 Thtr 300 Del from £105 to £165* **Services** Lift **Parking** 300 **Notes** ⊗ Civ Wed 200

STANSTED AIRPORT
Essex Map 6 TL52

See also Birchanger Green Motorway Service Area (M11)

Radisson Blu Hotel London Stansted Airport

★★★★ 78% HOTEL

☎ 01279 661012
Waltham Close, Stansted Airport CM24 1PP
e-mail: info.stansted@radissonblu.com
web: www.radissonblu.co.uk/hotel-stanstedairport
dir: M11 junct 8 onto A120. Follow London Stansted Airport signs

This modern glass-fronted hotel, linked to the airport terminal by a covered walkway, is particularly well appointed. Facilities include a wide choice of restaurants, a smart leisure club and spa, extensive conference and meeting rooms, and the much talked about wine tower, complete with wine angels. Bedrooms follow a contemporary theme and include a host of thoughtful extras.

Rooms 500 (42 fmly) (51 smoking) **Facilities** Spa STV FTV Wi-fi ⌕ ☜ Gym Steam room Sauna Solarium ♫ Xmas New Year **Conf** Class 180 Board 36 Thtr 400 **Services** Lift Air con **Parking** 220 **Notes** ⊗

STANTON ST QUINTIN
Wiltshire Map 4 ST97

Stanton Manor Hotel
★★★ 79% ◉ HOTEL

☎ 01666 837552
SN14 6DQ
e-mail: reception@stantonmanor.co.uk
web: www.stantonmanor.co.uk
dir: M4 junct 17, A429 Malmesbury/Cirencester, 200yds, 1st left signed Stanton St Quintin, hotel entrance on left after church

Set in five acres of lovely gardens that includes a short golf course, this charming manor house, mentioned in the Domesday Book, has easy access to the M4. Public areas are a delight offering both character and comfort. The restaurant offers a short carte of imaginative dishes and an interesting wine selection.

Rooms 23 (4 fmly) (8 GF) ♞ **S** £89-£99; **D** £95-£150 (incl. bkfst)* **Facilities** Wi-fi ⌕ Xmas New Year **Conf** Class 40 Board 32 Thtr 80 Del from £140 to £159 **Parking** 60 **Notes** Civ Wed 120

STEEPLE ASTON
Oxfordshire Map 11 SP42

The Holt Hotel
★★★ 73% HOTEL

☎ 01869 340259
Oxford Rd OX25 5QQ
e-mail: info@holthotel.co.uk
web: www.holthotel.co.uk
dir: At junct of B4030 & A4260

This attractive former coaching inn has given hospitality to many over the centuries, not least to Claude Duval, a notorious 17th-century highwayman. Today guests are offered well-equipped, modern bedrooms and attractive public areas, which include a relaxing bar, restaurant and a well-appointed lounge. A selection of meeting rooms is available.

Rooms 86 (19 fmly) (20 GF) (8 smoking) **S** £58.80-£82.80; **D** £70.80-£94.80 (incl. bkfst)* **Facilities** FTV Wi-fi Xmas New Year **Conf** Class 57 Board 32 Thtr 140 Del from £120 to £140* **Parking** 200 **Notes** Civ Wed 120

STEVENAGE
Hertfordshire Map 12 TL22

Holiday Inn Stevenage
★★★★ 73% HOTEL

☎ 01438 722727 & 346060
St George's Way SG1 1HS
e-mail: reservations@histevenage.com
dir: A1(M) junct 7 take A602 to Stevenage, across 1st rdbt, 1st exit at 2nd rdbt, 2nd exit at next rdbt along St George's Way. Hotel 100yds on right

Situated in the heart of the town centre and just 25 minutes from central London by train. Bedrooms are air conditioned and well equipped; ideal for business and leisure travellers. Public areas are smart, capacious and stylish, and as well as a comfortable bar and restaurant, there is a mini gym. Parking is limited.

Rooms 140 (8 fmly) **Facilities** STV FTV Wi-fi ⌕ Gym Xmas New Year **Conf** Class 180 Board 190 Thtr 400 **Services** Lift Air con **Parking** 23 **Notes** Civ Wed 400

Novotel Stevenage

★★★ 78% HOTEL

☎ 01438 346100
Knebworth Park SG1 2AX
e-mail: H0992@accor.com
web: www.novotel.com
dir: A1(M) junct 7, at entrance to Knebworth Park

Ideally situated just off the A1(M) is this purpose built hotel, which is a popular business and conference venue. Bedrooms are pleasantly decorated and equipped with a good range of useful extras. Public rooms include a large open plan lounge bar serving a range of snacks, and a smartly appointed restaurant.

Rooms 101 (20 fmly) (30 GF) **S** fr £49; **D** fr £49 **Facilities** STV Wi-fi ॐ Use of local health club New Year **Conf** Class 80 Board 70 Thtr 150 **Services** Lift **Parking** 120 **Notes** LB Civ Wed 120

Best Western Roebuck Inn

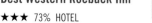

★★★ 73% HOTEL

☎ 01438 365445 & 365653
London Rd, Broadwater SG2 8DS
e-mail: hotel@roebuckinn.com
dir: A1(M) junct 7, right towards Stevenage. At 2nd rdbt take 2nd exit signed Roebuck-London/ Knebworth/B197. Hotel in 1.5m

Suitable for both the business and leisure traveller, this hotel provides spacious contemporary accommodation in well-equipped bedrooms. The older part of the building, where there is a restaurant and a cosy public bar with log fire and real ales, dates back to the 15th century.

Rooms 26 (8 fmly) (13 GF) ☞ **Facilities** STV FTV Wi-fi ॐ Xmas New Year **Conf** Class 20 Board 30 Thtr 50 Del from £125 to £175* **Parking** 50 **Notes** ⊗

Holiday Inn Express Stevenage

BUDGET HOTEL

☎ 01438 344300
Danestreet SG1 1XB
e-mail: gsm@hiexpressstevenage.co.uk
web: www.hiexpressstevenage.co.uk
dir: A1(M) junct 7, A72, bear left, 3rd exit onto A1070, then 2nd exit to Danestrete

A modern hotel ideal for families and business travellers. Fresh and uncomplicated, the spacious rooms include Sky TV, power shower and tea and coffee-making facilities. Continental buffet breakfast is included in the room rate; other meals may be taken at the nearby family pub or restaurant. See also the Hotel Groups pages.

Rooms 129 (100 fmly) (5 GF) (23 smoking) ☞ **S** fr £39; **D** fr £39 (incl. bkfst)* **Conf** Class 30 Board 20 Thtr 40

Ibis Stevenage Centre

BUDGET HOTEL

☎ 01438 779955
Danestrete SG1 1EJ
e-mail: H2794@accor.com
web: www.ibishotel.com
dir: In town centre adjacent to Tesco & Westgate multi storey car park

Modern, budget hotel offering comfortable accommodation in bright and practical bedrooms. Breakfast is self-service and dinner is available in the restaurant. See also the Hotel Groups pages.

Rooms 98 ☞ **S** £40-£75; **D** £40-£100*

Premier Inn Stevenage Central

BUDGET HOTEL

☎ 0871 527 9034
Six Hills Way, Horizon Technology Park SG1 2DD
web: www.premierinn.com
dir: A1(M) junct 7, follow Stevenage signs. Left into Gunnels Wood Rd. (NB do not use underpass). Left at next rdbt. Hotel in Horizon Technology Park on left

High quality, budget accommodation ideal for both families and business travellers. Spacious, en suite bedrooms feature tea and coffee making facilities, and Freeview TV in most hotels. Internet access and Wi-fi are available for a small fee. The adjacent family restaurant features a wide and varied menu. See also the Hotel Groups pages.

Rooms 115

Premier Inn Stevenage North

BUDGET HOTEL

☎ 0871 527 9036
Corey's Mill Ln SG1 4AA
web: www.premierinn.com
dir: A1(M) junct 8, at intersection with A602 (Hitchin Rd & Corey's Mill Lane)

Rooms 41

STEYNING　　　**Map 6 TQ11**
West Sussex

Best Western Old Tollgate Hotel & Restaurant

★★★ 78% HOTEL

☎ 01903 879494
The Street, Bramber BN44 3WE
e-mail: info@oldtollgatehotel.com
web: www.oldtollgatehotel.com
dir: From A283 at Steyning rdbt to Bramber. Hotel 200yds on right

As its name suggests, this well-presented hotel is built on the site of the old toll house. The spacious bedrooms are smartly designed and are furnished to a high standard; eight rooms are air conditioned and have smart power showers. Open for both lunch and dinner, the popular carvery-style restaurant offers an extensive choice of dishes.

Rooms 38 (28 annexe) (5 fmly) (14 GF) ☞ **Facilities** STV Wi-fi ॐ HL New Year **Conf** Class 32 Board 24 Thtr 50 Del from £119 to £144* **Services** Lift **Parking** 60 **Notes** ⊗ Civ Wed 70

S

STILLINGTON — Map 19 SE56
North Yorkshire

The Baytree

◉ RESTAURANT WITH ROOMS

☎ 01347 811394
High St YO61 1JU
e-mail: info@baytreestillington.com
web: www.baytreestillington.com
dir: A19 into Tollerton Rd (signed Huby, Public
Weighbridge, Sutton Park). In Huby left into Main St,
right into Stillington Rd. 1m, right into Roseberry Ln.
0.5m, left into Carr Ln (B1363), right into Main St

Just a 20-minute drive from York, The Baytree enjoys
a quiet country village location. It is spacious with
comfortable seating, a large conservatory restaurant,
and a small, private dining area - perfect for small
parties. The bar has open fires, stone-flagged floors
and a great ambiance. The accommodation includes
rooms suitable for families. The award-winning food
is the highlight of any stay; the outside eating areas
are delightful, and even if it's chilly, there are patio
heaters.

Rooms 4 (2 fmly)

STILTON — Map 12 TL18
Cambridgeshire

Bell Inn Hotel

★★★ 81% ◉ HOTEL

☎ 01733 241066
Great North Rd PE7 3RA
e-mail: reception@thebellstilton.co.uk
web: www.thebellstilton.co.uk
dir: A1(M) junct 16, follow Stilton signs. Hotel in
village centre

This delightful inn is steeped in history and retains
many original features, with imaginative food served
in both the character village bar/brasserie and the
elegant beamed first floor restaurant; refreshments
can be enjoyed in the attractive courtyard and rear
gardens when weather permits. Individually designed
bedrooms are stylish and equipped to a high
standard.

Rooms 22 (3 annexe) (1 fmly) (3 GF) ✦ **S** fr £78;
D £105-£138 (incl. bkfst)* **Facilities** STV FTV Wi-fi
Conf Class 46 Board 50 Thtr 130 Del from £143*
Parking 30 **Notes** ⊗ Closed 25 Dec (pm) RS 26 Dec
(pm) Civ Wed 130

STOCK — Map 6 TQ69
Essex

Greenwoods Hotel Spa & Retreat

★★★★ 75% HOTEL

☎ 01277 829990 & 829205
Stock Rd CM4 9BE
e-mail: info@greenwoodshotel.co.uk
web: www.greenwoodshotel.co.uk
dir: A12 junct 16 take B1007 signed Billericay. Hotel
on right on entering village

Greenwoods is a beautiful 17th-century, Grade II
listed manor house set in extensive landscaped
gardens. All bedrooms are tastefully appointed, have
marble bathrooms and a wide range of extras; the
premier rooms have spa baths and antique beds. The
spa facilities are impressive offering the latest
beauty treatments, together with saunas, a jacuzzi,
steam rooms, a monsoon shower and a 20-metre
pool.

Rooms 39 (6 GF) ✦ **S** £149-£205; **D** £229-£290*
Facilities Spa STV FTV Wi-fi ⊗ Gym Steam room
Sauna Monsoon shower New Year **Conf** Class 70
Board 52 Thtr 110 Del from £165 to £195
Services Lift **Parking** 100 **Notes** ⊗ No children 16yrs
Closed 24-26 Dec & 1 Jan Civ Wed 110

STOCKPORT — Map 16 SJ89
Greater Manchester

See also Manchester Airport

Bredbury Hall Hotel & Country Club

★★★ 80% HOTEL

☎ 0161 430 7421
Goyt Valley, Bredbury SK6 2DH
e-mail: reservations@bredburyhallhotel.com
dir: M60 junct 25 signed Bredbury, right at lights, left
onto Osbourne St, hotel 500mtrs on right

With views over open countryside, this large, modern
hotel is conveniently located for the M60. The well-
equipped bedrooms are spacious and comfortable,
and the restaurant serves a very wide range of freshly
prepared dishes. Additional facilities include a fitness
suite, complimentary Wi-fi and conference rooms
accommodating up to 200 delegates.

Rooms 148 (2 fmly) (50 GF) ✦ **Facilities** STV FTV
Wi-fi ⊗ Fishing Gym Night club (Fri & Sat eve) ♪
Xmas New Year **Conf** Class 120 Board 60 Thtr 200
Del from £120 to £125* **Services** Lift **Parking** 450
Notes ⊗ Civ Wed 80

Alma Lodge Hotel

★★★ 74% HOTEL

☎ 0161 483 4431
149 Buxton Rd SK2 6EL
e-mail: reception@almalodgehotel.com
web: www.almalodgehotel.com
dir: M60 junct 1 at rdbt take 2nd exit under rail
viaduct at lights opposite. At Debenhams turn right
onto A6. Hotel approx 1.5m on left

A large hotel located on the main road close to the
town, offering modern and well-equipped bedrooms.
It is family owned and run and serves a good range of
quality Italian cooking in Luigi's restaurant. Good
function rooms and free internet access are also
available.

Rooms 52 (32 annexe) (2 fmly) **S** £47-£65; **D** £65-£75
(incl. bkfst) **Facilities** FTV Wi-fi **Conf** Class 100
Board 60 Thtr 250 **Parking** 120 **Notes** ⊗ RS BHs
Civ Wed 200

Save on hotels. Book at **theAA.com/hotel**

STI – STO 441 ENGLAND

The Wycliffe Hotel

★★★ 74% HOTEL

☎ 0161 477 5395

74 Edgeley Rd, Edgeley SK3 9NQ

e-mail: reception@wycliffe-hotel.com

web: www.wycliffe-hotel.com

dir: M60 junct 2, follow A560 Stockport signs, right at
1st lights, hotel 0.5m on left

A family-run hotel close to the town centre and also
convenient for Manchester airport. The contemporary
bedrooms are very well maintained and equipped,
with LCD TVs and data ports provided. There is a well
stocked bar and a popular restaurant where the menu
has an Italian bias. There is also a large car park.

Rooms 14 (3 fmly) (2 GF) **S** £67.50-£78; **D** £73-£89
(incl. bkfst)* **Facilities** FTV Wi-fi **Conf** Class 20
Board 20 Thtr 30 Del from £100* **Parking** 46
Notes ⊗ Closed 25-27 Dec RS BHs

Premier Inn Manchester Airport Heald Green

BUDGET HOTEL

☎ 0871 527 8734

Finney Ln, Heald Green SK8 3QH

web: www.premierinn.com

dir: M56 junct 5 follow signs to Terminal 1, at rdbt
take 2nd exit, at next rdbt follow Cheadle signs. Left
at lights, right at next lights

High quality, budget accommodation ideal for both
families and business travellers. Spacious, en suite
bedrooms feature tea and coffee making facilities,
and Freeview TV in most hotels. Internet access and
Wi-fi are available for a small fee. The adjacent
family restaurant features a wide and varied menu.
See also the Hotel Groups pages.

Rooms 66

Premier Inn Stockport Central

BUDGET HOTEL

☎ 0871 527 9040

Churchgate SK1 1YG

web: www.premierinn.com

dir: M60 junct 27, A626 towards Marple. Right at
Spring Gardens

Rooms 46

Premier Inn Stockport South

BUDGET HOTEL

☎ 0871 527 9042

Buxton Rd, Heaviley SK2 6NB

web: www.premierinn.com

dir: On A6, 1.5m from town centre

Rooms 40

STOCKTON-ON-TEES   **Map 19 NZ41**
Co Durham

Best Western Parkmore Hotel & Leisure Club

★★★ 79% HOTEL

☎ 01642 786815

636 Yarm Rd, Eaglescliffe TS16 0DH

e-mail: enquiries@parkmorehotel.co.uk

dir: Exit A19 at Crathorne, A67 to Yarm. Through
Yarm right onto A135 to Stockton. Hotel 1m on left

Set in its own gardens, this smart hotel has grown
from its Victorian house origins to provide stylish
public areas, as well as extensive leisure and beauty
facilities including a hydrotherapy pool and
conference facilities. The well-equipped bedrooms
include junior suites. The restaurant known as
J's@636 has a reputation for creative meals. Service
is friendly and obliging.

Rooms 55 (8 fmly) (9 GF) **Facilities** Spa STV Wi-fi ⏱
supervised Gym Beauty salon Badminton Aerobics
studio Hydrotherapy Xmas New Year **Conf** Class 40
Board 40 Thtr 130 **Parking** 90 **Notes** Civ Wed 130

Premier Inn Stockton-on-Tees/ Hartlepool

BUDGET HOTEL

☎ 0871 527 9044

Coal Ln, Wolviston TS22 5PZ

web: www.premierinn.com

dir: A1(M) junct 60, A689, follow Teeside then
Hartlepool signs. Hotel on left at A89 & A19 junct

High quality, budget accommodation ideal for both
families and business travellers. Spacious, en suite
bedrooms feature tea and coffee making facilities,
and Freeview TV in most hotels. Internet access and
Wi-fi are available for a small fee. The adjacent
family restaurant features a wide and varied menu.
See also the Hotel Groups pages.

Rooms 49

Premier Inn Stockton-on-Tees/ Middlesbrough

BUDGET HOTEL

☎ 0871 527 9048

Whitewater Way, Thornaby TS17 6QB

web: www.premierinn.com

dir: A19, A66 towards Stockton & Darlington. Take 1st
exit signed Teeside Park/Teesdale. Right at lights over
viaduct bridge rdbt & Tees Barrage

Rooms 62

Premier Inn Stockton-on-Tees West

BUDGET HOTEL

☎ 0871 527 9046

Yarm Rd TS18 3RT

web: www.premierinn.com

dir: A1(M) junct 60, A689 towards Teeside. Follow
Hartlepool signs. Hotel on left at A689 & A19
interchange

Rooms 40

STOKE-BY-NAYLAND   **Map 13 TL93**
Suffolk

The Crown

★★★ 86% ◉◉ SMALL HOTEL

☎ 01206 262001 & 262346

CO6 4SE

e-mail: reservations@crowninn.net

web: www.crowninn.net

dir: Follow Stoke-by-Nayland signs from A12 & A134.
Hotel in village off B1068 towards Higham

Situated in a picturesque village this establishment,
with an award-winning restaurant, has a reputation
for making everyone feel welcome. It offers quiet,
individually decorated rooms that look out over the
countryside. Ground floor rooms, including three with
a terrace, are of a contemporary design while upstairs
rooms are in a country-house style; each room has
Wi-fi, DVDs and luxury toiletries.

Rooms 11 (1 fmly) (8 GF) ⏲ **S** £90-£220;
D £120-£220 (incl. bkfst)* **Facilities** FTV Wi-fi ⏱ New
Year **Conf** Board 10 Del from £162 to £174
Parking 49 **Notes** LB ⊗

S

STOKE D'ABERNON
Surrey   **Map 6 TQ15**

Woodlands Park Hotel

★★★★ 81% ◉◉ HOTEL

☎ 01372 843933 & 0845 072 7581
Woodlands Ln KT11 3QB
e-mail: woodlandspark@handpicked.co.uk
web: www.handpickedhotels.co.uk/woodlandspark
dir: A3 exit at Cobham. Through town centre & Stoke
D'Abernon, left at garden centre into Woodlands Lane,
hotel 0.5m on right

Originally built for the Bryant family, of the
matchmaker firm Bryant & May, this lovely Victorian
mansion enjoys an attractive parkland setting in ten
and a half acres of Surrey countryside. Bedrooms in
the wing are contemporary in style while those in the
main house are more traditionally decorated. The
hotel boasts two dining options, Benson's Brasserie
and the Oak Room Restaurant. Hand Picked Hotels –
AA Hotel Group of the Year 2012-13.

Rooms 57 (4 fmly) ☞ **S** £199; **D** £209 (incl. bkfst)*
Facilities STV Wi-fi HL ⚓ ⚓ Xmas New Year
Conf Class 20 Board 50 Thtr 150 Del £259*
Services Lift Air con **Parking** 150 **Notes** LB ⊗
Civ Wed 200

STOKE-ON-TRENT
Staffordshire   **Map 10 SJ84**

Quality Hotel Stoke
★★★ 74% HOTEL

☎ 01782 202361
66 Trinity St, Hanley ST1 5NB
e-mail: enquiries@qualityhotelsstoke.co.uk
dir: M6 junct 15(S)/16(N) then A500 to city centre &
Festival Park. A53 to Leek, keep in left lane, 3rd exit
at rdbt for Hanley/City Centre/Cultural Quarter. Hotel
on left at top of hill

This large city centre hotel provides a range of
bedrooms and extensive public areas including a
choice of popular bars. A well lit spacious car park
and modern leisure facilities are additional benefits.

Rooms 136 (8 annexe) (54 fmly) (5 GF)
Facilities Wi-fi ⓢ supervised Gym Sports massage
Hair salon Xmas New Year **Conf** Class 125 Board 60
Thtr 300 **Services** Lift **Parking** 150
Notes Civ Wed 250

Holiday Inn Express Stoke-on-Trent
BUDGET HOTEL

☎ 01782 377000
Sir Stanley Matthews Way, Trentham Lakes ST4 4EG
e-mail: info@expressstoke.co.uk
web: www.expressstoke.co.uk
dir: M6 junct 15, follow signs for Uttoxeter/Derby to
A50. Hotel adjacent to Britannia Stadium

A modern hotel ideal for families and business
travellers. Fresh and uncomplicated, the spacious
rooms include Sky TV, power shower and tea and
coffee-making facilities. Continental buffet breakfast
is included in the room rate; other meals may be
taken at the nearby family pub or restaurant. See also
the Hotel Groups pages.

Rooms 123 (73 fmly) (21 GF) ☞ **D** £49-£89 (incl.
bkfst)* **Conf** Class 16 Board 16 Thtr 35

Premier Inn Stoke (Trentham Gardens)

BUDGET HOTEL

☎ 9871 527 9050
Stone Rd, Trentham ST4 8JG
web: www.premierinn.com
dir: M6 junct 15, A500, follow Trentham signs. At rdbt
3rd exit onto A34, 2m to hotel on right in Trentham
Gardens

High quality, budget accommodation ideal for both
families and business travellers. Spacious, en suite
bedrooms feature tea and coffee making facilities,
and Freeview TV in most hotels. Internet access and
Wi-fi are available for a small fee. The adjacent
family restaurant features a wide and varied menu.
See also the Hotel Groups pages.

Rooms 119

Weathervane
OldEngl⚓sh
BUDGET HOTEL

☎ 01782 388799
Lysander Rd ST3 7WA
e-mail: 5305@greenking.co.uk
web: www.oldenglish.co.uk

A few minutes from the A50 and convenient for both
the city and industrial areas, this popular, modern
pub and restaurant, under the 'Hungry Horse' brand,
provides hearty, well-cooked food at reasonable
prices. Adjacent bedrooms are furnished for both
commercial and leisure customers.

Rooms 39 (8 fmly) (18 GF) **Conf** Class 20 Board 20
Thtr 20

STOKE POGES
Buckinghamshire   **Map 6 SU98**

Stoke Park
★★★★★ 85% ◉◉◉ HOTEL

☎ 01753 717171
Park Rd SL2 4PG
e-mail: info@stokepark.com
dir: M4 junct 6, A355 towards Slough, B416 (Park
Rd). Hotel 1.25m on right

Located within 350 acres of beautiful parkland
created by 'Capability' Brown and Humphry Repton,
this hotel offers outstanding leisure and sporting
facilities. Inside the stunning mansion house,
designed by George III's architect, the public areas
display lavish opulence throughout and the bedrooms
have a luxurious and classic feel. In contrast, the
Pavilion features more contemporary bedrooms and
public areas; here also are extensive state-of-the-art
health and beauty facilities. The hotel has a
championship golf course, tennis courts, and four
restaurants, including the award-winning Dining
Room and the more informal Italian brasserie, San
Marco. There are bars, lounges and meeting rooms as
well.

Rooms 49 (28 annexe) (6 fmly) ☞ **Facilities** Spa STV
FTV Wi-fi ⓢ ⚓ 27 ⚓ Putt green Fishing ⚓ Gym New
Year Child facilities **Conf** Class 30 Board 34 Thtr 80
Del £360* **Services** Lift **Parking** 460 **Notes** ⊗ Closed
24-26 Dec Civ Wed 120

Save on hotels. Book at **theAA.com/hotel**

STO 443 ENGLAND

Stoke Place

★★★★ 79% ◎ ◎ HOTEL

☎ 01753 534790
Stoke Green SL2 4HT
e-mail: enquiries@stokeplace.co.uk
dir: A355, right onto A4. At rdbt 2nd exit into Stoke
Rd. B416 to Stoke Green. Hotel 200mtrs

Originally built in 1690 and set in 26 acres of
'Capability' Brown designed gardens, this is a
delightful William and Mary style manor house. It
offers a range of stylish modern bedrooms that are
equipped to a very high standard; rear-facing rooms
have fantastic view of the garden. Guests can relax in
the peaceful lounge and enjoy afternoon tea if they
wish. The award-winning Garden Restaurant serves
imaginative dishes and the tranquil bar area is ideal
for post-dinner drinks.

Rooms 39 (15 annexe) (14 GF) ↟ **S** £130-£400;
D £130-£400 (incl. bkfst)* **Facilities** STV FTV Wi-fi ↧
Fishing ⬥ Gym Outdoor jogging track Bicycles Boule
pitch Giant kids' games Xmas New Year
Conf Class 100 Board 60 Thtr 200 Del from £230 to
£350* **Parking** 120 **Notes** LB ⊗ Civ Wed 150

STONE
Staffordshire
Map 10 SJ93

Stone House Hotel

★★★ 70% HOTEL

OXFORD
HOTELS & INNS

☎ 01785 815531 & 0844 414 6580
Stafford Rd ST15 0BQ
e-mail: reservations.stone@ohiml.com
web: www.oxfordhotelsandinns.com
dir: M6 junct 14 (N) or junct 15 (S). Hotel on A34

This former country house, set in attractive grounds,
is located within easy reach of the M6. Attractive
comfortable bedrooms and tastefully appointed
public areas together with leisure and conference
facilities make the hotel popular with both corporate
and leisure guests. A light menu is offered in the bar
and lounge areas, or guests can choose to dine in the
stylish restaurant.

Rooms 50 (1 fmly) (15 GF) **Facilities** FTV Wi-fi ⏣
supervised Gym New Year **Conf** Class 50 Board 40
Thtr 120 **Parking** 100 **Notes** ⊗ Civ Wed 60

STON EASTON
Somerset
Map 4 ST65

INSPECTORS' CHOICE

Ston Easton Park Hotel

★★★★ ◎ ◎ COUNTRY HOUSE HOTEL

☎ 01761 241631
BA3 4DF
e-mail: info@stoneaston.co.uk
web: www.stoneaston.co.uk
dir: On A37

Surrounded by The Mendips, this outstanding
Palladian mansion lies in extensive parklands that
were landscaped by Humphrey Repton. The
architecture and decorative features are stunning;
the state rooms include one of England's earliest
surviving Print Rooms, and the Palladian Saloon
considered one of Somerset's finest rooms. There is
even an Edwardian kitchen that guests might like
to take a look at. The helpful and attentive team
provide a very efficient service, and the award-
winning cuisine uses organic produce from the
hotel's own kitchen garden. The bedrooms and
bathrooms are all appointed to an excellent
standard.

Rooms 22 (3 annexe) (2 fmly) ↟ **S** £125-£250;
D £150-£490 (incl. bkfst)* **Facilities** FTV Wi-fi ↧ ⚘
Fishing ⬥ Archery Clay pigeon shooting Quad bikes
Hot air ballooning Xmas New Year **Conf** Class 60
Board 30 Thtr 100 Del from £150 to £250*
Parking 120 **Notes** LB Civ Wed 120

STOURPORT-ON-SEVERN
Worcestershire
Map 10 SO87

Menzies Stourport Manor

MenziesHotels

★★★★ 77% HOTEL

☎ 01299 289955
35 Hartlebury Rd DY13 9JA
e-mail: stourport@menzieshotels.co.uk
web: www.menzieshotels.co.uk
dir: M5 junct 6, A449 towards Kidderminster, B4193
towards Stourport. Hotel on right

Once the home of Prime Minister Sir Stanley Baldwin,
this much extended country house is set in attractive
grounds. A number of bedrooms and suites are
located in the original building, although the majority
are in a more modern, purpose-built section.
Spacious public areas include a range of lounges, a
popular restaurant, a leisure club and conference
facilities.

Rooms 68 (17 fmly) (31 GF) (10 smoking)
Facilities FTV Wi-fi ↧ ⚘ ⚘ Putt green Gym Squash
Xmas New Year **Conf** Class 110 Board 100 Thtr 400
Parking 300 **Notes** Civ Wed 300

STOWMARKET
Suffolk
Map 13 TM05

Cedars Hotel

THE INDEPENDENTS
HOTEL ASSOCIATION

★★★ 75% HOTEL

☎ 01449 612668
Needham Rd IP14 2AJ
e-mail: info@cedarshotel.co.uk
dir: A14 junct 15, A1120 towards Stowmarket. At
junct with A1113 turn right. Hotel on right

Expect a friendly welcome at this privately owned
hotel, which is situated just off the A14 within easy
reach of the town centre. Public rooms are full of
charm and character with features such as exposed
beams and open fireplaces. Bedrooms are pleasantly
decorated and thoughtfully equipped with modern
facilities.

Rooms 25 (3 fmly) (9 GF) ↟ **S** £69.50; **D** £77 (incl.
bkfst)* **Facilities** Wi-fi **Conf** Class 60 Board 40
Thtr 150 Del from £100* **Parking** 75 **Notes** LB Closed
25 Dec-1 Jan

S

STOW-ON-THE-WOLD
Gloucestershire
Map 10 SP12

Number Four at Stow Hotel & Restaurant

★★★★ 77% ◉◉ SMALL HOTEL

☎ 01451 830297
Fosseway GL54 1JX
e-mail: reservations@hotelnumberfour.co.uk

This hotel is situated in one of the most picturesque areas of the Cotswolds. Service is relaxed and friendly, and the bedrooms are very stylish and beautifully presented. The award-winning Cutler's Restaurant serves imaginative dishes using the finest in local produce. Public areas include a contemporary lounge area and a well-equipped business suite.

Rooms 18 (5 fmly) (12 GF) **S** fr £100; **D** fr £120 (incl. bkfst) **Facilities** FTV Wi-fi **Conf** Class 15 Board 28 Thtr 50 Del from £180* **Services** Air con **Parking** 50 **Notes** ⊗

The Wyck Hill House Hotel

★★★★ 74% ◉◉ HOTEL

☎ 01451 831936
Burford Rd GL54 1HY
e-mail: info.wyckhillhouse@bespokehotels.com
dir: Exit A429. Hotel 1m on right

This charming 18th-century house enjoys superb views across the Windrush Valley and is ideally positioned for a relaxing weekend exploring the Cotswolds. The spacious and thoughtfully equipped bedrooms provide high standards of comfort and quality, located both in the main house and also the original coach house. Elegant public rooms include a cosy bar, library and the magnificent front hall with crackling log fire. The imaginative cuisine makes extensive use of local produce.

Rooms 60 (4 GF) **Facilities** Spa FTV Wi-fi ⬥ Sauna Steam room Xmas New Year **Conf** Class 50 Board 50 Thtr 150 **Services** Lift **Parking** 100 **Notes** ⊗ Civ Wed 120

Fosse Manor

★★★ 80% ◉◉ HOTEL

☎ 01451 830354
GL54 1JX
e-mail: enquiries@fossemanor.co.uk
web: www.fossemanor.co.uk
dir: 1m S on A429, 300yds past junct with A424

Deriving its name from the historic Roman Fosse Way, this popular hotel is ideally situated for exploring the many delights of this picturesque area. Bedrooms, located both in the main building and the adjacent coach house, offer high standards of comfort and quality. Public areas include a small lounge, spacious bar and light and airy restaurant. Classy cuisine is on offer with quality produce used to create imaginative dishes.

Rooms 19 (8 annexe) (3 fmly) (5 GF) ⬥ **D** £80-£200 (incl. bkfst)* **Facilities** FTV Wi-fi ⬥ Xmas New Year **Conf** Class 40 Board 40 Thtr 100 Del from £125 to £140* **Parking** 30 **Notes** LB ⊗ Civ Wed 70

Stow Lodge Hotel

★★★ 77% SMALL HOTEL

☎ 01451 830485
The Square GL54 1AB
e-mail: enquiries@stowlodge.com
web: www.stowlodge.com
dir: In town centre

Situated in smart grounds, this family-run hotel has direct access to the market square and provides high standards of customer care. Bedrooms are offered both within the main building and in the converted coach house, all of which provide similar standards of homely comfort. Extensive menus and an interesting wine list make for an enjoyable dining experience.

Rooms 21 (10 annexe) (1 fmly) ⬥ **S** £70-£130; **D** £90-£170 (incl. bkfst)* **Facilities** Wi-fi **Parking** 30 **Notes** LB ⊗ No children 5yrs Closed Xmas-end Jan

Old Stocks Hotel

★★ 72% SMALL HOTEL

☎ 01451 830666
The Square GL54 1AF
e-mail: aa@oldstockshotel.co.uk
web: www.oldstockshotel.co.uk
dir: A429 to town centre

Overlooking the old market square, this Grade II listed, mellow Cotswold-stone building is a comfortable and friendly base from which to explore this picturesque area. There's lots of character throughout, and the bedrooms offer individuality and charm. Facilities include a guest lounge, restaurant and bar, whilst outside, the patio is a popular summer venue for refreshing drinks and good food.

Rooms 18 (3 annexe) (5 fmly) (4 GF) ⬥ **S** £40-£55; **D** £92-£112 (incl. bkfst)* **Facilities** FTV Wi-fi New Year **Parking** 10 **Notes** LB

STRATFORD-UPON-AVON
Warwickshire
Map 10 SP25

INSPECTORS' CHOICE

Ettington Park Hotel

HandPICKED HOTELS
BUILT FOR PLEASURE

★★★★ ◉◉
COUNTRY HOUSE HOTEL

☎ 01789 450123 & 0845 072 7454
CV37 8BU
e-mail: ettingtonpark@handpicked.co.uk
web: www.handpickedhotels.co.uk/ettingtonpark

(For full entry see Alderminster)

The Arden Hotel

★★★★ 83% ◉◉ HOTEL

☎ 01789 298682
Waterside CV37 6BA
e-mail: enquiries@theardenhotelstratford.com
web: www.theardenhotelstratford.com
dir: M40 junct 15 follow signs to town centre. At Barclays Bank rdbt left into High St, 2nd left into Chapel Lane. Hotel car park in 40yds

This property is on the same road as the world famous Royal Shakespeare and Swan theatres, and just a short walk from the town centre. The bedrooms and bathrooms have been tastefully designed and have quality fixtures and fittings. The dedicated team provide polite and professional service. Award-winning cuisine is served in the popular restaurant.

Rooms 45 (6 fmly) (17 GF) **Facilities** FTV Wi-fi Xmas New Year **Conf** Class 18 Board 28 Thtr 50 **Parking** 50 **Notes** ⊗ Civ Wed 50

Menzies Welcombe Hotel Spa & Golf Club

★★★★ 83% ◉◉ HOTEL

☎ 01789 295252
Warwick Rd CV37 0NR
e-mail: welcombe@menzieshotels.co.uk
web: www.menzieshotels.co.uk
dir: M40 junct 15, A46 towards Stratford-upon-Avon, at rdbt follow signs for A439. Hotel 3m on right

This Jacobean manor house is set in 157 acres of landscaped parkland. Public rooms are impressive, especially the lounge with its wood panelling and ornate marble fireplace, and the gentleman's club-style bar. Bedrooms in the original building are stylish and gracefully proportioned; those in the garden wing are comfortable and thoughtfully equipped. The spa development incorporates advanced, luxurious facilities and treatments.

Rooms 78 (12 fmly) (11 GF) (6 smoking)
Facilities Spa STV FTV Wi-fi ↕ ⓑ ♨ 18 ⚑ Putt green Gym Xmas New Year **Conf** Class 75 Board 40 Thtr 200 **Parking** 200 **Notes** ⊗ Civ Wed 120

Billesley Manor Hotel

★★★★ 79% ◉◉ HOTEL

☎ 01789 279955
Billesley, Alcester B49 6NF
e-mail: billesleymanor@pumahotels.co.uk
web: www.pumahotels.co.uk
dir: A46 towards Evesham. Over 3 rdbts, right for Billesley after 2m

This 16th-century manor is set in peaceful grounds and parkland with a delightful yew topiary garden and fountain. The spacious bedrooms and suites, most in traditional country-house style, are thoughtfully designed and well equipped. Conference facilities and some of the bedrooms are found in the cedar barns. Public areas retain many original features, such as oak panelling, fireplaces and exposed stone.

Rooms 72 (29 annexe) (5 GF) **Facilities** Spa ⓑ supervised ♨ ♨ Gym Steam room Beauty treatments Yoga studio Xmas New Year **Conf** Class 60 Board 50 Thtr 100 **Parking** 100 **Notes** Civ Wed 75

Macdonald Alveston Manor

★★★★ 79% ◉ HOTEL

☎ 0844 879 9138
Clopton Bridge CV37 7HP
e-mail: sales.alvestonmanor@macdonald-hotels.co.uk
web: www.macdonald-hotels.co.uk
dir: On rdbt south of Clopton Bridge

A striking red-brick and timbered façade, well-tended grounds, and a giant cedar tree all contribute to the charm of this well-established hotel, just five minutes from Stratford. The bedrooms vary in size and character - the coach house conversion offers an impressive mix of full and junior suites. The superb leisure complex offers a 20-metre swimming pool, steam room, sauna, a high-tech gym and a host of beauty treatments.

Rooms 113 (8 fmly) (45 GF) **Facilities** Spa FTV Wi-fi ⓑ supervised Gym Techno-gym Beauty treatments New Year **Conf** Class 80 Board 40 Thtr 140 **Services** Air con **Parking** 150 **Notes** Civ Wed 110

The Stratford

★★★★ 78% HOTEL

☎ 01789 271000 & 271007
Arden St CV37 6QQ
e-mail: thestratfordreservations@qhotels.co.uk
web: www.qhotels.co.uk
dir: A439 into Stratford. In town follow A3400/Birmingham, at lights left into Arden St, hotel 150yds on right

Situated adjacent to the hospital, this eye-catching modern hotel with its red-brick façade is within walking distance of the town centre. The hotel offers modern, well-equipped and spacious bedrooms. The open-plan public areas include a comfortable lounge, a small, atmospheric bar and a spacious restaurant with exposed beams.

Rooms 102 (7 fmly) (14 GF) **Facilities** STV Wi-fi ↕ Gym Free use of Stratford Manor's leisure facilities Xmas New Year **Conf** Class 66 Board 54 Thtr 132 **Services** Lift Air con **Parking** 92 **Notes** ⊗ Civ Wed 132

Stratford Manor

★★★★ 77% HOTEL

☎ 01789 731173
Warwick Rd CV37 0PY
e-mail: stratfordmanor@qhotels.co.uk
web: www.qhotels.co.uk
dir: M40 junct 15, A46 signed Stratford. At 2nd rdbt take A439 signed Stratford Town Centre. Hotel 1m on left. Or from Stratford centre take A439 signed Warwick & M40. Hotel 3m on right

Just outside Stratford, this hotel is set against a rural backdrop with lovely gardens and ample parking. Public areas include a stylish lounge bar and a contemporary restaurant. Service is both professional and helpful. Bedrooms are smartly appointed, spacious and have generously sized beds and a range of useful facilities. The leisure centre boasts a large indoor pool.

Rooms 104 (8 fmly) (24 GF) ↑ **Facilities** Spa Wi-fi ↕ ⓑ ♨ Gym Sauna Steam room Archery Falconry Xmas New Year **Conf** Class 120 Board 100 Thtr 350 **Del** from £125 to £169* **Services** Lift **Parking** 220 **Notes** Civ Wed 150

Holiday Inn Stratford-upon-Avon

★★★★ 74% HOTEL

☎ 0871 942 9270 & 01789 279988
Bridgefoot CV37 6YR
e-mail: histratford@qmh-hotels.com
web: www.holidayinn.co.uk
dir: A439 to Stratford-upon-Avon. On entering town bear left, hotel 200mtrs on left

This large modern hotel sits beside the River Avon in landscaped grounds and has ample parking. Bedrooms have a light contemporary feel and are equipped with a good range of facilities that include air conditioning and Wi-fi. Day rooms include a terrace lounge and bar, a carvery restaurant and the Club Moativation health and fitness facility that proves popular with both corporate and leisure guests.

Rooms 259 (8 fmly) **Facilities** STV Wi-fi ⓑ supervised Gym Sauna Steam room Solarium Beauty Salon Xmas New Year **Conf** Class 340 Board 42 Thtr 550 **Services** Lift Air con **Parking** 350 **Notes** ⊗

S

STRATFORD-UPON-AVON *continued*

Macdonald Swan's Nest Hotel

★★★★ 74% HOTEL

☎ 0844 879 9140
Bridgefoot CV37 7LT
e-mail: sales.swansnest@macdonald-hotels.co.uk
web: www.macdonald-hotels.co.uk/swansnest
dir: A439 towards Stratford, follow one-way system, left over bridge (A3400), hotel on right

Dating back to the 17th century, this hotel is said to be one of the earliest brick-built houses in Stratford. It occupies a prime position on the banks of the River Avon and is ideally situated for exploring the town. Bedrooms and bathrooms are appointed to a high standard with some thoughtful guest extras provided.

Rooms 68 (2 fmly) (25 GF) **Facilities** FTV Wi-fi Use of facilities at Macdonald Alveston Manor New Year **Conf** Class 100 Board 60 Thtr 150 **Parking** 80 **Notes** Civ Wed 150

The Legacy Falcon Hotel

★★★★ 73% HOTEL

☎ 08444 119005 & 0330 333 2805
Chapel St CV37 6HA
e-mail: res-falcon@legacy-hotels.co.uk
web: www.legacy-hotels.co.uk
dir: M40 junct 15, A46, A349, A3400 towards Stratford. Into one-way system into right lane marked Town Centre. At rdbt (Barclays Bank facing) left into High St. 2nd right into Scholars Lane

Situated in the heart of the town just a short walk from all the Shakespeare properties. The hotel dates back to 1500, and in the 17th century an extra storey was added. Bedrooms provide contemporary accommodation and the public areas are cosy. Service is provided by a friendly team. The restaurant provides good quality cuisine using fresh, local ingredients.

Rooms 83 (11 annexe) (6 fmly) (3 GF) 🐾 **Facilities** STV Wi-fi ♺ Xmas New Year **Conf** Class 80 Board 50 Thtr 150 **Services** Lift **Parking** 120 **Notes** Civ Wed 150

Mercure Stratford-upon-Avon Shakespeare Hotel

★★★★ 71% ⍟ HOTEL

☎ 01789 294997
Chapel St CV37 6ER
e-mail: h6630@accor.com
web: www.mercure.com
dir: M40 junct 15. Follow signs for Stratford town centre on A439. Follow one-way system into Bridge St. Left at rdbt, hotel 200yds on left opposite HSBC bank

Dating back to the early 17th century, The Shakespeare is one of the oldest hotels in this historic town. The hotel name represents one of the earliest exploitations of Stratford as the birthplace of one of the world's leading playwrights. With exposed beams and open fires, the public rooms retain an ambience reminiscent of this era. Bedrooms are appointed to a good standard and remain in keeping with the style of the property.

Rooms 78 (11 annexe) (3 GF) **S** £69-£149; **D** £79-£159 (incl. bkfst)* **Facilities** Wi-fi Xmas New Year **Conf** Class 45 Board 40 Thtr 90 **Services** Lift **Parking** 31 **Notes** LB Civ Wed 100

Best Western Grosvenor Hotel

★★★ 78% HOTEL

☎ 01789 269213
Warwick Rd CV37 6YT
e-mail: res@bwgh.co.uk
web: www.bwgh.co.uk
dir: M40 junct 15, follow Stratford signs to A439 (Warwick Rd). Hotel 7m, on one-way system

This hotel is a short distance from the town centre and many of the historic attractions. Bedroom styles and sizes vary, and the friendly staff offer an efficient service. Refreshments are served in the lounge all day, and room service is available. The Garden Room restaurant offers a choice of dishes from set priced and carte menus.

Rooms 73 (16 fmly) (25 GF) **Facilities** STV FTV Wi-fi ♺ Xmas New Year **Conf** Class 45 Board 50 Thtr 100 **Parking** 46 **Notes** ⊗ Civ Wed 100

Premier Inn Stratford-upon-Avon Central

BUDGET HOTEL

☎ 0871 527 9282
Payton Rd CV37 6UQ
web: www.premierinn.com
dir: A439, A4300 signed Stratford-upon-Avon. Hotel on left

High quality, budget accommodation ideal for both families and business travellers. Spacious, en suite bedrooms feature tea and coffee making facilities, and Freeview TV in most hotels. Internet access and Wi-fi are available for a small fee. The adjacent family restaurant features a wide and varied menu. See also the Hotel Groups pages.

Rooms 87

STREATLEY	Map 5 SU58
Berkshire	

The Swan at Streatley

★★★★ 73% ⍟⍟ HOTEL

☎ 01491 878800
High St RG8 9HR
e-mail: sales@swan-at-streatley.co.uk
web: www.swanatstreatley.co.uk
dir: From S right at lights in Streatley, hotel on left before bridge

A stunning location set beside the Thames, ideal for an English summer's day. The bedrooms are well appointed and many enjoy the lovely views. The hotel offers a range of facilities including meeting rooms, and the Magdalen Barge is moored beside the hotel making an unusual, yet perfect meeting venue. Motor launches are available for hire from April to October. The spa includes an indoor heated mineral pool and offers a range of treatments. Cuisine is accomplished and dining here should not be missed.

Rooms 45 (12 GF) **Facilities** Spa STV Wi-fi ♺ ⍟ supervised Fishing 🛶 Gym Electric motor launches for hire Apr-Oct Xmas New Year **Conf** Class 80 Board 60 Thtr 140 **Parking** 170 **Notes** Civ Wed 130

Save on hotels. Book at **theAA.com/hotel**

STR – STU 447 ENGLAND

STREET
Somerset   Map 4 ST43

Wessex Hotel

★★★ 64% HOTEL

☎ 01458 443383
High St BA16 0EF
e-mail: info@wessexhotel.com
dir: From A303, onto B3151 to Somerton. Then 7m, pass lights by Millfield School. Left at mini-rdbt

Centrally located in this popular town, with easy access to all the shops and attractions. The bedrooms and bathrooms vary slightly in size but most rooms provide good levels of quality and comfort. A wide range of snacks and refreshments is available throughout the day, including a regular carvery at dinner. Entertainment is often offered in the main season.

Rooms 51 (9 fmly) **Facilities** FTV Wi-fi ♫ Xmas New Year **Conf** Class 120 Board 80 Thtr 400 **Services** Lift **Parking** 70 **Notes** ⊗

STROUD
Gloucestershire   Map 4 SO80

The Bear of Rodborough

COTSWOLD
INNS & HOTELS

★★★ 80% HOTEL

☎ 01453 878522
Rodborough Common GL5 5DE
e-mail: info@bearofrodborough.info
web: www.cotswold-inns-hotels.co.uk/bear
dir: M5 junct 13, A419 to Stroud. Follow signs to Rodborough. Up hill, left at top at T-junct. Hotel on right

This popular 17th-century coaching inn is situated high above Stroud in acres of National Trust parkland. Character abounds in the lounges and cocktail bar, and in the Box Tree Restaurant where the cuisine utilises fresh local produce. Bedrooms offer equal measures of comfort and style with plenty of extra touches. There is also a traditional and well-patronised public bar. Cotswold Inns & Hotels — AA Small Hotel Group of the Year 2012-13.

Rooms 46 (2 fmly) **Facilities** STV Wi-fi Putt green ⛳ Xmas New Year **Conf** Class 35 Board 30 Thtr 60 **Parking** 70 **Notes** Civ Wed 70

Burleigh Court Hotel

★★★ 79% ◉◉ HOTEL

☎ 01453 883804
Burleigh, Minchinhampton GL5 2PF
e-mail: burleighcourt@aol.com
web: www.burleighcourthotel.co.uk
dir: From Stroud A419 towards Cirencester. Right after 2.5m signed Burleigh & Minchinhampton. Left after 500yds signed Burleigh Court. Hotel 300yds on right

Dating back to the 18th century, this former gentleman's manor house is in a secluded and elevated, though accessible, position with some wonderful countryside views. Public rooms are elegantly styled and include an oak-panelled bar for pre-dinner drinks beside a crackling fire. Combining comfort and quality, no two bedrooms are alike; some are in an adjoining coach house.

Rooms 18 (7 annexe) (2 fmly) (3 GF) 🐾 **S** £90-£125; **D** £140-£200 (incl. bkfst)* **Facilities** Wi-fi 🎣 ⛳ New Year Child facilities **Conf** Class 30 Board 30 Thtr 50 Del £280* **Parking** 40 **Notes** LB Closed 24-26 Dec Civ Wed 50

Premier Inn Stroud

Premier Inn

BUDGET HOTEL

☎ 0871 527 9052
Stratford Lodge, Stratford Rd GL5 4AF
web: www.premierinn.com
dir: M5 junct 13, A419 to town centre, follow Leisure Centre signs. Hotel adjacent to Tesco superstore

High quality, budget accommodation ideal for both families and business travellers. Spacious, en suite bedrooms feature tea and coffee making facilities, and Freeview TV in most hotels. Internet access and Wi-fi are available for a small fee. The adjacent family restaurant features a wide and varied menu. See also the Hotel Groups pages.

Rooms 32

STUDLEY
Warwickshire   Map 10 SP06

Best Western Studley Castle

Best Western

★★★ 74% HOTEL

☎ 01527 853111 & 855200
Castle Rd B80 7AJ
e-mail: bookings@studleycastle.com
dir: A435 S into Studley, left at castle sign, hotel 1m on right

This hotel has a delightful parkland location close to Stratford. Specialising in providing meeting room venues, the hotel has an impressive range of public areas. The restaurant also offers a relaxing environment and lovely views across the countryside. Bedrooms are available in a range of sizes and all are well equipped.

Rooms 57 (2 fmly) 🐾 **Facilities** STV Wi-fi Gym Sauna Xmas New Year **Conf** Class 66 Board 20 Thtr 150 **Services** Lift **Parking** 150 **Notes** Civ Wed 150

S

SUDBURY
Derbyshire   Map 10 SK13

The Boars Head Hotel

★★★ 75% HOTEL

☎ 01283 820344
Lichfield Rd DE6 5GX
e-mail: enquiries@boars-head-hotel.co.uk
web: www.boars-head-hotel.co.uk
dir: A50 onto A515 towards Lichfield, hotel 1m on right

This popular hotel offers comfortable accommodation in well-equipped bedrooms. There is a relaxed atmosphere in the public rooms, which consists of a several bars and dining options. The beamed lounge bar provides informal dining thanks to a popular carvery, while the restaurant and cocktail bar offer a more formal environment.

Rooms 23 (1 annexe) (14 GF) **Facilities** STV Wi-fi Beauty salon Xmas New Year **Parking** 85

See advert on page 109

SUNBURY
Surrey

See **LONDON SECTION** plan A1

Premier Inn Sunbury (Kempton Park)

BUDGET HOTEL

☎ 0871 527 9054
Staines Road West, Sunbury Cross TW16 7AT
web: www.premierinn.com
dir: M25 junct 12, onto M3 signed London & Richmond. Exit at junct 1, take 1st exit at rdbt into Staines Road West (A308). 1st left into Crossways. Hotel on right

High quality, budget accommodation ideal for both families and business travellers. Spacious, en suite bedrooms feature tea and coffee making facilities, and Freeview TV in most hotels. Internet access and Wi-fi are available for a small fee. The adjacent family restaurant features a wide and varied menu. See also the Hotel Groups pages.

Rooms 109

SUNDERLAND
Tyne & Wear   Map 19 NZ35

Sunderland Marriott Hotel

Marriott HOTELS & RESORTS

★★★★ 71% HOTEL

☎ 0191 529 2041
Queen's Pde, Seaburn SR6 8DB
e-mail: mhrs.nclsl.frontoffice@marriotthotels.com
web: www.sunderlandmarriott.co.uk
dir: A19, A184 (Boldon/Sunderland North), 3m. At rdbt left, then right. At rdbt left, follow to coast. Turn right, hotel on right

Comfortable and spacious accommodation, some with fabulous views of the North Sea and vast expanses of sandy beach, is provided at this seafront hotel. Public rooms are bright and modern and a number of meeting rooms are available. The hotel is conveniently located for access to the local visitor attractions.

Rooms 82 (6 fmly) **Facilities** STV Wi-fi ⌂ Gym Xmas New Year **Conf** Class 120 Board 70 Thtr 300 Del from £130 to £150 **Services** Lift **Parking** 110 **Notes** ⊗ Civ Wed 100

Best Western Roker Hotel

★★★ 78% HOTEL

☎ 0191 567 1786
Roker Ter, Roker SR6 9ND
e-mail: info@rokerhotel.co.uk

This modern hotel offers stunning views of the coastline. Well-equipped bedrooms come in a variety of sizes, and several have feature bathrooms. Functions, conferences and weddings are all well catered for in the function suite. A choice of dining options is available including Restaurant Italia and Restaurant China, as well as an impressive range of bar meals in the R-bar.

Rooms 43 (8 fmly) (3 GF) S £55-£125; D £75-£175 (incl. bkfst) **Facilities** STV FTV Wi-fi ⌂ ♫ Xmas New Year **Conf** Class 150 Board 100 Thtr 300 Del from £95 to £165 **Services** Lift Air con **Parking** 150 **Notes** LB ⊗ Civ Wed 350

Premier Inn Sunderland A19/A1231

BUDGET HOTEL

☎ 0871 527 9058
Wessington Way, Castletown SR5 3HR
web: www.premierinn.com
dir: From A19 take A1231 towards Sunderland. Hotel 100yds

High quality, budget accommodation ideal for both families and business travellers. Spacious, en suite bedrooms feature tea and coffee making facilities, and Freeview TV in most hotels. Internet access and Wi-fi are available for a small fee. The adjacent family restaurant features a wide and varied menu. See also the Hotel Groups pages.

Rooms 61

Premier Inn Sunderland North West

BUDGET HOTEL

☎ 0871 527 9056
Timber Beach Rd, off Wessington Way, Castletown SR5 3XG
web: www.premierinn.com
dir: A1(M) junct 65, A1231 towards Sunderland, (cross over A19)

Rooms 63

S

Save on hotels. Book at **theAA.com/hotel**

SUD – SUT 449 ENGLAND

SURBITON
Greater London

See London plan 1 C1

Holiday Inn London - Kingston South

★★★★ 75% HOTEL

☎ 020 8786 6565 & 8786 6500
Kingston Tower, Portsmouth Rd KT6 5QQ
e-mail: enquiries@hikingston.co.uk
dir: M25 junct 10, A3, left onto A243, 3rd exit at rdbt. At lights left onto A307

This hotel occupies a convenient location overlooking the River Thames just outside Kingston-upon-Thames and close to Surbiton. Many front-facing bedrooms have beautiful river views; all are comfortable and stylish. The public areas include a small yet well-equipped fitness room. Complimentary parking and Wi-fi are also available.

Rooms 116 (2 fmly) ★ S £79-£199; D £79-£199
Facilities STV FTV Wi-fi ⌨ Gym **Conf** Class 125 Board 60 Thtr 250 Del from £145 to £195
Services Lift Air con **Parking** 120 **Notes** LB Civ Wed 300

SUTTON
Greater London
Map 6 TQ26

Holiday Inn London - Sutton

★★★ 77% HOTEL

☎ 020 8234 1100 & 8234 1104
Gibson Rd SM1 2RF
e-mail: sales-sutton@ihg.com
web: www.hilondonsuttonhotel.co.uk
dir: M25 junct 8, A217, B2230. Pass rail station, follow one-way system in right lane. At lights, right then immediately left, left into Gibson Rd

Well located for many famous attractions such as Chessington World of Adventure, the All England Tennis Club at Wimbledon and Epsom Racecourse. This hotel offers air-conditioned bedrooms ranging from standard to executive, a variety of conference rooms, and leisure facilities with a swimming pool.

Rooms 119 (4 fmly) **S** £70-£200; **D** £75-£205*
Facilities Spa STV Wi-fi ⌨ HL ⌨ supervised Gym Xmas New Year **Conf** Class 100 Board 70 Thtr 180
Services Lift Air con **Parking** 105 **Notes** LB ⊗ Civ Wed 160

SUTTON COLDFIELD
West Midlands
Map 10 SP19

New Hall Hotel & Spa

★★★★ 80% ◉◉ HOTEL

☎ 08450 727577
Walmley Rd B76 1QX
e-mail: newhall@handpicked.co.uk
web: www.handpickedhotels.co.uk/newhall
dir: M42 junct 9, A4097, 2m to rdbt, take 2nd exit signed Walmley. Take 2nd exit from next 5 rdbts follow Sutton Coldfield signs. At 6th rdbt take 3rd exit follow Sutton Coldfield signs. Hotel on left

Situated in 26 acres of beautiful grounds this hotel is reputed to be the oldest inhabited, moated house in the country. The house's medieval charm and character combine well with 21st-century guest facilities. Executive and luxury suites are available. Public areas, with their fine panelling and mullioned stained-glass windows include the magnificent Great Chamber. Hand Picked Hotels – AA Hotel Group of the Year 2012-13.

Rooms 60 (14 fmly) (25 GF) ★ **Facilities** Spa STV FTV Wi-fi ⌨ supervised ⌨ 9 ⌨ Fishing ⌨ Gym Steam room Pitch & putt Xmas New Year **Conf** Class 75 Board 35 Thtr 150 **Parking** 80 **Notes** LB ⊗ Civ Wed 70

Best Western Premier Moor Hall Hotel & Spa

★★★★ 77% HOTEL

☎ 0121 308 3751
Moor Hall Dr, Four Oaks B75 6LN
e-mail: mail@moorhallhotel.co.uk
web: www.moorhallhotel.co.uk
dir: A38 onto A453 towards Sutton Coldfield, right at lights into Weeford Rd. Hotel 150yds on left

Although only a short distance from the city centre this hotel enjoys a peaceful setting, overlooking extensive grounds and an adjacent golf course. Bedrooms are well equipped and executive rooms are particularly spacious. Public rooms include the formal Oak Room Restaurant, and the informal Country Kitchen which offers a carvery and blackboard specials. The hotel also has a well-equipped spa with pool, sauna, steam room, jacuzzi and treatment rooms.

Rooms 82 (5 fmly) (33 GF) ★ S £55-£149; D £88-£169 (incl. bkfst)* **Facilities** Spa FTV Wi-fi ⌨ HL ⌨ Gym Aerobics studio Sauna Steam room **Conf** Class 120 Board 45 Thtr 250 Del from £139 to £160* **Services** Lift **Parking** 170 **Notes** LB ⊗ Civ Wed 180

Ramada Birmingham, Sutton Coldfield

★★★ 74% HOTEL

☎ 0121 351 3111
Penns Ln, Walmley B76 1LH
e-mail: enquiries@ramadasuttonhotel.co.uk
web: www.ramadasuttonhotel.co.uk
dir: From S: M6 junct 5 A452, 3rd rdbt right into Eachelhurst Rd, left at lights into Penns Lane. From N and W: M6 junct 6, Sutton Coldfield A5127, follow signs, 2m on at lights (Macdonalds) 4th right into Penns Lane

This hotel offers comfortable bedrooms which are fully equipped with a range of thoughtful accessories. The public areas provide a leisure facility with a well-equipped gym, alongside a smart lounge bar and function rooms.

Rooms 170 (23 annexe) (26 fmly) (48 GF) ★ S £59-£169; D £59-£239* **Facilities** Spa STV FTV Wi-fi ⌨ Fishing Gym Squash Sauna Steam room Studio Hair salon New Year **Conf** Class 200 Board 80 Thtr 600 Del from £99 to £179* **Services** Lift **Parking** 500 **Notes** LB Civ Wed 200

S

SUTTON COLDFIELD *continued*

Premier Inn Birmingham North (Sutton Coldfield)

BUDGET HOTEL

☎ 0871 527 8088
Whitehouse Common Rd B75 6HD
web: www.premierinn.com
dir: M42 junct 9, A446 towards Lichfield, then A453 to Sutton Coldfield. Left into Whitehouse Common Rd, hotel on left

High quality, budget accommodation ideal for both families and business travellers. Spacious, en suite bedrooms feature tea and coffee making facilities, and Freeview TV in most hotels. Internet access and Wi-fi are available for a small fee. The adjacent family restaurant features a wide and varied menu. See also the Hotel Groups pages.

Rooms 42

| **SUTTON ON SEA** | **Map 17 TF58** |
| Lincolnshire | |

The Grange & Links Hotel
★★★ 73% HOTEL

☎ 01507 441334
Sea Ln, Sandilands LN12 2RA
e-mail: grangeandlinkshotel@btconnect.com
web: www.grangeandlinkshotel.co.uk
dir: A1111 to Sutton-on-Sea, follow signs to Sandilands

This friendly, family-run hotel sits in five acres of grounds, close to both the beach and its own 18-hole links golf course. Bedrooms are pleasantly appointed and are well equipped for both business and leisure guests. Public rooms include ample lounge areas, a formal restaurant and a traditional bar, serving a wide range of meals and snacks.

Rooms 23 (10 fmly) (3 GF) **Facilities** Wi-fi ⚑ 18 🏌
Putt green ⚑ Gym Xmas New Year **Conf** Class 200 Board 100 Thtr 200 **Parking** 60 **Notes** Civ Wed 150

| **SUTTON SCOTNEY** | **Map 5 SU43** |
| Hampshire | |

Norton Park
★★★★ 76% HOTEL

☎ 0845 074 0055 & 01962 763000
SO21 3NB
e-mail: nortonpark@qhotels.co.uk
web: www.qhotels.co.uk
dir: From A303 & A34 junct follow signs to Sutton Scotney. Hotel on Micheldever Station Rd (old A30), 1m from Sutton Scotney

Set in 54 acres of beautiful parkland in the heart of Hampshire, Norton Park offers both business and leisure guests a great range of amenities. Dating from the 16th century, the hotel is complemented by extensive buildings housing the bedrooms, and public areas which include a superb leisure club and numerous conference facilities. Ample parking is available.

Rooms 175 (11 fmly) (80 GF) **Facilities** Spa Wi-fi ☺ supervised ⚑ Gym Steam room Sauna Experience shower Ice fountain Xmas New Year **Conf** Class 250 Board 80 Thtr 340 **Services** Lift **Parking** 220 **Notes** Civ Wed 340

| **SWAFFHAM** | **Map 13 TF80** |
| Norfolk | |

Best Western George Hotel
★★★ 77% ◉ HOTEL

☎ 01760 721238
Station Rd PE37 7LJ
e-mail: georgehotel@bestwestern.co.uk
web: www.arlingtonhotelgroup.co.uk
dir: Exit A47 signed Swaffham. Hotel opposite St Peter & St Paul church

A Georgian hotel situated in the heart of this bustling market town, which is ideally placed for touring north Norfolk. Bedrooms vary in size and style; each one is pleasantly decorated and well equipped. Public rooms include a cosy restaurant, a lounge and a busy bar where a range of drinks and snacks is available.

Rooms 29 (1 fmly) (8 GF) **S** £70-£85; **D** £80-£95 (incl. bkfst) **Facilities** FTV Wi-fi New Year **Conf** Class 70 Board 70 Thtr 150 Del from £95 to £135 **Parking** 80 **Notes** LB RS 24-26 Dec

---

| **SWANAGE** | **Map 5 SZ07** |
| Dorset | |

The Pines Hotel
★★★ 79% HOTEL

☎ 01929 425211
Burlington Rd BH19 1LT
e-mail: reservations@pineshotel.co.uk
web: www.pineshotel.co.uk
dir: A351 to seafront, left then 2nd right. Hotel at end of road

Enjoying a peaceful location with spectacular views over the cliffs and sea, The Pines is a pleasant place to stay. Many of the comfortable bedrooms have sea views. Guests can take tea in the lounge, enjoy appetising bar snacks in the attractive bar, and interesting cuisine in the restaurant.

Rooms 41 (26 fmly) (6 GF) ⚑ **S** £68; **D** £136-£176 (incl. bkfst)* **Facilities** FTV Wi-fi ♫ Xmas New Year **Conf** Class 80 Board 80 Thtr 80 Del from £84 to £104.70* **Services** Lift **Parking** 60 **Notes** LB

See advert on opposite page

Grand Hotel
★★★ 67% HOTEL

☎ 01929 423353
Burlington Rd BH19 1LU
e-mail: reservations@grandhotelswanage.co.uk
web: www.grandhotelswanage.co.uk

Dating back to 1898, this hotel is located on the Isle of Purbeck and has spectacular views across Swanage Bay and Peveril Point. Bedrooms are individually decorated and well equipped; public rooms offer a number of choices from relaxing lounges to extensive leisure facilities. The hotel also has its own private beach.

Save on hotels. Book at **theAA.com/hotel**

SUT – SWI 451 ENGLAND

Rooms 30 (2 fmly) **S** £55-£80; **D** £110-£160 (incl. bkfst)* **Facilities** FTV Wi-fi 🕲 supervised Fishing Gym Table tennis Beauty treatment room Sauna Solarium Xmas New Year **Conf** Class 40 Board 40 Thtr 120 Del from £83 to £108* **Services** Lift **Parking** 15

SWANLEY
Kent

Map 6 TQ56

Premier Inn Swanley

BUDGET HOTEL

☎ 0871 527 9288
London Rd BR8 7QD
web: www.premierinn.com
dir: M25 junct 3, B2173 towards Swanley. At rdbt 2nd exit onto B258 (High St). At next rdbt 4th exit into Swanley Ln, 1st exit into Bartholomew Way, at next rdbt 3rd exit into London Rd

High quality, budget accommodation ideal for both families and business travellers. Spacious, en suite bedrooms feature tea and coffee making facilities, and Freeview TV in most hotels. Internet access and Wi-fi are available for a small fee. The adjacent family restaurant features a wide and varied menu. See also the Hotel Groups pages.

Rooms 61

SWAY
Hampshire

Map 5 SZ29

Sway Manor Restaurant & Hotel

★★★ 77% HOTEL

☎ 01590 682754
Station Rd SO41 6BA
e-mail: info@swaymanor.com
web: www.swaymanor.com
dir: Exit B3055 (Brockenhurst/New Milton road) into village centre

Built at the turn of the 20th century, this attractive mansion is set in its own grounds, and conveniently located in the village centre. Bedrooms are well appointed and generously equipped; most have views over the gardens and pool. The bar and conservatory restaurant, both with views over the gardens, are popular with locals.

Rooms 15 (3 fmly) **Facilities** FTV Wi-fi ⌘ ⚡ ♫ Xmas New Year **Conf** Class 20 Board 15 **Services** Lift **Parking** 40 **Notes** Civ Wed 80

SWINDON
Wiltshire

Map 5 SU18

See also Wootton Bassett (Royal)

Swindon Marriott Hotel

★★★★ 74% HOTEL

Marriott
HOTELS & RESORTS

☎ 01793 512121
Pipers Way SN3 1SH
e-mail: mhrs.swidt.frontdesk@marriotthotels.com
web: www.swindonmarriott.co.uk
dir: M4 junct 15, A419, A4259 to Coate rdbt & B4006 signed 'Old Town'

With convenient access to the motorway, this hotel is a good venue for meetings, and an ideal base from which to explore Wiltshire and the Cotswolds. The hotel offers a good range of public rooms, including a well-equipped leisure centre, Chats café bar and the informal, brasserie-style Mediterrano restaurant.

Rooms 156 (42 fmly) **Facilities** Spa Wi-fi 🕲 ♨ Gym Aerobics studio Hairdresser Health & beauty salon Sauna Steam room **Conf** Class 100 Board 40 Thtr 280 **Services** Lift Air con **Parking** 300 **Notes** ⊗ Civ Wed 280

SWINDON *continued*

Best Western Premier Blunsdon House Hotel

★★★★ 72% HOTEL

☎ 01793 721701
Blunsdon SN26 7AS
e-mail: reservations@blunsdonhouse.co.uk
web: www.blunsdonhouse.co.uk
dir: M4 junct 15, A419 towards Cirencester. Exit at Turnpike junct, right, follow brown hotel signs

Located just to the north of Swindon, Blunsdon House is set in 30 acres of well-kept grounds, and offers extensive leisure facilities and spacious day rooms. The hotel has a choice of eating and drinking options in three bars and two restaurants; the lively and informal Christopher's, and Nichols for fine dining. Bedrooms are comfortably furnished, and include family rooms with bunk beds and the contemporary spacious Pavilion rooms.

Rooms 108 (15 fmly) (27 GF) ➽ **S** £79-£149; **D** £79-£149 **Facilities** Spa STV FTV Wi-fi ⌨ HL ⏱ ♨ 9 ⛳ Putt green Gym Squash Beauty therapy Woodland walk Xmas New Year Child facilities **Conf** Class 200 Board 55 Thtr 300 Del from £99 to £165 **Services** Lift **Parking** 300 **Notes** ⊗ Civ Wed 200

Menzies Swindon

★★★★ 71% HOTEL

☎ 01793 528282
Fleming Way SN1 1TN
e-mail: swindon@menzieshotels.co.uk
web: www.menzieshotels.co.uk
dir: M4 junct 15/16, follow town centre signs

This modern hotel is conveniently located in the centre of the town with the added advantage of nearby parking. The hotel offers bedrooms and bathrooms that are well equipped with plenty of useful extras. The brasserie serves an exciting selection of dishes. There are also various conference and event facilities available.

Rooms 95 (2 fmly) **Facilities** FTV Wi-fi ⌨ Xmas New Year **Conf** Class 80 Board 60 Thtr 200 **Services** Lift **Notes** ⊗ Civ Wed 200

The Pear Tree at Purton

★★★ 81% ⚜⚜ HOTEL

☎ 01793 772100
Church End SN5 4ED
e-mail: stay@peartreepurton.co.uk

(For full entry see Purton)

Stanton House Hotel

★★★ 77% HOTEL

☎ 0870 084 1388
The Avenue, Stanton Fitzwarren SN6 7SD
e-mail: reception@stantonhouse.co.uk
web: www.stantonhouse.co.uk
dir: A419 onto A361 towards Highworth, left towards Stanton Fitzwarren about 600yds past business park, hotel on left

Extensive grounds and superb gardens surround this Cotswold-stone manor house: the park and Stanton Lake are accessible to guests and provide great walks. Smart, well-maintained bedrooms have been equipped with modern comforts. Public areas include a conservatory, a bar and two eating options - The Rosemary Restaurant offering a wide choice of Japanese and European dishes, and the Mt Fuji Restaurant specialising in authentic Japanese food in traditional surroundings. The friendly, multi-lingual staff create a relaxing atmosphere for their guests.

Rooms 78 (27 GF) ➽ **Facilities** STV Wi-fi Xmas New Year **Conf** Class 70 Board 40 Thtr 110 Del from £105* **Services** Lift **Parking** 110 **Notes** ⊗ Civ Wed 110

Chiseldon House Hotel

★★★ 75% ⚜ HOTEL

☎ 01793 741010
New Rd, Chiseldon SN4 0NE
e-mail: welcome@chiseldonhouse.com
web: www.chiseldonhouse.com
dir: M4 junct 15, A346 signed Marlborough. In 0.5m right onto B4500, 0.25m, hotel on right

Conveniently located for access to the M4, Chiseldon House is in a quiet location and has a relaxed ambience. Bedrooms include a number of larger rooms but all are comfortably furnished. The award-winning restaurant offers a selection of carefully prepared dishes utilising high quality produce. Guests are welcome to enjoy the pleasant garden with outdoor seating.

Rooms 21 ➽ **Facilities** FTV Wi-fi ⌨ **Conf** Class 20 Board 32 Thtr 65 **Notes** ⊗ Civ Wed 85

Holiday Inn Swindon

★★★ 74% HOTEL

☎ 01793 817000 & 0871 942 9079
Marlborough Rd SN3 6AQ
e-mail: swindon@ihg.com
web: www.holidayinn.co.uk
dir: M4 junct 15, A419 towards Swindon. Take A4259 for 1m. Hotel on right opposite Sun Inn

With convenient access to both the M4 and Swindon's centre, this hotel provides an ideal base for business or leisure guests. Bedrooms are well decorated and have a good range of useful extras. Guests can enjoy the facilities of The Spirit Health and Fitness Club and then relax in the comfortable bar. A good selection of dishes is available whether by way of room service, lounge snacks or the welcoming, informal restaurant.

Rooms 99 (25 fmly) (48 GF) (9 smoking) **Facilities** STV FTV Wi-fi ⌨ supervised Gym **Conf** Class 30 Board 30 Thtr 60 **Services** Air con **Parking** 120 **Notes** ⊗ Civ Wed 80

Marsh Farm Hotel

★★★ 72% HOTEL

☎ 01793 842800 & 848044
Coped Hall, Royal Wootton Bassett SN4 8ER
e-mail: info@marshfarmhotel.co.uk
web: www.marshfarmhotel.co.uk
dir: M4 junct 16 onto A3102, straight on at 1st rdbt, right at 2nd rdbt. Hotel 200yds on left

The well decorated and comfortably furnished bedrooms at this hotel are situated in converted barns and extensions around the original farmhouse, which is set in its own grounds less than a mile from the M4. A relaxed and welcoming atmosphere prevails especially at dinner, when an extensive range of dishes to suit all tastes, is offered in the conservatory restaurant.

Rooms 50 (39 annexe) (1 fmly) (16 GF) **Facilities** FTV Wi-fi Putt green Beauty salon Use of nearby leisure centre New Year **Conf** Class 60 Board 50 Thtr 120 **Parking** 100 **Notes** ⊗ Closed 26-30 Dec RS 25 Dec Civ Wed 100

Mercure Swindon South Marston Hotel & Spa

★★★ 72% HOTEL

☎ 01793 833700
Old Vicarage Ln, South Marston SN3 4SH
e-mail: info@southmarstonhotel.com
web: www.southmarstonhotel.com
dir: M4 junct 15, A419 N to Cirencester. Exit 2nd junct signed A420 Oxford, left to South Marston. Hotel past pub on left

Located just outside Swindon, this hotel offers smart, modern, well-appointed bedrooms and spacious public areas. Leisure facilities include a spa with health and beauty treatments, a well-equipped gym and a 23-metre pool. The light and airy restaurant serves modern British cuisine. Free Wi-fi is available throughout.

Rooms 60 (7 fmly) (30 GF) **Facilities** Spa FTV Wi-fi ☼ ⓢ Gym Squash Sauna Steam room Fitness studio Spinning room Xmas New Year **Conf** Class 75 Board 60 Thtr 150 **Parking** 200 **Notes** ⊗ Civ Wed 120

Campanile Swindon

BUDGET HOTEL

☎ 01793 514777
Delta Business Park, Great Western Way SN5 7XG
e-mail: swindon@campanile.com
web: www.campanile-swindon.co.uk
dir: M4 junct 16, A3102 towards Swindon. After 2nd rdbt, 2nd exit onto Welton Rd (Delta Business Park), 1st left

This modern building offers accommodation in smart, well-equipped bedrooms, all with en suite bathrooms. Refreshments may be taken at the informal bistro. See also the Hotel Groups pages.

Rooms 120 (6 fmly) (22 GF) **Conf** Class 40 Board 40 Thtr 70

Holiday Inn Express Swindon City Centre

BUDGET HOTEL

☎ 01793 602000
Bridge St SN1 5BT
e-mail: info@exhiswindon.co.uk
web: www.exhiswindon.co.uk

A modern hotel ideal for families and business travellers. Fresh and uncomplicated, the spacious rooms include Sky TV, power shower and tea and coffee-making facilities. Continental buffet breakfast is included in the room rate; other meals may be taken at the nearby family pub or restaurant. See also the Hotel Groups pages.

Rooms 134 (71 fmly) ⌂ **D** £44-£79 (incl. bkfst)*
Conf Class 30 Board 24 Thtr 50

Holiday Inn Express Swindon West M4 Jct 16

BUDGET HOTEL

☎ 01793 818800
Frankland Rd, Blagrove SN5 8UD
e-mail: swindon@expressholidayinn.co.uk
web: www.hiexpress.com/swindonwest
dir: M4 junct 16, follow signs for town centre (A3102), 1st left after rdbt

Rooms 121 (85 fmly) (10 GF) (10 smoking)
Conf Class 30 Board 27 Thtr 56

Premier Inn Swindon Central

BUDGET HOTEL

☎ 0871 527 9064
Kembrey Business Park, Kembrey St SN2 8YS
web: www.premierinn.com
dir: M4 junct 15, A419 (Swindon bypass) towards Cirencester. In 6m at Turnpike Rdbt 1st left. Hotel on left in 2m

High quality, budget accommodation ideal for both families and business travellers. Spacious, en suite bedrooms feature tea and coffee making facilities, and Freeview TV in most hotels. Internet access and Wi-fi are available for a small fee. The adjacent family restaurant features a wide and varied menu. See also the Hotel Groups pages.

Rooms 50

Premier Inn Swindon North

BUDGET HOTEL

☎ 0871 527 9066
Broad Bush, Blunsdon SN26 8DJ
web: www.premierinn.com
dir: N of Swindon. 5m from M4 junct 15. At junct of A419 & B4019

Rooms 62

Premier Inn Swindon West

BUDGET HOTEL

☎ 0871 527 9068
Great Western Way SN5 8UY
web: www.premierinn.com
dir: M4 junct 16, A3102 to Lydiard Fields. Past Hilton, entrance on left. (NB for Sat Nav use SN5 8UB)

Rooms 63

SWINTON
Greater Manchester   Map 15 SD70

Premier Inn Manchester (Worsley East/A580)

BUDGET HOTEL

☎ 0871 527 8724
East Lancs Rd M27 0AA
web: www.premierinn.com
dir: M60 junct 13 (Swinton/Leigh), A580

High quality, budget accommodation ideal for both families and business travellers. Spacious, en suite bedrooms feature tea and coffee making facilities, and Freeview TV in most hotels. Internet access and Wi-fi are available for a small fee. The adjacent family restaurant features a wide and varied menu. See also the Hotel Groups pages.

Rooms 27

S

TADWORTH
Surrey · Map 6 TQ25

Premier Inn Epsom South

BUDGET HOTEL

☎ 0871 527 8382

Brighton Rd, Burgh Heath KT20 6BW

web: www.premierinn.com

dir: Just off M25 junct 8 on A217 towards Sutton

High quality, budget accommodation ideal for both families and business travellers. Spacious, en suite bedrooms feature tea and coffee making facilities, and Freeview TV in most hotels. Internet access and Wi-fi are available for a small fee. The adjacent family restaurant features a wide and varied menu. See also the Hotel Groups pages.

Rooms 76

TAMWORTH
Staffordshire · Map 10 SK20

Drayton Court Hotel

★★ 83% HOTEL

☎ 01827 285805

65 Coleshill St, Fazeley B78 3RG

e-mail: draytoncthotel@yahoo.co.uk

web: www.draytoncourthotel.co.uk

dir: M42 junct 9, A446 to Lichfield, at next rdbt right onto A4091. 2m, Drayton Manor Theme Park on left. Hotel on right

Conveniently located close to the M42, this lovingly restored hotel offers bedrooms that are elegant and have been thoughtfully equipped to suit both business and leisure guests. Beds are particularly comfortable, and one room has a four-poster. Public areas include a panelled bar, a relaxing lounge and an attractive restaurant.

Rooms 19 (3 fmly) **Facilities** Wi-fi **Conf** Board 12 **Parking** 23 **Notes** ⊗ Closed 22 Dec-1 Jan

Holiday Inn Express Tamworth

BUDGET HOTEL

☎ 01827 303220

Leisure Island, River Dr B79 7ND

e-mail: info@express-tamworth.com

dir: M42 junct 10, A5 to Tamworth. Hotel adjacent to Snowdome

A modern hotel ideal for families and business travellers. Fresh and uncomplicated, the spacious rooms include Sky TV, power shower and tea and coffee-making facilities. Continental buffet breakfast is included in the room rate; other meals may be taken at the nearby family pub or restaurant. See also the Hotel Groups pages.

Rooms 120 (83 fmly) (14 smoking) ⚓ **S** £49-£115; **D** £49-£115 (incl. bkfst)* **Conf** Class 35 Board 36 Thtr 80

Premier Inn Tamworth Central

BUDGET HOTEL

☎ 0871 527 9070

Bonehill Rd, Bitterscote B78 3HQ

web: www.premierinn.com

dir: M42 junct 10, A5 towards Tamworth. Left in 3m onto A51 signed Tamworth. Straight on at 1st rdbt. At next rdbt 3rd exit. Hotel adjacent to Ladybridge Beefeater

High quality, budget accommodation ideal for both families and business travellers. Spacious, en suite bedrooms feature tea and coffee making facilities, and Freeview TV in most hotels. Internet access and Wi-fi are available for a small fee. The adjacent family restaurant features a wide and varied menu. See also the Hotel Groups pages.

Rooms 58

Premier Inn Tamworth South

BUDGET HOTEL

☎ 0871 527 9072

Watling St, Wilnecote B77 5PN

web: www.premierinn.com

dir: M42 junct 10, A5 towards Tamworth. Left in 200yds signed Wilnecote/B5404. Left at next rdbt, hotel on left

Rooms 58

TANKERSLEY
South Yorkshire · Map 16 SK39

Tankersley Manor

★★★★ 77% HOTEL

☎ 01226 744700

Church Ln S75 3DQ

e-mail: tankersleymanor@qhotels.co.uk

web: www.qhotels.co.uk

dir: M1 junct 36, A61 (Sheffield road)

High on the moors with views over the countryside, this 17th-century residence is well located for major cities, tourist attractions and motorway links. Where appropriate, bedrooms retain original features such as exposed beams or Yorkshire-stone window sills. The hotel has its own traditional country pub, complete with old beams and open fires, alongside the more formal restaurant and bar. A well-equipped leisure centre is also available.

Rooms 99 (10 fmly) (16 GF) ⚓ **S** £65-£129; **D** £65-£129 **Facilities** Spa STV FTV Wi-fi ❦ ⌕ Gym Swimming lessons Beauty treatments Xmas New Year **Conf** Class 200 Board 100 Thtr 400 Del from £109 to £173 **Services** Lift **Parking** 350 **Notes** LB Civ Wed 250

Premier Inn Sheffield/ Barnsley M1 Jct 36

BUDGET HOTEL

☎ 0871 527 8968

Maple Rd S75 3DL

web: www.premierinn.com

dir: M1 junct 35A (N'bound exit only), A616 for 2m. From M1 junct 36, A61 towards Sheffield

High quality, budget accommodation ideal for both families and business travellers. Spacious, en suite bedrooms feature tea and coffee making facilities, and Freeview TV in most hotels. Internet access and Wi-fi are available for a small fee. The adjacent family restaurant features a wide and varied menu. See also the Hotel Groups pages.

Rooms 62

Save on hotels. Book at **theAA.com/hotel**

TAD – TAU 455 ENGLAND

TAPLOW
Buckinghamshire   Map 6 SU98

INSPECTORS' CHOICE

Cliveden

★★★★★ ◎◎ COUNTRY HOUSE HOTEL

☎ 01628 668561
SL6 0JF
e-mail: info@clivedenhouse.co.uk
web: www.clivedenhouse.co.uk
dir: M4 junct 7, A4 towards Maidenhead, 1.5m, onto B476 towards Taplow, 2.5m, hotel on left

This wonderful stately home stands at the top of a gravelled boulevard. Visitors are treated as house-guests and staff recapture the tradition of fine hospitality. Bedrooms have individual quality and style, and reception rooms retain a timeless elegance. Exceptional leisure facilities include cruises along Cliveden Reach and massages in the Pavilion. The Terrace Restaurant with its delightful views has been awarded two AA Rosettes.

Rooms 39 (16 fmly) (10 GF) 🐾 **S** £252-£2094; **D** £252-£2094 (incl. bkfst)* **Facilities** Spa STV FTV Wi-fi ⊙ ⌇ ♨ ♨ Gym Squash Full range of beauty treatments 3 vintage boats ♫ Xmas New Year **Conf** Class 48 Board 60 Thtr 80 Del from £255 to £425* **Services** Lift **Parking** 60 **Notes** LB Civ Wed 150

Taplow House Hotel

★★★★ 75% ◎◎ HOTEL

☎ 01628 670056
Berry Hill SL6 0DA
e-mail: reception@taplowhouse.com
dir: Exit A4 onto Berry Hill, hotel 0.5m on right

This elegant Georgian manor is set amid beautiful gardens and has been skilfully restored. Character public rooms are pleasing and include a number of air-conditioned conference rooms and an elegant restaurant. Comfortable bedrooms are individually decorated and furnished to a high standard.

Rooms 32 (4 fmly) (2 GF) 🐾 **Facilities** STV FTV Wi-fi ⤵ Complimentary use of private leisure facilities

---

(1m) Xmas New Year **Conf** Class 50 Board 50 Thtr 120 Del from £155 to £205 **Services** Air con **Parking** 100 **Notes** ⊗ Civ Wed 100

TARPORLEY
Cheshire   Map 15 SJ56

Macdonald Portal Hotel Golf & Spa

★★★★ 78% ◎◎ HOTEL

☎ 0844 879 9082
Cobblers Cross Ln CW6 0DJ
e-mail: general.portal@macdonaldhotels.co.uk
dir: M6 junct 18, A54 towards Middlewich/Winsford. Left onto A49, through Cotebrook. In approx 1m follow signs for hotel

This hotel is located in beautiful rolling countryside and provides a luxury base for both the leisure and business guest. The spacious and well-equipped bedrooms have bathrooms with baths and power showers. Extensive leisure facilities include a superb spa, state-of-the-art fitness equipment, three golf courses and a golf academy. The Ranulf Restaurant delivers skilfully prepared, innovative cooking, as well as an excellent breakfast. Staff throughout are very friendly and nothing is too much trouble.

Rooms 85 (29 GF) 🐾 **S** £79-£189; **D** £94-£204 **Facilities** Spa STV FTV Wi-fi ⤵ HL ⊙ ♪ 45 Putt green Gym Golf academy Outdoor pursuits New Year **Conf** Class 180 Board 60 Thtr 250 Del from £130 to £165 **Services** Lift **Parking** 250 **Notes** LB Civ Wed 250

TAUNTON
Somerset   Map 4 ST22

The Mount Somerset Hotel

★★★ 83% ◎◎ HOTEL

☎ 01823 442500
Lower Henlade TA3 5NB
e-mail: info@mountsomersethotel.co.uk
dir: M5 junct 25, A358 towards Chard/Ilminster, at Henlade right into Stoke Rd, left at T-junct at end, then right into drive

From its elevated and rural position, this impressive Regency house has wonderful views over Taunton Vale. There are impressive quality and comfort levels throughout in the stylish bedrooms and bathrooms. The elegant public rooms combine elegance and flair with an engaging and intimate atmosphere. In addition to the daily-changing, fixed-price menu, a carefully selected seasonal carte is available in the restaurant.

Rooms 19 (1 fmly) 🐾 **S** £99-£150; **D** £129-£350 (incl. bkfst) **Facilities** Spa FTV Wi-fi ⤵ Gym Hydrotherapy pool Sauna Steam room Experience showers Xmas

---

New Year **Conf** Class 60 Board 35 Thtr 70 Del from £125 to £165* **Services** Lift **Parking** 100 **Notes** LB ⊗ Civ Wed 80

Farthings Country House Hotel and Restaurant

★★★ 74% ◎ SMALL HOTEL

☎ 01823 480664 & 0785 668 8128
Village Rd, Hatch Beauchamp TA3 6SG
e-mail: farthingshotel@yahoo.co.uk
web: www.farthingshotel.co.uk
dir: From A358 (between Taunton & Ilminster) into Hatch Beauchamp. Hotel in village centre

This delightful hotel, set in its own extensive gardens in a peaceful village location, offers comfortable accommodation, combined with all the character and charm of a building dating back over 200 years. The calm atmosphere makes this a great place to relax and unwind. Dinner service is attentive, and menus feature best quality local ingredients prepared and presented with care.

Rooms 12 (2 annexe) (2 fmly) (3 GF) 🐾 **S** £55-£155; **D** £65-£195 (incl. bkfst) **Facilities** STV FTV Wi-fi ⤵ ⤵ Xmas New Year **Conf** Class 25 Board 24 Thtr 50 **Parking** 25 **Notes** LB Civ Wed 175

Holiday Inn Taunton M5 Jct 25

★★★ 74% HOTEL   Holiday Inn

☎ 0871 942 9080 & 01823 281600
Deane Gate Av TA1 2UA
web: www.hitauntonhotelm5.co.uk
dir: Adjacent to M5 junct 25, hotel before Harvester on right at entrance to business park

Handily located close to the M5, this is a popular choice for both business and leisure travellers. The open-plan public areas have a light and airy feel and include extensive leisure facilities. Bedrooms are well equipped and contemporary, with executive rooms also available. A choice of menus, with daily specials, is served in the relaxed restaurant.

Rooms 99 (68 fmly) (48 GF) (8 smoking) **Facilities** Wi-fi ⊙ Gym Xmas New Year **Conf** Class 100 Board 30 Thtr 280 **Services** Lift Air con **Parking** 300 **Notes** ⊗ Civ Wed 200

T

TAUNTON *continued*

Corner House Hotel

★★★ 71% HOTEL

☎ 01823 284683
Park St TA1 4DQ
e-mail: res@corner-house.co.uk
web: www.corner-house.co.uk
dir: 0.3m from town centre. Hotel on junct of Park St & A38 (Wellington Rd)

The unusual Victorian façade of the Corner House, with its turrets and stained-glass windows, belies a wealth of innovation, quality and style to be found inside. The contemporary bedrooms have state-of-the-art facilities including flat-screen TVs, ample working space, and fridges with complimentary water and fresh milk. The smart public areas include the convivial bar and the relaxed and enjoyable 'Wine & Sausage' eating rooms. Free Wi-fi is available throughout the hotel.

Rooms 44 (9 annexe) (4 fmly) (5 GF) **Facilities** FTV Wi-fi **Conf** Class 30 Board 28 Thtr 50 **Parking** 30 **Notes** ⊗

Salisbury House Hotel

★★ 79% HOTEL

☎ 01823 272083
14 Billetfield TA1 3NN
e-mail: res@salisburyhousehotel.co.uk
web: www.salisburyhousehotel.co.uk

Centrally and conveniently located, this elegant establishment dates back to the 1850s and retains many original features such as stained-glass windows and a wonderful oak staircase. Bedrooms provide impressive levels of comfort and quality with well-equipped, modern bathrooms. Public areas reflect the same high standards that are a hallmark throughout this hotel.

Rooms 17 (4 fmly) (6 GF) (2 smoking) ✿ **S** £65-£90; **D** £69-£99 (incl. bkfst) **Facilities** FTV Wi-fi ⌂ **Parking** 17 **Notes** ⊗

Holiday Inn Express Taunton M5 Jct 25

BUDGET HOTEL

☎ 01823 624000
Blackbrook Business Park, Blackbrook Park Av TA1 2PX
e-mail: managertaunton@expressholidayinn.co.uk
web: www.hiexpress.com/taunton
dir: M5 junct 25. Follow signs for Blackbrook Business Park. Hotel 100yds on right

A modern hotel ideal for families and business travellers. Fresh and uncomplicated, the spacious rooms include Sky TV, power shower and tea and coffee-making facilities. Continental buffet breakfast is included in the room rate; other meals may be taken at the nearby family pub or restaurant. See also the Hotel Groups pages.

Rooms 92 (55 fmly) (22 GF) (8 smoking)
Conf Class 24 Board 16 Thtr 30

Premier Inn Taunton Central (North)

BUDGET HOTEL

☎ 0871 527 9076
Massingham Park, Priorswood Rd TA2 7RX
web: www.premierinn.com
dir: M5 junct 25, A358 into Taunton, at 2nd rdbt right onto Obridge Viaduct. Hotel at next rdbt

High quality, budget accommodation ideal for both families and business travellers. Spacious, en suite bedrooms feature tea and coffee making facilities, and Freeview TV in most hotels. Internet access and Wi-fi are available for a small fee. The adjacent family restaurant features a wide and varied menu. See also the Hotel Groups pages.

Rooms 40

Premier Inn Taunton East

BUDGET HOTEL

☎ 0871 527 9080
81 Bridgwater Rd TA1 2DU
web: www.premierinn.com
dir: M5 junct 25 follow signs to Taunton. Straight on at 1st rdbt, keep left at Creech Castle lights, hotel 200yds on right

Rooms 40

Premier Inn Taunton (Ruishton)

BUDGET HOTEL

☎ 0871 527 9074
Ruishton Ln, Ruishton TA3 5LU
web: www.premierinn.com
dir: Just off M5 junct 25 on A38

Rooms 38

The Horn of Plenty

★★★ 85% ⊛ ⊛ HOTEL

☎ 01822 832528
Gulworthy PL19 8JD
e-mail: enquiries@thehornofplenty.co.uk
web: www.thehornofplenty.co.uk
dir: From Tavistock take A390 W for 3m. Right at Gulworthy Cross. In 400yds turn left, hotel in 400yds on right

With stunning views over the Tamar Valley, The Horn of Plenty maintains its reputation as one of Britain's best country-house hotels. Bedrooms are well equipped and have many thoughtful extras. The garden rooms offer impressive levels of both quality and comfort, while award-winning cuisine is served with accomplished skill and a passion for local produce.

Rooms 10 (6 annexe) (3 fmly) (4 GF) ✿ **S** £85-£215; **D** £95-£225 (incl. bkfst)* **Facilities** FTV Wi-fi ⌂ HL Xmas New Year **Conf** Class 22 Board 14 Thtr 22 Del from £180 to £351* **Parking** 25 **Notes** LB Civ Wed 80

Bedford Hotel

★★★ 76% ⊛ HOTEL

☎ 01822 613221
1 Plymouth Rd PL19 8BB
e-mail: enquiries@bedford-hotel.co.uk
web: www.bedford-hotel.co.uk
dir: M5 junct 31, A30 (Launceston/Okehampton). Then A386 to Tavistock, follow town centre signs. Hotel opposite church

Built on the site of a Benedictine abbey, this impressive castellated building has been welcoming visitors for over 200 years. Very much a local landmark, the hotel offers comfortable and relaxing public areas, all reflecting charm and character throughout. Bedrooms are traditionally styled with contemporary comforts, whilst the Woburn Restaurant provides a refined setting for enjoyable cuisine.

Rooms 31 (2 fmly) (5 GF) **S** £45-£70; **D** £90-£140 (incl. bkfst)* **Facilities** FTV Wi-fi ⌂ Xmas New Year **Conf** Class 100 Board 60 Thtr 160 Del from £115 to £135 **Parking** 45 **Notes** LB Civ Wed 120

TEBAY
Cumbria　　　Map 18 NY60

Westmorland Hotel
★★★ 83% ◉ HOTEL

☎ 015396 24351
Westmorland Place, Orton CA10 3SB
e-mail: reservations@westmorlandhotel.com
web: www.westmorlandhotel.com
dir: Signed from Westmorland Services between M6 junct 38 & 39 N'bound & S'bound

With fine views over rugged moorland, this modern and friendly hotel is ideal for conferences and meetings. Bedrooms are spacious and comfortable, with the executive rooms being particularly well equipped. Open-plan public areas provide a Tyrolean touch and include a split-level restaurant.

Rooms 51 (5 fmly) (12 GF) 🐾 **S** £90; **D** £110 (incl. bkfst)* **Facilities** FTV Wi-fi HL Xmas New Year **Conf** Class 24 Board 30 Thtr 120 Del from £132 to £145* **Services** Lift **Parking** 60 **Notes** LB RS 1 Jan Civ Wed 120

TEIGNMOUTH
Devon　　　Map 3 SX97

Cliffden Hotel
★★★ 74% HOTEL

☎ 01626 770052
Dawlish Rd TQ14 8TE
e-mail: cliffden.hotel@visionhotels.co.uk
dir: M5 junct 31, A380, B3192 to Teignmouth. Down hill on Exeter Rd to lights, left to rdbt (station on left). Left, follow Dawlish signs. Up hill. Hotel next right

Whilst this hotel mainly caters for visually impaired guests, their families, friends and guide dogs, it offers a warm welcome to all. This establishment is a listed Victorian building set in six acres of delightful gardens overlooking a small valley. Bedrooms are comfortable, very spacious and thoughtfully equipped. There's also leisure facilities and, of course, special provision for guide dogs.

Rooms 47 (5 fmly) (10 GF) 🐾 **Facilities** FTV Wi-fi 🏊 supervised 🎵 Xmas New Year **Conf** Class 30 Board 30 Thtr 50 **Services** Lift **Parking** 25 **Notes** Civ Wed 60

TELFORD
Shropshire　　　Map 10 SJ60

Telford Hotel & Golf Resort
QHOTELS
★★★★ 77% HOTEL

☎ 01952 429977
Great Hay Dr, Sutton Heights TF7 4DT
e-mail: telford@qhotels.co.uk
web: www.qhotels.co.uk
dir: M54 junct 4, A442. Follow signs for Telford Golf Club

Set on the edge of Telford with panoramic views of the famous Ironbridge Gorge, this hotel offers excellent standards. Smart bedrooms are complemented by spacious public areas, large conference facilities, a spa with treatment rooms, a golf course and a driving range. Ample parking is available.

Rooms 114 (8 fmly) (50 GF) 🐾 **S** £92-£196; **D** £125-£223 (incl. bkfst & dinner)* **Facilities** Spa STV Wi-fi 🏊 ⚽ 18 Putt green Gym Xmas New Year **Conf** Class 220 Board 100 Thtr 350 Del from £115 to £149* **Services** Lift **Parking** 200 **Notes** LB Civ Wed 250

Best Western Valley Hotel
Best Western
★★★ 82% ◉◉ HOTEL

☎ 01952 432247
Ironbridge TF8 7DW
e-mail: info@thevalleyhotel.co.uk
dir: M6, M54 junct 6 onto A5223 to Ironbridge

This privately owned hotel is situated in attractive gardens, close to the famous Iron Bridge. It was once the home of the Maws family who manufactured ceramic tiles, and fine examples of their craft are found throughout the house. Bedrooms vary in size and are split between the main house and a mews development; imaginative meals are served in the attractive Chez Maws restaurant.

Rooms 44 (3 fmly) (6 GF) **S** £49-£101; **D** £72-£138 (incl. bkfst)* **Facilities** FTV Wi-fi 🏊 **Conf** Class 80 Board 60 Thtr 150 Del from £120 to £160 **Services** Lift **Parking** 80 **Notes** LB ⊗ Closed 24 Dec-2 Jan RS 25 Dec Civ Wed 150

Hadley Park House
★★★ 81% ◉ HOTEL

☎ 01952 677269
Hadley Park TF1 6QJ
e-mail: info@hadleypark.co.uk
dir: Off Hadley Park Island exit A442 to Whitchurch

Located in Telford, but close to Ironbridge this elegant Georgian mansion is situated in three acres of its own grounds. Bedrooms are spacious and well equipped. There is a comfortable bar and lounge and meals are served in the attractive conservatory-style restaurant.

Rooms 22 (6 fmly) (5 GF) **Facilities** STV FTV Wi-fi Xmas New Year **Conf** Class 80 Board 45 Thtr 200 **Parking** 60 **Notes** ⊗ Civ Wed 200

Mercure Telford Madeley Court Hotel
Mercure
★★★ 75% HOTEL

☎ 01952 680068
Castlefields Way, Madeley TF7 5DW
e-mail: enquiries@hotels-telford.com
web: www.hotels-telford.com
dir: A464 to Telford then A442, A4169 to Castlefields rdbt, 1st exit onto B4373. Hotel 200yds on left

This beautifully restored 16th-century manor house is set in extensive grounds and gardens. Bedrooms vary between character rooms and the newer annexe rooms. Public areas consist of two wood-panelled lounges, a lakeside bar and at the centre of the original manor house, The Priory restaurant. The 16th-century Grade I listed mill house makes a lovely location for wedding receptions.

Rooms 49 (49 annexe) (4 fmly) (21 GF) **S** £85-£125; **D** £95-£175 **Facilities** FTV Wi-fi Xmas New Year **Conf** Class 150 Board 50 Thtr 175 Del from £99 to £155* **Parking** 150 **Notes** LB Civ Wed 175

T

TELFORD *continued*

Park Inn by Radisson, Telford

★★★ 67% HOTEL

☎ 01952 429988
Forgegate TF3 4NA
e-mail: info.telford@rezidorparkinn.com
dir: M54 junct 5

In a convenient location just off the motorway this is a comfortable place to stay. The facilities include a spa, indoor swimming pool and conference rooms, an on-site car valet service as well as secure parking. The restaurant provides a relaxing setting with lots of natural daylight. Bedrooms are comfortably appointed.

Rooms 153 (1 fmly) (17 GF) (17 smoking)
S £37-£124; D £37-£124* Facilities Wi-fi ⚲ ☺ Gym Weights room Beauty treatment rooms Xmas New Year Conf Class 200 Board 100 Thtr 400 Services Lift Parking 300 Notes LB Civ Wed 400

Premier Inn Telford Central

BUDGET HOTEL

☎ 0871 527 9082
Euston Way TF3 4LY
web: www.premierinn.com
dir: M54 junct 5 follow Central Railway Station signs. Hotel at 2nd exit off rdbt signed railway station

High quality, budget accommodation ideal for both families and business travellers. Spacious, en suite bedrooms feature tea and coffee making facilities, and Freeview TV in most hotels. Internet access and Wi-fi are available for a small fee. The adjacent family restaurant features a wide and varied menu. See also the Hotel Groups pages.

Rooms 62

Premier Inn Telford North (Donnington)

BUDGET HOTEL

☎ 0871 527 9084
Donnington Wood Way, Donnington TF2 8LE
web: www.premierinn.com
dir: From Telford M54 junct 4, B5060 (Redhill Way) signed Donnington. At rdbt straight on (becomes Donnington Wood Way then School Rd). At mini rdbt take 1st left into Wellington Rd (hotel adjacent to McDonalds & Shell garage)

Rooms 20

Days Inn Telford - M54

BUDGET HOTEL

☎ 01952 238400
Telford Services, Priorslee Rd TF11 8TG
e-mail: telford.hotel@welcomebreak.co.uk
web: www.welcomebreak.co.uk
dir: At M54 junct 4

This modern building offers accommodation in smart, spacious and well-equipped bedrooms, suitable for families and business travellers, and all with en suite bathrooms. Continental breakfast is available, and other refreshments may be taken at the nearby family restaurant. See also the Hotel Groups pages.

Rooms 48 (45 fmly) (21 GF) (8 smoking) Conf Board 8

Cameley Lodge

★★★ 75% SMALL HOTEL

☎ 01761 452790
Cameley BS39 5AH
e-mail: john@cameleylodge.co.uk
dir: Exit A37 at Temple Cloud, 1m, hotel signed

A peacefully located property with views over a lake and surrounded by pleasant countryside. Being a small hotel, friendly and personal service is delivered by the resident proprietors and their staff. The bedrooms and bathrooms have been appointed to provide very good levels of quality and comfort. The modern and stylish restaurant offers a good selection of carefully prepared dishes, and the conference and wedding facilities are popular.

Rooms 9 (2 fmly) Facilities Wi-fi Fishing Clay pigeon shooting Conf Class 64 Board 24 Thtr 80 Services Lift Parking 48 Notes ⊗ Civ Wed 100

Temple Sowerby House Hotel & Restaurant

★★★ 87% ◉◉ COUNTRY HOUSE HOTEL

☎ 017683 61578
CA10 1RZ
e-mail: stay@templesowerby.com
web: www.templesowerby.com
dir: 7m from M6 junct 40, midway between Penrith & Appleby, in village centre

The hotel is set in the heart of the Eden Valley, ideal for exploring the northern Lake District and Pennine Fells. Bedrooms are comfortable and stylish, most feature ultra-modern bathrooms, and there is a choice of pleasant lounges. The restaurant, with picture windows overlooking the beautiful walled garden, is a splendid place to enjoy the award-winning cuisine. Staff throughout are friendly and keen to please.

Rooms 12 (4 annexe) (2 GF) ⟨ S £95-£110; D £135-£160 (incl. bkfst) Facilities FTV Wi-fi ⚑ New Year Conf Class 20 Board 20 Thtr 30 Del from £170 to £185 Parking 15 Notes LB ⊗ No children 12yrs Closed 20-29 Dec Civ Wed 40

Cadmore Lodge Hotel & Country Club

★★ 74% ◉ HOTEL

☎ 01584 810044
Berrington Green, St Michaels WR15 8TQ
e-mail: reception.cadmore@cadmorelodge.com
web: www.cadmorelodge.com
dir: From A4112 (Leominster-Tenbury Wells road), follow signs for Berrington

Cadmore Lodge is situated in an idyllic rural location overlooking a private lake. The 70-acre private estate features a 9-hole golf course and two fishing lakes. The traditionally styled bedrooms have modern amenities, and a large function room with lake views is popular for weddings and special occasions. The hotel has a well deserved reputation for its food.

Rooms 15 (1 fmly) Facilities ☺ ♪ 9 Fishing Gym Bowling green Steam room Nature reserve Xmas New Year Conf Class 40 Board 20 Thtr 100 Parking 100 Notes ⊗ Civ Wed 160

TENTERDEN
Kent
Map 7 TQ83

Little Silver Country Hotel

★★★ 79% HOTEL

☎ 01233 850321 & 0845 166 2516
Ashford Rd, St Michael's TN30 6SP
e-mail: enquiries@little-silver.co.uk
web: www.little-silver.co.uk
dir: M20 junct 8, A274 signed Tenterden

Located just outside the charming town of Tenterden and within easy reach of many local Kent attractions, this charming hotel is ideal for leisure and business guests as well as being a popular wedding venue. Bedrooms are spaciously appointed and well equipped; many boast spa baths. There is a spacious lounge, small bar and the modern restaurant overlooks beautifully tended gardens.

Rooms 16 (2 fmly) (6 GF) 🐾 **S** £62-£100; **D** £97-£199 (incl. bkfst) **Facilities** FTV Wi-fi ⅋ Xmas **Conf** Class 50 Board 25 Thtr 75 Del £123.50 **Parking** 70 **Notes** LB ⊗ Civ Wed 120

London Beach Country Hotel, Spa & Golf Club

★★★ 71% HOTEL

☎ 01580 766279
Ashford Rd TN30 6HX
e-mail: enquiries@londonbeach.com
web: www.londonbeach.com
dir: M20 junct 9, A28 follow signs to Tenterden (10m). Hotel on right 1m before Tenterden

A modern purpose-built hotel situated in mature grounds on the outskirts of Tenterden. The spacious bedrooms are smartly decorated, have co-ordinated soft furnishings and most rooms have balconies with superb views over the golf course. The open-plan public rooms feature a brasserie-style restaurant, where a good choice of dishes is served.

Rooms 26 (2 fmly) (3 smoking) **Facilities** Spa Wi-fi ⅋ 9 Putt green Fishing Driving range Health club Xmas New Year **Conf** Class 75 Board 40 Thtr 100 **Services** Lift **Parking** 100 **Notes** ⊗ Civ Wed 100

TETBURY
Gloucestershire
Map 4 ST89

Calcot Manor

★★★★ ◉ ◉ HOTEL

☎ 01666 890391
Calcot GL8 8YJ
e-mail: reception@calcotmanor.co.uk
web: www.calcotmanor.co.uk
dir: 3m W of Tetbury at A4135 & A46 junct

Cistercian monks built the ancient barns and stables around which this lovely English farmhouse is set. No two rooms are identical, and each is beautifully decorated in a variety of styles and equipped with the contemporary comforts. Sumptuous sitting rooms, with crackling log fires in the winter, look out over immaculate gardens. There are two dining options: the elegant conservatory restaurant and the informal Gumstool Inn. There are also ample function rooms. The superb health and leisure spa includes an indoor pool, high-tech gym, massage tables, complementary therapies and much more. For children, a supervised crèche and 'playzone' are a great attraction.

Rooms 35 (23 annexe) (13 fmly) (17 GF) 🐾 **S** £248-£515; **D** £275-£525 (incl. bkfst)* **Facilities** Spa STV Wi-fi ⅋ 🐾 ⅋ Gym Clay pigeon shooting Archery Cycling Running track Xmas New Year Child facilities **Conf** Class 40 Board 35 Thtr 120 Del from £290 to £315* **Parking** 150 **Notes** LB ⊗ Civ Wed 100

Hare & Hounds Hotel

★★★★ 78% ◉ ◉ HOTEL

COTSWOLD INNS & HOTELS

☎ 01666 880233 & 881000
Westonbirt GL8 8QL
e-mail: reception@hareandhoundshotel.com
web: www.hareandhoundshotel.com
dir: 2.5m SW of Tetbury on A433

This popular hotel, set in extensive grounds, is situated close to Westonbirt Arboretum and has remained under the same ownership for over 50 years. The stylish bedrooms are individually designed; those in the main house are more traditional and the cottage rooms are contemporary. The public rooms include an informal bar and light, airy lounges - one with a log fire lit in colder months. Guests can eat either in the bar or the attractive Beaufort Restaurant. Cotswold Inns & Hotels – AA Small Hotel Group of the Year 2012-13.

Rooms 42 (21 annexe) (8 fmly) (13 GF) **Facilities** FTV Wi-fi ⅋ ⅋ Xmas New Year **Conf** Class 80 Board 40 Thtr 120 **Parking** 85 **Notes** Civ Wed 200

The Priory Inn

★★★ 77% SMALL HOTEL

☎ 01666 502251
London Rd GL8 8JJ
e-mail: info@theprioryinn.co.uk
web: www.theprioryinn.co.uk
dir: On A433 (Cirencester to Tetbury road). Hotel 200yds from Market Square

A warm welcome is assured at this attractive inn where friendly service is a high priority to the team. Public areas and bedrooms have a contemporary style that mixes well with more traditional features, such as an open fireplace in the cosy bar dining room. Cuisine, using locally sourced produce, is offered on the menu that will suit all tastes.

Rooms 14 (1 fmly) (4 GF) **S** £85; **D** £109-£135 (incl. bkfst)* **Facilities** FTV Wi-fi Beauty treatment rooms 🎵 **Conf** Class 28 Board 28 Thtr 30 Del £125* **Parking** 35 **Notes** ⊗

T

TETBURY *continued*

Snooty Fox

★★★ 73% SMALL HOTEL

☎ 01666 502436
Market Place GL8 8DD
e-mail: res@snooty-fox.co.uk
web: www.snooty-fox.co.uk
dir: In town centre

Centrally situated this 16th-century coaching inn retains original features and is a popular venue for weekend breaks. The relaxed and friendly atmosphere, the high standard of accommodation, and the food offered in the bar and restaurant, are all very good reasons why many guests return here time and again.

Rooms 12 **Facilities** FTV Wi-fi ↻ Xmas New Year **Conf** Class 12 Board 16 Thtr 24 Del from £100 to £120

The Ormond at Tetbury

★★★ 70% HOTEL

☎ 01666 505690
23 Long St GL8 8AA
e-mail: info@theormond.co.uk
dir: Exit A433 from Cirencester into Long St. Hotel approx 100yds on left

Located on the main street of this charming town, The Ormond provides a choice of individually styled and comfortably furnished bedrooms in a variety of shapes and sizes. The ambience is relaxed and friendly, and guests may choose to dine in either the popular bar area or in the adjoining restaurant. In warmer weather, outdoor seating is available in the courtyard.

Rooms 15 (3 fmly) **S** £60-£90; **D** £75-£140 (incl. bkfst)* **Facilities** FTV Wi-fi Xmas New Year Child facilities **Conf** Class 20 Board 20 Thtr 40 **Notes** LB Civ Wed 80

TEWKESBURY
Gloucestershire Map 10 SO83

Premier Inn Tewkesbury Central

BUDGET HOTEL

☎ 0871 527 9088
Shannon Way, Ashchurch GL20 8ND
web: www.premierinn.com
dir: M5 junct 9, A438 towards Tewkesbury, hotel 400yds on right

High quality, budget accommodation ideal for both families and business travellers. Spacious, en suite bedrooms feature tea and coffee making facilities, and Freeview TV in most hotels. Internet access and Wi-fi are available for a small fee. The adjacent family restaurant features a wide and varied menu. See also the Hotel Groups pages.

Rooms 40

THETFORD
Norfolk Map 13 TL88

Premier Inn Thetford

BUDGET HOTEL

☎ 0871 527 9090
Lynn Wood, Maine St IP24 3PG
web: www.premierinn.com
dir: From A11 N follow Thetford signs. At 3rd rdbt 1st exit for town centre into Brandon Rd. 1st exit into Maine St

High quality, budget accommodation ideal for both families and business travellers. Spacious, en suite bedrooms feature tea and coffee making facilities, and Freeview TV in most hotels. Internet access and Wi-fi are available for a small fee. The adjacent family restaurant features a wide and varied menu. See also the Hotel Groups pages.

Rooms 40

THORNBURY
Gloucestershire Map 4 ST69

INSPECTORS' CHOICE

Thornbury Castle

★★★ ◎ ◎
COUNTRY HOUSE HOTEL

☎ 01454 281182
Castle St BS35 1HH
e-mail: info@thornburycastle.co.uk
web: www.thornburycastle.co.uk
dir: On A38 N'bound from Bristol take 1st turn to Thornbury. At end of High St left into Castle St, follow brown sign, entrance to Castle on left behind St Mary's Church

Henry VIII ordered the first owner of this castle to be beheaded! Guests today have the opportunity of sleeping in historical surroundings fitted out with all the modern amenities. Most rooms have four-poster or coronet beds and real fires, and guests can even choose to sleep in the Duke's Bedchamber where King Henry and Anne Boleyn once slept, or in the Tower Suite that has reputedly the widest four-poster bed in England. Tranquil lounges enjoy views over the wonderful gardens, while elegant, wood-panelled dining rooms make memorable settings for a leisurely award-winning meal. Activities include falconry and archery and there is a 500-year-old vineyard. The castle is, of course, a popular wedding venue.

Rooms 27 (3 fmly) (4 GF) ♠ **Facilities** STV FTV Wi-fi ↻ ✈ Archery Helicopter rides Clay pigeon shooting Massage treatment Xmas New Year Child facilities **Conf** Class 40 Board 30 Thtr 70 Del from £200* **Parking** 50 **Notes** Civ Wed 70

THORNTON HOUGH Map 15 SJ38
Merseyside

Thornton Hall Hotel and Spa

★★★★ 81% ◉◉◉ HOTEL

☎ 0151 336 3938 & 353 3717
Neston Rd CH63 1JF
e-mail: reservations@thorntonhallhotel.com
web: www.thorntonhallhotel.com
dir: M53 junct 4, B5151/Neston onto B5136 to
Thornton Hough (signed)

Dating back to the mid 1800s, this country-house
hotel has been carefully extended and restored. Public
areas include an impressive leisure spa boasting
excellent facilities, a choice of restaurants and a
spacious bar. Bedrooms vary in style and include
feature rooms in the main house and more
contemporary rooms in the garden wing. Delightful
grounds and gardens, and impressive function
facilities make this a popular wedding venue.

Rooms 63 (6 fmly) (28 GF) ➶ **Facilities** Spa STV FTV
Wi-fi ⓒ ☞ Gym Outdoor spa pools **Conf** Class 225
Board 80 Thtr 650 **Parking** 250 **Notes** ⊗ Closed 1
Jan Civ Wed 500

THORPENESS Map 13 TM45
Suffolk

Thorpeness Hotel T|A|HOTEL COLLECTION

★★★ 82% ◉ HOTEL

☎ 01728 452176
Lakeside Av IP16 4NH
e-mail: info@thorpeness.co.uk
web: www.thorpeness.co.uk
dir: A1094 towards Aldeburgh, take coast road N for
2m

Ideally situated in an unspoilt, tranquil setting close
to Aldeburgh and Snape Maltings. The extensive
public rooms include a choice of lounges, a
restaurant, a smart bar, a snooker room and
clubhouse. The spacious bedrooms are pleasantly
decorated, tastefully furnished and equipped with
modern facilities. An 18-hole golf course and tennis
courts are also available.

Rooms 36 (36 annexe) (10 fmly) (10 GF) **S** £80-£135;
D £98-£180 (incl. bkfst)* **Facilities** Wi-fi ఈ 18 ⌁
Putt green Fishing Cycle hire Rowing boat hire
Birdwatching Xmas New Year **Conf** Class 30 Board 24
Thtr 130 **Parking** 80 **Notes** LB Civ Wed 130

THURLASTON Map 11 SP47
Warwickshire

Draycote Hotel

★★★ 64% ◉ HOTEL

☎ 01788 521800
London Rd CV23 9LF
e-mail: mail@draycotehotel.co.uk
web: www.draycotehotel.co.uk
dir: M1 junct 17 onto M45, A45. Hotel 500mtrs on left

Located in the picturesque Warwickshire countryside
and within easy reach of motorway networks, this
hotel offers modern, comfortable and well-equipped
accommodation with a relaxed and friendly welcome.
The hotel has a challenging golf course.

Rooms 49 (24 fmly) (24 GF) **Facilities** FTV Wi-fi
ఈ 18 Putt green Golf driving range Chipping green
New Year **Conf** Class 78 Board 72 Thtr 250
Parking 150 **Notes** ⊗ Civ Wed 180

THURLESTONE Map 3 SX64
Devon

Thurlestone Hotel

★★★★ 83% ◉ HOTEL

☎ 01548 560382
TQ7 3NN
e-mail: enquiries@thurlestone.co.uk
web: www.thurlestone.co.uk
dir: A38, A384 into Totnes, A381 towards Kingsbridge,
A379 towards Churchstow, onto B3197. Into lane
signed to Thurlestone

This perennially popular hotel has been in the same
family-ownership since 1896 and continues to go
from strength to strength. A vast range of facilities is
available for all the family including indoor and
outdoor pools, a golf course and a beauty salon.
Bedrooms are equipped to ensure a comfortable stay
with many having wonderful views of the south Devon
coast. The range of eating options includes the
elegant and stylish restaurant with its stunning
views.

Rooms 65 (23 fmly) ➶ **S** £75-£140; **D** £150-£280
(incl. bkfst)* **Facilities** STV Wi-fi ⓒ ⓒ ➹ supervised
ఈ 9 ⌁ Putt green ☞ Gym Squash Badminton Games
room Toddler room Snooker room ♫ Xmas New Year
Conf Class 100 Board 40 Thtr 150 Del from £150 to
£300* **Services** Lift **Parking** 121 **Notes** LB Closed
1-2 wks Jan Civ Wed 160

THURSFORD Map 13 TF93
Norfolk

The Old Forge Seafood Restaurant

◉ RESTAURANT WITH ROOMS

☎ 01328 878345
Seafood Restaurant, Fakenham Rd NR21 0BD
e-mail: sarah.goldspink@btconnect.com
dir: On A148 (Fakenham to Holt road)

Expect a warm welcome at this delightful relaxed
restaurant with rooms. The open-plan public areas
include a lounge bar area with comfy sofas, and an
intimate restaurant with pine tables. Bedrooms are
pleasantly decorated and equipped with a good range
of useful facilities.

Rooms 3

TICEHURST Map 6 TQ63
East Sussex

Dale Hill Hotel & Golf Club

★★★★ 80% ◉ HOTEL

☎ 01580 200112
TN5 7DQ
e-mail: info@dalehill.co.uk
web: www.dalehill.co.uk
dir: M25 junct 5, A21. 5m after Lamberhurst right at
lights onto B2087 to Flimwell. Hotel 1m on left

This modern hotel is situated just a short drive from
the village. Extensive public rooms include a lounge
bar, a conservatory brasserie, a formal restaurant
and the Spike Bar, which is mainly frequented by golf
club members and has a lively atmosphere. The hotel
also has two superb 18-hole golf courses, a
swimming pool and gym.

Rooms 35 (8 fmly) (23 GF) **S** fr £70; **D** fr £100 (incl.
bkfst)* **Facilities** STV Wi-fi ⓒ ఈ 36 Putt green Gym
Covered driving range Pool table Xmas New Year
Conf Class 50 Board 50 Thtr 120 Del from £150
Services Lift **Parking** 220 **Notes** LB ⊗ Civ Wed 150

TINTAGEL
Cornwall
Map 2 SX08

Atlantic View Hotel
★★ 78% SMALL HOTEL

☎ 01840 770221
Treknow PL34 0EJ
e-mail: atlantic-view@eclipse.co.uk
web: www.holidayscornwall.com
dir: B3263 to Tregatta, turn left into Treknow, hotel on road to Trebarwith Strand Beach

Conveniently located for all the attractions of Tintagel, this family-run hotel has a wonderfully relaxed and welcoming atmosphere. Public areas include a bar, comfortable lounge, TV/games room and heated swimming pool. Bedrooms are generally spacious and some have the added advantage of distant sea views.

Rooms 9 (1 fmly) ♦ **S** £70-£80; **D** £136-£140 (incl. bkfst & dinner)* **Facilities** FTV 🔍 Pool table **Parking** 10 **Notes** LB ⊗ Closed Nov-Feb RS Mar

TITCHWELL
Norfolk
Map 13 TF74

Titchwell Manor Hotel
★★★ 87% ◉◉ HOTEL

☎ 01485 210221
PE31 8BB
e-mail: margaret@titchwellmanor.com
web: www.titchwellmanor.com
dir: On A149 (coast road) between Brancaster & Thornham

Friendly family-run hotel ideally placed for touring the north Norfolk coastline. The tastefully appointed bedrooms are very comfortable; some in the adjacent annexe offer ground floor access. Smart public rooms include a lounge area, relaxed informal bar and a delightful conservatory restaurant, overlooking the walled garden. Imaginative menus feature quality local produce and fresh fish.

Rooms 26 (18 annexe) (4 fmly) (16 GF) **S** £55-£250; **D** £90-£500 (incl. bkfst)* **Facilities** FTV Wi-fi Xmas New Year **Conf** Class 50 Board 30 Thtr 30 **Parking** 50 **Notes** LB Civ Wed 80

TOLLESHUNT KNIGHTS
Essex
Map 7 TL91

Crowne Plaza Resort Colchester - Five Lakes
★★★★ 77% ◉ HOTEL

☎ 01621 868888
Colchester Rd CM9 8HX
e-mail: enquiries@cpcolchester.co.uk
web: www.cpcolchester.co.uk
dir: Exit A12 at Kelvedon, follow brown signs through Tiptree to hotel

This hotel is set amidst 320 acres of open countryside, featuring two golf courses. The spacious bedrooms are furnished to a high standard and have excellent facilities. The public rooms offer a high degree of comfort and include five bars, two restaurants and a large lounge. The property also boasts extensive leisure facilities.

Rooms 194 (80 annexe) (4 fmly) (40 GF) ♦ **Facilities** Spa STV FTV Wi-fi 🔍 ♨ 36 ⛳ Putt green Gym Squash Sauna Steam room Health & beauty spa Badminton Aerobics Studio Hairdresser ♫ Xmas New Year **Conf** Class 700 Board 60 Thtr 2000 Del from £160* **Services** Lift **Parking** 550 **Notes** ⊗ Civ Wed 250

TONBRIDGE
Kent
Map 6 TQ54

Rose & Crown Hotel
★★★ 78% HOTEL

☎ 01732 357966
125 High St TN9 1DD
e-mail: rose.crown@bestwestern.co.uk

A 15th-century coaching inn situated in the heart of this bustling town centre. The public areas are light and airy yet still retain much original character such as oak beams and Jacobean panelling. Food is served throughout the day in the Oak Room Bar & Grill. Bedrooms are stylishly decorated, spacious and well presented; amenities include free Wi-fi.

Rooms 56 (3 fmly) (10 GF) ♦ **S** £60-£80; **D** £90-£160 **Facilities** FTV Wi-fi ♨ **Conf** Class 60 Board 60 Thtr 125 Del from £99 to £175 **Parking** 43 **Notes** ⊗ Civ Wed 60

Premier Inn Tonbridge

BUDGET HOTEL

☎ 0871 527 9096
Pembury Rd TN11 0NA
web: www.premierinn.com
dir: 11m from M25 junct 5. Follow A21 towards Hastings, pass A26 (Tunbridge Wells) junct. Exit at next junct, 1st exit at rdbt

High quality, budget accommodation ideal for both families and business travellers. Spacious, en suite bedrooms feature tea and coffee making facilities, and Freeview TV in most hotels. Internet access and Wi-fi are available for a small fee. The adjacent family restaurant features a wide and varied menu. See also the Hotel Groups pages.

Rooms 40

Premier Inn Tonbridge North
BUDGET HOTEL

☎ 0871 527 9098
Hilden Manor, London Rd TN10 3AN
web: www.premierinn.com
dir: From A21 follow Seven Oaks & Hildenborough signs. At rdbt take 2nd exit onto B245 signed Hildenborough. In 2m hotel on right

Rooms 41

TORBAY

See Brixham, Paignton & Torquay

Save on hotels. Book at **theAA.com/hotel**

TIN – TOR 463 **ENGLAND**

TORQUAY
Devon

Map 3 SX96

The Imperial Hotel

PUMA HOTELS COLLECTION

★★★★ 81% HOTEL

☎ 01803 294301
Park Hill Rd TQ1 2DG
e-mail: imperialtorquay@pumahotels.co.uk
web: www.pumahotels.co.uk
dir: A380 towards seafront. Turn left to harbour, right at clocktower. Hotel 300yds on right

This hotel has an enviable location with extensive views of the coastline. Traditional in style, the public areas are elegant and offer a choice of dining options including the Regatta Restaurant, with its stunning views over the bay. Bedrooms are spacious, most with private balconies, and the hotel has an extensive range of indoor and outdoor leisure facilities.

Rooms 152 (14 fmly) **Facilities** Spa STV Wi-fi ⊕ ⊰ supervised ⊛ Gym Squash Beauty salon Hairdresser Steam room ♫ Xmas New Year **Conf** Class 200 Board 30 Thtr 350 **Services** Lift **Parking** 140 **Notes** Civ Wed 250

Grand Hotel

RICHARDSON HOTELS
Where Memories are Made

★★★★ 76% ⊛ HOTEL

☎ 01803 296677
Sea Front TQ2 6NT
e-mail: reservations@grandtorquay.co.uk
web: www.grandtorquay.co.uk
dir: A380 to Torquay. At seafront turn right, then 1st right. Hotel on corner, entrance 1st on left

Within level walking distance of the town, this large Edwardian hotel overlooks the bay and offers modern facilities. Many of the bedrooms, some with balconies, enjoy the best of the views; all are very well equipped. Boaters Bar also benefits from the hotel's stunning position and offers an informal alternative to the Gainsborough Restaurant.

Rooms 132 (32 fmly) (3 GF) ⊰ **S** £53-£112; **D** £69-£149 (incl. bkfst)* **Facilities** FTV Wi-fi ⊕ ⊰ supervised ⊛ Gym Beauty clinic Car valeting ♫ Xmas New Year **Conf** Class 150 Board 60 Thtr 250 Del from £110 to £140* **Services** Lift **Parking** 57 **Notes** LB Civ Wed 250

Palace Hotel

★★★★ 72% HOTEL

☎ 01803 200200
Babbacombe Rd TQ1 3TG
e-mail: info@palacetorquay.co.uk
web: www.palacetorquay.co.uk
dir: Towards harbour, left by clocktower into Babbacombe Rd, hotel on right after 1m

Set in 25 acres of stunning, beautifully tended wooded grounds, the Palace offers a tranquil environment. Suitable for business and leisure, the hotel boasts a huge range of well-presented indoor and outdoor facilities. Much of the original charm and grandeur is still in evidence, particularly in the dining room. Many of the bedrooms enjoy views of the magnificent gardens.

Rooms 141 (7 fmly) **Facilities** Wi-fi ⊕ ⊰ ⌘ 9 ⊛ Putt green ⌘ Gym Squash Table tennis Snooker Childrens' play area Xmas New Year **Conf** Class 800 Board 40 Thtr 1000 **Services** Lift **Parking** 140 **Notes** ⊗

Best Western Hotel Gleneagles

Best Western

★★★ 80% HOTEL

☎ 01803 293637
Asheldon Rd, Wellswood TQ1 2QS
e-mail: enquiries@hotel-gleneagles.com
dir: A380 onto A3022 to A379, follow to St Mathias Church, turn right into Asheldon Rd

From its hillside location, looking out over Anstey's Cove towards Lyme Bay, this peacefully located hotel is appointed to an impressive standard. Stylish public areas combine comfort, flair and quality with ample space in which to find a quiet spot to unwind. Bedrooms also have a contemporary feel; many have balconies or patios. The pool area has a real Riviera feel with elegant Lloyd Loom sun loungers and palm trees.

Rooms 41 (2 fmly) (5 GF) ⊰ **Facilities** FTV Wi-fi ⊱ ⊰ Xmas New Year **Services** Lift **Parking** 21

Corbyn Head Hotel

★★★ 77% HOTEL

☎ 01803 213611
Torbay Rd, Sea Front TQ2 6RH
e-mail: info@corbynhead.com
web: www.corbynhead.com
dir: Follow signs to Torquay seafront, turn right on seafront. Hotel on right with green canopies

This hotel occupies a prime position overlooking Torbay, and offers well-equipped bedrooms, many with sea views and some with balconies. The staff are friendly and welcoming, and a well-stocked bar and comfortable lounge are available. Guests can enjoy fine dining in the Harbour View Restaurant, with attentive service assured.

Rooms 45 (4 fmly) (9 GF) **Facilities** FTV Wi-fi ⊰ Gym Squash ♫ Xmas New Year **Conf** Class 30 Board 30 Thtr 50 **Parking** 50 **Notes** Civ Wed 85

T

TORQUAY *continued*

Livermead House Hotel

★★★ 74% HOTEL

☎ 01803 294361 & 294363
Torbay Rd TQ2 6QJ
e-mail: info@livermead.com
web: www.livermead.com
dir: From seafront turn right, follow A379 towards
Paignton & Livermead, hotel opposite Institute Beach

Having a splendid waterfront location, this hotel
dates back to the 1820s and is where Charles
Kingsley is said to have written *The Water Babies*.
Bedrooms vary in size and style, excellent public
rooms are popular for private parties and meetings,
and a range of leisure facilities is provided. Enjoyable
cuisine is served in the impressive restaurant.

Rooms 67 (6 fmly) (2 GF) **Facilities** ⚡ Gym Squash
♫ Xmas **Conf** Class 175 Board 80 Thtr 320
Services Lift **Parking** 131

Best Western Livermead Cliff Hotel

Best Western

★★★ 71% HOTEL

☎ 01803 299666
Torbay Rd TQ2 6RQ
e-mail: enquiries@livermeadcliff.co.uk
web: www.livermeadcliff.co.uk
dir: A379, A3022 to Torquay, towards seafront, turn
right towards Paignton. Hotel 600yds on seaward side

Situated at the water's edge, this long-established
hotel offers friendly service and traditional

hospitality. The splendid views can be enjoyed from
the lounge, bar and dining room. Alternatively, guests
can take advantage of refreshment on the wonderful
terrace and enjoy one of the best outlooks in the bay.
Bedrooms, many with sea views and some with
balconies, are comfortable and well equipped; a
range of room sizes is available.

Rooms 65 (21 fmly) **Facilities** FTV Wi-fi Fishing Use
of facilities at sister hotel Xmas New Year
Conf Class 60 Board 40 Thtr 120 **Services** Lift
Parking 80 **Notes** Civ Wed 200

Abbey Lawn Hotel

★★★ 66% HOTEL

☎ 01803 299199 & 203181
Scarborough Rd TQ2 5UQ
e-mail: nicky@holdsworthhotels.freeserve.co.uk

Conveniently located for both the seafront and town
centre, this is an ideal base for visiting the
attractions of the 'English Riviera'. Many of the
bedrooms, including the four-poster suite, benefit
from lovely sea views. Facilities include a health club
with extensive leisure activities, plus indoor and
outdoor pools. Traditional cuisine is served in the
elegant restaurant, and evening entertainment is a
regular feature in the ballroom.

Rooms 57 (3 fmly) **Facilities** ⊛ supervised ⚡
supervised Gym Steam room ♫ Xmas New Year
Services Lift **Parking** 20 **Notes** ⊗ Closed Jan

Anchorage Hotel

★★ 74% HOTEL

☎ 01803 326175
Cary Park, Aveland Rd, Babbacombe TQ1 3PT
e-mail: enquiries@anchoragehotel.co.uk

Quietly located in a residential area and providing a
friendly welcome, this family-run establishment
enjoys a great deal of repeat business. Bedrooms
come in a range of sizes but all rooms are neatly
presented. Evening entertainment is provided
regularly in the large and comfortable lounge.

Rooms 56 (5 fmly) (17 GF) **S** £32.50-£52; **D** £65-£104
(incl. bkfst & dinner)* **Facilities** FTV Wi-fi ⚡ ♫
Xmas New Year **Services** Lift **Parking** 26 **Notes** LB

Albaston House Hotel

★★ 69% HOTEL

☎ 01803 296758
27 St Marychurch Rd TQ1 3JF
e-mail: albastonhousehotel@hotmail.com
dir: A380 left at lights then B3199, follow signs for
Plainmoor to Westhill Rd. Right at lights. Hotel 0.5m
on left

The Albaston is situated close to the town centre and
is also convenient for the quieter attractions of
Babbacombe. Public areas and bedrooms alike
combine comfort and quality. Many guests return
time after time to this welcoming, family-run hotel.

Rooms 13 (2 fmly) **S** £25-£36; **D** £50-£72 (incl.
bkfst)* **Facilities** FTV Wi-fi ⅍ **Parking** 6 **Notes** LB ⊗
Closed 30 Nov-28 Feb

The Heritage Hotel

★★ 68% HOTEL

☎ 01803 299332
Seafront, Shedden Hill TQ2 5TY
e-mail: enquiries@heritagehoteltorquay.co.uk
web: www.heritagehoteltorquay.co.uk
dir: A380 to Torquay follow signs to seafront. Hotel on
left

In an elevated position overlooking Tor Abbey Sands,
this hotel is a short walk from both the harbour and
the shops. The bedrooms are traditionally furnished
and come in various sizes; all have sea views except
one. There is a variety of eating options based on
American food themes and a large sun deck for
relaxation in summer.

Rooms 24 (24 fmly) (4 GF) ⚡ **S** £40-£50; **D** £70-£90
(incl. bkfst) **Facilities** STV FTV Wi-fi ⊛ **Services** Lift
Parking 40 **Notes** LB ⊗

Save on hotels. Book at **theAA.com/hotel**

TOR – TRI 465 ENGLAND

Maycliffe Hotel

★★ 68% HOTEL

☎ 01803 294964
St Lukes Road North TQ2 5DP
e-mail: bob.west1@virgin.net
web: www.maycliffehotel.co.uk
dir: Left from Kings Dr, along seafront keep in left
lane, at next lights (Belgrave Rd) up Shedden Hill,
2nd right into St Lukes Rd then 1st left

Set in a quiet and elevated position which is
convenient for the town centre and attractions, the
Maycliffe is a popular choice for leisure breaks. The
bedrooms are individually decorated and equipped
with modern facilities; there are two rooms on the
ground floor suitable for less able guests. There is a
quiet lounge for relaxation, and the bar hosts a
cabaret on certain nights during the season.

Rooms 28 (1 fmly) (2 GF) **Facilities** ♫ Xmas
Services Lift **Parking** 10 **Notes** ✪ No children 4yrs
Closed 2 Jan-12 Feb

Regina Hotel

★★ 68% HOTEL

☎ 01803 292904
Victoria Pde TQ1 2BE
e-mail: regina.torquay@alfatravel.co.uk
web: www.leisureplex.co.uk
dir: Into Torquay, follow harbour signs, hotel on outer
corner of harbour

This hotel enjoys a pleasant and convenient location
right on the harbourside, a short stroll from the
town's attractions. Bedrooms, some with harbour
views, vary in size. Entertainment is provided on most
nights and there is a choice of bars.

Rooms 68 (5 fmly) **Facilities** FTV ♫ Xmas New Year
Services Lift **Parking** 6 **Notes** ✪ Closed Jan & part
Feb RS Nov-Dec (ex Xmas) & Feb-Mar

Shelley Court Hotel

★★ 68% HOTEL

☎ 01803 295642
29 Croft Rd TQ2 5UD
e-mail: shelleycourthotel@hotmail.com
dir: From B3199 up Shedden Hill Rd, 1st left into
Croft Rd

This hotel, popular with groups, is located in a
pleasant, quiet area that overlooks the town towards
Torbay. With a friendly team of staff, many guests
return here time and again. Entertainment is provided
most evenings in the season. Bedrooms come in a
range of sizes and there is a large and comfortable
lounge bar.

Rooms 27 (3 fmly) (6 GF) **Facilities** FTV ✦ Pool table
Indoor skittle alley ♫ Xmas New Year **Parking** 20
Notes Closed 4 Jan-10 Feb

Ashley Court Hotel

★★ 64% HOTEL

☎ 01803 292417
107 Abbey Rd TQ2 5NP
e-mail: reception@ashleycourt.co.uk
web: www.ashleycourt.co.uk
dir: A380 to seafront, left to Shedden Hill to lights,
hotel opposite

Located close to the town centre and within easy
strolling distance of the seafront, this hotel offers a
warm welcome to guests. Bedrooms are pleasantly
appointed and some have sea views. The outdoor pool
and patio are popular with guests wishing to soak up
some sunshine. Live entertainment is provided every
night throughout the season.

Rooms 83 (12 fmly) (8 GF) (14 smoking) ✦
Facilities ✦ Games room ♫ Xmas New Year
Services Lift **Parking** 51 **Notes** ✪ Closed 3 Jan-1
Feb

Premier Inn Torquay

BUDGET HOTEL

☎ 0871 527 9102
Seafront, Belgrave Rd TQ2 5HE
web: www.premierinn.com
dir: On A380 into Torquay, continue to lights (Torre
Station on right). Right into Avenue Road to Kings
Drive. Left at seafront, hotel at lights

High quality, budget accommodation ideal for both
families and business travellers. Spacious, en suite
bedrooms feature tea and coffee making facilities,
and Freeview TV in most hotels. Internet access and
Wi-fi are available for a small fee. The adjacent
family restaurant features a wide and varied menu.
See also the Hotel Groups pages.

Rooms 83

TRING
Hertfordshire

Map 6 SP91

Pendley Manor Hotel

★★★★ 78% ❀❀ HOTEL

☎ 01442 891891
Cow Ln HP23 5QY
e-mail: info@pendley-manor.co.uk
web: www.pendley-manor.co.uk
dir: M25 junct 20, A41 (Tring exit). At rdbt follow
Berkhamsted/London signs. 1st left signed Tring
Station & Pendley Manor

This impressive Victorian mansion is set in extensive
and mature landscaped grounds where peacocks
roam. The spacious bedrooms are situated in both the
manor house and the wing, and offer a useful range
of facilities. Public areas include a cosy bar, a
conservatory lounge and an intimate restaurant as
well as a leisure centre.

Rooms 73 (17 fmly) (17 GF) **S** £90-£140;
D £100-£150 (incl. bkfst)* **Facilities** Spa FTV Wi-fi ⟨
⟨ ✦ Gym Steam room Dance Studio Sauna Snooker
room **Conf** Class 80 Board 80 Thtr 250 Del £230*
Services Lift **Parking** 150 **Notes** LB ✪ Civ Wed 160

Premier Inn Tring

BUDGET HOTEL

☎ 0871 527 9104
Tring Hill HP23 4LD
web: www.premierinn.com
dir: M25 junct 20, A41 towards Aylesbury, at end of
Hemel Hempstead/Tring bypass straight on at rdbt,
hotel approx 100yds on right

High quality, budget accommodation ideal for both
families and business travellers. Spacious, en suite
bedrooms feature tea and coffee making facilities,
and Freeview TV in most hotels. Internet access and
Wi-fi are available for a small fee. The adjacent
family restaurant features a wide and varied menu.
See also the Hotel Groups pages.

Rooms 30

T

TROWBRIDGE   Map 4 ST85
Wiltshire

Fieldways Hotel & Health Club
★★ 67% SMALL HOTEL

☎ 01225 768336
Hilperton Rd BA14 7JP
e-mail: fieldwayshotel@yahoo.co.uk
dir: A361 from Trowbridge towards Melksham, Chippenham, Devizes. Hotel last property on left

Originally part of a Victorian mansion this hotel is quietly set in well-kept grounds and provides a pleasant combination of spacious, comfortably furnished bedrooms. There are two splendid wood-panelled dining rooms, one of which is impressively finished in oak, pine, rosewood and mahogany. The indoor leisure facilities include a gym, a pool and treatment rooms; 'Top to Toe' days are especially popular.

Rooms 13 (5 annexe) (2 fmly) (2 GF) **S** £60; **D** £80-£90 (incl. bkfst)* **Facilities** Spa Wi-fi ✪ Gym Range of beauty treatments/massage Pampering days **Conf** Class 40 Board 20 Thtr 40 **Parking** 70 **Notes** LB

TRURO   Map 2 SW84
Cornwall

Mannings Hotel
★★★ 85% HOTEL

☎ 01872 270345
Lemon St TR1 2QB
e-mail: reception@manningshotels.co.uk
web: www.manningshotels.co.uk
dir: A30 to Carland Cross then Truro. Follow brown signs to hotel in city centre

A smart and friendly Georgian townhouse in the centre of Truro which is both stylish and contemporary. The bedrooms are tastefully designed and furnished, and the modern airy interior blends well with the charm of the original architecture. The bar and brasserie are popular with residents and locals alike, and menus change to reflect the best of what's seasonally and locally available. An extensive wine list is on offer along with a range of authentic cocktails.

Rooms 43 (9 annexe) (4 fmly) (3 GF) ➜ **S** £79-£129; **D** £79-£129 (incl. bkfst)* **Facilities** FTV Wi-fi **Parking** 43 **Notes** ⊗ Closed 25-26 Dec

Alverton Manor
Ⓤ

☎ 01872 276633
Tregolls Rd TR1 1ZQ
e-mail: reception@alvertonmanor.co.uk
web: www.alvertonmanor.co.uk
dir: From A30 at Carland Cross take A39 to Truro. At lights right onto A39 (Tregolls Rd) signed Truro/Falmouth

Currently the rating for this establishment is not confirmed. This may be due to a change of ownership or because it has only recently joined the AA rating scheme. For further details please see the AA website: theAA.com

Rooms 33 (3 GF) ➜ **S** £80-£125; **D** £130-£160 (incl. bkfst)* **Facilities** FTV Wi-fi Xmas **Conf** Class 40 Board 60 Thtr 120 Del from £140 to £200* **Parking** 120 **Notes** LB Closed 28 Dec RS 4 Jan Civ Wed 80

Premier Inn Truro
BUDGET HOTEL

☎ 0871 527 9106
Old Carnon Hill, Carnon Downs TR3 6JT
web: www.premierinn.com
dir: On A39 (Truro to Falmouth road), 3m SW of Truro

High quality, budget accommodation ideal for both families and business travellers. Spacious, en suite bedrooms feature tea and coffee making facilities, and Freeview TV in most hotels. Internet access and Wi-fi are available for a small fee. The adjacent family restaurant features a wide and varied menu. See also the Hotel Groups pages.

Rooms 62

TUNBRIDGE WELLS (ROYAL)   Map 6 TQ53
Kent

The Spa Hotel
★★★★ 80% ◉ HOTEL

☎ 01892 520331
Mount Ephraim TN4 8XJ
e-mail: reservations@spahotel.co.uk
web: www.spahotel.co.uk
dir: A21 to A26, follow A264 East Grinstead signs, hotel on right

Set in 14 acres of beautifully tended grounds, this imposing 18th-century mansion offers spacious, modern bedrooms that are stylishly decorated and thoughtfully equipped. The public rooms include the Chandelier Restaurant, a champagne bar and the Orangery which complements the traditional lounge. There are extensive meeting and health club facilities, and the spa offers treatment rooms and is licensed for civil wedding ceremonies.

Rooms 70 (4 fmly) (1 GF) **S** £110-£135; **D** £125-£180* **Facilities** Spa STV FTV Wi-fi ✪ ➳ ➲ Gym ♫ Xmas New Year **Conf** Class 90 Board 90 Thtr 300 **Services** Lift **Parking** 150 **Notes** LB ⊗ Civ Wed 150

The Brew House Hotel

★★★★ 77% ◉ HOTEL

☎ 01892 520587
1 Warwick Park TN2 5TA
e-mail: reception@brewhousehotel.com
web: www.brewhousehotel.com
dir: A267, 1st left onto Warwick Park, hotel immediately on left

Located adjacent to The Pantiles and a short walk from the historic town centre with its interesting boutiques, restaurants and bars. Built in the 18th-century and appointed in a contemporary style, this hotel offers accommodation of the highest quality including impressive bathrooms and hi-tech amenities. The popular, modern restaurant, brasserie and bar has mood lighting and chic furnishings creating an relaxed atmosphere.

Rooms 15 (5 annexe) (2 fmly) **S** £155-£199; **D** £155-£199 (incl. bkfst) **Facilities** STV FTV Wi-fi ◈ Gym ♫ Xmas New Year **Conf** Class 100 Board 50 Thtr 120 Del £180 **Services** Lift Air con **Parking** 8 **Notes** LB ⊗

Hotel du Vin Tunbridge Wells

★★★★ 72% ◉
TOWN HOUSE HOTEL

☎ 01892 526455
Crescent Rd TN1 2LY
e-mail: reception.tunbridgewells@hotelduvin.com
web: www.hotelduvin.com
dir: Follow town centre, to main junct of Mount Pleasant Rd & Crescent Rd/Church Rd. Hotel 150yds on right just past Phillips House

This impressive Grade II listed building dates from 1762, and as a princess, Queen Victoria often stayed here. The spacious bedrooms are available in a range of sizes, beautifully and individually appointed, and equipped with a host of thoughtful extras. Public rooms include a bistro-style restaurant, two elegant lounges and a small bar.

Rooms 34 ♟ **Facilities** STV Wi-fi Boules court in garden **Conf** Class 40 Board 25 Thtr 60 **Services** Lift **Parking** 30 **Notes** Civ Wed 84

Mercure Tunbridge Wells

★★★★ 71% HOTEL

☎ 0844 815 9074
8 Tonbridge Rd, Pembury TN2 4QL
e-mail: sales.mercuretunbridgewells@jupiterhotels.co.uk
web: www.jupiterhotels.co.uk
dir: M25 junct 5, A21 S. Left at 1st rdbt signed Pembury Hospital. Hotel on left, 400yds past hospital

Built in the style of a traditional Kentish oast house, this well presented hotel is conveniently located just off the A21 with easy access to the M25. Bedrooms are comfortably appointed for both business and leisure guests. Public areas include a leisure club and a range of meeting rooms.

Rooms 84 (8 fmly) (40 GF) ♟ **Facilities** STV FTV Wi-fi ◈ HL ◈ Steam room Sauna Xmas New Year **Conf** Class 80 Board 50 Thtr 150 **Parking** 200 **Notes** Civ Wed 150

Russell Hotel

★★ 65% METRO HOTEL

☎ 01892 544833
80 London Rd TN1 1DZ
e-mail: sales@russell-hotel.com
web: www.russell-hotel.com
dir: At A26 & A264 junct at lights, uphill on A26, hotel on right

This detached Victorian property is situated just a short walk from the centre of town. The generously proportioned bedrooms in the main house are pleasantly decorated and well equipped. In addition, there are several smartly appointed self-contained suites in an adjacent building. The public rooms include a lounge and cosy bar.

Rooms 26 (5 annexe) (5 fmly) (1 GF) **S** £55-£85; **D** £65-£98 (incl. bkfst)* **Facilities** FTV Wi-fi **Conf** Class 10 Board 10 Thtr 10 **Parking** 14 **Notes** LB ⊗

TURNERS HILL   Map 6 TQ33
West Sussex

Alexander House Hotel & Utopia Spa

★★★★★ 86% ◉◉ HOTEL

☎ 01342 714914
East St RH10 4QD
e-mail: info@alexanderhouse.co.uk
web: www.alexanderhouse.co.uk
dir: 6m from M23 junct 10, on B2110 between Turners Hill & East Grinstead

Set in 175 acres of parkland and landscaped gardens, this delightful country house hotel dates back to the 17th century. Most of the bedrooms are very spacious and all have luxurious bathrooms; the rooms in the most recent wing are particularly stunning. There are two options for dining - the AG's Grill which has been awarded AA Rosettes, or the lively Reflections which is set around an open courtyard, ideal for eating alfresco. The Utopia Spa has a state-of-the-art pool and gym, as well as specialised treatments.

Rooms 38 (12 fmly) (1 GF) ♟ **D** £125-£550* **Facilities** Spa STV Wi-fi ◈ ◈ ◈ Gym Clay shooting Archery Mountain bikes Pony trekking Xmas New Year **Conf** Class 70 Board 40 Thtr 150 Del from £195 to £280* **Services** Lift **Parking** 100 **Notes** LB ⊗ Civ Wed 100

TWICKENHAM
Greater London

See London plan 1 B2

London Marriott Hotel Twickenham

Marriott. HOTELS & RESORTS

★★★★ 77% HOTEL

☎ 020 8891 8200
198 Whitton Rd TW2 7BA
dir: A316, exit Whitton Rd rdbt towards stadium.
Hotel within South Stand of stadium

This purpose-built hotel occupies an area of the South Stand of the Twickenham Rugby Club Stadium. The bedrooms have the latest Marriott innovations including flat-screen LCD TVs and state-of-the-art technology; six suites even overlook the pitch. There is a popular Twenty Two South restaurant, the Side Step sports bar and a café lounge. Guests can use the health club and there's a wide range of meeting rooms and conference facilities. Hampton Court Palace, Kew Gardens and the River Thames are all close by.

Rooms 156 (76 fmly) **Facilities** STV FTV Wi-fi HL supervised Gym Sauna Steam room Soft climbing wall Xmas New Year **Conf** Class 100 Board 30 Thtr 240 **Services** Lift Air con **Parking** 150 **Notes** ⊗

Premier Inn Twickenham East

Premier Inn

BUDGET HOTEL

☎ 0871 527 9108
Corner Sixth Cross, Staines Rd TW2 5PE
web: www.premierinn.com
dir: M25 junct 12 onto M3, follow Central London signs, at end of M3 becomes A316. Straight on at 1st rdbt. Hotel 500yds on left

High quality, budget accommodation ideal for both families and business travellers. Spacious, en suite bedrooms feature tea and coffee making facilities, and Freeview TV in most hotels. Internet access and Wi-fi are available for a small fee. The adjacent family restaurant features a wide and varied menu. See also the Hotel Groups pages.

Rooms 17

Premier Inn Twickenham Stadium

BUDGET HOTEL

☎ 0871 527 9110
Chertsey Rd, Whitton TW2 6LS
web: www.premierinn.com
dir: From M3 onto A316, then A305 signed Twickenham. At Hospital Bridge Rdbt 3rd exit into Hospital Bridge Rd. Take B358 signed Teddington. Becomes Sixth Cross Rd. Hotel on left

Rooms 31

TWO BRIDGES
Devon   Map 3 SX67

Two Bridges Hotel

★★★ 78% HOTEL

☎ 01822 892300
PL20 6SW
e-mail: enquiries@twobridges.co.uk
web: www.twobridges.co.uk
dir: At junct of B3212 & B3357

This wonderfully relaxing hotel is set in the heart of the Dartmoor National Park, in a beautiful riverside location. Three standards of comfortable rooms provide every modern convenience, and include four-poster rooms. There is a choice of lounges and fine dining is available in the restaurant, where menus feature local game and other seasonal produce.

Rooms 33 (2 fmly) (6 GF) **Facilities** STV Wi-fi Fishing Xmas New Year **Conf** Class 60 Board 40 Thtr 130 **Parking** 100 **Notes** Civ Wed 130

TYNEMOUTH
Tyne & Wear   Map 21 NZ36

Grand Hotel

★★★ 79% HOTEL

☎ 0191 293 6666
Grand Pde NE30 4ER
e-mail: info20@grandhotel-uk.com
web: www.grandhotel-uk.com
dir: A1058 for Tynemouth. At coast rdbt turn right. Hotel on right approx 0.5m

This grand Victorian building offers stunning views of the coast. Bedrooms come in a variety of styles and are well equipped, tastefully decorated and have impressive bathrooms. In addition to the restaurant there are two bars; the elegant and imposing staircase is a focal point, and is a favourite spot for the bride and groom to have their photograph taken after their wedding here.

Rooms 45 (5 annexe) (11 fmly) (10 smoking) **Facilities** STV Wi-fi Xmas New Year **Conf** Class 40 Board 40 Thtr 130 **Services** Lift **Parking** 16 **Notes** ⊗ RS Sun evening Civ Wed 120

UCKFIELD
East Sussex   Map 6 TQ42

INSPECTORS' CHOICE

Buxted Park Hotel

HandPICKED HOTELS BUILT FOR PLEASURE

★★★★ ◉◉ HOTEL

☎ 01825 733333 & 0845 458 0901
Buxted TN22 4AY
e-mail: buxtedpark@handpickedhotels.co.uk/
buxtedpark
web: www.handpickedhotels.co.uk/buxtedpark
dir: From A26 (Uckfield bypass) take A272 signed Buxted. Through lights, hotel 1m on right

An attractive Grade II listed Georgian mansion dating back to the 17th century. The property is set amidst 300 acres of beautiful countryside and landscaped gardens. The stylish, thoughtfully equipped bedrooms are split between the main house and the modern Garden Wing. An interesting choice of dishes is served in the restaurant. Hand Picked Hotels – AA Hotel Group of the Year 2012-13.

Rooms 44 (7 fmly) (16 GF) **Facilities** FTV Wi-fi Fishing Gym Orienteering Walking trail Snooker room Xmas New Year **Conf** Class 80 Board 42 Thtr 180 Del from £140 to £190* **Services** Lift **Parking** 100 **Notes** ⊗ Civ Wed 120

East Sussex National Golf Resort & Spa

★★★★ 77% ◉ HOTEL

☎ 01825 880088
Little Horsted TN22 5ES
e-mail: reception@eastsussexnational.co.uk
dir: M25 junct 6, A22 signed East Grinstead & Eastbourne. Straight on at rdbt junct of A22 & A26 (Little Horsted). At next rdbt right to hotel

This modern hotel is located in a lovely country location and offers a super range of facilities with

Save on hotels. Book at **theAA.com/hotel**

TWI – UPP 469 ENGLAND

two golf courses and an impressive leisure suite. In addition there are also conference and meeting facilities. The bedrooms are spacious and have good facilities; all have delightful views across the golf course to the countryside beyond. The cuisine is enjoyable; particularly at breakfast, which is served in the restaurant that overlooks the course.

Rooms 104 (3 fmly) (36 GF) ↻ **Facilities** Spa STV FTV Wi-fi ↻ ⑬ ↧ 36 ⑲ Putt green ⤳ Gym Academy of Golf Xmas New Year **Conf** Class 200 Board 50 Thtr 450 Del from £130 to £170* **Services** Lift Air con **Parking** 500 **Notes** ⊗ Civ Wed 250

Horsted Place

★★★ ⑯ HOTEL

☎ 01825 750581
Little Horsted TN22 5TS
e-mail: hotel@horstedplace.co.uk
dir: From Uckfield 2m S on A26 towards Lewes

This property is one of Britain's finest examples of Gothic revivalist architecture, and much of the 1850s building was designed by Augustus Pugin. The hotel is situated in extensive landscaped grounds, with a tennis court and croquet lawn, and is adjacent to the East Sussex National Golf Club. The spacious bedrooms, of ranging sizes and designs, are attractively decorated, tastefully furnished and equipped with many thoughtful touches such as flowers and books; most bedrooms also have a separate sitting area. Formal dining can be enjoyed in the elegant dining room (no children after 7pm) where the menus are based the quality seasonal produce. Pre-dinner drinks and after-dinner coffees can be enjoyed either in the Drawing Room or on the terrace overlooking the garden.

Rooms 20 (3 annexe) (5 fmly) (2 GF) ↻
S £145-£360; **D** £145-£360 (incl. bkfst)*
Facilities STV FTV Wi-fi ↧ 36 ⑲ ⤳ Free use of gym & indoor pool at nearby hotel ♫ Xmas New Year **Conf** Class 50 Board 40 Thtr 80 Del from £170* **Services** Lift **Parking** 32 **Notes** LB ⊗ No children 7yrs Civ Wed 100

ULLESTHORPE — Map 11 SP58
Leicestershire

Best Western Ullesthorpe Court Hotel & Golf Club

★★★★ 78% HOTEL

☎ 01455 209023
Frolesworth Rd LE17 5BZ
e-mail: bookings@ullesthorpecourt.co.uk
web: www.bw-ullesthorpecourt.co.uk
dir: M1 junct 20 towards Lutterworth. Follow brown tourist signs

Complete with its own golf club, this impressively equipped hotel is within easy reach of the motorway network, NEC and Birmingham airport. Public areas include both formal and informal eating options and extensive conference and leisure facilities. Spacious bedrooms are thoughtfully equipped for both the business and leisure guests, and a four-poster room is available.

Rooms 72 (3 fmly) (16 GF) ↻ **S** £69-£104; **D** £69-£104* **Facilities** Spa STV Wi-fi ↻ ⑬ supervised ↧ 18 ⑲ Putt green Gym Beauty room Steam room Sauna Snooker room New Year **Conf** Class 48 Board 30 Thtr 80 Del from £105 to £145* **Services** Lift **Parking** 280 **Notes** LB ⊗ RS 25-26 Dec Civ Wed 120

ULLSWATER

See Glenridding & Patterdale

UPPER SLAUGHTER — Map 10 SP12
Gloucestershire

Lords of the Manor

★★★★ ⑯⑯⑯
COUNTRY HOUSE HOTEL

☎ 01451 820243
GL54 2JD
e-mail: reservations@lordsofthemanor.com
web: www.lordsofthemanor.com
dir: 2m W of A429. Exit A40 onto A429, take 'The Slaughters' turn. Through Lower Slaughter for 1m to Upper Slaughter. Hotel on right

This wonderfully welcoming 17th-century manor house hotel sits in eight acres of gardens and parkland surrounded by Cotswold countryside. A relaxed atmosphere, underpinned by professional and attentive service is the hallmark here, so that guests are often reluctant to leave. The hotel has elegant public rooms that overlook the immaculate lawns, and the restaurant is the venue for consistently impressive cuisine. Bedrooms have much character and charm, combined with the extra touches expected of a hotel of this stature.

Rooms 26 (4 fmly) (9 GF) **S** £150-£550; **D** £199-£550 (incl. bkfst)* **Facilities** FTV Wi-fi Fishing ⤳ Xmas New Year **Conf** Class 20 Board 20 Thtr 30 Del from £185 to £335* **Parking** 40 **Notes** LB Civ Wed 80

U

UPPINGHAM
Rutland — Map 11 SP89

The Lake Isle

◎◎ RESTAURANT WITH ROOMS

☎ 01572 822951
16 High Street East LE15 9PZ
e-mail: info@lakeisle.co.uk
web: www.lakeisle.co.uk
dir: From A47, turn left at 2nd lights, 100yds on right

This attractive townhouse centres round a delightful restaurant and small elegant bar. There is also an inviting first-floor guest lounge, and the bedrooms are extremely well appointed and thoughtfully equipped; spacious split-level cottage suites situated in a quiet courtyard are also available. The imaginative cooking and an extremely impressive wine list are highlights.

Rooms 12 (3 annexe) (1 fmly)

UPTON UPON SEVERN
Worcestershire — Map 10 SO84

White Lion Hotel

★★★ 73% ◎ HOTEL

☎ 01684 592551
21 High St WR8 0HJ
e-mail: reservations@whitelionhotel.biz
dir: A422, A38 towards Tewkesbury. In 8m take B4104, after 1m cross bridge, turn left to hotel, past bend on left

Famed for being the inn depicted in Henry Fielding's novel *Tom Jones*, this 16th-century hotel is a reminder of 'Old England' with features such as exposed beams and wall timbers still remaining. The quality furnishing and the decor throughout enhance its character; the bedrooms are smart and include one four-poster room.

Rooms 13 (2 annexe) (2 fmly) (2 GF) ☖ **S** £70-£80; (incl. bkfst)* **Facilities** FTV Wi-fi **Parking** 14 **Notes** LB Closed 1 Jan RS 25 Dec

UTTOXETER
Staffordshire — Map 10 SK03

Premier Inn Uttoxeter

BUDGET HOTEL

☎ 0871 527 9112
Derby Rd ST14 5AA
web: www.premierinn.com
dir: At junct of A50 & B5030 on outskirts of Uttoxeter, 7m S of Alton Towers Theme Park

High quality, budget accommodation ideal for both families and business travellers. Spacious, en suite bedrooms feature tea and coffee making facilities, and Freeview TV in most hotels. Internet access and Wi-fi are available for a small fee. The adjacent family restaurant features a wide and varied menu. See also the Hotel Groups pages.

Rooms 41

UXBRIDGE

See Ruislip

VENTNOR
Isle of Wight — Map 5 SZ57

The Royal Hotel

★★★★ 79% ◎◎ HOTEL

☎ 01983 852186
Belgrave Rd PO38 1JJ
e-mail: enquiries@royalhoteliow.co.uk
web: www.royalhoteliow.co.uk
dir: A3055 into Ventnor follow one-way system, after lights left into Belgrave Rd. Hotel on right

This smart hotel enjoys a central yet peaceful location in its own gardens, complete with an outdoor pool. Spacious, elegant public areas include a bright conservatory, bar and lounge. Bedrooms, appointed to a high standard, vary in size and style. Staff are friendly and efficient, particularly in the smart restaurant, where modern British cuisine is offered.

Rooms 53 (9 fmly) **S** £105-£120; **D** £175-£195 (incl. bkfst)* **Facilities** Wi-fi ✲ Xmas New Year **Conf** Class 40 Board 24 Thtr 100 **Services** Lift **Parking** 50 **Notes** ⊗ Closed 1st 2 wks Jan Civ Wed 120

Eversley Hotel

★★★ 74% HOTEL

☎ 01983 852244 & 852462
Park Av PO38 1LB
e-mail: eversleyhotel@yahoo.co.uk
web: www.eversleyhotel.com
dir: On A3055 W of Ventnor, next to Ventnor Park

Located west of Ventnor, this hotel enjoys a quiet location and has some rooms with garden and pool views. The spacious restaurant is sometimes used for local functions, and there is a bar, television room, lounge area, a card room as well as a jacuzzi and gym. Bedrooms are generally a good size.

Rooms 30 (8 fmly) (2 GF) **Facilities** ✲ Gym Xmas **Conf** Class 40 Board 20 **Parking** 23 **Notes** Closed 30 Nov-22 Dec & 2 Jan-8 Feb

Ventnor Towers Hotel

★★★ 70% HOTEL

☎ 01983 852277
54 Madeira Rd PO38 1QT
e-mail: reservations@ventnortowers.com
web: www.ventnortowers.com
dir: From E, 1st left off A3055 just before pelican crossing

This mid-Victorian hotel, set in spacious grounds from where a path leads down to the shore, is high above the bay and enjoys splendid sea views. Many potted plants and fresh flowers grace the day rooms, which include two lounges and a spacious bar. Bedrooms include two four-poster rooms and some that have their own balconies.

Rooms 25 (4 fmly) (6 GF) **Facilities** Wi-fi ✲ ♨ 9 ♦ Putt green Xmas New Year **Conf** Class 60 Board 44 Thtr 100 **Parking** 20 **Notes** Civ Wed 150

The Wellington Hotel

★★★ ▲ HOTEL

☎ 01983 856600
Belgrave Rd PO38 1JH
e-mail: enquiries@thewellingtonhotel.net
web: www.thewellingtonhotel.net

Rooms 28 (5 fmly) (7 GF) (14 smoking) **Facilities** STV Wi-fi Xmas New Year **Conf** Class 28 Board 28 Thtr 28 **Parking** 10 **Notes** ⊗ Civ Wed 60

Save on hotels. Book at **theAA.com/hotel**

UPP – WAK 471 ENGLAND

INSPECTORS' CHOICE

The Hambrough

◉ ◉ ◉ RESTAURANT WITH ROOMS

☎ 01983 856333
Hambrough Rd PO38 1SQ
e-mail: reservations@robert-thompson.com
dir: Telephone for directions

A former Victorian villa set on the hillside above Ventnor and with memorable views out to sea, The Hambrough has a modern, stylish interior with well equipped and boutique style accommodation. The kitchen team's passion for food is clearly evident in the superb cuisine served in the minimalistic styled restaurant.

Rooms 7 (3 fmly)

| VERYAN | Map 2 SW93 |
| Cornwall | |

INSPECTORS' CHOICE

The Nare Hotel

★★★★ ◉
COUNTRY HOUSE HOTEL

☎ 01872 501111
Carne Beach TR2 5PF
e-mail: stay@narehotel.co.uk
web: www.narehotel.co.uk
dir: A3078 from Tregony, approx 1.5m. Left at Veryan sign, through village towards sea & hotel

This delightful hotel offers a relaxed, country-house atmosphere in a spectacular coastal setting. The elegantly designed bedrooms, many with balconies, have fresh flowers, carefully chosen artwork and antiques that contribute to their engaging individuality. A choice of dining options is available, from light snacks to superb local seafood.

Rooms 37 (7 fmly) (7 GF) ↱ **S** £140-£268;
D £270-£768 (incl. bkfst)* **Facilities** Spa FTV Wi-fi
🌀 ⌁ ♨ 🏊 Gym Health & beauty clinic Sauna Steam room Hotel sailing boat Shooting Xmas New Year **Services** Lift **Parking** 80 **Notes** LB

| WADDESDON | Map 11 SP71 |
| Buckinghamshire | |

The Five Arrows

RESTAURANT WITH ROOMS

☎ 01296 651727
High St HP18 0JE
e-mail: five.arrows@nationaltrust.org.uk
dir: On A41 in Waddesdon. Into Baker St for car park

This Grade II listed building with elaborate Elizabethan chimney stacks, stands at the gates of Waddesdon Manor and was named after the Rothschild family emblem. Individually styled en suite bedrooms are comfortable and well appointed. Friendly staff are on hand to offer a warm welcome. Alfresco dining is possible in the warmer months.

Rooms 11

| WAKEFIELD | Map 16 SE32 |
| West Yorkshire | |

See also Liversedge

Waterton Park Hotel

★★★★ 78% ◉ HOTEL

CLASSIC BRITISH HOTELS

☎ 01924 257911 & 249800
Walton Hall, The Balk, Walton WF2 6PW
e-mail: info@watertonparkhotel.co.uk
web: www.watertonparkhotel.co.uk
dir: 3m SE off B6378. Exit M1 junct 39 towards Wakefield. At 3rd rdbt right for Crofton. At 2nd lights right & follow signs

This Georgian mansion, built on an island in the centre of a 26-acre lake is in an idyllic setting. The main house contains many feature bedrooms, and the annexe houses more spacious rooms, all equally well equipped with modern facilities; most of the bedrooms have views over the lake or the 18-hole golf course. The delightful beamed restaurant, two bars and leisure club are located in the old hall, and there is a licence for civil weddings.

Rooms 65 (43 annexe) (5 fmly) (23 GF) ↱
Facilities STV FTV Wi-fi ⌁ ⊛ supervised Fishing Gym Steam room Sauna New Year **Conf** Class 80 Board 80 Thtr 150 **Services** Lift **Parking** 200 **Notes** ⊗
Civ Wed 130

Cedar Court Hotel Wakefield

THE INDEPENDENTS HOTEL ASSOCIATION

★★★★ 73% HOTEL

☎ 01924 276310
Denby Dale Rd WF4 3QZ
e-mail: sales@cedarcourthotels.co.uk
web: www.cedarcourthotels.co.uk
dir: Adjacent to M1 junct 39

This hotel enjoys a convenient location just off the M1. Traditionally styled bedrooms offer a good range of facilities while open-plan public areas include a busy bar and restaurant operation. Conferences and functions are extremely well catered for and a modern leisure club completes the picture.

Rooms 149 (2 fmly) (74 GF) (6 smoking) ↱
S £55-£99; **D** £65-£140 (incl. bkfst)* **Facilities** FTV
Wi-fi ⌁ ⊛ supervised Gym Sauna Steam room Beauty treatment room Xmas New Year **Conf** Class 140 Board 80 Thtr 400 Del from £99 to £145*
Services Lift **Parking** 350 **Notes** LB Civ Wed 250

Holiday Inn Leeds - Wakefield

Holiday Inn

★★★ 75% HOTEL

☎ 0871 942 9082
Queen's Dr, Ossett WF5 9BE
e-mail: reception-wakefield@ihg.com
web: www.holidayinn.co.uk/wakefield
dir: M1 junct 40 follow signs for Wakefield. Hotel on right in 200yds

Situated close to major motorway networks, this modern hotel offers well-equipped and comfortable bedrooms. Public areas include the popular Traders restaurant and a comfortable lounge where a menu is available throughout the day. Conference facilities are also available.

Rooms 104 (32 fmly) (35 GF) (9 smoking)
Facilities STV Wi-fi ⌁ Xmas New Year **Conf** Class 80 Board 80 Thtr 160 **Services** Lift Air con **Parking** 105 **Notes** Civ Wed 160

W

WAKEFIELD *continued*

Campanile Wakefield

Campanile

BUDGET HOTEL

☎ 01924 201054
Monckton Rd WF2 7AL
e-mail: wakefield@campanile.com
web: www.campanile.com
dir: M1 junct 39, A636, 1m towards Wakefield, left
into Monckton Rd, hotel on left

This modern building offers accommodation in smart,
well-equipped bedrooms, all with en suite bathrooms.
Refreshments may be taken at the informal bistro.
See also the Hotel Groups pages.

Rooms 76 (76 annexe) (4 fmly) (25 GF) **Conf** Class 15
Board 15 Thtr 25

Premier Inn Wakefield Central

Premier Inn

BUDGET HOTEL

☎ 0871 527 9114
Thornes Park, Denby Dale Rd WF2 8DY
web: www.premierinn.com
dir: M1 junct 41, A650 towards Wakefield. Approx
1.5m. Hotel on right

High quality, budget accommodation ideal for both
families and business travellers. Spacious, en suite
bedrooms feature tea and coffee making facilities,
and Freeview TV in most hotels. Internet access and
Wi-fi are available for a small fee. The adjacent
family restaurant features a wide and varied menu.
See also the Hotel Groups pages.

Rooms 42

Premier Inn Wakefield South M1 Jct 39

BUDGET HOTEL

☎ 0871 527 9118
Calder Park, Denby Dale Rd WF4 3BB
web: www.premierinn.com
dir: M1 junct 39, A636 towards Wakefield. At 1st rdbt
1st exit into Calder Park. Hotel on right

Rooms 74

WALLASEY　　　　Map 15 SJ29
Merseyside

Grove House Hotel

★★★　81%　HOTEL

☎ 0151 639 3947　& 630 4558
Grove Rd CH45 3HF
e-mail: reception@thegrovehouse.co.uk
web: www.thegrovehouse.co.uk
dir: M53 junct 1, A554 (Wallasey New Brighton), right
after church into Harrison Drive, left after Windsors
Garage into Grove Rd

Ideally situated for Liverpool and the M53, this
friendly hotel offers a high level of comfort to guests.
Attractive bedrooms are comfortable and provide a
wealth of extras. Well-cooked meals are served in the
elegant panelled dining room. Weddings and
conferences also catered for.

Rooms 14 (7 fmly) 🐾 **S** £69-£79; **D** £90-£139 (incl.
bkfst)* **Facilities** FTV Wi-fi **Conf** Class 30 Board 50
Thtr 50 Del from £104.90 to £114.90* **Parking** 28
Notes LB ⊗ RS BHs Civ Wed 50

WALLINGFORD　　　　Map 5 SU68
Oxfordshire

The Springs Hotel & Golf Club

★★★　80%　⊛　HOTEL

☎ 01491 836687
Wallingford Rd, North Stoke OX10 6BE
e-mail: info@thespringshotel.com
web: www.thespringshotel.com
dir: A4074 (Oxford-Reading road) onto B4009
(Goring). Hotel approx 1m on right

Set on its own 18-hole, par 72 golf course, this
Victorian mansion has a timeless and peaceful
atmosphere. The generously equipped, individually
styled bedrooms vary in size but many are spacious.
Some bedrooms overlook the pool and grounds while
others have views of the spring-fed lake as does the
elegant restaurant. There is also a comfortable
lounge, with original features, to relax in.

Rooms 32 (3 fmly) (10 GF) **Facilities** FTV Wi-fi ⟲ ⌁
18 Putt green Fishing ⛵ Boat trips on Thames Xmas
New Year **Conf** Class 16 Board 26 Thtr 60
Parking 150 **Notes** Civ Wed 150

W

Save on hotels. Book at **theAA.com/hotel**

WAK – WAL 473 ENGLAND

The George

★★★ 77% HOTEL

☎ 01491 836665
High St OX10 0BS
e-mail: info@george-hotel-wallingford.com
web: www.peelhotels.co.uk
dir: E side of A329, N end of Wallingford

Old world charm and modern facilities merge seamlessly in this former coaching inn. Bedrooms in the main house have character in abundance. Those in the wing have a more contemporary style, but all are well equipped and attractively decorated. Diners can choose between the restaurant and bistro, or relax in the cosy bar.

Rooms 39 (1 fmly) (9 GF) **S** £90-£132; **D** £110-£160 (incl. bkfst)* **Facilities** STV Wi-fi Xmas New Year **Conf** Class 60 Board 50 Thtr 150 Del from £135 to £148.50* **Parking** 60 **Notes** LB ⊗ Civ Wed 100

WALSALL
West Midlands　　　　　Map 10 SP09

Fairlawns Hotel & Spa

★★★ 86% ◎ ◎ HOTEL

☎ 01922 455122
178 Little Aston Rd WS9 0NU
e-mail: reception@fairlawns.co.uk
web: www.fairlawns.co.uk
dir: Exit A452 towards Aldridge at x-roads with A454. Hotel 600yds on right

In a rural location with immaculate landscaped grounds, this constantly improving hotel offers a wide range of facilities and modern, comfortable bedrooms. Family rooms, one with a four-poster bed, and suites are also available. The Fairlawns Restaurant serves a wide range of award-winning seasonal dishes. The extensive, comprehensively equipped leisure complex is mainly for adult use as there is restricted availability to young people.

Rooms 58 (8 fmly) (1 GF) (3 smoking) ℉ **S** £75-£175; **D** £95-£245 (incl. bkfst) **Facilities** Spa STV FTV Wi-fi ↕ ⓣ supervised ⌣ ⌣ Gym Dance studio Beauty salon Bathing suite Floatation suite Sauna

Aromatherapy room New Year **Conf** Class 40 Board 30 Thtr 80 Del from £117.50 to £217.50 **Services** Lift **Parking** 150 **Notes** LB RS 24 Dec-2 Jan Civ Wed 100

Beverley Hotel

★★★ 74% HOTEL

☎ 01922 622999
58 Lichfield Rd WS4 2DJ
e-mail: info@beverley-hotel.com
dir: 1m N of town centre on A461 to Lichfield

This privately owned hotel dates back to 1880. Bedrooms are comfortably appointed, and the tastefully decorated public areas include a spacious bar combined with a conservatory. The restaurant offers guests a choice of carefully prepared, appetising dishes.

Rooms 31 (2 fmly) (4 GF) ℉ **S** £45-£65; **D** £55-£75 (incl. bkfst) **Facilities** FTV Wi-fi ↕ New Year **Conf** Class 30 Board 30 Thtr 80 Del from £90 to £135 **Parking** 68 **Notes** LB Civ Wed 80

Holiday Inn Express Walsall M6 Jct 10

BUDGET HOTEL

☎ 01922 705250
Tempus Ten, Tempus Dr WS2 8TJ
e-mail: admin@hiexwalsall.com
web: www.hiexpress.co.uk
dir: M6 junct 10/A454 to Walsall. Right at 1st lights, hotel 200mtrs on right

A modern hotel ideal for families and business travellers. Fresh and uncomplicated, the spacious rooms include Sky TV, power shower and tea and coffee-making facilities. Continental buffet breakfast is included in the room rate; other meals may be taken at the nearby family pub or restaurant. See also the Hotel Groups pages.

Rooms 120 (77 fmly) (30 GF) (19 smoking) ℉ **S** fr £49; **D** fr £49 (incl. bkfst) **Conf** Class 45 Board 36 Thtr 60 Del from £75*

Premier Inn Walsall M6 Jct 10

BUDGET HOTEL

☎ 0871 527 9120
Bentley Green, Bentley Road North WS2 0WB
web: www.premierinn.com
dir: M6 junct 10, A454 signed Wolverhampton. 2nd exit (Ansons junct). Left at rdbt, 1st left at next rdbt, hotel on right

High quality, budget accommodation ideal for both families and business travellers. Spacious, en suite

bedrooms feature tea and coffee making facilities, and Freeview TV in most hotels. Internet access and Wi-fi are available for a small fee. The adjacent family restaurant features a wide and varied menu. See also the Hotel Groups pages.

Rooms 40

WALTHAM ABBEY
Essex　　　　　Map 6 TL30

Waltham Abbey Marriott Hotel

★★★★ 76% HOTEL

☎ 01992 717170
Old Shire Ln EN9 3LX
web: www.walthamabbeymarriott.co.uk
dir: M25 junct 26

This hotel benefits from convenient access to London and the major road networks. The air-conditioned bedrooms are spacious, tastefully decorated and offer a range of facilities for the modern business traveller. The hotel also provides a range of meeting rooms, a substantial parking area and a well-equipped indoor leisure centre.

Rooms 162 (16 fmly) (80 GF) **Facilities** STV Wi-fi ↕ ⓣ Gym Sauna Steam room ♫ Xmas New Year **Conf** Class 120 Board 50 Thtr 280 **Services** Air con **Parking** 250 **Notes** ⊗ Civ Wed 250

Premier Inn Waltham Abbey

BUDGET HOTEL

☎ 0871 527 9122
Sewardstone Rd EN9 3QF
web: www.premierinn.com
dir: M25 junct 26, A121 towards Waltham Abbey. Left onto A112, hotel 0.5m on left

High quality, budget accommodation ideal for both families and business travellers. Spacious, en suite bedrooms feature tea and coffee making facilities, and Freeview TV in most hotels. Internet access and Wi-fi are available for a small fee. The adjacent family restaurant features a wide and varied menu. See also the Hotel Groups pages.

Rooms 93

W

WANSFORD
Cambridgeshire   Map 12 TL09

The Haycock Hotel
★★★ 86% ◉ HOTEL

THE INDEPENDENTS
HOTEL ASSOCIATION

☎ 01780 782223 & 781124
PE8 6JA
e-mail: sales@thehaycock.co.uk
dir: A1 junct to A47 Leicester

A charming 17th-century coaching inn set amidst attractive landscaped grounds in a peaceful village location. The smartly decorated bedrooms are tastefully furnished and thoughtfully equipped. Public rooms include a choice of restaurants, a lounge bar, a cocktail bar and a stylish lounge. The hotel has a staffed business centre, and banqueting facilities are also available.

Rooms 48 (14 GF) Facilities FTV Wi-fi ⋈
Conf Class 100 Board 45 Thtr 300 Parking 300
Notes Civ Wed

WANTAGE
Oxfordshire   Map 5 SU38

La Fontana Restaurant with Accommodation

RESTAURANT WITH ROOMS

☎ 01235 868287
Oxford Rd, East Hanney OX12 0HP
e-mail: anna@la-fontana.co.uk
dir: A338 from Wantage towards Oxford. Restaurant on right in East Hanney

Guests are guaranteed a warm welcome at this family-run Italian restaurant which is located on the outskirts of the busy town of Wantage. The stylish bedrooms are individually designed, well equipped and very comfortable. Dinner should not to be missed - the menu features a wide range of regional Italian specialities.

Rooms 15 (7 annexe) (2 fmly)

WARE
Hertfordshire   Map 6 TL31

Hanbury Manor, A Marriott Hotel & Country Club

★★★★★ 81% ◉ ◉
COUNTRY HOUSE HOTEL

☎ 01920 487722 & 0870 400 7222
SG12 0SD
e-mail: mhrs.stngs.guestrelations@marriotthotels.com
web: www.marriotthanburymanor.co.uk
dir: M25 junct 25, A10 N for 12m, take A1170, right at rdbt, hotel on left

Set in 200 acres of landscaped grounds, this impressive Jacobean-style mansion boasts an enviable range of leisure facilities, including an excellent health club and championship golf course. Bedrooms are traditionally and comfortably furnished in the country-house style and have lovely marbled bathrooms. There are a number of food and drink options, including the renowned Zodiac and Oakes restaurants.

Rooms 161 (27 annexe) (60 fmly) Facilities Spa STV FTV Wi-fi ⓢ supervised ⅃ 18 ⅋ Putt green ⇘ Gym Health & beauty treatments Aerobics Yoga Dance class Xmas New Year Conf Class 86 Board 36 Thtr 150 Services Lift Parking 200 Notes Civ Wed 120

WARMINSTER
Wiltshire   Map 4 ST84

The Bishopstrow Hotel & Spa
Ⓤ

☎ 01985 212312
Borenam Rd BA12 9HH
dir: From rdbt on A36 take B3414 towards Warminster. Follow brown hotel signs

Currently the rating for this establishment is not confirmed. This may be due to a change of ownership or because it has only recently joined the AA rating scheme. For further details please see the AA website: theAA.com

Rooms 32 S £110-£170; D £140-£200 (incl. bkfst)*
Conf Class 40 Board 36 Thtr 80

WARRINGTON
Cheshire   Map 15 SJ68

The Park Royal
★★★★ 78% HOTEL

☎ 01925 730706
Stretton Rd, Stretton WA4 4NS
e-mail: parkroyalreservations@qhotels.co.uk
web: www.qhotels.co.uk
dir: M56 junct 10, A49 to Warrington, at lights turn right to Appleton Thorn, 1st right into Spark Hall Close, hotel on left

This modern hotel enjoys a peaceful setting, yet is conveniently located just minutes from the M56. The bedrooms are contemporary, well furnished and attractively co-ordinated. Spacious, stylish public areas include extensive conference and function facilities and a comprehensive leisure centre complete with outdoor tennis courts and a spa. Complimentary Wi-fi is also provided.

Rooms 146 (32 fmly) (34 GF) Facilities Spa FTV Wi-fi ⓢ ⅋ Gym Dance studio Xmas New Year Conf Class 180 Board 90 Thtr 400 Services Lift Parking 400 Notes Civ Wed 300

Best Western Fir Grove Hotel
★★★ 78% HOTEL

☎ 01925 267471
Knutsford Old Rd WA4 2LD
e-mail: firgrove@bestwestern.co.uk
web: www.bw-firgrovehotel.co.uk
dir: M6 junct 20, follow signs for A50 to Warrington for 2.4m, before swing bridge over canal, turn right & right again

Situated in a quiet residential area, this hotel is convenient for both the town centre and the motorway network. Comfortable, smart bedrooms, including spacious executive rooms, offer some excellent extra facilities such as PlayStations and CD players. Public areas include a smart lounge/bar, a neatly appointed restaurant and excellent function and meeting facilities.

Rooms 52 (3 fmly) (20 GF) Facilities STV FTV Wi-fi Xmas New Year Conf Class 150 Board 50 Thtr 200 Parking 100 Notes Civ Wed 200

W

Holiday Inn Warrington

★★★ 73% HOTEL *Holiday Inn*

☎ 0871 942 9087

Woolston Grange Av, Woolston WA1 4PX
e-mail: paul.ellison@ihg.com
web: www.hiwarringtonhotel.co.uk
dir: M6 junct 21, follow signs for Birchwood

Ideally located within the M62 and M56 interchange, this hotel provides the ideal base for all areas of the north-west region for both corporate and leisure guests. Rooms are spacious and well equipped, and a wide choice of meals is available in the comfortable restaurant and cosy bar. Meeting and conference facilities are also available.

Rooms 96 (41 fmly) (9 GF) **D** £25-£129 **Facilities** STV FTV Wi-fi ⌧ HL Xmas New Year **Conf** Board 20 Thtr 30 Del from £125 to £145* **Services** Lift Air con **Parking** 101

Ramada Encore Warrington

★★★ 71% HOTEL

☎ 01925 847050

Aston Avene, Birchwood Business Park WA3 6ZN
e-mail: gm@encorewarrington.co.uk
dir: M6 junct 21a, M62 junct 11. Follow signs for Birchwood Park on A574

This purpose-built hotel makes a good base for both business and leisure guests. The bedrooms are spacious and bright with en suite power-shower rooms. Public areas include a restaurant, bar and lounge. Secure parking is available on site.

Rooms 103 (16 fmly) (7 GF) ⌧ **S** £49-£109; **D** £49-£109 **Facilities** FTV Wi-fi ⌧ **Conf** Class 30 Board 18 Thtr 40 Del from £99 to £149 **Services** Lift Air con **Parking** 94 **Notes** ⊗

Villaggio

★★ 63% HOTEL

☎ 01925 630106

5-9 Folly Ln WA5 0LZ
e-mail: villaggiowarrington@hotmail.co.uk
dir: M62 junct 9, A49, through 2 rdbts to x-rds. Left at McDonalds, through lights, hotel on left

Conveniently located close to northwest motorway networks and only half a mile from the town centre. Bedrooms are simply furnished in a contemporary style with good quality accessories such as flat-screen TVs and complimentary Wi-fi. An extensive choice of meals is served in the spacious restaurant. Off-road parking is available.

Rooms 19 (2 fmly) ⌧ **S** fr £49.95; **D** fr £55 (incl. bkfst)* **Facilities** FTV Wi-fi Xmas New Year **Conf** Class 180 Board 100 Thtr 230 **Parking** 30

Premier Inn Warrington A49/M62 Jct 9

BUDGET HOTEL

☎ 0871 527 9128

Winwick Rd WA2 8RN
web: www.premierinn.com
dir: M62 junct 9 towards Warrington, hotel 100yds

High quality, budget accommodation ideal for both families and business travellers. Spacious, en suite bedrooms feature tea and coffee making facilities, and Freeview TV in most hotels. Internet access and Wi-fi are available for a small fee. The adjacent family restaurant features a wide and varied menu. See also the Hotel Groups pages.

Rooms 74

Premier Inn Warrington Centre

BUDGET HOTEL

☎ 0871 527 9126

1430 Centre Park, Park Boulevard WA1 1PR
web: www.premierinn.com
dir: Take A49 to Brian Beven Island Rdbt, into Park Boulevard (Centre Park). Over bridge. Hotel on right

Rooms 42

Premier Inn Warrington (M6 Jct 21)

BUDGET HOTEL

☎ 0871 527 9124

Manchester Rd, Woolston WA1 4GB
web: www.premierinn.com
dir: Just off M6 junct 21 on A57 to Warrington

Rooms 105

Premier Inn Warrington North

BUDGET HOTEL

☎ 0871 527 9128

Winwick Rd WA2 8RN
web: www.premierinn.com
dir: M62 junct 9, A49 signed Warrington. At next rdbt follow Town Centre signs. Straight on at next rdbt, left into Warrington Collegiate Camp

Rooms 74

Premier Inn Warrington North East

BUDGET HOTEL

☎ 0871 527 9130

Golborne Rd, Winwick WA2 8LF
web: www.premierinn.com
dir: M6 junct 22, A573 towards Newton-le-Willows. Dual carriageway to end, take 3rd exit at rdbt. Hotel adjacent to church

Rooms 42

Premier Inn Warrington South

BUDGET HOTEL

☎ 0871 527 9134

Tarporley Rd, Stretton WA4 4NB
web: www.premierinn.com
dir: Just off M56 junct 10. Follow A49 to Warrington, left at 1st lights

Rooms 29

WARWICK   Map 10 SP26
Warwickshire

See also Leamington Spa (Royal) & Wroxall

Ardencote Manor Hotel, Country Club & Spa

★★★★ 80% ◉◉ HOTEL

☎ 01926 843111

The Cumsey, Lye Green Rd, Claverdon CV35 8LT
e-mail: hotel@ardencote.com
web: www.ardencote.com

(For full entry see Claverdon)

Chesford Grange

★★★★ 78% HOTEL QHOTELS

☎ 01926 859331

Chesford Bridge CV8 2LD
e-mail: chesfordreservations@qhotels.co.uk
web: www.qhotels.co.uk

(For full entry see Kenilworth)

W

WARWICK *continued*

Holiday Inn Express Warwick

BUDGET HOTEL

☎ 01926 483000
Stratford Rd CV34 6TW
e-mail: info@expresswarwick.co.uk
web: www.expresswarwick.co.uk
dir: M40 junct 15, follow signs A429 to Warwick. Take 1st right

A modern hotel ideal for families and business travellers. Fresh and uncomplicated, the spacious rooms include Sky TV, power shower and tea and coffee-making facilities. Continental buffet breakfast is included in the room rate; other meals may be taken at the nearby family pub or restaurant. See also the Hotel Groups pages.

Rooms 138 (35 fmly) (36 GF) **Conf** Class 16 Board 16 Thtr 35

WARWICK MOTORWAY SERVICE AREA (M40) Warwickshire	Map 10 SP35

Days Inn Warwick North - M40

BUDGET HOTEL

☎ 01926 651681
Warwick Services, M40 Northbound Junction 12-13, Banbury Rd CV35 0AA
e-mail: warwick.north.hotel@welcomebreak.co.uk
web: www.welcomebreak.co.uk
dir: M40 northbound between junct 12 & 13

This modern building offers accommodation in smart, spacious and well-equipped bedrooms, suitable for families and business travellers, and all with en suite bathrooms. Continental breakfast is available and other refreshments may be taken at the nearby family restaurant. See also the Hotel Groups pages.

Rooms 54 (45 fmly) (8 smoking) **Conf** Board 30

Days Inn Warwick South - M40

BUDGET HOTEL

☎ 01926 650168
Warwick Services, M40 Southbound, Banbury Rd CV35 0AA
e-mail: warwick.south.hotel@welcomebreak.co.uk
web: www.welcomebreak.co.uk
dir: M40 southbound between junct 14 & 12

Rooms 40 (38 fmly) (5 smoking)

WASHINGTON Tyne & Wear	Map 19 NZ35

Mercure Newcastle George Washington Hotel

★★★ 81% HOTEL

☎ 0191 402 9988
Stone Cellar Rd, High Usworth NE37 1PH
e-mail: reservations@georgewashington.co.uk
web: www.georgewashington.co.uk
dir: A1(M) junct 65 onto A194(M). Take A195 signed Washington North. Take last exit from rdbt for Washington then right at mini-rdbt. Hotel 0.5m on right

Popular with business and leisure guests, this purpose-built hotel boasts two golf courses and a driving range. Bedrooms are stylish and modern, generally spacious and comfortably equipped. Public areas include extensive conference facilities, a business centre and fitness club.

Rooms 103 (9 fmly) (41 GF) **S** £59-£129; **D** £59-£159 **Facilities** Spa STV FTV Wi-fi 🕉 supervised ᵴ 18 Putt green Gym Squash Golf driving range Beauty salon Xmas **Conf** Class 80 Board 80 Thtr 200 **Parking** 180 **Notes** LB ⊗ Civ Wed 180

Holiday Inn Washington

★★★ 79% HOTEL

☎ 0871 942 9084
Emerson District 5 NE37 1LB
e-mail: washingtonhi@ihg.com
web: www.holidayinn.co.uk
dir: Just off A1(M) junct 64. Left at rdbt, hotel on left

This is an ideally located hotel, just off the A1(M), and located near historic Durham, Sunderland and Newcastle's city centre. It is a well established hotel noted for its friendly staff. Bedrooms are air conditioned, and executive rooms are available. The eating options are Traders Restaurant and the lounge bar area.

Rooms 136 (6 GF) (4 smoking) **D** £44-£110 **Facilities** STV FTV Wi-fi 🗘 Discounted leisure facilities at nearby club Xmas New Year **Conf** Class 60 Board 50 Thtr 100 Del from £79 to £135 **Services** Lift Air con **Parking** 200 **Notes** LB Civ Wed 150

Campanile Washington

BUDGET HOTEL

☎ 0191 416 5010
Emerson Rd, District 5 NE37 1LE
e-mail: washington@campanile.com
web: www.campanile.com
dir: A1(M) junct 64, A195 to Washington, 1st left at rdbt into Emerson Rd. Hotel 800yds on left

This modern building offers accommodation in smart, well-equipped bedrooms, all with en suite bathrooms. Refreshments may be taken at the informal bistro. See also the Hotel Groups pages.

Rooms 79 (79 annexe) (1 fmly) (28 GF) **Conf** Class 15 Board 25 Thtr 40

Premier Inn Newcastle (Washington)

BUDGET HOTEL

☎ 0871 527 9136
Emerson Rd NE37 1LB
web: www.premierinn.com
dir: A1(M) junct 64, A195, follow Emerson signs. Left at rdbt, hotel 250yds left

High quality, budget accommodation ideal for both families and business travellers. Spacious, en suite bedrooms feature tea and coffee making facilities, and Freeview TV in most hotels. Internet access and Wi-fi are available for a small fee. The adjacent family restaurant features a wide and varied menu. See also the Hotel Groups pages.

Rooms 74

W

Save on hotels. Book at **theAA.com/hotel**

WAR – WAT 477 **ENGLAND**

WATERMILLOCK
Cumbria

Map 18 NY42

Macdonald Leeming House

★★★★ 76% ◉ HOTEL

☎ 0844 879 9142
CA11 0JJ
e-mail: sales/oldengland@macdonald-hotels.co.uk
web: www.macdonald-hotels.co.uk
dir: M6 junct 40, A66 to Keswick. At rdbt take A592
(Ullswater). 5m to T-junct, right (A592). Hotel on left
in 3m

This hotel enjoys a superb location, being set in 20
acres of mature wooded gardens in the Lake District
National Park, and overlooking Ullswater and the
towering fells. Many rooms offer views of the lake and
the rugged mountains beyond, with more than half
having their own balcony. Public rooms include three
sumptuous lounges, a cosy bar and library.

Rooms 41 (1 fmly) (10 GF) **Facilities** Wi-fi Fishing ⬥
Xmas New Year **Conf** Class 40 Board 30 Thtr 80
Parking 50 **Notes** Civ Wed 80

INSPECTORS' CHOICE

Rampsbeck Country House Hotel

★★★ ◉◉◉ HOTEL

☎ 017684 86442
CA11 0LP
e-mail: enquiries@rampsbeck.co.uk
web: www.rampsbeck.co.uk
dir: M6 junct 40, A592 to Ullswater, at T-junct (with
lake opposite) turn right, hotel 1.5m

This fine country house lies in 18 acres of parkland
on the shores of Lake Ullswater, and is furnished
with many period and antique pieces. There are
three delightful lounges, an elegant restaurant and
a traditional bar. Bedrooms come in three grades;
the most spacious rooms are spectacular and

overlook the lake. Service is attentive and the
award-winning cuisine a real highlight.

Rampsbeck Country House Hotel

Rooms 19 (1 fmly) (1 GF) ⬥ **S** £97.50-£200;
D £145-£300 (incl. bkfst)* **Facilities** STV FTV Wi-fi
Putt green ⬥ Private boat trips on Lake Ullswater
Xmas New Year **Conf** Class 10 Board 15 Thtr 15
Del from £160 to £300* **Parking** 25 **Notes** LB
Civ Wed 60

See advert on this page

W

WATFORD
Hertfordshire — Map 6 TQ19

Best Western White House
★★★ 73% HOTEL

☎ 01923 237316
Upton Rd WD18 0JF
e-mail: info@whitehousehotel.co.uk
web: www.whitehousehotel.co.uk
dir: From centre ring road into Exchange Rd, exit left into Upton Rd, hotel on left

This popular commercial hotel is situated within easy walking distance to the town centre. Bedrooms are pleasantly decorated and offer a good range of facilities that include interactive TV with internet. The public areas are open plan; they include a comfortable lounge/bar, cosy snug and an attractive conservatory restaurant with a sunny open terrace for summer dining. Functions suites are also available.

Rooms 57 (8 GF) **Facilities** STV FTV Wi-fi **Conf** Class 80 Board 50 Thtr 200 **Services** Lift **Parking** 50 **Notes** ⊗ RS 25 Dec-2 Jan Civ Wed 120

Park Inn Watford
★★★ 64% HOTEL

☎ 01923 429988 & 429900
30-40 St Albans Rd WD17 1RN
e-mail: info.watford@rezidorparkinn.com
web: www.watford.parkinn.co.uk
dir: On A412 between Town Hall & Watford Junction Station

Located within walking distance of Watford Junction main station, which has easy connections to London. This modern hotel has contemporary bedrooms and bathrooms providing comfortable accommodation for both the leisure or business guest. The larger bedroom range is particularly suitable for visiting executives and for families. The restaurant and lounge areas offer a substantial menu. Up-to-date conference rooms are available, and secure parking is an asset.

Rooms 100 (6 fmly) **Facilities** FTV Wi-fi Gym Xmas New Year **Conf** Class 90 Board 40 Thtr 180 **Services** Lift Air con **Parking** 92 **Notes** Civ Wed 180

Holiday Inn Express London - Watford Junction
BUDGET HOTEL

☎ 01923 288600
19 Bridle Path WD17 1UE
e-mail: info@express-watford.com
dir: Telephone for directions

A modern hotel ideal for families and business travellers. Fresh and uncomplicated, the spacious rooms include Sky TV, power shower and tea and coffee-making facilities. Continental buffet breakfast is included in the room rate; other meals may be taken at the nearby family pub or restaurant. See also the Hotel Groups pages.

Rooms 98 (60 fmly) (14 smoking) **S** £49.95-£199.95; **D** £49.95-£199.95 (incl. bkfst)* **Conf** Class 14 Board 14 Thtr 24 Del from £120 to £200*

Premier Inn Watford Centre
BUDGET HOTEL

☎ 0871 527 9140
Timms Meadow, Water Ln WD17 2NJ
web: www.premierinn.com
dir: M1 junct 5, A41 into town centre. At rdbt take 3rd exit, stay in left lane through lights. Take 1st left into Water Ln. Hotel on left

High quality, budget accommodation ideal for both families and business travellers. Spacious, en suite bedrooms feature tea and coffee making facilities, and Freeview TV in most hotels. Internet access and Wi-fi are available for a small fee. The adjacent family restaurant features a wide and varied menu. See also the Hotel Groups pages.

Rooms 105

Premier Inn Watford (Croxley Green)
BUDGET HOTEL

☎ 0871 527 9138
2 Ascot Rd WD18 8AD
web: www.premierinn.com
dir: M25 junct 18, A404 signed Watford/ Rickmansworth, left at 1st rdbt signed A412 Watford. Follow Croxley Green Business Park/Watford signs, at 4th rdbt, 3rd exit. M1 junct 5, A41 towards Watford, follow Watford West & Rickmansworth A412 signs. Then Croxley Green Business Park signs

Rooms 121

Premier Inn Watford North
BUDGET HOTEL

☎ 0871 527 9142
859 St Albans Rd, Garston WD25 0LH
web: www.premierinn.com
dir: M1 junct 6, A405 towards Watford. At 2nd lights onto A412 (St Albans Rd). Into TGI Friday's car park. Hotel directly behind

Rooms 45

WATTON
Norfolk — Map 13 TF90

Broom Hall Country Hotel
★★★ 77% COUNTRY HOUSE HOTEL

☎ 01953 882125
Richmond Rd, Saham Toney IP25 7EX
e-mail: enquiries@broomhallhotel.co.uk
web: www.broomhallhotel.co.uk
dir: From A11 at Thetford onto A1075 to Watton (12m), B1108 towards Swaffham, in 0.5m at rdbt turn right to Saham Toney, hotel 0.5m on left. From A47 take A1075, left onto B1108

A delightful Victorian country house situated down a private drive and set in mature landscaped gardens surrounded by parkland. The well-equipped bedrooms are split between the main house and an adjacent building. Public rooms include a relaxing lounge, a brasserie restaurant, a lounge bar, a conservatory and a smart restaurant. There is an indoor swimming pool.

Rooms 15 (5 annexe) (3 fmly) (5 GF) **S** £75-£125; **D** £95-£160 (incl. bkfst) **Facilities** FTV Wi-fi Massage Beauty treatments **Conf** Class 30 Board 22 Thtr 80 Del from £110 to £150 **Parking** 30 **Notes** LB Closed 24 Dec-4 Jan Civ Wed 70

WELLESBOURNE
Warwickshire
Map 10 SP25

Walton Hall

★★★★ 81% ◎◎ HOTEL

PUMA HOTELS
COLLECTION

☎ 01789 842424
Walton CV35 9HU
e-mail: waltonhall.mande@pumahotels.co.uk
dir: A429 through Barford towards Wellesbourne,
right after watermill, follow signs to hotel

Sitting in 65 acres of beautiful countryside, this hotel
is just 10 minutes from the M40. It has a fascinating
history, with parts dating back to the 1500s. The
property has been appointed in a style that combines
both the traditional and the modern. The individually
designed bedrooms, many with stunning views over
the lake and garden, have plasma screen TVs, DVD
players and lap top-sized safes. Premium rooms and
suites are available. The award-winning Moncreiffe
Restaurant is situated in the hall and has views over
the lovely gardens.

Rooms 56 (19 annexe) (11 GF) **Facilities** Spa STV FTV
Wi-fi ⓢ supervised Gym Dance studio Beauty salon
Xmas New Year **Conf** Class 60 Board 36 Thtr 240
Services Air con **Parking** 240 **Notes** ⊗ Civ Wed 240

WELLINGBOROUGH
Northamptonshire
Map 11 SP86

Ibis Wellingborough

BUDGET HOTEL

☎ 01933 228333
Enstone Court NN8 2DR
e-mail: H3164@accor-hotels.com
web: www.ibishotel.com
dir: At junct of A45 & A509 towards Kettering, SW
outskirts of Wellingborough

Modern, budget hotel offering comfortable
accommodation in bright and practical bedrooms.
Breakfast is self-service and dinner is available in
the restaurant. See also the Hotel Groups pages.

Rooms 78 (20 fmly) (2 GF)

Premier Inn
Wellingborough

BUDGET HOTEL

☎ 0871 527 9144
London Rd NN8 2DP
web: www.premierinn.com
dir: 0.5m from town centre on A5193, near
Dennington Industrial Estate

High quality, budget accommodation ideal for both
families and business travellers. Spacious, en suite
bedrooms feature tea and coffee making facilities,
and Freeview TV in most hotels. Internet access and
Wi-fi are available for a small fee. The adjacent
family restaurant features a wide and varied menu.
See also the Hotel Groups pages.

Rooms 40

WELLS
Somerset
Map 4 ST54

Best Western Plus Swan Hotel

★★★ 86% ◎◎ HOTEL

☎ 01749 836300
Sadler St BA5 2RX
e-mail: info@swanhotelwells.co.uk
web: www.swanhotelwells.co.uk
dir: A39, A371, on entering Wells follow signs for
Hotels & Deliveries. Hotel on right opposite cathedral

Situated in the shadow of Wells Cathedral, this
privately owned hotel enjoys a truly stunning location
and extends a genuinely friendly welcome. Full of
character and with a rich history, the hotel has been
restored and extended to provide high levels of quality
and comfort. Guests can choose between the larger,
period bedrooms in the main building or the more
contemporary coach house rooms. Dinner in the oak-
panelled restaurant should not be missed.

Rooms 51 (3 fmly) (4 GF) ⓝ **S** £110-£135;
D £144-£194 (incl. bkfst)* **Facilities** FTV Wi-fi Gym
Xmas New Year **Conf** Class 45 Board 40 Thtr 120
Del £135* **Parking** 25 **Notes** LB ⊗ Civ Wed 90

White Hart Hotel

THE INDEPENDENTS
HOTEL ASSOCIATION

★★ 78% HOTEL

☎ 01749 672056
Sadler St BA5 2RR
e-mail: info@whitehart-wells.co.uk
web: www.whitehart-wells.co.uk
dir: Sadler St at start of one-way system. Hotel
opposite cathedral

A former coaching inn dating back to the 15th
century, this hotel offers comfortable, modern
accommodation. Some bedrooms are in an adjoining
former stable block and two are at ground-floor level.
Public areas include a guest lounge, a bar and the
popular restaurant, Brufani's, where delicious steaks
and gourmet burgers are in high demand.

Rooms 15 (3 fmly) (2 GF) **S** £90-£100; **D** £110-£115
(incl. bkfst)* **Facilities** Wi-fi Xmas New Year
Conf Class 50 Board 35 Thtr 150 Del from £125 to
£140* **Parking** 17 **Notes** LB Civ Wed 100

W

WELLS *continued*

Ancient Gate House Hotel

★★ 69% ⊛ HOTEL

☎ 01749 672029
20 Sadler St BA5 2SE
e-mail: info@ancientgatehouse.co.uk
web: www.ancientgatehouse.co.uk
dir: 1st hotel on left on cathedral green

Guests are treated to good old-fashioned hospitality in a friendly informal atmosphere at this charming hotel. Bedrooms, many with unrivalled cathedral views and four-poster beds, are well equipped and furnished in keeping with the age and character of the building. The Rugantino Restaurant remains popular, offering typically Italian specialities and traditional English dishes.

Rooms 9 **Facilities** FTV Wi-fi Xmas New Year
Notes Closed 27-29 Dec

Coxley Vineyard Hotel

★★ 67% HOTEL

☎ 01749 670285
Coxley BA5 1RQ
e-mail: max@orofino.freeserve.co.uk
dir: A39 from Wells signed Coxley. Village halfway between Wells & Glastonbury. Hotel at end of village

This privately owned and personally run hotel was built on the site of an old cider farm. It was later part of a commercial vineyard and some of the vines are still in evidence. It provides well equipped, modern bedrooms; most are situated on the ground floor. There is a comfortable bar and a spacious restaurant with an impressive lantern ceiling. The hotel is a popular venue for conferences and other functions.

Rooms 9 (5 fmly) (8 GF) **Facilities** FTV Wi-fi ↯ ↯
Xmas **Conf** Class 50 Board 40 Thtr 90 **Parking** 50

The White Hart Hotel

★★★ 75% ⊛ HOTEL

☎ 01438 715353
2 Prospect Place AL6 9EN
e-mail: bookings@thewhitehart.net
web: www.thewhitehart.net
dir: A1(M) junct 6. From N: take 3rd exit at rdbt, follow road under motorway bridge, keep left passing fire station, hotel on right at T-junct. From S: 1st exit, 1st right after BP petrol station, hotel 0.25m ahead

Enjoying a prominent position in the heart of the pretty village of Welwyn, this 17th-century coaching inn offers a very good choice of well-appointed bedrooms. The very popular bar serves a good choice of Cask Marque traditional real ales The bar is used for casual dining and the restaurant has a warm, welcoming atmosphere.

Rooms 13 (4 annexe) (4 GF) **S** £70-£165; **D** £80-£175 (incl. bkfst)* **Facilities** STV FTV Wi-fi ↯ Discounts available at local gym, spa & golf course Xmas New Year **Conf** Class 22 Board 18 Thtr 48 Del from £150 to £195 **Parking** 20 **Notes** ⊗ RS 25-26 Dec & 1 Jan

Tewin Bury Farm Hotel

★★★★ 77% ⊛⊛ HOTEL

☎ 01438 717793
Hertford Road (B1000) AL6 0JB
e-mail: reservations@tewinbury.co.uk
dir: From N: A1(M) junct 6, 1st exit signed A1000, at next rdbt 1st exit towards Digswell. 0.1m straight on at rdbt. 1m on B100. Hotel on left

Situated not far from the A1(M) and within easy reach of Stevenage and Knebworth House, this delightful country-house hotel is part of a thriving farm. Stylish, well-equipped bedrooms of varying sizes are perfectly suited for both leisure and business guests. An award-winning restaurant and meeting rooms are all part of this family-run establishment.

Rooms 39 (30 annexe) (6 fmly) (26 GF) **Facilities** STV FTV Wi-fi Fishing Cycling New Year **Conf** Class 180 Board 40 Thtr 500 **Services** Lift **Parking** 400 **Notes** ⊗ Civ Wed 150

Premier Inn Welwyn Garden City

BUDGET HOTEL

☎ 0871 527 9146
Stanborough Rd AL8 6DQ
web: www.premierinn.com
dir: A1(M) junct 4, A6129

High quality, budget accommodation ideal for both families and business travellers. Spacious, en suite bedrooms feature tea and coffee making facilities, and Freeview TV in most hotels. Internet access and Wi-fi are available for a small fee. The adjacent family restaurant features a wide and varied menu. See also the Hotel Groups pages.

Rooms 90

See London plan 1 C4

Quality Hotel Wembley London & Conference Centre

★★★ 71% HOTEL

☎ 020 8733 9000
Empire Way HA9 0NH
e-mail: sales@hotels-wembley.com
dir: M1 junct 6, A406, right onto A404. Right onto Empire Way, after rdbt at lights. Hotel on right

Conveniently situated within walking distance of both the Arena and conference centres this modern hotel offers smart, comfortable, spacious bedrooms; many are air conditioned. All rooms offer an excellent range of amenities. Air-conditioned public areas include a large restaurant serving a wide range of contemporary dishes.

Rooms 165 (70 fmly) (3 GF) (48 smoking) **S** £75-£325; **D** £80-£350* **Facilities** STV FTV Wi-fi ↯ **Conf** Class 90 Board 90 Thtr 150 Del from £135 to £145* **Services** Lift Air con **Parking** 65 **Notes** ⊗

Save on hotels. Book at **theAA.com/hotel**

WEL – WES 481 **ENGLAND**

Ibis London Wembley

BUDGET HOTEL

☎ 020 8453 5100
Southway HA9 6BA
e-mail: H3141@accor.com
web: www.ibishotel.com
dir: From Hanger Lane on A40, take A406 N, exit at Wembley. A404 to lights junct with Wembley Hill Rd, right, 1st right into Southway. Hotel 75mtrs on left

Modern, budget hotel offering comfortable accommodation in bright and practical bedrooms. Breakfast is self-service and dinner is available in the restaurant. See also the Hotel Groups pages.

Rooms 210 (44 fmly)

Premier Inn London Wembley Stadium

BUDGET HOTEL

☎ 0871 527 8682
151 Wembley Park Dr HA9 8HQ
web: www.premierinn.com
dir: A406 (North Circular) take A404 towards Wembley. 2m right into Wembley Hill Rd, keep right into Empire Way (B4565), pass Wembley Arena on right, keep right around petrol station. Hotel 200yds on left

High quality, budget accommodation ideal for both families and business travellers. Spacious, en suite bedrooms feature tea and coffee making facilities, and Freeview TV in most hotels. Internet access and Wi-fi are available for a small fee. The adjacent family restaurant features a wide and varied menu. See also the Hotel Groups pages.

Rooms 154

WEST AUCKLAND   Map 19 NZ12
Co Durham

The Manor House Hotel

★★★ 80% HOTEL

☎ 01388 834834
The Green DL14 9HW
e-mail: enquiries@manorhousehotelcountydurham.co.uk
web: www.manorhousehotelcountydurham.co.uk
dir: A1(M) junct 58, A68 to West Auckland. At T-junct left, hotel 150yds on right

This historic manor house, dating back to the 14th century, is full of character. Welcoming log fires await guests on cooler evenings. Comfortable bedrooms are individual in style, tastefully furnished and well equipped. The brasserie and Juniper's restaurant both offer an interesting selection of freshly prepared dishes. Well-equipped leisure facilities are available.

Rooms 35 (11 annexe) (6 fmly) (3 GF) **Facilities** FTV Wi-fi ⊗ Gym Steam room Sauna Xmas New Year **Conf** Class 80 Board 50 Thtr 100 **Parking** 150 **Notes** Civ Wed 120

WEST BAY

See Bridport

WEST BROMWICH   Map 10 SP09
West Midlands

Park Inn by Radisson Birmingham West

★★★ 72% HOTEL

☎ 0121 609 9988 & 609 9931
Birmingham Rd B70 6RS
e-mail: info.birminghamwest@rezidorparkinn.com
dir: Birmingham Rd towards town centre, 1st right into Beechs Rd, 2nd right into Europa Ave. Hotel on right

Convenient for the M5, M42 and M6, this large, purpose-built hotel provides versatile and well-equipped contemporary accommodation. Facilities include a spacious restaurant, comfortable lounge areas, a bar and secure parking, as well as meeting rooms and function suites. There is also a modern leisure complex.

Rooms 168 (16 fmly) (33 GF) (9 smoking) 🐾 **S** £39–£110; **D** £49–£120* **Facilities** STV FTV Wi-fi ⊗ ⊛ supervised Gym Beauty treatment room Sauna Dance studio **Conf** Class 80 Board 60 Thtr 180 Del from £79 to £160 **Services** Lift Air con **Parking** 300 **Notes** LB

Premier Inn West Bromwich

BUDGET HOTEL

☎ 0871 527 9148
New Gas St B70 0NP
web: www.premierinn.com
dir: M5 junct 1, A41 (Expressway) towards Wolverhampton. At 3rd rdbt, hotel on right

High quality, budget accommodation ideal for both families and business travellers. Spacious, en suite bedrooms feature tea and coffee making facilities, and Freeview TV in most hotels. Internet access and Wi-fi are available for a small fee. The adjacent family restaurant features a wide and varied menu. See also the Hotel Groups pages.

Rooms 40

Premier Inn West Bromwich Central

BUDGET HOTEL

☎ 0871 527 9150
144 High St B70 6JJ
web: www.premierinn.com
dir: M5 junct 1 towards town centre, hotel 2m

Rooms 85

W

WEST DRAYTON

Hotels are listed under Heathrow Airport

WEST LULWORTH   Map 4 SY88
Dorset

Cromwell House

★★ 75% HOTEL

☎ 01929 400253 & 400332
Lulworth Cove BH20 5RJ
e-mail: catriona@lulworthcove.co.uk
web: www.lulworthcove.co.uk
dir: 200yds beyond end of West Lulworth, left onto high slip road, hotel 100yds on left opposite beach car park

Built in 1881 by the Mayor of Weymouth, specifically as a guest house, this family-run hotel now provides visitors with an ideal base for touring the area and for exploring the beaches and coast. The house enjoys spectacular views across the sea and countryside. Bedrooms, many with sea views, are comfortable and some have been specifically designed for family use.

Rooms 18 (1 annexe) (3 fmly) (2 GF) 🐾 **S** fr £45; **D** fr £130 (incl. bkfst) **Facilities** FTV Wi-fi ➰ ➘ Access to Dorset coastal footpath & Jurassic Coast **Parking** 17 **Notes** LB Closed 22 Dec-3 Jan RS Xmas & New Year

WEST THURROCK   Map 6 TQ57
Essex

Ibis London Thurrock

BUDGET HOTEL

☎ 01708 686000
Weston Av RM20 3JQ
e-mail: H2176@accor.com
web: www.ibishotel.com
dir: M25 junct 31 to West Thurrock Services, right at 1st & 2nd rdbts, left at 3rd rdbt. Hotel on right in 500yds

Modern, budget hotel offering comfortable accommodation in bright and practical bedrooms. Breakfast is self-service and dinner is available in the restaurant. See also the Hotel Groups pages.

Rooms 102 (18 GF) 🐾

Premier Inn Thurrock East

BUDGET HOTEL

☎ 0871 527 9092
Fleming Rd, Unicorn Estate, Chafford Hundred RM16 6YJ
web: www.premierinn.com
dir: From A13 follow Lakeside Shopping Centre signs. Right at 1st rdbt, straight on at next rdbt, then 1st slip road. Left at next rdbt

High quality, budget accommodation ideal for both families and business travellers. Spacious, en suite bedrooms feature tea and coffee making facilities, and Freeview TV in most hotels. Internet access and Wi-fi are available for a small fee. The adjacent family restaurant features a wide and varied menu. See also the Hotel Groups pages.

Rooms 62

Premier Inn Thurrock West

BUDGET HOTEL

☎ 0871 527 9094
Stonehouse Ln RM19 1NS
web: www.premierinn.com
dir: From N: M25 junct 31, A1090 to Purfleet. (NB do not cross Dartford Bridge or follow signs for Lakeside). From S: M25 junct 31. On approach to Dartford Tunnel, bear far left signed Dagenham. After tunnel, hotel at top of slip road

Rooms 161

WEST WITTON   Map 19 SE08
North Yorkshire

The Wensleydale Heifer

◉◉ RESTAURANT WITH ROOMS

☎ 01969 622322
Main St DL8 4LS
web: www.wensleydaleheifer.co.uk
dir: A1 to Leeming Bar junct, A684 towards Bedale for approx 10m to Leyburn, then towards Hawes 3.5m to West Witton

Describing itself as 'boutique style', this 17th-century former coaching inn is very much in the 21st century. The bedrooms, with Egyptian cotton linen and Molton Brown toiletries as standard, are each designed with a unique and interesting theme - for example, Black Sheep, Night at the Movies, True Romantics and Shooters, and for chocolate lovers there's a bedroom where they can eat as much chocolate as they like! The food is very much the focus here in both the informal fish bar and the contemporary style restaurant. The kitchen prides itself on sourcing the freshest fish and locally reared meats.

Rooms 13 (4 annexe) (2 fmly)

WESTBURY   Map 4 ST85
Wiltshire

The Cedar Hotel & Restaurant

★★★ 66% HOTEL

☎ 01373 822753
114 Warminster Rd BA13 3PR
e-mail: info@cedarhotel-wiltshire.co.uk
dir: On A350, 0.5m S of town towards Warminster

Popular with both business and leisure guests, this hotel is located on the main Warminster Road with easy access to many local attractions. Bedrooms and bathrooms offer a variety of shapes and sizes and the hotel has a relaxed and traditional feel. A good range of options is available at dinner from the well chosen restaurant menu with a range of bar snacks also available. The hotel has a car park and pleasant garden to the rear.

Rooms 20 (12 annexe) **Notes** Closed 25 Dec-2 Jan

WESTLETON   Map 13 TM46
Suffolk

The Westleton Crown

★★★ 79% ◉◉ HOTEL

☎ 01728 648777
The Street IP17 3AD
e-mail: info@westletoncrown.co.uk
web: www.westletoncrown.co.uk
dir: A12 N, turn right for Westleton just after Yoxford. Hotel opposite on entering Westleton

A charming coaching inn situated in a peaceful village location just a few minutes from the A12. Public rooms include a smart, award-winning restaurant, comfortable lounge, and busy bar with exposed beams and open fireplaces. The stylish bedrooms are tastefully decorated and equipped with many thoughtful little extras.

Rooms 34 (22 annexe) (5 fmly) (13 GF) 🐾 **S** £80-£100; **D** £90-£215 (incl. bkfst) **Facilities** FTV Wi-fi ➘ Xmas New Year **Conf** Class 40 Board 30 Thtr 60 **Parking** 34 **Notes** Civ Wed 90

WESTON-SUPER-MARE
Somerset   Map 4 ST36

The Royal Hotel
★★★ 77% HOTEL

☎ 01934 423100
1 South Pde BS23 1JP
e-mail: reservations@royalhotelweston.com
web: www.royalhotelweston.com
dir: M5 junct 21, follow signs to seafront. Hotel next to Winter Gardens Pavillion

The Royal, which opened in 1810, was the first hotel in Weston and occupies a prime seafront position. It is a grand building and many of the bedrooms, including some with sea views, are spacious and comfortable; family apartments are also available. Public areas include a choice of bars and a restaurant which offers a range of dishes to meet all tastes. Entertainment is provided during the season.

The Royal Hotel

Rooms 43 (3 annexe) (8 fmly) ⚓ **S** £73-£93; **D** £105-£169 (incl. bkfst)* **Facilities** FTV Wi-fi HL Beauty room Hair salon ♫ **Conf** Class 100 Board 60 Thtr 200 Del from £145 to £155* **Services** Lift **Parking** 152 **Notes** LB ⊗ Civ Wed 200

See advert on this page

Beachlands Hotel
★★★ 70% HOTEL

☎ 01934 621401
17 Uphill Road North BS23 4NG
e-mail: info@beachlandshotel.com
web: www.beachlandshotel.com
dir: M5 junct 21, follow signs for hospital. At hospital rdbt follow signs for beach, hotel 300yds before beach

This popular hotel is very close to the 18-hole links course and a short walk from the seafront. Elegant public areas include a bar, a choice of lounges and a bright dining room. Bedrooms vary slightly in size, but all are well equipped for both the business and leisure guest. There is the added bonus of a 10-metre indoor pool and a sauna.

Rooms 21 (6 fmly) (11 GF) ⚓ **S** £65-£92; **D** £99-£135.95 (incl. bkfst) **Facilities** FTV Wi-fi ⊗ Sauna Beauty treatment room New Year **Conf** Class 20 Board 30 Thtr 60 Del from £92.25 to £108.75 **Parking** 28 **Notes** LB ⊗ Closed 23-29 Dec Civ Wed 110

W

WESTON-SUPER-MARE continued

Lauriston Hotel

★★★ 70% HOTEL

☎ 01934 620758
6-12 Knightstone Rd BS23 2AN
e-mail:
lauriston.hotel@actionforblindpeople.org.uk
dir: 1st right after Winter Gardens, hotel entrance
opposite Cabot Court Hotel

A friendly welcome is assured at this pleasant hotel,
located right on the seafront, just a few minutes'
stroll from the pier. The hotel extends a warm
welcome to everyone but caters especially for the
visually impaired, their families, friends and guide
dogs. There are comfortable and well-appointed
bedrooms; special facilities for the guide dogs are, of
course, available.

Rooms 37 (2 fmly) (8 GF) ₪ **Facilities** FTV Wi-fi HL ♫
Xmas New Year **Conf** Class 12 Board 10 Thtr 18
Services Lift **Parking** 16

Anchor Head Hotel

★★ 67% HOTEL

☎ 01934 620880
19 Claremont Crescent, Birnbeck Rd BS23 2EE
e-mail: anchor.weston@alfatravel.co.uk
web: www.leisureplex.co.uk
dir: M5 junct 21, A370 to seafront, right, past Grand
Pier towards Brimbeck Pier. Hotel at end of terrace on
left

Enjoying a very pleasant location with views across
the bay, the Anchor Head offers a varied choice of
comfortable lounges and a relaxing outdoor patio
area. Bedrooms and bathrooms are traditionally
furnished and include several ground-floor rooms.
Dinner and breakfast are served in the spacious
dining room that also benefits from sea views.

Rooms 52 (1 fmly) (5 GF) **Facilities** FTV ♫ Xmas New
Year **Services** Lift **Notes** ⊗ Closed Dec-Feb (ex
Xmas) RS Mar & Nov

Premier Inn
Weston-Super-Mare East

BUDGET HOTEL

☎ 0871 527 9156
Hutton Moor Rd BS22 8LY
web: www.premierinn.com
dir: M5 junct 21, A370 towards Weston-Super-Mare.
After 3rd rbt right at lights into Hutton Moor Leisure
Centre. Left, into car park

High quality, budget accommodation ideal for both
families and business travellers. Spacious, en suite
bedrooms feature tea and coffee making facilities,
and Freeview TV in most hotels. Internet access and
Wi-fi are available for a small fee. The adjacent
family restaurant features a wide and varied menu.
See also the Hotel Groups pages.

Rooms 88

WESTON-UNDER-REDCASTLE   Map 15 SJ52
Shropshire

Hawkstone Park Hotel   *principal hayley*

★★★ 75% HOTEL

☎ 01948 841700
SY4 5UY
e-mail: enquiries@hawkstone.co.uk
dir: 1m E of A49 between Shrewsbury & Whitchurch

Built in the 1700 this splendid former coaching inn is
set in 400 acres of lovely scenery which includes two
championship golf courses and the much remarked
upon, 18th-century follies. The bedrooms are
comfortably appointed and well equipped for both
leisure and business guests, and the public areas
include conference facilities and a pleasant dining
room.

Rooms 67 (19 annexe) (2 fmly) (26 GF) **S** £45-£89;
D £55-£109 (incl. bkfst)* **Facilities** STV Wi-fi ₪ ♨ 42
Putt green ⛳ Xmas New Year **Conf** Class 90
Board 50 Thtr 200 **Parking** 200 **Notes** LB Civ Wed 200

WETHERBY   Map 16 SE44
West Yorkshire

Wood Hall Hotel & Spa   *Hand PICKED HOTELS*

★★★★ ◎◎ HOTEL

☎ 01937 587271
Trip Ln, Linton LS22 4JA
e-mail: woodhall@handpicked.co.uk
web: www.handpickedhotels.co.uk/woodhall
dir: From Wetherby take Harrogate road N (A661)
for 0.5m, left to Sicklinghall & Linton. Cross bridge,
left to Linton & Wood Hall. Turn right opposite
Windmill Inn, 1.25m to hotel

A long sweeping drive leads to this delightful
Georgian house situated in 100 acres of parkland.
Spacious bedrooms are appointed to an impressive
standard and feature comprehensive facilities,
including large plasma-screen TVs. Public rooms
reflect the same elegance and include a smart
drawing room and dining room, both with fantastic
views. A state-of-the-art technogym is available.
Hand Picked Hotels — AA Hotel Group of the Year
2012-13.

Rooms 44 (30 annexe) (5 fmly) **S** £111-£194;
D £121-£204 (incl. bkfst)* **Facilities** Spa STV FTV
Wi-fi ₪ ☼ Fishing Gym Beauty spa Xmas New Year
Conf Class 70 Board 40 Thtr 100 **Services** Lift
Parking 200 **Notes** LB ⊗ Civ Wed 100

Save on hotels. Book at **theAA.com/hotel**

WES – WEY 485 ENGLAND

The Bridge Hotel & Spa

★★★★ 77% HOTEL

☎ 01937 580115
Walshford LS22 5HS
e-mail: info@bridgewetherby.co.uk
web: www.bridgewetherby.co.uk
dir: From N exit A1(M) at junct 47 (York) or S junct 46 (Wetherby Race Centre), 1st left Walshford, follow brown tourist signs

A very conveniently located hotel close to the A1 with spacious public areas and a good range of services make this an ideal venue for business or leisure. The stylish bedrooms are comfortable and well equipped. The Bridge offers a choice of bars and a large open-plan restaurant. Conference and banqueting suites are also available.

Rooms 30 (2 fmly) (10 GF) **S** £60-£90; **D** £75-£130 (incl. bkfst) **Facilities** Spa FTV Wi-fi ◊ Gym Xmas New Year **Conf** Class 50 Board 50 Thtr 200 Del from £100 to £140 **Parking** 150 **Notes** LB Civ Wed 150

Days Inn Wetherby

BUDGET HOTEL

☎ 01937 547557
Junction 46 A1(M), Kirk Deighton LS22 5GT
e-mail: reservations@daysinnwetherby.co.uk
dir: A1(M) junct 46 at Moto Service Area

This modern building offers accommodation in smart, spacious and well-equipped bedrooms, suitable for families and business travellers, and all with en suite bathrooms. Continental breakfast is available and other refreshments may be taken at the nearby family restaurant. See also the Hotel Groups pages.

Rooms 129 (33 fmly) (35 GF) ◊ **Conf** Class 20 Board 20 Thtr 20

WEYBRIDGE — Map 6 TQ06
Surrey

Brooklands Hotel

★★★★ 79% ◉ HOTEL

☎ 01932 335700
Brooklands Dr KT13 0SL
e-mail: info@brooklandshotelsurrey.com
dir: Telephone for detailed directions

Overlooking the historic motoring racing circuit, this hotel has stunning design that reflects the art deco style and that of the Mercedes Benz racetrack's heyday in the 1920 and 30s. The bedrooms are notably spacious and very comfortable with many contemporary facilities; all have floor-to-ceiling windows, and many come with balconies overlooking the racetrack. There is a wealth of public areas including leisure and meeting rooms as well as a spa. The contemporary 1907 Restaurant, Bar and Grill offers imaginative menus.

Rooms 120 (16 fmly) ◊ **S** £120-£275; **D** £120-£275* **Facilities** Spa STV FTV Wi-fi ◊ Gym New Year **Conf** Class 86 Board 90 Thtr 174 Del from £225 to £350* **Services** Lift Air con **Parking** 120 **Notes** ⊗ Civ Wed 174

OATLANDS PARK HOTEL

BEDROOMS **144** · MEETING ROOMS **6** · SYNDICATE ROOMS **6** · MAX CAPACITY **300**

Oatlands Park Hotel, Weybridge

- 10 Acres of secluded gardens
- 144 en-suite bedrooms offering very modern facility
- 6 main meeting rooms-
  10- 300 delegates theatre style
  6 syndicate rooms to seat up to 10 boardroom style
- The Foyer Area is home to a lounge bar where guests can enjoy light snacks and beverages as well as afternoon tea

- Free broadband access in all our bedroom accommodation. Free Wi-Fi internet access in all public areas and meeting rooms
- 9 hole golf course, tennis court, fully equipped gymnasium
- 4 rooms licensed for Civil Wedding Ceremonies. Wedding receptions ranging from 10- 220 guests
- The Broadwater Restaurant offers excellent and imaginative cuisine

Oatlands Drive, Weybridge, Surrey KT13 9HB
Tel: +44 (0)1932 847242 • Fax: +44 (0)1932 821413
Email: events@oatlandsparkhotel.com • www.oatlandsparkhotel.com

W

WEYBRIDGE *continued*

Oatlands Park Hotel

★★★★ 76% HOTEL

☎ 01932 847242
146 Oatlands Dr KT13 9HB
e-mail: info@oatlandsparkhotel.com
web: www.oatlandsparkhotel.com
dir: Through High Street to Monument Hill mini rdbt.
Left into Oatlands Drive. Hotel 500yds on left

Once a palace for Henry VIII, this impressive building
sits in extensive grounds encompassing tennis
courts, a gym and a 9-hole golf course. The spacious
lounge and bar create a wonderful first impression
with tall marble pillars and plush comfortable
seating. Most of the bedrooms are very spacious, and
all are well equipped.

Rooms 144 (24 fmly) (39 GF) (8 smoking)
Facilities STV Wi-fi ↕ HL ⌧ 9 ◔ Putt green ⛳ Gym
Jogging course Fitness suite Xmas New Year
Conf Class 150 Board 80 Thtr 300 Del from £165 to
£225 **Services** Lift Air con **Parking** 144
Notes Civ Wed 220

See advert on page 485

Best Western Ship Hotel

★★★ 77% HOTEL

☎ 01932 848364
Monument Green KT13 8BQ
e-mail: reservations@desboroughhotels.com
dir: M25 junct 11, at 3rd rdbt left into High St. Hotel
300yds on left

A former coaching inn retaining much period charm
that is now a spacious and comfortable hotel.
Bedrooms, some overlooking a delightful courtyard,
are spacious and cheerfully decorated. Public areas
include a lounge and cocktail bar, restaurant and a
popular pub. The high street location and private
parking are a bonus.

Rooms 76 (2 fmly) **Facilities** Wi-fi **Conf** Class 70
Board 60 Thtr 180 **Services** Lift **Parking** 65

WEYMOUTH	Map 4 SY67
Dorset	

Hotel Prince Regent

★★★ 74% HOTEL

☎ 01305 771313
139 The Esplanade DT4 7NR
e-mail: info@princeregentweymouth.co.uk
web: www.princeregentweymouth.co.uk
dir: From A354 follow seafront signs. Left at Jubilee
Clock, 25mtrs on seafront

Dating back to 1855, this welcoming resort hotel
boasts splendid views over Weymouth Bay from the
majority of public rooms and front-facing bedrooms.
It is conveniently close to the town centre and
harbour, and is opposite the beach. The restaurant
offers a choice of menus, and entertainment is
regularly provided in the ballroom during the season.

Rooms 70 (12 fmly) (5 GF) ↖ **S** £45-£119;
D £65-£159 (incl. bkfst)* **Facilities** STV Wi-fi Xmas
New Year **Conf** Class 150 Board 150 Thtr 180
Del from £95 to £105* **Services** Lift **Parking** 10
Notes LB ⊗ Civ Wed 200

Best Western Hotel Rembrandt

★★★ 72% HOTEL

☎ 01305 764000
12-18 Dorchester Rd DT4 7JU
e-mail: reception@hotelrembrandt.co.uk
web: www.hotelrembrandt.co.uk
dir: On A354 from Dorchester, turn left at Manor rdbt
& proceed for 0.75m

Only a short distance from the seafront and the town
centre, this hotel is ideal for visiting the many local
attractions. Facilities include indoor leisure, a bar
and extensive meeting rooms. The restaurant offers
an impressive carvery and carte menu which proves
popular with locals and residents alike.

Rooms 78 (27 fmly) (5 GF) ↖ **S** £55-£92; **D** £75-£145
(incl. bkfst)* **Facilities** STV FTV Wi-fi ↕ ◔ Gym
Steam room Sauna Beautician Beauty treatment room
Conf Class 100 Board 60 Thtr 200 Del from £95 to
£125* **Services** Lift **Parking** 80 **Notes** LB ⊗
Civ Wed 100

Hotel Rex

★★★ 71% HOTEL

☎ 01305 760400
29 The Esplanade DT4 8DN
e-mail: rex@kingshotels.co.uk
web: www.kingshotels.co.uk
dir: On seafront opposite Alexandra Gardens

Originally built as the summer residence for the Duke
of Clarence, this hotel benefits from a seafront
location with stunning views across Weymouth Bay.
Bedrooms, including several sea-facing rooms, are
well equipped. A wide range of imaginative dishes is
served in the popular and attractive restaurant.

Rooms 31 (2 fmly) ↖ **Facilities** FTV Wi-fi New Year
Conf Class 30 Board 25 Thtr 40 **Services** Lift
Parking 10 **Notes** ⊗ Closed Xmas

W

Crown Hotel

★★ 74% HOTEL

☎ 01305 760800

51-53 St Thomas St DT4 8EQ

e-mail: crown@kingshotels.co.uk

web: www.kingshotels.co.uk

dir: From Dorchester, A354 to Weymouth. Follow Back Water on left & cross 2nd bridge

This popular hotel is conveniently located adjacent to the old harbour and is ideal for shopping, local attractions and transportation links, including the ferry. Public areas include an extensive bar, ballroom and comfortable residents' lounge on the first floor. Themed events, such as mock cruises, are a speciality.

Rooms 86 (15 fmly) **S** £57-£63; **D** £108-£118 (incl. bkfst)* **Facilities** ♫ New Year **Services** Lift **Parking** 14 **Notes** LB ⊗ Closed Xmas

Hotel Central

★★ 71% HOTEL

☎ 01305 760700

17-19 Maiden St DT4 8BB

e-mail: central@kingshotels.co.uk

dir: In town centre

Well located for the town, the beach and the ferries to the Channel Islands, and with off-road parking, this privately owned hotel has friendly staff. The bedrooms are comfortable, and three are designed for guests with limited mobility. The pleasant dining room offers a varied menu. Live entertainment is provided during the season.

Rooms 28 (5 fmly) (4 GF) (9 smoking) **S** £56-£60; **D** £95-£99 (incl. bkfst)* **Facilities** ♫ **Services** Lift **Parking** 16 **Notes** LB ⊗ Closed mid Dec-1 Mar

Fairhaven Hotel

★★ 69% HOTEL

☎ 01305 760200

37 The Esplanade DT4 8DH

e-mail: fairhaven@kingshotels.co.uk

dir: On right just before Alexandra Gardens

A popular sea-facing, family-run hotel which has a friendly young team of staff. Bedrooms are comfortable and well maintained, and the hotel boasts two bars, one with panoramic views of the bay. Entertainment is provided most nights during the season.

Rooms 82 (23 fmly) (1 GF) (60 smoking) **S** £56-£60; **D** £95-£99 (incl. bkfst)* **Facilities** ♫ **Services** Lift **Parking** 16 **Notes** LB ⊗ Closed Nov-1 Mar

Premier Inn Weymouth

BUDGET HOTEL

☎ 0871 527 9158

Lodmoor Country Park, Preston Beach Rd, Green Hill DT4 7SX

web: www.premierinn.com

dir: Follow signs to Weymouth then brown route signs to Lodmoor Country Park (height restriction 9' 4" at barrier). Hotel adjacent to Lodmoor Brewers Fayre (NB for Sat Nav use DT4 7SL)

High quality, budget accommodation ideal for both families and business travellers. Spacious, en suite bedrooms feature tea and coffee making facilities, and Freeview TV in most hotels. Internet access and Wi-fi are available for a small fee. The adjacent family restaurant features a wide and varied menu. See also the Hotel Groups pages.

Rooms 64

WHITBY　　　　　**Map 19 NZ81**
North Yorkshire

Dunsley Hall

★★★ 82% ◉ COUNTRY HOUSE HOTEL

☎ 01947 893437

Dunsley YO21 3TL

e-mail: reception@dunsleyhall.com

web: www.dunsleyhall.com

dir: 3m N of Whitby, signed off A171

Friendly service is found at this fine country mansion set in a quiet hamlet with coastal views north of Whitby. The house has Gothic overtones and boasts fine woodwork and panelling, particularly in the magnificent lounge. Two lovely dining rooms offer imaginative dishes and there is also a cosy bar.

Rooms 26 (2 fmly) (10 GF) ⚘ **Facilities** Wi-fi ⛳ Putt green Xmas New Year **Conf** Class 50 Board 40 Thtr 95 **Parking** 30 **Notes** ⊗ Civ Wed 100

The Cliffemount Hotel

★★★ 80% ◉◉ SMALL HOTEL

☎ 01947 840103

Bank Top Ln, Runswick Bay TS13 5HU

e-mail: info@cliffemounthotel.co.uk

dir: Exit A174, 8m N of Whitby, 1m to end

Overlooking Runswick Bay this property offers a relaxed and romantic atmosphere with open fires and individual, carefully designed bedrooms; some have a private balcony overlooking the bay. Dining is recommended; the food is modern British in style and uses locally sourced fresh seafood, and game from nearby estates.

Rooms 20 (4 fmly) (5 GF) **S** £75-£115; **D** £115-£180 (incl. bkfst)* **Facilities** FTV Wi-fi Xmas New Year **Conf** Class 25 Board 16 Thtr 25 Del from £95 to £215* **Parking** 25 **Notes** LB

Saxonville Hotel

★★★ 77% HOTEL

☎ 01947 602631

Ladysmith Av, Argyle Rd YO21 3HX

e-mail: newtons@saxonville.co.uk

web: www.saxonville.co.uk

dir: A174 to North Promenade. Turn inland at large four-towered building visible on West Cliff, into Argyle Rd, then 1st right

The friendly service is noteworthy at this long-established holiday hotel. Well maintained throughout it offers comfortable bedrooms and inviting public areas that include a well-proportioned restaurant where quality dinners are served.

Rooms 23 (2 fmly) (1 GF) **S** £45-£65; **D** £90-£150 (incl. bkfst)* **Facilities** Wi-fi **Conf** Class 40 Board 40 Thtr 100 **Parking** 20 **Notes** ⊗ Closed Dec-Jan RS Feb-Mar

Estbek House

◉◉ RESTAURANT WITH ROOMS

☎ 01947 893424

East Row, Sandsend YO21 3SU

e-mail: info@estbekhouse.co.uk

dir: From Whitby take A174. In Sandsend, left into East Row

A speciality seafood restaurant on the first floor is the focus of this listed building in a small coastal village north west of Whitby. There is also a small bar and breakfast room, and four individually appointed bedrooms offering luxury and comfort.

Rooms 4

W

WHITCHURCH Map 15 SJ54
Shropshire

Macdonald Hill Valley Spa, Hotel & Golf

★★★★ 76% HOTEL

☎ 0844 879 9049
Tarporley Rd SY13 4JH
e-mail:
general.hillvalley@macdonald-hotels.co.uk
web: www.macdonald-hotels.co.uk/hillvalley
dir: 2nd exit off A41 towards Whitchurch

Located in rural surroundings on the town's outskirts, this modern hotel is surrounded by two golf courses and very well equipped leisure spa is also available. Spacious bedrooms, with country views, are furnished in minimalist style and public areas include a choice of bar lounges and extensive conference facilities.

Rooms 80 (15 fmly) (27 GF) ↖ **Facilities** Spa STV FTV Wi-fi ↕ ⊗ ⅃ 36 Putt green Gym Mud Rasul Xmas New Year **Conf** Class 150 Board 150 Thtr 300 Del from £130 to £169* **Services** Lift **Parking** 300 **Notes** Civ Wed 300

WHITEHAVEN Map 18 NX91
Cumbria

Premier Inn Whitehaven

BUDGET HOTEL

☎ 0871 527 9160
Howgate CA28 6PL
web: www.premierinn.com
dir: On A595 just outside Whitehaven

High quality, budget accommodation ideal for both families and business travellers. Spacious, en suite bedrooms feature tea and coffee making facilities, and Freeview TV in most hotels. Internet access and Wi-fi are available for a small fee. The adjacent family restaurant features a wide and varied menu. See also the Hotel Groups pages.

Rooms 47

WHITSTABLE Map 7 TR16
Kent

Premier Inn Whitstable

BUDGET HOTEL

☎ 0871 527 9162
Thanet Way CT5 3DB
web: www.premierinn.com
dir: 2m W of town centre on B2205

High quality, budget accommodation ideal for both families and business travellers. Spacious, en suite bedrooms feature tea and coffee making facilities, and Freeview TV in most hotels. Internet access and Wi-fi are available for a small fee. The adjacent family restaurant features a wide and varied menu. See also the Hotel Groups pages.

Rooms 41

WHITTLEBURY Map 11 SP64
Northamptonshire

Whittlebury Hall

★★★★ 79% ◉◉ HOTEL

☎ 01327 857857
NN12 8QH
e-mail: reservations@whittleburyhall.co.uk
web: www.whittleburyhall.co.uk
dir: A43, A413 towards Buckingham, through Whittlebury, turn for hotel on right (signed)

A purpose-built, Georgian-style country house hotel with excellent spa and leisure facilities and pedestrian access to the Silverstone circuit. Grand public areas include F1 car racing memorabilia and the accommodation includes some lavishly appointed suites. Food is a strength, with a choice of various dining options. Particularly noteworthy are the afternoon teas in the spacious, comfortable lounge and the fine dining in Murray's Restaurant.

Rooms 212 (4 fmly) (13 smoking) **S** £200-£250; **D** £260-£370 (incl. bkfst)* **Facilities** Spa FTV Wi-fi ↕ ⊗ Gym Beauty treatments Relaxation room Hair studio Heat & Ice experience Leisure club ♫ Xmas New Year **Conf** Class 175 Board 40 Thtr 500 Del from £0* **Services** Lift **Parking** 450 **Notes** LB ⊗

WICKHAM Map 5 SU51
Hampshire

Old House Hotel & Restaurant

★★★ 80% ◉◉ HOTEL

☎ 01329 833049
The Square PO17 5JG
e-mail: enquiries@oldhousehotel.co.uk
web: www.oldhousehotel.co.uk
dir: M27 junct 10, N on A32 for 2m towards Alton

This hotel, a Grade II listed building, occupies a convenient location in the heart of historic Wickham, which is not far from Portsmouth and Southampton. Bedrooms and bathrooms are smartly co-ordinated, and include stylish Garden Suites that look out on the delightful garden. The public areas have much character and charm, and the service is attentive and friendly. The award-winning cuisine utilises seasonal, local produce.

Rooms 12 (4 annexe) (1 fmly) (4 GF) **S** £70; **D** £95-£170 (incl. bkfst)* **Facilities** STV FTV Wi-fi Xmas New Year **Conf** Board 14 Thtr 24 Del from £220* **Parking** 8 **Notes** LB ⊗ Civ Wed 70

W

Save on hotels. Book at **theAA.com/hotel**

WHI – WIL 489 ENGLAND

WIGAN
Greater Manchester | Map 15 SD50

Wrightington Hotel & Country Club

★★★★ 75% HOTEL

☎ 01257 425803
Moss Ln, Wrightington WN6 9PB
e-mail: info@wrightingtonhotel.co.uk
dir: M6 junct 27, 0.25m W, hotel on right after church

Situated in open countryside close to the M6, this privately owned hotel offers friendly hospitality. Accommodation is well equipped and spacious, and public areas include an extensive leisure complex complete with hair salon, boutique and sports injury lab. Blazers Restaurant, two bars and air-conditioned banqueting facilities appeal to a broad market.

Rooms 73 (6 fmly) (36 GF) **Facilities** Spa STV FTV Wi-fi ☜ Gym Squash Hairdressing salon Sports injury clinic New Year **Conf** Class 120 Board 40 Thtr 200 Del from £120 to £140* **Services** Lift **Parking** 240 **Notes** Civ Wed 100

Macdonald Kilhey Court Hotel

★★★★ 73% HOTEL

☎ 0844 879 9045 & 01257 472100
Chorley Rd, Standish WN1 2XN
e-mail: general.kilheycourt@macdonald-hotels.co.uk
web: www.macdonaldhotels.co.uk/kilheycourt
dir: M6 junct 27, A5209 Standish, over at lights, past church on right, left at rdbt (1st exit), hotel on right 350yds. M61 junct 6, signed Wigan & Haigh Hall. 3m & right at rdbt (2nd exit). Hotel 0.5m on right

Peacefully located in its own grounds yet convenient for the motorway network. Bedrooms are divided between the Victorian house and the modern extension, while public areas have original features and the split-level restaurant has views over the Worthington Lakes. There are eleven meeting rooms, ideal for exhibitions, and extensive landscaped grounds available for weddings. Facilities also include an indoor pool and spa.

Rooms 62 (18 fmly) (8 GF) **Facilities** Spa STV FTV Wi-fi ☜ HL ☜ Gym Aerobics classes Beauty treatments Xmas New Year **Conf** Class 180 Board 60 Thtr 400 **Services** Lift **Parking** 200 **Notes** Civ Wed 300

Mercure Wigan Oak Hotel

★★★ 75% HOTEL

☎ 01942 826888
Orchard St WN1 3SS
e-mail: enquiries@hotels-wigan.com
web: www.hotels-wigan.com
dir: From S: M6 junct 25, A49 signed Wigan then B5238, right after Grand Arcade Shopping. From N: M6 junct 27, A5209, right onto A49, left at lights, hotel opposite Tesco

This modern and stylish hotel is situated in the centre of Wigan; easily accessed from the M6 and M61 and well positioned for public transport. The bedrooms are both comfortable and well equipped and public rooms include the restaurant, conservatory and popular bar. There is free Wi-fi throughout, and conference and events facilities are available. Ample parking is a plus in this central location.

Rooms 88 (7 fmly) (16 GF) ☜ **Facilities** FTV Wi-fi ☜ New Year **Conf** Class 80 Board 40 Thtr 160 **Services** Lift **Parking** 100 **Notes** Civ Wed 50

Premier Inn Haydock Park (Wigan South)

BUDGET HOTEL

☎ 0871 527 8502
53 Warrington Rd, Ashton-in-Makerfield WN4 9PJ
web: www.premierinn.com
dir: Just off M6 junct 23, A49 towards Wigan

High quality, budget accommodation ideal for both families and business travellers. Spacious, en suite bedrooms feature tea and coffee making facilities, and Freeview TV in most hotels. Internet access and Wi-fi are available for a small fee. The adjacent family restaurant features a wide and varied menu. See also the Hotel Groups pages.

Rooms 30

Premier Inn Wigan M6 Jct 25

BUDGET HOTEL

☎ 0871 527 9164
Warrington Rd, Marus Bridge WN3 6XB
web: www.premierinn.com
dir: M6 junct 25 (N'bound). At rdbt left, hotel on left

Rooms 40

Premier Inn Wigan West

BUDGET HOTEL

☎ 0871 527 9168
Orrell Rd, Orrell WN5 8HQ
web: www.premierinn.com
dir: M6 junct 26 follow signs for Upholland & Orrell. At 1st lights turn left. Hotel on right behind Priory Wood Beefeater

Rooms 40

The Beeches

RESTAURANT WITH ROOMS

☎ 01257 426432 & 421316
School Ln, Standish WN6 0TD
e-mail: mail@beecheshotel.co.uk
dir: M6 junct 27, A5209 into Standish & into School Ln

Located a short drive from M6, this elegant Victorian house has been appointed to provide high standards of comfort. Bedrooms are equipped with practical and homely extras, and public areas include spacious lounges, a popular brasserie, and a self-contained function suite.

Rooms 10 (4 fmly)

WILLERBY
East Riding of Yorkshire | Map 17 TA03

Best Western Willerby Manor Hotel

★★★ 83% HOTEL

☎ 01482 652616
Well Ln HU10 6ER
e-mail: willerbymanor@bestwestern.co.uk
web: www.willerbymanor.co.uk
dir: Exit A63, signed Humber Bridge. Right at rdbt by Waitrose. At next rdbt hotel signed

Set in a quiet residential area, amid well-tended gardens, this hotel was originally a private mansion; it has now been thoughtfully extended to provide very comfortable bedrooms, equipped with many useful extras. There are extensive leisure facilities and a wide choice of meals offered in the contemporary Figs Brasserie which has an impressive heated outdoor area.

Rooms 63 (6 fmly) (20 GF) (1 smoking) **S** £66-£99; **D** £107-£127 (incl. bkfst)* **Facilities** STV FTV Wi-fi ☜ supervised ☜ Gym Steam room Beauty therapist Aerobic classes New Year **Conf** Class 200 Board 100 Thtr 500 Del £160* **Parking** 300 **Notes** LB Closed 24-26 Dec Civ Wed 150

W

WILMINGTON
East Sussex　　　　　　　　　Map 6 TQ50

Crossways
◎ ◎ RESTAURANT WITH ROOMS

☎ 01323 482455
Lewes Rd BN26 5SG
e-mail: stay@crosswayshotel.co.uk
web: www.crosswayshotel.co.uk
dir: On A27 between Lewes & Polegate, 2m E of Alfriston rdbt

Amidst stunning gardens and attractively tended grounds sits this well-established, popular restaurant. The well-presented bedrooms are tastefully decorated and provide an abundance of thoughtful amenities including free Wi-fi. Guest comfort is paramount and the naturally warm hospitality ensures guests often return.

Rooms 7

WILMSLOW

See Manchester Airport

WIMBORNE MINSTER
Dorset　　　　　　　　　　　Map 5 SZ06

Les Bouviers Restaurant with Rooms
◎ ◎ RESTAURANT WITH ROOMS

☎ 01202 889555
Arrowsmith Rd, Canford Magna BH21 3BD
e-mail: info@lesbouviers.co.uk
web: www.lesbouviers.co.uk
dir: A31 onto A349. Left in 0.6m. In approx 1m right into Arrowsmith Rd. Establishment approx 100yds on right

An excellent restaurant with rooms in a great location, set in five and a half acres of grounds. Food is a highlight of any stay here as is the friendly, attentive service. Chef patron James Coward's team turn out impressive cooking, which has been recognised with 2 AA Rosettes. Bedrooms are extremely well equipped and beds are supremely comfortable. Cream tea can be taken on the terrace.

Rooms 6 (4 fmly)

WINCANTON
Somerset　　　　　　　　　　Map 4 ST72

Holbrook House
★★★ 82% ◎ ◎ COUNTRY HOUSE HOTEL

☎ 01963 824466 & 828844
Holbrook BA9 8BS
e-mail: enquiries@holbrookhouse.co.uk
web: www.holbrookhouse.co.uk
dir: From A303 at Wincanton left onto A371 towards Castle Cary & Shepton Mallet

This handsome country house offers a unique blend of quality and comfort combined with a friendly atmosphere. Set in 17 acres of peaceful gardens and wooded grounds, Holbrook House makes a perfect retreat. The restaurant provides a selection of innovative dishes prepared with enthusiasm and served by a team of caring staff.

Rooms 21 (5 annexe) (2 fmly) (5 GF) 🐾 **Facilities** Spa FTV Wi-fi 🏊 🕐 🧖 💆 Gym Beauty treatment Exercise classes Sauna Steam room Fitness suite 🎵 Xmas New Year **Conf** Class 50 Board 55 Thtr 200 Del from £120 to £160* **Parking** 100 **Notes** Civ Wed 250

WINCHCOMBE
Gloucestershire　　　　　　　Map 10 SP02

Wesley House
◎ ◎ RESTAURANT WITH ROOMS

☎ 01242 602366
High St GL54 5LJ
e-mail: enquiries@wesleyhouse.co.uk
web: www.wesleyhouse.co.uk
dir: In town centre

This 15th-century, half-timbered property is named after John Wesley, founder of the Methodist Church, who stayed here while preaching in the town. Bedrooms are small but full of character. In the rear dining room, a unique lighting system changes colour to suit the mood required, and also highlights the various floral creations by a world-renowned flower arranger. A glass atrium covers the outside terrace.

Rooms 5

WINCHESTER
Hampshire　　　　　　　　　Map 5 SU42

Lainston House Hotel

★★★★★ 85% ◎ ◎ ◎ HOTEL

☎ 01962 776088
Sparsholt SO21 2LT
e-mail: enquiries@lainstonhouse.com
web: www.lainstonhouse.com
dir: 2m NW off B3049 towards Stockbridge

This graceful example of a William and Mary House enjoys a countryside location amidst mature grounds and gardens. Staff provide good levels of courtesy and care with a polished, professional service. Bedrooms are tastefully appointed and include some spectacular, spacious rooms with stylish handmade beds and stunning bathrooms. Public rooms include a cocktail bar built entirely from a single cedar and stocked with an impressive range of rare drinks and cigars.

Rooms 49 (6 fmly) (18 GF) 🐾 **D** £165-£745* **Facilities** STV FTV Wi-fi 🏊 🧖 Fishing 💆 Gym Archery Clay pigeon shooting Cycling Hot air ballooning Onsite falconer 🎵 Xmas New Year **Conf** Class 80 Board 40 Thtr 166 Del £375* **Parking** 200 **Notes** LB Civ Wed 200

Holiday Inn Winchester
★★★★ 77% HOTEL　　　　　　*Holiday Inn*

☎ 01962 670700 & 0871 942 9188
Telegraph Way, Morn Hill SO21 1HZ
e-mail: info@hiwinchester.co.uk
dir: M3 junct 9, A31 signed Alton, A272 & Petersfield. 1st exit at rdbt onto A31, 1.6m, take 1st exit into Alresford Rd, left into Telegraph Way

Located a few miles from the historic city of Winchester and within easy reach of the south's

W

transport links, this modern, purpose-built property is presented to a high standard. Bedrooms are spacious and well-equipped for both the business and leisure guest. Enjoyable cuisine is served in the restaurant and there is a very good range of freshly prepared dishes to choose from. Conference facilities and ample parking are available.

Rooms 141 (7 fmly) (60 GF) 🐾 **Facilities** STV FTV Wi-fi HL Xmas New Year **Conf** Class 110 Board 120 Thtr 250 **Services** Lift Air con **Parking** 167 **Notes** ❂ Civ Wed 200

The Winchester Hotel

★★★★ 76% ⑧ HOTEL

☎ 01962 709988
Worthy Ln SO23 7AB
e-mail: info@thewinchesterhotel.co.uk
web: www.thewinchesterhotel.co.uk
dir: A33 then A3047, hotel 1m on right

This hotel is just a few minutes' walk from the city centre, is very smartly appointed throughout, and includes a great leisure centre. The staff are extremely friendly and helpful, and praiseworthy food is served in the contemporary Hutton's Brasserie.

Rooms 96 (2 fmly) (6 GF) **S** £79-£155; **D** £79-£155 (incl. bkfst)* **Facilities** Spa FTV Wi-fi ⌕ ⊙ Gym Sauna Steam room Xmas New Year **Conf** Class 100 Board 40 Thtr 200 Del from £120 to £180* **Services** Lift Air con **Parking** 60 **Notes** LB ❂ Civ Wed 180

Hotel du Vin Winchester

★★★★ 74% ⑧⑧

TOWN HOUSE HOTEL

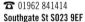

☎ 01962 841414
Southgate St SO23 9EF
e-mail: info@winchester.hotelduvin.com
web: www.hotelduvin.com
dir: M3 junct 11 towards Winchester, follow signs. Hotel in approx 2m on left just past cinema

Continuing to set high standards, this inviting hotel is best known for its high profile bistro. The individually designed bedrooms have all the Hotel du Vin signature touches including fine Egyptian cotton linen, power showers and Wi-fi. The bistro serves imaginative yet simply cooked dishes from a seasonal, daily-changing menu.

Rooms 24 (4 annexe) (4 GF) 🐾 **D** £125-£295* **Facilities** STV Wi-fi ⌕ Xmas New Year **Conf** Class 30 Board 20 Thtr 40 Del from £200 to £240* **Services** Air con **Parking** 35 **Notes** LB Civ Wed 60

Mercure Winchester Wessex Hotel

★★★★ 69% HOTEL

☎ 01962 861611
Paternoster Row SO23 9LQ
e-mail: H6619@accor.com
web: www.mercure.com
dir: M3 junct 10, 2nd exit at rdbt signed Winchester/B3330. Right at lights, left at 2nd rdbt. Over small bridge, straight on at next rdbt into Broadway. Past Guildhall, 1st left into Colebrook St. Hotel 50yds on right

Occupying an enviable location in the centre of this historic city and adjacent to the spectacular cathedral, this hotel is quietly situated on a side street. Inside, the atmosphere is restful and welcoming, with public areas and some bedrooms enjoying unrivalled views of the hotel's centuries-old neighbour.

Rooms 94 (6 fmly) **S** £69-£149; **D** £79-£159* **Facilities** STV Wi-fi Xmas New Year **Conf** Class 25 Board 40 Thtr 100 Del from £125 to £155 **Services** Lift **Parking** 42 **Notes** LB Civ Wed 120

Marwell Hotel

★★★ 73% HOTEL

☎ 01962 777681
Thompsons Ln, Colden Common, Marwell SO21 1JY
e-mail: info@marwellhotel.co.uk
web: www.marwellhotel.co.uk
dir: B3354 through Twyford. 1st exit at rdbt (B3354), left onto B2177 signed Bishop Waltham. Left into Thomsons Ln after 1m, hotel on left

Taking its theme from the adjacent zoo, this unusual hotel is based on the famous TreeTops safari lodge in Kenya. The well-equipped bedrooms, split between four lodges, convey a safari style, while the smart public areas include an airy lobby bar and an 'Out of Africa' themed restaurant. There is also a selection of meeting and leisure facilities.

Rooms 68 (10 fmly) (36 GF) **Facilities** FTV Wi-fi ⌕ ⊙ ⚓ 36 Putt green Gym Sauna New Year **Conf** Class 60 Board 60 Thtr 175 **Parking** 120 **Notes** ❂ Civ Wed 150

INSPECTORS' CHOICE

Gilpin Hotel & Lake House

★★★★ ⑧⑧⑧ HOTEL　

☎ 015394 88818
Crook Rd LA23 3NE
e-mail: hotel@gilpinlodge.co.uk
web: www.gilpinlodge.co.uk
dir: M6 junct 36, A590, A591 to rdbt N of Kendal, onto B5284, hotel 5m on right

This smart Victorian residence is set amidst delightful gardens leading to the fells, and is just a short drive from the lake. The individually designed bedrooms are stylish and a number benefit from private terraces; all are spacious and thoughtfully equipped, and each has a private sitting room. In addition there are luxury Garden Suites that lead onto private gardens with cedar wood hot tubs. The welcoming atmosphere is notable and the attractive day rooms are perfect for relaxing, perhaps beside a real fire. Eating in any of the quartet of dining rooms is a must.

Rooms 26 (12 annexe) (1 fmly) (12 GF) 🐾 **S** £200-£550; **D** £310-£590 (incl. bkfst & dinner)* **Facilities** Wi-fi ⌕ ⚓ Free membership at local leisure club In-room spa treatment Xmas New Year **Parking** 40 **Notes** LB ❂ No children 7yrs

W

WINDERMERE *continued*

Holbeck Ghyll Country House Hotel

★★★★ ◎◎◎ COUNTRY HOUSE HOTEL

☎ 015394 32375
Holbeck Ln LA23 1LU
e-mail: stay@holbeckghyll.com
dir: 3m N of Windermere on A591, right into Holbeck Lane (signed Troutbeck), hotel 0.5m on left

Holbeck Ghyll sits high up overlooking the majestic Lake Windermere surrounded by well maintained grounds. The original house was bought in 1888 by Lord Lonsdale, the first president of the AA, who used it as a hunting lodge. Guests today will find that this is a delightful place where the service is professional and attentive. There are beautifully designed, spacious bedrooms situated in the main house and also in lodges in the grounds; each has lake views and some have patios. There are also The Shieling and Miss Potter suites. Each bedroom has Egyptian cotton linens, fresh flowers, LCD satellite TV, CD & DVD players, bathrobes and a decanter of damson gin. The restaurant impresses with its award-winning cuisine. The hotel also has a health spa, gym and boutique store.

Rooms 26 (13 annexe) (5 fmly) (11 GF)
D £160-£380 (incl. bkfst) **Facilities** Spa FTV Wi-fi
🍸 ❄ Sauna Steam room Beauty treatment rooms Beauty massage Xmas New Year **Conf** Class 40 Board 30 Thtr 60 Del £199* **Parking** 34 **Notes** LB Civ Wed 60

Linthwaite House Hotel & Restaurant

★★★★ ◎◎ COUNTRY HOUSE HOTEL

☎ 015394 88600
Crook Rd LA23 3JA
e-mail: stay@linthwaite.com
web: www.linthwaite.com
dir: A591 towards The Lakes for 8m to large rdbt, take 1st exit (B5284), 6m, hotel on left. 1m past Windermere golf club

Linthwaite House is set in 14 acres of hilltop grounds and enjoys stunning views over Lake Windermere. Inviting public rooms include an attractive conservatory and adjoining lounge, and an elegant restaurant which occupies three rooms and offers menus based on the finest local ingredients. Bedrooms, which are individually decorated, combine contemporary furnishings with classical styles; all are thoughtfully equipped and include CD players, radios and free Wi-fi. There is also a Garden Suite and the luxurious Loft Suite which even has a retractable roof and telescope for star gazing. Service and hospitality are attentive and friendly.

Rooms 30 (1 fmly) (7 GF) 🐾 **S** £141-£320;
D £282-£640 (incl. bkfst & dinner)* **Facilities** STV FTV Wi-fi 🐾 Putt green Fishing 🦆 Beauty treatments Massage Access to nearby spa with pool & gym Xmas New Year **Conf** Class 22 Board 25 Thtr 54 **Parking** 40 **Notes** Civ Wed 64

Macdonald Old England Hotel & Spa

★★★★ 84% ◎◎ HOTEL

☎ 0844 879 9144
Church St, Bowness LA23 3DF
e-mail: sales.oldengland@macdonald-hotels.co.uk
web: www.macdonaldhotels.co.uk
dir: Through Windermere to Bowness, straight across at mini-rdbt. Hotel behind church on right

This hotel stands right on the shore of England's largest lake and boasts superb views, especially through the floor-to-ceiling windows in the Vinand Restaurant. There are several bedroom types; standard, executive and suites; some rooms have been designed for wheelchairs users. The spa has a 20-metre pool, a gym, sauna and steam room.

Rooms 106 (6 fmly) (14 GF) 🐾 **Facilities** Spa STV Wi-fi 🐾 supervised Gym Private jetties Rock sauna Aromatherapy shower Steam room Ice room Xmas New Year **Conf** Class 60 Board 25 Thtr 150 **Services** Lift **Parking** 90 **Notes** ⊗ Civ Wed 100

Lindeth Howe Country House Hotel & Restaurant

★★★★ 79% ◎◎ COUNTRY HOUSE HOTEL

☎ 015394 45759
Lindeth Dr, Longtail Hill LA23 3JF
e-mail: hotel@lindeth-howe.co.uk
web: www.lindeth-howe.co.uk
dir: Exit A592, 1m S of Bowness onto B5284 (Longtail Hill) signed Kendal & Lancaster, hotel last driveway on right

Historic photographs commemorate the fact that this delightful house was once the family home of Beatrix Potter. Secluded in landscaped grounds, it enjoys views across the valley and Lake Windermere. Public rooms are plentiful and inviting, with the restaurant being the perfect setting for modern country-house cooking. Deluxe and superior bedrooms are spacious and smartly appointed.

Rooms 34 (3 fmly) (2 GF) **Facilities** STV Wi-fi 🐾 Gym Sauna Fitness room Xmas New Year **Conf** Class 20 Board 18 Thtr 30 **Parking** 50 **Notes** ⊗

Save on hotels. Book at **theAA.com/hotel**

WIN 493 ENGLAND

Storrs Hall Hotel

English Lakes
Hotels Resorts & Venues

★★★★ 78% ◎◎ HOTEL

☎ 015394 47111
Storrs Park LA23 3LG
e-mail: storrshall@elhmail.co.uk
web: www.elh.co.uk/hotels/storrshall
dir: On A592, 2m S of Bowness, on Newby Bridge road

Set in 17 acres of landscaped grounds by the lakeside, this imposing Georgian mansion is delightful. There are numerous lounges to relax in, furnished with fine art and antiques. Individually styled bedrooms are generally spacious and boast impressive bathrooms. Imaginative cuisine is served in the elegant restaurant, which offers fine views across the lawn to the lake and fells beyond.

Rooms 30 **Facilities** FTV Wi-fi Fishing ⛵ Use of nearby sports/beauty facilities Xmas New Year **Conf** Class 35 Board 24 Thtr 50 **Parking** 50 **Notes** No children 12yrs Civ Wed 94

Low Wood Bay

English Lakes
Hotels Resorts & Venues

★★★★ 77% HOTEL

☎ 015394 33338 & 0845 850 3502
LA23 1LP
e-mail: lowwoodbay@englishlakes.co.uk
dir: M6 junct 36, A590, A591 to Windermere, then 3m towards Ambleside, hotel on right

Benefiting from a lakeside location, this hotel offers an excellent range of leisure and conference facilities. Bedrooms, many with panoramic lake views, are attractively furnished, and include a number of larger executive rooms and suites. There is a choice of bars, a spacious restaurant and the more informal Café del Lago. The poolside bar offers internet access.

Rooms 111 (13 fmly) (21 GF) 🐾 **Facilities** Spa FTV Wi-fi ♨ ⊗ supervised Fishing Gym Squash Water skiing Canoeing Beauty salon Marina Xmas New Year **Conf** Class 180 Board 150 Thtr 340 **Services** Lift **Parking** 200 **Notes** Civ Wed 280

Beech Hill Hotel

★★★★ 74% ◎ HOTEL

☎ 015394 42137
Newby Bridge Rd LA23 3LR
e-mail: reservations@beechhillhotel.co.uk
web: www.beechhillhotel.co.uk
dir: M6 junct 36, A591 to Windermere. Left onto A592 towards Newby Bridge

Located on the edge of Lake Windermere, the panoramic views across the lake to the Cumbrian fells beyond are impressive. The bedrooms are well appointed and some have balconies overlooking the lake. The open areas, for enjoying coffee or drinks, prove very popular in the summer. There are cosy lounges with log fires, a fine restaurant, leisure facilities and landscaped gardens. High standards of service can be expected from the attentive, informative and very friendly staff.

Rooms 57 (5 fmly) (4 GF) 🐾 **Facilities** FTV Wi-fi ⊗ Fishing Solarium ♫ Xmas New Year **Parking** 70 **Notes** ⊗ Civ Wed 130

INSPECTORS' CHOICE

The Samling

★★★ ◎◎ HOTEL

☎ 015394 31922
Ambleside Rd LA23 1LR
e-mail: info@thesamlinghotel.co.uk
web: www.thesamlinghotel.co.uk
dir: M6 junct 36, A591 towards Ambleside. 2m. 300yds past Water Sports Centre right after bend

This stylish house, built in the late 1700s, is situated in 67 acres of grounds and enjoys an elevated position overlooking Lake Windermere. The

spacious, beautifully furnished bedrooms and suites, some in adjacent buildings, are thoughtfully equipped and all have superb bathrooms. Public rooms include a sumptuous drawing room, a small library and an elegant dining room where imaginative, skilfully prepared food is served.

Rooms 11 (6 annexe) (6 fmly) (6 GF) 🐾 **D** £190-£470 (incl. bkfst)* **Facilities** STV FTV Wi-fi ⛵ Xmas New Year **Conf** Board 14 Thtr 30 Del from £330* **Parking** 20 **Notes** Civ Wed 50

Miller Howe Hotel

★★★ 86% ◎◎ COUNTRY HOUSE HOTEL

☎ 015394 42536
Rayrigg Rd LA23 1EY
e-mail: info@millerhowe.com
dir: M6 junct 36 , A591 past Windermere, left at rdbt towards Bowness

This long established hotel of much character enjoys a lakeside setting amidst delightful landscaped gardens. The bright and welcoming day rooms include sumptuous lounges, a conservatory and an opulently decorated restaurant. Imaginative dinners make use of fresh, local produce where possible and there is an extensive, well-balanced wine list. Stylish bedrooms, many with fabulous lake views, include well-equipped cottage rooms and a number with whirlpool baths.

Rooms 15 (3 annexe) (1 GF) 🐾 **S** £125-£190; **D** £210-£320 (incl. bkfst & dinner) **Facilities** FTV Wi-fi ♨ HL Xmas New Year **Parking** 35 **Notes** LB Civ Wed 75

Lindeth Fell Country House Hotel

★★★ 85% COUNTRY HOUSE HOTEL

☎ 015394 43286 & 44287
Lyth Valley Rd, Bowness-on-Windermere LA23 3JP
e-mail: kennedy@lindethfell.co.uk
web: www.lindethfell.co.uk
dir: 1m S of Bowness on A5074

Enjoying delightful views, this smart Edwardian residence stands in seven acres of glorious, landscaped gardens. Bedrooms, which vary in size and style, are comfortably equipped. Skilfully prepared dinners are served in the spacious dining room that commands fine views. The resident owners and their attentive, friendly staff provide high levels of hospitality and service.

Rooms 14 (2 fmly) (1 GF) 🐾 **S** £65-£85; **D** £130-£210 (incl. bkfst)* **Facilities** Wi-fi Putt green Fishing ⛵ Bowling Xmas New Year **Conf** Class 12 Board 12 **Parking** 20 **Notes** LB ⊗ Closed 3-29 Jan

W

WINDERMERE *continued*

Windermere Manor Hotel

★★★ 78% HOTEL

☎ 01539 445801
Rayrigg Rd LA23 1ES
e-mail: windermere@actionforblindpeople.org.uk
dir: A591 towards Ambleside. At mini-rdbt turn left, hotel 1st on left

Set above the shores of Lake Windermere in wooded landscaped gardens, this former manor house has been restored to its original splendour. The bedrooms and suites are smart and well appointed. The attractive dining room has an unusual barrel-vaulted wooden roof and serves delicious home cooking. The hotel extends a warm welcome to everyone but caters especially for the visually impaired, their families, friends and guide dogs. Special facilities for guide dogs are provided.

Rooms 35 (7 annexe) (2 fmly) (10 GF) ⚓ **S** £39–£69; **D** £89–£159 (incl. bkfst)* **Facilities** FTV Wi-fi HL ⊗ supervised Gym Xmas New Year **Conf** Class 30 Board 15 Thtr 40 Del from £95 to £125 **Services** Lift **Parking** 28 **Notes** LB Civ Wed 40

Craig Manor

★★★ 77% HOTEL

☎ 015394 88877
Lake Rd LA23 2JF
e-mail: info@craigmanor.co.uk
dir: A590, then A591 into Windermere, left at Windermere Hotel, through village, pass Magistrates' Court, hotel on left

Situated in the heart of the Lake District, Craig Manor has is a relaxed and friendly atmosphere with professional staff providing attentive service. Bedrooms are comfortable and well equipped, and some rooms offer stunning views across the lake. The attractive and elegant lake-facing restaurant serves an excellent choice of quality dishes. The large car park is a further benefit in this popular tourist resort.

Rooms 16

Cedar Manor Hotel & Restaurant

★★ 85% ◉◉ HOTEL

☎ 015394 43192 & 45970
Ambleside Rd LA23 1AX
e-mail: info@cedarmanor.co.uk
dir: From A591 follow signs to Windermere. Hotel on left just beyond St Mary's Church

Built in 1854 as a country retreat this lovely old house enjoys a peaceful location that is within easy walking distance of the town centre. Bedrooms, some on the ground floor, are attractive and well equipped, with two bedrooms in the adjacent coach house. There is a comfortable lounge bar where guests can relax before enjoying dinner in the well-appointed dining room.

Rooms 10 (1 annexe) (1 fmly) (3 GF) ⚓ **S** £70–£175; **D** £100–£350 (incl. bkfst)* **Facilities** FTV Wi-fi New Year **Conf** Board 10 Del from £160 to £190* **Parking** 11 **Notes** LB ⊗ Closed 3-21 Jan

The Hideaway at Windermere

◉◉ RESTAURANT WITH ROOMS

☎ 015394 43070
Phoenix Way LA23 1DB
e-mail:
eatandstay@thehideawayatwindermere.co.uk
web: www.thehideawayatwindermere.co.uk
dir: Exit A591 at Ravensworth B&B, into Phoenix Way, The Hideaway 100mtrs on right

Tucked away quietly this beautiful Victorian Lakeland house is personally run by owners Richard and Lisa. Delicious food, individually designed bedrooms and warm hospitality ensure an enjoyable stay. There is a beautifully appointed lounge looking out to the garden, and the restaurant is split between two light and airy rooms; here guests will find the emphasis is on fresh, local ingredients and attentive, yet friendly service. Bedrooms vary in size and style - the larger rooms feature luxury bathrooms.

Rooms 11 (1 annexe)

Jerichos

◉◉ RESTAURANT WITH ROOMS

☎ 015394 42522
College Rd LA23 1BX
e-mail: info@jerichos.co.uk
dir: A591 to Windermere, 2nd left into Elleray Rd then 1st right into College Rd

Dating back to around 1870, this property has been lovingly restored. All the elegant bedrooms are en suite. The comfortable lounge has a real fire to relax by on chillier days. The chef/proprietor has established a strong reputation for his creative menus that use the best local and seasonal produce.

Rooms 10

INSPECTORS' CHOICE

Macdonald Windsor Hotel

★★★★ ◉ HOTEL

☎ 0844 879 9101
23 High St SL4 1LH
e-mail: gm.windsor@macdonaldwindsor.com

Just across the street from Windsor Castle, this hotel is an ideal base for visiting not only the castle, but all the other famous attractions of the town. It has well-appointed contemporary, designer-led bedrooms, some overlooking the castle, that are decorated in soft shades to create a calm atmosphere, and include flat-screen TVs and Bose iPod docks. The Scottish Steak Club @ Caleys restaurant offers a relaxed and informal dining venue, and 24-hour room service is also available. There is complimentary Wi-fi in the bedrooms and the conference rooms.

Rooms 120 (4 fmly) ⚓ **S** £100–£375; **D** £100–£375* **Facilities** FTV Wi-fi ⚓ HL ♫ **Conf** Class 80 Board 35 Thtr 100 Del from £199 to £300 **Services** Lift Air con **Parking** 42 **Notes** LB Civ Wed 100

Save on hotels. Book at **theAA.com/hotel**

WIN 495 ENGLAND

Oakley Court Hotel

★★★★ 78% HOTEL

☎ 01753 609988 & 609900
Windsor Rd, Water Oakley SL4 5UR
e-mail: oakley.reservations@principal-hayley.com
web: www.principal-hayley.com/theoakleycourt
dir: M4 junct 6, A355, then A332 towards Windsor,
right onto A308 towards Maidenhead. Pass
racecourse, hotel 2.5m on right

Built in 1859 this splendid Victorian Gothic mansion
is enviably situated in extensive grounds that lead
down to the Thames. All bedrooms are spacious,
beautifully furnished and many enjoy river views.
Extensive public areas include a range of comfortable
lounges and the Oakleaf Restaurant. The
comprehensive leisure facilities include a 9-hole golf
course.

Rooms 118 (108 annexe) (6 fmly) **S** £96-£206;
D £106-£216* **Facilities** FTV Wi-fi HL 🕲 ⚓ 9 ⚴ Putt
green ⚴ Gym Boating Sauna Steam room Snooker
Xmas New Year **Conf** Class 90 Board 50 Thtr 170
Del from £180 to £330* **Services** Air con **Parking** 120
Notes LB ⊗ Civ Wed 120

Mercure Windsor Castle Hotel

★★★★ 77% ◉◉ HOTEL

☎ 01753 851577
18 High St SL4 1LJ
e-mail: h6618@accor.com
web: www.mercure.com
dir: M4 junct 6/M25 junct 15, follow signs to Windsor
town centre & castle. Hotel at top of hill opposite
Guildhall

This is one of the oldest hotels in Windsor, beginning
life as a coaching inn in the 16th century. Located
opposite Windsor Castle, it is an ideal base from
which to explore the town and its royal connections.
Stylish bedrooms are thoughtfully equipped and
include four-poster and executive rooms. Public areas
are spacious and tastefully decorated.

Rooms 108 (70 annexe) (18 fmly) (3 GF) ➤
S £119-£250; **D** £129-£260 (incl. bkfst) **Facilities** STV
FTV Wi-fi Xmas New Year **Conf** Class 150 Board 50
Thtr 400 Del from £195 to £300 **Services** Lift Air con
Parking 135 **Notes** LB ⊗ Civ Wed 300

Sir Christopher Wren Hotel and Spa

★★★★ 76% ◉ HOTEL

☎ 01753 442400
Thames St SL4 1PX
e-mail: wrens@sarova.co.uk
dir: M4 junct 6, at 1st exit follow signs to Windsor,
1st major exit on left, left at lights

Located by the side of the Thames and close to the
Eton Bridge stands this well presented hotel.
Bedrooms vary - with both traditional and
contemporary tastes catered for. There are
comfortable lounges, a popular restaurant with great
views of the river and a well-equipped leisure club is
also available. Limited parking is available.

Rooms 93 (36 annexe) (5 fmly) (10 GF) **S** £95-£250;
D £115-£270* **Facilities** Spa STV Wi-fi ⚴ Gym Sauna
🎵 Xmas New Year **Conf** Class 50 Board 45 Thtr 100
Del from £195 to £270* **Parking** 14 **Notes** LB ⊗
Civ Wed 100

Best Western Royal Adelaide Hotel

★★★★ 72% HOTEL

☎ 01753 863916 & 07710 473130
46 Kings Rd SL4 2AG
e-mail: info@theroyaladelaide.com
web: www.theroyaladelaide.com
dir: M4 junct 6, A322 to Windsor. 1st left at rdbt into
Clarence Rd. At 4th lights right into Sheet St, then
Kings Rd. Hotel on right

This attractive Georgian-style hotel enjoys a quiet
location yet is only a short walk from the town centre.
Bedrooms vary in size. Public areas are tastefully
appointed and include a range of meeting rooms, a
bar and an elegant restaurant. Off-street parking is
available.

Rooms 42 (4 annexe) (6 fmly) (8 GF) (5 smoking) ➤
S £99-£109; **D** £145-£165 (incl. bkfst)* **Facilities** STV
FTV Wi-fi Xmas **Conf** Class 80 Board 50 Thtr 100
Del from £155 to £165* **Services** Air con **Parking** 16
Notes Civ Wed 110

Christopher Hotel

★★★ 79% HOTEL

☎ 01753 852359
110 High St, Eton SL4 6AN
e-mail: reservations@thechristopher.co.uk
web: www.thechristopher.co.uk
dir: M4 junct 5 (Slough E), Colnbrook Datchet Eton
(B470). At rdbt 2nd exit for Datchet. Right at mini
rdbt (Eton), left into Eton Rd (3rd rdbt). Left, hotel on
right

This hotel benefits from an ideal location in Eton,
being only a short stroll across the pedestrian bridge
from historic Windsor Castle and the many other
attractions the town has to offer. The hotel has
comfortable and smartly decorated accommodation,
and a wide range of dishes is available in the
informal bar and grill. A stylish room is available for
private dining or for meetings.

Rooms 34 (23 annexe) (10 fmly) (22 GF) ➤
S £108-£144; **D** £150-£200* **Facilities** FTV Wi-fi ⚴
Xmas New Year **Conf** Board 10 Thtr 30 **Parking** 19

WINTERINGHAM
Lincolnshire

Map 17 SE92

INSPECTORS' CHOICE

Winteringham Fields

◉◉ RESTAURANT WITH ROOMS

☎ 01724 733096
DN15 9ND
e-mail: reception@winteringhamfields.co.uk
dir: In village centre at x-rds

This highly regarded restaurant with rooms, located
deep in the countryside in the village of
Winteringham, is just six miles west of the Humber
Bridge. Public rooms and bedrooms, some of which
are housed in renovated barns and cottages, are
delightfully cosseting. Award-winning food is
served in the restaurant.

Rooms 11 (7 annexe) (2 fmly)

W

WISBECH
Cambridgeshire   Map 12 TF40

Crown Lodge Hotel
THE INDEPENDENTS
HOTEL ASSOCIATION

★★★ 85% ⊛ HOTEL

☎ 01945 773391 & 772206
Downham Rd, Outwell PE14 8SE
e-mail: office@thecrownlodgehotel.co.uk
web: www.thecrownlodgehotel.co.uk
dir: On A1122, approx 5m from Wisbech

A friendly, privately owned hotel situated in a peaceful location on the banks of Well Creek a short drive from Wisbech. The bedrooms are pleasantly decorated, have co-ordinated fabrics and modern facilities. The public areas are very stylish; they include a lounge bar, brasserie restaurant and a large seating area with plush leather sofas.

Rooms 10 (1 fmly) (10 GF) 🐾 **S** £79; **D** £99 (incl. bkfst)* **Facilities** FTV Wi-fi ⤸ Squash **Conf** Class 60 Board 40 Thtr 80 **Services** Air con **Parking** 55 **Notes** LB Closed 25-26 Dec & 1 Jan

Elme Hall Hotel

★★★ 73% HOTEL

☎ 01945 475566
Elm High Rd PE14 0DQ
e-mail: elmehallhotel@btconnect.com
web: www.elmehall.co.uk
dir: A47 onto A1101 towards Wisbech. Hotel on right

An imposing, Georgian-style property conveniently situated on the outskirts of the town centre just off the A47. Individually decorated bedrooms are tastefully furnished with quality reproduction pieces and equipped to a high standard. Public rooms include a choice of attractive lounges, as well as two bars, meeting rooms and a banqueting suite.

Rooms 42 (34 annexe) (3 fmly) (21 GF) 🐾 **S** £69; **D** £78-£245 (incl. bkfst)* **Facilities** FTV Wi-fi ♫ **Conf** Class 200 Board 20 Thtr 350 **Parking** 200 **Notes** Civ Wed 350

WITHAM
Essex   Map 7 TL81

Rivenhall Hotel
★★★ 77% HOTEL

☎ 01376 516969
Rivenhall End CM8 3HB
e-mail: info@rivenhallhotel.com
web: www.rivenhallhotel.com
dir: M25 junct 28 towards Chelmsford on A12, take exit for Silver End/Great Braxted. At T-junct turn right, then 1st right, hotel directly ahead

This modern hotel is ideally situated just off the A12 between Chelmsford and Colchester. Bedrooms are pleasantly decorated and equipped with modern facilities. Public rooms include a large restaurant and a comfortable lounge bar; conference and leisure facilities are also available.

Rooms 55 (37 annexe) (6 fmly) (42 GF) **S** £55-£65; **D** £65-£79 (incl. bkfst)* **Facilities** STV FTV Wi-fi ☉ Gym Sauna Steam room Xmas New Year **Conf** Class 70 Board 50 Thtr 150 Del from £120 to £130* **Parking** 150 **Notes** ⊗ Closed 26 Dec RS Xmas Civ Wed 150

WITNEY
Oxfordshire   Map 5 SP31

Oxford Witney Four Pillars Hotel
FOUR PILLARS HOTELS

★★★★ 71% HOTEL

☎ 0800 374692 & 01993 779777
Ducklington Ln OX28 4TJ
e-mail: witney@four-pillars.co.uk
web: www.four-pillars.co.uk/witney
dir: M40 junct 9, A34 to A40, exit A415 Witney/Abingdon. Hotel on left, 2nd exit for Witney

This attractive modern hotel is close to Oxford and Burford and offers spacious, well-equipped bedrooms. The cosy Spinners Bar has comfortable seating areas and the popular Weavers Restaurant offers a good range of dishes. Other amenities include extensive function and leisure facilities, complete with indoor swimming pool.

Rooms 87 (14 fmly) (21 GF) 🐾 **S** £70-£140; **D** £70-£140 **Facilities** FTV Wi-fi ⤸ ☉ Gym Steam room Sauna Beauty treatment room Xmas New Year **Conf** Class 76 Board 44 Thtr 150 Del from £99 to £145 **Parking** 120 **Notes** LB ⊗ Civ Wed 150

W

WOBURN
Bedfordshire   Map 11 SP93

The Inn at Woburn
★★★ 81% ◉◉ HOTEL

☎ 01525 290441
George St MK17 9PX
e-mail: inn@woburn.co.uk
web: www.woburn.co.uk/inn
dir: M1 junct 13, towards Woburn. In Woburn left at T-junct , hotel in village

This inn provides a high standard of accommodation. Bedrooms are divided between the original house, a modern extension and some stunning cottage suites. Public areas include the beamed, club-style Tavistock Bar, a range of meeting rooms and an attractive restaurant with interesting dishes on offer.

Rooms 55 (7 annexe) (4 fmly) (21 GF) **Facilities** FTV Wi-fi ⚓ 54 Putt green Concessionary rate to access Woburn Safari Park & Woburn Abbey **Conf** Class 40 Board 40 Thtr 60 **Parking** 80 **Notes** ⊗ Civ Wed 60

WOKING
Surrey   Map 6 TQ05

Holiday Inn Woking
★★★ 79% HOTEL

☎ 01483 221000
Victoria St GU21 8EW
e-mail: reservations@wokingholiday-inn.com
web: www.hiwoking.co.uk
dir: A320 to Woking. After last rdbt to town centre take slip road off dual carriageway. Hotel on left

Situated in a convenient town centre location with parking facilities and only ten minutes from Woking main line train station. Public areas are stylish and comfortable; dining options include bar snacks, a substantial restaurant meal or choices from room service. Bedrooms and bathrooms are generally spacious and offer good levels of comfort.

Rooms 161 (30 fmly) (17 smoking) **Facilities** FTV Wi-fi ⚓ Gym **Conf** Class 180 Board 40 Thtr 300 **Services** Lift Air con **Parking** 50 **Notes** ⊗ Civ Wed 60

Premier Inn Woking
BUDGET HOTEL

☎ 0871 527 9182
Bridge Barn Ln, Horsell GU21 6NL
web: www.premierinn.com
dir: From A324 at rdbt into Parley Drive. Left at next rdbt into Goldsworth Rd

High quality, budget accommodation ideal for both families and business travellers. Spacious, en suite bedrooms feature tea and coffee making facilities, and Freeview TV in most hotels. Internet access and Wi-fi are available for a small fee. The adjacent family restaurant features a wide and varied menu. See also the Hotel Groups pages.

Rooms 34

WOLVERHAMPTON
West Midlands   Map 10 SO99

See also Pattingham

Novotel Wolverhampton
★★★ 80% HOTEL

☎ 01902 871100
Union St WV1 3JN
e-mail: H1188@accor.com
web: www.novotel.com
dir: 6m from M6 junct 10. A454 to Wolverhampton. Hotel on main ring road

This large, modern, purpose-built hotel stands close to the town centre. It provides spacious, smartly presented and well-equipped bedrooms, all of which contain convertible bed settees for family occupancy. In addition to the open-plan lounge and bar area, there is an attractive brasserie-style restaurant, which overlooks an attractive patio garden.

Rooms 132 (9 fmly) **Facilities** STV Wi-fi **Conf** Class 100 Board 80 Thtr 200 **Del** from £99 to £135* **Services** Lift **Parking** 120 **Notes** RS 23 Dec-4 Jan Civ Wed 200

Holiday Inn Wolverhampton
★★★ 73% HOTEL

☎ 01902 390004
Dunstall Park WV6 0PE
e-mail: holidayinn@wolverhampton-racecourse.com
web: www.holidayinn.co.uk
dir: Off A449, 1.5m from city centre. Follow brown sign for Dunstall Park

Located at Wolverhampton Racecourse, which is a floodlit racecourse with afternoon and evening meets, this modern hotel provides a range of well-equipped bedrooms and an open-plan public area with bar, lounge and brasserie-style restaurant.

Rooms 54 (18 fmly) **Facilities** STV Wi-fi **Services** Lift **Parking** 1500

Mercure Wolverhampton Goldthorn Hotel
★★★ 72% HOTEL

☎ 01902 429216
126 Penn Rd WV3 0ER
e-mail: enquiries@hotels-wolverhampton.com
web: www.hotels-wolverhampton.com
dir: A454 then A449 signed Kidderminster. Hotel 1m on right

This hotel is situated just on the outskirts of the old town and offers easy access to major motorway networks. The bedrooms are comfortable and well equipped; free Wi-fi available throughout the hotel. The leisure facilities include a health club with a swimming pool, gym, steam room and sauna. There is also free on-site parking.

Rooms 74 (16 annexe) (12 fmly) (4 GF) **S** £37-£50; **D** £58-£90* **Facilities** FTV Wi-fi ❄ Gym Sauna Steam room Xmas New Year **Conf** Class 70 Board 40 Thtr 140 **Del** from £105 to £135* **Parking** 100 **Notes** LB Civ Wed 100

W

WOLVERHAMPTON *continued*

The Connaught Hotel

★★★ 67% HOTEL

☎ 01902 424433
Tettenhall Rd WV1 4SW
e-mail: info@theconnaughthotel.net
dir: A41 junct 3, 1st exit at rdbt. Follow signs for
Tettenhall. In Tettenhall Rd, hotel on left

This hotel is located a short walk from the city centre
and the railway station, with convenient access to the
motorway networks. Bedrooms provide modern
comfort with a contemporary decor. Complimentary
Wi-fi is available throughout the hotel. The Americano
steakhouse and bar offers American-style dishes,
with exotic meats a speciality. There are seven air-
conditioned conference and banqueting suites.

Rooms 87 (8 fmly) (3 GF) **Facilities** STV FTV Wi-fi
Xmas New Year **Conf** Class 300 Board 60 Thtr 500
Services Lift **Parking** 120 **Notes** ⊛ Civ Wed 500

Premier Inn
Wolverhampton City Centre

BUDGET HOTEL

☎ 0871 527 9186
Broad Gauge Way WV10 0BA
web: www.premierinn.com
dir: M6 junct 10, A454 signed Wolverhampton for
approx 2m. Right into Neachalls Ln (signed
Wednesfield). 0.75m. At rdbt 1st exit onto A4124
(Wednesfield Way). 1st exit at next rdbt. 2nd exit at
3rd rdbt. At 2nd lights left into Sun St. 1st right, hotel
at end of road

High quality, budget accommodation ideal for both
families and business travellers. Spacious, en suite
bedrooms feature tea and coffee making facilities,
and Freeview TV in most hotels. Internet access and
Wi-fi are available for a small fee. The adjacent
family restaurant features a wide and varied menu.
See also the Hotel Groups pages.

Rooms 88

Premier Inn Wolverhampton North

BUDGET HOTEL

☎ 0871 527 9184
Greenfield Ln, Stafford Rd WV10 6TA
web: www.premierinn.com
dir: M54 junct 2. Hotel at lights in approx 100yds

Rooms 77

Premier Inn Barnsley
(Dearne Valley)

BUDGET HOTEL

☎ 0871 527 8050
Meadow Gate, Dearne Valley S73 0UN
web: www.premierinn.com
dir: M1 junct 36 E'bound, A6195 towards Doncaster
(5m). Hotel at rdbt adjacent to Meadows Brewers
Fayre

High quality, budget accommodation ideal for both
families and business travellers. Spacious, en suite
bedrooms feature tea and coffee making facilities,
and Freeview TV in most hotels. Internet access and
Wi-fi are available for a small fee. The adjacent
family restaurant features a wide and varied menu.
See also the Hotel Groups pages.

Rooms 41

Chequers Inn

★★★ 78% ⊛ HOTEL

☎ 01628 529575
Kiln Ln, Wooburn HP10 0JQ
e-mail: info@chequers-inn.com
web: www.chequers-inn.com
dir: M40 junct 2, A40 through Beaconsfield Old Town
towards High Wycombe. 2m from town left into Broad
Ln. Inn 2.5m

This 17th-century inn enjoys a peaceful, rural location
beside the common. Bedrooms feature stripped-pine
furniture, co-ordinated fabrics and an excellent range
of extra facilities. The bar, with its massive oak post,
beams and flagstone floor, and the restaurant, which
overlooks a pretty patio, are very much focal points
here.

Rooms 17 (8 GF) **S** £85-£99.50; **D** £90-£107.50*
Facilities FTV Wi-fi **Conf** Class 30 Board 20 Thtr 50
Del from £155* **Parking** 60 **Notes** LB ⊛

Days Inn Sheffield - M1

BUDGET HOTEL

☎ 0114 248 7992
Woodall Service Area S26 7XR
e-mail: woodall.hotel@welcomebreak.co.uk
web: www.welcomebreak.co.uk
dir: M1, between juncts 30 & 31 S'bound, at Woodall
Services

This modern building offers accommodation in smart,
spacious and well-equipped bedrooms, suitable for
families and business travellers, and all with en suite
bathrooms. Continental breakfast is available and
other refreshments may be taken at the nearby family
restaurant. See also the Hotel Groups pages.

Rooms 38 (32 fmly) (16 GF) (6 smoking)
Conf Board 10

Seckford Hall Hotel

★★★★ 76% ⊛⊛ HOTEL   CLASSIC BRITISH HOTELS

☎ 01394 385678
IP13 6NU
e-mail: reception@seckford.co.uk
web: www.seckford.co.uk
dir: Signed on A12. (NB do not follow signs for town
centre)

An elegant Tudor manor house set amid landscaped
grounds just off the A12. It is reputed that Queen
Elizabeth I visited this property, and it retains much
of its original character. Public rooms include a
superb panelled lounge, a cosy bar and an intimate
restaurant. The spacious bedrooms are attractively
decorated, tastefully furnished and thoughtfully
equipped.

Rooms 32 (10 annexe) (4 fmly) (7 GF) **S** £85-£95;
D £140-£230* **Facilities** Wi-fi ⟳ Putt green Fishing
Gym Beauty salon & treatment room New Year
Conf Class 46 Board 40 Thtr 100 Del from £170 to
£190* **Parking** 100 **Notes** LB Closed 25 Dec
Civ Wed 120

W

Save on hotels. Book at **theAA.com/hotel**

WOL – WOO 499 ENGLAND

The Crown at Woodbridge

T|A|HOTEL
COLLECTION

★★★ 87% ◉◉ HOTEL

☎ 01394 384242
2 Thoro'fare IP12 1AD
e-mail: info@thecrownatwoodbridge.co.uk
dir: A12 follow signs for Woodbridge onto B1438.
1.25m from rdbt left into Quay St. Hotel on right
approx 100yds

This 17th-century property offers contemporary-style
accommodation throughout. The open-plan public
areas are tastefully appointed and include a large
lounge bar, a restaurant and a private dining room.
The stylish bedrooms are tastefully appointed and
equipped with modern facilities.

Rooms 10 (2 fmly) **Facilities** STV Wi-fi **Parking** 40
Notes ⊗

Ufford Park Hotel Golf & Spa

★★★ 82% HOTEL

☎ 01394 383555
Yarmouth Rd, Ufford IP12 1QW
e-mail: enquiries@uffordpark.co.uk
web: www.uffordpark.co.uk
dir: A12 N to A1152, in Melton left at lights, follow
B1438, hotel 1m on right

A modern hotel set in open countryside boasting
superb leisure facilities including a challenging golf
course. The spacious public rooms provide a wide
choice of areas in which to relax and include a busy
lounge bar, a carvery restaurant and the Vista
Restaurant. Bedrooms are smartly appointed and
pleasantly decorated; each is thoughtfully equipped
and many overlook the golf course.

Rooms 87 (20 fmly) (32 GF) ⌇ **S** £79–£109;
D £89–£159 (incl. bkfst)* **Facilities** Spa FTV Wi-fi ⌇
⊛ supervised ⌇ 18 Putt green Fishing ⌇ Gym Golf
Academy with PGA tuition 2 storey floodlit driving
range Dance Studio Xmas New Year **Conf** Class 120
Board 120 Thtr 300 Del from £109 to £119*
Services Lift **Parking** 250 **Notes** LB Civ Wed 120

Woodbury Park Hotel and Golf Club

★★★★ 75% ◉ HOTEL

☎ 01395 233382
Woodbury Castle EX5 1JJ
e-mail: enquiries@woodburypark.co.uk
web: www.woodburypark.co.uk
dir: M5 junct 30, A376 then A3052 towards Sidmouth,
onto B3180, hotel signed

Situated in 500 acres of beautiful and unspoilt
countryside, yet within easy reach of Exeter and the
M5, this hotel offers smart, well-equipped and
immaculately presented accommodation together
with a host of sporting and banqueting facilities.
There is a choice of golf courses, a Bodyzone beauty
centre and enjoyable dining in the Atrium Restaurant.

Rooms 60 (4 annexe) (4 fmly) (28 GF) **S** fr £69.95;
D fr £84.95 (incl. bkfst)* **Facilities** Spa STV FTV Wi-fi
⌇ ⊛ ⌇ 27 ⌇ Putt green Fishing Gym Squash Beauty
salon Football pitch Driving range Fitness Studio
Xmas New Year **Conf** Class 100 Board 40 Thtr 250
Del from £145* **Services** Lift **Parking** 400 **Notes** LB
⊗ Civ Wed 150

Menzies Prince Regent

Ⓜ MenziesHotels

★★★★ 70% HOTEL

☎ 020 8505 9966
Manor Rd IG8 8AE
e-mail: princeregent@menzieshotels.co.uk
web: www.menzieshotels.co.uk
dir: From A113 (Chigwell Rd) S of Chigwell into B173
(Manor Rd)

Situated on the edge of Woodford Bridge and
Chigwell, this hotel with delightful rear gardens,
offers easy access into London as well as the M11
and M25. There is a good range of spacious, well-
equipped bedrooms. Extensive conference and
banqueting facilities are particularly well appointed,
and are very suitable for weddings and for business
events.

Rooms 61 (4 fmly) (15 GF) (10 smoking)
Facilities STV FTV Wi-fi ⌇ Xmas New Year
Conf Class 180 Board 80 Thtr 400 **Services** Lift
Parking 225 **Notes** Civ Wed 350

Petwood

★★★ 74% HOTEL

☎ 01526 352411
Stixwould Rd LN10 6QG
e-mail: reception@petwood.co.uk
web: www.petwood.co.uk
dir: From Sleaford take A153 (signed Skegness). At
Tattershall turn left on B1192. Hotel is signed from
village

This lovely Edwardian house, set in 30 acres of
gardens and woodlands, is adjacent to Woodhall Golf
Course. Built in 1905, the house was used by 617
Squadron, the famous Dambusters, as an officers'
mess during World War II. Bedrooms and public areas
are spacious and comfortable, and retain many
original features. Weddings and conferences are well
catered for in modern facilities.

Rooms 53 (3 GF) ⌇ **S** £70; **D** £100-£130 (incl.
bkfst)* **Facilities** FTV Wi-fi HL Putt green ⌇ ♫ Xmas
New Year **Conf** Class 100 Board 50 Thtr 250
Del £120* **Services** Lift **Parking** 140 **Notes** LB
Civ Wed 200

W

WOODHALL SPA *continued*

Golf Hotel

★★★ 72% HOTEL

☎ 01526 353535
The Broadway LN10 6SG
e-mail: reception@thegolf-hotel.com
web: www.thegolf-hotel.com
dir: From Lincoln take B1189 to Metheringham onto B1191 towards Woodhall Spa. Hotel on left in approx 500yds from rdbt

Located near the centre of the village, this traditional hotel is ideally situated to explore the Lincolnshire countryside and coast. The adjacent golf course makes this a popular venue for golfers, and the hotel's hydrotherapy suite uses the original spa water supplies. Bedrooms vary in size.

Rooms 50 (2 fmly) (8 GF) (3 smoking) **Facilities** Spa FTV Wi-fi Xmas New Year **Conf** Class 50 Board 50 Thtr 150 **Services** Lift **Parking** 100 **Notes** Civ Wed 150

WOODSTOCK
Oxfordshire
Map 11 SP41

The Feathers Hotel

★★★★ 80% ◉ ◉
TOWN HOUSE HOTEL

☎ 01993 812291
Market St OX20 1SX
e-mail: enquiries@feathers.co.uk
dir: From A44 (Oxford to Woodstock), 1st left after lights. Hotel on left

This intimate and unique hotel enjoys a town centre location with easy access to nearby Blenheim Palace. Public areas are elegant and full of traditional character from the cosy drawing room to the atmospheric restaurant. Individually styled bedrooms are appointed to a high standard and are furnished with attractive period and reproduction furniture.

Rooms 21 (5 annexe) (4 fmly) (2 GF) **S** £104-£199; **D** £134-£409 (incl. bkfst) **Facilities** FTV Wi-fi ♪ Xmas New Year **Conf** Class 18 Board 20 Thtr 40 **Notes** LB

Macdonald Bear Hotel

★★★★ 77% ◉ ◉ HOTEL

☎ 0844 879 9143
Park St OX20 1SZ
e-mail: gm.bear@macdonaldhotels.co.uk
web: www.macdonaldhotels.co.uk
dir: M40 junct 9 follow signs for Oxford & Blenheim Palace. A44 to town centre, hotel on left

With its ivy-clad façade, oak beams and open fireplaces, this 13th-century coaching inn exudes charm and cosiness. The bedrooms are decorated in a modern style that remains in keeping with the historic character of the building. Public rooms include a variety of function rooms, an intimate bar area and an attractive restaurant where attentive service and good food are offered.

Rooms 54 (18 annexe) (1 fmly) (8 GF) ↑ **S** £100-£250; **D** £100-£250* **Facilities** FTV Wi-fi Xmas New Year **Conf** Class 12 Board 24 Thtr 40 **Parking** 40

Kings Arms Hotel

★★★ 79% ◉ HOTEL

☎ 01993 813636
19 Market St OX20 1SU
e-mail: stay@kingshotelwoodstock.co.uk
web: www.kings-hotel-woodstock.co.uk
dir: In town centre, on corner of Market St & A44

This appealing and contemporary hotel is situated in the centre of town just a short walk from Blenheim Palace. Public areas include an attractive bistro-style restaurant and a smart bar. Bedrooms and bathrooms are comfortably furnished and well equipped, and appointed to a high standard.

Rooms 15 ↑ **S** £80-£85; **D** £150-£160 (incl. bkfst)* **Facilities** FTV Wi-fi Xmas New Year **Notes** LB ⊗ No children 12yrs

---

WOODY BAY
Devon
Map 3 SS64

Woody Bay Hotel

★★ 78% HOTEL

☎ 01598 763264 & 763563
EX31 4QX
e-mail: info@woodybayhotel.co.uk
dir: Signed from A39 between Blackmoor Gate & Lynton

Popular with walkers, this Victorian country style hotel is perfectly situated to enjoy sweeping views over Woody Bay. Bedrooms vary in style and size, but all boast truly magnificent views across dense woodland to the sea beyond. The same views can be enjoyed from the restaurant where local fish features prominently on the imaginative menus.

Rooms 7 (1 fmly) **Parking** 7 **Notes** ⊗ No children 5yrs Closed Dec-Jan RS Nov & Feb

---

WOOKEY HOLE
Somerset
Map 4 ST54

Wookey Hole Hotel

★★ 74% HOTEL

☎ 01749 672243
BA5 1BB
e-mail: witch@wookey.co.uk

This impressive hotel is located in the heart of the pretty village, famous for its magnificent cave system and just a couple of miles from the historic cathedral city of Wells. The bedrooms are modern, spacious and comfortable with both family and connecting rooms available. Additional facilities include a bar and restaurant; there is extensive parking provision.

Rooms 58 (37 fmly) (27 GF) **Facilities** FTV Wi-fi ♪ 9 hole adventure golf course **Services** Lift **Parking** 800 **Notes** ⊗

W

WOOLACOMBE　　Map 3 SS44
Devon

The Woolacombe Bay Hotel
★★★★ 74% HOTEL

☎ 01271 870388
South St EX34 7BN
e-mail: enquiries@woolacombebayhotel.co.uk
web: www.woolacombebayhotel.com
dir: A361 onto B3343 to Woolacombe. Hotel in centre

This family-friendly hotel is adjacent to the beach and the village centre, and has a welcoming environment. The public areas are spacious and comfortable, and many of the well-equipped bedrooms have balconies with splendid views over the bay. In addition to the elegant surroundings of Doyle's Restaurant, The Bay Brasserie is available for an informal alternative. Extensive leisure facilities are also provided.

Rooms 69 (26 fmly) (2 GF) ✿ **S** £100-£150; **D** £200-£300 (incl. bkfst)* **Facilities** Spa FTV Wi-fi HL ⟨⟩ ⟨⟩ ♨ 9 ♨ Gym Squash Paddling pool Table tennis Snooker Steam room Sauna Outdoor short mat bowls Xmas New Year Child facilities **Conf** Class 150 Board 150 Thtr 200 Del from £105 to £200* **Services** Lift **Parking** 150 **Notes** ⊗ Closed 2 Jan-10 Feb Civ Wed 150

Watersmeet Hotel
★★★ 87% ⊛ HOTEL

☎ 01271 870333
Mortehoe EX34 7EB
e-mail: info@watersmeethotel.co.uk
web: www.watersmeethotel.co.uk
dir: B3343 into Woolacombe, right onto esplanade, hotel 0.75m on left

With magnificent views, and steps leading directly to the beach, this popular hotel offers guests attentive service and a relaxing atmosphere. Bedrooms benefit from the wonderful sea views and some have private balconies. Diners in the attractive tiered restaurant can admire the beautiful sunsets while enjoying an innovative range of dishes offered on the fixed-price menu. Both indoor and outdoor pools are available.

Rooms 25 (4 fmly) (3 GF) ✿ **S** £76-£156; **D** £90-£340 (incl. bkfst & dinner)* **Facilities** FTV Wi-fi ⟨⟩ ⟨⟩ ⟨⟩ ⟨⟩ Steam room ♫ Xmas New Year **Conf** Board 20 Thtr 20 **Services** Lift **Parking** 38 **Notes** ⊗ Civ Wed 60

Trimstone Manor Country House Hotel
★★★ Ⓐ

☎ 01271 862841 & 868050
Trimstone EX34 8NR
e-mail: info@trimstone.co.uk
web: www.trimstone.co.uk
dir: M5 junct 27 towards Barnstaple, A361, through Braunton & Knowle. Left into Trimstone Lane after 1m, hotel 300yds on left

Rooms 15 (2 fmly) (3 GF) ✿ **S** £42-£65; **D** £86-£139 (incl. bkfst)* **Facilities** FTV Wi-fi ⟨⟩ ♨ Gym Sauna Games room Xmas New Year **Conf** Class 45 Board 40 Thtr 100 Del £130* **Parking** 20 **Notes** Civ Wed 179

WOOTTON BASSETT (ROYAL)　Map 5 SU08
Wiltshire

The Wiltshire
★★★ 75% HOTEL

☎ 01793 849999
SN4 7PB
e-mail: reception@the-wiltshire.co.uk
dir: M4 junct 16 follow Royal Wootton Bassett signs. Hotel 1m S of Royal Wootton Bassett on left of A3102 towards Lyneham

Surrounded by 220 acres of rolling countryside, this hotel, with easy access to the M4, offers golf enthusiasts two splendid courses - the 18-hole Lakes Course and the 9-hole Garden Course. The hotel has contemporary bedrooms with Freeview and free Wi-fi, and purpose-designed disabled access rooms are available. The air-conditioned Pavilion Restaurant & Lounge open onto a large patio overlooking the 18th green, and there are splendid leisure facilities including a techno-gym, 18-metre swimming pool, sauna and steam room.

Rooms 58 (29 GF) ✿ **S** £75-£125; **D** £75-£125 (incl. bkfst) **Facilities** FTV Wi-fi ⟨⟩ ♨ 27 Putt green Gym Sauna Steam room Beauty treatment rooms New Year **Conf** Class 120 Board 30 Thtr 250 **Services** Lift **Parking** 250 **Notes** LB ⊗ Closed 24-25 Dec Civ Wed 140

WORCESTER　　Map 10 SO85
Worcestershire

Pear Tree Inn & Country Hotel
★★★ 79% HOTEL

☎ 01905 756565
Smite WR3 8SY
e-mail: info@thepeartree.co.uk
dir: M5 junct 6, A4538 towards Droitwich. In 200yds 3rd exit at island (Brown Pear Tree sign), over canal bridge, up hill, hotel on left

Located close to M5 in pretty landscaped grounds, this traditional English inn and country hotel has spacious, air-conditioned bedrooms with attractive colour schemes and good facilities. Four suites are available. Guests can enjoy good food and a drink in relaxed surroundings; there is an excellent range of conference and function rooms.

Rooms 24 (2 fmly) (12 GF) **Facilities** Wi-fi Fishing **Conf** Class 150 Board 40 Thtr 250 **Services** Lift Air con **Parking** 200 **Notes** ⊗ Closed 25-26 Dec RS 1 Jan Civ Wed 120

W

WORCESTER continued

Premier Inn Worcester
BUDGET HOTEL

☎ 0871 527 9188
Wainwright Way, Warndon WR4 9FA
web: www.premierinn.com
dir: M5 junct 6. At entrance of Warndon commercial development area

High quality, budget accommodation ideal for both families and business travellers. Spacious, en suite bedrooms feature tea and coffee making facilities, and Freeview TV in most hotels. Internet access and Wi-fi are available for a small fee. The adjacent family restaurant features a wide and varied menu. See also the Hotel Groups pages.

Rooms 60

WORKINGTON Map 18 NY02
Cumbria

Washington Central Hotel
★★★★ 74% HOTEL

☎ 01900 65772
Washington St CA14 3AY
e-mail: kawildwchotel@aol.com
web: www.washingtoncentralhotelworkington.com
dir: M6 junct 40, A66 to Workington. Left at lights, hotel on right

Enjoying a prominent town centre location, this modern hotel boasts memorably hospitable staff. The well-maintained and comfortable bedrooms are equipped with a range of thoughtful extras. Public areas include numerous lounges, a spacious bar, Caesars leisure club, a smart restaurant and a popular coffee shop. The comprehensive conference facilities are ideal for meetings and weddings.

Rooms 46 (4 fmly) **S** £95-£115; **D** £140-£220 (incl. bkfst) **Facilities** FTV Wi-fi ⏱ ⊞ supervised Gym Sauna Steam room Sunbed **New Year Conf** Class 200 Board 100 Thtr 300 Del £145 **Services** Lift **Parking** 25 **Notes** LB ⊗ Civ Wed 300

WORKSOP Map 16 SK57
Nottinghamshire

Clumber Park Hotel and Spa
"bespoke"
★★★ 78% HOTEL

☎ 01623 835333
Clumber Park S80 3PA
e-mail: enquiries@clumberparkhotel.com
dir: M1 junct 30/31 follow signs to A57 & A1. From A1 take A614 towards Nottingham. Hotel 2m on left

Beside the A614, this hotel is situated in open countryside, edging on to Sherwood Forest and Clumber Park. Bedrooms are comfortably furnished and well equipped and public areas include a choice of formal and informal eating options. A wide choice of dishes and a relaxed atmosphere are offered in the Normanton Inn, while The Courtyard Restaurant has a more traditional style of service.

Rooms 73 (5 fmly) (27 GF) **S** fr £69; **D** £79-£240 (incl. bkfst)* **Facilities** Spa FTV Wi-fi ⏱ Gym Sauna Steam room Xmas New Year **Conf** Class 90 Board 40 Thtr 250 Del from £120 to £155* **Parking** 200 **Notes** LB Civ Wed 160

WORSLEY Map 15 SD70
Greater Manchester

Novotel Manchester West
★★★ 72% HOTEL
NOVOTEL

☎ 0161 799 3535
Worsley Brow M28 2YA
e-mail: H0907@accor.com
web: www.novotel.com
dir: Adjacent to M60 junct 13

Well placed for access to the Peak District and the Lake District, as well as Manchester, this modern hotel successfully caters for both families and business guests. The spacious bedrooms have sofa beds and a large work area; the hotel has an outdoor swimming pool, children's play area and secure parking.

Rooms 119 (10 fmly) (41 GF) ⚓ **Facilities** STV Wi-fi ⏱ Gym Xmas New Year **Conf** Class 130 Board 60 Thtr 220 **Services** Lift **Parking** 95 **Notes** Civ Wed 140

WORTHING Map 6 TQ10
West Sussex

Ardington Hotel
★★★ 80% HOTEL

☎ 01903 230451
Steyne Gardens BN11 3DZ
e-mail: reservations@ardingtonhotel.co.uk
web: www.ardingtonhotel.co.uk
dir: A27 to Lancing, to seafront. Follow signs for Worthing. Left at church into Steyne Gardens

Overlooking Steyne Gardens adjacent to the seafront, this popular hotel offers well-appointed bedrooms with a good range of facilities. There's a stylishly modern lounge/bar with ample seating, where a light menu is available throughout the day. The popular restaurant offers local seafood and a choice of modern dishes. Wi-fi is available in lounge/bar.

Rooms 45 (4 fmly) (12 GF) **S** £55-£76; **D** £75-£170 (incl. bkfst)* **Facilities** STV FTV Wi-fi **Conf** Class 60 Board 35 Thtr 140 Del from £80 to £140* **Notes** LB Closed 25 Dec-4 Jan

Findon Manor Hotel
★★★ 70% HOTEL

☎ 01903 872733
High St, Findon BN14 0TA
e-mail: hotel@findonmanor.com
dir: 500yds off A24 between Worthing & Horsham. At sign for Findon follow signs to Findon Manor into village

Located in the centre of the village, Findon Manor was built as a rectory and has a beamed lounge which doubles as the reception area. Bedrooms, several with four-poster beds, are attractively decorated in a traditional style. The cosy bar offers the very good range of bar food, and is popular with locals, while the restaurant overlooks the garden and offers modern and traditional dishes.

Rooms 11 (2 GF) **Facilities** Wi-fi 🎱 Boules Xmas New Year **Conf** Class 18 Board 25 Thtr 50 **Parking** 25 **Notes** ⊗ RS 24-30 Dec Civ Wed 60

W

Kingsway Hotel

★★ 74% HOTEL

☎ 01903 237542
Marine Pde BN11 3QQ
e-mail: accounts@kingswayhotel-worthing.co.uk
dir: A27 to Worthing seafront follow signs 'Hotel
West'. Hotel 0.75m west of pier

Ideally located on the seafront and close to the town
centre, this family-owned property extends a warm
welcome to guests. Bedrooms vary in size, and some
are very spacious with impressive sea views.
Comfortable public areas include two modern
lounges, a bright, stylish bar and well appointed
restaurant.

Rooms 36 (7 annexe) (4 fmly) (3 GF) ✿ **Facilities** FTV
Wi-fi Xmas **Conf** Class 25 Board 25 Thtr 50
Services Lift **Parking** 9

WOTTON-UNDER-EDGE   Map 4 ST79
Gloucestershire

Tortworth Court Four Pillars Hotel

★★★★ 78% ◎ HOTEL

☎ 0800 374 692 & 01454 263000
Tortworth GL12 8HH
e-mail: tortworth@four-pillars.co.uk
web: www.four-pillars.co.uk/tortworth
dir: M5 junct 14, B4509 towards Wotton. 1st right
into Tortworth Rd next right, hotel 0.5m on right

Set within 30 acres of parkland, this Gothic mansion
displays original features cleverly combined with
contemporary additions. Elegant public rooms include
a choice of dining options, one housed within the
library, another in the atrium and the third in the
orangery. Bedrooms are well equipped, and additional
facilities include a host of conference rooms and a
leisure centre.

Rooms 190 (25 fmly) (74 GF) **S** £79-£149;
D £79-£149 (incl. bkfst) **Facilities** Spa FTV Wi-fi ⓣ
⛱ Gym Beauty suite Steam room Sauna Xmas New
Year **Conf** Class 200 Board 80 Thtr 400 Del from £130
to £189 **Services** Lift **Parking** 200 **Notes** LB ⊗
Civ Wed 400

The Park Hotel

★★ 71% HOTEL

☎ 01454 260550
Whitfield GL12 8DR
e-mail: info@parkhotelfalfield.co.uk
web: www.parkhotelfalfield.co.uk
dir: M5 junct 14, A38, through Falfield. Hotel on left in
0.5m

Not far from the A38 and with easy access to the M5,
this family-run hotel offers friendly service.
Bedrooms, which vary in size, are located either in the
main house or in the cottage annexe, just yards away.
There is an informal bar where drinks and bar meals
are served, and dinner, featuring home made dishes,
is available in the pleasant restaurant. The garden
may be enjoyed during the warmer weather.

Rooms 18 (7 annexe) (2 fmly) (3 GF) **Facilities** Wi-fi
⛱ Xmas New Year **Conf** Class 60 Board 40 Thtr 80
Parking 80 **Notes** Civ Wed 118

WROTHAM   Map 6 TQ65
Kent

Holiday Inn Maidstone Sevenoaks

Holiday Inn

★★★ 77% HOTEL

☎ 0871 942 9054 & 01732 781510
London Rd, Wrotham Heath TN15 7RS
e-mail: reservations-maidstone@ihg.com
web: www.holidayinn.co.uk
dir: M26 junct 2A onto A20. Hotel on left

This purpose-built hotel is located within easy reach
of the world famous Brands Hatch racing circuit as
well as historic Leeds and Hever Castles. Bedrooms
are very spacious and comfortably furnished with
many accessories. A bar, restaurant and lounges are
also available as well as a range of modern meeting
rooms and a fully equipped leisure centre.

Rooms 105 (16 fmly) (6 GF) (10 smoking)
Facilities STV Wi-fi ⓣ supervised Gym Steam room
Sauna New Year **Conf** Class 35 Board 30 Thtr 70
Services Air con **Parking** 120 **Notes** ⊗ Civ Wed 60

Premier Inn Sevenoaks/ Maidstone

Premier Inn

BUDGET HOTEL

☎ 0871 527 8962
London Rd, Wrotham Heath TN15 7RX
web: www.premierinn.com
dir: M26 junct 2a, A20 S. At light left onto A20
towards West Malling. Hotel on right.

High quality, budget accommodation ideal for both
families and business travellers. Spacious, en suite
bedrooms feature tea and coffee making facilities,
and Freeview TV in most hotels. Internet access and
Wi-fi are available for a small fee. The adjacent
family restaurant features a wide and varied menu.
See also the Hotel Groups pages.

Rooms 40

WROXALL   Map 10 SP27
Warwickshire

Wroxall Abbey Estate

★★★★ 75% HOTEL

☎ 01926 484470 & 486730
Birmingham Rd CV35 7NB
e-mail: info@wroxall.com
dir: Between Solihull & Warwick on A4141

Situated in 27 acres of open parkland, yet only 10
miles from the NEC and Birmingham International
Airport, this hotel is a magnificent Victorian mansion.
Some of the individually designed bedrooms have
traditional decor but there are some modern loft
rooms as well; some rooms have four-posters.
Sonnets Restaurant, with its impressive fireplace and
oak panelling, makes the ideal setting for fine dining.

Rooms 70 (22 annexe) (10 GF) ✿ **S** £89-£199;
D £99-£399* **Facilities** Spa STV Wi-fi ⓣ ⛱ Fishing
⛱ Gym Ten-pin bowling Walking & jogging trail ♪
Xmas New Year **Conf** Class 80 Board 60 Thtr 160
Del from £139 to £169* **Services** Lift **Parking** 200
Notes LB ⊗ No children 12yrs Civ Wed 200

W

WROXHAM
Norfolk   Map 13 TG31

Hotel Wroxham

★★ 71% HOTEL

☎ 01603 782061
The Bridge NR12 8AJ
e-mail: reservations@hotelwroxham.co.uk
web: www.arlingtonhotelgroup.co.uk
dir: From Norwich, A1151 signed Wroxham & The
Broads, approx 7m. Over bridge at Wroxham, 1st
right, sharp right. Hotel car park on right

Perfectly placed for touring the Norfolk Broads this
hotel is in the heart of the bustling town centre. The
bedrooms are pleasantly decorated and well
equipped; some rooms have balconies with lovely
views of the busy waterways. The open-plan public
rooms include the lively riverside bar, lounge, large
sun terrace and restaurant.

Rooms 18 (2 fmly) **S** £69.50-£79.45; **D** £98.50-£120
(incl. bkfst)* **Facilities** FTV Wi-fi Fishing Boating
facilities (by arrangement) **Conf** Class 50 Board 20
Thtr 200 Del from £100 to £140 **Parking** 45 **Notes** ⊗
Civ Wed 40

WYBOSTON
Bedfordshire   Map 12 TL15

Wyboston Lakes Hotel

★★★ 80% ◉ HOTEL

☎ 0333 700 7666   & 01480 479300
Wyboston Lakes, Great North Rd MK44 3BA
e-mail: reservations@wybostonlakes.co.uk
dir: From A1, A428, follow brown Cambridge signs.
Wyboston Lakes & hotel on right, marked by flags

Ideally located adjacent to the A1 on the
Cambridgeshire/Bedfordshire border, Wyboston Lakes
is easily accessible. The hotel is located within an
extensive conference and leisure complex that
includes a golf course. Bedrooms are tastefully
decorated in a contemporary style, and offer a range
of amenities to suit both the business and leisure
traveller. The dining room overlooks the idyllic lake.

Rooms 103 (39 annexe) (18 fmly) (50 GF)
S £62-£130; **D** £62-£130* **Facilities** Spa FTV Wi-fi ↳
🏊 ᠘ 18 Putt green Fishing Gym Golf driving range

Conf Class 56 Board 40 Thtr 130 Del from £115 to
£125* **Services** Lift **Parking** 200 **Notes** ⊗ Closed
24-26 & 31 Dec & 1 Jan Civ Wed 100

YARM
North Yorkshire   Map 19 NZ41

Judges Country House Hotel

★★★ ◉◉◉ HOTEL

☎ 01642 789000
Kirklevington Hall TS15 9LW
e-mail: enquiries@judgeshotel.co.uk
web: www.judgeshotel.co.uk
dir: 1.5m from A19. At A67 junct, follow Yarm road,
hotel on left

Formerly a lodging for local circuit judges, this
gracious mansion lies in landscaped grounds
through which a stream runs. Stylish bedrooms are
individually decorated and come with 101 extras;
four-poster bedrooms and suites are available. The
Conservatory restaurant serves award-winning
cuisine, and private dining for a small number of
guests is available in the wine cellar. Judges is a
popular wedding venue. The genuinely caring and
attentive service from the staff is truly memorable.

Rooms 21 (3 fmly) (5 GF) 🐾 **S** £99-£180;
D £110-£210* **Facilities** STV FTV Wi-fi ↳ 🚣 Gym
Mountain bikes Nature trails Beauty treatment
room Xmas New Year **Conf** Class 120 Board 80
Thtr 200 Del from £210 to £240* **Parking** 102
Notes LB ⊗ Civ Wed 200

YARMOUTH
Isle of Wight   Map 5 SZ38

George Hotel

★★★ ◉◉ HOTEL

☎ 01983 760331
Quay St PO41 0PE
e-mail: res@thegeorge.co.uk
dir: Between castle & pier

This delightful 17th-century hotel enjoys a
wonderful location at the water's edge, adjacent to
the castle and the quay. Public areas include a
bright brasserie where organic and local produce
are utilised, a cosy bar and an inviting lounge.
Individually styled bedrooms, with many thoughtful
extras, are beautifully appointed; some benefit from
spacious balconies. The hotel's motor yacht is
available for guests to hire.

Rooms 19 (1 GF) **S** £99-£137.50; **D** £190-£287
(incl. bkfst)* **Facilities** STV Wi-fi Sailing from
Yarmouth Mountain biking Xmas New Year
Conf Class 20 Board 20 Thtr 40 Del from £185*
Notes LB ⊗ No children 10yrs

YATELEY
Hampshire   Map 5 SU86

Casa dei Cesari Restaurant & Hotel

★★★ 73% HOTEL

☎ 01252 873275
Handford Ln GU46 6BT
e-mail: reservations@casadeicesari.co.uk
dir: M3 junct 4a, follow signs for town centre. Hotel
signed

This delightful hotel where a warm welcome is
guaranteed is ideally located for transport networks.
It boasts rooms with quality and comfort, and the
Italian-themed restaurant, which is very popular
locally, serves an extensive traditional menu.

Rooms 63 (2 fmly) (15 GF) (33 smoking)
Facilities Wi-fi ↳ Xmas New Year **Conf** Class 60
Board 60 Thtr 150 **Services** Lift **Parking** 80 **Notes** ⊗
Civ Wed 150

Save on hotels. Book at **theAA.com/hotel**

WRO – YEO 505 ENGLAND

YATTON
Somerset
Map 4 ST46

Bridge Inn
BUDGET HOTEL

☎ 01934 839100 & 839101
North End Rd BS49 4AU
e-mail: bridge.yatton@newbridgeinns.co.uk
web: www.oldenglish.co.uk
dir: M5 junct 20, B3133 to Yatton. 1st left at rdbt, 1st left at 2nd rdbt. Hotel 2.5m on right

This establishment offers spacious, well-equipped bedrooms, and the bar/restaurant serves a variety of dishes throughout the day in a relaxed and informal environment. Breakfast is a self-service buffet plus a full English breakfast served at the table. There is also a play zone area for children.

Rooms 41 (4 fmly) (20 GF) ➧ **D** £35-£49*
Conf Class 30 Board 50 Thtr 100 Del from £99.99*

YAXLEY
Suffolk
Map 13 TM17

The Auberge
◉ ◉ RESTAURANT WITH ROOMS

☎ 01379 783604
Ipswich Rd IP23 8BZ
e-mail: aubmail@the-auberge.co.uk
web: www.the-auberge.co.uk
dir: On A140 between Norwich & Ipswich at x-rds with B1117

A warm welcome awaits at this charming 15th-century property, which has been lovingly converted by the present owners from a rural pub into a smart restaurant with rooms. The restaurant has gained AA Rosettes for the good use of fresh, quality produce. The public areas have a wealth of character, such as exposed brickwork and beams, and the grounds are particularly well-kept and attractive. The spacious bedrooms are tastefully appointed and have many thoughtful touches; one bedroom has a four-poster.

Rooms 11 (11 annexe) (2 fmly)

YEOVIL
Somerset
Map 4 ST51

Lanes
★★★ 82% ◉◉ HOTEL

☎ 01935 862555
West Coker BA22 9AJ
e-mail: stay@laneshotel.net
web: www.laneshotel.net
dir: 2m W of Yeovil on A30 in centre of West Coker

This splendid building, once a rectory, has a cleverly designed, contemporary extension. Guests are assured of a relaxed and friendly stay. The stylish, modern bedrooms, with their superb bathrooms, are equipped with many extras. The brasserie-style restaurant offers an imaginative range of dishes, using local produce whenever possible. There is also a luxury jacuzzi, sauna and small gym.

Rooms 27 (17 annexe) (3 fmly) (8 GF) ➧ **S** £90;
D £130-£150 (incl. bkfst) **Facilities** FTV Wi-fi ➧ ➧
Gym Sauna Spa pool Beauty treatment room Xmas
New Year **Conf** Class 40 Board 20 Thtr 60
Services Lift **Parking** 40 **Notes** LB

The Yeovil Court Hotel & Restaurant
★★★ 78% ◉◉ HOTEL

☎ 01935 863746
West Coker Rd BA20 2HE
e-mail: unwind@yeovilhotel.com
web: www.yeovilcourthotel.com
dir: 2.5m W of town centre on A30

This comfortable, family-run hotel offers a very relaxed and caring atmosphere. Bedrooms are well equipped and neatly presented; some are located in an adjacent building. Public areas consist of a smart lounge, a popular bar and an attractive restaurant. Menus combine an interesting selection that includes lighter options and dishes suited to special occasion dining.

The Yeovil Court Hotel & Restaurant

Rooms 30 (12 annexe) (3 fmly) (11 GF) **S** £67-£120;
D £93-£120 (incl. bkfst)* **Facilities** FTV Wi-fi ➧
Conf Class 18 Board 30 Thtr 50 **Parking** 65 **Notes** LB
RS Sat lunch, 25 Dec eve & 26 Dec Civ Wed 70

Premier Inn Yeovil
BUDGET HOTEL

☎ 0871 527 9192
Alvington Ln, Brympton BA22 8UX
web: www.premierinn.com
dir: M5 junct 25, A358, A303 follow Yeovil signs. At rdbt onto A3088. At next rdbt 1st left, at next rdbt turn left. Hotel on left

High quality, budget accommodation ideal for both families and business travellers. Spacious, en suite bedrooms feature tea and coffee making facilities, and Freeview TV in most hotels. Internet access and Wi-fi are available for a small fee. The adjacent family restaurant features a wide and varied menu. See also the Hotel Groups pages.

Rooms 20

INSPECTORS' CHOICE

Little Barwick House
◉ ◉ ◉ RESTAURANT WITH ROOMS

☎ 01935 423902
Barwick Village BA22 9TD
e-mail: littlebarwick@hotmail.com
dir: From Yeovil A37 towards Dorchester, left at 1st rdbt, 1st left, 0.25m on left

Situated in a quiet hamlet in three and half acres of gardens and grounds, this listed Georgian dower house is an ideal retreat for those seeking peaceful surroundings and good food. Just one of the highlights of a stay here is a meal in the restaurant, where good use is made of local ingredients. Each of the bedrooms has its own character, and a range of thoughtful extras such as fresh flowers, bottled water and magazines is provided.

Rooms 6

Y

YORK
North Yorkshire   **Map 16 SE65**

See also Aldwark & Escrick

Cedar Court Grand Hotel & Spa
★★★★★ 86% ◉◉ HOTEL

☎ 01904 380038
Station Rise YO1 6HT
e-mail: info@cedarcourtgrand.co.uk
web: www.cedarcourtgrand.co.uk
dir: In city centre, near station

Located in the heart of the city, this majestic Edwardian building, originally built in 1908, has been transformed into a luxury hotel. Spacious, air-conditioned accommodation offers deeply comfortable rooms with luxurious bathrooms. Public areas are equally impressive with a range of delightful lounges, a modern spa in the former vaults, and excellent meeting rooms. The Grill offers a high standard of cooking with modern, classic dishes on the menus, plus afternoon tea. Valet parking is a great asset given the hotel's central location.

Rooms 107 (14 GF) ↖ **S** £135–£285; **D** £135–£285* **Facilities** Spa FTV Wi-fi ↕ ⊡ supervised Gym Sauna Steam room Xmas New Year **Conf** Class 60 Board 50 Thtr 120 Del from £215 to £365 **Services** Lift Air con **Notes** ⊗ Civ Wed 120

INSPECTORS' CHOICE

Middlethorpe Hall & Spa
★★★★ ◉◉ HOTEL

☎ 01904 641241
Bishopthorpe Rd, Middlethorpe YO23 2GB
e-mail: info@middlethorpe.com
dir: A1, A64 follow York West (A1036) signs, then Bishopthorpe, Middlethorpe racecourse signs

This fine house, dating from the reign of William and Mary, sits in acres of beautifully landscaped gardens. The bedrooms vary in size but all are comfortably furnished; some are located in the main house, and others are in a cottage and converted courtyard stables. Public areas include a small spa and a stately drawing room where afternoon tea is quite an event. The delightful

---

panelled restaurant is a perfect setting for enjoying the imaginative cuisine.

Rooms 29 (19 annexe) (2 fmly) (10 GF) ↖ **S** fr £129; **D** £199–£269 (incl. bkfst)* **Facilities** Spa FTV Wi-fi ↕ ⊡ ⤳ Gym Xmas New Year **Conf** Class 30 Board 25 Thtr 56 Del from £175 to £195* **Services** Lift **Parking** 71 **Notes** LB No children 6yrs RS 25 & 31 Dec Civ Wed 56

Hotel du Vin York
★★★★ 81% ◉ HOTEL

☎ 01904 557350
89 The Mount YO24 1AX
e-mail: info.york@hotelduvin.com
web: www.hotelduvin.com
dir: A1036 towards city centre, 6m. Hotel on right through lights.

This Hotel du Vin offers luxury and quality that will cosset even the most discerning guest. Bedrooms are decadent in design and the bathrooms have huge monsoon showers and feature baths. Dinner in the bistro provides a memorable highlight thanks to exciting menus and a superb wine list. Staff throughout are naturally friendly, nothing is too much trouble.

Rooms 44 (3 fmly) (14 GF) **Facilities** STV FTV Wi-fi **Conf** Class 8 Board 22 Thtr 22 **Services** Lift Air con **Parking** 18 **Notes** Civ Wed 50

The Grange Hotel
★★★★ 78% ◉◉ HOTEL

☎ 01904 644744
1 Clifton YO30 6AA
e-mail: info@grangehotel.co.uk
web: www.grangehotel.co.uk
dir: On A19 York/Thirsk road, approx 500yds from city centre

This bustling Regency town house is just a few minutes' walk from the centre of York. A professional service is efficiently delivered by caring staff in a very friendly and helpful manner. Public rooms are comfortable and have been stylishly furnished; these include two dining options, the popular and informal Cellar Bar, and main hotel restaurant The Ivy

---

Brasserie, which offers fine dining in a lavishly decorated environment. The individually designed bedrooms are comfortably appointed and have been thoughtfully equipped.

Rooms 36 (6 GF) **S** £125–£227; **D** £140–£242 (incl. bkfst)* **Facilities** STV FTV Wi-fi Use of nearby health club (chargeable) Xmas New Year **Conf** Class 24 Board 24 Thtr 50 Del from £156 to £174* **Parking** 26 **Notes** LB Civ Wed 90

York Marriott Hotel
★★★★ 77% HOTEL

Marriott HOTELS & RESORTS

☎ 01904 701000
Tadcaster Rd YO24 1QQ
e-mail: mhrs.qqyyk.dos@marriott.com
web: www.yorkmarriott.co.uk
dir: From A64 at York 'West' onto A1036, follow signs to city centre. Approx 1.5m, hotel on right after church and lights

Overlooking the racecourse and Knavesmire Parkland, the hotel offers modern accommodation, including family rooms, all with comfort cooling. Within the hotel, guests enjoy the use of extensive leisure facilities including indoor pool, putting green and tennis court. For those wishing to explore the historic and cultural attractions, the city is less than a mile away.

Rooms 151 (14 fmly) (27 GF) (10 smoking) ↖ **Facilities** Spa STV Wi-fi ⊡ ⤳ Putt green Gym Beauty treatment New Year **Conf** Class 90 Board 40 Thtr 190 **Services** Lift Air con **Parking** 140 **Notes** ⊗ Civ Wed 140

Best Western Plus Dean Court Hotel
★★★★ 76% ◉ HOTEL

Best Western PLUS

☎ 01904 625082
Duncombe Place YO1 7EF
e-mail: sales@deancourt-york.co.uk
web: www.deancourt-york.co.uk
dir: In city centre opposite York Minster

This smart hotel enjoys a central location overlooking The Minster, and guests will find the service is particularly friendly and efficient. Bedrooms are stylishly appointed and vary in size. Public areas are

Y

Save on hotels. Book at **theAA.com/hotel**

YOR 507 **ENGLAND**

elegant in a contemporary style and include the popular D.C.H. restaurant which enjoys wonderful views of the cathedral, and The Court café-bistro and bar where a more informal, all-day menu is offered. Valet parking is available.

Best Western Plus Dean Court Hotel

Rooms 37 (4 fmly) 🐾 **S** £95-£145; **D** £125-£245 (incl. bkfst)* **Facilities** FTV Wi-fi ⓦ Xmas New Year **Conf** Class 12 Board 32 Thtr 50 **Services** Lift **Parking** 30 **Notes** LB ⊗ Civ Wed 50

The Royal York Hotel & Events Centre

PH | principal hayley

★★★★ 75% HOTEL

☎ 01904 653681
Station Rd YO24 1AA
e-mail: royalyork.reservations@principal-hayley.com
web: www.principal-hayley.com
dir: Adjacent to railway station

Situated in three acres of landscaped grounds in the very heart of the city, this Victorian railway hotel has views over the city and York Minster. Contemporary bedrooms are divided between those in the main hotel and the air-conditioned garden mews. There is also a leisure complex and state-of-the-art conference centre.

Rooms 167 (8 fmly) **Facilities** Wi-fi ⓦ Gym Steam room Weights room Xmas New Year **Conf** Class 250 Board 80 Thtr 410 Del from £129 to £159* **Services** Lift **Parking** 80 **Notes** ⊗ Civ Wed 160

Marmadukes Hotel

★★★★ 74% TOWN HOUSE HOTEL

☎ 01904 623716
4-5 St Peters Grove, Bootham YO30 6AQ
e-mail: reservations@marmadukesyork.com
web: www.marmadukesyork.com
dir: A1036 signed York for approx 6m past train station then signed Inner Ring Rd. Over Lendal bridge, at lights left onto A19 (Bootham Bar) for 0.4m, right into St Peters Grove

Quietly situated just a short walk from the Minster, Marmadukes is a classically furnished, period property with all the expected modern amenities. Steeped in history and with a Roman burial ground

underneath the lawn, it also has a sauna and spa bath in the grounds. The bedrooms have antique furniture and many of the bathrooms have roll-top baths. The public areas, including the conservatory-style breakfast room, are equally impressive with an air of spaciousness.

Rooms 21 (2 fmly) (2 GF) 🐾 **Facilities** FTV Wi-fi ⓦ Sauna **Conf** Class 20 Board 16 Thtr 20 **Parking** 14 **Notes** ⊗ Civ Wed 50

Mercure York Fairfield Hotel

 Mercure

★★★★ 73% COUNTRY HOUSE HOTEL

☎ 0844 815 9038
Shipton Rd, Skelton YO30 1XW
e-mail: gm.mercureyorkfairfieldmanor@jupiterhotels.co.uk
web: www.jupiterhotels.co.uk
dir: Exit A1237 onto A19, hotel 0.5m on left

This stylish Georgian mansion stands in six acres of private grounds on the outskirts of the city. The contemporary bedrooms, styled in reds or blues, have broadband access and flat-screen TVs; some rooms have garden and courtyard views. The suites have either four-poster or king-size beds and a separate seating area. Kilby's Restaurant serves bistro food, and 24-hour room service is available. There are good conference facilities.

Rooms 89 (20 fmly) (24 GF) 🐾 **Facilities** Wi-fi ⓦ HL Xmas New Year **Conf** Class 72 Board 60 Thtr 180 **Services** Lift **Parking** 130 **Notes** ⊗ Civ Wed 150

The Churchill Hotel

★★★ 82% ◉◉ HOTEL

☎ 01904 644456
65 Bootham YO30 7DQ
e-mail: info@churchillhotel.com
dir: On A19 (Bootham), W from York Minster, hotel 250yds on right

A late Georgian manor house set in its own grounds, just a short walk from the Minster and other attractions. Period features and interesting artefacts relating to Winston Churchill are incorporated into smart contemporary design and up-to-date technology. Public areas include the Piano Bar & Restaurant, where innovative menus feature high quality, local produce.

Rooms 32 (4 fmly) (5 GF) **Facilities** Wi-fi 🎵 Xmas New Year **Conf** Class 50 Board 30 Thtr 100 **Services** Lift **Parking** 40 **Notes** Civ Wed 70

Holiday Inn York

 Holiday Inn

★★★ 81% HOTEL

☎ 0871 942 9085
Tadcaster Rd YO24 1QF
e-mail: reservations-york@ihg.com
web: www.hiyorkhotel.co.uk
dir: From A1(M) take A64 towards York. In 7m take A1036 to York. Straight over at rdbt to city centre. Hotel 0.5m on right

Located in a suburban area close to the city centre and overlooking York race course, this modern hotel caters equally well for business and leisure guests. Public areas include the spacious family friendly Junction Restaurant, lounge bar and the Cedar Tree Terrace. Seven function rooms are also available for meetings and social events.

Rooms 142 (50 fmly) (12 GF) **S** £49-£199; **D** £49-£199 (incl. bkfst) **Facilities** STV Wi-fi ⓦ HL Xmas New Year **Conf** Class 45 Board 55 Thtr 100 Del from £99 to £139 **Services** Lift Air con **Parking** 160 **Notes** LB

Novotel York Centre

 NOVOTEL

★★★ 80% HOTEL

☎ 01904 611660
Fishergate YO10 4FD
e-mail: H0949@accor.com
web: www.novotel.com
dir: A19 north to city centre, hotel set back on left

Set just outside the ancient city walls, this modern, family-friendly hotel is conveniently located for visitors to the city. Bedrooms feature bathrooms with a separate toilet room, plus excellent desk space and sofa beds. Four rooms are equipped for less able guests. The hotel's facilities include indoor and outdoor children's play areas and an indoor pool.

Rooms 124 (124 fmly) **Facilities** STV Wi-fi ⓦ HL ⓦ Xmas New Year **Conf** Class 100 Board 120 Thtr 210 Del from £130 to £180* **Services** Lift **Parking** 140

The Parsonage Country House Hotel

★★★ 79% ◉ COUNTRY HOUSE HOTEL

☎ 01904 728111
York Rd YO19 6LF
e-mail: reservations@parsonagehotel.co.uk
web: www.parsonagehotel.co.uk

(For full entry see Escrick)

Y

YORK *continued*

Best Western Monkbar Hotel

★★★ 79% HOTEL

☎ 01904 638086
Monkbar YO31 7JA
e-mail: sales@monkbarhotel.co.uk
web: www.monkbarhotel.co.uk
dir: A64 onto A1079 to city, turn right at city walls, take middle lane at lights. Hotel on right

This smart hotel enjoys a prominent position adjacent to the city walls, and just a few minutes' walk from the cathedral. Individually styled bedrooms are well equipped for both business and leisure guests. Spacious public areas include comfortable lounges, an American-style bar, an airy restaurant and impressive meeting and training facilities.

Rooms 99 (8 fmly) (2 GF) ☝ **S** £90-£125; **D** £95-£160 (incl. bkfst)* **Facilities** STV FTV Wi-fi ॐ Xmas New Year **Conf** Class 80 Board 50 Thtr 140 Del from £115 to £155* **Services** Lift **Parking** 66 **Notes** LB Civ Wed 80

Mount Royale

★★★ 79% HOTEL

☎ 01904 628856
The Mount YO24 1GU
e-mail: reservations@mountroyale.co.uk
web: www.mountroyale.co.uk
dir: W on A1036, 0.5m after racecourse. Hotel on right after lights

This friendly hotel, a William IV listed building, offers comfortable bedrooms in a variety of styles, several leading onto the delightful gardens. Public rooms include a lounge, a meeting room and a cosy bar; the hotel has an outdoor pool, a sauna and a hot tub plus a beauty therapist. There is a separate restaurant called One 19 The Mount and a cocktail lounge overlooking the gardens (all meals and drinks can be charged to room accounts).

Rooms 24 (3 fmly) (6 GF) **Facilities** Spa FTV Wi-fi ॐ supervised Beauty treatment centre Sauna Steam room ♫ Xmas New Year **Conf** Board 25 Thtr 35 Del from £85 to £165 **Parking** 27

Best Western Kilima Hotel

★★★ 77% HOTEL

☎ 01904 625787
129 Holgate Rd YO24 4AZ
e-mail: sales@kilima.co.uk
web: www.kilima.co.uk
dir: On A59, on W outskirts

This establishment, a former rectory, is conveniently situated within easy walking distance of the city centre. There is a relaxed and friendly atmosphere with professional, friendly staff providing attentive service. Bedrooms are comfortable and well equipped. There is an indoor pool, a fitness centre and a Turkish steam room.

Rooms 26 (2 fmly) (10 GF) **Facilities** FTV Wi-fi ॐ Gym Leisure complex Steam room Fitness suite Xmas New Year **Conf** Board 14 **Parking** 26 **Notes** ⊗

Best Western York Pavilion Hotel

★★★ 77% HOTEL

☎ 01904 622099 & 239900
45 Main St, Fulford YO10 4PJ
e-mail: reservations@yorkpavilionhotel.com
web: www.yorkpavilionhotel.com
dir: Exit A64 (York ring road) at A19 junct towards York. Hotel 0.5m on right opposite Pavilion Court

An attractive Georgian hotel situated in its own grounds. All the bedrooms are individually designed to a high specification; some are in the old house and some in the converted stables set around a garden terrace. There is a comfortable lounge, a conference centre and an inviting brasserie-style restaurant with a regularly changing menu.

Rooms 57 (4 fmly) (11 GF) **Facilities** FTV Wi-fi ॐ Xmas New Year **Conf** Class 120 Board 68 Thtr 250 **Parking** 55 **Notes** ⊗ Civ Wed 250

Park Inn by Radisson York

★★★ 73% HOTEL

☎ 01904 459988 & 459900
North St YO1 6JF
e-mail: info.york@rezidorparkinn.com
dir: A64/A1063 follow signs for city centre, into North St, hotel 250yds on right

Boasting spectacular views over the River Ouse in the heart of York this hotel is just minutes away from all the attractions of this historic, walled city. There are impressive conference rooms and leisure facilities, and the RBG Lounge Bar, overlooking the river, serves a wide-ranging menu throughout the day. Private parking is available.

Rooms 200 (8 fmly) **Facilities** FTV Wi-fi Gym Sauna Dance studio Exercise classes Beauty treatments Reflexology Sports therapy Xmas New Year **Conf** Class 150 Board 75 Thtr 400 **Services** Lift Air con **Parking** 92 **Notes** ⊗

Knavesmire Manor Hotel

★★ 75% SMALL HOTEL

☎ 01904 702941
302 Tadcaster Rd YO24 1HE
e-mail: enquire@knavesmire.co.uk
dir: A1036 into city centre. Hotel on right, overlooking racecourse

Commanding superb views across York's famous racecourse, this former manor house offers comfortable, well-equipped bedrooms, either in the main house or the garden rooms to the rear. Comfortable day rooms are stylishly furnished, whilst the heated indoor pool provides a popular addition.

Rooms 20 (9 annexe) (3 fmly) **S** £60-£95; **D** £69-£140 (incl. bkfst)* **Facilities** FTV Wi-fi ॐ ⊕ New Year **Conf** Class 36 Board 30 Thtr 40 Del from £99 to £150* **Services** Lift **Parking** 28 **Notes** Closed 23-27 Dec

Y

Lady Anne Middleton's Hotel

★★ 72% HOTEL

☎ 01904 611570
Skeldergate YO1 6DS
e-mail: bookings@ladyannes.co.uk
web: www.ladyannes.co.uk
dir: From A64 (Leeds) A1036 towards city centre.
Right at City Walls lights, keep left, 1st left before
bridge, then 1st left into Cromwell Rd. Hotel on right.
(NB for Sat Nav use YO1 6DU)

This hotel has been created from several listed
buildings and is very well located in the centre of
York. Bedrooms are comfortably equipped. Among its
amenities is a bar-lounge and a dining room where a
satisfying range of food is served. An extensive
fitness club is also available along with private
parking.

Rooms 57 (20 annexe) (15 fmly) (17 GF) ⚕
Facilities FTV Wi-fi ⌚ Gym Fitness centre Beauty
treatments Massage **Conf** Class 30 Board 30 Thtr 100
Parking 40 **Notes** ⊗ Closed 24-29 Dec

Holiday Inn Express York

BUDGET HOTEL

☎ 01904 438660
Malton Rd YO32 9TE
web: www.hiexpressyorkeast.co.uk
dir: From A64 take A1036 towards York centre. Hotel
on left behind The Hopgrove Toby Carvery

A modern hotel ideal for families and business
travellers. Fresh and uncomplicated, the spacious
rooms include Sky TV, power shower and tea and
coffee-making facilities. Continental buffet breakfast
is included in the room rate; other meals may be
taken at the nearby family pub or restaurant. See also
the Hotel Groups pages.

Rooms 49 (20 fmly) (21 GF) ⚕ **S** £55-£120;
D £55-£120 (incl. bkfst)*

Ibis York Centre

BUDGET HOTEL

☎ 01904 658301
77 The Mount YO24 1BN
e-mail: H6390@accor.com
dir: A64/A1036 follow signs to city centre, hotel on
right

Modern, budget hotel offering comfortable
accommodation in bright and practical bedrooms.
Breakfast is self-service and dinner is available in
the restaurant. See also the Hotel Groups pages.

Rooms 91 **Conf** Class 16 Board 16 Thtr 24

Premier Inn York City (Blossom St North)

BUDGET HOTEL

☎ 0871 527 9196
20 Blossom St YO24 1AJ
web: www.premierinn.com
dir: 12m from A1 junct 47, off A59

High quality, budget accommodation ideal for both
families and business travellers. Spacious, en suite
bedrooms feature tea and coffee making facilities,
and Freeview TV in most hotels. Internet access and
Wi-fi are available for a small fee. The adjacent
family restaurant features a wide and varied menu.
See also the Hotel Groups pages.

Rooms 86

Premier Inn York City (Blossom St South)

BUDGET HOTEL

☎ 0871 527 9194
28-40 Blossom St YO24 1AJ
web: www.premierinn.com
dir: From S, E & W: A64, A1036 (signed York West).
From N: A1 (or A19), A59, follow city centre signs. At
lights left onto A1036. Hotel on left just after cinema.
(NB no drop-off point, parking at NCP, Queens St)

Rooms 91

Premier Inn York North

BUDGET HOTEL

☎ 0871 527 9198
Shipton Rd YO30 5PA
web: www.premierinn.com
dir: From A1237 (ring road), A19 (Shipton Road
South) signed York Centre. Hotel on right in Clifton
Park

Rooms 49

Premier Inn York North West

BUDGET HOTEL

☎ 0871 527 9200
**White Rose Close, York Business Park, Nether
Poppleton YO26 6RL**
web: www.premierinn.com
dir: On A1237 between A19 (Thirsk road) & A59
(Harrogate road)

Rooms 64

Premier Inn York South West

BUDGET HOTEL

☎ 0871 527 9202
Bilbrough Top, Colton YO23 3PP
web: www.premierinn.com
dir: On A64 between Tadcaster & York

Rooms 61

YOXFORD   **Map 13 TM36**
Suffolk

Satis House Hotel

★★★ 88% ◉◉ COUNTRY HOUSE HOTEL

☎ 01728 668418
IP17 3EX
e-mail: enquiries@satishouse.co.uk
web: www.satishouse.co.uk
dir: Off A12 between Ipswich & Lowestoft. 9m E
Aldeburgh & Snape

Expect a warm welcome from the caring hosts at this
delightful 18th-century, Grade II listed property set in
three acres of parkland. The stylish public areas have
a really relaxed atmosphere; they include a choice of
dining rooms, a smart bar and a cosy lounge. The
individually decorated bedrooms are tastefully
appointed and thoughtfully equipped.

Rooms 10 (2 annexe) (1 fmly) (2 GF) **Facilities** STV
FTV Wi-fi ⌚ Xmas New Year **Conf** Class 40 Board 20
Thtr 40 **Parking** 30 **Notes** Civ Wed 50

Y

Sefton Hotel

★★★★ 81% ◉◉ HOTEL

☎ 01624 645500
Harris Promenade IM1 2RW
e-mail: info@seftonhotel.co.im
web: www.seftonhotel.co.im
dir: 500yds from ferry dock on promenade

This Victorian hotel, extended over the years offers comfortably furnished bedrooms; many are spacious. Some have balconies overlooking the atrium water garden, while others enjoy sweeping views across the bay. Nine, individually designed, themed suites provide even greater luxury. A choice of comfortable lounges is available and freshly prepared dishes are served in the Gallery Restaurant.

Rooms 96 (3 fmly) **Facilities** Wi-fi ⊗ Gym Cycle hire Steam room Library ♫ New Year **Conf** Class 30 Board 50 Thtr 150 **Services** Lift **Parking** 36 **Notes** ⊗

Mount Murray Hotel and Country Club

★★★★ 74% HOTEL

☎ 01624 661111
Santon IM4 2HT
e-mail: hotel@mountmurray.com
web: www.mountmurray.com
dir: 4m from Douglas towards airport. Hotel signed at Santon

This large, modern hotel and country club offers a wide range of sporting and leisure facilities, and a superb health and beauty salon. The attractively appointed public areas provide a choice of bars and eating options, including the Mallards Restaurant. The spacious bedrooms are well equipped and many enjoy fine views over the
200-acre grounds and golf course. There is a very large conference suite.

Rooms 103 (4 fmly) (27 GF) ☝ **Facilities** FTV Wi-fi ⊗ ⊗ ⅃ 18 Putt green Gym Squash Driving range New Year **Conf** Class 200 Board 100 Thtr 300 Del from £118* **Services** Lift **Parking** 400 **Notes** ⊗ Civ Wed 120

Admiral House Hotel

★★★ 74% ◉◉ HOTEL

☎ 01624 629551
12 Loch Promenade IM1 2LX
e-mail: enquiries@admiralhouse.com
dir: 2 mins from ferry terminal

A grand Victorian building with stunning views over Douglas Bay. Spacious bedrooms and public areas combine period features with contemporary style. JAR Restaurant is a highlight, offering excellent food, a stylish setting and professional service. There is also a modern champagne and cocktail bar and IGI's Café serves snacks and light meals throughout the day. Complimentary Wi-fi is provided throughout.

Rooms 23 (3 fmly) ☝ **S** £70-£85; **D** £75-£90 (incl. bkfst)* **Facilities** STV FTV Wi-fi ⊗ Xmas New Year **Services** Lift **Notes** LB ⊗ Civ Wed

Falcon's Nest

★★ 72% HOTEL

☎ 01624 834077
The Promenade IM9 6AF
e-mail: falconsnest@enterprise.net
web: www.falconsnesthotel.co.uk
dir: Follow coast road S from airport or ferry. Hotel on seafront, immediately after steam railway station

Situated overlooking the bay and harbour, this Victorian hotel offers generally spacious bedrooms. There is a choice of bars, one of which attracts many locals. Meals can be taken in the lounge bar, the conservatory or in the attractively decorated main restaurant.

Rooms 39 (9 fmly) (15 smoking) **Facilities** FTV Wi-fi Xmas New Year **Conf** Class 50 Board 50 Thtr 50 **Parking** 20

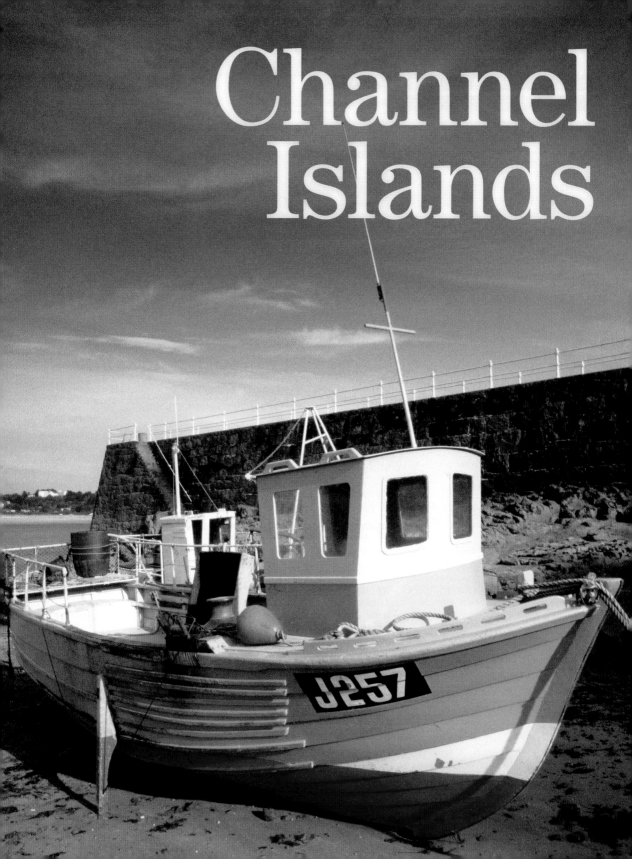

Channel Islands

ALDERNEY

ALDERNEY — Map 24

Braye Beach Hotel

★★★★ 71% ⬡ HOTEL

☎ 01481 824300
Braye St GY9 3XT
e-mail: reception@brayebeach.com
web: www.brayebeach.com
dir: Follow coast road from airport

Situated just a stone's throw from Braye's harbour and beach, this hotel provides comfortable yet stylish accommodation where many guest rooms have sea views; all bedrooms are well appointed and generously equipped. Public rooms include the popular bar and lounge, spacious terrace for the summer months and even a cinema. The well-appointed restaurant offers a varied seasonal menu often showcasing locally caught fish. Private dining can be catered for in the vaulted wine cellar.

Rooms 27 (2 fmly) ⬥ **Facilities** FTV Wi-fi Cinema Xmas New Year **Conf** Class 12 Board 16 Thtr 19 **Services** Lift **Notes** ⊗ Civ Wed 80

GUERNSEY

CASTEL — Map 24

La Grande Mare Hotel Golf & Country Club

★★★★ 71% ⬡ HOTEL

☎ 01481 256576
The Coast Rd, Vazon Bay GY5 7LL
e-mail: reservations@lagrandemare.com
web: www.lgm.guernsey.net
dir: From airport turn right. At Coast Rd turn right

This hotel is located by a sandy bay and is set in 110 acres of private grounds that incorporates an 18-hole golf course and has a health suite. Bedrooms range from spacious studios to deluxe suites, and feature handcrafted furniture and impressive decor. The health suite features a 40ft-swimming pool that has dedicated children's swimming times.

Rooms 24 (13 fmly) (5 GF) ⬥ **D** £100-£260 (incl. bkfst) **Facilities** FTV Wi-fi ⬥ ⬡ supervised ⬥ ⬦ 18 ⬥ Putt green Fishing Gym ⬥ Xmas New Year **Conf** Class 21 Board 22 Thtr 48 **Services** Lift **Parking** 200 **Notes** LB

Cobo Bay Hotel

★★★ 82% ⬡⬡ HOTEL

☎ 01481 257102
Coast Rd, Cobo GY5 7HB
e-mail: reservations@cobobayhotel.com
web: www.cobobayhotel.com
dir: From airport turn right, follow road to W coast at L'Eree. Turn right onto coast road for 3m to Cobo Bay. Hotel on right

A popular hotel situated on the seafront overlooking Cobo Bay. The well-equipped bedrooms are pleasantly decorated; many of the front rooms have balconies and there is a secluded sun terrace to the rear. Public rooms include the Chesterfield Bar with its leather sofas and armchairs and a welcoming award-winning restaurant and terrace with stunning views of the bay.

Rooms 34 (4 fmly) ⬥ **S** £59-£195; **D** £75-£195 (incl. bkfst)* **Facilities** STV FTV Wi-fi ⬥ Gym 2 exercise bikes Sauna Steam room **Conf** Class 30 Board 30 Thtr 100 Del from £99 to £195* **Services** Lift **Parking** 60 **Notes** LB ⊗ Closed Jan-Feb

FOREST — Map 24

Le Chene Hotel

★★ 71% HOTEL

☎ 01481 235566
Forest Rd GY8 0AH
e-mail: info@lechene.co.uk
web: www.lechene.co.uk
dir: Between airport & St Peter Port. From airport left to St Peter Port. Hotel on right after 1st lights

This Victorian manor house is well located for guests wishing to explore Guernsey's spectacular south coast. The building has been skilfully extended to house a range of well-equipped, modern bedrooms. There is a swimming pool, a cosy cellar bar and a varied range of enjoyable freshly cooked dishes at dinner.

Rooms 26 (2 fmly) (1 GF) (1 smoking) **Facilities** Wi-fi ⬥ Library Xmas New Year **Parking** 20 **Notes** ⊗

ST MARTIN — Map 24

La Barbarie Hotel

★★★ 81% ⬡ HOTEL

☎ 01481 235217
Saints Rd, Saints Bay GY4 6ES
e-mail: reservations@labarbariehotel.com
web: www.labarbariehotel.com

This former priory dates back to the 17th century and retains much charm and style. Staff provide a very friendly and attentive atmosphere, and the modern facilities offer guests a relaxing stay. Excellent choices and fresh local ingredients form the basis of the interesting menus in the attractive restaurant and bar.

Rooms 30 (8 GF) **S** £62.50-£103; **D** £79-£152* **Facilities** Wi-fi ⬥ **Parking** 50 **Notes** ⊗ Closed Nov-11 Mar

Hotel Jerbourg

★★★ 78% HOTEL

☎ 01481 238826
Jerbourg Point GY4 6BJ
e-mail: stay@hoteljerbourg.com
dir: From airport turn left to St Martin, right at filter, straight on at lights, hotel at end of road on right

This hotel boasts excellent sea views from its cliff-top location. Public areas are smartly appointed and include an extensive bar/lounge and bright conservatory-style restaurant. In addition to the fairly extensive carte, a daily-changing menu is available. Bedrooms are well presented and comfortable, and the luxury bay rooms are generally more spacious.

Rooms 32 (4 fmly) (5 GF) **S** £74-£119; **D** £89-£129 (incl. bkfst)* **Facilities** STV Wi-fi ⚡ Petanque Xmas New Year **Parking** 50 **Notes** LB ⊗ Closed 5 Jan-1 Mar

Saints Bay Hotel

★★★ 77% HOTEL

☎ 01481 238888
Icart Rd GY4 6JG
e-mail: info@saintsbayhotel.com
dir: From St Martin take Saints Rd into Icart Rd

Ideally situated in an elevated position near Icart Point headland and above the fishing harbour at Saints Bay, this hotel has superb views. The spacious public rooms include a smart lounge bar, a first-floor lounge and a smart conservatory restaurant that overlooks the swimming pool. Bedrooms are pleasantly decorated and thoughtfully equipped.

Rooms 35 (2 fmly) (13 GF) **Facilities** FTV Wi-fi ⚡ Xmas New Year **Parking** 15 **Notes** ⊗

La Villette Hotel & Leisure Suite

★★★ 75% HOTEL

☎ 01481 235292
GY4 6QG
e-mail: reservations@lavillettehotel.co.uk
dir: Turn left from airport. Follow road past La Trelade Hotel. Take next right, hotel on left

Set in spacious grounds, this peacefully located, family-run hotel has a friendly atmosphere. The well-equipped bedrooms are spacious and comfortable. Live music is a regular feature in the large bar, while in the separate restaurant a fixed-price menu is provided. Residents have use of the excellent indoor leisure facilities, and there are also beauty treatments and a hairdressing salon.

Rooms 35 (3 fmly) (14 GF) **Facilities** STV Wi-fi ⓢ supervised ⚡ Gym Steam room Leisure suite Beauty salon Hairdresser Petanque Xmas New Year **Conf** Board 40 Thtr 80 **Services** Lift **Parking** 50 **Notes** ⊗

Hotel La Michele

★★ 81% HOTEL

☎ 01481 238065
Les Hubits GY4 6NB
e-mail: info@lamichelehotel.com
web: www.lamichelehotel.com
dir: Approx 1.5m from St Peter Port

Expect a warm welcome from the caring hosts at this friendly family-run hotel, which is situated in a peaceful location. Bedrooms are particularly well equipped; each one is pleasantly decorated and has co-ordinated fabrics. Public areas include a conservatory and a cosy bar, and guests can relax in the well-tended gardens or around the pool.

Rooms 16 (2 fmly) (6 GF) 🏃 **S** £49-£69; **D** £98-£138 (incl. bkfst & dinner)* **Facilities** FTV Wi-fi ⚡ **Parking** 16 **Notes** ⊗ No children 10yrs Closed Nov-Mar

---

ST PETER PORT   Map 24

INSPECTORS' CHOICE

Old Government House Hotel & Spa

THE RED CARNATION HOTEL COLLECTION

★★★★ ◉◉ HOTEL

☎ 01481 724921
St Ann's Place GY1 2NU
e-mail: ogh@theoghhotel.com
web: www.theoghhotel.com
dir: At junct of St Julian's Ave & St Anns Place

The affectionately known OGH is one of the island's leading hotels. Located in the heart of St Peter Port, it is the perfect base to explore Guernsey and the other islands of the Bailiwick. Bedrooms vary in size but are comfortable and offer high quality accommodation. There is an indulgent health club and spa, and the eating options are the OGH Brasserie, and award-winning Governor's that offers local produce with a French twist.

Rooms 62 (3 annexe) (6 fmly) **Facilities** Spa STV Wi-fi ⓢ ⚡ Gym Steam room Sauna Aerobics studio 🎵 Xmas New Year **Conf** Class 100 Board 80 Thtr 200 **Services** Lift Air con **Parking** 20

Fermain Valley Hotel

★★★★ 79% ◉◉ HOTEL

☎ 0800 316 0314 & 01481 235666
Fermain Ln GY1 1ZZ
e-mail: info@fermainvalley.com
dir: Turn left from airport, follow Forest Rd, right into Le Route de Sausmarez, right into Fermain Lane at Fermain Tavern. Hotel 100mtrs on left

This hotel occupies an amazing location high above Fermain Bay with far reaching views out to sea; there are lovely walks along the cliff or down the lanes from the hotel. The delightfully furnished bedrooms, some with balconies, have either views of the sea, the valley or the well tended gardens. Informal eating is available in the stylish Rock Garden bar, and in summer on the terrace, the Valley Restaurant is the fine dining option. The leisure facilities include a pool, a sauna and a private cinema. The well-trained staff provide warm and friendly service.

Rooms 43 (11 annexe) (2 fmly) 🏃 **S** £85-£150; **D** £100-£165 (incl. bkfst)* **Facilities** FTV Wi-fi ⓢ Cinema Sauna Xmas New Year **Conf** Class 70 Board 45 Thtr 100 **Services** Lift **Notes** LB ⊗

St Pierre Park Hotel

★★★★ 73% HOTEL

☎ 01481 728282
Rohais GY1 1FD
e-mail: reservations@stpierrepark.co.uk
web: www.stpierrepark.co.uk
dir: From harbour straight over rdbt, up hill through 3 sets of lights. Right at filter, to lights. Straight ahead, hotel 100mtrs on left

Peacefully located on the outskirts of town amidst 45 acres of grounds, this well established hotel also features a 9-hole golf course. Most of the bedrooms overlook the pleasant gardens and have either a balcony or a terrace. Public areas include a choice of restaurants and a stylish bar which opens onto a spacious terrace, overlooking an elegant water feature.

Rooms 131 (5 fmly) (20 GF) 🏃 **Facilities** Spa STV Wi-fi ⓢ ⓢ 🏌 9 ⛳ Putt green ⚡ Gym Bird watching Children's playground Crazy golf Xmas New Year **Conf** Class 120 Board 70 Thtr 200 **Services** Lift **Parking** 150 **Notes** ⊗

CHANNEL ISLANDS

ST PETER PORT *continued*

La Frégate Hotel & Restaurant

★★★★ 72% SMALL HOTEL

☎ 01481 724624
Les Cotils GY1 1UT
e-mail: enquiries@lafregatehotel.com

This intimate hotel enjoys a fabulous location with unobstructed views overlooking St Peter Port and is just a few minutes walk from the centre of town. Bedrooms are appointed to a high standard; all are spacious and all have a sea view. Public areas are cosy and the dining room menus feature good use of local produce.

Rooms 22 (4 fmly) ☎ **S** £99.50; **D** £180-£227 (incl. bkfst)* **Facilities** STV FTV Wi-fi Xmas New Year **Conf** Class 20 Board 20 Thtr 40 Del from £169.50 to £199.50* **Services** Lift **Parking** 20 **Notes** LB ⊗

Les Rocquettes Hotel

★★★ 79% ◉ HOTEL

☎ 01481 722146
Les Gravees GY1 1RN
e-mail: rocquettes@sarniahotels.com
dir: From ferry terminal take 2nd exit at rdbt, through 5 sets of lights. After 5th lights into Les Gravees. Hotel on right opposite church

This late 18th-century country mansion is in a good location close to St Peter Port and Beau Sejour. Bedrooms come in three grades - Deluxe, Superior and Standard, but all have plenty of useful facilities. Guests can eat in Oaks restaurant and bar. The hotel has attractive lounge areas on three levels; there is a health suite with a gym and swimming pool with an integrated children's pool.

Les Rocquettes Hotel

Rooms 51 (5 fmly) **S** £54-£110; **D** £90-£150 (incl. bkfst)* **Facilities** FTV Wi-fi ⊠ ⊗ supervised Gym Beauty treatment rooms Sauna Steam room Xmas New Year **Conf** Class 60 Board 60 Thtr 100 Del from £110 to £180* **Services** Lift **Parking** 60 **Notes** LB ⊗

The Duke of Richmond Hotel

RED CARNATION
HOTEL COLLECTION

★★★ 79% HOTEL

☎ 01481 726221
Cambridge Park GY1 1UY
e-mail: manager@dukeofrichmond.com
web: www.dukeofrichmond.com
dir: On corner of Cambridge Park & L'Hyvreuse Ave, opposite leisure centre

Peacefully located in a mainly residential area overlooking Cambridge Park, this hotel has comfortable, well-appointed bedrooms that vary in size. Public areas include a spacious lounge, a terrace and the unique Sausmarez Bar, with its nautical theme. The smartly uniformed team of staff provide professional standards of service.

Rooms 75 (7 fmly) ☎ **S** £130; **D** £210 (incl. bkfst)* **Facilities** STV Wi-fi ⊹ Xmas New Year **Conf** Class 50 Board 36 Thtr 200 **Services** Lift **Parking** 10 **Notes** LB ⊗

Best Western Hotel de Havelet

Best Western

★★★ 78% HOTEL

☎ 01481 722199
Havelet GY1 1BA
e-mail: havelet@sarniahotels.com
dir: From airport follow signs for St Peter Port through St. Martins. At bottom of 'Val de Terres' hill turn left at top of hill, hotel on right

This extended Georgian hotel looks over the harbour to Castle Cornet. Many of the well-equipped bedrooms are set around a pretty colonial-style courtyard. Day rooms in the original building have period elegance;

the restaurant and bar are on the other side of the car park in converted stables.

Rooms 34 (4 fmly) (8 GF) (10 smoking) ☎ **S** £55-£130; **D** £94-£160 (incl. bkfst)* **Facilities** FTV Wi-fi ⊗ Sauna Steam room Xmas New Year **Conf** Class 20 Board 18 Thtr 30 Del from £120 to £180* **Parking** 40 **Notes** LB ⊗

Best Western Moores Hotel

Best Western

★★★ 77% HOTEL

☎ 01481 724452
Pollet GY1 1WH
e-mail: moores@sarniahotels.com
dir: Left at airport, follow signs to St Peter Port. Fort Road to seafront, straight on, turn left before rdbt, to hotel

An elegant granite town house situated in the heart of St Peter Port amidst the shops and amenities. Public rooms feature a smart conservatory restaurant which leads out onto a first-floor terrace for alfresco dining; there is also a choice of lounges and bars as well as a patisserie. Bedrooms are pleasantly decorated and thoughtfully equipped.

Rooms 49 (3 annexe) (8 fmly) (10 smoking) ☎ **S** £56-£198; **D** £100-£240 (incl. bkfst)* **Facilities** FTV Wi-fi ⊠ Gym Sauna Xmas New Year **Conf** Class 20 Board 18 Thtr 40 Del from £120 to £180* **Services** Lift **Notes** LB ⊗

Duke of Normandie Hotel

★★★ 75% HOTEL

☎ 01481 721431
Lefebvre St GY1 2JP
e-mail: enquiries@dukeofnormandie.com
web: www.dukeofnormandie.com
dir: From harbour rdbt St Julians Ave, 3rd left into Anns Place, continue to right, up hill, then left into Lefebvre St, archway entrance on right

An 18th-century hotel situated close to the high street and just a short stroll from the harbour. Bedrooms vary in style and include some that have their own access from the courtyard. Public areas feature a smart brasserie, a contemporary lounge/lobby area and a busy bar with beams and an open fireplace.

Rooms 37 (17 annexe) (8 GF) ☎ **S** £49-£65; **D** £100-£140 (incl. bkfst) **Facilities** STV Wi-fi ⊠ **Conf** Class 30 Board 20 Thtr 40 **Parking** 15 **Notes** LB ⊗

Save on hotels. Book at **theAA.com/hotel**

ST (GUERNSEY) 515 ENGLAND

Sunnycroft Hotel

★★ 72% METRO HOTEL

☎ 01481 723008 & 0800 316 0314
5 Constitution Steps GY1 2PN
e-mail: sunnycrofthotel@cwgsy.com
dir: In centre of town, past Salvation Army Building
on left down Constitution steps

This property is located in one of St Peter Port's
cobbled, stepped alleyways and has great views
overlooking the marina. The bedrooms are cosy and
provide a good level of comfort; many have sea views.
An honesty bar is available and breakfast is served in
the rooftop dining room. Access to the property is by
foot only and might be unsuitable for those who are
less steady on their feet.

Rooms 14 (7 GF) **S** £52-£71; **D** £81-£117 (incl.
bkfst)* **Facilities** FTV Wi-fi

ST SAVIOUR   **Map 24**

The Farmhouse Hotel

★★★★ 84% ◉ SMALL HOTEL

☎ 01481 264181
Route Des Bas Courtils GY7 9YF
e-mail: enquiries@thefarmhouse.gg
web: www.thefarmhouse.gg
dir: From airport, left to 1st lights. Left then left
again around runway perimeter. After 1m left at
x-rds. Hotel 100mtrs on right

This hotel provides spacious accommodation with
amazingly comfortable beds and state-of-the-art

bathrooms with under-floor heating. Guests can
choose from various stylish dining options including
alfresco eating in the warmer months. The outdoor
swimming pool is available to guests in the summer
and there are lots of countryside walks to enjoy.

The Farmhouse Hotel

Rooms 14 (7 fmly) 🐾 **D** £84-£230 (incl. bkfst)*
Facilities STV Wi-fi �Χ ⛳ 🎵 Xmas New Year
Conf Class 130 Board 30 Thtr 150 Del from £245 to
£445 **Services** Air con **Parking** 80 **Notes** LB ⊗

See advert on this page

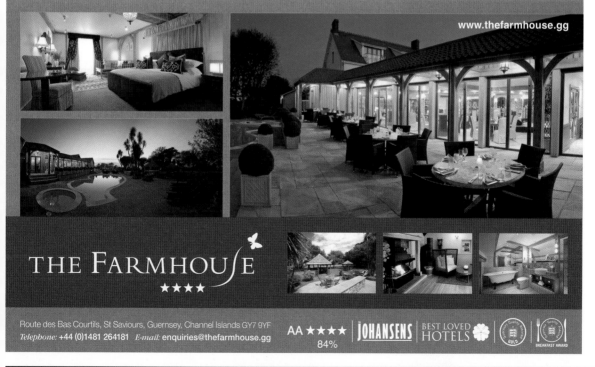

CHANNEL ISLANDS

VALE Map 24

Peninsula Hotel

★★★ 77% HOTEL

☎ 01481 248400
Les Dicqs GY6 8JP
e-mail: peninsula@guernsey.net
dir: On coast road at Grand Havre Bay

Adjacent to the sandy beach and set in five acres of grounds, this modern hotel provides comfortable accommodation. Bedrooms have an additional sofa bed to suit families and good workspace for the business traveller. Both fixed-price and carte menus are served in the restaurant, or guests can eat informally in the bar.

Rooms 99 (99 fmly) (25 GF) (5 smoking) 🐾
S £74.50-£94.50; **D** £121-£159 (incl. bkfst)*
Facilities STV Wi-fi 🎣 Putt green Petanque Children's playground Xmas New Year **Conf** Class 140 Board 105 Thtr 250 Del from £104.45 to £122.45*
Services Lift **Parking** 120 **Notes** LB ⊗ Closed Jan

HERM

HERM Map 24

White House Hotel

★★★ 77% ◉ HOTEL

☎ 01481 750075
GY1 3HR
e-mail: hotel@herm.com
web: www.herm.com
dir: Transport to island by catamaran ferry from St Peter Port, Guernsey

Enjoying a unique island setting, this attractive hotel is just 20 minutes from Guernsey by sea. Set in well-tended gardens, the hotel offers neatly decorated bedrooms, located in either the main house or adjacent cottages; the majority of rooms have sea views. Guests can relax in one of several lounges, enjoy a drink in one of two bars and choose from two dining options.

Rooms 40 (23 annexe) (23 fmly) (7 GF) **S** £95-£166;
D £190-£292 (incl. bkfst & dinner)* **Facilities** Wi-fi

🎣 🚣 ⛵ Fishing trips Yacht & motor boat charters Child facilities **Conf** Board 10 Thtr 50 Del from £145 to £165* **Notes** LB ⊗ Closed Nov-Mar

---

JERSEY

GOREY Map 24

The Moorings Hotel & Restaurant

★★★ 79% ◉ HOTEL

☎ 01534 853633
Gorey Pier JE3 6EW
e-mail: reservations@themooringshotel.com
web: www.themooringshotel.com
dir: At foot of Mont Orgueil Castle

Enjoying an enviable position by the harbour, the heart of this hotel is the restaurant where a selection of menus offers an extensive choice of dishes. Other public areas include a bar, coffee shop and a comfortable first-floor residents' lounge. Bedrooms at the front have a fine view of the harbour; three have access to a balcony. A small sun terrace at the back of the hotel is available to guests.

Rooms 15 🐾 **S** £57.50-£75; **D** £115-£143 (incl. bkfst)* **Facilities** FTV Wi-fi 🐾 Xmas New Year **Conf** Class 20 Board 20 Thtr 20 Del from £100 to £150* **Notes** LB ⊗

Old Court House Hotel

★★★ 72% HOTEL

☎ 01534 854444
JE3 9FS
e-mail: ochhotel@itl.net
web: www.ochhoteljersey.com

Situated on the east of the island, a short walk from the beach, this long established hotel continues to have a loyal following for its relaxed atmosphere and friendly staff. Bedrooms are of similar standard throughout and some have balconies overlooking the gardens. Spacious public areas include a comfortable, quiet lounge, a restaurant, and a large bar with a dance floor.

Rooms 58 (4 fmly) (9 GF) **S** £53-£80; **D** £106-£160 (incl. bkfst)* **Facilities** FTV Wi-fi 🎣 **Services** Lift **Parking** 40 **Notes** LB Closed Oct-Apr

---

The Dolphin Hotel and Restaurant

★★ 74% HOTEL

☎ 01534 853370
Gorey Pier JE3 6EW
e-mail: dolphinhotel@jerseymail.co.uk
dir: At foot of Mont Orgueil Castle

Located on the main harbour at Gorey, many bedrooms at this popular hotel enjoy views over the sea and beaches. The relaxed and friendly style is apparent from the moment of arrival, and the busy restaurant and bar are popular with locals and tourists alike. Outdoor seating is available in season, and fresh fish and seafood are included on the menu.

Rooms 16 **S** £43-£56; **D** £86-£112 (incl. bkfst)*
Facilities STV Wi-fi 🎵 Xmas New Year **Conf** Class 20 Board 20 Thtr 20 Del from £150 to £190* **Notes** LB ⊗

Maison Gorey

★★ 69% HOTEL

☎ 01534 857775 & 07797 715051
Gorey Village Main Rd JE3 9EP
e-mail: maisongorey@jerseymail.co.uk
dir: Adjacent to Jersey Pottery

Located in the middle of Gorey this small, relaxing hotel provides well-equipped bedrooms and bathrooms. In addition to a spacious bar, a small TV lounge is available for guests. Some off-street parking is available in front of the hotel.

Rooms 26 (26 annexe) (2 fmly) **Facilities** FTV Wi-fi 🎣 Xmas New Year **Parking** 6 **Notes** ⊗ No children 5yrs Civ Wed 85

GROUVILLE Map 24

The Beausite Hotel

★★★ 71% HOTEL

☎ 01534 857577
Les Rue des Pres, Grouville Bay JE3 9DJ
e-mail: beausite@jerseymail.co.uk
web: www.southernhotels.com
dir: Opposite Royal Jersey Golf Course

This hotel is situated on the south-east side of the island; a short distance from the picturesque harbour at Gorey. With parts dating back to 1636, the public rooms retain original character and charm; bedrooms are generally spacious and modern in design. The indoor swimming pool, fitness room, saunas and spa bath are all added bonuses.

Rooms 75 (5 fmly) (18 GF) **S** £42-£96.75; **D** £84-£129 (incl. bkfst)* **Facilities** STV FTV Wi-fi ⊕ Gym **Parking** 60 **Notes** LB Closed Oct-Mar

---

Save on hotels. Book at theAA.com/hotel

VA (GUERNSEY) – ST (JERSEY) 517 ENGLAND

ROZEL Map 24

INSPECTORS' CHOICE

Château la Chaire
★★★ ◎◎ HOTEL

☎ 01534 863354
Rozel Bay JE3 6AJ
e-mail: res@chateau-la-chaire.co.uk
web: www.chateau-la-chaire.co.uk
dir: From St Helier on B38 turn left in village by
Rozel Bay Inn, hotel 100yds on right

Built as a gentleman's residence in 1843, Château
la Chaire is a haven of peace and tranquillity, set
in a secluded wooded valley. Picturesque Rozel
Harbour is within easy walking distance and the
house is surrounded by terraced gardens and
woods. There is a wonderful atmosphere here and
the helpful staff deliver high standards of guest
care. Imaginative menus, making the best use of
local produce, are served in the oak-panelled dining
room, in the conservatory or on the terrace when the
weather permits. Bedroom and suite styles and
sizes vary, but all are beautifully appointed and
include many nice touches such as towelling robes,
slippers, flowers and DVD players. Free Wi-fi is
available throughout the hotel.

Rooms 14 (2 fmly) (1 GF) **S** £75-£145;
D £105-£280 (incl. bkfst) **Facilities** FTV Wi-fi ৬
Xmas New Year **Conf** Class 20 Board 20 Thtr 20
Parking 30 **Notes** LB ⊗ No children 7yrs
Civ Wed 60

ST BRELADE Map 24

INSPECTORS' CHOICE

The Atlantic Hotel
★★★★ ◎◎◎◎ HOTEL

☎ 01534 744101
Le Mont de la Pulente JE3 8HE
e-mail: info@theatlantichotel.com
web: www.theatlantichotel.com
dir: From Petit Port turn right into Rue de la
Sergente, right again, hotel signed

Adjoining the manicured fairways of La Moye
championship golf course, this hotel enjoys a
peaceful setting with breathtaking views over
St Ouen's Bay. Stylish bedrooms look onto the
course or the sea, and offer a blend of high quality
and reassuring comfort. An air of understated
luxury is apparent throughout, and the attentive
service achieves the perfect balance of friendliness
and professionalism. The Ocean restaurant's very
talented chef, Mark Jordan, uses the best island
produce to create outstanding and impeccably
modern cuisine.

Rooms 50 (8 GF) ✎ **S** £110-£210; **D** £160-£360
(incl. bkfst)* **Facilities** STV Wi-fi ৬ ⊛ ⤳ ⤳ Gym
Saunas Xmas New Year **Conf** Class 40 Board 20
Thtr 60 Del from £210 to £260* **Services** Lift
Parking 60 **Notes** LB ⊗ Closed 2 Jan-1 Feb
Civ Wed 80

L'Horizon Hotel & Spa
★★★★ 85% ◎◎ HOTEL

☎ 01534 743101
St Brelade's Bay JE3 8EF
e-mail: lhorizon@handpicked.co.uk
web: www.handpickedhotels.co.uk/lhorizon
dir: From airport right at rdbt towards St Brelades &
Red Houses. Through Red Houses, hotel 300mtrs on
right in centre of bay

The combination of a truly wonderful setting on the
golden sands of St Brelade's Bay, a relaxed
atmosphere and excellent facilities prove a winning
formula here. Bedrooms are stylish and have a real
contemporary feel, all with plasma TVs and a host of
extras; many have balconies or terraces and superb
sea views. Spacious public areas include a spa and
leisure club, a choice of dining options and relaxing
lounges. Hand Picked Hotels – AA Hotel Group of the
Year 2012-13.

Rooms 105 (1 fmly) (15 GF) ✎ **S** £59-£145;
D £118-£290 (incl. bkfst)* **Facilities** Spa STV FTV
Wi-fi ৬ ⊛ ⤳ Gym Windsurfing Water skiing Sailing
Sauna Steam room Beauty treatment rooms ♬ Xmas
New Year **Conf** Class 100 Board 50 Thtr 250
Del from £130 to £220* **Services** Lift **Parking** 125
Notes LB ⊗ Civ Wed 240

ST BRELADE *continued*

St Brelade's Bay Hotel

★★★★ 80% HOTEL

☎ 01534 746141
JE3 8EF
web: www.stbreladesbayhotel.com
dir: SW corner of island

The hotel, in five-acre gardens, enjoys a fabulous location with unobstructed views overlooking St Brelade's Bay and with the sandy beach right on the doorstep. The bedrooms are beautifully presented and equipped to a very high standard; they include two-bedroom suites, family rooms and superb penthouse suites that have large balconies, and even telescopes. The relaxing public areas include a stylish, comfortable lounge along with a spacious bar. The gardens feature a pool area, terraces for relaxing and eating, and a tennis court for the more energetic. Attentive friendly service is guaranteed in the elegant restaurant with its sea views.

Rooms 77 (8 fmly) ✿ **S** £93-£142; **D** £140-£284 (incl. bkfst)* **Facilities** STV Wi-fi ⊗ ₹ ⌣ Beauty treatment rooms ♫ **Conf** Board 12 **Services** Lift **Parking** 90 **Notes** ⊗ Closed 12 Oct-2 Apr Civ Wed

Hotel La Place

★★★★ 73% ® HOTEL

☎ 01534 744261
Route du Coin, La Haule JE3 8BT
e-mail: reservations@hotellaplacejersey.com
dir: Off main St Helier/St Aubin coast road at La Haule Manor (B25). Up hill, 2nd left (to Red Houses), 1st right. Hotel 100mtrs on right

Developed around a 17th-century farmhouse, this hotel is well placed for exploration of the island. Attentive, friendly service is very much part of the ethos here. Many of the bedrooms have been refurbished and offer high levels of quality and comfort; some have private patios and direct access to the pool area. The cocktail bar is popular for pre-dinner drinks, and the stylish lounge is a perfect place to sit back and enjoy the tranquil delights of this peaceful setting. Cuisine is also an important feature here with the menu offering a good range of local, seasonal produce, served within the elegant restaurant.

Rooms 42 (1 fmly) (10 GF) **Facilities** STV Wi-fi ₹ Discount at Les Ormes Country Club Xmas **Conf** Class 40 Board 40 Thtr 100 **Parking** 100 **Notes** Civ Wed 100

Beau Rivage Hotel

★★★ 77% HOTEL

☎ 01534 745983
St Brelade's Bay JE3 8EF
e-mail: beau@jerseyweb.demon.co.uk
web: www.jersey.co.uk/hotels/beau
dir: Sea side of coast road in centre of St Brelade's Bay, 1.5m S of airport

With direct access to one of Jersey's most popular beaches, residents and non-residents alike are welcome to this hotel's bar and terrace. All of the well-equipped bedrooms are now suites, most have wonderful sea views, and some have the bonus of balconies. Residents have a choice of lounges, plus a sun deck exclusively for their use. A range of dishes, featuring English and Continental cuisine, is available from a selection of menus in either the bar or the main bistro restaurant.

Rooms 12 (12 fmly) (12 smoking) **Facilities** STV FTV Wi-fi Games room **Services** Lift **Parking** 16 **Notes** ⊗ RS Nov-Mar Civ Wed 80

Hotel Miramar

★★ 72% HOTEL

☎ 01534 743831
Mont Gras d'Eau JE3 8ED
e-mail: reservations@miramarjersey.com
web: www.miramarjersey.com
dir: From airport take B36 at lights, turn left onto A13, 1st right into Mont Gras d'Eau

A friendly welcome awaits at this family-run hotel set in delightful sheltered gardens, overlooking the beautiful bay. Accommodation is comfortable with well-appointed bedrooms; some are on the ground

floor, and there are two on the lower ground with their own terrace overlooking the outdoor heated pool. The restaurant offers a varied set menu.

Rooms 38 (2 fmly) (12 GF) ✿ **S** £36-£53.45; **D** £72-£106.90 (incl. bkfst)* **Facilities** FTV Wi-fi ₹ **Parking** 30 **Notes** LB Closed Oct-mid Apr

ST CLEMENT　　　　　　　　Map 24

Pontac House Hotel

★★★ 77% HOTEL

☎ 01534 857771
St Clements Bay JE2 6SE
e-mail: info@pontachouse.com
web: www.pontachouse.com
dir: 10 mins from St Helier

Overlooking the sandy beach of St Clement's Bay, this hotel is located on the south eastern corner of Jersey. Many guests return on a regular basis to experience the friendly, relaxed style of service. The bedrooms, most with splendid views, are comfortable and well equipped. Varied menus, featuring local seafood, are on offer each evening.

Rooms 27 (1 fmly) (5 GF) ✿ **Facilities** FTV Wi-fi ₹ **Parking** 35 **Notes** Closed 18 Dec-1 Mar

The Samares Coast Hotel

★★★ 72% HOTEL

☎ 01534 723411 ＆ 873006
St Clement's Coast Rd JE2 6SB
e-mail: admin@morvanhotels.com
dir: On main esplanade

This hotel is situated on the south coast in a prime seafront location with delightful views from the restaurant and many of the bedrooms. All the bedrooms

Save on hotels. Book at **theAA.com/hotel**

ST (JERSEY) 519 ENGLAND

are well appointed and the sea-facing; balcony rooms prove especially popular. Facilities include a leisure complex with swimming pool and gym, and there are pleasant gardens. Carefully prepared dishes are offered in the comfortable restaurant.

Rooms 52 (4 annexe) (5 fmly) (14 GF) **Facilities** STV FTV Wi-fi 🕲 ⚡ Gym Steam room **Services** Lift **Parking** 35 **Notes** ⊗ Closed Nov-Mar

ST HELIER — Map 24

Grand Jersey

★★★★★ 82% ⊛⊛⊛ HOTEL

☎ 01534 722301
The Esplanade JE2 3QA
e-mail: reservations@grandjersey.com

A local landmark, the Grand Hotel has pleasant views across St Aubin's Bay to the front and the bustling streets of St Helier to the rear. The hotel is elegant and contemporary in design with a real touch of grandeur throughout. The air-conditioned bedrooms, including six suites, come in a variety of designs, but all have luxurious beds, ottomans and LCD TVs. The spacious public areas include the popular Champagne Lounge, the Victorias brasserie, and the impressive Tassili fine-dining restaurant. There is a large terrace for alfresco eating in the summer months, and the spa offers an indoor pool, gym and treatment rooms.

Rooms 123 (18 fmly) (6 GF) ⚲ **Facilities** Spa STV FTV Wi-fi ↳ 🕲 Gym 🎵 Xmas New Year **Conf** Class 100 Board 50 Thtr 180 **Services** Lift Air con **Parking** 27 **Notes** ⊗ Civ Wed 180

INSPECTORS' CHOICE

The Club Hotel & Spa
CLASSIC BRITISH HOTELS

★★★★ ⊛⊛⊛⊛
TOWN HOUSE HOTEL

☎ 01534 876500
Green St JE2 4UH
e-mail: reservations@theclubjersey.com
web: www.theclubjersey.com
dir: 5 mins walk from main shopping centre

This swish, town house hotel is conveniently located close to the centre of town and features stylish,

contemporary decor throughout. All the guest rooms and suites have power showers and state-of-the-art technology including wide-screen LCD TV, DVD and CD systems. The choice of restaurants includes Bohemia, a sophisticated eating option that continues to offer outstanding cuisine. For relaxation there is an elegant spa with a luxurious range of treatments.

Rooms 46 (4 fmly) (4 GF) **S** £99-£445; **D** £99-£445 (incl. bkfst) **Facilities** Spa STV FTV Wi-fi 🕲 ⚡ Sauna Steam room Salt cabin Hydrothermal bench Rasul room New Year **Conf** Class 60 Board 34 Thtr 80 Del from £195 to £215 **Services** Lift Air con **Parking** 32 **Notes** LB ⊗ Closed 24-30 Dec Civ Wed 84

Pomme d'Or Hotel

★★★★ 80% HOTEL

☎ 01534 880110
Liberation Square JE1 3UF
e-mail: enquiries@pommedorhotel.com
dir: Opposite harbour

This historic hotel overlooks Liberation Square and the marina and offers comfortably furnished, well-equipped bedrooms. Popular with the business fraternity, a range of conference facilities and meeting rooms are available. Dining options include The Harbour Room Carvery, and the new Gills and Grills, a café bar.

Rooms 143 (3 fmly) ⚲ **S** £79-£290; **D** £79-£290 (incl. bkfst)* **Facilities** STV FTV Wi-fi ↳ Use of Aquadome at Merton Hotel Xmas New Year **Conf** Class 100 Board 50 Thtr 220 Del from £145 to £195* **Services** Lift Air con **Notes** LB ⊗ Civ Wed 100

Radisson Blu Waterfront Hotel, Jersey

★★★★ 80% HOTEL

☎ 01534 671100 & 671173
The Waterfront, La Rue de L'Etau JE2 3WF
e-mail: info.jersey@radissonblu.com
web: www.radissonblu.com/hotel-jersey
dir: Follow signs to St Helier. From A2 follow signs to harbour. At rdbt just before harbour take 2nd exit, continue to hotel

Most of the bedrooms at this purpose-built hotel have fabulous views of the coastline. There is a popular brasserie, cocktail bar, lounges, indoor heated pool, gym, sauna and steam room. A wide range of meeting rooms provides conference facilities for delegates; parking is extensive.

Rooms 195 ⚲ **S** £89-£169; **D** £89-£169* **Facilities** Spa STV Wi-fi ↳ HL 🕲 Gym Sauna Steam

room 🎵 Xmas New Year **Conf** Class 184 Board 30 Thtr 400 Del from £155 to £195* **Services** Lift Air con **Parking** 70 **Notes** ⊗ Civ Wed 400

Hotel Savoy

★★★★ 75% ⊛ HOTEL

☎ 01534 727521
37 Rouge Bouillon JE2 3ZA
e-mail: info@thesavoy.biz
web: www.thesavoy.biz
dir: From airport 1st exit at rdbt. At next rdbt 2nd exit right, down Beaumont Hill. At bottom left, along coast onto dual carriageway. At 3rd lights 1st left. Right at end. Remain in right lane, into left lane before hospital. Hotel on left opposite police station

This family-run hotel, a manor house dating from the 19th century, sits peacefully in its own grounds, just a short walk from the main shopping area in St Helier. It offers spacious, comfortable accommodation and smart public rooms. The Montana Restaurant serves carefully prepared, imaginative cuisine. A car park and leisure facilities are also available.

Rooms 56 (2 fmly) (10 GF) ⚲ **S** £80-£100; **D** £120-£140 (incl. bkfst)* **Facilities** STV FTV Wi-fi ↳ ⚡ Gym 🎵 **Conf** Class 70 Board 12 Thtr 120 Del from £125 to £180* **Services** Lift **Parking** 46 **Notes** LB ⊗ Civ Wed 80

Best Western Royal Hotel

★★★ 79% ⊛ HOTEL

Best Western

☎ 01534 726521 & 873006
David Place JE2 4TD
e-mail: enquiries@royalhoteljersey.com
web: www.royalhoteljersey.com
dir: From Airport: In St Helier on Victoria Ave, left by Grand Hotel into Peirson Rd. Follow one-way system into Cheapside. Left at filter, follow Ring Rd signs into Rouge Boullion (A14). At rdbt right, stay in right lane, right at lights into Midvale Rd. Through 2 lights, hotel on left

This long established hotel is located in the centre of town and is within walking distance of the business district and shops. Seasons Restaurant offers a modern approach to dining, and the adjoining bar provides a relaxed venue for residents and locals alike. The bedrooms are individually styled. Extensive conference facilities are available.

Rooms 89 (4 fmly) (9 smoking) **Facilities** Wi-fi Gym Xmas New Year **Conf** Class 120 Board 80 Thtr 300 **Services** Lift **Parking** 15 **Notes** ⊗ Civ Wed 30

CHANNEL ISLANDS

ST HELIER *continued*

The Monterey Hotel

★★★ 73% HOTEL

☎ 01534 724762 & 873006
St Saviour's Rd JE2 7LA
e-mail: admin@morvanhotels.com

Conveniently located for the town, this comfortable hotel has the added benefit of ample parking and a range of leisure facilities including an indoor pool. Bedrooms are well decorated and furnished, and include a number of superior rooms. The relaxing bar area is open all day, and a good range of freshly prepared dishes is offered each evening.

Rooms 73 (6 fmly) (9 GF) **Facilities** STV FTV Wi-fi 🕏 ⌇ Gym Xmas New Year **Conf** Class 12 Board 22 Thtr 40 **Services** Lift **Parking** 40 **Notes** ⊗

The Hotel Revere

★★★ 72% HOTEL

☎ 01534 611111
Kensington Place JE2 3PA
e-mail: reservations@revere.co.uk
web: www.revere.co.uk
dir: From Esplanade left after De Vere Grand Hotel

Situated on the west side of the town and convenient for the centre and harbour side, this hotel dates back to the 17th century and retains many period features. The style here is engagingly different, and bedrooms are individually decorated. There are three dining options and a small sun terrace.

Rooms 56 (2 fmly) (4 GF) 🖝 **S** £40-£75; **D** £80-£150 (incl. bkfst)* **Facilities** STV Wi-fi ⌇ ♫ Xmas New Year **Notes** LB ⊗ Civ Wed 50

Hampshire Hotel

★★★ 71% HOTEL

☎ 01534 724115
53 Val Plaisant JE2 4TB
e-mail: info@hampshirehotel.je

Located a short walk from the town centre, this hotel features spacious public areas and comfortable bedrooms. There are premier, standard and family rooms, each with a flat-screen TV. The spacious restaurant features a seasonal changing menu of popular dishes at dinner; and at breakfast a wide choice is offered. The outdoor swimming pool and sun terrace are popular in the summer months.

Rooms 42 (2 fmly) (5 GF) **S** £40-£79; **D** £74-£119 (incl. bkfst)* **Facilities** STV Wi-fi ⌇ ♫ Xmas New Year **Services** Lift **Parking** 30 **Notes** LB ⊗

The Norfolk Lodge Hotel

★★★ 71% HOTEL

☎ 01534 722950 & 873006
Rouge Bouillon JE2 3ZB
e-mail: admin@morvanhotels.com

Centrally located and just a short walk to the main town, this popular hotel has a large number of regularly returning guests. Bedrooms are well decorated and equipped, and include some on the ground floor. In addition to an indoor swimming pool, the hotel offers regular evening entertainment during the main season. A range of well-prepared dishes is offered at dinner in the spacious restaurant.

Rooms 101 (11 annexe) (8 fmly) (22 GF) **Facilities** FTV Wi-fi 🕏 Children's pool Cycling machine ♫ **Services** Lift **Parking** 50 **Notes** ⊗ Closed Nov-Mar

Uplands Hotel

★★★ 70% HOTEL

☎ 01534 730151 & 873006
St John's Rd JE2 3LE
e-mail: admin@morvanhotels.com
dir: From main esplanade (A1) into Pierson Rd by Grand Hotel, follow ring road, 200mtrs, 3rd left into St John's Rd, hotel 0.5m

This hotel is situated on twelve acres of farmland just one mile from the centre of St Helier. The bedrooms are modern, spacious and comfortable; some overlook the swimming pool while others have country views. Plenty of parking and spacious public areas add to the attraction of this friendly and popular hotel.

Rooms 43 (3 fmly) (24 GF) **Facilities** STV FTV Wi-fi ⌇ **Parking** 35 **Notes** ⊗ Closed Nov-Mar

Apollo Hotel

★★★ 55% HOTEL

☎ 01534 725441
St Saviours Rd JE2 4GJ
e-mail: reservations@huggler.com
web: www.huggler.com
dir: On St Saviours Rd at junct with La Motte St

Centrally located, this popular hotel has a relaxed, informal atmosphere. Bedrooms are comfortably furnished and include useful extras. Many guests return regularly to enjoy the variety of leisure facilities including an outdoor pool with water slide and indoor pool with separate jacuzzi. The separate cocktail bar is an ideal place for a pre-dinner drink.

Rooms 85 (5 fmly) **S** £75-£117; **D** £80-£122 (incl. bkfst)* **Facilities** FTV Wi-fi 🕏 supervised ⌇

supervised Gym Xmas New Year **Conf** Class 100 Board 80 Thtr 150 Del from £120 to £170* **Services** Lift **Parking** 40 **Notes** LB ⊗

Millbrook House Hotel

★★ 76% HOTEL

☎ 01534 733036
Rue De Trachy, Millbrook JE2 3JN
e-mail: millbrook.house@jerseymail.co.uk
web: www.millbrookhousehotel.com
dir: 1.5m W of town off A1

Peacefully located within its own grounds, this small, personally run hotel offers a friendly welcome and relaxing ambience. Bedrooms and bathrooms vary in size; many have pleasant, countryside views. In addition to outdoor seating in the warmer months, guests can relax in the library, maybe with a drink before dinner.

Rooms 24 (2 fmly) (6 GF) **Services** Lift **Parking** 20 **Notes** ⊗ Closed Oct-13 May

Westhill Country Hotel

★★ 74% COUNTRY HOUSE HOTEL

☎ 01534 723260
Mont-a-l'abbe JE2 3HB
e-mail: info@westhillhoteljersey.com
web: www.westhillhoteljersey.com
dir: Telephone for detailed directions

Set in its own beautifully landscaped gardens this hotel enjoys a prominent position just on the outskirts of St Helier. Service is attentive and guests are guaranteed a warm welcome and genuine hospitality throughout the hotel. The bedrooms are spacious and well equipped; several rooms have commanding views over the gardens to the countryside beyond. Public areas include a stylish lounge bar and popular restaurant. Free Wi-fi is available in the public areas and the swimming pool proves very popular with guests.

Rooms 90 (20 fmly) (16 GF) 🖝 **Facilities** FTV Wi-fi ⌇ ♫ **Parking** 75 **Notes** ⊗ Closed early Oct-early Apr Civ Wed 75

Sarum Hotel

★★ 65% METRO HOTEL

☎ 01534 731340
19/21 New St Johns Rd JE2 3LD
e-mail: sarum@jerseyweb.demon.co.uk
dir: On NW edge of St Helier, 0.5m from town centre

This hotel, just 600yds from the beach, offers self-catering bedrooms and a number of suites. The friendly staff provide a warm welcome, and there is a spacious recreational lounge with pool tables, plasma-screen TV and internet access. A garden and

CHANNEL ISLANDS

outdoor pool are also available. Local restaurants are just a short walk away, and bar snacks are available throughout the day.

Rooms 52 (5 annexe) (6 fmly) (2 GF) (52 smoking) **Facilities** STV FTV Wi-fi Games room **Services** Lift **Parking** 10 **Notes** ⊗

ST MARY   Map 24

West View Hotel

★★ 72% HOTEL

☎ 01534 481643
La Grande Rue JE3 3BD
e-mail: westview@jerseymail.co.uk
web: www.westviewhoteljersey.com
dir: At junct of B33 & C103

Located in the quiet parish of St Mary, this welcoming hotel is close to the delightful walks and cycle routes of the north coast. Bedrooms here are well equipped especially the larger, superior rooms. Entertainment is provided in the lounge bar during the summer months, when guests can also enjoy a swim in the heated outdoor pool.

Rooms 42 (3 fmly) (18 GF) **S** £37-£48; **D** £64-£94 (incl. bkfst)* **Facilities** Wi-fi ⚡ **Parking** 38 **Notes** ⊗ Closed Nov-Apr

ST PETER   Map 24

Greenhills Country Hotel

★★★★ 74% ⊚ COUNTRY HOUSE HOTEL

☎ 01534 481042
Mont de L'Ecole JE3 7EL
e-mail: reserve@greenhillshotel.co.uk
dir: From A1 signed St Peter's Valley (A11), in 4m right onto E112

Centrally located on the island, this relaxing country-house hotel, with delightful gardens, has a lovely atmosphere. Bedrooms extend from the main building around the courtyard; all are comfortable and well equipped with satellite LED TVs, luxurious bathrobes, white duck down duvets and cotton linen. A varied menu, based on fresh local produce, is served in the spacious restaurant.

Rooms 31 (2 fmly) (9 GF) **S** £60-£100; **D** £79-£230 (incl. bkfst)* **Facilities** STV FTV Wi-fi ⚡ **Conf** Class 12 Board 16 Thtr 20 Del from £75 to £150* **Parking** 40 **Notes** ⊗ Closed mid Dec-early Feb Civ Wed 40

ST SAVIOUR   Map 24

Longueville Manor Hotel

★★★★★ ⊚⊚⊚ HOTEL

☎ 01534 725501
JE2 7WF
e-mail: info@longuevillemanor.com
web: www.longuevillemanor.com
dir: A3 E from St Helier towards Gorey. Hotel 1m on left

Dating back to the 13th century, there is something very special about Longueville Manor, which is why so many guests return time and again. It is set in 16 acres of grounds including woodland walks, a spectacular rose garden, Victorian kitchen garden and a lake. Bedrooms have great style and individuality boasting fresh flowers, fine embroidered bed linen and a host of extras. The very accomplished cuisine is also a highlight of any stay. In summer the pool and terrace are popular spots, plus there's croquet and tennis courts. Families are particular welcome and there are extra activities arranged for children, an adventure zone to explore, and they have their own menus and DVD library. The committed team of staff create a welcoming atmosphere and every effort is made to ensure a memorable stay.

Rooms 30 (1 annexe) (7 GF) **S** £75-£225; **D** £150-£550 (incl. bkfst)* **Facilities** STV Wi-fi ⚡ ⚡ ⚡ ⚡ Xmas New Year **Conf** Class 30 Board 30 Thtr 45 Del from £160 to £320* **Services** Lift **Parking** 40 **Notes** LB Civ Wed 40

SARK

SARK   Map 24

Hotel Petit Champ

★★ 79% ⊚⊚ SMALL HOTEL

☎ 01481 832046
GY10 1SF
e-mail: info@hotelpetitchamp.co.uk
web: www.hotelpetitchamp.com
dir: Ferry from St Peter Port, Guernsey. From harbour through village, right at Gallery Stores. Pass church, left at x-rds. To Methodist Church, right, follow hotel signs

Guests can expect a warm welcome from the caring staff at this delightful small hotel, situated within a 20-minute walk of the main street. Wonderful views of the sea and neighbouring islands can be enjoyed from the lounges, the gardens and most of the bedrooms. A five-course dinner is included in the half-board terms, and a there's a well-stocked wine cellar and bar. An outdoor solar-heated swimming pool is available to residents.

Rooms 10 (2 fmly) **S** £75; **D** £145-£186 (incl. bkfst)* **Facilities** Wi-fi ⚡ ⚡ ⚡ Xmas New Year **Notes** ⊗ No children 10yrs

CHANNEL ISLANDS

Scotland

Falkirk Wheel

A

ABERDEEN
City of Aberdeen   Map 23 NJ90

See also Aberdeen Airport

Norwood Hall Hotel

★★★★ 81% ◉ HOTEL

☎ 01224 868951
Garthdee Rd, Cults AB15 9FX
e-mail: info@norwood-hall.co.uk
web: www.norwood-hall.co.uk
dir: Off A90, at 1st rdbt cross Bridge of Dee, left at rdbt onto Garthdee Rd (B&Q & Sainsburys on left) continue to hotel sign

This imposing Victorian mansion has retained many of its original features, most notably the fine oak staircase, stained glass and ornately decorated walls and ceilings. Accommodation varies in style from individually designed bedrooms in the main house to the newest contemporary bedrooms. The extensive grounds ensure the hotel is popular as a wedding venue.

Rooms 73 (14 GF) **Facilities** STV FTV Wi-fi ⬓ Xmas
New Year **Conf** Class 100 Board 70 Thtr 200
Services Lift **Parking** 140 **Notes** ⊗ Civ Wed 150

Holiday Inn Aberdeen West

★★★★ 76% ◉ HOTEL

☎ 01224 270300
Westhill Dr, Westhill AB32 6TT
e-mail: info@hiaberdeenwest.co.uk
web: www.holidayinn.co.uk
dir: On A944 in Westhill

In a good location at the west side of the city, this modern hotel caters well for the needs of both business and leisure guests. The nicely appointed bedrooms and bathrooms have a contemporary feel. Luigi's restaurant serves modern Italian food, and the popular lounge offers more informal dining. There is a separate pub operation with wide-screen TVs showing a range of sporting events.

Rooms 86 (30 fmly) ⤣ **Facilities** STV FTV Wi-fi ⬓ Gym
Conf Class 150 Board 80 Thtr 300 **Services** Lift
Air con **Parking** 90 **Notes** Civ Wed 250

Mercure Aberdeen Ardoe House Hotel & Spa

★★★★ 74% ◉ HOTEL

☎ 01224 860600
South Deeside Rd, Blairs AB12 5YP
e-mail: h6626@accor.com
web: www.mercure.com
dir: 4m W of city off B9077

From its elevated position on the banks of the River Dee, this 19th-century baronial-style mansion commands excellent countryside views. Beautifully decorated, thoughtfully equipped bedrooms are located in the main house, and in the more modern extension. Public rooms include a spa and leisure club, a cosy lounge and cocktail bar and impressive function facilities.

Rooms 119 **D** £89-£250* **Facilities** Spa STV Wi-fi ⬓
⬔ ⬒ Gym Aerobics studio Xmas New Year
Conf Class 200 Board 150 Thtr 600 Del from £165 to
£195* **Services** Lift **Parking** 220 **Notes** ⊗
Civ Wed 250

A

Copthorne Hotel Aberdeen

MILLENNIUM
HOTELS AND RESORTS
MILLENNIUM · COPTHORNE

★★★★ 73% HOTEL

☎ 01224 630404
122 Huntly St AB10 1SU
e-mail: reservations.aberdeen@millenniumhotels.co.uk
web: www.millenniumhotels.co.uk/aberdeen
dir: West end of city centre, off Union St, up Rose St, hotel 0.25m on right on corner with Huntly St

Situated just outside of the city centre, this hotel offers friendly, attentive service. The smart bedrooms are well proportioned and guests will appreciate the added quality of the Connoisseur rooms. The West End Bistro and Bar provides a relaxed atmosphere in which to enjoy a drink or a meal; a great traditional steak and grill selection is on offer.

Rooms 89 (15 fmly) S £60-£295; D £60-£295*
Facilities STV FTV Wi-fi HL New Year **Conf** Class 100 Board 70 Thtr 200 Del from £105 to £250*
Services Lift **Parking** 15 **Notes** LB RS 24-26 Dec Civ Wed 180

Maryculter House Hotel

★★★★ 71% ⊚ HOTEL

☎ 01224 732124
South Deeside Rd, Maryculter AB12 5GB
e-mail: info@maryculterhousehotel.com
web: www.maryculterhousehotel.com
dir: Exit A90 S of Aberdeen onto B9077. Hotel 8m on right, 0.5m beyond Lower Deeside Caravan Park

Set in grounds on the banks of the River Dee, this charming Scottish mansion dates back to medieval times and is now a popular wedding and conference venue. Exposed stonework and open fires feature in the oldest parts, which house the cocktail bar and Priory Restaurant. Lunch and breakfast are taken overlooking the river; bedrooms are equipped especially with business travellers in mind.

Rooms 40 (1 fmly) (16 GF) S £120-£140; D £140-£200 (incl. bkfst)* **Facilities** STV FTV Wi-fi Fishing Clay pigeon shooting Archery Xmas New Year **Conf** Class 100 Board 50 Thtr 200 **Parking** 150 **Notes** LB Civ Wed 220

The Caledonian, Aberdeen
thistle

★★★★ 71% HOTEL

☎ 0871 376 9003
10-14 Union Ter AB10 1WE
e-mail: aberdeencaledonian@thistle.co.uk
web: www.thistlehotels.com/thecaledonian
dir: Follow signs to city centre & Union St. Turn into Union Terrace. Hotel on left, parking behind hotel in Diamond St

Centrally located just off Union Street and overlooking Union Terrace Gardens this traditional hotel offers comfortable and well-appointed bedrooms, and public areas in keeping with the age of the building. The upbeat Café Bar Caley serves informal food, but for a more formal dining experience there's the Restaurant on the Terrace. A small car park is available to the rear.

Rooms 83 (5 fmly) **Facilities** FTV Wi-fi **Conf** Class 40 Board 30 Thtr 80 **Services** Lift **Parking** 22 **Notes** ⊛ Civ Wed 40

Thistle Aberdeen Altens
thistle

★★★★ 71% HOTEL

☎ 0871 376 9002
Souter Head Rd, Altens AB12 3LF
e-mail: aberdeenaltens@thistle.co.uk
web: www.thistle.com/aberdeenaltens
dir: A90 onto A956 signed Aberdeen Harbour. Hotel just off rdbt

Popular with oil industry personnel, this large purpose-built hotel lies in the Altens area, south east of the city. It's worth asking for one of the executive bedrooms that provide excellent space. A wide choice of meals are available in the Restaurant or the Cairngorm Bar where there is a relaxed atmosphere.

Rooms 216 (96 fmly) (48 GF) **Facilities** FTV Wi-fi HL ⊙ Gym Sauna Steam room Solarium Aerobic studio New Year **Conf** Class 144 Board 30 Thtr 400 **Services** Lift **Parking** 300 **Notes** ⊛ Civ Wed 150

Malmaison Aberdeen
Malmaison
hotels that dare to be different

★★★ 86% ⊚ HOTEL

☎ 01224 327370
49-53 Queens Rd AB15 4YP
e-mail: info.aberdeen@malmaison.com
dir: A90, 3rd exit into Queens Rd at 3rd rdbt, hotel on right

Popular with business travellers and as a function venue, this well-established hotel lies east of the city centre. Public areas include a reception lounge and an intimate restaurant, plus the extensive bar menu which remains a popular choice for many regulars. There are two styles of accommodation, with the

superior rooms being particularly comfortable and well equipped.

Rooms 79 (8 fmly) (10 GF) **Facilities** Spa STV FTV Wi-fi Gym Steam room Xmas New Year **Conf** Class 30 Board 20 Thtr 40 **Services** Lift **Parking** 50

The Craighaar Hotel

★★★ 80% HOTEL

☎ 01224 712275
Waterton Rd, Bucksburn AB21 9HS
e-mail: info@craighaar.co.uk
dir: From A96 (Airport/Inverness) onto A947, hotel signed

Conveniently located for the airport, this welcoming hotel is a popular base for business people and tourists alike. Guests can make use of a quiet library lounge, and enjoy meals in the bar or restaurant. All bedrooms are well equipped, plus there is a wing of duplex suites that provide additional comfort.

Rooms 53 (6 fmly) (16 GF) S £55-£109; D £65-£139 (incl. bkfst)* **Facilities** STV FTV Wi-fi Library **Conf** Class 33 Board 30 Thtr 90 Del £129.50* **Parking** 80 **Notes** ⊛ Closed 25-26 Dec Civ Wed 40

The Mariner Hotel

★★★ 79% HOTEL

☎ 01224 588901
349 Great Western Rd AB10 6NW
e-mail: info@themarinerhotel.co.uk
dir: E off Anderson Drive (A90) at Great Western Rd. Hotel on right on corner of Gray St

This well maintained, family operated hotel is located west of the city centre. The smart, spacious bedrooms are well equipped and particularly comfortable, with executive suites available. The public rooms are restricted to the lounge bar, which is food driven, and the Atlantis Restaurant that showcases the region's wide choice of excellent seafood and meats.

Rooms 25 (8 annexe) (4 GF) S £90; D £130 (incl. bkfst)* **Facilities** FTV Wi-fi New Year **Parking** 51 **Notes** ⊛

A

ABERDEEN *continued*

Holiday Inn Express Aberdeen City Centre

BUDGET HOTEL

☎ 01224 623500
Chapel St AB10 1SQ
e-mail: info@hieaberdeen.co.uk
web: www.hiexpress.com/exaberdeencc
dir: In west end of city, just off Union Street

A modern hotel ideal for families and business travellers. Fresh and uncomplicated, the spacious rooms include Sky TV, power shower and tea and coffee-making facilities. Continental buffet breakfast is included in the room rate; other meals may be taken at the nearby family pub or restaurant. See also the Hotel Groups pages.

Rooms 155 (102 fmly) (30 smoking) ♦ S £59-£149; **D** £59-£149 (incl. bkfst)* **Conf** Class 18 Board 16 Thtr 35

Holiday Inn Express Aberdeen - Exhibition Centre

BUDGET HOTEL

☎ 01224 706878
Exhibition & Conference Centre, Parkway East, Bridge of Don AB23 8AJ
e-mail: info@hieaberdeenexhibitioncentre.co.uk

Rooms 135 (100 fmly) **Conf** Class 20 Board 24 Thtr 50

Premier Inn Aberdeen Central West

BUDGET HOTEL

☎ 0871 527 8006
North Anderson Dr AB15 6DW
web: www.premierinn.com
dir: Into Aberdeen from S on A90 follow airport signs. Hotel 1st left after fire station. (NB for Sat Nav use AB15 6TP)

High quality, budget accommodation ideal for both families and business travellers. Spacious, en suite bedrooms feature tea and coffee making facilities, and Freeview TV in most hotels. Internet access and Wi-fi are available for a small fee. The adjacent family restaurant features a wide and varied menu. See also the Hotel Groups pages.

Rooms 62

Premier Inn Aberdeen City Centre

BUDGET HOTEL

☎ 0871 527 8008
Inverlair House, West North St AB24 5AS
web: www.premierinn.com
dir: A90 onto A9013 into city centre. Take A956 towards King St, 1st left into Meal Market St

Rooms 162

Premier Inn Aberdeen North (Murcar)

BUDGET HOTEL

☎ 0871 527 8010
Ellon Rd, Murcar, Bridge of Don AB23 8BP
web: www.premierinn.com
dir: From city centre take A90 N follow Peterhead signs. At rdbt 2m after Aberdeen Exhibition & Conference Centre, left onto B999. Hotel on right

Rooms 40

Premier Inn Aberdeen South

BUDGET HOTEL

☎ 0871 527 8012
Mains of Balquharn, Portlethen AB12 4QS
web: www.premierinn.com
dir: From A90 follow Portlethen & Badentoy Park signs. Hotel on right

Rooms 40

Premier Inn Aberdeen (Westhill)

BUDGET HOTEL

☎ 0871 527 8004
Straik Rd, Westhill AB32 6HF
web: www.premierinn.com
dir: On A944 towards Alford, hotel adjacent to Tesco

Rooms 61

Thistle Aberdeen Airport thistle

★★★★ 78% HOTEL

☎ 0871 376 9001
Aberdeen Airport, Argyll Rd AB21 0AF
e-mail: aberdeenairport@thistle.co.uk
web: www.thistle.com/aberdeenairport
dir: Adjacent to Aberdeen Airport

Ideally located at the entrance to the airport this hotel offers ample parking plus a courtesy bus service to the terminal. This is a well presented establishment that benefits from good-sized bedrooms and comfortable public areas. Just Gym offers a good variety of exercise equipment.

Rooms 147 (3 fmly) (74 GF) (18 smoking)
Facilities FTV Wi-fi ⓑ HL Gym **Conf** Class 350 Board 100 Thtr 600 Del from £165 to £225*
Parking 300 **Notes** ⊗

Aberdeen Marriott Hotel **Marriott** HOTELS & RESORTS

★★★★ 76% HOTEL

☎ 01224 770011
Overton Circle, Dyce AB21 7AZ
e-mail: reservations.scotland@marriotthotels.com
web: www.aberdeenmarriott.co.uk
dir: Follow A96 to Bucksburn, right at rdbt onto A947. Hotel in 2m at 2nd rdbt

Close to the airport and conveniently located for the business district, this purpose-built hotel is a popular conference venue. The well-proportioned bedrooms come with many thoughtful extras. Public areas include an informal bar and lounge, a split-level restaurant and a leisure centre that can be accessed directly from a number of bedrooms.

Rooms 155 (81 fmly) (61 GF) (10 smoking)
S £59-£205; **D** £59-£205* **Facilities** STV Wi-fi HL ⓑ supervised Gym Saunas (male & female) Solarium New Year **Conf** Class 200 Board 60 Thtr 400 Del from £150 to £250* **Services** Air con **Parking** 180 **Notes** LB ⊗ Civ Wed 90

Menzies Dyce Aberdeen Airport

MenziesHotels

★★★ 78% HOTEL

☎ 01224 723101
Farburn Ter, Dyce AB21 7DW
e-mail: dyce@menzieshotels.co.uk
dir: A96/A947 airport E after 1m turn left at lights. Hotel in 250yds

This hotel is very convenient for air travellers and for those wishing to explore this lovely Highland area. The spacious, well-equipped bedrooms have all the expected up-to-date amenities. The public areas are welcoming and include a contemporary brasserie. Secure parking and Wi-fi are also provided.

Rooms 208 (208 annexe) (3 fmly) (107 GF) (54 smoking) **Facilities** STV FTV Wi-fi Xmas New Year **Conf** Class 160 Board 120 Thtr 400 **Parking** 150 **Notes** Civ Wed 220

| ABERDOUR | Map 21 NT18 |
| Fife | |

The Woodside Hotel

★★★ 🅰 HOTEL

☎ 01383 860328
High St KY3 0SW
e-mail: reception@thewoodsidehotel.co.uk
web: www.thewoodsidehotel.co.uk
dir: M90 junct 1, E on A291 for 5m, hotel on left

Rooms 20 (3 fmly) 🐾 **Facilities** FTV Wi-fi **Conf** Class 80 Thtr 60 Del £125* **Parking** 22 **Notes** ⊗ Closed 25 Dec & 1 Jan

| ABERFOYLE | Map 20 NN50 |
| Stirling | |

Macdonald Forest Hills Hotel & Resort

MACDONALD
HOTELS & RESORTS

★★★★ 76% ◉ HOTEL

☎ 0844 879 9057 & 01877 389500
Kinlochard FK8 3TL
e-mail: forest_hills@macdonald-hotels.co.uk
web: www.macdonald-hotels.co.uk/foresthills
dir: A84, A873, A81 to Aberfoyle onto B829

Situated in the heart of The Trossachs with wonderful views of Loch Ard, this popular hotel forms part of a resort complex offering a range of indoor and outdoor facilities. The main hotel has relaxing lounges and a restaurant that all overlook the landscaped gardens. A separate building houses the leisure centre, lounge bar and bistro.

Rooms 49 (16 fmly) (12 GF) **Facilities** Spa STV FTV Wi-fi ⊛ 🏊 Gym Children's club Snooker Watersports

Quad biking Archery Clay pigeon shooting 🎵 Xmas New Year **Conf** Class 60 Board 45 Thtr 150 Del from £95 to £165 **Services** Lift **Parking** 100 **Notes** ⊗ Civ Wed 100

| ABERLADY | Map 21 NT47 |
| East Lothian | |

Ducks at Kilspindie

◉◉ RESTAURANT WITH ROOMS

☎ 01875 870682
Main St EH32 0RE
e-mail: kilspindie@ducks.co.uk
web: www.ducks.co.uk
dir: A1 (Bankton junct), take 1st exit to North Berwick. At next rdbt 3rd exit onto A198 signed Longniddry, left towards Aberlady. At T-junct, facing river, right to Aberlady

The name of this restaurant with rooms is referenced around the building - Ducks restaurant for award-winning cuisine; Donald's Bistro and the Ducklings informal coffee shop. The warm and welcoming public areas include a great bar offering real ales and various objets d'art. The bedrooms are comfortable and well appointed with well-presented en suites. The team are informal, friendly and take the time to chat to their guests.

Rooms 23 (1 fmly)

ABINGTON MOTORWAY	Map 21 NS92
SERVICE AREA (M74)	
South Lanarkshire	

Days Inn Abington - M74

BUDGET HOTEL

☎ 01864 502782
ML12 6RG
e-mail: abington.hotel@welcomebreak.co.uk
web: www.welcomebreak.co.uk
dir: M74 junct 13, accessible from N'bound and S'bound carriageways

This modern building offers accommodation in smart, spacious and well-equipped bedrooms, suitable for families and business travellers, and all with en suite bathrooms. Continental breakfast is available and other refreshments may be taken at the nearby family restaurant. See also the Hotel Groups pages.

Rooms 52 (50 fmly) (8 smoking) **Conf** Board 10

| ARCHIESTOWN | Map 23 NJ24 | A |
| Moray | | |

Archiestown Hotel

★★★ 79% ◉ SMALL HOTEL

☎ 01340 810218
AB38 7QL
e-mail: jah@archiestownhotel.co.uk
web: www.archiestownhotel.co.uk
dir: A95 Craigellachie, B9102, 4m to Archiestown

Set in the heart of this Speyside village this small hotel is popular with anglers and locals alike. It is rightly noted for its great hospitality, attentive service and good food. Cosy and comfortable public rooms include a choice of lounges (there is no bar as such) and a bistro offering an inviting choice of dishes at both lunch and dinner.

Rooms 11 (1 fmly) **S** £80-£90; **D** £80-£90 (incl. bkfst)* **Facilities** FTV Wi-fi 🐾 🏊 New Year **Conf** Board 12 Thtr 20 **Parking** 20 **Notes** LB ⊗ Closed 24-27 Dec & 3 Jan-9 Feb

| ARDUAINE | Map 20 NM71 |
| Argyll & Bute | |

Loch Melfort Hotel

★★★ 83% ◉◉ HOTEL

☎ 01852 200233
PA34 4XG
e-mail: reception@lochmelfort.co.uk
web: www.lochmelfort.co.uk
dir: On A816, midway between Oban & Lochgilphead

Enjoying one of the finest locations on the West Coast, this popular, family-run hotel has outstanding views across Asknish Bay towards the Islands of Jura, Scarba and Shuna. Accommodation is provided in either the balconied rooms of the Cedar wing or the more traditional rooms in the main hotel. Dining options include the main restaurant with stunning views or the more informal bistro.

Rooms 25 (20 annexe) (2 fmly) (10 GF) 🐾 **S** £128-£346; **D** £196-£306 (incl. bkfst & dinner)* **Facilities** Wi-fi 4 moorings Childrens' play park Xmas New Year Child facilities **Conf** Class 40 Board 20 Thtr 50 **Parking** 50 **Notes** LB Closed 2 wks mid Jan RS Winter Civ Wed 100

A

AUCHENCAIRN — Map 21 NX75
Dumfries & Galloway

Balcary Bay Hotel
★★★ 87% ◉◉ HOTEL

☎ 01556 640217 & 640311
DG7 1QZ
e-mail: reservations@balcary-bay-hotel.co.uk
web: www.balcary-bay-hotel.co.uk
dir: On A711 between Dalbeattie & Kirkcudbright, hotel 2m from Auchencairn

Taking its name from the bay on which it lies, this hotel has lawns running down to the shore. The larger bedrooms enjoy stunning views over the bay, whilst others overlook the gardens. The comfortable public areas invite relaxation. Imaginative dishes feature at dinner, accompanied by a good wine list.

Rooms 20 (1 fmly) (3 GF) ☛ **S** £78; **D** £142-£174 (incl. bkfst) **Facilities** FTV **Parking** 50 **Notes** Closed 1st Sun Dec-last Fri in Jan

AUCHTERARDER — Map 21 NN91
Perth & Kinross

INSPECTORS' CHOICE

The Gleneagles Hotel

★★★★★ ◉◉◉◉ HOTEL

☎ 01764 662231
PH3 1NF
e-mail: resort.sales@gleneagles.com
web: www.gleneagles.com
dir: Exit A9 onto A823 follow signs for Gleneagles Hotel

With its international reputation for high standards, this grand hotel provides something for everyone. Set in 850 acres of glorious countryside, Gleneagles offers a peaceful retreat, as well as many sporting activities, including the famous championship golf courses. All bedrooms are appointed to a high standard and offer both traditional and contemporary styles. Stylish public areas include various dining options - the Deseo 'Mediterranean Food Market' eaterie, The Strathearn, with two AA Rosettes, as well as inspired cooking at Andrew Fairlie at Gleneagles, a restaurant with four AA Rosettes. There's also the Clubhouse and many bars. The award-winning EPSA spa offers the very latest treatments to restore both body and soul. Service is always professional - the staff are friendly and nothing is too much trouble.

Rooms 232 (115 fmly) (11 GF) **Facilities** Spa STV FTV Wi-fi ↳ ☜ supervised ↳ supervised ↕ 54 ☞ Putt green Fishing ↯ Gym Falconry Off-road driving Golf Archery Clay target shooting Gundog School Xmas New Year **Conf** Class 240 Board 60 Thtr 360 **Services** Lift **Parking** 277 **Notes** Civ Wed 360

AVIEMORE — Map 23 NH81
Highland

Macdonald Highlands Hotel

★★★★ 74% HOTEL

☎ 01479 815100
Aviemore Highland Resort PH22 1PN
e-mail: general@aviemorehighlandresort.com
web: www.aviemorehighlandresort.com
dir: From N: Exit A9 to Aviemore (B970). Right at T-junct, through village. Right (2nd exit) at 1st rdbt into Macdonald Aviemore Highland Resort, follow reception signs. From S: Exit A9 to Aviemore, left at T-junct. Immediately after Esso garage, turn left into Resort

This hotel is part of the Aviemore Highland Resort which boasts a wide range of activities including a championship golf course. The modern, well-equipped bedrooms suit business, leisure guests and families, and Aspects Restaurant is the fine dining option. In addition there is a state-of-the-art gym, spa treatments and a 25-metre pool with a wave machine and flume.

Rooms 151 (10 fmly) (44 GF) **S** £65-£144; **D** £75-£159 (incl. bkfst)* **Facilities** Spa STV FTV Wi-fi ↳ ☜ supervised ↕ 18 Putt green Fishing Gym Steam room Sauna Children's indoor & outdoor playgrounds Xmas New Year **Conf** Class 610 Board 38 Thtr 1000 **Services** Lift **Parking** 500 **Notes** LB ⊗ Civ Wed 300

AYR — Map 20 NS32
South Ayrshire

The Western House Hotel
★★★★ 82% ◉◉ HOTEL

☎ 0870 055 5510
2 Whitletts Rd KA8 0HA
e-mail: info@westernhousehotel.co.uk
dir: From Glasgow M77 then A77 towards Ayr. At Whitletts rdbt take A719 towards town centre

This impressive hotel is located in its own attractive gardens on the edge of Ayr racecourse. Bedrooms in the main house are superbly appointed, and the courtyard rooms offer much comfort too. Nicely appointed day rooms include the light and airy restaurant with views across the course. The staff are attentive and welcoming.

Rooms 49 (39 annexe) (39 fmly) (16 GF) **Facilities** STV Wi-fi Xmas New Year **Conf** Class 300 Board 50 Thtr 1200 **Services** Lift **Parking** 250 **Notes** ⊗ Civ Wed 200

Save on hotels. Book at **theAA.com/hotel**

AUC – BAL 529 SCOTLAND

Fairfield House Hotel

★★★★ 78% ◉◉ HOTEL

☎ 01292 267461
12 Fairfield Rd KA7 2AR
e-mail: reservations@fairfieldhotel.co.uk
dir: From A77 towards Ayr South (A30). Follow town
centre signs, down Miller Rd, left, then right into
Fairfield Rd

Situated in a leafy cul-de-sac close to the esplanade,
this hotel enjoys stunning seascapes towards to the
Isle of Arran. Bedrooms are in either modern or
classical styles, the latter featuring impressive
bathrooms. Public areas provide stylish, modern
rooms in which to relax. Skilfully prepared meals are
served in the casual brasserie or elegant restaurant.

Rooms 44 (4 annexe) (3 fmly) (9 GF) **Facilities** FTV
Wi-fi ↕ 🖎 supervised Gym Fitness room Sauna Steam
room Xmas New Year **Conf** Class 80 Board 40 Thtr 120
Services Lift **Parking** 50 **Notes** ⊗ Civ Wed 150

Enterkine Country House

★★★★ 77% ◉◉ COUNTRY HOUSE HOTEL

☎ 01292 520580
Annbank KA6 5AL
e-mail: mail@enterkine.com
dir: 5m E of Ayr on B743

This luxurious art deco country mansion dates from
the 1930s and retains many original features, notably
some splendid bathroom suites. The focus is very
much on dining, and in country house tradition there
is no bar, drinks being served in the elegant lounge
and library. The well-proportioned bedrooms are
furnished and equipped to high standards, many with
lovely countryside views.

Rooms 14 (8 annexe) (2 fmly) (3 GF) ⬧ **S** £50–£100;
D £60–£160 (incl. bkfst) **Facilities** FTV Wi-fi Xmas New
Year **Conf** Class 140 Board 140 Thtr 200 Del from £145
to £210 **Parking** 40 **Notes** LB Civ Wed 250

Holiday Inn Express Ayr

BUDGET HOTEL

☎ 01292 272300
Wheatpark Place KA8 9RT
e-mail: info@hiexpressayr.com
web: www.hiexpress.co.uk

A modern hotel ideal for families and business
travellers. Fresh and uncomplicated, the spacious
rooms include Sky TV, power shower and tea and
coffee-making facilities. Continental buffet breakfast
is included in the room rate; other meals may be
taken at the nearby family pub or restaurant. See also
the Hotel Groups pages.

Rooms 84 (44 fmly) (3 GF) **Conf** Class 12 Board 12
Thtr 23

Premier Inn Ayr/Prestwick Airport

BUDGET HOTEL

☎ 0871 527 8038
Kilmarnock Rd, Monkton KA9 2RJ
web: www.premierinn.com
dir: At Dutch House Rdbt (at junct of A77 & A78) at
Monkton

High quality, budget accommodation ideal for both
families and business travellers. Spacious, en suite
bedrooms feature tea and coffee making facilities,
and Freeview TV in most hotels. Internet access and
Wi-fi are available for a small fee. The adjacent
family restaurant features a wide and varied menu.
See also the Hotel Groups pages.

Rooms 64

BALLANTRAE   Map 20 NX08
South Ayrshire

INSPECTORS' CHOICE

Glenapp Castle

★★★★★ ◉◉◉◉ HOTEL

☎ 01465 831212
KA26 0NZ
e-mail: enquiries@glenappcastle.com
web: www.glenappcastle.com
dir: S through Ballantrae, cross bridge over River
Stinchar, 1st right, hotel gates 1m

Friendly hospitality and attentive service prevail at
this stunning Victorian castle, set in extensive
private grounds to the south of the village.
Impeccably furnished bedrooms are graced with
antiques and period pieces, and include two master
rooms and a ground-floor family suite. Breathtaking
views of Arran and Ailsa Craig can be enjoyed from
the delightful, sumptuous day rooms and from
many of the bedrooms. The outstanding cuisine is a
real draw here; dinner is offered on a well crafted
and imaginative fixed six-course menu. Much of the
fruit, vegetables and herbs come from the hotel's
own garden. Guests should make a point of walking
round the wonderful 36-acre grounds, and take a

---

look at the azalea pond, walled vegetable gardens
and restored Victorian greenhouses.

Rooms 17 (2 fmly) (7 GF) ⬧ **S** £265–£285;
D £415–£620 (incl. bkfst & dinner)* **Facilities** STV
FTV Wi-fi ↕ 🖎 New Year **Conf** Class 12 Board 17
Thtr 17 **Services** Lift **Parking** 20 **Notes** LB Closed
Jan-mid Mar & Xmas week Civ Wed 40

B

BALLATER   Map 23 NO39
Aberdeenshire

INSPECTORS' CHOICE

Darroch Learg Hotel

★★★ ◉◉◉ SMALL HOTEL

☎ 013397 55443
Braemar Rd AB35 5UX
e-mail: enquiries@darrochlearg.co.uk
web: www.darrochlearg.co.uk
dir: On A93, W of Ballater

Set high above the road in extensive wooded
grounds, this long-established hotel offers superb
views over the hills and countryside of Royal
Deeside. Nigel and Fiona Franks are caring and
attentive hosts who improve their hotel every year.
Bedrooms, some with four-poster beds, are
individually styled, bright and spacious. Food is a
highlight of any visit, whether it is a freshly
prepared breakfast or the fine cuisine served in the
delightful conservatory restaurant.

Rooms 12 (1 GF) **S** £130–£195; **D** £210–£320 (incl.
bkfst & dinner)* **Facilities** New Year
Conf Board 12 Thtr 25 Del from £150 to £220*
Parking 15 **Notes** Closed Xmas & Jan (ex New Year)

BALLATER *continued*

Loch Kinord Hotel

★★★ 78% ☻ HOTEL

☎ 013398 85229
Ballater Rd, Dinnet AB34 5JY
e-mail: stay@lochkinord.com
web: www.lochkinord.com
dir: Between Aboyne & Ballater, on A93, in Dinnet

Family-run, this roadside hotel is well located for leisure and sporting pursuits. It has lots of character and a friendly atmosphere. There are two bars, one outside and a cosy one inside, plus a dining room with a bold colour scheme. Bedrooms are stylish and have smart bathrooms.

Rooms 20 (3 fmly) (4 GF) ⌇ **S** £55-£95; **D** £70-£110*
Facilities FTV Wi-fi ♗ Xmas **Conf** Class 30 Board 30 Thtr 40 **Parking** 20 **Notes** LB Civ Wed 50

The Green Inn

☻ ☻ ☻ RESTAURANT WITH ROOMS

☎ 013397 55701
9 Victoria Rd AB35 5QQ
e-mail: info@green-inn.com
web: www.green-inn.com
dir: In village centre

A former temperance hotel, the Green Inn enjoys a central location in the pretty village of Ballater. Bedrooms are of a high standard and attractively presented. The kitchen has a strong reputation for its excellent cuisine, which can be enjoyed in the stylish conservatory restaurant. The head chef is Chris O'Halloran, son of owners Trevor and Evelyn. Breakfast is equally enjoyable and should also not be missed. Genuine hospitality from the enthusiastic proprietors is a real feature of any stay.

Rooms 2

The Auld Kirk

☻ ☻ RESTAURANT WITH ROOMS

☎ 01339 755762 & 07918 698000
Braemar Rd AB35 5RQ
e-mail: info@theauldkirk.com
dir: From Aboyne on A93 into Ballater, establishment on right just before village centre

A Victorian Scottish Free Church building that is now a contemporary restaurant with rooms, boasting well-appointed bedrooms and bathrooms. Many original features of this kirk have been restored and incorporated in the design. The Spirit Restaurant with its high ceilings and tall windows provides a wonderful setting to enjoy the award-winning, seasonal food. There is a stylish bar with a good selection of malts and a terrace for alfresco eating when the weather permits.

Rooms 7 (1 fmly)

BALLOCH   **Map 20 NS38**
West Dumbartonshire

Cameron House on Loch Lomond

DE VERE
Hotels & Resorts

★★★★★ 83% ☻ HOTEL

☎ 01389 755565
G83 8QZ
e-mail: reservations@cameronhouse.co.uk
web: www.devere.co.uk
dir: M8 (W) junct 30 for Erskine Bridge. A82 for Crainlarich. 14m, at rdbt signed Luss, hotel on right

Enjoying an idyllic location on the banks of Loch Lomond in over 100 acres of wooded parkland, this stylish hotel offers an excellent range of leisure facilities. These include two golf courses, a world-class spa and a host of indoor and outdoor sporting activities. A choice of restaurants and bars cater for all tastes and include the Scottish-themed Cameron Grill and a fine dining operation, Martin Wishart at Loch Lomond (3 AA Rosettes). Bedrooms are stylish, well equipped and many boast wonderful loch views.

Rooms 96 (9 fmly) **Facilities** ⌸ ♨ 9 ♨ Fishing ⌇ Gym Squash Outdoor sports Motor boat on Loch Lomond Hairdresser Xmas **Conf** Class 80 Board 80 Thtr 300 **Services** Lift **Parking** 200 **Notes** ⊗ Civ Wed 200

BANCHORY   **Map 23 NO69**
Aberdeenshire

Raemoir House Hotel

★★★ 85% ☻ ☻ COUNTRY HOUSE HOTEL

☎ 01330 824884
Raemoir AB31 4ED
e-mail: hotel@raemoir.com

A beautiful country house set in 11 acres of secluded, peaceful grounds, close to Aberdeen and perfectly situated for the whisky and castle trails. The new owners have refurbished the property, and the individually styled bedrooms feature modern comforts including Wi-fi access. Cooking is a highlight with delicious meals served in the wood-panelled dining room. The hotel has a helicopter pad.

Rooms 20 (6 annexe) (2 fmly) (3 GF) ⌇ **S** £105-£115; **D** £150-£210 (incl. bkfst) **Facilities** FTV Wi-fi Putt green ⌇ Xmas New Year **Conf** Class 50 Board 40 Thtr 80 **Parking** 30 **Notes** LB No children 12yrs Civ Wed 50

Best Western Burnett Arms Hotel

Best Western

★★★ 70% SMALL HOTEL

☎ 01330 824944
25 High St AB31 5TD
e-mail: theburnett@btconnect.com
web: www.bw-burnettarms.co.uk
dir: Town centre on N side of A93

This popular hotel is located in the heart of the town centre and gives easy access to the many attractions of Royal Deeside. Public areas include a choice of eating and drinking options, with food served in the restaurant, bar and foyer lounge. Bedrooms are thoughtfully equipped and comfortably modern.

Save on hotels. Book at **theAA.com/hotel**

BAL – BEA 531 SCOTLAND

Best Western Burnett Arms Hotel

Rooms 18 (1 fmly) 🐾 **S** £69-£79; **D** £84-£98 (incl. bkfst)* **Facilities** STV FTV Wi-fi Xmas New Year **Conf** Class 50 Board 50 Thtr 100 Del from £100 to £120* **Parking** 23 **Notes** LB Civ Wed 100

See advert on this page

BATHGATE Map 21 NS96
West Lothian

Premier Inn Livingston (Bathgate)

BUDGET HOTEL

☎ 0871 527 8630
Starlaw Rd EH48 1LQ
web: www.premierinn.com
dir: M8 junct 3A. At 1st rdbt 1st exit (Bathgate). Over bridge, at 2nd rdbt take 1st exit. Hotel 200yds on left

High quality, budget accommodation ideal for both families and business travellers. Spacious, en suite

bedrooms feature tea and coffee making facilities, and Freeview TV in most hotels. Internet access and Wi-fi are available for a small fee. The adjacent family restaurant features a wide and varied menu. See also the Hotel Groups pages.

Rooms 74

BEAULY Map 23 NH54
Highland

Priory Hotel

★★★ 73% HOTEL

☎ 01463 782309
The Square IV4 7BX
e-mail: reservations@priory-hotel.com
web: www.priory-hotel.com
dir: Signed from A832, into Beauly, hotel in square on left

This popular hotel occupies a central location in the town square. Standard and executive rooms are on offer, both providing a good level of comfort and range of facilities. Food is served throughout the day in the open-plan public areas, with menus offering a first rate choice.

Rooms 37 (3 fmly) (1 GF) 🐾 **S** £65-£75; **D** £70-£95 (incl. bkfst)* **Facilities** STV FTV Wi-fi Xmas New Year **Conf** Class 40 Board 30 Thtr 40 Del from £75 to £95 **Services** Lift **Parking** 20 **Notes** LB ⊗

The Lovat Arms

★★★ 71% HOTEL

B

☎ 01463 782313
IV4 7BS
e-mail: info@lovatarms.com
web: www.lovatarms.com
dir: From The Square past Royal Bank of Scotland, hotel on right

This fine family run hotel enjoys a prominent position in this charming town which is a short drive from Inverness. The bedrooms are comfortable and well appointed. The spacious foyer has a real fire and comfortable seating, while the Strubag lounge is ideal for informal dining.

Rooms 33 (12 annexe) (4 fmly) (6 GF) 🐾 **S** £59-£67.50; **D** £80-£120 (incl. bkfst)* **Facilities** STV FTV Wi-fi ⌕ Xmas New Year **Conf** Class 26 Board 40 Thtr 80 **Parking** 25 **Notes** LB Civ Wed 60

B

BOAT OF GARTEN   Map 23 NH91
Highland

Boat Hotel

★★★ 80% ◉◉ HOTEL

☎ 01479 831258 & 831696
PH24 3BH
e-mail: info@boathotel.co.uk
dir: Exit A9 N of Aviemore onto A95, follow signs to Boat of Garten

A well established hotel situated in the heart of this pretty village. Public areas include a choice of comfortable lounges and The Osprey Bistro & Bar is inviting and relaxed, with appealing menus and a well deserved reputation for food. Individually styled bedrooms reflect the unique character of the hotel; all are comfortable and well equipped.

Rooms 34 (2 fmly) **Facilities** FTV Wi-fi Xmas New Year **Conf** Class 30 Board 25 Thtr 40 **Parking** 36 **Notes** Civ Wed 40

BOTHWELL   Map 20 NS75
South Lanarkshire

Bothwell Bridge Hotel

★★★ 79% HOTEL

☎ 01698 852246
89 Main St G71 8EU
e-mail: reception@bothwellbridge-hotel.com
web: www.bothwellbridge-hotel.com
dir: M74 junct 5 & follow signs to Uddingston, right at mini-rdbt. Hotel just past shops on left

This red-sandstone mansion house is a popular business, function and conference hotel and is conveniently placed for the motorway. Most bedrooms are spacious and all are well equipped. The conservatory is a bright and comfortable restaurant serving an interesting variety of Italian influenced dishes. The lounge bar offers a comfortable seating area that proves popular as a stop for coffee.

Rooms 90 (14 fmly) (13 GF) **S** £55-£95; **D** £65-£190 (incl. bkfst)* **Facilities** STV FTV Wi-fi ✈ HL ♫ Xmas New Year **Conf** Class 80 Board 50 Thtr 200 Del from £85 to £103* **Services** Lift **Parking** 125 **Notes** ⊗ Civ Wed 250

BRACHLA   Map 23 NH53
Highland

Loch Ness Lodge

◉◉ RESTAURANT WITH ROOMS

☎ 01456 459469
Loch Ness-Side IV3 8LA
e-mail: escape@loch-ness-lodge.com
dir: A9 from Inverness onto A82 signed Fort William, 9m, at 30mph sign. Lodge on right immediately after Clansman Hotel

This house enjoys a prominent position overlooking Loch Ness, and each of the individually designed bedrooms enjoys views of the loch. The bedrooms are of the highest standard, and are beautifully presented with a mix of traditional luxury and up-to-date technology, including Wi-fi. There is a spa with a hot tub, sauna and a therapy room offering a variety of treatments. Award-winning evening meals are served in the restaurant, and guests have a choice of attractive lounges which feature real fires in the colder months.

Rooms 7

BRORA   Map 23 NC90
Highland

Royal Marine Hotel, Restaurant & Spa

CLASSIC BRITISH HOTELS

★★★★ 77% ◉ HOTEL

☎ 01408 621252
Golf Rd KW9 6QS
e-mail: info@royalmarinebrora.com
web: www.royalmarinebrora.com
dir: Off A9 in village towards beach & golf course

A distinctive Edwardian residence sympathetically extended, the Royal Marine attracts a mixed market. Its leisure centre is popular, and the restaurant, Hunters Lounge and café bar offer three contrasting eating options. A modern bedroom wing complements the original bedrooms, which retain period style. There are also luxury apartments just a short walk away.

Rooms 21 (1 fmly) (2 GF) ✿ **Facilities** FTV Wi-fi ✈ ⊗ ✿ Putt green Fishing ⬤ Gym Steam room Sauna Xmas New Year **Conf** Class 40 Board 40 Thtr 70 Del £135 **Parking** 40 **Notes** Civ Wed 60

CALLANDER   Map 20 NN60
Stirling

INSPECTORS' CHOICE

Roman Camp Country House Hotel

★★★ ◉◉◉ COUNTRY HOUSE HOTEL

☎ 01877 330003
FK17 8BG
e-mail: mail@romancamphotel.co.uk
web: www.romancamphotel.co.uk
dir: N on A84, left at east end of High Street. 300yds to hotel

Built in the 17th century and originally used as a shooting lodge, this charming country house has a rich history; it has been in the same ownership of over two decades. Twenty acres of gardens and grounds lead down to the River Teith, and the town centre and its attractions are only a short walk away. Each bedroom is individually and elegantly designed, and offers much pampering comfort. Food is a highlight of any stay and menus are dominated by high-quality Scottish produce that is sensitively treated by the talented kitchen team. Real fires warm the atmospheric public areas and service is friendly yet professional.

Rooms 15 (4 fmly) (7 GF) **Facilities** STV FTV Wi-fi ✈ Fishing Xmas New Year **Conf** Class 60 Board 30 Thtr 120 **Parking** 80 **Notes** Civ Wed 150

Save on hotels. Book at **theAA.com/hotel**

BOA – CON 533 | SCOTLAND

Callander Meadows

◉ RESTAURANT WITH ROOMS

☎ 01877 330181
24 Main St FK17 8BB
e-mail: mail@callandermeadows.co.uk
web: www.callandermeadows.co.uk
dir: M9 junct 10, A84 to Callander, house on main
street just past A81 junct

Located on the high street in Callander, this family-
run business offers comfortable accommodation and
a restaurant that has quickly become very popular
with the locals. The bedrooms have been appointed to
a high standard. Private parking is available to the
rear.

Rooms 3

CARNOUSTIE Map 21 NO53
Angus

Carnoustie Golf Hotel & Spa

OXFORD
HOTELS & INNS

★★★★ 73% ◉ HOTEL

☎ 0844 414 6520
The Links DD7 7JE
e-mail: reservations.carnoustie@ohiml.com
web: www.oxfordhotelsandinns.com
dir: Adjacent to Carnoustie Golf Links

This fine hotel enjoys an enviable location and is
adjacent to the 1st and 18th green of the famous
Championship Course of Carnoustie. All bedrooms are
spacious and attractively presented; most overlook
the magnificent course and enjoy breathtaking
coastal views. Fine dining can be enjoyed in the
restaurant with more informal meals served in the
comfortable bar.

Rooms 85 (11 fmly) **Facilities** Spa STV FTV Wi-fi ↕ ③
Putt green Gym Xmas New Year **Conf** Class 200
Board 100 Thtr 350 **Services** Lift Air con **Parking** 100
Notes ⊗ Civ Wed 325

CLYDEBANK Map 20 NS47
West Dumbartonshire

Beardmore Hotel

★★★★ 77% ◉ HOTEL

☎ 0141 951 6000
Beardmore St G81 4SA
e-mail: info@beardmore.scot.nhs.uk
web: www.thebeardmore.com
dir: M8 junct 19, follow signs for Clydeside
Expressway to Glasgow road, then A814 (Dumbarton
road), then follow Clydebank Business Park signs.
Hotel on left

Attracting much business and conference custom,
this stylish modern hotel lies beside the River Clyde
and shares an impressive site with a hospital
(although the latter does not intrude). Spacious and
imposing public areas include the stylish Arcoona
Restaurant providing innovative contemporary
Scottish cooking. The lounge bar offers a more
extensive choice of lighter dishes. The leisure
facilities include a 15-metre swimming pool, sauna
and steam room.

Rooms 166 **Facilities** STV Wi-fi ③ supervised Gym
Sauna Steam room Whirlpool Xmas New Year
Conf Class 84 Board 27 Thtr 240 **Services** Lift Air con
Parking 300 **Notes** ⊗ Civ Wed 170

COMRIE Map 21 NN72
Perth & Kinross

Royal Hotel

★★★ 83% ◉ HOTEL

☎ 01764 679200
Melville Square PH6 2DN
e-mail: reception@royalhotel.co.uk
web: www.royalhotel.co.uk
dir: Exit A9 on A822 to Crieff, then B827 to Comrie.
Hotel in main square on A85

The traditional façade gives little indication of the
style and elegance to be found inside this long-
established hotel located in the village centre. Public
areas include a bar and library, a bright modern
restaurant and a conservatory-style brasserie. The
bedrooms are tastefully appointed and furnished with
smart reproduction antiques.

Rooms 13 (2 annexe) **S** fr £85; **D** fr £140 (incl. bkfst)*
Facilities STV Wi-fi Fishing Shooting arranged New
Year **Conf** Class 10 Board 20 Thtr 20 Del from £135*
Parking 22 **Notes** LB Closed 25-26 Dec

CONNEL Map 20 NM93
Argyll & Bute

Falls of Lora Hotel

THE INDEPENDENTS
HOTEL ASSOCIATION

★★★ 77% HOTEL

C

☎ 01631 710483
PA37 1PB
e-mail: enquiries@fallsoflora.com
web: www.fallsoflora.com
dir: From Glasgow take A82, A85. Hotel 0.5m past
Connel sign (5m before Oban)

Personally run and welcoming, this long-established
and thriving holiday hotel enjoys inspiring views over
Loch Etive. The spacious ground floor takes in a
comfortable, traditional lounge and a cocktail bar
with over a hundred whiskies and an open log fire.
Guests can eat in the popular, informal bistro, which
is open all day. Bedrooms come in a variety of styles,
ranging from the cosy standard rooms to high quality
luxury rooms.

Rooms 30 (4 fmly) (4 GF) (30 smoking) ⌇
S £49.50-£69.50; **D** £59-£159 (incl. bkfst)*
Facilities FTV Wi-fi Child facilities **Conf** Class 20
Board 15 Thtr 45 **Parking** 40 **Notes** LB Closed mid
Dec & Jan

See advert on page 565

CRAIGELLACHIE — Map 23 NJ24
Moray

Craigellachie Hotel

★★★★ 72% ◉ HOTEL

OXFORD HOTELS & INNS

☎ 01340 881204
AB38 9SR
e-mail: reservations.craigellachie@ohiml.com
web: www.oxfordhotelsandinns.com
dir: On A95 between Aberdeen & Inverness

This impressive and popular hotel is located in the heart of Speyside, so it is no surprise that malt whisky takes centre stage in the Quaich Bar with over 700 varieties featured. Bedrooms come in various sizes but all are tastefully decorated and bathrooms are of a high specification. Creative dinners showcase local ingredients in the traditionally styled dining room.

Rooms 26 (1 fmly) (6 GF) **Facilities** Wi-fi Xmas New Year **Conf** Class 35 Board 30 Thtr 60 **Parking** 30 **Notes** Civ Wed 60

CRAIL — Map 21 NO60
Fife

Balcomie Links Hotel

★★ 75% SMALL HOTEL

☎ 01333 450237
Balcomie Rd KY10 3TN
e-mail: mikekadir@balcomie.co.uk
web: www.balcomie.co.uk
dir: A917 into Crail to village shops, right into Market Gate, becomes Balcomie Rd, hotel on left

Especially popular with visiting golfers, this family-run hotel on the east side of the village represents good value for money and has a relaxing atmosphere. Bedrooms come in a variety of sizes and styles and offer all the expected amenities. Food is served from midday in the attractive lounge bar, and also in the bright cheerful dining room in the evening.

Rooms 14 (2 fmly) **S** £55-£85; **D** £75-£99 (incl. bkfst)* **Facilities** FTV Wi-fi Games room Xmas New Year **Parking** 20 **Notes** LB ⊗ Closed Jan-Feb Civ Wed 45

CRIANLARICH — Map 20 NN32
Stirling

The Crianlarich Hotel

★★★ 77% ◉ HOTEL

Best Western

☎ 01838 300272
FK20 8RW
e-mail: info@crianlarich-hotel.co.uk
web: www.crianlarich-hotel.co.uk
dir: At junct of A85 & A82

Standing at what has been an important transport junction for many years, this hotel continues to cater to travellers' needs. The ground-floor areas are impressive, and the pleasant bedrooms are smartly appointed and offer all the usual amenities. Friendly relaxed service and high quality food makes this an enjoyable place to stay especially as it is close to Loch Lomond and the Trossachs National Park.

Rooms 36 (5 fmly) ⚲ **S** £38.50-£105; **D** £54.50-£115 (incl. bkfst) **Facilities** FTV Wi-fi ⌂ ♫ Xmas New Year **Conf** Class 60 Board 40 Thtr 100 Del from £105 to £135 **Services** Lift **Parking** 30 **Notes** LB Civ Wed 100

CULLEN — Map 23 NJ56
Moray

Cullen Bay Hotel

★★★ 75% SMALL HOTEL

☎ 01542 840432
A98 AB56 4XA
e-mail: stay@cullenbayhotel.com
web: www.cullenbayhotel.com
dir: On A98, 1m west of Cullen

This family-run hotel sits on the hillside west of the town and has lovely views of the golf course, beach and Moray Firth. The spacious restaurant, which offers a selection of fine dishes, makes the most of the view, as do many of the bedrooms. There is a comfortable modern bar, a quiet lounge and a second dining room where breakfasts are served.

Rooms 14 (3 fmly) **Facilities** FTV Wi-fi New Year **Conf** Class 80 Board 80 Thtr 200 **Parking** 100 **Notes** ⊗ Civ Wed 200

CUMBERNAULD — Map 21 NS77
North Lanarkshire

The Westerwood Hotel & Golf Resort

QHOTELS

★★★★ 81% ◉ HOTEL

☎ 01236 457171
1 St Andrews Dr, Westerwood G68 0EW
e-mail: westerwood@qhotels.co.uk
web: www.qhotels.co.uk

This stylish, contemporary hotel enjoys an elevated position within 400 acres at the foot of the Campsie Hills. Accommodation is provided in spacious, bright bedrooms, many with super bathrooms, and day rooms include sumptuous lounges and an airy restaurant; extensive golf, fitness and conference facilities are available.

Rooms 148 (15 fmly) (49 GF) **Facilities** Spa STV Wi-fi ⌂ ⓣ ♨ 18 ♣ Putt green Gym Beauty salon Relaxation room Sauna Steam room Xmas New Year **Conf** Class 120 Board 60 Thtr 400 **Services** Lift **Parking** 250 **Notes** Civ Wed 350

Premier Inn Glasgow (Cumbernauld)

Premier Inn

BUDGET HOTEL

☎ 0871 527 8424
4 South Muirhead Rd G67 1AX
web: www.premierinn.com
dir: From A80, A8011 follow Cumbernauld & town centre signs. Hotel opposite Asda & McDonalds

High quality, budget accommodation ideal for both families and business travellers. Spacious, en suite bedrooms feature tea and coffee making facilities, and Freeview TV in most hotels. Internet access and Wi-fi are available for a small fee. The adjacent family restaurant features a wide and varied menu. See also the Hotel Groups pages.

Rooms 37

Tulloch Castle Hotel

★★★★ 74% HOTEL   OXFORD
HOTELS & INNS

☎ 01349 861325
Tulloch Castle Dr IV15 9ND
e-mail: reservations.tulloch@ohiml.com
web: www.oxfordhotelsandinns.com
dir: A9 N, Tore rdbt 2nd left signed Dingwall. On to
A862 at 3rd lights through Dingwall, left, hotel signed

Overlooking the town of Dingwall this 12th-century
castle is still the gathering place of the Clan
Davidson and boasts its own ghost in the shape of
the Green Lady. The friendly team are very helpful and
love to tell you about the history of the castle; the
ghost tour after dinner is a must. The hotel has a self
contained suite and a number of bedrooms with four-
posters.

Rooms 20 (2 fmly) ☏ **Facilities** FTV Wi-fi Xmas New
Year **Conf** Class 70 Board 70 Thtr 120 **Parking** 50
Notes Civ Wed 110

Dornoch Castle Hotel

★★★ 75% ⊕ HOTEL

☎ 01862 810216
Castle St IV25 3SD
e-mail: enquiries@dornochcastlehotel.com
web: www.dornochcastlehotel.com
dir: 2m N of Dornoch Bridge on A9, turn right to
Dornoch. Hotel in village centre

Situated opposite the cathedral, this fully restored
ancient castle has become a popular wedding venue.
Within the original castle are some splendid themed
bedrooms, and elsewhere the more modern bedrooms
have all of the expected facilities. There is a
character bar and a delightful conservatory
restaurant overlooking the garden.

Rooms 23 (3 fmly) (4 GF) ☏ **S** £65-£250; **D** £96-£250
(incl. bkfst)* **Facilities** FTV Wi-fi New Year
Conf Class 40 Board 30 Thtr 60 **Parking** 16 **Notes** LB
⊗ Closed 24-26 Dec & 2nd wk Jan

Best Western Buchanan Arms Hotel & Spa

★★★ 79% HOTEL

☎ 01360 660588
23 Main St G63 0BQ
e-mail: info@buchananarms.co.uk

This former coaching inn is located in the quiet
conservation village of Drymen, and provides a
perfect base for touring this area, with Loch Lomond
just a few miles away. There are well-appointed
bedrooms and welcoming public areas. Good leisure
facilities are an added benefit.

Rooms 52 (9 fmly) (3 GF) **S** £40-£160; **D** £50-£240
(incl. bkfst) **Facilities** Spa FTV Wi-fi ↕ ⟳ supervised
Gym Squash Xmas New Year **Conf** Class 140
Board 60 Thtr 250 Del from £90 to £155 **Parking** 120
Notes LB ⊗ Civ Wed 160

Winnock Hotel

★★★ 75% HOTEL

☎ 01360 660245
The Square G63 0BL
e-mail: info@winnockhotel.com
web: www.winnockhotel.com
dir: From S: M74 onto M8 junct 16b through Glasgow.
Follow A809 to Aberfoyle

Occupying a prominent position overlooking the
village green, this popular hotel offers well-equipped
bedrooms of various sizes and styles. The public
rooms include a bar, a lounge and an attractive
formal dining room that serves dishes of good, locally
sourced food.

Rooms 73 (18 fmly) (19 GF) **Facilities** FTV Wi-fi ↕
Xmas New Year **Conf** Class 60 Board 70 Thtr 140
Parking 60 **Notes** ⊗ Civ Wed 100

Premier Inn Dumbarton

BUDGET HOTEL   Premier Inn

☎ 0871 527 9274
Lomondgate Dr G82 2QU
web: www.premierinn.com
dir: From Glasgow follow A82 towards Crainlarich,
right at Lomondgate rdbt onto A813, hotel on right.
From N: A82 towards Glasgow, left at Lomondgate
rdbt onto A813, hotel on right

High quality, budget accommodation ideal for both
families and business travellers. Spacious, en suite
bedrooms feature tea and coffee making facilities,

and Freeview TV in most hotels. Internet access and
Wi-fi are available for a small fee. The adjacent
family restaurant features a wide and varied menu.
See also the Hotel Groups pages.

Rooms 60

See also Kirkbean

Cairndale Hotel & Leisure Club

★★★ 80% HOTEL

☎ 01387 254111
English St DG1 2DF
e-mail: sales@cairndalehotel.co.uk
web: www.cairndalehotel.co.uk
dir: From S on M6 take A75 to Dumfries, left at 1st
rdbt, cross rail bridge to lights, hotel 1st building on
left

Within walking distance of the town centre, this hotel
provides a wide range of amenities, including leisure
facilities and an impressive conference and
entertainment centre. Bedrooms range from stylish
suites to cosy singles. There's a choice of eating
options in the evening. The Reivers Restaurant is
smartly modern with food to match.

Rooms 91 (22 fmly) (5 GF) **S** £59-£99; **D** £79-£139*
Facilities Wi-fi ⟳ supervised Gym Steam room Sauna
♫ Xmas New Year **Conf** Class 150 Board 50 Thtr 300
Del from £79 to £119 **Services** Lift **Parking** 100
Notes Civ Wed 200

DUMFRIES *continued*

Best Western Station Hotel

★★★ 79% HOTEL

☎ 01387 254316
49 Lovers Walk DG1 1LT
e-mail: info@stationhotel.co.uk
web: www.stationhoteldumfries.co.uk
dir: A75, follow signs to town centre, hotel opposite railway station

This friendly hotel built in the Victorian era offers stylish, well-equipped bedrooms that feature satellite TVs and free Wi-fi; three rooms have four-poster beds and spa baths. The Courtyard restaurant creates an informal atmosphere where, each evening, guests can enjoy a popular range of dishes; in addition good-value meals are served at lunchtime in either the lounge bar or on the patio in warmer weather. There is a delightful small garden to relax in.

Rooms 32 ☝ **S** £59-£79; **D** £87-£107 (incl. bkfst)*
Facilities Wi-fi Use of local gym **Conf** Class 35
Board 30 Thtr 80 Del from £100 to £135 **Services** Lift
Parking 34 **Notes** LB Closed 26 Dec & 2 Jan
Civ Wed 50

Premier Inn Dumfries

BUDGET HOTEL

☎ 0871 527 8316
Annan Rd, Collin DG1 3JX
web: www.premierinn.com
dir: At rdbt junct of Euroroute bypass (A75) & A780

High quality, budget accommodation ideal for both families and business travellers. Spacious, en suite bedrooms feature tea and coffee making facilities, and Freeview TV in most hotels. Internet access and Wi-fi are available for a small fee. The adjacent family restaurant features a wide and varied menu. See also the Hotel Groups pages.

Rooms 40

DUNBAR — East Lothian — Map 21 NT67

Rossborough Hotel

★★★ 70% HOTEL

☎ 01368 862356
Queens Rd EH42 1LG
e-mail: info@therossborough.com
web: www.therossborough.com
dir: From A1 onto A1087 towards Dunbar, or from rdbt on A1 into Spott Rd. Hotel on corner of Spott Rd & A1087 (Queens Rd)

This hotel was built in 1902 and opened as a temperance establishment. Many original features have been retained, and bedrooms are comfortable with many useful extras. Wi-fi is available throughout the hotel. A well-balanced menu is served in both bar and restaurant.

Rooms 19 (1 GF) **S** £45-£58; **D** £70-£110 (incl. bkfst)
Facilities FTV Wi-fi **Conf** Class 50 Board 50 Thtr 120
Del £80 **Parking** 24 **Notes** LB Closed 25-26 Dec
Civ Wed 120

DUNDEE — City of Dundee — Map 21 NO43

Apex City Quay Hotel & Spa

★★★★ 77% HOTEL

☎ 0845 365 0000 & 01382 202404
1 West Victoria Dock Rd DD1 3JP
e-mail: dundee.reservations@apexhotels.co.uk
web: www.apexhotels.co.uk
dir: A85/Riverside Drive to Discovery Quay. Exit rdbt for City Quay

This stylish, purpose-built hotel occupies an enviable position at the heart of Dundee's regenerated quayside. Bedrooms, including a number of smart suites, feature the very latest in design. Warm hospitality and professional service are an integral part of the hotel's appeal. Public areas are open-plan with panoramic windows and contemporary dining options. The luxurious Yu Spa completes the package.

Rooms 151 (17 fmly) ☝ **Facilities** Spa FTV Wi-fi ⌂ HL
⌂ Gym Steam room Sauna Xmas New Year
Conf Class 180 Board 120 Thtr 375 **Services** Lift
Parking 150 **Notes** ⊗ Civ Wed 300

The Landmark Hotel

★★★★ 76% ◉ HOTEL

☎ 01382 641122
Kingsway West DD2 5JT
e-mail: sales@thelandmarkdundee.co.uk
web: www.thelandmarkdundee.co.uk
dir: From A90 (Kingsway) at rdbt junct with A85, follow hotel signs

Well located off Kingsway West with ample parking, this hotel offers contemporary bedrooms that are equipped with many thoughtful extras. The restaurant overlooks the gardens which are a feature at this hotel. A good leisure club includes a gym, steam room and sauna. The hotel is a popular wedding venue.

Rooms 95 (11 fmly) (45 GF) ☝ **S** £59-£89;
D £69-£129* **Facilities** STV FTV Wi-fi ⌂ supervised
Gym Sauna Steam room Xmas New Year
Conf Class 50 Board 45 Thtr 100 Del from £119 to
£200* **Parking** 140 **Notes** LB ⊗ Civ Wed 100

Holiday Inn Express Dundee

BUDGET HOTEL

☎ 01382 314330
Dock St DD1 3DR
e-mail: dm1@hiexpressdundee.com
dir: Telephone for directions

A modern hotel ideal for families and business travellers. Fresh and uncomplicated, the spacious rooms include Sky TV, power shower and tea and coffee-making facilities. Continental buffet breakfast is included in the room rate; other meals may be taken at the nearby family pub or restaurant. See also the Hotel Groups pages.

Rooms 95 (49 fmly) **Conf** Class 25 Board 25 Thtr 30

Premier Inn Dundee Centre

BUDGET HOTEL

☎ 0871 527 8320
Discovery Quay, Riverside Dr DD1 4XA
web: www.premierinn.com
dir: Follow signs for Discovery Quay, hotel on waterfront

High quality, budget accommodation ideal for both families and business travellers. Spacious, en suite bedrooms feature tea and coffee making facilities, and Freeview TV in most hotels. Internet access and Wi-fi are available for a small fee. The adjacent family restaurant features a wide and varied menu. See also the Hotel Groups pages.

Rooms 40

Save on hotels. Book at **theAA.com/hotel**

DUM – DUN 537 SCOTLAND

D

Premier Inn Dundee East

BUDGET HOTEL

☎ 0871 527 8322

115-117 Lawers Dr, Panmurefield Village, Broughty Ferry DD5 3UP

web: www.premierinn.com

dir: From N: A92 (Dundee & Arbroath). Hotel 1.5m after Sainsbury's. From S: A90. At end of dual carriageway follow Dundee to Arbroath signs

Rooms 60

Premier Inn Dundee (Monifieth)

BUDGET HOTEL

☎ 0871 527 8318

Ethiebeaton Park, Arbroath Rd, Monifieth DD5 4HB

web: www.premierinn.com

dir: From A90 (Kingsway Rd) follow Carnoustie/Arbroath (A92) signs

Rooms 40

Premier Inn Dundee North

BUDGET HOTEL

☎ 0871 527 8324

Camperdown Leisure Park, Dayton Dr, Kingsway DD2 3SQ

web: www.premierinn.com

dir: 2m N of city centre on A90 at junct with A923, adjacent to cinema. At entrance to Camperdown Country Park

Rooms 78

Premier Inn Dundee West

BUDGET HOTEL

☎ 0871 527 8326

Kingsway West DD2 5JU

web: www.premierinn.com

dir: On A90 towards Aberdeen adjacent to Technology Park rdbt

Rooms 64

DUNFERMLINE Map 21 NT08
Fife

Pitbauchlie House Hotel

★★★ 79% HOTEL

☎ 01383 722282

Aberdour Rd KY11 4PB

e-mail: info@pitbauchlie.com

web: www.pitbauchlie.com

dir: M90 junct 2, A823, then B916. Hotel 0.5m on right

Situated in three acres of wooded grounds this hotel is just a mile south of the town and has a striking modern interior. The bedrooms are well equipped, and the deluxe rooms have 32-inch LCD satellite TVs and CD micro systems; there is one bedroom designed for less able guests. The eating options include Harvey's Conservatory bistro and Restaurant 47 where Scottish and French influenced cuisine is offered.

Rooms 50 (3 fmly) (19 GF) **Facilities** STV FTV Wi-fi Gym **Conf** Class 80 Board 60 Thtr 150 **Parking** 80 **Notes** Civ Wed 150

King Malcolm Hotel

★★★ 73% HOTEL

☎ 01383 722611

Queensferry Rd KY11 8DS

e-mail: info@kingmalcolm-hotel-dunfermline.com

web: www.peelhotels.co.uk

dir: On A823, S of town

Located to the south of the city, this purpose-built hotel remains popular with business clientele and is convenient for access to both Edinburgh and Fife. Public rooms include a smart foyer lounge and a conservatory bar, as well as a restaurant. Bedrooms, although not large, are well laid out and well equipped.

Rooms 48 (2 fmly) (24 GF) **Facilities** Wi-fi ♬ Xmas New Year **Conf** Class 60 Board 50 Thtr 150 **Parking** 60 **Notes** Civ Wed 120

Holiday Inn Express Dunfermline

BUDGET HOTEL

☎ 01383 748220

Lauder College, Halbeath KY11 8DY

e-mail: info@hiexpressdunfermline.co.uk

web: www.hiexpress.com/dunfermline

dir: M9 junct 7 signed A994/A907, 3rd exit Lynebank rdbt or M90 junct 3, 2nd exit for A907, next rdbt 3rd exit, next rdbt 1st exit

A modern hotel ideal for families and business travellers. Fresh and uncomplicated, the spacious rooms include Sky TV, power shower and tea and coffee-making facilities. Continental buffet breakfast is included in the room rate; other meals may be taken at the nearby family pub or restaurant. See also the Hotel Groups pages.

Rooms 82 (34 fmly) (12 GF) ☎ **Conf** Class 8 Board 16 Thtr 25

Premier Inn Dunfermline

BUDGET HOTEL

☎ 0871 527 8328

4-12 Whimbrel Place, Fife Leisure Park KY11 8EX

web: www.premierinn.com

dir: M90 junct 3 (Forth Road Bridge exit) 1st left at lights signed Duloch Park. 1st left into Fife Leisure Park

High quality, budget accommodation ideal for both families and business travellers. Spacious, en suite bedrooms feature tea and coffee making facilities, and Freeview TV in most hotels. Internet access and Wi-fi are available for a small fee. The adjacent family restaurant features a wide and varied menu. See also the Hotel Groups pages.

Rooms 40

DUNOON
Argyll & Bute — Map 20 NS17

Selborne Hotel
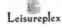

★★ 74% HOTEL

☎ 01369 702761
Clyde St, West Bay PA23 7HU
e-mail: selborne.dunoon@alfatravel.co.uk
web: www.leisureplex.co.uk
dir: From Caledonian MacBrayne pier. Past castle, left into Jane St, right into Clyde St

This holiday hotel is situated overlooking the West Bay and provides unrestricted views of the Clyde Estuary towards the Isles of Cumbrae. Tour groups are especially well catered for in this good-value establishment, which offers entertainment most nights. Bedrooms are comfortable and many have sea views.

Rooms 98 (6 fmly) (14 GF) **Facilities** FTV Pool table Table tennis ♫ Xmas New Year **Services** Lift **Parking** 30 **Notes** ⊗ Closed Dec-Feb (ex Xmas) RS Nov & Mar

EAST KILBRIDE
South Lanarkshire — Map 20 NS65

Macdonald Crutherland House

★★★★ 74% ◉◉ HOTEL

☎ 0844 879 9039
Strathaven Rd G75 0QZ
e-mail: crutherland@macdonald-hotels.co.uk
web: www.macdonaldhotels.co.uk/crutherland
dir: Follow A726 signed Strathaven, straight over Torrance rdbt, hotel on left after 250yds

This mansion is set in 37 acres of landscaped grounds two miles from the town centre. Behind its Georgian façade is a very relaxing hotel with elegant public areas plus extensive banqueting and leisure facilities. The bedrooms are spacious and comfortable. Staff provide good levels of attention and enjoyable meals are served in the restaurant.

Rooms 75 (16 fmly) (16 GF) **S** £65-£185; **Facilities** Spa STV Wi-fi ☉ Gym Sauna Steam room Xmas New Year **Conf** Class 100 Board 50 Thtr 500 Del from £130 to £225* **Services** Lift **Parking** 200 **Notes** LB ⊗ Civ Wed 300

Premier Inn Glasgow East Kilbride

BUDGET HOTEL

☎ 0871 527 8446
5 Lee's Burn Court, Nerston G74 3XB
web: www.premierinn.com
dir: M74 junct 5, follow East Kilbride/A725 signs. Into right lane, follow Glasgow/A749 signs. At lights left onto A749 signed East Kilbride Town Centre (A725). Take slip road to Lee's Burn Court

High quality, budget accommodation ideal for both families and business travellers. Spacious, en suite bedrooms feature tea and coffee making facilities, and Freeview TV in most hotels. Internet access and Wi-fi are available for a small fee. The adjacent family restaurant features a wide and varied menu. See also the Hotel Groups pages.

Rooms 44

Premier Inn Glasgow East Kilbride Central

BUDGET HOTEL

☎ 0871 527 8450
Brunel Way, The Murray G75 0LD
web: www.premierinn.com
dir: M74 junct 5, follow East Kilbride A725 signs, then Paisley A726 signs, left at Murray Rdbt, left into Brunel Way

Rooms 40

Premier Inn Glasgow East Kilbride (Peel Park)

BUDGET HOTEL

☎ 0871 527 8448
Eaglesham Rd G75 8LW
web: www.premierinn.com
dir: 8m from M74 junct 5 on A726 at rdbt of B764

Rooms 42

EDDLESTON
Scottish Borders — Map 21 NT24

The Horseshoe Inn

◉◉ RESTAURANT WITH ROOMS

☎ 01721 730225
EH45 8QP
e-mail: reservations@horseshoeinn.co.uk
web: www.horseshoeinn.co.uk
dir: A703, 5m N of Peebles

This inn is five miles north of Peebles and only 18 miles south of Edinburgh. Originally a blacksmith's shop, it has a very good reputation for its delightful atmosphere and excellent cuisine. The bedrooms are luxuriously appointed and individually designed.

Rooms 8 (1 fmly)

EDINBURGH
City of Edinburgh — Map 21 NT27

INSPECTORS' CHOICE

The Balmoral

★★★★★ ◉◉◉ TOWN HOUSE HOTEL

☎ 0131 556 2414
1 Princes St EH2 2EQ
e-mail: reservations.balmoral@roccofortecollection.com
web: www.roccofortecollection.com
dir: Follow city centre signs. Hotel at E end of Princes St, adjacent to Waverley Station

This elegant hotel enjoys a prestigious address at the top of Princes Street, with fine views over the city and the castle. Bedrooms and suites are stylishly furnished and decorated, all boasting a thoughtful range of extras and impressive marble bathrooms. Hotel amenities include a Roman-style health spa, extensive function facilities, a choice of bars and two very different dining options - Number One offers inspired fine dining whilst Hadrians is a bustling, informal brasserie.

Rooms 188 (22 fmly) (15 smoking) **Facilities** Spa STV Wi-fi ☉ Gym ♫ Xmas New Year **Conf** Class 180 Board 60 Thtr 350 **Services** Lift Air con **Parking** 100 **Notes** ⊗ Civ Wed 120

E

INSPECTORS' CHOICE

Prestonfield

★★★★★ ◎◎ TOWN HOUSE HOTEL

☎ 0131 225 7800
Priestfield Rd EH16 5UT
e-mail: reservations@prestonfield.com
web: www.prestonfield.com
dir: A7 towards Cameron Toll. 200mtrs beyond Royal Commonwealth Pool, into Priestfield Rd

This centuries-old landmark has been lovingly restored and enhanced to provide deeply comfortable and dramatically furnished bedrooms. The building demands to be explored: from the tapestry lounge and the whisky room to the restaurant, where the walls are adorned with pictures of former owners. Facilities and services are up-to-the-minute, and carefully prepared meals are served in the award-winning Rhubarb restaurant.

Rooms 23 (6 GF) ↟ **S** £295; **D** £295 (incl. bkfst)*
Facilities STV FTV Wi-fi ↘ ⚘ 18 Putt green ➴ Free bike hire Xmas New Year **Conf** Class 500 Board 40 Thtr 700 **Services** Lift **Parking** 250 **Notes** LB Civ Wed 350

Hotel Missoni Edinburgh

★★★★★ 85% ◎◎ HOTEL

☎ 0131 220 6666
1 George IV Bridge EH1 1AD
e-mail: info.edinburgh@hotelmissoni.com
dir: At corner of Royal Mile & George IV Bridge

Located on the corner of the George IV Bridge and the Royal Mile in the heart of the old town, this hotel's design is strikingly different. Bold use of black and white and vivid colours together with strong patterns creates a stunning impression. Stylish bedrooms, some with great city views, have iPod/AV hook-up, Wi-fi, coffee machines, and bathrooms with walk-in showers as standard. The buzzing cocktail bar and Cucina Missoni, for modern Italian cuisine, attract locals and residents alike.

Rooms 136 **Facilities** Spa STV FTV Wi-fi ↘ Gym Xmas New Year **Conf** Class 24 Board 24 Thtr 63 **Services** Lift Air con **Parking** 13

The Howard

★★★★★ 83% ◎ TOWN HOUSE HOTEL

☎ 0131 537 3500
34 Great King St EH3 6QH
e-mail: reserve@thehoward.com
web: www.thehoward.com
dir: E on Queen St, 2nd left, Dundas St. Through 3 lights, right, hotel on left

Quietly elegant and splendidly luxurious, The Howard provides an intimate and high quality experience for the discerning traveller. It comprises three linked Georgian houses and is situated just a short walk from Princes Street. The sumptuous bedrooms and spacious suites, in a variety of styles, have well-equipped bathrooms and a host of thoughtful touches. Ornate chandeliers and lavish drapes adorn the drawing room, while the Atholl Dining Room contains unique hand-painted murals dating from the 19th century.

Rooms 18 (3 fmly) (2 GF) ↟ **S** £100-£185; **D** £195-£300* **Facilities** STV FTV Wi-fi ↘ HL Xmas New Year **Conf** Class 28 Board 28 Thtr 28 Del from £150 to £580* **Services** Lift **Parking** 12 **Notes** ⊗ Civ Wed 28

The Scotsman

★★★★★ 83% ◎ TOWN HOUSE HOTEL

☎ 0131 556 5565
20 North Bridge EH1 1TR
e-mail:
reservations@thescotsmanhotelgroup.co.uk
web: www.thescotsmanhotel.co.uk
dir: A8 to city centre, left onto Charlotte St. Right into Queen St, right at rdbt onto Leith St. Straight on, left onto North Bridge, hotel on right

Formerly the headquarters of The Scotsman newspaper this is a stunning hotel conversion. The classical elegance of the public areas, complete with a marble staircase, blends seamlessly with the contemporary bedrooms and their state-of-the-art technology. The superbly equipped leisure club includes a stainless steel swimming pool and large gym. Dining arrangements can be made in the popular North Bridge Brasserie where afternoon tea is also served.

Rooms 69 (4 GF) **Facilities** Spa STV Wi-fi ↘ ⊙ supervised Gym Beauty treatments Xmas New Year **Conf** Class 50 Board 40 Thtr 100 **Services** Lift **Notes** ⊗ Civ Wed 70

The Sheraton Grand Hotel & Spa

★★★★★ 78% HOTEL

☎ 0131 229 9131
1 Festival Square EH3 9SR
e-mail: grandedinburgh@sheraton.com
dir: Follow City Centre signs (A8). Through Shandwick Place, right at lights into Lothian Rd. Right at next lights. Hotel on left at next lights

This modern hotel boasts one of the best spas in Scotland - the external top floor hydro pool is definitely worth a look whilst the thermal suite provides a unique venue for serious relaxation. The spacious bedrooms are available in a variety of styles, and the suites prove very popular. There is a wide range of eating options including Santini's, which has a loyal local following, and One Spa Café for light meals and snacks.

Rooms 269 ↟ **D** £160-£315 (incl. bkfst)*
Facilities Spa STV FTV Wi-fi ↘ ⊙ ⚘ Gym Indoor/outdoor hydropool Kinesis studio Thermal suite Fitness studio ♬ Xmas New Year **Conf** Class 350 Board 120 Thtr 500 Del from £215 to £344* **Services** Lift Air con **Parking** 122 **Notes** LB ⊗ Civ Wed 485

E

EDINBURGH *continued*

Norton House Hotel & Spa

★★★★ ◉◉◉ HOTEL

☎ 0131 333 1275
Ingliston EH28 8LX
e-mail: nortonhouse@handpicked.co.uk
web: www.handpickedhotel.co.uk/nortonhouse
dir: Off A8, 5m W of city centre

This extended Victorian mansion, set in 55 acres of parkland, is peacefully situated just outside the city and is convenient for the airport. The original building dates from 1840, and it was bought nearly 40 years later by John Usher of the Scottish brewing family. Today both the contemporary bedrooms and the very spacious, traditional ones have an impressive range of accessories including large flat-screen satellite TVs, DVD/CD players and free high speed internet access; executive rooms have more facilities, of course, including MP3 connection and 'tilevision' TVs at the end of the baths. Public areas take in a choice of lounges as well as dining options, with a popular brasserie and Ushers Restaurant, the intimate award-winning restaurant. There is a health club, and a spa which offers a long list of treatments. Hand Picked Hotels – AA Hotel Group of the Year 2012-13.

Rooms 83 (10 fmly) (20 GF) **S** £86-£675;
D £96-£685 (incl. bkfst)* **Facilities** Spa STV Wi-fi
◉ Gym Archery Laser Clay shooting Quad biking
Xmas New Year **Conf** Class 100 Board 60 Thtr 300
Del from £134 to £210 **Services** Lift **Parking** 200
Notes LB ⊗ Civ Wed 140

Marriott Dalmahoy Hotel & Country Club

★★★★ 81% ◉ HOTEL

☎ 0131 333 1845
Kirknewton EH27 8EB
e-mail: mhrs.edigs.frontdesk@marriotthotels.com
web: www.marriottdalmahoy.co.uk
dir: A720 (Edinburgh City Bypass) onto A71 towards Livingston, hotel on left in 2m

The rolling Pentland Hills and beautifully kept parkland provide a stunning setting for this imposing Georgian mansion. With two championship golf courses and a health and beauty club, there is plenty here to occupy guests. Bedrooms are spacious and most have fine views, while public rooms offer a choice of formal and informal drinking and dining options.

Rooms 215 (172 annexe) (59 fmly) (6 smoking) ☛
S £130-£170; **D** £130-£170 (incl. bkfst)*
Facilities Spa STV Wi-fi ◉ HL ◉ ♨ 36 ⚑ Putt green
Gym Health & beauty treatments Steam room Dance studio Driving range Golf lessons Xmas New Year
Conf Class 200 Board 120 Thtr 300 Del £180
Services Lift Air con **Parking** 350 **Notes** LB ⊗
Civ Wed 250

Hotel du Vin Edinburgh

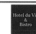

★★★★ 80% ◉
TOWN HOUSE HOTEL

☎ 0131 247 4900
11 Bristo Place EH1 1EZ
dir: M8 junct 1, A720 (signed Kilmarnock/W Calder/Edinburgh W). Right at fork, follow A720 signs, merge onto A720. Take exit signed A703. At rdbt take A702/Biggar Rd. 3.5m. Right into Lauriston Pl which becomes Forrest Rd. Right at Bedlam Theatre. Hotel on right

This hotel offers very stylish and comfortable accommodation; all bedrooms display the Hotel du Vin trademark facilities - air conditioning, free Wi-fi, plasma TVs, monsoon showers and Egyptian cotton linen to name but a few. Public areas include a whisky snug, a mezzanine bar that overlooks the brasserie where modern Scottish cuisine is served. For the wine connoisseur there's La Roche tasting room where wines from around the world can be appreciated.

Rooms 47 **Facilities** STV Wi-fi **Services** Lift Air con

Apex International Hotel

★★★★ 79% ◉◉ HOTEL

☎ 0845 365 0000 & 0131 300 3456
31/35 Grassmarket EH1 2HS
e-mail: edinburgh.reservations@apexhotels.co.uk
web: www.apexhotels.co.uk
dir: Into Lothian Rd at west end of Princes St, 1st left into King Stables Rd, leads into Grassmarket

A sister to the Apex City Hotel close by, the International lies in a historic yet trendy square in the shadow of Edinburgh Castle. It has a versatile business and conference centre, and also Yu Time leisure and fitness facility with a stainless steel ozone pool. Bedrooms are contemporary in style and very well equipped. The fifth-floor restaurant boasts stunning views of the castle.

Rooms 169 (99 fmly) ☛ **Facilities** FTV Wi-fi ◉ Gym Tropicarium Xmas New Year **Conf** Class 80 Board 40 Thtr 200 **Services** Lift **Parking** 60 **Notes** ⊗ Civ Wed 200

George Hotel Edinburgh

★★★★ 79% HOTEL

☎ 0131 225 1251
19-21 George St EH2 2PB
e-mail: enquiries.thegeorge@principal-hayley.com
web: www.principal-hayley.com/thegeorge
dir: In city centre

A long-established hotel, the George enjoys a city centre location. The splendid public areas have many original features such as intricate plasterwork, a marble-floored foyer and chandeliers. The Tempus Bar offers menus that feature a wide range of dishes to suit most tastes. The elegant, modern bedrooms come in a mix of sizes and styles; the upper ones having fine city views.

Rooms 249 (20 fmly) (4 GF) **Facilities** STV Wi-fi ◉ HL Xmas New Year **Conf** Class 120 Board 50 Thtr 300 **Services** Lift **Notes** ⊗ Civ Wed 300

Edinburgh Marriott Hotel

★★★★ 78% HOTEL

☎ 0131 334 9191
111 Glasgow Rd EH12 8NF
e-mail: edinburgh@marriotthotels.com
web: www.edinburghmarriott.co.uk
dir: M8 junct 1 for Gogar, at rdbt turn right for city centre, hotel on right

This smart, modern hotel is located on the city's western edge which is convenient for the bypass, airport, showground and business park. Public areas include an attractive marbled foyer, extensive conference facilities and a restaurant serving a range

Save on hotels. Book at **theAA.com/hotel**

EDI 541 SCOTLAND

of international dishes. The air-conditioned bedrooms are spacious and equipped with a range of extras.

Rooms 245 (76 fmly) (64 GF) **Facilities** STV FTV Wi-fi ↷ ☜ Gym Steam room Sauna Massage & beauty treatment room Xmas New Year **Conf** Class 120 Board 50 Thtr 250 **Del** from £130 to £200 **Services** Lift Air con **Parking** 300 **Notes** LB Civ Wed 80

Apex City Hotel

★★★★ 77% ◉ HOTEL

☎ 0845 365 0000 & 0131 243 3456
61 Grassmarket EH1 2JF
e-mail: edinburgh.reservations@apexhotels.co.uk
web: www.apexhotels.co.uk
dir: Into Lothian Rd at west end of Princes St, 1st left into King Stables Rd. Leads into Grassmarket

This modern, stylish hotel lies in a historic yet trendy square dominated by Edinburgh Castle above. The design-led bedrooms are fresh and contemporary and each has artwork by Richard Demarco. Agua Bar and Restaurant is a smart open-plan area in dark wood and chrome that serves a range of meals and cocktails. Residents can use the spa at a sister hotel, Apex International, which is nearby.

Rooms 119 ♖ **Facilities** FTV Wi-fi ↷ Complimentary use of leisure facilities at Apex International Hotel Xmas **Conf** Class 30 Board 34 Thtr 70 **Services** Lift **Notes** ⊗ Civ Wed 60

Novotel Edinburgh Park

★★★★ 77% HOTEL

☎ 0131 446 5600
15 Lochside Av EH12 9DJ
e-mail: h6515@accor.com
dir: Near Hermiston Gate shopping area

Located just off the city by-pass and within minutes of the airport, this modern hotel offers bedrooms that are spacious and comfortable. The public areas include the open-plan lobby, bar and a restaurant where some tables have their own TVs.

Rooms 170 (130 fmly) **Facilities** Wi-fi ☜ Gym **Conf** Class 60 Board 40 Thtr 150 **Del** from £140 to £180* **Services** Lift **Parking** 96 **Notes** Civ Wed 90

Radisson Blu Hotel Edinburgh

★★★★ 77% HOTEL

☎ 0131 557 9797 & 557 6523
80 High St, The Royal Mile EH1 1TH
e-mail: sales.edinburgh@radissonblu.com
web: www.radissonblu.com/hotel-edinburgh
dir: On Royal Mile

Centrally located in the heart of the old town on the Royal Mile, the spacious and comfortable bedrooms cater well for both leisure and corporate guests. The staff provide very attentive service. Leisure facilities, parking and complimentary Wi-fi are all assets at this hotel.

Rooms 238 (5 fmly) **Facilities** STV FTV Wi-fi ☜ supervised Gym Saunas **Conf** Class 105 Board 52 Thtr 240 **Services** Lift Air con **Parking** 131 **Notes** ⊗ Civ Wed 180

The Royal Terrace Hotel

★★★★ 76% ◉ HOTEL

☎ 0131 557 3222
18 Royal Ter EH7 5AQ
e-mail: sales@royalterracehotel.co.uk
web: www.royalterracehotel.co.uk
dir: A8 to city centre, follow one-way system, left into Charlotte Sq. At end right into Queens St. Left at rdbt. At next island right into London Rd, right into Blenheim Place leading to Royal Terrace

Forming part of a quiet Georgian terrace in the heart of the city, this hotel offers bedrooms that successfully blend the historic architecture of the building with state-of-the-art facilities. Although most rooms afford lovely views, the top floor rooms provide excellent panoramas over the city to the Firth of Forth; for something unusual book an Ambassador Suite with a glass bathroom. The hotel's leisure club has a swimming pool, sauna and steam room, and award-winning dinners are served in the Terrace Brasserie.

Rooms 107 (13 fmly) (7 GF) **Facilities** Wi-fi ☜ Gym Steam room Sauna Aromatherapy shower Xmas New Year **Conf** Class 40 Board 40 Thtr 100 **Services** Lift **Notes** ⊗ Civ Wed 80

Apex Waterloo Place Hotel

★★★★ 76% HOTEL

☎ 0845 365 0000 & 0131 523 1819
23-27 Waterloo Place EH1 3BH
e-mail: edinburgh.reservations@apexhotels.co.uk
dir: At E end of Princes St. Telephone for detailed directions

This stunning hotel provides a state-of-the-art experience with slick interior design. Bedrooms, many with city views, are well appointed for both the business and leisure guest; stunning duplex suites provide extra space, surround-sound TV systems and luxurious feature bathrooms. The restaurant provides an appealing menu both at dinner and breakfast. There is also a well-equipped fitness centre and indoor pool. The hotel has direct, pedestrian access to Edinburgh's Waverley Station.

Rooms 186 (5 fmly) (15 GF) ♖ **Facilities** FTV Wi-fi ↷ ☜ Gym Sauna Steam rooms Xmas New Year **Conf** Class 70 Board 40 Thtr 150 **Services** Lift Air con **Notes** ⊗ Civ Wed 80

Holiday Inn Edinburgh

★★★★ 76% HOTEL

Holiday Inn

☎ 0871 942 9026
Corstorphine Rd EH12 6UA
e-mail: edinburghhi@ihg.com
web: www.hiedinburghhotel.co.uk
dir: On A8, adjacent to Edinburgh Zoo

A modern hotel situated three miles west of Edinburgh and near Edinburgh Business Park. The hotel enjoys panoramic views of the Pentland Hills and makes a good base for visiting the attractions of the city. Bedrooms include family and executive rooms. The eating options are Traders Restaurant or Sampans Oriental Restaurant, as well as a café and bar. The Spirit Health and Fitness Club has a gym, swimming pool, sauna, spa and beauty treatments. There is also a conference centre.

Rooms 303 (76 fmly) (41 smoking) **S** £49-£220; **D** £59-£250* **Facilities** Spa STV FTV Wi-fi ↷ HL ☜ supervised Gym New Year **Conf** Class 60 Board 45 Thtr 120 **Del** from £120 to £185* **Services** Lift Air con **Parking** 105 **Notes** LB ⊗ Civ Wed 80

E

EDINBURGH *continued*

Macdonald Holyrood Hotel

★★★★ 76% HOTEL

☎ 0870 1942106
Holyrood Rd EH8 8AU
e-mail: general.holyrood@macdonald-hotels.co.uk
web: www.macdonaldhotels.co.uk/holyrood
dir: Parallel to Royal Mile, near Holyrood Palace & Dynamic Earth

Situated just a short walk from Holyrood Palace, this impressive hotel lies next to the Scottish Parliament building. Air-conditioned bedrooms are comfortably furnished, whilst the Club floor boasts a private lounge. Full business services complement the extensive conference suites.

Rooms 156 (16 fmly) (13 GF) **Facilities** Spa STV Wi-fi ⌕ Gym Beauty treatment rooms Sauna Steam room Library ♫ Xmas New Year **Conf** Class 100 Board 80 Thtr 200 **Services** Lift Air con **Parking** 38 **Notes** Civ Wed 100

Novotel Edinburgh Centre

★★★★ 76% HOTEL

☎ 0131 656 3500
Lauriston Place, Lady Lawson St EH3 9DE
e-mail: H3271@accor.com
web: www.novotel.com
dir: From Edinburgh Castle right onto George IV Bridge from Royal Mile. Follow to junct, then right into Lauriston Place. Hotel 700mtrs on right

This modern hotel is located in the centre of the city, close to Edinburgh Castle. Smart and stylish public areas include a cosmopolitan bar, brasserie-style restaurant and indoor leisure facilities. The air-conditioned bedrooms feature a comprehensive range of extras and bathrooms with baths and separate shower cabinets.

Rooms 180 (146 fmly) ⌕ **Facilities** STV Wi-fi ⌕ ⌕ Gym Sauna Steam room Xmas **Conf** Class 50 Board 32 Thtr 80 **Services** Lift Air con **Parking** 15

Channings

★★★★ 75% ⊛ TOWN HOUSE HOTEL

☎ 0131 315 2226
15 South Learmonth Gardens EH4 1EZ
e-mail: reserve@channings.co.uk
web: www.channings.co.uk
dir: From A90 & Forth Road Bridge, follow signs for city centre

Just minutes from the city centre, this elegant hotel occupies five Edwardian terraced houses. The public areas include sumptuous, inviting lounges whilst the restaurant and bar are places to relax in the evening. The attractive and individually designed bedrooms offer a mix of modern and contemporary features.

Rooms 41 (4 GF) ⌕ **S** £85-£145; **D** £120-£240 (incl. bkfst)* **Facilities** STV FTV Wi-fi Xmas New Year **Conf** Class 40 Board 30 Thtr 60 Del £125* **Services** Lift **Notes** ⊗ Civ Wed 50

The King James, Edinburgh

thistle

★★★★ 75% HOTEL

☎ 0871 376 9016
107 Leith St EH1 3SW
e-mail: edinburgh@thistle.co.uk
web: www.thistlehotels.com/edinburgh
dir: M8/M9 onto A8 signed city centre. Hotel at end of Princes St adjacent to St James shopping centre

This purpose-built hotel adjoins one of Edinburgh's premier shopping malls at the east end of Princes Street. The friendly team of staff are keen to please whilst stylish, well-equipped bedrooms provide excellent levels of comfort and good facilities. Public areas include a spacious restaurant, popular bar and an elegant lobby lounge.

Rooms 143 (12 fmly) ⌕ **S** £50-£250; **D** £50-£250 **Facilities** STV FTV Wi-fi HL Xmas New Year **Conf** Class 160 Board 50 Thtr 250 Del from £110 to £190 **Services** Lift **Parking** 18 **Notes** ⊗

The Roxburghe Hotel

★★★★ 75% HOTEL

☎ 0844 879 9063 & 0131 240 5500
38 Charlotte Square EH2 4HQ
e-mail: general.roxburghe@macdonald-hotels.co.uk
web: www.macdonaldhotels.co.uk/roxburghe
dir: On corner of Charlotte Sq & George St

This long-established hotel lies in the heart of the city overlooking Charlotte Square Gardens. Public areas are inviting and include relaxing lounges, a choice of bars (in the evening) and an inner concourse that looks onto a small lawned area. Smart bedrooms come in both classic and contemporary styles. There is a secure underground car park.

Rooms 199 (3 fmly) **Facilities** Spa STV FTV Wi-fi ⌕ Gym Dance studio Sauna Steam room Xmas New Year **Conf** Class 160 Board 50 Thtr 300 **Services** Lift Air con **Parking** 20 **Notes** ⊗ Civ Wed 280

The Carlton Hotel

★★★★ 74% HOTEL

☎ 0131 472 3000
North Bridge EH1 1SD
e-mail: carlton@pumahotels.co.uk
web: www.pumahotels.co.uk
dir: On North Bridge which links Princes St to The Royal Mile

The Carlton occupies a city centre location just off the Royal Mile. Inside, it is modern and stylish in design, with an impressive open-plan reception/lobby, spacious first-floor lounge, bar and restaurant, plus a basement leisure club. Bedrooms, many air-conditioned, are generally spacious, with an excellent range of accessories.

Rooms 189 (20 fmly) **Facilities** STV Wi-fi ⌕ supervised Gym Squash Table tennis Dance studio Exercise classes Beauty treatment rooms Crèche ♫ Xmas New Year **Conf** Class 110 Board 60 Thtr 220 **Services** Lift **Notes** Civ Wed 160

Malmaison Edinburgh

★★★ 86% ⊛ HOTEL

☎ 0131 468 5000
One Tower Place EH6 7DB
e-mail: edinburgh@malmaison.com
web: www.malmaison.com
dir: A900 from city centre towards Leith, at end of Leith Walk, through 3 sets of lights, left into Tower St. Hotel on right at end of road

The trendy Port of Leith is home to this stylish Malmaison. Inside, bold contemporary designs create a striking effect. Bedrooms are comprehensively equipped with CD players, mini-bars and loads of individual touches. Ask for one of the stunning superior rooms for a really memorable stay. The smart brasserie and a café bar are popular with the local clientele.

Rooms 100 (18 fmly) **Facilities** STV Wi-fi Gym Xmas New Year **Conf** Class 30 Board 40 Thtr 55 Del from £150 to £195* **Services** Lift **Parking** 50 **Notes** Civ Wed

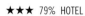

Apex European Hotel
★★★ 83% HOTEL

☎ 0845 365 0000 & 0131 474 3456
90 Haymarket Ter EH12 5LQ
e-mail: edinburgh.reservations@apexhotels.co.uk
web: www.apexhotels.co.uk
dir: A8 to city centre, 100m from Haymarket Railway Station

Lying just west of the city centre, close to Haymarket Station and handy for the Conference Centre, this modern hotel is popular with business travellers. Smart, stylish bedrooms offer an excellent range of facilities and have been designed with work requirements in mind. Public areas include Metro, an informal bistro. Service is friendly and pro-active.

Rooms 66 (3 GF) (8 smoking) **Facilities** FTV Wi-fi
New Year **Conf** Class 30 Board 36 Thtr 80
Services Lift **Parking** 10 **Notes** ⊗ Closed 24-27 Dec

Dalhousie Castle and Aqueous Spa
★★★ 82% ◉◉ HOTEL

☎ 01875 820153
Bonnyrigg EH19 3JB
e-mail: info@dalhousiecastle.co.uk
web: www.dalhousiecastle.co.uk
dir: A7 S from Edinburgh through Lasswade/Newtongrange, right at Shell Garage (B704), hotel 0.5m from junct

A popular wedding venue, this imposing medieval castle sits amid lawns and parkland and even has a falconry. Bedrooms offer a mix of styles and sizes, including richly decorated themed rooms named after various historical figures. The Dungeon restaurant provides an atmospheric setting for dinner, and the less formal Orangery serves food all day. The spa offers many relaxing and therapeutic treatments and hydro facilities.

Rooms 36 (7 annexe) (3 fmly) **Facilities** Spa FTV Wi-fi Fishing Falconry Clay pigeon shooting Archery Laserday Xmas New Year **Conf** Class 60 Board 45 Thtr 120 Del £180* **Parking** 110 **Notes** Civ Wed 100

Best Western Braid Hills Hotel
★★★ 82% HOTEL

☎ 0131 447 8888 & 446 3003
134 Braid Rd EH10 6JD
e-mail: bookings@braidhillshotel.co.uk
web: www.braidhillshotel.co.uk
dir: 2.5m S A702, opposite Braid Burn Park

From its elevated position on the south side, this long-established hotel enjoys splendid panoramic views of the city and castle. Bedrooms are smart, stylish and well equipped. The public areas are comfortable and inviting, and guests can dine in either the restaurant or popular bistro/bar.

Rooms 67 (14 fmly) (14 GF) **S** £50-£130;
D £65-£200* **Facilities** STV FTV Wi-fi Xmas New Year **Conf** Class 50 Board 30 Thtr 100 **Parking** 38 **Notes** LB ⊗ Civ Wed 100

The Point Hotel, Edinburgh
★★★ 80% HOTEL

☎ 0131 221 5555
34 Bread St EH3 9AF
e-mail: enquiries@pointhoteledinburgh.co.uk
dir: A71 to Haymarket Station. Straight on at junct & right on Torphichen St, left onto Morrison St, straight on to Bread St, hotel on right

Built in 1892 as a Co-op which once employed Sean Connery as a milkman, the hotel has won many awards for its design and presentation. Bedrooms are spacious and cater well for the needs of the modern guest. Open-plan public areas are enhanced with coloured lighting and an array of artwork. The Point Restaurant offers imaginative dishes. The Glass Box Penthouse conference room affords fantastic views of the city.

Rooms 139 **Facilities** FTV Wi-fi **Conf** Class 60 Board 40 Thtr 120 **Services** Lift **Notes** ⊗ Civ Wed 90

Best Western Kings Manor
★★★ 79% HOTEL

☎ 0131 669 0444 & 468 8003
100 Milton Road East EH15 2NP
e-mail: reservations@kingsmanor.com
web: www.kingsmanor.com
dir: A720 E to Old Craighall junct, left into city, right at A1/A199 junct, hotel 400mtrs on right

Lying on the eastern side of the city and convenient for the by-pass, this hotel is popular with business guests, tour groups and for conferences. It boasts a fine leisure complex and a bright modern bistro, which complements the quality, creative cooking in the main restaurant.

Rooms 95 (8 fmly) (13 GF) **S** £45-£105;
D £60-£195* **Facilities** Spa STV FTV Wi-fi Gym Health & beauty salon Steam room Sauna **Conf** Class 80 Board 60 Thtr 160 Del from £85 to £145* **Services** Lift **Parking** 130 **Notes** LB Civ Wed 100

Holiday Inn Edinburgh West
★★★ 78% HOTEL *Holiday Inn*

☎ 0871 942 9025
107 Queensferry Rd EH4 3HL
e-mail: reservations-edinburghcitywest@ihg.com
web: www.holidayinn.co.uk
dir: On A90 approx 1m from city centre

Situated on the north-west side of the city, close to Murrayfield Stadium and just five miles from the airport, this purpose-built hotel has a bright contemporary look. The colourful, modern bedrooms are well equipped and three specifications are available - with two double beds; with a double bed and sofa; or with a double bed and separate lounge. Some have great views of the city too. There is limited free parking.

Rooms 101 (65 fmly) **Facilities** STV FTV Wi-fi HL New Year **Conf** Class 60 Board 50 Thtr 140 **Services** Lift Air con **Parking** 80 **Notes** ⊗ Civ Wed 120

E

EDINBURGH *continued*

Old Waverley Hotel

★★★ 78% HOTEL

☎ 0131 556 4648
43 Princes St EH2 2BY
e-mail: reservations@oldwaverley.co.uk
web: www.oldwaverley.co.uk
dir: In city centre, opposite Scott Monument, Waverley Station & Jenners

Occupying a commanding position opposite Sir Walter Scott's famous monument on Princes Street, this hotel lies right in the heart of the city close to the station. The comfortable public rooms are all on first-floor level and along with front-facing bedrooms enjoy the fine views.

Rooms 85 (5 fmly) **Facilities** Wi-fi Leisure facilities at sister hotel **Services** Lift **Notes** ⊗

Royal Over-Seas League Hotel

Ⓤ

☎ 0131 225 1501
100 Princes St EH2 3AB
e-mail: daniel@ros1-edinburgh.org
dir: In city centre. Nearest car park accessed via Leith St

Currently the rating for this establishment is not confirmed. This may be due to a change of ownership or because it has only recently joined the AA rating scheme. For further details please see the AA website: theAA.com

Rooms 20 **S** £89-£99; **D** £110-£215 (incl. bkfst)*

Holiday Inn Express Edinburgh City Centre

BUDGET HOTEL

☎ 0131 558 2300
Picardy Place EH1 3JT
e-mail: info@hieedinburgh.co.uk
web: www.hiexpress.com/edinburghctyct
dir: Follow signs to city centre & Greenside NCP. Hotel near E end of Princes St

A modern hotel ideal for families and business travellers. Fresh and uncomplicated, the spacious rooms include Sky TV, power shower and tea and coffee-making facilities. Continental buffet breakfast is included in the room rate; other meals may be taken at the nearby family pub or restaurant. See also the Hotel Groups pages.

Rooms 161 (53 fmly) (27 GF) (13 smoking) 🐾
S £59-£299; **D** £59-£299 (incl. bkfst)* **Conf** Class 8 Board 18 Thtr 20 Del from £138 to £399

Holiday Inn Express Edinburgh Royal Mile

BUDGET HOTEL

☎ 0131 524 8400
South Grays Close, Cowgate EH1 1NA
e-mail: info@hiexpressedinburgh.co.uk
web: www.hiexpressedinburgh.co.uk

Rooms 78 (50 fmly) (10 GF) **Conf** Class 20 Board 20 Thtr 40

Holiday Inn Express Edinburgh Waterfront

BUDGET HOTEL

☎ 0131 555 4422
Britannia Way, Ocean Dr, Leith EH6 6JJ
e-mail: info@hiex-edinburgh.com
web: www.hiexpress.com/exedinburghwat
dir: Follow signs for Royal Yacht Britannia. Hotel just before Britannia on right

Rooms 145 (36 fmly) **Conf** Class 15 Board 18 Thtr 35

Ibis Edinburgh Centre

BUDGET HOTEL

☎ 0131 240 7000
6 Hunter Square, off The Royal Mile EH1 1QW
e-mail: H2039@accor.com
web: www.ibishotel.com
dir: M8/M9/A1 over North Bridge (A7) & High St, take 1st right off South Bridge, into Hunter Sq

Modern, budget hotel offering comfortable accommodation in bright and practical bedrooms. Breakfast is self-service and dinner is available in the restaurant. See also the Hotel Groups pages.

Rooms 99 (2 GF)

Premier Inn Edinburgh Airport (Newbridge)

BUDGET HOTEL

☎ 0871 527 9284
2A Kirkliston Rd, Newbridge EH28 8SL
web: www.premierinn.com
dir: M9 junct 1, A89 signed Broxburn. At lights turn right, then 2nd right

High quality, budget accommodation ideal for both families and business travellers. Spacious, en suite bedrooms feature tea and coffee making facilities, and Freeview TV in most hotels. Internet access and Wi-fi are available for a small fee. The adjacent family restaurant features a wide and varied menu. See also the Hotel Groups pages.

Rooms 119

Premier Inn Edinburgh City Centre (Haymarket)

BUDGET HOTEL

☎ 0871 527 8368
1 Morrison Link EH3 8DN
web: www.premierinn.com
dir: Adjcent to Edinburgh International Conference Centre

Rooms 281

Premier Inn Edinburgh City Lauriston Place

BUDGET HOTEL

☎ 0871 527 8366
82 Lauriston Place, Lady Lawson St EH3 9DG
web: www.premierinn.com
dir: A8 onto A702 (Lothian Rd). Left into Lauriston Place. Hotel on left

Rooms 112

Premier Inn Edinburgh East

BUDGET HOTEL

☎ 0871 527 8370
228 Willowbrae Rd EH8 7NG
web: www.premierinn.com
dir: M8 junct 1, A720 S for 12m, then A1. At Asda rdbt turn left. In 2m, hotel on left before Esso garage

Rooms 39

Premier Inn Edinburgh (Inveresk)

BUDGET HOTEL

☎ 0871 527 8358
Carberry Rd, Inveresk, Musselburgh EH21 8PT
web: www.premierinn.com
dir: From A1 follow Dalkeith (A6094) signs. At rdbt turn right, hotel 300yds on right

Rooms 40

Premier Inn Edinburgh (Leith)

BUDGET HOTEL

☎ 0871 527 8360
51-53 Newhaven Place, Leith EH6 4TX
web: www.premierinn.com
dir: From A1 follow coast road through Leith. Pass Ocean Terminal, straight ahead at mini-rdbt, 2nd exit signed Harry Ramsden's car park

Rooms 60

21212

◎◎◎ RESTAURANT WITH ROOMS

☎ 0131 523 1030 & 0845 222 1212
3 Royal Ter EH7 5AB
e-mail: reservations@21212restaurant.co.uk

A real gem in Edinburgh's crown, this establishment takes its name from the numbers of choices at each course on the five-course dinner menu. Located on the prestigious Royal Terrace this is a light and airy, renovated Georgian townhouse stretching over four floors. The four individually designed bedrooms epitomise luxury living and the bathrooms certainly have the wow factor. At the heart of this restaurant with rooms is the creative, award-winning cooking of Paul Kitching. Service throughout is friendly and very attentive.

Rooms 4

INSPECTORS' CHOICE

The Witchery by the Castle

◎ RESTAURANT WITH ROOMS

☎ 0131 225 5613
352 Castlehill, The Royal Mile EH1 2NF
e-mail: mail@thewitchery.com
web: www.thewitchery.com
dir: Top of Royal Mile at gates of Edinburgh Castle

Originally built in 1595, The Witchery by the Castle is situated in a historic building at the gates of Edinburgh Castle. The two luxurious and theatrically decorated suites, known as the Inner Sanctum and the Old Rectory are located above the restaurant and are reached via a winding stone staircase. Filled with antiques, opulently draped beds, large roll-top baths and a plethora of memorabilia, this ancient and exciting establishment is often described as one of the country's most romantic destinations.

Rooms 8 (5 annexe)

ELGIN   **Map 23 NJ26**
Moray

Mansion House Hotel

★★★ 79% HOTEL

☎ 01343 548811
The Haugh IV30 1AW
e-mail: reception@mhelgin.co.uk
web: www.mansionhousehotel.co.uk
dir: Exit A96 into Haugh Rd, then 1st left

Set in grounds by the River Lossie, this baronial mansion is popular with leisure and business guests as well as being a popular wedding venue. Bedrooms are spacious and many have views of the river. Extensive public areas include a choice of restaurants, with the bistro contrasting with the classical main restaurant. There is an indoor pool and a beauty and hair salon.

Rooms 23 (2 fmly) (5 GF) ☛ **S** £97-£113; **D** £154-£202 (incl. bkfst)* **Facilities** STV FTV Wi-fi ⏳ ☙ supervised Fishing Gym Hair studio New Year **Conf** Thtr 180 **Parking** 50 **Notes** LB ⊗ Civ Wed 160

Premier Inn Elgin

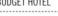

BUDGET HOTEL

☎ 0871 527 8372
15 Linkwood Way IV30 1HY
web: www.premierinn.com
dir: On A96, 1.5m E of city centre

High quality, budget accommodation ideal for both families and business travellers. Spacious, en suite bedrooms feature tea and coffee making facilities, and Freeview TV in most hotels. Internet access and Wi-fi are available for a small fee. The adjacent family restaurant features a wide and varied menu. See also the Hotel Groups pages.

Rooms 40

ERISKA   **Map 20 NM94**
Argyll & Bute

INSPECTORS' CHOICE

Isle of Eriska Hotel, Spa & Golf

★★★★★ ◎◎◎ COUNTRY HOUSE HOTEL

☎ 01631 720371
PA37 1SD
e-mail: office@eriska-hotel.co.uk
dir: Exit A85 at Connel, onto A828, 4m, follow hotel signs from N of Benderloch

Situated on its own private island with delightful beaches and walking trails, this hotel is in a tranquil setting, perfect for total relaxation. The spacious bedrooms are very comfortable and boast some fine antique pieces. The restaurant is now under the auspices of Simon McKenzie and he has hit the ground running. Dinner is served in the dining room made up of a series of spaces including a conservatory. Simon's cooking matches the mood of the place perfectly - refined and classy, maintaining the integrity of the regional produce. Local seafood, meats and game feature prominently on the award-winning menus, as do vegetables and herbs grown in the hotel's kitchen garden. Leisure facilities include an indoor pool, gym and spa treatment rooms.

Rooms 23 (6 fmly) (2 GF) **Facilities** Spa FTV Wi-fi ⏳ ☙ supervised ⅃ 9 ☙ Putt green Fishing ⚲ Gym Squash Sauna Steam room Skeet shooting Nature trails Xmas New Year **Conf** Class 30 Board 30 Thtr 30 **Parking** 40 **Notes** Closed Jan Civ Wed 50

E

FALKIRK
Falkirk
Map 21 NS88

Premier Inn Falkirk Central
BUDGET HOTEL

☎ 0871 527 8388
Main St, Camelon FK1 4DS
web: www.premierinn.com
dir: From Falkirk A803 signed Glasgow. At mini-rdbt right, continue on A803. At Rosebank rdbt 2nd exit signed Glasgow & Stirling

High quality, budget accommodation ideal for both families and business travellers. Spacious, en suite bedrooms feature tea and coffee making facilities, and Freeview TV in most hotels. Internet access and Wi-fi are available for a small fee. The adjacent family restaurant features a wide and varied menu. See also the Hotel Groups pages.

Rooms 31

Premier Inn Falkirk (Larbert)
BUDGET HOTEL

☎ 0871 527 8390
Glenbervie Business Park, Bellsdyke Rd, Larbert FK5 4EG
web: www.premierinn.com
dir: Just off A88. Approx 1m from M876 junct 2

Rooms 60

FINTRY
Stirling
Map 20 NS68

Culcreuch Castle Hotel & Estate
★★★ 80% HOTEL

☎ 01360 860555 & 860228
Kippen Rd G63 0LW
e-mail: info@culcreuch.com
web: www.culcreuch.com
dir: On B822, 17m W of Stirling

Peacefully located in 1,600 acres of parkland, this ancient castle dates back to 1296. Tastefully restored accommodation is in a mixture of individually themed castle rooms, some with four-poster beds, and more modern courtyard rooms which are suitable for families. Period style public rooms include a bar, serving light meals, an elegant lounge and a wood-panelled dining room.

Rooms 14 (4 annexe) (4 fmly) (4 GF) ⌂ **S** £76-£120; **D** £102-£190 (incl. bkfst) **Facilities** STV FTV Wi-fi ☝ Fishing New Year **Conf** Class 70 Board 30 Thtr 140 Del from £119 to £129 **Parking** 100 **Notes** LB ⊗ Closed 4-18 Jan & 25-26 Dec Civ Wed 110

FORT AUGUSTUS
Highland
Map 23 NH30

The Lovat, Loch Ness
★★★ 87% ◉◉ HOTEL

☎ 01456 459250 & 0845 450 1100
Loch Ness Side PH32 4DU
e-mail: info@thelovat.com
web: www.thelovat.com
dir: A82 between Fort William & Inverness

This charming hotel enjoys an elevated position in the pretty town of Fort Augustus with views over Loch Ness. It has impressively styled bedrooms with a host of thoughtful extras. Inviting public areas include a comfortable lounge with a log fire, a stylish bar, and contemporary restaurant were food is cooked with skill and care. The hospitality and commitment to guest care will leave a lasting impression.

Rooms 28 (7 GF) **S** £65-£195; **D** £70-£265 (incl. bkfst)* **Facilities** FTV Wi-fi ☝ Beauty treatment room Xmas New Year **Conf** Class 32 Board 24 Thtr 70 Del from £145 to £176* **Services** Lift **Parking** 30 **Notes** LB Civ Wed 150

Inchnacardoch Lodge Hotel
★★★ 73% ◉ SMALL HOTEL

☎ 01456 450900
Inchnacardoch Bay PH32 4BL
e-mail: happy@inchhotel.com

This 150-year-old former hunting lodge is set on the hillside looking over the south end of Loch Ness, making it a perfect base for exploring the Highlands. Guests can expect the finest hospitality here from staff that are always eager to please. The bedrooms are very individual in style; the Bridal Suite is a very well appointed room with stunning views. The award-winning Yard Restaurant serves dishes based on the plentiful supply of local game and seafood.

Rooms 14 (2 fmly) **S** £55-£135; **D** £80-£135 (incl. bkfst) **Facilities** FTV Wi-fi Fishing Xmas New Year **Conf** Class 30 Board 26 Thtr 45 Del from £80 to £250 **Parking** 30 **Notes** Civ Wed 35

FORTINGALL
Perth & Kinross
Map 20 NN74

Fortingall Hotel
★★★★ 82% ◉◉ SMALL HOTEL

☎ 01887 830367 & 830368
PH15 2NQ
e-mail: hotel@fortingallhotel.com
dir: B846 from Aberfeldy for 6m, left signed Fortingall for 3m. Hotel in village centre

Appointed to a very high standard, this hotel has plenty of charm. It lies at the foot of wooded hills in the heart of Glen Lyon. All the bedrooms are very well equipped and have an extensive range of thoughtful extras. The comfortable lounge, with its log fire, is ideal for pre-dinner drinks, and the small bar is full of character.

Rooms 10 (1 fmly) **S** £90-£135; **D** £120-£270 (incl. bkfst & dinner)* **Facilities** STV Wi-fi Fishing Deer stalking ♫ Xmas New Year **Conf** Board 16 Thtr 30 **Parking** 20 **Notes** Civ Wed 30

FORT WILLIAM
Highland
Map 22 NN17

Inverlochy Castle Hotel
★★★★★ ◉◉◉
COUNTRY HOUSE HOTEL

☎ 01397 702177
Torlundy PH33 6SN
e-mail: info@inverlochy.co.uk
web: www.inverlochycastlehotel.com
dir: Accessible from either A82 (Glasgow-Fort William) or A9 (Edinburgh-Dalwhinnie). Hotel 3m N of Fort William on A82, in Torlundy

With a backdrop of Ben Nevis, this imposing and gracious castle sits amidst extensive gardens and grounds overlooking the hotel's own loch. Lavishly appointed in classic country-house style, spacious bedrooms are extremely comfortable and boast flat-screen TVs and laptops with internet access. The sumptuous main hall and lounge provide the perfect setting for afternoon tea or a pre-dinner cocktail, while imaginative modern British cuisine is served in one of three dining rooms. A snooker room and DVD library are also available.

Rooms 17 (6 fmly) ⌂ **S** £265-£695; **D** £320-£695 (incl. bkfst)* **Facilities** STV Wi-fi ☝ ☝ Fishing on loch Massage Riding Hunting Stalking Clay pigeon shooting Archery ♫ Xmas New Year **Conf** Class 20 Board 20 Thtr 50 Del £320* **Parking** 17 **Notes** Civ Wed 80

Moorings Hotel

★★★ 82% ◉ HOTEL

☎ 01397 772797
Banavie PH33 7LY
e-mail: reservations@moorings-fortwilliam.co.uk
web: www.moorings-fortwilliam.co.uk
dir: Take A830 (N from Fort William), cross
Caledonian Canal, 1st right

Located on the Caledonian Canal next to a series of
locks known as Neptune's Staircase and close to
Thomas Telford's house, this hotel with its dedicated
team offers friendly service. Accommodation comes in
two distinct styles and the newer rooms are
particularly appealing. Meals can be taken in the
bars or the spacious dining room.

Rooms 27 (2 fmly) (1 GF) ↑ **S** £80-£143; **D** £90-£153
(incl. bkfst)* **Facilities** STV Wi-fi Gym New Year
Conf Class 60 Board 40 Thtr 140 Del from £105 to
£125* **Parking** 60 **Notes** LB Closed 24-26 Dec
Civ Wed 120

Lime Tree Hotel & Restaurant

★★★ 79% ◉◉ SMALL HOTEL

☎ 01397 701806
Lime Tree Studio, Achintore Rd PH33 6RQ
e-mail: info@limetreefortwilliam.co.uk
dir: On A82 at entrance to Fort William

A charming small hotel with an inspirational art
gallery on the ground floor, with lots of original
artwork displayed throughout. Evening meals can be
enjoyed in the restaurant which has a loyal following.
The hotel's comfortable lounges with their real fires
are ideal for pre or post dinner drinks or maybe just to
relax in. Individually designed bedrooms are spacious
with some nice little personal touches courtesy of the
artist owner.

Rooms 9 (4 fmly) **S** £60-£110; **D** £80-£120 (incl.
bkfst)* **Facilities** FTV Wi-fi New Year **Conf** Class 40
Board 30 Thtr 60 **Parking** 9 **Notes** Closed 24-26 Dec

Alexandra Hotel

★★★ 75% HOTEL

☎ 01397 702241
The Parade PH33 6AZ
e-mail: salesalexandra@strathmorehotels.com
dir: Off A82. Hotel opposite railway station

This charming old hotel enjoys a prominent position
in the town centre and is just a short walk from all
the major attractions. Front-facing bedrooms have
views over the town and the spectacular Nevis
mountain range. There is a choice of restaurants,
including a bistro serving meals until late, along with
several stylish and very comfortable lounges.

Rooms 93 (2 fmly) **Facilities** Wi-fi Free use of nearby
leisure club ♫ Xmas New Year **Conf** Class 100
Board 40 Thtr 120 **Services** Lift **Parking** 50
See advert on page 524

Ben Nevis Hotel & Leisure Club

★★ 75% HOTEL

☎ 01397 702331
North Rd PH33 6TG
e-mail: bennevismanager@strathmorehotels.com
dir: Off A82

This popular hotel is ideally situated on the outskirts
of Fort William. It provides comfortable, well equipped
bedrooms; many with views of the impressive Nevis
mountains. The hotel's leisure centre is a firm
favourite with guests at the hotel.

Rooms 119 (3 fmly) (30 GF) **Facilities** Wi-fi ⊗
supervised Gym Beauty salon ♫ Xmas New Year
Conf Class 60 Board 40 Thtr 150 **Parking** 100
Notes Civ Wed 60
See advert on page 524

Croit Anna Hotel

★★ 71% HOTEL

☎ 01397 702268
Achintore Rd, Drimarben PH33 6RR
e-mail: croitanna.fortwilliam@alfatravel.co.uk
web: www.leisureplex.co.uk
dir: From Glencoe on A82 into Fort William, hotel 1st
on right

Located on the edge of Loch Linnhe, just two miles
out of town, this hotel offers some spacious
bedrooms, many with fine views over the loch. There
is a choice of two comfortable lounges and a large
airy restaurant. The hotel appeals to coach parties
and independent travellers alike.

Rooms 92 (5 fmly) (13 GF) **Facilities** FTV Pool table
♫ Xmas New Year **Parking** 25 **Notes** ⊗ Closed Dec-
Jan (ex Xmas) RS Nov, Feb, Mar

Premier Inn Fort William

BUDGET HOTEL

☎ 0871 527 8402
Loch Iall, An Aird PH33 6AN
web: www.premierinn.com
dir: N end of Fort William Shopping Centre, just off
A82 (ring road)

High quality, budget accommodation ideal for both
families and business travellers. Spacious, en suite
bedrooms feature tea and coffee making facilities,
and Freeview TV in most hotels. Internet access and
Wi-fi are available for a small fee. The adjacent
family restaurant features a wide and varied menu.
See also the Hotel Groups pages.

Rooms 40

F

F

FOYERS — Highland — Map 23 NH52

Craigdarroch House

RESTAURANT WITH ROOMS

☎ 01456 486400
IV2 6XU
e-mail: info@hotel-loch-ness.co.uk
dir: Take B862 from either end of loch, then B852
signed Foyers

Craigdarroch is located in an elevated position high
above Loch Ness on the south side. Bedrooms vary in
style and size but all are comfortable and well
equipped; those that are front-facing have wonderful
views. The award-winning food is well worth staying
in for, and breakfasts are also memorable.

Rooms 8 (1 fmly)

GALASHIELS — Scottish Borders — Map 21 NT43

Kingsknowes Hotel

★★★ 77% HOTEL

☎ 01896 758375
Selkirk Rd TD1 3HY
e-mail: enq@kingsknowes.co.uk
web: www.kingsknowes.co.uk
dir: Exit A7 at Galashiels/Selkirk rdbt

An imposing turreted mansion, this hotel lies in
attractive gardens on the outskirts of town close to
the River Tweed. It boasts elegant public areas and
many spacious bedrooms, some with excellent views.
There is a choice of bars, one with a popular menu to
supplement the restaurant.

Rooms 12 (2 fmly) ✆ **S** fr £69; **D** fr £99 (incl. bkfst)*
Facilities FTV Wi-fi HL **Conf** Class 40 Board 30
Thtr 80 **Parking** 65 **Notes** LB Civ Wed 75

GATEHOUSE OF FLEET — Dumfries & Galloway — Map 20 NX55

Cally Palace Hotel

★★★★ 76% COUNTRY HOUSE HOTEL

☎ 01557 814341
DG7 2DL
e-mail: info@callypalace.co.uk
web: www.callypalace.co.uk
dir: From M6 & A74, signed A75 Dumfries then
Stranraer. At Gatehouse-of-Fleet right onto B727, left
at Cally

A resort hotel with extensive leisure facilities, this
grand 18th-century building is set in 500 acres of
forest and parkland that incorporates its own golf
course. Bedrooms are spacious and well equipped,
whilst public rooms retain a quiet elegance. The short
dinner menu focuses on freshly prepared dishes; a
pianist plays most nights and the wearing of jacket
and tie is obligatory.

Rooms 55 (7 fmly) **Facilities** STV FTV Wi-fi ⚅ ⚘ 18
⚘ Putt green Fishing ⚘ Gym Table tennis Practice
fairway Xmas New Year **Conf** Class 40 Board 25
Thtr 40 **Services** Lift **Parking** 100 **Notes** ⊗ Closed
Jan-early Feb

GLASGOW — City of Glasgow — Map 20 NS56

See also Clydebank & Uplawmoor

Blythswood Square

★★★★★ 88% ◉◉ HOTEL

☎ 0141 248 8888
11 Blythswood Square G2 4AD
e-mail: reserve@blythswoodsquare.com

Built in 1821, and restored to its former glory, this
was the headquarters of the Royal Scottish
Automobile Club which was the official start point for
the 1955 Monte Carlo Rally. The bedrooms and
bathrooms are sumptuous, and include suites and a
penthouse. Afternoon tea and cocktails are served in
the 35-metre, first-floor Salon Lounge, and the
award-winning restaurant occupies the old RSAC's
ballroom. The spa includes a fantastic thermal suite.

Rooms 100 ✆ **S** £120-£200; **D** £160-£260 (incl.
bkfst)* **Facilities** Spa Wi-fi ⚅ ⚘ **Conf** Board 80
Thtr 130 Del £235* **Services** Lift Air con

Hotel du Vin at One Devonshire Gardens

Hotel du Vin & Bistro

★★★★ ◉◉◉ TOWN HOUSE HOTEL

☎ 0141 339 2001
1 Devonshire Gardens G12 0UX
e-mail: reservations.odg@hotelduvin.com
web: www.hotelduvin.com
dir: M8 junct 17, follow signs for A82, in 1.5m left
into Hyndland Rd, 1st right, right at mini rdbt, right
at end

Situated in a tree lined Victorian terrace this luxury
'boutique' hotel has stunning, individually designed
bedrooms and suites that have the trademark
Egyptian linens and seriously good showers. The
oak-panelled Bistro offers daily-changing menus
that use the finest Scottish produce. Naturally, wine
is an important part of the equation here, and the
sommelier and the knowledgeable staff can guide
guests around the impressive wine list.

Rooms 49 (7 GF) ✆ **D** £185-£525 **Facilities** STV
Wi-fi Gym Beauty treatment room Tennis & Squash
facilities at nearby club Xmas New Year
Conf Class 30 Board 30 Thtr 50 Del from £165 to
£275 **Notes** LB Civ Wed 70

Beardmore Hotel

★★★★ 77% ◉ HOTEL

☎ 0141 951 6000
Beardmore St G81 4SA
e-mail: info@beardmore.scot.nhs.uk
web: www.thebeardmore.com

(For full entry see Clydebank)

Menzies Glasgow

MenziesHotels

★★★★ 77% ◉ HOTEL

☎ 0141 222 2929 & 270 2323
27 Washington St G3 8AZ
e-mail: glasgow@menzieshotels.co.uk
web: www.menzieshotels.co.uk
dir: M8 junct 19, follow signs for SECC & Broomielaw.
Left at lights

Centrally located, this modern hotel is a short drive from the airport and a short walk from the centre of the city. Bedrooms are generally spacious and boast a range of facilities, including high-speed internet access. Facilities include a brasserie restaurant and an impressive indoor leisure facility.

Rooms 141 (16 fmly) (15 smoking) **Facilities** STV FTV Wi-fi ♨ ⏱ supervised Gym Sauna Steam room Hair & beauty salon Xmas New Year **Conf** Class 60 Board 70 Thtr 160 **Services** Lift Air con **Parking** 50 **Notes** Civ Wed 150

Glasgow Marriott Hotel

Marriott.
HOTELS & RESORTS

★★★★ 76% HOTEL

☎ 0141 226 5577
500 Argyle St, Anderston G3 8RR
e-mail: cork.regional.reservations@marriott.com
web: www.glasgowmarriott.co.uk
dir: M8 junct 19, turn left at lights, then left into hotel

Conveniently located for all major transport links and the city centre, this hotel benefits from extensive conference and banqueting facilities and a spacious car park. Public areas include an open-plan lounge/ bar and a Mediterranean style restaurant. High quality, well-equipped bedrooms benefit from air conditioning and generously sized beds; the suites are particularly comfortable.

Rooms 300 (89 fmly) **Facilities** Wi-fi ⏱ Gym Beautician Poolside steam room Sauna New Year **Conf** Class 300 Board 50 Thtr 800 **Services** Lift Air con **Parking** 180 **Notes** ⊗

Thistle Glasgow

thistle

★★★★ 76% HOTEL

☎ 0871 376 9043
36 Cambridge St G2 3HN
e-mail: glasgow@thistle.co.uk
web: www.thistle.com/glasgow
dir: In city centre, just off Sauchiehall St

Ideally located within the centre of Glasgow and with ample parking, this hotel is well presented with the lobby area that gives a great impression on arrival. It also benefits from having a well-presented leisure club along with the largest ballroom in Glasgow. Service is friendly and attentive.

Rooms 300 (38 fmly) (1 smoking) ⏻ **Facilities** STV FTV Wi-fi ⏱ HL ⏲ Gym Sauna Steam room Beauty treatment room New Year **Conf** Class 800 Board 15 Thtr 1000 **Del** from £99 to £179* **Services** Lift Air con **Parking** 216 **Notes** ⊗ Civ Wed 720

Grand Central Hotel

 principal hayley

★★★★ 75% HOTEL

☎ 0141 240 3700
99 Gordon St G1 3SF
e-mail: grandcentralhotel@principal-hayley.com
dir: M8 junct 19 towards city centre turn left at Hope St. Hotel 200mtrs on right

This is the place where John Logie Baird transmitted the world's first long-distance television pictures in 1927, and this 'grand old lady' of the Glasgow hotel scene is appointed to a very good standard. The decor is a blend of contemporary, art deco and original Victorian styles. Bedrooms are well equipped and suit business travellers especially. There is Champagne Central, a glamorous bar, the Tempus Bar and Restaurant, and Deli Central (with direct access to the Central Station) which is an eat-in deli and a take-away. Ample meeting facilities are available, and NCP car parks are nearby.

Rooms 186 (13 fmly) ⏻ **S** £79-£269; **D** £79-£269 **Facilities** FTV Wi-fi ♫ **Conf** Class 350 Board 60 Thtr 500 **Del** from £125 to £195 **Services** Lift **Notes** ⊗ Civ Wed 500

Millennium Hotel Glasgow

MILLENNIUM
HOTELS AND RESORTS
MILLENNIUM · COPTHORNE

★★★★ 74% HOTEL

☎ 0141 332 6711
George Square G2 1DS
e-mail: glasgow.reservations@millenniumhotels. co.uk
web: www.millenniumhotels.co.uk
dir: M8 junct 15 through 4 sets of lights, at 5th left into Hanover St. George Sq directly ahead, hotel on right

Right in the heart of the city, this hotel has pride of place overlooking George Square. Inside, the property has a contemporary air, with a spacious reception concourse and a glass veranda overlooking the square. There is a stylish brasserie and separate lounge bar, and bedrooms come in a variety of sizes.

Rooms 116 (17 fmly) ⏻ **Facilities** STV Wi-fi New Year **Conf** Class 24 Board 32 Thtr 40 **Del** from £130 to £185 **Services** Lift **Notes** ⊗ Closed 25 Dec Civ Wed 120

Novotel Glasgow Centre

NOVOTEL

★★★★ 71% HOTEL

☎ 0141 222 2775
181 Pitt St G2 4DT
e-mail: H3136@accor.com
web: www.novotel.com
dir: M8 junct 18 for Charing Cross. Follow to Sauchiehall St. 3rd right

Enjoying a convenient city centre location and with limited parking spaces, this hotel is ideal for both business and leisure travellers. Well-equipped bedrooms are brightly decorated and offer functional design. Modern public areas include a small fitness club and a brasserie serving a range of meals all day.

Rooms 139 (139 fmly) **Facilities** Wi-fi Gym Sauna Steam room Xmas **Conf** Class 20 Board 20 Thtr 40 **Services** Lift Air con **Parking** 19

G

GLASGOW *continued*

Malmaison Glasgow

★★★ 82% ⊛ HOTEL

☎ 0141 572 1000
278 West George St G2 4LL
e-mail: glasgow@malmaison.com
web: www.malmaison.com
dir: From S & E: M8 junct 18 (Charing Cross). From W & N: M8 city centre

Built around a former church in the historic Charing Cross area, this hotel is a smart, contemporary establishment offering impressive levels of service and hospitality. Bedrooms are spacious and feature a host of modern facilities, such as CD players and mini bars. Dining is a treat here, with French brasserie-style cuisine, backed up by an excellent wine list, served in the original crypt.

Rooms 72 (4 fmly) (19 GF) **Facilities** STV Wi-fi ☼ Gym Cardiovascular equipment New Year **Conf** Board 22 Thtr 30 **Services** Lift **Notes** Civ Wed 60

Uplawmoor Hotel

★★★ 81% ⊛ SMALL HOTEL

☎ 01505 850565
Neilston Rd G78 4AF
e-mail: info@uplawmoor.co.uk
web: www.uplawmoor.co.uk

(For full entry see Uplawmoor)

Holiday Inn Glasgow City Centre - Theatreland

★★★ 80% ⊛ HOTEL

☎ 0141 352 8300
161 West Nile St G1 2RL
e-mail: reservations@higlasgow.com
web: www.holidayinn.co.uk
dir: M8 junct 16, follow signs for Royal Concert Hall, hotel opposite

Built on a corner site close to the Theatre Royal Concert Hall and the main shopping areas, this contemporary hotel features the popular La Bonne Auberge French restaurant, a bar area and conservatory. Bedrooms are well equipped and comfortable; suites are available. Staff are friendly and attentive.

Rooms 113 (20 fmly) (10 smoking) **Facilities** STV FTV Wi-fi **Conf** Class 60 Board 60 Thtr 100 **Services** Lift Air con **Notes** ⊗

Best Western Glasgow City Hotel

★★★ 73% TOWN HOUSE HOTEL

☎ 0141 227 2772
27 Elmbank St G2 4PB
e-mail: manager@cityhotelsglasgow.co.uk
dir: M8 junct 18, Charing Cross into Sauciehall St, 1st right into Elmbank St, pass petrol station, hotel on right

Situated in the heart of the city, this hotel offers spacious and well-equipped accommodation suitable for both families and business guests. Staff are friendly and helpful, and are mindful of the needs of the modern traveller. There is a secure pay car park close to the hotel.

Rooms 52 (4 fmly) (12 GF) ☁ S £59-£109; D £59-£129 **Facilities** FTV Wi-fi ☼ Xmas **Notes** LB ⊗

Argyll Hotel

★★★ 70% HOTEL

☎ 0141 337 3313
973 Sauchiehall St G3 7TQ
e-mail: info@argyllhotelglasgow.co.uk
web: www.argyllhotelglasgow.co.uk
dir: M8 junct 18, stay in right lane, to 2nd lights. Right into Berkley St, right into Elderslie St, 1st left into Sauchiehall St

Enjoying a prime city-centre location this popular hotel is within easy reach of the main shopping district, the university and the Scottish Exhibition & Conference Centre. The bedrooms are attractively presented with a good range of facilities including flat-screen TVs and free Wi-fi. The public areas include Sutherlands Restaurant and a cosy basement bar.

Rooms 38 (8 fmly) (5 GF) **Facilities** FTV Wi-fi **Conf** Class 16 Board 20 Thtr 25 **Services** Lift Parking 5 **Notes** ⊗

Campanile Glasgow

BUDGET HOTEL

☎ 0141 287 7700
10 Tunnel St G3 8HL
e-mail: glasgow@campanile.com
web: www.campanile.com
dir: M8 junct 19, follow signs to SECC. Hotel adjacent to SECC

This modern building offers accommodation in smart, well-equipped bedrooms, all with en suite bathrooms. Refreshments may be taken at the informal bistro. See also the Hotel Groups pages.

Rooms 106 (2 fmly) (21 GF) **Conf** Class 60 Board 90 Thtr 150

Holiday Inn Express Glasgow City Centre - Riverside

BUDGET HOTEL

☎ 0141 548 5000
122 Stockwell St G1 4LT
e-mail: info@expressglasgow.co.uk
web: www.expressglasgow.co.uk
dir: M8 (E & S) junct 19 SECC, left at end of exit, follow river under Central Station bridge to Stockwell St

A modern hotel ideal for families and business travellers. Fresh and uncomplicated, the spacious rooms include Sky TV, power shower and tea and coffee-making facilities. Continental buffet breakfast is included in the room rate; other meals may be taken at the nearby family pub or restaurant. See also the Hotel Groups pages.

Rooms 128 (79 fmly) (13 smoking) **Conf** Class 16 Board 16 Thtr 30

Holiday Inn Express - Glasgow Theatreland

BUDGET HOTEL

☎ 0141 331 6800
165 West Nile St G1 2RL
e-mail: frontoffice.exp@higlasgow.com
web: www.hiexpressglasgow.co.uk
dir: Follow signs to Royal Concert Hall

Rooms 118 (34 fmly) (17 smoking) **Conf** Board 12 Thtr 20

Ibis Glasgow

BUDGET HOTEL

☎ 0141 225 6000
220 West Regent St G2 4DQ
e-mail: H3139@accor-hotels.com
web: www.ibishotel.com

Modern, budget hotel offering comfortable accommodation in bright and practical bedrooms. Breakfast is self-service and meals are also available in the café-bar 24 hours. See also the Hotel Groups pages.

Rooms 141 ☁ S £55-£140; D £55-£140*

Premier Inn Glasgow (Bearsden)

BUDGET HOTEL

☎ 0871 527 8418
279 Milngavie Rd G61 3DQ
web: www.premierinn.com
dir: M8 junct 16, A81. Pass Asda on right. Hotel on left, behind The Burnbrae

High quality, budget accommodation ideal for both families and business travellers. Spacious, en suite bedrooms feature tea and coffee making facilities, and Freeview TV in most hotels. Internet access and Wi-fi are available for a small fee. The adjacent family restaurant features a wide and varied menu. See also the Hotel Groups pages.

Rooms 61

Premier Inn Glasgow (Bellshill)

BUDGET HOTEL

☎ 0871 527 8421
New Edinburgh Rd, Bellshill ML4 3PD
web: www.premierinn.com
dir: M74 junct 5, A725. Follow Bellshill A721 signs, bear left. At rdbt left, follow Tannochside sign. At next rdbt left into Bellziehill Rd. Hotel on right

Rooms 40

Premier Inn Glasgow (Cambuslang/M74 Jct 1)

BUDGET HOTEL

☎ 0871 527 8422
Cambuslang Investment Park, Off London Rd G32 8YX
web: www.premierinn.com
dir: At end of M74, turn right at rdbt. At 1st lights turn right, at 2nd lights straight ahead. Hotel on right

Rooms 40

Premier Inn Glasgow City Centre Argyle St

BUDGET HOTEL

☎ 0871 527 8436
377 Argyle St G2 8LL
web: www.premierinn.com
dir: From S: M8 junct 19, at pedestrian lights left into Argyle St. Hotel 200yds on right

Rooms 121

Premier Inn Glasgow City Centre (Charing Cross)

BUDGET HOTEL

☎ 0871 527 8438
10 Elmbank Gardens G2 4PP
web: www.premierinn.com
dir: Telephone for directions

Rooms 278

Premier Inn Glasgow City Centre (George Square)

BUDGET HOTEL

☎ 0871 527 8440
187 George St G1 1YU
web: www.premierinn.com
dir: M8 junct 15, into Stirling Rd. Right into Cathedral St. At 1st lights left into Montrose St. Hotel after 1st lights

Rooms 239

Premier Inn Glasgow City Centre South

BUDGET HOTEL

☎ 0871 527 8442
80 Ballater St G5 0TW
web: www.premierinn.com
dir: M8 junct 21 follow East Kilbride signs, right onto A8 into Kingston St. Right into South Portland St, left into Norfolk St, through Gorbals St into Ballater St

Rooms 114

Premier Inn Glasgow East

BUDGET HOTEL

☎ 0871 527 8444
601 Hamilton Rd, Uddington G71 7SA
web: www.premierinn.com
dir: At entrance to Glasgow Zoo, adjacent to junct 4 of M73 & M74

Rooms 66

GLASGOW AIRPORT　　Map 20 NS46
Renfrewshire

Holiday Inn Glasgow Airport

★★★ 79% HOTEL

☎ 0871 942 9031 & 0141 887 1266
Abbotsinch PA3 2TR
e-mail: operations-glasgow@ihg.com
web: www.holidayinn.co.uk
dir: From E: M8 junct 28, follow hotel signs. From W: M8 junct 29, airport slip road to hotel

Located within the airport grounds and within walking distance of the terminal. Bedrooms are well appointed and cater for the needs of the modern traveller; all have mini bars. The open-plan public areas are relaxing as is the restaurant which offers a wide ranging a la carte menu. Wi-fi is available in the public areas.

Rooms 300 (6 fmly) (18 smoking) **Facilities** STV FTV Wi-fi ॐ **Conf** Class 150 Board 75 Thtr 300 Del from £79 to £159 **Services** Lift Air con **Parking** 56 **Notes** Civ Wed 250

Holiday Inn Express Glasgow Airport

BUDGET HOTEL

☎ 0141 842 1100
St Andrews Dr PA3 2TJ
e-mail: info@expressglasgowairport.co.uk
web: www.expressglasgowairport.co.uk
dir: M8 junct 28, at 1st rdbt turn right, hotel on right

A modern hotel ideal for families and business travellers. Fresh and uncomplicated, the spacious rooms include Sky TV, power shower and tea and coffee-making facilities. Continental buffet breakfast is included in the room rate; other meals may be taken at the nearby family pub or restaurant. See also the Hotel Groups pages.

Rooms 143 (65 fmly) (11 GF) **Conf** Class 20 Board 30 Thtr 70

G

GLASGOW AIRPORT *continued*

Premier Inn Glasgow Airport

BUDGET HOTEL

☎ 0871 527 8434
Whitecart Rd, Glasgow Airport PA3 2TH
web: www.premierinn.com
dir: M8 junct 28, follow airport signs for Long Stay & Car Park 3 (Premier Inn signed). At 1st rdbt right into St Andrews Drive. At next rdbt right into Whitecart Rd. Under motorway. Left at garage. Hotel on right

High quality, budget accommodation ideal for both families and business travellers. Spacious, en suite bedrooms feature tea and coffee making facilities, and Freeview TV in most hotels. Internet access and Wi-fi are available for a small fee. The adjacent family restaurant features a wide and varied menu. See also the Hotel Groups pages.

Rooms 104

Premier Inn Glasgow (Paisley)

BUDGET HOTEL

☎ 0871 527 8432
Phoenix Retail Park PA1 2BH
web: www.premierinn.com
dir: M8 junct 28a, A737 signed Irvine, take 1st exit signed Linwood, left at 1st rdbt to Phoenix Park

Rooms 40

GLENEAGLES

See Auchterarder

GLENFINNAN   Map 22 NM98
Highland

The Prince's House

★★★ 75% ◉◉ SMALL HOTEL

☎ 01397 722246
PH37 4LT
e-mail: princeshouse@glenfinnan.co.uk
web: www.glenfinnan.co.uk
dir: On A830, 0.5m on right past Glenfinnan Monument. 200mtrs from railway station

This delightful hotel enjoys a well deserved reputation for fine food and excellent hospitality. The hotel has inspiring views and sits close to where 'Bonnie' Prince Charlie raised the Jacobite standard. Comfortably appointed bedrooms offer pleasing decor. Excellent local game and seafood can be enjoyed in the restaurant and the bar.

Rooms 9 ☎ **S** £65-£75; **D** £95-£145 (incl. bkfst)*
Facilities STV FTV Wi-fi Fishing New Year
Conf Class 20 Thtr 40 **Parking** 18 **Notes** LB Closed Xmas & Jan-Feb (ex New Year) RS Nov-Dec & Mar

GLENROTHES   Map 21 NO20
Fife

Holiday Inn Express Glenrothes

BUDGET HOTEL

☎ 01592 745509
Leslie Roundabout, Leslie Rd KY6 3EP
e-mail: reservations@hiexpressglenrothes.co.uk
web: www.hiexpress.com/glenrothes
dir: M90 junct 2A, onto A911 for Leslie. Through 4 rdbts, hotel on left

A modern hotel ideal for families and business travellers. Fresh and uncomplicated, the spacious rooms include Sky TV, power shower and tea and coffee-making facilities. Continental buffet breakfast is included in the room rate; other meals may be taken at the nearby family pub or restaurant. See also the Hotel Groups pages.

Rooms 49 (40 fmly) (21 GF) ☎ **S** £49.95-£99;
D £49.95-£99 (incl. bkfst)* **Conf** Class 16 Board 16 Thtr 30

Premier Inn Glenrothes

BUDGET HOTEL

☎ 0871 527 8454
Beaufort Dr, Bankhead Roundabout KY7 4UJ
web: www.premierinn.com
dir: M90 junct 2a N'bound, A92 to Glenrothes. At 2nd rbt (Bankhead) take 3rd exit. Hotel on left

High quality, budget accommodation ideal for both families and business travellers. Spacious, en suite bedrooms feature tea and coffee making facilities, and Freeview TV in most hotels. Internet access and Wi-fi are available for a small fee. The adjacent family restaurant features a wide and varied menu. See also the Hotel Groups pages.

Rooms 41

GRANGEMOUTH   Map 21 NS98
Falkirk

The Grange Manor

★★★★ 77% HOTEL

☎ 01324 474836
Glensburgh FK3 8XJ
e-mail: info@grangemanor.co.uk
web: www.grangemanor.co.uk
dir: E: M9 junct 6, hotel 200mtrs to right. W: M9 junct 5, A905 for 2m

Located south of town and close to the M9, this stylish hotel, popular with business and corporate clientele, benefits from hands-on family ownership. It offers spacious, high quality accommodation with superb bathrooms. Public areas include a comfortable foyer area, a lounge bar and a smart restaurant. Wallace's bar and restaurant is adjacent to the main house in the converted stables. Staff throughout are very friendly.

Rooms 36 (30 annexe) (6 fmly) (15 GF) **S** £60-£100;
D £60-£140* **Facilities** FTV Wi-fi New Year
Conf Class 68 Board 40 Thtr 120 Del from £123 to £154* **Services** Lift **Parking** 154 **Notes** LB ⊗ Civ Wed 120

GRANTOWN-ON-SPEY   Map 23 NJ02
Highland

Grant Arms Hotel

★★★ 79% HOTEL

☎ 01479 872526
25-27 The Square PH26 3HF
e-mail: info@grantarmshotel.com
web: www.grantarmshotel.com
dir: Exit A9 N of Aviemore onto A95

Conveniently located in the centre of the town, this fine hotel is appointed to a high standard yet still retains the building's traditional character. The spacious bedrooms are stylishly presented and very well equipped. The Garden Restaurant is a popular venue for dinner, and lighter snacks can be enjoyed in the comfortable bar. Modern conference facilities are available and the hotel is very popular with birdwatchers and wildlife enthusiasts.

Rooms 50 (7 fmly) ☎ **S** £50-£75; **D** £100-£150 (incl. bkfst) **Facilities** FTV Wi-fi ↳ Birdwatching & Wildlife Club ♫ Xmas New Year **Conf** Class 30 Board 16 Thtr 70 Del from £90 to £125 **Services** Lift **Notes** LB

Save on hotels. Book at **theAA.com/hotel**

GLA – HAM 553 SCOTLAND

GREENOCK
Inverclyde   Map 20 NS27

Holiday Inn Express Greenock

BUDGET HOTEL

☎ 01475 786666
Cartsburn PA15 1AE
e-mail: greenock@holidayinnexpress.org.uk
web: www.hiexpressgreenock.co.uk
dir: M8 junct 31, A8 to Greenock, right at 5th rdbt, hotel on right

A modern hotel ideal for families and business travellers. Fresh and uncomplicated, the spacious rooms include Sky TV, power shower and tea and coffee-making facilities. Continental buffet breakfast is included in the room rate; other meals may be taken at the nearby family pub or restaurant. See also the Hotel Groups pages.

Rooms 71 (15 fmly) (6 GF) (20 smoking)
Conf Class 48 Board 32 Thtr 70

Premier Inn Greenock

BUDGET HOTEL

☎ 0871 527 8476
The Point, 1-3 James Watt Way PA15 2AD
web: www.premierinn.com
dir: A8 to Greenock. At rdbt junct of East Hamilton St & Main St (McDonalds visable on right) take 3rd exit. Hotel on left

High quality, budget accommodation ideal for both families and business travellers. Spacious, en suite bedrooms feature tea and coffee making facilities, and Freeview TV in most hotels. Internet access and Wi-fi are available for a small fee. The adjacent family restaurant features a wide and varied menu. See also the Hotel Groups pages.

Rooms 17

GRETNA
SERVICE AREA (A74(M))
Dumfries & Galloway   Map 21 NY36

Days Inn Gretna Green - M74

BUDGET HOTEL

☎ 01461 337566
Welcome Break Service Area DG16 5HQ
e-mail: gretna.hotel@welcomebreak.co.uk
web: www.welcomebreak.co.uk
dir: Between junct 21 & 22 of A74(M) - accessible from both N'bound & S'bound carriageways

This modern building offers accommodation in smart, spacious and well-equipped bedrooms suitable for families and business travellers, and all with en suite bathrooms. Continental breakfast is available and other refreshments may be taken at the nearby family restaurant. See also the Hotel Groups pages.

Rooms 64 (54 fmly) (64 GF) **S** £39.95-£65.95; **D** £49.95-£89.95*

GRETNA (WITH GRETNA GREEN) Map 21 NY36
Dumfries & Galloway

Smiths at Gretna Green

★★★★ 78% ◉ ◉ HOTEL   CLASSIC BRITISH HOTELS

☎ 01461 337007
Gretna Green DG16 5EA
e-mail: info@smithsgretnagreen.com
web: www.smithsgretnagreen.com
dir: From M74 junct 22 follow signs to Old Blacksmith's Shop. Hotel opposite

Located next to the World Famous Old Blacksmith's Shop Centre just off the motorway linking Scotland and England. The bedrooms offer a spacious environment, complete with flat-screen TVs, DVD players and broadband. Family rooms feature a separate children's area with bunk beds, each with its own TV. Three suites and a penthouse apartment are also available. Open-plan contemporary day rooms lead to the brasserie restaurant; impressive conference and banqueting facilities are provided.

Rooms 50 (8 fmly) ⚓ **Facilities** STV FTV Wi-fi ⚓ HL New Year **Conf** Class 100 Board 40 Thtr 250 Del from £95 to £145* **Services** Lift Air con **Parking** 115 **Notes** Civ Wed 150

The Gables Hotel

★★★ 75% HOTEL

☎ 01461 338300
1 Annan Rd DG16 5DQ
e-mail: reservations@gables-hotel-gretna.co.uk
dir: M74 S or M6/M74 N follow signs for Gretna. At rdbt at Gretna Gateway take exit onto Annan Rd, hotel 200yds on right

This Grade II listed hotel is located close to the Gretna Gateway and is ideally located to explore both Galloway and the Border City of Carlisle. Bedrooms offer comfortable and well-appointed accommodation. The main restaurant offers a carte menu with a range of freshly prepared dishes, whilst Saddlers bar provides light snacks and meals.

Rooms 31 (5 fmly) (10 GF) ⚓ **S** £59-£89; **D** £79-£130 (incl. bkfst) **Facilities** FTV Wi-fi Xmas New Year **Conf** Class 60 Board 48 Thtr 100 **Parking** 60 **Notes** ⊗ Civ Wed 100

H

HAMILTON
South Lanarkshire   Map 20 NS75

Holiday Inn Express Hamilton

BUDGET HOTEL

☎ 01698 456300
Keith St ML3 7BL
e-mail: hamilton@holidayinnexpress.org.uk
web: www.hiexpress.com/hamilton
dir: 0.25m from M74 junct 6, in town centre

A modern hotel ideal for families and business travellers. Fresh and uncomplicated, the spacious rooms include Sky TV, power shower and tea and coffee-making facilities. Continental buffet breakfast is included in the room rate; other meals may be taken at the nearby family pub or restaurant. See also the Hotel Groups pages.

Rooms 104 (68 fmly) (26 smoking) ⚓ **D** £39-£99 (incl. bkfst)* **Conf** Class 32 Board 36 Thtr 60 Del from £75 to £109*

H

HAWICK   Map 21 NT51
Scottish Borders

Mansfield House Hotel

★★★ 81% HOTEL

☎ 01450 360400
Weensland Rd TD9 8LB
e-mail: reception@themansfieldhousehotel.co.uk
dir: A7 to Hawick onto A698 (Weensland Rd). Hotel
0.75m on right

This hotel is set in its own mature grounds at the top
of a hill with spectacular views over Hawick. The
bedrooms, located on the basement level and the first
floor, differ in size and include the fantastic Tower
Room accessed via a steep, narrow staircase - but
the climb is well worth the effort! Public areas are
welcoming and the style is in keeping with the age of
the building. The restaurant proudly uses local,
quality ingredients for the menus.

Rooms 16 (2 fmly) **Facilities** FTV Wi-fi ⓘ Xmas New
Year **Conf** Class 160 Board 60 Thtr 160 Del from £75
to £120 **Parking** 25 **Notes** ⊗ Civ Wed 120

HOWWOOD   Map 20 NS36
Renfrewshire

Bowfield Hotel & Country Club

★★★ 80% ⑧ HOTEL

☎ 01505 705225
PA9 1DZ
e-mail: enquiries@bowfieldhotel.co.uk
web: www.bowfieldhotel.co.uk
dir: M8 junct 28a/29, A737 for 6m, left onto B787,
right in 2m, 1m to hotel

This former textile mill is now a popular hotel which
has become a convenient stopover for travellers using
Glasgow Airport. The leisure club offers very good
facilities. Public areas have beamed ceilings, brick
and white painted walls, and welcoming open fires.
Bedrooms are housed in a separate wing and offer
good modern comforts and facilities.

Rooms 23 (3 fmly) (7 GF) **S** £55-£75; **D** £60-£90 (incl.
bkfst)* **Facilities** Spa FTV Wi-fi ⓘ supervised Gym
Squash Children's soft play area Aerobics studio
Health & beauty Xmas New Year **Conf** Class 60
Board 40 Thtr 100 Del from £85 to £105*
Parking 120 **Notes** LB ⊗ Civ Wed 80

INVERGARRY   Map 22 NH30
Highland

Glengarry Castle Hotel

★★★ 82% ⑧ COUNTRY HOUSE HOTEL

☎ 01809 501254
PH35 4HW
e-mail: castle@glengarry.net
web: www.glengarry.net
dir: On A82, 0.5m from A82/A87 junct

This charming country-house hotel is set in 50 acres
of grounds on the shores of Loch Oich. The spacious
day rooms include comfortable sitting rooms with lots
to read and board games to play. The classical dining
room boasts an innovative menu that showcases
local Scottish produce. The smart bedrooms vary in
size and style but all boast magnificent loch or
woodland views.

Rooms 26 (2 fmly) **S** £70-£80; **D** £106-£188 (incl.
bkfst) **Facilities** FTV Wi-fi ⓘ Fishing **Parking** 30
Notes Closed mid Nov-mid Mar

INVERGORDON   Map 23 NH76
Highland

Kincraig Castle Hotel

★★★★ 77% ⑧ COUNTRY HOUSE HOTEL

☎ 01349 852587
IV18 0LF
e-mail: info@kincraig-house-hotel.co.uk
web: www.kincraig-house-hotel.co.uk
dir: Off A9 past Alness towards Tain. Hotel on left
0.25m past Rosskeen Church

This imposing castle is set in well-tended grounds in
an elevated position with views over the Cromarty
Firth. It offers smart, individually designed, well-
equipped bedrooms with satellite TVs, and inviting
public areas that retain the original features.
However, it is the friendly service and commitment to
guest care that will leave a lasting impression.

Rooms 15 (1 fmly) (1 GF) **S** £60-£130; **D** £80-£330
(incl. bkfst)* **Facilities** STV Wi-fi ⓘ Xmas New Year
Conf Class 30 Board 24 Thtr 50 Del from £150 to
£190 **Parking** 30 **Notes** LB Civ Wed 70

INVERKEILOR   Map 23 NO64
Angus

Gordon's

⑨ ⑨ ⑨ RESTAURANT WITH ROOMS

☎ 01241 830364
Main St DD11 5RN
e-mail: gordonsrest@aol.com
dir: Exit A92 between Arbroath & Montrose into
Inverkeilor

It's worth a detour off the main road to this family-
run restaurant with rooms set in the centre of the
village. It has earned AA Rosettes for dinner, and the
excellent breakfasts are equally memorable. A huge
fire dominates the restaurant on cooler evenings, and
there is a small lounge with limited seating. The
attractive bedrooms are tastefully decorated and
thoughtfully equipped; the larger two are furnished in
pine.

Rooms 5 (1 annexe)

INVERNESS   Map 23 NH64
Highland

Culloden House Hotel

★★★★ 83% ⑧ ⑧ HOTEL

☎ 01463 790461
Culloden IV2 7BZ
e-mail: info@cullodenhouse.co.uk
web: www.cullodenhouse.co.uk
dir: A96 from Inverness, right for Culloden. 1m after
2nd lights, left at church

Dating from the late 1700s this impressive mansion
is set in extensive grounds close to the famous
Culloden Battlefield. High ceilings and intricate
cornices are particular features of the public rooms,
including the elegant Adam dining room. Bedrooms
come in a range of sizes and styles, with a number
situated in a separate house.

Rooms 28 (5 annexe) (1 fmly) (3 GF) **S** £100-£175;
D £135-£270 (incl. bkfst)* **Facilities** FTV Wi-fi ⓘ
Putt green ⓘ Boules Badminton Golf driving net New
Year **Conf** Class 40 Board 30 Thtr 60 Del from £145 to
£315* **Parking** 50 **Notes** LB No children 10yrs Closed
24-28 Dec Civ Wed 65

Save on hotels. Book at **theAA.com/hotel**

HAW – INV 555 SCOTLAND

The New Drumossie Hotel

★★★★ 80% ◉◉ HOTEL

☎ 01463 236451 & 0870 194 2110
Old Perth Rd IV2 5BE
e-mail: stay@drumossiehotel.co.uk
dir: From A9 follow signs for Culloden Battlefield, hotel on left after 1m

Set in nine acres of landscaped hillside grounds south of Inverness, this hotel has fine views of the Moray Firth towards Ben Wyvis. Art deco style decoration together with a country-house atmosphere are found throughout. Service is friendly and attentive, the food imaginative and enjoyable and the bedrooms spacious and well presented. The main function room is probably the largest in this area.

Rooms 44 (10 fmly) (6 GF) **Facilities** STV Wi-fi HL Fishing New Year **Conf** Class 200 Board 40 Thtr 500 **Services** Lift **Parking** 200 **Notes** ⊗ Civ Wed 400

Loch Ness Country House Hotel

★★★★ 79% ◉◉ SMALL HOTEL

☎ 01463 230512
Loch Ness Rd IV3 8JN
e-mail: info@lochnesscountryhousehotel.co.uk
web: www.lochnesscountryhousehotel.co.uk
dir: On A82, 1m from Inverness town boundary

Built in the Georgian era, this fine house is perfectly situated in its own six acre private Highland estate. The hotel has luxurious bedrooms, four of which are in the garden suite cottages. The stylish restaurant serves the best of local produce and guests have a choice of cosy well-appointed lounges for after dinner drinks. The terrace has splendid views over the landscaped gardens towards Inverness.

Rooms 13 (2 annexe) (8 fmly) (3 GF) **S** £70-£145; **D** £80-£250 (incl. bkfst)* **Facilities** FTV Wi-fi Xmas New Year **Conf** Class 40 Board 40 Thtr 100 Del from £120 to £180* **Parking** 50 **Notes** LB Civ Wed 150

Glenmoriston Town House Hotel

★★★★ 76% HOTEL

☎ 01463 223777
20 Ness Bank IV2 4SF
e-mail: reception@glenmoristontownhouse.com
web: www.glenmoristontownhouse.com
dir: On riverside opposite theatre

Bold contemporary designs blend seamlessly with the classical architecture of this stylish hotel, situated on the banks of the River Ness. Delightful day rooms include a piano bar and two eating options. Abstract Restaurant features accomplished modern French cuisine based on the finest Scottish produce, and Contrast Brasserie is ideal for relaxed meals from breakfast through to dinner, and when possible for eating alfresco when the weather warms up. The sleek, modern, individually designed bedrooms have many facilities including free Wi-fi, DVD players and flat-screen TVs.

Rooms 30 (15 annexe) (1 fmly) (6 GF) **Facilities** STV Wi-fi ♫ Xmas New Year **Conf** Class 10 Board 10 Thtr 15 **Parking** 40 **Notes** ⊗ Closed 26-28 Dec & 4-6 Jan Civ Wed 70

Bunchrew House Hotel

★★★★ 75% ◉◉ COUNTRY HOUSE HOTEL

☎ 01463 234917
Bunchrew IV3 8TA
e-mail: welcome@bunchrewhousehotel.com
web: www.bunchrewhousehotel.com
dir: W on A862. Hotel 2m after canal on right

Overlooking the Beauly Firth this impressive mansion house dates from the 17th century and retains much original character. Individually styled bedrooms are spacious and tastefully furnished. A wood-panelled restaurant is the setting for artfully constructed cooking and there is a choice of comfortable lounges complete with real fires.

Rooms 16 (4 fmly) (1 GF) ☞ **S** £99-£155; **D** £98-£230 (incl. bkfst)* **Facilities** FTV Wi-fi Fishing New Year **Conf** Class 30 Board 30 Thtr 80 Del from £160 to £240* **Parking** 40 **Notes** LB Closed 24-27 Dec Civ Wed 92

The Columba Hotel

★★★★ 74% HOTEL

 OXFORD
HOTELS & INNS

☎ 08444 146 522
Ness Walk IV3 5NF
e-mail: reservations.columba@ohiml.com
web: www.oxfordhotelsandinns.com
dir: From A9, A96 follow signs to town centre, pass Eastgate shopping centre into Academy St, at bottom left into Bank St, right over bridge, hotel 1st left

Originally built in 1881 and with many original features retained, the Columba Hotel lies in the heart of Inverness overlooking the fast flowing River Ness. The bedrooms are very stylish, and public areas include a first-floor restaurant and lounge. A second dining option is the ever popular McNabs bar bistro, which is ideal for less formal meals.

Rooms 76 (4 fmly) **Facilities** FTV Wi-fi ♫ Xmas New Year **Conf** Class 100 Board 60 Thtr 200 **Services** Lift **Notes** Civ Wed 120

Best Western Palace Hotel & Spa

★★★ 77% HOTEL

☎ 01463 223243
8 Ness Walk IV3 5NG
e-mail: palace@miltonhotels.com
web: www.invernesspalacehotel.co.uk
dir: A82 Glenurquhart Rd onto Ness Walk. Hotel 300yds on right opposite Inverness Castle

Set on the north side of the River Ness close to the Eden Court theatre and a short walk from the town, this hotel has a contemporary look. Bedrooms offer good levels of comfort and equipment, and a smart leisure centre attracts a mixed market.

Rooms 88 (48 annexe) (3 fmly) **S** £89.90-£199.90; **D** £99.90-£269.90* **Facilities** Spa FTV Wi-fi ⊗ supervised Gym Beautician Sauna Steam room Xmas New Year **Conf** Class 40 Board 30 Thtr 80 Del from £142.90 to £214.90* **Services** Lift **Parking** 38 **Notes** LB Civ Wed 40

INVERNESS *continued*

Royal Highland Hotel

★★★ 77% HOTEL

☎ 01463 231926 & 251451
Station Square, Academy St IV1 1LG
e-mail: info@royalhighlandhotel.co.uk
web: www.royalhighlandhotel.co.uk
dir: From A9 into town centre. Hotel next to rail
station & Eastgate Retail Centre

Built in 1858 adjacent to the railway station, this
hotel has the typically grand foyer of the Victorian era
with comfortable seating. The contemporary ASH
Brasserie and bar is a refreshing venue for both
eating and drinking throughout the day. The generally
spacious bedrooms are comfortably equipped
especially for the business traveller.

Rooms 85 (12 fmly) (2 GF) (25 smoking) 🐾
Facilities FTV Wi-fi Xmas New Year **Conf** Class 80
Board 80 Thtr 200 **Services** Lift **Parking** 8
Notes Civ Wed 200

Thistle Inverness

★★★ 77% HOTEL

☎ 0871 376 9023
Millburn Rd IV2 3TR
e-mail: reception.inverness@thistle.co.uk
web: www.thistlehotels.com/inverness
dir: From A9 take Raigmore Interchange exit (towards
Aberdeen), 3rd left towards centre. Hotel opposite

Well located within easy distance of the town centre.
This well presented hotel offers modern bedrooms
including three suites. There is a well equipped
leisure centre along with an informal brasserie and
open-plan bar and lounge. Ample parking is an added
benefit.

Rooms 118 **Facilities** Wi-fi HL 🕙 supervised Gym
Sauna Steam room Xmas New Year **Conf** Class 70
Board 50 Thtr 120 **Services** Lift **Parking** 80 **Notes** ⊗
Civ Wed 120

Ramada Encore Inverness City Centre

★★★ 75% HOTEL

☎ 01463 228850
63 Academy St IV1 1LU
e-mail: reservations@encoreinverness.co.uk
dir: A9, A82, B865, hotel on right

This hotel is ideally located, as its name suggests,
close to the main shopping district, railway station
and the tourist attractions of Inverness. The
contemporary bedrooms have a bright stylish design
and all rooms are equipped with Wi-fi along with an
extensive choice of TV channels and movies. Public

areas include a modern restaurant and a light-filled
lounge area with comfortable seating. There is a
choice of ground-floor business suites which makes
the hotel very popular with corporate guests.

Rooms 90 (20 fmly) **Facilities** STV FTV Wi-fi
Conf Class 20 Board 20 Thtr 34 **Services** Lift
Notes ⊗

Holiday Inn Express Inverness

BUDGET HOTEL

☎ 01463 732700
Stoneyfield IV2 7PA
e-mail: info@expressinverness.co.uk
web: www.hiexpress.com/inverness
dir: From A9 follow A96 & Inverness Airport signs,
hotel on right

A modern hotel ideal for families and business
travellers. Fresh and uncomplicated, the spacious
rooms include Sky TV, power shower and tea and
coffee-making facilities. Continental buffet breakfast
is included in the room rate; other meals may be
taken at the nearby family pub or restaurant. See also
the Hotel Groups pages.

Rooms 94 (43 fmly) (24 GF) 🐾 **Conf** Class 20
Board 15 Thtr 35

Premier Inn Inverness Centre (Milburn Rd)

BUDGET HOTEL

☎ 0871 527 8544
Millburn Rd IV2 3QX
web: www.premierinn.com
dir: From A9 & A96 junct (Raigmore Interchange,
signed Airport/Aberdeen), take B865 towards town
centre, hotel 100yds after next rdbt

High quality, budget accommodation ideal for both
families and business travellers. Spacious, en suite
bedrooms feature tea and coffee making facilities,
and Freeview TV in most hotels. Internet access and
Wi-fi are available for a small fee. The adjacent
family restaurant features a wide and varied menu.
See also the Hotel Groups pages.

Rooms 55

Premier Inn Inverness East

BUDGET HOTEL

☎ 0871 527 8546
Beechwood Business Park IV2 3BW
web: www.premierinn.com
dir: From A9 follow Raigmore Hospital, Police HQ &
Inshes Retail Park signs

Rooms 60

| **INVERURIE** | **Map 23 NJ72** |
| Aberdeenshire | |

Macdonald Pittodrie House

★★★★ 75% ⊛ HOTEL

☎ 0870 1942111 & 01467 681744
Chapel of Garioch, Pitcaple AB51 5HS
e-mail: pittodrie@macdonald-hotels.co.uk
web: www.macdonald-hotels.com/pittodrie
dir: From A96 towards Inverness, pass Inverurie under
bridge with lights. Turn left & follow signs

Set in extensive grounds this house dates from the
15th century and retains many historic features.
Public rooms include a gracious drawing room,
restaurant, and a cosy bar boasting an impressive
selection of whiskies. The well-proportioned bedrooms
are found in both the original house and in the
extension that was designed to match the existing
building.

Rooms 27 (3 fmly) **Facilities** STV FTV Wi-fi Clay
pigeon shooting Quad biking Outdoor activities Xmas
New Year **Conf** Class 75 Board 50 Thtr 150
Parking 200 **Notes** Civ Wed 120

| **IRVINE** | **Map 20 NS33** |
| North Ayrshire | |

Menzies Irvine

★★★★ 76% HOTEL

☎ 01294 274272
46 Annick Rd KA11 4LD
e-mail: irvine@menzieshotels.co.uk
web: www.menzieshotels.co.uk
dir: From A78 at Warrix Interchange follow Irvine
Central signs. At rdbt 2nd exit (town centre). At next
rdbt right onto A71/Kilmarnock. Hotel 100mtrs on left

Situated on the edge of Irvine with good
transportation links (including Prestwick Airport just
seven miles away), this is a well-presented hotel that
has an extremely friendly team with good customer
care awareness. The decor is contemporary
throughout, and there is a brasserie-style restaurant,
cocktail bar and spacious lounge.

Rooms 128 (14 fmly) (64 GF) **Facilities** STV FTV Wi-fi
⅋ Fishing Xmas New Year **Conf** Class 140 Board 100
Thtr 280 **Parking** 220 **Notes** Civ Wed 200

Save on hotels. Book at **theAA.com/hotel**

INV – KIL 557 SCOTLAND

KELSO
Scottish Borders
Map 21 NT73

The Roxburghe Hotel & Golf Course
★★★★ 79% ® COUNTRY HOUSE HOTEL

☎ 01573 450331
Heiton TD5 8JZ
e-mail: hotel@roxburghe.net
web: www.roxburghe-hotel.com
dir: From A68 Jedburgh take A698 to Heiton, 3m SW of Kelso

Outdoor sporting pursuits are popular at this impressive Jacobean mansion owned by the Duke of Roxburghe, and set in 500 acres of woods and parkland bordering the River Teviot. Gracious public areas are the perfect settings for afternoon teas and carefully prepared meals. The elegant bedrooms are individually designed, some by the Duchess herself, and include superior rooms, some with four posters and log fires.

Rooms 22 (6 annexe) (3 fmly) (8 GF) **S** £120-£270; **D** £150-£300 (incl. bkfst)* **Facilities** Spa STV FTV Wi-fi ⚓ 18 Putt green Fishing ⛵ Clay shooting Health & beauty salon Mountain bike hire Falconry Archery Xmas New Year **Conf** Class 20 Board 20 Thtr 50 Del from £169 to £229* **Parking** 150 **Notes** LB Civ Wed 60

KENMORE
Perth & Kinross
Map 21 NN74

Kenmore Hotel
★★★ 79% ® HOTEL

☎ 01887 830205
The Square PH15 2NU
e-mail: reception@kenmorehotel.co.uk
web: www.kenmorehotel.com
dir: Exit A9 at Ballinluig onto A827, through Aberfeldy to Kenmore, hotel in village centre

Dating back to 1572, this riverside hotel is Scotland's oldest inn and has a rich and interesting history. Bedrooms have tasteful decor, and meals can be enjoyed in the restaurant which has panoramic views of the River Tay. The choice of bars includes one with real fires.

Rooms 40 (13 annexe) (4 fmly) (7 GF) **Facilities** STV Wi-fi Salmon fishing on River Tay Xmas New Year **Conf** Class 60 Board 50 Thtr 80 **Services** Lift **Parking** 40 **Notes** Civ Wed 150

KILCHRENAN
Argyll & Bute
Map 20 NN02

Taychreggan Hotel
★★★★ 76% ®® COUNTRY HOUSE HOTEL

☎ 01866 833211 & 833366
PA35 1HQ
e-mail: info@taychregganhotel.co.uk
web: www.taychregganhotel.co.uk
dir: W from Crianlarich on A85 to Taynuilt, S for 7m on B845 (single track) to Kilchrenan

K

Surrounded by stunning Highland scenery this stylish and superbly presented hotel, once a drover's cottage, enjoys an idyllic setting in 40 acres of wooded grounds on the shores of Loch Awe. The hotel has a smart bar with adjacent courtyard Orangerie and a choice of quiet lounges with deep, luxurious sofas. A well earned reputation has been achieved by the kitchen for the skilfully prepared dinners that showcase the local and seasonal Scottish larder. Families, and also dogs and their owners, are welcome.

Rooms 18 (1 fmly) **Facilities** FTV Wi-fi Fishing ⛵ Air rifle range Archery Clay pigeon shooting Falconry Mock deer stalk Xmas New Year **Conf** Class 15 Board 20 **Parking** 40 **Notes** Closed 3 Jan-9 Feb Civ Wed 70

KILCHRENAN *continued*

The Ardanaiseig Hotel

★★★ ◎◎ COUNTRY HOUSE HOTEL

☎ 01866 833333
by Loch Awe PA35 1HE
e-mail: info@ardanaiseig.com
dir: A85 at Taynuilt onto B845 to Kilchrenan. Left in front of pub (road very narrow) signed 'Ardanaiseig Hotel' & 'No Through Road'. Continue for 3m

Set amid lovely gardens and breathtaking scenery beside the shore of Loch Awe, this peaceful country-house hotel was built in a Scottish baronial style in 1834. Many fine pieces of furniture are evident in the bedrooms and charming day rooms, which include a drawing room, a library bar and an elegant dining room. The bedrooms are individually designed including some with four posters, some with loch views and some with access to the garden; standing on its own by the water is the Boat Shed, a delightful one bedroom suite. Guests can certainly look forward to the award-winning, skilfully cooked dishes that make excellent use of local, seasonal produce.

Rooms 18 (4 fmly) (5 GF) ♠ **Facilities** FTV Wi-fi ⇗ Fishing ⇘ Boating Clay pigeon shooting Bikes for hire In house massage treatments Xmas New Year **Parking** 20 **Notes** Civ Wed 50

KILLIECRANKIE Map 23 NN96
Perth & Kinross

Killiecrankie House Hotel

★★★ ◎◎ SMALL HOTEL

☎ 01796 473220
PH16 5LG
e-mail: enquiries@killiecrankiehotel.co.uk
dir: Exit A9 at Killiecrankie onto B8079. Hotel 3m on right

Originally built in the 1840s, Killiecrankie sits in fours acres of wooded grounds with beautifully landscaped gardens; it enjoys a tranquil location by the Pass of Killiecrankie and the River Garry. Public areas include a wood-panelled bar and a cosy sitting room with original artwork and a blazing fire in colder months. Each of the bedrooms is individually decorated, well equipped and have wonderful countryside views.

Rooms 10 (2 GF) **Facilities** FTV Wi-fi ⇘ Xmas New Year **Parking** 20 **Notes** Closed 3 Jan-12 Mar

---

KILMARNOCK Map 20 NS43
East Ayrshire

The Fenwick Hotel

★★★ 82% HOTEL

☎ 01560 600478
Fenwick KA3 6AU
e-mail: info@thefenwickhotel.co.uk
web: www.thefenwickhotel.co.uk
dir: M77 junct 8, B7061 towards Fenwick, follow hotel signs

Benefiting from a great location alongside the M77 and offering easy links to Ayr, Kilmarnock and Glasgow. The spacious bedrooms are thoughtfully equipped; complimentary Wi-fi is available throughout the hotel. The bright restaurant offers both formal and informal dining and there are two bars to choose from.

Rooms 30 (1 fmly) (9 GF) ♠ **Facilities** STV FTV Wi-fi ⇘ Xmas New Year **Conf** Class 280 Board 150 Thtr 280 **Services** Lift **Parking** 64 **Notes** Civ Wed 110

Premier Inn Kilmarnock

BUDGET HOTEL

☎ 0871 527 8566
Moorfield Roundabout, Annadale KA1 2RS
web: www.premierinn.com
dir: M74 junct 8 signed Kilmarnock (A71). From M77 onto A71 to Irvine. At next rdbt right onto B7064 signed Crosshouse Hospital. Hotel on right

High quality, budget accommodation ideal for both families and business travellers. Spacious, en suite bedrooms feature tea and coffee making facilities, and Freeview TV in most hotels. Internet access and Wi-fi are available for a small fee. The adjacent family restaurant features a wide and varied menu. See also the Hotel Groups pages.

Rooms 40

KINCARDINE Map 21 NS98
Fife

Premier Inn Falkirk North

BUDGET HOTEL

☎ 0871 527 8394
Bowtrees Roundabout, Houghs of Airth FK2 8PJ
web: www.premierinn.com
dir: From N: M9 junct 7 (or from S: M876) towards Kincardine Bridge. On rdbt at end of slip road

High quality, budget accommodation ideal for both families and business travellers. Spacious, en suite bedrooms feature tea and coffee making facilities, and Freeview TV in most hotels. Internet access and Wi-fi are available for a small fee. The adjacent family restaurant features a wide and varied menu. See also the Hotel Groups pages.

Rooms 40

KINCLAVEN Map 21 NO13
Perth & Kinross

Ballathie House Hotel

★★★★ 78% ◎◎ COUNTRY HOUSE HOTEL

☎ 01250 883268
PH1 4QN
e-mail: email@ballathiehousehotel.com
web: www.ballathiehousehotel.com
dir: From A9, 2m N of Perth, take B9099 through Stanley, follow signs. Or from A93 at Beech Hedge follow signs for hotel, 2.5m

Set in delightful grounds, this splendid Scottish mansion house combines classical grandeur with modern comfort. Bedrooms range from well-proportioned master rooms to modern standard rooms, and many boast antique furniture and art deco bathrooms. It might be worth requesting one of

K

Save on hotels. Book at **theAA.com/hotel**

KIL – KIR 559 SCOTLAND

the Riverside Rooms, a purpose-built development right on the banks of the river, complete with balconies and terraces. The elegant restaurant has views over the River Tay.

Rooms 41 (16 annexe) (2 fmly) (10 GF) 🐾 **S** £95-£135; **D** £190-£300 (incl. bkfst)* **Facilities** FTV Wi-fi Fishing 🏊 Xmas New Year **Conf** Class 20 Board 30 Thtr 50 Del from £140 to £170* **Services** Lift **Parking** 50 **Notes** Civ Wed 90

KINGUSSIE
Highland
Map 23 NH70

INSPECTORS' CHOICE

The Cross at Kingussie

◉◉◉ RESTAURANT WITH ROOMS

☎ 01540 661166
Tweed Mill Brae, Ardbroilach Rd PH21 1LB
e-mail: relax@thecross.co.uk
dir: From lights in Kingussie centre take Ardbroilach Rd, 300yds left into Tweed Mill Brae

Situated in the valley near Kingussie, this former tweed mill sits next to a river, with wild flower gardens and a sunny terrace. Hospitality and food are clearly highlights of any stay at this special restaurant with rooms. Locally sourced produce is carefully prepared with passion and skill. Bedrooms are spacious and airy, with little touches such as fluffy towels and hand-made toiletries providing extra luxury.

Rooms 8 (1 fmly)

KINLOCH RANNOCH
Perth & Kinross
Map 23 NN65

Dunalastair Hotel

★★★ 75% ◉ HOTEL

☎ 01882 632323 & 632218
PH16 5PW
e-mail: info@dunalastair.co.uk
dir: A9 to Pitlochry, on N side take B8019 to Tummel Bridge then A846 to Kinloch Rannoch

Surrounded by unspoilt and beautiful countryside, this family-owned hotel, offers a warm and friendly welcome and great hospitality. The public areas are inviting, and fires are lit on colder days. The restaurant offers a fine dining experience whilst the lounge and conservatory have a more informal and relaxed atmosphere. The bedrooms are well appointed.

Rooms 28 (4 fmly) (9 GF) **Facilities** Fishing 4x4 safaris Rafting Clay pigeon shooting Bike hire Archery Xmas New Year **Conf** Class 35 Board 30 Thtr 60 **Parking** 33 **Notes** Civ Wed 70

Macdonald Loch Rannoch Hotel

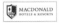

★★★ 75% HOTEL

☎ 0844 879 9059 & 01882 632201
PH16 5PS
e-mail: loch_rannoch@macdonald-hotels.co.uk
web: www.macdonald-hotels.co.uk
dir: Exit A9 onto B847 Calvine. Follow signs to Kinloch Rannoch, hotel 1m from village

Set deep in the countryside with elevated views across Loch Rannoch, this hotel is built around a 19th-century hunting lodge and provides a great base for exploring this beautiful area. The superior bedrooms have views over the loch. There is a choice of eating options - The Ptarmigan Restaurant and the Schiehallan Bar for informal eating. The hotel provides both indoor and outdoor activities.

Rooms 48 (25 fmly) **Facilities** FTV Wi-fi 🏂 Fishing Gym Xmas New Year **Conf** Class 80 Board 50 Thtr 160 **Services** Lift **Parking** 52 **Notes** Civ Wed 130

KINROSS
Perth & Kinross
Map 21 NO10

The Green Hotel Golf & Leisure Resort

★★★★ 74% ◉ HOTEL

☎ 01577 863467
2 The Muirs KY13 8AS
e-mail: reservations@green-hotel.com
web: www.green-hotel.com
dir: M90 junct 6, follow Kinross signs onto A922 for hotel

A long-established hotel offering a wide range of indoor and outdoor activities. Public areas include a classical restaurant, a choice of bars and a well-stocked gift shop. The comfortable, well-equipped bedrooms, most of which are generously proportioned, boast attractive colour schemes and smart modern furnishings.

Rooms 46 (3 fmly) (12 GF) **Facilities** Spa STV Wi-fi ⌨ 🎾 supervised 🏌 36 ⛳ Putt green Fishing 🏊 Gym Petanque Curling (Sep-Apr) Cycling Shooting (Oct-Feb) Cycle hire Falconry 🎵 Xmas New Year **Conf** Class 75 Board 60 Thtr 130 Del from £100 to £200* **Parking** 60 **Notes** Civ Wed 100

The Windlestrae Hotel

★★★ 🅰 HOTEL

☎ 01577 863217
The Muirs KY13 8AS
e-mail: reservations@green-hotel.com
web: www.green-hotel.com
dir: M90 junct 6 into Kinross, left at 2nd mini rdbt. Hotel 400yds on right

Rooms 47 (12 GF) **Facilities** Spa STV Wi-fi ⌨ 🎾 supervised 🏌 36 ⛳ Putt green Fishing 🏊 Gym Curling (Sep-Apr) Steam room Toning tables Cycle hire Falconry Xmas New Year **Conf** Class 100 Board 80 Thtr 250 Del from £100 to £200* **Parking** 80 **Notes** Civ Wed 100

KIRKBEAN
Dumfries & Galloway
Map 21 NX95

INSPECTORS' CHOICE

Cavens

★★★ ◉ COUNTRY HOUSE HOTEL

☎ 01387 880234
DG2 8AA
e-mail: enquiries@cavens.com
web: www.cavens.com
dir: Enter Kirkbean on A710, hotel signed

Set in 20 acres of parkland gardens, Cavens encapsulates all the virtues of an intimate country-house hotel. Quality is the keynote, and the proprietors spared no effort when they renovated the house. The bedrooms are delightfully individual and very comfortably equipped, and now have free Wi-fi; there are Country rooms or the more spacious Estate rooms. The charming lounges invite peaceful relaxation. The menu at dinner offers dishes using the best local and home-made produce.

Rooms 6 (2 fmly) (1 GF) **Facilities** FTV Wi-fi 🏊 Shooting Fishing Horse riding New Year **Conf** Class 20 Board 20 Thtr 20 **Parking** 20 **Notes** Closed Jan Civ Wed 100

KIRKCALDY
Fife Map 21 NT29

Dean Park Hotel
★★★ 78% HOTEL

☎ 01592 261635
Chapel Level KY2 6QW
e-mail: reception@deanparkhotel.co.uk
dir: Signed from A92 (Kirkcaldy West junct)

Popular with both business and leisure guests, this hotel has extensive conference and meeting facilities. Executive bedrooms are spacious and comfortable, and all are well equipped with modern decor and amenities. Twelve direct access, chalet-style rooms are set in the grounds and equipped to the same specification as main bedrooms. Public areas include a choice of bars and a restaurant.

Rooms 34 (2 fmly) (5 GF) (12 smoking) **Facilities** STV FTV Wi-fi **Conf** Class 125 Board 54 Thtr 250 **Services** Lift **Parking** 250 **Notes** ⊗ Civ Wed 200

KIRKCUDBRIGHT
Dumfries & Galloway Map 20 NX65

Arden House Hotel
★★ 75% HOTEL

☎ 01557 330544
Tongland Rd DG6 4UU
dir: Exit A75, 4m W of Castle Douglas onto A711. Follow Kirkcudbright signs, over Telford Bridge. Hotel 400mtrs on left

Set well back from the main road in extensive grounds on the northeast side of town, this spotlessly maintained hotel offers attractive bedrooms, a lounge bar and adjoining conservatory serving a range of popular dishes, which are also available in the dining room. It boasts an impressive function suite in its grounds.

Rooms 9 (7 fmly) (5 smoking) ⚓ **S** £60-£65; **D** £75-£80 (incl. bkfst)* **Conf** Class 175 Board 120 Thtr 175 Del from £100 to £125* **Parking** 70 **Notes** LB

LANARK
South Lanarkshire Map 21 NS84

Best Western Cartland Bridge Hotel

★★★ 75% COUNTRY HOUSE HOTEL

☎ 01555 664426
Glasgow Rd ML11 9UF
e-mail: sales@cartlandbridge.co.uk
dir: A73 through Lanark towards Carluke. Hotel in 1.25m

Situated in wooded grounds on the edge of the town, this Grade I listed mansion continues to be popular with both business and leisure guests. Public areas feature wood panelling, a gallery staircase and a magnificent dining room. The well-equipped bedrooms vary in size.

Rooms 18 (2 fmly) ⚓ **Facilities** FTV Wi-fi Xmas New Year **Conf** Class 180 Board 50 Thtr 250 **Parking** 120 **Notes** ⊗ Civ Wed 200

LANGBANK
Renfrewshire Map 20 NS37

Best Western Gleddoch House Hotel
OXFORD HOTELS & INNS

★★★★ 73% HOTEL

☎ 01475 540711
PA14 6YE
e-mail: reservations.gleddochhouse@ohiml.com
web: www.oxfordhotelsandinns.com
dir: M8 to Greenock, onto A8, left at rdbt onto A789, follow for 0.5m, turn right, 2nd on left

This hotel is set in spacious, landscaped grounds high above the River Clyde with fine views. The period house is appointed to a very high standard. The modern extension is impressive and offers spacious and very comfortable bedrooms. Warm hospitality and attentive service are noteworthy along with the hotel's parkland golf course and leisure club.

Rooms 70 (22 fmly) (17 GF) **Facilities** Spa FTV Wi-fi ⚓ ⚲ ♪ 18 Putt green Gym Steam room Sauna Xmas New Year **Conf** Class 70 Board 40 Thtr 150 Del from £125 to £150* **Parking** 150 **Notes** Civ Wed 120

LARGS
North Ayrshire Map 20 NS25

Willowbank Hotel
★★★ 73% HOTEL

☎ 01475 672311 & 675435
96 Greenock Rd KA30 8PG
e-mail: iaincsmith@btconnect.com
dir: On A78

A relaxed, friendly atmosphere prevails at this well maintained hotel where hanging baskets are a feature in summer months. The nicely decorated bedrooms are, in general, spacious and offer comfortable modern appointments. The public areas include a large, well-stocked bar, a lounge and a dining room.

Rooms 30 (4 fmly) **Facilities** STV ♪ Xmas New Year **Conf** Class 100 Board 40 Thtr 200 **Parking** 40

LIVINGSTON
West Lothian Map 21 NT06

Premier Inn Livingston M8 Jct 3

BUDGET HOTEL

☎ 0871 527 8632
Deer Park Av, Deer Park, Knightsbridge EH54 8AD
web: www.premierinn.com
dir: At M8 junct 3. Hotel opposite rdbt

High quality, budget accommodation ideal for both families and business travellers. Spacious, en suite bedrooms feature tea and coffee making facilities, and Freeview TV in most hotels. Internet access and Wi-fi are available for a small fee. The adjacent family restaurant features a wide and varied menu. See also the Hotel Groups pages.

Rooms 83

LOCHGILPHEAD
Argyll & Bute Map 20 NR88

Cairnbaan Hotel
★★★ 78% ⊛ HOTEL

☎ 01546 603668
Crinan Canal, Cairnbaan PA31 8SJ
e-mail: info@cairnbaan.com
web: www.cairnbaan.com
dir: 2m N, A816 from Lochgilphead, hotel off B841

Located on the Crinan Canal, this small hotel offers relaxed hospitality in a delightful setting. Bedrooms are thoughtfully equipped, generally spacious and benefit from stylish decor. Fresh seafood is a real feature in both the formal restaurant and the comfortable bar area. Alfresco dining is popular in the warmer months.

Rooms 12 **Facilities** Xmas **Conf** Class 100 Board 80 Thtr 160 **Parking** 53 **Notes** Civ Wed 120

K

Save on hotels. Book at **theAA.com/hotel**

KIR – LUS 561 SCOTLAND

LOCHINVER — Map 22 NC02
Highland

Inver Lodge Hotel
★★★★ ◎◎ HOTEL

☎ 01571 844496
IV27 4LU
e-mail: stay@inverlodge.com
web: www.inverlodge.com
dir: A837 to Lochinver, through village, left after village hall, follow private road for 0.5m

Genuine hospitality is a noteworthy at this delightful, purpose-built hotel, set high on the hillside above the village. All bedrooms and public rooms enjoy stunning views. There is a choice of lounges and a restaurant where the chefs make use of the abundant local produce. Bedrooms are spacious, stylish and come with an impressive range of accessories. There is no night service between 11pm and 7am.

Rooms 21 (11 GF) ⚒ **S** £115-£120; **D** £215-£220 (incl. bkfst)* **Facilities** FTV Wi-fi Sauna **Parking** 30 **Notes** LB Closed Nov-Mar Civ Wed 50

LOCKERBIE — Map 21 NY18
Dumfries & Galloway

Best Western Dryfesdale Country House Hotel
★★★★ 74% HOTEL

☎ 01576 202427
Dryfebridge DG11 2SF
e-mail: reception@dryfesdalehotel.co.uk
web: www.dryfesdalehotel.co.uk
dir: From M74 junct 17 follow Lockerbie North signs, 3rd left at 1st rdbt, 1st exit left at 2nd rdbt, hotel 200yds on left

Conveniently situated for the M74, yet discreetly screened from it, this friendly hotel provides attentive service. Bedrooms, some with access to patio areas, vary in size and style; all offer good levels of comfort and are well equipped. Creative, good value dinners make use of local produce and are served in the airy restaurant that overlooks the manicured gardens and rolling countryside.

Rooms 29 (5 fmly) (20 GF) **Facilities** STV FTV Wi-fi Putt green ⚒ Clay pigeon shooting Fishing ♫ Xmas New Year **Conf** Class 100 Board 100 Thtr 150 Del from £109 to £129 **Parking** 60 **Notes** Civ Wed 150

Kings Arms Hotel
★★ 80% HOTEL

☎ 01576 202410
High St DG11 2JL
e-mail: reception@kingsarmshotel.co.uk
web: www.kingsarmshotel.co.uk
dir: A74(M), 0.5m into town centre, hotel opposite town hall

Dating from the 17th century this former inn lies in the town centre. Now a family-run hotel, it provides attractive well-equipped bedrooms with Wi-fi access. At lunch a menu ranging from snacks to full meals is served in both the cosy bars and the restaurant at dinner.

Rooms 13 (2 fmly) ⚒ **S** £55; **D** £87 (incl. bkfst) **Facilities** FTV Wi-fi Xmas New Year **Conf** Class 40 Board 30 Thtr 80 **Parking** 8

Ravenshill House Hotel
★★ 74% HOTEL

☎ 01576 202882
12 Dumfries Rd DG11 2EF
e-mail: aaenquiries@ravenshillhotellockerbie.co.uk
web: www.ravenshillhotellockerbie.co.uk
dir: From A74(M) Lockerbie junct onto A709. Hotel 0.5m on right

Set in spacious gardens on the fringe of the town, this friendly, family-run hotel offers cheerful service and good value, home-cooked meals. Bedrooms are generally spacious and comfortably equipped, including a two-room unit ideal for families.

Rooms 8 (2 fmly) ⚒ **S** £45-£60; **D** £75-£80 (incl. bkfst)* **Facilities** FTV Wi-fi **Conf** Class 20 Board 12 Thtr 30 **Parking** 35 **Notes** LB Closed 1-7 Jan & 2 wks in Feb

LUSS — Map 20 NS39
Argyll & Bute

The Lodge on Loch Lomond Hotel
★★★★ 76% ◎◎ HOTEL

L

☎ 01436 860201
G83 8PA
e-mail: res@loch-lomond.co.uk
web: www.loch-lomond.co.uk
dir: Off A82, follow sign for hotel

This hotel is idyllically set on the shores of Loch Lomond. Public areas consist of an open-plan, split-level bar and fine dining restaurant overlooking the loch. The pine-finished bedrooms also enjoy the views and are comfortable, spacious and well equipped; some with saunas, DVDs and all with internet access. There is a stunning state-of-the-art leisure suite.

Rooms 47 (17 annexe) (20 fmly) (13 GF) **Facilities** Spa STV FTV Wi-fi ⌚ Fishing Boating Xmas New Year **Conf** Class 80 Board 60 Thtr 150 **Parking** 120 **Notes** Civ Wed 100

M

Burt's Hotel

★★★ 78% ◉◉ HOTEL

☎ 01896 822285
Market Square TD6 9PL
e-mail: enquiries@burtshotel.co.uk
web: www.burtshotel.co.uk
dir: A6091, 2m from A68 3m S of Earlston

Recognised by its distinctive black and white façade and colourful window boxes, in the heart of a small market town, this hotel has been under the same family ownership for almost 40 years. The genuine warmth of hospitality is notable. The smart bedrooms have been individually styled and include Wi-fi. Food is important at Burt's and the elegant restaurant is well complemented by the range of tasty meals in the bar.

Rooms 20 🔥 **S** £70-£90; **D** £100-£140 (incl. bkfst)*
Facilities STV FTV Wi-fi Salmon fishing Shooting New Year **Conf** Class 20 Board 20 Thtr 38 Del from £100 to £140* **Parking** 40 **Notes** Closed 24-26 Dec & 2-8 Jan

Premier Inn Glasgow (Milngavie)

BUDGET HOTEL

☎ 0871 527 8428
103 Main St G62 6JQ
web: www.premierinn.com
dir: M8 junct 16, follow Milngavie (A879) signs. Approx. 5m. Pass Murray Park Training Ground. Left at lights. Hotel on A81adjacent to West Highland Gate Beefeater

High quality, budget accommodation ideal for both families and business travellers. Spacious, en suite bedrooms feature tea and coffee making facilities, and Freeview TV in most hotels. Internet access and Wi-fi are available for a small fee. The adjacent family restaurant features a wide and varied menu. See also the Hotel Groups pages.

Rooms 60

Annandale Arms Hotel

★★★ 78% ◉ HOTEL

☎ 01683 220013
High St DG10 9HF
e-mail: reception@annandalearmshotel.co.uk
web: www.annandalearmshotel.co.uk
dir: M74 junct 15, A701. Hotel on west side of central square that forms High St

With a history dating back 250 years old, this family run hotel in the heart of Moffat provides well-appointed, modern bedrooms and bathrooms, located away from the hustle and bustle of the high street. There is a welcoming bar and restaurant serving real ales and quality food. Wi-fi and off-road parking are added benefits.

Rooms 16 (2 fmly) (5 GF) 🔥 **S** fr £75; **D** fr £115 (incl. bkfst) **Facilities** FTV Wi-fi 🐾 New Year **Conf** Class 40 Board 40 Thtr 60 **Parking** 20 **Notes** Closed 25-26 Dec

Alona Hotel

★★★★ 77% HOTEL

☎ 01698 333888
Strathclyde Country Park ML1 3RT
e-mail: gm@alonahotel.co.uk
web: www.alonahotel.co.uk
dir: M74 junct 5, hotel approx 250yds on left

Alona is a Celtic word meaning 'exquisitely beautiful'. This hotel is situated within the idyllic beauty of Strathclyde Country Park, with tranquil views over the picturesque loch and surrounding forests. There is a very contemporary feel, from the open-plan public areas to the spacious and well-appointed bedrooms. Wi-fi is available throughout. M&D's, Scotland's Family Theme Park, is just next door.

Rooms 51 (24 fmly) (17 GF) 🔥 **Facilities** FTV Wi-fi 🎵 Xmas New Year **Conf** Class 100 Board 76 Thtr 400 **Services** Lift Air con **Parking** 100 **Notes** ⊗ Civ Wed 250

Holiday Inn Express Strathclyde Park

BUDGET HOTEL

☎ 01698 858585
Hamilton Rd, Hamilton ML1 3RB
e-mail: isabella.little@ichotelsgroup.com
web: www.hiexpress.com/strathclyde
dir: M74 junct 5 follow signs for Strathclyde Country Park

A modern hotel ideal for families and business travellers. Fresh and uncomplicated, the spacious rooms include Sky TV, power shower and tea and coffee-making facilities. Continental buffet breakfast is included in the room rate; other meals may be taken at the nearby family pub or restaurant. See also the Hotel Groups pages.

Rooms 120 (58 fmly) **Conf** Class 10 Board 18 Thtr 30

Premier Inn Glasgow (Motherwell)

BUDGET HOTEL

☎ 0871 527 8430
Edinburgh Rd, Newhouse ML1 5SY
web: www.premierinn.com
dir: From S: M74 junct 5, A725 towards Coatbridge. Take A8 towards Edinburgh, exit at junct 6, follow Lanark signs. Hotel 400yds on right

High quality, budget accommodation ideal for both families and business travellers. Spacious, en suite bedrooms feature tea and coffee making facilities, and Freeview TV in most hotels. Internet access and Wi-fi are available for a small fee. The adjacent family restaurant features a wide and varied menu. See also the Hotel Groups pages.

Rooms 40

Save on hotels. Book at **theAA.com/hotel**

MEL – NAI 563 | SCOTLAND

MUIR OF ORD
Highland   **Map 23 NH55**

Ord House Hotel

★★ 74% ◉ SMALL HOTEL   THE CIRCLE

☎ 01463 870492
IV6 7UH
e-mail: admin@ord-house.co.uk
dir: Exit A9 at Tore rdbt onto A832. 5m, through Muir of Ord. Left towards Ullapool (A832). Hotel 0.5m on left

Dating back to 1637, this country-house hotel is situated peacefully in wooded grounds and offers brightly furnished and well-proportioned accommodation. Comfortable day rooms reflect the character and charm of the house, with inviting lounges, a cosy snug bar and an elegant dining room where wide-ranging, creative menus are offered.

Rooms 12 (3 GF) ☜ **S** £60; **D** £130 (incl. bkfst)*
Facilities Wi-fi Putt green ⛳ Clay pigeon shooting
Parking 30 **Notes** LB Closed Nov-Apr

MUTHILL
Perth & Kinross   **Map 21 NN81**

Barley Bree Restaurant with Rooms

◉◉ RESTAURANT WITH ROOMS

☎ 01764 681451
6 Willoughby St PH5 2AB
e-mail: info@barleybree.com
dir: A9 onto A822 in centre of Muthill

Situated in the heart of the small village of Muthill, and is just a short drive from Crieff, genuine hospitality and quality food are obvious attractions at this charming restaurant with rooms. The property has been transformed by the current owners, and the stylish bedrooms are appointed to a very high standard. The restaurant has a rustic feel with exposed stonework, wooden floors and a log-burning fire in the centre. Choices range from set, carte and tasting menus. Children are welcome too.

Rooms 6 (1 fmly)

NAIRN
Highland   **Map 23 NH85**

Newton Hotel

★★★★ 74% ◉ HOTEL   OXFORD HOTELS & INNS

☎ 01667 453144
Inverness Rd IV12 4RX
e-mail: newton.frontdesk@ohiml.com
web: www.oxfordhotelsandinns.com
dir: A96 from Inverness to Nairn, through 3 sets of lights, at 4th right to Newton Gate

This former mansion house, set in 21 acres of mature parkland and bordering Nairn's championship golf course, was a favourite with the actor Charlie Chaplin who often visited with his family. Originally built as a family home in 1872 the hotel has been extensively refurbished over the years, including the addition of the Highland Conference Centre. Bedrooms are of a high standard, and many of the front-facing rooms having splendid sea views.

Rooms 56 (4 fmly) **Facilities** STV Wi-fi ⌨ Xmas New Year **Conf** Class 220 Board 90 Thtr 450 Del from £125 to £135* **Services** Lift **Parking** 150
Notes Civ Wed 250

Golf View Hotel & Leisure Club

★★★★ 72% ◉ HOTEL

☎ 01667 452301
The Seafront IV12 4HD
e-mail: golfview@crerarhotels.com
dir: Off A96 into Seabank Rd, hotel at end on right

This fine hotel has wonderful sea views and overlooks the Morey Firth and the Black Isle beyond. The championship golf course at Nairn is adjacent to the hotel and guests have direct access to the long sandy beaches. Bedrooms are of a very high standard and the public areas are charming. A well-equipped leisure complex and swimming pool are also available.

Rooms 42 (6 fmly) **Facilities** Spa FTV Wi-fi ⌨ supervised ⌨ Gym Sauna Steam room Xmas New Year **Conf** Class 40 Board 40 Thtr 100 **Services** Lift **Parking** 40 **Notes** Civ Wed 100

Boath House

★★★ ◉◉◉◉ HOTEL

☎ 01667 454896
Auldearn IV12 5TE
e-mail: info@boath-house.com
web: www.boath-house.com
dir: 2m past Nairn on A96, E towards Forres, signed on main road

Standing in its own 20-acre grounds, this splendid Georgian mansion was built in 1825 for the Dunbar family but there has been has been occupation on is site since the 16th century. Guests are welcome to stroll around the gardens which have an ornamental lake, walled garden and secluded seating areas to relax in. The hospitality here is first class; the owners are passionate about what they do, and have an ability to establish a special relationship with their guests that will be particularly remembered. The food is also very memorable; head chef Charlie Lockley is devotee of slow and organic cooking which also includes using foraged produce. The five-course dinners are a culinary adventure, matched only by the excellence of breakfasts. The house itself is delightful, with inviting lounges and a dining room overlooking a trout loch. The bedrooms, with lake and woodland views, are striking and very comfortable; Orangerie Rooms have their own conservatory.

Rooms 8 (1 fmly) (1 GF) ☜ **S** £190-£260; **D** £230-£335 (incl. bkfst) **Facilities** FTV Wi-fi ⌨ Fishing ⛳ Beauty salon & treatment room Xmas New Year **Conf** Class 10 Board 10 Thtr 15 Del from £300 to £370 **Parking** 20 **Notes** LB Civ Wed 28

N

NETHY BRIDGE   Map 23 NJ02
Highland

Nethybridge Hotel
★★★ 68% HOTEL

☎ 01479 821203
PH25 3DP
e-mail: salesnethybridge@strathmorehotels.com
dir: A9 onto A95, onto B970 to Nethy Bridge

This popular tourist and coaching hotel enjoys a central location amidst the majestic Cairngorm Mountains. Bedrooms are stylishly furnished in bold tartans whilst traditionally styled day rooms include two bars and a popular snooker room. Staff are friendly and keen to please.

Rooms 69 (3 fmly) (7 GF) **Facilities** Putt green Bowling green Beauty therapy room ♬ Xmas New Year **Conf** Thtr 100 Del £75* **Services** Lift **Parking** 80

See advert on page 524

NEW LANARK   Map 21 NS84
South Lanarkshire

New Lanark Mill Hotel
★★★ 83% HOTEL

☎ 01555 667200
Mill One, New Lanark Mills ML11 9DB
e-mail: hotel@newlanark.org
web: www.newlanark.org
dir: Signed from major roads, M74 junct 7 & M8

Originally built as a cotton mill in the 18th century, this hotel forms part of a fully restored village, now a UNESCO World Heritage Site. There's a bright modern style throughout which contrasts nicely with features from the original mill. There is a comfortable foyer-lounge with a galleried restaurant above. The hotel enjoys stunning views over the River Clyde.

Rooms 38 (5 fmly) (6 smoking) **S** £49-£89; **D** £59-£109 (incl. bkfst)* **Facilities** STV Wi-fi ⊗ Gym Beauty room Steam room Sauna Aerobics studios Xmas New Year **Conf** Class 60 Board 40 Thtr 200 Del from £99 to £139 **Services** Lift **Parking** 75 **Notes** LB ⊗ Civ Wed 120

NEWTON STEWART   Map 20 NX46
Dumfries & Galloway

Kirroughtree House
★★★ ◉◉ COUNTRY HOUSE HOTEL

☎ 01671 402141
Minnigaff DG8 6AN
e-mail: info@kirroughtreehouse.co.uk
web: www.kirroughtreehouse.co.uk
dir: A75 onto A712, hotel entrance 300yds on left

This imposing mansion enjoys a peaceful location in eight acres of landscaped gardens near Galloway Forest Park. It is said that Robert Burns, a friend of the Heron family who owned the house at the time, sat on the staircase and recited his poems. The inviting day rooms comprise a choice of lounges, and two elegant dining rooms where guests can enjoy the delightful cuisine which is firmly based on top quality, locally sourced ingredients. Well-proportioned, individually styled bedrooms include some suites and mini-suites and many rooms enjoy lovely views. The service is very friendly and attentive. Stargazing and garden breaks are available.

Rooms 17 ⟨ **S** £90-£105; **D** £180-£210 (incl. bkfst)* **Facilities** FTV Wi-fi ⊌ 9-hole pitch & putt Xmas New Year **Conf** Class 20 Board 20 Thtr 30 Del from £130 to £165* **Services** Lift **Parking** 50 **Notes** LB No children 10yrs Closed 2 Jan-1 Feb

The Bruce Hotel
★★★ 73% HOTEL

☎ 01671 402294
88 Queen St DG8 6JL
e-mail: mail@the-bruce-hotel.com
web: www.the-bruce-hotel.com
dir: Exit A75 at Newton Stewart rdbt towards town. Hotel 800mtrs on right

Named after the Scottish patriot Robert the Bruce, this welcoming hotel is just a short distance from the A75. One of the well-appointed bedrooms features a four-poster bed, and popular family suites contain separate bedrooms for children. Public areas include

a traditional lounge, a formal restaurant and a lounge bar, both offering a good choice of dishes.

Rooms 20 (3 fmly) **Facilities** FTV Wi-fi New Year **Conf** Class 50 Board 14 Thtr 100 **Parking** 14

NORTH BERWICK   Map 21 NT58
East Lothian

Macdonald Marine Hotel & Spa

★★★★ 82% ◉◉ HOTEL

☎ 0844 879 9130
Cromwell Rd EH39 4LZ
e-mail: sales.marine@macdonald-hotels.co.uk
web: www.macdonaldhotels.co.uk
dir: From A198 turn into Hamilton Rd at lights then 2nd right

This imposing hotel commands stunning views across the local golf course to the Firth of Forth. Stylish public areas provide a relaxing atmosphere; creative dishes are served in the restaurant and lighter bites in the lounge/bar. Bedrooms come in a variety of sizes and styles, all are well equipped and some are impressively large. The hotel boasts extensive leisure and conference facilities.

Rooms 83 (4 fmly) (4 GF) **Facilities** Spa STV Wi-fi ⊗ supervised Putt green Gym Indoor & outdoor salt water hydro pool Xmas New Year **Conf** Class 120 Board 60 Thtr 300 **Services** Lift **Parking** 50 **Notes** Civ Wed 150

OBAN   Map 20 NM82
Argyll & Bute

Best Western The Queens Hotel

★★★★ Ⓐ HOTEL

☎ 01631 562505 & 570230
Corran Esplanade PA34 5AG
e-mail: thequeenshoteloban@hotmail.co.uk
dir: Into Oban on A85, down hill to mini rdbt. 2nd exit towards seafront. At next rdbt follow Ganavan Sands sign. Hotel 0.4m on right just after cathedral

Rooms 46 (2 fmly) **Facilities** FTV Wi-fi New Year **Services** Lift **Parking** 15 **Notes** Closed 3 -31 Jan Civ Wed 60

Save on hotels. Book at **theAA.com/hotel**

NET – OBA 565 SCOTLAND

Manor House Hotel

★★★ 83% ⚜ HOTEL

☎ 01631 562087
Gallanach Rd PA34 4LS
e-mail: info@manorhouseoban.com
web: www.manorhouseoban.com
dir: Follow MacBrayne Ferries signs, pass ferry
entrance for hotel on right

Handy for the ferry terminal and with views of the bay
and harbour, this elegant Georgian residence was
built in 1780 as the dower house for the family of the
Duke of Argyll. Comfortable and attractive public
rooms invite relaxation, whilst most of the well-
equipped bedrooms are furnished with period pieces.

Rooms 11 (1 GF) ☞ **S** £105-£210; **D** £115-£225 (incl.
bkfst)* **Facilities** FTV Wi-fi New Year **Parking** 20
Notes No children 12yrs Closed 25-26 Dec Civ Wed 30

Falls of Lora Hotel

THE INDEPENDENTS
HOTEL ASSOCIATION

★★★ 77% HOTEL

☎ 01631 710483
PA37 1PB
e-mail: enquiries@fallsoflora.com
web: www.fallsoflora.com

(For full entry see Connel; see advert below)

Royal Hotel

★★★ 74% HOTEL

☎ 01631 563021
Argyll Sqaure PA34 4BE
e-mail: salesroyaloban@strathmorehotels.com
dir: A82 from Glasgow towards Loch Lomond &
Crianlarich then A85 (pass Loch Awe) to Oban

Well situated in the heart of Oban, just minutes from
the ferry terminal and with all the shops on its

doorstep, this hotel really is central. The comfortable
and well-presented bedrooms differ in size, and all
public areas are smart. There is a first-floor
restaurant overlooking the town square.

Rooms 91 (5 fmly) **S** £30-£60; **D** £80-£124 (incl.
bkfst)* **Facilities** Wi-fi ♫ Xmas New Year
Conf Class 60 Board 30 Thtr 140 **Services** Lift
Parking 25 **Notes** Civ Wed 70

See advert on page 524

The Columba Hotel

★★★ 70% HOTEL

☎ 01631 562183
The Esplanade PA34 5QD
e-mail: columba@mckeverhotels.co.uk
dir: A85 to Oban, at 1st lights turn right

One of Oban's landmarks, this Victorian hotel is
located on the seafront with stunning views out over
the Firth of Lorne to the Isle of Mull. The well-
appointed, contemporary bedrooms offer guests
comfortable accommodation. Alba Restaurant
provides a menu of modern Scottish dishes.

Rooms 49 (5 fmly) **Facilities** FTV Wi-fi ♫ Xmas New
Year **Services** Lift **Parking** 6 **Notes** ⊗

O

O

OLDMELDRUM
Aberdeenshire   Map 23 NJ82

Meldrum House Country Hotel & Golf Course

★★★★ 79% ◉◉ COUNTRY HOUSE HOTEL

☎ 01651 872294
AB51 0AE
e-mail: enquiries@meldrumhouse.co.uk
web: www.meldrumhouse.com
dir: 11m from Aberdeen on A947 (Aberdeen to Banff road)

Set in 350 acres of wooded parkland this imposing baronial country mansion has a golf course as its centrepiece. Tastefully restored to highlight its original character it provides a peaceful retreat. Bedrooms are massive, and like the public rooms, transport guests back to a bygone era, but at the same time provide stylish modern amenities including smart bathrooms.

Rooms 24 (13 annexe) (1 fmly) (6 GF) 📶
Facilities FTV Wi-fi ♨ 18 Putt green ♨ Xmas New Year **Conf** Class 20 Board 30 Thtr 80 Del from £160 to £175* **Parking** 70 **Notes** Civ Wed 100

ONICH
Highland   Map 22 NN06

Onich Hotel

★★★ 77% HOTEL

☎ 01855 821214
PH33 6RY
e-mail: enquiries@onich-fortwilliam.co.uk
web: www.onich-fortwilliam.co.uk
dir: Beside A82, 2m N of Ballachulish Bridge

Genuine hospitality is part of the appeal of this hotel, which lies right beside Loch Linnhe with gardens extending to its shores. Nicely presented public areas include a choice of inviting lounges and contrasting bars, and views of the loch can be enjoyed from the attractive restaurant. Bedrooms, with pleasing colour schemes, are comfortably modern.

Rooms 26 (6 fmly) **Facilities** STV Wi-fi Games room ♫ Xmas New Year **Conf** Board 40 Thtr 150 **Parking** 50 **Notes** Civ Wed 120

PEAT INN
Fife   Map 21 NO40

The Peat Inn

◉◉◉ RESTAURANT WITH ROOMS

☎ 01334 840206
KY15 5LH
e-mail: stay@thepeatinn.co.uk
dir: At junct of B940 & B941, 5m SW of St Andrews

This 300-year-old former coaching inn enjoys a rural location, yet is close to St Andrews. The spacious restaurant with rooms is very well appointed and all rooms have lounge areas. The inn is steeped in history and for years has proved a real haven for food lovers. The three dining areas create a romantic setting, and chef/owner Geoffrey Smeddle produces excellent, award-winning dishes. Expect welcoming open fires and a relaxed ambiance.

Rooms 8 (8 annexe) (3 fmly)

Save on hotels. Book at **theAA.com/hotel**

OLD – PER 567   SCOTLAND

PEEBLES
Scottish Borders   Map 21 NT24

Cringletie House

★★★★ ◉◉◉ COUNTRY HOUSE HOTEL

☎ 01721 725750
Edinburgh Rd EH45 8PL
e-mail: enquiries@cringletie.com
web: www.cringletie.com
dir: 2m N on A703

This romantic baronial mansion, built in 1861, is set in 28 acres of beautiful gardens and woodland; there is a walled garden with a 400-year-old yew hedge (perhaps the oldest in Scotland), a waterfall, sculptures and croquet lawn. In 1971 Scottish Heritage granted the property a Grade B listing, and in the same year the house became a hotel. The delightful public rooms, with welcoming fires, include a cocktail lounge with adjoining conservatory, and there are service bells in each room which still work. The award-winning, first-floor restaurant has a magnificent hand-painted ceiling. The individually designed bedrooms have grace and charm, and for the ultimate luxury there's the Selkirk Suite.

Rooms 13 (2 GF) 🐾 **S** £85-£286; **D** £99-£300 (incl. bkfst)* **Facilities** FTV Wi-fi HL Putt green 🏌 Petanque Giant chess & draughts In room therapy treatments Xmas New Year **Conf** Class 20 Board 24 Thtr 45 Del from £169* **Services** Lift **Parking** 30 **Notes** LB Closed 2-27 Jan Civ Wed 60

Macdonald Cardrona Hotel, Golf & Spa

★★★★ 77% ◉ HOTEL

☎ 01896 833600
Cardrona EH45 8NE
e-mail: general.cardrona@macdonald-hotels.co.uk
web: www.macdonald-hotels.co.uk/cardrona
dir: On A72, 3m S of Peebles

The rolling hills of the Scottish Borders are a stunning backdrop for this modern, purpose-built hotel. Spacious bedrooms are traditional in style, equipped with a range of extras, and most enjoy fantastic countryside. The hotel features some impressive leisure facilities, including an 18-hole golf course, 18-metre indoor pool and state-of-the-art gym.

Rooms 99 (24 fmly) (16 GF) **S** £105-£175; **D** £115-£185 (incl. bkfst)* **Facilities** Spa STV Wi-fi 🕃 ఓ 18 Putt green Fishing Gym Sauna Steam room Xmas New Year **Conf** Class 120 Board 90 Thtr 250 Del from £125 to £155* **Services** Lift **Parking** 200 **Notes** LB Civ Wed 200

The Tontine Hotel

★★★ 80% HOTEL

☎ 01721 720892
High St EH45 8AJ
e-mail: info@tontinehotel.com
web: www.tontinehotel.com
dir: In town centre

Conveniently situated in the main street, this long-established hotel offers comfortable public rooms including the elegant Adam Restaurant and an inviting lounge and 'clubby' bar. Bedrooms, contained in the original house and the river-facing wing, offer a smart, classical style of accommodation. The lasting impression is of the excellent level of hospitality and guest care.

Rooms 36 (3 fmly) 🐾 **S** £55-£65; **D** £80-£110 (incl. bkfst)* **Facilities** STV FTV Wi-fi Xmas New Year **Conf** Class 24 Board 24 Thtr 40 Del from £100 to £120 **Parking** 24 **Notes** LB

PERTH
Perth & Kinross   Map 21 NO12

Murrayshall House Hotel & Golf Course

★★★★ 76% ◉◉ HOTEL

☎ 01738 551171
New Scone PH2 7PH
e-mail: info@murrayshall.co.uk
web: www.murrayshall.co.uk
dir: From Perth take A94 (Coupar Angus), 1m from Perth, right to Murrayshall just before New Scone

This imposing country house is set in 350 acres of grounds, including two golf courses, one of which is of championship standard. Bedrooms come in two distinct styles: modern suites in a purpose-built building contrast with more classic rooms in the main building. The Clubhouse bar serves a range of meals all day, whilst more accomplished cooking can be enjoyed in the Old Masters Restaurant.

Rooms 41 (14 annexe) (17 fmly) (5 GF) 🐾 **S** fr £120; **D** fr £160 (incl. bkfst)* **Facilities** STV FTV Wi-fi HL ఓ 36 🏌 Putt green Driving range New Year **Conf** Class 60 Board 30 Thtr 150 Del £149* **Parking** 120 **Notes** LB Civ Wed 130

Parklands Hotel

★★★★ 73% ◉◉ SMALL HOTEL

☎ 01738 622451
2 St Leonards Bank PH2 8EB
e-mail: info@theparklandshotel.com
web: www.theparklandshotel.com
dir: M90 junct 10, in 1m left at lights at end of park

Ideally located close to the centre of town with open views over the South Inch. The enthusiastic proprietors continue to invest heavily in the business and the bedrooms have a smart contemporary feel. Public areas include a choice of restaurants with a fine dining experience offered in Acanthus.

Rooms 15 (3 fmly) (4 GF) 🐾 **S** £89-£129; **D** £109-£179 (incl. bkfst)* **Facilities** STV Wi-fi **Conf** Class 18 Board 20 Thtr 24 Del from £124 to £139.50* **Parking** 30 **Notes** LB Closed 26 Dec-7 Jan Civ Wed 40

The New County Hotel

★★★ 77% ◉◉ HOTEL

☎ 01738 623355
22-30 County Place PH2 8EE
e-mail: enquiries@newcountyhotel.com
web: www.newcountyhotel.com
dir: A9 junct 11 (Perth). Follow signs for town centre. Hotel on right after library

This is a smart hotel in the heart of the beautiful garden city of Perth. The bedrooms have a modern and stylish appearance and public areas include a popular bar and contemporary lounge area. No stay here is complete without a visit to the award-winning Opus One Restaurant, which has a well deserved reputation for fine dining.

Rooms 23 (4 fmly) 🐾 **S** £50-£75; **D** £80-£140 (incl. bkfst) **Facilities** STV FTV Wi-fi New Year **Conf** Class 80 Board 24 Thtr 120 Del from £85* **Parking** 10 **Notes** LB ⊗

Best Western Queens Hotel

★★★ 75% HOTEL

☎ 01738 442222
Leonard St PH2 8HB
e-mail: enquiry@queensperth.co.uk
dir: From M90 follow to 2nd lights, turn left. Hotel on right, opposite railway station

This popular hotel benefits from a central location close to both the bus and rail stations. Bedrooms vary in size and style with top floor rooms offering extra space and excellent views of the town. Public rooms include a smart leisure centre and versatile conference space. A range of meals is served in both the bar and restaurant.

continued

P

PERTH *continued*

Rooms 50 (4 fmly) **Facilities** STV FTV Wi-fi 🕲 Gym Steam room Xmas New Year **Conf** Class 70 Board 50 Thtr 200 **Services** Lift **Parking** 50 **Notes** ⊗ Civ Wed 220

Salutation Hotel

★★★ 70% HOTEL

☎ 01738 630066
South St PH2 8PH
e-mail: salessalutation@strathmorehotels.com
dir: At end of South St on right before River Tay

Situated in heart of Perth, the Salutation is reputed to be one of the oldest hotels in Scotland and has been welcoming guests through its doors since 1699. It offers traditional hospitality with all the modern comforts. Bedrooms vary in size and are thoughtfully equipped. An extensive menu is available in the Adam Restaurant with its impressive barrel vaulted ceiling and original features.

Rooms 84 (5 fmly) 🐾 **S** £40-£95; **D** £60-£120 (incl. bkfst) **Facilities** Wi-fi 🎵 Xmas New Year **Conf** Class 180 Board 60 Thtr 300 Del from £90 to £120 **Services** Lift **Notes** LB Civ Wed 100

See advert on page 524

Holiday Inn Express Perth

BUDGET HOTEL

☎ 01738 636666
200 Dunkeld Rd, Inveralmond PH1 3AQ
e-mail: info@hiexpressperth.co.uk
web: www.hiexpressperth.co.uk
dir: Exit A9 (Inverness to Stirling road) at Inveralmond rdbt onto A912 signed Perth. Right at 1st rdbt, follow signs for hotel

A modern hotel ideal for families and business travellers. Fresh and uncomplicated, the spacious rooms include Sky TV, power shower and tea and coffee-making facilities. Continental buffet breakfast is included in the room rate; other meals may be taken at the nearby family pub or restaurant. See also the Hotel Groups pages.

Rooms 81 (43 fmly) (19 GF) (8 smoking)
Conf Class 15 Board 16 Thtr 30

Buchan Braes Hotel

★★★★ 75% ⑧ HOTEL

☎ 01779 871471
Boddam AB42 3AR
e-mail: info@buchanbraes.co.uk
dir: From Aberdeen take A90, follow Peterhead signs. 1st right in Stirling signed Boddam. 50mtrs, 1st right

A contemporary hotel located in Boddam that is an excellent base for exploring the attractions of this wonderful part of Scotland. There is an open-plan lounge for drinks and snacks and the Grill Room with an open kitchen that offers a weekly changing, seasonal menu of locally sourced produce. All the bedrooms, including three suites, have 32" flat-screen TVs with satellite channels, king-sized beds and free Wi-fi.

Rooms 47 (1 fmly) (26 GF) 🐾 **S** £95-£130; **D** £105-£130 (incl. bkfst)* **Facilities** Wi-fi Xmas New Year **Conf** Class 100 Board 130 Thtr 250 Del from £150 to £170* **Services** Lift **Parking** 40 **Notes** ⊗ Civ Wed 220

Palace Hotel

★★★ 81% HOTEL

☎ 01779 474821
Prince St AB42 1PL
e-mail: info@palacehotel.co.uk
web: www.palacehotel.co.uk
dir: A90 from Aberdeen, follow signs to Peterhead, on entering town turn into Prince St, then right into main car park

This town centre hotel is popular with business travellers and for social events. Bedrooms come in two styles, with the executive rooms being particularly smart and spacious. Public areas include a themed bar, an informal diner reached via a spiral staircase, and a brasserie restaurant and cocktail bar.

Rooms 64 (1 fmly) (14 GF) 🐾 **S** £70-£85; **D** £80-£95 (incl. bkfst)* **Facilities** Wi-fi Snooker & pool table 🎵 New Year **Conf** Class 100 Board 60 Thtr 250 Del from £125 to £150* **Services** Lift **Parking** 50 **Notes** Civ Wed 250

See also Kinloch Rannoch

Knockendarroch House Hotel

★★★★ 74% ⑧ SMALL HOTEL

☎ 01796 473473
Higher Oakfield PH16 5HT
e-mail: bookings@knockendarroch.co.uk
dir: Just off A9

This secluded hotel has outstanding views over the town and surrounding hills. The individually styled bedrooms are spacious and very well appointed - all have plasma TVs. The traditional, country-style public rooms have large sofas, welcoming open fires and an excellent whisky cabinet. Dinner is served every evening in the award-winning restaurant with only the best of Scottish produce being used. The staff are friendly and attentive.

Rooms 12 (1 GF) 🐾 **D** £148-£208 (incl. bkfst & dinner)* **Facilities** FTV Wi-fi **Parking** 12 **Notes** LB No children 10yrs Closed Dec-Jan

Green Park Hotel

★★★ 87% ⑧ COUNTRY HOUSE HOTEL

☎ 01796 473248
Clunie Bridge Rd PH16 5JY
e-mail: bookings@thegreenpark.co.uk
web: www.thegreenpark.co.uk
dir: Exit A9 at Pitlochry, follow signs 0.25m through town

Guests return year after year to this lovely hotel that is situated in a stunning setting on the shores of Loch Faskally. Most of the thoughtfully designed bedrooms, including a splendid wing, the restaurant and the comfortable lounges enjoy these views. Dinner utilises fresh produce, much of it grown in the kitchen garden.

Rooms 51 (3 fmly) (16 GF) 🐾 **S** £72-£105; **D** £144-£210 (incl. bkfst & dinner)* **Facilities** FTV Wi-fi Putt green New Year **Services** Lift **Parking** 51

Dundarach Hotel

★★★ 78% HOTEL

☎ 01796 472862
Perth Rd PH16 5DJ
e-mail: inbox@dundarach.co.uk
web: www.dundarach.co.uk
dir: S of town centre on main road

This welcoming, family-run hotel stands in mature grounds at the south end of town. Bedrooms come in a variety of styles, including a block of large purpose-built rooms that will appeal to business guests. Well-proportioned public areas feature inviting lounges and a conservatory restaurant giving fine views of the Tummel Valley.

Rooms 39 (19 annexe) (7 fmly) (12 GF) ♠ **S** £45-£70; **D** £90-£110 (incl. bkfst)* **Facilities** FTV Wi-fi **Conf** Class 40 Board 40 Thtr 60 **Parking** 39 **Notes** LB ⊗ Closed Jan RS Dec & early Feb

PLOCKTON   Map 22 NG83
Highland

The Plockton Hotel

★★★ 77% SMALL HOTEL

☎ 01599 544274
41 Harbour St IV52 8TN
e-mail: info@plocktonhotel.co.uk
web: www.plocktonhotel.co.uk
dir: A87 towards Kyle of Lochalsh. At Balmacara follow Plockton signs, 7m

This very popular hotel occupies an idyllic position on the waterfront of Loch Carron. Stylish bedrooms offer individual, pleasing decor and many have spacious balconies or panoramic views. There is a choice of three dining areas and seafood is very much a speciality. The staff and owners provide a relaxed and informal style of attentive service. A self-contained cottage is available for group bookings.

The Plockton Hotel

Rooms 15 (4 annexe) (1 fmly) (1 GF) ♠ **S** £40-£90; **D** £80-£130 (incl. bkfst)* **Facilities** STV Wi-fi ♌ Pool table ♫ New Year **Notes** ⊗ Closed 25 Dec & 1 Jan

POLMONT   Map 21 NS97
Falkirk

Macdonald Inchyra Hotel and Spa

 MACDONALD HOTELS & RESORTS

★★★★ 75% HOTEL

☎ 01324 711911
Grange Rd FK2 0YB
e-mail: inchyra@macdonald-hotels.co.uk
web: www.macdonaldhotels.co.uk
dir: Just beyond BP Social Club on Grange Rd

Ideally placed for the M9 and Grangemouth terminal, this former manor house has been tastefully extended. It provides extensive conference facilities and a choice of eating options: the relaxed atmosphere of the Café Crema or the Opus 504 Restaurant, which provides a more formal dining experience. Bedrooms are comfortable and mostly spacious.

Rooms 98 (6 annexe) (35 fmly) (33 GF) **Facilities** Spa STV ⊗ ♨ Gym Steam room Sauna New Year **Conf** Class 300 Board 80 Thtr 750 **Services** Lift **Parking** 500 **Notes** Civ Wed 450

Premier Inn Falkirk East

 Premier Inn

BUDGET HOTEL

☎ 0871 527 8392
Beancross Rd FK2 0YS
web: www.premierinn.com
dir: M9 junct 5, Polmont A9 signs. Hotel on left

High quality, budget accommodation ideal for both families and business travellers. Spacious, en suite bedrooms feature tea and coffee making facilities, and Freeview TV in most hotels. Internet access and Wi-fi are available for a small fee. The adjacent family restaurant features a wide and varied menu. See also the Hotel Groups pages.

Rooms 40

PORT APPIN   Map 20 NM94
Argyll & Bute

INSPECTORS' CHOICE

Airds Hotel

 RELAIS & CHATEAUX

★★★★ ⑳⑳⑳ SMALL HOTEL

☎ 01631 730236
PA38 4DF
e-mail: airds@airds-hotel.com
web: www.airds-hotel.com
dir: From A828 (Oban to Fort William road), turn at Appin signed Port Appin. Hotel 2.5m on left

The views are stunning from this small, luxury hotel on the shores of Loch Linnhe and where the staff are delightful and nothing is too much trouble. The well-equipped bedrooms provide style and luxury whilst many bathrooms are furnished in marble and have power showers. Chef Robert Macpherson creates award-winning contemporary Scottish dishes. First-rate regional ingredients play a starring role, and Robert's acute technical ability and sound culinary judgement are hallmarks of the refined cuisine. Comfortable lounges with deep sofas and roaring fires provide the ideal retreat for relaxation. This hotel is a real get-away-from-it-all experience.

Rooms 11 (3 fmly) (2 GF) ♠ **S** £202-£412; **D** £270-£480 (incl. bkfst & dinner)* **Facilities** STV FTV Wi-fi ♌ Putt green ⛳ Xmas New Year **Conf** Class 16 Board 16 Thtr 16 **Parking** 20 **Notes** LB RS Nov-Jan Civ Wed 40

P

PORT APPIN *continued*

The Pierhouse Hotel

★★★ 80% ◉ SMALL HOTEL

☎ 01631 730302 & 730622
PA38 4DE
e-mail: reservations@pierhousehotel.co.uk
web: www.pierhousehotel.co.uk
dir: A828 from Ballachulish to Oban. In Appin right at
Port Appin & Lismore ferry sign. After 2.5m left after
post office, hotel at end of road

Originally the residence of the Pier Master, with parts
of the building dating back to the 19th century, this
hotel is located on the shores of Loch Linnhe with
picture-postcard views to the islands of Lismore and
Mull. The beautifully appointed, individually designed
bedrooms have Wi-fi access and include Arran
Aromatics toiletries. The hotel has a Finnish sauna,
and also offers a range of treatments. Babysitting
can be arranged.

Rooms 12 (2 fmly) (6 GF) ⚓ **S** £75-£130;
D £130-£185 (incl. bkfst)* **Facilities** FTV Wi-fi ⌂
Aromatherapy Massage Sauna New Year
Conf Class 20 Board 20 Thtr 20 Del from £105 to
£160* **Parking** 20 **Notes** LB Closed 25-26 Dec
Civ Wed 80

PORT OF MENTEITH Map 20 NN50
Stirling

The Lake of Menteith Hotel

★★★ 74% ◉◉ SMALL HOTEL

☎ 01877 385258
FK8 3RA
e-mail: enquiries@lake-hotel.com
web: www.lake-hotel.com
dir: M9 junct 10, A84. At Blairdrummond take A873.
Left onto A81 to Port of Mentieth. Left onto B8034,
hotel 200yds on right

This hotel is situated on the shores of the Lake of
Menteith in the Trossachs National Park, within an
hour's drive from either Glasgow or Edinburgh. The
converted 19th-century manse house has stylish
bedrooms with great views over the lake or the
countryside; all offer a very good range of accessories.
Dining is a highlight with two dining options on offer.
There's the fine dining restaurant with spectacular
views, and also the Port Bar that has outdoor seating
for the summer months; both menus are based on
well-sourced produce.

Rooms 17 (5 GF) ⚓ **S** £95-£155; **D** £130-£195 (incl.
bkfst)* **Facilities** FTV Wi-fi Xmas New Year
Conf Board 18 Thtr 30 Del from £120 to £140*
Parking 50 **Notes** LB ⊗ Civ Wed 50

PORTPATRICK Map 20 NW95
Dumfries & Galloway

INSPECTORS' CHOICE

Knockinaam Lodge

★★★ ◉◉◉ HOTEL

☎ 01776 810471
DG9 9AD
e-mail: reservations@knockinaamlodge.com
web: www.knockinaamlodge.com
dir: From A77 or A75 follow signs to Portpatrick.
Through Lochans. After 2m left at signs for hotel

Any tour of Dumfries & Galloway would not be
complete without a stay at this haven of tranquillity
and relaxation. Knockinaam Lodge is an extended
Victorian house set in an idyllic cove with its own
pebble beach (ideal for a private swim in the
summer) and sheltered by majestic cliffs and
woodlands. Surrounded by 30 acres of delightful
grounds, the lodge was the location for a meeting
between Churchill and General Eisenhower in World
War II. Today, a warm welcome is assured from the
proprietors and their committed team, and much
emphasis is placed on providing a sophisticated
but intimate home-from-home experience. There
are just ten suites - each individually designed and
all with flat-screen TVs with DVD players, luxury
toiletries and complimentary bottled water. The
cooking is a real treat and showcases prime
Scottish produce on the daily-changing, four-course
set menus; guests can always discuss the choices
in advance if they wish.

Rooms 10 (1 fmly) ⚓ **S** £170-£340; **D** £275-£440
(incl. bkfst & dinner)* **Facilities** FTV Wi-fi Fishing
⌂ Shooting Walking Sea fishing Clay pigeon
shooting Xmas New Year **Conf** Class 10 Board 16
Thtr 30 **Parking** 20 **Notes** Civ Wed 40

POWFOOT Map 21 NY16
Dumfries & Galloway

Powfoot Golf Hotel

★★★ 75% HOTEL

☎ 01461 700254 & 207580
Links Av DG12 5PN
e-mail: reception@thepowfootgolfhotel.co.uk
dir: A75 onto B721, through Annan. B724, approx 3m,
left onto unclassified road

This hotel has well presented and comfortable
modern bedrooms, many of which overlook the
championship golf course. Public areas have
panoramic views onto the Solway Firth and the
Lakeland hills beyond. The service is friendly and
relaxed, and quality food is served in a choice of
locations.

Rooms 24 (9 fmly) (5 GF) **Facilities** STV FTV Wi-fi Putt
green Xmas New Year **Conf** Class 80 Board 80 Thtr 80
Parking 30 **Notes** ⊗ Civ Wed 100

PRESTWICK Map 20 NS32
South Ayrshire

Parkstone Hotel

★★★ 77% HOTEL

☎ 01292 477286
Esplanade KA9 1QN
e-mail: info@parkstonehotel.co.uk
web: www.parkstonehotel.co.uk
dir: From Main St (A79) W to seafront, hotel in 600yds

Situated on the seafront in a quiet residential area
only one mile from Prestwick Airport, this family-run
hotel caters for business visitors as well as golfers.
Bedrooms come in a variety of sizes; all are furnished
in a smart, contemporary style. The attractive,
modern look of the bar and restaurant is matched by
an equally up-to-date menu.

Rooms 30 (2 fmly) (7 GF) ⚓ **S** £59-£79; **D** £86-£96
(incl. bkfst)* **Facilities** FTV Wi-fi Xmas New Year
Conf Thtr 100 **Parking** 34 **Notes** LB ⊗ Civ Wed 100

Save on hotels. Book at **theAA.com/hotel**

POR – ST 571 SCOTLAND

RHU Map 20 NS28
Argyll & Bute

Rosslea Hall Hotel

★★★ 79% HOTEL

☎ 01436 439955
Ferry Rd G84 8NF
dir: On A814, opposite church

Overlooking the Firth of the Clyde and close to Helensburgh, this imposing mansion is set in its own well tended gardens. Bedrooms and bathrooms are of a good size, well appointed and cater well for the modern traveller. The eating options include the Conservatory Restaurant, overlooking the grounds and the Clyde, which offers dishes cooked with imagination and flair. The hotel is a popular wedding venue.

Rooms 30 (3 fmly) (2 GF) **Facilities** FTV Wi-fi Xmas New Year **Conf** Class 60 Board 80 Thtr 150 **Parking** 30 **Notes** ⊗ Civ Wed 110

ROY BRIDGE Map 22 NN28
Highland

Best Western Glenspean Lodge Hotel

★★★ 83% HOTEL

☎ 01397 712223
PH31 4AW
e-mail: reservations@glenspeanlodge.co.uk
web: www.glenspeanlodge.com
dir: 2m E of Roy Bridge, exit A82 at Spean Bridge onto A86

With origins as a hunting lodge dating back to the Victorian era, this hotel sits in gardens in an elevated position in the Spean Valley. Accommodation is provided in well laid out bedrooms, some suitable for families. Inviting public areas include a comfortable lounge bar and a restaurant that enjoys stunning views of the valley.

Rooms 17 (4 fmly) **Facilities** Wi-fi Gym Sauna Xmas New Year **Conf** Class 16 **Parking** 60 **Notes** Civ Wed 60

The Stronlossit Inn

★★★ 77% SMALL HOTEL

☎ 01397 712253
PH31 4AG
e-mail: stay@stronlossit.co.uk
web: www.stronlossit.co.uk
dir: Exit A82 at Spean Bridge onto A86, signed Roy Bridge. Hotel on left

Appointed to modern standards with the character and hospitality of a traditional hostelry, The Stronlossit Inn is quite a draw for the discerning Highland tourist. The spacious bar is the focal point, with a peat burning fire providing a warm welcome in cooler months; guests can eat in the attractive restaurant. Bedrooms come in a mix of sizes and styles, most being smartly modern and well equipped.

Rooms 10 (5 GF) **Facilities** Wi-fi ↘ **Conf** Class 12 Board 10 Thtr 20 **Parking** 30 **Notes** ⊗ No children 17yrs Closed 1-15 Dec

ST ANDREWS Map 21 NO51
Fife

INSPECTORS' CHOICE

The Old Course Hotel, Golf Resort & Spa

★★★★★ ◉◉◉ HOTEL

☎ 01334 474371
KY16 9SP
e-mail: reservations@oldcoursehotel.co.uk
dir: M90 junct 8, A91 to St Andrews

A haven for golfers, this internationally renowned hotel sits adjacent to the 17th hole of the championship course. Bedrooms vary in size and style but all provide decadent levels of luxury. Day rooms include intimate lounges, a bright conservatory, a spa and a range of pro golf shops. The fine dining Road Hole Restaurant, the Sands Grill specialising in seafood and steaks, and the informal Jigger Inn are all popular eating venues. Staff throughout are friendly and services are impeccably delivered.

Rooms 144 (5 fmly) (3 GF) **Facilities** Spa STV FTV Wi-fi ↘ ⒮ ♪ 18 Putt green Gym Thermal suite ♬ Xmas New Year **Conf** Class 473 Board 259 Thtr 950 **Services** Lift **Parking** 125 **Notes** ⊗ Civ Wed 180

Fairmont St Andrews, Scotland

★★★★★ 85% ◉◉ HOTEL

☎ 01334 837000
KY16 8PN
e-mail: standrews.scotland@fairmont.com
dir: Approx 2m from St Andrews on A917 towards Crail

Sitting just a few miles from St Andrews, overlooking the rugged Fife coastline and the championship golf courses, The Fairmont is situated on a 520-acre estate. There are spacious bedrooms and bathrooms. The eating options are The Squire for brasserie-style food, Esperante for Mediterranean dishes, and The Clubhouse and The Atrium with all-day menus. The hotel has an impressive spa and health club. Good standards of service are found throughout.

Rooms 209 (209 fmly) (68 GF) ↖ **S** £159-£299; **D** £159-£299 (incl. bkfst)* **Facilities** Spa STV FTV Wi-fi ↘ ⒮ ♪ 36 Putt green Gym 106-seat cinema Nail salon Xmas New Year Child facilities **Conf** Class 450 Board 168 Thtr 500 **Services** Lift Air con **Parking** 150 **Notes** LB Civ Wed 350

S

ST ANDREWS *continued*

INSPECTORS' CHOICE

Rufflets Country House

★★★★ ◉◉ HOTEL

☎ 01334 472594
Strathkinness Low Rd KY16 9TX
e-mail: reservations@rufflets.co.uk
web: www.rufflets.co.uk
dir: 1.5m W on B939

Built in 1924 for a Dundee jute baron, this charming property is set in extensive gardens a few minutes' drive from the town centre. The stylish, spacious bedrooms are individually decorated, and includes the Gilroy Suite, The Orchard Suite (separate from the main building), and Turret Rooms that have their own seating areas. Public rooms include a well-stocked bar, a choice of inviting lounges and the delightful Terrace Restaurant that serves imaginative, carefully prepared cuisine based on seasonal produce. Impressive conference and banqueting facilities are available in the adjacent Garden Suite. Families are very welcome, and the hotel is a popular wedding venue.

Rooms 24 (5 annexe) (2 fmly) (5 GF) 🐾
S £145-£180; **D** £215-£275 (incl. bkfst)*
Facilities STV FTV Wi-fi ♨ Putt green ⛳ Golf driving net Children's outdoor games New Year
Conf Class 60 Board 60 Thtr 200 Del from £180 to £300* **Parking** 50 **Notes** Civ Wed 130

Macdonald Rusacks Hotel

★★★★ 75% ◉◉◉ HOTEL

☎ 0844 879 9136 & 01334 474321
Pilmour Links KY16 9JQ
e-mail: general.rusacks@macdonald-hotels.co.uk
web: www.macdonald-hotels.co.uk
dir: From A91 W, straight on at rdbt into St Andrews. Hotel 220yds on left

This long-established hotel enjoys an almost unrivalled location with superb views across the famous golf course. Bedrooms, though varying in size, are comfortably appointed and well equipped. Classically styled public rooms include an elegant reception lounge are contrasted with a modern Rocca Bar & Grill bar where award-winning classic Scottish cuisine, with an Italian slant, is served. It is a spacious room with panoramic views over the 18th green towards the beach. Other eating options are the One Under Gastro Pub, and the refurbished R Bar for lunch and afternoon tea.

Rooms 70 (1 annexe) 🐾 **S** £90-£310; **D** £90-£510 (incl. bkfst)* **Facilities** STV FTV Wi-fi New Year **Conf** Class 35 Board 20 Thtr 80 Del from £135 to £350* **Services** Lift **Parking** 21 **Notes** LB Civ Wed 60

Best Western Scores Hotel

★★★ 81% HOTEL

☎ 01334 472451
76 The Scores KY16 9BB
e-mail: reception@scoreshotel.co.uk
web: www.bw-scoreshotel.co.uk
dir: M90 junct 2a, A92 E. Follow Glenrothes signs then St Andrews signs. Straight on at next 2 rdbts, left into Golf Place, right into The Scores

Enjoying views over St Andrews Bay, this well presented hotel is situated only a short pitch from the first tee of the famous Old Course. Bedrooms are impressively furnished and come in various sizes; many are quite spacious. Smart public areas include Champions Grill offering food all day from breakfast to dinner; Scottish High Teas are served here from 4.30-6.30pm. Alexander's Restaurant opens Thursday, Friday and Saturday evenings.

Rooms 36 (1 fmly) 🐾 **S** £94-£219; **D** £140-£350 (incl. bkfst) **Facilities** FTV Wi-fi Xmas New Year **Conf** Class 60 Board 40 Thtr 180 Del from £144 to £203 **Services** Lift **Parking** 12 **Notes** LB ⊗ Civ Wed 100

Russell Hotel

★★ 82% ◉ HOTEL

☎ 01334 473447
26 The Scores KY16 9AS
e-mail: russellhotel@talk21.com
web: www.russellhotelstandrews.co.uk
dir: From A91 left at 2nd rdbt into Golf Place, right in 200yds into The Scores, hotel in 300yds on left

Lying on the east bay, this friendly, family-run Victorian terrace hotel provides well appointed bedrooms in varying sizes; some enjoy fine sea views. Cosy public areas include a popular bar and an intimate restaurant, both offering a good range of freshly prepared dishes. Situated in St Andrews, said to be 'The Home of Golf', this hotel offers a comprehensive range of golfing breaks, and is convenient for visits to the castle, cathedral and university.

Rooms 10 (3 fmly) **Facilities** New Year **Notes** ⊗

ST BOSWELLS   Map 21 NT53
Scottish Borders

Dryburgh Abbey Hotel

★★★★ 73% ◉◉ COUNTRY HOUSE HOTEL

☎ 01835 822261
TD6 0RQ
e-mail: enquiries@dryburgh.co.uk
web: www.dryburgh.co.uk
dir: Exit A68 at St Boswells. B6356 signed Scott's View & Earlston. Through Clintmains, 1.8m to hotel

Found in the heart of the Scottish Borders, and sitting beside to the ancient ruins of Dryburgh Abbey and the majestic River Tweed. This country house hotel, dating from the mid-19th century, offers comfortable public areas and an array of bedrooms and suites, each still displaying original features. The award-winning Tweed Restaurant, overlooking the river, showcases the chef's dedication to producing modern Scottish cuisine, and The Abbey Bistro offers food from noon until 9pm.

Rooms 38 (31 fmly) (8 GF) ⬧ **S** £60–£205; **D** £120–£372 (incl. bkfst)* **Facilities** FTV Wi-fi ⬧ ⬧ Putt green Fishing ⬧ Sauna Xmas New Year **Conf** Class 80 Board 60 Thtr 150 Del from £80 to £240* **Services** Lift **Parking** 70 **Notes** Civ Wed 120

ST FILLANS   Map 20 NN62
Perth & Kinross

The Four Seasons Hotel

★★★ 85% ◉ ◉ HOTEL

☎ 01764 685333
Loch Earn PH6 2NF
e-mail: info@thefourseasonshotel.co.uk
web: www.thefourseasonshotel.co.uk
dir: On A85, towards W of village

Set on the edge of Loch Earn, this welcoming hotel and many of its bedrooms benefit from fine views. There is a choice of lounges, including a library, warmed by log fires during winter. Local produce is used to good effect in both the Meall Reamhar restaurant and the more informal Tarken Room.

Rooms 18 (6 annexe) (7 fmly) **S** £54–£97; **D** £108–£166 (incl. bkfst) **Facilities** FTV Wi-fi Xmas New Year **Conf** Class 45 Board 38 Thtr 95 Del from £115.50 to £154.50 **Parking** 40 **Notes** LB Closed 2 Jan-mid Feb RS Nov, Dec, Mar Civ Wed 80

SANQUHAR   Map 21 NS70
Dumfries & Galloway

Blackaddie House Hotel

★★★ 79% ◉ ◉ COUNTRY HOUSE HOTEL

☎ 01659 50270
Blackaddie Rd DG4 6JJ
e-mail: ian@blackaddiehotel.co.uk
dir: Exit A76 just N of Sanquhar at Burnside Service Station. Take private road to hotel 300mtrs on right

Overlooking the River Nith and in two acres of secluded gardens, this family run country house hotel offers friendly and attentive hands-on service. The bedrooms and suites, including family accommodation, are all well presented and comfortable with many useful extras provided as standard. The award-winning food, served in the restaurant, with its lovely garden views, is based on prime Scottish ingredients.

Rooms 9 (3 annexe) (2 fmly) (3 GF) ⬧ **S** £65–£170; **D** £110–£190 (incl. bkfst) **Facilities** FTV Wi-fi Xmas New Year **Conf** Class 12 Board 16 Thtr 20 Del from £148 to £188* **Parking** 20 **Notes** LB Civ Wed 24

SCOURIE   Map 22 NC14
Highland

Scourie Hotel

★★★ 73% SMALL HOTEL

☎ 01971 502396
IV27 4SX
e-mail: patrick@scourie-hotel.co.uk
dir: N'bound on A894. Hotel in village on left

This well-established hotel is an angler's paradise with extensive fishing rights available on a 25,000-acre estate. Public areas include a choice of comfortable lounges, a cosy bar and a smart dining room offering wholesome fare. The bedrooms are comfortable and generally spacious. The resident proprietors and their staff create a relaxed and friendly atmosphere.

Rooms 20 (2 annexe) (2 fmly) (5 GF) **S** £43–£54; **D** £82–£102 (incl. bkfst)* **Facilities** Wi-fi Fishing **Parking** 30 **Notes** LB Closed mid Oct-end Mar

---

SELKIRK   Map 21 NT42
Scottish Borders

Best Western Philipburn Country House Hotel

★★★★ 🅰 COUNTRY HOUSE HOTEL

☎ 01750 20747
Linglie Rd TD7 5LS
e-mail: info@philipburnhousehotel.co.uk
dir: From A7 follow signs for A72/A707/Peebles/Moffat. Hotel 1m from town centre

Rooms 12 (2 fmly) **S** £90–£150; **D** £110–£180 (incl. bkfst) **Facilities** FTV Wi-fi ⬧ Xmas New Year **Conf** Class 12 Board 24 Thtr 40 Del from £148 to £168 **Parking** 52 **Notes** LB ⊗ Closed 4-19 Jan Civ Wed 85

SHIEL BRIDGE   Map 22 NG91
Highland

Grants at Craigellachie

◉ RESTAURANT WITH ROOMS

☎ 01599 511331
Craigellachie, Ratagan IV40 8HP
e-mail: info@housebytheloch.co.uk
dir: From A87 exit for Glenelg, 1st right to Ratagan, opposite Youth Hostel sign

Sitting on the tranquil shores of Loch Duich and overlooked by the Five Sisters Mountains, Grants really does occupy a stunning location. The restaurant has a well deserved reputation for its cuisine, and the bedrooms are stylish and have all the creature comforts. Guests are guaranteed a warm welcome at this charming house.

Rooms 4 (2 annexe)

S

SHIELDAIG
Highland   Map 22 NG85

Tigh an Eilean
★ ◉◉ SMALL HOTEL

☎ 01520 755251
IV54 8XN
e-mail: tighaneilean@keme.co.uk
dir: Exit A896 into Shieldaig, hotel in village centre

A splendid location by the sea, with views over the bay, is the icing on the cake for this delightful small hotel. It can be a long drive to reach Sheildaig but guests remark that the journey is more than worth the effort. The brightly decorated bedrooms are comfortable though don't expect television, except in one of the lounges. For many, it's the food that attracts, with fish and seafood featuring strongly.

Rooms 11 (1 fmly) **Facilities** Wi-fi ⌨ Birdwatching Kayaks Astronomical telescope Xmas New Year **Parking** 15 **Notes** RS late Oct-mid Mar

SORN
East Ayrshire   Map 20 NS52

The Sorn Inn
◉◉ RESTAURANT WITH ROOMS

☎ 01290 551305
35 Main St KA5 6HU
e-mail: craig@sorninn.com
dir: A70 from S or A76 from N onto B743 to Sorn

Centrally situated in a rural village, which is convenient for many of Ayrshire's attractions, this inn has a fine dining restaurant with a cosy lounge area. There is also a popular chop house with a pub-like environment. The freshly decorated bedrooms have comfortable beds and good facilities.

Rooms 4 (1 fmly)

SOUTH QUEENSFERRY
City of Edinburgh   Map 21 NT17

Premier Inn Edinburgh (Newcraighall)

BUDGET HOTEL

☎ 0871 527 8362
91 Newcraighall Rd, Newcraighall EH21 8RX
web: www.premierinn.com
dir: At junct of A1 & A6095 towards Musselburgh

High quality, budget accommodation ideal for both families and business travellers. Spacious, en suite bedrooms feature tea and coffee making facilities, and Freeview TV in most hotels. Internet access and Wi-fi are available for a small fee. The adjacent family restaurant features a wide and varied menu. See also the Hotel Groups pages.

Rooms 42

Premier Inn Edinburgh (South Queensferry)

BUDGET HOTEL

☎ 0871 527 8364
Builyeon Rd EH30 9YJ
web: www.premierinn.com
dir: M8 junct 2 follow M9 Stirling signs, exit at junct 1a take A8000 towards Forth Road Bridge, at 3rd rdbt 2nd exit into Builyeon Rd (NB do not go onto Forth Road Bridge)

Rooms 70

SPEAN BRIDGE
Highland   Map 22 NN28

Smiddy House
◉◉ RESTAURANT WITH ROOMS

☎ 01397 712335
Roy Bridge Rd PH34 4EU
e-mail: enquiry@smiddyhouse.com
web: www.smiddyhouse.com
dir: In village centre, A82 onto A86

Set in the Great Glen which stretches from Fort William to Inverness, this was once the village smithy, and is now a very friendly establishment. The attractive bedrooms, named after places in Scotland, are comfortably furnished and well equipped. A relaxing garden room is available for guest use. Delicious evening meals are served in Russell's restaurant.

Rooms 4 (1 fmly)

STEPPS
North Lanarkshire   Map 20 NS66

Premier Inn Glasgow North East (Stepps)

BUDGET HOTEL

☎ 0871 527 8452
Crowwood Roundabout, Cumbernauld Rd G33 6HN
web: www.premierinn.com
dir: M8 junct 12, A80 (becomes dual carriageway) to Crowwood rdbt, 4th exit back onto A80, hotel 1st left. Or exit M80 at Crowwood rdbt, 3rd exit signed A80 West. Hotel 1st left

High quality, budget accommodation ideal for both families and business travellers. Spacious, en suite bedrooms feature tea and coffee making facilities, and Freeview TV in most hotels. Internet access and Wi-fi are available for a small fee. The adjacent family restaurant features a wide and varied menu. See also the Hotel Groups pages.

Rooms 80

STIRLING
Stirling   Map 21 NS79

The Stirling Highland Hotel

★★★★ 76% HOTEL

☎ 01786 272727
Spittal St FK8 1DU
e-mail: stirling@pumahotels.co.uk
web: www.pumahotels.co.uk
dir: A84 into Stirling. Follow Stirling Castle signs to Albert Hall. Left, left again, follow Castle signs

Enjoying a location close to the castle and historic town, this atmospheric hotel was previously a high school. Public rooms have been converted from the original classrooms and retain many interesting features. Bedrooms are more modern in style and comfortably equipped. Scholars Restaurant serves traditional and international dishes, and the Headmaster's Study is the ideal venue for enjoying a drink.

Rooms 96 (4 fmly) **Facilities** Spa STV Wi-fi ⌨ supervised Gym Squash Steam room Dance studio Beauty therapist Xmas New Year **Conf** Class 80 Board 60 Thtr 100 **Services** Lift **Parking** 96 **Notes** Civ Wed 100

Holiday Inn Express - Stirling

BUDGET HOTEL

☎ 01786 449922
Springkerse Business Park FK7 7XH
e-mail: reservations@expressstirling.co.uk
web: www.hiexpress.com/stirling
dir: M9, M80 junct 9, A91, Stirling/St Andrews exit. 2.8m, at 4th rdbt, 2nd exit to sports stadium, 3rd exit to hotel

A modern hotel ideal for families and business travellers. Fresh and uncomplicated, the spacious rooms include Sky TV, power shower and tea and coffee-making facilities. Continental buffet breakfast is included in the room rate; other meals may be taken at the nearby family pub or restaurant. See also the Hotel Groups pages.

Rooms 80 (36 fmly) (16 GF) ☜ **S** £49-£150; **D** £49-£150 (incl. bkfst)* **Conf** Class 14 Board 18 Thtr 30

Premier Inn Stirling

BUDGET HOTEL

☎ 0871 527 9038
Glasgow Rd, Whins of Milton FK7 8EX
web: www.premierinn.com
dir: On A872, 0.25m from M9/M80 junct 9

High quality, budget accommodation ideal for both families and business travellers. Spacious, en suite bedrooms feature tea and coffee making facilities, and Freeview TV in most hotels. Internet access and Wi-fi are available for a small fee. The adjacent family restaurant features a wide and varied menu. See also the Hotel Groups pages.

Rooms 60

STRACHUR　　　**Map 20 NN00**
Argyll & Bute

The Creggans Inn

★★★ 80% ◉◉ HOTEL

☎ 01369 860279
PA27 8BX
e-mail: info@creggans-inn.co.uk
web: www.creggans-inn.co.uk
dir: A82 from Glasgow, at Tarbet take A83 towards Cairndow, left onto A815 to Strachur

Benefiting from a superb location on the shores of Loch Fyne, this well established family-run hotel caters well for both the leisure and corporate market. Many of the bedrooms are generous in size and enjoy wonderful views of the loch. During the cooler months open log fires are lit in the bar lounge and restaurant. Wi-fi is available throughout.

The Creggans Inn

Rooms 14 (2 fmly) ☜ **Facilities** FTV Wi-fi New Year **Parking** 16 **Notes** Civ Wed 80

See advert on this page

STRANRAER　　　**Map 20 NX06**
Dumfries & Galloway

Corsewall Lighthouse Hotel

★★★ 80% ◉ HOTEL

☎ 01776 853220
Corsewall Point, Kirkcolm DG9 0QG
e-mail: lighthousehotel@btinternet.com
web: www.lighthousehotel.co.uk
dir: A718 from Stranraer to Kirkcolm (approx 8m). Follow hotel signs for 4m

Looking for something completely different? This is a unique hotel converted from buildings that adjoin a Grade A listed, 19th-century lighthouse set on a rocky coastline. Situated on the headland to the west of Loch Ryan, the lighthouse beam still functions to warn approaching ships. Bedrooms come in a variety of sizes, some reached by a spiral staircase, and like the public areas, are cosy and atmospheric. The cottage suites in the grounds offer greater space. The

continued

S

STRANRAER *continued*

restaurant menus are based on Scottish produce such as venison and salmon.

Rooms 11 (5 annexe) (4 fmly) (2 GF) (3 smoking) **Facilities** FTV Wi-fi Xmas New Year **Conf** Thtr 20 **Parking** 20 **Notes** ⊗ Civ Wed 28

STRATHAVEN	Map 20 NS74
South Lanarkshire	

Rissons at Springvale

⊚ RESTAURANT WITH ROOMS

☎ 01357 521131 & 520234
18 Lethame Rd ML10 6AD
e-mail: rissons@msn.com
dir: A71 into Strathaven, W of town centre off Townhead St

Guests are assured of a warm welcome at this charming establishment close to the town centre. The bedrooms and bathrooms are stylish and well equipped. The main attraction here is the food - a range of interesting, well-prepared dishes served in Rissons Restaurant.

Rooms 9 (1 fmly)

STRATHBLANE	Map 20 NS57
Stirling	

Strathblane Country House

★★★ 78% COUNTRY HOUSE HOTEL

☎ 01360 770491
Milngavie Rd G63 9EH
e-mail: info@strathblanecountryhouse.co.uk
dir: On A81 (Milngavie Rd) S of Strathblane. Hotel 0.75m past Mugdock Country Park on right

Set in 10-acre grounds looking out on the beautiful Campsie Fells, this majestic property, built in 1874, offers a get-away-from-it-all experience, yet is just a 20-minute drive from Glasgow. Lunch and dinner are served in the relaxed Brasserie Restaurant, and guests can visit the falconry or just kick back and relax in front of the fire with a book and a dram of whisky. Weddings are especially well catered for.

Rooms 10 (3 fmly) **S** £59-£89; **D** £75-£150 (incl. bkfst)* **Facilities** FTV Wi-fi Falconry ♫ Xmas New Year **Conf** Class 60 Board 60 Thtr 180 Del from £100 to £150* **Parking** 120 **Notes** LB ⊗ Civ Wed 180

STRATHYRE	Map 20 NN51
Stirling	

Creagan House

⊚ ⊚ RESTAURANT WITH ROOMS

☎ 01877 384638
FK18 8ND
e-mail: eatandstay@creaganhouse.co.uk
web: www.creaganhouse.co.uk
dir: 0.25m N of Strathyre on A84

Originally a farmhouse dating from the 17th century, Creagan House has operated as a restaurant with rooms for many years. The baronial-style dining room provides a wonderful setting for the cuisine which is classic French with some Scottish influences. The warm hospitality and attentive service are noteworthy.

Rooms 5 (1 fmly)

STRONTIAN	Map 22 NM86
Highland	

Kilcamb Lodge Hotel

★★★ ⊚ ⊚ COUNTRY HOUSE HOTEL

☎ 01967 402257
PH36 4HY
e-mail: enquiries@kilcamblodge.co.uk
web: www.kilcamblodge.co.uk
dir: Off A861, via Corran Ferry

This historic house on the shores of Loch Sunart was one of the first stone buildings in the area, and was used as military barracks around the time of the Jacobite uprising. It is situated on the beautiful and peaceful Ardamurchan Peninsula where otters, red squirrels and eagles can be spotted. The suites and bedrooms, with either loch or garden views, are stylishly decorated using designer fabrics and have flat-screen TVs, DVD/CD players, plus bath robes, iced water and even guest umbrellas. Accomplished cooking, utilising much local produce, can be

---

enjoyed in the stylish dining room. Warm hospitality is assured.

Rooms 10 (2 fmly) **Facilities** FTV Wi-fi ⇘ Fishing Boating Hiking Bird/whale/otter watching Stalking Clay pigeon shooting Xmas New Year **Conf** Class 18 Board 18 Thtr 18 **Parking** 20 **Notes** No children 10yrs Closed 2 Jan-1 Feb Civ Wed 120

TAIN	Map 23 NH78
Highland	

The Glenmorangie Highland Home at Cadboll

★★★ ⊚ ⊚ COUNTRY HOUSE HOTEL

☎ 01862 871671
Cadboll, Fearn IV20 1XP
e-mail: relax@glenmorangie.co.uk
web: www.theglenmorangiehouse.com
dir: A9 onto B9175 towards Nigg. Follow tourist signs

This historic highland home superbly balances top class service with intimate customer care. Evenings are dominated by the highly successful 'house party' where guests are introduced in the drawing room, sample whiskies then take dinner (a set six-course meal) together around one long table. Conversation can extend well into the evening. Stylish bedrooms are divided between the traditional main house and some cosy cottages in the grounds. This is an ideal base from which to enjoy the world famous whisky tours.

Rooms 9 (3 annexe) (4 fmly) (3 GF) ⋔ **Facilities** FTV Wi-fi ⇘ Archery Beauty treatments Clay pigeon shooting Falconry Xmas New Year **Conf** Board 12 Del from £175 to £225* **Parking** 60 **Notes** ⊗ No children 15yrs Civ Wed 60

Save on hotels. Book at theAA.com/hotel

STR – TRO 577 SCOTLAND

TARBERT LOCH FYNE
Argyll & Bute
Map 20 NR86

Stonefield Castle Hotel
★★★★ 74% ◉ HOTEL

☎ 01880 820836
PA29 6YJ
e-mail: reservations.stonefieldcastle@ohiml.com
web: www.oxfordhotelsandinns.com
dir: From Glasgow take M8 towards Erskine Bridge onto A82, follow Loch Lomond signs. From Arrochar follow A83 signs through Inveraray & Lochgilphead, hotel on left 2m before Tarbert

This fine baronial castle commands a superb lochside setting amidst beautiful woodland gardens renowned for their rhododendrons - visit in late spring to see them at their best. Elegant public rooms are a feature, and the picture-window restaurant offers unrivalled views across Loch Fyne. Bedrooms are split between the main house and a purpose-built wing.

Rooms 32 (2 fmly) (10 GF) **Facilities** Wi-fi Xmas New Year **Conf** Class 40 Board 50 Thtr 120 **Services** Lift **Parking** 50 **Notes** Civ Wed 100

THURSO
Highland
Map 23 ND16

Forss House Hotel
★★★★ 76% ◉◉ SMALL HOTEL

☎ 01847 861201
Forss KW14 7XY
e-mail: anne@forsshousehotel.co.uk
web: www.forsshousehotel.co.uk
dir: On A836 between Thurso & Reay

This delightful country house is set in its own 20 acres of woodland and was originally built in 1810. The hotel offers a choice of bedrooms from the traditional styled rooms in the main house to the more contemporary annexe rooms in the grounds. All rooms are very well equipped and well appointed. The beautiful River Forss runs through the grounds and is a firm favourite with fishermen.

Rooms 14 (6 annexe) (1 fmly) (7 GF) ✆ **S** £97-£115; **D** £130-£165 (incl. bkfst)* **Facilities** FTV Wi-fi

Fishing **Conf** Class 12 Board 14 Thtr 20 Del from £160 to £175* **Parking** 14 **Notes** LB Closed 23 Dec-3 Jan Civ Wed 26

TORRIDON
Highland
Map 22 NG95

HOTEL OF THE YEAR
INSPECTORS' CHOICE

The Torridon
★★★★ ◉◉◉
COUNTRY HOUSE HOTEL

☎ 01445 791242
By Achnasheen, Wester Ross IV22 2EY
e-mail: info@thetorridon.com
web: www.thetorridon.com
dir: From A832 at Kinlochewe, A896 towards Torridon. (NB do not turn into village) 1m, hotel on right

Delightfully set amidst inspiring loch and mountain scenery, this elegant Victorian shooting lodge has been beautifully appointed to make the most of its many original features, and the 58 acres of surrounding parkland make it a perfect getaway destination. The attractive bedrooms are individually furnished and most enjoy stunning Highland views; expect to find Egyptian cotton sheets, duck down duvets, flat-screen satellite TVs, FM radios and iPod docks plus Victorian-style bathrooms; for complete privacy choose The Boathouse on the loch shore. Comfortable day rooms feature fine wood panelling and roaring fires in cooler months. Head chef Bruno Birckbeck creates award-winning menus based as much as possible on the locally sourced ingredients; the hotel has its own herd of cattle. The whisky bar is aptly named, boasting over 300 malts and in-depth tasting notes. Outdoor activities include shooting, cycling and walking. AA Hotel of the Year for Scotland 2012-13.

Rooms 18 (2 GF) **D** £220-£455 (incl. bkfst)* **Facilities** STV Wi-fi Fishing ⚓ Abseiling Archery Climbing Falconry Kayaking Mountain biking Xmas New Year **Conf** Board 16 Thtr 42 **Services** Lift **Parking** 20 **Notes** ⊗ Closed 2 Jan-9 Feb RS Nov-14 Mar Civ Wed 42

TROON
South Ayrshire
Map 20 NS33

INSPECTORS' CHOICE

Lochgreen House Hotel
★★★★ ◉◉◉ COUNTRY HOUSE HOTEL

☎ 01292 313343
Monktonhill Rd, Southwood KA10 7EN
e-mail: lochgreen@costley-hotels.co.uk
web: www.costley-hotels.co.uk
dir: From A77 follow Prestwick Airport signs. 0.5m before airport take B749 to Troon. Hotel 1m on left

Set in immaculately maintained grounds, Lochgreen House is graced by tasteful extensions which have created stunning public rooms and spacious, comfortable and elegantly furnished bedrooms. Extra facilities include a coffee shop, gift shop and beauty treatments in The Retreat. The magnificent Tapestry Restaurant provides the ideal setting for dinners that are immaculately presented.

Rooms 38 (7 annexe) (17 GF) **Facilities** STV Wi-fi Beauty treatments Xmas New Year **Conf** Class 50 Board 50 Thtr 70 **Services** Lift **Parking** 50 **Notes** ⊗ Civ Wed 140

T

TROON *continued*

The Marine Hotel

★★★★ 78% ◉◉ HOTEL PUMA HOTELS COLLECTION

☎ 01292 314444
Crosbie Rd KA10 6HE
e-mail: marine@pumahotels.co.uk
web: www.pumahotels.co.uk
dir: A77, A78, A79 onto B749. Hotel on left after golf course

A favourite with conference and leisure guests, this hotel overlooks Royal Troon's 18th fairway. The cocktail lounge and split-level restaurant enjoy panoramic views of the Firth of Clyde across to the Isle of Arran. Bedrooms and public areas are attractively appointed.

Rooms 89 **Facilities** Spa STV Wi-fi ✆ supervised Gym Squash Steam room Beauty room Xmas New Year **Conf** Class 100 Board 40 Thtr 200 **Services** Lift **Parking** 200 **Notes** ⊗ Civ Wed 100

TURNBERRY Map 20 NS20
South Ayrshire

INSPECTORS' CHOICE

Turnberry Resort, Scotland

★★★★★ ◉◉◉ HOTEL

☎ 01655 331000
KA26 9LT
e-mail: turnberry@luxurycollection.com
web: www.turnberryresort.co.uk
dir: From Glasgow take A77, M77 S towards Stranraer, 2m past Kirkoswald follow signs for A719 & Turnberry. Hotel 500mtrs on right

Golf probably springs to mind when this hotel is mentioned. This famous establishment enjoys magnificent views over to Arran, Ailsa Craig, and the Mull of Kintyre. Facilities include a world-renowned golf course, the excellent Colin Montgomerie Golf Academy, a luxurious spa with pool, ESPA treatments and a techno fitness studio, and a host of outdoor pursuits for both adults and children. Both the superbly appointed modern rooms and the more traditional, elegant bedrooms and suites are located in the main hotel, while

adjacent lodges provide more space. The stunning public areas include the Grand Tea Lounge, Ailsa Bar and Lounge, the Duel in the Sun sports bar, 1906 restaurant (3 AA Rosettes) serving Escoffier inspired dishes with a modern twist , and the fine-dining James Miller Room and chef's table (2 AA Rosettes).

Rooms 157 (40 annexe) (2 fmly) (12 GF) 🐾 **S** £120-£395; **D** £140-£415 (incl. bkfst)*
Facilities Spa STV FTV Wi-fi ☇ ✆ supervised ⚓ 45 Putt green Fishing Gym Leisure club Outdoor activity centre Colin Montgomerie Golf Academy Xmas New Year **Conf** Class 145 Board 80 Thtr 300 Del from £195 to £345* **Services** Lift **Parking** 200 **Notes** LB Civ Wed 220

Malin Court

★★★ 83% HOTEL

☎ 01655 331457
KA26 9PB
e-mail: info@malincourt.co.uk
web: www.malincourt.co.uk
dir: On A74 to Ayr then A719 to Turnberry & Maidens

Forming part of the Malin Court Residential and Nursing Home Complex, this friendly and comfortable hotel enjoys delightful views over the Firth of Clyde and Turnberry golf courses. Standard and executive rooms are available; all are well equipped. Public areas are plentiful, with the restaurant serving high teas, dinners and light lunches.

Rooms 18 (9 fmly) **S** £70-£75; **D** £110-£120 (incl. bkfst) **Facilities** STV Wi-fi Putt green **Conf** Class 60 Board 30 Thtr 200 Del from £115 to £125 **Services** Lift **Parking** 110 **Notes** ⊗ RS Oct-Mar Civ Wed 80

UPHALL Map 21 NT07
West Lothian

Macdonald Houstoun House

★★★★ 78% ◉ HOTEL MACDONALD HOTELS & RESORTS

☎ 0844 879 9043
EH52 6JS
e-mail: houstoun@macdonald-hotels.co.uk
web: www.macdonaldhotels.co.uk
dir: M8 junct 3 follow Broxburn signs, straight over rdbt, at mini-rdbt turn right towards Uphall, hotel 1m on right

This historic 17th-century tower house lies in beautifully landscaped grounds and gardens, and features a modern leisure club and spa, a choice of dining options, a vaulted cocktail bar and extensive conference and meeting facilities. Stylish bedrooms, some located around a courtyard, are comfortably furnished and well equipped.

Rooms 73 (47 annexe) (12 fmly) (12 GF) 🐾 **S** £79-£200; **D** £79-£200* **Facilities** Spa STV FTV Wi-fi ☇ ✆ 🏊 Gym Health & beauty salon Xmas New Year **Conf** Class 80 Board 80 Thtr 400 Del from £125 to £170* **Parking** 250 **Notes** Civ Wed 200

UPLAWMOOR Map 20 NS45
East Renfrewshire

Uplawmoor Hotel

★★★ 81% ◉ SMALL HOTEL THE CIRCLE

☎ 01505 850565
Neilston Rd G78 4AF
e-mail: info@uplawmoor.co.uk
web: www.uplawmoor.co.uk
dir: M77 junct 2, A736 signed Barrhead & Irvine. Hotel 4m beyond Barrhead

Originally a coaching inn, this friendly hotel is set in a village off the Glasgow to Irvine road. The relaxed restaurant (with cocktail lounge adjacent) features imaginative dishes, whilst the separate lounge bar is popular for freshly prepared bar meals. The modern bedrooms are both comfortable and well equipped.

Save on hotels. Book at **theAA.com/hotel**

TRO – WIC 579 SCOTLAND

Uplawmoor Hotel

Rooms 14 (1 fmly) (2 smoking) **S** £60-£70; **D** £85-£95 (incl. bkfst)* **Facilities** STV Wi-fi **Conf** Class 12 Board 20 Thtr 40 Del from £75 to £95* **Parking** 40 **Notes** LB ⊗ Closed 26 Dec & 1 Jan

See advert on this page

WHITEBRIDGE
Highland   Map 23 NH41

Whitebridge Hotel

★★ 68% HOTEL

☎ 01456 486226
IV2 6UN
e-mail: info@whitebridgehotel.co.uk
dir: A9 onto B851, follow signs to Fort Augustus. Or A82 onto B862 at Fort Augustus

Close to Loch Ness and set amid rugged mountain and moorland scenery, this hotel is popular with tourists, fishermen and deerstalkers. Guests have a choice of more formal dining in the restaurant or lighter meals in the popular cosy bar. Bedrooms are thoughtfully equipped and brightly furnished.

Rooms 12 (3 fmly) **S** £50-£60; **D** £80-£90 (incl. bkfst) **Facilities** Wi-fi Fishing **Parking** 32 **Notes** Closed 11 Dec-9 Jan

---

WICK
Highland   Map 23 ND35

Mackay's Hotel

★★★ 74% HOTEL

☎ 01955 602323
Union St KW1 5ED
e-mail: info@mackayshotel.co.uk
dir: Opposite Caithness General Hospital

This well-established hotel is situated just outside the town centre overlooking the River Wick. MacKay's provides well-equipped, attractive accommodation, suited to both the business and leisure guest. There is a stylish bistro offering food throughout the day and the main bar offers a wide selection of whiskies.

Rooms 30 (2 fmly) **Facilities** FTV Wi-fi ♫ **Conf** Class 100 Board 60 Thtr 100 **Services** Lift **Notes** ⊗ Closed 24-26 Dec & 1-3 Jan

---

W

Scottish
Islands

Tobermory Bay, Isle of Mull

ISLE OF ARRAN

BLACKWATERFOOT — Map 20 NR92

Best Western Kinloch Hotel

★★★ 80% HOTEL

☎ 01770 860444
KA27 8ET
e-mail: reservations@kinlochhotel.eclipse.co.uk
web: www.bw-kinlochhotel.co.uk
dir: Ferry from Ardrossan to Brodick, follow signs for Blackwaterfoot, hotel in village centre

Well known for providing an authentic island experience, this long established stylish hotel is in an idyllic location. Smart public areas include a choice of lounges, popular bars and well-presented leisure facilities. Bedrooms vary in size and style but most enjoy panoramic sea views and several family suites offer excellent value. The spacious restaurant provides a wide ranging menu, and in winter when the restaurant is closed, the bar serves a choice of creative dishes.

Rooms 37 (7 fmly) (7 GF) 🐾 **S** £25–£70; **D** £50–£140 (incl. bkfst)* **Facilities** STV Wi-fi ↘ 🌀 Gym Squash Beauty therapy 🎵 New Year **Conf** Class 20 Board 40 Thtr 120 Del from £80 to £110* **Services** Lift **Parking** 2 **Notes** LB Civ Wed 150

BRODICK — Map 20 NS03

INSPECTORS' CHOICE

Kilmichael Country House Hotel

★★★ ◉◉ COUNTRY HOUSE HOTEL

☎ 01770 302219
Glen Cloy KA27 8BY
e-mail: enquiries@kilmichael.com
web: www.kilmichael.com
dir: From Brodick ferry terminal towards Lochranza for 1m. Left at golf course, follow signs

Reputed to be the oldest on the island, this lovely house lies in attractive gardens in a quiet glen less than five minutes' drive from the ferry terminal. It is a stylish, elegant country house, adorned with ornaments from around the world. The delightful bedrooms are furnished in classical style; some are

contained in a pretty courtyard conversion. There are two inviting drawing rooms and a bright dining room where award-winning contemporary cuisine is served. The dishes include fresh eggs laid by the hotel's own ducks and hens; vegetables, fruit and herbs from the kitchen garden, and mushrooms and berries foraged in season from the estate.

Rooms 8 (3 annexe) (7 GF) 🐾 **S** £76–£95; **D** £128–£205 (incl. bkfst)* **Facilities** Wi-fi **Parking** 14 **Notes** LB No children 12yrs Closed Nov-Feb (ex for prior bookings)

ISLE OF HARRIS

SCARISTA (SGARASTA BHEAG) — Map 22 NG09

Scarista House

◉◉ RESTAURANT WITH ROOMS

☎ 01859 550238
HS3 3HX
e-mail: timandpatricia@scaristahouse.com
dir: On A859, 15m S of Tarbert

A former manse, Scarista House is a haven for food lovers who seek to explore this magnificent island. It enjoys breathtaking views of the Atlantic and is just a short stroll from miles of golden sandy beaches. The house is run in a relaxed country-house manner by the friendly hosts. Expect wellies in the hall and masses of books and CDs in one of two lounges. Bedrooms are cosy, and delicious set dinners and memorable breakfasts are provided.

Rooms 6 (3 annexe) (1 fmly)

TARBERT — Map 22 NB10

Hotel Hebrides

★★★★ 78% ◉ HOTEL

☎ 01859 502364
Pier Rd HS3 3DG
e-mail: stay@hotel-hebrides.com
dir: To Tarbert via ferry from Uig (Isle of Skye); or ferry from Ullapool to Stornaway, A859 to Tarbert; or by plane to Stornaway from Glasgow, Edinburgh or Inverness

Benefiting from an elevated position overlooking the town this hotel is just a few minutes' walk from the centre. The small, hands-on team extend wonderful hospitality and customer care. The bedrooms are stylishly designed and include Wi-fi, high speed internet access and flat-screen TVs; the deluxe rooms have iPod docking stations and some rooms have loch and harbour views. Award-winning food is served in the Pierhouse Restaurant. A complimentary bus service is provided to the theatre in the summer months.

Rooms 21 (2 fmly) **S** £55–£80; **D** £110–£160 (incl. bkfst) **Facilities** FTV Wi-fi ↘ 🎵 **Conf** Class 35 Board 35 Del from £100 to £150 **Notes** ⊗

ISLE OF ISLAY

PORT ASKAIG — Map 20 NR46

Port Askaig Hotel

★★ 63% SMALL HOTEL

☎ 01496 840245
PA46 7RD
e-mail: hotel@portaskaig.co.uk
web: www.portaskaig.co.uk
dir: At ferry terminal

The building of this endearing family-run hotel dates back to the 18th-century. The lounge provides fine views over the Sound of Islay to Jura, and there is a choice of bars that are popular with locals. Traditional dinners are served in the bright restaurant and a full range of bar snacks and meals is also available. The bedrooms are smart and comfortable.

Rooms 8 (1 fmly) (8 GF) **Parking** 21

ISLE OF MULL

TOBERMORY   Map 22 NM55

INSPECTORS' CHOICE

Highland Cottage

★★★ ◎◎   SMALL HOTEL

☎ 01688 302030
Breadalbane St PA75 6PD
e-mail: davidandjo@highlandcottage.co.uk
web: www.highlandcottage.co.uk
dir: A848 Craignure/Fishnish ferry terminal, pass Tobermory signs, straight on at mini rdbt across narrow bridge, turn right. Hotel on right opposite fire station

Providing the highest level of natural and unassuming hospitality, this delightful little gem lies high above the island's capital. Don't be fooled by its side street location, a stunning view over the bay is just a few metres away. 'A country house hotel in town' it is an Aladdin's Cave of collectables and treasures, as well as masses of books and magazines. There are two inviting lounges, one with an honesty bar. The cosy dining room offers memorable dinners and splendid breakfasts. Bedrooms are individual; some have four-posters and all are comprehensively equipped to include TVs and music centres.

Rooms 6 (1 GF) **Facilities** FTV Wi-fi ⌇ **Parking** 6
Notes No children 10yrs Closed Nov-Mar

ORKNEY

ST MARGARET'S HOPE   Map 24 ND49
Orkney

The Creel Restaurant with Rooms

◎◎   RESTAURANT WITH ROOMS

☎ 01856 831311
Front Rd KW17 2SL
e-mail: alan@thecreel.freeserve.co.uk
web: www.thecreel.co.uk
dir: A961 into village, establishment on seafront

With wonderful sea views, The Creel enjoys a prominent position in the pretty fishing village of St Margaret's Hope. The award-winning restaurant has a well deserved reputation for the quality of its seafood and a window seat is a must in the charming restaurant. The stylish bedrooms are appointed to a high standard and most enjoy views over the bay. Breakfasts should not be missed, with local Orkney produce and freshly baked breads on the menu.

Rooms 3

SHETLAND

LERWICK   Map 24 HU44

Shetland Hotel

★★★ 73%   HOTEL

☎ 01595 695515
Holmsgarth Rd ZE1 0PW
e-mail: reception@shetlandhotel.co.uk
dir: Opposite ferry terminal, on main road N from town centre

This purpose-built hotel, situated opposite the main ferry terminal, offers spacious and comfortable bedrooms on three floors. Two dining options are available - the informal Oasis bistro and Ninians Restaurant. Service is prompt and friendly.

Rooms 64 (4 fmly) ⌇ **S** £89; **D** £120 (incl. bkfst)*
Facilities FTV Wi-fi **Conf** Class 75 Board 50 Thtr 300
Services Lift **Parking** 150 **Notes** ⊗

ISLE OF SKYE

ARDVASAR   Map 22 NG60

Ardvasar Hotel

★★★ 74%   SMALL HOTEL

☎ 01471 844223
Sleat IV45 8RS
e-mail: richard@ardvasar-hotel.demon.co.uk
web: www.ardvasarhotel.com
dir: From ferry, 500mtrs, left signed Ardvasar

The Isle of Skye is dotted with cosy, welcoming hotels that make touring the island easy and convenient. This hotel ranks highly amongst its peers thanks to great hospitality and a preservation of community spirit. The hotel sits less than five minutes' drive from the Mallaig ferry and provides comfortable bedrooms and a cosy bar lounge for residents. Seafood is prominent on menus, and meals can be enjoyed in either the popular bar or the attractive dining room.

Rooms 10 (4 fmly) **Facilities** FTV Wi-fi ♫ Xmas New Year **Conf** Board 24 Thtr 50 **Parking** 30

See advert on page 585

SCOTTISH ISLANDS

COLBOST — Map 22 NG24

INSPECTORS' CHOICE

The Three Chimneys and House Over-By

◉◉◉ RESTAURANT WITH ROOMS

☎ 01470 511258
IV55 8ZT
e-mail: eatandstay@threechimneys.co.uk
dir: 4m W of Dunvegan village on B884 signed Glendale

A visit to this delightful property will make a trip to Skye even more memorable. The stunning food is the result of a deft approach using quality local ingredients. Breakfast is an impressive array of local fish, meats and cheeses, served with fresh home baking and home-made preserves. The stylish lounge-breakfast area has the real wow factor. Bedrooms, in the House Over-By, are creative and thoughtfully equipped - all have spacious en suites and wonderful views across Loch Dunvegan.

Rooms 6 (1 fmly) (6GF)

ISLEORNSAY — Map 22 NG71

Duisdale House Hotel

★★★★ 81% ◉◉ SMALL HOTEL

☎ 01471 833202
IV43 8QW
e-mail: info@duisdale.com
web: www.duisdale.com
dir: 7m S of Bradford on A851 towards Armadale. 7m N of Armadale ferry

This grand Victorian house stands in its own landscaped gardens overlooking the Sound of Sleat. The hotel has a contemporary and chic style which complements the original features of the house. Each bedroom is individually designed and the superior rooms have four-poster beds. The elegant lounge has sumptuous sofas, original artwork and blazing log fires in the colder months.

Duisdale House Hotel

Rooms 18 (1 fmly) (1 GF) 🐾 S £69.50-£150;
D £69.50-£155 (incl. bkfst)* **Facilities** STV Wi-fi 🏌
Private yacht Outdoor hydropool Xmas New Year
Conf Board 28 Thtr 50 Del from £99 to £175*
Parking 30 **Notes** LB ⊗ Civ Wed 58

See advert on opposite page

INSPECTORS' CHOICE

Kinloch Lodge

★★★ ◉◉◉ COUNTRY HOUSE HOTEL

☎ 01471 833214 & 833333
IV43 8QY
e-mail: reservations@kinloch-lodge.co.uk
web: www.kinloch-lodge.co.uk
dir: 6m S of Broadford on A851, 10m N of Armadale on A851

Owned and ran in a hands-on fashion by Lord and Lady MacDonald and their family, this hotel enjoys a picture postcard location surrounded by hills and a sea loch. Bedrooms and bathrooms are well appointed and comfortable, and public areas boast numerous open fires and relaxing areas to sit. There is a cookery school run by Claire MacDonald and a shop that sells her famous cookery books and produce.

Rooms 15 (8 annexe) (1 GF) 🐾 **Facilities** STV FTV
Wi-fi Fishing Beauty treatment room Xmas New
Year **Conf** Class 20 Board 20 Thtr 20 **Parking** 40

Toravaig House Hotel

★★★ 81% ◉◉ SMALL HOTEL

☎ 01471 820200 & 833231
Knock Bay, Sleat IV44 8RE
e-mail: info@skyehotel.co.uk
web: www.skyehotel.co.uk
dir: From Skye Bridge, left at Broadford onto A851, hotel 11m on left. Or from ferry at Armadale take A851, hotel 6m on right

Set in two acres and enjoying panoramic views to the Knoydart Hills, this hotel is a haven of peace, with stylish, well-equipped and beautifully decorated bedrooms. There is an inviting lounge complete with deep sofas and an elegant dining room where delicious meals are the order of the day. The hotel provides a sea-going yacht for guests' exclusive use from April to September.

Rooms 9 🐾 S £69-£150; **D** £69.50-£120 (incl.
bkfst)* **Facilities** STV Wi-fi 🏌 Daily excursions (Apr-Sep) on hotel yacht Xmas New Year **Conf** Board 10
Thtr 15 Del from £99 to £175* **Parking** 15 **Notes** LB
⊗ Civ Wed 25

See advert on opposite page

Save on hotels. Book at **theAA.com/hotel**

ISLE OF SKYE 585 SCOTLAND

SCOTTISH ISLANDS

ISLEORNSAY *continued*

Hotel Eilean Iarmain

★★★ 78% ◎◎ SMALL HOTEL

THE CIRCLE

☎ 01471 833332

IV43 8QR

e-mail: hotel@eileaniarmain.co.uk
web: www.eileaniarmain.co.uk
dir: From Skye Bridge take A87 towards Broadford.
Left onto A851 signed Armadale. 8m, left to hotel. Or
from Armadale ferry take A851 signed Broadford. 7m
to hotel

A hotel of charm and character, this 19th-century
former inn sits by the pier and enjoys fine views
across the sea loch towards Isleornsay lighthouse and
the Knoydart Hills. Bedrooms are individual and
retain a traditional style, and a stable block has been
converted into four delightful suites. Public rooms are
cosy and inviting, and the restaurant offers award-
winning menus showcasing the island's best
produce, especially seafood and game.

Rooms 16 (10 annexe) (4 fmly) (3 GF) **S** £75-£135;
D £100-£250 (incl. bkfst)* **Facilities** FTV Wi-fi
Fishing Shooting Art exhibitions Whisky tasting Shop
Tweed Shop ♫ Xmas New Year **Conf** Class 10
Board 14 Thtr 25 **Parking** 20 **Notes** LB Civ Wed 30

See advert on opposite page

PORTREE Map 22 NG44

Cuillin Hills Hotel

★★★★ 77% ◎◎ HOTEL

☎ 01478 612003

IV51 9QU

e-mail: info@cuillinhills-hotel-skye.co.uk
web: www.cuillinhills-hotel-skye.co.uk
dir: Right 0.25m N of Portree off A855. Follow hotel
signs

This imposing building enjoys a superb location
overlooking Portree Bay and the Cuillin Hills.
Accommodation is provided in smart, well-equipped
rooms that are generally spacious; some rooms are
found in an adjacent building. Public areas include a
split-level restaurant that takes advantage of the
views. Service is particularly attentive.

Rooms 29 (7 annexe) (4 fmly) (10 GF) ↖ **S** £80-£160;
D £110-£200 (incl. bkfst)* **Facilities** STV FTV Wi-fi HL
Xmas New Year **Parking** 56 **Notes** LB Civ Wed 45

Rosedale Hotel

★★★ 75% HOTEL

☎ 01478 613131

Beaumont Crescent IV51 9DF

e-mail: rosedalehotelsky@aol.com
web: www.rosedalehotelskye.co.uk
dir: Follow directions to village centre & harbour

The atmosphere is wonderfully warm at this delightful
family-run waterfront hotel. A labyrinth of stairs and
corridors connects the comfortable lounges, bar and
charming restaurant - all are set on different levels.
The restaurant has fine views of the bay. The modern
bedrooms offer a good range of amenities.

Rosedale Hotel

Rooms 18 (1 fmly) (3 GF) **S** £45-£65; **D** £70-£150
(incl. bkfst)* **Facilities** FTV Wi-fi **Parking** 2 **Notes** ⊗
Closed Nov-mid Mar

SKEABOST BRIDGE Map 22 NG44

Skeabost Country House

★★★ 75% ◎

COUNTRY HOUSE HOTEL

OXFORD
HOTELS & INNS

☎ 01470 532202 & 08444 146572

IV51 9NP

e-mail: manager.skeabost@ohiml.com
web: www.oxfordhotelsandinns.com
dir: From Skye Bridge on A87, through Portree towards
Uig. Left onto A850, hotel on right

This delightful property stands in mature, landscaped
grounds at the edge of Loch Snizort. Originally built
as a hunting lodge by the MacDonalds and steeped in
history, Skeabost offers a welcoming environment
from the caring and helpful staff. The hotel provides
award-winning food, charming day rooms and well
appointed accommodation. The pretty grounds
include a challenging 9-hole golf course, and there is
salmon and trout fishing nearby. Wi-fi is available.

Rooms 14 (5 GF) ↖ **S** £60-£145; **D** £160-£255*
Facilities FTV Wi-fi ♿ 9 Fishing Xmas New Year
Conf Class 20 Board 20 Thtr 40 Del from £100 to
£185* **Parking** 40 **Notes** LB Civ Wed 100

Save on hotels. Book at **theAA.com/hotel**

ISLE OF SKYE 587 SCOTLAND

STAFFIN
Map 22 NG46

Flodigarry Country House Hotel

★★★ 78% COUNTRY HOUSE HOTEL

☎ 01470 552203
IV51 9HZ
e-mail: info@flodigarry.co.uk
web: www.flodigarry.co.uk
dir: A855 from Portree, through Staffin to Flodigarry, hotel signed on right

This hotel is located in woodlands on The Quiraing in north-east Skye overlooking the sea towards the Torridon Mountains. The dramatic scenery is a real inspiration here, and this charming house was once the home of the Scotland's heroine, Flora MacDonald. Guests are assured of real Highland hospitality and there is an easy going atmosphere throughout. A full range of activities is offered, with mountain walks, fishing and boat trips proving to be the most popular.

Rooms 18 (7 annexe) (3 fmly) (4 GF) **Facilities** FTV Wi-fi Xmas New Year **Parking** 40 **Notes** Closed Nov-15 Dec & Jan Civ Wed 80

The Glenview

◉ ◉ RESTAURANT WITH ROOMS

☎ 01470 562248
Culnacnoc IV51 9JH
e-mail: enquiries@glenviewskye.co.uk
dir: 12m N of Portree on A855

The Glenview is located in one of the most beautiful parts of Skye with stunning sea views; it is close to the famous rock formation, the Old Man of Storr. The individually styled bedrooms are very comfortable and front-facing rooms enjoy the dramatic views. Evening meals should not to be missed as the restaurant has a well deserved reputation for its locally sourced produce.

Rooms 5

STRUAN
Map 22 NG33

INSPECTORS' CHOICE

Ullinish Country Lodge

◉ ◉ ◉ RESTAURANT WITH ROOMS

☎ 01470 572214
IV56 8FD
e-mail: ullinish@theisleofskye.co.uk
dir: Take A863 N. Lodge signed on left

Set in some of Scotland's most dramatic landscape, with views of the Black Cuillin and MacLeod's Tables, this lodge has lochs on three sides. Samuel Johnson and James Boswell stayed here in 1773 and were impressed with the hospitality even then. Hosts Brian and Pam hope to extend the same welcome to their guests today. As you would expect, all bedrooms have amazing views, and come with half-tester beds. The cuisine in the restaurant is impressive and uses the best of Skye's produce including locally sourced seafood and game.

Rooms 6

SCOTTISH ISLANDS

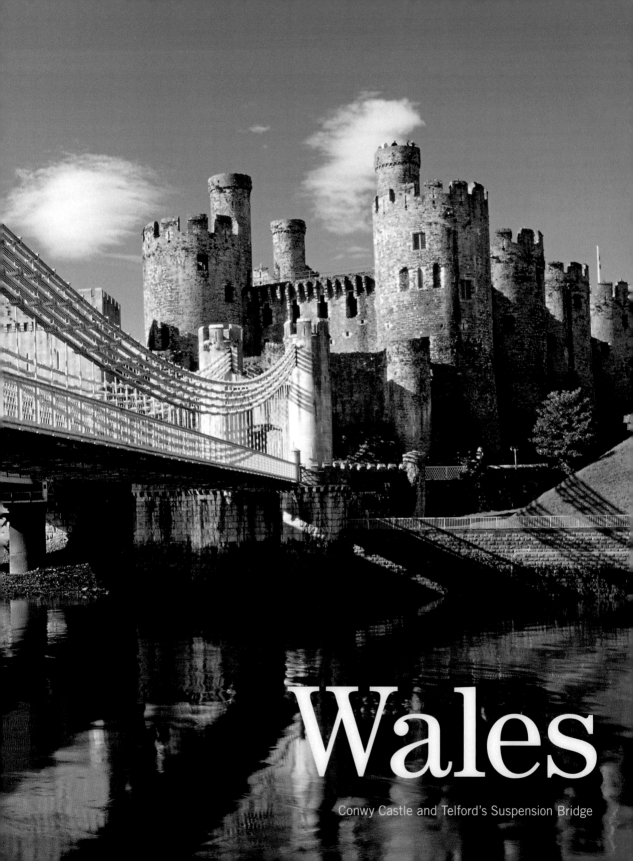

Wales

Conwy Castle and Telford's Suspension Bridge

A

ABERAERON
Ceredigion   Map 8 SN46

Ty Mawr Mansion

◉◉ RESTAURANT WITH ROOMS

☎ 01570 470033
Cilcennin SA48 8DB
e-mail: info@tymawrmansion.co.uk
web: www.tymawrmansion.co.uk
dir: On A482 (Lampeter to Aberaeron road), 4m from Aberaeron

Surrounded by rolling countryside in its own naturally beautiful gardens, this fine country mansion house is a haven of peace and tranquillity. Careful renovation has restored it to its former glory and, combined with lush fabrics, top quality beds and sumptuous furnishings, the accommodation is spacious, superbly equipped and very comfortable. Award-winning chefs create mouth-watering dishes from local and seasonal produce. There is also a 27-seat cinema with all the authenticity of the real thing. Martin and Cath McAlpine offer the sort of welcome which makes every visit to Ty Mawr a memorable one.

Rooms 9 (1 annexe) (1 fmly)

ABERDARE
Rhondda Cynon Taff   Map 9 SO00

Premier Inn Aberdare

BUDGET HOTEL

☎ 0871 527 8002
Riverside Retail Park, Tirfounders Field CF44 0AH
web: www.premierinn.com
dir: M4 junct 32, A470 signed Merthyr Tydfil. In approx 10m take A4059 signed Aberdare. Straight on at 1st rdbt, 3rd exit at next rdbt into Ffordd Tirwaun signed Riverside Retail Park, hotel in park

High quality, budget accommodation ideal for both families and business travellers. Spacious, en suite bedrooms feature tea and coffee making facilities, and Freeview TV in most hotels. Internet access and Wi-fi are available for a small fee. The adjacent family restaurant features a wide and varied menu. See also the Hotel Groups pages.

Rooms 28

ABERGAVENNY
Monmouthshire   Map 9 SO21

Llansantffraed Court Hotel
WELSH *RAREBITS* Hotels of Distinction

★★★★ 78% ◉◉
COUNTRY HOUSE HOTEL

☎ 01873 840678
Llanvihangel Gobion, Clytha NP7 9BA
e-mail: reception@llch.co.uk
web: www.llch.co.uk
dir: At A465 & A40 Abergavenny junct take B4598 signed Usk (NB do not join A40). Towards Raglan, hotel on left in 4.5m

In a commanding position and in its own extensive grounds, this very impressive property, a privately owned country-house hotel, has enviable views of the Brecon Beacons. Extensive public areas include a relaxing lounge and a spacious restaurant offering imaginative and enjoyable award-winning dishes. Bedrooms vary in size and reflect the individuality of the building; all are comfortably furnished and provide some thoughtful extras. Extensive parking is available.

Rooms 21 (1 fmly) ⟐ **S** £90-£110; **D** £130-£180 (incl. bkfst)* **Facilities** STV FTV Wi-fi ↘ Putt green Fishing ⚓ Clay pigeon shooting school Child facilities **Conf** Class 120 Board 100 Thtr 220 Del from £150 to £220* **Services** Lift **Parking** 250 **Notes** LB Civ Wed 150

Angel Hotel

★★★ 80% ◉ HOTEL

☎ 01873 857121
15 Cross St NP7 5EN
e-mail: mail@angelabergavenny.com
web: www.angelabergavenny.com
dir: From A40 & A465 junct follow town centre signs, S of Abergavenny, past rail & bus stations

Once a coaching inn this has long been a popular venue for both local people and visitors; the two traditional function rooms and a ballroom are in regular use. In addition there is a comfortable lounge, a relaxed bar and a smart restaurant. In warmer weather there is a central courtyard that is ideal for alfresco eating. The bedrooms include a four-poster room and some that are suitable for families.

Rooms 35 (4 annexe) (2 fmly) ⟐ **S** fr £89; **D** £111-£210 (incl. bkfst)* **Facilities** FTV Wi-fi ⏃ New Year **Conf** Class 60 Board 60 Thtr 180 Del from £168* **Services** Lift **Parking** 30 **Notes** LB Closed 25 Dec RS 24 & 26-30 Dec Civ Wed 180

ABERGELE
Conwy   Map 14 SH97

Kinmel Manor Hotel
THE INDEPENDENTS HOTEL ASSOCIATION

★★★ 75% HOTEL

☎ 01745 832014
St George's Rd LL22 9AS
e-mail: reception@kinmelmanorhotel.co.uk
dir: A55 junct 24, hotel entrance on rdbt

Rurally located at the end of a long drive leading from the A55, parts of this notable, family-run hotel date from the 16th century. The smart bedrooms vary from standard to superior and executive rooms. The public areas include a popular lounge bar, the stylish Seasons Brasserie, and leisure facilities which include a gym, indoor pool, jacuzzi, steam room and sauna.

Rooms 51 (3 fmly) (22 GF) ⟐ **S** £65-£90; **D** £80-£120 (incl. bkfst)* **Facilities** FTV Wi-fi ⓈⓇ Gym Steam room Sauna Spa bath Xmas New Year **Conf** Class 100 Board 100 Thtr 250 **Services** Lift **Parking** 120 **Notes** LB Civ Wed 250

The Kinmel Arms

◉◉ RESTAURANT WITH ROOMS

☎ 01745 832207
The Village, St George LL22 9BP
e-mail: info@thekinmelarms.co.uk
dir: From A55 junct 24a to St George. E on A55, junct 24. 1st left to Rhuddlan, 1st right into St George. 2nd right

This converted 17th-century coaching inn stands close to the church in the village of St George, in the beautiful Elwy Valley. The popular restaurant specialises in produce from Wales and north-west England, and friendly and helpful staff ensure you will have an enjoyable stay. The four attractive suites are luxuriously furnished and feature stunning bathrooms. Substantial continental breakfasts are served in the rooms.

Rooms 4

Save on hotels. Book at **theAA.com/hotel**

ABE – BED **591** WALES

B

ABERSOCH
Gwynedd
Map 14 SH32

Porth Tocyn Hotel

★★★ 80% ◉ ◉ COUNTRY HOUSE HOTEL

☎ 01758 713303 & 07789 994942
Bwlch Tocyn LL53 7BU
e-mail: bookings@porthtocyn.fsnet.co.uk
web: www.porthtocynhotel.co.uk
dir: 2.5m S of Abersoch follow Porth Tocyn signs after Sarnbach

Located above Cardigan Bay with fine views over the area, Porth Tocyn is set in attractive gardens. Several elegantly furnished sitting rooms are provided and bedrooms are comfortably furnished. Children are especially welcome and a playroom is provided. Award-winning food is served in the restaurant.

Rooms 17 (1 fmly) (3 GF) **S** £74-£90; **D** £100-£180 (incl. bkfst)* **Facilities** FTV Wi-fi ⌇ ⌓ Table tennis **Conf** Class 15 **Parking** 50 **Notes** LB Closed mid Nov-week before Easter

ABERYSTWYTH
Ceredigion
Map 8 SN58

Richmond Hotel

★★★ 78% SMALL HOTEL

☎ 01970 612201
44-45 Marine Ter SY23 2BX
e-mail: reservations@richmondhotel.uk.com
web: www.richmondhotel.uk.com
dir: On entering town follow signs for Promenade

This privately owned and personally run, friendly hotel offers good sea views from its day rooms and many of the bedrooms. Good standards of comfort and facilities are found throughout; bedrooms have smart, modern bathrooms. An attractive dining room is the setting for imaginative dinners and comprehensive breakfasts.

Rooms 15 (2 fmly) **Facilities** FTV Wi-fi **Conf** Class 22 Board 28 Thtr 60 **Parking** 22 **Notes** ⊗ Closed 20 Dec-3 Jan

Nanteos Mansion

Ⓤ

☎ 01970 600522
Rhydyfelin SY23 4LU
e-mail: info@nanteos.com
web: www.nanteos.com
dir: SE of Aberystwyth take A420 signed Devil's Bridge. Immediately right onto B4340 signed Trewscoed. Take narrow unclassified road at hotel sign on left

Currently the rating for this establishment is not confirmed. This may be due to a change of ownership or because it has only recently joined the AA rating scheme. For further details please see the AA website: theAA.com

Rooms 14 (5 annexe) (1 fmly) (2 GF) ⌇ **S** £100-£180; **D** £180-£270 (incl. bkfst)* **Facilities** FTV Wi-fi HL ⌣ Xmas New Year **Conf** Class 24 Board 24 Thtr 50 Del £180* **Parking** 60 **Notes** LB Civ Wed 100

BANGOR
Gwynedd
Map 14 SH57

Premier Inn Bangor

BUDGET HOTEL

☎ 0871 527 8046
Parc Menai, Ffordd Y Parc LL57 4FA
web: www.premierinn.com
dir: A55 junct 9 (Holyhead, Ysbyty Gwynedd Hospital). Take 3rd exit off rdbt. Hotel next left

High quality, budget accommodation ideal for both families and business travellers. Spacious, en suite bedrooms feature tea and coffee making facilities, and Freeview TV in most hotels. Internet access and Wi-fi are available for a small fee. The adjacent family restaurant features a wide and varied menu. See also the Hotel Groups pages.

Rooms 40

BEAUMARIS
Isle of Anglesey
Map 14 SH67

Best Western Bulkeley Hotel

★★★ 78% HOTEL

☎ 01248 810415
Castle St LL58 8AW
e-mail: reception@bulkeleyhotel.co.uk
web: www.bulkeleyhotel.co.uk
dir: A55 junct 8a to Beaumaris. Hotel in town centre

A Grade I listed hotel built in 1832, the Bulkeley is just 100 yards from the 13th-century Beaumaris Castle in the centre of town; the friendly staff create a relaxed atmosphere. Many rooms, including 18 of the bedrooms, have fine panoramic views across the Menai Straits to the Snowdonian Mountains. The well-equipped bedrooms and suites, some with four-posters, are generally spacious, and have pretty furnishings. There is a choice of bars, a coffee shop, a restaurant and bistro.

Rooms 43 (5 fmly) ⌇ **S** £50-£100; **D** £95-£138 (incl. bkfst)* **Facilities** FTV Wi-fi Xmas New Year **Conf** Class 40 Board 25 Thtr 180 Del from £95 to £105* **Services** Lift **Parking** 25 **Notes** Civ Wed 140

Bishopsgate House Hotel

★★ 85% ◉ SMALL HOTEL

☎ 01248 810302
54 Castle St LL58 8BB
e-mail: hazel@bishopsgatehotel.co.uk
dir: From Menai Bridge onto A545 to Beaumaris. Hotel on left in main street

This immaculately maintained, privately owned and personally run small hotel dates back to 1760. It features fine examples of wood panelling and a Chinese Chippendale staircase. Thoughtfully furnished bedrooms are attractively decorated and two have four-poster beds. Quality cooking is served in the elegant restaurant and guests have a comfortable lounge and cosy bar to relax in.

Rooms 9 **Facilities** FTV Wi-fi ↳ Xmas New Year **Parking** 8

BEDDGELERT
Gwynedd
Map 14 SH54

The Royal Goat Hotel

★★★ 78% HOTEL

THE CIRCLE

☎ 01766 890224
LL55 4YE
e-mail: info@royalgoathotel.co.uk
web: www.royalgoathotel.co.uk
dir: On A498 at Beddgelert

An impressive building steeped in history, the Royal Goat provides well-equipped accommodation, and carries out an annual programme of refurbishment. Attractively appointed, comfortable public areas include a choice of bars and restaurants, a residents' lounge and function rooms.

Rooms 32 (4 fmly) **S** fr £53; **D** fr £75 (incl. bkfst)* **Facilities** FTV Wi-fi Fishing Xmas New Year **Conf** Class 40 Board 30 Thtr 70 **Services** Lift **Parking** 100 **Notes** Closed Jan-14 Feb

B

See also Llanrwst

Craig-y-Dderwen Riverside Hotel

★★★★ 78% ⚜ COUNTRY HOUSE HOTEL

☎ 01690 710293
LL24 0AS
e-mail: info@snowdoniahotel.com
web: www.snowdoniahotel.com
dir: A5 to Betws-y-Coed, cross Waterloo Bridge, take 1st left

This Victorian country-house hotel is set in well-maintained grounds alongside the River Conwy, at the end of a tree-lined drive. Views down the river can be enjoyed from the restaurant and deck. Many of the bedrooms have balconies, and the feature rooms include a four-poster bed and a hot tub. There are comfortable lounges and the atmosphere throughout is tranquil and relaxing.

Rooms 18 (2 fmly) (1 GF) (1 smoking) 🐾
S £105-£115; **D** £120-£230 (incl. bkfst)*
Facilities STV FTV Wi-fi ॐ Fishing ⚓ Badminton Volleyball New Year **Conf** Class 50 Board 50 Thtr 100 Del from £148 to £198* **Parking** 50 **Notes** LB Closed 23-26 Dec & 2 Jan-1 Feb Civ Wed 100

Royal Oak Hotel

★★★ 86% ⚜ HOTEL

☎ 01690 710219
Holyhead Rd LL24 0AY
e-mail: royaloakmail@btopenworld.com
web: www.royaloakhotel.net
dir: On A5 in town centre, adjacent to St Mary's Church

Centrally situated in the village, this elegant, privately owned hotel started life as a coaching inn and now provides very comfortable bedrooms with smart, modern en suite bathrooms. The extensive public areas retain original charm and character. The choice of eating options includes the Grill Bistro, the Stables Bar which is much frequented by locals, and the more formal Llugwy Restaurant.

Royal Oak Hotel

Rooms 27 (1 fmly) 🐾 **S** £70-£120; **D** £95-£185 (incl. bkfst)* **Facilities** FTV Wi-fi ॐ 🎵 New Year **Conf** Class 40 Board 20 Thtr 80 Del from £80 to £140* **Parking** 90 **Notes** LB ⊗ Closed 25-26 Dec Civ Wed 60

See advert on opposite page

Best Western Waterloo Hotel

★★★ 80% HOTEL

☎ 01690 710411
LL24 0AR
e-mail: reservations@waterloo-hotel.info
web: www.waterloo-hotel.info
dir: On A5, S of village centre

This long-established hotel, named after the nearby Waterloo Bridge, is ideally located for visiting Snowdonia. Stylish accommodation is split between rooms in the main hotel and modern, cottage-style rooms located in buildings to the rear. The attractive Garden Room Restaurant serves traditional Welsh specialities, and the vibrant Bridge Inn provides a wide range of food and drink throughout the day and evening.

Rooms 47 (36 annexe) (13 fmly) (33 GF) 🐾
S £80-£95; **D** £120-£150 (incl. bkfst)* **Facilities** FTV

Wi-fi ॐ 🕑 Gym Steam room Sauna Hair & beauty salon New Year **Conf** Class 18 Board 12 Thtr 40 Del from £130.75 to £158* **Parking** 100 **Notes** LB Closed 24-26 Dec

Bodelwyddan Castle Hotel

Warner Leisure Hotels
JUST FOR GROWN-UPS

★★★ 73% HOTEL

☎ 01745 585088
LL18 5YA
dir: At A55 junct 25

This Grade II listed Victorian castle is located on the north Wales coast less than an hour from the Snowdonian mountains. The famous Bodelwyddan marble church, set in the valley below, can be seen from the grounds and The National Portrait Gallery is also situated on site. The hotel offers a great range of leisure facilities and numerous daily in-house and external activities. Packages range from a minimum two-night, half board stay. Please note that this is an adults-only (over 21 years) hotel.

Rooms 186 (51 GF) 🐾 **Facilities** Spa FTV Wi-fi ॐ HL 🕑 supervised ⛳ Putt green ⚓ Gym 🎵 Xmas New Year **Services** Lift **Notes** ⊗ No children 21yrs

The Castle of Brecon Hotel

★★★ 75% HOTEL

☎ 01874 624611
Castle Square LD3 9DB
e-mail: hotel@breconcastle.co.uk
dir: In town centre

This former coaching inn occupies an elevated position overlooking the town and the River Usk, with the ruins of the 11th-century castle in the grounds. Lovely views can be enjoyed from the restaurant and some of the bedrooms. The remaining public areas are roomy and relaxed in a contemporary style. Function and meeting rooms are available and even incorporate one of the castle walls. There is ample parking to the front of the property.

Rooms 38 (8 annexe) (9 fmly) (2 GF) 🐾 **S** fr £55; **D** fr £170 (incl. bkfst)* **Facilities** STV FTV Wi-fi New Year **Conf** Class 100 Board 40 Thtr 140 Del £120* **Parking** 35 **Notes** LB ⊗ RS 24-26 Dec Civ Wed 120

Save on hotels. Book at **theAA.com/hotel**

BET – BRI 593 WALES

Peterstone Court

RESTAURANT WITH ROOMS

☎ 01874 665387
Llanhamlach LD3 7YB
e-mail: info@peterstone-court.com
dir: 3m from Brecon on A40 towards Abergavenny

Situated on the edge of the Brecon Beacons, this establishment affords stunning views overlooking the River Usk. The atmosphere is friendly and informal; without any unnecessary fuss. No two bedrooms are alike, but all share comparable levels of comfort, quality and elegance. Public areas reflect similar standards, eclectically styled with a blend of the contemporary and the traditional. Quality produce is cooked with care in a range of enjoyable dishes.

Rooms 12 (4 annexe) (2 fmly)

BRIDGEND
Bridgend
Map 9 SS97

Best Western Heronston Hotel

★★★ 75% HOTEL

☎ 01656 668811
Ewenny Rd CF35 5AW
e-mail: reservations@bestwesternheronstonhotel.co.uk
web: www.bw-heronstonhotel.co.uk
dir: M4 junct 35, follow signs for Porthcawl, at 5th rdbt left towards Ogmore-by-Sea (B4265), hotel 200yds on left

Situated within easy reach of the town centre and the M4, this large modern hotel offers spacious well-equipped accommodation, including ground floor rooms. Public areas include an open-plan lounge/bar, attractive restaurant and a smart leisure and fitness club. The hotel also has a choice of function and conference rooms, and ample parking is available.

Rooms 75 (4 fmly) (37 GF) 🐾 **S** £69-£120; **D** £79-£130 (incl. bkfst) **Facilities** STV Wi-fi ⚓ HL 🌀 Gym Steam room Sauna Spa pool New Year **Conf** Class 80 Board 60 Thtr 250 Del from £99 to £120 **Services** Lift **Parking** 160 **Notes** LB Civ Wed 200

Court Colman Manor

★★★ 72% ◉ COUNTRY HOUSE HOTEL

☎ 01656 720212
Pen-y-Fai CF31 4NG
e-mail: experience@court-colman-manor.com
dir: M4 junct 36, A4063 towards Maesteg, after lights 1st exit to Bridgend, under motorway, next right, follow hotel signs

Dating back to the Tudor times this fine mansion is set in its own peaceful grounds outside Bridgend, and is just a short distance from the M4. The spacious, comfortable bedrooms include ten themed rooms inspired by an exotic location - India, Japan, Morocco etc. The award-winning food served in Bokhara Brasserie is imaginative, and Indian and Mediterranean dishes are included in the choices. Diners can view their meals being prepared in the open-plan kitchen.

Rooms 30 (2 fmly) 🐾 **Facilities** FTV Wi-fi ⚓ Xmas New Year **Conf** Class 60 Thtr 100 **Parking** 180 **Notes** ⊗ Civ Wed 150

Premier Inn Bridgend Central

BUDGET HOTEL

☎ 0871 527 8146
The Derwen CF32 9ST
web: www.premierinn.com
dir: M4 junct 36, A4061 (signed Bridgend & Pen-y-Bont). Hotel at next rdbt

High quality, budget accommodation ideal for both families and business travellers. Spacious, en suite bedrooms feature tea and coffee making facilities, and Freeview TV in most hotels. Internet access and Wi-fi are available for a small fee. The adjacent family restaurant features a wide and varied menu. See also the Hotel Groups pages.

Rooms 68

Premier Inn Bridgend M4 Jct 35

BUDGET HOTEL

☎ 0871 527 8144
Pantruthyn Farm, Pencoed CF35 5HY
web: www.premierinn.com
dir: At M4 junct 35, behind petrol station & McDonalds

Rooms 40

BUILTH WELLS
Map 9 SO05
Powys

Caer Beris Manor Hotel
THE INDEPENDENTS
HOTEL ASSOCIATION

★★★ 77% COUNTRY HOUSE HOTEL

☎ 01982 552601
LD2 3NP
e-mail: caerberis@btconnect.com
web: www.caerberis.com
dir: From town centre follow A483/Llandovery signs. Hotel on left

Guests can expect a relaxing stay at this friendly and privately owned hotel that has extensive landscaped grounds. Bedrooms are individually decorated and furnished to retain an atmosphere of a bygone era. The spacious and comfortable lounge and a lounge bar continue this theme, and there's an elegant restaurant, complete with 16th-century panelling.

Rooms 23 (2 fmly) (3 GF) **Facilities** FTV Wi-fi Fishing ♨ Clay pigeon shooting Birdwatching Xmas New Year **Conf** Class 75 Board 50 Thtr 100 **Parking** 100 **Notes** Civ Wed 200

BURTON
Map 8 SM90
Pembrokeshire

Beggars Reach

★★★ 79% HOTEL

☎ 01646 600700
SA73 1PD
e-mail: stay@beggars-reach.com
web: www.beggars-reach.com
dir: 8m S of Haverfordwest, 6m N of Pembroke, off A477

This privately owned and personally run hotel was a rectory in Georgian times; it stands in eight acres of grounds peacefully located close to the village of Burton. It provides modern, well-equipped bedrooms; two located in former stables which date back to the 14th century. Milford Haven and the ferry terminal at Pembroke Dock are both within easy reach.

Rooms 30 (16 annexe) (4 fmly) (8 GF) (1 smoking) **S** £81.50-£102; **D** £120-£175 (incl. bkfst)* **Facilities** STV FTV Wi-fi ♨ **Conf** Class 80 Board 80 Thtr 160 Del from £100 to £120* **Parking** 80 **Notes** LB ⊗ Civ Wed 180

CAERNARFON
Map 14 SH46
Gwynedd

Seiont Manor Hotel
HandPICKED
HOTELS
BUILT FOR PLEASURE

★★★ ◉ ◉
COUNTRY HOUSE HOTEL

☎ 01286 673366
Llanrug LL55 2AQ
e-mail: seiontmanor@handpicked.co.uk
web: www.handpickedhotels.co.uk/seiontmanor
dir: E on A4086, 2.5m from Caernarfon

A splendid hotel created from authentic farm buildings, set in the tranquil countryside near Snowdonia; the River Seiont flows through the 150-acre grounds. The bedrooms, including junior suites, are individually decorated and have luxurious extra touches; each has either a balcony or patio. The comfortable public rooms are cosy and furnished in country-house style. The kitchen team use the best local produce to provide exciting takes on traditional dishes, and guests can choose to eat in either the award-winning Llwyn y Brain Restaurant or the conservatory brasserie. Hand Picked Hotels — AA Hotel Group of the Year 2012-13.

Rooms 28 (2 fmly) (14 GF) 🐾 **S** £79-£169; **D** £89-£179 (incl. bkfst)* **Facilities** STV FTV Wi-fi ♨ HL 🕭 Fishing Gym Xmas New Year **Conf** Class 40 Board 40 Thtr 100 Del from £115 to £155* **Parking** 60 **Notes** LB ⊗ Civ Wed 100

Celtic Royal Hotel

★★★ 80% HOTEL

☎ 01286 674477
Bangor St LL55 1AY
e-mail: reservations@celtic-royal.co.uk
web: www.celtic-royal.co.uk
dir: Exit A55 at Bangor, take A487 towards Caernarfon

This large, impressive, privately owned hotel is situated in the town centre. It provides attractively appointed accommodation, which includes family rooms and bedrooms for less able guests. The spacious public areas include a bar, a choice of lounges and a pleasant split-level restaurant. Guests also have the use of the impressive health club.

Rooms 110 (12 fmly) 🐾 **S** £59-£99; **D** £69-£135 (incl. bkfst) **Facilities** Wi-fi 🕭 Gym Steam room Sauna ♫ Xmas New Year **Conf** Class 120 Board 120 Thtr 300 Del from £99 to £135 **Services** Lift **Parking** 180 **Notes** LB ⊗ Civ Wed 200

Premier Inn Caernarfon

Premier Inn

BUDGET HOTEL

☎ 0871 527 8180
Victioria Dock, Balaclava Rd LL55 1SQ
web: www.premierinn.com
dir: A55 junct 9, at rdbt 1st exit follow Caernarfon signs. In Caernarfon at rdbt (Morrisons on right) 1st exit, keep in right lane, at next rdbt 4th exit to mini rdbt, hotel opposite

High quality, budget accommodation ideal for both families and business travellers. Spacious, en suite bedrooms feature tea and coffee making facilities, and Freeview TV in most hotels. Internet access and Wi-fi are available for a small fee. The adjacent family restaurant features a wide and varied menu. See also the Hotel Groups pages.

Rooms 49

Save on hotels. Book at **theAA.com/hotel**

BUI – CAR 595 WALES

Rhiwafallen Restaurant with Rooms

@@ RESTAURANT WITH ROOMS

☎ 01286 830172

Rhiwafallen, LLandwrog LL54 5SW

e-mail: ktandrobjohn@aol.com

dir: A487 from Caernarfon. Right onto A499. Establishment signed

Located south of Caernarfon on the Llyn Peninsula link, this former farmhouse is appointed to provide high levels of comfort and facilities. Quality bedrooms are furnished in minimalist style with a wealth of thoughtful extras. The original modern art in public areas adds vibrancy to the interior. Warm hospitality and imaginative cooking ensure a memorable stay at this owner-managed establishment.

Rooms 3

Premier Inn Caerphilly (Corbetts Lane)

BUDGET HOTEL

☎ 0871 527 8182

Corbetts Ln CF83 3HX

web: www.premierinn.com

dir: M4 junct 32, A470, 2nd left signed Caerphilly. At rdbt 4th exit, at next rdbt 2nd exit. Straight on at next rdbt & at Pwllypant Rdbt, hotel on left

High quality, budget accommodation ideal for both families and business travellers. Spacious, en suite bedrooms feature tea and coffee making facilities, and Freeview TV in most hotels. Internet access and Wi-fi are available for a small fee. The adjacent family restaurant features a wide and varied menu. See also the Hotel Groups pages.

Rooms 42

Premier Inn Caerphilly (Crossways)

BUDGET HOTEL

☎ 0871 527 8184

Crossways Business Park, Pontypandy CF83 3NL

web: www.premierinn.com

dir: M4 junct 32, A470 towards Merthyr Tydfil (junct 4 take A458 towards Caerphilly). At Crossways Business Park (5th rdbt). Hotel on right at McDonald's rdbt

Rooms 40

The Talkhouse

@@ RESTAURANT WITH ROOMS

☎ 01686 688919 & 07876 086183

Pontdolgoch SY17 5JE

e-mail: info@talkhouse.co.uk

dir: 1.5m NW of Caersws on A470

A highlight of this delightful 19th-century restaurant with rooms is the food - home-made dishes make good use of local produce. The bedrooms offer luxury in every area and the cosy lounge, filled with sofas, is the place to while away some time with a glass of wine or a pot of tea. The bar features a large fireplace.

Rooms 3

Cobdens Hotel

 ★★ 62% SMALL HOTEL

☎ 01690 720243

LL24 0EE

e-mail: info@cobdens.co.uk

dir: On A5, 4m N of Betws-y-Coed

Situated in the heart of Snowdonia, this hotel has been a centre for mountaineering and other outdoor pursuits for many years. A wide range of meals using local produce is served in the restaurant. There are two bars including the aptly named Mountain Bar, built in the side of the mountain. A sauna room is also available.

Rooms 17 (4 fmly) **S** £32.50-£37.50; **D** £65-£75 (incl. bkfst)* **Facilities** STV FTV Wi-fi ↴ Fishing Sauna Pool table New Year **Conf** Class 25 Board 30 Thtr 50 Del from £75 to £100* **Parking** 40 **Notes** LB Closed Jan RS 24-25 & 31 Dec

---

The St David's Hotel & Spa

PH principal hayley

★★★★★ 78% HOTEL

☎ 029 2045 4045

Havannah St CF10 5SD

e-mail: stdavids.reservations@principal-hayley.com

web: www.thestdavidshotel.com

dir: M4 junct 33, A4232 for 9m, follow Cardiff Bay signs, then Techniquest signs, at top exit slip road, 1st left at rdbt, 1st right

This imposing contemporary building sits in a prime position on Cardiff Bay and has a seven-storey atrium creating a dramatic impression. Leading from the atrium are the practically designed and comfortable bedrooms. Tides Restaurant, adjacent to the stylish cocktail bar, has views across the water to Penarth, and there is a quiet first-floor lounge for guests seeking peace and quiet. A well-equipped spa and extensive business areas complete the package.

Rooms 142 ✎ **D** £105-£495* **Facilities** Spa FTV Wi-fi ↴ ⓒ Gym Fitness studio Hydrotherapy pool Aerobics studio ♫ Xmas New Year **Conf** Class 110 Board 76 Thtr 270 Del from £150 to £195* **Services** Lift Air con **Parking** 80 **Notes** ⊗ Civ Wed 270

The Parc Hotel, Cardiff

thistle

★★★★ 85% @@ HOTEL

☎ 0871 376 9011

Park Place CF10 3UD

e-mail: cardiff@thistle.co.uk

web: www.thistle.com/theparchotel

dir: M4 junct 29, A48(M), 4th exit signed City Centre/A470. At rdbt 2nd exit signed City Centre/A470

Ideally located in the very centre of Cardiff, this bustling hotel retains an exterior of Victorian splendour while the interior is contemporary. The bedrooms are spacious, modern and well equipped, and a range of dining options is available including the Harlech Lounge & Bar and the modern Crown Social Restaurant which offers quality food with efficient service.

Rooms 140 (5 fmly) ✎ **Facilities** STV Wi-fi Xmas New Year **Conf** Class 100 Board 50 Thtr 225 **Services** Lift Air con **Parking** 60 **Notes** ⊗ Civ Wed 225

CARDIFF *continued*

Cardiff Marriott Hotel

★★★★ 80% ◉ HOTEL

☎ 029 2039 9944
Mill Ln CF10 1EZ
web: www.cardiffmarriott.co.uk
dir: M4 junct 29, A48(M) E follow signs city centre &
Cardiff Bay. 3m, right into Mill Lane

Centrally located in the Café Quarter of the city, this
modern hotel has spacious public areas and a good
range of services to suit both business and leisure
guests. The eating options include the informal Chats
Café Bar, and the Brasserie Centrale for contemporary
French cuisine that uses locally sourced ingredients.
The well-equipped bedrooms are comfortable and air
conditioned. The leisure suite includes a multi-gym
and a good size swimming pool.

Rooms 184 (68 fmly) ⋒ **Facilities** STV Wi-fi ⋫ ⓒ
Gym Steam room Sauna Spa bath Xmas New Year
Conf Class 200 Board 100 Thtr 400 Del from £145 to
£175* **Services** Lift Air con **Parking** 146 **Notes** ⊗
Civ Wed 200

Park Plaza Cardiff

★★★★ 80% HOTEL

☎ 029 2011 1111 & 2011 1101
Greyfriars Rd CF10 3AL
e-mail: ppcres@parkplazahotels.co.uk
web: www.parkplazacardiff.com
dir: From M4 follow city centre (A470) signs. Left into
Boulevard de Nantes immediately left into Greyfriars
Rd. Hotel on left by New Theatre

A smart hotel located in the city centre that features
eye-catching, contemporary decor, a state-of-the-art
indoor leisure facility, extensive conference and
banqueting facilities and the spacious Laguna
Kitchen and Bar. The bedrooms are also up-to-the-
minute in style and feature a host of extras including
a private bar, a safe and modem points.

Rooms 129 (20 fmly) ⋒ **S** £89-£210; **D** £99-£220*
Facilities Spa FTV Wi-fi ⋫ ⓒ Gym Dance studio
Steam room New Year **Conf** Class 80 Board 60
Thtr 150 Del from £149 to £199* **Services** Lift Air con
Notes LB ⊗ Closed 24-25 Dec Civ Wed 120

Novotel Cardiff Central

★★★★ 77% HOTEL

☎ 029 2047 5000
Schooner Way, Atlantic Wharf CF10 4RT
e-mail: h5982@accor.com
web: www.novotel.com
dir: M4 junct 29 onto A48(M), follow signs for city
centre

Situated in the heart of the city's development area,
this hotel is equally convenient for the centre and
Cardiff Bay. Bedrooms vary between standard rooms
in the modern extension and executive rooms in the
original wing. There is good seating space in public
rooms, and the hotel has a popular leisure club and
the Elements Restaurant innovative dining concept.

Rooms 138 (100 fmly) ⋒ **Facilities** FTV Wi-fi ⋫ ⓒ
Gym Sauna Steam room Xmas New Year
Conf Class 90 Board 65 Thtr 250 **Services** Lift Air con
Parking 120 **Notes** Civ Wed 250

Copthorne Hotel Cardiff-Caerdydd

★★★★ 75% ◉ HOTEL

☎ 029 2059 9100
Copthorne Way, Culverhouse Cross CF5 6DH
e-mail: reservations.cardiff@millenniumhotels.co.uk
web: www.millenniumhotels.co.uk
dir: M4 junct 33, A4232 for 2.5m towards Cardiff
West. Take A48 W to Cowbridge

A comfortable, popular and modern hotel,
conveniently located for the airport and city.
Bedrooms are a good size and some have a private
lounge. Public areas are smartly presented and
include a gym, pool, meeting rooms and a
comfortable restaurant with views of a lake.

Rooms 135 (7 fmly) (27 GF) **S** £65-£80; **D** £65-£95*
Facilities STV Wi-fi ⓒ Gym Sauna Steam room
Beauty treatment room Xmas New Year
Conf Class 140 Board 80 Thtr 300 Del from £110 to
£180* **Services** Lift **Parking** 225 **Notes** LB
Civ Wed 200

Mercure Cardiff Holland House Hotel & Spa

★★★★ 75% HOTEL

☎ 029 2043 5000
24/26 Newport Rd CF24 0DD
e-mail: h6622@accor.com
web: www.mercure.com
dir: M4 junct 33, A4232 to city centre, right at lights
facing prison, straight through next lights, hotel car
park end of lane facing Magistrates Court

Conveniently located just a few minutes' walk from
the city centre, this exciting hotel combines
contemporary styling with a genuinely friendly
welcome. Bedrooms, including five luxurious suites,
are spacious and include many welcome extras. A
state-of-the-art leisure club and spa is available in
addition to a large function room. An eclectic menu
provides a varied range of freshly prepared, quality
dishes.

Rooms 165 (80 fmly) (8 smoking) **Facilities** Spa STV
Wi-fi ⓒ supervised Gym **Conf** Class 140 Board 42
Thtr 700 **Services** Lift Air con **Parking** 90
Notes Civ Wed 500

The Angel Hotel

★★★★ 68% HOTEL

☎ 029 2064 9200
Castle St CF10 1SZ
e-mail: angel@pumahotels.co.uk
web: www.pumahotels.co.uk
dir: Opposite Cardiff Castle

This well-established hotel is in the heart of the city
overlooking the famous castle and almost opposite
the Millennium Stadium. All bedrooms offer air
conditioning and are appointed to a good standard.
Public areas include an impressive lobby, a modern
restaurant and a selection of conference rooms. There
is limited parking at the rear of the hotel.

Rooms 102 (3 fmly) **Facilities** STV Wi-fi Xmas New
Year **Conf** Class 120 Board 50 Thtr 300 **Services** Lift
Air con **Parking** 60 **Notes** Civ Wed 200

Holiday Inn Cardiff City

★★★ 80% HOTEL

☎ 0800 40 50 60 & 0871 942 9240
Castle St CF10 1XD
e-mail: cardiffcity@ihg.com
web: www.hicardiffcitycentre.co.uk
dir: M4 junct 29 E/A48(M), follow city centre signs,
onto A470. Turn left to hotel

This hotel has a fantastic location in the heart of the
city and is just a short walk from the Millennium
Stadium, Cardiff Castle and Cardiff Bay. There are

state-of-the-art conference and meeting facilities available as well as banqueting. The air-conditioned accommodation is modern with many guest extras provided. The restaurant offers a good menu choice or guests can take a snack in the lounge/bar area.

Rooms 157 (20 fmly) (10 smoking) **Facilities** Wi-fi ⇘ ♫ Xmas New Year **Conf** Class 60 Board 50 Thtr 180 **Services** Lift Air con **Parking** 85 **Notes** ⊗ Civ Wed 100

Park Inn by Radisson Cardiff City Centre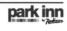

★★★ 77% HOTEL

☎ 029 2034 1441 & 2072 7026
Mary Ann St CF10 2JH
e-mail: info.cardiff-city@rezidorparkinn.com
dir: In city centre adjacent to John Lewis building & Motorpoint Arena Cardiff. Follow signs to St Davids car park adjacent to hotel

This hotel is ideal for both business travellers and leisure guests being situated in the centre of the city, and close to the shops and the Millennium Stadium. The accommodation has been appointed in a contemporary style, with guest comfort as the key consideration. The friendly restaurant provides a good range of contemporary dishes, including grill specialities. Limited (secure) parking is available.

Rooms 146 (9 fmly) **Facilities** STV Wi-fi ⇘ Arrangement with local gym nearby ♫ Xmas New Year **Conf** Class 120 Board 50 Thtr 300 **Services** Lift **Parking** 40 **Notes** ⊗ Civ Wed 300

Park Inn by Radisson Cardiff North

★★★ 72% HOTEL

☎ 029 2058 9988
Circle Way East, Llanedeyrn CF23 9XF
e-mail: info.cardiff@rezidorparkinn.com
web: www.cardiff.parkinn.co.uk

This hotel is ideal for both business travellers and leisure guests, being situated just a short distance from the M4 and convenient for city-centre shopping and the Millennium Stadium. The accommodation has been appointed in a contemporary style, with comfort as the key consideration. The friendly restaurant provides a good range of dishes including their specialities. There is a complimentary gym and parking is extensive and secure.

Rooms 132 (16 fmly) (20 GF) **Facilities** STV FTV Wi-fi ⇘ supervised Gym Beauty treatment room Xmas New Year **Conf** Class 160 Board 160 Thtr 200 **Services** Lift Air con **Parking** 200 **Notes** ⊗ Civ Wed

Best Western St Mellons Hotel & Country Club

★★★ 70% HOTEL

☎ 01633 680355
Castleton CF3 2XR
e-mail: reservations.stmellons@ohiml.com
web: www.oxfordhotelsandinns.com
dir: M4 junct 28 follow A48 Castleton/St Mellons signs. Hotel on left after garage

This Regency mansion has been tastefully converted into an elegant hotel with an adjoining leisure complex that attracts a strong local following. Bedrooms, some in purpose-built wings, are spacious and smart. The public areas retain pleasing architectural proportions and include relaxing lounges and a restaurant serving a varied choice of carefully prepared, enjoyable dishes.

Rooms 41 (20 annexe) (9 fmly) (5 GF) **Facilities** Spa FTV Wi-fi ⇘ ⊛ Gym Squash Beauty salon Xmas New Year **Conf** Class 80 Board 80 Thtr 220 Del from £99 to £150* **Parking** 100 **Notes** Civ Wed 160

The Legacy Cardiff International Hotel

★★★ 70% HOTEL

☎ 08444 119074 & 029 2052 9988
Merthyr Rd, Tongwynlais CF15 7LD
e-mail: res-cardiffinternational@legacy-hotels.co.uk
dir: M4 junct 32, follow Tongwynlais A4054 signs at large rdbt, hotel on right

This modern hotel is conveniently located off the M4 and has easy access to Cardiff and the Millennium Stadium. Guests can enjoy the spacious open-plan public areas and relax in the well-proportioned and well-equipped bedrooms, which include some suites. A good range of meeting rooms makes this hotel a popular conference venue. There is ample parking in the area around the hotel.

Rooms 95 (38 fmly) (20 GF) **Facilities** FTV Wi-fi Xmas New Year **Conf** Class 120 Board 60 Thtr 180 **Services** Lift **Parking** 180 **Notes** ⊗

Sandringham Hotel

★★ 71% HOTEL

☎ 029 2023 2161
21 St Mary St CF10 1PL
e-mail: mm@sandringham-hotel.com
dir: M4 junct 29, follow 'city centre' signs. Opposite castle left into High St; leads to St Mary St (pedestrianised). Hotel on left

This friendly, privately owned and personally run hotel is near the Millennium Stadium and offers a convenient base for access to the city centre. Bedrooms are well equipped, and diners can relax in Café Jazz, the hotel's adjoining restaurant, where live music is provided most week nights. There is also a separate lounge/bar for residents, and an airy breakfast room.

Rooms 28 (1 fmly) **S** £35-£110; **D** £38-£155 (incl. bkfst) **Facilities** FTV Wi-fi ♫ **Conf** Class 70 Board 60 Thtr 100 Del from £50 to £95 **Notes** LB ⊗ Closed 24-26 Dec (pm) & 1 Jan (pm)

Mercure Cardiff Centre Hotel

Ⓤ

☎ 029 2089 4000
Wharf Road East, Tyndall St CF10 4BB
e-mail: h6623@accor.com
web: www.mercure.com
dir: M4 juncts 29 & 33 follow city centre signs

Currently the rating for this establishment is not confirmed. This may be due to a change of ownership or because it has only recently joined the AA rating scheme. For further details please see the AA website: theAA.com

Rooms 100 (48 fmly) (27 GF) (5 smoking) **Facilities** STV Wi-fi ⇘ Leisure facilities at Mercure Holland House **Services** Lift Air con **Parking** 90

Campanile Cardiff

BUDGET HOTEL

☎ 029 2054 9044
Caxton Place, Pentwyn CF23 8HA
e-mail: cardiff@campanile.com
web: www.campanile.com
dir: Take Pentwyn exit from A48(M), follow signs for hotel

This modern building offers accommodation in smart, well-equipped bedrooms, all with en suite bathrooms. Refreshments may be taken at the informal bistro. See also the Hotel Groups pages.

Rooms 47 (47 annexe) **Conf** Class 18 Board 16 Thtr 35

CARDIFF *continued*

Holiday Inn Express Cardiff Airport

BUDGET HOTEL

☎ 01446 711117
Port Rd, Rhoose CF62 3BT
e-mail: sales@exhicardiffairport.co.uk
web: www.hiexpress.com/cardiffairport
dir: M4 junct 33, follow signs for Barry & Cardiff Airport. Hotel adjacent to airport terminal

A modern hotel ideal for families and business travellers. Fresh and uncomplicated, the spacious rooms include Sky TV, power shower and tea and coffee-making facilities. Continental buffet breakfast is included in the room rate; other meals may be taken at the nearby family pub or restaurant. See also the Hotel Groups pages.

Rooms 111 (60 fmly) (22 GF) (7 smoking) ⊱
S £42.25-£69.95; **D** £42.25-£69.95 (incl. bkfst)*
Conf Class 20 Board 20 Thtr 40

Holiday Inn Express Cardiff Bay

BUDGET HOTEL

☎ 029 2044 9000
Atlantic Wharf CF10 4EE
e-mail: reservations@exhicardiff.co.uk
web: www.hiexpresscardiff.co.uk
dir: M4 junct 33, A4232 through Queensgate Tunnel. Left at rdbt, into Hemmingway Rd, right into Schooner Way, 2nd right

Rooms 87 (49 fmly) (15 GF) ⊱ **S** £59-£250;
D £59-£250 (incl. bkfst) **Conf** Class 12 Board 20 Thtr 30 Del from £75

Ibis Cardiff City Centre

BUDGET HOTEL

☎ 029 2064 9250
Churchill Way CF10 2HA
e-mail: H2936@accor.com
web: www.ibishotel.com
dir: M4 junct 29, to junct 29A, A48(M), A48, 2nd exit A4232. Follow signs to City Centre on Newport Rd, left after rail bridge, left after Queen St station

Modern, budget hotel offering comfortable accommodation in bright and practical bedrooms. Breakfast is self-service and dinner is available in the restaurant. See also the Hotel Groups pages.

Rooms 102 (19 GF)

Ibis Cardiff Gate

BUDGET HOTEL

☎ 029 2073 3222
Malthouse Av, Cardiff Gate Business Park, Pontprennau CF23 8RA
e-mail: H3159@accor.com
web: www.ibishotel.com
dir: M4 junct 30, follow Cardiff Service Station signs. Hotel on left

Rooms 78 (19 fmly) (22 GF) (7 smoking)
Conf Class 24 Thtr 25

Premier Inn Cardiff City Centre

BUDGET HOTEL

☎ 0871 527 8196
Helmont House, 10 Churchill Way CF10 2NB
web: www.premierinn.com
dir: M4 junct 29 onto A48(M) towards Cardiff (East & South), 4.5m. Follow Cardiff (East), Docks & A4232 signs. Left at A4161 (Eastern Avenue North). At rdbt 2nd exit onto A4161 (Newport Rd). 2m, left into Station Terrace. Right into Churchill Way

High quality, budget accommodation ideal for both families and business travellers. Spacious, en suite bedrooms feature tea and coffee making facilities, and Freeview TV in most hotels. Internet access and Wi-fi are available for a small fee. The adjacent family restaurant features a wide and varied menu. See also the Hotel Groups pages.

Rooms 200

Premier Inn Cardiff City South

BUDGET HOTEL

☎ 0871 527 8198
Keen Rd CF24 5JT
web: www.premierinn.com
dir: Follow Cardiff Docks & Bay signs from A48(M), over flyover. At 5th rdbt 3rd exit. Hotel 1st right, 1st right again

Rooms 77

Premier Inn Cardiff East

BUDGET HOTEL

☎ 0871 527 8200
Newport Rd, Castleton CF3 2UQ
web: www.premierinn.com
dir: M4 junct 28, A48 signed Castleton. 3m, hotel on right

Rooms 49

Premier Inn Cardiff North

BUDGET HOTEL

☎ 0871 527 8202
Pentwyn Rd, Pentwyn CF23 7XH
web: www.premierinn.com
dir: W'bound: M4 junct 29, A48(M). (E'bound: M4 junct 30, A4232 signs, A48(M) towards Cardiff). Follow Pentwyn signs, 3rd exit at rdbt. Hotel 200yds on right

Rooms 142

Premier Inn Cardiff (Roath)

BUDGET HOTEL

☎ 0871 527 8194
Ipswich Rd, Roath CF23 9AQ
web: www.premierinn.com
dir: W'bound: M4 junct 29, A48(M) (or E'bound: M4 junct 30 A48(M)). Follow Cardiff (E) Docks & Cardiff Bay signs. Then follow brown signs for David Lloyd Tennis Centre. Into David Lloyd Leisure Club car park, follow hotel signs

Rooms 75

Premier Inn Cardiff West

BUDGET HOTEL

☎ 0871 527 8204
Port Rd, Nantisaf, Wenvoe CF5 6DD
web: www.premierinn.com
dir: M4 junct 33, S on A4232. Take 2nd exit (signed Airport), 3rd exit at Culverhouse Cross rdbt. Hotel 0.5m on Barry Rd (A4050)

Rooms 39

Save on hotels. Book at **theAA.com/hotel**

CAR – CRI 599 WALES

CARMARTHEN
Carmarthenshire

Map 8 SN42

Ivy Bush Royal Hotel
★★★ 77% HOTEL

☎ 01267 235111
Spilman St SA31 1LG
e-mail: reception@ivybushroyal.co.uk
web: www.ivybushroyal.co.uk
dir: A48 to Carmarthen, over 1st rdbt, at 2nd rdbt right onto A4242. Straight over next 2 rdbts. Left at lights. Hotel on right at top of hill

This hotel offers spacious, well-equipped bedrooms and bathrooms, a relaxing lounge with outdoor patio seating and a comfortable restaurant serving a varied selection of carefully prepared meals. Weddings, meetings and conferences are all well catered for at this friendly, family-run establishment.

Rooms 70 (4 fmly) ☞ **S** £60-£115; **D** £80-£150 (incl. bkfst)* **Facilities** FTV Wi-fi ⓑ Gym Xmas New Year **Conf** Class 50 Board 40 Thtr 200 Del from £89.50 to £125* **Services** Lift **Parking** 83 **Notes** LB ⊗ Civ Wed 150

Falcon Hotel
★★★ 74% HOTEL

☎ 01267 234959 & 237152
Lammas St SA31 3AP
e-mail: reception@falconcarmarthen.co.uk
web: www.falconcarmarthen.co.uk
dir: In town centre pass bus station, left, hotel 200yds on left

This friendly hotel has been owned and run by the Exton family for over 45 years, and it is well placed in the centre of the town. Bedrooms, some with four-poster beds, are tastefully decorated with good facilities. There is a comfortable lounge with adjacent bar, and the restaurant offers a varied selection of enjoyable dishes at both lunch and dinner.

Rooms 16 (1 fmly) **Facilities** FTV ⓑ **Conf** Class 50 Board 40 Thtr 80 **Parking** 36 **Notes** Closed 26 Dec RS Sun

CHEPSTOW
Monmouthshire

Map 4 ST59

St Pierre, A Marriott Hotel & Country Club

★★★★ 79% ⓢ COUNTRY HOUSE HOTEL

☎ 01291 625261
St Pierre Park NP16 6YA
e-mail: mhrs.cwlgs.frontdesk@marriotthotels.com
web: www.marriottstpierre.co.uk
dir: M48 junct 2, A466 for Chepstow. At next rdbt 1st exit signed Caerwent A48. Hotel approx 2m on left

This 14th-century property offers an extensive range of leisure and conference facilities. The comfortable bedrooms are well equipped and located in adjacent wings or in a lakeside cottage complex. The main bar, popular with golfers, overlooks the 18th green; diners can choose between an elegant, traditional restaurant or a modern brasserie.

Rooms 148 (16 fmly) (75 GF) **S** £79-£139; **D** £79-£139* **Facilities** Spa STV Wi-fi ⓑ ⓛ 36 ⓢ Putt green Fishing ⓛ Gym Chipping green Floodlit driving range Sauna Steam room Xmas New Year **Conf** Class 120 Board 90 Thtr 240 Del from £130 to £155* **Parking** 440 **Notes** LB ⊗ Civ Wed 220

CHIRK
Wrexham

Map 15 SJ23

Moreton Park Hotel
★★★ 77% HOTEL

☎ 01691 776666
Moreton Park, Gledrid LL14 5DG
e-mail: reservations@moretonpark.com
web: www.moretonpark.com
dir: 200yds from rdbt junct of A5 & B5070

Located on the town's outskirts and convenient for the A5, this very well maintained property provides a range of spacious, well-equipped bedrooms ideal for both business and leisure guests. Breakfast, lunch and dinner are available in the adjacent Lord Moreton Bar & Restaurant. Service is friendly and attentive.

Rooms 45 (20 fmly) **Facilities** STV Wi-fi Free use of facilities at sister hotel (0.5m) **Conf** Class 50 Board 20 Thtr 60 **Parking** 200 **Notes** ⊗

CONWY
Conwy

Map 14 SH77

Castle Hotel Conwy
★★★★ 79% ⓢⓢ TOWN HOUSE HOTEL

☎ 01492 582800
High St LL32 8DB
e-mail: mail@castlewales.co.uk
web: www.castlewales.co.uk
dir: A55 junct 18, follow town centre signs, cross estuary (castle on left). Right then left at mini-rdbts onto one-way system. Right at Town Wall Gate, right into Berry St then High St

This family-run, 16th-century hotel is one of Conwy's most distinguished buildings and offers a relaxed and friendly atmosphere. Bedrooms are appointed to an impressive standard and include a stunning suite. Public areas include a popular modern bar and the award-winning Shakespeare's restaurant.

Rooms 28 (2 fmly) ☞ **S** £82-£95; **D** £130-£270 (incl. bkfst) **Facilities** FTV Wi-fi ⓑ Xmas New Year **Conf** Class 20 Board 20 Thtr 30 Del from £115 to £175 **Parking** 34 **Notes** LB

CRICCIETH
Gwynedd

Map 14 SH43

Bron Eifion Country House Hotel
★★★★ 77% ⓢ COUNTRY HOUSE HOTEL

☎ 01766 522385
LL52 0SA
e-mail: enquiries@broneifion.co.uk
dir: A497 between Porthmadog & Pwllheli, 0.5m from Criccieth, on right towards Pwhelli

This delightful country house built in 1883, is set in extensive grounds to the west of Criccieth. Now a privately owned and personally run hotel, it provides warm and very friendly hospitality as well as attentive service. The interior style highlights the many retained period features; there is a choice of lounges and the very impressive central hall features a minstrels' gallery.

Rooms 18 (1 fmly) (1 GF) ☞ **S** £95-£135; **D** £135-£185 (incl. bkfst)* **Facilities** FTV Wi-fi ⓑ Xmas New Year **Conf** Class 150 Board 60 Thtr 150 **Parking** 50 **Notes** LB ⊗ Civ Wed 150

C

CRICCIETH *continued*

George IV Hotel

★★ 65% HOTEL

☎ 01766 522168
23-25 High St LL52 0BS
e-mail: georgeiv.criccieth@alfatravel.co.uk
web: www.leisureplex.co.uk
dir: On A497 in town centre

This hotel stands back from the A497 in the town centre. The bedrooms, which in general are spacious, are attractively furnished and well equipped to meet the needs of both business guests and holidaymakers. George's Brasserie serves a menu based on locally sourced ingredients.

Rooms 47 (11 fmly) **Facilities** FTV ♫ Xmas New Year **Services** Lift **Parking** 16 **Notes** ⊗ Closed Jan RS Nov & Feb-Mar

| CRICKHOWELL | Map 9 SO21 |
| Powys | |

Bear Hotel

WELSH RAREBITS
Hotels of Distinction

★★★ 75% ◉ HOTEL

☎ 01873 810408
NP8 1BW
e-mail: bearhotel@aol.com
dir: On A40 between Abergavenny & Brecon

A favourite with locals as well as visitors, the character and friendliness of this 15th-century coaching inn are renowned. The bedrooms come in a variety of sizes and standards including some with four-posters. The bar and restaurant are furnished in keeping with the style of the building and provide comfortable areas in which to enjoy some of the very popular dishes that use the finest locally-sourced ingredients.

Rooms 34 (13 annexe) (6 fmly) (6 GF) **Facilities** STV FTV Wi-fi ⇗ **Conf** Class 20 Board 20 Thtr 40 **Parking** 45 **Notes** RS 25 Dec

Manor Hotel

★★★ 75% ◉ HOTEL

☎ 01873 810212
Brecon Rd NP8 1SE
e-mail: info@manorhotel.co.uk
web: www.manorhotel.co.uk
dir: On A40, 0.5m from Crickhowell

This impressive manor house, set in a stunning location, was the birthplace of Sir George Everest. The bedrooms and public areas are elegant, and there are extensive leisure facilities. The restaurant, with panoramic views, is the setting for exciting modern cooking.

Rooms 23 (2 fmly) **S** £69-£80; **D** £85-£120 (incl. bkfst)* **Facilities** STV FTV Wi-fi ⇗ ⊗ Gym Fitness assessment Sunbed Xmas New Year **Conf** Class 250 Board 150 Thtr 300 Del from £120 to £140* **Parking** 200 **Notes** LB Civ Wed 150

| CWMBRAN | Map 9 ST29 |
| Torfaen | |

Best Western Parkway Hotel

★★★★ 79% HOTEL

☎ 01633 871199
Cwmbran Dr NP44 3UW
e-mail: enquiries@parkwayhotel.co.uk
web: www.bw-parkwayhotel.co.uk
dir: M4 junct 25a & 26, A4051 follow Cwmbran-Llantarnam Park signs. Right at rdbt, right to hotel

This purpose-built hotel, in over seven acres of grounds, offers comfortable bedrooms and public areas that will suit a wide range of guests. The coffee shop is an informal eating option throughout the day, and there is fine dining in Ravello's Restaurant. The bedrooms, including suites, interconnecting family rooms and wheelchair access rooms, are stylishly appointed. Additional facilities include a sports centre and conference and meeting facilities.

Rooms 70 (4 fmly) (34 GF) **S** £60-£120; **D** £70-£150 (incl. bkfst) **Facilities** STV Wi-fi ⊗ Gym Steam room Sauna Solaria Spa bath ♫ Xmas New Year **Conf** Class 240 Board 100 Thtr 500 Del from £111 to £169 **Parking** 350 **Notes** LB ⊗ Closed 27-30 Dec Civ Wed 250

Premier Inn Cwmbran

BUDGET HOTEL

☎ 0870 111 2851
Avondale Rd, Pontrhydyrun NP44 1DE
web: www.premierinn.com
dir: M4 junct 26, A4501 signed Cwmbran, straight on at next 5 rdbts. At 6th take Pontrhydyrun Rd exit, left into Avondale Rd

High quality, budget accommodation ideal for both families and business travellers. Spacious, en suite bedrooms feature tea and coffee making facilities, and Freeview TV in most hotels. Internet access and Wi-fi are available for a small fee. The adjacent family restaurant features a wide and varied menu. See also the Hotel Groups pages.

Rooms 40

| DEGANWY | Map 14 SH77 |
| Conwy | |

Quay Hotel & Spa

★★★★ 84% ◉ HOTEL

☎ 01492 564100
Deganwy Quay LL31 9DJ
e-mail: info@quayhotel.com
web: www.quayhotel.co.uk
dir: M56, A494, A55 junct 18, straight across 2 rdbts. At lights bear left into The Quay. Hotel on right

This boutique hotel occupies a stunning position beside the estuary on Deganwy's Quay. What was once an area for railway storage is now a property of modern architectural design offering hotel-keeping of the highest standard. Spacious bedrooms, many with balconies and wonderful views, are decorated in neutral colours and boast a host of thoughtful extras, including up-to-the-minute communication systems. The friendly staff provide a fluent service in a charmingly informal manner.

Rooms 74 (15 fmly) (30 GF) **Facilities** Spa Wi-fi ⊗ supervised Gym Steam & sauna room Hydro therapy pool Xmas New Year **Conf** Class 240 Board 90 Thtr 240 **Services** Lift **Parking** 96 **Notes** ⊗ Civ Wed 150

Save on hotels. Book at **theAA.com/hotel**

CRI – EGL 601 WALES

E

DEVIL'S BRIDGE — Map 9 SN77
Ceredigion

The Hafod Hotel

★★★ 68% HOTEL

☎ 01970 890232
SY23 3JL
e-mail: hafodhotel@btconnect.com
dir: Exit A44 in Ponterwyd signed Devil's Bridge/
Pontarfynach onto A4120, 3m, over bridge. Hotel
opposite

This former hunting lodge dates back to the 17th
century and is situated in six acres of grounds. Now a
family-owned and run hotel, it provides
accommodation suitable for both business and
leisure guests. Family rooms and a four-poster room
are available. In addition to the dining area and
lounge, there are tea rooms.

Rooms 17 (2 fmly) **Facilities** Wi-fi Xmas New Year
Conf Class 70 Board 40 Thtr 100 **Parking** 200
Notes Civ Wed 40

DOLGELLAU — Map 14 SH71
Gwynedd

INSPECTORS' CHOICE

Penmaenuchaf Hall Hotel

WELSH
RAREBITS
*Hotels of
Distinction*

★★★ ◉ COUNTRY HOUSE HOTEL

☎ 01341 422129
Penmaenpool LL40 1YB
e-mail: relax@penhall.co.uk
web: www.penhall.co.uk
dir: A470 onto A493 to Tywyn. Hotel approx 1m on
left

Built in 1860, this impressive hall stands in 20
acres of formal gardens, grounds and woodland,
and enjoys magnificent views across the River
Mawddach. Sympathetic restoration has created a
comfortable and welcoming hotel with spacious day
rooms and thoughtfully furnished bedrooms, some
with private balconies. Fresh produce cooked in
modern British style is served in an elegant

conservatory restaurant, overlooking the
countryside.

Penmaenuchaf Hall Hotel

Rooms 14 (2 fmly) ✆ **S** £115-£180; **D** £170-£260
(incl. bkfst)* **Facilities** STV FTV Wi-fi ⊱ ⥼
Complimentary salmon & trout fishing Coracling
Xmas New Year **Conf** Class 30 Board 22 Thtr 50
Del from £132 to £214* **Parking** 30 **Notes** LB No
children 6yrs Civ Wed 65

EBBW VALE — Map 9 SO10
Blaenau Gwent

Premier Inn Ebbw Vale

BUDGET HOTEL

☎ 0871 527 8356
Victoria Business Park, Waunllwyd NP23 8AN
web: www.premierinn.com
dir: M4 junct 28, A467 signed Risca, then Brynmawr.
At rdbt at Brynithel 1st exit onto A4046, signed Ebbw
Vale. At rdbt 3rd exit towards Waunllwyd. At rdbt 1st
exit, next left. Hotel adjacent

High quality, budget accommodation ideal for both
families and business travellers. Spacious, en suite
bedrooms feature tea and coffee making facilities,
and Freeview TV in most hotels. Internet access and
Wi-fi are available for a small fee. The adjacent
family restaurant features a wide and varied menu.
See also the Hotel Groups pages.

Rooms 44

EGLWYS FACH — Map 14 SN69
Ceredigion

INSPECTORS' CHOICE

Plas Ynyshir Hall Hotel

RELAIS &
CHATEAUX

★★★ ◉◉◉ COUNTRY HOUSE HOTEL

☎ 01654 781209 & 781268
SY20 8TA
e-mail: ynyshir@relaischateaux.com
web: www.ynyshirhall.co.uk
dir: Exit A487, 5.5m S of Machynlleth, signed from
main road

Set in beautifully landscaped grounds and
surrounded by the RSPB Ynys-hir Nature Reserve,
Plas Ynyshir Hall is a haven of calm. The house was
once owned by Queen Victoria and it is surrounded
by mountain scenery. Lavishly styled bedrooms,
each individually themed around a great painter,
provide high standards of luxury and comfort. The
lounge and bar, adorned with an abundance of
fresh flowers, have different moods. The dining
room offers highly accomplished cooking using the
best, locally sourced ingredients including herbs,
soft fruit and vegetables from the hotel's own
kitchen garden and wild foods gathered nearby. The
hotel makes an idyllic location for weddings.

Rooms 9 (2 annexe) (2 GF) ✆ **D** £295-£405 (incl.
bkfst)* **Facilities** Wi-fi ⊱ ⥼ Xmas New Year
Conf Class 20 Board 18 Thtr 25 Del from £245 to
£275* **Parking** 20 **Notes** LB No children 9yrs
Civ Wed 40

FISHGUARD
Pembrokeshire   **Map 8 SM93**

The Cartref Hotel

★★ 65% HOTEL

☎ 01348 872430 & 0781 330 5235
15-19 High St SA65 9AW
e-mail: cartrefhotel@btconnect.com
web: www.cartrefhotel.co.uk
dir: On A40 in town centre

Personally run by the proprietor, this friendly hotel offers convenient access to the town centre and ferry terminal. Bedrooms are well maintained and include some family rooms. There is also a cosy lounge bar and a welcoming restaurant that looks out onto the high street.

Rooms 10 (2 fmly) ⚡ **S** £35-£42; **D** £65-£72 (incl. bkfst)* **Facilities** FTV Wi-fi **Parking** 4 **Notes** LB

GWBERT-ON-SEA
Ceredigion   **Map 14 SN69**

The Cliff Hotel

★★★ 75% HOTEL

☎ 01239 613241
SA43 1PP
e-mail: reservations@cliffhotel.com
web: www.cliffhotel.com
dir: A487, into Cardigan, take B4548 towards Gwbert, 2m to hotel

Set in 30 acres of grounds with a 9-hole golf course, this hotel commands superb sea views from its cliff-top location overlooking Cardigan Bay. Bedrooms in the main building have excellent views and there is also a wing of modern rooms. Public areas are spacious and comprise a choice of bars, lounges and a fine dining restaurant. The spa offers a wide range of up-to-the-minute leisure facilities.

Rooms 70 (6 fmly) (5 GF) ⚡ **S** £60-£85; **D** £75-£150 (incl. bkfst)* **Facilities** Spa FTV ⛳ ⛳ 9 Putt green Fishing Gym Xmas New Year **Conf** Class 150 Board 140 Thtr 250 Del from £89 to £145* **Services** Lift **Parking** 100 **Notes** LB Civ Wed 200

HAY-ON-WYE
Powys   **Map 9 SO24**

The Swan-at-Hay Hotel

★★★ 74% HOTEL

☎ 01497 821188
Church St HR3 5DQ
e-mail: stay@swanathay.co.uk
web: www.swanathay.co.uk
dir: In town centre, on Brecon Road opposite cinema bookshop

This former coaching inn, now a privately owned hotel, has plenty of character and overlooks well-tended gardens. The bedrooms are comfortable and a good range of guest extras are provided. The food, based on fresh local ingredients, is offered on a well-balanced menu. The Swan's location, between The Black Mountains and the Brecon Beacons, is ideal for walkers of course, but also convenient for leisure and business guests visiting the area. Wi-fi is available.

Rooms 17 (1 fmly) (2 GF) **Facilities** FTV Wi-fi Xmas New Year **Conf** Class 80 Board 60 Thtr 120 **Parking** 17 **Notes** RS Jan Civ Wed 80

HENSOL
Vale of Glamorgan   **Map 9 ST07**

Vale Resort

★★★★ 85% ◉ HOTEL   **CLASSIC** BRITISH HOTELS

☎ 01443 667800
Hensol Park CF72 8JY
e-mail: reservations@vale-hotel.com
web: www.vale-hotel.com
dir: M4 junct 34 towards Pendoylan, hotel signed from junct

A wealth of leisure facilities is offered at this large and modern, purpose-built complex, including two golf courses and a driving range plus an extensive health spa with a gym, swimming pool, squash courts, orthopaedic clinic and a range of treatments. Public areas are spacious and attractive, whilst bedrooms, many with balconies, are well appointed. Meeting and conference facilities are available. Guests can dine in the traditional Vale Grill, a brasserie-style restaurant serving quality fresh ingredients.

Vale Resort

Rooms 143 (114 annexe) (15 fmly) (36 GF) **Facilities** Spa STV Wi-fi ⛳ ⛳ 36 ⛳ Putt green Fishing Gym Squash Children's club (Sat am & school hols) Xmas New Year **Conf** Class 280 Board 60 Thtr 700 Del from £140 to £160* **Services** Lift Air con **Parking** 450 **Notes** ⊗ Civ Wed 700

See advert on opposite page

KNIGHTON
Powys   **Map 9 SO27**

Milebrook House Hotel

WELSH RAREBITS
Hotels of Distinction

★★★ 79% ◉ ◉
COUNTRY HOUSE HOTEL

☎ 01547 528632
Milebrook LD7 1LT
e-mail: hotel@milebrook.co.uk
web: www.milebrookhouse.co.uk
dir: 2m E of Knighton, on A4113

Set in three acres of grounds and gardens in the Teme Valley, this charming house dates back to 1760. Over the years since its conversion into a hotel, it has acquired a well-deserved reputation for its warm hospitality, comfortable accommodation and the quality of its cuisine, that uses local produce and home-grown vegetables.

Rooms 10 (2 fmly) (2 GF) **S** £77-£83.25; **D** £121-£133 (incl. bkfst)* **Facilities** Wi-fi ⛳ Table tennis Trout fly fishing Xmas New Year **Conf** Class 30 **Parking** 21 **Notes** LB ⊗ No children 8yrs RS Mon lunch

Save on hotels. Book at **theAA.com/hotel**

FIS – LLA 603 WALES

LAMPETER	Map 8 SN54
Ceredigion	

The Falcondale Hotel & Restaurant

WELSH RAREBITS
Hotels of Distinction

★★★★ 76% ◉◉ COUNTRY HOUSE HOTEL

☎ 01570 422910
SA48 7RX
e-mail: info@thefalcondale.co.uk
web: www.thefalcondale.co.uk
dir: 800yds W of High St (A475) or 1.5m NW of Lampeter (A482)

Built in the Italianate style, this charming Victorian property is set in extensive grounds and beautiful parkland. The individually-styled bedrooms are generally spacious, well equipped and tastefully decorated. Bars and lounges are similarly well appointed with additional facilities including a conservatory and terrace. The award-winning restaurant, with a relaxed and friendly atmosphere, offers menus based on the best seasonal, locally sourced produce.

Rooms 19 (2 fmly) **S** £109-£169; **D** £139-£209 (incl. bkfst)* **Facilities** FTV Wi-fi ⬥ ⬥ Xmas New Year **Conf** Class 26 Board 26 Thtr 60 Del from £139 to £209* **Services** Lift **Parking** 60 **Notes** LB Civ Wed 200

LLANBEDR	Map 14 SH52
Gwynedd	

Ty Mawr Hotel

★★ 78% SMALL HOTEL

☎ 01341 241440 & 07717 080171
LL45 2NH
e-mail: info@tymawrhotel.com
web: www.tymawrhotel.com
dir: From Barmouth A496 (Harlech road). In Llanbedr turn right after bridge, hotel 50yds on left, follow brown tourist sigs

Ty Mawr means 'Big House' in Welsh. Located in a picturesque village within Snowdonia National Park, this family-run hotel has a relaxed, friendly atmosphere. The attractive grounds, opposite the River Artro, provide a popular beer garden during fine weather. The attractive, rustically furnished bar offers a blackboard selection of food and a good choice of real ales; a more formal menu is available in the restaurant. Bedrooms are smart and brightly decorated.

Rooms 10 (2 fmly) ⬥ **S** £50-£60; **D** £80-£90 (incl. bkfst) **Facilities** STV FTV Wi-fi **Conf** Class 25 **Parking** 30 **Notes** Closed 24-26 Dec

LLANBERIS	Map 14 SH56
Gwynedd	

The Legacy Royal Victoria Hotel

 LEGACY HOTELS

★★★ 68% HOTEL

☎ 08444 119 003 & 0330 333 2803
LL55 4TY
e-mail: res-royalvictoria@legacy-hotels.co.uk
web: www.legacy-hotels.co.uk
dir: On A4086 (Caernarfon to Llanberis road), directly opposite Snowdon Mountain Railway

This well-established hotel sits near the foot of Snowdon, between the Peris and Padarn lakes. Pretty gardens and grounds make an attractive setting for the many weddings held here. Bedrooms are well equipped. There are spacious lounges and bars, and a large dining room with a conservatory looking out over the lakes.

Rooms 106 (14 annexe) (7 fmly) ⬥ **Facilities** FTV Wi-fi ♫ Xmas New Year **Conf** Class 60 Board 50 Thtr 100 **Services** Lift **Parking** 107 **Notes** Civ Wed 100

L

LLANDEILO	Map 8 SN62
Carmarthenshire	

The Plough Inn

★★★★ 77% ⊛ HOTEL

☎ 01558 823431
Rhosmaen SA19 6NP
e-mail: info@ploughrhosmaen.com
web: www.ploughrhosmaen.com
dir: 0.5m N of Llandeilo on A40

This privately owned hotel has memorable views over the Towy Valley and the Black Mountains. Bedrooms, situated in a separate wing, are tastefully furnished, spacious and comfortable. The public lounge bar is popular with locals, as is the spacious restaurant where freshly prepared food can be enjoyed. There are also conference facilities, a gym and a sauna.

Rooms 23 (11 fmly) (8 GF) **S** fr £70; **D** fr £90 (incl. bkfst)* **Facilities** FTV Wi-fi Gym Sauna Xmas New Year **Conf** Class 60 Board 30 Thtr 100 Del from £97.95* **Services** Air con **Parking** 70 **Notes** LB Civ Wed 120

White Hart Inn

★★ 72% HOTEL

☎ 01558 823419
36 Carmarthen Rd SA19 6RS
e-mail: info@thewhitehartinnwales.co.uk
web: www.whitehartinnwales.co.uk
dir: A40 onto A483, hotel 200yds on left

This privately owned, 19th-century roadside hostelry is on the outskirts of town. The modern bedrooms are well equipped and tastefully furnished, and family rooms are available. Public areas include a choice of bars where a wide range of grilled dishes is available. There are several function rooms, including a large self-contained suite.

Rooms 11 (6 fmly) ☌ **S** £40-£45; **D** £60-£70 (incl. bkfst)* **Facilities** STV FTV Wi-fi New Year **Conf** Class 80 Board 40 Thtr 100 **Parking** 50 **Notes** ⊗ Civ Wed 70

LLANDRILLO	Map 15 SJ03
Denbighshire	

Tyddyn Llan Restaurant

⊛ ⊛ RESTAURANT WITH ROOMS

☎ 01490 440264
LL21 0ST
e-mail: info@tyddynllan.co.uk
web: www.tyddynllan.co.uk
dir: Off A4 at Corwen onto B4401, through villages of Cynwyd & Llandrillo. On right leaving village

Tyddyn Llan is a very well appointed property set in the Edeyrnion Valley at the gateway to Snowdonia. Whilst not all the individually styled bedrooms are spacious, they do offer many home comforts. The public areas are beautifully furnished and have open fires in the colder months. Susan runs the front of the house with friendly informed staff; service is formal and in keeping with the style of the establishment. Husband and chef Bryan sources ingredients as locally as possible and his cooking is sympathetic to the produce. An extensive breakfast menu is available.

Rooms 13

LLANDRINDOD WELLS	Map 9 SO06
Powys	

The Metropole

★★★★ 77% ⊛ HOTEL

CLASSIC BRITISH HOTELS

☎ 01597 823700
Temple St LD1 5DY
e-mail: info@metropole.co.uk
web: www.metropole.co.uk
dir: On A483 in town centre

The centre of this famous spa town is dominated by this large Victorian hotel, which has been personally run by the same family for well over 100 years. The lobby leads to Spencers Bar and Brasserie and to the comfortable and elegantly styled lounge. Bedrooms vary in style, but all are spacious and well equipped. Facilities include an extensive range of modern conference and function rooms, as well as the impressive leisure centre. Extensive parking is provided to the rear of the hotel.

Rooms 114 (11 fmly) **S** £85-£123; **D** £110-£156 (incl. bkfst) **Facilities** Spa FTV Wi-fi ↳ ⒮ Gym Beauty & holistic treatments Sauna Steam room Xmas New Year **Conf** Class 200 Board 80 Thtr 300 **Services** Lift **Parking** 150 **Notes** LB Civ Wed 300

LLANDUDNO	Map 14 SH78
Conwy	

INSPECTORS' CHOICE

Bodysgallen Hall and Spa

★★★★ ⊛ ⊛ ⊛ COUNTRY HOUSE HOTEL

☎ 01492 584466
LL30 1RS
e-mail: info@bodysgallen.com
web: www.bodysgallen.com
dir: A55 junct 19, A470 towards Llandudno. Hotel 2m on right

Situated in idyllic surroundings of its own parkland and formal gardens, this 17th-century house is in an elevated position, with views towards Snowdonia and across to Conwy Castle. The lounges and dining room have fine antiques and great character. Accommodation is provided in the house, but also in delightfully converted cottages, together with a superb spa. Friendly and attentive service is discreetly offered, whilst the restaurant features fine local produce prepared with great skill. AA Hotel of the Year for Wales 2012-13.

Rooms 31 (16 annexe) (4 fmly) (4 GF) **S** £159-£195; **D** £179-£425 (incl. bkfst)* **Facilities** Spa STV Wi-fi ↳ ⒮ ⚘ Gym Beauty treatments Steam room Relaxation room Sauna Xmas New Year **Conf** Class 30 Board 22 Thtr 50 Del £174* **Parking** 50 **Notes** LB ⊗ No children 6yrs Civ Wed 50

Imperial Hotel

★★★★ 81% ® HOTEL

☎ 01492 877466
The Promenade LL30 1AP
e-mail: reception@theimperial.co.uk
web: www.theimperial.co.uk
dir: A470 to Llandudno

The Imperial is a large and impressive hotel, situated on the promenade with lovely views out over the blue flag beaches to the bay, and within easy reach of the town centre and other amenities. Many of the bedrooms have the sea views and there are also several suites available. The elegant Chantrey's Restaurant offers a fixed-price, monthly-changing menu that utilises local produce, and The Terrace is the place to relax and enjoy a leisurely lunch or a snack during the day.

Imperial Hotel

Rooms 98 (10 fmly) **Facilities** FTV Wi-fi ✈ Gym Beauty therapist Hairdressing ♫ Xmas New Year **Conf** Class 50 Board 50 Thtr 150 **Services** Lift **Parking** 25 **Notes** ® Civ Wed 150

See advert on this page

St George's Hotel

★★★★ 80% ® HOTEL

☎ 01492 877544 & 862184
The Promenade LL30 2LG
e-mail: sales@stgeorgeswales.co.uk
web: www.stgeorgeswales.co.uk
dir: A55, A470, follow to promenade, 0.25m, hotel on corner

This large and impressive seafront property was the first hotel to be built in the town. Restored it to its former glory, the accommodation is of very high quality. The many Victorian features include the splendid, ornate Wedgwood Room restaurant. The terrace restaurant and main lounges overlook the bay; hot and cold snacks are available all day. Many of the thoughtfully equipped bedrooms enjoy sea views.

St George's Hotel

Rooms 76 (13 fmly) ✦ **S** £90-£120; **D** £115-£180 (incl. bkfst) **Facilities** STV FTV Wi-fi ♧ In room beauty treatments Xmas New Year **Conf** Class 200 Board 45 Thtr 250 **Services** Lift Air con **Parking** 36 **Notes** LB ® Civ Wed 200

See advert on page 601

Empire Hotel & Spa

★★★★ 77% ® HOTEL

☎ 01492 860555
Church Walks LL30 2HE
e-mail: reservations@empirehotel.co.uk
web: www.empirehotel.co.uk
dir: From Chester, A55 junct 19 for Llandudno. Follow signs to Promenade, turn right at war memorial & left at rdbt. Hotel 100yds on right

Run by the same family for over almost 60 years, the Empire offers luxuriously appointed bedrooms with every modern facility. The 'Number 72' rooms in an

continued

L

L

LLANDUDNO *continued*

adjacent house are particularly sumptuous. The indoor pool is overlooked by a lounge area where snacks are served all day, and in summer an outdoor pool and roof garden are available. The Watkins restaurant offers an interesting fixed-price menu.

Rooms 58 (8 annexe) (1 fmly) (2 GF) ↗
S £72.50-£87.50; **D** £102.50-£130 (incl. bkfst)*
Facilities Spa STV FTV Wi-fi ↕ HL ⊕ ↖ Gym Sauna Steam room Fitness suite New Year **Conf** Class 20 Board 20 Thtr 24 Del from £100 to £130*
Services Lift Air con **Parking** 47 **Notes** LB Closed 20-30 Dec

---

INSPECTORS' CHOICE

Osborne House

★★★ ◉ TOWN HOUSE HOTEL

☎ 01492 860330
17 North Pde LL30 2LP
e-mail: sales@osbornehouse.com
web: www.osbornehouse.com
dir: Exit A55 junct 19. Follow signs for Llandudno then Promenade. Continue to junct, turn right. Hotel on left opposite pier entrance

Built in 1832, this Victorian house was restored and converted into a luxurious townhouse by the Maddocks family. Spacious suites offer unrivalled comfort and luxury, combining antique furnishings with state-of-the-art technology and facilities. Each suite provides super views over the pier and bay. Osborne's café grill is open throughout the day and offers high quality food, whilst the bar blends elegance with plasma screens, dazzling chandeliers and gilt framed mirrors.

Rooms 7 (1 fmly) ↗ **S** £143.50-£164;
D £143.50-£164 (incl. bkfst)* **Facilities** STV FTV Wi-fi ↕ Use of swimming pool & sauna at Empire Hotel (100yds) New Year **Services** Air con **Parking** 6 **Notes** ⊗ No children 11yrs Closed 16-30 Dec

---

Dunoon Hotel

★★★ 82% HOTEL

☎ 01492 860787
Gloddaeth St LL30 2DW
e-mail: reservations@dunoonhotel.co.uk
web: www.dunoonhotel.co.uk
dir: Exit Promenade at war memorial by pier into Gladdaeth St. Hotel 200yds on right

This impressive, privately owned hotel is centrally located and offers a variety of well-equipped bedrooms. Elegant public areas include a tastefully appointed restaurant where competently prepared dishes are served together with a good choice of notable, reasonably priced wines. The caring and attentive service is also noteworthy.

Rooms 49 (4 fmly) ↗ **S** £80-£115; **D** £142-£162 (incl. bkfst & dinner) **Facilities** FTV Wi-fi Pool table **Services** Lift **Parking** 24 **Notes** LB Closed 17 Dec-early Mar

---

St Tudno Hotel and Restaurant

WELSH RAREBITS
Hotels of Distinction

★★★ 82% ◉ HOTEL

☎ 01492 874411
The Promenade LL30 2LP
e-mail: sttudnohotel@btinternet.com
web: www.st-tudno.co.uk
dir: On Promenade towards pier, hotel opposite pier entrance

An excellent family-owned hotel with friendly and attentive staff, that enjoys fine sea views. The stylish bedrooms are well equipped with mini-bars, robes,

---

satellite TVs and many other thoughtful extras. Public rooms include a lounge, a welcoming bar and a small indoor pool. The Terrace Restaurant, where seasonal and daily-changing menus are offered, has a delightful Mediterranean atmosphere. Afternoon tea is a real highlight.

Rooms 18 (4 fmly) ↗ **S** £75-£110; **D** £98-£220 (incl. bkfst) **Facilities** FTV Wi-fi HL ⊕ ♫ Xmas New Year **Conf** Class 25 Board 20 Thtr 40 **Services** Lift **Parking** 12 **Notes** LB Civ Wed 70

Tynedale Hotel

★★★ 80% HOTEL

☎ 01492 877426
Central Promenade LL30 2XS
e-mail: enquiries@tynedalehotel.co.uk
web: www.tynedalehotel.co.uk
dir: On Promenade opposite bandstand

Tour groups are well catered for at this privately owned and personally run hotel, and regular live entertainment is a feature. Vibrant modern public areas create a unique and comfortable setting, and an attractive seafront patio garden is an additional asset. Bedrooms provide good comfort levels, and the staff offer friendly and efficient service.

Rooms 54 (1 fmly) (10 GF) ↗ **S** £42-£64; **D** £84-£128 (incl. bkfst)* **Facilities** FTV Wi-fi ↕ ♫ Xmas New Year **Services** Lift **Parking** 15 **Notes** LB ⊗

Save on hotels. Book at **theAA.com/hotel**

LLA 607 WALES

Merrion Hotel

★★★ 76% HOTEL

☎ 01492 860022
Promenade, South Pde LL30 2LN
e-mail: enquiries@merrion-hotel.co.uk
dir: From A55 follow Llandudno signs onto
Promenade, towards pier

Located on the seafront opposite The Victorian Pier
and close to the town centre, this constantly
improving owner-managed hotel offers comfortable,
well-equipped accommodation; many rooms have sea
views. Stylish air-conditioned public areas provide
high standards of comfort and regular evening
entertainment is a feature.

Rooms 65 (6 fmly) (3 GF) 🕯 **S** £45-£71.50;
D £90-£123 (incl. bkfst)* **Facilities** STV FTV Wi-fi ♬
Xmas **Conf** Class 40 Board 20 Thtr 30 Del from £100
to £120* **Services** Lift **Parking** 24 **Notes** LB ⊗
Closed Jan

Cae Mor Hotel

★★★ 75% HOTEL

☎ 01492 878101
5-6 Penrhyn Crescent LL30 1BA
e-mail: info@caemorhotel.co.uk
dir: Exit A55 junct 19, follow A470/Llandudno/Town
Centre signs. Straight on at 3 rdbts, right at 4th. Into
right lane, right at next rdbt, follow Promenade signs.
Straight on at next rdbt, left at next rdbt onto
Promenade. 200yds, pass Venue Cymru

Located in a stunning seafront position adjacent to
Venue Cymru, this tastefully renovated Victorian hotel

provides a range of thoughtfully furnished bedrooms
in minimalist style with smart modern bathrooms.
Public areas include a choice of lounges and a stylish
restaurant, the setting for imaginative dinners
featuring the best of local seasonal produce.

Rooms 23 (2 fmly) (2 GF) 🕯 **S** £64-£75; **D** £85-£140
(incl. bkfst) **Facilities** FTV Wi-fi Xmas New Year
Conf Board 28 Thtr 60 **Services** Lift **Parking** 26
Notes LB Civ Wed 50

Hydro Hotel

★★ 72% HOTEL

☎ 01492 870101
Neville Crescent LL30 1AT
e-mail: hydro.llandudno@alfatravel.co.uk
web: www.leisureplex.co.uk
dir: Follow signs for theatre to seafront, towards pier

This large hotel is situated on the promenade
overlooking the sea, and offers good, value-for-
money, modern accommodation. Public areas are
quite extensive and include a choice of lounges, a
games/snooker room and a ballroom where
entertainment is provided every night. The hotel is a
popular venue for coach tour parties.

Rooms 120 (4 fmly) (9 GF) **Facilities** Table tennis
Snooker ♬ Xmas New Year **Services** Lift **Parking** 10
Notes ⊗ Closed Jan-mid Feb RS Nov-Dec (ex Xmas)
& mid Feb-Mar

The Broadway Hotel

★★ 🄰 HOTEL

☎ 01492 876398
Mostyn Broadway LL30 1YL
e-mail: sales@thebroadwayhotel.com
web: www.thebroadwayhotel.com
dir: A55 junct 19, A470 towards Llandudno, follow
signs to town centre. Approaching town centre into
right lane, right into Mostyn Broadway, hotel on left

Rooms 29 (4 fmly) 🕯 **S** £40; **D** £80 (incl. bkfst)*
Facilities FTV ♧ Xmas New Year **Conf** Class 12
Board 16 Thtr 30 Del from £80 to £105* **Services** Lift
Parking 4 **Notes** LB Closed 2 & 31 Jan

Premier Inn Llandudno North (Little Orme)

BUDGET HOTEL

☎ 0871 527 8636
Colwyn Rd LL30 3AL
web: www.premierinn.com
dir: A55 junct 20 follow Rhos-on-Sea/Llandrillo-Yn-
Rhos/B5115 signs. Onto B5115 (Brompton Ave).
Straight on at next 2 rdbts. Hotel on left

High quality, budget accommodation ideal for both
families and business travellers. Spacious, en suite
bedrooms feature tea and coffee making facilities,
and Freeview TV in most hotels. Internet access and
Wi-fi are available for a small fee. The adjacent
family restaurant features a wide and varied menu.
See also the Hotel Groups pages.

Rooms 19

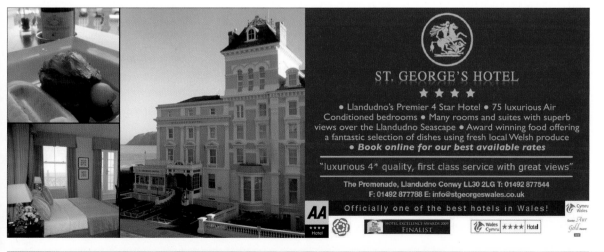

LLANDUDNO *continued*

The Lilly Restaurant with Rooms

◉ RESTAURANT WITH ROOMS

☎ 01492 876513
West Pde, West Shore LL30 2BD
e-mail: thelilly@live.co.uk
dir: Telephone for detailed directions

Located on the seafront on the West Shore with views over the Great Orme, this establishment has bedrooms that offer high standards of comfort and good facilities. Children are very welcome here, and a relaxed atmosphere can be found in Madhatters Brasserie, which takes its name from Lewis Caroll's Alice in Wonderland which was written on the West Shore. A fine dining restaurant is also available.

Rooms 12 (2 fmly)

LLANDUDNO JUNCTION   Map 14 SH77
Conwy

Premier Inn Llandudno (Glan-Conwy)

BUDGET HOTEL

☎ 0871 527 8634
Afon Conwy LL28 5LB
web: www.premierinn.com
dir: A55 junct 19. Exit rdbt at A470 (Betws-y-Coed). Hotel immediately on left, opposite petrol station

High quality, budget accommodation ideal for both families and business travellers. Spacious, en suite bedrooms feature tea and coffee making facilities, and Freeview TV in most hotels. Internet access and Wi-fi are available for a small fee. The adjacent family restaurant features a wide and varied menu. See also the Hotel Groups pages.

Rooms 41

LLANELLI   Map 8 SN50
Carmarthenshire

Best Western Diplomat Hotel and Spa

★★★ 79% HOTEL

☎ 01554 756156
Felinfoel SA15 3PJ
e-mail: reservations@diplomat-hotel-wales.com
web: www.diplomat-hotel-wales.com
dir: M4 junct 48, A4138 then B4303, hotel 0.75m on right

This Victorian mansion, set in mature grounds, has been extended over the years to provide a comfortable and relaxing hotel. The well-appointed bedrooms are located in the main house and there is also a wing of

equally comfortable modern rooms. Public areas include Trubshaw's Restaurant, a large function suite and a modern leisure centre.

Rooms 50 (8 annexe) (2 fmly) (4 GF) **Facilities** FTV Wi-fi ⓐ ⓢ supervised Gym Sauna Steam room Sun beds Hairdresser ♫ Xmas New Year **Conf** Class 150 Board 100 Thtr 450 **Services** Lift **Parking** 250 **Notes** Civ Wed 300

Ashburnham Hotel

★★ 76% HOTEL

☎ 01554 834343 & 834455
Ashburnham Rd, Pembrey SA16 0TH
e-mail: info@ashburnham-hotel.co.uk
web: www.ashburnham-hotel.co.uk
dir: M4 junct 48, A4138 to Llanelli, A484 W to Pembrey. Follow brown information signs

Amelia Earhart stayed at this friendly hotel after finishing her historic trans-Atlantic flight in 1928. Public areas include the brasserie restaurant and the conservatory lounge bar that serve an extensive range of bar meals. Bedrooms, varying from standard to superior, have modern furnishings and facilities. The hotel is licensed for civil ceremonies, and function and conference facilities are also available.

Rooms 13 (2 fmly) **S** £45-£55; **D** £50-£70 (incl. bkfst) **Facilities** FTV Wi-fi ⓐ **Conf** Class 150 Board 80 Thtr 150 **Parking** 100 **Notes** ⊗ RS 24-26 Dec Civ Wed 130

Premier Inn Llanelli Central East

BUDGET HOTEL

☎ 0871 527 8638
Llandafen Rd SA14 9BD
web: www.premierinn.com
dir: M4 junct 48, A4138, approx 3m. Hotel on left

High quality, budget accommodation ideal for both families and business travellers. Spacious, en suite bedrooms feature tea and coffee making facilities, and Freeview TV in most hotels. Internet access and Wi-fi are available for a small fee. The adjacent family restaurant features a wide and varied menu. See also the Hotel Groups pages.

Rooms 50

LLANGAMMARCH WELLS   Map 9 SN94
Powys

The Lake Country House & Spa

★★★ ◉◉ COUNTRY HOUSE HOTEL

☎ 01591 620202
LD4 4BS
e-mail: info@lakecountryhouse.co.uk
web: www.lakecountryhouse.co.uk
dir: W from Builth Wells on A483 to Garth (approx 6m). Left for Llangammarch Wells, follow hotel signs

Expect good old-fashioned values and hospitality at this Victorian country house hotel. In fact, the service is so traditionally English, guests may believe they have their own butler! The establishment offers a 9-hole, par 3 golf course, 50 acres of wooded grounds and a spa with a hot tub that overlooks the lake. Bedrooms, some located in an annexe, and some at ground-floor level, are individually styled and have many extra comforts. Traditional afternoon teas are served in the lounge, and award-winning cuisine is provided in the spacious and elegant restaurant.

Rooms 30 (7 GF) ♞ **S** £145-£210; **D** £195-£260 (incl. bkfst)* **Facilities** Spa FTV Wi-fi ⓐ ♨ 9 ⓢ Putt green Fishing ⛳ Gym Archery Horse riding Mountain biking Quad biking Xmas New Year **Conf** Class 30 Board 25 Thtr 80 Del £156* **Parking** 70 **Notes** LB No children 8yrs Civ Wed 100

LLANGATTOCK — Map 9 SO21
Powys

The Old Rectory Hotel & Golf Club
★★★ 75% ⊛ HOTEL

☎ 01873 810373
NP8 1PH
e-mail: oldrectoryhotel@live.com
dir: In village turn 60mtrs after Horseshoe Inn, follow narrow lane for approx 0.25m. Hotel on right

Dating back to the 16th century this house was once the home of poet Henry Vaughan. It retains all the character of an elegant country house whilst offering contemporary bedrooms and bathroom facilities; there are ground-floor bedrooms, family rooms and suites. Guests receive complimentary use of the 9-hole, par 3 golf course which forms part of the extensive grounds. This hotel is a popular choice for weddings, and the large function room also caters for corporate events.

Rooms 23 **Facilities** STV Wi-fi ⬧ 9 **Conf** Class 80 Board 30 Thtr 100 **Parking** 50 **Notes** Civ Wed

LLANRWST — Map 14 SH86
Conwy

See also Betws-y-Coed

Maenan Abbey
★★★ 77% HOTEL

☎ 01492 660247
Maenan LL26 0UL
e-mail: reservations@manab.co.uk
dir: 3m N on A470

Set in its own spacious grounds, this privately owned hotel was built as an abbey in 1850 on the site of a 13th-century monastery. It is now a popular venue for weddings as the grounds and magnificent galleried staircase make ideal settings for photographs. Bedrooms include a large suite and are equipped with modern facilities. Meals are served in the bar and restaurant.

Rooms 14 (3 fmly) (4 smoking) **Facilities** Wi-fi Fishing Guided mountain walks Xmas New Year **Conf** Class 30 Board 30 Thtr 50 **Parking** 60 **Notes** Civ Wed 55

LLANTRISANT — Map 9 ST39
Monmouthshire

Premier Inn Llantrisant

BUDGET HOTEL

☎ 0871 527 8640
Gwaun Elai, Magden Park CF72 8LL
web: www.premierinn.com
dir: M4 junct 34, A4119 towards Llantrisant & Rhondda. At 1st rdbt take 2nd exit. At 2nd rdbt take 1st exit

High quality, budget accommodation ideal for both families and business travellers. Spacious, en suite bedrooms feature tea and coffee making facilities, and Freeview TV in most hotels. Internet access and Wi-fi are available for a small fee. The adjacent family restaurant features a wide and varied menu. See also the Hotel Groups pages.

Rooms 51

LLANWDDYN — Map 15 SJ01
Powys

Lake Vyrnwy Hotel & Spa
★★★★ 76% ⊛
COUNTRY HOUSE HOTEL

☎ 01691 870692
Lake Vyrnwy SY10 0LY
e-mail: info@lakevyrnwyhotel.co.uk
web: www.lakevyrnwy.com
dir: On A4393, 200yds past dam, sharp right into drive

This elegant Victorian country-house hotel lies in 26,000 acres of woodland above Lake Vyrnwy, and provides a wide range of bedrooms, most with superb views and many with four-poster beds and balconies. Extensive public rooms retain many period features, and informal dining is available in the popular Tower Tavern. Relaxing and rejuvenating treatments are a feature of the stylish health spa.

Rooms 52 (12 fmly) **S** £100-£200; **D** £125-£225 (incl. bkfst)* **Facilities** Spa STV FTV Wi-fi ⬧ ⬧ Gym Archery Birdwatching Canoeing Kayaking Clay shooting Sailing Fly fishing Cycling Xmas New Year **Conf** Class 80 Board 60 Thtr 200 **Services** Lift **Parking** 70 **Notes** LB Civ Wed 200

LLANWRTYD WELLS — Map 9 SN84
Powys

Carlton Riverside
⊛ ⊛ RESTAURANT WITH ROOMS

☎ 01591 610248
Irfon Crescent LD5 4SP
e-mail: info@carltonriverside.com
dir: In town centre beside bridge

Guests become part of the family at this character property, set beside the river in Wales's smallest town. Carlton Riverside offers award-winning cuisine which Mary Ann Gilchrist produces using the very best of local ingredients. The set menu is complemented by a well-chosen wine list and dinner is served in the stylish restaurant which offers a memorable blend of traditional comfort, modern design and river views. Four comfortable bedrooms have tasteful combinations of antique and contemporary furniture, along with welcome personal touches.

Rooms 4

Lasswade Country House
⊛ ⊛ RESTAURANT WITH ROOMS

☎ 01591 610515
Station Rd LD5 4RW
e-mail: info@lasswadehotel.co.uk
dir: Exit A483 into Irfon Terrace, right into Station Rd, 350yds on right

This friendly establishment on the edge of the town has impressive views over the countryside. Bedrooms are comfortably furnished and well equipped, while the public areas consist of a tastefully decorated lounge, an elegant restaurant with a bar, and an airy conservatory which looks towards the neighbouring hills. The kitchen utilises fresh, local produce to provide an enjoyable dining experience.

Rooms 8

L

L

LLYSWEN
Powys
Map 9 SO13

Llangoed Hall

★★★★ 85% ◎◎ COUNTRY HOUSE HOTEL

☎ 01874 754525
LD3 0YP
e-mail: drayson.kohli@llangoedhall.co.uk

Set against the stunning backdrop of the Black Mountains and the Wye Valley, this imposing country house is a haven of peace and quiet. The interior is no less impressive, with a noteworthy art collection complementing the many antiques in day rooms and bedrooms. Comfortable, spacious bedrooms and suites are matched by equally inviting lounges.

Rooms 23 ♠ **S** fr £95; **D** £190-£295 (incl. bkfst)* **Facilities** FTV Wi-fi ↳ ⍦ Snooker table Xmas New Year **Conf** Class 30 Board 30 Thtr 80 **Parking** 50 **Notes** LB ⊗ Civ Wed 80

MAESYCWMMER
Caerphilly
Map 9 ST19

Bryn Meadows Golf, Hotel & Spa

★★★★ 80% HOTEL

☎ 01495 225590
CF82 7SN
e-mail: reception@brynmeadows.co.uk
web: www.brynmeadows.com
dir: M4 junct 28, A467 signed Brynmawr, 10m to Newbridge. Take A472 signed Ystrad Mynach. Hotel off Crown rdbt signed 'golf course'. (NB for Sat Nav use NP12 2BR)

Surrounded by its own mature parkland and 18-hole golf course, this impressive hotel, golf, leisure and function complex provides a range of high quality, well-equipped bedrooms; several have their own balconies or patio areas. The attractive public areas include a pleasant restaurant which, like many of the bedrooms, enjoys striking views of the golf course and beyond. There are impressive function facilities and the hotel is a popular venue for weddings.

Rooms 42 (4 fmly) (21 GF) **S** £60-£150; **D** £75-£165 (incl. bkfst)* **Facilities** Spa FTV Wi-fi ⍦ supervised ⌀ 18 Putt green Gym Sauna Steam room Aromatherapy suite Xmas New Year **Conf** Class 70 Board 60 Thtr 120 Del from £120 to £160 **Services** Air con **Parking** 120 **Notes** LB ⊗ Civ Wed 250

MANORBIER
Pembrokeshire
Map 8 SS09

Castlemead

RESTAURANT WITH ROOMS

☎ 01834 871358
SA70 7TA
e-mail: castlemeadhotel@aol.com
web: www.castlemeadhotel.com
dir: A4139 towards Pembroke, B4585 into village, follow signs to beach & castle, establishment on left

Benefiting from a superb location with spectacular views of the bay, the Norman church and Manorbier Castle, this family-run business is friendly and welcoming. Bedrooms, which include some in a converted former coach house at ground floor level, are generally quite spacious and have modern facilities. Public areas include a sea-view residents' lounge and a restaurant accessed by stairs, which is available to non-residents, along with a cosy bar. There are extensive gardens to the rear of the property.

Rooms 8 (3 annexe) (2 fmly)

MERTHYR TYDFIL
Merthyr Tydfil
Map 9 SO00

Premier Inn Merthyr Tydfil

BUDGET HOTEL

☎ 0871 527 8768
Pentrebach CF48 4BB
web: www.premierinn.com
dir: M4 junct 32, A470 to Merthyr Tydfil. At rdbt right to Pentrebach (A4060). At next rdbt 3rd exit signed Abergavenny, (dual carriageway). Double back at next rdbt by Pentrebach Co-op onto A4060 towards Pentrebach. Left after layby, hotel adjacent to Pentrebach House

High quality, budget accommodation ideal for both families and business travellers. Spacious, en suite bedrooms feature tea and coffee making facilities, and Freeview TV in most hotels. Internet access and Wi-fi are available for a small fee. The adjacent family restaurant features a wide and varied menu. See also the Hotel Groups pages.

Rooms 40

MISKIN
Rhondda Cynon Taff
Map 9 ST08

Miskin Manor Country Hotel

★★★★ 75% ◎◎ COUNTRY HOUSE HOTEL

☎ 01443 224204
Pendoylan Rd CF72 8ND
e-mail: reservations@miskin-manor.co.uk
web: www.miskin-manor.co.uk
dir: M4 junct 34, A4119, signed Llantrisant, hotel 300yds on left

This historic manor house is peacefully located in 22-acre grounds, yet is only minutes away from the M4. Bedrooms are furnished to a high standard and include some located in converted stables and cottages. Public areas are spacious and comfortable and include a variety of function rooms. The relaxed atmosphere and the surroundings ensure this hotel remains popular for wedding functions as well as with business guests. There is a separate modern health and fitness centre which includes a gym, sauna, steam room and swimming pool.

Rooms 43 (9 annexe) (2 fmly) (7 GF) **Facilities** FTV Wi-fi ⍟ ⍦ Gym **Conf** Class 80 Board 65 Thtr 160 **Parking** 200 **Notes** Civ Wed 120

MOLD
Flintshire
Map 15 SJ26

Beaufort Park Hotel

★★★ 77% HOTEL

☎ 01352 758646
Alltami Rd, New Brighton CH7 6RQ
e-mail: info@beaufortparkhotel.co.uk
web: www.beaufortparkhotel.co.uk
dir: A55, A494, through Alltami lights, over mini rdbt by petrol station towards Mold, A5119. Hotel 100yds on right

This large, modern hotel is conveniently located a short drive from the North Wales Expressway and offers various styles of spacious accommodation. There are extensive public areas, and several meeting and function rooms are available. There is a wide choice of meals in the formal restaurant and in the popular Arches bar.

Rooms 106 (8 fmly) (32 GF) **Facilities** FTV Wi-fi Squash ♫ Xmas New Year **Conf** Class 120 Board 120 Thtr 250 Del from £100 to £120 **Parking** 200 **Notes** Civ Wed 250

Save on hotels. Book at **theAA.com/hotel**

LLY – NEW 611 WALES

NARBERTH
Pembrokeshire   Map 8 SN11

The Grove
◉◉ RESTAURANT WITH ROOMS

☎ 01834 860915
Molleston SA67 8BX
e-mail: info@thegrove-narberth.co.uk
web: www.thegrove-narberth.co.uk
dir: A48 to Carmarthen, then A40 to Haverfordwest. At A478 rdbt 1st exit to Narberth, through town towards Tenby. At bottom of hill right, 1m, The Grove on right

The Grove is an elegant 18th-century country house set on a hillside in 24 acres of rolling countryside. The owners have lovingly restored this building with care, combining period features with excellent modern decor. There are bedrooms in the main house and additional rooms in separate buildings; all are appointed with quality and comfort. Some bedrooms are on the ground floor, and most have fantastic views out over the Preseli Hills. There are two sumptuous lounge areas, one with an open fire and a small bar, and two separate dining rooms that offer award-winning cuisine. Self-catering cottages are available.

Rooms 20 (6 annexe) (3 fmly)

NEATH
Neath Port Talbot   Map 9 SS79

Castle Hotel
★★★ 73% HOTEL

☎ 01639 641119
The Parade SA11 1RB
e-mail: info@castlehotelneath.co.uk
web: www.castlehotelneath.co.uk
dir: M4 junct 43, follow signs for Neath, 500yds past rail station, hotel on right. Car park on left in 50yds

Situated in the town centre, this Georgian property, once a coaching inn, has a wealth of history and much character. Lord Nelson and Lady Hamilton are reputed to have stayed here, and it is where the Welsh Rugby Union was founded in 1881. The hotel provides well-equipped accommodation and pleasant public areas. Bedrooms include family bedded rooms and one with a four-poster. Green's restaurant provides a good range of dishes at both lunch and dinner. Function and meeting rooms are available.

Rooms 29 (3 fmly) (14 smoking) **S** £40-£100; **D** £45-£110 **Facilities** STV FTV Wi-fi ♫ Xmas New Year **Conf** Class 75 Board 50 Thtr 160 Del from £70 to £95 **Parking** 26 **Notes** LB ⊗ Civ Wed 120

NEWCASTLE EMLYN
Carmarthenshire   Map 8 SN34

Gwesty'r Emlyn Hotel
★★★ 79% HOTEL

☎ 01239 710317
Bridge St SA38 9DU
e-mail: reception@gwestyremlynhotel.co.uk
web: www.gwestyremlynhotel.co.uk
dir: In town centre

This hotel, in the heart of a busy market town, dates back some 300 years. Appointed to a high standard, the stylish and comfortable bedrooms have luxury bathrooms. The public areas comprise a choice of bars, a cosy seating area and a modern restaurant offering dishes created from good, locally sourced ingredients. There is a gym, sauna and spa pool plus a large function suite for weddings and parties.

Rooms 24 (3 fmly) (1 GF) **S** £75-£95; **D** £85-£135 (incl. bkfst)* **Facilities** FTV Wi-fi Gym Sauna Splash pool Xmas New Year **Conf** Class 100 Board 50 Thtr 150 Del from £90 to £155* **Parking** 25 **Notes** LB ⊗ Civ Wed

NEWPORT
Newport   Map 9 ST38

See also Cwmbran

The Celtic Manor Resort
★★★★★ 85% ◉◉◉ HOTEL

☎ 01633 413000
Coldra Woods NP18 1HQ
e-mail: bookings@celtic-manor.com
web: www.celtic-manor.com
dir: M4 junct 24, take B4237 towards Newport. Hotel 1st on right

This hotel is in the outstanding Celtic Manor Resort. Here there are three challenging golf courses including the Twenty Ten Course specifically designed for the 2010 Ryder Cup, a huge convention centre, superb leisure clubs and two hotels. This hotel has excellent bedrooms, including suites and two Presidential suites, offering good space and comfort; stylish extensive public areas are set around a spectacular atrium lobby that includes several eating options; Terry M is the award-winning, fine dining restaurant. There is a choice of shops and boutiques as well.

Rooms 400 (34 fmly) **S** £230-£1500; **D** £230-£1500 (incl. bkfst) **Facilities** Spa STV FTV Wi-fi ♪ ♀ ⅃ 54 ♨ Putt green Gym Golf Academy Clay pigeon shooting Mountain bike trails Games room ♫ Xmas New Year Child facilities **Conf** Class 150 Board 60 Thtr 1200 **Services** Lift Air con **Parking** 1300 **Notes** LB ⊗ Civ Wed 100

The Manor House
★★★★ 74% ◉ HOTEL

☎ 01633 413000
The Celtic Manor Resort, Coldra Woods NP18 1HQ
e-mail: bookings@celtic-manor.com
web: www.celtic-manor.com
dir: M4 junct 24, B4237 towards Newport. Hotel 1st on right

Part of the complex of the Celtic Manor Resort (see previous entry), this hotel, built in the 19th century, offers country house charm combined with modern comforts. Sitting in beautiful landscaped gardens it has traditionally styled bedrooms, three with four-posters. Several eating options are available both at Manor House and at the Celtic Manor Resort, where guests have access to all the hotel and leisure facilities; three challenging golf courses and superb leisure clubs among them.

Rooms 69 **S** fr £92; **D** fr £111 (incl. bkfst)* **Facilities** Spa STV FTV Wi-fi ♀ supervised ⅃ 54 (at Celtic Manor Resort) ♨ Putt green Fishing Gym ♫ Xmas New Year **Conf** Class 80 Thtr 200 **Services** Lift Air con **Notes** LB ⊗ Civ Wed

NEWPORT *continued*

Holiday Inn Newport
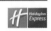
★★★ 70% HOTEL

☎ 01633 412777
The Coldra NP6 2YG
web: www.holidayinn.co.uk
dir: M4 junct 24, follow signs for B4237 towards Newport. Hotel 200yds on left

A modern, purpose-built hotel, in a very convenient location near to the M4, that caters equally well for leisure and business guests. The public areas include Harpers, an informal restaurant, a small leisure complex and a business centre.

Rooms 119 (5 fmly) (22 smoking) ⚭ **S** £48–£185; **D** £48–£185 (incl. bkfst)* **Facilities** STV Wi-fi Ⓢ Gym ♫ Xmas New Year **Conf** Class 250 Board 200 Thtr 500 Del from £124 to £132* **Services** Air con **Parking** 300 **Notes** LB ⊗ Civ Wed 400

Holiday Inn Express Newport

BUDGET HOTEL

☎ 01633 819850
Lakeside Dr, Coedkernew NP10 8BB
e-mail: gm@expressnewport.co.uk
web: www.hiexpress.com/exnewport
dir: M4 junct 28 at junct take St Mellons/Castleton exit. Remain in right lane, at lights turn right. Hotel on left

A modern hotel ideal for families and business travellers. Fresh and uncomplicated, the spacious rooms include Sky TV, power shower and tea and coffee-making facilities. Continental buffet breakfast is included in the room rate; other meals may be taken at the nearby family pub or restaurant. See also the Hotel Groups pages.

Rooms 125 (70 fmly) (34 GF) **Conf** Class 15 Board 15 Thtr 50

Premier Inn Newport South Wales
BUDGET HOTEL

☎ 0871 527 8814
Coldra Junction, Chepstow Rd, Langstone NP18 2NX
web: www.premierinn.com
dir: M4 junct 24, A48 to Langstone, at next rdbt return towards junct 24. Hotel 50mtrs on left

High quality, budget accommodation ideal for both families and business travellers. Spacious, en suite bedrooms feature tea and coffee making facilities, and Freeview TV in most hotels. Internet access and Wi-fi are available for a small fee. The adjacent

family restaurant features a wide and varied menu. See also the Hotel Groups pages.

Rooms 63

NEWPORT   Map 8 SN03
Pembrokeshire

Llysmeddyg
 RESTAURANT WITH ROOMS

☎ 01239 820008
East St SA42 0SY
e-mail: contact@llysmeddyg.com
dir: On A487 in centre of town

Llysmeddyg is a Georgian townhouse offering a blend of old and new, with elegant furnishings, deep sofas and a welcoming fire. The owners of this property employed local craftsmen to create a lovely interior that has an eclectic style. The focus of the quality restaurant menu is the use of fresh, seasonal, locally sourced ingredients. The spacious bedrooms are comfortable and contemporary in design; bathrooms vary in style.

Rooms 8 (3 annexe) (3 fmly)

NORTHOP HALL   Map 15 SJ26
Flintshire

Holiday Inn A55 Chester West
★★★ 74% HOTEL

☎ 01244 550011
Westbound A55, Mold Nr Chester CH7 6HB
e-mail: bookings@holidayinnchesterwest.co.uk
web: www.holidayinnchesterwest.co.uk
dir: M6 junct 20, M56 to Queensferry, follow signs for A55/Conwy. Hotel 500yds past A494 slip road

This modern hotel is ideally situated to explore north Wales, and offers comfortable accommodation and warm hospitality. Facilities include a well-equipped gym. Hearty meals are served in the conservatory restaurant.

Rooms 81 (29 fmly) (31 GF) (5 smoking) **S** £39–£74; **D** £39–£74* **Facilities** STV Wi-fi ⓗ HL Gym New Year **Conf** Class 130 Board 55 Thtr 220 Del from £99 to £105* **Services** Lift Air con **Parking** 200 **Notes** LB Closed 24-25 Dec Civ Wed 100

PARKMILL (NEAR SWANSEA)   Map 8 SS58
Swansea

Maes-Yr-Haf Restaurant with Rooms
◉ RESTAURANT WITH ROOMS

☎ 01792 371000
SA3 2EH
e-mail: enquiries@maes-yr-haf.com
dir: A4118 W from Swansea

Set in the peaceful location on The Gower in the small village of Parkmill, this property is well situated for easy access to Swansea and the coast. It offers contemporary, individually styled bedrooms with a very good range of guest extras, where comfort is the key. Bathrooms have both bath and shower. The food is created from high quality, locally sourced ingredients; dinner is a highlight, served in the modern restaurant, and breakfast provides a very good start to the day.

Rooms 5

PEMBROKE   Map 8 SM90
Pembrokeshire

Best Western Lamphey Court Hotel & Spa

★★★★ 73% ◉ HOTEL

☎ 01646 672273
Lamphey SA71 5NT
e-mail: info@lampheycourt.co.uk
web: www.lampheycourt.co.uk
dir: A477 to Pembroke. Left at Milton for Lamphey, hotel on right

This Georgian mansion, on an elevated site, is set in attractive countryside and is perfectly situated for exploring the stunning Pembrokeshire coast, the beaches and the Preseli Hills. Well-appointed bedrooms and family suites are situated in a converted coach house within the grounds. The elegant public areas include both formal and informal dining rooms that feature dishes inspired by the local produce. Leisure facilities include a state-of-the-art spa with a swimming pool, gym, sauna, treatment rooms and much more.

Save on hotels. Book at **theAA.com/hotel**

NEW – PON 613 WALES

Best Western Lamphey Court Hotel & Spa

Rooms 38 (12 annexe) (7 fmly) (6 GF) **Facilities** Spa FTV Wi-fi 🐾 🌊 Gym Yacht charter Xmas New Year **Conf** Class 40 Board 30 Thtr 60 **Parking** 50 **Notes** Civ Wed 80

Lamphey Hall Hotel

★★★ 77% HOTEL

☎ 01646 672394 & 07791 896191
Lamphey SA71 5NR
e-mail: andrewjones1990@aol.com
dir: From Carmarthen A40 to St Clears. Follow signs for A477, left at Milton

Set in a delightful village, this very friendly, privately owned and efficiently run hotel offers an ideal base from which to explore the surrounding countryside.

Bedrooms are well equipped, comfortably furnished and include family rooms and ground floor rooms. Diners have a choice of three restaurant areas offering an extensive range of dishes. There is also a small lounge, a bar and attractive gardens.

Rooms 10 (1 fmly) (2 GF) **S** £55-£59.50; **D** £80-£89.50 (incl. bkfst) **Facilities** FTV Wi-fi **Parking** 32

PONTYPOOL Map 9 SO20
Torfaen

Premier Inn Pontypool

BUDGET HOTEL

☎ 0871 527 8890
Tyr'felin, Lower Mill Field NP4 0RH
web: www.premierinn.com
dir: At junct of A4042 & A472

High quality, budget accommodation ideal for both families and business travellers. Spacious, en suite bedrooms feature tea and coffee making facilities, and Freeview TV in most hotels. Internet access and Wi-fi are available for a small fee. The adjacent family restaurant features a wide and varied menu. See also the Hotel Groups pages.

Rooms 49

PONTYPRIDD Map 9 ST08
Rhondda Cynon Taff

Llechwen Hall Hotel

★★★ 74% ⚜ COUNTRY HOUSE HOTEL

☎ 01443 742050 & 743020
Llanfabon CF37 4HP
e-mail: enquiries@llechwenhall.co.uk
dir: A470 N towards Merthyr Tydfil. At large rdbt take 3rd exit. At mini rdbt take 3rd exit, hotel signed 0.5m on left

Set on top of a hill with a stunning approach, this country house hotel has served many purposes in its 200-year-old history including a private school and a magistrates' court. The spacious, individually

continued

P

PONTYPRIDD *continued*

decorated bedrooms are well equipped; some are situated in the separate coach house nearby. There are ground-floor, twin, double and family bedrooms on offer. The Victorian-style public areas are attractively appointed and the hotel is a popular venue for weddings.

Llechwen Hall Hotel

Rooms 20 (8 annexe) (6 fmly) (4 GF) **Facilities** FTV Wi-fi ♨ Xmas New Year **Conf** Class 80 Board 40 Thtr 200 **Parking** 150 **Notes** Civ Wed 80

See advert on page 613

PORTHCAWL	**Map 9 SS87**
Bridgend	

Seabank Hotel

★★ 64% HOTEL

☎ 01656 782261
Esplanade CF36 3LU
e-mail: seabank@alfatravel.co.uk
web: www.leisureplex.co.uk
dir: M4 junct 37, A4229 to Porthcawl seafront

This large hotel stands in a prime location on the promenade of this seaside town, with panoramic sea views from the majority of bedrooms. Porthcawl has several beaches and coastal walks; the world famous Royal Porthcawl golf course is within easy distance and the cities of Swansea and Cardiff only a short drive. The spacious bedrooms are all en suite and there is a lift which serves most bedrooms. There is a spacious restaurant, a lounge bar and a choice of lounges with sea views. The hotel is a popular venue for coach tour parties, as well as weddings and conferences. There is ample parking around the hotel.

Rooms 89 (5 GF) ✧ **S** £37-£53; **D** £60-£92 (incl. bkfst)* **Facilities** STV ♫ Xmas New Year **Services** Lift **Parking** 100 **Notes** ⊗ Closed 2 Jan-10 Feb

---

PORTHMADOG	**Map 14 SH53**
Gwynedd	

Royal Sportsman Hotel

★★★ 82% ◉◉ HOTEL

☎ 01766 512015
131 High St LL49 9HB
e-mail: enquiries@royalsportsman.co.uk
dir: At rdbt junct of A497 & A487

Ideally located in the centre of Porthmadog, this former coaching inn dates from the Victorian era and is a friendly, privately owned and personally run hotel. Bedrooms are tastefully decorated and well equipped, and some are in an annexe close to the hotel. There is a large comfortable lounge and a wide range of meals is served in the bar or restaurant.

Rooms 28 (9 annexe) (7 fmly) (9 GF) ✧ **S** £62-£86; **D** £88-£102* **Facilities** STV FTV Wi-fi Xmas New Year **Conf** Class 50 Board 30 Thtr 50 **Parking** 17

PORTMEIRION	**Map 14 SH53**
Gwynedd	

The Hotel Portmeirion

WELSH
RAREBITS
*Hotels of
Distinction*

★★★★ 79% ◉◉ HOTEL

☎ 01766 770000
LL48 6ET
e-mail: hotel@portmeirion-village.com
web: www.portmeirion-village.com
dir: 2m W, Portmeirion village is S off A487

Saved from dereliction in the 1920s by Clough Williams-Ellis, the elegant Hotel Portmeirion enjoys one of the finest settings in Wales, located beneath the wooded slopes of the village, overlooking the sandy estuary towards Snowdonia. Many bedrooms have private sitting rooms and balconies with spectacular views. The staff, mostly Welsh-speaking, provide a good mix of warm hospitality and efficient service.

Rooms 42 (28 annexe) (4 fmly) ✧ **S** £119-£199; **D** £159-£250 (incl. bkfst)* **Facilities** Spa STV FTV Wi-fi ♨ ⌇ ☃ Xmas New Year **Conf** Class 40 Board 30 Thtr 100 **Services** Lift **Parking** 40 **Notes** LB ⊗ Civ Wed 130

Castell Deudraeth

WELSH
RAREBITS
*Hotels of
Distinction*

★★★★ 77% ◉ HOTEL

☎ 01766 770000
LL48 6EN
e-mail: castell@portmeirion-village.com
web: www.portmeirion-village.com
dir: Exit A4212 for Trawsfynydd/Porthmadog. 1.5m beyond Penrhyndeudraeth, hotel on right

A castellated mansion that overlooks Snowdonia and the famous Italianate village featured in the 1960's cult series *The Prisoner*. An original concept, Castell Deudraeth combines traditional materials, such as oak and slate, with state-of-the-art technology and design. Dynamically styled bedrooms boast underfloor heating, real-flame gas fires, wide-screen TVs with DVDs and cinema surround-sound. The brasserie-themed dining room provides an informal option at dinner.

Rooms 11 (5 fmly) **Facilities** Spa STV FTV Wi-fi ♨ ⌇ ☃ Xmas New Year **Conf** Class 18 Board 25 Thtr 30 **Services** Lift **Parking** 30 **Notes** ⊗ Civ Wed 30

PORT TALBOT	**Map 9 SS78**
Neath Port Talbot	

Best Western Aberavon Beach Hotel

★★★ 80% HOTEL

☎ 01639 884949
Neath SA12 6QP
e-mail: sales@aberavonbeach.com
web: www.aberavonbeachhotel.com
dir: M4 junct 41, A48 & follow signs for Aberavon Beach & Hollywood Park

This friendly, purpose-built hotel enjoys a prominent position on the seafront overlooking Swansea Bay. Bedrooms, many with sea views, are comfortably appointed and thoughtfully equipped. Public areas include an all-weather leisure suite with swimming pool, open-plan bar and restaurant plus a choice of function rooms.

Rooms 52 (6 fmly) ✧ **S** £60-£80; **D** £65-£95 (incl. bkfst) **Facilities** FTV Wi-fi ☃ Sauna ♫ Xmas New Year **Conf** Class 200 Board 100 Thtr 300 Del from £95 to £120 **Services** Lift **Parking** 150 **Notes** LB Civ Wed 300

Save on hotels. Book at **theAA.com/hotel**

PON – ROC 615 WALES

Premier Inn Port Talbot

BUDGET HOTEL

☎ 0871 527 8896
Baglan Rd, Baglan SA12 8ES
web: www.premierinn.com
dir: M4 junct 41 W'bound. Hotel just off 4th exit at
rdbt. M4 junct 42 E'bound, left towards Port Talbot.
Take 2nd exit off 2nd rdbt

High quality, budget accommodation ideal for both
families and business travellers. Spacious, en suite
bedrooms feature tea and coffee making facilities,
and Freeview TV in most hotels. Internet access and
Wi-fi are available for a small fee. The adjacent
family restaurant features a wide and varied menu.
See also the Hotel Groups pages.

Rooms 42

RAGLAN
Monmouthshire
Map 9 SO40

The Beaufort Arms Coaching Inn & Brasserie

WELSH RAREBITS
Hotels of Distinction

★★★ 77% ◉ HOTEL

☎ 01291 690412
High St NP15 2DY
e-mail: enquiries@beaufortraglan.co.uk
web: www.beaufortraglan.co.uk
dir: M4 junct 24, A449/A40 junct Monmouth/
Abergavenny, 0.5m into village opposite church

This friendly, family-run village inn dating back to the
15th century has historic links with nearby Raglan
Castle. The bright, stylish and beautifully appointed
bedrooms in the main house are suitably equipped for
both tourists and business guests. Food is served in
either The Brasserie restaurant or traditional lounge,
and both offer a relaxed service with an enjoyable
selection of carefully prepared dishes.

Rooms 15 (5 annexe) (1 fmly) (5 GF) **Facilities** Wi-fi
Use of facilities at golf club in village **Conf** Class 60
Board 30 Thtr 120 **Parking** 30 **Notes** ⊗ RS 25-26
Dec

REYNOLDSTON
Swansea
Map 8 SS48

INSPECTORS' CHOICE

Fairyhill

◉ ◉ RESTAURANT WITH ROOMS

☎ 01792 390139
SA3 1BS
e-mail: postbox@fairyhill.net
web: www.fairyhill.net
dir: M4 junct 47, A483, at next rdbt right onto A484.
At Gowerton take B4295 for 10m

Peace and tranquillity are never far away at this
charming Georgian mansion set in the heart of the
beautiful Gower peninsula. Bedrooms are furnished
with care and are filled with many thoughtful
extras. There is also a range of comfortable seating
areas, with crackling log fires, to choose from, and
the smart restaurant offers menus based on local
produce and complemented by an excellent wine
list.

Rooms 8

RHUDDLAN
Denbighshire
Map 15 SJ07

Premier Inn Rhuddlan

BUDGET HOTEL

☎ 0871 527 8932
Castle View Retail Park, Marsh Rd LL18 5UA
web: www.premierinn.com
dir: A55 junct 27, A525 signed Rhyl. At next rdbt 3rd
exit into Station Rd. Next left into Marsh Rd. Hotel on
left

High quality, budget accommodation ideal for both
families and business travellers. Spacious, en suite
bedrooms feature tea and coffee making facilities,
and Freeview TV in most hotels. Internet access and
Wi-fi are available for a small fee. The adjacent
family restaurant features a wide and varied menu.
See also the Hotel Groups pages.

Rooms 44

RHYL
Denbighshire
Map 14 SJ08

Barratt's at Ty'n Rhyl

◉ ◉ RESTAURANT WITH ROOMS

☎ 01745 344138 & 0773 095 4994
Ty'n Rhyl, 167 Vale Rd LL18 2PH
e-mail: ebarratt5@aol.com
dir: A55 onto A525 to Rhyl, pass Sainsburys & B&Q,
pass Roger Jones on left, 50yds on right

This delightful 16th-century house lies in a secluded
location surrounded by attractive gardens. The quality
of the food reflects the skill of the owner-chef. Public
areas are smartly furnished and include a panelled
lounge, cosy library and an attractive conservatory.
Bedrooms are comfortable and equipped with lots of
thoughtful extras.

Rooms 3

ROCKFIELD
Monmouthshire
Map 9 SO41

The Stonemill & Steppes Farm Cottages

◉ ◉ RESTAURANT WITH ROOMS

☎ 01600 775424
NP25 5SW
e-mail: bookings@thestonemill.co.uk
dir: A48 to Monmouth, take B4233 to Rockfield. 2.6m

Located in a small hamlet just west of Monmouth,
close to the Forest of Dean and the Wye Valley, this
operation offers six very well-appointed cottages. The
comfortable rooms (for self-catering or on a B&B
basis) are architect designed and has been lovingly
restored to retain many original features. In a
separate, converted 16th-century barn is Stonemill
Restaurant with oak beams, vaulted ceilings and an
old cider press. Breakfast is served in the cottages on
request. This establishment's location proves handy
for golfers with a choice of many courses in the area.

Rooms 6 (6 fmly)

R

ROSSETT
Wrexham — Map 15 SJ35

Best Western Llyndir Hall Hotel

★★★ 81% HOTEL

☎ 01244 571648
Llyndir Ln LL12 0AY
e-mail: llyndirhallhotel@feathers.uk.com
dir: 5m S of Chester on B5445 follow Pulford signs

Located on the English/Welsh border within easy reach of Chester and Wrexham, this elegant manor house lies in several acres of mature grounds. The hotel is popular with both business and leisure guests, and facilities include conference rooms, an impressive leisure centre, a choice of comfortable lounges and a brasserie-style restaurant.

Rooms 48 (3 fmly) (17 GF) S £49-£139; D £49-£149* **Facilities** Spa FTV Wi-fi HL supervised Gym Beauty salon Sauna Xmas New Year **Conf** Class 60 Board 40 Thtr 120 Del from £119 to £149 **Parking** 80 **Notes** LB Civ Wed 120

ST ASAPH
Denbighshire — Map 15 SJ07

The Oriel
★★★★ 74% HOTEL

☎ 01745 582716
Upper Denbigh Rd LL17 0LW
e-mail: mail@theorielhotel.com
web: www.theorielhotel.com
dir: A55 onto A525, right at cathedral, 1m on right

Set in several acres of mature grounds south of St Asaph, Oriel House offers generally spacious, well-equipped bedrooms and has a friendly and hospitable staff. The Terrace restaurant serves imaginative food with an emphasis on local produce. Extensive function facilities cater for business meetings and weddings, and the leisure club is available to guests.

Rooms 33 (3 fmly) (13 GF) **Facilities** Spa STV FTV Wi-fi Gym Steam room Sauna Xmas New Year **Conf** Class 100 Board 50 Thtr 220 **Parking** 200 **Notes** Civ Wed 200

ST DAVIDS
Pembrokeshire — Map 8 SM72

Warpool Court Hotel
WELSH RAREBITS
Hotels of Distinction

★★★ 83% ◉ ◉
COUNTRY HOUSE HOTEL

☎ 01437 720300
SA62 6BN
e-mail: info@warpoolcourthotel.com
web: www.warpoolcourthotel.com
dir: At Cross Square left by The Bishops Restaurant (Goat St). Pass Farmers Arms pub, left in 400mtrs, follow hotel signs, entrance on right

Originally the cathedral choir school, this hotel is set in landscaped gardens looking out to sea and is within easy walking distance of the Pembrokeshire Coastal Path. The lounges are spacious and comfortable, and the bedrooms are well furnished and equipped with modern facilities. The restaurant offers delightful cuisine.

Rooms 22 (3 fmly) S £115-£215; D £140-£340 (incl. bkfst)* **Facilities** Wi-fi Table tennis Pool table Xmas New Year **Conf** Class 25 Board 25 Thtr 40 **Parking** 100 **Notes** LB Closed Nov & 1st half Dec Civ Wed 120

SARN PARK MOTORWAY SERVICE AREA (M4)
Bridgend — Map 9 SS98

Days Inn Bridgend Cardiff - M4
Welcome Break
BUDGET HOTEL

☎ 01656 659218
Sarn Park Services, M4 Junct 36 CF32 9RW
e-mail: sarn.hotel@welcomebreak.co.uk
web: www.welcomebreak.co.uk
dir: M4 junct 36

This modern building offers accommodation in smart, spacious and well-equipped bedrooms, suitable for families and business travellers, and all with en suite bathrooms. Continental breakfast is available and other refreshments may be taken at the nearby family restaurant. See also the Hotel Groups pages.

Rooms 40 (39 fmly) (20 GF) (5 smoking)

SAUNDERSFOOT
Pembrokeshire — Map 8 SN10

St Brides Spa Hotel
WELSH RAREBITS
Hotels of Distinction

★★★★ 83% ◉ HOTEL

☎ 01834 812304
St Brides Hill SA69 9NH
e-mail: reservations@stbridesspahotel.com
web: www.stbridesspahotel.com
dir: A478 onto B4310 to Saundersfoot. Hotel above harbour

Set overlooking Carmarthen Bay this contemporary hotel and spa takes prime position. Many of the stylish, modern bedrooms enjoy sea views and have balconies; there are also luxury apartments in the grounds. The hotel is open plan and has excellent views of the bay from the split-level lounge areas. Fresh local seafood is a speciality in the modern airy restaurant which has a terrace for eating alfresco when the weather allows. The destination spa enjoys some of the very best views from the double treatment room and spa pool.

Rooms 46 (12 annexe) (6 fmly) (9 GF) S £125-£230; D £150-£360 (incl. bkfst)* **Facilities** Spa FTV Wi-fi Gym Thermal suite Hydrotherapy pool Xmas New Year **Conf** Class 40 Board 34 Thtr 100 Del from £170 to £200* **Services** Lift **Parking** 65 **Notes** LB Civ Wed 90

See advert on opposite page

Save on hotels. Book at **theAA.com/hotel**

ROS – SWA 617 WALES

INSPECTORS' CHOICE

The Bell at Skenfrith

◎ ◎ RESTAURANT WITH ROOMS

☎ 01600 750235
NP7 8UH
e-mail: enquiries@skenfrith.co.uk
web: www.skenfrith.co.uk
dir: On B4521 in Skenfrith, opposite castle

The Bell is a beautifully restored, 17th-century former coaching inn which still retains much original charm and character. It is peacefully situated on the banks of the Monnow, a tributary of the River Wye, and is ideally placed for exploring the numerous delights of the area. Natural materials have been used to create a relaxing atmosphere, while the bedrooms, which include full suites and rooms with four-poster beds, are stylish, luxurious and equipped with DVD players. The garden produces many of the fresh ingredients used in the kitchen where award-winning quality food is produced for relaxed dining in the welcoming restaurant.

Rooms 11 (2 fmly)

See also Port Talbot

Swansea Marriott Hotel

Marriott
HOTELS & RESORTS

★★★★ 80% HOTEL

☎ 0870 400 7282
The Maritime Quarter SA1 3SS
web: www.swanseamarriott.co.uk
dir: M4 junct 42, A483 to city centre past Leisure Centre, then follow signs to Maritime Quarter

Just opposite City Hall in the bustling Maritime Quarter, this busy hotel enjoys fantastic views over the bay and marina. The air-conditioned bedrooms are spacious and equipped with a range of extras. Public rooms include a popular leisure club with a gym, whirlpool, sauna and swimming pool, and The Bayside Grill restaurant which overlooks the marina. It is worth noting, however, that lounge seating is limited.

Rooms 119 (49 fmly) (11 GF) **Facilities** STV Wi-fi ⓢ Gym New Year **Conf** Class 120 Board 30 Thtr 300 **Services** Lift Air con **Parking** 122 **Notes** ⊗ Civ Wed 220

The Dragon Hotel

CLASSIC
BRITISH HOTELS

★★★★ 77% ◎ HOTEL

☎ 01792 657100 & 0870 4299 848
The Kingsway Circle SA1 5LS
e-mail: info@dragon-hotel.co.uk
web: www.dragon-hotel.co.uk
dir: A483 follow signs for city centre. After lights at Sainsbury's right onto The Strand then left. Hotel straight ahead

This privately owned hotel is located in the city centre and offers spacious modern accommodation with

well-equipped, comfortable bedrooms. There is a bar and lounge facility on the first floor along with the dining room for breakfast. On the ground floor, the Dragons Brasserie provides award-winning food from a vibrant continental menu for both residents and non-residents. The health and fitness club offers an excellent choice of facilities and there is a good range of conference rooms.

Rooms 106 (5 fmly) ⓟ **Facilities** STV Wi-fi ⓢ ⓢ supervised Gym Beauty therapist Xmas New Year **Conf** Class 120 Board 60 Thtr 230 **Services** Lift Air con **Parking** 52 **Notes** ⊗ Civ Wed 200

Holiday Inn Express Swansea - West

Holiday Inn Express

BUDGET HOTEL

☎ 01792 818700
Neath Rd, Llandarcy SA10 6JQ
e-mail: gm.swansea@expressholidayinn.co.uk
web: www.expressswansea.co.uk
dir: Off M4 junct 43

A modern hotel ideal for families and business travellers. Fresh and uncomplicated, the spacious rooms include Sky TV, power shower and tea and coffee-making facilities. Continental buffet breakfast is included in the room rate; other meals may be taken at the nearby family pub or restaurant. See also the Hotel Groups pages.

Rooms 91 (60 fmly) (18 GF) **Conf** Class 20 Board 16 Thtr 25

S

St BRIDES
spa hotel

SWANSEA continued

Premier Inn Swansea City Centre

BUDGET HOTEL

☎ 0871 527 9060
Salubrious Place, Wind St SA1 1EE
web: www.premierinn.com
dir: M4 junct 42, A483 towards the city centre. Pass Sainsburys on left, right into Salubrious Place, 2nd right, then 3rd exit at mini rdbt

High quality, budget accommodation ideal for both families and business travellers. Spacious, en suite bedrooms feature tea and coffee making facilities, and Freeview TV in most hotels. Internet access and Wi-fi are available for a small fee. The adjacent family restaurant features a wide and varied menu. See also the Hotel Groups pages.

Rooms 116

Premier Inn Swansea North

BUDGET HOTEL

☎ 0871 527 9062
Upper Forest Way, Morriston SA6 8WB
web: www.premierinn.com
dir: M4 junct 45, A4067 towards Swansea. In 0.5m at 2nd exit left into Clase Rd. Hotel 400yds on left

Rooms 40

Premier Inn Swansea Waterfront

BUDGET HOTEL

☎ 0871 577 9212
The Waterfront Development, Langdon Rd SA1 8PL
web: www.premierinn.com
dir: M4 junct 42, A483 towards Swansea/Abertawe (signed Fabian Way). Approx 4.5m. At 2nd lights, left into SA1 Waterfront development. At rdbt take 2nd exit into Langdon Rd. Hotel on left

Rooms 132

TENBY
Pembrokeshire   Map 8 SN10

Atlantic Hotel

★★★ 81% HOTEL

☎ 01834 842881
The Esplanade SA70 7DU
e-mail: enquiries@atlantic-hotel.uk.com
web: www.atlantic-hotel.uk.com
dir: A478 into Tenby, follow town centre signs (keep town walls on left) right at Esplanade, hotel on right

This privately owned and personally run, friendly hotel has an enviable position looking out over South Beach

towards Caldy Island. Bedrooms vary in size and style, but all are well equipped and tastefully appointed. The comfortable public areas include a choice of restaurants and, in fine weather guests can also enjoy the cliff-top gardens.

Rooms 42 (11 fmly) (4 GF) **S** £82-£93; **D** £114-£195 (incl. bkfst) **Facilities** FTV Wi-fi ⊗ Steam room Spa bath **Conf** Board 8 **Services** Lift **Parking** 25 **Notes** LB Closed early Dec-late Jan

Clarence House

★★ 64% HOTEL

☎ 01834 844371
Esplanade SA70 7DU
e-mail: clarencehotel@freeuk.com
web: www.clarencehotel-tenby.co.uk
dir: From South Parade (by town walls) into St Florence Parade & Esplanade

Owned by the same family for over 50 years, this hotel has superb views from its elevated position. Many of the bedrooms have sea views and all are comfortably furnished. The bar leads to a sheltered rose garden and a number of lounges. Entertainment is provided in high season, and this establishment is particularly popular with coach tour parties.

Rooms 76 (6 fmly) **Facilities** ♫ **Services** Lift **Notes** Closed 18-28 Dec

See advert on opposite page

TINTERN PARVA
Monmouthshire   Map 4 SO50

Best Western Royal George Hotel

★★★ 78% HOTEL

☎ 01291 689205
Wye Valley Rd NP16 6SF
e-mail: royalgeorgetintern@hotmail.com
web: www.bw-royalgeorgehotel.co.uk
dir: M48 junct 2, A466, 5m to Tintern, 2nd left

This privately owned and personally run hotel provides comfortable, spacious accommodation, including bedrooms with balconies overlooking the well-tended garden; there are also a number of ground-floor bedrooms. The public areas include a lounge bar and a large function room, and a varied and popular menu is available in either the bar or restaurant. This hotel is an ideal base for exploring the counties of Monmouthshire and Herefordshire.

Rooms 15 (14 annexe) (6 fmly) (10 GF) **S** £65-£100; **D** £75-£110 (incl. bkfst)* **Facilities** FTV Wi-fi ♂ Xmas New Year **Conf** Class 40 Board 30 Thtr 100 Del from £95 to £135 **Parking** 50 **Notes** LB Civ Wed 70

Tintern Abbey Hotel

★★★ 67% HOTEL

☎ 01291 680020
1 Monmouth Rd NP16 6SF
e-mail: abbeyhotel@live.com
dir: Opposite Tintern Abbey, off A466

Situated in the heart of the Wye Valley, this hotel offers many bedrooms that have views of Tintern Abbey. In addition to the main restaurant, a comfortable bar area is available for lighter dining options. Two function rooms are available and the hotel is a popular venue for weddings.

Rooms 22 (2 fmly) **Facilities** FTV Wi-fi Xmas New Year **Conf** Class 80 Board 40 Thtr 100 **Parking** 60 **Notes** Civ Wed 120

Save on hotels. Book at **theAA.com/hotel**

SWA – USK 619 **WALES**

TREARDDUR BAY
Isle of Anglesey

Map 14 SH27

Trearddur Bay Hotel

★★★ 82% HOTEL

☎ 01407 860301
LL65 2UN
e-mail: enquiries@trearddurbayhotel.co.uk
web: www.trearddurbayhotel.co.uk
dir: A55 junct 2, left, over 1st rdbt, left at 2nd rdbt,
left after approx 2m

This seaside hotel stands 100 yards from the Blue
Flag beach, offering stunning views of the bay. The
very comfortable bedrooms are well appointed and
have flat-screen TVs. Guests have a choice of dining
options, the more formal Bay Restaurant, or the Inn at
The Bay, which also has an outdoor area for summer
dining. Facilities include an indoor swimming pool
and a children's play area.

Rooms 42 (6 annexe) (6 fmly) (3 GF) ✆ **S** £60-£120;
D £80-£250 (incl. bkfst) **Facilities** FTV Wi-fi ↕ ☜
Conf Class 80 Board 60 Thtr 200 Del from £100 to
£180 **Parking** 200 **Notes** LB Civ Wed 140

USK
Monmouthshire

Map 9 SO30

Glen-yr-Afon House Hotel

★★★ 80% HOTEL

☎ 01291 672302 & 673202
Pontypool Rd NP15 1SY
e-mail: enquiries@glen-yr-afon.co.uk
web: www.glen-yr-afon.co.uk
dir: A472 through High St, over river bridge, follow to
right. Hotel 200yds on left

On the edge of this delightful old market town,
Glen-yr-Afon, a unique Victorian villa, offers all the
facilities expected of a modern hotel combined with
the warm atmosphere of a family home. Bedrooms are
furnished to a high standard and several overlook the
well-tended gardens. There is a choice of comfortable
sitting areas and a stylish and spacious banqueting
suite.

Rooms 28 (1 annexe) (2 fmly) ✆ **S** £99-£123;
D £136-£159 (incl. bkfst)* **Facilities** STV FTV Wi-fi ⟲
Complimentary access to Usk Tennis Club New Year
Conf Class 200 Board 30 Thtr 100 Del from £110 to
£140* **Services** Lift **Parking** 151 **Notes** LB
Civ Wed 150

The Three Salmons Hotel

★★★ 78% ◉◉ HOTEL

☎ 01291 672133
Bridge St NP15 1RY
e-mail: general@threesalmons.co.uk
dir: M4 junct 24, A449, 1st exit signed Usk. On
entering town, hotel on main road

A 17th-century coaching inn located in the centre of a
small market town with friendly, efficient staff who
help create a welcoming atmosphere. Many changes
have taken place these past years with quality and
comfort the key to any guest stay. The food in the
contemporary restaurant proves popular. Bedrooms
are comfortable and a good range of extras are
provided. There is a large function suite ideal for
weddings and parties. Parking is secure.

Rooms 24 (14 annexe) (3 fmly) (7 GF) **S** £80-£95;
D £90-£115 (incl. bkfst)* **Facilities** FTV Wi-fi
Conf Class 80 Board 40 Thtr 110 Del from £125 to
£150* **Parking** 25 **Notes** Civ Wed 100

Newbridge on Usk

◎◎ RESTAURANT WITH ROOMS

☎ 01633 451000 & 410262
Tredunnock NP15 1LY
e-mail: newbridgeonusk@celtic-manor.com
web: www.celtic-manor.com
dir: M4 junct 24, signed Newport, onto B4236. At Ship
Inn turn right, over mini-rdbt onto Llangybi/Usk road.
Turn right opposite Cwrt Bleddyn Hotel, signed
Tredunnock, through village & down hill

This cosy, gastro-pub is tucked away in a beautiful
village setting with the River Usk nearby. The well-
equipped bedrooms, in a separate building, provide
comfort and a good range of extras. Guests can eat at
rustic tables around the bar or in the upstairs dining
room where award-winning, seasonal food is served;
there is also a small private dining room. Breakfast is
one of the highlights of a stay with quality local
ingredients offered in abundance.

Rooms 6 (2 fmly)

U

WELSHPOOL — Map 15 SJ20
Powys

Royal Oak Hotel
WELSH RAREBITS
Hotels of Distinction

★★★ 77% HOTEL

☎ 01938 552217
The Cross SY21 7DG
e-mail: relax@royaloakhotel.info
web: www.royaloakhotel.info
dir: By lights at junct of A483 & A458

This traditional market town hotel dates back over 350 years. The public areas are furnished in a minimalist style that highlight the many retained period features, including exposed beams and open fires. Three different bedroom styles provide good comfort levels and imaginative food is served in the elegant Red Room or in the adjacent all-day café/bar.

Rooms 25 (3 fmly) **Facilities** FTV Wi-fi Xmas New Year **Conf** Class 60 Board 60 Thtr 150 **Parking** 19 **Notes** ⊗ Civ Wed

WHITEBROOK — Map 4 SO50
Monmouthshire

INSPECTORS' CHOICE

The Crown at Whitebrook
◉◉◉ RESTAURANT WITH ROOMS

☎ 01600 860254
NP25 4TX
e-mail: info@crownatwhitebrook.co.uk
dir: 4m from Monmouth on B4293, left at sign to Whitebrook, 2m on unclassified road, Crown on right

In a secluded spot in the wooded valley of the River Wye, this former drover's cottage dates back to the 17th century. Individually decorated bedrooms boast a contemporary feel with smart modern facilities. The restaurant and lounge combine many original features with a bright fresh look. The memorable cuisine features locally sourced ingredients, skilfully prepared; the dishes are marked by their clear, fresh flavours and razor-sharp timing.

Rooms 8

WOLF'S CASTLE — Map 8 SM92
Pembrokeshire

Wolfscastle Country Hotel
WELSH RAREBITS
Hotels of Distinction

★★★ 79% ◉
COUNTRY HOUSE HOTEL

☎ 01437 741225 & 741688
SA62 5LZ
e-mail: enquiries@wolfscastle.com
web: www.wolfscastle.com
dir: On A40 in village at top of hill. 6m N of Haverfordwest

This large stone house, a former vicarage, dates back to the mid-19th century and is now a friendly, privately-owned and personally-run hotel. It provides stylish, modern, well-maintained and well-equipped bedrooms. There is a pleasant bar and an attractive restaurant, which has a well deserved reputation for its food.

Rooms 20 (2 fmly) 🏃 **S** £82-£105; **D** £118-£150 (incl. bkfst)* **Facilities** STV Wi-fi New Year **Conf** Class 100 Board 30 Thtr 100 Del £122.50* **Parking** 60 **Notes** LB Closed 24-26 Dec Civ Wed 70

WREXHAM — Map 15 SJ35
Wrexham

Best Western Cross Lanes Hotel & Restaurant

Best Western

★★★ 79% HOTEL

☎ 01978 780555
Cross Lanes, Bangor Rd, Marchwiel LL13 0TF
e-mail: guestservices@crosslanes.co.uk
dir: 3m SE of Wrexham, on A525, between Marchwiel & Bangor-on-Dee

This hotel was built as a private house in 1890 and stands in over six acres of beautiful grounds. The bedrooms are well equipped and meet the expected needs of today's guest; two rooms have four-poster beds. A fine selection of well prepared food is available in Lanes Bar Restaurant.

Rooms 16 (1 fmly) **Facilities** FTV Wi-fi Putt green ⛳ New Year **Conf** Class 60 Board 40 Thtr 120 **Parking** 80 **Notes** ⊗ Closed 25-26 Dec (nights) Civ Wed 120

Premier Inn Wrexham
Premier Inn

BUDGET HOTEL

☎ 0871 527 9190
Chester Rd, Gresford LL12 8PW
web: www.premierinn.com
dir: On B5445, just off A483 (dual carriageway) near Gresford

High quality, budget accommodation ideal for both families and business travellers. Spacious, en suite bedrooms feature tea and coffee making facilities, and Freeview TV in most hotels. Internet access and Wi-fi are available for a small fee. The adjacent family restaurant features a wide and varied menu. See also the Hotel Groups pages.

Rooms 38

W

Save on hotels. Book at **theAA.com/hotel**

621 WALES

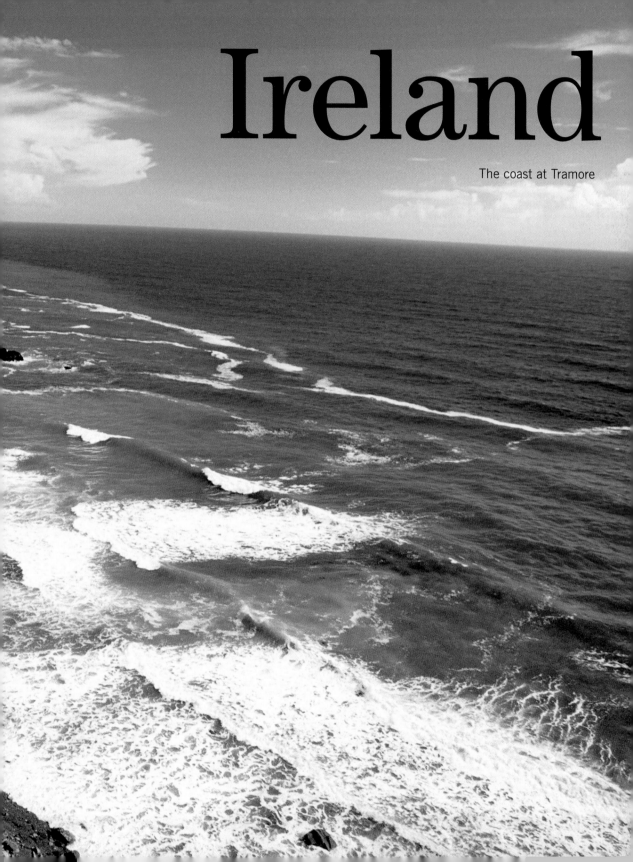

Ireland

The coast at Tramore

Additional Information for Northern Ireland & the Republic of Ireland

Licensing Regulations

Northern Ireland: Public houses open Mon-Sat 11.30-23.00. Sun 12.30-22.00. Hotels can serve residents without restriction. Non-residents can be served 12.30-22.00 on Christmas Day. Children under 18 are not allowed in the bar area and may neither buy nor consume liquor in hotels.

Republic of Ireland: General licensing hours are Mon-Thu 10.30-23.30, Fri & Sat 10.30-00.30. Sun 12.30-23.00 (or 00.30 if the following day is a Bank Holiday). There is no service (except for hotel residents) on Christmas Day or Good Friday.

The Fire Services (NI) Order 1984

This covers establishments accommodating more than six people, which must have a certificate from the Northern Ireland Fire Authority. Places accommodating fewer than six people need adequate exits. AA inspectors check emergency notices, fire fighting equipment and fire exits here.

The Republic of Ireland safety regulations are a matter for local authority regulations. For your own and others' safety, read the emergency notices and be sure you understand them.

Telephone numbers

Area codes for numbers in the Republic of Ireland apply only within the Republic. If dialling from outside check the telephone directory (from the UK the international dialling code is 00 353). Area codes for numbers in Britain and Northern Ireland cannot be used directly from the Republic.

For the latest information on the Republic of Ireland visit the AA Ireland's website: www.AAireland.ie

---

NORTHERN IRELAND

NORTHERN IRELAND

AGHADOWEY
Co Londonderry
Map 1 C6

Brown Trout Golf & Country Inn

IRISH COUNTRY HOTELS

★★★ 73% HOTEL

☎ 028 7086 8209
209 Agivey Rd BT51 4AD
e-mail: jane@browntroutinn.com
dir: At junct of A54 & B66 junct on road to Coleraine

Set alongside the Agivey River and featuring its own 9-hole golf course, this welcoming inn offers a choice of spacious accommodation. Comfortably furnished bedrooms are situated around a courtyard area whilst the cottage suites also have lounge areas. Home-cooked meals are served in the restaurant and lighter fare is available in the charming lounge bar which has entertainment at weekends.

Rooms 15 (11 fmly) (15 GF) ✎ **S** £50-£70; **D** £70-£110 (incl. bkfst) **Facilities** STV FTV Wi-fi ♨ ﹠ 9 Putt green Gym Game fishing ♫ Xmas New Year **Conf** Class 24 Board 28 Thtr 40 Del from £60 to £75 **Parking** 80 **Notes** LB

ANTRIM
Co Antrim
Map 1 D5

Holiday Inn Express Antrim M2 Jct 1

BUDGET HOTEL

☎ 028 9442 5500
Ballymena Rd BT4 1LL
e-mail: reception.antrim@holidayinnexpress.org.uk
web: www.hiexpress.com/antrim
dir: At Junction One Shopping Outlet

A modern hotel ideal for families and business travellers. Fresh and uncomplicated, the spacious rooms include Sky TV, power shower and tea and coffee-making facilities. Continental buffet breakfast is included in the room rate; other meals may be taken at the nearby family pub or restaurant. See also the Hotel Groups pages.

Rooms 90 (52 fmly) (10 GF) **Conf** Class 20 Board 20 Thtr 40

BALLYMENA
Co Antrim
Map 1 D5

Galgorm Resort & Spa

★★★★ 82% ◉◉ HOTEL

☎ 028 2588 1001
BT42 1EA
e-mail: mail@galgorm.com
dir: 1m from Ballymena on A42, between Galgorm & Cullybackey

Standing in 85 acres of private woodland and sweeping lawns beside the River Maine, this 19th-century mansion offers spacious, comfortable bedrooms. Public areas include a welcoming cocktail bar and elegant restaurant, as well as Gillies, a lively and atmospheric locals' bar. Also on the estate is an equestrian centre and a conference hall.

Rooms 75 (14 fmly) (8 GF) ✎ **S** £105-£155; **D** £135-£185 (incl. bkfst)* **Facilities** Spa FTV Wi-fi Fishing Clay pigeon shooting Archery Horseriding ♫ Xmas New Year **Conf** Class 170 Board 30 Thtr 500 Del from £150 to £175* **Services** Lift **Parking** 300 **Notes** LB ⊗ Civ Wed 500

Save on hotels. Book at **theAA.com/hotel**

AGH – BEL 625 IRELAND

BANGOR
Co Down

Map 1 D5

The Old Inn
★★★★ 82% ◉ ◉ HOTEL

☎ 028 9185 3255
15 Main St BT19 1JH
e-mail: info@theoldinn.com
web: www.theoldinn.com
dir: A2 from Belfast (pass Belfast City Airport & Transport Museum). 2m, left at lights onto B20. 1.2m to hotel

This delightful hotel enjoys a peaceful rural setting just a short drive from Belfast. The property dates from 1614, and many of the day rooms exude charm and character. Individually styled, comfortable bedrooms, some with feature beds, offer modern facilities. The popular bar and intimate restaurant both offer creative menus, and staff throughout are keen to please.

Rooms 31 (1 annexe) (7 fmly) (6 GF) ☏ **Facilities** STV FTV Wi-fi ♨ In room spa/massage treatments ♫ Xmas New Year **Conf** Class 120 Board 40 Thtr 150 **Services** Lift **Parking** 84 **Notes** ⊗ Civ Wed 100

BELFAST
Belfast

Map 1 D5

The Merchant Hotel
★★★★★ 83% ◉ HOTEL

☎ 028 9023 4888
16 Skipper St BT1 2DZ
e-mail: info@themerchanthotel.com
dir: In city centre, 2nd left at Albert Clock into Waring St. Hotel on left

A magnificent hotel situated in the historic Cathedral Quarter of the city centre. This Grade I listed building has been lovingly and sensitively restored to reveal its original architectural grandeur and interior opulence. All the bedrooms, including five suites, have air-conditioning, hi-speed internet access, flat-screen TVs and luxury bathrooms. There are several eating options including the grand and beautifully decorated Great Room Restaurant.

Rooms 62 (17 fmly) ☏ S £160-£240; D £180-£260 (incl. bkfst) **Facilities** Spa FTV Wi-fi ♨ Gym ♫ Xmas New Year **Conf** Class 100 Board 60 Thtr 200 **Services** Lift Air con **Parking** 35 **Notes** LB ⊗ Civ Wed 130

Radisson Blu Hotel Belfast

★★★★ 75% HOTEL

☎ 028 9043 4065 & 9082 0107
3 Cromac Place BT7 2JB
e-mail: reservations.belfast@radissonblu.com
dir: On corner of Ormeau Rd & Cromac St

This modern hotel is in the centre of the regenerated urban area close to the city centre. The bedrooms are stylishly presented, well equipped and all have are air conditioning; there is a choice of business suites. Public areas include a spacious lounge bar and the Filini Restaurant, which serves good Italian and Sardinian cuisine. Ample secure parking, and free Wi-Fi (throughout the hotel) are available.

Rooms 120 (11 fmly) (4 smoking) **Facilities** FTV Wi-fi ♨ Access to LA Fitness Xmas New Year **Conf** Class 70 Board 50 Thtr 150 **Services** Lift Air con **Parking** 120 **Notes** Civ Wed 90

Malone Lodge Hotel
★★★★ 74% ◉ HOTEL

☎ 028 9038 8000
60 Eglantine Av BT9 6DY
e-mail: info@malonelodgehotel.com
web: www.malonelodgehotelbelfast.com
dir: At hospital rdbt exit towards Bouchar Rd, left at 1st rdbt, right at lights at top, then 1st left

Situated in the leafy suburbs of the university area of south Belfast, this stylish hotel forms the centrepiece of an attractive row of Victorian terraced properties. The unassuming exterior belies an attractive and spacious interior with a smart lounge, popular bar and stylish Green Door restaurant. The hotel also has a small, well-equipped fitness room.

Rooms 46 (5 fmly) (1 GF) **Facilities** FTV Wi-fi Gym **Conf** Class 90 Board 40 Thtr 150 **Services** Lift **Parking** 35 **Notes** ⊗ Civ Wed 120

Malmaison Belfast

★★★ 85% ◉ HOTEL

☎ 028 9022 0200
34-38 Victoria St BT1 3GH
e-mail: lsteele@malmaison.com
web: www.malmaison.com
dir: M1 along Westlink to Grosvenor Rd. Follow city centre signs. Pass City Hall on right, left onto Victoria St. Hotel on right

Situated in a former seed warehouse, this luxurious, contemporary hotel is ideally located for the city centre. Comfortable bedrooms, boast a host of modern facilities, whilst the deeply comfortable, stylish public areas include a popular bar lounge. The 'Home Grown and Local' menu in the brasserie showcases local seasonal ingredients. The warm hospitality is notable.

Rooms 64 (8 fmly) **Facilities** STV Wi-fi Gym **Conf** Board 22 **Services** Lift

Holiday Inn Belfast

★★★ 81% HOTEL

☎ 0871 942 9005
22 Ormeau Av BT2 8HS
e-mail: belfast@ihg.com
web: www.holidayinn.co.uk
dir: M1/M2 onto West Link at Grosvenor Rd rdbt, follow city centre signs. 1st right, 2nd left into Hope St, at 2nd lights left into Bedford St, at next lights right into Ormeau Ave, hotel on right

This contemporary hotel is located in the heart of the city centre's 'golden mile' which makes it ideal for business visitors, for shopping and for exploring the tourist attractions. The air-conditioned bedrooms are modern in style and offer a comprehensive range of facilities. Public rooms include a staffed business centre and state-of-the-art health club.

Rooms 170 **Facilities** Spa Wi-fi ☺ Gym ♫ **Services** Lift Air con

NORTHERN IRELAND

BELFAST *continued*

Ramada Encore Belfast City Centre

★★★ 79% HOTEL

☎ 028 9026 1800 & 028 9026 1809
20 Talbot St BT1 2LD
e-mail: reception@encorebelfast.co.uk
dir: On Dunbar Link behind St Annes Cathedral

This stylish modern hotel is ideally located in the city's Cathedral Quarter and is a short walk from the main shopping and business district. The open-plan public areas feature the SQ Bar & Grill, which is ideal for a relaxed lunch or an intimate dinner. The popular Hub Bar serves an extensive choice of cocktails and there's free Wi-fi in the bar area. The spacious bedrooms are very well appointed and have bathrooms with power showers.

Rooms 165 (20 fmly) ✿ **Facilities** FTV Wi-fi ➟ HL ♫ Xmas New Year **Conf** Class 75 Board 30 Thtr 110 **Services** Lift **Notes** ⊗

Park Inn by Radisson Belfast

★★★ 77% HOTEL

☎ 028 9067 7700
4 Clarence Street West BT2 7GP
e-mail: info.belfast@rezidorparkinn.com
dir: M1 into Belfast, which becomes A12 (Westlink). Right into Grosvenor Rd (B38), follow City Centre signs. Right into Durnham St (B503), left into Hope St, which becomes Bruce St. Left into Bedford St (A1). Left into Clarence St, hotel on left

This hotel is well located in the city centre and a short walk from the main shopping, entertainment and business districts. The contemporary bedrooms are stylishly presented and the ten spacious business rooms have complimentary
Wi-fi. The hotel also provides the RBG Bar and Grill, a sauna, steam room and conference facilities.

Rooms 145 (5 fmly) **Facilities** FTV Wi-fi Gym Sauna Steam room ♫ Xmas New Year **Conf** Class 60 Board 44 Thtr 120 **Services** Lift Air con **Parking** 15 **Notes** ⊗

Fitzwilliam Hotel

Ⓤ

☎ 028 9044 2080
Great Victoria St BT2 7BQ
e-mail: enq@fitzwilliamhotelbelfast.com
dir: In city centre, adjacent to Grand Opera House

Currently the rating for this establishment is not confirmed. This may be due to a change of ownership or because it has only recently joined the AA rating

scheme. For further details please see the AA website: theAA.com

Rooms 130 **S** fr £190; **D** fr £200 **Facilities** STV FTV Wi-fi ➟ Gym ♫ Xmas New Year **Conf** Class 20 Board 25 Thtr 55 **Services** Lift Air con **Parking** 35 **Notes** ⊗

Premier Inn Belfast City Cathedral Quarter

BUDGET HOTEL

☎ 0871 527 8070
2-6 Waring St BT1 1XY
web: www.premierinn.com
dir: M1 or M2 to Westlink to Grosvenor Rd rdbt, signed city centre. Into Grosvenor Rd. At 2nd lights left, take right lane, right (pass City Hall on right). At end of Chichester St left into Victoria St. Through next 2 lights, left into Waring St. Hotel 300yds on right

High quality, budget accommodation ideal for both families and business travellers. Spacious, en suite bedrooms feature tea and coffee making facilities, and Freeview TV in most hotels. Internet access and Wi-fi are available for a small fee. The adjacent family restaurant features a wide and varied menu. See also the Hotel Groups pages.

Rooms 171

Premier Inn Belfast City Centre Alfred St

BUDGET HOTEL

☎ 0871 527 8068
Alfred St BT2 8ED
web: www.premierinn.com
dir: M1 or M2 to Westlink. Follow city centre signs. 1st right, 2nd left into Hope St. At 2nd lights left into Bedford St. At next lights right into Ormeau Ave. Left into Alfred St. Underground car park (chargeable) on left

Rooms 148

Premier Inn Belfast Titanic Quarter

BUDGET HOTEL

☎ 0871 527 9210
2A Queens Rd BT3 9FB
web: www.premierinn.com
dir: From all major routes follow Odyssey Arena signs. From M3 junct 1 exit onto Queens Island, to lights. Hotel on left

Rooms 102

BUSHMILLS
Co Antrim
Map 1 C6

Bushmills Inn Hotel

★★★★ 79% ◉ HOTEL

☎ 028 2073 3000 & 2073 2339
9 Dunluce Rd BT57 8QG
e-mail: mail@bushmillsinn.com
web: www.bushmillsinn.com
dir: On A2 in village centre

Enjoying a prominent position in the heart of the village, this hotel offers a range of bedroom styles including spacious, creatively designed rooms that have the latest technology and a small dressing room. The charming public areas feature inglenook turf-burning fires, cosy snugs along with a very popular traditional bar. The restaurant has a well deserved reputation for its food. The hotel is very popular with golfers; it is close to the Giants Causeway, Bushmills Distillery and the stunning scenery of the Antrim Coast.

Rooms 41 (2 fmly) (20 GF) **Facilities** STV Wi-fi ♫ New Year **Conf** Class 30 Board 18 Thtr 40 **Services** Lift **Parking** 70 **Notes** ⊗ Closed 25 Dec

CARNLOUGH
Co Antrim
Map 1 D6

Londonderry Arms Hotel

IRISH COUNTRY HOTELS

★★★ 73% ◉ HOTEL

☎ 028 2888 5255
20 Harbour Rd BT44 0EU
e-mail: lda@glensofantrim.com
dir: 14m N from Larne on A2 (coast road)

This delightful hotel was built in the mid-19th century by Lady Londonderry, whose grandson, Winston Churchill, also owned it at one time. Today the hotel's Georgian architecture and rooms are still evident, and spacious bedrooms can be found in the modern extension. The hotel enjoys a prime location in this pretty fishing village overlooking the Antrim coast.

Rooms 35 (15 fmly) **S** £45-£50; **D** £50-£100 (incl. bkfst) **Facilities** Wi-fi Fishing New Year **Conf** Class 60 Board 40 Thtr 120 Del from £80 to £100 **Services** Lift **Parking** 50 **Notes** ⊗ Closed 24-25 Dec Civ Wed 60

NORTHERN IRELAND

Save on hotels. Book at **theAA.com/hotel**

BEL – ENN 627 **IRELAND**

NORTHERN IRELAND

CARRICKFERGUS   Map 1 D5
Co Antrim

Premier Inn Carrickfergus

BUDGET HOTEL

☎ 0871 527 8214
The Harbour, Alexandra Pier BT38 8BE
web: www.premierinn.com
dir: Exit at M2 junct 2, take M5 N onto A2 towards Carrickfergus. Follow Castle/Maritime Area signs. Right at rdbt adjacent to castle. Hotel straight ahead, adjacent to harbour

High quality, budget accommodation ideal for both families and business travellers. Spacious, en suite bedrooms feature tea and coffee making facilities, and Freeview TV in most hotels. Internet access and Wi-fi are available for a small fee. The adjacent family restaurant features a wide and varied menu. See also the Hotel Groups pages.

Rooms 49

CLOGHER   Map 1 C5
Co Tyrone

Corick House Hotel

★★★ 80% COUNTRY HOUSE HOTEL

☎ 028 8554 8216
20 Corick Rd BT76 0BZ
e-mail: reservations@corickcountryhouse.com
dir: Off A4 (Augher & Clogher road)

A warm welcome is guaranteed at Corick House, a charming 17th-century William and Mary house set amid meandering streams and winding country roads in the heart of the beautiful Clogher Valley. The bedrooms are very spacious and many have breathtaking views of the valley and mountains. Public areas reflect much period charm and include a large dining room, a sun lounge and a cosy bar.

Rooms 19 (9 fmly) (3 GF) 🐾 S fr £80; **D** £110-£120 (incl. bkfst)* **Facilities** STV FTV Wi-fi 🏊 Xmas New Year **Conf** Class 150 Board 60 Thtr 400 **Parking** 200 **Notes** LB ⊗ Civ Wed 350

COLERAINE   Map 1 C6
Co Londonderry

Premier Inn Coleraine

BUDGET HOTEL

☎ 0871 527 8262
3 Riverside Park North, Castleroe Rd BT51 3GE
web: www.premierinn.com
dir: A26 towards Colraine. At rdbt left on A29 (ring road) signed Cookstown/Garragh. At rdbt A54 (Castleroe Rd). Hotel on right

High quality, budget accommodation ideal for both families and business travellers. Spacious, en suite bedrooms feature tea and coffee making facilities, and Freeview TV in most hotels. Internet access and Wi-fi are available for a small fee. The adjacent family restaurant features a wide and varied menu. See also the Hotel Groups pages.

Rooms 49

DUNGANNON   Map 1 C5
Co Tyrone

The Cohannon Inn & Auto Lodge

★★ 72% HOTEL

☎ 028 8772 4488
212 Ballynakilly Rd BT71 6HJ
e-mail: info@cohannon.com
dir: 400yds from M1 junct 14

Handy for the M1 and the nearby towns of Dungannon and Portadown, this hotel offers well-maintained bedrooms, located behind the inn complex in a smart purpose-built wing. Public areas are smartly furnished and wide-ranging menus are served throughout the day.

Rooms 42 (20 fmly) (21 GF) (5 smoking) **S** £39.95; **D** £49.95* **Facilities** FTV Wi-fi Hair & beauty salon New Year **Conf** Class 100 Board 40 Thtr 160 **Parking** 160 **Notes** RS 25 Dec

---

ENNISKILLEN   Map 1 C5
Co Fermanagh

Lough Erne Resort

★★★★★ 86% ◉◉ HOTEL

☎ 028 6632 3230
Belleek Rd BT93 7ED
e-mail: info@lougherneresort.com
web: www.lougherneresort.com
dir: A46 from Enniskillen towards Donegal, hotel in 3m

This delightful resort enjoys a peaceful and idyllic setting and boasts championship golf courses, a wonderful Thai spa and a host of outdoor and leisure pursuits. Bedrooms and en suites are spacious, particularly well appointed and include a number of luxury suites. Day rooms are spacious, luxurious and include lounges, bars and restaurants with splendid views. Service is friendly and extremely attentive.

Rooms 120 (61 annexe) **Facilities** Spa STV Wi-fi 🕸 ⅃ 18 Fishing Gym ♫ Xmas New Year **Conf** Class 200 Board 80 Thtr 400 **Services** Lift **Parking** 240 **Notes** ⊗ Civ Wed 300

Manor House Country Hotel

★★★★ 80% ◉◉ COUNTRY HOUSE HOTEL

☎ 028 6862 2200
Killadeas BT94 1NY
e-mail: info@manorhouseresorthotel.com

This charming country house hotel enjoys a stunning location on the banks of Lower Lough Erne and is a short drive from the busy town of Enniskillen. Bedrooms are equipped to a very high standard with front-facing rooms having the fabulous lough views. There is a choice of restaurants, and afternoon tea is served in the comfortable lounge with its open fire. The hotel has first-class business, conference and leisure facilities including its own air-conditioned cruiser for tours and corporate events.

Rooms 81 (12 fmly) (12 GF) **Facilities** FTV Wi-fi 🕸 Gym Sauna ♫ Xmas New Year **Conf** Class 120 Board 100 Thtr 400 **Services** Lift **Parking** 300 **Notes** ⊗ Civ Wed

NORTHERN IRELAND

ENNISKILLEN *continued*

Killyhevlin Hotel & Health Club

IRISH
COUNTRY
HOTELS

★★★★ 80% HOTEL

☎ 028 6632 3481
BT74 6RW
e-mail: info@killyhevlin.com
web: www.killyhevlin.com
dir: 2m S of Enniskillen, off A4

This modern, stylish hotel is situated on the shores of Lough Erne, south of the town. The well-equipped bedrooms are particularly spacious and enjoy fine views of the gardens and lake. The restaurant, informal bar and comfortable lounges all share the views. Staff are friendly and helpful. There are extensive leisure facilities and a spa.

Rooms 70 (42 fmly) (22 GF) **Facilities** Spa STV Wi-fi ⓣ supervised Fishing Gym Aerobic studio Steam room Sauna Hydrotherapy area 🎵 New Year **Conf** Class 160 Board 100 Thtr 500 **Services** Lift **Parking** 500 **Notes** Closed 25 Dec RS 24 & 26 Dec Civ Wed 250

LIMAVADY   Map 1 C6
Co Londonderry

Roe Park Resort

★★★★ 75% ◉ HOTEL

☎ 028 7772 2222
BT49 9LB
e-mail: reservations@roeparkresort.com
web: www.roeparkresort.com
dir: On A2 (Londonderry-Limavady road), 1m from Limavady

This impressive, popular hotel is part of a modern golf resort. The spacious, contemporary bedrooms are well equipped and many have excellent views of the fairways and surrounding estate. The Greens Restaurant provides a refreshing dining experience and the Coach House brasserie offers a lighter menu. The leisure options are extensive.

Rooms 118 (15 fmly) (37 GF) (5 smoking) **Facilities** Spa FTV Wi-fi ⓣ supervised ⌢ 18 Putt green Fishing Gym Driving range Indoor golf academy 🎵 Xmas New Year **Conf** Class 190 Board 140 Thtr 450 **Services** Lift **Parking** 350 **Notes** ⊗ Civ Wed 300

LISBURN   Map 1 D5
Co Antrim

Premier Inn Lisburn

Premier Inn

BUDGET HOTEL

☎ 0871 527 8606
136-144 Hillsborough Rd BT27 5QY
web: www.premierinn.com
dir: M1 onto A1 (Sprucefield Rd). Left into Hillsborough Rd. Approx 1.5m, hotel on left

High quality, budget accommodation ideal for both families and business travellers. Spacious, en suite bedrooms feature tea and coffee making facilities, and Freeview TV in most hotels. Internet access and Wi-fi are available for a small fee. The adjacent family restaurant features a wide and varied menu. See also the Hotel Groups pages.

Rooms 60

LONDONDERRY   Map 1 C5
Co Londonderry

City Hotel

★★★★ 74% HOTEL

☎ 028 7136 5800
Queens Quay BT48 7AS
e-mail: reservations@cityhotelderry.com
dir: Follow city centre signs. Hotel on waterfront

In a central position overlooking the River Foyle, this stylish, contemporary hotel will appeal to business and leisure guests alike. All bedrooms have excellent facilities including internet access; the executive rooms make particularly good working environments. Meeting and function facilities are extensive and there are good leisure options.

Rooms 146 (16 fmly) (11 smoking) **Facilities** Wi-fi ⓣ supervised Gym Steam room 🎵 New Year **Conf** Class 150 Board 80 Thtr 350 **Services** Lift Air con **Parking** 48 **Notes** ⊗ Closed 25 Dec Civ Wed 350

REPUBLIC OF IRELAND

ADARE   Map 1 B3
Co Limerick

Dunraven Arms Hotel

MANOR HOUSE HOTELS

★★★★ 82% ◉◉ HOTEL

☎ 061 605900
e-mail: reservations@dunravenhotel.com
dir: On N21, follow signs Cork & Tralee. 1st hotel on right

This charming hotel, established in 1792, is a traditional country inn situated in the heart of one of Ireland's prettiest villages. The comfortable lounges have log fires and most of the spacious bedrooms and suites have four-poster beds. The lovely gardens, leisure and beauty facilities, a conference centre and good cuisine all add up to creating an enjoyable visit. Golf, horse racing and equestrian sports are available nearby.

Rooms 86 (6 fmly) (40 GF) 🐾 **Facilities** STV FTV Wi-fi ⓣ supervised Fishing Gym Beauty salon Xmas New Year **Conf** Class 60 Board 12 Thtr 180 **Services** Lift **Parking** 90 **Notes** LB Civ Wed 250

ARDMORE   Map 1 C2
Co Waterford

The Cliff House Hotel

★★★★ 83% ◉◉◉ HOTEL

☎ 024 87800 & 87801
e-mail: info@thecliffhousehotel.com
dir: From Dungarvan: N25, signed Cork. Left onto R673. From Youghal: N25 signed Waterford. Right onto R673 signed Ardmore. In Ardmore take Middle Rd to hotel

This unique property, virtually sculpted into the cliff face overlooking Ardmore Bay, is just a few minutes' walk from the village. Most of the individually designed bedroom suites and the public rooms enjoy the spectacular views, as do the stunning spa and leisure facilities. Dinner in the award-winning House Restaurant is a particular highlight - the menus feature imaginatively cooked, seasonal and local produce.

Rooms 39 (8 fmly) (7 GF) **Facilities** Spa STV FTV Wi-fi ⓣ Fishing Gym Sauna Steam room Relaxation room Outdoor pursuits New Year **Conf** Class 30 Board 20 Thtr 50 **Services** Lift Air con **Parking** 52 **Notes** ⊗ Closed 2 wks in Jan

ATHY
Co Kildare | Map 1 C3

Clanard Court Hotel

★★★★ 77% HOTEL

☎ 059 8640666
Dublin Rd
e-mail: sales@clanardcourt.ie
web: www.clanardcourt.ie
dir: N7 from Naas/M7 junct 11/M9/N78 signed Athy. Continue for 8km, take 3rd exit at rdbt. Hotel approx 500mtrs on left

Located just one kilometre from Athy on the Dublin road, this family owned hotel enjoys a well earned reputation for hosting weddings and family celebrations. Concerts and events are also a regular feature here. Bedrooms are spacious, attractively decorated and very comfortable. Bailey's Bar & Brasserie is a popular bar serving food throughout the day, with full dinner in the evenings.

Rooms 38 (2 fmly) (17 GF) (5 smoking) ☏
S €69-€129; **D** €89-€170 (incl. bkfst) **Facilities** STV FTV Wi-fi ⌘ Putt green Use of leisure facilities at affiliated club ♫ New Year **Conf** Class 300 Board 20 Thtr 450 Del from €143 to €188* **Services** Lift **Parking** 250 **Notes** LB ⊗ Closed 25-26 Dec Civ Wed 250

BALLINA
Co Mayo | Map 1 B4

Mount Falcon Estate

★★★★ 83% ◉◉ HOTEL

☎ 096 74472
Mount Falcon Estate
e-mail: info@mountfalcon.com
web: www.mountfalcon.com
dir: On N26, 6m from Foxford & 3m from Ballina. Hotel on left

Dating from 1876, this house has been lovingly restored to its former glory, and has a bedroom extension that is totally in keeping with the original design. Relaxing lounges look out on the 100-acre estate, which has excellent salmon fishing on The Moy plus well-stocked trout lakes. Dinner is served in the original kitchen with choices from a varied and interesting menu; for lunch there is also the Boathole Bar. An air-conditioned gym is available.

Rooms 32 (3 fmly) **Facilities** Spa STV Wi-fi ⌘ ⓧ supervised Fishing Gym Sauna Steam room New Year **Conf** Class 120 Board 80 Thtr 200 **Services** Lift **Parking** 260 **Notes** ⊗ Closed 24-27 Dec Civ Wed 200

The Ice House

★★★★ 79% ◉◉ HOTEL

☎ 096 23500
The Quay
e-mail: chill@theicehouse.ie
dir: On Sligo road turn right at Judge's Garage into Riverside Estate. Right at T-junct into Quay Rd. Hotel on left

With a fascinating history, this property, a mile or so from the town centre, is a stunning mix of old and new. The contemporary decor features lots of wood, steel and glass creating a very light and airy interior, contrasted with a Victorian features and furnishing in the original house. The stylish bedrooms include suites that have river views from their balconies. An interesting menu is offered at dinner in the vaulted Pier Restaurant, once the ice store for the Moy fishery, with lighter fare offered during the day in the bright riverside bar.

Rooms 32 (7 fmly) (10 GF) ☏ **S** €110-€190; **D** €150-€250 (incl. bkfst)* **Facilities** Spa STV Wi-fi Laconium Steam room New Year Child facilities **Conf** Class 35 Board 30 Thtr 70 **Services** Lift **Parking** 32 **Notes** Closed 25-26 Dec Civ Wed 150

Belleek Castle

★★★ 71% ◉ HOTEL

☎ 096 22400
Belleek
e-mail: info@belleekcastle.com
dir: In Belleek woods N of Ballina

This lovely manor house, formerly the ancestral home of the Earl of Arran, is set in wonderful parkland at the head of Belleek Wood on the River Moy estuary. The cosy public lounges are welcoming, and are complemented by a series of banqueting suites that are decorated in a nautical theme. Bedroom accommodation varies in style; all rooms are comfortably appointed. Dinner is the highlight of any visit, offered from a choice of Market or Gourmet set menus. The food is all locally sourced, and the chef has a keen eye for seasonality. The hotel is a popular wedding venue. There is also a museum specialising in armoury and memorabilia from the Spanish Armada.

Rooms 13 (1 fmly) **S** €70-€220; **D** €160-€220* **Facilities** STV FTV Wi-fi New Year **Conf** Class 60 Board 30 Thtr 100 **Parking** 200 **Notes** ⊗ Civ Wed 200

Ballina Manor Hotel

Ⓤ

☎ 096 80900
At the Moy Ridgepool
e-mail: info@ballinamanorhotel.ie

Currently the rating for this establishment is not confirmed. This may be due to a change of ownership or because it has only recently joined the AA rating scheme. For further details please see the AA website: theAA.com

Rooms 66 (4 fmly) (10 smoking) **Facilities** STV Wi-fi ⌘ ⓧ Gym Beauty treatment rooms ♫ New Year **Conf** Class 110 Board 150 Thtr 220 Del from €90 to €160* **Services** Lift **Parking** 70 **Notes** LB ⊗ Closed 25-26 Dec RS 24 & 27 Dec Civ Wed 160

BALLINASLOE — Map 1 B4
Co Galway

Carlton Shearwater Hotel

★★★★ 76% HOTEL

☎ 090 9630400
Marina Point
e-mail: info.shearwater@carlton.ie
dir: N6 junct 14 or 15 to Ballinasloe, hotel at marina

Striking in its design, this hotel is situated at Marine Point in Ballinasloe. The spacious public areas are contemporary in style with a range of lounges to relax in, a bar, and an outdoor patio where bistro-style food is served throughout the day. The Carvery is popular at lunch time, and dinner is served in Marengo's Restaurant. Bedrooms are comfortably furnished, and the deluxe and Presidential Suites are particularly stylish. There are extensive conference, meeting and banqueting facilities, plus a spa and leisure centre. Ample underground parking is available.

Rooms 104 (44 fmly) (8 smoking) **Facilities** Spa STV FTV Wi-fi 🕹 🖎 Gym Aerobics studio 🎵 New Year **Conf** Class 440 Board 96 Thtr 900 Del €89* **Services** Lift Air con **Parking** 303 **Notes** ⊗ Closed 23-26 Dec Civ Wed 160

BALLINGEARY — Map 1 B2
Co Cork

Gougane Barra Hotel

★★★ 75% 🏵 HOTEL

☎ 026 47069
Gougane Barra
e-mail: gouganebarrahotel@eircom.net
dir: On L4643. Exit R584 between N22 at Macroom & N71 at Bantry

Picturesquely situated on the shore of Gougane Barra Lake and at the entrance to the National Park, the Lucey family have run this hotel for five generations. The bedrooms are very comfortable. Dinner is a treat, and there are lounges and a cosy, traditional bar. Guests can enjoy a unique theatre during high season, and bikes and boats are available together with action-packed activity weekends. Winner of AA Ireland's Courtesy & Care Award 2012-13.

Rooms 26 (12 GF) **Facilities** STV FTV Wi-fi Fishing Boating Cycling 🎵 **Parking** 26 **Notes** ⊗ Closed 10 Oct-18 Apr

BALLYBOFEY — Map 1 C5
Co Donegal

Jackson's Hotel

Ⓤ

☎ 074 9131021
e-mail: enquiry@jacksons-hotel.ie

Currently the rating for this establishment is not confirmed. This may be due to a change of ownership or because it has only recently joined the AA rating scheme. For further details please see the AA website: theAA.com

Rooms 138 (55 fmly) (68 smoking) **Facilities** Spa STV FTV Wi-fi 🖎 supervised ⛲ Gym 🎵 Xmas New Year **Conf** Class 800 Board 60 Thtr 1500 **Services** Lift **Parking** 550 **Notes** Civ Wed 800

BALLYCOTTON — Map 1 C2
Co Cork

Bayview Hotel

★★★ 🏵🏵 HOTEL

☎ 021 4646746
e-mail: res@thebayviewhotel.com
dir: Exit N25 at Castlemartyr, through Ladysbridge & Garryvoe to Ballycotton

The gardens of this hotel seem to hang onto the cliffs overlooking the fishing port and Ballycotton Bay. The comfortable public rooms and bedrooms with balconies take in the breathtaking coastline views. Dinner in the Capricho Room is a special delight with menus based on fresh, seasonal and locally sourced ingredients, including locally landed fish. The warm and friendly team certainly impress with their standards of customer care. Guests have complimentary use of the health club at the sister hotel, The Garryvoe Hotel, just a five-minute drive away.

Rooms 35 (5 GF) (10 smoking) **S** €80-€145; **D** €80-€145* **Facilities** STV Wi-fi Pitch and putt Sea angling Use of swimming pool at sister hotel **Conf** Class 30 Board 24 Thtr 60 Del €135* **Services** Lift Air con **Parking** 40 **Notes** LB ⊗ Closed Nov-Apr Civ Wed 100

BALLYLICKEY — Map 1 B2
Co Cork

Sea View House Hotel

★★★ 🏵🏵 HOTEL

☎ 027 50073 & 50462
e-mail: info@seaviewhousehotel.com
web: www.seaviewhousehotel.com
dir: 5km from Bantry, 11km from Glengarriff on N71

Colourful gardens and glimpses of Bantry Bay through the mature trees frame this delightful country house. Owner Kathleen O'Sullivan's team of staff are exceptionally pleasant and there is a relaxed atmosphere in the cosy lounges. Guest comfort and good cuisine are the top priorities. Bedrooms are spacious and individually styled; some on the ground floor are appointed to suit less able guests.

Rooms 25 (3 fmly) (5 GF) **S** €75-€95; **D** €120-€150 (incl. bkfst)* **Facilities** STV FTV Wi-fi **Conf** Class 30 Board 25 Thtr 25 Del from €100 to €125* **Parking** 32 **Notes** LB Closed mid Nov-mid Mar Civ Wed 75

Save on hotels. Book at **theAA.com/hotel**

BAL – BAN 631 IRELAND

BALLYLIFFIN Map 1 C6
Co Donegal

Ballyliffin Lodge & Spa

★★★★ 77% HOTEL

☎ 074 9378200
Shore Rd
e-mail: info@ballyliffinlodge.com
dir: From Derry take A2 towards Moville, exit for Carndonagh at Quigleys Point. Ballyliffin 10km

Located in the heart of the village, this property offers a range of very comfortable bedrooms, many of which enjoy panoramic views of Malin Head and the famed Ballyliffin Golf Club. The Holly Tree offers a menu of the best local produce presented with international flair. The popular bar serves less formal meals throughout the day. Guests are welcome to use the leisure facilities in the adjoining Crystal Rock Spa.

Rooms 40 (28 fmly) **Facilities** Spa STV Wi-fi ⓢ supervised Gym ♫ New Year **Conf** Class 200 Board 100 Thtr 300 **Services** Lift **Parking** 80 **Notes** ⊗ Civ Wed 150

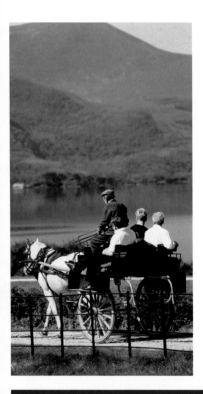

BALLYVAUGHAN Map 1 B3
Co Clare

Gregans Castle

★★★ ◉◉◉
COUNTRY HOUSE HOTEL

☎ 065 7077005
e-mail: stay@gregans.ie
dir: 3.5m S of Ballyvaughan on N67

This hotel is a hidden gem in The Burren area, and the delightful restaurant and bedrooms enjoy splendid views towards Galway Bay. The Haden family, together with their welcoming staff, offer a high level of personal service. Bedrooms are individually decorated; superior rooms and suites are particularly comfortable; some are on the ground floor and have patio gardens. There are welcoming fires in the comfortable drawing room and the cosy cocktail bar where afternoon tea is served. Dinner is a highlight of any visit; the chef shows a real passion for food which is evident in his cooking of top quality local and organic produce. The area is rich in archaeological, geological and botanical interest, and cycling and walking tours can be organised. There is a beautiful garden to relax in.

Rooms 20 (3 fmly) (7 GF) **Facilities** Wi-fi ⓢ ♫ **Conf** Class 25 Board 14 Thtr 25 **Parking** 25 **Notes** Closed Jan-12 Feb & 30 Nov-Dec Civ Wed 65

BALTIMORE Map 1 B1
Co Cork

Rolfs Country House

◉ RESTAURANT WITH ROOMS

☎ 028 20289
Baltimore Hill
e-mail: info@rolfscountryhouse.com
dir: Before village sharp left up hill. House signed

Situated on a hill above the fishing village of Baltimore, are the 400-year-old stone buildings that the Haffner family converted into accommodation. Available are ten traditionally furnished en suite bedrooms in annexe building, a cosy bar with an open fire, and a rustic restaurant on two levels. Dinner is served nightly during the high season and at weekends in the winter months; the menu features quality meats, artisan cheeses and fish landed at the busy pier. This is a lovely place to stay and the hosts are very friendly.

Rooms 10 (10 annexe)

BANTRY Map 1 B2
Co Cork

Westlodge Hotel

★★★ 77% HOTEL

☎ 027 50360
e-mail: reservations@westlodgehotel.ie
web: www.westlodgehotel.ie
dir: N71 to Bantry

With a superb leisure and wellness centre and good children's facilities, this hotel is very popular with families; the friendly team of staff ensure a memorable visit. The bedrooms include standard and family rooms and there is one superior suite. Dinner menus include organic and local seafood. The hotel's location on the outskirts of Bantry makes it an ideal base for touring west Cork and south Kerry, and there are lovely walks in the grounds. Historical and archaeology tours of the Bantry can be booked.

Rooms 90 (20 fmly) (20 GF) **S** €60-€75; **D** €120-€140 (incl. bkfst)* **Facilities** STV Wi-fi ⓢ supervised ⌁ Putt green Gym Squash 2 beauty treatment rooms Pitch & putt ♫ New Year **Conf** Class 200 Board 24 Thtr 400 **Services** Lift Air con **Parking** 400 **Notes** LB ⊗ Closed 23-27 Dec Civ Wed 300

BARNA (BEARNA) — Map 1 B3
Co Galway

The Twelve
★★★★ 80% ◉◉ HOTEL

☎ 091 597000
Barna Village
e-mail: enquire@thetwelvehotel.ie
dir: On outskirts of Barna on coast road

Located just ten minutes west of Galway city, this hotel looks as if it has been on the site for decades. However, once inside the decor is striking and contemporary. The bedrooms come in a number of different sizes, but all are furnished with taste and with guest comfort in mind. The Pins is a vibrant and popular bar and bistro where food is served throughout the day. West Restaurant opens during the evening, and offers fine dining from a well-compiled menu of local and seasonal produce. Le Petit Spa provides treatments based on seaweed products.

Rooms 47 (12 fmly) ✦ **S** €80-€140; **D** €89-€165 (incl. bkfst) **Facilities** STV FTV Wi-fi ✎ Beauty treatment room Children's cookery programme Art classes Wine classes ♪ Xmas New Year **Conf** Class 70 Board 60 Thtr 80 Del from €210 to €390 **Services** Lift Air con **Parking** 140 **Notes** LB RS 22-27 Dec Civ Wed 100

See advert on opposite page

BLARNEY — Map 1 B2
Co Cork

Blarney Golf Resort
★★★★ 77% ◉ HOTEL

☎ 021 4384477
Tower
e-mail: reservations@blarneygolfresort.com
dir: Exit N20 for Blarney, 4km to Tower, right into Old Kerry Rd. Hotel 2km on right

This resort includes a John Daly designed golf course. The hotel is situated close to Tower village and the famous Blarney Castle. Bedrooms are well equipped and comfortable; some have balconies and spacious lounges. Early Bird and carte dinner menus are served nightly in the Inniscarra Restaurant, with more casual dining available in the golf club bar. There are excellent leisure facilities in the Sentosa Spa.

Rooms 117 (56 annexe) (56 fmly) (30 GF) **Facilities** Spa FTV Wi-fi ✎ supervised ♨ 18 Putt green Gym Steam room Sauna ♪ Xmas New Year **Conf** Class 150 Board 40 Thtr 300 **Services** Lift Air con **Parking** 250 **Notes** ✪

BRAY — Map 1 D4
Co Wicklow

Royal Hotel & Leisure Centre
★★★ 71% HOTEL

☎ 01 2862935 & 2724900
Main St
e-mail: royal@regencyhotels.com
dir: From N11, 1st exit for Bray, 2nd exit from rdbt, through 2 sets of lights, across bridge, hotel on left

Located in the town centre and walking distance from the seafront at Bray and close to Dun Laoighaire ferry port. Public areas offer comfortable lounges, a traditional bar and The Heritage Restaurant. Bedrooms vary in size but all are well appointed. There is a well-equipped leisure centre and a supervised car park.

Rooms 130 (10 fmly) **Facilities** Wi-fi ✎ supervised Gym Massage & beauty clinic Creche ♪ Xmas New Year **Conf** Class 300 Board 200 Thtr 500 **Services** Lift **Parking** 60 **Notes** ✪ Civ Wed 300

BUNCLODY — Map 1 D3
Co Wexford

Carlton Millrace Hotel
★★★★ 79% HOTEL

CARLTON
HOTEL GROUP

☎ 053 9375100 & 1890 288288
Riversedge
e-mail: reservations.millrace@carlton.ie
dir: On N80 (Carlow to Wexford road) in town

Located on the edge of the picturesque town of Bunclody, this modern hotel offers spacious well-appointed bedrooms that have comfort in mind. The public rooms are smartly presented, not least of which is the rooftop Lady Lucy restaurant where dinner and breakfast are served. Less formal dining takes place throughout the day in the Mill Bistro and bar. The hotel is popular for leisure breaks and has a good reputation for wedding celebrations.

Rooms 72 (12 annexe) (15 fmly) **Facilities** Spa STV FTV Wi-fi ✎ supervised Gym Sauna Steam room ♪ Xmas New Year **Conf** Class 125 Board 80 Thtr 350 **Services** Lift Air con **Parking** 120 **Notes** ✪ Closed 24-25 Dec Civ Wed 120

CAHERDANIEL (CATHAIR DÓNALL) — Map 1 A2
Co Kerry

Derrynane Hotel
★★★ 75% ◉ HOTEL

☎ 066 9475136
e-mail: info@derrynane.com
dir: Just off N70

This family run hotel has a super cliff top location overlooking Derrynane Bay on the Ring of Kerry. Many of the comfortable bedrooms have spectacular views as do the relaxing lounge and open-plan restaurant. The outdoor leisure facilities include cliff top walks, a heated 15-metre pool (in season), tennis court and gardens overlooking the ocean. Indoors there is a gym, natural seaweed bath, plus a steam and sauna room. Guests can also use the laundry and drying facility.

Rooms 50 (30 fmly) (32 GF) **Facilities** Wi-fi ✦ supervised ♨ Gym Seaweed therapy room ♪ **Parking** 60 **Notes** ✪ Closed 4 Oct-15 Apr

Save on hotels. Book at **theAA.com/hotel**

BAR – CAR 633 IRELAND

CARLOW   Map 1 C3
Co Carlow

Seven Oaks Hotel

★★★ 78% HOTEL

☎ 059 9131308
Athy Rd
e-mail: info@sevenoakshotel.com

This hotel is conveniently situated within walking distance of the town centre. Public areas include comfortable lounges, library, bar and a restaurant where food is available all day. There is a traditional Irish music session on Monday nights in the Oak Bar. Bedrooms are spacious and very well appointed. There are extensive leisure and banqueting facilities and a secure car park.

Rooms 89 (5 fmly) (7 GF) ⚡ **S** €60-€90; **D** €90-€140 (incl. bkfst) **Facilities** STV Wi-fi ⓦ ⓔ supervised Gym Aerobic studio Steam room ♫ **Conf** Class 150 Board 80 Thtr 400 Del from €105 to €120 **Services** Lift Air con **Parking** 200 **Notes** LB ⊗ Closed 25-26 Dec RS Good Fri Civ Wed 200

CARRICKMACROSS   Map 1 C4
Co Monaghan

Nuremore Hotel

★★★★ 80% ⦿⦿ HOTEL

☎ 042 9661438
e-mail: info@nuremore.com
web: www.nuremore.com
dir: M1 junct 14, N2. Hotel 3km S of Carrickmacross

Set in rolling Monaghan countryside, overlooking its own golf course and lakes, the Nuremore Hotel is a quiet retreat with excellent facilities. Bedrooms are comfortably appointed and spacious, with several having views of the well-tended gardens. Public areas are relaxing and include a leisure centre and Vida spa. The kitchen has a well earned reputation for its modern interpretation of classical dishes with many of the ingredients coming from local and artisan producers.

Rooms 72 (6 fmly) (42 smoking) **Facilities** Spa STV FTV Wi-fi ⓦ ⓔ supervised ⓛ 18 ⓟ Putt green Fishing Gym Beauty treatments Aromatherapy Massage ♫ Xmas New Year **Conf** Class 300 Board 50 Thtr 600 **Services** Lift **Parking** 200 **Notes** ⊗ Civ Wed 200

Shirley Arms Hotel

★★★★ 76% HOTEL

☎ 042 9673100
Main St
e-mail: reception@shirleyarmshotel.ie
dir: N2 to Derry, take Ardee Rd to Carrickmacross

Set at the top of the town, this long established hotel is an imposing stone building with a contemporary interior. Bedrooms, in a purpose-built block, are spacious and have clean, modern lines; there is also a comfortable suite in the original house overlooking the square. Food is an important element of the business here, with options available throughout the day.

Rooms 25 (2 fmly) ⚡ **S** €75-€105; **D** €110-€160 (incl. bkfst)* **Facilities** STV Wi-fi ⓦ ♫ New Year **Conf** Class 150 Board 200 Thtr 200 Del from €120 to €180* **Services** Lift **Parking** 80 **Notes** LB ⊗ Closed 24-26 Dec RS 6 Apr Civ Wed 150

REPUBLIC OF IRELAND

CASHEL
Co Galway

Map 1 A4

INSPECTORS' CHOICE

Cashel House Hotel

★★★ ◉◉ COUNTRY HOUSE HOTEL

☎ 095 31001
e-mail: res@cashel-house-hotel.com
web: www.cashel-house-hotel.com
dir: S off N59, 1.5km W of Recess, well signed

Cashel House is a mid-19th century property, standing at the head of Cashel Bay in the heart of Connemara, and set amidst secluded, award-winning gardens with woodland walks. Attentive service comes with the perfect balance of friendliness and professionalism from McEvilly family and their staff. The comfortable lounges have turf fires and antique furnishings. The restaurant offers local produce such as the famous Connemara lamb, and fish from the nearby coast.

Rooms 29 (4 fmly) (6 GF) (4 smoking) 🐾
Facilities STV FTV Wi-fi Garden school Cookery classes Xmas New Year **Parking** 40 **Notes** Closed Jan-10 Feb Civ Wed 80

Zetland Country House Hotel

★★★ 78% HOTEL

MANOR HOUSE HOTELS

☎ 095 31111
Cashel Bay
e-mail: info@zetland.com
dir: N59 from Galway towards Clifden, right after Recess onto R340, left in 4m onto R341, hotel 1m on right

Standing on the edge of Cashel Bay in Connemara, this former sporting lodge dating from the early 1800s, is a cosy and relaxing hotel that exudes charm. Many of the comfortable bedrooms have sea views, as has the restaurant where country-house and seafood cooking is a particular feature. Johnny O'Loughlins is atmospheric bistro and bar which stocks a very large range of Irish whiskey. This property is a popular base for fishing and shooting parties, with access to over 17,000 acres of diverse countryside.

Rooms 19 (10 fmly) (3 GF) **Facilities** STV FTV Wi-fi 🦢 Fishing 🎣 Shooting Cycling Xmas New Year **Conf** Class 40 Board 20 Thtr 80 **Parking** 32

CASTLEMARTYR
Co Cork

Map 1 C2

Castlemartyr Resort

★★★★★ 89% ◉ HOTEL

☎ 021 4219000
e-mail: reception@castlemartyrresort.ie
dir: N25, 3rd exit signed Rosslare. Continue past Carrigtwohill & Midleton exits. Right at lights in village

Castlemartyr Resort is an impressively restored 18th-century property, where old world grandeur and contemporary styles marry well. The individually decorated bedrooms in the Manor House make luxurious retreats, while the modern wing rooms are furnished in a more contemporary style to a very high standard. The hotel offers fine dining in the Bell Tower Restaurant featuring modern Irish cuisine and more casual eating options in Knights Bar and the Golf Clubhouse nearby. The estate grounds of over 220 acres offer a myriad of outdoor pursuits including golf on the Ron Kirby designed inland links style course, cycling and boating on the lake. There are walking and jogging routes along the nature trails, and also a stunning wellness and leisure facility.

Rooms 109 (98 annexe) (6 fmly) (30 GF)
Facilities Spa STV FTV Wi-fi 🦢 🖎 supervised 🏊 18 🏌 Gym Bicycles Horse & carriage rides Target archery Clay pigeon shooting 🎵 New Year **Conf** Class 150 Board 75 Thtr 250 **Services** Lift Air con **Parking** 200 **Notes** Closed 16-27 Dec Civ Wed 190

CAVAN
Co Cavan

Map 1 C4

Cavan Crystal Hotel

★★★★ 80% ◉◉ HOTEL

☎ 049 4360600
Dublin Rd
e-mail: info@cavancrystalhotel.com
web: www.cavancrystalhotel.com
dir: N3 towards Cavan, at 1st rdbt take N55 signed Athlone

Contemporary design using native timber and handcrafted brickwork together with crystal chandeliers make this a particularly distinctive hotel. Expect excellent hospitality from all the highly trained staff. Located on the southern edge of the town, the hotel also features a well-equipped health plus beauty clinic and extensive banquet and conference facilities.

Rooms 85 (2 fmly) (9 GF) **Facilities** Wi-fi 🖎 supervised Gym Beauty & massage treatment Salon 🎵 New Year **Conf** Class 300 Board 100 Thtr 500 **Services** Lift **Parking** 216 **Notes** ⊗ Closed 24-25 Dec

CLAREMORRIS
Co Mayo

Map 1 B4

McWilliam Park Hotel

★★★★ 78% HOTEL

☎ 094 9378000
e-mail: info@mcwilliamparkhotel.ie
dir: Take Castlebar/Claremorris exit from N17, straight over rdbt. Hotel on right

This fine hotel is situated on the outskirts of Claremorris which is close to the Knock Shrine and the airport. Public areas offer comfortable lounges, together with extensive conference, leisure and health facilities. The bedrooms are spacious and well appointed. Food is served all day in Kavanagh's bar, and dinner nightly in J.G's restaurant. Traditional music and social dancing evenings are held regularly in the McWilliam Suite.

Rooms 103 (19 fmly) (15 GF) (44 smoking) 🐾
S €60-€95; **D** €80-€160 (incl. bkfst) **Facilities** Spa STV FTV Wi-fi 🦢 🖎 Gym 🎵 Xmas New Year **Conf** Class 250 Board 80 Thtr 600 Del from €75 to €130 **Services** Lift **Parking** 320 **Notes** LB ⊗ Civ Wed 200

CLIFDEN
Co Galway

Map 1 A4

Abbeyglen Castle Hotel

★★★★ 80% ◉ HOTEL

☎ 095 21201
Sky Rd
e-mail: info@abbeyglen.ie
dir: N59 from Galway towards Clifden. Hotel 1km from Clifden on Sky Road

The tranquil setting overlooking Clifden, matched with the dedication of the Hughes's father and son team and their attentive staff, combine to create a magical atmosphere here. Now into its 5th decade, Abbeyglen Castle has a well earned reputation, with

Save on hotels. Book at **theAA.com/hotel**

CAS – CON 635 IRELAND

many guests returning year after year. Well-appointed rooms and very comfortable suites are available, together with a range of relaxing lounge areas. The restaurant features a daily-changing menu of traditional and more modern dishes; many guests enjoy impromptu sessions around the piano in the bar following dinner. Treatment rooms are available.

Rooms 45 (9 GF) 📞 **S** €125-€150; **D** €190-€240 (incl. bkfst)* **Facilities** STV Wi-fi 🏊 Putt green Beauty treatment & relaxation centre 🎵 Xmas New Year **Conf** Class 50 Board 40 Thtr 100 Del from €190 to €220* **Services** Lift **Parking** 50 **Notes** LB ⊗ No children 10yrs Closed 6 Jan-1 Feb

---

CLONAKILTY
Co Cork
Map 1 B2

Inchydoney Island Lodge & Spa
★★★★ 83% ◉◉ HOTEL

☎ 023 8833143
e-mail: reservations@inchydoneyisland.com
dir: Follow N71 (West Cork road) to Clonakilty. At rdbt in Clonakilty take 2nd exit, follow signs to hotel

Benefiting from a stunning location on Inchydoney Island, this welcoming hotel has much to offer guests that are looking for a truly relaxing experience. All of the comfortably appointed bedrooms and suites have sea views with balconies or terraces. The public rooms are spacious and decorated with an interesting range of specially commissioned furniture and artwork. Guests can choose between the informal atmosphere of the popular Dunes pub and bistro, or The Gulfstream Restaurant where the emphasis is on locally landed seafood cooked with care. The Island Spa offers a range of thalassotherapy treatments, featuring sea water pumped daily from the shore.

Rooms 67 (24 fmly) (18 GF) **S** €129-€175; **D** €158-€250 (incl. bkfst)* **Facilities** Spa Wi-fi 🐦 supervised Fishing Gym Sauna Steam room Snooker room Surfing Ocean safari 🎵 **Conf** Board 50 Thtr 300 **Services** Lift **Parking** 200 **Notes** LB ⊗ Closed 24-25 Dec Civ Wed 300

Quality Hotel & Leisure Club, Clonakilty
★★★ 75% HOTEL

☎ 023 883 6400
Skibbereen Rd
e-mail: info.clonakilty@qualityhotels.ie
web: www.qualityhotelclonakilty.com
dir: In Clonakilty take 2nd exit at mini rdbt into Skibbereen Bypass Rd. Hotel on left, approx 1m

Situated on the by-pass of the vibrant town of Clonakilty this family friendly hotel has a variety of activities for children including a supervised Kids Klub, leisure centre and treatment rooms and gym for the adults. There is a choice of bedroom sizes all are spacious and well appointed. Oscars is a lively bar with entertainment nightly during the summer and at weekends in the winter months. Dinner is served nightly in Flanagan's Restaurant and offers a range of menus to suite all ages. There is also a cinema in the grounds.

Rooms 96 (63 fmly) (41 GF) (4 smoking) 📞 **S** €62-€124; **D** €78-€198 (incl. bkfst) **Facilities** Spa STV Wi-fi 🦢 supervised Gym 3-screen cinema Sauna Steam room Jungle gym Teen zone 🎵 New Year Child facilities **Conf** Class 75 Board 40 Thtr 140 Del from €99 to €130 **Services** Lift **Parking** 200 **Notes** LB ⊗ Closed 24-26 Dec

---

CLONMEL
Co Tipperary
Map 1 C2

Hotel Minella
★★★★ 79% HOTEL

IRISH COUNTRY HOTELS

☎ 052 6122388
e-mail: frontdesk@hotelminella.ie
web: www.hotelminella.ie
dir: S of river in town

This family-run hotel is set in nine acres of well-tended gardens on the banks of the Suir River. The hotel originates from the 1860s, and the public areas include a cocktail bar and a range of lounges; some of the bedrooms are particularly spacious. The leisure centre in the grounds is noteworthy. Two-bedroom holiday homes are also available.

Rooms 90 (8 fmly) (14 GF) (10 smoking) 📞 **S** €100-€120; **D** €120-€160 (incl. bkfst) **Facilities** FTV Wi-fi 🐦 🦢 Fishing 🏊 Gym Beauty treatment room Sauna Steam room **Conf** Class 300 Board 20 Thtr 500 Del from €120 to €150 **Services** Lift **Parking** 100 **Notes** LB ⊗ Closed 24-28 Dec

---

CONG
Co Mayo
Map 1 B4

Ashford Castle
★★★★★ 86% ◉◉ HOTEL

☎ 094 9546003
e-mail: ashford@ashford.ie
web: www.ashford.ie
dir: In Cross left at church onto R345 signed Cong. Left at hotel sign, through castle gates

Set in over 300 acres of rolling parklands, this magnificent castle, dating from 1228, occupies a stunning position on the edge of Lough Corrib. Bedrooms and suites vary in style but all benefit from a pleasing combination of character, charm and modern comforts. Dinner in the elegant George V Dining Room is a treat, with creative cookery using seasonal ingredients. Less formal dining is available in other locations on the estate during peak periods. The hotel offers an extensive range of both indoor and outdoor leisure pursuits including falconry, golf, shooting, fishing and an equestrian centre.

Rooms 83 (6 fmly) (22 GF) 📞 **D** €275-€980 (incl. bkfst) **Facilities** Spa STV Wi-fi ⚡ 9 🏊 Putt green Fishing Gym Archery Clay pigeon shooting Falconry Horse riding Bike hire Lake cruises 🎵 Xmas New Year **Conf** Class 65 Thtr 110 **Services** Lift **Parking** 200 **Notes** ⊗ Civ Wed 150

REPUBLIC OF IRELAND

CONG *continued*

The Lodge at Ashford

★★★★ 77% HOTEL

☎ 094 9545400
The Quay
e-mail: lodge@lisloughrey.ie
dir: N84 from Galway to Cross. Left at Cong sign. Left at hotel sign

Situated in an elevated position overlooking the quay and Lough Corrib, this delightful property combines contemporary luxury with a traditional country house setting. The individually-styled bedrooms and suites are in a quiet courtyard linked to the main house; each is named after a French wine region. The rooms have flat-screen TVs, goose down duvets and en suites with under floor heating. Equestrian pursuits, fishing and falconry are among the activities that can be arranged in the locality. Dinner in Wilde's is the highlight of any visit. This makes a popular and ideal location for small wedding and intimate family celebrations.

Rooms 50 (44 annexe) (5 fmly) (21 GF) **Facilities** Spa STV FTV Wi-fi Fishing Gym Outdoor sauna Beauty salon Screening room New Year **Conf** Class 70 Board 40 Thtr 180 **Services** Lift **Parking** 100 **Notes** Closed 24-26 Dec & 1 Jan Civ Wed 150

COOTEHILL Map 1 C4
Co Cavan

Errigal Country House Hotel

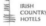 IRISH COUNTRY HOTELS

★★★★ 77% HOTEL

☎ 049 5556901
Cavan Rd
e-mail: info@errigalhotel.com
web: www.errigalhotel.com
dir: 1km from town centre on R188 (Cavan Rd)

This modern hotel is located in landscaped gardens and within walking distance of Cootehill. Bedrooms are appointed to a high standard and public areas are very comfortable and attractively decorated. Reynards Restaurant serves dinner each evening, and a more informal fare is available in The Brewery Bar. The Eden Health & Wellness suite offers a range of treatments.

Rooms 29 (2 fmly) **Facilities** Spa STV Wi-fi New Year **Conf** Class 215 Board 130 Thtr 420 **Services** Lift Air con **Parking** 350 **Notes** ⊗ Civ Wed 350

CORK Map 1 B2
Co Cork

Maryborough Hotel & Spa

★★★★ 80% ◉ HOTEL

☎ 021 4365555
Maryborough Hill, Douglas
e-mail: info@maryborough.com
dir: From Jack Lynch Tunnel 2nd exit signed Douglas. Right at 1st rdbt, follow Rochestown signs to fingerpost rdbt. Left, hotel on left in 0.5m

Dating from 1715, this house was renovated and extended to become a fine hotel with beautifully landscaped grounds featuring rare plant species. There are stylish suites in the main house and the bedrooms in the wing are comfortably furnished. The bar and lounge are very popular for the range of food served throughout the day; Zings restaurant offers a mix of classic and contemporary dishes. There are impressive spa, leisure and conference facilities, plus activities for children.

Rooms 93 (6 fmly) **Facilities** Spa STV Wi-fi supervised Gym Sauna Steam room New Year **Conf** Class 250 Board 60 Thtr 500 **Services** Lift **Parking** 300 **Notes** ⊗ Closed 24-26 Dec Civ Wed 100

Silver Springs Moran Hotel

 MORAN HOTELS

★★★★ 78% HOTEL

☎ 021 4507533
Tivoli
e-mail: silverspringsres@moranhotels.com
web: www.silverspringshotel.ie
dir: N8 S, take Silver Springs exit. Right, then right again, hotel on left

Located on the main approach to the city this hotel has spacious, contemporary public areas. The lobby lounge is very popular for all-day dining, with more formal meals served in the Watermarq Restaurant. Bedrooms and suites are comfortable, many offering good views over the River Lee. Excellent conference and leisure facilities are available in separate buildings in the grounds.

Rooms 109 (29 fmly) (12 smoking) **Facilities** Wi-fi supervised Gym Squash Aerobics classes New Year **Conf** Class 400 Board 30 Thtr 800 **Services** Lift **Parking** 325 **Notes** ⊗ Closed 24-27 Dec Civ Wed 800

CURRY Map 1 B4
Co Sligo

Yeats County Inn Hotel

★★ 74% HOTEL

☎ 094 9255050
e-mail: mail@yeatscountyinn.com
dir: On N17, S of Sligo

Located in the village of Curry, near the town of Charlestown, this family-run hotel offers a relaxing and friendly atmosphere. The popular traditional bar, with its open and welcoming fire, is comfortably furnished and serves a selection of food throughout the day. The bedrooms are attractively decorated and well appointed. The international airport at Knock, the Marian Shrine and Foxford Woollen Mills are all close by, as are a number of golf courses.

Rooms 11 (2 fmly) (2 smoking) **S** €40-€55; **D** €80-€100 (incl. bkfst) **Facilities** STV FTV Wi-fi Xmas New Year **Conf** Class 150 Board 100 Thtr 200 Del from €87.50 to €100 **Services** Lift **Parking** 120 **Notes** LB ⊗ Civ Wed 100

DELGANY Map 1 D3
Co Wicklow

Glenview Hotel

★★★★ 77% HOTEL

☎ 01 2873399
Glen O' the Downs
e-mail: sales@glenviewhotel.com
dir: From Dublin city centre follow signs for N11, past Bray on N11 S'bound

This hotel is set in lovely terraced gardens overlooking the Glen o' the Downs. The comfortable bedrooms are spacious, and many enjoy the great views over the valley. The impressive public areas include a conservatory bar, lounge and choice of dining options including the first-floor Woodlands Restaurant where dinner is served. The hotel has an excellent range of leisure and conference facilities. A championship golf course and horse riding can be found nearby.

Rooms 70 (11 fmly) (16 GF) **Facilities** Spa STV Wi-fi supervised Gym Aerobics studio Massage Beauty treatment room Xmas New Year **Conf** Class 100 Board 80 Thtr 270 **Services** Lift **Parking** 200 **Notes** ⊗ Civ Wed 120

Save on hotels. Book at **theAA.com/hotel**

CON – DON 637 | **IRELAND**

DINGLE (AN DAINGEAN)
Co Kerry — Map 1 A2

Dingle Skellig Hotel & Peninsula Spa
★★★★ 80% HOTEL

☎ 066 9150200
e-mail: reservations@dingleskellig.com
dir: N86 to Dingle, hotel on harbour

This modern hotel, close to the town, overlooks Dingle Bay and has spectacular views from many of the comfortably furnished bedrooms and suites. Public areas offer a spacious bar and lounge and a bright, airy restaurant. There are extensive health and leisure facilities, and many family activities are organised in the Fungi Kids Club.

Rooms 113 (10 fmly) (31 GF) **Facilities** Spa STV FTV Wi-fi ⓑ supervised Gym ♪ New Year **Conf** Class 120 Board 100 Thtr 250 **Services** Lift **Parking** 110 **Notes** ⊗ Closed Jan RS Nov-Dec Civ Wed 230

Dingle Benners Hotel
★★★ 70% HOTEL

☎ 066 9151638
Main St
e-mail: info@dinglebenners.com
dir: In town centre

Located in the centre of the town with parking to the rear, this long-established property has an old world charm. There are a selection of relaxing lounges, open turf fires and comfortable bedrooms that are furnished with antique pine; some have four-poster beds. Food is available in Mrs Benner's traditional bar.

Rooms 52 (2 fmly) (9 GF) **Facilities** STV FTV Wi-fi **Services** Lift **Parking** 32 **Notes** ⊗ Closed 19-27 Dec Civ Wed 90

DONABATE
Co Dublin — Map 1 D4

The Waterside House Hotel
★★★ 73% HOTEL

☎ 01 8436153
e-mail: info@watersidehousehotel.ie
web: www.watersidehousehotel.ie
dir: Exit M1 junct 4 (Donabate/Portrane), 3rd exit at rdbt, pass Newbridge House Demesne on left, continue over rail bridge, right at sign for golf courses & hotel. Hotel on left

This family run hotel is situated in an enviable position right on Donabate Beach. Overlooking Lambay Island, the public areas and bedrooms are appointed in a contemporary style, with the comfortable lounge bar and terrace taking advantage of the breathtaking views. The Signal Restaurant offers evening dining in a cosy environment at weekends and during peak seasons. Entertainment is provided on a regular basis, with tribute shows during the summer months. A popular wedding venue, it is close to Dublin Airport and a number of golf courses.

Rooms 35 (8 fmly) (8 GF) ⌇ **S** €48-€80; **D** €65-€130 (incl. bkfst) **Facilities** STV FTV Wi-fi ♪ Xmas New Year **Conf** Class 150 Board 100 Thtr 400 Del from €69 to €130 **Services** Lift Air con **Parking** 100 **Notes** LB ⊗ Civ Wed 250

DONEGAL
Co Donegal — Map 1 B5

Harvey's Point Country Hotel
★★★★ 87% ⍟⍟ HOTEL

☎ 074 9722208
Lough Eske
e-mail: sales@harveyspoint.com
web: www.harveyspoint.com
dir: N56 from Donegal, then 1st right (Loch Eske/Harvey's Point)

Situated by the lake shore, this hotel is an oasis of relaxation; comfort and attentive guest care are the norm here. A range of particularly spacious suites and bedrooms is available, together with smaller rooms in the courtyard annexe. The kitchen brigade maintains consistently high standards in The Restaurant, with less formal dining in The Steakhouse at peak periods. A very popular Sunday buffet lunch is served weekly, with dinner entertainment on selected dates.

Rooms 70 (34 GF) **Facilities** Wi-fi Beauty treatment rooms Pitch 'n' putt Bicycle hire Walking tours ♪ **Conf** Class 200 Board 50 Thtr 200 **Services** Lift **Parking** 300 **Notes** Closed Mon & Tue Nov-Mar Civ Wed 250

The Central Hotel Conference & Leisure Centre
★★★ 77% HOTEL

☎ 074 9721027
The Diamond
e-mail: info@centralhoteldonegal.com
dir: In town centre

Located in the centre of the town, this long established hotel is a gem. The public rooms are decorated to a high standard; a popular carvery lunch is served in The Just William, and an all-day menu of European dishes and authentic Thai specialities is available in the atmospheric Upper Deck Bar. Afternoon tea is served on the first-floor mezzanine from where guests can look down on the bustling town below. Bedrooms vary in style and many have views over Donegal Bay. There is also a contemporary banqueting suite where occasional concerts are held.

Rooms 112 (26 fmly) **Facilities** STV FTV Wi-fi ⓑ supervised Gym ♪ Xmas New Year **Conf** Class 160 Board 70 Thtr 380 **Services** Lift **Notes** ⊗ Civ Wed

Mill Park Hotel
Ⓤ

☎ 074 9722880
The Mullins
e-mail: info@millparkhotel.com
dir: Take N15 signed Lifford. 2nd exit at rdbt to N56 signed Killybegs. Hotel on right

Currently the rating for this establishment is not confirmed. This may be due to a change of ownership or because it has only recently joined the AA rating scheme. For further details please see the AA website: theAA.com

Rooms 100 (10 fmly) (44 GF) (12 smoking) **Facilities** Spa Wi-fi ⓑ supervised Gym **Conf** Class 100 Board 30 Thtr 450 **Services** Lift **Parking** 250 **Notes** ⊗ Civ Wed 300

REPUBLIC OF IRELAND

DUBLIN
Dublin   Map 1 D4

The Merrion Hotel

★★★★★ ◉◉◉◉ HOTEL

☎ 01 6030600
Upper Merrion St
e-mail: info@merrionhotel.com
dir: At top of Upper Merrion St on left, beyond
Government buildings on right

This terrace of gracious Georgian buildings, reputed
to have been the birthplace of the Duke of
Wellington, embraces the character of many
changes of use over 200 years. Bedrooms and
suites are spacious, some in the original house;
others are in a modern wing overlooking the
gardens. They all offer great comfort and a wide
range of extra facilities. The lounges retain the
charm and opulence of days gone by, while the
Cellar bar area is a popular meeting point. Dining
options include The Cellar Restaurant specialising
in prime local ingredients and, for that very special
occasion, the award-winning Restaurant Patrick
Guilbaud is Dublin's finest. Art Tea is an afternoon
tea experience with a difference - the delightful
pastries are inspired by the hotel's vast art
collection.

Rooms 142 (21 GF) (20 smoking) ⚡ **S** €460-€3000;
D €480-€3000* **Facilities** Spa STV FTV Wi-fi ⅄ ⊛
Gym Steam room Xmas New Year **Conf** Class 25
Board 25 Thtr 60 **Services** Lift Air con **Parking** 60
Notes ⊗ Civ Wed 50

The Shelbourne Dublin, a
Renaissance Hotel

RENAISSANCE.
HOTELS & RESORTS

★★★★★ 88% ◉◉ HOTEL

☎ 01 6634500
27 St Stephen's Green
e-mail: rhi.dubbr.reservations@renaissancehotels.
com
web: www.theshelbourne.ie
dir: M1 to city centre, along Parnell St to O'Connell St
towards Trinity College, 3rd right into Kildare St, hotel
on left

This Dublin landmark exudes elegance and a real
sense of history, having been established in 1824.
The public areas are spacious and offer a range of
dining and bar options. There is a selection of
bedroom styles and suites available, many with
commanding views over St. Stephen's Green. No 27 is
a popular bar and lounge where casual dining takes
place. The Saddle Room is the main restaurant
featuring a steak and seafood menu with a
contemporary twist, while afternoon tea is served in
the elegant Lord Mayor's Lounge.

Rooms 265 (20 smoking) **S** €198-€2500;
D €219-€2500 **Facilities** Spa STV FTV Wi-fi ⅄ ⊛ Gym
Salt cave Aerobics studio Nail bar Sauna Steam room
♫ Xmas **Conf** Class 180 Board 60 Thtr 500
Del from €285 to €600 **Services** Lift Air con **Notes** LB
⊗ Civ Wed 350

The Westbury Hotel

★★★★★ 87% ◉◉ HOTEL

☎ 01 6791122
Grafton St
e-mail: westbury@doylecollection.com
dir: Adjacent to Grafton St, half way between Trinity
College & Stephen's Green

Located just off Grafton Street, Dublin's premier
shopping district, this is an oasis of calm; guests are
well cared for the amid smart, contemporary

surroundings. Spacious public areas include the
relaxing Gallery Lounge where afternoon tea is
popular with shoppers taking a break. Café Novo is
the hotel's buzzing street-level brasserie bar, while
Wilde-The Restaurant is an elegant grill with an
emphasis on seasonal and artisan fare. A range of
stylish suites and bedrooms is offered; many overlook
the roofs of the city. Valet parking is available.

Rooms 205 (9 fmly) ⚡ **S** €169-€499; **D** €169-€499*
Facilities STV FTV Wi-fi ⅄ Gym **Conf** Class 100
Board 46 Thtr 200 Del from €315 to €649*
Services Lift Air con **Parking** 100 **Notes** LB ⊗
Civ Wed 120

The Clarence

★★★★ ◉◉ HOTEL

☎ 01 4070800
6-8 Wellington Quay
e-mail: reservations@theclarence.ie
web: www.theclarence.ie
dir: From O'Connell Bridge, W along Quays, through
1st lights (at Ha'penny Bridge), hotel 500mtrs

Located on the banks of the River Liffey in the
Temple Bar area, The Clarence is within walking
distance of the shops and visitor attractions. This
is a very distinctive property - the character of the
1850 building has been successfully combined with
contemporary design in the bedrooms and suites.
The friendly service team provides unobtrusive yet
professional and personable service. The eating
options include The Tea Room, a spectacularly
bright and airy room with a 20-foot high ceiling
that serves innovative dishes cooked with flair and
based on excellent ingredients. More casual dining
can be found in the Octagon Bar, or in the cosy
Study Café with its log fire.

Rooms 49 (3 fmly) (7 smoking) **Facilities** STV Wi-fi
Gym Beauty treatment & massage room New Year
Conf Class 24 Board 35 Thtr 50 **Services** Lift
Parking 15 **Notes** ⊗ Closed 24-26 Dec Civ Wed 50

Save on hotels. Book at **theAA.com/hotel**

DUB 639 IRELAND

Castleknock Hotel & Country Club

FBD Hotels

★★★★ 81% ⊛ HOTEL

☎ 01 6406300
Porterstown Rd, Castleknock
e-mail: info@chcc.ie
web: www.castleknockhotel.com
dir: From airport/Blanch exit, left, right, right again into Castleknock. At Myos pub left, right at x-rds, follow signs

This modern hotel is set on a golf course yet it is only 15 minutes from Dublin. The bedrooms are very comfortable, with all the expected modern guest facilities. The spacious public rooms have an airy feel, and some rooms open onto a terrace that overlooks the golf course. The range of food and beverage outlets includes The Park Room, a steak house, a busy all-day brasserie, and The Lime Tree which is open in the evening. Excellent conference and banqueting facilities are available, together with a popular leisure centre.

Rooms 143 (6 fmly) (25 smoking) **Facilities** Spa FTV Wi-fi ⊗ supervised ♨ 18 Gym Sauna Steam room ♪ Xmas New Year **Conf** Class 200 Board 80 Thtr 500 **Services** Lift **Parking** 200 **Notes** ⊗ Closed 24-25 Dec Civ Wed 200

Clontarf Castle Hotel

★★★★ 80% HOTEL

☎ 01 8332321 & 8534336
Castle Av, Clontarf
e-mail: mlong@clontarfcastle.ie
dir: M1 towards centre, left at Whitehall Church, left at T-junct, straight on at lights, right at next lights into Castle Ave, hotel on right at rdbt

Dating back to the 12th century, this castle retains many historic architectural features which have been combined with contemporary styling in the well-equipped bedrooms. Public areas offer relaxing lounges, and modern cuisine is served in Fahrenheit Grill, Indigo Lounge and Knights Bar. The Great Hall is a versatile venue for banqueting and conferences.

Rooms 111 (7 fmly) (11 GF) (23 smoking) ♠ **S** €89-€236; **D** €89-€236* **Facilities** STV Wi-fi ♘ Gym Xmas New Year **Conf** Class 250 Board 90 Thtr 600 **Services** Lift Air con **Parking** 134 **Notes** LB ⊗ Civ Wed 400

Crowne Plaza Hotel

CROWNE PLAZA
HOTELS & RESORTS

★★★★ 79% ⊛ HOTEL

☎ 01 8977777
The Blanchardstown Centre
e-mail: info@cpireland.crowneplaza.com
dir: M50 junct 6 (Blanchardstown)

This landmark building is on the doorstep of a wide range of shops in Blanchardstown. Bedrooms are stylishly decorated with generously sized beds and well appointed en suites. The Sanctuary Bar serves an international range of informal dishes from lunchtime through to the evening, with Italian specialities (pasta dishes and pizzas) served in the evenings in Forchetta Restaurant. There is a floor of dedicated boardrooms and meeting facilities, together with banqueting rooms. Secure underground parking is complimentary to resident guests.

Rooms 188 (60 fmly) (15 smoking) ♠ **S** €59-€259; **D** €59-€259 **Facilities** STV FTV Wi-fi ♘ HL Gym Sauna ♪ New Year **Conf** Class 300 Board 300 Thtr 500 **Services** Lift Air con **Parking** 200 **Notes** ⊗ Civ Wed 300

Carlton Hotel Blanchardstown

CARLTON
HOTEL GROUP

★★★★ 78% HOTEL

☎ 01 8275600
Tyrrelstown
e-mail: info.blanch@carlton.ie
dir: Take Blanchardstown exit from M50 onto N3. Follow signs for Tyrrelstown

Easily accessed from both the airport and Dublin city, this contemporary hotel offers a fine range of spacious and comfortable bedrooms that are air conditioned and offer good work space. The en suites are well appointed with separate shower cubicles and baths. It is a property that was built with meetings and conferences in mind, and also enjoys an excellent reputation for wedding receptions. All-day dining is available in the smart Hourglass Bistro Bar, with evening dining in the Time restaurant, where a fine buffet breakfast is also served. There is a well-equipped gym.

Rooms 155 (22 fmly) (20 smoking) ♠ **S** €70-€250; **D** €80-€260 **Facilities** STV Wi-fi ♘ Gym New Year **Conf** Class 400 Board 100 Thtr 500 Del from €119 to €290 **Services** Lift Air con **Parking** 200 **Notes** LB ⊗ Closed 25-26 Dec Civ Wed 300

Stillorgan Park Hotel

★★★★ 77% ⊛ HOTEL

☎ 01 2001800
Stillorgan Rd, Stillorgan
e-mail: sales@stillorganpark.com
web: www.stillorganpark.com
dir: From N11 follow Wexford signs (pass RTE studios on left) through 5 sets of lights. Hotel on left

This modern hotel is situated on the southern outskirts of the city, close to UCD, Dundrum and Stillorgan shopping centres. Comfortable public areas include a spacious lobby, The Purple Sage Restaurant and a traditional style bar. There are extensive air-conditioned banqueting and conference facilities, a gym and a spa with treatment rooms.

Rooms 150 (8 fmly) (4 smoking) ♠ **S** €86-€219; **D** €86-€350* **Facilities** Spa STV Wi-fi ♘ Gym Beauty treatment room ♪ New Year **Conf** Class 220 Board 130 Thtr 500 Del from €138 to €195* **Services** Lift Air con **Parking** 300 **Notes** LB ⊗ Closed 25 Dec RS 24 Dec Civ Wed 300

Ashling Hotel, Dublin

★★★★ 77% HOTEL

☎ 01 6772324
Parkgate St
e-mail: info@ashlinghotel.ie
dir: Opposite Heuston Station

Situated on the banks of the River Liffey close to the city centre, railway station and law courts, this hotel is on the tram route and just a five-minute walk from the Phoenix Park. The property is appointed to a high standard in a contemporary style. The bedrooms are comfortably furnished; the newer ones are more spacious. Food is available in the Iveagh Bar throughout the day and a popular carvery is served at lunchtime; Chesterfield's Brasserie offers a carte menu in the evening. Staff are very friendly and service is attentive and professional. Secure multi-storey parking is available.

Rooms 225 (23 fmly) (10 smoking) ♠ **S** €79-€250; **D** €89-€360 **Facilities** STV Wi-fi **Conf** Class 110 Board 50 Thtr 220 **Services** Lift **Parking** 100 **Notes** LB ⊗ Closed 24-26 Dec

REPUBLIC OF IRELAND

DUBLIN *continued*

Red Cow Moran Hotel

★★★★ 76% HOTEL

☎ 01 4593650
Red Cow Complex, Naas Rd
e-mail: redcowres@moranhotels.com
web: www.moranhotels.com
dir: At junct of M50 & N7 on city side of motorway

Located just off the M50, this hotel is 20 minutes from the airport and only minutes away from the city centre via the Luas light rail system. The dedicated team of staff show a genuine willingness to create a memorable stay. Bedrooms are well equipped and comfortable, and the public areas and conference rooms are spacious. Ample free parking is available.

Rooms 123 (21 fmly) (48 smoking) **Facilities** FTV Wi-fi ♪ New Year **Conf** Class 350 Board 150 Thtr 750 **Services** Lift Air con **Parking** 700 **Notes** ⊗ Closed 24-26 Dec Civ Wed 200

Bewleys Hotel Ballsbridge

★★★ 77% HOTEL

☎ 01 6681111
Merrion Rd, Ballsbridge
e-mail: ballsbridge@bewleyshotels.com
dir: On corner of Merrion Rd & Simmonscourt Rd

This stylish hotel is a restored 19th-century Masonic school situated near the RDS, Aviva Stadium and the city centre. It offers comfortable, good-value, well-appointed accommodation. The Brasserie serves an interesting menu with a very popular carvery lunch and breakfast; snacks are available in Tom's Bar throughout the day. There is secure underground parking, and Thomas Prior Hall is a unique venue for banquets and conferences.

Rooms 304 (64 fmly) (45 GF) (25 smoking) 📶 **Facilities** Wi-fi ♪ Xmas New Year **Conf** Class 150 Board 80 Thtr 250 **Services** Lift **Parking** 220 **Notes** ⊗ Civ Wed 250

Bewleys Hotel Leopardstown
★★★ 75% HOTEL

☎ 01 2935000 & 2935001
Central Park, Leopardstown
e-mail: leop@bewleyshotels.com
dir: M50 juncts 13 & 14, follow signs for Leopardstown. Hotel on right

This hotel is conveniently situated close to the Central Business Park and Leopardstown Racecourse and serviced by the Luas light rail system and Aircoach.

The bedrooms are spacious and well appointed. Contemporary in style, the open-plan public areas include a spacious lounge bar with snack food available throughout the day; both lunch and dinner are served in the brasserie. There is a gym and a choice of conference rooms including the Power Suite. Underground parking is available.

Rooms 354 (70 fmly) (50 smoking) 📶 **Facilities** STV FTV Wi-fi ♪ Gym **Conf** Class 50 Board 50 Thtr 160 **Services** Lift **Parking** 228 **Notes** ⊗ Closed 23-25 Dec

Cassidys Hotel
★★★ 75% HOTEL

☎ 01 8780555
6-8 Cavendish Row, Upper O'Connell St
e-mail: stay@cassidyshotel.com
dir: In city centre at N end of O'Connell St

This family-run hotel is located at the top of O'Connell Street, in a terrace of red-brick Georgian townhouses, directly opposite the famed Gate Theatre. The warm and welcoming atmosphere created by the hospitable team in Groomes Bar and Bistro adds to the traditional atmosphere. Bedrooms are individually styled and well appointed; many have air conditioning. A residents' gym, conference facilities and limited parking are all available.

Rooms 113 (26 annexe) (3 fmly) (12 GF) (30 smoking) **Facilities** STV Wi-fi Gym Fitness suite **Conf** Class 45 Board 45 Thtr 80 **Services** Lift **Parking** 8 **Notes** ⊗ Closed 24-26 Dec

Sandymount Hotel
★★★ 75% HOTEL

☎ 01 614 2000
Herbert Rd, Sandymount
e-mail: info@sandymounthotel.ie
dir: Adjacent to Aviva Stadium, 200mtrs from Dart Rail Station

This hotel has been run by the Loughran family for three generations, and is located close to the Aviva Stadium, the RDS and Sandymount village. The comfortable bedrooms are well appointed, as are the lounge areas. The bistro restaurant and bar overlook the lovely garden. There are conference facilities and ample free parking is available.

Rooms 168 (3 fmly) (56 GF) **Facilities** STV Wi-fi **Conf** Class 60 Board 40 Thtr 100 **Services** Lift **Parking** 90 **Notes** ⊗ Closed 21-27 Dec

Temple Bar Hotel

★★★ 74% HOTEL

☎ 01 6773333
Fleet St, Temple Bar
e-mail: reservations@tbh.ie
web: www.templebarhotel.com
dir: From Trinity College towards O'Connell Bridge. 1st left onto Fleet St. Hotel on right

This hotel is situated right in the heart of Dublin's Temple Bar area, and is close to the main shopping districts, restaurants and the nightlife of the city. Bedrooms are comfortable and well equipped, with more spacious executive rooms available. Food is served throughout the day in Buskers themed bar, with the Rendezvous a more peaceful option. Alchemy is the smart night club which becomes a music venue at weekends and at other peak periods. Parking is available in a multi-storey opposite at a reduced rate for hotel guests.

Rooms 129 (6 fmly) (30 smoking) **S** €70-€240; **D** €70-€310 (incl. bkfst)* **Facilities** STV Wi-fi ♪ **Conf** Class 40 Board 40 Thtr 70 Del €120* **Services** Lift **Notes** LB ⊗ Closed 23-25 Dec RS Good Fri

Bewleys Hotel Newlands Cross
★★★ 73% HOTEL

☎ 01 4640140 & 4123301
Newlands Cross, Naas Rd
e-mail: newlands@bewleyshotels.com
web: www.bewleyshotels.com
dir: M50 junct 9, N7 (Naas road). Hotel near junct of N7 & Belgard Rd

This modern hotel is situated on the N7 and close to the M50 and Luas light rail to the city. Bedrooms are spacious and the pricing structure proves popular with families. The Brasserie restaurant is open through the day for casual dining and serves a carvery lunch; more formal meals are served in the evening. The hotel also has a comfortable bar where snacks are available, conference rooms, a gym and ample free parking.

Rooms 299 (176 fmly) (63 GF) **Facilities** Wi-fi ♪ **Conf** Class 18 Board 14 Thtr 50 **Services** Lift **Parking** 200 **Notes** ⊗ Closed 24-26 Dec

Save on hotels. Book at **theAA.com/hotel**

DUB – DUN 641 IRELAND

West County Hotel

★★ 74% HOTEL

☎ 01 6264011 & 6264647
Chapelizod
e-mail: info@westcountyhotel.ie
dir: From city centre follow signs for N4(W), 4m from city centre between Palmerstown & Ballyfermot on N4

This family run hotel is situated just off the N4 and is within walking distance of Chapelizod. The bedrooms are well appointed, and public areas include a comfortable lobby lounge and bar where carvery lunches are served daily; dinner is available in the Pine Restaurant.

Rooms 48 (10 fmly) (18 smoking) **Facilities** Wi-fi ♫ New Year **Conf** Class 100 Board 60 Thtr 200 **Services** Lift **Parking** 200 **Notes** ⊗ Closed 24-26 Dec Civ Wed 80

Ibis Hotel Dublin West

BUDGET HOTEL

☎ 01 464 1480
Naas Rd, Monastery Rd, Clondalkin
e-mail: H0595@accor.com
dir: Exit M50 junct 9 (Red Cow rdbt)

Close to Dublin airport and the M50, this hotel is modern in style. Bedrooms have contemporary furnishings including large desks. Public rooms include a restaurant and a lounge. Breakfast is self-service and a 24-hour snack service is also available.

Rooms 150 (39 fmly) (35 GF) **S** €40-€99; **D** €40-€99 **Conf** Class 25 Board 18 Thtr 35

Crowne Plaza Dublin Northwood

CROWNE PLAZA
HOTELS & RESORTS

★★★★ 80% ⊛ HOTEL

☎ 01 8628888
Northwood Park, Santry Demesne, Santry
e-mail: info@crowneplazadublin.ie
web: www.cpdublin.crowneplaza.com
dir: M50 junct 4, left into Northwood Park, 1km, hotel on left

Located within minutes of Dublin Airport, and served by a complimentary shuttle service, this modern hotel is located in Northwood Park, and benefits from an idyllic location overlooking 85 acres of mature woodlands of the former Santry Demesne. Bedrooms come in a variety of styles, and each is comfortable and well appointed. Guests in executive rooms have the use of a lounge facility where light breakfast is served. The hotel offers a range of dining options, including full room service and a lobby café. There are extensive conference and event rooms at this property, together with a secure multi storey car park. Guests also have use of a well equipped gym.

Rooms 204 (17 fmly) (5 smoking) ♠ **S** €75-€280; **D** €75-€280* **Facilities** STV FTV Wi-fi ♫ Gym Xmas New Year **Conf** Class 450 Board 100 Thtr 850 Del from €89 to €129* **Services** Lift Air con **Parking** 400 **Notes** LB ⊗ Civ Wed 300

Carlton Hotel Dublin Airport

CARLTON
HOTEL GROUP

★★★★ 76% HOTEL

☎ 01 8667500 & 8667501
Old Airport Rd
e-mail: info.dublin@carlton.ie
dir: From city centre take M1 to airport rdbt then 1st exit S towards Santry. Hotel 800mtrs on right

Conveniently located next to Dublin Airport this modern hotel offers every facility for business and leisure guests. The spacious air-conditioned bedrooms are well appointed; some have balconies. Public areas include a comfortable lobby lounge, Kittyhawks Bar and Bistro where food is served throughout the day. There is extensive banqueting and conference facilities and a fitness centre. Ample parking is available, and a complimentary, 24-hour shuttle coach service operates to and from the airport.

Rooms 100 (10 fmly) (13 GF) (13 smoking) ♠ **S** €150; **D** €190 **Facilities** STV Wi-fi ♫ Gym **Conf** Class 150 Board 80 Thtr 400 **Services** Lift Air con **Parking** 270 **Notes** LB Civ Wed 200

Premier Inn Dublin Airport

Premier Inn

BUDGET HOTEL

☎ 0871 527 8312
Airside Retail Park
web: www.premierinn.com
dir: M1 junct 2 for Dublin Airport. At main airport rdbt 3rd exit, follow Drogheda & Belfast signs. 2nd exit at Cloghran rdbt. Right at lights signed Airside Industrial Estate/Retail Park. Hotel on right

High quality, budget accommodation ideal for both families and business travellers. Spacious, en suite bedrooms feature tea and coffee making facilities, and Freeview TV in most hotels. Internet access and Wi-fi are available for a small fee. The adjacent family restaurant features a wide and varied menu. See also the Hotel Groups pages.

Rooms 155

Ballymascanlon House Hotel

★★★★ 80% HOTEL

☎ 042 9358200
e-mail: info@ballymascanlon.com
dir: M1 junct 18 onto N52 signed Dundalk North/R173 at Carlingford. Exit at Faughart rdbt. 1st left at next rdbt. Hotel in approx 1km on left

This Victorian mansion is set in 130 acres of woodland and landscaped gardens at the foot of the Cooley Mountains. The elegant house and the modern extension make this a very comfortable hotel that has really stylish bedrooms. Public areas include a spacious restaurant, lounge and bar, together with relaxing reading rooms that retain many original architectural features. There is a well-equipped leisure centre, and The Oak Room banqueting facility proves to be very popular for weddings and family occasions.

Rooms 90 (11 fmly) (5 GF) (34 smoking) ♠ **Facilities** STV FTV Wi-fi ♫ ⊙ supervised ⚐ 18 ⚑ Putt green Gym Steam room Sauna Plunge pool ♫ Xmas New Year **Conf** Class 220 Board 100 Thtr 400 **Services** Lift **Parking** 250 **Notes** Civ Wed 200

Arnold's Hotel

IRISH
COUNTRY
HOTELS

★★★ 75% ⊛ HOTEL

☎ 074 9136208
e-mail: enquiries@arnoldshotel.com
dir: N56 from Letterkenny, hotel on left on entering village

This family owned and run hotel, situated in a coastal village overlooking sandy beaches and beautiful scenery, is noted for its warm welcome and good food. The public areas and bedrooms are very comfortable; there is a traditional cosy bar with turf fires, a popular bistro that serves food throughout the day, and Seascapes Restaurant where dinner is a treat with local seafood featuring on the menus. There are stables attached to the hotel, with preferential terms for residents. Photographic and painting breaks are available as is links based golf.

Rooms 30 (10 fmly) ♠ **S** €50-€70; **D** €90-€130 (incl. bkfst)* **Facilities** FTV Wi-fi Fishing ♫ New Year **Parking** 60 **Notes** LB ⊗ RS Nov-Apr Civ Wed 80

REPUBLIC OF IRELAND

DUNGARVAN
Co Waterford
Map 1 C2

Lawlors Hotel

★★★ 70% HOTEL

☎ 058 41122
e-mail: info@lawlorshotel.com
dir: Off N25

This town centre hotel has very attractive and comfortable public areas with a busy bar where food is served throughout the day. A good value dinner menu is available in Davit's Restaurant. The bedrooms vary in size but all are well appointed. Conference and meeting rooms plus secure parking are available.

Rooms 89 (8 fmly) **Facilities** Wi-fi ♫ New Year **Conf** Class 215 Board 420 Thtr 420 **Services** Lift **Notes** Closed 25 Dec

DUNKINEELY
Co Donegal
Map 1 B5

Castle Murray House and Restaurant

◉ RESTAURANT WITH ROOMS

☎ 074 973 7022
St Johns Point
e-mail: info@castlemurray.com
dir: From Donegal take N56 towards Killybegs. Left to Dunkineely

Situated on the coast road of St Johns Point, this charming family-run restaurant with rooms overlooks McSwynes Bay and the castle. The bedrooms are individually decorated and appointed with guest comfort very much in mind, as is the cosy bar and sun lounge. There is a strong French influence in the cooking; locally landed fish, and prime lamb and beef are featured on the menus. Dates when this establishment is closed are subject to change, please telephone for details.

Rooms 10 (2 fmly)

DURRUS
Co Cork
Map 1 B2

Blairscove House & Restaurant

◉◉ RESTAURANT WITH ROOMS

☎ 027 61127
e-mail: mail@blairscove.ie
dir: From Durrus on R591 towards Crookhaven, 2.4km, house (blue gate) on right

Blairscove comprises four elegant suites located in the courtyard of a Georgian country house outside the pretty village of Durrus near Bantry; each room is individually decorated in a contemporary style and has stunning views over Dunmanus Bay and the

mountains. The restaurant is renowned for its wide range of hors d'oeuvres and its open wood-fire grill. The piano playing and candle light add to a unique dining experience.

Rooms 4 (4 annexe) (1 fmly)

ENNIS
Co Clare
Map 1 B3

Temple Gate Hotel

★★★ 80% ◉ HOTEL

☎ 065 6823300
The Square
e-mail: info@templegatehotel.com
dir: Exit N18 onto Tulla Rd for 0.25m, hotel on left

This smart hotel is owned and run by the Madden family and is located in the centre of the town. It incorporates a 19th-century, Gothic-style Great Hall banqueting room. The public areas are well planned and include a comfortable library lounge, popular traditional pub and Legends Restaurant. Bedrooms are attractive and well equipped with some executive rooms and suites available.

Rooms 70 (3 fmly) (11 GF) (20 smoking) **Facilities** STV FTV Wi-fi ♪ ♫ New Year **Conf** Class 100 Board 80 Thtr 250 **Services** Lift **Parking** 52 **Notes** ⊗ Closed 25-26 Dec RS 24 Dec Civ Wed 200

ENNISKERRY
Co Wicklow
Map 1 D3

The Ritz Carlton Powerscourt

★★★★★ 88% ◉◉ HOTEL

☎ 01 2748888
Powerscourt Estate
e-mail: powerscourtreservations@ritzcarlton.com
dir: From Dublin take M50, M11, then N11, follow Enniskerry signs. In Enniskerry left up hill, hotel on right

This very stylish hotel, built in the Palladian style, has a tranquil setting with stunning views over the gardens and woodlands to the Sugar Loaf. The bedrooms and suites are particularly spacious and well appointed with very impressive bathrooms that have TVs, deep tubs and walk-in showers. The luxuriously appointed public areas are airy and spacious with a variety of food options that includes the Gordon Ramsay at Powerscourt restaurant. The hotel also has a stunning spa, two golf courses, and includes fly fishing and equestrian pursuits among its many leisure facilities.

Rooms 200 (39 GF) **Facilities** Spa STV Wi-fi ♪ ◉ ♨ 36 Putt green Fishing ⤴ Gym Cycling Mega chess Xmas New Year **Conf** Class 240 Board 72 Thtr 500 **Services** Lift Air con **Parking** 384 **Notes** Civ Wed 400

GALWAY
Co Galway
Map 1 B3

The G Hotel

★★★★★ 87% ◉◉ HOTEL

☎ 091 865200
Wellpark, Dublin Rd
e-mail: info@theg.ie
dir: Telephone for detailed directions

Designed in association with the acclaimed milliner Philip Treacy, this hotel is the epitome of contemporary styling. The public areas comprise a series of eclectically furnished lounges, each with its own identity. The cutting-edge design is also apparent in the bedrooms and suites, which are very comfortable and appointed to a high standard. An interesting menu is on offer at dinner each evening in the atmospheric restaurant, and a very popular all-day menu is served in the lounges. The hotel has a number of boardrooms, and an Espa spa facility. Underground and valet parking is available.

Rooms 101 (2 fmly) ♠ **S** €140-€440; **D** €140-€440 (incl. bkfst)* **Facilities** Spa STV FTV Wi-fi HL Gym New Year **Conf** Class 42 Board 40 Thtr 120 Del from €165* **Services** Lift Air con **Parking** 349 **Notes** ⊗ Closed 23-26 Dec Civ Wed 90

Ardilaun Hotel & Leisure Club

★★★★ 81% ◉ HOTEL

☎ 091 521433
Taylor's Hill
e-mail: info@theardilaunhotel.ie
web: www.theardilaunhotel.ie
dir: M6 to Galway City West, then follow signs for N59 Clifden, then N6 towards Salthill

This very smart country-house style hotel, appointed to a high standard, is located on the outskirts of the city near Salthill and has lovely landscaped gardens. The bedrooms have been thoughtfully appointed and the deluxe rooms and suites are particularly spacious. Public areas include a selection of comfortable lounges, the Camilaun Restaurant that overlooks the garden, Blazers bistro and bar, and extensive banqueting and leisure facilities.

Rooms 125 (17 fmly) (8 GF) (16 smoking) ♠ **S** €69-€280; **D** €89-€390 (incl. bkfst)* **Facilities** Spa STV Wi-fi ♨ supervised Gym Beauty treatment & analysis rooms Beauty salon ♫ New Year **Conf** Class 300 Board 100 Thtr 650 Del from €140 to €175* **Services** Lift **Parking** 380 **Notes** LB Closed 24-26 Dec RS Closed 23 Dec pm Civ Wed 650

Save on hotels. Book at **theAA.com/hotel**

DUN – GOR 643 IRELAND

Park House Hotel & The Park Restaurant

★★★★ 78% HOTEL

☎ 091 564924
Forster St, Eyre Square
e-mail: parkhousehotel@eircom.net
web: www.parkhousehotel.ie
dir: In city centre

Situated just off Eyre Square, this well established hotel offers comfortable facilities to suite business or leisure guests. Public areas and bedrooms are well appointed and attractively decorated. The Park Restaurant has been a popular spot for the people of Galway for many years; less formal food is available throughout the day in Boss Doyle's bar. Parking for hotel guests is available at the rear.

Rooms 84 (4 smoking) ↾ **S** €109-€245; **D** €169-€295 (incl. bkfst & dinner)* **Facilities** STV FTV Wi-fi ♘ ♫ **Conf** Class 15 Board 15 Thtr 15 Del €169* **Services** Lift Air con **Parking** 48 **Notes** LB ⊗ Closed 24-26 Dec

Claregalway Hotel

 IRISH COUNTRY HOTELS

★★★ 79% HOTEL

☎ 091 738300 & 738302
Claregalway Village
e-mail: stay@claregalwayhotel.ie
dir: At junct of N17 (Galway/Sligo) & N18 (Dublin/Limerick)

Just 12 kilometres from Galway, this modern hotel offers comfortable bedrooms and spacious public areas. Run by the Gill family and their dedicated team, guests are sure to feel welcome and at home here. Food is served throughout the day in the popular Ti Cusack's Bar and Grill. Leisure facilities are complimentary to residents.

Rooms 48 (8 fmly) (3 smoking) **Facilities** Spa Wi-fi ⊛ supervised Gym Sauna Steam room Sunbeds ♫ New Year **Conf** Class 250 Board 100 Thtr 400 **Services** Lift Air con **Parking** 160 **Notes** ⊗ Closed 23-26 Dec Civ Wed 300

Carlton Hotel Galway City

CARLTON HOTEL GROUP

★★★ 77% HOTEL

☎ 091 381200
Dublin Rd
e-mail: reservations.galwaycity@carlton.ie
dir: M6 onto R446, last exit at Martin rdbt onto R338. Straight on at Steritt rdbt, hotel on left

This hotel is located a short drive from the city centre. It features a wide range of bedroom styles, many interconnected and suitable for family groups. The food options include all-day dining in Bar Solo, with

---

dinner in Reubens Restaurant. There are a number of conference and meeting rooms for up to 120 delegates, and Active Fitness is available to resident guests.

Rooms 363 (150 fmly) (80 GF) (80 smoking) **Facilities** STV FTV Wi-fi ♘ ⊛ supervised Gym Sauna Steam room Aerobics studio ♫ New Year **Services** Lift **Notes** ⊗ Closed 20-26 Dec

GARRYVOE **Map 1 C2**
Co Cork

Garryvoe Hotel

 IRISH COUNTRY HOTELS

★★★★ 79% HOTEL

☎ 021 4646718
Ballycotton Bay, Castlemartyr
e-mail: res@garryvoehotel.com
web: www.garryvoehotel.com
dir: N25 onto L72 at Castlemartyr (between Midleton & Youghal). 6km to hotel

In a delightful location facing the beach and overlooking Ballycotton Island and Bay, this is a comfortable, family-run hotel with caring staff. The bedrooms are appointed to a very high standard; some have balconies. The popular bar serves light meals throughout the day, and a more formal dinner menu is available in the dining room. There are extensive banqueting facilities and an excellent health club.

Rooms 82 (17 fmly) (5 smoking) **Facilities** STV Wi-fi ♘ ⊛ supervised Putt green Gym Sauna Steam room ♫ **Conf** Class 150 Board 12 Thtr 300 **Services** Lift **Parking** 100 **Notes** ⊗ Closed 24-25 Dec Civ Wed 150

GLASLOUGH **Map 1 C5**
Co Monaghan

The Lodge at Castle Leslie Estate

★★★★ 80% HOTEL

☎ 047 88100
e-mail: info@castleleslie.com
dir: M1 junct 14, N2 to Monaghan, N12 to N185 to Glaslough

Set in 1,000 acres of rolling countryside dotted with mature woodland, the lodge is the social hub of the Castle Leslie Estate which has been in the Leslie family since the 1660s. The comfortably furnished

---

bedrooms are in the original hunting lodge and the converted stable block. Resident guests have two dining options - Snaffles Restaurant and Connors Bar. There is a Victorian spa, a successful equestrian centre and a private fishing lake. For those who enjoy country pursuits this hotel is ideal for the many walks and interesting flora and fauna that the area has to offer.

Rooms 29 (2 fmly) (9 GF) ↾ **Facilities** Spa STV FTV Wi-fi ⌂ Fishing Equestrian centre **Conf** Class 25 Board 24 Thtr 40 **Services** Lift **Parking** 100 **Notes** ⊗ Closed 22-28 Dec Civ Wed 40

GLENDALOUGH **Map 1 D3**
Co Wicklow

The Glendalough Hotel

★★★ 73% HOTEL

☎ 0404 45135
e-mail: info@glendaloughhotel.ie
dir: N11 to Kilmacongue, right onto R755, straight on at Laragh, right onto R756

Mountains and forest provide the setting for this long-established hotel at the edge of the famed monastic site, and many of the comfortably appointed bedrooms have superb forest views. Food is served daily in the very popular bar and on the terrace when weather permits; the renovated Glendasan River Restaurant is a stylish bistro where dinner is served. The atmospheric Glendalough Tavern is a popular meeting place for visitors and locals alike.

Rooms 44 (3 fmly) **Facilities** STV Wi-fi Fishing ♫ **Conf** Class 150 Board 50 Thtr 200 **Services** Lift **Parking** 100 **Notes** ⊗ RS Dec-Jan, Mon-Fri

GOREY **Map 1 D3**
Co Wexford

Amber Springs Hotel

★★★★ 79% HOTEL

☎ 053 9484000
Wexford Rd
e-mail: info@ambersprings.ie
dir: 500mtrs from Gorey by-pass at junct 23

This hotel, on the Wexford road, is within walking distance of the town. Bedrooms are spacious and very comfortable, and guests have full use of the leisure facilities. Dining in Kelby's Bistro is a highlight of a visit, with a combination of interesting food and really friendly service.

Rooms 80 (34 fmly) (24 GF) ↾ **S** €65-€120; **D** €110-€170 (incl. bkfst)* **Facilities** Spa STV Wi-fi ⊛ supervised Gym ♫ New Year Child facilities **Conf** Class 450 Board 30 Thtr 700 **Services** Lift Air con **Parking** 178 **Notes** LB ⊗ Closed 25-26 Dec Civ Wed 700

GOREY *continued*

Seafield Golf & Spa Hotel

★★★★ 78% ◉ HOTEL

☎ 053 942 4000
Ballymoney
e-mail: reservations@seafieldhotel.com
dir: M11 junct 22

This ultra-modern hotel is part of a village style resort that includes an 18-hole championship golf course, courtyard family suites and the award-winning Oceo Spa. Set in 225 acres of parkland with mature trees, river-side walks and access onto Ballymoney Beach, the hotel offers contemporary, spacious bedrooms and suites which have views of either the coastline or the golf course. There are two dining options - fine dining in the restaurant and a more casual option in the bar or on the terrace.

Rooms 101 **S** €135-€155; **D** €210-€250 (incl. bkfst)* **Facilities** Spa STV Wi-fi ♨ ⟲ ♨ 18 Putt green Gym Playground ♫ New Year **Conf** Class 220 Board 40 Thtr 300 **Services** Lift **Parking** 200 **Notes** LB ⊗

Ashdown Park Hotel

★★★★ 76% ◉ HOTEL

☎ 053 9480500
The Coach Rd
e-mail: info@ashdownparkhotel.com
web: www.ashdownparkhotel.com
dir: N11 junct 22, on approaching Gorey, 1st left (before railway bridge), hotel on left

Situated on an elevated position overlooking the town, this modern hotel has excellent health, leisure and banqueting facilities. There are comfortable lounge areas and two dining options - Ivy, a popular carvery bar, and The Rowan Tree, the first-floor fine dining restaurant open in the evenings. Bedrooms are available in a number of styles; all are spacious and well equipped. Close to a number of golf courses, this property is popular with golfers, and also with families as it is near the beaches.

Rooms 79 (12 fmly) (20 GF) **S** €65-€120; **D** €110-€170 (incl. bkfst)* **Facilities** FTV Wi-fi ⟲ supervised Gym Leisure centre Massage rooms ♫ New Year **Conf** Class 315 Board 100 Thtr 800 **Services** Lift **Parking** 150 **Notes** LB ⊗ Closed 25 Dec Civ Wed 300

Marlfield House Hotel

★★★ ◉ ◉

COUNTRY HOUSE HOTEL

☎ 053 9421124
e-mail: info@marlfieldhouse.ie
web: www.marlfieldhouse.com
dir: N11 junct 23, follow signs for Courtown. At Courtown Rd rdbt left for Gorey. Hotel 1m on left

This Regency-style building has been gracefully extended and developed into an excellent hotel. An atmosphere of elegance and luxury permeates every corner of the house, underpinned by truly friendly and professional service led by the Bowe family who are always in evidence. The bedrooms are decorated in keeping with the style of the house, with some really spacious rooms and suites on the ground floor. Dinner in the restaurant is always a highlight of a stay at Marlfield.

Rooms 19 (3 fmly) (6 GF) ➤ **S** €75-€115; **D** €190-€650 (incl. bkfst) **Facilities** FTV Wi-fi ♨ ⟲ Beauty treatment room **Conf** Board 24 Thtr 60 Del from €185 to €250 **Parking** 100 **Notes** LB Closed 2 Jan-28 Feb RS Nov-Dec & Mar-Apr Civ Wed 120

KENMARE
Co Kerry
Map 1 B2

Sheen Falls Lodge

★★★★★ ◉ ◉ COUNTRY HOUSE HOTEL

☎ 06466 41600
e-mail: info@sheenfallslodge.ie
dir: From Kenmare take N71 to Glengarriff over suspension bridge, take 1st left

This former fishing lodge has been developed into a beautiful hotel with a friendly team of professional staff. The cascading Sheen Falls are floodlit at night, forming a romantic backdrop to the enjoyment of award-winning cuisine in La Cascade Restaurant. Less formal dining is available in Oscar's Bistro, and the Sun Lounge serves refreshments and light snacks throughout the day. The bedrooms are very comfortably appointed; many of the suites are particularly spacious. The leisure centre and beauty therapy facilities offer a number of exclusive treatments, and the outdoor pursuits include walking, fishing, tennis, horse riding and clay pigeon shooting.

Rooms 66 (14 fmly) (14 GF) ➤ **S** €150-€350; **D** €178-€450 (incl. bkfst)* **Facilities** Spa STV Wi-fi ♨ supervised ♨ Fishing ⟲ Gym Table tennis Steam room Clay pigeon shooting Cycling Vintage car rides Library ♫ Xmas New Year **Conf** Class 65 Board 50 Thtr 120 Del from €245* **Services** Lift **Parking** 76 **Notes** LB ⊗ Closed 2 Jan-1 Feb RS Midwk in Feb, Mar, Nov & Dec Civ Wed 100

KILKENNY
Co Kilkenny   Map 1 C3

Kilkenny River Court Hotel

★★★★ 78% ◉ HOTEL

☎ 056 7723388
The Bridge, John St
e-mail: reservations@rivercourthotel.com
dir: In town centre, opposite castle

Hidden behind archways on John Street, this is a very comfortable and welcoming establishment. The restaurant, bar and many of the well-equipped bedrooms command great views of Kilkenny Castle and the River Nore. Attentive, friendly staff ensure good service throughout the hotel. Excellent corporate and leisure facilities are provided.

Rooms 90 (4 fmly) **Facilities** Spa Wi-fi ⓘ supervised Gym Beauty salon & treatment rooms **Conf** Class 110 Board 45 Thtr 260 **Services** Lift **Parking** 84 **Notes** ⊗ Closed 23-26 Dec Civ Wed 250

Pembroke Hotel

★★★★ 77% HOTEL

☎ 056 7783500
Patrick St
e-mail: info@pembrokekilkenny.com

This hotel enjoys an ideal location right at the heart of the city. Bedrooms are spacious and furnished to a high standard, some with views of the famed Kilkenny Castle. Stathams bar and grill is open throughout the day; the menu features firm favourites, together with a range of home-made desserts and bakery items. Bright, airy meeting and training rooms are located in the courtyard and secure parking is complimentary to residents.

Rooms 74 (16 fmly) (5 GF) **Facilities** STV FTV Wi-fi Gym New Year **Services** Lift Air con **Parking** 80 **Notes** ⊗ Civ Wed 100

Langton House Hotel

★★★ 78% HOTEL

☎ 056 7765133 & 5521728
69 John St
e-mail: reservations@langtons.ie
dir: N9 & N10 from Dublin, follow city centre signs on outskirts of Kilkenny, left to Langtons. Hotel 500mtrs on left after lights

This hotel has a long and well-founded reputation for its genuine hospitality as an entertainment venue, nightclub and bar. The most recent addition is the much talked about Set Theatre, where leading performers take to the stage. There is a range of bedroom options, many in the garden annexe; all are very comfortable, tastefully decorated and well appointed. The eating options include The Langton, a busy restaurant serving dinner, and the more casual, all-day '67', a lively bar that is popular with visitors and locals alike.

Rooms 34 (16 annexe) (4 fmly) (8 GF) (22 smoking) **Facilities** STV Wi-fi ♪ New Year **Conf** Class 250 Board 30 Thtr 400 **Services** Air con **Parking** 60 **Notes** Closed 24-25 Dec Civ Wed 100

KILLARNEY
Co Kerry   Map 1 B2

Muckross Park Hotel & Cloisters Spa

★★★★ 84% HOTEL

☎ 064 6623400
Lakes of Killarney
e-mail: info@muckrosspark.com
dir: From Killarney take N71 towards Kenmare

Dating originally from 1795, this fine property offers spacious accommodation and excellent public areas. Most of the bedrooms are in a block to the rear, but some are in the original building which retains many original features. All of the bedrooms and suites are beautifully appointed, with high quality fabrics and furnishings. Casual dining is available throughout the day in the old world atmosphere of Molly Darcy's pub, with more formal dining in the Blue Pool or GB Shaw's Restaurants. The Cloisters Spa is an oasis of calm and tranquillity, with a wide range of treatments available.

Rooms 68 (3 fmly) **S** €79-€329; **D** €119-€369 (incl. bkfst) **Facilities** Spa STV Wi-fi ⓘ ⓘ supervised Fishing ➤ Gym Cycling Yoga Pilates ♪ New Year **Conf** Class 280 Board 30 Thtr 350 Del from €150 to €230 **Services** Lift Air con **Parking** 80 **Notes** LB ⊗ Closed Nov-Jan weekdays Civ Wed 250

Cahernane House Hotel

★★★★ 80% ◉◉ HOTEL

☎ 064 6631895
Muckross Rd
e-mail: info@cahernane.com
web: www.cahernane.com
dir: On N22 to Killarney, 1st exit at rdbt, left at church, 1st exit at next rdbt to Muckross Rd

This fine country mansion, the former home of the Earls of Pembroke, has a magnificent mountain backdrop and panoramic views from its lakeside setting, yet is only a ten-minute walk from the town centre. Elegant period furniture is complemented by more modern pieces to create a comfortable hotel offering a warm atmosphere with a particularly friendly team dedicated to guest care. There are a number of accommodation options, some in the original house, others in a building accessed via a stunning conservatory. Dinner in the Herbert Room is a highlight of any stay, with more casual fare on offer in the cosy Cellar Bar.

Rooms 38 (26 annexe) ⌂ **S** €75-€145; **D** €120-€250 (incl. bkfst) **Facilities** Wi-fi ⓘ Fishing ➤ **Conf** Class 10 Board 10 Thtr 15 Del from €135 to €175 **Services** Lift Air con **Parking** 50 **Notes** LB ⊗ Closed 21 Dec-Jan Civ Wed 60

Randles Court Hotel

★★★★ 80% HOTEL

☎ 064 6635333
Muckross Rd
e-mail: info@randlescourt.com
dir: N22 towards Muckross, right at T-junct. From N72 3rd exit on 1st rdbt into town, follow signs for Muckross, hotel on left

Owned and run by the Randles family, this charming hotel is situated close to the town, the lakes and Killarney National Park. The Drawing Room and Wiggs Bar are elegantly furnished and very relaxing. Bedrooms are spacious, and great care has been taken in the choice of furnishings and decor. Dinner is served nightly in Checkers Restaurant. There is a swimming pool, spa treatment rooms and secure underground parking.

Rooms 78 (4 fmly) (6 GF) **Facilities** Spa STV Wi-fi ⓘ ⓘ supervised Sauna Steam room Hydrotherapy suite New Year **Conf** Class 50 Board 40 Thtr 90 **Services** Lift **Parking** 110 **Notes** Closed 22-27 Dec Civ Wed 140

REPUBLIC OF IRELAND

KILLARNEY *continued*

The Lake Hotel

★★★★ 75% ⬡ HOTEL

☎ 064 6631035
Lake Shore, Muckross Rd
e-mail: info@lakehotel.com
dir: N22 to Killarney. Hotel 2km from town on Muckross Rd

Enjoying a delightful location on the shores of Killarney's lake shore, this hotel is run by the second generation of the Huggard family together with a dedicated and friendly team. There is a relaxed atmosphere with log fires and stunning views from the lounges and restaurant, and guests could be lucky enough to see a herd of red deer wander by. The smartly furnished bedrooms have either lake or woodland views; some have balconies and four-poster beds. The spa offers good facilities, and there are cycle paths and lovely walks to enjoy.

Rooms 130 (6 fmly) (23 GF) **S** €75–€240;
D €105–€360 (incl. bkfst) **Facilities** Spa STV FTV Wi-fi ⬡ Fishing ⬡ Gym Sauna Steam room ♫
Conf Class 60 Board 40 Thtr 80 **Services** Lift **Parking** 140 **Notes** LB ⊗ Closed 6 Dec-Jan Civ Wed 60

Castlerosse Hotel & Golf Resort

★★★ 79% HOTEL

☎ 064 6631144
Lakes of Killarney
e-mail: res@castlerosse.ie
web: www.castlerosse.ie
dir: From Killarney take R562 signed Killorglin & The Ring of Kerry. Hotel 2.5km on left

This hotel is situated on 6,000 acres overlooking the Lakes of Killarney with the Magillycuddy Mountains as a backdrop. At times guests will be able to spot deer in Killarney National Park. Bedrooms and junior suites are well appointed and comfortable. There is live entertainment most nights in Mulligan's pub. Leisure facilities include a 9-hole parkland golf course, tennis courts, a leisure centre and treatment rooms.

Rooms 120 (27 fmly) **S** €60–€100; **D** €90–€180 (incl. bkfst)* **Facilities** Spa STV FTV Wi-fi ⬡ supervised ⬡ 9 ⬡ Putt green Gym Golf & horse riding arranged ♫ **Conf** Class 100 Board 40 Thtr 200 **Services** Lift **Parking** 100 **Notes** LB ⊗ Closed Nov-Mar Civ Wed 80

Killeen House Hotel

★★★ 78% ⬡ HOTEL

☎ 064 6631711 & 6631773
Lakes of Killarney, Aghadoe
e-mail: charming@indigo.ie
dir: In Aghadoe, just outside Killarney

Dating back to 1838 this charming Victorian country house is situated close to Killarney National Park and lakes. Stylishly decorated public areas include a cosy sitting room and bar where 'golf' is spoken! Good cuisine is served in the restaurant which overlooks the beautifully manicured garden. Bedrooms are well appointed and comfortable. The Rosney family and their staff take particular pride in extending a warm welcome to their guests.

Rooms 23 (8 fmly) (10 GF) (10 smoking) **Facilities** STV FTV Wi-fi **Parking** 30 **Notes** Closed 21 Oct-19 Apr Civ Wed 50

KILLENARD   Map 1 C3
Co Laois

The Heritage Golf & Spa Resort

Ⓤ

☎ 057 8645500
e-mail: info@theheritage.com
dir: From Dublin M7 to Cork. Exit at Monesterevin, through village, in 3km right at Bollands Pub. Killenard in 3km

Currently the rating for this establishment is not confirmed. This may be due to a change of ownership or because it has only recently joined the AA rating scheme. For further details please see the AA website: theAA.com

Rooms 98 (10 fmly) (20 GF) (23 smoking) **Facilities** Spa Wi-fi ⬡ ⬡ 0 ⬡ Putt green Fishing ⬡ Gym ♫ **Conf** Class 250 Board 50 Thtr 400 **Services** Lift Air con **Parking** 600 **Notes** ⊗ Closed 19-26 Dec Civ Wed 170

KILLINEY   Map 1 D4
Co Dublin

Fitzpatrick Castle Hotel

★★★★ 81% ⬡ HOTEL

☎ 01 2305400
e-mail: reservations@fitzpatricks.com
web: www.fitzpatrickcastle.com
dir: From Dun Laoghaire port turn left, on coast road right at lights, left at next lights. Follow to Dalkey, right at Ivory Pub, immediate left, up hill, hotel at top

This family-owned, 18th-century castle is situated in lovely gardens with mature trees and spectacular views over Dublin Bay. The original castle rooms are appointed to a high standard and have four-poster beds, while the rooms in the modern wing are spacious and some have balconies. Lounges are comfortably furnished and PJ's restaurant serves dinner on certain days of the week; more casual fare is available each night in the trendy Dungeon bar and grill. There are extensive leisure and conference facilities.

Rooms 113 (36 fmly) (12 smoking) **S** €120–€200; **D** €150–€300 **Facilities** STV Wi-fi ⬡ supervised Gym Beauty/hairdressing salon Sauna Steam room Fitness centre ♫ Xmas New Year **Conf** Class 250 Board 80 Thtr 500 **Services** Lift **Parking** 300 **Notes** ⊗ RS 25-Dec Civ Wed 400

KILMESSAN   Map 1 C/D4
Co Meath

The Station House Hotel
★★★ 75% ⊛ HOTEL

☎ 046 9025239 & 9025586
e-mail: info@thestationhousehotel.com
web: www.thestationhousehotel.com
dir: M50, N3 towards Navan. At Dunshaughlin left at
end of village, follow signs

While the Station House saw its last train in the early
sixties, it still retains much of its railway history and
atmosphere. Some of the accommodation is located
in the old carriage house, and the signal box is the
bridal suite; the station itself hosts diners in the
station master's office. The bedrooms are comfortably
appointed, and the lounge areas are very relaxing. Set
in attractively landscaped gardens and woodlands,
this is a popular wedding venue. Dinner is always a
highlight, featuring well-sourced ingredients cooked
with both flair and care.

Rooms 20 (14 annexe) (3 fmly) (5 GF) **Facilities** Wi-fi
♫ Xmas New Year **Conf** Class 300 Board 100
Thtr 400 **Parking** 200 **Notes** ⊗ Civ Wed 100

KILTIMAGH   Map 1 B4
Co Mayo

Kiltimagh Park Hotel

★★★ 77% HOTEL

☎ 094 9374922
e-mail: info@parkhotelmayo.com
dir: N17 onto R322 or R323 (or N60 onto R320) to
Kiltimagh

This smart hotel overlooks the Wetlands Wildlife Park
and is within walking distance of Kiltimagh, and just
15 minutes from Ireland West Knock Airport and
Knock Marian Shrine. The spacious bedrooms are well
appointed. Public areas are attractively decorated
and include comfortable lounges, Café Bar, Park
Restaurant and banqueting facilities. The Aroma
Beauty Spa offers a range of treatments and there is
also a fitness centre and steam room. A shuttle coach
service operates to the airport, and for guests using
the airport, parking can be arranged at the hotel.

Rooms 46 (40 fmly) **Facilities** Spa Wi-fi ♫ Gym New
Year **Conf** Class 120 Board 60 Thtr 450 **Services** Lift
Parking 300 **Notes** Civ Wed 350

Cill Aodain Court Hotel
★★★ 70% HOTEL

☎ 094 9381761
Main St
e-mail: info@cillaodain.ie
dir: In town centre opposite Market Square

Situated in the heart of historic Kiltimagh and close
to Marian Shrine at Knock and also the airport, this
smart, contemporary hotel offers comfortable well-
appointed bedrooms. Public areas include The Gallery
Restaurant, Court Bar & Bistro. Off-street parking is
available opposite the hotel.

Rooms 17 (4 fmly) (7 smoking) **Facilities** STV Wi-fi ♫
New Year **Conf** Class 30 Board 25 Thtr 50 **Notes** ⊗
Closed 24-25 Dec

KINGSCOURT   Map 1 C4
Co Cavan

Cabra Castle Hotel
[U]

☎ 042 9667030
e-mail: sales@cabracastle.com
dir: R165 between Kingscourt & Carrickmacross

Currently the rating for this establishment is not
confirmed. This may be due to a change of ownership
or because it has only recently joined the AA rating
scheme. For further details please see the AA website:
theAA.com

Rooms 98 **Conf** Class 100 Board 50 Thtr 300
Notes Closed 24-26 Dec

KINSALE   Map 1 B2
Co Cork

Carlton Hotel Kinsale
★★★★ 79% ⊛ HOTEL

☎ 021 4706000
Rathmore Rd
e-mail: reservations.kinsale@carlton.ie
dir: R600 to Kinsale, turn left signed Charles Fort.
3kms, (pass rugby club), hotel on left

This hotel is set on an elevated position overlooking
Oysterhaven Bay in 90 acres of mature parkland,
approximately five kilometres from the town centre.
All of the bedrooms are spacious and well appointed;
many have spectacular views over the bay. Two-
bedroom holiday apartment options are available in
the grounds. The contemporary public rooms are on
the first floor, with spacious terraces. They include the
Rockpool Restaurant where guests can cook fine
Angus steaks on lava stones at their table. The team
at this property are all very guest focused, and make
families particularly welcome.

Rooms 130 (20 fmly) (24 GF) **Facilities** Spa STV FTV
Wi-fi ♫ ⊗ supervised Gym New Year **Conf** Class 120
Board 40 Thtr 300 **Services** Lift Air con **Parking** 140
Notes ⊗ Closed 23-27 Dec Civ Wed 200

Blue Haven
★★★ 75% HOTEL

☎ 021 4772209
3 Pearse St
e-mail: info@bluehavenkinsale.com
web: www.bluehavenkinsale.com
dir: In town centre

At the heart of this historic town, this vibrant hotel
offers a comfortable lounge and café, a very popular
and stylish bar with an airy bistro plus an elegant
restaurant. Live music is a feature seven days a week
in high season, and there is a pizza and disco bar at
the rear. Bedrooms vary in size and are furnished to a
high standard.

Rooms 17 ♥ S €59-€95; D €70-€170 (incl. bkfst)*
Facilities FTV Wi-fi ♫ New Year **Conf** Class 35
Board 25 Thtr 100 **Notes** LB ⊗ Closed 25 Dec
Civ Wed 70

The White House
⊛ RESTAURANT WITH ROOMS

☎ 021 4772125
Pearse St, The Glen
e-mail: whitehse@indigo.ie
dir: In town centre

Centrally located among the narrow, twisting streets
of the charming town of Kinsale, this restaurant with
rooms dates from 1850, and is a welcoming hostelry
with modern, smart, comfortable bedrooms. The bar
and bistro are open for lunch and dinner, and the
varied menu features local fish and beef. The
courtyard makes a perfect setting in summer and
there is traditional music in the bar most nights.

Rooms 10 (2 fmly)

REPUBLIC OF IRELAND

LEENANE
Co Galway — Map 1 A4

Delphi Mountain Resort

☎ 095 42208
e-mail: info@delphiescape.com

Currently the rating for this establishment is not confirmed. This may be due to a change of ownership or because it has only recently joined the AA rating scheme. For further details please see the AA website: theAA.com

Rooms 39 (4 fmly) (12 GF) **Facilities** Spa ♨ Thermal suite Xmas **Conf** Class 40 Board 60 Thtr 80 **Services** Lift **Parking** 40 **Notes** ⊗ Closed Jan Civ Wed 150

LETTERKENNY
Co Donegal — Map 1 C5

Radisson Blu Hotel Letterkenny

Radisson BLU HOTELS & RESORTS

★★★★ 79% ⊚ HOTEL

☎ 074 9194444
Paddy Harte Rd
e-mail: info.letterkenny@radissonblu.com
dir: N14 into Letterkenny. At Polestar Rdbt take 1st exit, to hotel

Letterkenny is an ideal base for visiting the many peninsulas of County Donegal. Within walking distance of the town and the retail parks, this hotel offers a range very comfortable rooms, with all the facilities that today's traveller expects. Guests can dine throughout the day in the popular Oakk Bar & Grill, or, in the evening, enjoy seafood delights and other good dishes in Brasserie TriBeCa, where there is a live TV link to the kitchen to see the action! Well-equipped meeting rooms are available, together with a large conference and banqueting hall. The leisure facilities are complimentary to resident guests.

Rooms 114 (5 fmly) (6 smoking) **S** €84-€135; **D** €99-€155 (incl. bkfst)* **Facilities** STV Wi-fi ⊙ Gym Sauna Steam room Sunbed Olympic weights room Xmas New Year **Conf** Class 270 Thtr 600 Del from €120* **Services** Lift **Parking** 150 **Notes** LB ⊗ Civ Wed 600

Downings Bay Hotel

★★★ 74% HOTEL

☎ 074 9155586 & 9155770
Downings
e-mail: info@downingsbayhotel.com
dir: 23m N of Letterkenny on R245. Hotel in village centre

This hotel is situated on Sheephaven Bay in the picturesque village of Downings. There is a cosy lounge, traditional style bar and a restaurant where food is available all day. The bedrooms are comfortable and well appointed. Guests have complimentary use of the local leisure centre, and the night club is open at weekends.

Rooms 40 (8 fmly) (4 smoking) ♥ **S** €50-€80; **D** €80-€140 (incl. bkfst)* **Facilities** Wi-fi ♫ ⊙ supervised Gym Sauna Steam room Indoor adventure play area ♫ New Year **Conf** Class 175 Board 50 Thtr 350 Del from €70 to €110* **Services** Lift Air con **Parking** 40 **Notes** LB ⊗ Closed 25-26 Dec Civ Wed 80

LIMERICK
Co Limerick — Map 1 B3

Carlton Castletroy Park Hotel

★★★★ 79% ⊚ HOTEL

☎ 061 335566 & 508700
Dublin Rd
e-mail: reservations.castletroy@carlton.ie
dir: On Dublin road, 3km from city, opposite University of Limerick

This modern hotel is close to the University of Limerick. The attractively decorated public areas include the atmospheric Merry Pedler Bar & Bistro that serves food throughout the day, and the fine-dining McLaughlin's Restaurant overlooking the gardens and which opens in the evening. Bedrooms are very well equipped to suit both leisure and business guests. The banqueting and conference facilities are extensive. Complimentary underground parking is available opposite the hotel.

Rooms 107 (80 fmly) (5 smoking) **S** €89-€199; **D** €98-€259 (incl. bkfst) **Facilities** Spa STV FTV Wi-fi ♫ ⊙ supervised ♨ Gym Sauna Steam room Xmas New Year **Conf** Class 270 Board 80 Thtr 400 Del from €143 to €170 **Services** Lift **Parking** 150 **Notes** ⊗ Civ Wed 300

Limerick Strand Hotel

★★★★ 79% ⊚ HOTEL

☎ 061 421800
Ennis Rd
e-mail: info@strandlimerick.ie
dir: From Shannon/Galway follow N18 to Limerick. At Coonagh rdbt follow Ennis road into city centre. Hotel on right on banks of river

This hotel enjoys stunning views over the River Shannon, and all bedrooms are spacious and fitted to a high standard. The public areas make the most of the views, with meeting rooms on the penthouse level. All-day dining is available in the bar, with innovative evening meals served in the River Restaurant. Secure parking is available at a reduced rate for residents.

Rooms 184 (13 fmly) ♥ **S** €99-€179; **D** €99-€179* **Facilities** Spa STV Wi-fi ♫ ⊙ supervised Gym ♫ Xmas New Year **Conf** Class 400 Board 50 Thtr 600 **Services** Lift Air con **Parking** 203 **Notes** LB Civ Wed 450

LISDOONVARNA
Co Clare — Map 1 B3

Sheedys Country House Hotel

★★★ 78% ⊚⊚ HOTEL

☎ 065 7074026
e-mail: info@sheedys.com
dir: 200mtrs from The Square in town centre

Dating in part from the 17th century and set in an unrivalled town centre location on the edge of The Burren, this house is full of character and has an intimate atmosphere. Fine cuisine can be enjoyed in the contemporary restaurant. The bedrooms are spacious and well appointed. This makes an ideal base for touring as it is close to Doolin, Lahinch Golf Course, and the Cliffs of Moher.

Rooms 11 (1 fmly) (5 GF) ♥ **S** €70-€90; **D** €100-€170 (incl. bkfst)* **Facilities** STV FTV Wi-fi **Parking** 40 **Notes** LB ⊗ Closed mid Oct-Apr

LUCAN
Co Dublin — Map 1 D4

Finnstown Country House Hotel

★★★ 79% ⊚ HOTEL

☎ 01 6010700 & 6010708
Newcastle Rd
e-mail: edwina@finnstown-hotel.ie
dir: From M1 onto M50 S'bound. 1st exit for N4. Take slip road signed Newcastle/Adamstown. Straight on at rdbt, through lights, hotel on right

Set in 45 acres of wooded grounds and paddocks, Finnstown House is a calm and peaceful country property in an urban setting. The elegant bar and drawing room is where informal meals are served throughout the day, with more formal dining at lunch and dinner in the Peacock Restaurant. There is a wide choice of bedroom styles, situated both in the main house and in the annexes. The staff members are very guest focused with a warm and friendly approach. This is a very popular venue for small conferences and family celebrations. A fitness centre is available to resident guests.

Rooms 81 (54 annexe) (6 fmly) (9 GF) (12 smoking) S €65–€200; D €65–€250 (incl. bkfst) **Facilities** STV Wi-fi Gym Steam room New Year **Conf** Class 150 Board 50 Thtr 300 Del from €120 to €220 **Services** Lift Air con **Parking** 300 **Notes** LB Closed 24-26 Dec Civ Wed 200

Lucan Spa Hotel
★★★ 64% HOTEL

☎ 01 6280494
e-mail: info@lucanspahotel.ie
web: www.lucanspahotel.ie
dir: At N4 junct 4a, approx 11km from city centre

Set in its own grounds and 20 minutes from Dublin Airport, close to the M50, the Lucan Spa is a lovely Georgian house with a modern extension. Bedrooms vary in size and are well equipped. There are two dining options; dinner is served in Honora D Restaurant, and The Earl Bistro is for more casual dining. A conference centre is also available.

Rooms 71 (15 fmly) (9 GF) (12 smoking) **Facilities** STV FTV Wi-fi New Year **Conf** Class 250 Board 80 Thtr 600 **Services** Lift Air con **Parking** 200 **Notes** Closed 24-25 Dec Civ Wed 100

MACREDDIN Map 1 D3
Co Wicklow

BrookLodge & Wells Spa
★★★★ 87% HOTEL

☎ 0402 36444
e-mail: info@brooklodge.com
web: www.brooklodge.com
dir: N11 to Rathnew, R752 to Rathdrum, R753 to Aughrim, follow signs to Macreddin Village

A luxury country-house hotel in a village-style setting which includes an 18-hole golf course, a pub, café and food shop. There is a choice of dining options - the award-winning Strawberry Tree Restaurant specialising in organic and wild foods and a more casual Italian restaurant. Bedrooms and lounges in the original house are very comfortable; there are also bedrooms in Brookhall, tailored for guests attending weddings and conferences. The Wells Spa offers extensive treatments and leisure facilities, and there are many outdoor activities including horse riding and off-road driving.

Rooms 86 (32 annexe) (27 fmly) (4 GF) **Facilities** Spa STV FTV Wi-fi 18 Putt green Gym Archery Clay pigeon shooting Off road driving New Year **Conf** Class 170 Board 150 Thtr 300 **Services** Lift Air con **Parking** 200 **Notes** Closed 24-25 Dec Civ Wed 200

MALAHIDE

Grand Hotel
★★★★ 80% HOTEL

☎ 018 450000
e-mail: info@thegrand.ie
dir: In town overlooking marina

Established in 1835, this fine hotel is in a vibrant and bustling coastal town. Family owned and operated, there is a very friendly and welcoming atmosphere throughout the hotel. It offers a range of spacious and well-appointed bedrooms and suites, including a penthouse. The hotel is well established for hosting conference and banqueting events, with an array of meeting rooms including a tiered auditorium. Coast Restaurant is the main dining room with picture windows overlooking the estuary; less formal dining is available in the Palm Court Carvery, and all day in Ryan's Bar. Guests are welcome to use the Arena Leisure Centre in the grounds

Rooms 203 (107 fmly) (14 smoking) S €90–€245; D €109–€308 (incl. bkfst)* **Facilities** STV Wi-fi supervised Gym New Year **Conf** Class 285 Board 90 Thtr 500 Del from €140 to €195* **Services** Lift **Parking** 400 **Notes** LB Closed 24-26 Dec Civ Wed 190

MALLOW Map 1 B2
Co Cork

Springfort Hall Country House Hotel
★★★ 77% HOTEL

☎ 022 21278
e-mail: stay@springfort-hall.com
web: www.springfort-hall.com
dir: N20 onto R581 at Two Pot House, hotel 500mtrs on right

This 18th-century country manor is tucked away amid tranquil woodlands located just six kilometres from Mallow. There is an attractive oval dining room, a cosy drawing room and lounge bar where bistro-style food is served. The spacious bedrooms are comfortably furnished. There are extensive banqueting and conference facilities. Local amenities include championship golf courses, fishing on the Blackwater and Ballyhass Lakes, and horse racing at Cork Racecourse.

Rooms 49 (5 fmly) (17 GF) **Facilities** STV FTV **Conf** Class 200 Board 50 Thtr 300 **Parking** 200 **Notes** Closed 23-26 Dec Civ Wed 250

MOHILL Map 1 C4
Co Leitrim

Lough Rynn Castle
★★★★ 78% HOTEL

☎ 071 9632700 & 9632714
e-mail: enquiries@loughrynn.ie

Once the ancestral home of Lord Leitrim, set in 300 acres of parkland, the castle offers a range of luxurious rooms and suites. The award-winning Sandstone Restaurant is an elegant dining option, and the many lounges are individually decorated; some feature antique furniture.

Rooms 43 (16 annexe) (5 fmly) (6 GF) S €99–€159; D €109–€180 (incl. bkfst)* **Facilities** STV FTV Wi-fi Xmas New Year **Conf** Class 200 Board 30 Thtr 450 Del from €129 to €179* **Services** Air con **Notes** LB Civ Wed 320

MOVILLE
Co Donegal

Redcastle Hotel, Golf & Spa Resort

★★★★ 78% HOTEL

☎ 074 9385555
Inishowen Peninsula
e-mail: info@redcastlehotel.com
dir: On R238 between Derby & Greencastle

Perched beside the sea in mature parkland just outside Redcastle, this hotel has an enviable position on the Inishowen Peninsula with great views over Lough Foyle. Now refurbished, it offers spacious bedrooms that are well equipped; some on the ground floor and some with balconies. The public areas include a range of relaxing lounges with an atmospheric bar where food is served throughout the day, and a large terrace for relaxing when the weather permits. The Edge Restaurant is right on the water's edge, and offers a well thought out menu with interesting options. There is a conference centre and an extensive leisure club offering spa treatments. The hotel has its own private 9-hole golf course, with sea fishing available from the shore.

Rooms 93 (17 fmly) (16 GF) (8 smoking)
Facilities Spa STV FTV Wi-fi ◊ ⑤ ↧ 9 Putt green Fishing ◓ Gym Thalasso therapy pool 刀 New Year **Conf** Class 150 Board 50 Thtr 300 **Services** Lift **Parking** 200 **Notes** ⊗ Civ Wed 250

MULLINGAR   Map 1 C4
Co Westmeath

Bloomfield House Hotel, Leisure Club & Spa

★★★ 75% HOTEL

☎ 044 93440894
Belvedere
e-mail: info@bloomfieldhouse.com
dir: N4 junct 15, N52 signed Tullamore/Belvedere. Take exit for Belvedere House, 0.5km. Hotel on left

Located in lovely parkland overlooking Lough Ennell, Bloomfield House is next to the Belvedere Estate on the outskirts of Mullingar. Bedrooms vary in style with the wing and suites enjoying the spectacular views. Public areas include comfortable and relaxing lounges with open fires. Informal food is available from the bar and carvery, while the smart restaurant serves dinner nightly. There are extensive leisure and banqueting facilities.

Rooms 111 (21 fmly) (26 smoking) **Facilities** Spa STV Wi-fi ⑤ supervised Gym Sauna Steam room Free kids club 刀 New Year **Conf** Class 200 Board 60 Thtr 450 **Services** Lift **Parking** 400 **Notes** LB ⊗ Closed 25 Dec Civ Wed 400

MULRANY   Map 1 B4
Co Mayo

Mulranny Park Hotel

★★★★ 79% ◉ HOTEL

☎ 098 36000
e-mail: info@mulrannyparkhotel.ie
dir: R311 from Castlebar to Newport onto N59. Hotel on right

Set on an elevated site, this property has commanding views over Clew Bay. Originally a railway hotel dating from the late 1800s, it has a range of smart public rooms that retain many of the period features. Bedrooms vary in size but are comfortable and decorated in a contemporary style. Dinner in the Nephin Restaurant is a highlight of any stay, with casual dining available throughout the day in the Waterfront Bar. A programme of activities is offered weekly for resident guests, in addition to a well appointed leisure club.

Rooms 61 (25 fmly) **S** €60-€125; **D** €100-€170 (incl. bkfst) **Facilities** Wi-fi ◊ ⑤ supervised Gym Steam room Health & beauty Hairdressing Cycling 刀 New Year **Conf** Class 140 Board 50 Thtr 400 Del from €125 to €150 **Services** Lift **Parking** 200 **Notes** LB ⊗ Closed 4-21 Jan Civ Wed 150

NAAS   Map 1 D3
Co Kildare

Maudlins House Hotel

★★★ 79% ◉◉ HOTEL

☎ 045 896999
Dublin Rd
e-mail: info@maudlinshousehotel.ie
web: www.maudlinshousehotel.ie
dir: M7 junct 9, R445 towards Naas. Hotel on right 200mtrs from Globe rdbt

Situated on the outskirts of Naas, this is a modern property that incorporates the original country house. Bedrooms are well appointed with a choice of classic and deluxe rooms; the annexed coach rooms are popular with long stay guests. The Virginia Restaurant, a series of comfortable rooms to the front of the house, offers fine dining from a creative menu; less formal options are served in the bar throughout the day. This hotel is located near two racecourses and many of the bloodstock agencies of County Kildare.

Rooms 25 (5 annexe) (5 GF) **Facilities** STV FTV Wi-fi Hair salon 刀 New Year **Conf** Class 50 Board 50 Thtr 100 **Services** Lift Air con **Parking** 70 **Notes** ⊗ Closed 24-25 Dec

NEWMARKET-ON-FERGUS   Map 1 B3
Co Clare

INSPECTORS' CHOICE

Dromoland Castle Hotel

★★★★★ ◎◎ HOTEL

☎ 061 368144
e-mail: sales@dromoland.ie
dir: N18 to Ennis/Galway from Shannon for 8km to 'Dromoland Interchange' signed Quin. Take slip road left, 4th exit at 1st rdbt, 2nd exit at 2nd rdbt. Hotel 500mtrs on left

Dromoland Castle, dating from the early 18th century, stands on a 375-acre estate and offers extensive indoor leisure activities and outdoor pursuits. The team are wholly committed to caring for guests. The thoughtfully equipped bedrooms and suites vary in style but all provide excellent levels of comfort, and the magnificent public rooms, warmed by log fires, are no less impressive. The hotel has several dining options - the elegant fine-dining Earl of Thomond, the less formal Fig Tree in the golf clubhouse, and The Gallery which offers a menu all day.

Rooms 99 (20 fmly) ◗ **S** €230-€1350; **D** €230-€1350* **Facilities** Spa STV Wi-fi ◊ ⑤ supervised ↧ 18 ⛳ Putt green Fishing Gym Archery Clay shooting Mountain bikes Driven shoots Falconry Pony & trap 刀 New Year **Conf** Class 220 Board 80 Thtr 450 Del from €340 to €560* **Services** Lift **Parking** 120 **Notes** ⊗ Closed 25-26 Dec Civ Wed 70

Save on hotels. Book at **theAA.com/hotel**

MOV – SAL 651 IRELAND

RATHMULLAN
Co Donegal   Map 1 C6

Rathmullan House

★★★★ 80% ◉ ◉   COUNTRY HOUSE HOTEL

☎ 074 9158188

e-mail: info@rathmullanhouse.com

dir: From Letterkenny, to Ramelton then Rathmullan, R243. Left at Mace shop, through village, hotel gates on right

Dating from the 18th century, this fine property has been operating as a country-house hotel for the last 50 years under the stewardship of the Wheeler family. It is in a magical setting leading right on the shores of Lough Swilly. Guests are welcome to wander around the well-planted grounds and the walled garden, from where much of the ingredients for the Weeping Elm Restaurant's seasonal menus are grown. The numerous lounges are relaxing and comfortable, many have welcoming log and turf fires. The bedrooms vary in size, but they are furnished to a high standard; many feature balconies and patio areas.

Rooms 34 (4 fmly) (9 GF) **S** €70-€170; **D** €140-€250 (incl. bkfst)* **Facilities** Wi-fi ⊗ ⚲ ⚲ Beauty treatment room New Year **Conf** Class 90 Board 40 Thtr 135 Del from €125 to €165* **Parking** 80 **Notes** LB Closed 11 Jan-5 Feb RS 15 Nov-12 Mar Civ Wed 135

RATHNEW
Co Wicklow   Map 1 D3

Tinakilly Country House & Restaurant

★★★★ 76% ◉ ◉   HOTEL

☎ 0404 69274 & 61258

e-mail: info@tinakilly.ie

dir: Follow N11/M11 to Rathnew, then R750 towards Wicklow. Entrance to hotel approx 500mtrs from village on left

An elegant oak-lined avenue leads to Tinakilly House, a Victorian mansion steeped in history. It was built in 1884 for Captain Robert Halpin, Master Mariner and Commander of *SS Great Eastern* who laid the telegraphic cable joining Europe to America. There are lovely garden views from the lounges that have open log fires. Some of the comfortable bedrooms and suites enjoy views over the Irish Sea and bird sanctuary at Broadlough Costal Lagoon. Furnishings throughout reflect the Victorian period yet providing all modern comforts. Fine dining is available in the dining room, and snacks and afternoon tea are served in the drawing room.

Rooms 51 (15 fmly) (14 GF) ⚲ **S** €60-€90; **D** €80-€220 (incl. bkfst) **Facilities** STV Wi-fi ⚲ ⚲ ♫

Xmas New Year **Conf** Class 70 Board 35 Thtr 100 Del from €120 to €170 **Services** Lift **Parking** 60 **Notes** LB ⊗ Civ Wed 100

Hunter's Hotel

★★★ 77% ◉   HOTEL

☎ 0404 40106

e-mail: reception@hunters.ie

dir: 1.5km from village off N11

One of Ireland's oldest coaching inns, this charming country house was built in 1720 and is full of character and atmosphere. The comfortable bedrooms have wonderful views over prize-winning gardens that border the River Vartry. The restaurant has a good reputation for carefully prepared dishes which make the best use of high quality local produce, including fruit and vegetables from the hotel's own garden.

Rooms 16 (2 fmly) (2 GF) **Conf** Class 40 Board 16 Thtr 40 **Parking** 50 **Notes** ⊗ Closed 24-26 Dec

RECESS (SRAITH SALACH)
Co Galway   Map 1 A4

INSPECTORS' CHOICE

Lough Inagh Lodge Hotel

★★★ ◉   COUNTRY HOUSE HOTEL

☎ 095 34706 & 34694

Inagh Valley

e-mail: inagh@iol.ie

dir: From Recess take R344 towards Kylemore

Dating from 1880, this former fishing lodge is akin to a family home, where guests are encouraged to relax and enjoy the peace. Overlooking Lough Inagh, and situated amid the mountains of Connemara, it is in an ideal location for those who enjoy walking and fishing. Bedrooms are individually decorated, some with spacious seating areas, and each is dedicated to an Irish literary figure. There are two cosy lounges where welcoming turf fires are often lit. Informal dining from a bar menu is available during the day. Dinner is a highlight of a visit to

the lodge; the menus feature locally sourced produce cooked with care - seafood is a speciality.

Rooms 13 (1 fmly) (4 GF) **Facilities** Fly fishing Cycling **Conf** Class 20 Board 20 Thtr 20 **Services** Air con **Parking** 16 **Notes** Closed mid Dec-mid Mar

ROSSLARE
Co Wexford   Map 1 D2

INSPECTORS' CHOICE

Kelly's Resort Hotel & Spa

★★★★ ◉   HOTEL

☎ 053 9132114

e-mail: info@kellys.ie

dir: N25 onto Rosslare/Wexford road, signed Rosslare Strand

The Kelly family have been offering hospitality here since 1895, and today together with a dedicated team they provide very professional and friendly service. The resort overlooks the sandy beach and is within minutes of the ferry port at Rosslare. Bedrooms are thoughtfully equipped and comfortably furnished. The extensive leisure facilities include a smart spa, swimming pools, a crèche, young adults' programme and spacious well-tended gardens. Both the eating options, La Marine Bistro and Beaches restaurant, have been awarded an AA Rosette for the quality of their cuisine.

Rooms 118 (15 fmly) (20 GF) **Facilities** Spa STV FTV Wi-fi ⊗ supervised ⚲ ⚲ Putt green ⚲ Gym Bowls Badminton Crazy golf Table tennis Snooker ♫ **Conf** Class 30 Board 20 Thtr 30 **Services** Lift **Parking** 120 **Notes** ⊗ Closed mid Dec-late Feb

SALTHILL

See Galway

SKIBBEREEN

West Cork Hotel

★★★ 75% HOTEL

☎ 028 21277
Ilen St
e-mail: info@westcorkhotel.com
dir: In Skibbereen, N71 into Bridge St, with Baby Hannah's pub on left turn right into Ilen St, hotel on right. From Cork road, N71 to Schull, left at next rdbt towards town centre, hotel on left

This charming hotel was built in 1902 and is family owned and run. Located in the centre of town beside the River Ilen. There is a cosy lounge with log fire and furnishings and decor that are a successfully mix the best of old and new. Food is available throughout the day in the Railway Bar and dinner in the evening in Kennedy's Restaurant; guests can also enjoy a drink while sitting on the historic old West Cork railway bridge. Bedrooms vary in size and are comfortably furnished; some have river views. There is extensive banqueting facilities.

Rooms 34 (4 fmly) ↝ **S** €60-€85; **D** €79-€139 (incl. bkfst) **Facilities** FTV Wi-fi Use of facilities at Skibbereen Sports Centre **Conf** Class 20 Board 24 Thtr 250 **Services** Lift **Parking** 100 **Notes** LB ⊗ Closed 24-28 Dec Civ Wed 300

SLIGO
Co Sligo   Map 1 B5

Radisson Blu Hotel & Spa Sligo

★★★★ 79% HOTEL

☎ 071 9140008
Rosses Point Rd, Ballincar
e-mail: info.sligo@radissonblu.com
dir: From N4 into Sligo to main bridge. Take R291 on left. Hotel 1.5m on right

Located three kilometres north of the town overlooking Sligo Bay, this contemporary hotel offers standard and business class bedrooms which are all appointed with up-to-date facilities. The Benwiskin bar offers tasty casual dining throughout the day, and for formal dining in the evening there's Classiebawn Restaurant. Residents are welcome to use Healthstyles leisure club during their stay, and spa treatment facilities are also available. A range of eleven rooms are provided for meetings and events.

Rooms 132 (13 fmly) (32 GF) (19 smoking)
Facilities Spa STV Wi-fi ⊙ Gym Steam room Beauty treatment rooms Thermal suite Xmas New Year **Conf** Class 420 Board 40 Thtr 750 **Del** from €120 to €150 **Services** Lift Air con **Parking** 320 **Notes** ⊗ Civ Wed 750

The Glasshouse

★★★★ 78% ⊛ HOTEL

☎ 071 9194300
Swan Point
e-mail: info@theglasshouse.ie
dir: From N4 right at 2nd junct. Left at Post Office into Wine St. Hotel on right

This landmark building in the centre of town makes a bold statement with its cutting edge design and contemporary decor. Cheerful colours are used throughout the hotel; the bedrooms have excellent facilities including LCD TVs, workspace and internet access. There is a first-floor café bar, a ground-floor bar and a Mediterranean-style restaurant with great river views. Secure underground parking is complimentary to residents.

Save on hotels. Book at **theAA.com/hotel**

SKI – THO 653 IRELAND

The Glasshouse

Rooms 116 **Facilities** STV FTV Wi-fi New Year **Conf** Class 100 Board 60 Thtr 120 **Services** Lift **Parking** 250 **Notes** ⊗ Closed 24-25 Dec Civ Wed 120

See advert on opposite page

Sligo Park Hotel & Leisure Club
★★★★ 76% HOTEL

☎ 071 9190400
Pearse Rd
e-mail: sligo@leehotels.com
dir: N4 to Sligo take exit S2 (Sligo Sth) Carrowroe/R287. Follow signs for Sligo. Hotel 1m on right

Set in seven acres on the southern side of town, this hotel is well positioned for visiting the many attractions of the north west and Yeats' Country. Bedrooms are spacious and appointed to a high standard. There are two dining options, plus good leisure and banqueting facilities.

Rooms 136 (10 fmly) (52 GF) (23 smoking) **S** €65-€195; **D** €65-€195* **Facilities** Wi-fi supervised Gym Holistic treatment suite Plunge pool Steam room Xmas New Year **Conf** Class 290 Board 80 Thtr 520 Del from €95 to €115 **Services** Lift **Parking** 200 **Notes** LB ⊗ RS 24-26 Dec Civ Wed 520

STRAFFAN Map 1 D4
Co Kildare

INSPECTORS' CHOICE
The K Club
★★★★★ COUNTRY HOUSE HOTEL

☎ 01 6017200
e-mail: sales@kclub.ie
dir: From Dublin take N4, exit for R406, hotel on right in Straffan

The K Club is set in 550 acres of rolling woodland. There are two magnificent championship golf courses, and a spa facility that complements the truly luxurious hotel that is the centrepiece of the resort. Public areas, suites and bedrooms are opulently furnished, and many have views of the formal gardens that lead down to the banks of the River Liffey. Dining options include the elegant River Room, with more informal dining options offered in Legends in the Golf Pavilion. There is also a Thai restaurant in the resort.

Rooms 69 (10 fmly) **Facilities** Spa Wi-fi supervised 36 Putt green Fishing Gym Beauty salon Fishing tuition Clay pigeon shooting Horse riding Falconry Xmas New Year **Conf** Class 300 Board 160 Thtr 300 **Services** Lift **Parking** 205 **Notes** ⊗

Barberstown Castle
★★★★ 80% HOTEL

☎ 01 6288157
e-mail: info@barberstowncastle.ie
web: www.barberstowncastle.ie
dir: R406, follow signs for Barberstown

With parts dating from the 13th century, this castle hotel provides the very best in standards of comfort. The inviting public areas range from the original keep, which houses one of the restaurant areas, to the warmth of the drawing room and its cocktail bar. Bedrooms, some in a purpose-built wing, are elegantly appointed with relaxing seating areas. The airy Tea Room serves light meals throughout the day. The Castle is a popular venue for weddings and other family occasions.

Rooms 57 (21 GF) **S** €150-€200; (incl. bkfst) **Facilities** STV Wi-fi New Year **Conf** Class 100 Board 70 Thtr 200 Del from €185 to €240 **Services** Lift **Parking** 200 **Notes** ⊗ Closed 24-26 Dec & Jan Civ Wed 300

THOMASTOWN Map 1 C3
Co Kilkenny

INSPECTORS' CHOICE
Mount Juliet Hotel
★★★★ COUNTRY HOUSE HOTEL

☎ 056 7773000
e-mail: info@mountjuliet.ie
dir: M7 from Dublin, M9 towards Waterford, exit at junct 9/Danesfort for hotel

Mount Juliet is set in 1,500 acres of parkland with a Jack Nicklaus designed golf course and an equestrian centre. The elegant and spacious public areas retain much of the original architectural features including ornate plasterwork and Adam fireplaces. Bedrooms in the main house are elegant and comfortably appointed to a high standard with more compact rooms available in the Clubhouse annexe. Fine dining is on offer in the ornate Lady Helen restaurant overlooking the river; with French brasserie cuisine in Kendal's located in the golf clubhouse. The President's Bar is the location for all day dining. The hotel has an excellent spa and health club, with equestrian and other activities also available.

Rooms 58 (27 annexe) (14 GF) **S** €79-€369; **D** €79-€369 **Facilities** Spa STV Wi-fi supervised 18 Putt green Fishing Gym Archery Cycling Clay pigeon shooting Equestrian Xmas New Year Child facilities **Conf** Class 40 Board 20 Thtr 75 **Parking** 200 **Notes** LB ⊗ Closed Sun-Wed eve Nov-1st wk Dec & Jan-Mar Civ Wed 60

REPUBLIC OF IRELAND

THURLES
Co Tipperary — Map 1 C3

Horse & Jockey Hotel
★★★★ 79% HOTEL

☎ 0504 44192
Horse & Jockey
e-mail: info@horseandjockeyhotel.com
dir: 800mtrs from M8 junct 6

Located just off the motorway, this hotel offers smart and well-appointed bedrooms which are very comfortable. Dining options are the Enclosure Bar with a varied menu, and for more formal dining in the evening there is Silks Restaurant. There is also a well-equipped leisure centre with spa treatments and an equestrian themed gift shop. The conference facilities include ten self-contained meeting rooms and a tiered auditorium seating 200 delegates.

Rooms 67 (4 fmly) (15 GF) (7 smoking) **S** €70-€90; **D** €99-€139 (incl. bkfst) **Facilities** Spa STV FTV Wi-fi ⓢ supervised Gym Sauna Steam room Hydrotherapy area **Conf** Class 24 Board 25 Thtr 200 **Services** Lift **Parking** 450 **Notes** LB ⊗ Closed 25 Dec RS 24 & 26 Dec

TRALEE
Co Kerry — Map 1 A2

Ballygarry House Hotel and Spa
★★★★ 80% HOTEL

☎ 066 7123322
Killarney Rd
e-mail: info@ballygarryhouse.com
web: www.ballygarryhouse.com
dir: 1.5km from Tralee, on N21

This charming hotel offers the complete country house experience, where courtesy and care is paramount from the friendly team. Located a short drive from the town centre, there are comfortably furnished lounges with open log fires. Food is served throughout the day in the Leebrook Lounge and fine dining is available in the evening in Brooks Restaurant which overlooks the lovely six-acre gardens. Bedrooms and suites are spacious and elegantly decorated. Spa treatments and relaxation areas are offered in the Nadur Spa. The Pavilion provides a party venue where the outdoors is seamlessly brought indoors.

Rooms 64 (10 fmly) (16 GF) **Facilities** Spa STV Wi-fi Steam room Sauna ♫ New Year **Conf** Class 100 Board 50 Thtr 200 **Services** Lift **Parking** 200 **Notes** ⊗ Closed 20-26 Dec Civ Wed 350

Carlton Hotel Tralee
★★★★ 78% HOTEL

CARLTON
HOTEL GROUP

☎ 066 7199100
Fels Point, Dan Spring Rd
e-mail: reservations.tralee@carlton.ie
dir: On N86 from Tralee towards Dingle

This contemporary hotel is situated on the ring road and is within walking distance of the town centre. Public areas include a stylish lobby lounge where a grand piano is played at weekends. Bistro food is served in Clarets Bar all day, with fine dining available in Morels Restaurant at night. The smart bedrooms are air conditioned and have LCD TVs and high-speed internet connections. There are extensive conference, banqueting and leisure facilities.

Rooms 165 (12 fmly) (29 smoking) ⓢ **S** €59-€139; **D** €79-€139 **Facilities** STV FTV Wi-fi ⓢ Gym ♫ New Year **Conf** Class 100 Board 60 Thtr 350 Del from €160 to €200 **Services** Lift Air con **Parking** 227 **Notes** LB ⊗ Closed 24-26 Dec Civ Wed 150

INSPECTORS' CHOICE
Ballyseede Castle
★★★ ◉ HOTEL

☎ 066 7125799
e-mail: info@ballyseedecastle.com
dir: On N21 just after junct of N21/N22

Ballyseede Castle is steeped in history dating back to 1590 and has been fought over, lived in and lovingly restored to a high standard which still pays homage to its ancient grandeur. The spacious bedrooms are elegantly decorated; some have four-poster beds and antique furnishings. There are gracious receptions rooms with original ornamental cornices and marble fireplaces, a carved oak library, a cosy bar and a splendid banqueting hall. The castle stands in its own grounds at the end of a winding drive through formal gardens and woodland.

Rooms 23 (4 fmly) (10 GF) **S** €85-€125; **D** €109-€189 (incl. bkfst)* **Facilities** STV FTV Wi-fi **Parking** 180 **Notes** LB ⊗ Closed Jan-3 Mar Civ Wed 130

TRAMORE
Co Waterford — Map 1 C2

Majestic Hotel
★★★ 78% HOTEL

☎ 051 381761
e-mail: info@majestic-hotel.ie
dir: Exit N25 through Waterford onto R675 to Tramore. Hotel on right, opposite lake

A warm welcome awaits visitors to this long established, family friendly hotel in the holiday resort of Tramore. Many of the comfortable and well-equipped bedrooms have sea views; some have balconies. Public areas offer relaxing comfortable lounges, a smartly decorated bar, a garden patio and a spacious restaurant where guests can enjoy the spectacular sea views. A discounted rate at Splashworld across from the hotel is available to residents.

Rooms 60 (8 fmly) ⓢ **S** €80-€100; **D** €80-€140 (incl. bkfst) **Facilities** STV FTV Wi-fi ⓢ ♫ New Year Child facilities **Conf** Class 100 Board 50 Thtr 100 Del €110 **Services** Lift **Parking** 10 **Notes** LB ⊗ Civ Wed 250

TULLOW
Co Carlow — Map 1 D3

Mount Wolseley Hotel, Spa & Country Club
★★★★ 80% ◉ HOTEL

☎ 059 9180100
e-mail: info@mountwolseley.ie
dir: N7 from Dublin. In Naas, take N9 towards Carlow. In Castledermot left for Tullow

Located on a vast, well landscaped estate long associated with the Wolseley family of motoring fame, this hotel has much to offer. Public areas are very spacious with a large range of suites and bedrooms. Leisure pursuits include a championship golf course together with a popular health centre and Sanctuary Spa facilities. The hotel offers a number of dining options including Aaron's lounge, Fredrick's (1 AA Rosette), and The Wolseley Lounge in the Golf Pavillion.

Rooms 143 (10 fmly) (5 smoking) **Facilities** Spa STV Wi-fi ⓢ ⓢ supervised ↓ 18 ⅃ Putt green Gym Childrens' play area ♫ New Year **Conf** Class 288 Board 70 Thtr 750 **Services** Lift Air con **Parking** 160 **Notes** ⊗ Closed 25-26 Dec Civ Wed 400

VIRGINIA
Co Cavan   Map 1 C4

The Park Hotel
★★★ 73% ⊛ HOTEL

☎ 049 8546100
Virginia Park
e-mail: info@parkhotelvirginia.com
web: www.parkhotelvirginia.com
dir: Exit N3 onto R194 to Virginia. Hotel 500yds on left

A charming hotel, built in 1750 as the summer retreat of the Marquis of Headford. Situated overlooking Lake Ramor on a 100-acre estate, it has a 9-hole golf course, lovely mature gardens and woodland. This hotel brings together generous hospitality and a relaxed, leisurely way of life. The Marquis Dining room is renowned for good food, and fruit, herbs and vegetables are grown in the estate's organic gardens.

Rooms 26 (1 fmly) (8 GF) **Facilities** Wi-fi ⅃ 9 Fishing ♫ New Year **Conf** Class 40 Board 40 Thtr 100 **Parking** 150 **Notes** ⊗ Closed 25 Dec Civ Wed 100

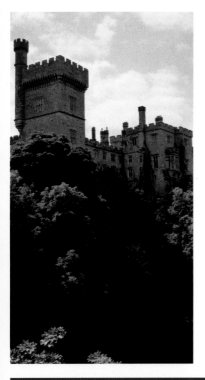

WATERFORD
Co Waterford   Map 1 C2

INSPECTORS' CHOICE

Waterford Castle Hotel and Golf Resort
★★★★ ⊛⊛ HOTEL

☎ 051 878203
The Island
e-mail: info@waterfordcastle.com
dir: From city centre into Dunmore East Rd, 1.5m, pass hospital, 0.5m left after lights. Ferry at bottom of road

This enchanting and picturesque castle dates back to Norman times and is located on a 320-acre island just a five-minute journey from the mainland by chain-link ferry. Bedrooms vary in style and size, but all are individually decorated and offer high standards of comfort. Dinner is served in the oak-panelled Munster Room, with breakfast taken in the conservatory. The 18-hole golf course is set in beautiful parkland where deer can be seen.

Rooms 19 (2 fmly) (4 GF) **Facilities** Wi-fi ⅃ 18 ⊗ Putt green ⅃ Boules Archery Clay pigeon shooting ♫ New Year **Conf** Board 15 Thtr 30 **Services** Lift **Parking** 50 **Notes** ⊗ Closed 24-26 Dec Civ Wed 120

Faithlegg House Hotel   FBD Hotels
★★★★ 78% ⊛ HOTEL

☎ 051 382000
Faithlegg
e-mail: reservations@fhh.ie
web: www.faithlegg.com
dir: From Waterford follow Dunmore East Rd then Cheekpoint Rd

This hotel is surrounded by a parkland championship golf course and overlooks the estuary of the River Suir. The house has 14 original bedrooms, and the others in a more contemporary style are in an adjacent modern block. There is a range of comfortable lounges together with comprehensive meeting facilities. The leisure and treatment rooms are the perfect way to work off the excesses of the food offered in the Roseville Restaurant. Lighter options are served throughout the day in the Piano Bar and in the golf clubhouse.

Rooms 82 (6 fmly) (30 GF) (16 smoking) **Facilities** FTV Wi-fi ⊗ supervised ⅃ 18 ⊗ Putt green Gym Sauna Steam room New Year **Conf** Class 90 Board 44 Thtr 180 **Services** Lift **Parking** 100 **Notes** ⊗ Closed 20-27 Dec Civ Wed

Granville Hotel
★★★ 80% HOTEL

☎ 051 305555
The Quay
e-mail: stay@granville-hotel.ie
web: www.granville-hotel.ie
dir: N25 to waterfront, hotel opposite clock tower

Centrally located on the quayside, this long established hotel was originally a coaching house. It is appointed to a very high standard, and retains much of its original character. The bedrooms come in a choice of standard or executive grades; all are well equipped and very comfortable. The Meagher Bar offers food throughout the day, and is a popular lunch venue with shoppers and the business community of Waterford. The Bianconi is an elegant restaurant where evening dinner is served. Friendliness and hospitality are hallmarks of a stay here.

Rooms 100 (5 fmly) (10 smoking) **S** €80-€120; **D** €90-€180 (incl. bkfst) **Facilities** STV ♫ New Year **Conf** Class 150 Board 30 Thtr 200 Del from €100 to €150 **Services** Lift **Parking** 300 **Notes** LB ⊗ Closed 25-26 Dec Civ Wed 200

WATERFORD *continued*

Tower Hotel
★★★ 79% HOTEL

☎ 051 862300
The Mall
e-mail: info@thw.ie
web: www.fbdhotels.com
dir: Opposite Reginald's Tower in town centre. Hotel at end of quay

With a commanding position on The Mall opposite Reginald's Tower, this well established hotel has much to offer. The spacious public areas include conference suites, a choice of dining options and a popular leisure club. Health and beauty treatments are available. A range of bedrooms is on offer; all are comfortably appointed and stylishly decorated. Secure parking is provided to the rear of the building.

Rooms 136 (9 fmly) ⚓ **S** €65-€140; **D** €89-€250 (incl. bkfst)* **Facilities** STV FTV Wi-fi 🕙 supervised Gym Beauty treatment rooms 🎵 New Year **Conf** Class 250 Board 80 Thtr 500 **Services** Lift **Parking** 100 **Notes** LB ⊗ Closed 24-28 Dec Civ Wed 400

Dooley's Hotel
★★★ 78% HOTEL

☎ 051 873531
30 The Quay
e-mail: hotel@dooleys-hotel.ie
dir: Adjacent to N25, on the Quay

This hotel has been family run for three generations. It is situated on the quay overlooking the River Suir at the harbour's mouth. Dinner is served in New Ship Restaurant and casual dining is available in the Dry Dock Bar. Bedrooms are attractively decorated and offer a good standard of comfort. There is a convenient public car park opposite the hotel.

Rooms 110 (3 fmly) (29 smoking) **S** €70-€140; **D** €80-€198* **Facilities** STV Wi-fi ⧉ 🎵 New Year **Conf** Class 150 Board 100 Thtr 240 Del from €110* **Services** Lift **Notes** ⊗ Closed 25-27 Dec

---

WESTPORT
Map 1 B4

HOTEL OF THE YEAR

Knockranny House Hotel
★★★★ 84% ⚜⚜ HOTEL

☎ 098 28600
e-mail: info@khh.ie
web: www.khh.ie
dir: On N5 (Westport-Castlebar road)

Perched on a height overlooking Westport, with Clew Bay and Croagh Patrick in the distance, this fine family-run property is set in well landscaped grounds. The reception rooms take full advantage of the stunning views, and include The Brehon, a lounge where food is served throughout the day, and La Fougére, the award-winning restaurant that is a real treat to visit. The comfortable furnishings create an inviting and relaxing atmosphere throughout the lounges, bar and restaurant. Bedrooms are very well appointed and come in a number of styles, with the newer ones being particularly spacious. Guests have complimentary use of extensive leisure facilities, with wellbeing treatments on offer in Spa Salveo. There are extensive banqueting and conference facilities. AA Hotel of the Year for the Republic of Ireland 2012-13.

Rooms 97 (4 fmly) (18 GF) ⚓ **Facilities** Spa STV Wi-fi ⧉ HL 🕙 Gym 🎵 New Year **Conf** Class 350 Board 40 Thtr 600 **Services** Lift **Parking** 150 **Notes** ⊗ Closed 24-26 Dec Civ Wed 250

Hotel Westport Leisure, Spa & Conference
★★★★ 79% ⚜ HOTEL

☎ 098 25122 & 0870 876 5432
Newport Rd
e-mail: reservations@hotelwestport.ie
web: www.hotelwestport.ie
dir: N5 to Westport. Right at end of Castlebar St, 1st right before bridge, right at lights, left before church. Follow to end of street

Located in seven acres of woodlands and just a short riverside walk to the town, this hotel offers spacious public areas, including The Islands restaurant and the all-day Maple Bar. Bedrooms come in a range of styles, and all are comfortable and well appointed. Both leisure and business guests are well catered for by the enthusiastic and friendly team who go to great lengths to ensure residents enjoy their stay. This hotel is a popular choice with special interest groups and also families, who enjoy the leisure facilities, and in summer time, the children's club.

Rooms 129 (67 fmly) (42 GF) (12 smoking) ⚓ **S** €59-€159; **D** €70-€270 (incl. bkfst) **Facilities** Spa STV Wi-fi ⧉ HL 🕙 supervised Gym Children's pool Lounger pool Steam room Sauna Fitness suite 🎵 Xmas New Year Child facilities **Conf** Class 150 Board 60 Thtr 500 Del from €79 to €199 **Services** Lift **Parking** 220 **Notes** LB ⊗ Civ Wed 350

Carlton Atlantic Coast Hotel
★★★★ 76% ⚜ HOTEL

☎ 098 29000
The Quay
e-mail: reservations.atlanticcoast@carlton.ie
dir: From N5 follow signs into Westport then Louisburgh on R335. 1m from Westport

This distinctive hotel is in a renovated mill that has been appointed to a good contemporary standard. It is located on the quay, a short drive from the town of Westport. Many of the rooms have sea views, as has the award-winning Blue Wave restaurant on the fourth floor. The ground floor has comfortable lounge areas and a lively bar, Fishworks, where food is served throughout the day. The leisure centre is complimentary to resident guests, and spa treatments are offered in the C Spa.

Rooms 85 (6 fmly) **S** €59-€125; **D** €98-€250 (incl. bkfst) **Facilities** Spa Wi-fi ⧉ 🕙 supervised Gym Beauty treatment rooms Sauna Steam room Fitness suite 🎵 New Year **Conf** Class 100 Board 70 Thtr 180 Del from €89 to €139 **Services** Lift **Parking** 140 **Notes** LB ⊗ Closed 23-27 Dec Civ Wed 140

The Wyatt Hotel

★★★ 73% HOTEL

☎ 098 25027
The Octagon
e-mail: info@wyatthotel.com
web: www.wyatthotel.com
dir: Follow one-way system in town. Hotel by tall monument at Octagon

This stylish, welcoming hotel is situated in the famous town-centre Octagon. Bedrooms are attractively decorated and well equipped. Public areas are very comfortable with open fires and include a lively, contemporary bar and the traditional Cobblers Bar is very cosy. JW Bistro serves food all day and in high season The Wyatt Restaurant offers more formal dining.

Rooms 51 (2 GF) (5 smoking) ⊀ **S** €39-€109; **D** €39-€199* **Facilities** Wi-fi Complimentary use of nearby leisure park ♫ New Year **Conf** Class 200 Board 80 Thtr 300 **Services** Lift **Parking** 20 **Notes** ⊗ Closed 25-26 Dec Civ Wed 200

Mill Times Hotel Westport

★★★ 71% HOTEL

☎ 098 29200 & 29130
Mill St
e-mail: info@milltimeshotel.ie
web: www.milltimeshotel.ie
dir: N59 signed town centre, in Bridge St keep in left lane, into Mill St, hotel on left

This family run hotel is situated in the centre of Westport, close to the shops and many pubs of this bustling town. It is ideal for visiting north Mayo with its many beaches and golf courses, or as a base for climbing the pilgrimage mountain of Croagh Patrick. Bedrooms are traditional in style and public areas are comfortable. Uncle Sam's café bar is a lively venue with entertainment at weekends. Temptations Restaurant offers good value meals during the evening, and is where a hearty breakfast is served. Underground parking is provided.

Rooms 34 (6 fmly) **Facilities** Wi-fi ♫ New Year **Conf** Class 60 Board 60 Thtr 200 **Services** Lift Air con **Parking** 25 **Notes** ⊗ Closed 24-25 Dec Civ Wed 100

Whitford House Hotel Health & Leisure Club

★★★★ 75% ◉ HOTEL

☎ 053 9143444
New Line Rd
e-mail: info@whitford.ie
web: www.whitford.ie
dir: Just off N25 (Duncannon rdbt) take exit for R733 (Wexford), hotel immediately left

This is a friendly family-run hotel just three kilometres from the town centre and within easy reach of the Rosslare Ferry. Comfortable bedrooms range from standard to the spacious deluxe rooms. Public areas include a choice of lounges and the popular Forthside Bar Bistro where a carvery is served at lunch. More formal meals are on offer during the evening in the award-winning Seasons Restaurant. Leisure and fitness facilities are complimentary to resident guests.

Rooms 36 (28 fmly) (18 GF) **S** €59-€130; **D** €98-€190 (incl. bkfst)* **Facilities** Spa FTV Wi-fi ♨ ⓢ supervised Gym Children's playground Football area Hairdresser ♫ Xmas New Year **Conf** Class 12 Board 25 Thtr 50 Del €110* **Parking** 200 **Notes** LB ⊗ RS 24-27 Dec Civ Wed 100

REPUBLIC OF IRELAND

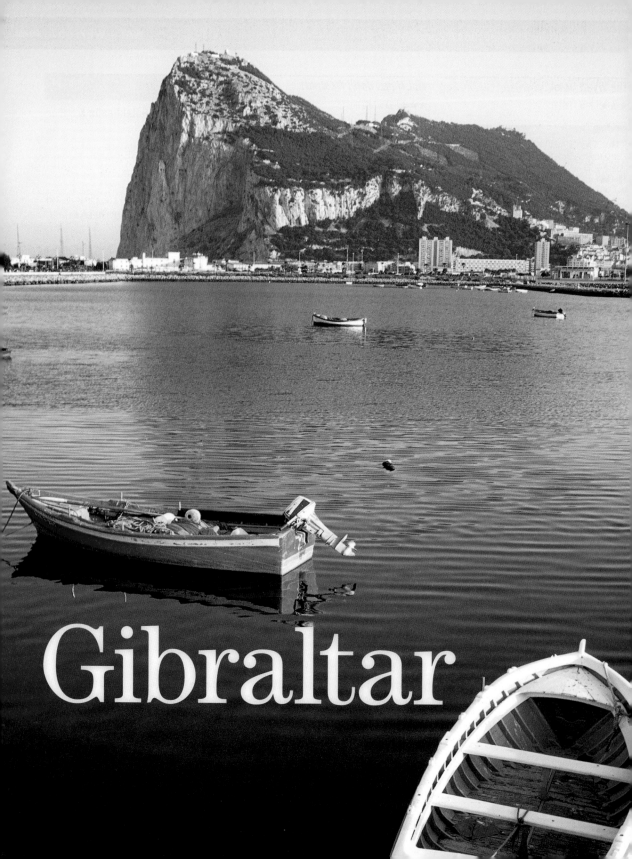

Gibraltar

Save on hotels. Book at **theAA.com/hotel**

GIBRALTAR 659

GIBRALTAR

GIBRALTAR

Caleta Hotel

★★★★ 79% ◉ ◉ HOTEL

☎ 00 350 200 76501
Sir Herbert Miles Rd, PO Box 73
e-mail: sales@caletahotel.gi
web: www.caletahotel.com
dir: Enter Gibraltar via Spanish border & cross
runway. At 1st rdbt turn left, hotel in 2kms

For travellers arriving in Gibraltar by plane, the
Caleta is an eye-catching coastal landmark that can
be spotted from the air if arriving from the east. This
imposing and stylish hotel sits on a cliff top and all
sea-facing rooms enjoy panoramic views across the
straights to Morocco. Bedrooms vary in size and style;
some have spacious balconies, flat-screen TVs and
mini bars. Several dining venues are available, but
Nunos provides an award-winning, fine dining Italian
experience. The staff are friendly and service is
professional.

Rooms 161 (89 annexe) (13 fmly) (80 smoking)
Facilities Spa STV FTV Wi-fi ⌕ ➘ supervised Gym
Health & beauty club Xmas New Year **Conf** Class 172
Board 85 Thtr 200 **Services** Lift Air con **Parking** 32
Notes ⊗ Civ Wed 300

O'Callaghan Eliott Hotel

★★★★ 77% HOTEL

☎ 00 350 200 70500 & 200 75905
2 Governor's Pde
e-mail: eliott@ocallaghanhotels.com
web: www.ocallaghanhotels.com

Located in the heart of the old town, this hotel
provides a convenient central base for exploring the
duty-free shopping district and other key attractions
on foot. The bedrooms are stylish, spacious and well
equipped. The roof-top restaurant provides stunning
bay views, whilst guests can also take a swim in the
roof-top pool.

Rooms 123 ☛ **S** £159-£400; **D** £169-£410*
Facilities STV Wi-fi ➘ Gym ♫ Xmas New Year
Conf Class 80 Board 70 Thtr 180 Del from £229 to
£329* **Services** Lift Air con **Parking** 17 **Notes** LB ⊗
Civ Wed 120

The Rock Hotel

Ⓤ

☎ 00 350 200 73000
Europa Rd
e-mail: rockhotel@gibtelecom.net
web: www.rockhotelgibraltar.com
dir: From airport follow tourist board signs. Hotel on
left half way up Europa Rd

At the time of going to press we learnt that The Rock
was embarking on a multi-million pound
refurbishment of the bedrooms, all public and food
and beverage areas as well as a considerable
makeover of the building, considered one of the
island's icons. The style will remain colonial but new
bedrooms will also feature cutting edge facilities
including iPod docks, spacious walk-in showers,
flat-screen TVs and Wi-fi, plus the introduction of a
number of energy saving concepts that will enhance
the hotel's green credentials. For further details
please see the AA website: theAA.com

Rooms 104 (25 smoking) **Facilities** STV Wi-fi ➘
supervised Xmas New Year **Conf** Class 24 Board 30
Thtr 70 **Services** Lift Air con **Parking** 40 **Notes** RS 5
Oct-1 Apr Civ Wed 40

GIBRALTAR

The Automobile Association would like to thank the following photographers, companies and picture libraries for their assistance in the preparation of this
book.

Abbreviations for the picture credits are as follows – (t) top; (b) bottom; (c) centre; (l) left; (r) right; (AA) AA World Travel Library

1b Roger Cracknell 01/classic/Alamy; 2l Aardvark/Alamy; 3tl AA/Nick Jenkins; 7r AA/Adam Burton; 9tl Courtesy Lime Wood; 9tr Courtesy Richard Waite/Four
Seasons Hotel Park Lane; 10tl Courtesy The Torridon;10tr Courtesy Bodysgallen Hotel; 11tl Courtesy Peter Moloney/Knockranny House Hotel; 11r AA/Mike Kipling;
12tr, 12c, 12br Courtesy Handpicked Hotels; 13tr, 13cr, 13b Courtesy Cotswold Inns & Hotels; 15 Courtesy Fawsley Hall; 17b Jeff Gilbert/Alamy; 18t John
Morrison/Alamy; 18b Adrian Houston/Loop Images; 19r AA/Anna Mockford and Nick Bonetti; 20 AA/Peter Wilson; 22l Stockbroker/Alamy; 22c Hemis /Alamy;
22r VIEW Pictures Ltd/Alamy; 23tl AA/Mike Kipling; 23bc AA/Sarah Montgomery; 23br AA/Michael Moody; 24t Sam Stephenson/Alamy; 25br AA/James Tims;
37 AA/Tom Mackie;143 AA/John Miller; 250 AA/James Tims;268 AA/James Tims; 511 AA/Peter Trenchard; 522 AA/Jonathan Smith; 566 AA/David W Robertson;
580 AA/Richard Elliot; 588 AA/Nick Jenkins;621 AA/Mark Bauer; 622 AA/Steve Day; 631 AA/Jamie Blandford; 655 AA/Jamie Blandford; 658 AA/Peter Wilson

Every effort has been made to trace the copyright holders, and we apologise in advance for any unintentional omissions or errors. We would be pleased to apply
any corrections in a following edition of this publication.

COUNTY MAPS

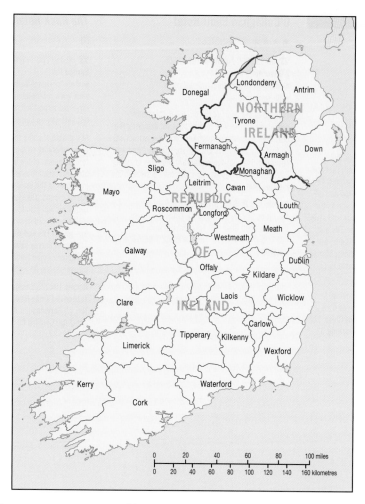

England

1 Bedfordshire
2 Berkshire
3 Bristol
4 Buckinghamshire
5 Cambridgeshire
6 Greater Manchester
7 Herefordshire
8 Hertfordshire
9 Leicestershire
10 Northamptonshire
11 Nottinghamshire
12 Rutland
13 Staffordshire
14 Warwickshire
15 West Midlands
16 Worcestershire

Scotland

17 City of Glasgow
18 Clackmannanshire
19 East Ayrshire
20 East Dunbartonshire
21 East Renfrewshire
22 Perth & Kinross
23 Renfrewshire
24 South Lanarkshire
25 West Dunbartonshire

Wales

26 Blaenau Gwent
27 Bridgend
28 Caerphilly
29 Denbighshire
30 Flintshire
31 Merthyr Tydfil
32 Monmouthshire
33 Neath Port Talbot
34 Newport
35 Rhondda Cynon Taff
36 Torfaen
37 Vale of Glamorgan
38 Wrexham

Na h-Eileanan
an Iar

Orkney Islands

Shetland Islands

Highland

Moray

Aberdeenshire

City of
Aberdeen

Angus

SCOTLAND

Perth &
Kinross

City of
Dundee

Argyll
& Bute

Stirling

Fife

East
Lothian

North
Ayrshire

Argyll
& Bute

Stirling

18

22

Fife

Inverclyde

25

20

Falkirk

City of
Edinburgh

23

17

North
Lanarkshire

West
Lothian

Midlothian

North
Ayrshire

21

Scottish
Borders

19

South Lanarkshire

24

19

Scottish
Borders

South
Ayrshire

Dumfries &
Galloway

Northumberland

Tyne & Wear

Isle
of Man

Cumbria

Durham

North
Yorkshire

East Riding
of Yorkshire

Isle of
Anglesey

Lancashire

West
Yorkshire

Merseyside

6

South
Yorkshire

Lincolnshire

Conwy

30

Cheshire

Derbyshire

29

38

11

Gwynedd

ENGLAND

13

Norfolk

Shropshire

9

12

WALES

15

Suffolk

Ceredigion

Powys

14

10

5

7

16

1

Pembrokeshire

Carmarthenshire

Gloucestershire

4

8

Essex

Swansea

Oxfordshire

Greater
London

26

32

31

36

3

2

Kent

33

35

28

34

Wiltshire

Surrey

27

Cardiff

Hampshire

37

Somerset

West
Sussex

East
Sussex

Devon

Dorset

Isle of
Wight

Cornwall

Isles of
Scilly

Guernsey

Jersey

| 0 | 20 | 40 | 60 | 80 | 100 miles |

| 0 | 20 | 40 | 60 | 80 | 100 | 120 | 140 | 160 kilometres |

KEY TO ATLAS

24 Shetland Islands

24 Orkney Islands

22

23

Inverness

Aberdeen

Fort William

Perth

20 Glasgow

21 Edinburgh

Stranraer

Newcastle upon Tyne

Carlisle

Middlesbrough

18 Kendal

19

Isle of Man

24

Leeds

York

Kingston upon Hull

1

Londonderry

Larne

Belfast

Galway

Dublin

Limerick

Rosslare

Cork

Holyhead

Liverpool

Manchester

16 Sheffield

17

Lincoln

14

15

Nottingham

Aberystwyth

Birmingham

Norwich

12

13

10

11

Cambridge

8

9

Gloucester

Colchester

Carmarthen

Oxford

Cardiff

Bristol

LONDON

Guildford

6

7

4

5

Maidstone

Dover

Barnstaple

Taunton

Southampton

Brighton

2

3

Bournemouth

Exeter

Plymouth

Penzance

Isles of Scilly

Channel Islands **24**

2

Legend

Symbol	Description
M6	Motorway/toll motorway
	Motorway junction full/restricted. Service area
A35	Primary route single/dual carriageway
A34	Other A road single/dual carriageway
B3400	B road
	Unclassified road
V	Vehicle ferry
C	Fast vehicle ferry or catamaran
• Stamford	Hotel
• Lyndhurst	AA Hotel of the Year
○ King's Cliffe	Town/Village name
	National boundary
ESSEX	English county name & boundary
CONWY	Welsh county name & boundary
MORAY	Scottish county name & boundary
	National Park

Lundy

Hartland Point
Hartland

Morwenstow

Kilkhampton

Bude
Bude Bay
Bude Str
Widemouth Bay

Crackington Haven
Week St Mary

Boscastle
Tintagel

Delabole
Camelford

Bolventor
BODMIN MOOR
St Tudy
Blisland

ISLES OF SCILLY
Bryher
New Grimsby
Tresco
St Martin's
Higher Town
Hugh Town
St Mary's
Old Town
St Agnes
Middle Town

SV

Port Isaac
Polzeath
Pendoggett

Harlyn
Rock
Padstow
Porthcothan
Wadebridge

SW

Mawgan Porth
St Mawgan
Newquay
West Pentire
St Columb Major
Fraddon
Roche
Summercourt
Bugle
St Blazey

CORNWALL
Bodmin
St Cleer
Lanivet
Dobwalls
Liske
St Keyne

Lostwithiel
Golant
Pelynt

Perranporth

St Agnes
Ladock
St Austell
Fowey
Polruan
Polperro

Porthtowan
Marazanvose
St Stephen
Pentewan

Portreath
Grampound
Mevagissey

St Ives Bay
Gwithian
St Day
Tregony
Gorran Haven

St Ives
Redruth
Camborne
Carnon Downs
Truro
Portloe

Zennor
Lelant
Hayle
St Just-in-Roseland
Veryan

Marazion
Penryn
Portscatho

St Just
PENZANCE
Falmouth
St Mawes

Penzance
Newlyn
Helston
Constantine

Land's End
Sennen
St Buryan
Praa Sands
Porthleven
Mawnan Smith

Land's End
Mousehole
Gweek
Manaccan

Porthcurno
Treen
St Keverne

Mullion
Coverack
Cadgwith

Lizard
Lizard Point

For continuation pages refer to numbered arrows

For continuation pages refer to numbered arrows

For continuation pages refer to numbered arrows

Cemaes
Amlwch

ISLE OF
ANGLESEY
Llanerchymedd

Holyhead

Llanfachraeth
Benllech
Red
Wharf Bay
Llangoed

Trearddur Bay
Pentraeth

Holy
Island
Llangefni
Penmaenmawr

Rhosneigr

Aberffraw
Menai
Bridge
Beaumaris
Bangor
Llanfairfechan

Llanfair
P.G
Llanllechid

Newborough
Y Felinheli
Bethesda
Tal-y-Bont

Caernarfon
Llanrug
Llanberis

Bontnewydd

Caernarfon
Bay
Llandwrog
Llanwnda
Capel Curig
Betws-y-Coed

Clynnog-fawr
Penygroes
Rhyd-Ddu
Dolwyddelan
Penmachno

Llanaelhaearn
SH
Beddgelert
SNOWDONIA
Blaenau Ffestiniog

Morfa Nefyn
Prenteg
Maentwrog
Ffestiniog

Nefyn
LLEYN
Bodfuan
Llanystumdwy
Tremadog
Porthmadog
Penrhyndeudraeth

Sarn
Criccieth
Portmeirion
Talsarnau
NATIONAL

Pwllheli
Borth-y-Gest
Trawsfynydd
GWYNEDD
Bala

Llanbedrog
Harlech
Llanuwchllyn

Aberdaron
Y Rhiw
Abersoch
Llanbedr
PARK

Bardsey
Island
Dyffryn Ardudwy
Ganllwyd

Tal-y-bont

Barmouth
Dolgellau
Dinas-Mawddwy

Fairbourne
Mallwyd

Llwyngwril
Corris

Cemmaes
Road
Llanbrynmair

Tywyn
Bryncrug
Pennal
Machynlleth

Carno

Aberdyfi
Eglwys Fach

SN

Borth
Tal-y-bont

Llandre

Llanidloes

CARDIGAN BAY
Aberystwyth
Capel
Bangor
Ponterwyd

Llandudno
Rhôs-
on-Sea

Deganwy
Colwyn Bay

Llandudno Junction
Llandulas

Conwy
Bodelwyd

Llansanffraid
Glan Conwy
Betws-yn-Rhos

Tal-y-Cafn
Llanfair
Talhaiarn

Trefriw
Llangernyw

Pentrefoelas
Cerrigydrudion

CONWY

Llanrwst

Bylcha

Hotel
AA Hotel of the Year
Town/Village name

0   10 miles

0   10   20 kilometres

9

For continuation pages refer to numbered arrows

C EDIN	City of Edinburgh
C GLAS	City of Glasgow
CLACKS	Clackmannanshire
C DUND	City of Dundee
E DUNS	East Dunbartonshire
E RENS	East Renfrewshire
INVER	Inverclyde
MDLOTH	Midlothian
N LANS	North Lanarkshire
RENS	Renfrewshire
W DUNS	West Dunbartonshire
W LOTH	West Lothian

For continuation pages refer to numbered arrows

NA

NB

Cape Wrath

Rudha Rhobhanais
(Butt of Lewis)
Port Nis
(Port of Ness)

Cellar
Head

Handa Island

Scourie

LEWIS

Great
Bernera

Carlabhagh
(Carloway)

OF

Steornabhagh
(Stornoway)

STORNOWAY

Tiumpan
Head

Lochinver

Inchnadam

NA H–EILEANAN
AN IAR

ISLE

Scarp

THE MINCH

Taransay

Tairbeart
(Tarbert)

Scalpay

Gruinard
Bay

Ullapool

Sgarasta Bheag
(Scarista)

HARRIS

Pabbay

THE LITTLE MINCH

Boreray

Berneray

Gairloch

Loch nam Madadh
(Lochmaddy)
NORTH UIST

Staffin

Kinlochewe

Achnasheen

Ronay

Uig

Torridon

NG

Wiay

Colbost

Shieldaig

Dunvegan

Skeabost
Bridge

Portree

ISLE

Inner Sound

NF

SOUTH
UIST

Struan

Raasay

Plockton

OF

Cannich

Drynoch

SKYE

Scalpay

Kyle of
Lochalsh

Loch Baghasdail
(Lochboisdale)

Broadford

Shiel
Bridge

Eriskay

Isleornsay

Soay

BARRA

Canna

Ardvasar

Sound of Sleat

Cuillin Sound

Invergarry

Bàgh a Chaisteil
(Castlebay)

Rùm

Mallaig

Sandray

Eigg

NORTH

Spean Bridge

Roy
Bridge

Mingulay

Muck

Glenfinnan

INNER HEBRIDES

Fort William

Kinlochleven

NL

Point of
Ardnamurchan

NM

Acharacle

Strontian

Onich

Ballachulish

Coll

Tobermory

South
Ballachulish

Arinagour

Port Appin

Tiree

Scarinish

20

Eriska

Lismore

ISLE

Lochaline

Connel

Ulva

OF

Oban

Iona
Fionnphort

MULL

Kerrera

Dalmally

Crian

Lorne

Kilchrenan

OUTER HEBRIDES

WEST HIGHLANDS

For continuation pages refer to numbered arrows

Readers' Report Form

Please send this form to:–
Editor, The Hotel Guide,
Lifestyle Guides,
AA Media,
Fanum House,
Basingstoke RG21 4EA

e-mail: lifestyleguides@theAA.com

Please use this form to recommend any hotel where you have stayed, whether it is included in the guide or not currently listed. You can also help us to improve the guide by completing the short questionnaire on the reverse.

Please note that the AA does not undertake to arbitrate between you and the hotel management, or to obtain compensation or engage in protracted correspondence.

Date

Your name (BLOCK CAPITALS)

Your address (BLOCK CAPITALS)

Post code

E-mail address

Name of hotel

Location

Comments

(please attach a separate sheet if necessary)

Please tick here ☐ if you DO NOT wish to receive details of AA offers or products

PTO

Readers' Report Form *continued*

Have you bought this guide before? ☐ YES ☐ NO

Do you regularly use any other, accommodation, restaurant, pub or food guides? ☐ YES ☐ NO
If YES, which ones?

_____

_____

Why did you buy this guide? (tick all that apply)

Holiday ☐   Short break ☐   Business travel ☐   Special occasion ☐
Overnight stop ☐   Find a venue for an event e.g. conference ☐
Other (please state) _____

How often do you stay in hotels? (tick one choice)

More than once a month ☐   Once a month ☐   Once in 2-3 months ☐
Once in six months ☐   Once a year ☐   Less than once a year ☐
Other (please state) _____

Please answer these questions to help us make improvements to the guide:
Which of these factors are the most important when choosing a hotel? (tick all that apply)

Price ☐   Location ☐   Awards/ratings ☐   Service ☐
Decor/surroundings ☐   Previous experience ☐   Recommendation ☐
Other (please state) _____

Do you read the editorial features in the guide? ☐ YES ☐ NO

Do you use the location atlas? ☐ YES ☐ NO

What elements of the guide do you find most useful when choosing somewhere to stay? (tick all that apply)

Description ☐   Photo ☐   Advertisement ☐   Star rating ☐

Is there any other information you would like to see added to this guide?

_____

_____

_____

_____